International Applied Computational Electromagnetics Society Symposium in Denver (ACES-Denver 2018)

Denver, Colorado, USA
25 - 29 March 2018

ISBN: 978-1-5108-6303-3

Printed from e-media with permission by:

Curran Associates, Inc.
57 Morehouse Lane
Red Hook, NY 12571

CURRAN ASSOCIATES INC.
proceedings
.com

Some format issues inherent in the e-media version may also appear in this print version.

Printed by Curran Associates, Inc. (2018)

For permission requests, please contact The Applied Computational Electromagnetics Society (ACES) at the address below.

The Applied Computational Electromagnetics Society (ACES)
www.aces-society.org

Additional copies of this publication are available from:

Curran Associates, Inc.
57 Morehouse Lane
Red Hook, NY 12571 USA
Phone: 845-758-0400
Fax: 845-758-2633
Email: curran@proceedings.com
Web: www.proceedings.com

2018 International Applied Computational Electromagnetics Society Symposium in Denver (ACES-Denver 2018)

Conference Proceedings
Table of Contents

Session 3: Computational Electromagnetics, Advanced Algorithms and Emerging Applications

03-01 "A Nystrom Discretization of an Augmented Muller Surface Integral Equation"
Nastaran Hendijani and Stephen D. Gedney 1

03-02 "An Adaptive Factorization Method for Inverse Scattering Problems"
Koung Hee Leem, Jun Liu, and George Pelekanos 3

03-03 "First Principles Model of Electric and Magnetic Cable Braid Penetrations"
Salvatore Campione, Larry K. Warne, and William L. Langston 5

03-04 "Flammer's Exact Solution for the Circular Conducting Disk: A Benchmark Problem for EM Software Validation" 7
Andrew F. Peterson and Malcolm M. Bibby

Session 4: Antenna Optimization for RFID Applications

04-01 "On Compact Wideband Antenna Design Using Topology Modifications"
Muhammad Aziz ul Haq and Slawomir Koziel 9

04-02 "Design Optimization of Novel Compact Circular Polarization Antenna"
Slawomir Koziel and Adrian Bekasiewicz 11

04-03 "PEEC-Based Multi-Objective Synthesis of NFC Antennas in the Presence of Conductive Structures"
Thomas Bauernfeind, Paul Baumgartner, Oszkar Biro, Christian Magele, Werner Renhart, and Riccardo Torchio 13

04-04 "Synthesis of NFC Antenna Structure under Multi Card Condition"
Paul Baumgartner, Thomas Bauernfeind, Oszkar Biro, Christian Magele, Werner Renhart, and Riccardo Torchio 15

04-05 "The Adaptive Wind Driven Optimization and its Application in Electromagnetics"
Jogender Nagar, Sawyer D. Campbell, Douglas H. Werner, Zikri Bayraktar, and Muge Komurcu 17

Session 5: Microwave/Millimeter Wave and Terahertz Devices and Applications – 1

05-01 "Dual-Band Microstrip Antenna for the Fifth Generation Indoor/Outdoor Wireless Applications"
Mourad S. Ibrahim 19

05-02 "Co-Simulations of DC Magnetic Bias Fields and RF Performance for Microwave Ferrite Circulators"
Laila Fighera Marzall, Mauricio Pinto, Andrea Ashley, Dimitra Psychogiou, and Zoya Popovic 21

05-03 "A Design Approach for Monolithically Integrated Broadband Circulators"
Mauricio Pinto, Laila Fighera Marzall, Andrea Ashley, Dimitra Psychogiou, and Zoya Popovic 23

05-04 "Terahertz Evanescent Wave Tunneling in Bianisotropic Thin Films"
Faroq Razzaz and Majeed A. S. Alkanhal 25

05-05 "Tuning the Resonant Frequency of Microstrip Patch Antenna in LWIR"
Shenjie Miao and Brian A. Lail 27

Session 6: Student Paper Competition – 1

06-01 "On the Conforming Combination of the Electric and Magnetic Field Integral Equations"
Ahmet F. Yilmaz and H. Arda Ulku 29

06-02 "A Volume Integral Equation Solver for Quantum-Corrected Transient Analysis of Scattering from Plasmonic Nanostructures"
Sadeed B. Sayed, Ismail Enes Uysal, H. Arda Ulku, and Hakan Bagci 31

06-03 "A Space-Time Domain Decomposition Method for High-fidelity Electromagnetic Simulation"
Shu Wang and Zhen Peng 33

06-04 "Analysis of Nonlinear Graphene Plasmonics Using Surface Integral Equations"
Ling Ling Meng, Xiaoyan Y. Z. Xiong, Tian Xia, Li Jun Jiang, and Weng Cho Chew 35
06-05 "Design of Ungrounded CPW GaN-on-Si MMICs"
Philip Zurek, Myles Foreman, Ryan Johnson, Christopher Galbraith, Jose Estrada, and Zoya Popovic 37

Session 7: Challenges of Antenna Designs for Integration in Extreme Environments
07-01 "Even-Arm Modulated Arm Width Spiral Properties"
W. Neill Kefauver and Dejan S. Filipovic 39
07-02 "High Temperature Electronics for Demanding Aircraft Applications"
Roger A. Brewer 41
07-03 "Radiation Modes of an Outside Fed 4-arm Conical Spiral"
Thomas P. Cencich, Jeannette C. McDonnell, and Timothy W. Samson 43
07-04 "On Matching Lossy Antennas for Maximum Power Absorption"
Ofer Markish, Daniel Silverstein, and Yehuda Leviatan 45
07-05 "Fast Computation of Back Scattered Fields for Large Scanned Array Antennas"
Arun K. Bhattacharyya and Nicholas D. Saiz 47

Session 8: Design, Analysis and Applications of EM Metasurfaces – 1
08-01 "Triple Fano Resonances in Plasmonic Heptamer Nanohole Arrays: Symmetric and Asymmetric Structures"
Akram Hajebifard and Pierre Berini 49
08-02 "Metagratings: A Novel Paradigm for Efficient Wavefront Control"
Dimitrios L. Sounas, Younes Ra'di, and Andrea Alu 51
08-03 "Metamaterial Enhanced Antenna Systems: A Review"
Daniel Binion, Pingjuan L. Werner, Douglas H. Werner, Erik Lier, and Thomas H. Hand 53
08-04 "A Dual Band-Reject FSS for WI-FI Application"
Mehdi Bahadorzadeh and Charles F. Bunting 55
08-05 "The Time-Bandwidth Limit in Optical Nanostructures and Its Relation to Nonreciprocity"
Dimitrios L. Sounas, Sander Mann, and Andrea Alu 57

Session 9: Microwave/Millimeter Wave and Terahertz Devices and Applications – 2
09-01 "Design of Ungrounded CPW GaN-on-Si MMICs"
Philip Zurek, Myles Foreman, Ryan Johnson, Christopher Galbraith, Jose Estrada, and Zoya Popovic 59
09-02 "Bandwidth Design of Ferrite-Based Circulators"
Andrea Ashley, Laila Fighera Marzall, Mauricio Pinto, Zoya Popovic, and Dimitra Psychogiou 61
09-03 "Amplitude-Equalized Microwave Phasers"
Mohamed K. Emara, Kimi Maheshwari, Jim S. Wight, and Shulabh Gupta 63

Session 10: Student Paper Competition – 2
10-01 "A Novel Stochastic Integral Equation Method for Wireless Communication in Diffuse Multipath Environments"
Shen Lin and Zhen Peng 65
10-02 "Surface Integral Computation for the Higher Order Surface Integral Equation Method of Moments"
Sanja B. Manic and Branislav M. Notaros 67
10-03 "Vector Parabolic Equation Modeling of Wireless Propagation in Tunnels with Statistically Rough Surface Walls"
Xingqi Zhang and Costas D. Sarris 69
10-04 "A DC to HF Volume PEEC Formulation Based on Hertz Potentials and the Cell Method"
Riccardo Torchio, Piergiorgio Alotto, Paolo Bettini, Dimitri Voltolina, and Federico Moro 71
10-05 "Recent Developments in the Application of Contactless Inductive Flow Tomography"
Matthias Ratajczak, Thomas Wondrak, and Frank Stefani 73

Session 11: Fast Methods for Radar Signature Prediction and Direction Finding Algorithms

11-01 "Parametric Models for Signature Prediction and Feature Extraction"
Julie Ann Jackson 75

11-02 "Sparse Recovery Method for Order-of-Magnitude Reduction in RCS Measurements"
Tayfun Özdemir, Kevin Bi, Santos Campos, and Robert J. Burkholder 77

11-03 "Analytic Solutions for the Bistatic Radar Signature of a Dihedral Target of Arbitrary Angle"
Robert J. Burkholder 79

11-04 "GNSS AoA Estimation Based on Dual-frequency Joint Processing"
Boyi Wang, Yafeng Li, Nagaraj Channarayapatna Shivaramaiah, and Dennis M. Akos 81

11-05 "Design of Platform-Based HF Direction Finding Antennas Using the Characteristic Mode Theory"
Ruyu Ma and Nader Behdad 84

11-06 "Impact of Flat Radomes on Amplitude-Only Direction Finding Performance"
Muhannad A. Al-Tarifi and Dejan S. Filipovic 86

11-07 "Directional of Arrival Tag Response for Reverse RFID Localization"
Allee D. Zarrini, Atef Elsherbeni, and Jurgen F. Brune 88

Session 12: Design, Analysis and Applications of EM Metasurfaces – 2

12-01 "Modal Analysis of Stacked Gratings using B-splines Basis"
Gerard Granet 90

12-02 "Resonant Nanoantennas for Enhancing the Interaction of Terahertz Radiation with Nanomaterials"
L. Razzari 92

12-03 "Bi-Anisotropic Homogenization for Efficient Metasurface Design"
Zhaxylyk A. Kudyshev, Ludmila J. Prokopeva, Maowen Song, Sajid Choudhury, and Alexander V. Kildishev 94

12-04 "The Constitutive Effective Parameters of Two-Dimensional Multilayered Dielectric Grating Slab"
Quang Nguyen, Amir I. Zaghloul, Mario J. Mencagli, and Nader Engheta 96

12-05 "Optimization of Plasmonic Metasurfaces for Subtractive Color Filtering"
Walied Sabra, Maowen Song, Shaimaa I. Azzam, Arafa H. Aly, and Alexander V. Kildishev 98

12-06 "Millimeter-Wave Electromagnetic Metasurfaces based on Perforated Dielectrics"
NaquashA. Sheikh, Khaled Madhoun, Sonya Stuhec-Leonard, and Shulabh Gupta 100

12-07 "Implicit and Explicit FDTD Methods for Modelling EM Metasurfaces"
Tom J. Smy, Scott A. Stewart, and Shulabh Gupta 103

Session 13: Radio Propagation Modeling and Channel Estimation

13-01 "28 GHz Propagation Channel Measurements for 5G Microcellular Environments"
C. Umit Bas, Rui Wang, Seun Sangodoyin, Sooyoung Hur, Kuyeon Whang, Jeongho Park, Jianzhong Zhang, and Andreas F. Molisch 105

13-02 "Improving Millimeter-Wave Channel Models for Suburban Environments with Site-Specific Geometric Features"
Yaguang Zhang, David J. Love, Nicolo Michelusi, James V. Krogmeier, Soumya Jyoti, Alex Sprintson, and Christopher R. Anderson 107

13-03 "Analysis of Radar Altimeter Interference due to Wireless Avionics Intra-Communication Systems by Using Large-Scale FDTD Method"
Shunichi Futatsumori, Kazuyuki Morioka, Akiko Kohmura, Naruto Yonemoto, Takashi Hikage, Tetsuya Sekiguchi, Manabu Yamamoto, and Toshio Nojima 109

13-04 "Recent Advances in Spatiotemporally-Modulated (STM) Magnetless Circulators"
Dimitrios L. Sounas, Ahmed Kord, and Andrea Alu 111

13-05 "Millimeter-wave Frequency FDTD Simulation for Error Vector Magnitude of Modulated Signals"
Joseph Elliott Diener, Jeanne Quimby, Kate A. Remley, and Atef Z. Elsherbeni 113

Session 14: Numerical Methods for Analysis, Design and Measurement of Antennas – 1

14-01 "Near-Field Far-Field Transformations for Automobile Antenna Measurements"
Thomas F. Eibert and Raimud A.M. Mauermayer 115

14-02 "Hierarchical Universal Matrices for Sensitivity Analysis by Curvilinear Finite Elements"
Laszlo Levente Toth and Romanus Dyczij-Edlinger 117

14-03 "Embedding the Shooting and Bouncing Rays Method in a Hybrid Solver Framework"
Benjamin Motz and Thomas Weiland 119

14-04 "Mode Tracking for Parametrized Eigenvalue Problems in Computational Electromagnetics"
Philipp Jorkowski and Rolf Schuhmann 121

14-05 "Estimation of Mutual Coupling in Irregular Planar Arrays"
Andrej Konforta, Thomas Bertuch, and Peter Knott 123

14-06 "Effects of Internal Reflections on the Performance of Lens-Integrated mmW and THz Antenna"
Burak Ozbey and Kubilay Sertel 125

14-07 "Ray Tracing Using Shooting-Bouncing Technique to Model Mine Tunnels: Theory and Verification for a PEC Waveguide"
Blake Troksa, Cam Key, Forest Kunkel, Slobodan V. Savic, Milan M. Ilic, and Branislav M. Notaros 127

Session 17: Time Domain Methods – 1

17-01 "Integral Accuracy and Experimental Evidence for the Stability of Time Domain Integral Equations"
Jielin Li, Daniel S. Weile, and David A. Hopkins 129

17-02 "A Novel Port Extraction Technique for Coupling Circuits with Full Wave Time Domain Integral Equation Solvers"
S. O'Connor, S. Hughey, and B. Shanker 131

17-03 "A Modified Streamline Upwind/Petrov-Galerkin Stabilization Matrix for Time-Domain FEM"
Srijith Rajamohan and William Kyle Anderson 133

17-04 "Using an Approximate Streamline Upwind/Petrov-Galerkin Stabilization Matrix for the Solution of Maxwell's Equations in Dispersive Materials"
Srijith Rajamohan and William Kyle Anderson 135

17-05 "Analysis of Transient Scattering from Impedance Surfaces using Physical Optics Approximation"
Huseyin A. Serim and H. Arda Ulku 137

Session 18: Advances in Electrical Impedance Tomography

18-01 "Physiologically Inspired Model of the Skin for Use in Electrical Impedance Tomography"
Michelle M. Mellenthin and Jennifer L. Mueller 139

18-02 "Reconstruction of Complex Conductivities by Calderón's Method on Subject-Specific Domains"
Peter Muller and Jennifer L. Mueller 141

18-03 "Spatial Priors in the D-bar Method for Human Thoracic Electrical Impedance Tomography Data"3
Melody Alsaker and Jennifer L. Mueller 143

18-04 "An Experimental Study of the Human Scapula Movement for the Development of an Anatomical Atlas for Electrical Impedance Tomography"
Tayran M. M. Olegário, Erick L. B. de Camargo, Marcelo B. P. Amato, and Raul Gonzalez Lima 145

18-05 "Introduction of Statistical Priors into the D-bar Method for Electrical Impedance Tomography"
Talles B. R. Santos, Erick L. B. de Camargo, Jennifer L. Mueller, and Raul Gonzalez Lima 147

Session 19: Broadband Antennas and Applications

19-01 "Wideband GCPW-Fed Dielectric Resonator Antenna for WLAN Applications"
Wei-Chung Weng, Min-Chi Chang, and Min-Sian Chen 149

19-02 "Design of Broadband Luneburg Lens Feed Manifold"
Maxim Ignatenko, Carlos A. Mulero Hernandez, and Dejan Filipovic 151

19-03 "Multioctave Antenna Array for Simultaneous Transmit and Receive Applications"
Mohamed A. Elmansouri, Jaegeun Ha, and Dejan Filipovic 153
19-04 "Wideband, Scanning Array for Simultaneous Transmit and Receive"
Alexander Hovsepian, Satheesh Bojja Venkatakrishnan, Elias A. Alwan, and John L. Volakis 155
19-05 "Hexagonal Waveguides: New Class of Waveguides for mm-wave Circularly Polarized Horns"
Shubhendu Bhardwaj and John Volakis 157

Session 20: Wideband and Multiband Antennas
20-01 "Size-Reduced Patch-Antenna Feedpoint Parametric Study"
Randall L. Musselman and James L. Vedral 159
20-02 "Multiband Antenna for Wireless Applications Including GSM/UMTS/LTE and 5G Bands"
Amirreza Jalali Khalilabadi and Ata Zadehgol 161
20-03 "2 to 18 GHz Ultra-Wideband Dual-Linear Polarized Phased Array with 60° Scanning"
Jingni Zhong, Elias A. Alwan, and John L. Volakis 163

Session 21: Optimization and Inverse Problems in Low-Frequency Electromagnetic Fields
21-01 "Biomedical Magnetic Induction Tomography: An Inhomogeneous Green's Function Approach"
Philippe De Tillieux and Yves Goussard 165
21-02 "Approaches for Magnetic Sources Reconstruction in Controlled Thermo-Nuclear Fusion Technology"
A. G. Chiariello, A. Formisano, R. Martone, and JET Contributors 167
21-03 "Resolution Limits of Near-field Electromagnetic Imaging"
Vijay Harid 169
21-04 "Perturbation Approach to Shape Reconstruction in a Rectangular Waveguide using Experimental Data"
Martin Norgren, Irene Ortiz de Saracho, and Mariana Dalarsson 171

Session 22: Building Blocks for Fast FEM and MoM Computation in Electromagnetics
22-01 "High-Order Moment-Matching MOR with Impedance Boundaries for Signal Integrity Analysis"
Matthew B. Stephanson 173
22-02 "Circuit-Based Model Order Reduction for EM-CAD"
Valentin de la Rubia and Sofia Tinoco-Galafate 175
22-03 "Necessary Conditions for the Diagonalizability of Maxwell's Equations in Inhomogeneous and Fully Bi-anisotropic Media"
A. R. Baghai-Wadji 177
22-04 "Diagonalizability of Thermo Electromagnetic Equations in Inhomogeneous and Fully Tri-anisotropic Media"
A. R. Baghai-Wadji 179

Session 23: EM Modeling Using FEKO – 1
23-01 "A Study of SAR on Child Passengers and Driver Due to Cellphone Connectivity Within Vehicle"
M. Lyell and Daniel Aloi 181
23-02 "Reduction of Coupling between Flush-Mounted Antennas"
Prathap Valale Prasannakumar, Mohamed A. Elmansouri, Maxim Ignatenko, and Dejan Filipovic 183
23-03 "Review of Selected New Features in FEKO 2018"
Ulrich Jakobus, Andrés Aguilar, Elia Attardo, Marlize Schoeman, Johann van Tonder, and Kitty Longtin 185
23-04 "FEKO™ Modeling Study of Passive UHF RFID Tags Embedded in Pavement"
Sourabh R. Walvekar and Robert J. Burkholder 187
23-05 "The Application of Design of Experiments to RF Systems"
Scott Burnside 189

Session 24: Wideband and Multiband Antenna Modeling and Applications
24-01 "System Modeling of a Quad-band Antenna Using the Singularity Expansion Method"
Sajjad Ur Rehman and Majeed A. S. Alkanhal 191
24-02 "Inverted P-Shaped UWB Antenna with Dual/Tri-Band-Notch Characteristics"
Asim Quddus, Rashid Saleem, M. Farhan Shafique, and Sabih ur Rehman 193
24-03 "Printed Cross-Slot Wideband Conformal Antenna for GPS Application"
Ratikanta Sahoo, D. Vakula, and NVSN Sarma 195

Session 25: Time Domain Methods – 2
25-01 "A Volume Integral Equation Solver for Quantum-Corrected Transient Analysis of Scattering from Plasmonic Nanostructures"
Sadeed B. Sayed, Ismail Enes Uysal, Hakan Bagci, and H. Arda Ulku 197
25-02 "Mixed Finite Element Methods for the Maxwell's Equations with Matrix Parameters"
Asad Anees and Lutz Angermann 199
25-03 "Time-Domain Magnetic Shielding Effectiveness of Planar Stratified Shields"
R. Araneo, G. Lovat, S. Celozzi, and P. Burghignoli 201
25-04 "Modeling Time Domain Multiphysics of Reverse Saturable Absorption"
Shaimaa I. Azzam and Alexander V. Kildishev 203
25-05 "Time Domain Finite Element Methods for Maxwell's Equations in Three Dimensions"
Asad Anees and Lutz Angermann 205
25-06 "Numerical Simulation of EMP Environment Radiated by X-rays inside a High-Power Laser Facility"
Zhiqian Xu and Cui Meng 207
25-07 "A Multiphysics Time-Dependent Model of Dielectric Breakdown in Solids"
Raymond A. Wildman and George A. Gazonas 209

Session 27: EM Modeling Using FEKO – 2
27-01 "Massive MIMO – Beyond 4G and a Basis for 5G"
Gopinath Gampala and C. J. Reddy 211
27-02 "Ultra-Wideband Antenna Performance Comparison"
William Coburn and Seth McCormick 213

Session 28: Computational Methods for Complex EM Domains, Integral Equation Methods
28-01 "A DC to HF Volume PEEC Formulation Based on Hertz Potentials and the Cell Method"
Riccardo Torchio, Piergiorgio Alotto, Paolo Bettini, Dimitri Voltolina, and Federico Moro 215
28-02 "Decoupled Potential Integral Equations for Electromagnetic Scattering"
J. Li and B. Shanker 217
28-03 "A Lagrange Multiplier Approach to Constraining Electromagnetic Surface Integral Equations"
Daniel L. Dault and Andrew J. Pray 219
28-04 "Sparse Direct Matrix Solvers of Finite Element Discretizations in Electromagnetics"
Marinos N. Vouvakis and Javad Moshfegh 221
28-05 "Fast Integral Equation Solvers based on the Randomized Cross Approximation"
Constantinos L. Zekios and Marinos N. Vouvakis 223
28-06 "Adjoint Methods for Uncertainty Quantification in Applied Computational Electromagnetics: FEM Scattering Examples"
Cam Key, Aaron Smull, Branislav M. Notaros, Donald Estep, and Troy Butler 225
28-07 "Numerical Validation of a Boundary Element Method With E and $\partial E/\partial N$ as the Boundary Unknowns"
Johannes Markkanen, Alex J. Yuffa, and Joshua A. Gordon 227

Session 31: Low Frequency Computational Electromagnetics – 1
31-01 "Locally Corrected Nystrom Discretization for Impressed Current Cathodic Protection Systems"
John C. Young, Robert Pfeiffer, Robert J. Adams, and Stephen D. Gedney 229

31-02 "A Huygens Surface Source Model for Field Prediction Valid from sub-ELF to High Frequencies"
Nastaran Hendijani, Stephen D. Gedney, John C. Young, and Robert J. Adams 231
31-03 "Micromagnetic Model Simulation of Spin-Torque Oscillator and Write Head for Microwave-Assisted Magnetic Recording – Spin Injection Layer with In-Plane Anisotropy"
Yasushi Kanai, Ryo Itagaki, Simon Greaves, and Hiroaki Muraoka 233
31-04 "A Finite-Difference Frequency Domain Solver for Quasi-TEM Applications"
J. Patrick Donohoe 235

Session 32: Advanced FDTD Methods
32-01 "SAR and Temperature Rise Distributions in a Human Head Due to a Multi-Frequency Antenna Source"
Fatih Kaburcuk and Atef Z. Elsherbeni 237
32-02 "Provably Stable Local Application of Crank-Nicolson Time Integration to the FDTD Method with Nonuniform Gridding and Subgridding"
A. Van Londersele, D. De Zutter, and D. Vande Ginste 239
32-03 "Model Order Reduction for Finite Difference Modeling of Cardiac Propagation using DMD modes"
Riasat Khan and Kwong T. Ng 241
32-04 "Numerical Dispersion Analysis for Spherical FDTD"
Ravi C. Bollimuntha, Mohammed F. Hadi, Melinda J. Piket-May, and Atef Z. Elsherbeni 243
32-05 "Improved FDTD Method around Dielectric and PEC Interfaces using RBFFD Techniques"
Brad Martin, Atef Elsherbeni, Gregory E. Fasshauer, and Mohammed Hadi 245

Session 33: Electromagnetic Simulation for RF and Microwave Design Optimization
33-01 "GA-MoM Optimization of Slot Arrays"
Sembiam R. Rengarajan 247
33-02 "Uniform Sampling Procedure for Constrained Surrogate Modeling of Antenna Structures"
Slawomir Koziel and Ari T. Sigurdsson 249
33-03 "Novel Structure and EM-Driven Design of Miniaturized Microstrip Rat-Race Coupler"
Adrian Bekasiewicz and Slawomir Koziel 251
33-04 "Coplanar Waveguide-based Lowpass Filters with Non-uniform Signal Trace and Ground Planes"
Qizhen Li, Khair Al Shamaileh, and Vijay Devabhaktuni 253
33-05 "Nonlinear Neural Network Equalizer for Metro Optical Fiber Communication Systems"
Mahmoud M.T. Maghrabi, Shiva Kumar, and Mohamed H. Bakr 255

Session 34: Wireless Implants for Biomedical Telemetry – 1
34-01 "Towards Batteryless Wearables and Implants"
Wei-Chuan Chen, Brock DeLong, Ramandeep Vilkhu, and Asimina Kiourti 257
34-02 "Optimizing Scattering Coefficients of Disordered Metamaterials Using the Finite-Difference Time-Domain Method"
Adam Mock and Sheldon Hewlett 259
34-03 "Dual-Band (2.4/4.8 GHz) Implantable Antenna for Biomedical Telemetry Applications"
John Blauert and Asimina Kiourti 261
34-04 "An RF-Driven Lightweight Implantable Insulin Pump"
Bingxi Yan, Brock DeLong, Duo An, Asimina Kiourti, Kathleen Dungan, John Volakis, Minglin Ma, and Liang Guo 263
34-05 "Miniature Implantable Antenna Design for Blood Glucose Monitoring"
Ayesha Ahmed, Masood Ur-Rehman, and Qammer Hussain Abbasi 265

Session 35: Low Frequency Computational Electromagnetics – 2
35-01 "Field-Plate Length Variation on GaN Devices for BV and On-Resistance Characterization"
Christopher R. Lashway, Alberto Berzoy, and Osama Mohammed 267

35-02 "Numerical Analysis of Mutual Transient Voltages in Grounding Systems of Offshore Wind Farms"
R. Araneo, G. Lovat, S. Celozzi, and P. Burghignoli 269
35-03 "Shielding Effectiveness of Finite Width Shields Against Low-impedance Magnetic Near-field Sources"
R. Araneo, G. Lovat, S. Celozzi, and P. Burghignoli 271
35-04 "CT Eccentricity Error Evaluation Model Based on the Actual Magnetization Curve"
Hao Zhang, Zeyao Huang, Xiao Zhang, and Abd A. Arkadan 273
35-05 "Field Analysis of a Moving Current-carrying Coil in OMOP Kibble Balances"
S. Li, M. Stock, F. Biesla, A. Kiss, and H. Fang 275

Session 36: Celebrating 50th Anniversary of Field Computation by Moment Methods
36-01 "Roger Harrington and Shielded Planar Microwave Electromagnetic Analysis"
James C. Rautio 277
36-02 "HODLR Direct MOM Solver"
John Shaeffer 279
36-03 "History of Developments Leading to the Method of Moments"
Donald R. Wilton 281
36-04 "A Novel Stochastic Integral Equation Method for Wireless Communication in Diffuse Multipath Environments"
Shen Lin and Zhen Peng 283
36-05 "Spectral Element Boundary Integral Method for Rapid and Accurate Simulations of Inhomogeneous Objects in Layered Media in Nanophotonics"
Yiqian Mao, Jun Niu, and Qing Huo Liu 285

Session 37: Advances in Electromagnetic Modeling by WIPL-D – 1
37-01 "Robust Feed Modeling of the Asymmetric Planar Mesh Dipole-Type Antenna"
Jennifer Rayno and Derek S. Linden 287
37-02 "Modeling and Validation of a mm-Wave Shaped Dielectric Lens Antenna"
David C. Mooradd, Alan J. Fenn, and Peter T. Hurst 289
37-03 "Higher Order Mode Analysis in WIPL-D"
J. Lyn Alford and Milos S. Pavlovic 291
37-04 "Full-Wave Modeling of RF Exciters Using WIPL-D: Road to Real-Time Simulation and Optimization"
Pranav S. Athalye, Branislav M. Notaros, and Milan M. Ilic.....293
37-05 "Efficient Modeling of Towel Bar Antennas Using Model of Distributed Loading Along Wires"
Milos M. Jovicic, Saad N. Tabet, and Branko M. Kolundzija 295

Session 39: Modeling Electromagnetic Waves in Plasma Environments
39-01 "Whistler Mode Wave Numerical Raytracing in a Finite Temperature Anisotropic Plasma Medium"
Marek Golkowski and Ashanthi Maxworth 297
39-02 "Spatial Distributions of Magnetospheric Radio Energy due to Lightning"
Austin P. Sousa and Robert A. Marshall 299
39-03 "FD-PIC Simulation of Broadband Whistler Mode Wave Interactions with Energetic Electrons in the Earth's Radiation Belts"
Poorya Hosseini, Mark Golkowski, and Vijay Harid 301
39-04 "Particle-In-CellMethods for Modeling Electromagnetic Propagation in Plasmas"
John R. Cary 303
39-05 "Late-time Instability in Finite Difference Modeling of Very-Low-Frequency Propagation in the Earth-Ionosphere Waveguide"
Robert A. Marshall, Wei Xu, and Austin P. Sousa 307

39-06 "Simplified FDTD Model of Electromagnetic Wave Propagation in Magnetized Plasma"
Santosh Pokhrel, Varun Shankar, and Jamesina J. Simpson 309
39-07 "Nonlinear FDTD Modeling of Ionospheric Cross-Modulation Experiments"
Robert C. Moore and Anthony J. Erdman.....311

Session 41: Advances in Electromagnetic Modeling by WIPL-D – 2
41-01 "Monostatic RCS for General Aviation Aircraft"
Dennis W. Richardson, Ruben P. Ortega, and Saad N. Tabet 313
41-02 "Comparison of Commercial Simulation Performance for Efficient RCS Analysis"
Dongeun Lee, Sung-Hwan Chi, Do-Young Jang, and Han-Kil Jung 315
41-03 "Polarimetric Weather Radar Calibration by Computational Electromagnetics"
Djordje Mirkovic and Dusan S. Zrnic 317
41-04 "On Synthetic Aperture Radar Simulations using WIPL-D Pro"
Nimrod Teneh and Branko Lj. Mrdakovic 319

Session 42: Wireless Implants for Biomedical Telemetry – 2
42-01 "A Wideband Antenna for Biotelemetry Applications: Design and Transmission Link Evaluation"
Ala Alemaryeen and Sima Noghanian 321
42-02 "Hybrid Power Transfer and Wireless Antenna System Design for Biomedical Implanted Devices"
Reem Shadid and Sima Noghanian 323
42-03 "Circuitry Design and Magnetic Susceptibility Evaluation of 7T fMRI Implantable RF Coil"
Rong Wang, Celia M. Dong, Ed X. Wu, Robert C. Roberts, and Li Jun Jiang 325
42-04 "Power Transfer Efficiency for Distance-Adaptive Wireless Power Transfer System"
D.-G. Seo, S.-H. Ahn, J.-H. Kim, W.-S. Lee, S.-T. Khang, S.-C. Chae, and J.-W. Yu 327
42-05 "Novel Multiband Flamenco Fractal Antenna for Wearable WBAN Off-Body Communication Applications"
Omar Masood Khan, Qamar Ul Islam, Raed M. Shubair, and Asimina Kiourti 329
42-06 "Multi-Bandwidth CPW-Fed Open End Square Loop Monopole Antenna for Energy Harvesting"
Nermeen A. Eltresy, Dalia M. Elsheakh, and Esmat A. Abdallah 331

Session 43: Computational Nanophotonics: Advanced Numerical Methods and Applications – 1
43-01 "Quantum Electrodynamics of Optical Metasurfaces"
Igor V. Bondarev and Vladimir M. Shalaev 333
43-02 "Asymmetric Band Structure Calculations Using the Plane Wave Expansion Method with Time-Modulated Permittivity"
Adam Mock 335
43-03 "Ultra-thin, High-efficiency Mid-Infrared Huygens Metasurface Optics"
Hanyu Zheng, Jun Ding, Li Zhang, Hongtao Lin, Sensong An, Tian Gu, Hualiang Zhang, and Juejun Hu 337
43-04 "A High-Order Accurate FDTD Scheme for Maxwell's Equations on Overset Grids"
Jordan B. Angel, Jeffrey W. Banks, and William D. Henshaw 339
43-05 "Challenges and Opportunities in Modeling and Optimization of 3D Optical Metasurfaces"
D. Bruce Burckel, Aaron J. Pung, and Salvatore Campione 341
43-06 "Inverse Design of Engineered Materials for Extreme Optical Devices"
Sawyer D. Campbell, Danny Z. Zhu, Jogender Nagar, Ronald P. Jenkins, John A. Easum, Douglas H. Werner, and Pingjuan L. Werner 343

Session 45: Electromagnetic Methods for Devices and Applications – 1
45-01 "Suppression of Anisotropic Birefringence in a Rectangular Waveguide"
Gregory Mitchell 345

45-02 "Performance Analysis for Linear Minimum Variance Adaptive Beamforming"
Zhitao Yang and Guanglei Zhang 347
45-03 "The Novel Normalized Method for Interference Suppression at Subarray Level"
Zhitao Yang and Guanglei Zhang 349
45-04 "The Sidelobe Power Suppression for the Aircraft Circle Phase Array Radar"
Dan Wang 351
45-05 "Supercapacitor Implementation for PV Power Generation System and Integration"
Tunir Dey, Kowshik Dey, Greg Whelan, and Abdullah Eroglu 353
45-06 "Design of Dual Band Rectifiers for Energy Harvesting Applications"
Kowshik Dey, Tunir Dey, Rezwan Hussain, and Abdullah Eroglu 355

Session 46: Wireless Energy Harvesting and Power Transfer
46-01 "A Highly Efficient Miniaturized Microwave Collector for Wireless Power Transmission"
Safiullah Khan and Thomas F. Eibert 357
46-02 "Harvesting of Aircraft Radar Altimeter Sidelobes for Low-Power Sensors"
Jose Estrada, Philip Zurek, and Zoya Popovic 359
46-03 "Focused Antenna Arrays for Wireless Power Transfer Applications"
Payam Nayeri 361
46-04 "A Multi-Linear Polarization Reconfigurable Plus Shaped Dipole Antenna for Wireless Energy Harvesting Applications"
Ami Desai and Payam Nayeri 363
46-05 "Compact 24GHz Half-slot Antenna for Energy Combining"
M. Aboualalaa, Adel B. Abdel-Rahman, A. Allam, Ramesh K. Pokharel, Kuniaki Yoshitomi, and H. Elsadek 365
46-06 "Analysis of Two/Four Coils WPT Systems for Embedded PLC Communications"
Sami Barmada and Mauro Tucci 367

Session 47: Integral Equation Solvers for Real-Life Applications – 1
47-01 "On the Conforming Combination of the Electric and Magnetic Field Integral Equations"
Ahmet F. Yilmaz and H. Arda Ulku 369
47-02 "Coupled EM-Structural Analysis in Convected Coordinates"
Daniel S. Weile, David A. Hopkins, and Brian M. Powers 371
47-03 "A Study of Near-Field Imaging and Diagnostic Applications of Surface Equivalent Current Methods"
Arslan Azhar, Thomas F. Eibert, and Li Li 373
47-04 "Mode Analysis of Waveguides in Layered Media"
Aytac Alparslan 375
47-05 "Scattering Analysis of Silver Nanoparticles for Solar Cell Applications using Integral Equations"
Ismail Enes Uysal, Huseyin Arda Ulku, Oguz Gulseren, and Hakan Bagci 377
47-06 "An FFT-Accelerated Inductance Extractor for Voxelized Structures"
Abdulkadir C. Yucel, Ioannis P. Georgakis, Athanasios G. Polimeridis, Hakan Bagci, and Jacob K. White 379

Session 48: Computational Nanophotonics: Advanced Numerical Methods and Applications – 2
48-01 "Versatile Nanoparticle Manipulation with Designer Thermoplasmonic Metasurface"
Justus C. Ndukaife 381
48-02 "Time Domain Modeling of Active Materials"
Shaimaa I. Azzam, Ludmila J. Prokopeva, and Alexander V. Kildishev 383
48-03 "Coupling Electron Transport with Maxwell Equations for Modelling Optically Tunable Photonic Elements"
Michael Povolotskyi, Ludmila Prokopeva, and Alexander Kildishev 385

48-04 "Efficient Multiphysics and Multiscale FDTD Methods for Terahertz Plasmonic Devices"
Shubhendu Bhardwaj 387
48-05 "Frequency-Domain versus Time-Domain Analysis of Slow-light Mesophotonic Waveguides: Theoretical Insights for Practically Realizable Devices"
Stavroula Foteinopoulou 389

Session 49: RF/Microwave Electromagnetics
49-01 "Estimation of 1090 MHz Signal Environment on Airport Surface by using Multilateration System"
Junichi Honda, Yasuyuki Kakubari, and Takuya Otsuyama 391
49-02 "A Novel Compact Microstrip Bandstop Filter (BSF) Using Spurline & Stepped-Impedance Resonator (SIR)"
Hamad G. Alrwuili and T. S. Kalkur 393
49-03 "High-density Compact Chipless RFID Tag for Item-level Tagging"
Ayesha Habib, Hafsa Anam, Yasar Amin, and Hannu Tenhunen 395
49-04 "Design Method for Wide-Beam Waveguide Antenna"
Chong-Hwan Park, Seung-Real Ryu, Jae-Yoon Shin, Dong-Su Choi, and Jong-Myung Woo 397

Session 50: Electromagnetic Methods for Devices and Applications – 2
50-01 "Recent Developments in the Application of Contactless Inductive Flow Tomography"
Matthias Ratajczak, Thomas Wondrak, and Frank Stefani 399
50-02 "Simulation Model to Predict EM Scattering due to Different Parameters of Dust/Sand Storms"
Sharif Iqbal Mitu Sheikh and Mahfuz Ullah 401
50-03 "Examination on a Self-Mixing Circuit"
Congying Chen, Adalbert Beyer, Winfried Simon, Rudiger Follmann, Peter Waldow, and Dominique Schreurs 404

Session 51: Integral Equation Solvers for Real-Life Applications – 2
51-01 "Circulant Preconditioning in the Volume Integral Equation Method for Nanophotonics"
Samuel Groth, Jacob White, and Athanasios Polimeridis 406
51-02 "On Complexity Reduction in Solution of Scattering Problems on Well-Conducting 3D Objects With Surface-Volume-Surface EFIE"
Jamiu Mojolagbe, Reza Gholami, and Vladimir Okhmatovski 408
51-03 "Linear-Complexity Direct Integral Equation Solver with Explicit Accuracy Control for Large-Scale Interconnect Extraction"
Miaomiao Ma and Dan Jiao 410
51-04 "Optical Couplers for Sharply Bended Nanowires: Sensitivity to Coupler Nanoparticles"
Askin Altinoklu and Ozgur Ergul 412
51-05 "Analytical Evaluation of Matrix Elements of Electromagnetic Integral Equations with RWG basis Functions for Arbitrarily Oriented Pairs of Triangular Surface Elements"
Elizabeth Bleszynski, Marek Bleszynski, and Thomas Jaroszewicz 414

Session 52: Biomedical Applications
52-01 "Coupled Modeling and Experimental Investigation of RF-Induced Heating near Ablation Catheters under 1.5T MRI"
Qi Zeng, Jingshen Liu, Jianfeng Zheng, Tom Lloyd, Leonardo M. Angelone, Wolfgang Kainz, and Ji Chen 416
52-02 "Hyperthermia Study in Cancer Treatment"
H. F. Guarnizo Mendez, J. J. Pantoja, and M. A. Polochè Arango 418
52-03 "Co-simulation of a Reactor Assisted by Microwaves"
Carlos Rivera, John J. Pantoja, and Felix Vega 420

Session 54: Tunable RF Filters
54-01 "Simulation and Fabrication of BST FBAR Resonator"
Abdulhamid Matoug, Daw Asderah, and T. S. Kalkur 422

54-02 "A Tunable Microstrip Bandstop Filter Using Compact Spiral Folded Spurline For RF Microwave Systems"
Hamad G. Alrwuili and T. S. Kalkur 424
54-03 "A Balanced Dual-Band Tunable Bandpass Filter"
Dubari Borah and Thottam S. Kalkur 426
54-04 "UHF-Band Bandpass Filters With Fully-Reconfigurable Transfer Function"
Dakotah J. Simpson, Roberto Gómez-García, and Dimitra Psychogiou 428

Session 55: Devices and Applications
55-01 "Investigation of the RCS of Wind Turbine Rotor Blades"
Sebastian Hegler, Klaus Wolf, Christoph Statz, Niels Neumann, and Dirk Plettemeier 430
55-02 "Design of a Cost-Effective Analog Lock-In Amplifier Using Phase Sensitive Detector"
Fardin Humayun, Riasat Khan, Shatil Saadman, and Rezwanul Haque 432
55-03 "The Novel Adaptive Method for Interference Suppression"
Zhitao Yang and Guanglei Zhang 434
55-04 "Advanced Subspace Projection Method for Interference Suppression in Phase Array Radar"
Zhitao Yang and Guanglei Zhang 436
55-05 "The Adaptive Interference Suppression Method Based on Householder at Subarray Level"
Dan Wang and Guanglei Zhang 438

Session 56: Parallel and GPU EM Comput
56-01 "Massively Parallel Frequency Domain Electromagnetic Simulation Codes"
William L. Langston, Joseph Kotulski, Rebecca Coats, Roy Jorgenson, S. Adam Blake, Salvatore Campione, Aaron Pung, and Brian Zinser 440
56-02 "The Parallel Implementation and Accuracy of Matrix Compression in the Method of Moments code EIGER"
Joseph D. Kotulski 442
56-03 "HIPERCONE FDTD: Vectorized Highly Scalable Full-Wave Electromagnetic Solver"
Sergei Belousov, Sergey Khilkov, Vadim Levchenko, Anastasia Perepelkina, and Ilya Valuev 444

Session 57: Design Simulation and Build Microwave Devices using Sonnet Suites
57-01 "Dual Resonance Proximity Coupled Patch Antenna"
Bahadir Kilic, Taha Imeci, Oguzhan Salih Gungor, Mustafa Imeci, Negar Majidi, and Mohammad Rahim Sobhani 446
57-02 "Design of a Quad Element Patch Antenna at 5.8 GHz"
Negar Majidi, Goksen Goksenin Yaralioglu, Mohammad Rahim Sobhani, and Taha Imeci 448
57-03 "Design and Analysis of a Bandpass Hairpin Filter"
Rafsan Ahmed, Shpetim Emiri, and S. Taha Imeci 450
57-04 "Microstrip Patch Antenna with Triangular Slits"
Anil Elakas, Gurhan Ali Imrak, Mert Sencan, S. Taha Imeci, and Tahsin Durak 452
57-05 "Circular Shaped Microstrip Patch Antenna at 14.6 GHz"
Furkan Atalah, Mustafa Imeci, Oguzhan Gungor, S. Taha Imeci, and Tahsin Durak 454
57-06 "E-Shaped Patch Antenna at 4.87 GHz"
Ezgi Kucuk, Burak Bayram, S. Taha Imeci, and Tahsin Durak 456
57-07 "Roof Shaped Rectangular Slotted Patch Antenna at 18.3 GHz"
Melis Ecem Koca, Tahsin Durak, and S. Taha Imeci 458

Session 59: Uncertainty Quantification and Modeling for Complex Applications
59-01 "Effect of Random Antenna Element Displacements on Sparse-UCA-Root-MUSIC Direction-of-Arrival Estimation"
Veronique Inghelbrecht, Jo Verhaevert, Tanja Van Hecke, Dries Vande Ginste, Hendrik Rogier, Marc Moeneclaey, and Herwig Bruneel 460
59-02 "Designing Experiments to Reduce Uncertainty in Point Source Locations in the Helmholtz Equation"
Troy Butler 462

59-03 "Accurate and Efficient Bayesian Parameter Inversion Based on Low-Fidelity Model Solutions"
Yaning Liu 464

59-04 "Multi-Fidelity Approach for Polynomial Chaos Based Statistical Analysis of Microwave Networks"
Aditi K. Prasad and Sourajeet Roy 466

59-05 "Augmented Surrogates for Predictive Extrapolation in Electromagnetics"
Varis Carey 468

59-06 "Vector Parabolic Equation Modeling of Wireless Propagation in Tunnels with Statistically Rough Surface Walls"
Xingqi Zhang and Costas D. Sarris 470

59-07 "Ridge Approximation and Dimension Reduction for an Acoustic Scattering Model"
Paul G. Constantine, Jeffrey M. Hokanson, and Drew P. Kouri 472

59-08 "Wavelet Model of Multivariate Prior Covariance"
Aime Fournier 474

Session 60: Numerical Methods for Analysis, Design and Measurement of Antennas – 2

60-01 "A Cost-Effective Far-Field Antenna Pattern Measurement System"
Kyle Patel, Robert Jones, and Atef Elsherbeni 476

60-02 "Efficient Modeling of Antennas with Finite Conductivity using Calderon Preconditioning"
Michiel Gossye, Dries Vande Ginste, Daniel De Zutter, and Hendrik Rogier 478

60-03 "Domain Decomposition Method for Scattering from an Aircraft with Jet Engine Inlet Cavity"
Miodrag Tasic, Branko Kolundzija, and Tomislav Milosevic 480

60-04 "Improved Shaping of Reflector Antennas using a New Minimax Initialization Strategy"
Anders Eltved, Martin S. Andersen, and Oscar Borries 482

60-05 "Fast and Rigorous Method for Solving Low-Frequency Breakdown in Full-Wave Finite-Element-Based Solution of General Lossy Problems"
Li Xue and Dan Jiao 484

60-06 "Design and Optimization of Two-Dimensional Nano-Arrays for Beam Steering"
Askin Altinoklu, N. Rasoolzadeh, and Ozgur Ergul 486

Session 61: Antenna Arrays

61-01 "Pattern Synthesis of Irregular Antenna Arrays with Small Element-Counts"
Robert P. Scheeler, James L. McDonald, Arian C. Lalezari, and Joseph R. Mruk 488

61-02 "The General Sidelobe Cancellation Based on Linear Minimum Variance at Subarray Level"
Dan Wang and Guanglei Zhang 490

61-03 "Design Concepts for Broadband Antenna Arrays with Constant Half-Power Beamwidth"
Christopher Gay, Matthew Cullen, and Dimitra Psychogiou 492

61-04 "Comparison of an Isotropic Point Source and a Spherically Distributed Antenna Array"
Kristopher Buchanan, Timi Adeyemi, Carlos Flores-Molina, Sara Wheeland, and Steven Weiss 494

2018 International Applied Computational Electromagnetics Society Symposium in Denver (ACES-Denver 2018)

March 25-29, 2018
Denver, Colorado, USA

Sponsors

Lockheed Martin
LGS Innovations
Altair
Custom Microwave Inc.
WiPL-D
TECH-X

A Nyström Discretization of an Augmented Müller Surface Integral Equation

Nastaran Hendijani
Dept. of Electrical Engineering
University of Colorado Denver
Denver, CO USA
nastaran.hendijani@ucdenver.edu

Stephen D. Gedney
Dept. of Electrical Engineering
University of Colorado-Denver
Denver, CO USA
stephen.gedney@ucdenver.edu

***Abstract*— A well-conditioned surface integral equation method for the scattering from the material objects is presented. The formulation incorporates surface electric and magnetic charges into the conventional Müller formulation and adds constraints on the normal components of the magnetic and electric fields. It is arranged as an augmented Müller (A-Müller) formulation and is discretized using the locally corrected Nyström (LCN) method. Numerical results confirm that the method is accurate, well-conditioned and stable over a wide frequency range, including zero frequency, for multiply connected and complex multiscale geometries.**

Keywords*— *Locally corrected Nyström method, Müller formulation, surface integral equations

I. INTRODUCTION

A major obstacle in developing accurate and stable surface integral equation formulations for scattering by perfect conducting and penetrable objects is the low frequency breakdown of the electric field integral equation L-operator. Different strategies have been developed to address the instability including methods using the Helmholtz decomposition and Calderón-based stabilization methods [1, 2]. However, these methods have been mainly designed for the perfect electric conductors and also produce some limitations such as global loops and complexity of implementation. Some methods such as Müller remove the low frequency break down by transforming the hyper-singular kernel to a lower singularity [3]. While Müller is well conditioned, it provides inaccurate solutions at low frequencies because of the catastrophic cancellation in reconstructing the fields.

Other techniques addressing the low frequency instability of L-operator are called augmented formulations and include surface charges as additional unknowns [4, 5]. In this paper, a new augmented formulation based on the conventional Müller for scattering by penetrable objects is presented, wherein constraints on tangential and normal components of the fields in the background and the scattering media are expressed in terms of surface currents and charges and are combined in Müller form. The resulting A- Müller formulation is accurate, well-conditioned and stable and does not include line charges, charge continuity constraints, and any frequency dependent scaling of unknowns.

This work was supported in part by Office of Naval Research Grant N00014-16-1-2941.

II. A- MÜLLER FORMULATION

An electromagnetic field radiated by sources in an unbounded region V_1 with material properties (μ_1, ε_1) is incident on a material object with homogeneous material properties (μ_2, ε_2) occupying a finite volume V_2 bound by the surface $S_{1,2}$. Equivalent magnetic $(\vec{M}_{1,2})$ and electric currents $(\vec{J}_{1,2})$ are introduced on $S_{1,2}$ [6]:

$$\vec{M}_{1,2} = \vec{E}_1 \times \hat{n}\Big|_{S_{1,2}},\ \vec{J}_{1,2} = \hat{n} \times \vec{H}_1\Big|_{S_{1,2}}, \tag{1}$$

where $\vec{E}_1$ and $\vec{H}_1$ are the total electric and magnetic fields on $S_{1,2}$ just inside V_1, and $\hat{n}$ is the unit normal directed into V_1. The magnetic current continuity equation states:

$$\nabla' \cdot \vec{M}_{1,2}(\vec{r}\,') = -j\omega\rho_{m_{1,2}}, \tag{2}$$

where $\rho_{m_{1,2}}$ is the magnetic surface charge density on $S_{1,2}$, which satisfies the boundary condition:

$$\rho_{m_{1,2}} = \hat{n} \cdot \mu_1 \vec{H}_1\Big|_{S_{1,2}}. \tag{3}$$

The electric current continuity equation is defined by applying duality theorem on (2) and (3) leading to the surface electric charge density $\rho_{e_{1,2}}$. Applying surface electric and magnetic charge continuity constraints to the conventional Müller formulation one can show:

$$\begin{aligned}
&\mu_{r_1}\eta_0\vec{T}(\vec{r}) \cdot \vec{H}_1^{inc} + \mu_{r_2}\eta_0\vec{T}(\vec{r}) \cdot \vec{H}_2^{inc} = \frac{\mu_{r_1} + \mu_{r_2}}{2}\vec{T}(\vec{r}) \cdot \tilde{\vec{J}}_{1,2}(\vec{r}) \times \hat{n} \\
&-\oint\!\!\!\oint_{S_{1,2}} \vec{T}(\vec{r}) \cdot \left(\mu_{r_1}\nabla G_1(\vec{r},\vec{r}\,') - \mu_{r_2}\nabla G_2(\vec{r},\vec{r}\,')\right) \times \tilde{\vec{J}}_{1,2}(\vec{r}\,')\,ds' \\
&+j\omega\eta_0\oint\!\!\!\oint_{S_{1,2}} \vec{T}(\vec{r}) \cdot \vec{M}_{1,2}(\vec{r}\,')\left(\mu_{r_1}\varepsilon_1 G_1(\vec{r},\vec{r}\,') - \mu_{r_2}\varepsilon_2 G_2(\vec{r},\vec{r}\,')\right)ds' \\
&+\eta_0\oint\!\!\!\oint_{S_{1,2}} \vec{T}(\vec{r}) \cdot \left(\nabla G_1(\vec{r},\vec{r}\,') - \nabla G_2(\vec{r},\vec{r}\,')\right)\tilde{\rho}_{m_{1,2}}(\vec{r}\,')\,ds',
\end{aligned} \tag{4}$$

where $\vec{H}_i^{inc}$ is the incident magnetic field inside V_i, and $\vec{T}(\vec{r})$ is a test vector tangential to $S_{1,2}$, with $\vec{r} \in S_{1,2}$. $G_i(\vec{r},\vec{r}\,')$ is the Green's function in V_i, and $\vec{r}$ is an observation point in V_1. $\tilde{\rho}_{m_{1,2}} = (1/\mu_o)\rho_{m_{1,2}}$ $\tilde{\rho}_{e_{1,2}} = (1/\varepsilon_o)\rho_{e_{1,2}}$, and $\tilde{\vec{J}}_{1,2} = \eta_0\vec{J}_{1,2}$

are the scaled charge and current unknowns. μ_o and ε_o are the permeability and permittivity of the free space, respectively. η_o is the impedance of the free space. This is referred to as the A-Müller Tangential Magnetic Field Integral Equation (TMFIE). Using (2) and (3), and combining the normal constraints on the fields in the two regions in a Müller form, one can show:

$$\begin{aligned}
&\mu_{r_1}\eta_0\hat{n}\cdot\vec{H}_1^{inc}+\mu_{r_2}\eta_0\hat{n}\cdot\vec{H}_2^{inc}=\eta_0\tilde{\rho}_{m_{1,2}}(\vec{r}) \\
&-\oiint_{S_{1,2}}\hat{n}(\vec{r})\cdot\left(\mu_{r_1}\nabla G_1(\vec{r},\vec{r}')-\mu_{r_2}\nabla G_2(\vec{r},\vec{r}')\right)\times\tilde{\vec{J}}_{1,2}(\vec{r}')ds' \\
&+j\omega\eta_0\oiint_{S_{1,2}}\hat{n}(\vec{r})\cdot\vec{M}_{1,2}(\vec{r}')\left(\mu_{r_1}\varepsilon_1 G_1(\vec{r},\vec{r}')-\mu_{r_2}\varepsilon_2 G_2(\vec{r},\vec{r}')\right)ds' \qquad (5) \\
&+\eta_0\oiint_{S_{1,2}}\hat{n}(\vec{r})\cdot\left(\nabla G_1(\vec{r},\vec{r}')-\nabla G_2(\vec{r},\vec{r}')\right)\tilde{\rho}_{m_{1,2}}(\vec{r}')ds'.
\end{aligned}$$

Equation (5) forms the A-Müller Normal MFIE (NMFIE). By duality, the A-Müller TEFIE, and NEFIE are also derived.

The TMFIE, NFMIE, TEFIE, and NEFIE establish the A-Müller formulation. The formulation is discretized using the high order LCN method. TMFIE and TEFIE are discretized using divergence conforming mixed-order bases [7]. NMFIE and NEFIE are discretized using scalar bases. The tangential test vectors $\vec{T}(\vec{r})$ are unitary vectors, sampled at the mixed-order quadrature points. The normal test vectors $\hat{n}(\vec{r})$ are sampled at the scalar quadrature points.

The A-Müller formulation has the advantage that it is frequency and mesh stable. It is valid even down to zero frequency, where it exactly decouples the electrostatic and magnetostatic problems. It models the quasi-static fields through explicit representation of the charge densities. Unlike the standard Müller formulation, the error is stable even for very high contrast materials.

III. Numerical Results

The proposed A-Müller formulation is evaluated by simulating scattering from a one-meter radius dielectric sphere. The incident field is a $-\hat{\mathbf{z}}$ traveling plane wave polarized along the $\hat{\mathbf{x}}$ direction. Fig. 1 demonstrates the root mean square (RMS) error in the scattered vector electric and magnetic fields calculated by A-Müller at frequencies 1 Hz and 50 MHz. The field samples are calculated on a semi-circle with radius 1.5 m at $\varphi = 0^\circ$ plane at angles $\theta_i = 0^\circ, 1^\circ, \ldots, 180^\circ$. The errors are plotted versus LCN basis order, *p,* for different values of the relative permittivity, $\varepsilon_r = 2.0, 64.0$, of the dielectric material. The RMS errors are computed with respect to the reference analytical Mie series solution. The figure demonstrates high order convergence of the scattered electric and magnetic fields computed by A-Müller at 1Hz and 50MHz for low and high contrast dielectric sphere.

The condition number of the same sphere was computed for both the A-Müller formulation and a Volume Integral Equation (VIE) formulation as a function of the permittivity of the sphere at 1 Hz. The plot of the condition number is presented in Fig. 2. What is seen is that the A-Müller condition number is stable with ε_r, but, the condition number of the VIE grows linearly with ε_r, as is expected.

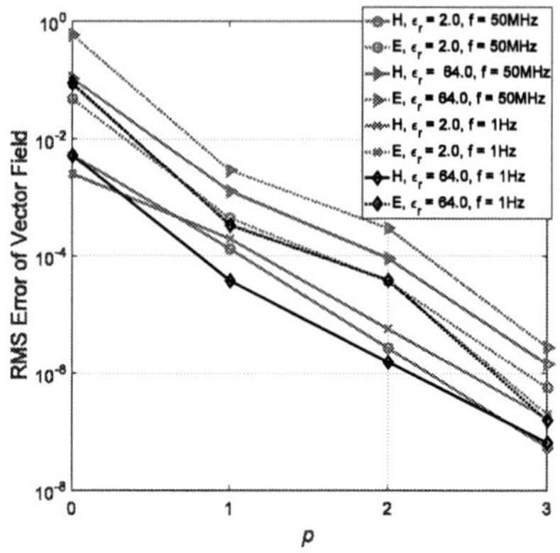

Fig. 1. The RMS error in vector magnetic (H) and electric (E) fields from A-Müller versus LCN order at 1Hz and 50MHz on the semicircle with radius 1.5 m located at $\varphi = 0^\circ$.

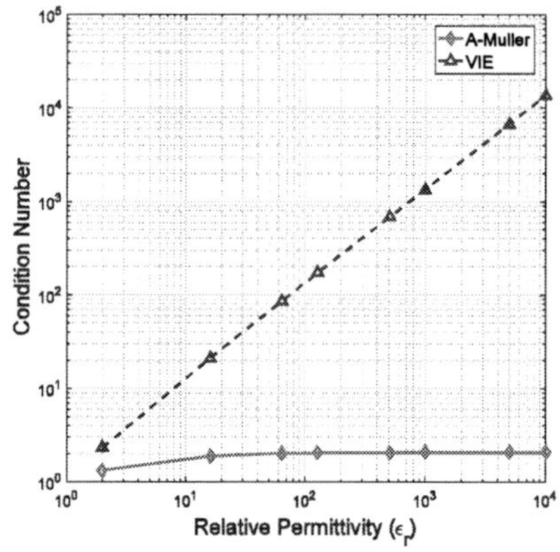

Fig. 2. Condition number of the A-Müller and VIE matrices versus relative permittivity, ε_r, for a 1 m sphere at 1Hz.

References

[1] G. Vecchi, "Loop-star decomposition of basis functions in the discretization of the EFIE," *IEEE Transactions on Antennas and Propagation,* vol. 47, pp. 339-346, Feb. 1999.

[2] F. P. Andriulli, et al., "A Multiplicative Calderon preconditioner for the electric field integral equation," *IEEE Transactions on Antennas and Propagation,* vol. 56, pp. 2398-2412, Aug. 2008.

[3] Z. Aiming, S. D. Gedney, and J. L. Visher, "A study of combined field formulations for material scattering for a locally corrected Nyström discretization," *IEEE Transactions on Antennas and Propagation,* vol. 53, pp. 4111-4120, Dec. 2005.

[4] M. Taskinen and P. Yla-Oijala, "Current and charge integral equation formulation," *IEEE Transactions on Antennas and Propagation,* vol. 54, pp. 58-67, Jan. 2006.

[5] T. Xia, et al., "An enhanced augmented electric-field integral equation formulation for dielectric objects," *IEEE Transactions on Antennas and Propagation,* vol. 64, pp. 2339-2347, June 2016.

[6] J. Stratton, "*Electromagnetic Theory*, 1st ed., New York, NY, USA: McGraw-Hill, 1941.

[7] S. D. Gedney, A. Zhu, and C. C. Lu, "Study of mixed-order basis functions for the locally-corrected nyström method," *IEEE Transactions on Antennas and Propagation,* vol. 52, pp. 2996-3004, Nov. 2004.

An Adaptive Factorization Method for Inverse Scattering Problems

Koung Hee Leem, Jun Liu, and George Pelekanos
Department of Mathematics and Statistics, Southern Illinois University Edwardsville,
Edwardsville, IL 62026, USA
kleem@siue.edu, juliu@siue.edu, gpeleka@siue.edu

***Abstract*—To drastically speed up Kirsch's factorization method for inverse scattering problems, we propose a novel adaptive algorithm that automatically generates nonuniform sampling points according to the shape of the obstacle. Built upon adaptive quadrature rules, our algorithm approximates the integral of an indicator function and yields reliable reconstructions significantly faster than the standard factorization method. Numerical tests are performed to validate the effectiveness of our algorithm.**

***Index Terms*—adaptive Simpson quadrature, inverse scattering, Kirsch's factorization method, linear sampling method.**

I. A Brief Review of Kirsch's Factorization Method

The factorization method (FM) [1], [2] provides an explicit and theoretically justified characterization for the support of a scattering object using far field measurements at fixed frequency. It is based on the idea that a point z belongs to the scatter if and only if a special test function belongs to the range of the square root of an operator that can be effortlessly computed from the far field data.

Based on the linear sampling method (LSM) [3], the factorization method (FM) solves the 'improved' far-field equation by computing the norm of a possible solution g_z of the equation below, using Pickard's criterion for many sampling points z from a grid covering a region of interest. Plotting of these norms yields a picture of the scattering object:

$$(F^*F)^{1/4}g_z = r_z := \frac{e^{i\pi/4}}{\sqrt{8\pi k}}e^{-ik\hat{x}\cdot z}.$$

In the equation above F denotes the far-field operator, k is the wavenumber, and $\hat{x} = x/|x|$ is on the unit sphere. In the finite dimensional framework, let F_n be the discretized far-field operator constructed by Nyström method [4], and let$\{\sigma_j, u_j, v_j\}_{j=1}^n$ be its singular system. Let $D \subset \mathbb{R}^2$ be the scatterer, then the standard FM is based on the following equivalence:

$$z \in D \iff r_z \in \text{Range}((F_n^*F_n)^{1/4}) \iff W(z)^{-1} < \infty,$$

where

$$W(z) := \left(\sum_{j=1}^{n} \frac{|v_j^\intercal r_z|}{\sigma_j}\right)^{-1},$$

The work of Jun Liu was supported in part by a Start-up Grant from the College of Arts and Sciences (CAS) at SIUE.

is the indicator function. The FM then determines the shape of the scatterer D as the location of those points z where $W(z)$ becomes significantly large, since the corresponding series fails to converge whenever $z \notin D$. In a standard implementation, one has to compute $W(z)$ over a uniformly spaced mesh that adequately covers the obstacle domain D. This process can be computationally very expensive, especially for those 3D applications involving large obstacles.

II. The Adaptive Factorization Method

The concept of adaptive discretization has been well studied and widely used in many fields of scientific computing, such as in numerical integration. Inspired by the fact that the indicator function $W(z)$ of the obstacle domain exploits very sharp changes across the boundary of the obstacle domain, we propose to treat the indicator function $W(z)$ as a virtual 2D function to be integrated over the global search domain S that contains the obstacle(s). To adaptively concentrate more sampling points near the to-be-determined boundary of the obstacle, we use a standard 2D adaptive Simpson's rule to perform the following global 2D integration:

$$I(W) = \iint_S W(z)\, dA,$$

where $S = [a, b] \times [c, d]$ is the initially estimated rectangle domain. It is important to mention here, that in our adaptive factorization method (AFM), we are only interested in obtaining the adaptively generated quadrature points and use them towards the approximation of I.

Let $e = (a + b)/2$ and $f = (c + d)/2$. Recall that the standard 2D Simpson's rule on $[a, b] \times [c, d]$ reads:

$$I(W) \approx S_{[a,b,c,d]}(W) := \frac{4(b-a)(d-c)}{9}\sum_{i=1}^{3}\sum_{j=1}^{3} s_{i,j}w_{i,j},$$

where $s = [s_{i,j}]$ and $w = [w_{i,j}]$ are given by:

$$s = \begin{bmatrix} 1 & 4 & 1 \\ 4 & 16 & 4 \\ 1 & 4 & 1 \end{bmatrix}, w = \begin{bmatrix} W(a,d) & W(e,d) & W(b,d) \\ W(a,f) & W(e,f) & W(b,f) \\ W(a,c) & W(e,c) & W(b,c) \end{bmatrix}.$$

The 2D adaptive Simpson's rule is based on the principle of divide and conquer, where each subdomain is recursively divided into four subdomains until the difference between two different quadrature approximations (with half step size) reaches a user-supplied tolerance tol. Following [5, p. 358], our AFM algorithm is summarized in Algorithm 1, where $I_0 = tol/\epsilon_{mach}$ where ϵ_{mach} is the machine precision. Upon getting the set $\mathcal{A}$ of computed sampling points, we can obtain the full-mesh profile via linear interpolation. The level of recursion depends on *tol* and the indicator function.

Algorithm 1 Our AFM based on 2D Simpson's rule:
Initialization: $I_H = S_{[a,b,c,d]}(W), I_0 = tol/\epsilon_{mach}$
Output: A set of sampling points $\mathcal{A} = \{(z_i, W(z_i))\}_{i=1}^N$

```
procedure Q=AFM(a, b, c, d, I_H)
    I_1 = S_[a,e,c,f](W); I_2 = S_[a,e,f,d](W)
    I_3 = S_[e,b,c,f](W); I_4 = S_[e,b,f,d](W)
    I_h = (I_1 + I_2 + I_3 + I_4)
    I_e = (16 I_h − I_H)/15                          ▷ Extrapolation
    Add newly computed points to A
    if I_0 + (I_e − I_h) == I_0 then                 ▷ Exit Recursion
        Q = I_e
    else                                             ▷ Enter Recursion
        Q_1 = AFM(a, e, c, f, I_1); Q_2 = AFM(a, e, f, d, I_2)
        Q_3 = AFM(e, b, c, f, I_3); Q_4 = AFM(e, b, f, d, I_4)
        Q = Q_1 + Q_2 + Q_3 + Q_4
    end if
end procedure
```

III. Numerical Results

In this section, we provide numerical examples to demonstrate the effectiveness of our proposed AFM. All simulations are performed using MATLAB R2016a on a laptop PC with i5 CPU@2.30GHz and 8GB RAM. The CPU time (in seconds) is estimated by timing functions *tic/toc*. To simulate noisy data, the discrete far-field matrix $F_n \in \mathbb{C}^{65\times 65}$ is perturbed into:

$$F_n^\delta = F_n + \epsilon(E_1 + iE_2)F_n,$$

where E_1 and E_2 are two random matrices with entries uniformly distributed in $[-1, 1]$, and $\epsilon > 0$ is chosen such that $\|F_n - F_n^\delta\|_2 \leq \delta = 2\%$. The Tikhonov regularization parameter is computed using the **fzero** function at each sampling point via Morozonv's discrepancy principle [6].

In Fig. 1, we compare two profiles obtained by the standard FM and our AFM, respectively, for a single kite. Our AFM used only less than 1% of the full mesh points. Here, the Structural Similarity Index (SSIM [7]) measures the similarity between two profiles. With the obtained SSIM value 0.999, the two profiles are indistinguishable to the human eye. In Table I,

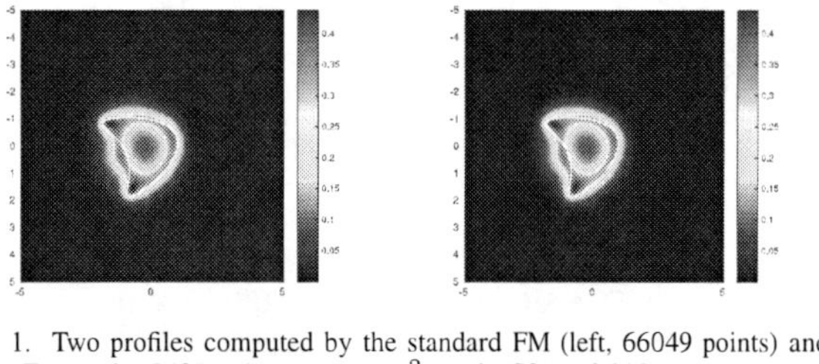

Fig. 1. Two profiles computed by the standard FM (left, 66049 points) and our AFM (right, 2437 points) on a 513^2 mesh (SSIM=0.999).

we further compare the CPU time and profile similarity from the standard FM and our AFM. Here, we also computed the Mean Squared Error (MSE) and Peak Signal-to-Noise Ratio (PSNR), which measure the difference between two profiles. The last row of Table I indicates that for a 513^2 mesh AFM is about 200 times faster than the standard FM. Moreover, in Fig. 2, we provide plots of generated nonuniform sampling points (with $n = 513$) and the comparison of CPU time between FM and AFM as a function of the mesh size n. Clearly, our AFM outperforms the traditional FM.

TABLE I
Comparison of the Standard FM and our AFM on Successively Refined Meshes with Decreasing $tol = 0.001/4^l, l = 0, 1, 2, 3, 4$.

	Standard FM		Our AFM		Profile Quality Metrics		
n	Points	CPU	Points	CPU	SSIM	MSE	PSNR
33	1089	0.8	557	0.3	0.9965	5.0e-05	43.0
65	4225	3.3	757	0.4	0.9987	8.0e-06	51.0
129	16641	13.2	1121	0.8	0.9982	8.7e-06	50.6
257	66049	53.4	2177	1.2	0.9997	8.8e-07	60.6
513	263169	200.9	3261	1.8	0.9999	1.9e-07	67.3

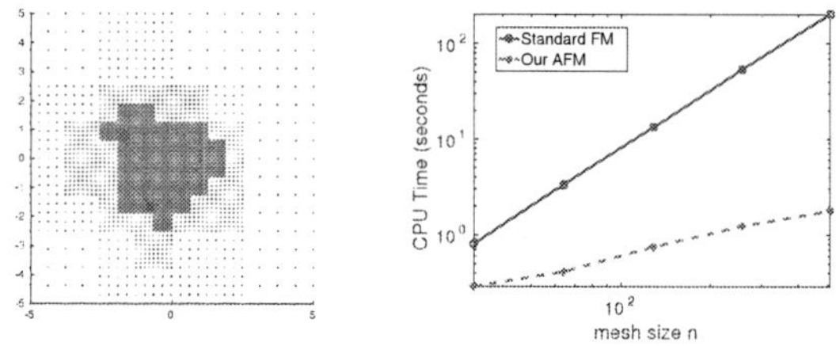

Fig. 2. The generated nonuniform sampling points of our AFM (left, $n = 513$) and the increasing CPU time as a function of the mesh size n (right).

IV. Conclusion

A novel adaptive factorization method (AFM) is proposed and the numerical results suggest a dramatic improvement over the computational efficiency of the standard factorization method. Extending this approach to three dimensional problems can be a natural continuation of this work. It is worthwhile to mention here that the multilevel linear sampling method (MLSM) [8] also demonstrates some adaptive behavior by recursively labeling and removing non-boundary cells in different levels. Comparison between our AFM and the MLSM will follow in future publications.

References

[1] A. Kirsch and N. Grinberg, *The Factorization Method for Inverse Problems*. OUP Oxford, 2008.
[2] X. Liu and B. Zhang, "Recent progress on the factorization method for inverse acoustic scattering problems," *SCIENTIA SINICA Mathematica*, vol. 45, pp. 873–890, 2015.
[3] F. Cakoni and D. Colton, *A Qualitative Approach to Inverse Scattering Theory*. Springer US, 2013.
[4] D. Colton and R. Kress, *Inverse Acoustic and Electromagnetic Scattering Theory*. Springer New York, 2012.
[5] M. Heath, *Scientific Computing: An Introductory Survey*. McGraw-Hill, 2002.
[6] D. Colton, M. Piana, and R. Potthast, "A simple method using morozov's discrepancy principle for solving inverse scattering problems," *Inverse Problems*, vol. 13, no. 6, pp. 1477–1493, 1997.
[7] Z. Wang, A. Bovik, H. Sheikh, and E. Simoncelli, "Image quality assessment: From error visibility to structural similarity," *IEEE Transactions on Image Processing*, vol. 13, no. 4, pp. 600–612, 2004.
[8] J. Li, H. Liu, and J. Zou, "Multilevel linear sampling method for inverse scattering problems," *SIAM Journal on Scientific Computing*, vol. 30, no. 3, pp. 1228–1250, 2008.

First Principles Model of Electric and Magnetic Cable Braid Penetrations

Salvatore Campione, Larry K. Warne, and William L. Langston
Electromagnetic Theory Department
Sandia National Laboratories
Albuquerque, NM, USA
sncampi@sandia.gov, lkwarne@sandia.gov, wllangs@sandia.gov

***Abstract*—In this paper, we report our recent findings about a first principles, multipole-based model of electric and magnetic cable braid penetrations. We consider for brevity a one-dimensional array of wires, but the model can be readily applied to realistic cable geometries. Comparisons between the first principles method and analytical formulas will be provided for both electric and magnetic penetration cases. These comparisons confirm that our first principles model works within the geometric characteristics of many commercial cables.**

Keywords*—*Cable braid; electric and magnetic penetration; first principles model; multipole moments.

I. Introduction

Limiting potential damage or upset of critical components due to electromagnetic coupling through electromagnetic pathways is a challenging task. One well-known pathway into components is electromagnetic penetration through braided shields used in cables.

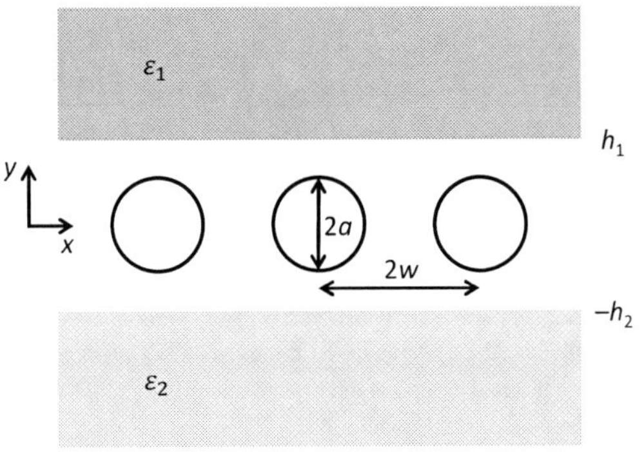

Fig. 1. A one-dimensional array of wires along the x direction with wire radius a and period $2w$. Note the wires are infinitely extended along the z direction.

Braided cables are generally modeled via transfer parameters (impedance Z_T and admittance Y_T, used to model the shield properties related to the braid weave characteristics and material) and self parameters (impedance Z_c and admittance Y_c, which are formed by the inner conductor and the shield) [1-7].

This paper discusses our recent results regarding a first principles, multipole-based cable braid electromagnetic (electric and magnetic) penetration model [5, 6, 8-10], which is able to provide estimates for all the canonical parameters of braided cables mentioned above. Our model delivers results based on the geometrical parameters of the cable in question and therefore also enables accounting for non-ideal geometry variations.

We will use our first principles model on the canonical structure [11] in Fig. 1, a one-dimensional array of wires, which can be modeled analytically through a multipole-conformal mapping expansion for the wire charges.

II. Electric Penetration

Consider the electric problem when dielectric materials are present around the array of wires as in Fig. 1. We take two dielectric half spaces with permittivities ε_1 and ε_2 above and below the wires, with the interfaces being at $y = h_1$ and $y = -h_2$, respectively. Note that the wires have radius a and period $2w$, and are in a material with permittivity ε_0 for $-h_2 < y < h_1$ and $a < h_1, h_2$.

The transfer elastance of the grid can be defined by $S_{c,j} = \phi_{c,j}/(wq) = \phi_{c,j}/(2wD_0 w)$, where D_0 is the vertical displacement field below or above the wires, q is the charge, and $\phi_{c,j}$ (the subscript j indicates internal, i, or external, e) is the difference of the electric potential at the point $y \to \pm\infty$ and a point on the wire, say at $x = 0$, $y = a$ or at $x = a$, $y = 0$. In a similar manner one could define the self elastance $S_{b,j}$ through the potential $\phi_{b,j}$, which is the counterpart of $\phi_{c,j}$ for the self-elastance computed as a limiting value in the illuminated half space with the uniform field contribution E_0 to the potential removed.

We want to compute the potentials ϕ_c and ϕ_b (both internal and external) that will be used to determine the transfer capacitance C_T and the self capacitance C_1. We decompose the total field into a uniform electric displacement plus a field generated by the multipolar charges. Because we are representing the braid wires by line multipole moment segments, these charge multipoles can be imaged in the dielectric interfaces to represent the potential in the various regions, as described in [10, 12]. Then, illuminating from below, for the shadow side of the structure, we evaluate a total potential far from the braid to find $\phi_{c,i}$. For the illuminated side of the structure, we evaluate the potential far from the braid to find $\phi_{b,e}$. When illuminating from above, for the shadow side of the structure, we evaluate a total potential far from the braid to find $\phi_{c,e}$. For the illuminated side of the structure, we evaluate the potential far from the braid to find $\phi_{b,i}$.

Consider now the case of $\varepsilon_1 = \varepsilon_0$ and $\varepsilon_2 = 2\varepsilon_0$, with $h_1 = h_2 = a$. Considering up to order $M = 2$ (quadrupole) and $M = 3$ (octopole), we plot in Fig. 2 the elastance computed using $\phi_{c,i}$ from the first principles model versus a/w as dark gray curves. We also report the analytical solution [10] as a red curve. One can notice that the agreement with the analytical conformal mapping solution is best when using up to the octopole moment, covering a dynamic range of up to $a/w = 0.6$. These results confirm that our first principles model works within the geometric characteristics of many commercial cables. More details will be shown during the presentation.

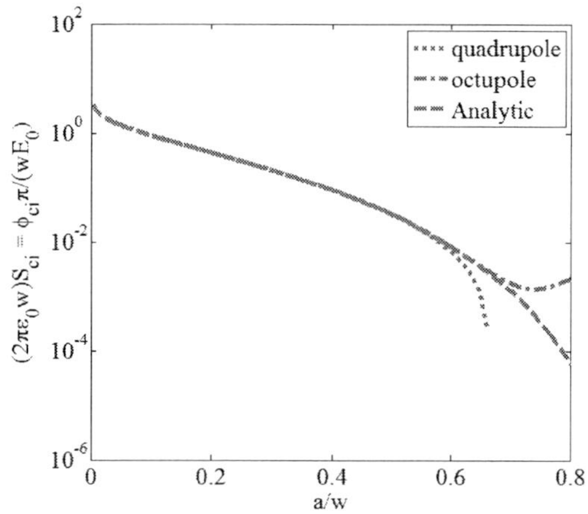

Fig. 2. The elastance $S_{c,i}$ of a one dimensional array of wires versus the ratio a/w when $\varepsilon_1 = \varepsilon_0$, $\varepsilon_2 = 2\varepsilon_0$, and $h_1 = h_2 = a$. The red dashed line corresponds to the analytical model. The dark gray lines correspond to the electric multipole penetration model up to order $M = 2$ (quadrupole) and $M = 3$ (octopole).

III. Magnetic Penetration

This is a dual problem to the electric penetration model of an array of wires discussed in the previous section [13]. One can again find analytical expressions for the one dimensional array of wires that can be compared to the first principles method solution [14]. Results will be shown during the presentation.

IV. Conclusion

We have reported recent results on electric and magnetic penetration using our first principles, multipole-based cable braid electromagnetic penetration model. The case of a one-dimensional array of wires was studied for brevity, but the model can be readily applied to realistic cable geometries. Comparisons of the transfer elastance from the first principles penetration model and the one obtained using an analytical method were shown. Magnetic penetration was also analyzed and results will be shown in the presentation. Our model is applicable within the characteristics of many commercial cables and takes into account the dependence on the actual cable geometry.

Acknowledgment

Sandia National Laboratories is a multimission laboratory managed and operated by National Technology and Engineering Solutions of Sandia, LLC, a wholly owned subsidiary of Honeywell International, Inc., for the U.S. Department of Energy's National Nuclear Security Administration under contract DE-NA-0003525.

References

[1] E. F. Vance, *Coupling to Shielded Cables*. R.E. Krieger, 1987.

[2] S. Celozzi, R. Araneo, and G. Lovat, *Electromagnetic Shielding*. John Wiley and Sons, 2008.

[3] K. S. H. Lee, *EMP Interaction: Principles, Techniques, and Reference Data*. Washington: Hemisphere Publishing Corp., 1986.

[4] F. M. Tesche, M. V. Ianoz, and T. Karlsson, *EMC Analysis Methods and Computational Models*. New York: John Wiley & Sons, Inc., 1997.

[5] L. K. Warne, W. L. Langston, L. I. Basilio, and W. A. Johnson, "Cable braid electromagnetic penetration model," *Sandia National Laboratories Report*, SAND2015-5019, Albuquerque, NM, 2015.

[6] L. K. Warne, W. L. Langston, L. I. Basilio, and W. A. Johnson, "First principles cable braid electromagnetic penetration model," *Progress in Electromagnetics Research B*, vol. 66, pp. 63-89, 2016.

[7] S. Campione, L. I. Basilio, L. K. Warne, H. G. Hudson, and W. L. Langston, "Shielding effectiveness of multiple-shield cables with arbitrary terminations via transmission line analysis," *Progress in Electromagnetics Research C*, vol. 65, pp. 93-102, 2016.

[8] W. A. Johnson, L. K. Warne, L. I. Basilio, R. S. Coats, J. D. Kotulski, and R. E. Jorgenson, "Modeling of Braided Shields," in *Proceedings of Joint 9th International Conference on Electromagnetics in Advanced Applications ICEAA 2005 and 11th European Electromagnetic Structures Conference EESE*, Torino, Italy, 2005, pp. 881-884.

[9] S. Campione, L. K. Warne, W. L. Langston, W. A. Johnson, R. S. Coats, and L. I. Basilio, "Multipole-based cable braid electromagnetic penetration model: Electric penetration case," *IEEE Transactions on Electromagnetic Compatibility*, vol. 60, pp. 444-452, 2018.

[10] S. Campione, L. K. Warne, W. L. Langston, and L. I. Basilio, "Multipole-based cable braid electromagnetic penetration model: Electric penetration pase with dielectrics," unpublished.

[11] T. Larsen, "A survey of the theory of wire grids," *IRE Transactions on Microwave Theory and Techniques*, vol. 10, pp. 191-201, 1962.

[12] T. Takashima and R. Ishibashi, "Electric fields in dielectric multi-layers calculated by digital computer," *IEEE Transactions on Electrical Insulation*, vol. EI-13, pp. 37-44, 1978.

[13] L. K. Warne, K. O. Merewether, and W. A. Johnson, "Approximations to Wire Grid Inductance," *Sandia National Laboratories Report*, SAND2007-8116, Albuquerque, NM, 2008.

[14] S. Campione, L. K. Warne, W. L. Langston, W. A. Johnson, R. S. Coats, and L. I. Basilio, "A First Principles, Multipole-Based Cable Braid Electromagnetic Penetration Model," presented at the 32nd URSI GASS, Montreal, Canada, 2017.

Flammer's Exact Solution for the Circular Conducting Disk: A Benchmark Problem for EM Software Validation

Andrew F. Peterson and Malcolm M. Bibby
School of Electrical and Computer Engineering
Georgia Institute of Technology
Atlanta, GA, USA
peterson@ece.gatech.edu, mbibby@ece.gatech.edu

***Abstract*—Flammer's exact solution for electromagnetic scattering from a circular, perfectly conducting disk is reviewed and used to assess the performance of singular basis functions within numerical solutions of the electric field integral equation. The error in both the scattering cross section and current density is computed to demonstrate that singular bases provide improved accuracy and efficiency.**

***Keywords*—electric field integral equation, numerical solution, singular basis functions, spheroidal wave functions.**

I. Introduction

A circular, perfectly conducting disk is one of only a few three-dimensional problems amenable to exact electromagnetic (EM) analysis. This makes it potentially useful as a benchmark geometry for validating EM analysis software. In addition, the induced tangential current components and charge density are singular at the disk edge, enabling the evaluation of basis functions that attempt to better model edge singularities [1].

Exact solutions for EM wave scattering from circular, perfectly conducting disks were first proposed by Andrejewski and Meixner [2] and Flammer [3-4] in the 1950s, in terms of oblate spheroidal functions. The problem of scattering from a disk is related to the problem of a circular aperture by Babinet's principle, and similar efforts were directed at the aperture problem. The vector Helmholtz equation is not separable in general spheroidal coordinates; however the disk is a special case (like the prolate spheroidal dipole antenna) where exact solutions may be constructed. The analysis includes an explicit enforcement of the edge condition on the disk rim. Because the solutions can be constructed in more than one way, the Andrejewski and Flammer solutions have very different forms.

A computer code for the radar cross section (RCS) of disks was developed by Mattson in 1970 [5], based on the Flammer formulation. In 1979, Hodge published disk RCS results and a code based on the Andrejewski formulation [6]. Those codes were subsequently used to evaluate asymptotic solutions for disk scattering and for measurement calibration [7]. Despite the fact the 1970s and 1980s also saw the development of method of moments (MoM) computational techniques that were applied to plates, circular disks, and similar structures [8-9], there appears to be no record of the disk solution used to validate computational results. Nor do there seem to be reports of computing the disk currents from the formulations of [2] or [3]. The authors have resurrected the RCS codes from [5] and [6] and have generated a new code that can also compute the current density induced on a disk by a normally-incident plane wave. A few results from the use of these tools are summarized below in connection with an assessment of singular basis functions. The exact solution and additional results will be reported in the presentation. Throughout this effort, spheroidal functions were computed using software from [10].

II. MoM Formulation

For illustration, we employ discretizations of the electric field integral equation (EFIE) on quadrilateral-cell meshes. Two discretization techniques are used to obtain numerical solutions. The first is the conventional approach using subsectional "rooftop" polynomial basis and testing functions ($p = 0.5$) [9]. The second uses the rooftop bases in conjunction with the lowest order singular vector bases from [11]. We employ an additive formulation where the singular bases are added to the representation in cells along the disk edge without removing any of the polynomial bases. Higher-order vector polynomial test functions are used in those cells (in addition to the rooftop test functions) to enforce the EFIE for the singular representation. The singular bases incorporate the leading order behavior of the current and charge singularity at that edge.

III. Results

Fig. 1 shows the convergence of the backscattered scattering cross section for a perfectly conducting disk with circumference $ka = 5$ wavelengths. Fig. 2 shows a plot of the current density induced along a cut through the disk center. Fig. 3 shows a plot of the current error versus the number of unknowns. The current error was sampled at the center of every mesh edge not having an endpoint on the disk boundary. While both MoM representations appear to converge to the exact solution, the singular bases produced more accurate results for a given number of unknowns than the conventional rooftop-basis discretization.

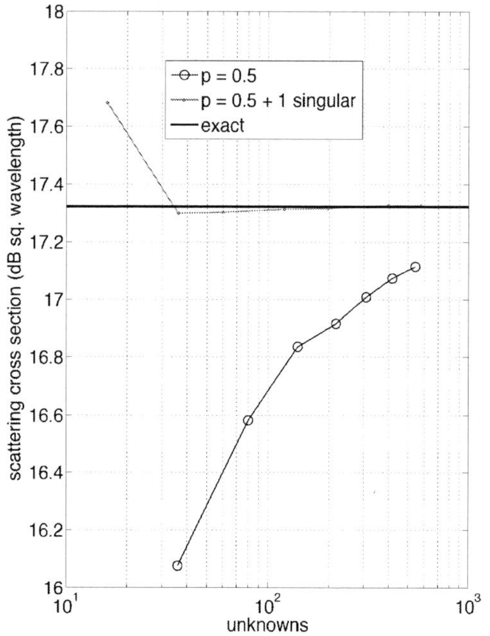

Fig. 1. Convergence of the backscattered scattering cross section for a disk with $ka = 5$. The two MoM results are compared with the exact solution.

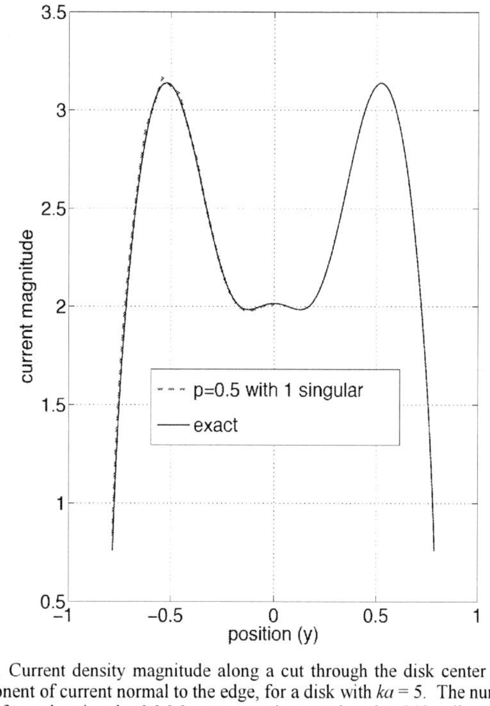

Fig. 2. Current density magnitude along a cut through the disk center for the component of current normal to the edge, for a disk with $ka = 5$. The numerical result from the singular MoM representation employed a 253-cell mesh and required 572 unknowns.

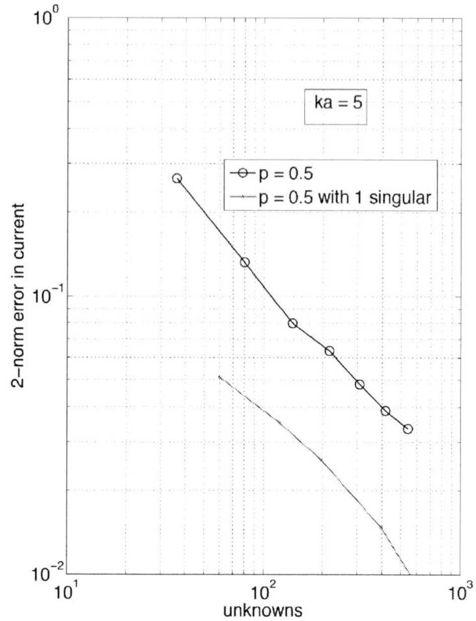

Fig. 3. Two-norm error in the current density for a disk with $ka = 5$.

REFERENCES

[1] A. F. Peterson and R. D. Graglia, "Basis functions for vertex, edge, and corner singularities: A review," IEEE J. Multiscale and Multiphysics Comp. Tech., vol. 1, pp. 161-175, December 2016.

[2] J. Meixner and W. Andrejewski, "Strenge theorie der beugung ebener elektromagnetischer wellen an der vollkommen leitenden kreisscheibe und an der kreisförmigen öffnung im vollkommen leitenden ebenen schirm," Ann. Physik, vol. 7, 157–168, 1950.

[3] C. Flammer, "The vector wave function solution of the diffraction of electromagnetic waves by circular disks and apertures. II. The diffraction problems," J. Applied Physics, vol. 24, pp. 1224-1231, September 1953.

[4] C. Flammer, Spheroidal Wave Functions. Stanford, CA: Stanford Univ. Press. 1957.

[5] G. R. Mattson, Electromagnetic Plane Wave Scattering by a Perfectly Conducting Disk. Ph.D. Dissertation, University of Michigan, 1970.

[6] D. B. Hodge, The calculation of far field scattering by a circular metallic disk, The Ohio State University ElectroScience Laboratory, Rep. 710816-2, February 1979.

[7] K. D. Trott, The Disk: A Comparison of Electromagnetic Scattering Solutions and its use as a Calibration Standard for Bistatic RCS Measurements, RADC-TR-88-16, Rome Air Development Center, February 1988.

[8] E. H. Newman and D. M. Pozar, "Electromagnetic modeling of composite wire and surface geometries," IEEE Trans. Antennas Propagat., vol. AP-26, pp. 784-788, November 1978.

[9] A. W. Glisson and D. R. Wilton, "Simple and efficient numerical methods for problems of electromagnetic radiation and scattering from surfaces," IEEE Trans. Antennas Propagat., vol. AP-28, pp. 593-603, September 1980.

[10] S. Zhang and J.-M. Jin, Computation of Special Functions. New York: Wiley, 1996.

[11] R. D. Graglia and G. Lombardi, "Singular higher order divergence-conforming bases of additive kind and moments method applications to 3D sharp-wedge structures," IEEE Trans. Antennas Propagat., vol. 56, pp. 3768-3788, December 2008.

On Compact Wideband Antenna Design Using Topology Modifications

Muhammad Aziz ul Haq and Slawomir Koziel

School of Science and Engineering, Reykjavik University, Reykjavik, Iceland
muhammadu16@ru.is, koziel@ru.is

***Abstract*—The most common way of designing compact wideband antennas is introduction of various topological modifications to the antenna radiator, feed line, or a ground plane. The claims of positive effects of such modifications (in terms of achieving better miniaturization rate) may or may not be justified. In this work, we indicate that rigorous numerical optimization of antenna parameters is mandatory in order to validate the relevance of any topology alterations. In particular, certain modifications may have minor or even negative effect on the obtainable miniaturization rate as illustrated using two case studies of UWB antennas.**

Keywords— antenna miniaturization, EM-driven design, topology modifications, wideband antennas.

I. Introduction

Small size has become one of the important criteria in the design of antennas for many applications, including wearable devices [1], internet of thigs (IoT) [2], or medical imaging [3]. In case of compact wideband antennas, reduction of the physical dimensions is typically obtained by means of various topological modifications of the basic structures (monopoles, slot antennas, etc.), applied to a radiator [4], the ground plane [5], or a feed line [6]. Clearly, a claim is made that particular modifications are important from the point of view achieving small size of the antenna. While in many cases such statements are correct, it is not always the case. The problem is that—in most publications—a comparison of the antenna structure before and after introducing modifications (some authors even provide the entire "evolution" of the topology, e.g., [7]) is meaningless because it is not based on rigorous optimization of antenna dimensions. In other words, the compared (before/after) structures are not optimal with respect to a particular set of specifications (e.g., minimum size with constraints of selected electrical/field parameters).

Here, two case studies are considered, pertinent to antenna structures proposed in the literature [8], [9]. We demonstrate that specific geometry modifications claimed to increase the miniaturization rate, are not beneficial whatsoever. In particular, the optimization process oriented towards size reduction leads to remove these modifications and the optimized antenna sizes are smaller than those reported in the literature.

II. Case Studies

Fig. 1 shows two antenna structures reported in [8] and [9], respectively. In both papers, particular modifications of the antenna radiator (C-shape slot and inverted L-strip in Antenna I, and rectangular slot in Antenna II) lead to a more compact design. The design parameters for Antenna I are $\boldsymbol{x}^{\mathrm{I}} = [l_{g1}, l_{g2}, w_{g2}, w_{g3}, w_{02}, w_{03}, l_{01}, l_{02}, l_{03}, l_{p1}, w_{p1}, w_{p2}, w_{p3}, l_1, w_1, s]^T$ (all dimensions in mm). The parameters of Antenna II are $\boldsymbol{x}^{\mathrm{II}} = [l_g, l_0, l_p, w_p, l_1, w_1, l_2, w_2, l_3, w_3, l_4, w_4, h_1, h_2]^T$. Both antennas are implemented on a 1.55-mm-thick FR-4 substrate (ε_r = 4.3). The lower bounds for parameters determining the aforementioned radiator modifications are set to zero so that the search space includes designs for which these modifications are removed altogether.

III. Results and Discussion

The antennas of Fig. 1 have been optimized for minimum size with a constraint on their reflection characteristic. In particular, the design problem was formulated as $\boldsymbol{x}^* = \mathrm{argmin}\{\boldsymbol{x} : A(\boldsymbol{x});\ S(\boldsymbol{x}) \leq -10\ \mathrm{dB}\}$, where $A(\boldsymbol{x})$ is an antenna footprint (as a function of its geometry parameters), whereas $S(\boldsymbol{x})$ is a maximum reflection level within the UWB frequency range. The problem is solved using a pattern search algorithm [10] with the reflection constrained handled explicitly. The benchmark designs are those reported in [8] and [9], respectively.

Table I shows the dimensions of Antennas I and II from [8] and [9] and those obtained as a result of the optimization process. Fig. 2 shows the topologies of the optimized antennas. Fig. 3 through 7 show the antenna reflection, total efficiency, realized gain, and radiation patterns.

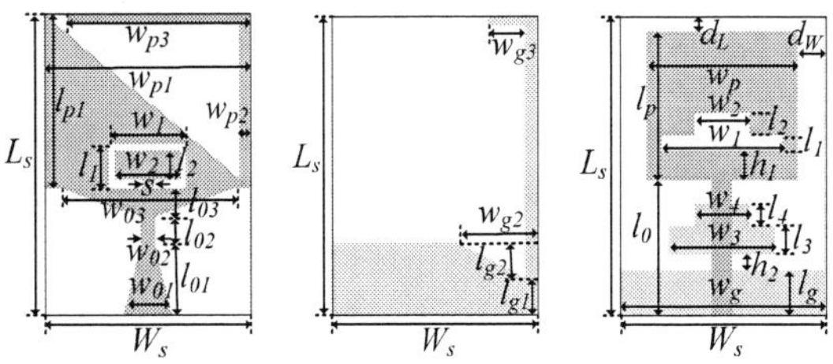

(a) (b) (c)

Fig. 1. UWB case studies considered: (a) Antenna I top [8], (b) Antenna I bottom, and (c) Antenna II [9].

TABLE I. GEOMETRY PARAMETERS OF ANTENNAS I AND II

	l_{g1}	l_{g2}	w_{g2}	w_{g3}	w_{02}	w_{03}	l_{01}	l_{02}	l_{03}	l_{p1}	w_{p1}	w_{p2}	w_{p3}	l_1	w_1	s
$\boldsymbol{x}^{\mathrm{I}}$	3	3.3	2.6	2.5	1	10.25	6	2.25	1.5	14	13	0.1	10.3	2.5	3	0.25
$\boldsymbol{x}^{*\mathrm{I}}$	3	3.3	1.9	2.5	0.9	10	6	2.2	1.5	13	12.8	0	10.3	2.5	3	0.25
	l_g	l_0	l_p	w_p	l_1	w_1	l_2	w_2	l_3	w_3	l_4	w_4	h_1	h_2		
$\boldsymbol{x}^{\mathrm{II}}$	3.5	7	10	10	0.5	8	2.5	4	1	5	0.5	4	1	1		
$\boldsymbol{x}^{*\mathrm{II}}$	6.3	10.3	11.5	9.6	0.4	1.9	0	0	0	0	0	0	2.7	0.5		

$\boldsymbol{x}^*$ denotes the optimized parametric values.

It can be observed that the radiator modifications of interest completely disappear in the course of the optimization process. This means that their incorporation into the antenna structures has actually a negative effect from the point of view of antenna miniaturization (leaving alone the fact that the obtained designs feature smaller footprints than those reported in the literature). The antenna characteristics shown in Figs. 3 through 7 also indicate that the minimum size designs have virtually identical electrical and field properties than those containing the said modifications. Obviously, rigorous numerical optimization is the only way of making such assessment.

The results of this paper allow us to draw a conclusion that proper optimization is necessary to identify the relevance of whatever topological modifications are introduced for a particular reason (here, size reduction). Unfortunately, such optimization is hardly ever executed for a bulk of reported antenna designs.

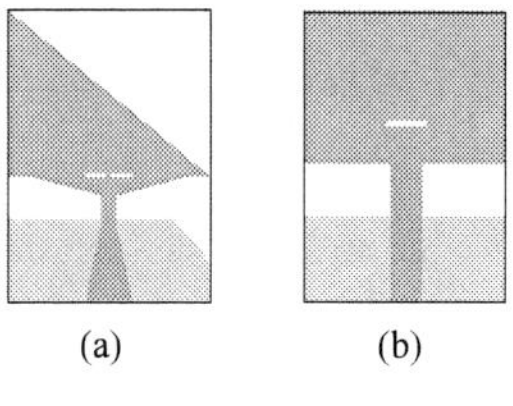

Fig. 2. Topologies of the size-optimized antennas of Fig. 1: (a) Antenna I, and (b) Antenna II. It can be observed that the radiator modifications (cf. Fig. 1) disappear in the course of the optimization process.

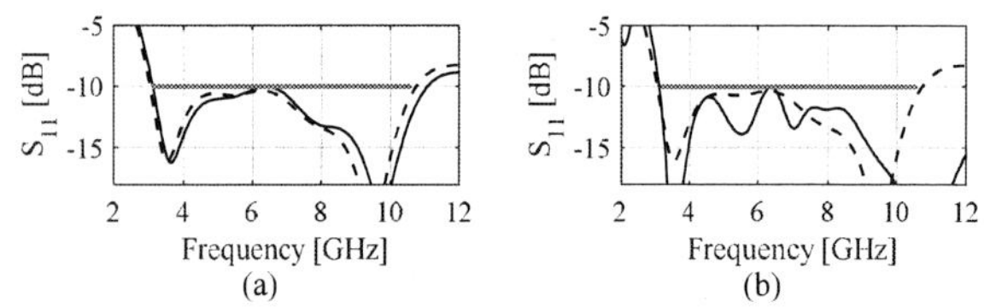

Fig. 3. Reflection responses of the antennas with the dimensions as reported in the literature (- - -) and size-optimized structure (—): (a) Antenna I, and (b) Antenna II.

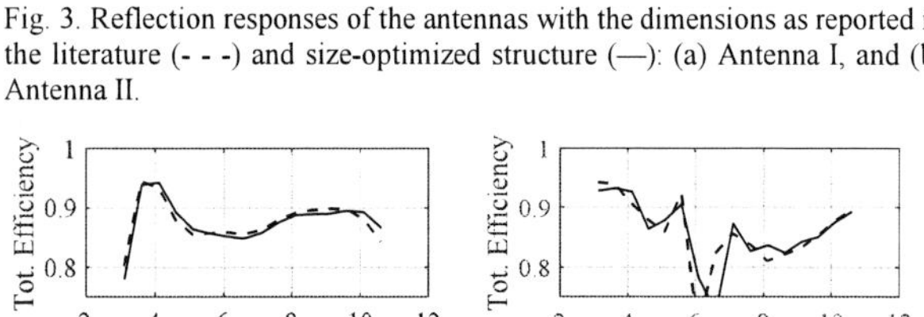

Fig. 4. Total efficiency characteristics of the antennas with the dimensions as reported in the literature (- - -) and size-optimized structure (—): (a) Antenna I, and (b) Antenna II.

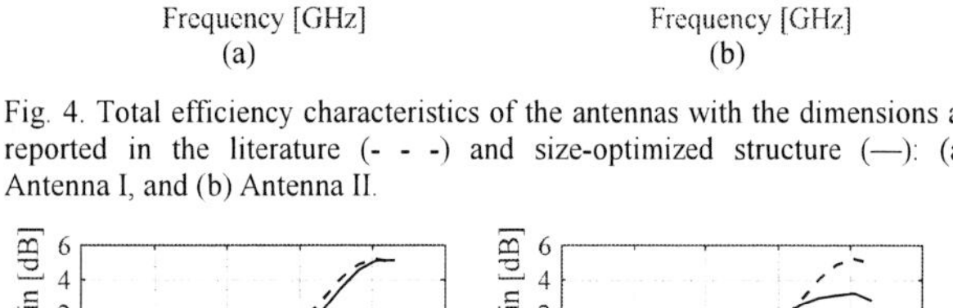

Fig. 5. Realized gain of the antennas with the dimensions as reported in the literature (- - -) and size-optimized structure (—): (a) Antenna I, and (b) Antenna II.

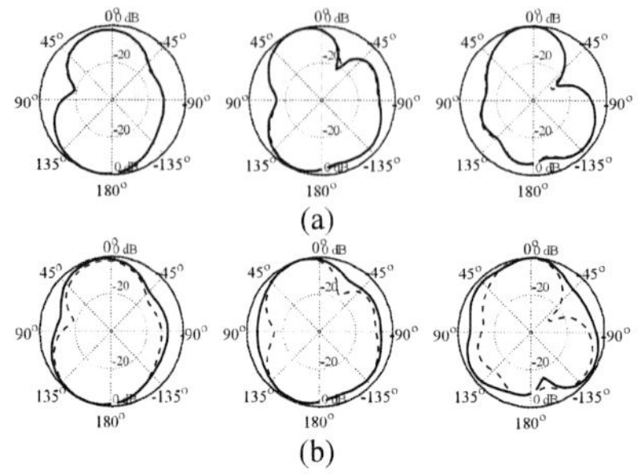

Fig. 6. E-plane radiation patterns of the antennas with the dimensions as reported in the literature (- - -) and size-optimized structure (—): (a) Antenna I, and (b) Antenna II. Left and right plots correspond to frequencies of 6 GHz, 8 GHz and 10 GHz, respectively.

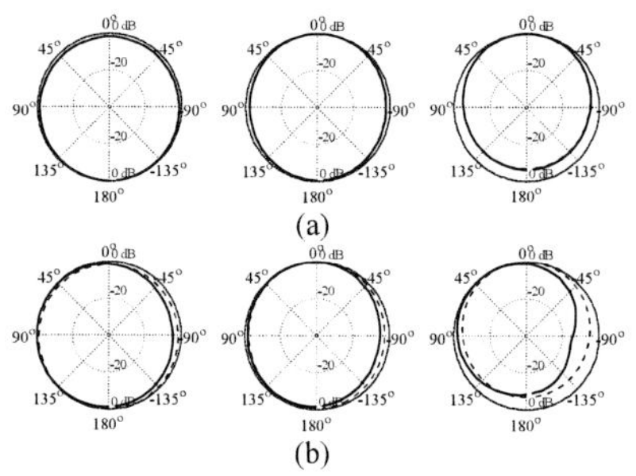

Fig. 7. H-plane radiation patterns of the antennas with the dimensions as reported in the literature (- - -) and size-optimized structure (—): (a) Antenna I, and (b) Antenna II. Left and right plots correspond to frequencies of 6 GHz, 8 GHz and 10 GHz, respectively.

ACKNOWLEDGMENT

This work is partially supported by the Icelandic Centre for Research (RANNIS) Grant 163299051.

REFERENCES

[1] A. Bekasiewicz and S. Koziel, "Structure and computationally-efficient simulation-driven design of compact UWB monopole antenna," *IEEE Ant. Wireless Prop. Lett.*, vol. 14, pp. 1282-1285, 2015.

[2] S. Koziel and A. Bekasiewicz, "A structure and simulation-driven design of compact CPW-fed UWB antenna," *IEEE Antennas and Wireless Propagation Letters*, pp. 750-753, 2016.

[3] T. Sugita, S. Kubo, A. Toya, X. Xiao, and T. Kikkawa, "A compact 4 x 4 planar UWB antenna array for 3-d breast cancer detection," *IEEE Antennas Wirel. Propag. Lett.*, vol. 12, pp. 733–736, 2013.

[4] R. N. Tiwari, P. Singh, and B. K. Kanaujia, "Dual U-slot loaded patch antenna with a modified L-probe feeding," *Journal Microw. Optoelectron. Electromagn. Appl.*, vol. 16, no. 3, pp. 646-663, 2017.

[5] M. G. N. Alsath and M. Kanagasabai, "Compact UWB monopole antenna for automotive communications," *IEEE Trans. Ant. Prop.*, vol. 63, no. 9, pp. 4204-4208, 2015.

[6] Y. Liu, P. Wang, and H. Qin, "Compact ACS-fed UWB monopole antenna with extra Bluetooth band," *Electr. Lett.*, vol. 50, no. 18, pp. 1263-1264, 2014.

[7] S. Mohammadi, J. Nourinia, C. Ghobadi, J. Pourahmadazar, and M. Shokri, "Compact broadband circularly polarized slot antenna using two linked elliptical slots for C-band applications," *IEEE Ant. Wireless Prop. Lett.*, vol. 12, pp. 1094-1097, 2013.

[8] S. Yadav, A. K. Gautam, B. K. Kanaujia, and K. Rambabu, "Design of band-rejected UWB planar antenna with integrated Bluetooth band," *IET Microwaves, Ant. Prop.*, vol. 10, No. 14, pp. 1528-1533, 2016.

[9] M. Ojaroudi, S. Yazdanifard, N. Ojaroudi, and M. N. Moghaddasi, "Small square monopole antenna with enhanced bandwidth by using inverted T-shaped slot and conductor-backed plane," *IEEE Trans. Ant. Prop.*, vol. 59, no. 2, pp. 670-674, 2011.

[10] S. Koziel, "Computationally efficient multi-fidelity multi-grid design optimization of microwave structures," *Applied Computational Electromagnetics Society Journal*, vol. 25, no. 7, pp. 578-586, 2010.

Design Optimization of Novel Compact Circular Polarization Antenna

Slawomir Koziel[1,2] and Adrian Bekasiewicz[1,2]

[1] School of Science and Engineering, Reykjavik University, Reykjavik, Iceland
[2] Faculty of Electronics, Telecommunications and Informatics, Gdansk University of Technology, 80-233 Gdansk, Poland
koziel@ru.is, bekasiewicz@ru.is

***Abstract*—The paper describes a structure and a design optimization procedure of a miniaturized circular polarization antenna with elliptical ground plane slots and feed line with stepped-impedance stubs. Constrained optimization of all antenna parameters is executed in order to explicitly reduce the antenna size while maintaining required impedance axial ratio bandwidth of 5 GHz to 7 GHz at the same time. The size of the optimized antenna is only 16.2 mm x 16.7 mm (footprint of 271 mm^2). At the same time, the electrical and field properties of the structure are competitive for state-of-the-art designs as indicated by the comparison provided in the paper.**

Keywords—axial ratio, circular polarization antennas, compact antennas, design optimization, EM-driven design.

I. Introduction

Circular polarization (CP) antennas are of high interest for contemporary mobile communication systems [1], [2] due to advantages of CP such as simplifying a TX/RX path, mitigation of the effects of weather conditions, or multipath reflections on the antenna performance. In case of planar antennas, the simplest way of establishing CP operation is utilization of appropriate feeding networks [3], which, however, hinders miniaturization attempts. Compact CP antennas can be realized using various geometrical modifications involving notches, stubs and slots [4], [5]. Clearly, proper adjustment of geometry parameters is necessary in order to achieve reduction of the physical dimensions of the structure while controlling the antenna reflection response and—even more importantly—the axial ratio (AR) bandwidth. A standard approach is parameter sweeping [6], [7], which fails to provide optimum results for miniaturization.

In this paper, we discuss a structure and a design procedure of a novel CP antenna which is a modification of the design proposed in [6]. In order to permit improved miniaturization, the asymmetrical stubs allocated on the opposite sides of the feed line are loaded with low-impedance lines and the ground plane structure is simplified by removing rectangular slots. Rigorous constrained optimization of all geometry parameters of the antenna allows to reduce its size to only 16.2 mm × 16.7 mm (footprint of 271 mm^2). At the same time, the required 3dB AR bandwidth of 5 GHz to 7 GHz is preserved, similarly as the impedance bandwidth. Comprehensive benchmarking indicates that the presented antenna is competitive to state-of-the-art CP structures reported in the literature. Given its operating bandwidth, the antenna may be suitable for C-band applications exploiting Industrial, Scientific and Medical (ISM) frequencies, as well as 5.2 GHz and 5.8 GHz WLAN.

II. CP Antenna Structure

The antenna structure is shown in Fig. 1. The substrate is Taconic RF-35 ($\varepsilon_r = 3.5$, $h = 0.762$ mm). The antenna is based on the design of [6], where CP operation is obtained by means of two stubs connected to the feed line. Here, to improve AR bandwidth, the low-impedance load is attached to one of the stubs. Also, the rectangular ground plane slots are removed. The antenna geometry is parameterized by fifteen variables $\boldsymbol{x} = [l_{fr}, l_{1r}, l_{2r}, l_3, l_4, l_5, w_{1r}, w_{11}, w_{2r}, w_3, w_{4r}, g_1, g_{11}, g_3, o]^T$, whereas $w_f = 1.7$ to ensure 50 ohm input impedance. Relative parameters are $l_f = (l_3 + 2l_5 + l_6 + o)l_{fr}$, $l_1 = (l_f - g_1)l_{1r}$, $l_2 = (l_f - g_2)l_{2r}$, $w_1 = 0.5(2w_3 + 2o - w_f)w_{2r}$, and $w_4 = 0.5(2w_3 + 2o)w_{4r}$. The computational model of the antenna is simulated in CST (1,700,000 mesh cells, evaluation time 10 min). The model contains an SMA connector. The desired bandwidth (reflection- and AR-wise) is 5 GHz to 7 GHz.

III. Design Optimization Methodology

The goal is to obtain the minimum antenna size $A(\boldsymbol{x})$ while satisfying the following two conditions: (i) $S(\boldsymbol{x}) \leq -10$ dB, and (ii) $AR(\boldsymbol{x}) \leq 3$ dB, where $S(\boldsymbol{x})$ is the maximum in-band reflection, and $AR(\boldsymbol{x})$ is the maximum axial ratio, both within the 5 GHz to 7 GHz frequency range. The design problem can be posed as a nonlinear minimization task of the form

$$\boldsymbol{x}^* = \arg\min_{\boldsymbol{x}} \{A(\boldsymbol{x})\}, \quad S(\boldsymbol{x}) \leq -10\,\text{dB}, \quad AR(\boldsymbol{x}) \leq 3\,\text{dB} \cdot \quad (1)$$

Because both constraints are expensive (in computational terms), they are handled implicitly using a penalty function approach. Thus, the design task is reformulated as

$$\boldsymbol{x}^* = \arg\min_{\boldsymbol{x}} U(\boldsymbol{x}) \, , \quad (2)$$

where the objective function U is defined as

$$U(\boldsymbol{x}) = A(\boldsymbol{x}) + \beta_1 \max\left\{\frac{S(\boldsymbol{x})+10}{10}, 0\right\}^2 + \beta_2 \max\left\{\frac{AR(\boldsymbol{x})-3}{3}, 0\right\}^2 \cdot \quad (3)$$

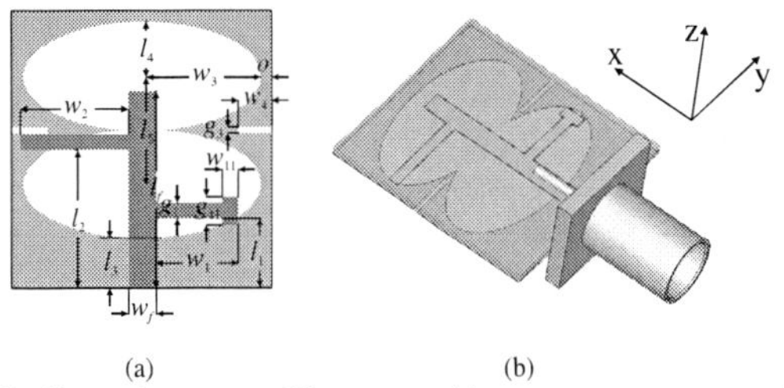

(a) (b)

Fig. 1. Proposed compact CP antenna: (a) structure geometry, and (b) visualization of the antenna EM model.

The penalty terms increase the objective function value if the reflection and AR thresholds are violated. The problem (2), (3) is solved using a trust-region gradient search [8] with derivatives of the antenna responses obtained using finite differentiation. Penalty coefficients β_1 and β_1 are set to 20.

IV. Results and Benchmarking

The antenna of Fig. 1 has been optimized using a technique of Section III. The final design is $x^* = [0.71, 0.38, 0.76, 2.99, 3.27, 6.45, 0.7, 1, 0.93, 7.38, 0.27, 0.93, 1.68, 0.36, 0.72]^T$. Another design has been obtained for comparison purposes with the optimization process oriented towards AR improvement with reflection constraints: $x^\# = [0.72, 0.4, 0.76, 3.1, 3.48, 6.58, 0.68, 1, 0.93, 7.6, 0.27, 0.93, 1.69, 0.36, 1.05]^T$. The reflection and AR characteristics are shown in Fig. 2. The antenna footprint is only 271 mm^2 versus 306 mm^2 for the structure optimized for minimum AR. At the same time, AR is below 3 dB and reflection does not exceed –10 dB for the entire frequency range of interest. For additional comparison, the antenna of [6] was re-optimized for the frequency range 5 GHz to 7 GHz, resulting in the maximum AR of 2.65 dB but much larger size of 396 mm^2. Fig. 3 shows comparison of the right- (RHCP) and left-handed circularly polarized patterns (LHCP) obtained in the xy-plane (cf. Fig. 1) at 5 GHz, 6 GHz, and 7 GHz. Fig. 4 shows realized gain in z-direction (see Fig. 1) and total efficiency of the antenna of Fig. 1 optimized for minimum size. The average in-band gain and efficiency are over 2.8 dB, and around –0.3 dB (or 93 percent), respectively.

Table I shows comparison between the proposed structure and several state-of-the-art CP antennas. For fair comparison, dimensions reported in Table I are expressed in terms of guided wavelength λ_g calculated at the low edge f_L of the bandwidth determined by –10 dB reflection for the substrate parameters. It is observed that our antenna offers the broadest AR bandwidth and the smallest size (in terms of λ_g) among the compared radiators. At the same time, it offers competitive impedance bandwidth. Note that re-optimized antenna of [6] features narrower AR bandwidth and larger size. This indicates the relevance (in the miniaturization and performance context) of the topological modifications introduced in the proposed antenna.

Acknowledgment

This work is partially supported by the Icelandic Centre for Research (RANNIS) Grant 174114051 and by National Science Centre of Poland Grant 2014/15/B/ST7/04683.

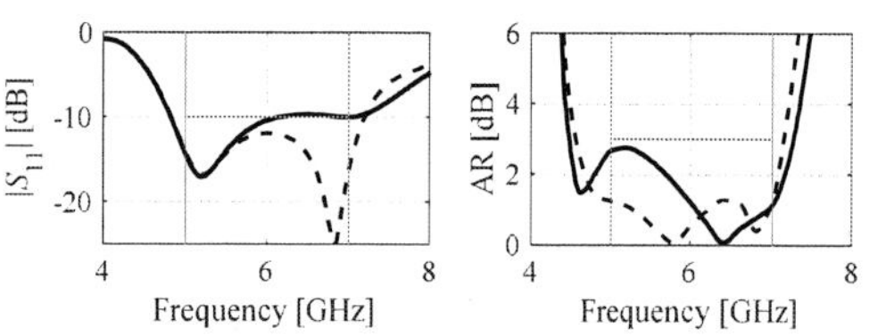

(a) (b)

Fig. 2. Responses of the proposed compact CP antenna, optimized for minimum size (—) and optimized for best in-band AR (- - -): (a) reflection and (b) axial-ratio.

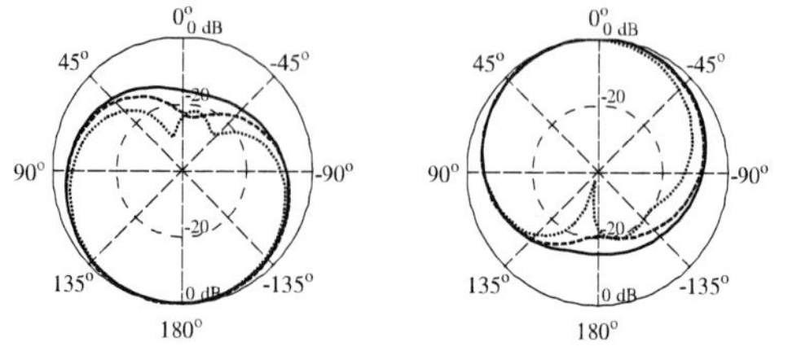

(a) (b)

Fig. 3. E-field radiation patterns obtained in xy-plane for the antenna optimized for minimum size at 5 GHz (—), 6 GHz (– –) and 7 GHz (····) frequencies: (a) LHCP and (b) RHCP.

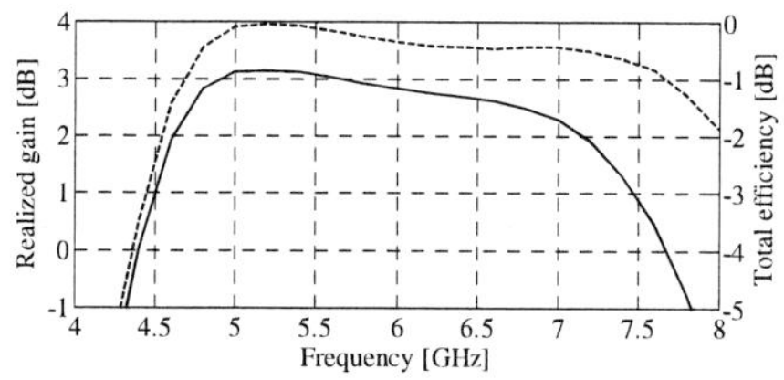

Fig. 4. Realized gain (—) obtained in z-direction and total efficiency (– –) of the size-optimized antenna of Fig. 1.

Table I. Comparison with State-of-the-Art CP Antennas

Structure	f_L [GHz]	AR BW [GHz]	$\lvert S_{11}\rvert$ BW [GHz]	Dimensions [mm]	Dimensions [λ_g]	Size [λ_g^2]
[9]	2.40	0.05	0.14	60.0 × 60.0	0.88 × 0.88	0.77
[10]	4.20	1.00	1.50	34.5 × 28.0	0.88 × 0.72	0.63
[11]	1.82	1.39	1.26	70.0 × 70.0	0.80 × 0.80	0.64
[6] (see Fig. 2)	4.66	2.10	3.10	20.5 × 19.2	0.53 × 0.49	0.26
[6]	4.41	2.27	3.52	20.0 × 20.0	0.54 × 0.54	0.29
This work	4.82	2.82	2.20	16.2 × 16.7	0.43 × 0.44	0.19

References

[1] M. Ur-Rehman, Q. H. Abbasi, M. Akram, and C. Parini, "Design of band-notched ultra wideband antenna for indoor and wearable wireless communications," *IET Micr., Ant. Prop.*, vol. 9, no. 3, pp. 243-251, 2015.

[2] L. Lizzi and F. Ferrero, "Use of ultra-narrow band miniature antennas for internet-of-things applications," *El. Lett.*, vol. 51, no. 24, pp. 1964-1966, 2015.

[3] W. Lin and H. Wong, "Wideband circular-polarization reconfigurable antenna with L-Shaped feeding probes," *IEEE Ant. Wireless Prop. Lett.*, vol. 16, pp. 2114-2117, 2017.

[4] C. J. Wang, M. H. Shih, and L. T. Chen, "A wideband open-slot antenna with dual-band circular polarization," *IEEE Ant. Wireless Prop. Lett.*, vol. 14, pp. 1306-1309, 2015.

[5] J. M. Kovitz, H. Rajagopalan, and Y. Rahmat-Samii, "Circularly polarised half E-shaped patch antenna: a compact and fabrication-friendly design," *IET Microwaves, Ant. Prop.*, vol. 10, no. 9, pp. 932-938, 2016.

[6] S. Mohammadi, J. Nourinia, C. Ghobadi, J. Pourahmadazar and M. Shokri, "Compact broadband circularly polarized slot antenna using two linked elliptical slots for C-band applications," *IEEE Ant. Wireless Prop. Lett.*, vol. 12, pp. 1094-1097, 2013.

[7] S. Ahdi Rezaeieh, A. Abbosh, and M.A. Antoniades, "Compact CPW-fed planar monopole antenna with wide circular polarization bandwidth," *IEEE Ant. Wireless Prop. Lett.*, vol. 12, pp. 1295-1298, 2013.

[8] A. Conn, N. I. M. Gould, P. L. Toint, *Trust-region methods*, MPS-SIAM Series on Optimization, Philadelphia, 2000.

[9] F. J. Huang, T. C. Yo, C. M. Lee, and C. H. Luo, "Design of circular polarization antenna with harmonic suppression for rectenna application," *IEEE Ant. Wireless Prop. Lett.*, vol. 11, pp. 592-595, 2012.

[10] Z. Wu, L. Li, Y. Li, and X. Chen, "Metasurface superstrate antenna with wideband circular polarization for satellite communication application," *IEEE Ant. Wireless Prop. Lett.*, vol. 15, pp. 374-377, 2016.

[11] T. Fujimoto and K. Jono, "Wideband rectangular printed monopole antenna for circular polarisation," *IET Microwaves, Ant. Prop.*, vol. 8, no. 9, pp. 649-656, 2014.

PEEC-Based Multi-Objective Synthesis of NFC Antennas in the Presence of Conductive Structures

Thomas Bauernfeind, Paul Baumgartner, Oszkar Biro, Christian Magele, and Werner Renhart
Institute of Fundamentals and Theory in Electrical Engineering
Graz University of Technology
Graz, Austria
t.bauernfeind@tugraz.at

Riccardo Torchio
Dipartimento di Ingegneria Industriale
Università degli Studi di Padova
Padova, Italy

***Abstract*—Near Field Communication (NFC) techniques are widely used within everyday activities, e.g., contactless payment systems or authentication. Regardless of the application typically the requirements on the antenna structure are manifold. Frequently limitations in the available space make the antenna design quite challenging especially if other conductive structures are close to the NFC antenna. In the present paper we propose to synthesize the geometry of proximity integrated circuit card (PICC) antennas according to class 6 in the presence of nearby metallic structures. The optimization relies on the differential evolution strategy. The computation of the forward problem is based on the partial element equivalent circuit (PEEC) method.**

Keywords*—*NFC antennas; numerical optimization; partial element equivalent circuit method.

I. Introduction

Within the contactless communication technologies the NFC services have found a mass market in the last decade. Nearly all new mobile devices like smart phones or tablet PCs are equipped with NFC technologies. Although the functionality of these devices has become very complex, they tend to become smaller in size. Hence, this leads to a reduced space for the certain services. Therefore, the requirements on the NFC antenna design are increasing. Typically the antenna designer has to find a suitable structure which enables the operation of the NFC device in the three dimensional NFC operating volume [1] which is defined by the NFC Forum.

Since the communication at the operating frequency of 13.56 MHz is established in the near field of the antennas, typically loop antennas like the one shown in Fig. 1 are utilized. Following the common design rules for the design of a PICC, the NFC transponder IC and the antenna structure should result in a resonant circuit at the operating frequency [2]. Typically the input capacitance of the NFC transponder IC is not sufficiently large to fulfill this recommendation, hence an external tuning capacitance is needed [2].

In addition to the tuning to the operating frequency, also the power transmission between the NFC devices has to be taken into account which is controlled by an additional matching circuitry. Especially in terms of standard compliance this behavior is essential. Typically the external matching circuit is developed subsequently to the design of the antenna structure [3], hence the NFC device does not necessarily result in an optimum design. Therefore, in the present paper we propose to optimize the antenna structure and the needed matching circuit in parallel during the numerical optimization process taking into account metallic structures which can be close to the NFC antenna structure. To enable this process the PEEC-method is applied since it permits a direct treatment of lumped components and the discretized antenna structure in a single system of equations.

It has been shown that stochastic optimization strategies deliver reasonable good results especially when the behavior of the objective function in the multi-dimensional parameter space is not very well known like it is the case for the present optimization task. For the present optimization task the differential evolution strategy [4] has been chosen.

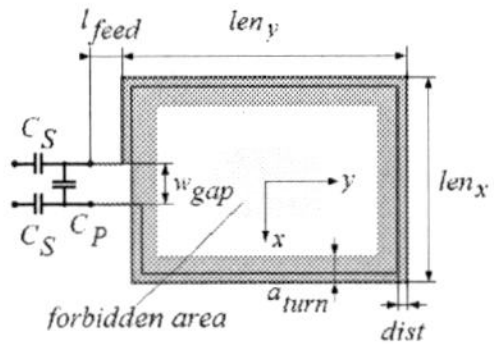

Fig. 1. Typical NFC antenna structure connected to a matching circuitry. For class 1 antennas a forbidden area is present; for class 6 no forbidden area is given.

II. Reader Power Requirements in the NFC Forum Operating Volume

A major test criterion within the standard compliance tests is the so called reader power requirements test. According to this test the NFC device is operated in reader mode (the device acts as polling device) and should conduct the communication to the NFC listening devices in card mode. Within this test the generated field strength of the polling device is measured with three standardized so called listener devices (Listener 1, 3 and 6) in the NFC Forum operating volume which is shown in Fig. 2. The field strength levels are measured in terms of voltages at specific load resistances at the defined points in the operating volume (see Table I). Please note that the load resistance values had to be modified to enable a frequency domain evaluation.

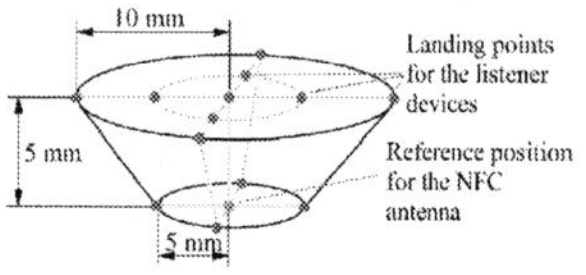

Fig. 2. NFC Operating Volume defined by the NFC Forum. Compliance tests have to be carried out at each point in the volume.

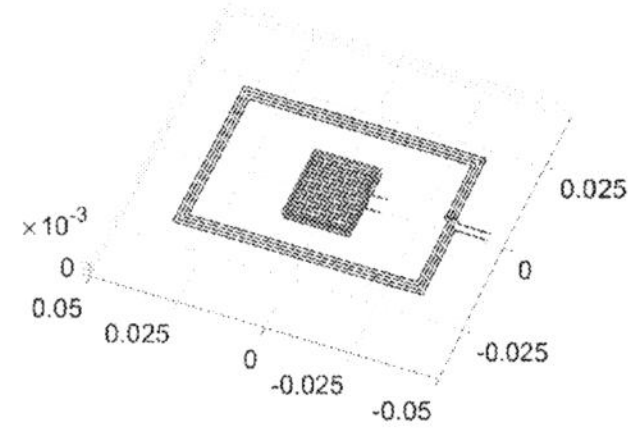

Fig. 3. PEEC-model for the numerical optimzation process; Test antenna (red) with metal grid and Listener 1 antenna (blue).

For the numerical optimization the NFC antenna under test as well as the listener devices has been modeled in terms of one-dimensional PEEC stick elements [5]. To take into account conductive material close to the antenna a dense grid structure is used. Fig. 3 shows such a test configuration. Numerical tests have shown that the strongest influence of the conductive structure is give when it has roughly the same dimensions as the antenna under test. Therefore, for the first investigations we decided to test such configurations. Naturally, the biggest influence of the metal grid is given when the grid is very close to the antenna under test. The design parameters for the first test case (class 6 antenna) are $\mathbf{p}_{cl6} = [len_x, len_y, dist, a_{turn}, C_S, C_P, R_P]$. The design parameters for the antenna geometry are limited according to the corresponding ISO/IEC definitions. For the test case it is assumed that the antenna is manufactured on a FR-4 substrate material with a thickness of 1.55 mm. In the PEEC model therefore the smallest distance between the metal structure and the antenna under test is mainly defined by the thickness of the substrate material. The objective set consists of the number of turns N_{turns}, the antennas quality factor Q_{Ant} as well as of the power levels at the listener devices computed from the voltages at the specific listener resistances ($H_{minList1}$, $H_{maxList1}$, $H_{minList3}$, $H_{maxList3}$, $H_{minList6}$, $H_{maxList6}$). Applying fuzzy functions [6] for all objectives a scalar objective function can be defined:

$$f(\mathbf{p}) = \mu_{N_{turns}}(\mathbf{p}) + \mu_{Q_{Ant}}(\mathbf{p}) + \sum_{i=1,3,6} \mu_{H_{min}L_i}(\mathbf{p}) + \sum_{i=1,3,6} \mu_{H_{max}L_i}(\mathbf{p}). \quad (1)$$

For our test problems (1) is minimized.

III. Results and Discussion

According to the standard, two requirements have to be fulfilled for all Listener devices: the so called H_{min} and the H_{max} test. For the H_{min} test the antenna under test must generate a field-strength which enables a voltage at the listener devices' load resistance which is above the limits presented in Table I.

TABLE I
Load Resistance Values and Voltage Levels

		Listener 1	Listener 3	Listener 6
H_{min}	R_{List} in Ω	620	505	380
	V_{Test} in V	4.1	3.14	3.79
H_{max}	R_{List} in Ω	62	53.5	41
	V_{Test} in V	2.85	2.5	2.23

For the H_{max} test the voltage must not exceed the limits in Table I. Due to the fact that for all points in the operating volume and for all listener devices the induced voltage has to be computed, a large number (3x14x2) of forward problems has to be computed for each population. For the class 6 test problem we have obtained a parameter set given to be $\mathbf{p}_{cl6} = [0.024m, 0.0175m, 336\mu m, 0.0628, 118pF, 372pF, 9.9k\Omega]$. The results have been obtained for a population size of $n = 20$ and $it_{max} = 100$ iterations. A similar optimization process for a class 6 antenna in the absence of conductive materials has been carried out, too. As can be seen from the post processing shown in Fig. 4 (a), a qualitatively similar behavior at the matching circuit can be obtained although e.g. N_{turns} is different. On the other hand as shown in Fig. 4 (b), the input impedance vary widely if the metal grid is removed for the optimized antenna (which is optimized provided that the metal is present).

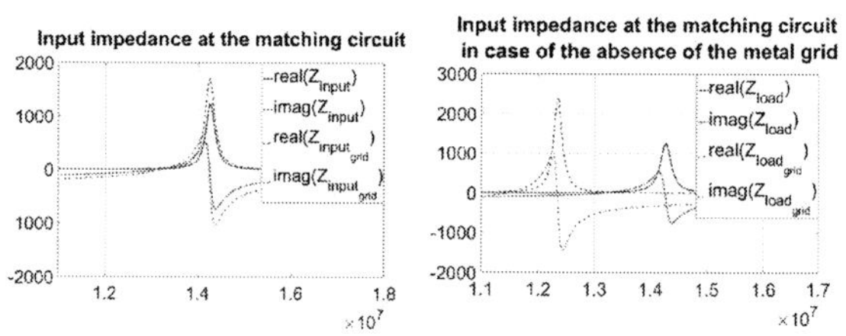

Fig. 4. (a) Input impedance at the matching circuit for class 6 antenna. Dashed lines give the antenna with the conductive structure. (b) Input impedance at the matching circuit in case of removing the conductive structure.

References

[1] M. Gebhart, R. Neubauer, M. Stark, and D. Warnez, "Design of 13.56 MHz smartcard stickers with ferrite for payment and authentication," 2011 3rd International Workshop on Near Field Communication, Hagenberg, 2011, pp. 59-64.

[2] T. Bauernfeind, K. Preis, W. Renhart, O. Bíró, and M. Gebhart, "Finite element simulation of impedance measurement effects of NFC antennas," *IEEE Trans. Magn.*, 51(3), pp. 1-4, 2015.

[3] M. Roland, H. Witschnig, E. Merlin, and C. Saminger, "Automatic impedance matching for 13.56 MHz NFC antennas," *2008 6th International Symposium on Communication Systems, Networks and Digital Signal Processing*, Graz, 2008, pp. 288-291.

[4] P. Alotto, "A hybrid multiobjective differential evolution method for electromagnetic device optimization," *COMPEL-The International Journal for Computation and Mathematics in Electrical and Electronic Engineering*, 30(6), pp. 1815-1828, 2011.

[5] T. Bauernfeind, P. Baumgartner, O. Bíró, C. A. Magele, K. Preis, and R. Torchio, "PEEC-based multi-objective synthesis of non-uniformly spaced linear antenna arrays," *IEEE Trans. Magn.*, 53(6), pp. 1-4, 2017.

[6] Ch. Magele, G. Fürntratt, B. Brandstätter, and K. R. Richter, "Self adaptive fuzzy sets in multi objective optimization using genetic algorithms," *Applied Computational Electromagnetics Society Journal*, 12(2), pp. 26-31, 1997.

Synthesis of NFC Antenna Structure under Multi-Card Condition

Paul Baumgartner, Thomas Bauernfeind, Oszkar Biro, Christian Magele, and Werner Renhart
Institute of Fundamentals and Theory in Electrical Engineering
Graz University of Technology
Graz, Austria
paul.baumgartner@tugraz.at

Riccardo Torchio
Dipartimento di Ingegneria Industriale
Università degli Studi di Padova
Padova, Italy

***Abstract*—Wireless communication technologies such as Near Field Communication (NFC) found its way into our everyday life. The antenna structures used in such systems have to comply with several standards to achieve all requirements defined for the specific application. However, in practice there are scenarios for such antennas which are not considered in standards or design guides, but mainly influence the antenna behavior. In the present paper the synthesis of an antenna used for NFC-cards in a contactless payment system under multi-card condition is presented. The optimization relies on the differential evolution (DE) strategy. The computation of the forward problem is based on the partial element equivalent circuit (PEEC) method.**

Keywords*—*Near field communication; numerical optimization; partial element equivalent circuit method.

I. Introduction

NFC applications, which belong to the contactless communication technologies, have become popular within the last decade. Especially for the usage of contactless payment systems a big increase is recognized. Although there are design guides and standards which describe the requirements and limits of the antennas for such systems, there are applications and use cases which are not covered by the standards but have significant impact on the overall system behavior.

One of those use cases for contactless payment is a wallet loaded with credit cards or cash cards of different providers, which should operate under those conditions. The standard for contactless payment EMVCo [1] only defines parameters for a system consisting of a Proximity Coupling Device (PCD), which provides the power to one Proximity IC Card (PICC). There are specific tests for the power and data transfer defined in a given three dimensional operating volume, as shown in Fig. 1. The simulation and antenna design under these standardized tests have been done by [2], but without considering, e.g., multi-card condition.

The communication of a NFC device is established at an operating frequency of 13.56 MHz in the near field surrounding the antennas, consequently loop antennas are utilized. For achieving optimal power transfer, the system

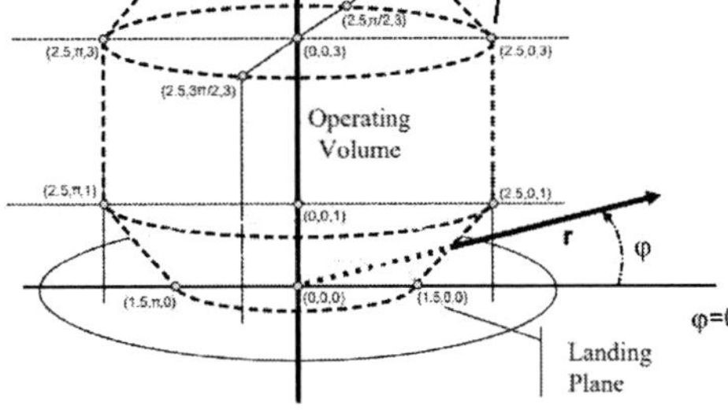

Fig. 1. Operating Volume defined by EMVCo [1]. Tests have to be carried out in different defined points of this volume.

consisting of the PCD and the PICC should result in a resonance frequency at 13.56 MHz.

In this paper the synthesis of a PICC-antenna with its corresponding matching network under the effect of multiple stacked PICC-cards is done. Aspects for conformance to the ISO/IEC14443 [3] as well as the EMVCo standard [1] are considered.

II. NFC Requirements

The tests for designing a PICC-antenna, with respect to the power transfer (defined in the EMVCo standard), forces to place the defined Poller-0 antenna [1] in the landing plane of the operating volume, as shown in Fig. 1. The PCD should be matched to an input impedance of Z=50 Ω at the operating frequency. To fulfill the resonance requirements, the PICC antenna is connected to a matching circuit, as shown in Fig. 2. To simulate the terminals of the card-IC, an input impedance is connected, which values were taken from [4]. The standardization test demands to place the PICC at given reference points in the operating volume. The measured voltage at R_{IC} have to be bigger than 100mV to guarantee the power supply of the reader-IC [4].

III. Antenna Optimization

Fig. 2 shows the geometry and matching circuit of the antenna design to be optimized. The antenna have to be placed in an area defined for ID1 cards [3], considering a forbidden space. The parameter vector **x** to be optimized consits of the lengths len_x and len_y for the antenna size and the capacitors C_s and C_p of the matching circuit. The whole problem has been computed in the presence of one to five PICCs. The optimization of the antenna design is done by a standard DE [5]. For solving the forward problem a one dimensional type of the PEEC method [6] is used. Due to the fact, that within this method the antenna structure is described in terms of lumped elements the matching circuit can easily be added to the system. Consequently, the combined system, consisting of the antenna structure and the matching circuit, can be solved within one step.

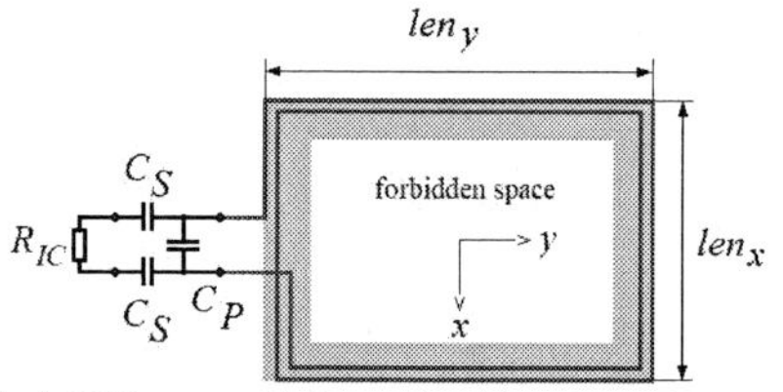

Fig. 2. Typical PICC-antenna design enclosed in an ID card.

In this work the power requirements for the PICC, in this case the voltage conditions U_{IC} defined in chapter II, in all fourteen positions and in the presence of one to five antennas were used for the quality function. Additionally, the area A_{ant} of the antenna was minimized.

Introducing sigmoidal membership functions μ for these parameters, a scalar quality function can be defined:

$$q = \sum_{N_{card}=1}^{5} \sum_{pos=1}^{14} \mu(U_{IC}) + \mu(A_{ant}). \qquad (1)$$

In Fig. 3 the input impedance of the PCD antenna with the optimized antenna design and different numbers of PICC antennas are shown. The detuning effect of the additional antennas can be seen. This effect results in a deterioration of the power transfer to the card system.

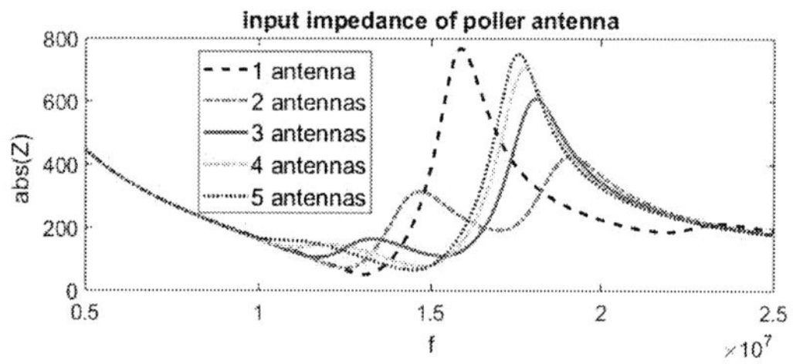

Fig. 3. Input impedance at the matching circuit of the PCD antenna for different numbers of PICC-antennas.

In Table I the voltages at the reader-IC's input resistance R_{IC} of the optimized and of the reference antenna design [1] is being compared. As can be seen for a one antenna system the reference design has higher voltages, which results in a better power transfer to the antenna system. In contrast, for the three and five antenna system, the optimized design outperforms the reference design. Especially for the system consisting of five PICC-antennas, the voltages of the reference design cannot comply with the voltage level defined in the datasheet of the supplier [4]. It can also be observed, that the optimized design has a higher voltage with the three card system than with the single card system. This effect can be described with a better tuning of this system.

TABLE I
Voltage at IC-Terminal of Card

	U_{IC} of	Position (0,0,0)	Position (2.5,0,3)	Position (1.5,π,3)
1 Card	Reference design	12.29 V	5.82 V	5.32 V
	Optimized design	7.18 V	1.32 V	1.18 V
3 Cards	Reference design	1.84 V	0.42 V	0.38 V
	Optimized design	14.87 V	3.52 V	3.15 V
5 Cards	Reference design	1.60 V	0.07 V	0.08 V
	Optimized design	5.12 V	1.07 V	0.95 V

Voltages at IC-terminal for different antenna designs and with different numbers of cards at specific positions as shown in Fig. 1.

IV. Conclusion

In this paper an approach for a design optimization of an antenna system, compliable to the EMVCo-standard and considering multi-card conditions has been presented. Since the PEEC method offers the possibility to directly connect lumped circuit elements, it therefore offers the possibility to integrate the matching circuit into the optimization process. As the typical usage of several cards in the wallet were considered, a more robust design for everyday life could be achieved.

References

[1] EMV Contactless Specifications for Payment Systems, Version 2.6, March 2016 (www.emvco.com/specifications.aspx?id=21).

[2] M. Gebhart, R. Neubauer, M. Stark, and D. Warnez, "Design of 13.56 MHz smartcard stickers with ferrite for payment and authentication," in *Proc. 3rd International Workshop on Near Field Communication*, February 2011.

[3] ISO/IEC 14443-1, Identification cards – Contactless integrated circuit cards – Proximity cards – Part 1: Physical characteristics.

[4] NXP, "NFC controller with integrated firmware, supporting all NFC Forum modes," PN7120 datasheet, October 2017.

[5] P. Alotto, "A hybrid multiobjective differential evolution method for electromagnetic device optimization," *COMPEL, Int. J. Comput. Math. Electr. Electron. Eng.*, vol. 30, no. 6, pp. 1815-1828, 2011.

[6] T. Bauernfeind, P. Baumgartner, O. Bíró, C. A. Magele, K. Preis and R. Torchio, "PEEC-based multi-objective synthesis of non-uniformly spaced linear antenna arrays," in *IEEE Transactions on Magnetics*, vol. 53, no. 6, pp. 1-4, June 2017.

The Adaptive Wind Driven Optimization and its Application in Electromagnetics

*Jogender Nagar,** Sawyer D. Campbell and *Douglas H. Werner*
Electrical Engineering and Computer Science
Penn State University
State College, PA, USA
*jun163@psu.edu

Zikri Bayraktar
Schlumberger-Doll Research Center
Cambridge, MA, USA

Muge Komurcu
Department of Earth, Atmosphere and Planetary Sciences
Massechusetts Institute of Technology
Cambridge, MA, USA

***Abstract*— In this paper, we analyze in detail the properties of the newly developed Adaptive Wind Driven Optimization (AWDO) method and demonstrate its efficiency on continuous-valued electromagnetic (EM) problems by comparing it to the performance of the classical Wind Driven Optimization (WDO) method. While WDO has proven to be competitive with similar algorithms such as Particle Swarm Optimization (PSO), there are a large number of inherent parameters in the WDO update equations which the user needs to fine tune for optimal performance. The newly developed AWDO method automatically determines these parameters, creating an adaptive algorithm which eliminates the need for the user to have apriori knowledge of the optimal values for the inherent parameters. Numerical optimization results on EM problems indicate that AWDO matches or surpasses the performance of WDO, yielding a self-adaptive algorithm which is both extremely efficient as well as easy to use.**

Keywords— ***adaptive wind drive optimization, antenna arrays, evolutionary optimization.***

I. Introduction

Wind Driven Optimization (WDO), introduced in 2010, is a population-based heuristic global optimizer inspired by the motion of air in the Earth's atmosphere [1, 2]. A randomly distributed population of air parcels traverse an N-dimensional search space to find the global optimum point, where the position and velocity of each parcel are updated based on the atmospheric momentum equations. The velocity and position update equations inherently contain four parameters which must be preset, including the gravitational constant and the temperature terms. This requires the user to study the algorithm as well as the problem's solution domain and pick the best values for the optimization problem at hand, a very difficult task for novice users. To alleviate this drawback of the WDO, we introduced the Adaptive Wind Driven Optimization (AWDO) in [3] to create a parameter-free adaptive algorithm where the inherent parameters are adaptively decided at each iteration by the Covariance Matrix Adaptation Evolutionary Strategy (CMA-ES) algorithm [4-6]. In [3], it was shown that the AWDO has improved performance over the WDO when tested on trivial numerical benchmark functions. However, up to this point, AWDO has not been tested on realistic engineering problems, which can be more complex and multi-modal. To this end, in this paper we compare the performance of AWDO against WDO when applied to real-world continuous-valued EM problems.

II. ADAPTIVE WIND DRIVE OPTIMIZATION

In WDO, the position and velocity update equations at iteration $n+1$ are given by:

$$x_{n+1} = x_n + u_{n+1}\Delta t$$
$$u_{n+1} = (1-\alpha)u_n - gx_n + \left|\frac{i-1}{i}\right| RT(x_{max} - x_n) + \frac{c * u_n^{other}}{i} \quad (1)$$

where u_n and x_n are the velocity and position at iteration n, respectively, x_{max} is the position of the highest pressure point that has been found, u_n^{other} is a velocity in one of the other dimensions and Δt is a time step, which is set to unity for this study. The inherent parameters which must be set by the user are α as the friction coefficient, g as the gravitational constant, c as a constant that represents the rotation of the Earth, R as the universal gas constant and T as the temperature. Note that R and T have been grouped together as a single inherent parameter since they always appear together in all equations governing WDO.

The AWDO combines the classical WDO with the CMA-ES [4] algorithm in order to select optimum values for its inherent terms. CMA-ES uses the same population size as the WDO and the optimization problem space is only limited to four dimensions for the inherent parameters; α, g, c and RT. At each iteration, CMA-ES returns new sets of inherent parameter values for each of the members of the WDO population. There is no need for additional cost function calls by the CMA-ES, since its operation is based on the pressure function computed by the WDO. It was shown in [3] that the AWDO eliminates the need for tuning the inherent parameters and provides improved performance when applied to simple numerical benchmark functions. The next section will apply the AWDO to a linear antenna array optimization problem and compare its performance to the classical WDO using the optimal settings provided in the literature.

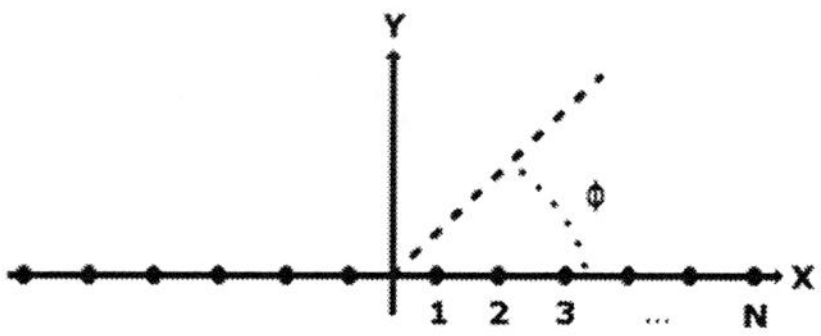

Fig. 1. Geometry of the $2N$-element linear antenna array positioned along the x-axis, where the array is symmetric with respect to the origin.

III. Linear Antenna Array Optimization

The optimization of linear arrays is a continuous-valued problem where the locations of the antenna array elements are determined by the optimization algorithm to achieve a desired radiation pattern. The problem considered here has been studied extensively and previously optimized via the classical WDO [2], Particle Swarm Optimization (PSO) [7], and Comprehensive Learning PSO (CLPSO) [8]. For this study, the goal is to achieve the best sidelobe level (SLL) suppression in the radiation pattern. The array factor (AF) for the linear antenna array with $2N$ elements is [9]:

$$AF(\varphi) = 2\sum_{i=1}^{N} \cos(kd_i \cos(\phi)), \quad (2)$$

where k is the free-space wavenumber and d_i is the location of the ith antenna element relative to the coordinate origin. The geometry of the $2N$-element linear array is illustrated in Fig. 1. The locations for an $N = 5$ element array are optimized by the WDO and AWDO to achieve a minimum SLL for angular ranges $\phi = [0°, 80°]$ and $\phi = [100°, 180°]$ [2, 7, 8]. The WDO and AWDO were run 100 times and the best 50 cases are utilized to compute the averages. Fig. 2 illustrates the results for both WDO and AWDO, where the red curves correspond to each run of AWDO and the green curves correspond to WDO. The average performance for the AWDO and the WDO are shown in blue and black, respectively. It can clearly be seen from Fig. 2 that on average the AWDO performs significantly better than the WDO, converging quicker. Fig. 3 shows an array factor comparison of the best results. It can be seen that

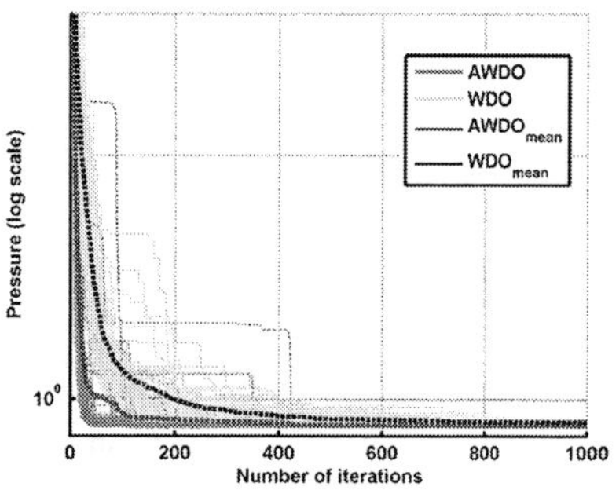

Fig. 2. Progress of best pressure versus the number of iterations for the best performing 50 runs for the optimization of the linear antenna array. The red and green curves correspond to each run of AWDO and WDO, respectively. The thick blue and black curves represent the average performance for AWDO and WDO, respectively.

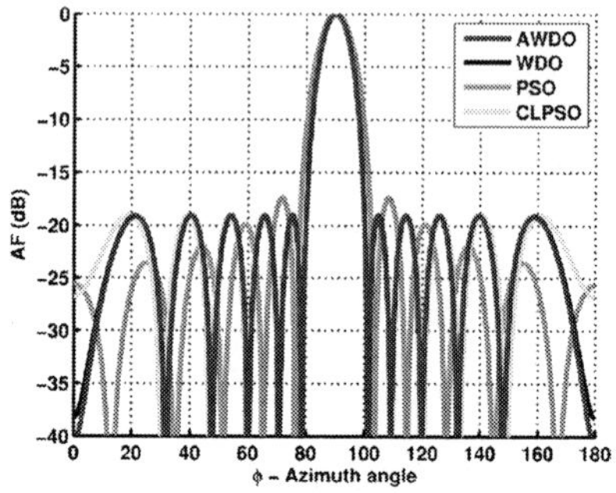

Fig. 3. Array factor comparison between AWDO, WDO, PSO and CLPSO.

AWDO, WDO and CLPSO arrive at similar results, while outperforming the standard PSO.

IV. Conclusion

In this paper, we compared the performance of the newly developed AWDO algorithm to the classical WDO method on a linear array synthesis problem. It was shown that the convergence performance of AWDO surpasses that of WDO. Further test cases were run including the optimization of both UWB and dual-band antennas where the function evaluations take a much longer time. The convergence parameters of these cases along with a discussion of how the parameters evolve over time will be presented.

References

[1] Z. Bayraktar, M. Komurcu, and D. H. Werner, "Wind driven optimization (WDO): A novel nature-inspired optimization algorithm and its application to electromagnetics," *Proceedings of the 2010 IEEE International Symposium on Antennas and Propagation and CNC/USNC/URSI Radio Science Meeting*, Toronto, Ontario, Canada, July 11-17, 2010.

[2] Z. Bayraktar, M. Komurcu, J. A. Bossard, and D. H. Werner, "The wind driven optimization technique and its application in electromagnetics," *IEEE Trans. Antennas Propag.*, vol. 61, no. 5, pp. 2745-2757, May 2013.

[3] Z. Bayraktar, and M. Komurcu, "Adaptive wind driven optimization," *Proceedings of the 9th EAI Int. Conf. on Bio-Inspired Information and Communications Technologies*, New York, NY, USA, Dec. 3-5, 2015.

[4] N. Hansen, and A. Ostermeier, "Adapting arbitrary normal mutation distributions in evolution strategies: The covariance matrix adaptation," *Proceedings of the 1996 IEEE Intern. Conf. on Evolutionary Computation*, pp. 312-317, 1996.

[5] M. D. Gregory, Z. Bayraktar, and D. H. Werner, "Fast optimization of electromagnetic design problems using the covariance matrix adaptation evolutionary strategy," *IEEE Trans. Antennas Propag.*, vol. 59, no. 4, pp. 1275-1285, Apr. 2011.

[6] M. D. Gregory, S. V. Martin and D. H. Werner, "Improved electromagnetics optimization: The covariance matrix adaptation evolutionary strategy," *IEEE Antennas and Propagation Magazine*, vol. 57, no. 3, pp. 48-59, 2015.

[7] M. M. Khodier and C. G. Christodoulou, "Linear array geometry synthesis with minimum sidelobe level and null control using particle swarm optimization," *IEEE Trans. Antennas Propag.*, vol. 53, no. 8, pp. 2674–2679, Aug. 2005.

[8] S. K. Goudos, V. Moysiadou, T. Samaras, K. Siakavara, and J. N. Sahalos, "Application of a comprehensive learning particle swarm optimizer to unequally spaced linear array synthesis with sidelobe level suppression and null control," *IEEE Trans. Antennas Propag.*, vol. 9, pp. 125–129, Sep. 2010.

[9] C. A. Balanis, *Antenna Theory*. New York: Wiley, 1997.

Dual-Band Microstrip Antenna for the Fifth Generation Indoor / Outdoor Wireless Applications

Mourad S. Ibrahim
College of Engineering
Prince Sultan University
Riyadh, KSA
mrizk@psu.edu.sa
On leave: College of Engineering, Modern Sciences and Arts University, 6th October, Egypt

Abstract— **In this paper a dual band monopole antenna with omnidirectional radiation pattern suitable for indoor and outdoor fifth generation (5G) applications at 28 GHz and 60 GHz systems is developed. The proposed monopole antenna is built up using a microstrip of two rectangular patches and a T-shaped folded patch. The analysis and optimization processes throughout this paper are carried out using a High Frequency Surface Structure (HFSS) that uses the Finite Element Method (FEM) numerical method, and CST Microwave Studio that uses the Finite Integral Technique (FIT) numerical method. Good agreement between the two methods is obtained. The bandwidth of the lower and upper bands is about 1.44 GHz (5.1%) and 39.24 GHz (60.6%), respectively. The antenna directivity is about 2.28 dBi at 28 GHz with a total efficiency of 93% and about 3.414 dBi with a total efficiency of 97.5% at 60 GHz.**

Keywords—Dual band, Fifth generation, LMDS, Omnidirectional pattern, WiGig.

I. Introduction

The exponential growth of telecommunication over the past three decades increases the amount of data the average person uses exponentially. This growth is more noteworthy especially with the evolution of wireless communications which requires the development of low cost, lightweight, and low profile antennas that are capable of maintaining high performance over a wide bandwidth [1]. The global bandwidth shortage facing wireless carriers has motivated the exploration of the underutilized millimeter wave (mm-wave) frequency spectrum for future broadband communication networks [2]. Due to the importance of multiband single feed patch antennas in enormous millimeter wave applications, various techniques can be found in literature for multiband planar antenna designs as in [3-6]. For example, multiband microstrip antennas operating at around 35 GHz using semi-insulating multilayer GaAs is described in [3]. In [4], dual band 24/60 GHz with bandwidth not exceed 1.2% and gain of -9 dB at the lower band and of 1 dB at the upper band is presented. A meta-resonator antenna in [5] with two operating frequencies (41 & 52.2) GHz using a pair of SRRs with 2% bandwidth, 3.76 dB gain, and 71% efficiency is proposed. In [6], two modes are excited to achieve a dual band (58 & 77) GHz with -2 dB and 0.3 dB gain respectively and nearly 6% bandwidth at both frequencies. A novel hybrid configuration, using coplanar patches and a slot in feed line, has been proposed in [7] to achieve dual band response at 83 and 94 GHz. In this paper, the design and the simulation of a dual band microstrip planar antenna are presented. The proposed antenna is operating at the 28 GHz (Ka-band) for LMDS which currently considered for 5G mobile cellular [8], and the 60 GHz (V-band) for Wireless Gigabit Alliance (WiGig) applications [4].

II. Antenna Structure and Design

The proposed monopole antenna structure geometry consists of a T-folded shape with two rectangular patches with partial ground plane [9]. The patch mounted on substrate FR4 with dielectric constant of 4.4. The dimensions of the antenna structure are shown in Fig. 1. The substrate dimension is W_s by L_s while the partial ground is W_s by L_g. The T-folded shape has dimensions W_t by L_t for the mid and L_{top} for top and L_{fold} for folded side. The two rectangular patches have dimensions W_p by L_p. The microstrip transmission line feeder dimesion is W_f by L_f. The characteristic parameters of the microstrip can be found in [10].

III. Antenna Simulation Results

In order to get optimized design dimensions a parametric analysis is carried out to achieve dual band antenna at 28 GHz and 60 GHz with acceptable performance. The optimized design dimensions are illustrated in Table I.

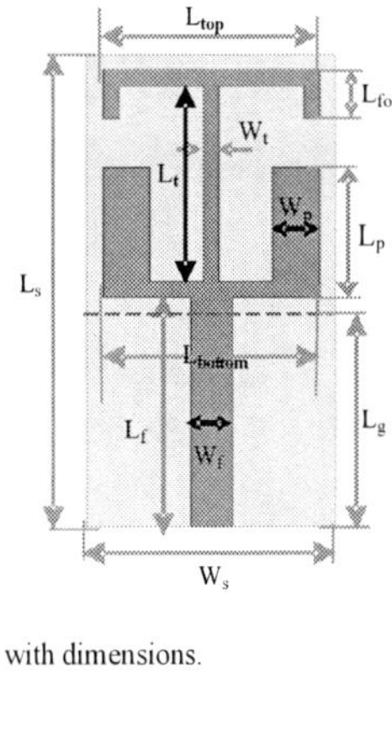

Fig. 1. Antenna structure with dimensions.

TABLE I. OPTIMIZED DIMENSIONS OF THE PROPOSED ANTENNA IN MM

Parameter	Value	Parameter	Value
W_s	1.6	W_p	0.3
L_s	2.9	L_p	0.7
L_g	1.3	W_t	0.1
W_f	0.2	L_t	1.2
L_f	1.4	L_{top}	1.2
L_{fold}	0.3	L_{bottom}	1.4

In order to verify our results, the proposed antenna is simulated using two different methods, FIT (commercial software CST) and FEM (commercial software HFSS). Fig. 2 shows the reflection coefficient for the proposed antenna using FIT, and FEM. Matching is better in FEM and there is a small deviation in the upper band between the two methods. It's noted in Fig. 2 that, the antenna achieve good impedance matching over the dual band and the impedance bandwidth for $S_{11} \leq -10$ dB in lower band is from 27.52 to 28.96 GHz which covers the LMDS frequency band, while in upper band is from 45.14 to 84.38 GHz which covers the WiGig frequency band. The center frequency of the lower band is 28.24 GHz with bandwidth 5.1% while the center frequency for the upper band is 64.76 GHz with bandwidth 60.6%. Fig. 3 shows the omnidirectional pattern at 28 and 60 GHz. Fig. 3 (a) shows the directivity pattern at 28 GHz with maximum directivity of 2.28 dBi and the total efficiency is 93%. While Fig. 3 (b) shows the directivity pattern at 60 GHz with maximum directivity of 3.414 dBi and the total efficiency is 97.5%.

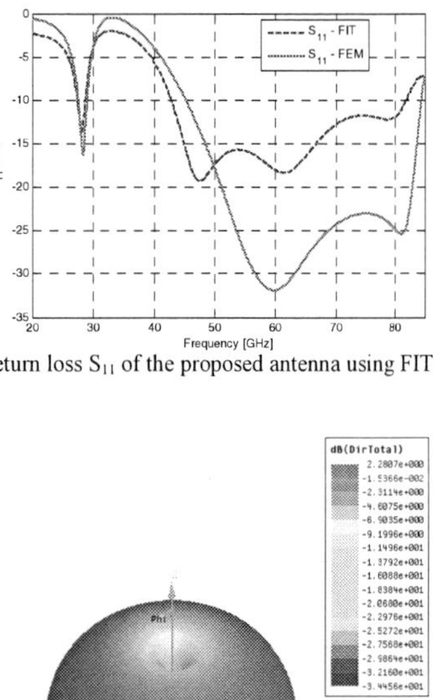

Fig. 2. Return loss S_{11} of the proposed antenna using FIT and FEM.

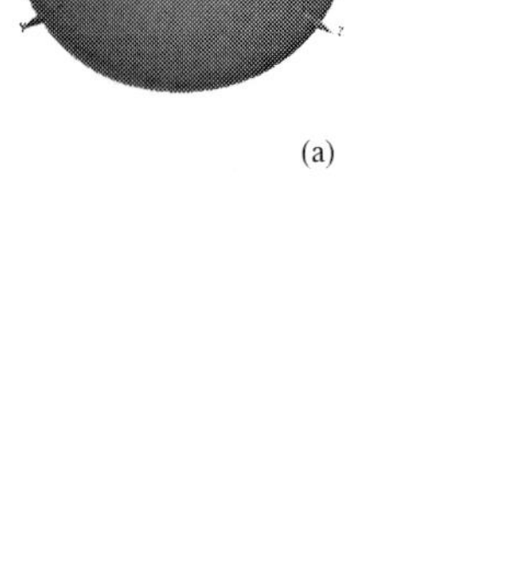

(a)

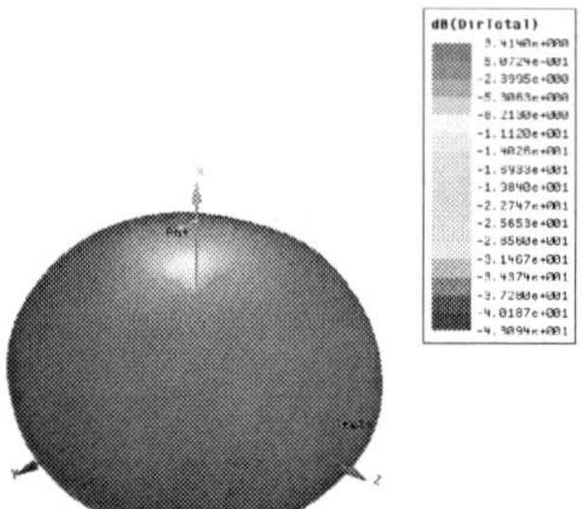

(b)

Fig. 3. Simulated directivity patterns at (a) 28 GHz and at (b) 60 GHz.

IV. CONCLUSION

In this paper, a monopole microstrip antenna with partial ground plane is designed and simulated. Dual bands centered at 28.24 GHz suitable for LDMS with bandwidth of 1.44 GHz (5.1%) and the upper band centered at 64.76 GHz with broad bandwidth suitable for WiGig of about 39.24 GHz (60.6%). The antenna radiation pattern is omnidirectional with maximum directivity of 2.28dBi and 3.414 dBi at 28 GHz and 60 GHz respectively with total efficiency exceeds 93%. Good agreement between the two methods is obtained.

ACKNOWLEDGMENT

The author gratefully acknowledges the support of Prince Sultan University.

REFERENCES

[1] S. S. Jaco du Preez, Millimeter-Wave Antennas: Configurations and Applications: Springer International Publishing Switzerland, 2016.

[2] T. S. Rappaport, S. Sun, R. Mayzus, H. Zhao, Y. Azar, K. Wang, G. N. Wong, J. K. Schulz, M. Samimi, and F. Gutierrez, "Millimeter wave mobile communications for 5G cellular: It Will Work!," IEEE Access, vol. 1, pp. 335-349, 2013.

[3] D. Sanchez-Hernandez, Q. H. Wang, A. A. Rezazadeh, and I. D. Robertson, "Millimeter-wave dual-band microstrip patch antennas using multilayer GaAs technology," IEEE Transactions on Microwave Theory and Techniques, vol. 44, pp. 1590-1593, 1996.

[4] H. Jie-Huang, W. Jin-Wei, C. Yi-Lin, and C. F. Jou, "A 24/60 GHz dual-band millimeter-wave on-chip monopole antenna fabricated with a 0.13-μm CMOS technology," in 2009 IEEE International Workshop on Antenna Technology, pp. 1-4, 2009.

[5] I. K. Kim and V. V. Varadan, "Electrically small, millimeter wave dual band meta-resonator antennas," IEEE Transactions on Antennas and Propagation, vol. 58, pp. 3458-3463, 2010.

[6] T. Y. Lin, T. Chiu, and D. C. Chang, "Design of dual-band millimeter-wave antenna-in-package using flip-chip assembly," IEEE Transactions on Components, Packaging and Manufacturing Technology, vol. 4, pp. 385-391, 2014.

[7] S. Agarwal, N. P. Pathak, and D. Singh, "Concurrent 83 GHz/94 GHz parasitically coupled defected microstrip feedline antenna for millimeter wave applications," in 2013 IEEE Applied Electromagnetics Conference (AEMC), pp. 1-2, 2013.

[8] N. Ashraf, O. Haraz, M. A. Ashraf, and S. Alshebeili, "28/38-GHz dual-band millimeter wave SIW array antenna with EBG structures for 5G applications," in 2015 International Conference on Information and Communication Technology Research (ICTRC), pp. 5-8, 2015.

[9] W. H. Yang J., Lv Z., Wang H., "Design of miniaturized dual-band microstrip antenna for WLAN application," Sensors, vol. 16, pp. 1-15, 2016.

[10] C. A. Balanis, Advanced Engineering Electromagnetics, Second Edition: John Wiley & Sons, New York, 2012.

Co-Simulations of DC Magnetic Bias Fields and RF Performance for Microwave Ferrite Circulators

Laila Fighera Marzall, Mauricio Pinto, Andrea Ashley, Dimitra Psychogiou and Zoya Popović
University of Colorado, Boulder, Colorado 80309-0425

Abstract—**This paper presents finite element co-simulations for DC magnetic field and microwave non-reciprocal performance of ferrite circulators. Permanent magnets provide a DC bias field, but need to be large for a uniform magnetic field distribution inside the ferrite material. Additionally, the ferrite effective permeability is a nonlinear function of magnetic bias. Smaller magnets give a non-uniform bias field distribution, which can be taken into account in the full-wave simulations. To demonstrate the effect of this nonuniform bias, a commercial ferrite material from Skyworks (TT105) is chosen for a circulator design around 3.9 GHz assuming first a uniform DC magnetic field that saturates the ferrite. A small commercial rare-earth permanent magnet is then simulated to obtain the nonuniform static magnetic field in the ferrite, and resulting HFSS simulations show that the effects of nonuniform bias field on circulator performance can be predicted using a combination of analysis methods.**

Index Terms—**Circulator, ferrite, permanent magnet, isolation**

I. Introduction

Circulators are non-reciprocal components that have been used for a long time in microwave systems to, e.g. isolate a receiver from a transmitter. Standard design approaches for circulators with saturated magnetic materials are described in [1]. Externally biased ferrite circulators were first examined in the 50's, e.g. [2]. Microstrip and stripline circulator design has been explored to a limited degree in, e.g., [3], [4]. However, although a few publications consider full-wave simulations using non-reciprocal materials [5], simulations of the external DC magnetic bias field are lacking.

In this work, we show in simulations how the DC magnetic bias field of small permanent magnets varies as a function of position and size. The resulting non-uniform field can be applied to a ferrite disk and microwave performance simulated. The geometry of such a circulator is shown in Fig.1. The ferrite disk is embedded in a microstrip substrate, with the permanent magnet placed directly above. Ansys Maxwell is used for the static simulations, while HFSS is used for the full-wave electromagnetic analysis. The nonlinearity of the ferrite is taken into account with a calculated effective permeability as a function of applied bias field. For a 3.9 GHz circulator design, a comparison is performed between a fully saturated ferrite and one with a non-uniform DC bias from a small permanent magnet.

II. B-field of a Cylindrical Permanent Magnet

Cylindrical magnets are easily found commercially and have a symmetry compatible with commercially available ferrite pucks, e.g. [6]. The estimate of the z-component of the magnetic flux density vector of a cylindrical permanent magnet shown in Fig.1 along its axis is given by [7]:

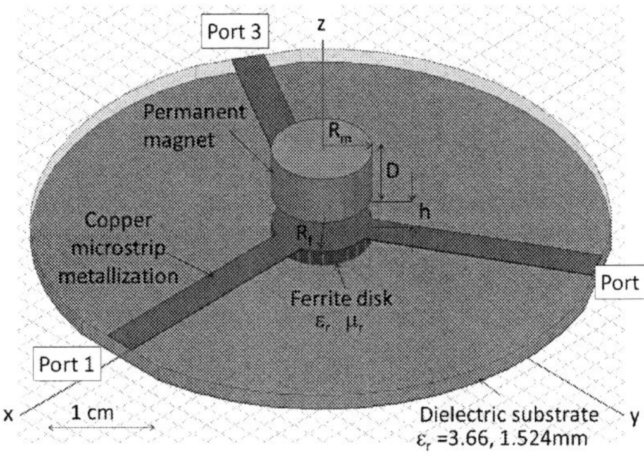

Fig. 1. Layout of microstrip circulator showing a permanent magnet that provides DC bias and a ferrite cylinder.

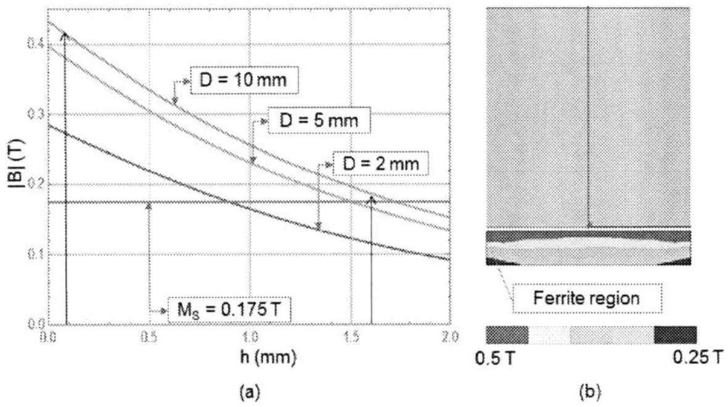

Fig. 2. (a) Calculated B-field magnitude versus distance for a permanent cylindrical magnet (embedded in air) with $D = 2, 5$ and $10\,\text{mm}$. (b) Simulated results for $D = 10\,\text{mm}$, $R_m = 5\,\text{mm}$ and $h = 0.1\,\text{mm}$.

$$B(z) = \frac{B_r}{2}\left(\frac{z}{\sqrt{z + R_m^2}}\right) - \left(\frac{z - D}{\sqrt{(z-D)^2 + R_m^2}}\right) \quad (1)$$

where B_r is the remnant flux density, and D and R_m are the magnet thickness and radius. Fig.2 shows $|B(z)|$ for different commercially available magnet thicknesses D, with $R_m = 5\,\text{mm}$ and $B_r = 1.2\,\text{T}$ [8]. The red line shows the magnetization M_s required to fully saturate the ferrite.

Starting from this one-dimensional theoretical estimate, three-dimensional static finite element simulations for $|\vec{B}|$ are performed in Ansys Maxwell. First, the nonlinear ferrite characteristics are taken into account by calculating the effective

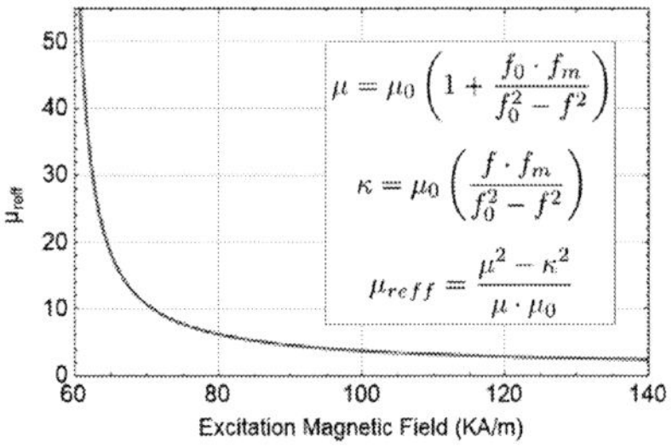

Fig. 3. Effective relative permeability versus magnetic bias field intensity. Relevant parameters: $f_0 = 3.8GHz$, $M_s = 0.175T$ [9].

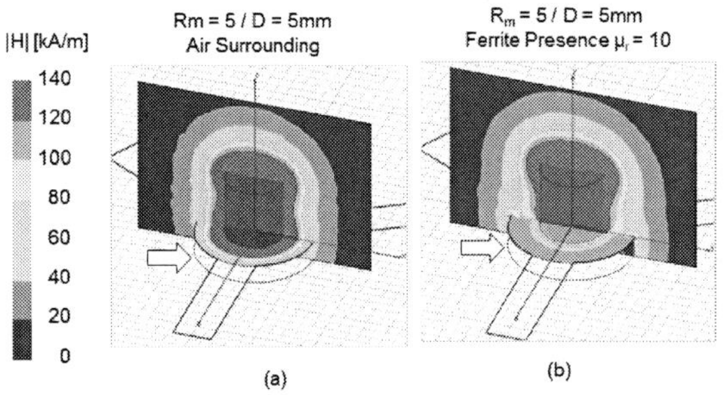

Fig. 4. Simulated magnitude of the H-Field produced by the permanent magnet (a) without ferrite (b) with the presence of ferrite puck. The relevant permanent magnet parameters are: remnant $B_r = 1.2\,\mathrm{T}$, cohercivity $H_c = 890\,\mathrm{kA/m}$, a conductivity $\sigma = \mathrm{S/m}$, ferrite $\mu_{reff} = 10$.

permeability μ_{reff} of the ferrite for a range of bias fields, Fig.3. Fig.4 shows an example field distribution with no ferrite and with a disk of $\mu_{reff} = 10$. A distribution for $\mu_{reff} = 2.5$ and a permanent magnet with $R_m = 3.5\,\mathrm{mm}$ and $D = 2\,\mathrm{mm}$ is used as input for full-wave high-frequency simulations.

III. Circulator Simulations and Performance

First, a microstrip circulator (Fig.1) is designed with a ferrite cylindrical puck for which the DC magnetic bias field is assumed to be uniform and above saturation. The magnetic saturation given for the Skyworks TT1-105 ferrite is $M_S = 0.175\,\mathrm{T}$ [6]. Assuming a saturated ferrite, $f_0 = 3.9\,\mathrm{GHz}$, $\mu_{reff} = 2.5$ and $\epsilon_r = 12.2$, the puck radius can be calculated from [1] to be $R_f = 4.49\,\mathrm{mm}$. After full-wave simulations in HFSS, the final radius is set to $R_f = 4.97\,\mathrm{mm}$. For 50-Ω ports and with no additional impedance matching, an isolation and match of better than 20 dB and an insertion loss of 1.8 dB are obtained around 3.9 GHz. The non-uniform field distribution in the ferrite is shown in Fig.5. This distribution is discretized with concentric circles, and within each hollow cylindrical volume, a uniform field is assumed for HFSS simulations. The resulting circulator performance is plotted in Fig.6 along with the baseline saturated design, with observed shift in frequency and increased loss and isolation. We conclude that the DC magnetic bias field nonuniformity needs to be taken into account for accurate modeling of circulators through co-simulation of the DC and high-frequency performance.

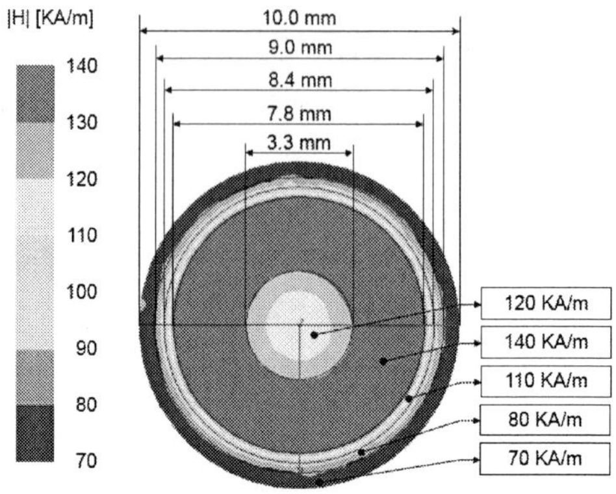

Fig. 5. Nonuniform DC B-field magnitude with discretization volumes for full-wave simulations of effects on circulator performance. Magnet dimensions $R_m = 3.5mm$, $D = 2mm$, $\mu_{rferrite} = 2.5$.

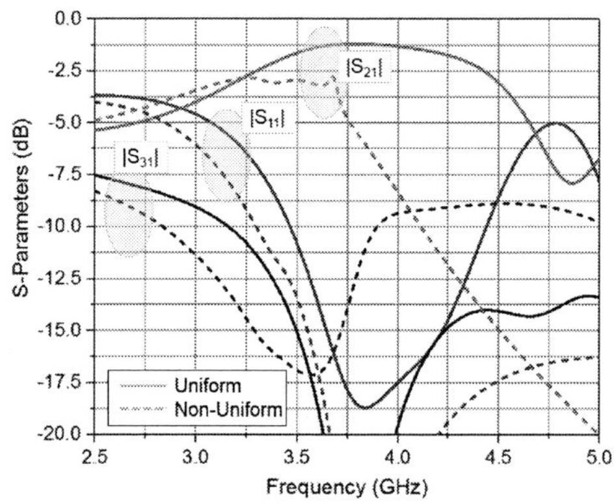

Fig. 6. Simulated S-parameters of the two circulators over frequency, showing that a nonuniform DC magnetic field from a small permanent magnet affects performance and can be taken into account by co-simulation.

References

[1] D. Linkhart, *Microwave circulator design*. Boston: Artech House, 2014.

[2] A. Fox, S. Miller and M. Weiss, "Behavior and Applications of Ferrites in the Microwave Region", *Bell System Technical Journal*, vol. 34, no. 1, pp. 5-103, 1955.

[3] H. Bosma, "On Stripline Y-Circulation at UHF", *IEEE Transactions on Microwave Theory and Techniques*, vol. 12, no. 1, pp. 61-72, 1964.

[4] B. Oneil and J. Young, "Experimental Investigation of a Self-Biased Microstrip Circulator," *IEEE Transactions on Microwave Theory and Techniques*, vol. 57, no. 7, pp. 1669-1674, 2009.

[5] F. Ghaffar and A. Shamim, "A Partially Magnetized Ferrite LTCC-Based SIW Phase Shifter for Phased Array Applications", *IEEE Transactions on Magnetics*, vol. 51, no. 6, pp. 1-8, 2015.

[6] "SKYWORKS:Products:TT1-105", *Skyworksinc.com*, 2017. [Online]. Available: http://www.skyworksinc.com/Product/3506/TT1-105. [Accessed: 11- Nov- 2017].

[7] J. Camacho, V. Sosa, "Alternative method to calculate the magnetic field of permanent magnets with azimuthal symmetry", *Revista mexicana de fisica*, E. 59, pp. 8-17, 2013.

[8] *Hkcm.de*, 2017. [Online]. Available: https://www.hkcm.de/HKCM_demag_data.php?l=en&gr=N35 [Accessed: 11- Nov- 2017].

[9] D. Pozar, *Microwave engineering*. Hoboken, NJ: Wiley, 2012.

A Design Approach for Monolithically Integrated Broadband Circulators

Mauricio Pinto, Laila Fighera Marzall, Andrea Ashley, Dimitra Psychogiou, and Zoya Popović
Department of Electrical, Computer and Energy Engineering
University of Colorado, Boulder, CO 80309, U.S.A.

***Abstract*—A design approach for self-biased monolithic microwave integrated circulators using a commercial computational electromagnetic code is presented. The nano-magnetic self-biased material is included in a microwave gallium nitride (GaN) on silicon carbide (SiC) integrated circuit process allowing for the design and realization of microstrip-type circulators. Simulated design performance showing >30% bandwidth, insertion loss of approximately 2.5 dB, and isolation greater than 9.3 dB from 16 to 23 GHz is compared between two commercial computational electromagnetic (EM) solvers.**

I. Introduction

Recent advancements in nano-magnetic materials have led to the possibility of self-biased circulators [1]. The materials can be deposited using several methods compatible with monolithic integration. Fig. 1 shows a photograph of a microstrip circulator fabricated on a 100-μm thick silicon carbide substrate used for gallium nitride (GaN) microwave integrated circuits (MMICs). Simulation and design challenges of integrated circulators lie in the iterative modeling with available process design kits (PDKs) used in MMIC fabrication. In many cases, it is not feasible nor time efficient to iteratively model a full MMIC design with a full-wave solver such as ANSYS HFSS.

This paper presents a design approach for monolithically integrated circulators using Qorvo's GaN-on-SiC PDK [2] and the magnetic material parameters of Argonne National Laboratory (ANL) such as the ones described in [1]. The circulator is designed starting from previous literature examples and then analyzed using an industry standard microwave circuit simulator (NI Microwave Office (MWO)) using passive matching elements from Qorvo's PDK. Scattering parameters for the circulator disk (puck) are extracted from full-wave HFSS simulations. The device performance using the combined full-wave and circuit analysis approach is then compared to a full-wave simulation of the full monolithically integrated circulator, validating the design approach.

II. Circulator Geometry and Simulation Setup

The circulator geometry discussed in this paper is of a conventional shape, e.g., presented in [3] and [4]. Fig. 2 shows the geometrical model using layout and materials compatible with the MMIC process that uses a thin GaN epitaxial layer on a 100μm thick SiC substrate [2]. The passive transmission lines and lumped elements are implemented in three layers of metal interconnects with TaN resistors and various capacitor

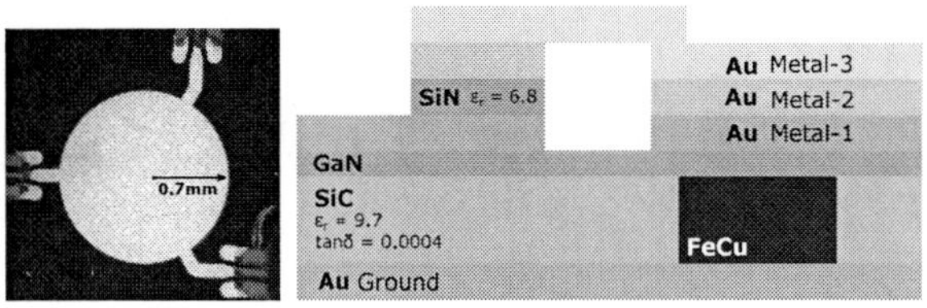

(a) (b)

Fig. 1. (a) Photo of fabricated unmatched microstrip circulator top metalization layer, and (b) cross-section of the Qorvo GaN-on-SiC MMIC process used for the design. The nano-magnetic material from ANL will be deposited in the cavity etched in the SiC under the microstrip metalization.

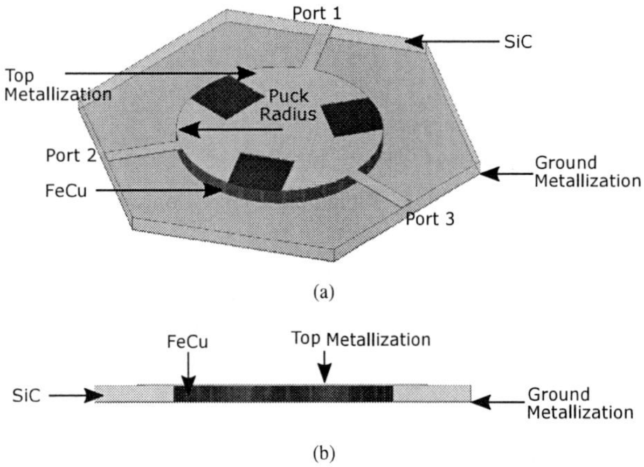

Fig. 2. Circulator geometry setup based on a 0.75mm radius puck. (a) Oblique view of three-port microstrip circulator geometry. (b) Side view of microstrip circulator configuration.

configurations with SiN dielectric. The stack-up of the process is shown in Fig.1 (b).

The full-wave simulation setup in HFSS for the geometry in Fig. 2 specifies the top trace and bottom ground as gold (thickness = 7 μm). The 100-μm thick SiC dielectric substrate has a relative permittivity of $\epsilon_r = 9.7$ and $\tan\delta = 0.0004$. It was found that the thin GaN epitaxial layer does not affect the results, while it substantially adds to the simulation time, so it is not included in the presented data. Wave ports are used on all three ports to excite the proper microstrip mode, with a radiation boundary condition. The magnetic material parameters assumed in the simulations are [1]: saturation magnetization $M_s = 0.5\,\mathrm{T}$; ratio of remnant to saturation

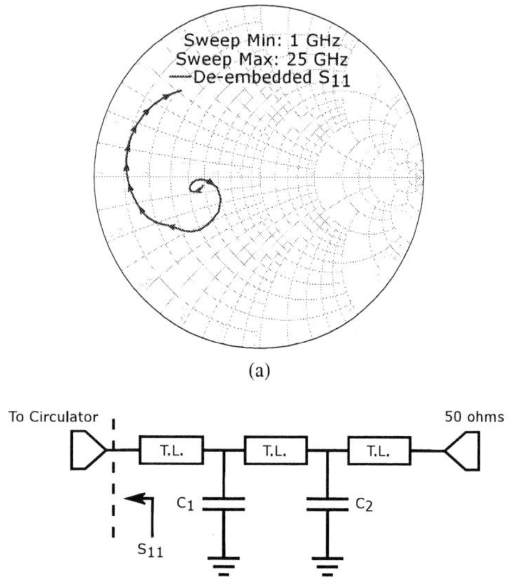

Fig. 3. (a) Circulator impedance de-embedded to the port of the circular circulator cavity. (b) Matching network topology used to match the circulator to 50-ohm impedance.

magnetization, $M_r/M_s = 0.5$; $\Delta H = 500\,\mathrm{Oe}$; $\mu_r = 2$; $\epsilon_r = 10$ and $\tan\delta = 0.002$. A uniform magnetic field excitation boundary condition is used for simulation of an internal, self-biased field of the magnetic material.

III. Circulator Design Approach

The initial circulator with only the magnetic puck is simulated in HFSS. All three ports are de-embedded to the plane of the puck and the scattering parameters normalized to $50\,\Omega$ are extracted and used for the design of the matching network with MWO and Qorvo's PDK. Fig. 3 (a) shows the de-embedded circulator impedance from 1 to 25 GHz. A low-Q matching network, Fig. 3 (b), provides increased bandwidth [5], and is implemented with capacitors and microstrip lines available in the process. EM simulations of the matching network using MWO's method of moment (MoM) solver are performed for the layout.

Finally, a full-wave simulation of the circulator together with its matching network is performed using HFSS. The model and simulation results of the bandwidth-optimized circulator are presented in Fig. 4 and Fig. 5, respectively. A comparison in Fig. 5 shows agreement between the design approach using only the magentic puck scattering parameters in conjunction with the planar MoM solver for the matching network and full-wave FEM simulations.

IV. Conclusion

In summary, this paper presents a simulation-based design approach for a miniature self-biased circulators using state-of-the-art MMIC integration. Predicted performance based on nano-magnetic material parameters result in a bandwidth of >30% with insertion loss and isolation of approximately 2.5 dB and >9.3 dB, respectively, from 16 to 23 GHz. Simulation results of the design approach show good agreement with the full-wave HFSS model.

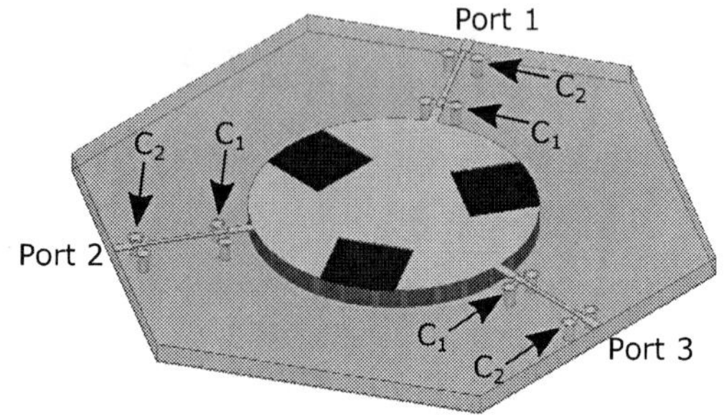

Fig. 4. Circulator geometry including matching network. The matching network including transmission lines and shunt capacitors are full-wave simulated together with the magnetic puck in HFSS.

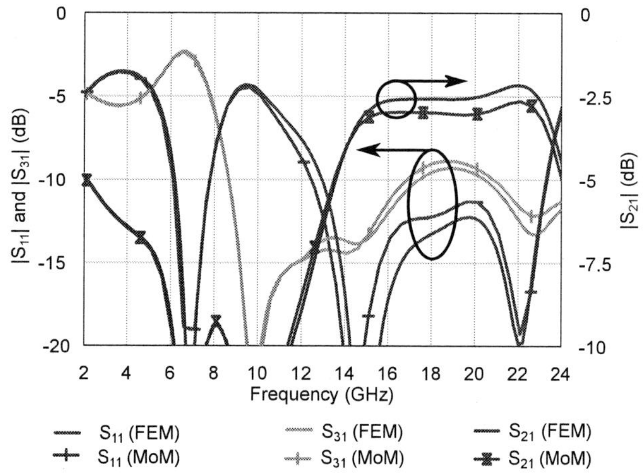

Fig. 5. Simulated performance of matched circulator. Insertion loss of approximately 2.5dB from 16-23GHz with isolation performance of greater than 9.3dB.

Acknowledgment

This work was funded by the DARPA M3IC program under a sub-contract to Qorvo. The authors would like to thank Qorvo and Argonne National Laboratory for the collaboration.

References

[1] X. Chen and Z. Zhou, "Magnetic nanofiber composite materials and devices using same." Apr. 11 2017, uS Patent 9,620,839. [Online]. Available: https://www.google.com/patents/US9620839

[2] Gallium nitride (gan). [Online]. Available: http://www.qorvo.com/innovation/technology/gan

[3] H. Bosma, "On stripline y-circulation at uhf," *IEEE Transactions on Microwave Theory and Techniques*, vol. 12, no. 1, pp. 61–72, Jan. 1964.

[4] C. E. Fay and R. L. Comstock, "Operation of the ferrite junction circulator," *IEEE Transactions on Microwave Theory and Techniques*, vol. 13, no. 1, pp. 15–27, Jan. 1965.

[5] J. L. Young, R. S. Adams, B. O'Neil, and C. M. Johnson, "Bandwidth optimization of an integrated microstrip circulator and antenna assembly. 1," *IEEE Antennas and Propagation Magazine*, vol. 48, no. 6, pp. 47–56, Dec. 2006.

Terahertz Evanescent Wave Tunneling in Bianisotropic Thin Films

Faroq Razzaz and Majeed A. S. Alkanhal
Department of Electrical Engineering, King Saud University, Riyadh, Saudi Arabia
fqaseem@ksu.edu.sa; Majeed@ksu.edu.sa

***Abstract*—This paper presents a theoretical investigation of electromagnetic wave tunneling through bianisotropic-bianisotropic interfaces. The dispersion relation and the conditions for terahertz evanescent wave tunneling in bianisotropic thin films are derived. The developed Berreman's matrix model is used to acquire the evanescent field characteristics through the bianisotropic layers. Fields incident with frequencies belong to the structure spectral interval will be tunneled effectively to the other side of the bianisotropic thin film via evanescent waves.**

Keywords— Bianisotropic, Terahertz, Thin film, Tunneling.

I. INTRODUCTION

Technologies established with optical and electromagnetic (EM) materials, recently, have made substantial evolution. Thin films fabricated from bianisotropic materials have become progressively significant in numerous electromagnetic and optical systems [1-2]. Bianisotropic media are very attractive for high frequency applications. Such media have been incorporated in many electromagnetic and optical encounters, such as in remote sensing and wave scattering and radiation, because of their numerous features [1-4]. Similar to anisotropic media [5], bianisotropic media can support two different propagating and evanescent wave modes simultaneously at the same frequency and the parallel wavevector components.

In this work, tunneling of electromagnetic fields by means of evanescent waves through a bianisotropic thin film inserted between two bianisotropic ambient media is explored. The dispersion relation and the (frequency) continuous spectral interval in which the electromagnetic fields can be tunneled to the other side of the thin film through the evanescent waves are determined.

II. ANALYSIS

To study evanescent and propagating waves in a layered bianisotropic structure where a lossless bianisotropic thin film is surrounded by a lossless bianisotropic ambient medium, the geometry model presented in Fig. 1 is considered. Both the bianisotropic ambient medium and the thin film layer support both evanescent and propagating modes simultaneously at the same frequency and parallel wavevectors. The constitutive relations that characterize the bianisotropic medium are given by:

$$\bar{D} = \bar{\bar{\varepsilon}}\bar{E} + \bar{\bar{\xi}}\bar{H}, \quad \bar{B} = \bar{\bar{\zeta}}\bar{E} + \bar{\bar{\mu}}\bar{H} \tag{1}$$

where $\bar{\bar{\varepsilon}}$ and $\bar{\bar{\mu}}$, and $\bar{\bar{\xi}}$ and $\bar{\bar{\zeta}}$ are the 3×3 permittivity, permeability, and magnetoelectric tensors for the bianisotropic material, respectively.

Considered a general obliquely incident plane wave with $\mathbf{E}(x,z)=\boldsymbol{E}_0\, exp(k_x x+k_z z)$ and $\mathbf{H}(x,z)=\boldsymbol{H}_0\, exp(k_x x+k_z z)$ with the time dependency $exp(-i\omega t)$, where k_x is the wavevector parallel to the bianisotropic thin layer, k_z is the wavevector component normal to the bianisotropic thin film, and ω is the frequency of the incident wave. A reduction of the Maxwell equations to a system of four first-order ordinary differential equations for the tangential fields can be obtained using the Berreman 4×4 matrix representation [6] as:

$$\frac{d\Psi(z)}{dz} = iJA\Psi(z), \tag{2}$$

where A is the 4×4 matrix that depends on the properties ($\bar{\bar{\varepsilon}}$, $\bar{\bar{\mu}}$, $\bar{\bar{\xi}}$, and $\bar{\bar{\zeta}}$) of the medium, the frequency of the incident wave, and the parallel wavevector components. Moreover, $\Psi(z)$ and J are, respectively, defined by,

$$\Psi(z) = \begin{bmatrix} E_x \\ E_y \\ H_x \\ H_y \end{bmatrix} \text{ and } J = \begin{bmatrix} 0 & 0 & 0 & 1 \\ 0 & 0 & -1 & 0 \\ 0 & -1 & 0 & 0 \\ 1 & 0 & 0 & 0 \end{bmatrix}.$$

In order to have two distinct normal wavevectors at the same frequency, namely TE and TM wavevectors, consider the lossless biaxial bianisotropic medium with the following properties:

$$\bar{\bar{\varepsilon}} = diag[\varepsilon_x, \varepsilon_y, \varepsilon_z] \text{ and } \bar{\bar{\mu}} = diag[\mu_x, \mu_y, \mu_z], \text{ and}$$

$$\bar{\bar{\xi}} = \bar{\bar{\zeta}} = j\begin{bmatrix} 0 & 0 & 0 \\ 0 & 0 & \xi \\ 0 & -\xi & 0 \end{bmatrix}.$$

Hence, the TE and TM z-directional wavevector components in the bianisotropic medium are given by:

$$k_z^{TE} = \pm\sqrt{\mu_x\left(\frac{\omega^2}{c^2}\varepsilon_y - \frac{k_x^2}{\mu_z} - \frac{\omega^2}{c^2}\xi^2\right)}, \tag{3}$$

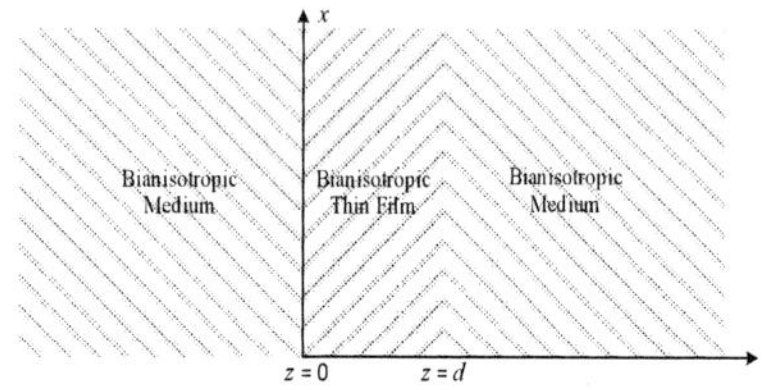

Fig. 1. Geometry of the problem.

$$k_z^{TM} = \pm\sqrt{\varepsilon_x\left(\frac{\omega^2}{c^2}\mu_y - \frac{k_x^2}{\varepsilon_z} - \frac{\omega^2}{c^2}\xi^2\right)}, \tag{4}$$

where the superscripts *TE* and *TM* refer to the transverse electric and the transverse magnetic wavevectors, respectively. These z-directional wave numbers are the eigenvalues of the matrix $M = iJA$ in (2). Corresponding to the properties of the medium, these two wavenumbers may be both real, imaginary, or one real and one imaginary corresponding to propagating and evanescent fields, respectively. The eigenfields (eigenvectors) associated with these eigenvalues are given by:

$$\left[0, \frac{\omega}{c}\mu_x, \mp k_z^{TE}, 0\right]^T, \tag{5}$$

$$\left[\pm k_z^{TM}, 0, 0, \frac{\omega}{c}\varepsilon_x\right]^T, \tag{6}$$

where the superscript T refers to vector-transpose. To examine the tunneling phenomenon in the bianisotropic thin film, consider that the TE fields propagating in the bianisotropic ambient medium (with real z-directional TE wavenumber in ambient medium) and evanescent in the bianisotropic thin film (with imaginary z-directional TE wavenumber in the thin film). To fulfil this situation, the following constraints must hold:

$$\frac{\varepsilon_y^f \mu_x^f - \xi^2}{\mu_x^f / \mu_z^f} < \frac{k_x^2}{(\omega/c)^2} < \frac{\varepsilon_y^a \mu_x^a - \xi^2}{\mu_x^a / \mu_z^a}. \tag{7}$$

The superscripts f and a refer to the material parameters of the film and the ambient media, respectively. The above TE wave tunneling constrain condition is satisfied within continuous frequency interval. This frequency interval can be determined from the dispersion relation between the z-directional TE wavenumbers and the frequency ω. The field distribution in the structure can be determined using the transfer matrix as follows

$$\Psi(z) = T(0,d)\Psi(0), \tag{8}$$

where $T(0,d) = exp[iJA_f d]$ is the transfer matrix of the bianisotropic thin film.

III. Results and Discussions

To illustrate the electromagnetic field tunneling through bianisotropic thin films, the permittivity and permeability tensors of the ambient medium is chosen as $\bar{\bar{\varepsilon}}_a = diag[2,6,1]$ and $\bar{\bar{\mu}}_a = diag[3,1,1]$, respectively while the permittivity and permeability tensors of the film material is given by $\bar{\bar{\varepsilon}}_f = [8,1,1]$ and $\bar{\bar{\mu}}_f = diag[1,3,1]$, respectively. The magnetoelectric parameter ξ is 0.5 in the both media. The dispersion relations of the real z-directional wavenumber and the normalized frequency ω ($\omega = \omega_r a/2\pi c$, where ω_r is the actual frequency and $a = 10^{-5}$) are shown in Fig. 2. The continuous spectral interval is confined by the black and red curves for $k_z = 0$. The field distribution across the thin film is depicted in Fig. 3. The TE fields tunneled to the other side of the thin film by means of the evanescent fields are illustrated.

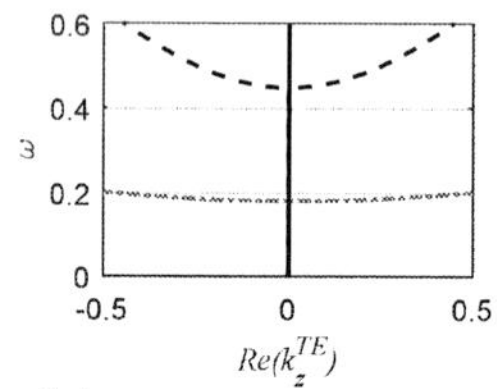

Fig. 2. The dispersion relations.

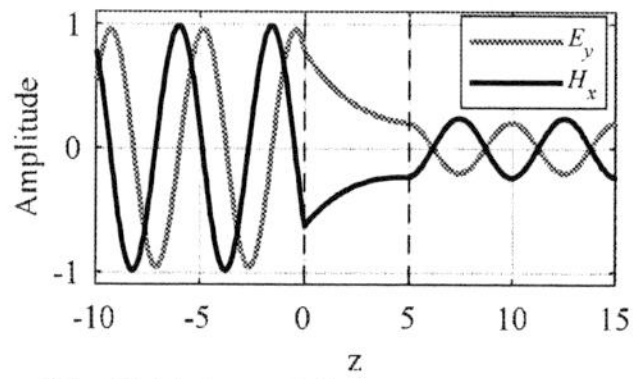

Fig. 3. Tunneling of the field at $\omega = 0.4$.

IV. Conclusions

This paper explores electromagnetic wave tunneling across bianisotropic films in the terahertz regime. The Berreman's matrix method is utilized to determine the evanescent and propagating field forms through the bianisotropic layers. The bianisotropic layers can support propagating and evanescent eigen-modes at the same frequency and parallel wavevectors. The propagating modes incident in the ambient medium can be feasibly tunneled to the other side via evanescent modes in the biaxial film when their frequencies belong to the continuum spectral interval determined by the material geometry of the layered structure.

References

[1] C. E. Kriegler, M. S. Rill, S. Linden, M. Wegener, "Bianisotropic photonic metamaterials", *IEEE J. Sel. Topics Quantum Electron.*, vol. 16, no. 2, pp. 367-375, Mar./Apr. 2010.

[2] S.-Y. Wang, W.-Y. Yin, L. Zhou, J. Chen, X.-Q. Gu, L.-F. Qiu, "THz wave interaction with planar structures consisting of multilayer graphene sheets and bianisotropic slabs", *Proc. IEEE Int. Wireless Symp.*, pp. 1-4, 2014.

[3] W.-Y. Yin, L.-W. Li, O. Ooi, P.-S. Kooi, M. Leong, "Interaction of EM waves with bianisotropic objects: Clarification of magnetic symmetry groups", *Proc. Antennas Propag. Soc. Int. Symp. 2001*, pp. 200-203, 2001.

[4] S. Rikte, G. Kristensson, M. Andersson, "Propagation in bianisotropic media reflection and transmission", *IEE Proc. Microw. Antennas Propag.*, vol. 148, pp. 29 36, 2001.

[5] S. P. Shipman and A. T. Welters, "Resonant electromagnetic scattering in anisotropic layered media," *J. Math. Phys.*, vol. 54, p. 103511, 2013.

[6] D. W. Berreman, "Optics in stratified and anisotropic media: 4×4-matrix formulation," *J. Opt. Soc. Am.*, vol. 62, 1972.

Tuning the Resonant Frequency of Microstrip Patch Antenna in LWIR

Shenjie Miao and Brian A. Lail
Department of Electrical & Computer Engineering
Florida Institute of Technology
Melbourne, Florida, USA
Smiao2012@my.fit.edu

***Abstract*—This paper proposes a new analytical method of tuning the resonant frequency of optical microstrip patch antennas. For this method, the changing of resonant frequency of microstrip patch antenna due to coupling additional reactance can be clearly determined. In this paper, this method verifies that the TM_{10} resonant frequency increases by adding a ridge with variable width and height under the patch antenna. A range of resonant frequencies tuning from 20.75 to 32.4THz, by varying ridge width from 0 to 0.5um and ridge height from 0.1 to 0.6um are demonstrated.**

***Keywords*—long-wave infrared, microstrip patch antenna, resonant frequency.**

I. Introduction

In the past decade, due to improved fabrication capability, there has been a flurry of activities and interests in optical antennas and their applications [1],[2]. Researchers mainly utilize radio frequency (RF) techniques and exploit the geometric shapes of optical antennas [3],[4] (e.g., dipole, bowtie and microstrip patch antenna) and their fundamental performance characteristics (e.g., radiation pattern, resonant frequency and input impedance) [5],[6].

Patch antennas are very common and one of the most studied types of antenna in RF. For optical applications, researchers are trying to translate the advantages of patch antennas in RF to the optical spectrum. The analytical model proposed in this paper provides a simple method of tuning the resonant frequency in LWIR.

II. Preliminary Patch Design

A patch antenna was first designed for TM_{10} mode resonant at 27.75THz. The design process includes monitoring the scattered electric field $|E_{Scatter}|$ in an optical cavity model and noting that resonance corresponds to maximum scattering [7]. Fig. 1 shows the normalized E field of TM_{10} mode with phase distribution at the resonant frequency.

The rectangular patch antenna made of gold (Au) is designed with dimensions 0.6um*1um*0.06um. A silicon substrate with $\varepsilon = 11.7$ and a ground plane under the rectangular patch form a resonant cavity. Gaussian beam illumination with beam-spot size equal to 10um is normally incident on the antenna plane.

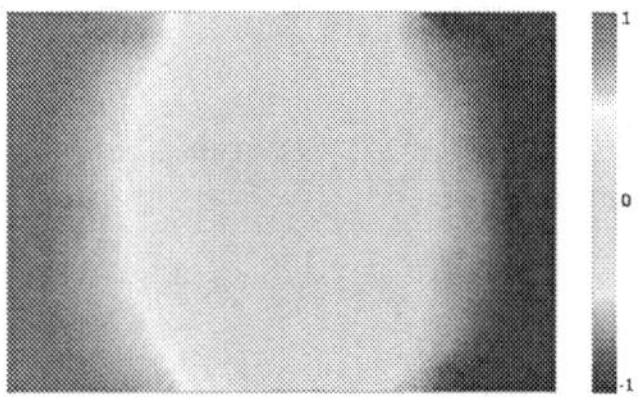

Fig. 1. The normalized electric field in Z direction at 27.75THz.

III. Ridge Effect and Analytical Method

A gold (Au) ridge with dimensions 8um*L_r*0.2um is placed under the patch in order to tune the capacitance in the resonant cavity, as shown in Fig. 2 denoted by the green color. Equation (1) shows the capacitance in the cavity:

$$C = \varepsilon \frac{L_r \times 8\mu m}{d}. \quad (1)$$

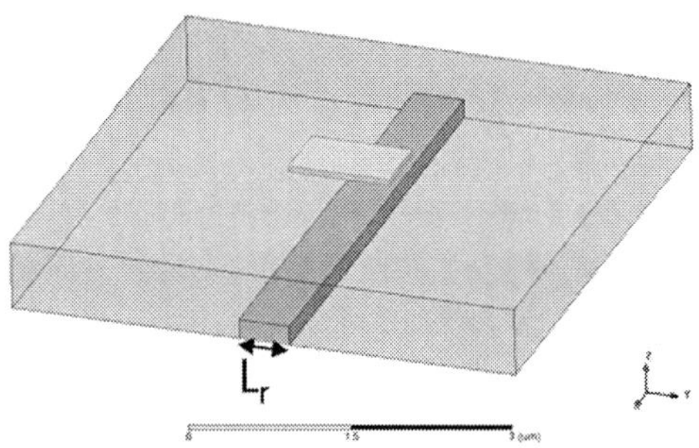

Fig. 2. Resonant frequencies with different Lr.

Here d is the vertical distance between the ridge and patch. The TM_{10} cavity model can be modeled as two parallel open circuit transmission lines [8]. The effective impedance with ridge can be determined by:

$$Z_{eff} = \frac{-j\frac{Z_0}{2}\cot(\beta_1\frac{L}{2})\times\frac{1}{j\omega C}}{-j\frac{Z_0}{2}\cot\left(\beta_1\frac{L}{2}\right)+\frac{1}{j\omega C}}. \quad (2)$$

where Z_0 is the characteristic impedance of transmission line model, $\beta_1 = \frac{2\pi}{\lambda_{eff}}$ and L is the length of patch in Y direction. When the width of the ridge L_r increases, the capacitance also increases, resulting in a new effective wavelength, thus resulting in a new resonant frequency. After considering the ridge effect, Z_{eff} becomes $-j\frac{Z_0}{2}\cot(\beta_2\frac{L}{2})$ where $\beta_2 = \frac{2\pi}{\lambda_{new}}$, giving the relation,

$$-j\frac{Z_0}{2}\cot(\beta_2\frac{L}{2}) = \frac{-j\frac{Z_0}{2}\cot(\beta_1\frac{L}{2})\times\frac{1}{j\omega C}}{-j\frac{Z_0}{2}\cot\left(\beta_1\frac{L}{2}\right)+\frac{1}{j\omega C}}. \quad (3)$$

After simplification we get,

$$\omega C\frac{Z_0}{2} = \frac{\cot\left(\beta_1\frac{L}{2}\right)-\cot\left(\beta_2\frac{L}{2}\right)}{\cot\left(\beta_1\frac{L}{2}\right)\cot\left(\beta_2\frac{L}{2}\right)}. \quad (4)$$

The left side of equation (4) is positive with a coupled ridge. Thus,

$$\cot\left(\beta_1\frac{L}{2}\right) > \cot\left(\beta_2\frac{L}{2}\right). \quad (5)$$

$$\frac{2\pi}{\lambda_{new}} > \frac{2\pi}{\lambda_{eff}}. \quad (6)$$

$$f_{new} > f_{eff}. \quad (7)$$

The equations (5)-(7) indicate that the new resonant frequency with a coupled ridge is larger than that without a coupled ridge.

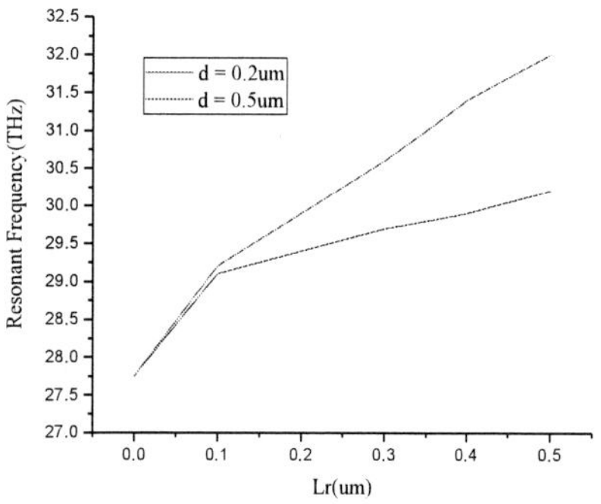

Fig. 3. Resonant frequencies with different Lr.

Ansys High Frequency Structure Simulator (HFSS) is implemented to predict the computational results. Fig. 3 and Fig. 4 contain simulated results of the new patch design including measured dispersive optical properties. Fig. 3 shows the blue shift of resonant frequencies with increasing width of the ridge. Fig. 4 show the red shift of resonant frequencies with 'd' increases in equation (1). These shifts due to the fact that the increase of L_r and decreasing 'd' causes the capacitance of ridge to increase.

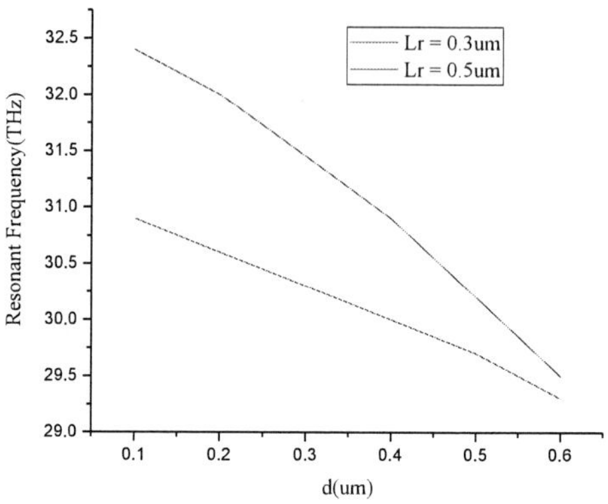

Fig. 4. Resonant frequencies with different d.

As shown in Fig. 3 and Fig. 4, manipulating the height and L_r of ridge can tune the capacitance of cavity then the resonant frequencies change as result. The analytical method predicts the results which are consistent with the simulation results.

This method demonstrates feasibility of tuning resonant frequencies by loading a microstrip patch cavity with a ridge. In optical antennas, graphene can be used as the ridge material. Tunable coupled capacitance can be achieved by biasing appropriate voltage on the graphene.

REFERENCES

[1] J. Farahani, D. Pohl, H. Eisler, and B. Hecht, "Single quantum dot coupled to a scanning optical antenna: A tunable superemitter," Physical Review Letters, vol. 95, no. 1, 2005.

[2] Y. Xu, E. Tucker, G. Boreman, M. Raschke, and B. Lail, "Optical nanoantenna input impedance," ACS Photonics, vol. 3, no. 5, pp. 881-885, 2016.

[3] G. Kino, "Optical antennas: Tuning in to optical wavelengths," Nature Photonics, vol. 2, no. 4, pp. 210-211, 2008.

[4] T. Taminiau, F. Stefani, F. Segerink, and N. van Hulst, "Optical antennas direct single-molecule emission," Nature Photonics, vol. 2, no. 4, pp. 234-237, 2008.

[5] H. Yang, R. Olmon, K. Deryckx, X. Xu, H. Bechtel, Y. Xu, B. Lail, and M. Raschke, "Accessing the optical magnetic near-field through Babinet's principle," ACS Photonics, vol. 1, no. 9, pp. 894-899, 2014.

[6] A. Alu and N. Engheta, "Theory, modeling and features of optical nanoantennas," IEEE Transactions on Antennas and Propagation, vol. 61, no. 4, pp. 1508-1517, 2013.

[7] G. Unal and M. Aksun, "Bridging the gap between RF and optical patch antenna analysis via the cavity model," Scientific Reports, vol. 5, no. 1, 2015.

[8] R. Garg, Microstrip Antenna Design Handbook. Boston: Artech House, 2001.

On the Conforming Combination of the Electric and Magnetic Field Integral Equations

Ahmet F. Yilmaz and H. Arda Ülkü
Department of Electronics Engineering
Gebze Technical University
Gebze, Kocaeli, 41400, Turkey
{a.yilmaz, haulku}@gtu.edu.tr

***Abstract*—A scheme to conformingly combine the electric and magnetic field integral equations (EFIE and MFIE) is presented. Particularly the range space of the method of moments (MoM) matrix system for the mixed discretized MFIE is projected to the range space of the classically discretized EFIE and then combined with EFIE. As a result, an accurate, interior resonance free, and ideally combination factor independent matrix system for the combined field integral equation (CFIE) is obtained. Numerical examples that demonstrate the accuracy and combination factor dependence are presented.**

***Index Terms*—combined field integral equation (CFIE), interior resonance problem, mixed discretization**

I. Introduction

The dependence of the accuracy of the combined field integral equation (CFIE) to the combination factor has been a problem [1]–[4]. Conventionally, EFIE, MFIE and CFIE are discretized using the divergence conforming Rao-Wilton-Glisson (RWG) functions as the testing and basis functions, which is called the classically discretized CFIE (C-CFIE). It is shown in [5] that the accuracy of MFIE is limited due to this discretization scheme because the conforming testing is not satisfied. This problem can be remedied using the curl conforming Buffa-Christiansen-Chen-Wilton (BCCW) functions [6], [7] for testing, which is called the mixed discretization of MFIE. Based on the mixed discretization scheme, combining the classically discretized EFIE and mixed discretized MFIE, which is called mixed CFIE (M-CFIE) in this work, is proposed in [2]. The solution of M-CFIE provides more accurate results compared to C-CFIE, however due to the nonconformity of the testing function (range) spaces of EFIE and MFIE, the resulting matrix system supports interior resonances [3], [4].

In this work, an alternative formulation of CFIE that is obtained by conformingly combining the classically discretized EFIE and mixed discretized MFIE is presented. This formulation is originally developed in [4] and applied to the marching on-in-time solution of the time domain integral equations. In this work, the same approach is applied to the MoM solution of CFIE and two implementations are presented and compared. First, the range function space of the mixed discretized MFIE, i.e., curl conforming BCCW function space, is projected onto the range function space of the classical discretization of EFIE, i.e., divergence conforming RWG function space, and then combined with EFIE. This implementation is called the conforming CFIE via range space projection (RSP-CFIE). As the second implementation, the range space projection is directly formulated as an auxiliary equation and the resulting equation system that doubles the unknowns is solved. This implementation is called the conforming CFIE via auxiliary equation (AE-CFIE). A scheme similar to the latter implementation is presented in [3] where the magnetic and electric currents are used and the combination factor should be 0.5.

II. Formulation

Let S denote the surface of a perfect electrically conducting (PEC) scatterer and the current induced on S is modelled using the RWG functions $\mathbf{f}_n(\mathbf{r})$: $\mathbf{J}(\mathbf{r}) = \sum_{n=1}^{N} \{\mathbf{I}\}_n \mathbf{f}_n(\mathbf{r})$, where $\mathbf{I}$ holds the unknown coefficients. Substituting this expansion in EFIE and MFIE, and testing the resulting equations yield the MoM matrix systems where $\bar{\mathbf{Z}}_{\mathbf{f}}^{\mathrm{E}}$ and $\bar{\mathbf{Z}}_{\hat{\mathbf{n}}\times\mathbf{g}}^{\mathrm{H}}$ are the MoM matrices, and $\mathbf{V}_{\mathbf{f}}^{\mathrm{E}}$ and $\mathbf{V}_{\hat{\mathbf{n}}\times\mathbf{g}}^{\mathrm{H}}$ are the vectors of the tested electric and magnetic fields for classically discretized EFIE and mixed discretized MFIE. The elements of $\bar{\mathbf{Z}}_{\mathbf{f}}^{\mathrm{E}}$, $\bar{\mathbf{Z}}_{\hat{\mathbf{n}}\times\mathbf{g}}^{\mathrm{H}}$, $\mathbf{V}_{\mathbf{f}}^{\mathrm{E}}$, and $\mathbf{V}_{\hat{\mathbf{n}}\times\mathbf{g}}^{\mathrm{H}}$ are:

$$\{\bar{\mathbf{Z}}_{\mathbf{f}}^{\mathrm{E}}\}_{m,n} = \langle \mathbf{f}_m(\mathbf{r}), \mathcal{T}\{\mathbf{f}_n(\mathbf{r})\}\rangle, \quad (1)$$

$$\{\bar{\mathbf{Z}}_{\hat{\mathbf{n}}\times\mathbf{g}}^{\mathrm{H}}\}_{m,n} = \langle \hat{\mathbf{n}}(\mathbf{r}) \times \mathbf{g}_m(\mathbf{r}), \mathcal{K}\{\mathbf{f}_n(\mathbf{r})\}\rangle, \quad (2)$$

$$\{\mathbf{V}_{\mathbf{f}}^{\mathrm{E}}\}_m = \langle \mathbf{f}_m(\mathbf{r}), \mathbf{E}^{\mathrm{inc}}(\mathbf{r})\rangle, \quad (3)$$

$$\{\mathbf{V}_{\hat{\mathbf{n}}\times\mathbf{g}}^{\mathrm{H}}\}_m = \langle \hat{\mathbf{n}}(\mathbf{r}) \times \mathbf{g}_m(\mathbf{r}), \hat{\mathbf{n}}(\mathbf{r}) \times \mathbf{H}^{\mathrm{inc}}(\mathbf{r})\rangle, \quad (4)$$

where $\langle \mathbf{a}(\mathbf{r}), \mathbf{b}(\mathbf{r})\rangle = \int \mathbf{a}(\mathbf{r}) \cdot \mathbf{b}(\mathbf{r}) d\mathbf{r}$, $\mathbf{E}^{\mathrm{inc}}(\mathbf{r})$ and $\mathbf{H}^{\mathrm{inc}}(\mathbf{r})$ are the incident electric and magnetic field intensities, $\hat{\mathbf{n}}(\mathbf{r})$ is the unit normal vector of S, and $\hat{\mathbf{n}}(\mathbf{r}) \times \mathbf{g}_m(\mathbf{r})$ is the curl conforming BCCW functions. Operators $\mathcal{T}\{\cdot\}$ and $\mathcal{K}\{\cdot\}$ are defined as:

$$\mathcal{T}\{\mathbf{f}_n(\mathbf{r})\} = \frac{-j\omega\mu_0}{4\pi} \int_{S_n} \mathbf{f}_n(\mathbf{r}') \frac{e^{-jkR}}{R} d\mathbf{r}' + \frac{1}{4\pi j\omega\varepsilon_0} \nabla \int_{S_n} \nabla' \cdot \mathbf{f}_n(\mathbf{r}') \frac{e^{-jkR}}{R} d\mathbf{r}', \quad (5)$$

$$\mathcal{K}\{\mathbf{f}_n(\mathbf{r})\} = \frac{1}{2}\mathbf{f}_n(\mathbf{r}) - \hat{\mathbf{n}}(\mathbf{r}) \times \nabla \times \int_{S_n} \mathbf{f}_n(\mathbf{r}') \frac{e^{-jkR}}{R} d\mathbf{r}'. \quad (6)$$

Here $R = |\mathbf{r} - \mathbf{r}'|$ is the distance between the observation point $\mathbf{r}$, and the source point $\mathbf{r}'$, μ_0 and ε_0 are the permeability and permittivity of the background medium, $k = 2\pi f\sqrt{\varepsilon_0\mu_0}$, and f is the frequency.

To project the function space, the range of the MFIE operator acting on the discretized current density is assumed to be expanded by RWG functions:

$$\sum_{n=1}^{N} \mathcal{K}\{\mathbf{f}_n(\mathbf{r})\}\{\mathbf{I}\}_n \approx \sum_{m=1}^{N} \mathbf{f}_m(\mathbf{r})\{\mathbf{b}\}_m. \quad (7)$$

Testing (7) with the curl conforming BCCW functions $\hat{\mathbf{n}}(\mathbf{r}) \times \mathbf{g}_m(\mathbf{r})$, results in a matrix equation and the coefficients of the range space projected MFIE operator $\mathbf{b}$ found as:

$$\mathbf{b} = \bar{\mathbf{G}}^{-1}_{\hat{\mathbf{n}}\times\mathbf{g},\mathbf{f}} \bar{\mathbf{Z}}^{\mathrm{H}}_{\hat{\mathbf{n}}\times\mathbf{g}}\mathbf{I}, \quad (8)$$

where the element of the Gram matrix $\{\bar{\mathbf{G}}_{\hat{\mathbf{n}}\times\mathbf{g},\mathbf{f}}\}_{m,n} = \langle \hat{\mathbf{n}} \times \mathbf{g}_m(\mathbf{r}), \mathbf{f}_n(\mathbf{r})\rangle$ [6]. The same procedure can be repeated for the tested magnetic field. Then the expansion at the right hand side of (7) can be combined with EFIE as

$$\begin{aligned} \mathbf{V}^{\mathrm{C}} &= -\alpha\bar{\mathbf{Z}}^{\mathrm{E}}_{\mathbf{f}}\mathbf{I} + \eta_0(1-\alpha)\bar{\mathbf{G}}_{\mathbf{f},\mathbf{f}}\mathbf{b} \\ &= [-\alpha\bar{\mathbf{Z}}^{\mathrm{E}}_{\mathbf{f}} + \eta_0(1-\alpha)\bar{\mathbf{G}}_{\mathbf{f},\mathbf{f}}\bar{\mathbf{G}}^{-1}_{\hat{\mathbf{n}}\times\mathbf{g},\mathbf{f}}\bar{\mathbf{Z}}^{\mathrm{H}}_{\hat{\mathbf{n}}\times\mathbf{g}}]\mathbf{I}, \end{aligned} \quad (9)$$

where, $\mathbf{V}^{\mathrm{C}} = -\alpha\mathbf{V}^{\mathrm{E}}_{\mathbf{f}} + \eta_0(1-\alpha)\bar{\mathbf{G}}_{\mathbf{f},\mathbf{f}}\bar{\mathbf{G}}^{-1}_{\hat{\mathbf{n}}\times\mathbf{g},\mathbf{f}}\mathbf{V}^{\mathrm{H}}_{\hat{\mathbf{n}}\times\mathbf{g}}$, η_0 is the intrinsic impedance and α is the combination factor of CFIE. The element of the Gram matrix $\{\bar{\mathbf{G}}_{\mathbf{f},\mathbf{f}}\}_{m,n} = \langle \mathbf{f}_m(\mathbf{r}), \mathbf{f}_n(\mathbf{r})\rangle$. (9) provides range function space conformity for the combination of EFIE and MFIE (RSP-CFIE). In addition this formulation eliminates the interior resonance problem and solution of (9) is less dependent to the combination factor. However, solution of (9) using an iterative solver requires nested matrix solver calls: one for $\bar{\mathbf{G}}^{-1}_{\hat{\mathbf{n}}\times\mathbf{g},\mathbf{f}}$, one for the resulting matrix system in (9). Even though the $\bar{\mathbf{G}}_{\hat{\mathbf{n}}\times\mathbf{g},\mathbf{f}}$ is well-conditioned and sparse, the nested operations might cause saturation in the error of the iterative solver. Instead of solving (9) directly, the first line in (9) as the range space conforming CFIE and matrix equation in (8) as the auxiliary equation can be combined in a single matrix system (AE-CFIE):

$$\begin{bmatrix} \mathbf{V}^{\mathrm{C}} \\ \mathbf{0} \end{bmatrix} = \begin{bmatrix} \bar{\mathbf{G}}_{\mathbf{f},\mathbf{f}} & -\alpha\bar{\mathbf{Z}}^{\mathrm{E}}_{\mathbf{f}} \\ \bar{\mathbf{G}}_{\hat{\mathbf{n}}\times\mathbf{g},\mathbf{f}} & -\eta_0(1-\alpha)\bar{\mathbf{Z}}^{\mathrm{H}}_{\hat{\mathbf{n}}\times\mathbf{g}} \end{bmatrix} \begin{bmatrix} \mathbf{b} \\ \mathbf{I} \end{bmatrix}. \quad (10)$$

This implementation doubles the unknowns, yet eliminates the nested matrix solver calls. In addition the matrix structure in (10) can be easily diagonally preconditioned.

III. Numerical Results

In this section a unit sphere discretized with 2430 RWG basis functions is analyzed to demonstrate the accuracy of the proposed scheme. An $\hat{\mathbf{x}}$ polarized plane wave propagating in $\hat{\mathbf{z}}$ direction is used as the excitation. A TFQMR iterative solver is employed to solve the MoM matrix systems. The tolerance is set to 10^{-10}. Note that for AE-CFIE the iterative solver saturates around 10^{-7} without reaching to 10^{-10}. In all figures, RMS errors are determined using the scattered electric fields in the far field obtained by the MoM solution and Mie series solution for $\theta \in [0, 180]^\circ$ and $\phi = 0^\circ$.

Fig. 1 plots the RMS error at $f = 130$ MHz for different values of the combination factor α. It is seen that the error values for RSP-CFIE (9) and AE-CFIE (10) are coinciding and do not vary drastically compared to the errors for C-CFIE and M-CFIE. Fig. 2 plots the RMS error for different frequencies. In this case the frequency is swept from 100 MHz to 200 MHz range and combination factor $\alpha = 0.5$. It is seen from Fig. 2 that the RSP-CFIE and AE-CFIE are resonance free and provide more accurate results. Although M-CFIE provides more accurate results than C-CFIE, solution is affected by interior resonances around 131 MHz and 186 MHz.

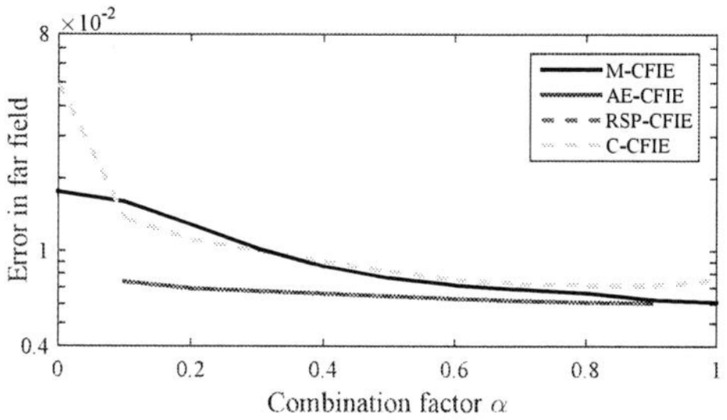

Fig. 1. The RMS error with respect to combination factor.

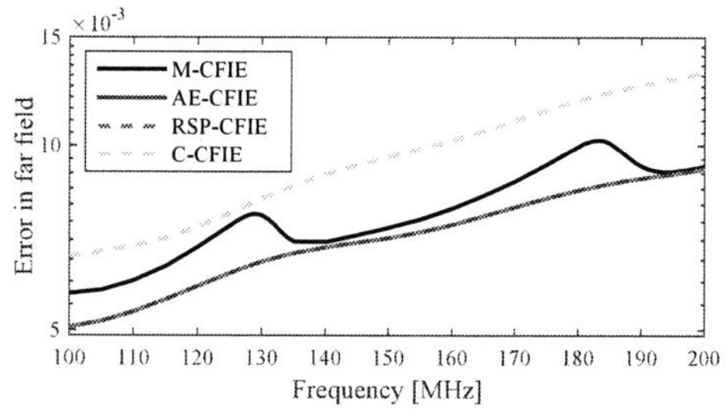

Fig. 2. The RMS error with respect to frequency.

Acknowledgement

This work is supported by the Scientific and Technical Research Council of Turkey (TUBITAK) under the Grant No. EEEAG-116E290.

References

[1] L. Gurel and O. Ergul, "Contamination of the accuracy of the combined-field integral equation with the discretization error of the magnetic-field integral equation," IEEE Trans. Antennas Propag., vol. 57, pp. 2650–2657, Sep. 2009.

[2] S. Yan, J. M. Jin, and Z. Nie, "Improving the accuracy of the second-kind Fredholm integral equations by using the Buffa-Christiansen functions," IEEE Trans. Antennas Propag., vol. 59, pp. 1299–1310, Apr. 2011.

[3] J. Kornprobst and T. F. Eibert, "An accurate combined source integral equation for perfect electrically conducting bodies," in Proc. IEEE Int. Symp. on Antennas and Propagation, pp. 1457–1458, July 2017.

[4] Y. Beghein *et al.*, "A space-time mixed Galerkin marching-on-in-time scheme for the time-domain combined field integral equation," IEEE Trans. Antennas Propag., vol. 61, pp. 1228–1238, Mar. 2013.

[5] K. Cools, F. P. Andriulli, D. D. Zutter, and E. Michielssen, "Accurate and conforming mixed discretization of the MFIE," IEEE Antennas Wireless Propag. Lett., vol. 10, pp. 528–531, 2011.

[6] F. P. Andriulli *et al.*, "A multiplicative Calderon preconditioner for the electric field integral equation," IEEE Trans. Antennas Propag., vol. 56, pp. 2398–2412, Aug. 2008.

[7] Q. Chen and D. R. Wilton, "Electromagnetic scattering by three-dimensional arbitrary complex material/conducting bodies," in Proc. IEEE Int. Symp. on Antennas and Propagation, pp. 590–593, vol.2, May 1990.

A Volume Integral Equation Solver for Quantum-Corrected Transient Analysis of Scattering from Plasmonic Nanostructures

Sadeed B. Sayed, Ismail Enes Uysal, and Hakan Bagci
Computer, Electrical and Mathematical Sciences and Engineering,
King Abdullah University of Science and Technology (KAUST),
Thuwal, 23955-6900, Saudi Arabia
Email: {sadeed.sayed, ismail.uysal, hakan.bagci}@kaust.edu.sa

H. Arda Ulku
Department of Electronics Engineering,
Gebze Technical University,
Kocaeli, 41400, Turkey
Email: haulku@gtu.edu.tr

***Abstract*—Quantum tunneling is observed between two nanostructures that are separated by a sub-nanometer gap. Electrons "jumping" from one structure to another create an additional current path. An auxiliary tunnel is introduced between the two structures as a support for this so that a classical electromagnetic solver can account for the effects of quantum tunneling. The dispersive permittivity of the tunnel is represented by a Drude model, whose parameters are obtained from the electron tunneling probability. The transient scattering from the connected nanostructures (i.e., nanostructures plus auxiliary tunnel) is analyzed using a time domain volume integral equation solver. Numerical results demonstrating the effect of quantum tunneling on the scattered fields are provided.**

I. Introduction

Recent advances in the fabrication of nanoparticles have paved the way to miniature electromagnetic devices to nanoscale. To accurately analyze electromagnetic scattering from such devices, quantum tunneling effects be accounted for. Quantum tunneling is observed between two structures when the gap between them is less than a nanometer. Electrons tunneled from one structure to the other one generate an additional current path that cannot be modeled by classical electromagnetic solvers. This results in errors in scattered field computations. In such cases, one could use a "full" quantum mechanical solver to obtain accurate results, but computational requirements of this solver would be prohibitively high. To alleviate this problem, one can use a (one dimensional) quantum mechanical solver for only the gap and obtain an effective permittivity for an auxiliary tunnel supporting the current generated by tunneled electrons [1]. Then, one can use a classical electromagnetic solver to compute scattered fields from the combined structure (nanostructures plus auxiliary tunnel).

Among several types of classical electromagnetic solvers, time domain volume integral equation (TD-VIE) solvers offer several advantages over their differential equation counterparts [2]. In this work, a time domain-electric field volume integral equation (TD-EFVIE) is developed for transient quantum-corrected analysis of scattering from plasmonic nanostructures. The dispersive permittivity of the auxiliary tunnel, which is introduced to support the currents generated by tunneled electrons, is represented by a Drude model whose parameters are computed from electron tunneling probability as described in [1]. The unknown electric flux density, field intensity and polarization density induced inside the nanostructures and the auxiliary tunnel are expanded in terms of full and half Schaubert-Wilton-Glisson (SWG) functions in space [3], [4] and approximate prolate spherical wave (APSW) functions [5] in time. These expansions are inserted into the TD-EFVIE and the constitutive relation (obtained by inverse Fourier transforming the Drude model) and the resulting coupled system of equations is Galerkin-tested in space. The final semi-discrete matrix system is cast in the form of an ordinary differential equation and integrated in time using a PE(CE)^{m} type linear multistep scheme [6] to yield the coefficients of the unknown expansions.

II. Formulation

Let V denote the volume of the combined structure (the plasmonic nanostructures plus the auxiliary tunnel) residing in an unbounded background medium with permittivity ε_0 and permeability μ_0. The combined structure is excited by band-limited electric field intensity $\mathbf{E}^{\mathrm{inc}}(\mathbf{r},t)$. Upon excitation, flux density $\mathbf{D}(\mathbf{r},t)$ and field intensity $\mathbf{E}(\mathbf{r},t)$ induced in V satisfy:

$$\mathbf{D}(\mathbf{r},t) = \varepsilon_0\varepsilon_\infty(\mathbf{r})\mathbf{E}(\mathbf{r},t) + \mathbf{P}(\mathbf{r},t), \quad (1)$$

$$\partial_t\mathbf{E}^{\mathrm{inc}}(\mathbf{r},t) = \partial_t\mathbf{E}(\mathbf{r},t) + \mathcal{L}\{\mathbf{E}(\mathbf{r},t)\} - \mathcal{L}\{\varepsilon_0^{-1}\mathbf{D}(\mathbf{r},t)\}, \quad (2)$$

for $\mathbf{r} \in V$. Here, the $\varepsilon_\infty(\mathbf{r})$ is the relative permittivity at infinite frequency, $\mathbf{P}(\mathbf{r},t)$ is the polarization density, and the integral operator $\mathcal{L}\{\cdot\}$ is:

$$\mathcal{L}\{\mathbf{X}(\mathbf{r},t)\} = -\frac{\varepsilon_0\mu_0}{4\pi}\int_V \frac{1}{R}\partial_{t'}^3\mathbf{X}(\mathbf{r}',t')\big|_{t'=t-R/c_0} d\mathbf{r}' + \frac{1}{4\pi}\nabla\int_V \frac{1}{R}[\nabla'\cdot\partial_{t'}\mathbf{X}(\mathbf{r}',t')]_{t'=t-R/c_0} d\mathbf{r}', \quad (3)$$

where $R = |\mathbf{r}-\mathbf{r}'|$ is the distance between source and observation points, $\mathbf{r}'$ and $\mathbf{r}$, and $c_0 = 1/\sqrt{\varepsilon_0\mu_0}$ is the speed of light in the background medium. When the permittivity in

V is represented using a Drude model [1], the $\mathbf{P}(\mathbf{r},t)$ satisfies:

$$\partial_t \mathbf{P}(\mathbf{r},t) = \hat{\mathbf{P}}(\mathbf{r},t),$$
$$\partial_t \hat{\mathbf{P}}(\mathbf{r},t) = -\gamma_{\rm p}(\mathbf{r})\mathbf{P}(\mathbf{r},t) + \varepsilon_0(\omega_{\rm p}(\mathbf{r}))^2\mathbf{E}(\mathbf{r},t), \quad (4)$$

where $\hat{\mathbf{P}}(\mathbf{r},t)$ is an intermediate variable, $\gamma_{\rm p}(\mathbf{r})$ is the damping factor, and $\omega_{\rm p}(\mathbf{r})$ is the plasmon frequency. To numerically solve the coupled equations (1), (2), and (4), V is discretized into tetrahedrons and unknowns $\mathbf{D}(\mathbf{r},t)$, $\mathbf{E}(\mathbf{r},t)$, $\mathbf{P}(\mathbf{r},t)$, and $\hat{\mathbf{P}}(\mathbf{r},t)$ are expanded:

$$\mathbf{D}(\mathbf{r},t) = \sum_{i=0}^{N_t}\sum_{n=1}^{N_{\rm F}} I_{n,i}^{\rm D} T_i(t)\mathbf{f}_n^{\rm F}(\mathbf{r}),$$
$$\mathbf{U}(\mathbf{r},t) = \sum_{i=0}^{N_t}\sum_{n=1}^{N_{\rm H}} I_{n,i}^{\rm U} T_i(t)\mathbf{f}_n^{\rm H}(\mathbf{r}), \mathrm{U} \in \{\mathrm{E,P,\hat{P}}\}. \quad (5)$$

Here, $\{\mathbf{f}_n^{\rm F}(\mathbf{r}), \mathbf{f}_n^{\rm H}(\mathbf{r})\}$ are the full and half SWG functions respectively [3], [4], $T_i(t) = T(t - i\Delta t)$, where $T(t)$ is the APSW function [5] and Δt is the time step, and $I_{n,i}^{\rm K}$, $\mathrm{K} \in \{\mathrm{E,D,P,\hat{P}}\}$ are unknown expansion coefficients. Inserting (5) into (1) and spatially testing the resulting equation with $\mathbf{f}_n^{\rm F}(\mathbf{r})$, $m = 1 : N_{\rm F}$, yields a matrix system at time step j:

$$\mathbf{G}^{\rm FF}\mathbf{I}_j^{\rm D} = \mathbf{G}^{\rm FH}\left(\varepsilon_0\varepsilon_\infty \mathbf{I}_j^{\rm E} + \mathbf{I}_j^{\rm P}\right). \quad (6)$$

Here, $\{\mathbf{I}_j^{\rm K}\}_n = I_{n,j}^{\rm K}$ and the elements of the $\mathbf{G}^{\rm AB}$, $\mathrm{A} \in \{\mathrm{F,H}\}$, $\mathrm{B} \in \{\mathrm{F,H}\}$:

$$\{\mathbf{G}^{\rm AB}\}_{m,n} = \int_{V_m} \mathbf{f}_m^{\rm A}(\mathbf{r}) \cdot \mathbf{f}_n^{\rm B}(\mathbf{r}) d\mathbf{r}. \quad (7)$$

Similarly, inserting (5) into (2), and (4) and testing the resulting equations with $\mathbf{f}_n^{\rm H}(\mathbf{r})$, $m = 1 : N_{\rm H}$, yield three coupled matrix systems at j:

$$\partial_t \mathbf{I}_j^{\rm P} = \mathbf{I}_j^{\rm \hat{P}},\ \partial_t \mathbf{I}_j^{\rm \hat{P}} = -\gamma_{\rm p}\mathbf{I}_j^{\rm \hat{P}} + \varepsilon_0\omega_{\rm p}^2\mathbf{I}_j^{\rm E}, \quad (8)$$
$$\mathbf{G}^{\rm HH}\partial_t \mathbf{I}_j^{\rm E} = \mathbf{V}_j^{\rm inc} - \mathbf{Z}_0^{\rm HH}\mathbf{I}_j^{\rm E} - \sum_{i=0}^{j-1}\mathbf{Z}_{j-i}^{\rm HH}\mathbf{I}_i^{\rm E} +$$
$$\varepsilon_0^{-1}\mathbf{Z}_0^{\rm HF}\mathbf{I}_j^{\rm D} + \varepsilon_0^{-1}\sum_{i=0}^{j-1}\mathbf{Z}_{j-i}^{\rm HF}\mathbf{I}_i^{\rm D}, \quad (9)$$

where $\{\mathbf{Z}_{j-i}^{\rm AB}\}_{m,n} = \int_{V_m} \mathbf{f}_m^{\rm A}(\mathbf{r}) \cdot \mathcal{L}\{\mathbf{f}_m^{\rm B}(\mathbf{r})T_i(t)\}\big|_{t=j\Delta t} d\mathbf{r}$. Coupled system of equations (6), (8) and (9) are integrated in time using a linear k-step PE(CE)$^{\rm m}$ scheme [6] to yield the unknown expansion coefficients $\mathbf{I}_j^{\rm K}$ for $j = 1 : N_t$.

III. Numerical Results

The proposed solver is used for analyzing scattering from a sodium dimer consisting of spheres with radius 2.17 nm. The separation between the spheres is 0.265 nm. The auxiliary tunnel is modeled using four concentric cylinders. The outer radius of the outermost shell is 0.8 nm. The Drude model parameters for the sodium and the tunnel are same as the ones in [1]. The dimer is excited using a plane wave with $\mathbf{E}^{\rm inc}(\mathbf{r},t) = \hat{\mathbf{x}}\cos[2\pi f_0(t - t_0 - \mathbf{r}\cdot\hat{\mathbf{z}}/c_0)]e^{-(t-t_0-\mathbf{r}\cdot\hat{\mathbf{z}}/c_0)^2/2\sigma^2}$, where $f_0 = 1200$ THz, $\sigma = 3.6/(2\pi f_0)$, and $t_0 = 6\sigma$. Discretization parameters $N^{\rm F} = 5330$, $N^{\rm H} = 10196$, $\Delta t = 0.01$ fs, and $N_t = 4000$. The predictor-corrector coefficients used for the PE(CE)$^{\rm m}$ scheme are the sixth order Adams-Bashforth and backward difference formula (BDF6) coefficients. For comparison, scattering from the dimer without the auxiliary tunnel is also studied under the same excitation.

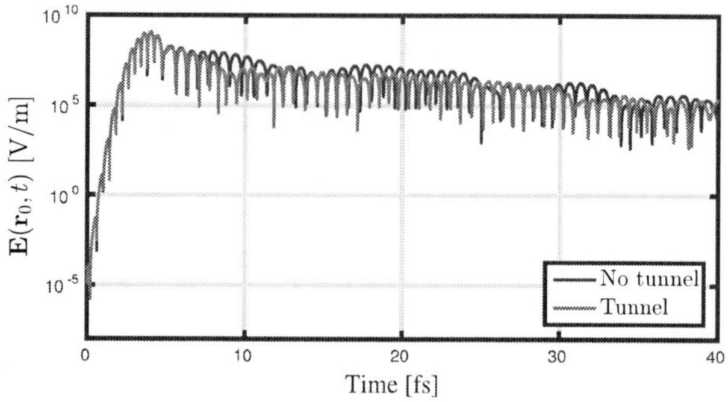

Fig. 1. $\mathbf{E}(\mathbf{r}_0,t)$ at $\mathbf{r}_0 = (2.3, 0.0, 0.0)$ nm.

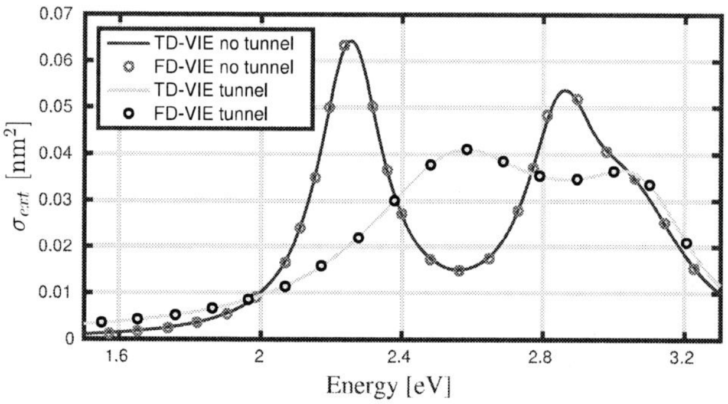

Fig. 2. Extinction cross section of the sodium dimer.

Fig. 1 compares $\mathbf{E}(\mathbf{r}_0,t)$ for $\mathbf{r}_0 = (2.3, 0.0, 0.0)$ nm computed for the dimers with and without the auxiliary tunnel. The result clearly shows that the solver provides stable results for both the cases. In Fig. 2, the extinction cross section of the dimers obtained by Fourier transforming the time domain solution is compared to that obtained directly by a frequency domain VIE solver. The results agree well. The figure also shows that introducing an auxiliary tunnel significantly changes the computed radiation pattern of the dimer.

References

[1] R. Esteban, A. G. Borisov, P. Nordlander, and J. Aizpurua, "Bridging quantum and classical plasmonics with a quantum-corrected model," Nat. Comm., vol. 3, 825, 2012.

[2] S. B. Sayed, H. A. Ulku, and H. Bagci, "A stable marching on-in-time scheme for solving the time domain electric field volume integral equation on high-contrast scatterers," IEEE Trans. Antennas Propag., vol. 63, no. 7, pp. 3098–3110, July 2015.

[3] D. H. Schaubert, R. W. Donald, and W. G. Allen, "A tetrahedral modeling method for electromagnetic scattering by arbitrarily shaped inhomogeneous dielectric bodies," IEEE Trans. Antennas Propag., vol. 32, no. 1, pp. 77–85, Jan. 1984.

[4] G. Kobidze, J. Gao, S. Balasubramaniam, and E. Michielssen, "A fast time domain integral equation based scheme for analyzing scattering from dispersive objects," IEEE Trans. Antennas Propag., vol. 53, no. 3, pp. 1215–1226, Mar. 2005.

[5] R. Wildman, G. Pisharody, D. S. Weile, S. Balasubramaniam, and E. Michielssen, "An accurate scheme for the solution of the time-domain integral equations of electromagnetics using higher order vector bases and bandlimited extrapolation," IEEE Trans. Antennas Propag., vol. 52, no. 11, pp. 2973–2984, Nov. 2004.

[6] H. A. Ulku, H. Bagci, and E. Michielssen, "Marching on-in-time solution of the time domain magnetic field integral equation using a predictor-corrector scheme," IEEE Trans. Antennas Propag., vol. 61, no. 8, pp. 4120–4131, Aug. 2013.

A Space-Time Domain Decomposition Method for High-fidelity Electromagnetic Simulation

Shu Wang and Zhen Peng
Electrical and Computer Engineering Department, University of New Mexico, Albuquerque, U.S.A.
shuwang12@unm.edu, pengz@unm.edu

***Abstract*—This paper addresses a growing need for space-time parallel simulation capability in electromagnetics (EM) applications. Currently time-dependent EM solvers are typically parallel only in space. The sequential-in-time nature of these solvers can achieve good parallel scaling when the number of spatial mesh points per core is large. But the parallel efficiency quickly deteriorates and even saturates if spatial parallelism has been fully exploited. We proposed a new time domain EM solver to harvest parallelism in both spatial and temporal dimension. The spatial parallelism is achieved by discontinuous Galerkin formulation, and the temporal parallelism is enabled by Krylov subspace method based exponential integrator. The improved parallel performance over space-only parallel time-domain solvers is validated by numerical examples.**

***Index Terms*— Domain Decomposition, Krylov Subspace Method, Space-time Paralle.**

I. Introduction

High-performance computing (HPC) architectures are rapidly evolving. With the advancements of massively parallel supercomputers and the flexible and general purpose families of multi-core processors, the era of exascale computing is on the horizon. Many of the currently used fast parallel algorithms become uncompetitive when mapped onto these latest HPC architectures. In particular, traditional time-dependent EM solvers [1]–[5] are structured to be parallel in space. The sequential-in-time nature of the solvers can achieve good parallel scaling when the number of spatial mesh points per core is large. But the parallel efficiency quickly deteriorates if spatial parallelism has been fully exploited, as shown in Fig. 1. Therefore, a futuristic question arises that if it is possible to parallelize the time dimension for Maxwell's Equations.

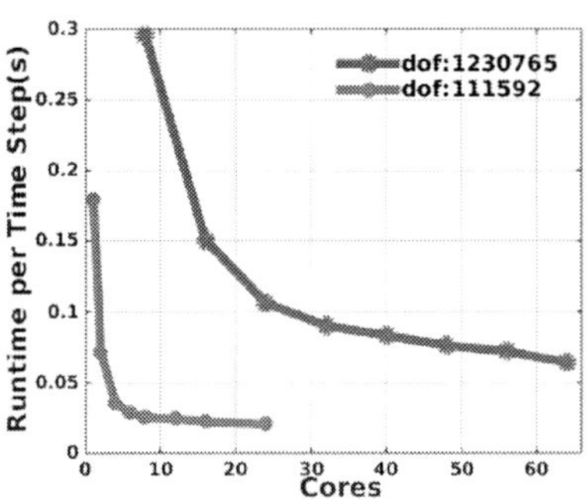

Fig. 1. Saturation of parallel efficiency.

This work proposes a space-time domain decomposition method for evolutional electromagnetic simulation. The technique ingredients include a discontinuous Galerkin discretization in space and Krylov subspace method based exponential integrator for the time dimension. This work has two major benefits: **(i)** it results in a highly scalable parallel time domain solver with flexible space and time decomposition scheme; **(ii)** it provides a natural way to integrated with many existing domain decomposition techniques. The capability and performance of the computational algorithms are illustrated and validated through numerical experiments.

II. Methodology

A. Problem Decomposition

The time-dependent Maxwell's Equations defined on $\Omega \times [0, T]$ can be written as:

$$\nabla \times \mathbf{E} = -\mu \frac{\partial \mathbf{H}}{\partial t}$$
$$\nabla \times \mathbf{H} = \epsilon \frac{\partial \mathbf{E}}{\partial t} + \sigma \mathbf{E} + \mathbf{J},$$

It can be abstracted as a first-order initial value problem (IVP):

$$u'(t) = Au(t) + g(t), u(0) = u_0, \tag{1}$$

where $u(t) = [\mathbf{E}, \mathbf{H}]^T$, A and $g(t)$ are operator discretization matrix and source term. Time period $[0, T]$ is divided into N time-windows $W_i = (t_{i-1}, t_i]$ with $i = 1, 2, ..., N$, $t_N = T$. Equation 1 can be decomposed into a superposition of source dependent subproblem on W_i:

$$v_i'(t) = Av_i(t) + g(t), \quad v_i(t_{i-1}) = 0, \tag{2}$$

and a source independent subproblem $y(t)$ on $[t_{i-1}, T]$ as:

$$y_i'(t) = Ay_i(t), \quad y_i(t_{i-1}) = v_{i-1}(t_{i-1}), \tag{3}$$

The original solution can be rewritten as $u_i(t) = v_i(t) + \sum_{j=1}^{i} y_j(t)$ [6]. Thus the simulation is carried out as following: the source dependent subproblem provides initial values for the source independent subproblem. Fig. 2 shows the computing grid partition for individual subproblems.

B. Parallelization of Source Dependent Subproblem

Consider the source-dependent subproblems, individual time windows are non-overlapping with zero initial values, we choose the internal penalty discontinuous Galerkin (IPDG) finite element method for spacial discretization and the stepping integrator (Leap Frog) to advance in time.

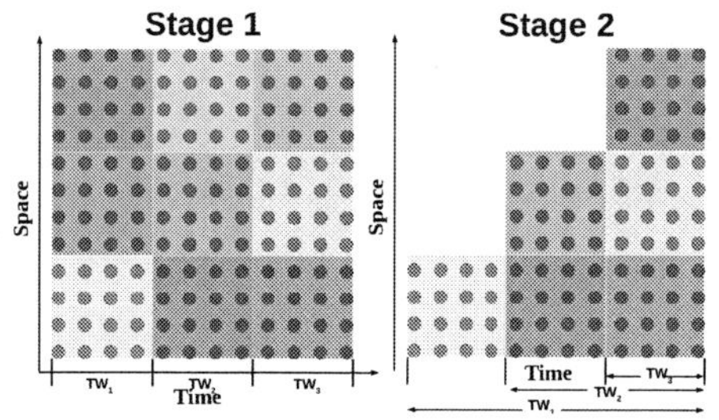

Fig. 2. Space-time domain decomposition.

C. Parallelization of Source Independent Subproblem

Source independent subproblems are homogeneous in time with non-zero initial values. Therefore, they can be calculated by evaluating the matrix exponential: $y_i(t) = e^{tA}v_{i-1}(t_{i-1}), \quad t \in [t_{i-1}, T]$. Evidently, the problem can be transformed into seeking for the reduced order model of e^{tA}. We have employed Rational Arnoldi decomposition (RAD) [7]. Sparse matrix A is projected onto a lower dimensional Rational Krylov (RK) space which can be constructed by:

$$AV_{m+1}\underline{K_m} = V_{m+1}\underline{H_m}, \quad (4)$$

where $\underline{K_m}, \underline{H_m}$ are upper Hessenberg matrices of size $(m+1)\times m$. Approximation to matrix exponential $y_i(t)$ is: $y_m(t) \approx V_m e^{tA_m} V_m^* v_{i-1}(t_{i-1})$, where $A_m := V_m^* A V_m \in \mathbb{C}^{m\times m}$.

III. Numerical Experiments

A. RAD for Source Independent Subproblem

We first study the performance of the RAD for source independent subproblem. The runtime is compared with the 2nd-order leap frog stepping method, as shown in Table I. As Krylov subspace method based exponential integrator breaks the limit of time step brought by CLF condition, it is much faster than the traditional time marching scheme.

TABLE I. Computational Statistics

RAD		Leap-Frog	
Period	4ns	Period	4ns
Orth	96s	Time Steps	32742
MxV+Solve	84s	Δt	0.12216ps
Total Time	180s	Total Time	2328s

B. Performance of Parallel Space-time DD Method

We proceed to evaluate the performance of space-time DD method on a practical application, a Gaussian pulse (temporal half-width 0.5ns) illuminating at a high-definition cavity (DOF=446,296). Time period $[0, 2ns]$ is divided into 2 even time windows. The geometry and electric fields at $t = 2$ns are illustrated in Fig. 3. If the time period was divided into more windows, we expect more efficiency gain since each time window would be assigned to fewer (spatial) processors. As shown in Fig. 4. We observe that the parallel scaling efficiency is 80% at 96 cores (8 time windows), compared with that less than 35% from space only parallel method.

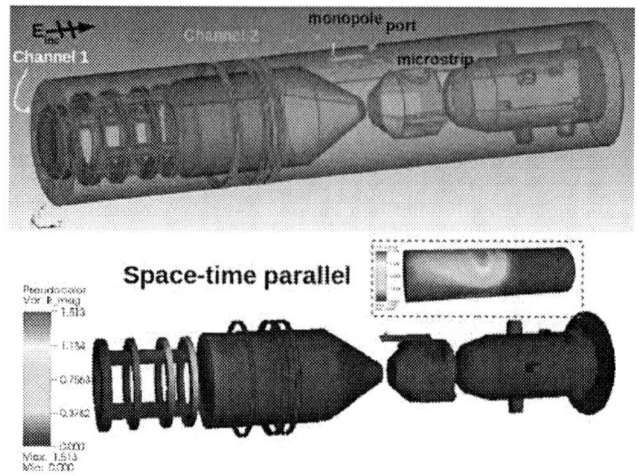

Fig. 3. Geometry of missile cavity and field distribution

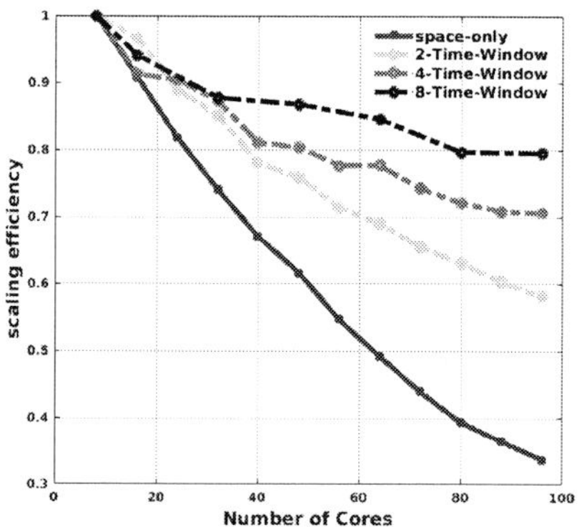

Fig. 4. Comparison of Parallel Scaling Efficiency

IV. Conclusion

A new space-time domain decomposition for time domain EM simulation has been presented. The results show that parallel efficiency gain is obtained by harvesting both temporal and spacial parallelism. This work demonstrates its potential in obtaining good parallel efficiency in massive parallel computing environment.

References

[1] T. Weiland, "Time domain electromagnetic field computation with finite difference methods," International Journal of Numerical Modeling: Electronic Networks, Devices and Fields. 9.4 (1996): 295-319.

[2] J.-F. Lee, R. Lee, and A. Cangellaris, "Time-domain finite-element methods," IEEE Trans. Antennas and Propagat., 45.3 (1997): 430-442.

[3] D. Jiao, et al., "Time-domain finite-element simulation of three-dimensional scattering and radiation problems ssing perfectly matched layers," IEEE Trans. Antennas and Propagat., 51.2 (2003): 296-305.

[4] A. Taflove and S. C. Hagness. Computational Electrodynamics: The Finite-Difference Time-Domain Method. Artech house, 2005.

[5] Z. Lou and J.-M. Jin, "A novel dual-field time-domain finite-element domain-decomposition method for computational electromagnetics," 54.6. 2006, 1850-1862.

[6] M. Gander and S. Guttel, "PARAEXP: A parallel integrator for linear initial-value problems," SIAM J. Sci. Comput., 35(2):C123-C142, 2013.

[7] A. Ruhe, "Rational Krylov: A practical algorithm for large sparse nonsymmetric matrix pencils," SIAM J. Sci. Comput., 19(5):1535-1551, 1998.

Analysis of Nonlinear Graphene Plasmonics Using Surface Integral Equations

1st Ling Ling Meng
and 3rd Tian Xia
*Dept. of Electrical
and Computer Engineering
University of Illinois at Urbana-Champaign*
Urbana, United States
lmeng9@illinois.edu, tianxia3@illinois.edu

2nd Xiaoyan Y. Z. Xiong
and 4th Li Jun Jiang
*Dept. of Electrical
and Electronic Engineering
The University of Hong Kong*
Hong Kong, China
xyxiong@eee.hku.hk, jianglj@hku.hk

5th Weng Cho Chew
*School of Electrical
and Computer Engineering
Purdue University*
West Lafayette, United States
wcchew@purdue.edu

***Abstract*—Graphene plasmonics have attracted significant attention in the past few years due to the remarkable optical and electrical properties of graphene. A highly effective method based on surface integral equations (SIE) in the frequency domain is proposed to describe both linear and nonlinear effects of graphene efficiently and accurately. Graphene, a centrosymmetric material, can possess second harmonic generation (SHG) when the conductivity is nonlocal. In this work, the fundamental harmonic (FH) of a graphene wrapped particle is studied as the first benchmark by introducing a conducting surface in SIE. Then it is modified to analyze a graphene-based patch antenna in both FH and SHG. This method can be extended to other two-dimensional materials easily, and fast multipole algorithm can be applied to accelerate the simulation.**

***Index Terms*—graphene, surface integral equation, nonlinear**

I. Introduction

Graphene, a monolayer of carbon atoms arranged in a hexagonal lattice, has aroused tremendous interest in the past years due to its remarkable optical and electrical properties. It has been proven to be an alternative platform for applications in confining light and guiding surface plasmon polaritons. Recent studies of the nonlinear optical properties of graphene make graphene as a competitive candidate in nonlinear optical devices. Optical Kerr effect due to large third-order susceptibilities has been observed in graphene [1]. Graphene is a centrosymmetric material with a vanishing second-order nonlinearity typically. This argument, however, breaks down when the conductivity is nonlocal [2]. The analysis of second harmonic generation (SHG) for graphene is still in semi-analytical stage that calls for numerical solutions [3].

Several numerical methods have been proposed to study the electromagnetic phenomena of graphene-based structures [4]. Compared to modeling graphene layer as a thin volume, it is more accurate to treat it as a conducting surface. The surface integral equation (SIE) formulation has inherent advantage to capture the layer feature of graphene. Furthermore, the analysis in the frequency domain can remove the cumbersome descriptions of material dispersion in the time domain. In this work, the SIE for graphene-involved structure is established for the studies of both the fundamental and second harmonic analysis.

II. SIE Formulation for Graphene-Based Structure

As aforementioned, the graphene layer is modeled as a surface current in the proposed method. The SHG problem of graphene-based structure is divided to two steps. First, the linear response is solved in the fundamental harmonic (FH). Then, the nonlinear effect is analyzed by using the nonlinear polarization induced by the fields in FH. The mutual coupling between fundamental and second harmonic field is obtained by iteratively solving the two processes.

A. Conductivity of Graphene

The surface conductivity of graphene is frequency dependent, which can be derived by random-phase approximation [5]. The linear part consists of intra-band and inter-band conductivities, expressed as:

$$\sigma_s = \sigma_{intra} + \sigma_{inter}. \tag{1}$$

The conductivity σ_s depends on electron charge, reduced Planck constant, Boltzmann constant, Fermi energy, electron-phonon relaxation time and temperature. The last three parameters can be tuned to change the property of graphene, providing more possible applications in optical and electronic devices. (Detailed expressions can be found in [5]). The current induced by second-order conductivity is:

$$\mathbf{J}_i^{(2)} = \sigma_{ijkl}^{(2)}(2\omega;\omega)E_j^{\omega}\nabla_k E_l^{\omega}, \tag{2}$$

where $ijkl$ denote in-plane vector indices and summation over repeated indices is implied. The nonlocal second order conductivity tensor can be found in [2].

B. SIE for FH Field

We consider the structure consisting of a monolayer graphene-wrapped dielectric sphere of radius a and permittivity ϵ_d, embedded in a homogeneous background medium with permittivity ϵ_b. We denote the background domain as V_1, the interior domain of particle as V_2, and the interface between them as S. On S^+, the equivalent surface currents $\{\mathbf{J}_1, \mathbf{M}_1\}$ generate $\{\mathbf{E}^{sca}, \mathbf{H}^{sca}\}$ in V_1 and $\{-\mathbf{E}^{inc}, -\mathbf{H}^{inc}\}$

in V_2. The equivalent currents are the discontinuities of the fields, therefore,

$$\begin{cases} \hat{\mathbf{n}} \times [\mathbf{E}^{sca} - (-\mathbf{E}^{inc})] = -\mathbf{M}_1 = \hat{\mathbf{n}} \times \mathbf{E}^{tot} \\ \hat{\mathbf{n}} \times [\mathbf{H}^{sca} - (-\mathbf{H}^{inc})] = \mathbf{J}_1 = \hat{\mathbf{n}} \times \mathbf{H}^{tot} \end{cases}. \tag{3}$$

On S^-, the equivalent surface currents $\{\mathbf{J}_2, \mathbf{M}_2\}$ generate $\{0, 0\}$ in V_1 and $\{\mathbf{E}_2^{tot}, \mathbf{H}_2^{tot}\}$ in V_2. Again, the boundary condition can be expressed as:

$$\hat{\mathbf{n}} \times [0 - \mathbf{E}_2^{tot}] = -\mathbf{M}_2, \quad \hat{\mathbf{n}} \times [0 - \mathbf{H}_2^{tot}] = \mathbf{J}_2. \tag{4}$$

Since there are no magnetic surface currents on graphene, $\hat{\mathbf{n}} \times [\mathbf{E}^{tot} - \mathbf{E}_2^{tot}] = 0$, i.e., $\mathbf{E}_{1t} = \mathbf{E}_{2t}$. Note that $\mathbf{E}_{2t} = -\hat{\mathbf{n}} \times \mathbf{M}_2$. The electric surface currents on graphene are not zero due to the conductivity of graphene, thus $\hat{\mathbf{n}} \times [\mathbf{H}^{tot} - \mathbf{H}_2^{tot}] = \mathbf{J}_\sigma$ and $\mathbf{J}_\sigma = \sigma_s \mathbf{E}_{2t} = -\sigma_s \hat{\mathbf{n}} \times \mathbf{M}_2$.

According to the above boundary conditions, a PMCHWT based matrix-vector product (MVP) form $\mathbf{C}\mathbf{x} = \mathbf{b}$ can be established as:

$$\mathbf{C} = \begin{pmatrix} \mathcal{L}_{1E} & \mathcal{K}'_{1E} + \mathcal{K}'_{2E} & -\mathcal{L}_{2E} \\ \mathcal{K}'_{1H} & \mathcal{L}_{1H} + \mathcal{L}_{2H} - \frac{1}{2}\sigma_s & -\mathcal{K}'_{2H} \\ \mathbf{I} & -\sigma_s \hat{\mathbf{n}} \times \mathbf{I} & \mathbf{I} \end{pmatrix}, \tag{5}$$

$$\mathbf{x} = \begin{pmatrix} \mathbf{J}_1 \\ \mathbf{M}_1 \\ \mathbf{J}_2 \end{pmatrix}, \quad \mathbf{b} = \begin{pmatrix} -\mathbf{E}^{inc} \\ -\mathbf{H}^{inc} \\ 0 \end{pmatrix}, \tag{6}$$

where $\mathcal{K}'$ represents the principle value for operator $\mathcal{K}$, I is the identity matrix. Detailed expressions for operators $\mathcal{L}$ and $\mathcal{K}$ can be found in [6]. The fast multipole algorithm can be applied to accelerate the MVP calculation [7] and accurate evaluations of lossy Green's function can be employed [8], making this method more efficient and accurate.

C. Calculation of SH Field

We denote $\mathbf{P}_{st}^{\Omega}$ and P_{sn}^{Ω} as the tangential and normal polarizations in second order separately. Here Ω is the frequency of the second harmonic. The relationships between currents and polarizations can be expressed as:

$$\begin{cases} \mathbf{J}_1^{\Omega} + \mathbf{J}_2^{\Omega} = -i\Omega \mathbf{P}_{st}^{\Omega} = \mathbf{J}_\sigma^{(2)} \\ \mathbf{M}_1^{\Omega} + \mathbf{M}_2^{\Omega} = 1/\epsilon' \hat{\mathbf{n}} \times \nabla_s P_{sn}^{\Omega} \end{cases}. \tag{7}$$

Since there are only tangential polarizations for graphene, $P_{sn} = 0$, thus $\mathbf{M}_1^{\Omega} = -\mathbf{M}_2^{\Omega}$. The second order electric current can be obtained from Eqn. (2).

III. Numerical Results

A graphene wrapped nanoparticle is studied in FH as a benchmark work. Afterwards, the SIE formulation is modified to analyze the graphene-based patch antenna.

Fig. 1 (a) shows the scattering cross section (SCS) of a graphene wrapped sphere with different radius at Fermi energy $E_F = 0.3eV$. The permittivity of background is the same as the dielectric sphere with $\epsilon_r = 2.25$. The results are consistent with data from [5]. The surface plasmon resonances are red-shifted with enhanced peaks, when the radius is increased.

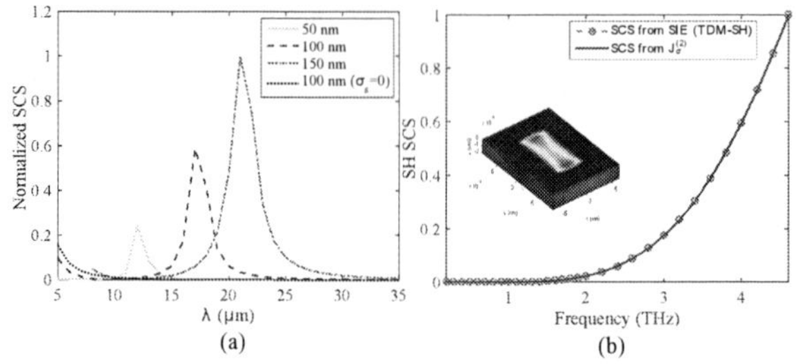

Fig. 1. (a) Scattering cross section (SCS) for graphene wrapped sphere in FH. (b) Benchmark of SCS for graphene-based patch antenna in SH. The inset is the electric current distribution of SH.

The terahertz radiation for a graphene-based patch antenna is studied using the proposed SIE. The dimension of the dielectric substrate is $13\mu m \times 18\mu m \times 2\mu m$ and the graphene pacth is $5\mu m \times 10\mu m$. To verify the SIE for SH, the permittivity of the substrate is set to 1, the same as the background of air. Then the SCS calculated directly from the second order current should be consistent with the SCS from the solutions of matrix-vector product of SIE. The results in Fig. 1 (b) demonstrate the validity of the proposed SIE formulations.

IV. Conclusion

The SIE formulation for graphene-based structures is proposed in both the fundamental and second harmonic calculations. It is highly effective to model the graphene layer as a conducting surface accurately. More complicated structures can be studied when semi-analytical solution vanishes. Furthermore, it is easy to extend this formulation to other two-dimensional materials, such as transition-metal dichalcogenide and black phosphorus.

References

[1] N. M. R. Peres, Y. V. Bludov, J. E. Santos, A. P. Jauho, and M. I. Vasilevskiy, "Optical bistability of graphene in the terahertz range," Phys. Rev. B, vol. 90, 2014.

[2] M. T. Manzoni, I. Silveiro, F. J. García de Abajo, and D. E. Chang, "Second-order quantum nonlinear optical processes in single graphene nanostructures and arrays," New J. Phys., vol. 17, no. 8, 2015.

[3] D. A. Smirnova, I. V. Shadrivov, A. E. Miroshnichenko, A. I. Smirnov, and Y. S. Kivshar, "Second-harmonic generation by a graphene nanoparticle," Phys. Rev. B, vol. 90, 2014.

[4] M. Weismann and N. C. Panoiu, "Theoretical and computational analysis of second-and third-harmonic generation in periodically patterned graphene and transition-metal dichalcogenide monolayers," Phys. Rev. B, vol. 94, 2016.

[5] K. Zhang, Y. Huang, A. E. Miroshnichenko, and L. Gao, "Tunable optical bistability and tristability in nonlinear graphene-wrapped nanospheres," J. Phys. Chem. C, 2017.

[6] W. C. Chew, M. S. Tong, and B. Hu, "Integral equation methods for electromagnetic and elastic waves," Synthesis Lectures on Computational Electromagnetics, 2008.

[7] L. L. Meng, X. Y. Z. Xiong, T. Xia, and L. J. Jiang, "The error control of mixed-form fast multipole algorithm based on the high order multipole rotation," IEEE Antennas Wireless Propag. Lett., vol. 16, 2017.

[8] T. Xia, H. Gan, M. Wei, W. C. Chew, H. Braunisch, Z. Qian, K. Aygün, and A. Aydiner, "An integral equation modeling of lossy conductors with the enhanced augmented electric field integral equation," IEEE Trans. Antennas Propag., vol. 65, no. 8, 2017.

Design of Ungrounded CPW GaN-on-Si MMICs

Philip Zurek*, Myles Foreman*, Ryan Johnson†, Christopher Galbraith†, José Estrada*, and Zoya Popovic*
*Department of Electrical, Computer, and Energy Engineering, University of Colorado, Boulder, Colorado 80309-0425
†MIT Lincoln Laboratory, Lexington, Massachusetts 02421-6426

Abstract—**This work presents a study of circuit component design in a new GaN-on-Si process being developed by the MIT Lincoln Laboratory. The process uses a thick silicon substrate with no through-vias with a multi-layer stack-up. Examples of components required for MMIC design include lines of various impedances, shorted and open stubs, tees, meander lines, and capacitors. Because the fabrication process requires the use of ungrounded CPW lines, underpasses are necessary to connect ground planes and a study of 50-Ohm lines with several underpass spacings is performed. The large range of dimensions and dielectric constants presents a challenge for full-wave simulations, and a comparison between Ansys HFSS and Sonnet Software is presented for a variety of passive circuit components implemented in the GaN-on-Si MMIC stack-up.**

I. Introduction

Gallium nitride (GaN) is established as a high-voltage semiconductor with broad applications, including those at microwave and millimeter-wave frequencies. At frequencies above UHF, MMIC passive and active circuit components with a GaN active layer are typically fabricated on a silicon carbide (SiC) substrate. However, SiC is expensive and not easily integrated with CMOS. To overcome this, GaN MMICs on silicon (Si) substrates are being developed that keep lag effects low [1], reduce the parasitic conduction layer [2], optimize device periphery [3], and integrate with CMOS [4].

In this work, we explore a different GaN-on-Si process under development at the MIT Lincoln Laboratory. A stack-up of the process is shown in Fig. 1, where a GaN active layer is epitaxially-grown on a high-resistivity Si substrate with three metal layers and no through-vias. AlGaN is used as a barrier layer (not shown). The fabrication process also includes high-electron mobility transistors (HEMTs) of varying gate lengths (from 120 to 200 nm), periphery, gate-source spacing, and gate-drain spacing. Metal structures are written using lithography. Several numerical challenges arise from the complex stack-up. The eight layer thickness ranges from 90 nm to 1.065 mm, while the guided wavelength at X-band is on the order of 15 mm. Appropriate port excitation and model de-embedding also need to be considered. In this paper, several CPW circuit components are designed and simulated using both Finite Element (FEM) Ansys HFSS and Method of Moments (MoM) Sonnet Software. Our goal is to establish which method agrees better with measurements.

Coplanar waveguide transmission lines can be evaluated using the conformal mapping method described in [5], which results in the characteristic impedance given by:

$$Z_{0cp} = \frac{30\pi}{\sqrt{\epsilon_{re}}} \frac{K'(k_1)}{K(k_1)}, \tag{1}$$

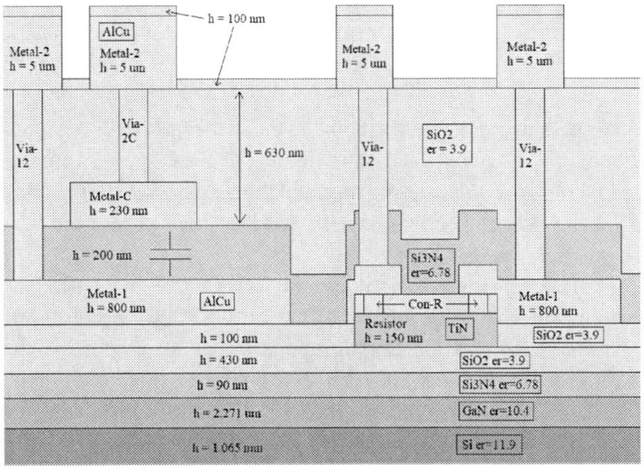

Fig. 1. GaN-on-Si process stack-up (not to scale). CPW lines are made in the Metal-2 layer (blue). Underpasses are made using the Metal-1 layer. Capacitors are made using Metal-C and Metal-1 layers. The various dielectrics and their permittivities are shown in green, GaN in purple and the Si substrate in orange. HEMT metal layers are omitted since this paper focuses on passive circuit components.

where K is the complete elliptic integral of the first kind (K' is its complement), k_1 is its argument, and ϵ_{re} is the effective dielectric constant. The constant ϵ_{re} can be determined as the weighted sum of each dielectric layer's filling factor and relative permittivity. This approach is used as a starting point in design, e.g., for a gap width of 34 μm and conductor line width of 40 μm, Z_{0cp} = 50 Ω. However, when simulated using HFSS, a gap width of 25 μm produced a 50-Ω line due to the influence of the conductor thickness, pointing to the need for detailed electromagnetic simulations.

II. Passive Component Design and Results

Because this GaN-on-Si process does not include through-vias to a ground plane, CPW transmission lines are used, whereas typical MMICs use microstrip transmission lines [1]. Along with the Metal-2 layer (see Fig. 1) used for the CPW lines, the Metal-1 layer is used to create underpasses to connect the CPW reference planes and for capacitor electrodes in conjunction with the Metal-C layer. An example ADS layout of a portion of a 50-Ω line with a λ/4 shunt shorted stub is included in Fig. 2. Because of the fringing fields associated with the inductive nature of the short, this line is modeled in ADS as having a length extension of 10 μm [5].

For a full stack-up model, Sonnet requires memory on the order of 30 GB for more complex circuit geometries, such as capacitors and meander lines, whereas HFSS requires 13 GB. In HFSS, lumped ports are used to excite the transmission

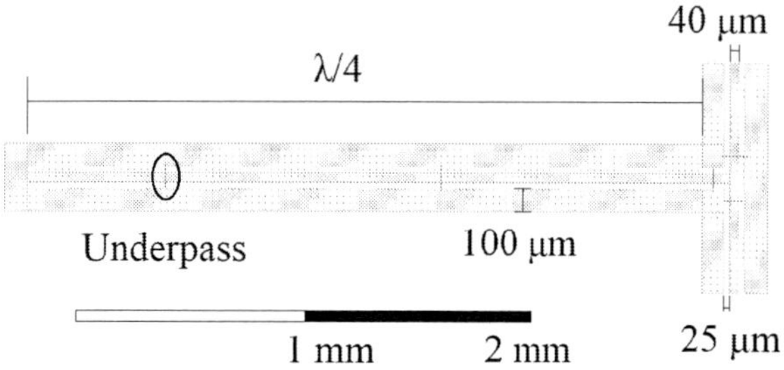

Fig. 2. ADS layout of a 50-Ω CPW line with λ/4 shunt shorted stub and λ/10 spaced underpasses, currently in fabrication. Labeled line width, gap width, and ground width are the same everywhere in this layout.

line so that the radiation boundary can be properly set up a distance λ/10 away. The shorted stub of Fig. 2, e.g., requires 8.35 hours to solve in Sonnet and 2.82 in HFSS with a full stack-up using a computer with 16 GB of RAM and an Intel i7 3.4 GHz processor.

To reduce simulation times, the stack-up is simplified by combining the two dielectric layers between Metal-2 and Metal-1 into a single homogeneous effective dielectric with a relative permittivity of 4.55 (1 % below weighted average). Similarly with the layers at Metal-1 and below, but not including Si, a second effective dielectric layer with relative permittivity 6.1 is included in the simulations (29 % below weighted average). The Si thickness was reduced to 600 μm by 44 %. These changes have little effect on performance, but decrease simulation times by about 95 % for complicated geometries.

Underpasses are added at varying intervals with necessary adjustments to produce varying impedance transmission lines, summarized in Table I. For the 50-Ω line with λ/10 spacing, plots of loss and $|S_{11}|$ for Z_L = 15 Ω are included in Fig. 3.

TABLE I. Varying Impedance Transmission Line Dimensions

ϵ_{re} HFSS	ϵ_{re} Sonnet	Underpass Spacing	Z_0	HFSS Line Width	HFSS Gap Width
4.96	5.06	none	50 Ω	40 μm	23 μm
5.61	5.38	∼ λ/20	50 Ω	40 μm	28 μm
5.20	5.18	∼ λ/10	50 Ω	40 μm	25 μm
5.11	5.01	∼ λ/4	50 Ω	40 μm	24 μm
4.83	5.05	∼ λ/10	30 Ω	74 μm	8 μm
4.83	4.95	∼ λ/10	75 Ω	16 μm	37 μm

Sonnet gives a resonant spike around 28 GHz due to the PEC boundaries imposed by the simulation method. The disagreement between the two simulations is about a 0.5 dB in $|S_{11}|$, 0.2 dB/mm in loss, with a nearly identical phase response (not plotted). It is found that each underpass adds about one effective degree of electrical line length. The ground plane width is also varied from 50 μm to 150 μm, with 100 μm chosen as the smallest distance that still gives expected performance.

The tee junction from Fig. 2 is simulated, separately from the entire circuit, in HFSS and Sonnet. Fig. 4 shows the tee and stub results. S-parameters demonstrate relatively good agreement between HFSS and Sonnet. Greater loss improves matching because more power is dissipated rather than reflected. Footprint miniaturization was studied on a four-turn

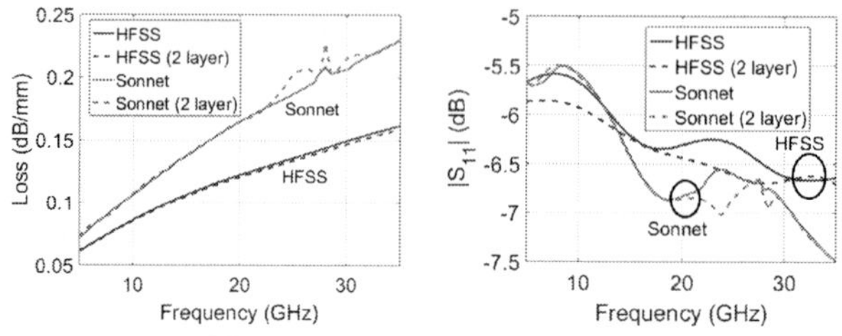

(a) (b)

Fig. 3. (a) Loss (dB/mm) and (b) $|S_{11}|$ comparison between HFSS (gap = 25 μm) and Sonnet (gap = 21 μm) of a 50-Ω line with λ/10 underpass spacing. (a) is terminated in a 50-Ω load and (b) in a 15-Ω load.

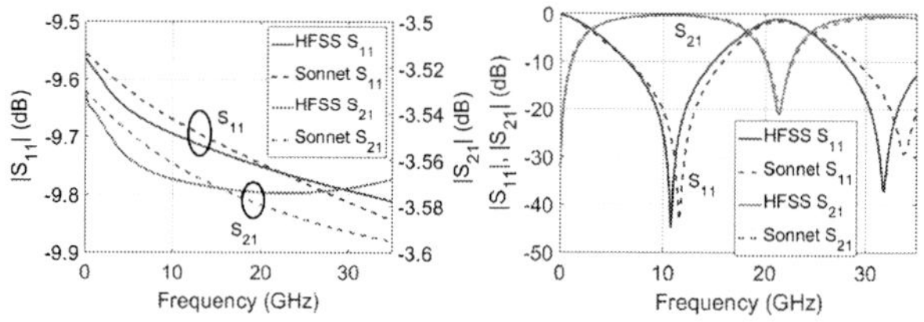

(a) (b)

Fig. 4. HFSS and Sonnet S-parameters of: (a) tee junction and (b) quarter-wave shorted stub.

half-wavelength meander line with 100 μm ground plane width between lines requiring a 28 μm gap width to maintain 50-Ω characteristic impedance. In addition, they are about 20 % shorter due to coupling. As width between lines increases, the meander line length approaches a half-wavelength, as expected. Lumped components are also investigated. Using the stack-up of Fig. 1, 0.3 fF/μm^2 is expected for the capacitors. An HFSS simulated 60 μm x 80 μm DC blocking capacitor, e.g., has a capacitance of 1.55 pF at DC (1.44 pF calculated) and 1.46 pF at 10 GHz. Sonnet results in a DC capacitance of 1.58 pF for the same capacitor.

ACKNOWLEDGMENT

This work is supported under the Assistant Secretary of Defense (ASD) for Research and Engineering Contract No. FA8721-05-C-0002 and/or FA8702-15-D-0001. Any opinions, findings, conclusions or recommendations expressed in this material are those of the authors and do not necessarily reflect the views of the ASD.

REFERENCES

[1] R. Leblanc, N. S. Ibeas, A. Gasmi, F. Auvray, J. Poulain. F. Lecourt, G. Dagher, and P. Frijlink, "6w ka band power amplifier and 1.2db nf x-band amplifier using a 100nm gan/si process," in 2016 IEEE CSICS, Oct. 2016, pp. 1–4.

[2] L. Pattison, T. Boles, N. Tuffy, and G. Lopes, "Improving gan on si power amplifiers through reduction of parasitic conduction layer," in 2014 9th EuMIC, Oct. 2014, pp. 92–95.

[3] J. Kim, H. Park, D. Kim. M. Lee. K. Seo. and Y. Kwon, "Rf parametric study on algan/gan hemts on si-substrate for millimeter-wave pa," in 2013 APMC Proceedings, Nov. 2013, pp. 775–777.

[4] T. E. Kazior, J. R. LaRoche, and W. E. Hoke, "More than moore: Gan hemts and si cmos get it together," in 2013 IEEE CSICS, Oct. 2013, pp. 1–4.

[5] K. C. Gupta, R. Garg, I. Bahl, and P. Bhartia, Microstrip Lines and Slotlines. Boston, MA: Artech House, 1996, pp. 375–451.

Even-Arm Modulated Arm Width Spiral Properties

W. Neill Kefauver
RF & Photonics, Advanced Technical Center
Lockheed Martin Space Systems Company
Littleton, CO, USA
w.neill.kefauver@lmco.com

Dejan S. Filipovic
Department of Electrical, Computer and Energy Engineering
University of Colorado
Boulder, CO, USA
dejan.filipovic@colorado.edu

Abstract— **Among Frequency Independent (FI) flush-mountable antennas the modulated arm width (MAW) spiral antenna provides the simplest architecture for measuring both polarization and direction of arrival instantaneously if frequency is known. Of interest is how the improvement in detection accuracy increases with additional arms. With additional modes, the polarization and direction of the incoming signal can be better estimated. In practical applications, this angle of arrival (AOA) capability with more channels for the MAW spiral antenna improves directional accuracy.**

*Keywords— **angle-of-arrival, beamformer, dual-polarization, frequency independent antennas, modulated arm width, spiral antennas, sum and difference modes.***

I. Introduction

Multi-polarized spiral antennas have several problems discussed previously including dispersion, loss and ambiguity [1-3]. MAW spirals reflect currents of the higher-order modes back towards the feed, simulating an outside feed but preserving frequency independence [4]. The geometry is still dispersive between modes preventing use without frequency detection. The MAW spiral also has the potential disadvantage of being dispersive by polarization, unlike the sinuous geometry [2]. For analog methods, the dispersive behavior would cause implementation difficulties, but in a system where digital post-processing can be done, the phenomenon is not a significant contributor to any system that has response times slower than that of the antennas rise time. The advantage of the MAW spiral sensor is extremely wide bandwidth even though the AoA is frequency dependent. This property eliminates the ambiguity at higher frequencies that arise from baseline interferometry by increasing accuracy of the direct detection of an incoming signal. However, without knowledge of polarization the directional accuracy is limited by the cross-product of the two modes used to estimate direction, before even considering noise, calibration or receiver linearity. In this paper we will discuss the ability of the even arm MAW spiral to filter orthogonal modes efficiently.

II. MAW Spiral Antenna Theory of Operation

The direction of the signal's origin requires an antenna with a pattern that is smooth and stable over both angle and frequency. In some applications multiple beam types are used to obtain direction. Once the signal is detected, and the location of the emitter is approximately known, additional information may then be extracted by more directive systems.

There are various technologies available to locate emitters, but one technique is angle of arrival (AOA) detection by a multimode antenna. The spiral antenna supports this capability by providing two modes, usually referred to a sum and difference. These modes can be frequency independent when the spiral has more than two arms. The ratio of the amplitude for these two modes without any other information provides a signal proportional to the off broadside angle. With the additional measurement of frequency or a compensation technique for frequency dispersion, the rotation angle about broadside can be derived from the measured phase of this ratio [3]. Only the quadrature voltage ratio is needed from the detection of the signal on two channels.

III. Multi-Arm Capabilities

A spiral antenna with six arms should have five useful modes. These modes would be expected to be ±1, ± 2 and 3, but not -3. The performance of the highest mode would degrade, primarily from the next higher mode. This behavior is because the opposite polarized mode has the same arm phasing and radiates at about the same circumference. In the six arm case both modes 3 and -3 have an 180° flip between arms and rely on the element alone for polarization control. The degradation of mode efficiency is much less for even arm counts. This improvement due to the preferred radiation mode being the nominal direction of propagation on the spiral arm.

Fig. 1 shows the self-complementary version of arm counts 6 and 8 with 8:1 modulation ratio and a slight increase in the growth rate from 1.5 for the six arms to 1.75 for the eight arms.

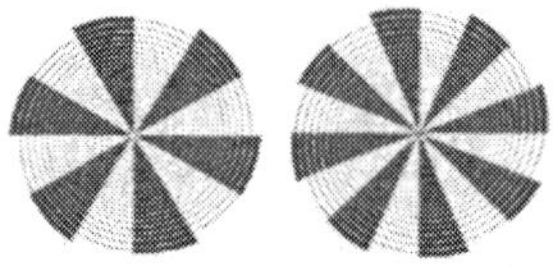

(a) six-arm (b) eight-arm

Fig. 1. Various arm count MAW spiral geometries.

Sponsored partly by office of Naval Research Grant #N00014-07-1-1161.

The choice of arm count is based on performance requirements. For example, a MAW spiral with more than four arms provides matched polarization response for performing AoA as recommended in many signal processing techniques, with independent orthogonal polarization detection [5]. With each additional arm, more pattern ambiguities were removed. Furthermore, with more collocated measurements of the detected signal, higher resolution of signal's properties were available using modal rather than baseline techniques. Both methods are more complex with additional channels of detection resulting in additional RF paths that track each other.

IV. Patterns of Multi-Arm MAW Spirals

The important characteristic of a multi-arm geometry is that it can control radiation patterns of the antenna through filtering modes of higher number proportional to the number of arms. Sensing is usually implemented by the Butler matrix beamformer, in which all power incident on the multi-port geometry can be converted into orthogonal modes corresponding to the number of arms [6]. Although, the behavior of the beamformer captures one component of the MAW spiral radiation properties, there is a second component that is the higher mode terms which can only be extracted from the patterns. This pattern component is of more practical application for distinguishing the different arm count geometries because it defines what power is delivered into modes that are not directly controlled by beamformers. We refer to this as modal efficiency. The following figures show total power controlled in the pattern versus total pattern radiated. The higher the efficiency, the less contribution to pattern ripple by the higher modes.

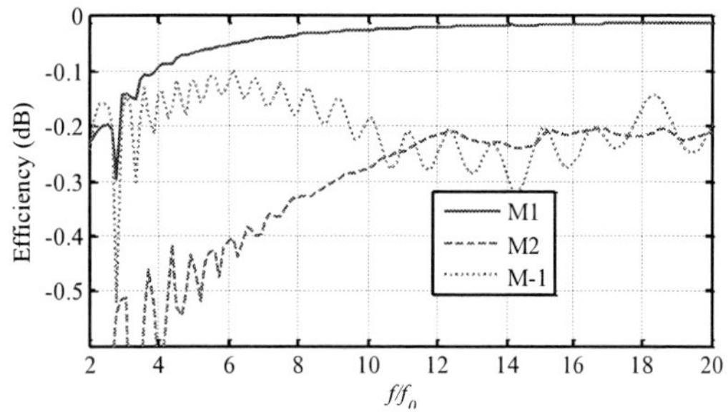

Fig. 2. Efficiency between beamformer mode and pattern mode for a four-arm MAW spiral.

To examine this phenomenon in more detail, consider the "highest" mode controlled by the beamformer. The efficiency of all controlled modes on even arm count MAW spirals are better than -10 dB contamination of the next mode. The spiral element has a preferential polarization for the highest mode in the 4, 6, and 8 cases in Fig. 2, 3, 4. The mode losses are tenths of a dB. The worst losses occur only in the mode that has its radiation region closest to the reverse mode with the same phasing. Otherwise, the bandstops work effectively for even arm count spirals. Furthermore, the highest mode does not reach maximum efficiency until twice its cutoff, unlike the lower modes, which reach full efficiency quickly. This reduced modal efficiency is because of the arm termination interacting with the bandstops preventing the reverse mode from being fully suppressed by the geometry.

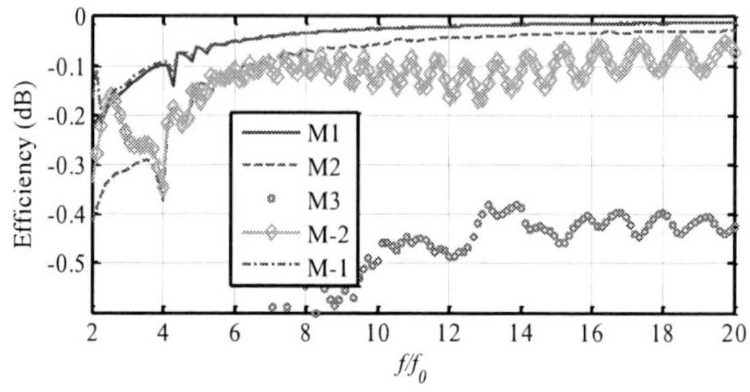

Fig. 3. Efficiency between beamformer mode and pattern mode for a six-arm MAW spiral.

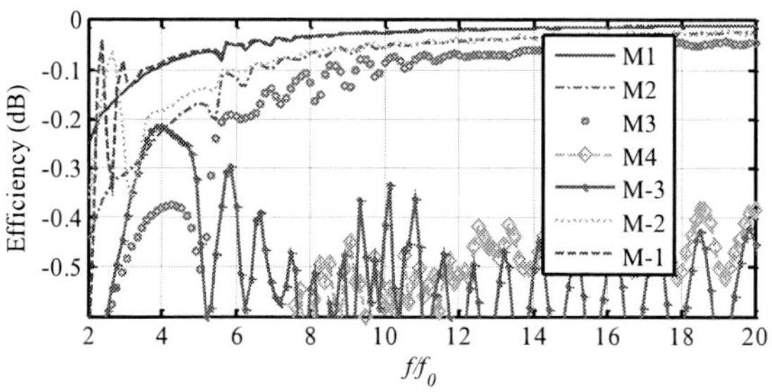

Fig. 4. Efficiency between beamformer mode and pattern mode for an eight-arm MAW spiral.

V. Conclusions

The even arm MAW spiral antenna can be used for many wideband applications. The MAW spiral with N arms has the following properties useful for a dual-polarized AOA sensor:

- Have N-1 useable modes, N-2 of which are reasonable free of modal contamination.
- The highest mode for even number arm antennas with a typical cross-polarization term of -10 dB.

References

[1] R. G. Corzine and J. A. Mosko, Four Arm Spiral Antennas, Norwood, MA, Artech House, 1990.

[2] R. H. DuHamel, "Dual polarized sinuous antennas," U. S. Patent 4658262, Ap. 14, 1987.

[3] J. Kaiser and J. Little, "Phase comparison properties of the dual mode spiral with application to direction finding," Antennas and Propagation Society International Symposium, pp. 67-72, 1964.

[4] P. G. Ingerson, "Modulated arm width spiral antenna," U. S. Patent 3,681,772, Aug. 1, 1972.

[5] E. Ferrara, T. Parks, "Direction finding with an array of antennas having diverse polarizations," IEEE Transactions on Antennas and Propagation, vol. 31, is. 2, pp. 231-236, Mar. 1983.

[6] W. Nester, "The fast Fourier transform and the Butler matrix," IEEE Transactions on Antennas and Propagation, Vol. 16, Issue 3, pp. 360, May 1968.

High Temperature Electronics for Demanding Aircraft Applications

Roger A. Brewer
Engineering & Technology, Air Vehicle Electrical Systems
Lockheed Martin Aeronautics Company
Ft. Worth, TX, USA
roger.brewer@lmco.com

Abstract — **This paper provides an overview of the evolving and challenging demands electronics systems must deal with when installed on an Aerospace platform. Environmental concerns related to heat and vibration, increased utilization system power usage and the need to install electronics in parts of an aircraft that might be remote from readily accessible forms of cooling are examples that combine to form the challenge. Wide Band Gap (WBG) technology is now evolving as a higher temperature, robust material that may address some of these challenges. However, while WBG materials address the active device material for a power switching device, processor, etc., other issues must be considered in creating a compliant higher temperature and environmentally robust packaged device or system. This paper will examine some of these various issues and create a roadmap for future technology development items of interest. A brief overview of a modern aircraft power system and the electrical usage needs that, in turn, drive thermal management challenges will first be provided as an Introduction and to set the stage.**

Keywords — Aircraft, Power Conditioning, Technology Roadmaps, Thermal Management Systems, Wide Band Gap.

I. INTRODUCTION

A typical aircraft electrical power system (EPS) architecture consists of multiple forms of power conversion (AC:DC, DC:DC, DC:AC) and conditioning. The reason behind this is typically the form of generated power on an aircraft, driven by a generator direct-mounted to a jet turbine or turboprop shaft, is not of the required form (voltage, frequency) and needed quality required by the utilization equipment. Fig. 1 [1] provides a typical illustration of an aircraft electrical power system from a modern commercial aircraft.

The power conditioning equipment on a modern aircraft can faces challenges, both in terms of increasing power usage demands while at the same time competing for precious aircraft cooling flow (liquid, forced air) and space in low vibration bays.

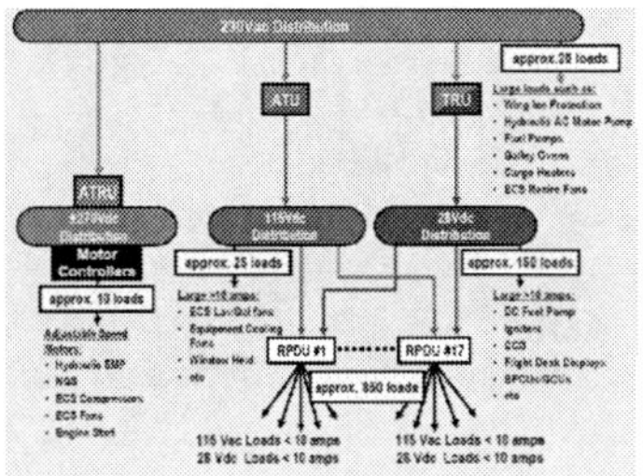

Fig. 1. An aircraft (commercial platform) power system.

At the same time environments can be challenging, power usage demands continue to rise as the figure below illustrates placing further demands on power conversion over the operating life of a typical aircraft. Fig. 2 illustrates a conceivable situation where the electronics used to condition the power generation may require derating (if for example installed in the engine bay collocated with the shaft driven generator). The final "nail in the coffin" is the increasing burden on the aircraft Thermal Management System (TMS) to cool the ever-increasing electrical loads (due to inefficiencies). The TMS requires its own electrical power resulting in a power usage "death spiral".

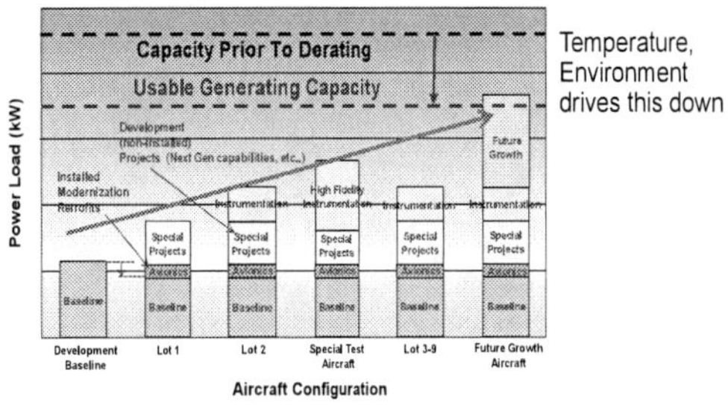

Fig. 2. A modern aircraft loading trend.

II. ANALOG ELECTRONICS & PROCESSING

Analog electronics and processors represent another challenging area for modern aircraft and installation in robust high temperature environments. Needs for additional speeds for ever-increasingly complex processing functions (radar mapping, high resolution systems, etc.) drive heat within the rack assembly. As another example, front end antenna analog electronics remotely located from the aircraft TMS result in lengthy (and difficult to maintain) plumbing. Engine controls are yet another example of electronics located in a high temperature, high vibration environment. It is clear more robust electronics solutions are required in the future.

III. WIDE BAND GAP ELECTRONICS & TECHNOLOGY ROADMAP

Wide Band Gap (WBG) devices represent a class of active materials possessing several inherent advantages that may address the evolving aerospace challenges, namely:

- Higher thermal conductivity (from active junction to case);
- Higher capable operating speed (due to less thermal dissipation);
- Higher stand-off voltage.

The potential benefits of WBG technology when being adopted in power, analog and digital aircraft electronics can now be extrapolated and include:

a) Increased power conditioning efficiency (reduce the TMS burden);
b) Higher system voltage (drive the voltage up and the current losses down, e.g., Power = Voltage x Current);
c) Improved reliability at higher temperatures (improved maintenance and life cycle costs);
d) Reduced weights/volumes for magnetic storage components (faster switching frequency), translates to improved power density (kW/kg and kW/liter) in power conditioning;
e) Widened temperature tolerance requirement at the box inlet from TMS (reduce TMS burden);
f) Expanded use of more readily available forms of cooling (ram air) or wider adoption of convectively cool boxes (may also translate to less of a power derating need at higher altitudes);
g) Flexibility in remotely locating electronics to the point of need without (or reduced) TMS infrastructure support (very high skin temperature fast moving vehicles).

The technology roadmap for a fully compliant, high temperature (>200 deg. C) enabled box should yet consider the many other components (passive devices) and packaging challenges as illustrated in Fig. 3. As seen from the typical power supply open view, tight volume constraints can drive risks due to radiated heat onto other more sensitive devices within the box.

Capacitor Technologies	(Typical) Upper Operating Temp Limit (°C)	Temperature Limiting Factors/Comments
Traditional Ceramic	125	Non uniform heating for large geometries, insulation resistance drops above the Curie point of the dielectric
Aluminum Electrolytic	125	Electrolyte, voltage derating implications vs. temp
High Temp Tantalum	230	Traditional tantalums limited by electrolyte and packaging
Traditional Film (polyethylene, polyphenylene)	150	Limitations in the film material (as plastic transition temperature is approached insulation properties lost)
Ultracapacitor Module (Electric Double Layer)	65	Electrolyte boiling point (80 deg. C), life of technology both temp and voltage dependent

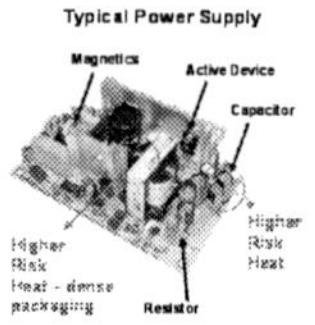

Fig. 3. Tight packaging, temp. limitations in capacitors.

Invoking multiphysics based modelling (or other approaches) is considered central in predicting the aircraft TMS impacts due to the new WBG device thermal properties and can form part of the roadmap for further exploration. All road-mapping areas are highlighted below:

- Higher temperature capable capacitors, passives;
- Higher temperature interconnect systems, connectors, solders;
- Higher temperature capable packaging;
- New approaches in system predictive models (Multiphysics based) where WBG is adopted.

IV. CONCLUSION

WBG represents a very hopeful step in the progression of creating high temperature capable electronics for challenging aircraft and aerospace systems and environments. In surveying the electronics industry, progress and novel techniques not only in Silicon Carbide (SiC) and Gallium Nitride (GaN) but other next generation WBG materials are likely moving the "technology needle" significantly including diamond CMOS. Wider use of WBG technology throughout the commercial sector (automotive, power grid, etc.) brings the hope that cost ($/kW) can continue to drop and bring not only the performance benefits discussed but cost competitive solutions (vs. the incumbent Silicon technology). As WBG technology begins to be employed in aircraft applications, more lessons learned are anticipated including the true effectiveness in creating more reliable hardware (reduced field returns).

REFERENCES

[1] Data taken from presentation by Tim Nelson of the Boeing Company at 2012 SAE Power Conference in Mesa AZ.

Radiation Modes of an Outside Fed 4-arm Conical Spiral

Thomas P. Cencich
Lockheed Martin Space Systems Company
Denver, Colorado, U.S.A.
Thomas.P.Cencich@LMCO.com

Jeannette C. McDonnell
Lockheed Martin Space Systems Company
Denver, Colorado, U.S.A.
Jeannette.C.McDonnell@LMCO.com

Timothy W. Samson
Lockheed Martin Space Systems Company
Denver, Colorado, U.S.A.
Timothy.W.Samson@LMCO.com

***Abstract*—The vast majority of spiral antennas are fed from the inside ports, near the center of the antenna. This paper will describe the radiation from a 4-arm conical spiral that is fed from its perimeter. It will be shown that higher order spiral modes can radiate over a significant bandwidth, and with good circular polarization. A rule of thumb for useful bandwidth will be provided.**

Keywords*— *Conical Spiral, Frequency Independent Antennas, Spiral Antennas, Spiral Modes, Beamformer.

I. Introduction

Spiral antennas [1-7] are known for their wide bandwidth and circular polarization. Here, to show other characteristics of a spiral antenna, we will investigate the modes from a 4-arm conical spiral when fed from the outside, not the inside. The first mode that is properly phased will radiate. Due to overmoding, the bandwidth will be decreased [1].

II. Spiral Antenna Theory

Several references explain the spiral antenna geometry and its theory of operation [1-5]. The spiral in Fig. 1 shows a radiation ring at mode 1 with a 1 λ circumference (left). The radiation circumference increases to 2 λ circumference for mode 2, etc. The radiation occurs when the spiral phases are the same on adjacent arms, as can be seen in both plots. Even though literature is typically for planar spiral, the theory applies to conical spirals as well.

This paper will focus on the modes of an outside fed conical spiral. Outside fed spirals have been discussed by Kuo [7] and others.

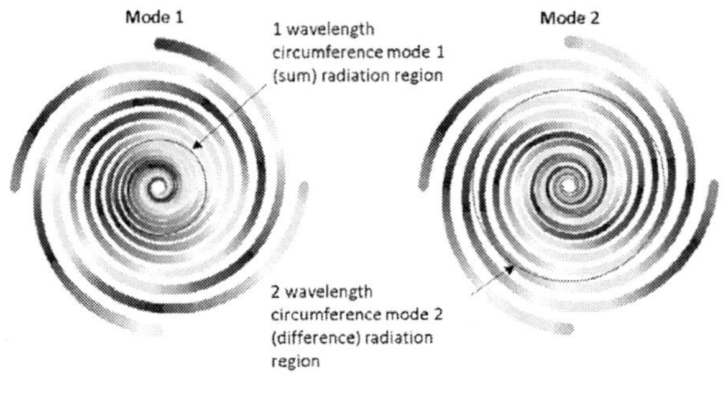

Fig. 1. Spiral antenna modes

The spiral antenna has great wideband circular polarization characteristics and is usually used in its planar form. The drawback to the planar geometry is its bidirectional radiation characteristics, where for wideband applications, one hemisphere is typically absorbed in a carbon loaded cavity resulting in a minimum of 3 dB loss. Here, we will use a conical spiral to reduce the backlobe losses

III. Modes from an Outside Fed 4-Arm Spiral

As in all spiral antenna theory, the first mode that is properly phased will radiate. When a spiral is fed from its inner ports, the lowest order mode will radiate first, so performance is wideband and typically well behaved. However, when fed from the outside or perimeter, this is no longer true. For example, let's look at a 4-arm conical spiral with a 3.76" diameter. The largest circumference will be ~11.8" which indicates the lowest frequency of ~ 1 GHz for mode 1, ~2 GHz for mode 2 and ~3 GHz for mode 3. If this antenna is excited in mode 1 where the antenna is large enough to support mode 5 radiation, or about 5 GHz for our conveniently selected example, mode 5 will predominately radiate rather than mode 1. In other words, Mode 1 will radiate from 1-4 GHz, mode 5 from 5-8 GHz, mode 9 from 9-12 GHz, mode 13 from 13-16 GHz, etc. Gaps exist in the frequency ranges listed as they will be a significant mixture of the two modes. These frequency ranges are not based on any specific performance criteria.

Mode 2 will have a similar situation, except this time Mode N + M will start at mode 6 for the 4-arm spiral. Mode 2 will exist from ~ 2-5 GHz, mode 6 from 6-9 GHz, mode 10 from 10-13 GHz, etc.

Bandwidth is determined using (1) where B is the bandwidth (f_{high}/f_{low}), N is the number of arms, M is the desired mode, Δ_{modal} reduces overmoding, and Δ_{base} increases the base mode radiating size. The values used for Δ_{modal} and Δ_{base} will change based on the criteria for the peak gain and modal purity. For the 4-arm case shown here, the gain criteria was to be within 3dB of the peak gain value and for the closest interfering modes to be at least 10dB down. By setting Δ_{modal} = 0.65 and Δ_{base} = 0.2, there is < 3.3% error between the equation and the model bandwidth when excited in modes 1 through 5 (these were the only modes in the study).

$$B = \frac{(M + N - \Delta_{modal})}{(M + \Delta_{base})} \quad (1)$$

IV. Conical Spiral Design

The spiral wrap was selected using the right hand rule for RCP. As mentioned earlier, a 3.76" diameter was selected to provide a convenient frequency range. A cone angle of 43.6 degrees was selected to provide a reasonable front to back ratio. The cone can also be truncated to reduce the height for radiation regions now used. An Archimedean spiral, with 5 turns, was used as an equiangular can have very wide traces near the perimeter and is more difficult to feed.

V. Model Performance

This antenna was modeled with the FEKO software code with MoM (Method of Moments). In this model, at each arm, ideal voltage sources were used between the arm ends and an annular ring used as a common ground. Mismatch losses are ignored (but are not extremely high) as the interest is in the far-field patterns. Modes for the patterns peak approximately at the angles shown in Table 1.

Table I. Spiral Antenna Mode Peak Direction and Directivity

	Spiral Mode								
	1	2	3	4	5	6	7	8	9
Beam Peak (deg)	0	35	40	47	50	53	55	57	59
Directivity (dBic)	9	6	6	6	6	6	6	6	6

Fig 2 shows the far-field patterns when fed in mode 1 from 1 to 6 GHz. The patterns are well behaved at peak at boresight until 6 GHz where mode 5 turns on, as expected.

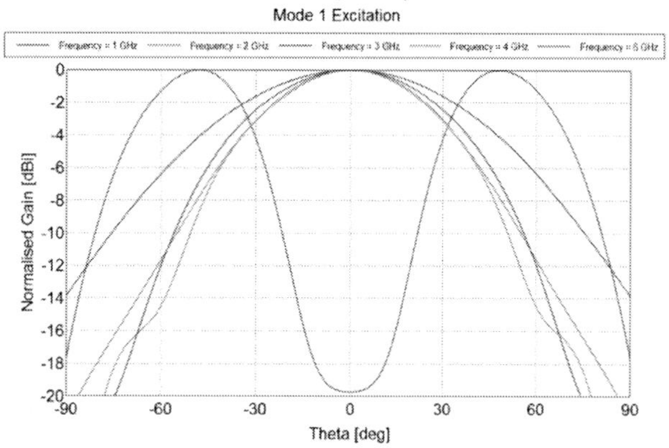

Fig. 2. Mode 1 phased patterns

As was predicted, when fed in mode 2 the typical difference pattern is seen working properly from 2 to 5 GHz, and falls apart a 6 GHz (now radiating mode 6). See Fig 3.

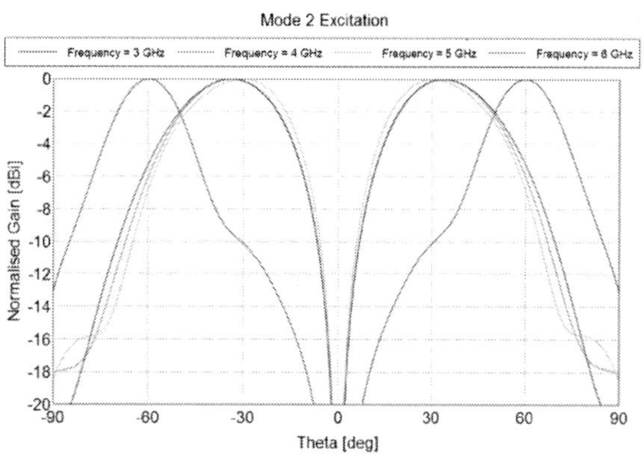

Fig. 3. Mode 2 phased patterns

In Fig 4, the Mode 3 peak moves a little with frequency, from ~ 40-50 degrees from 3 to 6 GHz. At 7 GHz, mode 7 is radiating and peaks near 60 degrees.

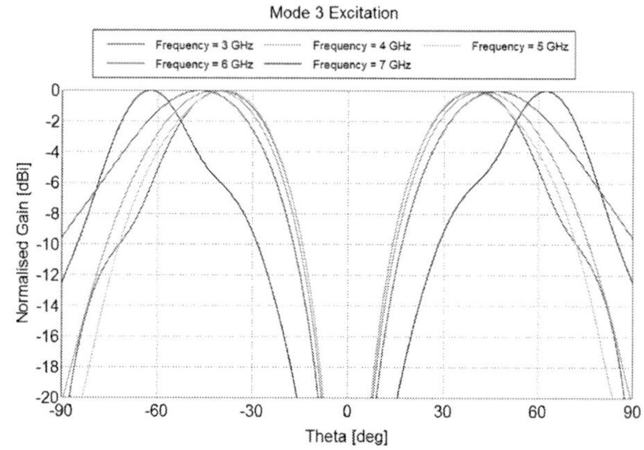

Fig. 4. Mode 3 phased patterns

VI. Conclusions

Modes of a 4-arm conical spiral were shown with the radiation ring explanation. These results can easily be extrapolated for a different number of arms and modes. Potential use for this type of antenna can be for higher order radiating structures at high frequencies (i.e., RCP gain required at 40 degrees at 90 GHz) where direct feeding from the inside may be problematic.

References

[1] R.H.DuHamel and J.P.Scherer, Frequency Independent Anteennas, Chap.14, Anrenna Engineering Handbook, Third Edition (New York: McGraw-Hill, 1993).

[2] R. G. Corzine and J. A. Mosko, Four Arm Spiral Antennas, Norwood, MA, Artech House, 1990.

[3] D. S. Filipovic and T.P. Cencich, Frequency Independent Antennas, in Antenna Engineering Handbook, 4th ed., J. L. Volakis, Ed. New York: McGraw-Hill, 2007, pp. 13-8.

[4] J. D. Dyson, "The unidirectional equiangular spiral antenna", IRE Trans. Anten. Propag., AP-7:329–334 (1959).

[5] T. Cencich and D. Filipovic, Spiral Antennas, Chapter in Wiley Encyclopedia of RF and Microwave Engineering, vol. 5, pp. 4853-4868, John Wiley & Sons, New York, March 2005.

[6] D. Filipovic, T. Cencich and M. Nuremburger, Frequency Independent Antennas, Chapter in Wiley Encyclopedia of RF and Microwave Engineering, vol. 2, pp. 1674-1690, John Wiley & Sons, New York, March 2005

[7] Kuo and Lin, Multiple Polarization Spiral Antenna, U.S. Patent 3,562,756 (Feb. 1971).

On Matching Lossy Antennas for Maximum Power Absorption

Ofer Markish, Daniel Silverstein, and Yehuda Leviatan
Department of Electrical Engineering
Technion - Israel Institute of Technology
Haifa 32000, Israel

***Abstract*—The impedance matching required for maximum absorption by a stand-alone lossy dipole and by an infinite array of lossy dipoles located in front of a ground plane is analyzed. In the case of the stand-alone terminal-loaded lossy dipole, we find an approximate analytical expression for the load impedance that maximizes the sum of the powers absorbed by the load and by the lossy material of which the dipole is made. Evidently, this load is different from the conjugate-matched load, which is required to maximize the load power alone. In the case of the infinite array of terminal-loaded lossy dipoles above a ground plane, we show that if the antennas are terminated with the proper load impedance, one can attain perfect absorption even when the array lies very close to the ground plane. In this case, we also identify the minimum height below which perfect absorption cannot be realized and the absorption efficiency rapidly drops.**

***Index Terms*—Antenna arrays, antennas, electromagnetic wave absorption, wire dipole.**

I. Introduction

The study of structures that absorb electromagnetic power efficiently is important in many application areas including metamaterial absorbers [1], radar cross section minimization [2], light enhancement by plasmonic particles [3], and detection by thermal bolometers [4]. The absorption by terminal-loaded lossy dipole particles can be found in [1]. Here, we extend the analysis of [1] to the case of terminal-loaded lossy dipole antennas that are of finite length. Specifically, we present an approximate analytical expression for the value of the load impedance that maximizes the combined absorption both by the load and by the lossy dipole structure. Since the dipole is lossy, the optimal load is different from the conjugate-matched load. We then extend the analysis of maximum absorption to the case of an infinite array of such dipoles above a ground plane. It is shown that by tuning the terminal loads of the dipoles correctly, perfect absorption can be attained.

II. Absorption by a Stand-Alone Lossy Dipole

A z-directed terminal-loaded dipole of finite conductivity σ, half-length l, and radius a, is illuminated by an obliquely incident uniform plane wave. The dipole geometry is shown in Fig. 1 (a). Without loss of generality, we set the azimuthal angle of incidence to $\varphi_{\text{inc}} = 0$. Hence, the z component of the incident field, which is exciting the dipole, is given by $E_z^{\text{inc}}(z) = E_0 \sin\theta_{\text{inc}} \exp(jk_0 z\cos\theta_{\text{inc}})$, where k_0 is the wavenumber, θ_{inc} is the polar angle of incidence, and E_0 is the complex amplitude of the field. The wire dipole is assumed to be thin such that $a \ll l$ and $a \ll \lambda_0$, where λ_0 is the wavelength. The total absorbed power by the dipole P_{abs}, is given by the sum of the load power P_{load} and the loss power P_{loss}. We have,

$$P_{\text{abs}} = P_{\text{load}} + P_{\text{loss}} = \frac{1}{2}\left|I_{\text{rx}}^{\sigma}(0)\right|^2 R_{\text{load}} + \frac{1}{2}\int_{-l}^{l} \frac{R_s}{2\pi a} \left| I_{\text{rx}}^{\sigma}(z')\right|^2 dz' \,. \quad (1)$$

Here, I_{rx}^{σ} is the current flowing along the lossy dipole in receiving-mode, R_{load} is the load resistance, and $R_s = 1/(\sigma\delta_{\text{skin}})$, with $\delta_{\text{skin}} = [2/(\omega\mu_0\sigma)]^{0.5}$ being the skin depth, is the surface resistance. We seek to find the optimal load $R_{\text{load}}^{\sigma,\text{opt}} + jX_{\text{load}}^{\sigma,\text{opt}}$ that maximizes P_{abs}. Following [5], we use a perturbation approach to account for the losses. Specifically, we express I_{rx}^{σ} in terms of the expressions for the short-circuit and transmitting-mode currents flowing along the corresponding lossless dipole, and in these expressions what we only do is replace the value of the dipole's input impedance by its value in the lossy case. We, in turn, substitute the expression for I_{rx}^{σ} into (1), differentiate (1) with respect to R_{load} and X_{load}, equate the result to zero, and arrive at a quartic equation. Solving this quartic equation approximately, we have [5]:

$$X_{\text{load}}^{\sigma,\text{opt}} \approx -X_{\text{ant}}^{\text{pec}},$$

$$R_{\text{load}}^{\sigma,\text{opt}} \approx \frac{\text{Re}(Z_{\text{ant}}^{\sigma})/2 - 2\text{Re}(C^{*}Z_{\text{ant}}^{\sigma})\text{Re}(Z_{\text{ant}}^{\sigma}) - 2D(X_{\text{ant}}^{\text{pec}})^2}{1/2 + 2\text{Re}(C^{*}Z_{\text{ant}}^{\sigma}) - 2D\text{Re}(Z_{\text{ant}}^{\sigma})}. \quad (2)$$

Here, $Z_{\text{ant}}^{\sigma} = R_{\text{rad}}^{\text{pec}} + R_{\text{loss}} + jX_{\text{ant}}^{\text{pec}}$ is the impedance of the lossy dipole, $R_{\text{loss}} = \frac{R_s}{2\pi a}\int_{-l}^{l} |\sin[k_0(l-|z'|)]/\sin k_0 l\,|^2 dz'$ is the loss resistance, and $R_{\text{rad}}^{\text{pec}}$ and $X_{\text{ant}}^{\text{pec}}$ denote the radiation resistance and antenna reactance of the corresponding lossless dipole, respectively. $R_{\text{rad}}^{\text{pec}}$ and $X_{\text{ant}}^{\text{pec}}$ and can be readily obtained assuming that the current distribution is sinusoidal, using the induced EMF method. Also in (2), the parameters C and D are given by:

$$C = \frac{R_s}{4\pi a\,|Z_{\text{ant}}^{\sigma}|^2}\left\{\frac{Ak_0 l\sin\theta_{\text{inc}}}{Ak_0\sin\theta_{\text{inc}} - 2E_0} + \frac{4E_0[\cos(k_0 l\cos\theta_{\text{inc}}) - \cos(k_0 l)]}{\sin(kl)(2E_0 k_0 - Ak_0^2\sin\theta_{\text{inc}})\sin^2\theta_{\text{inc}}}\right\},$$

$$D = \frac{R_s[2k_0 l - \sin(2k_0 l)]}{8\pi k_0 a\sin^2(k_0 l)\,|Z_{\text{ant}}^{\sigma}|^2}, \quad (3)$$

where

$$A = \frac{E_0[\exp(2jk_0 l\cos\theta_{\text{inc}}) + 1]}{k_0\sin\theta_{\text{inc}}\cos(k_0 l)\exp(jk_0 l\cos\theta_{\text{inc}})},\quad B = \frac{E_0[\exp(2jk_0 l\cos\theta_{\text{inc}}) - 1]}{k_0\sin\theta_{\text{inc}}\cos(k_0 l)\exp(jk_0 l\cos\theta_{\text{inc}})}. \quad (4)$$

Note that $R_{\text{load}}^{\sigma,\text{opt}}$ given by (2) is generally different from the conjugate-matched load resistance $R_{\text{load}}^{\sigma,\text{conj}} = R_{\text{rad}}^{\text{pec}} + R_{\text{loss}}$. In fact, $R_{\text{load}}^{\sigma,\text{opt}}$ approaches $R_{\text{load}}^{\sigma,\text{conj}}$ only when R_s (and hence C and and D) approach zero. The load, loss, and absorbed power

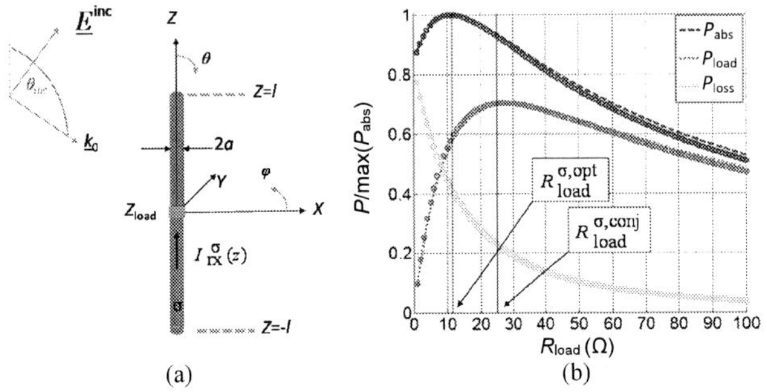

Fig. 1. (a) Stand-alone lossy dipole. (b) Load, loss, and absorbed power terms, calculated using the analytical model, for a lossy stand-alone dipole with $l = 0.15\lambda_0$, $a = 0.001\lambda_0$, $X_{load} = -X^{pec}_{ant}$, $\delta_{skin}/(2a) = 0.2$, and $\theta_{inc} = 90°$. MoM results are indicated by circles for comparison and validation purposes.

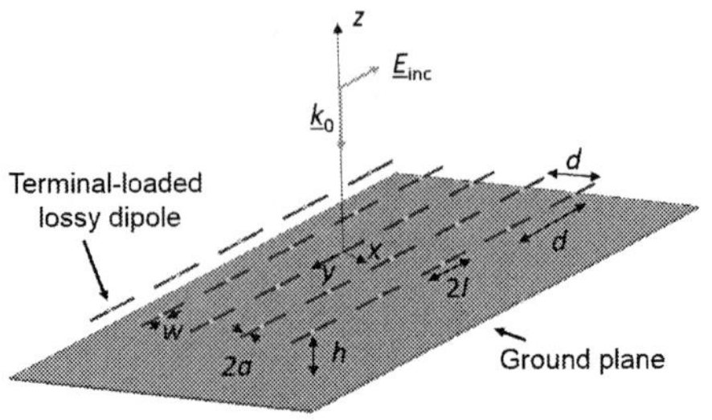

Fig. 2. Array of terminal-loaded lossy dipoles above a ground plane.

terms when $X_{load} = -X^{pec}_{ant}$ and for various load resistance values, are shown in Fig. 1 (b). For comparison and validation purposes, the corresponding Hellen's integral equation was solved by the method of moments (MoM) using pulse basis and testing functions, and the results are also shown in Fig. 1 (b). What is clearly evident is that the conjugate-matched load $R^{\sigma,conj}_{load}$ that maximizes P_{load} is different from $R^{\sigma,opt}_{load}$ that maximizes P_{abs}.

III. Absorption by an Array of Lossy Dipoles

We now extend the analysis of the stand-alone dipole to the case of an infinite array of terminal-loaded dipoles above a perfectly conducting ground plane shown in Fig. 2. The array is illuminated by a normally incident plane wave linearly polarized parallel to the axis of the dipoles. The height of the dipoles above the ground is h and we assume a square unit cell such that the distance between the centers of the dipoles is d in both lateral dimensions. Since the physical aperture (the unit cell area) is well defined, we can define the absorption efficiency as $\eta_{abs} = P_{abs}/P_{inc}$. Here, P_{abs} is the sum of the powers absorbed by the load and by the lossy dipole's material, and $P_{inc} = d^2|E_0|^2/(2Z_{free})$, with Z_{free} being the free space impedance, is the power incident upon a unit cell area. Fig. 3 shows the absorption efficiency as a function of h, simulated by ANSYS HFSS for $l = 0.235\lambda_0$, $2a = 0.005\lambda_0$, feed gap $w = 0.005\lambda_0$, $d = 0.5\lambda_0$, and σ such that $\delta_{skin}/(2a) = 0.2$. Results shown are for the case where each dipole is loaded with the optimal load for maximum power absorption $R^{\sigma,opt}_{load} + jX^{\sigma,opt}_{load}$, which was found, for each value of h, by numerical search in the complex impedance plane. It can be observed that perfect absorption is reached as long as h is larger than $h_{min} = \lambda_0/20$. It can be shown that for $h = h_{min}$, $R^{\sigma,opt}_{load}$ is zero and that for $h < h_{min}$, perfect absorption, with a passive load, cannot be attained. When $h = h_{min}$, the absorption bandwidth to a 90% level around the center frequency ω_0 is 4%, which is reasonable for narrow band applications. Also shown in Fig. 3 is the absorption efficiency when each dipole is loaded with an impedance $R^{\sigma,conj}_{load} + jX^{\sigma,conj}_{load}$ that is equal to the complex conjugate of the dipole's active impedance. It can be observed that for small values of h (when the losses are high), the efficiency with the conjugate-matched load impedance is suboptimal.

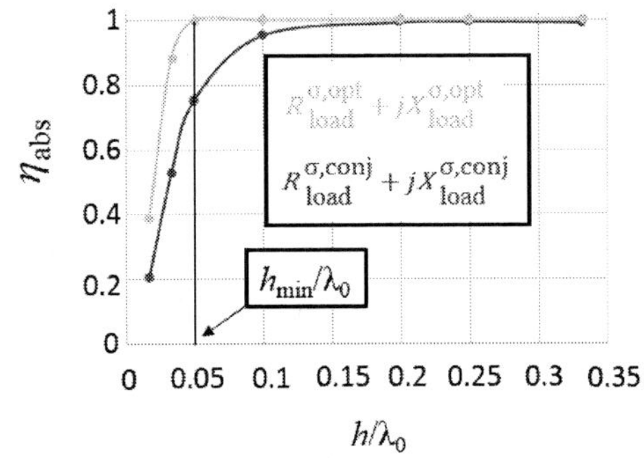

Fig. 3. Absorption efficiency of an array of lossy dipoles when the elements are terminated with the optimal load impedance and a conjugate-matched load impedance.

IV. Conclusion

The analysis of the impedance matching for maximum power absorption by a stand-alone lossy dipole has been extended to the case of an array of lossy dipoles. In contrast to an array of lossless dipoles above a ground plane, which can achieve perfect absorption for any height of the array above the ground [6], in the lossy case perfect absorption cannot be attained below a minimum height. However, we have demonstrated that the minimum height is still very small, and the proposed configuration can serve as a thin absorbing metastructure.

Acknowledgement

This work was supported in part by the Israel Science Foundation under Grant No. 141/17.

References

[1] S. Tretyakov, S. Maslovski, and P. A. Belov, "An analytical model of metamaterials based on loaded wire dipoles," *IEEE Trans. Antennas Propag.*, vol. 51, no. 10, pp. 2652-2658, 2003.

[2] P. D. Einziger, Y. Leviatan, and J. Remez, "Broad band optimization of RCS or wire dipole antenna," in Proc. 16th Conf. Elect. Electron. Eng. Israel, Mar. 1989, pp. 1–3.

[3] A. Normatov, B. Spektor, Y. Leviatan, and J. Shamir, "Absorption enhancement by matching the cross-section of plasmonic nanowires to the field structure of tightly focused beams," *Optics Express*, vol. 19, no. 9, pp. 8506-8513, 2011.

[4] O. Markish and Y. Leviatan, "Analysis and optimization of terahertz bolometer antennas," *IEEE Trans. Antennas Propag.*, vol. 64, no. 8, pp. 3302–3309, Aug. 2016.

[5] O. Markish and Y. Leviatan, "On maximum absorption by lossy finite-length dipole antennas," *IEEE Trans. Antennas Propag.*, vol. 65, no. 2, pp. 424-431, 2017.

[6] D.-H. Kwon and D. M. Pozar, "Optimal characteristics of an arbitrary receive antenna," *IEEE Trans. Antennas Propag.*, vol. 57, no. 12, pp. 3720–3727, Dec. 2009.

Fast computation of back scattered fields for large scanned array antennas

Arun K. Bhattacharyya and Nicholas D. Saiz
Lockheed Martin Space Systems
Littleton, CO

Abstract — Analysis of back scattered field of a large array antenna is presented. The induced current on the ground plane is obtained employing the equivalence principle and Galerkin's Method of Moment (MoM). For fast convergence a progressive wave type of basis function is proposed. Results for the scattered field intensities are shown for three cases and it is found that a tapered excitation reduces back scattered field significantly.

Index Terms — Array, back-scattered field, Galerkin's method of moments.

I. INTRODUCTION

In space and airborne communication systems phased arrays are gaining increasing popularity due to their beam flexibility and real time beam scanning advantages. Typically transmit and receive arrays are placed at two different locations in order to reduce the coupling between receive and transmit arrays. This reduction is particularly important for high power transmit arrays. It is sometimes possible to increase the isolation between the arrays by properly placing them within the available space. This necessitates a very accurate prediction of the field intensity much beyond the scan region. This is a huge computational challenge because the electrical volume of the array structure is very large. The MoM analysis, perhaps is the most efficient way to analyze such a structure. High frequency asymptotic methods, such as GTD and PTD are computationally fast, but they mostly work well in the far field region. For the near field coupling analysis, we believe, the MoM is the best option for this type of electrically large problems.

In this presentation we discuss the MoM analysis of an array antenna consisting of many identical elements. The element apertures are opened onto a finite ground plane. Employing the principle of equivalence [1] on the aperture we obtain the equivalent magnetic current. The magnetic current induces electric current on the ground plane. The induced electric current is computed rigorously using the spectral MoM. For a fast convergence, a progressive type of basis function is proposed. The scattered field is contributed by the magnetic current and induced electric current on the ground plane. The back-scattered field intensity is found to vary with the beam scanning. We present numerical results and discussion for few selective cases.

II. THEORY

Consider an array of radiating elements shown in Fig. 1. The elements are opened onto a ground plane and the ground plane is extended beyond the radiating aperture. We employ spectral Galerkin's MoM to analyze the structure. Toward that end we first set an integral equation based on the principle of equivalence. The total electric field produced by the equivalent source on the radiating apertures and by the induced current on the ground plane must vanish on the conducting ground plane. This condition leads to the following equation [2]:

$$\hat{n} \times \iint_{GP} \bar{I}.\bar{\bar{G}}\, ds = \frac{1}{2}\hat{n} \times \bar{E}_a \qquad (1)$$

In the above $\hat{n}$ is the unit normal vector, $\bar{I}$ is the induced surface current density on the ground plane (GP), $\bar{\bar{G}}$ is the dyadic Green's function and $\bar{E}_a$ is the electric field vector on the apertures of the radiating elements. In this development we assume that $\bar{E}_a$ is known a priory.

In (1) the induced surface current density is the only unknown to be solved. We use entire domain basis functions of two different kinds. The first kind is an orthogonal set of sine-cosine functions and the second kind is progressively phased functions that commensurate with the field distribution of a scanned beam. We will present numerical results with respect to the first kind basis functions. The results for the second kind will be considered during the presentation.

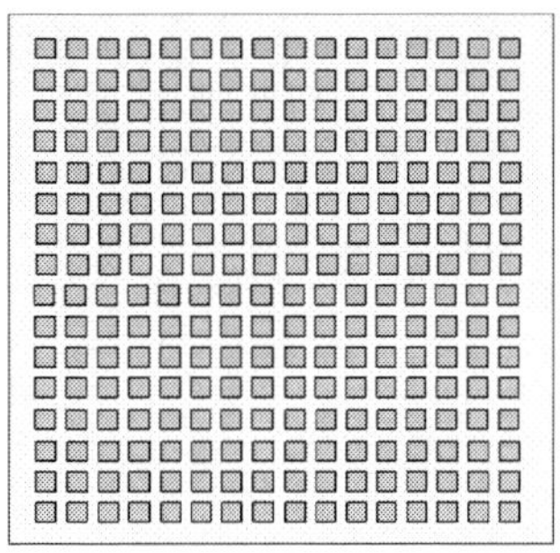

Fig. 1: Schematic of an array antenna. The element apertures open onto a ground plane.

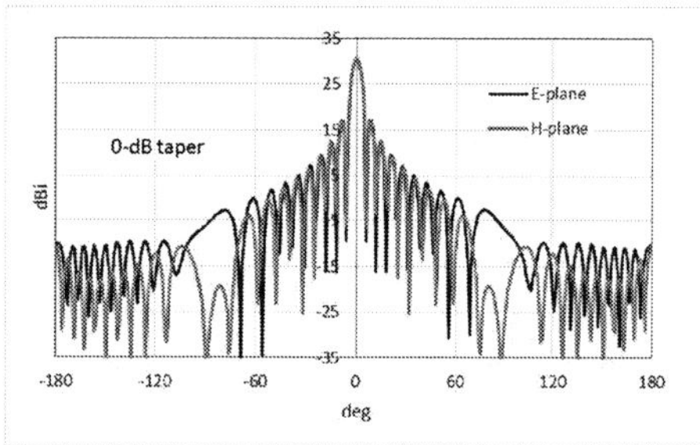

Fig. 2: Radiation patterns including back-scattered field of an array of 256 elements with uniform excitation. The element spacing is 0.6 wavelength. The ground plane size=10 wavelength x 10 wavelength.

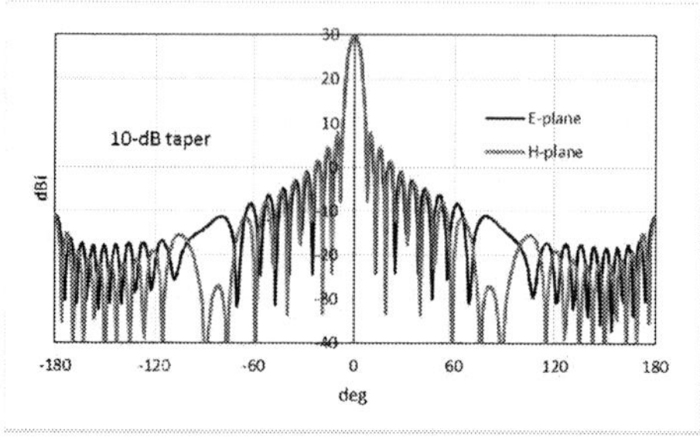

Fig. 3: The radiation patterns with 10-dB Gaussian taper on two principal planes. Other antenna parameters are same as in Fig. 2.

III. NUMERICAL RESULTS

We consider an array of 16 × 16 square elements with uniform aperture fields. The element spacing is 0.6 wavelength in a square grid. The ground plane size is about 100 square-wavelength. We found that for a reasonable convergence we need about 450 entire-domain basis functions for the induced current in two orthogonal directions. Figure 2 shows the array pattern with uniform excitation in both planes. The peak gain is about 30.6 dBi and the side lobe is about 13 dB below the beam peak as expected. It is found that near 90 degree look angle, the field intensity on H-plane is significantly lower than that on the E-plane. In fact, for an infinite ground plane the H-plane intensity should be zero ideally. The small intensity is due to the scattering from the ground-plane edge. In the back-lobe region, the E-plane intensity is higher than that of the H-plane. The peak intensity in the back-scattered region is about 37 dB below the beam-peak.

In figure 3 we compute the scattered field for the same array with 10 dB Gaussian taper on the two principal planes. Expectedly, the peak gain is reduced by about 0.8 dB due to the tapered excitation. Also, the peak side lobe is about 22 dB below the beam peak for this case. Interestingly, the peak intensity is about 44 dB below the beam peak in the back-scattered region, which is about 7 dB lower than that with uniform excitation. The induced current at the ground plane edge is mostly responsible for the back-scattered radiation. For the taper excitation, the induced edge current being small, the back-scattering intensity is small. Thus, a tapered excitation not only reduces the side lobe level, but also reduces the back scattered field for a small compromise of the peak gain.

Next we consider a scanned beam at 30 degree scan angle on E-plane. Figure 4 shows the scattered fields. For this case the back scattered field intensity deteriorates as compared with that for the bore-sight beam case. The peak back-scattered field is about 38 dB below the beam peak, which is significantly higher than that in Fig. 3. This is primarily due to the ground plane radiation, which is tilted to the right due to the phase progression. The induced current distribution for all three cases will be shown during presentation.

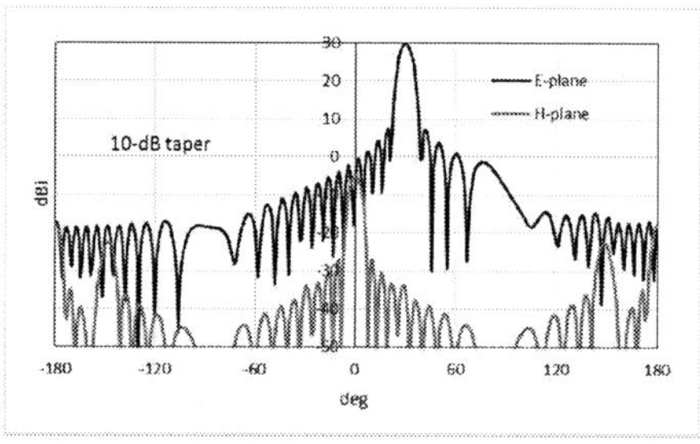

Fig. 4: The scanned radiation patterns (scan angle=30 deg). Other antenna parameters are same as in Fig. 3.

REFERENCES

[1] R. F. Harrington, *Time-Harmonic Electromagnetic Fields*, McGraw-Hill, New York, 1961.

[2] A.K. Bhattacharyya and G.Z. Rollins, "Accurate Radiation and Impedance Characteristics of Horn Antennas-A Moment-Method Model," *IEEE Trans. Antennas Propagat.*, vol. AP-44, pp. 523-531, 1996.

Triple Fano resonances in plasmonic heptamer nano-hole arrays: Symmetric and asymmetric structures

Akram Hajebifard[1,2]
[1]*Department of Physics,* [2]*Centre for Research in Photonics*
University of Ottawa
Ottawa, Canada
ahaje092@uottawa.ca

Pierre Berini[1,2,3]
[1]*Department of Physics,* [2]*Centre for Research in Photonics,*
[3]*School of Electrical Engineering and Computer Science*
University of Ottawa, Ottawa Canada
berini@eecs.uottawa.ca

Abstract— **The optical properties of gold heptamer-arranged nanoholes array have been studied numerically, for both symmetric and asymmetric structures. This array supports three Fano resonances arising from the excitation of localized surface plasmon polaritons (LSPPs), propagating surface plasmon polaritons (PSPPs), or/and waves related to Wood's anomaly (WA). To study the nature of each Fano resonance, electromagnetic near-field distributions have been computed, and the effects of the geometrical parameters has been carried out. In addition, the sensing performance of the structure has been examined, revealing that the highest bulk sensitivity (400 nm/RIU) and surface sensitivity (2 nm/nm) belong to LSPP Fano resonance, whereas, the highest figure of merit (24 RIU^{-1}) is obtained by a coupled WA-PSPP Fano resonance, which is only supported by the asymmetric structure.**

Keywords— Fano resonance, Wood's anomaly, Nanohole, surface plasmon polaritons

I. Introduction

Fano resonances supported in plasmonic structures have become a growing research topic due to their remarkable optical properties such as a narrow line-shape, and high sensitivity to changes in the surrounding media. While many studies have focused on exploring plasmonic nanoparticle arrangements [1], seeking Fano resonances in their spectral responses, far less attention has been paid to complementary structures - arrangements of nanoholes in metal films. Compared to nanoparticle arrangements, complementary structures can support various excitations, such as localized surface plasmon polaritons (LSPPs), propagating symmetric or asymmetric surface plasmon polaritons ($PSPP_s$, $PSPP_a$), and/or Wood's anomalies (WA). The interference between light indirectly scattered via these excitation, and light directly transmitted through the holes forms the Fano features in the spectral response of the structures. This increased number of resonances suggests broadband interrogation, and doubly-resonant Surface-enhanced Raman spectroscopy (SERS) applications [2]. In addition, the continuity of the metal layer can be useful in producing resonant Schottky contacts [3]. In this work, we investigate an array of gold heptamer nanoholes on a SiO_2 or CYTOP (a fluoropolymer) substrate, as sketched in Fig. 1. The physical mechanism underlying the formation of Fano resonances in such a structure is explained and their application to biosensors examined.

II. Proposed Structure and Numerical Model

The structure under study, shown in Fig. 1, is a 480 nm pitch ($P=P_x=P_y$) HNH array with surrounding holes of diameter (D) 100 nm, central holes of diameter (D_c) 100 nm, and of inter-hole spacing (G) 10 nm in a gold film of thickness (t) 60 nm. The gold film is covered by a dielectric medium (n_s = 1.33), and supported by a SiO_2 (asymmetric structure) or CYTOP (symmetric structure) substrate. COMSOL's implementation of the vectorial finite element method (FEM) was used to compute the optical spectra and the electromagnetic fields.

III. Results and Discussions

The optical responses of the HNH are plotted in Fig. 2. As observed, the asymmetric structure supports Fano features at λ_1 = 700, λ_2 = 780 and λ_3 = 884 nm, denoted WA-PSPPs(1,0), PSPPa(1,0) and LSPP, while the symmetric structure only supports two resonances denoted PSPPa(1,0) and LSPP at 760 nm and 782 nm, respectively.

To understand the characteristics of the resonances, electric and magnetic near-field distributions were computed at the spectral location of the resonances, for the asymmetric structure, as shown in Fig. 3.

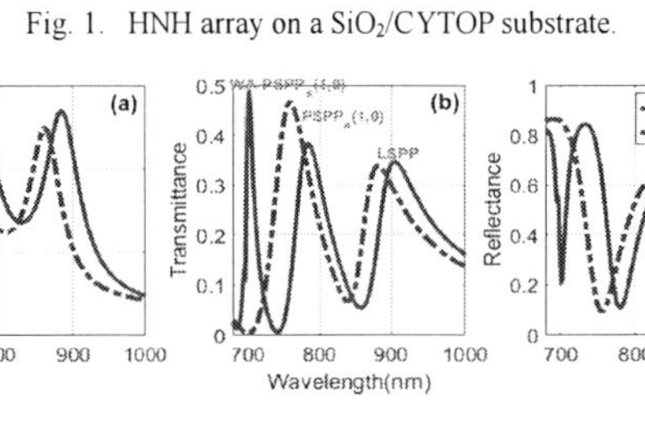

Fig. 1. HNH array on a SiO_2/CYTOP substrate.

Fig. 2. Optical response of an HNH array with the geometrical parameters of $D = D_c = 100$ nm, $G = 10$ nm, $t = 60$ nm and $P = 480$ nm on SiO_2 or CYTOP.

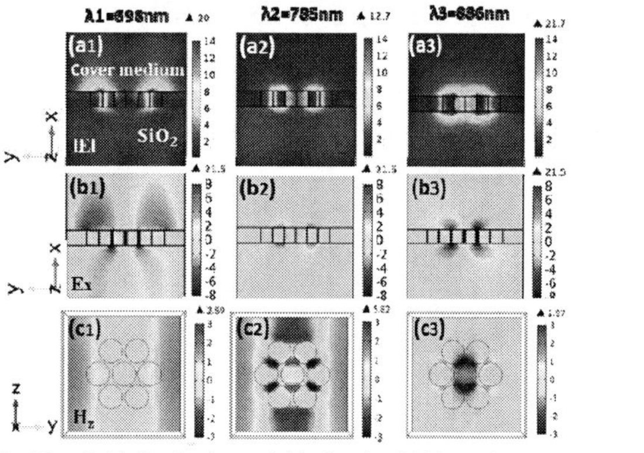

Fig. 3. Near-field distributions of (a) electric field intensity (|**E**|) on an xy plane, (b) E_x on an xy plane, and (c) H_z at the Au/cover interface, along the yz plane passing through the center of a unit cell, at λ_1, λ_2, and λ_3.

LSPP: The field distributions at λ_3, in Figs. 3(a3) and (c3), reveal that the fields are strongly localized to the center of the unit cell, which is a typical feature of a LSPP mode. **PSPPa:** The field distributions at λ_2, shown in Figs. 3(a2), (b2) (c2), show the characteristics of a propagating asymmetric SPP. E_x changes sign from one interface to the other, and |**E**| has maxima at the metal-dielectric interfaces while decaying exponentially away. Hz shows propagation of the mode along the y direction. **WA-PSPPs:** The narrowest resonance occurring at λ_1 is due to the coupling of a WA wave on one side of the metal film with the PSPPs mode. The E_x distribution, in Fig. 3(b1), reveals the excitation of a symmetric SPP mode, and of a WA wave in the SiO_2 as an extended plane wave propagating parallel to the metal film. The corresponding Hz, in Fig. 3(c1), also shows the propagation of the WA-PSPPs mode in the y direction. This mode is only supported by the asymmetric structure, in which both WA and PSPPs can occur at the same spectral position.

Another way of elucidating the nature of the resonances is by observing the evolution of the Fano resonances while altering structural parameters, such as periodicity and central hole diameter (D_c), as shown in Fig. 4. As expected, the WA-PSPP and PSPP-related Fano resonances are sensitive to the pitch P but not to D_c. However, the LSPP Fano resonance is strongly affected by altering D_c, but not by the pitch. In addition, increasing G increases the full size of the heptamer-shaped aperture and blue-shifts all resonances.

The sensing performance of all resonances for the symmetric and asymmetric cases was evaluated in terms of their bulk sensitivity (BS), figure of merit (FOM) and surface sensitivity (SS). The results for the asymmetric case are shown in Fig. 5. The LSPP Fano resonance exhibits the highest surface (2 nm/nm) and bulk sensitivities (400 nm/RIU), because the electromagnetic field of this mode is highly localized to the holes, where the sensing medium penetrates (RIU implies unity refractive index). The highest FOM (~24.5 RIU^{-1}) belongs to a WA-PSPPa resonance because it has the sharpest resonance.

In conclusion, the optical performance of gold heptamer arrays cladded symmetrically and asymmetrically has been assessed The excitation of LSPP, PSPP and coupled WA-PSPP modes produce several Fano resonances which can be useful for broadband interrogation, SERS applications, and producing resonant Schottky contacts. The high bulk and surface sensitivities of Fano resonances motivates sensing applications.

ACKNOWLEDGEMENTS

We acknowledge the Centre for Advanced Computing, for computational support, and the Natural Sciences and Engineering Research Council of Canada (RGPIN-2016-04197) for funding this project.

REFERENCES

[1] N. Papasimakis, Y. H. Fu, V. A. Fedotov, S. L. Prosvirnin, D. P. Tsai, and N. I. Zheludev, "Metamaterial with polarization and direction insensitive resonant transmission response mimicking electromagnetically induced transparency," Appl. Phys. Lett. **94**, 211902–211902 (2009).

[2] Z. Liu and J. Ye, "Highly controllable double Fano resonances in plasmonic metasurfaces," Nanoscale **8**, 17665–17674 (2016).

[3] M. Alavirad, S. S. Mousavi, L. Roy, and P. Berini, "Schottky-contact plasmonic dipole rectenna concept for biosensing," Opt. Express **21**, 4328–4347 (2013).

[4] A. Hajebifard, P. Berini, "Fano resonances in plasmonic heptamer nano-hole arrays," Optics Express **25**, pp. 18566-18580 (2017).

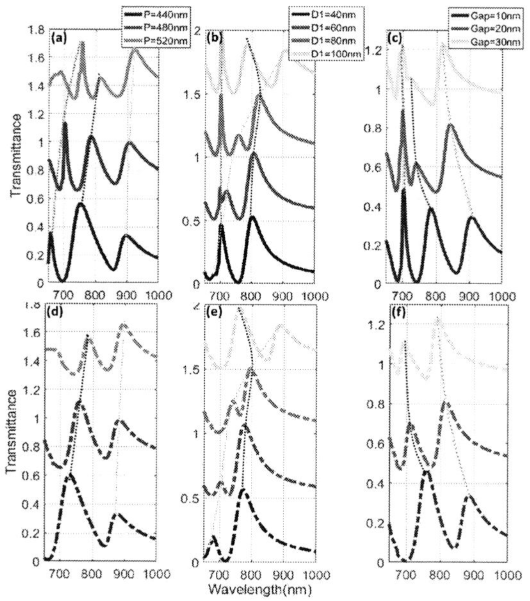

Fig. 4. Optical responses of the HNH arrays for symmetric (bottom, dashed-dot plots) and asymmetric (top, solid plots) claddings with the geometrical parameters of: D =100 nm, t = 60 nm. (a) and (d) $D_c = 100$ nm, G = 10 nm and varying P; (b) and (e) varying D_c, G = 10 nm and P = 480 nm; (c) and (f) $D_c = 100$ nm, varying G and P = 480 nm. Spectra are offset vertically for clarity. The Fano resonances associated with the LSPP, $PSPP_a$ and $WA\text{-}PSPP_s$ modes are highlighted by yellow, black and pink dashed lines, respectively.

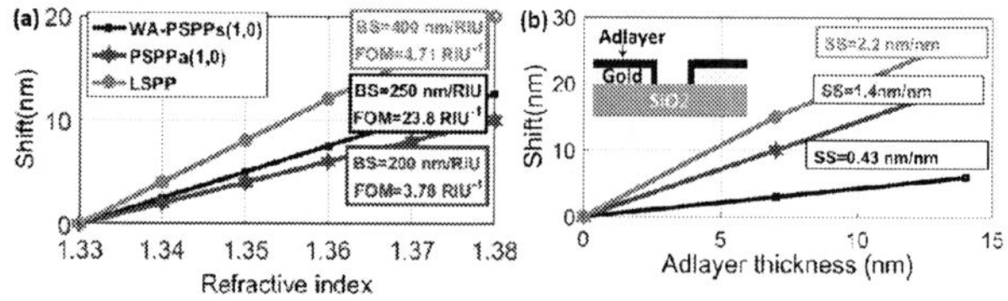

Fig. 5. Shift in the resonance wavelengths with respect to their nominal values at $n_s = 1.33$ (a) *vs.* the superstrate refractive index, and (b) *vs.* the adlayer thickness, for the case of the SiO_2 substrate.

Metagratings: A Novel Paradigm for Efficient Wavefront Control

Dimitrios L. Sounas, Younes Ra'di, and Andrea Alù

Department of Electrical and Computer Engineering
The University of Texas at Austin
Austin, U.S.A.
dimitrios.sounas@utexas.edu, younes.radi@utmail.utexas.edu, alu@mail.utexas.edu

Abstract—**Metasurfaces have recently gained a lot of attention in the context of beam steering, but they are subject to fundamental limitations regarding their efficiency, that cannot be overcome unless we use active or nonlocal materials. Here we show that these limitations can be overcome if we approach the problem of beam steering from a grating perspective. We show that by using metamaterial elements as the building blocks of a periodic lattice we can achieve extreme beam steering with unitary efficiency, if these elements are designed to cancel all the diffraction orders supported by the lattice apart from the one where we want to reroute an incident wave. We call such structures metagratings, in order to highlight the two main aspects of such structures, the grating principle and the metamaterial elements forming it.**

Keywords— *beam steering, gratings, metagratings, metamaterials, metasurfaces.*

I. INTRODUCTION

Metasusrfaces have recently attracted a lot of attention for the possibility of engineering the wavefront of impinging waves [1]-[7]. By imparting an appropriately selected reflection or transmission phase profile on a surface, it is possible to perform advanced operation on the wavefront, e.g., change its propagation direction or focusing it in space. This approach works quite well for small bending angles, when the difference between the wave impedances of the incident and transformed waves is small, but its efficiency drops dramatically as we go to more extreme beam steering cases. One solution to this problem is to design the metasurface to have the impedance profile required in order to achieve matching between the incident and refracted waves. However, this approach leads to locally active metasurfaces, which require increasingly large gain, as the beam steering angle increases [8]. The gain requirement can be removed if we use nonlocal metasurfaces, but with an obvious increase of complexity [9],[10]. Furthermore, when implementing any of the approaches mentioned above, it is necessary to discretize a continuous impedance or phase profile with rapid changes in space, which imposes stringent a small discretization step and subsequently significant implementation challenges.

Here, we show that these problems can be overcome if we approach the problem of beam steering from a grating perspective [11],[12]. Gratings are spatially periodic structures, which for a given incident wave support a discrete number of diffraction directions. In conventional gratings, most of the incident power is directed to the specular direction and the power distributed to other diffraction orders is usually small. We show that this fact can be changed up to the point of total rerouting of the incident signal to a non-specular direction, if the grating is realized as a periodic arrangement of appropriately designed resonant metamaterial elements. The main idea is to design these elements so that the radiated signal from these elements cancels the strong reflected signals along the specular direction and is also zero along all the other diffraction directions, apart from the one where we want to reroute the incident wave. Then, it follows from power conservation that for a passive structure the incident power is steered along the desired direction with unitary efficiency.

We demonstrate this approach in different beam-steering scenarios. We start from the simplest case of beam steering in the same quadrant as the incident wave and show that this operation can be achieved with 100% efficiency, even for extreme cases of beam-steering close to grazing direction, through an array of electric or magnetic dipoles at some distance from a metallic ground plane. We then move the more challenging and practically more interesting case of changing the direction of a normally incident wave to any other direction in space and demonstrate that this functionality can be achieved if we use bianisostropic elements for the grating inclusions. We discuss practical implementations of these structures at different parts of the spectrum, including microwaves, THz and optics. Furthermore, we show how we can design metagratings with tunable beam steering properties, if we use elements with externally controllable properties, such as graphene at THz frequencies. Our results show how we can design highly-efficient metasurfaces with extreme capabilities, with important applications as remote sensing and energy focusing.

ACKNOWLEDGMENT

This work was supported by the Air Force Office of Scientific Research under award No. FA9550-17-1-0002, the National Science Foundation, the Simons Foundation and the Welch Foundation with grant No. F-1802.

REFERENCES

[1] Na. Yu, P. Genevet, M. A. Kats, F. Aieta, J.-P. Tetienne, F. Capasso, and Z. Gaburr, "Light oropagation with phase discontinuities: Generalized laws of reflection and refraction," *Science*, vol. 334, p. 333-337, 2011.

[2] X. Ni, N. K. Emani, A. V. Kildishev, A. Boltasseva, V. M. Shalaev, "Broadband light bending with plasmonic nanoantennas," *Science*, vol. 335, p. 427, 2011.

[3] C. Pfeiffer and A. Grbic, "Metamaterial huygens' surfaces: Tailoring wave fronts with reflectionless sheets," *Phys. Rev. Lett.*, vol. 110, p. 197401, 2013.

[4] F. Monticone, N. M. Estakhri, and A. Alù, "Full control of nanoscale optical transmission with a composite metascreen," *Phys. Rev. Lett.*, vol. 110, p. 203903, 2013.

[5] M. Selvanayagam and G. V. Eleftheriades, "Discontinuous electromagnetic fields using orthogonal electric and magnetic currents for wavefront manipulation," *Opt. Express*, vol. 21, p. 14409-14429, 2013.

[6] V. S. Asadchy, Y. Ra'di, J. Vehmas, and S. A. Tretyakov, "Functional metamirrors using bianisotropic elements," *Phys. Rev. Lett.*, vol. 114, p. 095503, 2015.

[7] K. Achouri, M. A. Salem, and C. Caloz, "General metasurface synthesis based on susceptibility tensors," *IEEE Trans. Antennas Propag.*, vol. 63, no. 7, pp. 2977-2991, July 2015.

[8] N. Mohammadi Estakhri and A. Alù, "Wavefront transformation with gradient metasurfaces," *Phys. Rev. X*, vol. 6, p. 041008, 2016.

[9] A. Epstein and G. V. Eleftheriades, "Synthesis of passive lossless metasurfaces using auxiliary fields for reflectionless beam splitting and perfect reflection," *Phys. Rev. Lett.*, vol. 117, p. 256103, 2016.

[10] A. Díaz-Rubio, V. S. Asadchy, A. Elsakka, and S. Tretyakov, "From the generalized reflection law to the realization of perfect anomalous reflectors," *Science Advances*, vol. 3, no. 8, p. e1602714, 2017.

[11] D. L. Sounas, N. M. Estakhri, and A. Alù, "Metasurfaces with Engineered Reflection and Transmission: Optimal Designs Through Coupled-Mode Analysis," in 10th International Congress on Advanced Electro-magnetic Materials in Microwaves and Optics - Metamaterials 2016, Crete, Greece, Sept. 2016.

[12] Y. Ra'di, D. L. Sounas, and A. Alù, "Meta-gratings: Beyond the limits of graded metasurfaces for wavefront control," *Phys. Rev. Lett.*, vol. 119, p. 067404, 2017.

Metamaterial Enhanced Antenna Systems: A Review

Daniel Binion
Dept. of Electrical Engineering
Penn State University
University Park, PA, USA
jxb5879@psu.edu

Pingjuan L. Werner
Dept. of Electrical Engineering
Penn State University
University Park, PA, USA
plw7@psu.edu

Douglas H. Werner
Dept. of Electrical Engineering
Penn State University
University Park, PA, USA
dhw@psu.edu

Erik Lier
Lockheed Martin Space Systems Company
Littleton, CO, USA
erik.lier@lmco.com

Thomas H. Hand
Lockheed Martin Space Systems Company
Littleton, CO, USA
thomas.h.hand@lmco.com

***Abstract*—Recent advances in the field of metamaterial enhanced antenna systems are reviewed. The addition of metamaterial surfaces or lenses is shown to significantly improve antenna performance over what is achievable with conventional antennas. This includes soft horn antennas with low cross-polarization, short backfire antennas with high aperture efficiency and low cross-polarization, near-zero index metamaterial lenses for directivity enhancement, as well as capacitively loaded electromagnetic bandgap structures for broadband and omnidirectional surface wave suppression.**

Keywords—Electromagnetic bandgap, metamaterial, metasurface, short backfire antenna, soft horn.

I. INTRODUCTION

Metamaterials, consisting of a periodic lattice of subwavelength structures, can achieve electromagnetic properties not commonly found in natural materials. Their widespread use in a variety of antenna applications in recent years has been facilitated by the emergence of powerful computational tools and optimization algorithms. This paper reviews some recent work in the field of metamaterial enhanced antenna systems performed as part of an ongoing collaboration between Penn State University and Lockheed Martin [1]-[10].

II. METAMATERIAL LINED HORN ANTENNAS

A metamaterial-lined horn antenna was developed to counter some of the disadvantages of conventional horn antennas, offering low-cost lightweight hybrid-mode horns with low cross-polarization over a large bandwidth. The widely used soft corrugated horn suffers from high manufacturing cost and a relatively heavy weight. In contrast, including a metamaterial lining offers a low-cost, lightweight, and potentially wider bandwidth soft horn [1]-[5].

With the aid of a commercial solver and a material parameter inversion algorithm, the metamaterial in [1] was designed to achieve a particular surface reactance that would cancel the electric field on the E-plane wall of the rectangular horn and create a tapered aperture field distribution (soft horn). The metamaterial was realized using a wire-grid structure, which was manufactured and placed on the E-plane walls of a linearly polarized horn, operating in the super-extended C-band.

The measured results show that the metamaterial-coated horn antenna achieves much lower sidelobes than either a conventional or trifurcated horn. Additionally, the measured S_{11} was below -15 dB over most of the frequency band, and the cross polarization was below -25 dB over more than an octave bandwidth.

Fig. 1. Fabricated square Ku band horn with metamaterial lining [11].

To demonstrate the versatility of this design technique, a second metamaterial lining was designed for a square horn antenna operating in the K_u band [3]. The metamaterial was optimized to achieve a tapered aperture field distribution and enable polarization-independent, soft-horn radiation characteristics, which are typically realized with conical horns. The metamaterial was implemented using small metallic patches that were optimized using a genetic algorithm, and fabricated using printed circuit board (PCB) techniques (Fig. 1). Measured results show a symmetric radiation pattern, low cross polarization, and low sidelobes over a broad bandwidth.

III. METAMATERIAL ENHANCED SHORT BACKFIRE ANTENNAS

Short Backfire Antennas (SBFAs) consist of a feed antenna and a passive, conductive subreflector, placed within a metallic cavity. SBFAs offer low profile, high gain, and about 30° field of view, making them ideal candidates for space-based MEO (Medium Earth Orbit) applications such as GPS. To increase gain or aperture efficiency, a more uniform aperture field distribution is required, which can be achieved by modifying the cavity walls of the SBFA. In [6], hard walls consisting of vertical metallic strips were optimized to maximize aperture efficiencies at the GPS L1 and L2 frequency bands for a circular SBF antenna with a circularly polarized feed. Simulation results demonstrate that aperture efficiencies of 90% and 98% are simultaneously achievable at L1 and L2, respectively. In contrast, the SBFA without hard walls could only achieve aperture efficiencies of 67.4% and 82.2% respectively at L1 and L2.

The work presented in this paper was funded by Lockheed Martin.

In array applications, hexagonal SBFAs have the potential to achieve increased aperture efficiency over circular antennas due to greater packing efficiency. In [7], a design and optimization procedure similar to that in [6] was followed for a hexagonal SBFA. Rather than using metallic strips, however, the walls were instead modelled using anisotropic impedance surfaces that would eventually be realized with metamaterials. This gave the optimizer more degrees of freedom with which to find an optimal solution. Simulation results show that an average aperture efficiency of 90% was achieved at L1 and L2 for the optimized hexagonal antenna.

IV. Broadband, Low-Profile Metamaterial Lens For Directivity Enhancement

A vast body of research has demonstrated that near-zero index metamaterials have the capability of producing highly directive radiation from a low-profile structure. This principle is applied in [8]-[9] to design a low-profile lens to increase the directivity of a circularly-polarized crossed-dipole antenna. The performance achieved is comparable to that of an antenna array, but only a single feed antenna is required in this case.

To enable symmetric, polarization independent performance, both the permittivity and permeability in the direction of propagation must approach zero. To achieve this, an electric resonator element in the form of an end-loaded dipole and a magnetic resonator element in the form of a split-ring resonator were designed to resonate just below the frequency band of interest. The resonance tails of the effective ε and μ of these elements remain near zero over a wide bandwidth, enabling broad band collimation. The magnetic and electric resonating elements were combined into a single unit cell design and were fabricated using PCB manufacturing processes. Additionally, metal strips were placed around the outside of the lens to reduce energy leakage and ensure maximum broadside directivity.

The lens serves to distribute the amplitude and phase of the radiated field more uniformly over the lens aperture, resulting in a measured directivity increase greater than 6 dB compared to the crossed dipole feed alone. The lens performance was stable over a 15% bandwidth, and the overall thickness under 0.5λ.

V. Wideband and Multiband Gap Surfaces with Capacitive Loading

In many antenna systems the propagation of surface waves is highly undesirable and can lead to radiation from the edges of a grounded substrate, impairing radiation performance. Electromagnetic Band Gap (EBG) surfaces serve to suppress surface waves and can improve the isolation between antenna elements placed on a single substrate, leading to improved gain and radiation properties. Conventional EBG surfaces are relatively narrow band, but for many antenna applications a large bandwidth is required. This problem is addressed in [10] by proposing an EBG surface nonuniformly loaded with lumped capacitors to increase the degrees of freedom available in the design. The Covariance Matrix Adaptation Evolutionary Strategy (CMA-ES) is employed to optimize the value of each capacitor. Since the computational cost of running a full-wave simulation for each design during the optimization would be prohibitively large, the port reduction method is utilized, which enables each design to be evaluated within a fraction of a second, enabling rapid convergence to the optimal design.

This technique is employed to design both unidirectional wideband and multiband EBGs. An omnidirectional EBG with a hexagonal lattice connected by lumped capacitors was also successfully optimized. It was shown that the wideband EBG successfully reduces transmission below -20 dB over a 3:1 bandwidth and the multiband structure reduces transmission to less than -22 dB at three frequency bands. For the omnidirectional EBG, the transmission was reduced below -20 dB at two different angles.

VI. Conclusion

We have presented a number of metamaterial enhanced antenna systems that have been developed in collaboration between Lockheed Martin and Penn State University. Significant performance improvements over conventional antennas have been demonstrated, underscoring the practical importance of metamaterials for current and future antenna system designs.

References

[1] C. P. Scarborough, Q. Wu, D. H. Werner, E. Lier, R. K. Shaw, and B. G. Martin, "Demonstration of an octave-bandwidth negligible-loss metamaterial horn antenna for satellite applications," IEEE Trans. Antennas Propag., vol. 61, no. 3, pp. 1081–1088, Mar. 2013.

[2] Q. Wu, C. P. Scarborough, D. H. Werner, E. Lier, and X. Wang, "Design synthesis of metasurfaces for broadband hybrid-mode horn antennas with enhanced radiation pattern and polarization characteristics," IEEE Trans. Antennas Propag., vol. 60, no. 8, pp. 3594–3604, Aug. 2012.

[3] Q. Wu, C. P. Scarborough, B. G. Martin, R. K. Shaw, D. H. Werner, E. Lier, and X. Wang., "A Ku-band dual polarization hybrid-mode horn antenna enabled by printed-circuit-board metasurfaces," IEEE Trans. Antennas Propag., vol. 61, no. 3, pp. 1089–1098, Mar. 2013.

[4] Q. Wu, C. P. Scarborough, D. H. Werner, E. Lier, and R. K. Shaw, "Inhomogeneous metasurfaces with engineered dispersion for broadband hybrid-mode horn antennas," IEEE Trans. Antennas Propag., vol. 61, no. 10, pp. 4947–4956, Oct. 2013.

[5] E. Lier, D. H. Werner, C. P. Scarborough, Q. Wu, and J. A. Bossard, "An octave-bandwidth negligible-loss radiofrequency metamaterial," Nat Mater, vol. 10, no. 3, pp. 216–222, Mar. 2011.

[6] M. G. Bray and E. Lier, "High efficiency short backfire antenna using electromagnetically hard walls," IEEE Antennas and Wireless Propagation Letters, vol. 14, pp. 1614–1617, 2015.

[7] Z. H. Jiang, Z. C. P. O. Morgan, D. H. Werner, T. H. Hand, B. Martin, and E. Lier, "Anisotropic impedance metasurface enabled dual-band short backfire antennas with high aperture efficiency," Proceedings of the 2016 IEEE International Symposium on Antennas and Propagation (APSURSI), 2016, pp. 1305–1306.

[8] J. P. Turpin, Q. Wu, D. H. Werner, B. Martin, M. Bray, and E. Lier, "Low cost and broadband dual-polarization metamaterial lens for directivity enhancement," IEEE Trans. Antennas Propag., vol. 60, no. 12, pp. 5717–5726, Dec. 2012.

[9] J. P. Turpin, Q. Wu, D. H. Werner, B. Martin, M. Bray, and E. Lier, "Near-zero-index metamaterial lens combined with AMC metasurface for high-directivity low-profile antennas," IEEE Trans. Antennas Propag., vol. 62, no. 4, pp. 1928–1936, Apr. 2014.

[10] S. H. Martin, I. Martinez, J. P. Turpin, D. H. Werner, E. Lier, and M. G. Bray, "The synthesis of wide- and multi-bandgap electromagnetic surfaces with finite size and nonuniform capacitive loading," IEEE Transactions on Microwave Theory and Techniques, vol. 62, no. 9, pp. 1962–1972, Sep. 2014.

[11] B. G. Martin and E. Lier, "Printed circuit board based feed horn," US Patent No. 9,300,054.

A Dual Band-Reject FSS for WI-FI Application

Mehdi Bahadorzadeh
School of Electrical and Computer Engineering
Oklahoma State University
Stillwater, OK USA
Mehdi.bahadorzadeh@okstate.edu

Charles F. Bunting
School of Electrical and Computer Engineering
Oklahoma State University
Stillwater, OK USA
charles.bunting@okstate.edu

Abstract* — *A dual band FSS based on array of double square ring shaped resonators has been proposed. The proposed structure represents a wide-angle perfect rejection of incidence wave and polarization independency. The rejection occurs at two different resonant frequencies as high as 98% and 99%, at 2.45(GHz), 5 (GHz) respectively. The proposed Frequency Selective Surface has designated for blocking the WI-FI signals and screen room applications. Simulation results show polarization independency for both rejection bands.

Keywords*— *Dual Band-Rejection, Wide-angle Rejection, WI-FI Signal Blocker

I. Introduction

A Frequency Selective Surface (FSS) is a two-dimensional frequency filter exhibiting reflection and transmission properties that are analogous to electronic frequency filters. FSS characteristics can be engineered to represent band-pass, band-stop, low-pass, or high-pass characteristics depending on design [1].

The advantage of the symmetry of the structural has been implemented to create the polarization independent resonant filter. Basically, to design a FSS, we have to maximize the rejection level at the desired frequency. It is equivalent to minimize the transmission (T) and maximizing the reflection (R) coefficients. In this paper, a planar FSS has been proposed. It rejects the electromagnetic waves at nearly 2.45 (GHz) and 5 (GHz) with rejection rate of 98% and 99%, respectively. It is observed that the structure represents Single Negative Metamaterial (SNG) behaviors at rejection resonant frequencies. FSS is polarization insensitive for both transverse electric (TE) and transvers magnetic (TM) waves. The simulation results represent good stability for different radiation angles and polarization. Many proposed FSS filters are designed for single frequency [2], and most of them do not have the simplicity in construction and rejection independent from frequency like proposed metamaterial absorbers [3].

II. Design and Simulation

The proposed FSS is an array of unit cell, which is considered as a double ring square shape Fig. 1.

The metallic structures on the top of the substrate are chosen as copper, the electrical conductivity and thickness are $5.8\times10^{7}(s/m)$ and 0.04(mm), respectively. The substrate of absorber is FR4 ($\varepsilon_r = 4.38, \tan\delta = 0.025$) with 2 (mm) thickness.

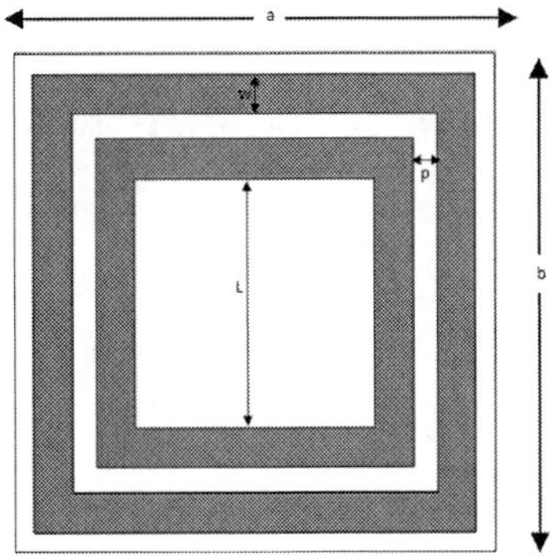

Fig. 1. Unit cell geometry and design parameters. a=b=25mm, L=12.25mm , w=2mm, p= 1mm.

The simulation is done by Full wave commercial software CST with periodic boundary conditions. The floquet boundary conditions perpendicular to the plane of the FSS are placed to simulate different incident angles Fig. 2.

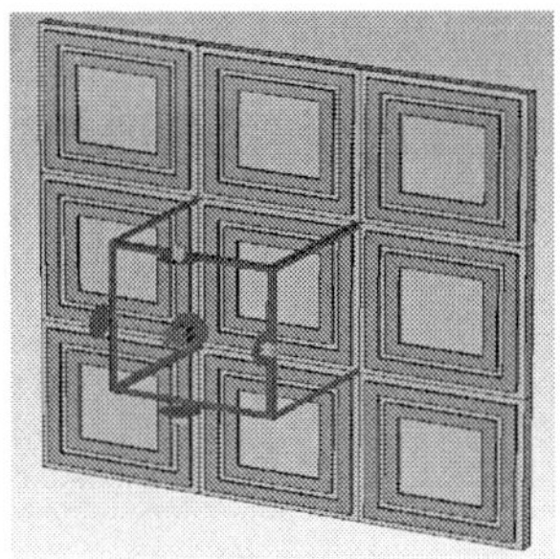

Fig. 2. Floquet boundary condition for unit cell geometry.

The S_{21} and S_{11} parameter which represent the the transmission and reflection respectively are shown in Fig.3.

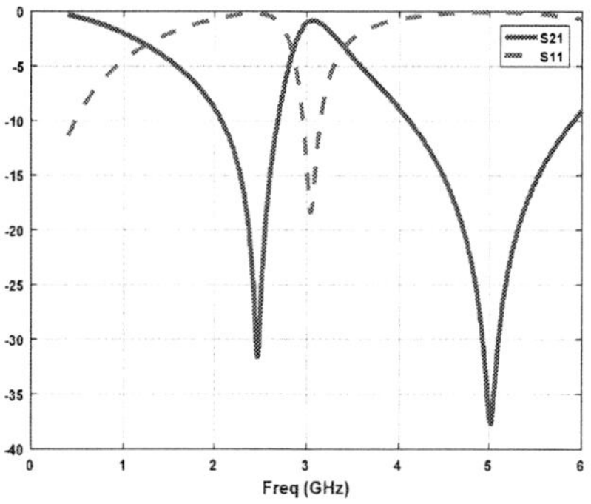

Fig. 3. Simulated reflection and transmission of the proposed metamaterial absorber.

The structure benefits from the symmetry so an independency of polarization and incident angle is expected. In order to investigate the influence of incident angle on the performance of the FSS, the absorption under different polarization incident wave for azimuth and elevation plane is presented in Fig. 4. The results show a good stability for different angle of incident and polarization.

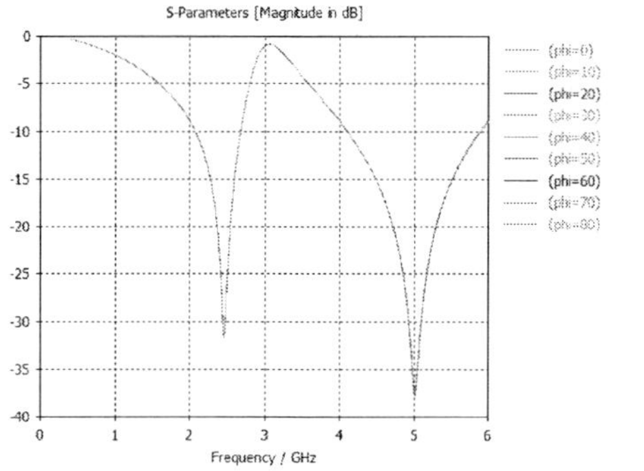

(a)

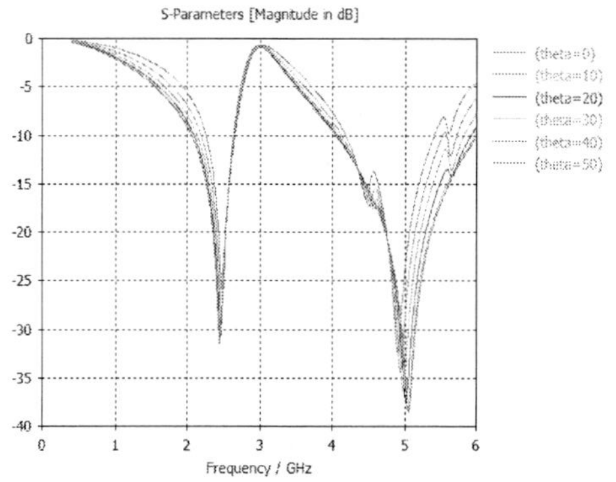

(b)

Fig. 4. Transmission at the different incident angles ranging from 0 to 80 Phi (a) and 0 for 50 Theta (b) with respect to FR4 plane.

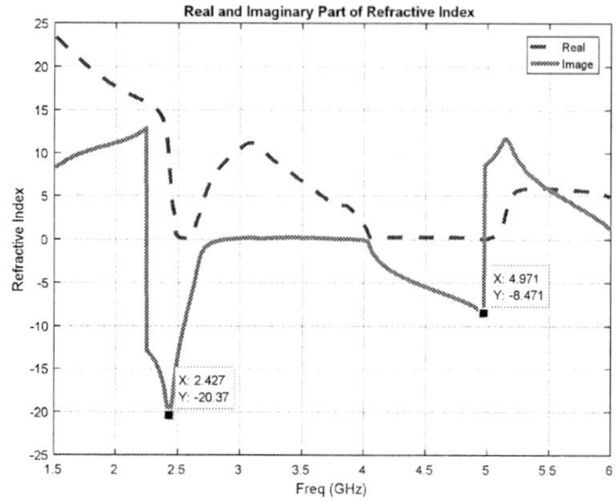

Fig. 5. Real and imaginary part of refractive index for normal incidence.

III. Theory

The structure shows maximum negative imaginary part of refractive index at resonant frequencies while the real part of refractive index is zero as shown in Fig. 5. Proposed FSS behaves like a SNG metamaterial at resonant frequencies and represents a high attenuation. Neglecting the losses, we see that when refractive index is purely imaginary at resonance frequencies the wave vector is also purely imaginary and the wave is strongly attenuated inside the slab [4]. This high attenuation constant results in a high mismatch and totally reflection of incident wave.

IV. Conclusion

The proposed symmetrical unit cell based on double square shapes represents a high level of rejection for dual WI-FI bands. Simulations demonstrated that due to the symmetry of structure the resonant frequency of rejection is independent of incident angles for a wide range both in azimuthal and elevation planes. In addition, FSS represents single negative metamaterial properties at resonance frequencies. The optimization of transmission bandwidth especially at five (GHz) can be a part of further research.

References

[1] B. A. Munk, Frequency Selective Surfaces: Theory and Design, Wiley-Interscience Publication, April 2000.

[2] S. Choudhary and H.S. Mewara, "A band-reject frequency selective surface with stable response for WLAN applications," Signal Processing and Communication Engineering Systems (SPACES), 2015 International Conference on, 2-3 January 2015.

[3] M. Bahdorzadeh, N. Feiz, and H. Bolandpour, "Design a multiband perfect metamaterial absorber based on hexagonal shapes," Applied Computational Electromagnetics (ACES), 2015 31st International Review of Progress in EM.

[4] N. Engheta and R. W. Ziolkowski, Metamaterials Physics and Engineering Explorations, Wiley-IEEE Press, July 2006.

The Time-Bandwidth Limit in Optical Nanostructures and Its Relation to Nonreciprocity

Dimitrios L. Sounas, Sander Mann, and Andrea Alù
Department of Electrical and Computer Engineering
The University of Texas at Austin
Austin, Texas, U.S.A.
dimitrios.sounas@utexas.edu, sandermann@utmail.utexas.edu, alu@mail.utexas.edu

Abstract—**The time-bandwidth limit refers to the trade-off between the time-delay that can be applied to a signal and the signal bandwidth. Recently, there have been several studies showing that this bound can be broken in nonreciprocal nano-structures, including nonreciprocal cavities and terminated unidirectional waveguides. Here, we clarify the nature of these claims and the physical mechanisms involved in such structures.**

Keywords— nonreciprocity, nonreciprocal cavities, time-bandwidth limit, unidirectional waveguides.

I. Introduction

The time-bandwidth limit is the bound between the bandwidth of a physical system and the time signals can interact with it (the time a signal can be stored in the system) [1],[2]. For example, the bandwidth of a resonator is inversely proportional to the decay time of the resonator, which is essentially the time a signal can stay in the resonator. The same bound can be extended to distributed systems, e.g., a system consisting of a series of resonators, in which case the time-bandwidth limit applies per unit length of the structure. Breaking this limit can be achieved through time-variant or nonlinear structures [3]-[9].

Recently, there have been several claims that the time-bandwidth limit can be overcome without modulation or nonlinear effects in nonreciprocal structures [10]. In particular, it was claimed that in a nonreciprocal resonator with different incoming and outgoing coupling coefficient, the decay time, which is proportional to the outgoing coupling coefficient, can be very different than the bandwidth, which was claimed to be determined by the incoming coupling coefficient. As a proof of this claim, Ref. [10] studied the properties of a unidirectional waveguide terminated at one side with an impenetrable wall. It was claimed that such a system forms a cavity that traps incident signals over the entire bandwidth of the waveguide for indefinitely long time, only determined by the material loss in the structure.

Here we show that the only physically possible way to realize a nonreciprocal cavity is by connecting a conventional cavity to an isolator/unidirectional waveguide. In this case, we show that the bandwidth of the signals in the cavity is always inversely proportional to the decay rate of the cavity. Although the bandwidth at the input port of the isolator/unidirectional waveguide can be large, the signals that lie outside the cavity bandwidth cannot enter the cavity and instead are absorbed at the edge between the waveguide and the cavity.

The second system presented in [10] is a terminated unidirectional waveguide. We first show that this system has no relation to conventional cavities, but instead it is equivalent to a waveguide that slows down signals as they approach the termination. A similar effect can be obtained in tapered waveguides, but it requires a long length in order to avoid reflections. On the other hand, a terminated unidirectional waveguide is always matched to incident signals, as a result of nonreciprocity, allowing to slow down the wave over small areas with large discontinuities along the propagation path. Therefore, as in the case of cavities, the role of nonreciprocity is to secure matching rather than breaking the time-bandwidth limit. Yet these structures can be attractive for their property to slow down waves over a small area. We support these claims with full-wave simulation results for the evolution of incident pulses as they approach the waveguide termination. Furthermore, we connect these results to works from the 1960's dealing with the thermodynamic paradox in nonreciprocal systems [11]-[15].

Our presentation will clarify some misconceptions regarding the time-bandwidth limit and its relation to non-reciprocity and shed light on what advantages we may expect to achieve by introducing nonreciprocity in delay systems.

Acknowledgment

This work was supported by the Air Force Office of Scientific Research, the Simons Foundation, and the National Science Foundation.

References

[1] D. A. B. Miller, "Fundamental limit to linear one-dimensional slow light structures," Phys. Rev. Lett., vol. 99, p. 203903, 2007.

[2] R. S. Tucker, P. C. Ku, and C. J. Chang-Hasnain, "Delay–bandwidth product and storage density in slow-light optical buffers," Electron. Lett., vol. 41, no. 4, pp. 208-209, 2005.

[3] M. F. Yanik and S. Fan, "Stopping light all optically," Phys. Rev. Lett., vol. 92, p. 83901, 2004.

[4] M. F. Yanik, W. Suh, Z. Wang, and S. Fan, "Stopping light in a waveguide with an all-optical analog of electromagnetically induced transparency," Phys. Rev. Lett., vol. 93, p. 149901, 2007.

[5] M. F. Yanik and S. Fan, "Stopping and storing light coherently," Phys. Rev. A, vol. 71, p. 13803, 2005.

[6] S. Sandhu, M. L. Povinelli, and S. Fan, "Stopping and time reversing a light pulse using dynamic loss tuning of coupled-resonator delay lines," Opt. Lett., vol. 32, no. 22, pp. 3333-3335, 2007.

[7] Q. Xu, P. Dong, and M. Lipson, "Breaking the delay-bandwidth limit in a photonic structure," Nat. Phys., vol. 3, pp. 406–410, 2007.

[8] M. F. Yanik and S. Fan, "Dynamic photonic structures: Stopping, storage, and time reversal of light," Stud. Appl. Math., vol. 115, pp. 233–253, 2005.

[9] S. Lannebère and M. Silveirinha, "Optical meta-atom for localization of light with quantized energy," Nature Commun., vol. 6, p. 8766, 2015.

[10] K. L. Tsakmakidis, et al., "Breaking Lorentz reciprocity to overcome the time-bandwidth limit in physics and engineering," Science, vol. 356, pp. 1260–1264, 2017.

[11] P. G. Barzilai and G. Gerosa, "Rectangular waveguides loaded with magnetised ferrite, and the so-called thermodynamic paradox," Proc. IEE, vol. 113, pp. 285–288, 1966.

[12] A. Ishimaru, "Unidirectional waves in anisotropic media and the resolution of the thermodynamic paradox," Technical Report, 1962.

[13] A. D. Bresler, "On the TEn0 modes of a ferrite slab loaded rectangular waveguide and the associated thermodynamic paradox," IRE Trans. Microw. Theory Tech., vol. 8, no. 1, pp. 81–95, 1960.

[14] R. R. J. Gagne, "The paradoxical surface wave (crack wave) in Ferrite-filled waveguides," IEEE Trans. Microw. Theory Tech., vol. 16, no. 4, pp. 241–250, 1968.

[15] A. V. Mrstik, Jr., "The resolution of the thermodynamic paradox and the theory of guided wave propagation in anisotropic media," 1968, (Caltech, 1968).

Design of Ungrounded CPW GaN-on-Si MMICs

Philip Zurek*, Myles Foreman*, Ryan Johnson†, Christopher Galbraith†, José Estrada*, and Zoya Popovic*
*Department of Electrical, Computer, and Energy Engineering, University of Colorado, Boulder, Colorado 80309-0425
†MIT Lincoln Laboratory, Lexington, Massachusetts 02421-6426

***Abstract*—This work presents a study of circuit component design in a new GaN-on-Si process being developed by the MIT Lincoln Laboratory. The process uses a thick silicon substrate with no through-vias with a multi-layer stack-up. Examples of components required for MMIC design include lines of various impedances, shorted and open stubs, tees, meander lines, and capacitors. Because the fabrication process requires the use of ungrounded CPW lines, underpasses are necessary to connect ground planes and a study of 50-Ohm lines with several underpass spacings is performed. The large range of dimensions and dielectric constants presents a challenge for full-wave simulations, and a comparison between Ansys HFSS and Sonnet Software is presented for a variety of passive circuit components implemented in the GaN-on-Si MMIC stack-up.**

I. Introduction

Gallium nitride (GaN) is established as a high-voltage semiconductor with broad applications, including those at microwave and millimeter-wave frequencies. At frequencies above UHF, MMIC passive and active circuit components with a GaN active layer are typically fabricated on a silicon carbide (SiC) substrate. However, SiC is expensive and not easily integrated with CMOS. To overcome this, GaN MMICs on silicon (Si) substrates are being developed that keep lag effects low [1], reduce the parasitic conduction layer [2], optimize device periphery [3], and integrate with CMOS [4].

In this work, we explore a different GaN-on-Si process under development at the MIT Lincoln Laboratory. A stack-up of the process is shown in Fig. 1, where a GaN active layer is epitaxially-grown on a high-resistivity Si substrate with three metal layers and no through-vias. AlGaN is used as a barrier layer (not shown). The fabrication process also includes high-electron mobility transistors (HEMTs) of varying gate lengths (from 120 to 200 nm), periphery, gate-source spacing, and gate-drain spacing. Metal structures are written using lithography. Several numerical challenges arise from the complex stack-up. The eight layer thickness ranges from 90 nm to 1.065 mm, while the guided wavelength at X-band is on the order of 15 mm. Appropriate port excitation and model de-embedding also need to be considered. In this paper, several CPW circuit components are designed and simulated using both Finite Element (FEM) Ansys HFSS and Method of Moments (MoM) Sonnet Software. Our goal is to establish which method agrees better with measurements.

Coplanar waveguide transmission lines can be evaluated using the conformal mapping method described in [5], which results in the characteristic impedance given by:

$$Z_{0cp} = \frac{30\pi}{\sqrt{\epsilon_{re}}} \frac{K'(k_1)}{K(k_1)}, \quad (1)$$

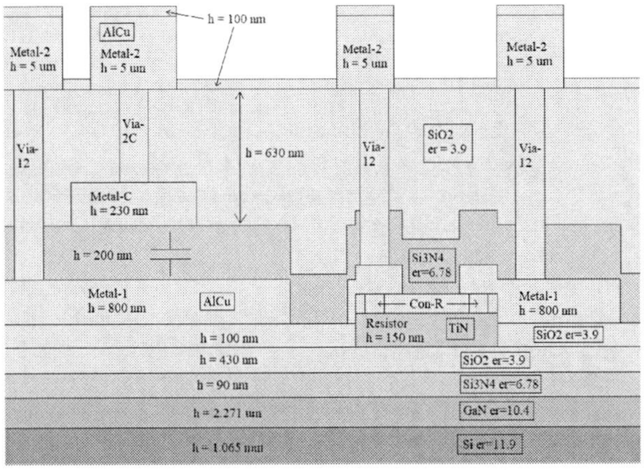

Fig. 1. GaN-on-Si process stack-up (not to scale). CPW lines are made in the Metal-2 layer (blue). Underpasses are made using the Metal-1 layer. Capacitors are made using Metal-C and Metal-1 layers. The various dielectrics and their permittivities are shown in green, GaN in purple and the Si substrate in orange. HEMT metal layers are omitted since this paper focuses on passive circuit components.

where K is the complete elliptic integral of the first kind (K' is its complement), k_1 is its argument, and ϵ_{re} is the effective dielectric constant. The constant ϵ_{re} can be determined as the weighted sum of each dielectric layer's filling factor and relative permittivity. This approach is used as a starting point in design, e.g., for a gap width of 34 μm and conductor line width of 40 μm, Z_{0cp} = 50 Ω. However, when simulated using HFSS, a gap width of 25 μm produced a 50-Ω line due to the influence of the conductor thickness, pointing to the need for detailed electromagnetic simulations.

II. Passive Component Design and Results

Because this GaN-on-Si process does not include through-vias to a ground plane, CPW transmission lines are used, whereas typical MMICs use microstrip transmission lines [1]. Along with the Metal-2 layer (see Fig. 1) used for the CPW lines, the Metal-1 layer is used to create underpasses to connect the CPW reference planes and for capacitor electrodes in conjunction with the Metal-C layer. An example ADS layout of a portion of a 50-Ω line with a $\lambda/4$ shunt shorted stub is included in Fig. 2. Because of the fringing fields associated with the inductive nature of the short, this line is modeled in ADS as having a length extension of 10 μm [5].

For a full stack-up model, Sonnet requires memory on the order of 30 GB for more complex circuit geometries, such as capacitors and meander lines, whereas HFSS requires 13 GB. In HFSS, lumped ports are used to excite the transmission

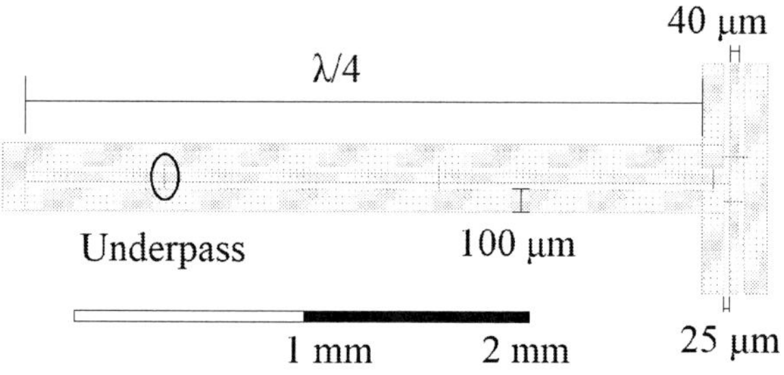

Fig. 2. ADS layout of a 50-Ω CPW line with λ/4 shunt shorted stub and λ/10 spaced underpasses, currently in fabrication. Labeled line width, gap width, and ground width are the same everywhere in this layout.

line so that the radiation boundary can be properly set up a distance λ/10 away. The shorted stub of Fig. 2, e.g., requires 8.35 hours to solve in Sonnet and 2.82 in HFSS with a full stack-up using a computer with 16 GB of RAM and an Intel i7 3.4 GHz processor.

To reduce simulation times, the stack-up is simplified by combining the two dielectric layers between Metal-2 and Metal-1 into a single homogeneous effective dielectric with a relative permittivity of 4.55 (1 % below weighted average). Similarly with the layers at Metal-1 and below, but not including Si, a second effective dielectric layer with relative permittivity 6.1 is included in the simulations (29 % below weighted average). The Si thickness was reduced to 600 μm by 44 %. These changes have little effect on performance, but decrease simulation times by about 95 % for complicated geometries.

Underpasses are added at varying intervals with necessary adjustments to produce varying impedance transmission lines, summarized in Table I. For the 50-Ω line with λ/10 spacing, plots of loss and $|S_{11}|$ for Z_L = 15 Ω are included in Fig. 3.

TABLE I. Varying Impedance Transmission Line Dimensions

ϵ_{re} HFSS	ϵ_{re} Sonnet	Underpass Spacing	Z_0	HFSS Line Width	HFSS Gap Width
4.96	5.06	none	50 Ω	40 μm	23 μm
5.61	5.38	∼ λ/20	50 Ω	40 μm	28 μm
5.20	5.18	∼ λ/10	50 Ω	40 μm	25 μm
5.11	5.01	∼ λ/4	50 Ω	40 μm	24 μm
4.83	5.05	∼ λ/10	30 Ω	74 μm	8 μm
4.83	4.95	∼ λ/10	75 Ω	16 μm	37 μm

Sonnet gives a resonant spike around 28 GHz due to the PEC boundaries imposed by the simulation method. The disagreement between the two simulations is about a 0.5 dB in $|S_{11}|$, 0.2 dB/mm in loss, with a nearly identical phase response (not plotted). It is found that each underpass adds about one effective degree of electrical line length. The ground plane width is also varied from 50 μm to 150 μm, with 100 μm chosen as the smallest distance that still gives expected performance.

The tee junction from Fig. 2 is simulated, separately from the entire circuit, in HFSS and Sonnet. Fig. 4 shows the tee and stub results. S-parameters demonstrate relatively good agreement between HFSS and Sonnet. Greater loss improves matching because more power is dissipated rather than reflected. Footprint miniaturization was studied on a four-turn

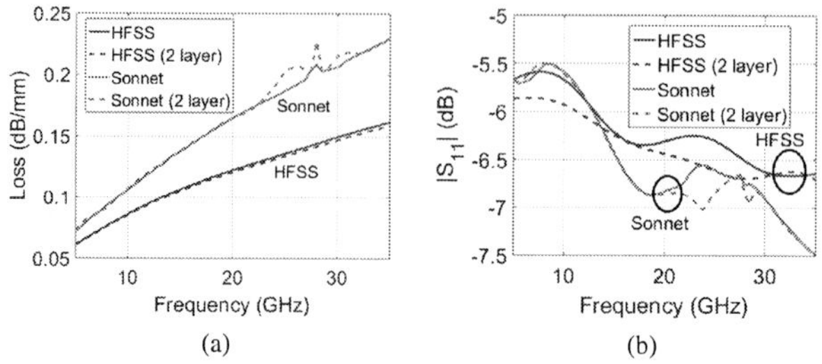

Fig. 3. (a) Loss (dB/mm) and (b) $|S_{11}|$ comparison between HFSS (gap = 25 μm) and Sonnet (gap = 21 μm) of a 50-Ω line with λ/10 underpass spacing. (a) is terminated in a 50-Ω load and (b) in a 15-Ω load.

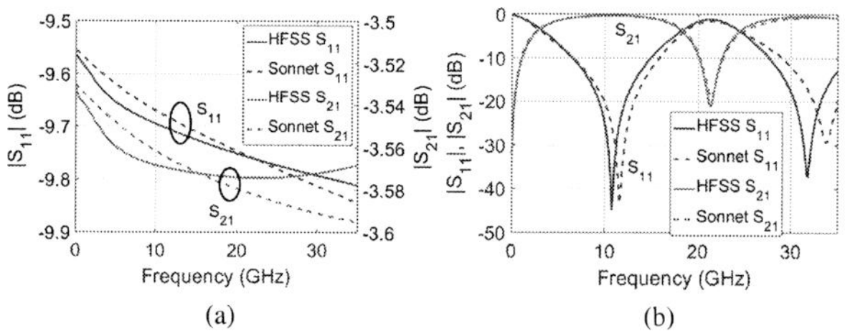

Fig. 4. HFSS and Sonnet S-parameters of: (a) tee junction and (b) quarter-wave shorted stub.

half-wavelength meander line with 100 μm ground plane width between lines requiring a 28 μm gap width to maintain 50-Ω characteristic impedance. In addition, they are about 20 % shorter due to coupling. As width between lines increases, the meander line length approaches a half-wavelength, as expected. Lumped components are also investigated. Using the stack-up of Fig. 1, 0.3 fF/μm^2 is expected for the capacitors. An HFSS simulated 60 μm x 80 μm DC blocking capacitor, e.g., has a capacitance of 1.55 pF at DC (1.44 pF calculated) and 1.46 pF at 10 GHz. Sonnet results in a DC capacitance of 1.58 pF for the same capacitor.

ACKNOWLEDGMENT

This work is supported under the Assistant Secretary of Defense (ASD) for Research and Engineering Contract No. FA8721-05-C-0002 and/or FA8702-15-D-0001. Any opinions, findings, conclusions or recommendations expressed in this material are those of the authors and do not necessarily reflect the views of the ASD.

REFERENCES

[1] R. Leblanc, N. S. Ibeas, A. Gasmi, F. Auvray, J. Poulain, F. Lecourt, G. Dagher, and P. Frijlink, "6w ka band power amplifier and 1.2db nf x-band amplifier using a 100nm gan/si process," in 2016 IEEE CSICS, Oct. 2016, pp. 1–4.

[2] L. Pattison, T. Boles, N. Tuffy, and G. Lopes, "Improving gan on si power amplifiers through reduction of parasitic conduction layer," in 2014 9th EuMIC, Oct. 2014, pp. 92–95.

[3] J. Kim, H. Park, D. Kim, M. Lee, K. Seo, and Y. Kwon, "Rf parametric study on algan/gan hemts on si-substrate for millimeter-wave pa," in 2013 APMC Proceedings, Nov. 2013, pp. 775–777.

[4] T. E. Kazior, J. R. LaRoche, and W. E. Hoke, "More than moore: Gan hemts and si cmos get it together," in 2013 IEEE CSICS, Oct. 2013, pp. 1–4.

[5] K. C. Gupta, R. Garg, I. Bahl, and P. Bhartia, Microstrip Lines and Slotlines. Boston, MA: Artech House, 1996, pp. 375–451.

Bandwidth Design of Ferrite-Based Circulators

Andrea Ashley, Laila Fighera Marzall, Mauricio Pinto, Zoya Popovic, and Dimitra Psychogiou
Department of Electrical, Computer and Energy Engineering
University of Colorado, Boulder, CO 80309, USA

***Abstract*—This paper reports on the RF design of planar ferrite-based RF circulators with bandwidth control through the height of the ferrite-puck and the DC magnetic biasing. The analysis is performed with the aid of a commercially-available finite-element solver for a design frequency of 3.9 GHz. The study reveals that by varying the ratio of ferrite height to substrate height within the circulator cavity from 0.1 to 1, the 1-dB bandwidth varies between 5 and 36.2%. While conventional RF circulators are designed for a fill factor equal to 1, this study shows that maximum bandwidth is obtained for a fill factor of 0.82.**

***Index Terms*— Circulator, fractional bandwidth, magnetic bias, insertion loss, isolation.**

I. Introduction

Recent advances in high power radar systems call for high levels of isolation between the transmit and received RF signals within a broad bandwidth of operation. In order to meet these requirements, low-profile and broadband RF circulators need to be developed [1]. However, the majority of commercially-available planar-based circulators exhibit fractional bandwidths (FBWs) below 20% [2]-[4]. Alternative RF design techniques have been developed with the purpose of increasing FBW. These include, adding multi-section matching networks at the input/outputs of the ferrite-puck or by routing the RF signal between inter-coupled ferrite-loaded cavities [4]. However, these techniques result in large physical size and excess of RF loss.

This paper examines the FBW design limits of microstrip-type circulators loaded by circular ferrite pucks. The proposed study focuses on single cavity circulators and analyzes the effects of altering the ferrite material fill factor H_P/H_S within the circulator cavity, as shown in Fig. 1. Commercially-available ferrite pucks from TransTech (TT1-105) and a dielectric substrate from Rogers (4350) are considered for all devices. The proposed study reveals that by altering the ferrite's fill factor, the FBW of the circulator can be tailored between 5-36.2% with the maximum FBW obtained for a fill factor of 0.82.

II. Fill Factor Study

The RF design of ferrite-based microstrip circulators has been widely discussed in the open technical literature and is summarized in this section. For a uniformly applied DC magnetic bias field— above magnetization saturation M_S —and a defined set of material parameters including: relative permittivity ε_r, relative permeability μ_r, linewidth of the ferromagnetic resonance ΔH and a desired design frequency f_0,

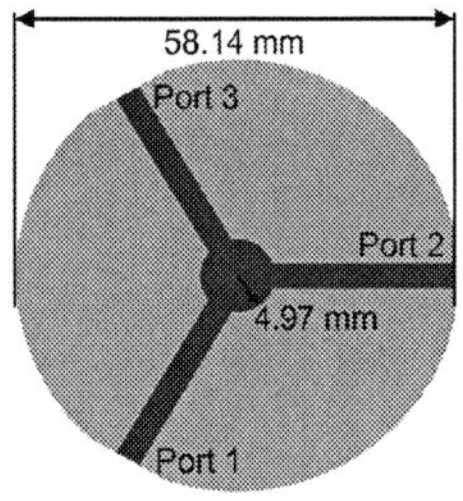

(a)

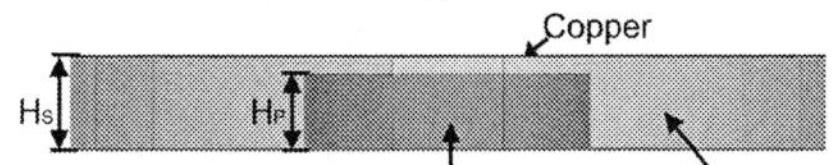

(b)

Fig. 1. (a) Top view. (b) Cross-sectional view of the microstrip-line type circulator. The material properties are summarized as follows: Dielectric substrate: Rogers 4350, ε_r=3.66, H_S=1.524 mm, Ferrite puck: TransTech TT1-105: M_S=0.175T, ε_r=12.2, μ_0=55, ΔH=220 Oe, $H_P \leq 1.524$ mm. The conceptual drawings of the circulator are not in scale.

the radius of the ferrite puck can be calculated using (1):

$$R_f = \frac{1.84}{2\pi f_0 \sqrt{\varepsilon_r \mu_{r,eff}}} \quad (1)$$

where $\mu_{r,eff}$ denotes the effective permeability that is a function of f_0 and magnetization.

For the sake of comparison, a baseline circulator architecture is designed for a frequency of 3.9 GHz and 50 Ω reference impedance using as a basis the material parameters in Fig. 1 and the design methodology in [1]. Furthermore, the ferrite's height H_P is set equal to the height of the dielectric substrate H_S,

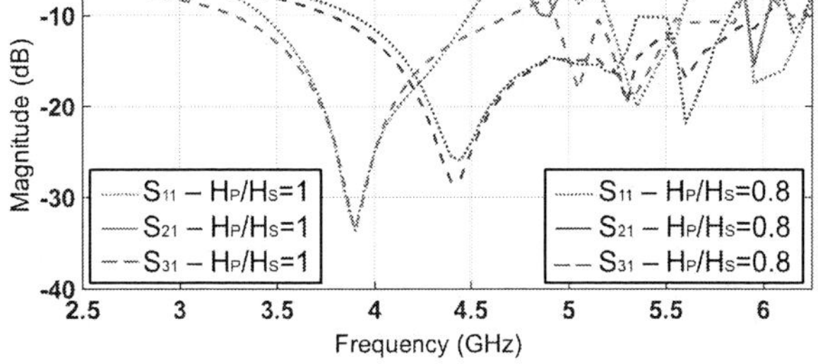

Fig. 2. Electromagnetically-simulated response in terms of S-parameters for alternative levels of H_P/H_S. The circulator dimensions and the applied DC magnetic bias field are identical for both designs.

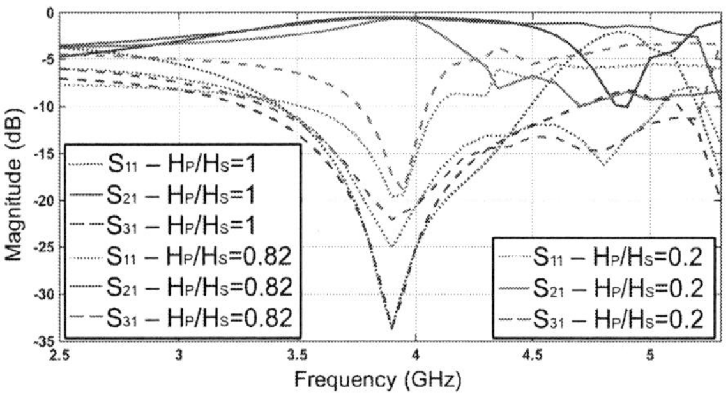

Fig. 3. Electromagnetically-simulated response in terms of S-parameters for alternative levels of H_P/H_S. The circulator dimensions are identical for both designs. The DC magnetic bias field is altered as shown in Fig. 4.

resulting in a fill factor of 1. Its simulated response is obtained using the commercially available finite-element-based software ANSYS HFSS and is illustrated in Fig. 2. It exhibits a 1-dB-bandwidth of 1.1 GHz, FBW of 28.1%, minimum insertion loss and maximum isolation of 0.51 dB and 33 dB respectively.

The ferrite fill factor effect is studied by altering the ratio of H_P/H_S whilst keeping the rest of the circulator dimensions constant. A comparison for two different values of the fill factor, 1 and 0.8 is shown in Fig. 2. It can be seen that by reducing the fill factor from 1 to 0.8, the operational frequency of the circulator shifts to higher frequencies whereas its bandwidth broadens. In order to better compare the circulator designs, they are redesigned for the same center frequency. This is achieved by altering the DC magnetic bias field from 142 KA/m to 108 KA/m (below M_S) which results in both designs operating at the same center frequency of 3.9 GHz.

The overall RF performance of the circulator for various fill factors H_P/H_S is shown in Figs. 3, 4 in terms of S-parameters, FBW and magnetic bias. It can be seen that by altering H_P/H_S from 0.1 to 1 and the magnetic bias between 108-142 KA/m, the FBWs can be designed between 5% and 36.2%. This effect proves that the proposed RF design technique is suitable for the realization of both narrowband and broadband circulators in which the resonator footprint is identical. It should be highlighted that although conventional circulator designs have $H_P/H_S=1$ [4], maximum FBW is obtained for $H_P/H_S <1$ which is 0.82 in this case. However, the maximum FBW state exhibits 10 dB less isolation than the baseline design ($H_P/H_S=1$). Furthermore, for fill factors that are set <0.82 (FBW maximum), the following trends can be observed. The FBW becomes narrower with the decrease of H_P/H_S, whereas the insertion loss increases and the isolation decreases.

III. Conclusion

This paper reports on the RF design of ferrite-based microstrip-type circulators with narrow and broadband width. The analysis considers ferrite-based pucks with fill factor ≤ 1 and alternative levels of DC magnetic biasing that was modified with the purpose of altering the circulator bandwidth, without affecting its operational frequency. The presented study reveals that by altering the ferrite fill factor within the circulator cavity from 0.1 to 1, the 1-dB bandwidth varies between 5 and 36.2%. While conventional RF circulators are designed for a fill factor equal to 1, this study shows that maximum bandwidth can be obtained for a fill factor <1. For the specific materials considered here, this value is 0.82.

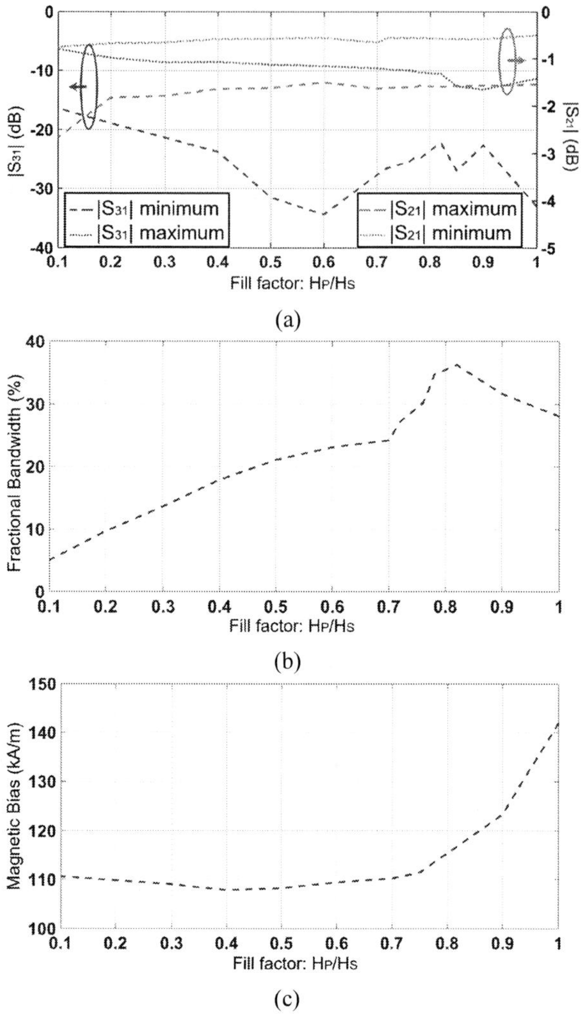

Fig. 4. Circulator performance for alternative levels of H_P/H_S. (a) Power transmission response: S_{21}, S_{31}, (b) FBW, and (c) DC magnetic bias.

Acknowledgement

This work was funded by the DARPA M3IC program under sub-contract to Qorvo.

References

[1] S. George, The Analysis of the Circulator Frequency Shift with the Temperature Variation. *1980 10th European Microwave Conference*, 1980.

[2] D. Linkhart, *Microwave Circulator Design*. Boston: Artech House, 2014, pp. 153-157.

[3] H. Bosma, "On stripline Y-circulation at UHF," IEEE Transactions on Microwave Theory and Techniques, vol. 12, no. 1, pp. 61-72, 1964.

[4] J. L. Young, R. S. Adams, B. O'Neil, and C. M. Johnson, "Bandwidth optimization of an integrated microstrip circulator and antenna assembly," IEEE Antennas and Propagation Magazine, vol. 48, no. 6, pp. 47–56, Dec. 2006.

Amplitude-Equalized Microwave Phasers

Mohamed K. Emara, Kimi Maheshwari, Jim S. Wight and Shulabh Gupta
Department of Electronics, Carleton University, 1125 Colonel by Drive,
Ottawa, Ontario, Canada, shulabh.gupta@carleton.ca

Abstract—**An active microwave C-section phaser is proposed which provides a flat magnitude transmission in a wide frequency band along with a frequency-dependent group delay response considering practical dissipation losses. The key lies in integrating a constant gain amplifier inside a microwave C-section, which perfectly compensates the distributed conductor and dielectric losses of the coupler, while preserving the intrinsic dispersion of the C-section. The operation of the proposed device is confirmed using numerical analysis and full-wave simulations.**

I. Introduction

A C-section represents a fundamental building unit of microwave dispersive devices such a wide-band phase shifters [1], equalizers [2] and real-time signal processors [3][4]. Recently, they have been used extensively to build dispersive devices exhibiting complex group delay profiles, owing to their all-pass transmission properties, which have found important applications in Real-Time Analog Signal Processing (R-ASP) technology [5]. A microwave C-section is 2-port device and is based on contra-directional TEM coupled-line couplers [2]. Under *ideal lossless conditions,* it provides a flat transmission [$|S_{21}(\omega)| = 1$] with a strongly dispersive frequency-dependent group delay response [$\tau = \tau(\omega)$]. However, all practical devices exhibit dissipation losses, and therefore, a flat transmission is never achieved in practice, i.e. $|S_{21}(\omega)| \neq 1$. Its magnitude transmission is always dependent on the dispersion response following Kramers-Kronig relations and the corresponding Bode gain-phase relations [6]. This frequency-dependent magnitude transmission subsequently leads to undesired signal distortion at the output of the corresponding dispersive devices.

To combat this issue, the concept of a *perfect dispersive medium* (PDM) was recently developed in [6] to decouple the magnitude and phase response of an electromagnetic device, while satisfying all causality requirements, i.e. achieving $|S_{21}(\omega)| = 1$ and $\tau = \tau(\omega)$, simultaneously. The 1-D counterpart of a PDM was demonstrated using microwave C-sections in [7], where each super-cell consisted of two separate loss and gain C-sections leading to amplitude-equalization of the super-cell and dispersion reconfigurability. While dispersion reconfigurability is specific to certain systems such as dispersion code multiple access (DCMA), amplitude equalization is a desired characteristic of any other dispersion based system such as real-time Fourier transformers [8][9], spectrum sniffers or frequency discriminators [10].

In this work, the same flat transmission response and frequency-dependent group delay are achieved simultaneously using a *single* microwave C-section. It will be shown that the losses of the C-section can be perfectly compensated in a wide band by integrating a gain-load inside a microwave C-section.

II. Proposed Active C-section

The analytical transfer function of a microwave C-section is given by [11][12]

$$S_{21}(\theta) = \left(\frac{1 - j\rho\tan\theta}{1 + j\rho\tan\theta}\right) \tag{1}$$

where $\rho = \sqrt{(1-k)/(1+k)}$, with k as the voltage coupling coefficient and $\text{Re}\{\theta(\omega)\} = \gamma(\omega)\ell$ as the electrical length of the transmission with γ as the complex propagation constant of the isolated line. The complex propagation constant $\gamma(\omega) = \beta(\omega) - j\alpha(\omega)$, where β and α are the per-unit propagation and attenuation constants of the isolated transmission lines, respectively. For a practical C-section with $\alpha \neq 0$, the transfer function can be re-written as [7]

$$S_{21}(\omega) = \left\{\frac{1 - \rho\tanh\alpha\ell - j(\rho - \tanh\alpha\ell)\tan\beta\ell}{1 + \rho\tanh\alpha\ell + j(\rho + \tanh\alpha\ell)\tan\beta\ell}\right\}, \tag{2}$$

It can be verified that the transmission magnitude $|S21(\omega)| \neq 1$, and is a strong function of frequency. In addition, the minimum transmission, $\min\{|S21(\omega)|\}$, is at the resonant frequency ω_0 of the coupler where its length ℓ is a quarter wavelength long

A C-section also exhibits a strong dispersion (frequency dependent group delay). Its group delay response $\tau(\omega) = -d\angle S_{21}(\omega)/d\omega$. It can be easily verified that the maximum delay τ occurs at the resonant frequency ω_0 of the coupler, and is given by

$$\max\{\tau(\omega)\} = \frac{2}{\rho}\frac{d\beta(\omega)}{d\omega}\ell. \tag{3}$$

III. Proposed Amplitude-Equalized Active C-section

To achieve a flat magnitude transmission from a microwave C-section preserving its strongly dispersive characteristic, let us modify the microwave C-section where the through and the isolated ports of the corresponding coupler are now connected through a matched load G, as shown in Fig. 1. Using the wave-interference approach, the transfer function of such a C-section is given by

$$S_{21}(\theta) = a(\theta) + \frac{G \cdot b^2(\theta)}{1 - a(\theta) \cdot G}, \tag{4}$$

which when $G = 1$, corresponds to a passive C-section, and reduces to (2), with $|S_{21}(\omega)| \neq 1$. This expression suggests that the load parameter G acts as a free parameter which maybe used to compensate for the frequency-dependent losses in a practical C-section. Let us intuitively enforce the amplitude-equalization at the fundamental resonant frequency ω_0 ($\beta\ell = \pi/2$) of the coupler, i.e.

$$a(\pi/2 - j\alpha\ell) + \frac{G \cdot b^2(\pi/2 - j\alpha\ell)}{1 - a(\pi/2 - j\alpha\ell) \cdot G} = \pm 1, \quad (5)$$

so that $|S_{21}(\omega_0)| = 1$. The $\pm$ signs on the RHS corresponds to resonant or anti-resonant conditions exhibiting the two group delay extrema. This equation can be easily solved for an optimum value of $G = G_0$, in closed-form to achieve a unity transmission across the C-section at the resonant frequency.

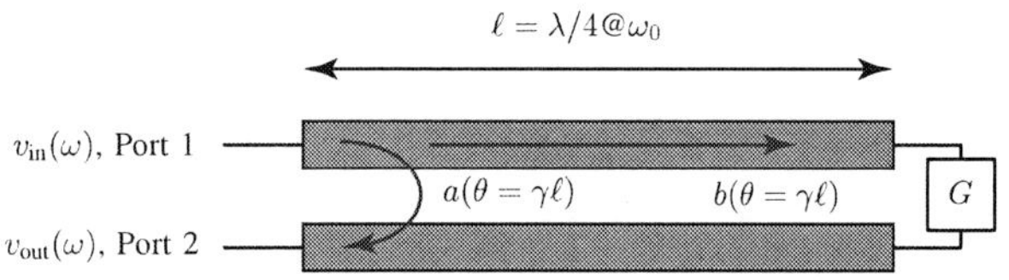

Fig. 1. Proposed configuration of an amplitude-equalized microwave C-section, where the through and isolated ports of the corresponding coupler is connected through a load G.

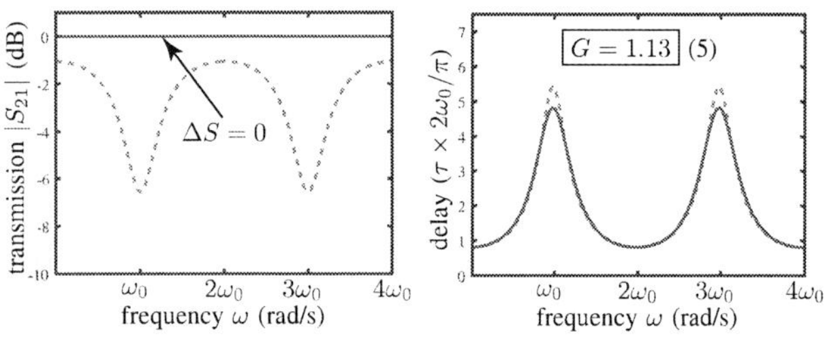

Fig. 2. The magnitude transmission and delay responses of an active microwave C-section of Fig. 1 computed using (4). The responses of a passive C-section is also shown using dashed curves for comparison. The design parameters are: $k = 0.71$, $\alpha\ell = 0.15$ and the gain G_0 calculated using (5).

Figure 2 shows the modified magnitude and delay responses of the amplitude-equalized C-section, following the optimum value of G_0. The transmission magnitude is now perfectly equalized to 0 dB. Naturally, the C-section maintains a strong dependence of the group delay on frequency, as desired. Fig. 3 confirms this feature of an active C-section, using full-wave simulations in FEM-HFSS, for a stripline structure (not shown here). The optimal gain load required agrees with the numerical value from (5), thereby confirming the operation of the active C-section.

IV. Conclusions

An active microwave C-section has been proposed which provides a flat magnitude transmission in a wide frequency band along with a frequency-dependent group delay response. It is based on integrating a constant gain amplifier inside a microwave C-section, which perfectly compensates the dissipation losses of the coupler, while preserving the intrinsic dispersion of the C-section. The proposed amplitude-equalized active C-section is compatible with standard MMIC processes and may find practical applications in wide range of phase shifting and dispersive devices for microwaves. Moreover, the proposed concept is also compatible with micro-ring resonators [13] which are based on co-directional coupled-line couplers, suitable for high-frequency devices and compatible with silicon photonic technologies for optics and THz applications.

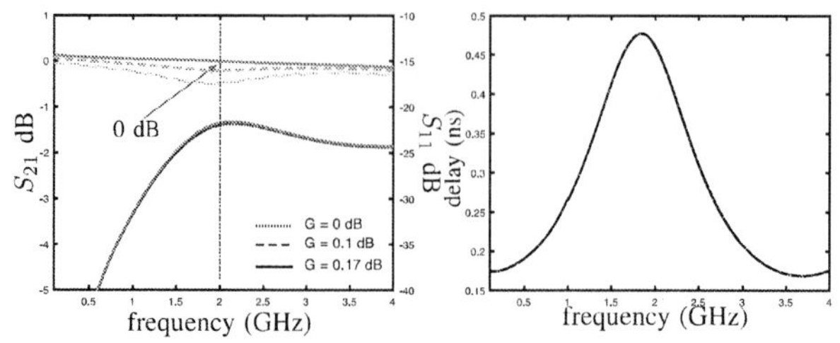

Fig. 3. FEM-HFSS Simulated S-parameters and delay response of an active C-section implemented in stripline technology, for different values of Gain load, including the optimum value $G_{\text{opt}} = 0.17$ dB.

References

[1] E. G. Cristal, "Theory and design of transmission line all-pass equalizers," *IEEE Trans. Microw. Theory Techn.*, vol. 17, no. 1, pp. 28–38, Jan. 1969.

[2] G. Matthaei, E. M. T. Jones, and L. Young, *Microwave Filters, Impedance-Matching Networks, and Coupling Structures*. Artech House Publishers, 1980.

[3] S. Gupta, D. L. Sounas, Q. Zhang, and C. Caloz, "All-pass dispersion synthesis using microwave C-sections," *Int. J. Circ. Theory Appl.*, May 2013.

[4] S. Gupta, Q. Zhang, L. Zou, L. J. Jiang, and C. Caloz, "Generalized coupled-line all-pass phasers," *IEEE Trans. Microw. Theory Techn.*, vol. 63, no. 3, pp. 1007 – 1018, Mar. 2015.

[5] C. Caloz, S. Gupta, Q. Zhang, and B. Nikfal, "Analog signal processing," *Microw. Mag.*, vol. 14, no. 6, pp. 87–103, Sept. 2013.

[6] S. Gupta and C. Caloz, "Perfect dispersive medium," *arXiv:1511.00671*, Nov 2015.

[7] L. Zou, S. Gupta, and C. Caloz, "Loss-gain equalized reconfigurable c-section analog signal processor," *IEEE Trans. Microw. Theory Techn.*, vol. 65, no. 2, pp. 555–564, Feb. 2017.

[8] T. Jannson, "Real-time Fourier transformation in dispersive optical fibers," *Opt. Lett.*, vol. 8, no. 4, pp. 232–234, Apr. 1983.

[9] M. A. G. Laso, T. Lopetegi, M. J. Erro, D. Benito, M. J. Garde, M. A. Muriel, M. Sorolla, and M. Guglielmi, "Real-time spectrum analysis in microstrip technology," *IEEE Trans. Microw. Theory Techn.*, vol. 51, no. 3, pp. 705–717, Mar. 2003.

[10] B. Nikfal, S. Gupta, and C. Caloz, "Increased group delay slope loop system for enhanced-resolution analog signal processing," *IEEE Trans. Microw. Theory Techn.*, vol. 59, no. 6, pp. 1622–1628, Jun. 2011.

[11] S. Gupta, D. L. Sounas, H. V. Nguyen, Q. Zhang, and C. Caloz, "CRLH-CRLH C-section dispersive delay structures with enhanced group delay swing for higher analog signal processing resolution," *IEEE Trans. Microw. Theory Techn.*, vol. 60, no. 21, pp. 3939–3949, Dec. 2012.

[12] S. Gupta, A. Parsa, E. Perret, R. V. Snyder, R. J. Wenzel, and C. Caloz, "Group delay engineered non-commensurate transmission line all-passnetwork for analog signal processing," *IEEE Trans. Microw. Theory Techn.*, vol. 58, no. 9, pp. 2392–2407, Sept. 2010.

[13] O. Schwelb, "Transmission, group delay, and dispersion in single-ring optical resonators and add/drop filters - a tutorial overview," *J. Lightwave Technol.*, vol. 22, no. 0, p. 1380, 2004.

A Novel Stochastic Integral Equation Method for Wireless Communication in Diffuse Multipath Environments

Shen Lin and Zhen Peng
Electrical and Computer Engineering Department, University of New Mexico, Albuquerque, U.S.A.
shenlin@unm.edu, pengz@unm.edu

***Abstract*—This paper investigates a novel stochastic integral equation method for the statistical characterization of wave propagation within diffuse multipath environments. The stochastic integral equation rigorously integrates coherent and incoherent propagations within a compact form, which does not appear to be available in the literature. Furthermore, it quantitatively describes universal statistical properties of the environment through random matrix theory. The theoretical research is evaluated and validated through semi-empirical statistical fading models.**

***Index Terms*—diffuse multipath, Green's function, integral equation, propagation, statistical analysis.**

I. Introduction

Transmission of information through complicated diffuse mulitpath environments is a topic of both fundamental and practical importance to wireless communication. Representative applications include indoor communications [1], [2], communications in metropolitan areas [3], transmission through diffusive random media [4], [5], etc. The complexity of the scattering environment creates an extremely large number of multiple paths between transmitters and receivers. Attributed to the distinguished characteristics and unique behaviors, applied scientists and engineers has found diverse applications, including multiple-input and multiple-output (MIMO) communications [6], [7], time-reversal systems [8], [9], wavefront shaping and focusing [10], [11], sensing and targeting [12], [13], et al. Yet, much potential is not fully exploited due to a lack of rigorous and versatile mathematical models.

II. Methodology

A. Stochastic Green's Function

We propose a novel theoretical solution to Maxwell's Equations in the diffuse multipath media, leveraging wave chaos theory and random statistical analysis [14]–[16]. The resulting stochastic Green's function (SGF), $G_{\rm S}$, can be written as a sum of a correlated component, $G_{\rm co}$, and an uncorrelated component, $G_{\rm uc}$. We obtain:

$$G_{\rm S}(\mathbf{r},\mathbf{r}') = \underbrace{\frac{1}{\pi}\sum_i \frac{\omega_i^2}{k^2-k_i^2}\frac{k\Delta}{k_i}\frac{\sin k_i|\mathbf{r}'-\mathbf{r}|}{4\pi|\mathbf{r}'-\mathbf{r}|}}_{\text{correlated},\ G_{\rm co}} + \underbrace{\sum_i \frac{\omega_i\omega_i'}{k^2-k_i^2}\frac{k\Delta}{4\pi^2}\frac{\sin k_i|\mathbf{r}'-\mathbf{r}_0'|}{k_i|\mathbf{r}'-\mathbf{r}_0'|}\frac{\sin k_i|\mathbf{r}-\mathbf{r}_0|}{k_i|\mathbf{r}-\mathbf{r}_0|}}_{\text{uncorrelated},\ G_{\rm uc}}. \quad (1)$$

In Eq. 1, ω_i and ω_i' are taken to be two independent Gaussian random variables with zero mean and unit variance. The eigenvalues k_i obey locally repulsion laws, which are distributed according to the random matrix hypotheses of Wigner. The $\mathbf{r}_0$ and $\mathbf{r}_0'$ are local expansion centers with respect to the source point, $\mathbf{r}$, and the receiving point $\mathbf{r}'$. In addition, Δ is the mean-spacing between adjacent eigenvalues of the Helmholtz operator predicted by Weyl Formula [15], [17].

B. Stochastic Integral Equation

Consider a Tx antenna array and a Rx antenna array in the chaotic environment. Each array contains three antenna elements. The exterior surfaces of the Tx and Rx antenna elements are denoted by $S_m^T, m=1,2,3$ and $S_n^R, n=1,2,3$, respectively, The basis and testing functions are introduced on the surfaces of the antennas, defined as λ_m^t on S_m^T and λ_n^r on S_n^R. We propose a new stochastic integral equation method using the SGF (SIE-SGF):

$$\mathcal{Z}^{\rm RT} = \sum_{n=1}^{3}\sum_{m=1}^{3}\int_{S_n^R}\int_{S_m^T}\lambda_n^r\cdot\mathcal{F}(G_{\rm S})\cdot\lambda_m^t dS_n^R dS_m^T. \quad (2)$$

In Eq. 2, the $\mathcal{F}$ is defined as a general differential operator on the proposed SGF. Taking the electric field integral operator as an example, $\mathcal{F}=\left(\bar{\bar{\mathbf{I}}}-\frac{\nabla\nabla}{k^2}\right)$ for vector EM fields.

In analogy to the standard fast multipole method [18], the discrete matrix of SIE-SGF can be decomposed as:

$$\mathbf{Z}^{\rm RT} = {\rm Re}\left[\mathbf{Z}_0^{\rm RT}\right] + j\mathbf{D}_0^{\rm R}\cdot\underbrace{\left[\mathbf{T}_0^{\rm RT}\mathbf{g}_{\rm co}+\mathbf{g}_{\rm uc}\right]}_{\text{Translation}}\cdot\mathbf{A}_0^{\rm T}. \quad (3)$$

where $\mathbf{Z}_0^{**}$, $\mathbf{A}_0^{*}$, $\mathbf{D}_0^{*}$ are the impedance matrix, aggregation matrix, and disaggregation matrix using free-space Green's function, respectively. The $\mathbf{T}_0^{**}$ is the free-space translation matrix, which corresponds to the direct trajectory contributions between the source and receiver. The $\mathbf{g}_{**}$ represents the effects of multipath chaotic rays with random phases, whose statistics are obtained from random matrix theory [19].

III. Experimental Verfication

We begin with the verification of the work with semi-empirical Rayleigh fading model, which is introduced for extremely multipath environments [20]. In the experimental verification, we consider two monopole antennas as transmitting (Tx) and receiving (Rx) inside the complex multipath environment. The two antennas are separated by $L = 20\lambda$. The SIE-SGF is employed at the exterior surfaces of two antennas, and the finite element method is used for the modeling of volume domain of antennas. The probability distribution function (PDF) of the normalized S-parameter of the Rx antenna is depicted in Fig. 1 (a). Since the Tx and Rx are well-separated, the SGF is dominated by the uncorrelated component, G_{uc}, which corresponds to the diffuse multipath propagator. The PDF indeed follows the Rayleigh distribution.

Next, we calculate the PDF of the channel capacity with respect to Signal-to-Noise ratio: $\rho = 2$ in Fig. 1 (b). We notice that the results are consistent with the expression given in the literature for the single-input single-output case (SISO) in presence of Rayleigh fading [20]. Nevertheless, there are no fitting parameters needed in the proposed work.

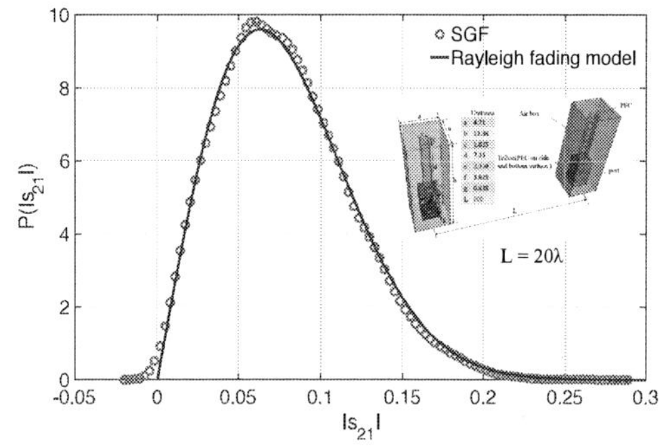

(a) Normalized S_{12} parameter

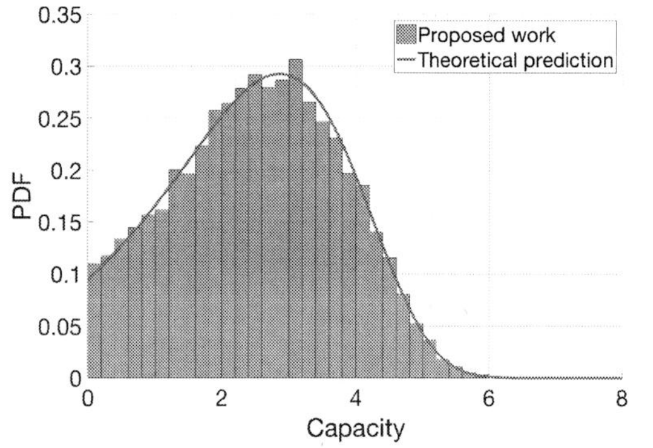

(b) Channel capacity

Fig. 1: Probability distribution functions

IV. Conclusion

The results verify that the proposed work leads to a competent statistical model for predicting the performance of wireless antennas in the multipath environment. The SGF statistically replicates the propagation phenomena that includes both direct orbits and uniform, isotropic multipath fading. Moreover, the computational costs are comparable to the free-space environment, since the SIE-SGF are placed only at the exterior surface of antennas. The advancements have diverse applications to wireless experimentation, time-reversal experiments, wavefront shaping, and sensing and targeting.

References

[1] A. O. Kaya, L. J. Greenstein, and W. Trappe, "Characterizing indoor wireless channels via ray tracing combined with stochastic modeling," *IEEE Transactions on Wireless Communications*, vol. 8, pp. 4165–4175, Aug. 2009.

[2] D. Micheli, M. Barazzetta, F. Moglie, and V. M. Primiani, "Power boosting and compensation during OTA testing of a real 4G LTE base station in reverberation chamber," *IEEE Transactions on Electromagnetic Compatibility*, vol. 57, pp. 623–634, Aug. 2015.

[3] P. Kyösti, J. Meinilä, L. Hentilä, X. Zhao, T. Jämsä, C. Schneider, M. Narandžić, M. Milojević, A. Hong, J. Ylitalo, M. A. V.-M. Holappa, R. Bultitude, Y. de Jong, and T. Rautiainen, "WINNER II channel models," tech. rep., European Commission, IST-WINNER, Technical Report D1.1.2, 2007.

[4] Z. Q. Zhang, I. P. Jones, H. P. Schriemer, J. H. Page, D. A. Weitz, and P. Sheng, "Wave transport in random media: The ballistic to diffusive transition," *Phys. Rev. E*, vol. 60, pp. 4843–4850, Oct. 1999.

[5] C. Jin, R. R. Nadakuditi, E. Michielssen, and S. C. Rand, "Iterative, backscatter-analysis algorithms for increasing transmission and focusing light through highly scattering random media," *J. Opt. Soc. Am. A*, vol. 30, pp. 1592–1602, Aug. 2013.

[6] S. H. Simon, A. L. Moustakas, M. Stoytchev, and H. Safar, "Communication in a disordered world," *Physics Today*, vol. 54, no. 9, pp. 38–43, 2001.

[7] A. L. Moustakas, H. U. Baranger, L. Balents, A. M. Sengupta, and S. H. Simon, "Communication through a diffusive medium: Coherence and capacity," *Science*, vol. 287, no. 5451, pp. 287–290, 2000.

[8] G. Lerosey, J. de Rosny, A. Tourin, A. Derode, G. Montaldo, and M. Fink, "Time reversal of electromagnetic waves," *Phys. Rev. Lett.*, vol. 92, p. 193904, May 2004.

[9] M. Frazier, B. Taddese, T. Antonsen, and S. M. Anlage, "Nonlinear time reversal in a wave chaotic system," *Phys. Rev. Lett.*, vol. 110, p. 063902, Feb. 2013.

[10] C. W. Hsu, S. F. Liew, A. Goetschy, H. Cao, and A. Douglas Stone, "Correlation-enhanced control of wave focusing in disordered media," *Nature Physics*, vol. 13, pp. 497–502, 2017.

[11] P. Ambichl, A. Brandstttter, J. Bhm, M. Khmayer, U. Kuhl, and S. Rotter, "Focusing inside disordered media with the generalized Wigner-Smith operator," *Phys. Rev. Lett.*, vol. 119, p. 033903, 2017.

[12] L. Carin, D. Liu, W. Lin, and B. Guo, "Compressive sensing for multi-static scattering analysis," *Journal of Computational Physics*, vol. 228, no. 9, pp. 3464 – 3477, 2009.

[13] S. D. Cohen, H. L. D. de S. Cavalcante, and D. J. Gauthier, "Subwavelength position sensing using nonlinear feedback and wave chaos," *Phys. Rev. Lett.*, vol. 107, p. 254103, Dec. 2011.

[14] M. V. Berry, "Regular and irregular semiclassical wavefunctions," *Journal of Physics A: Mathematical and General*, vol. 10, no. 12, p. 2083, 1977.

[15] E. Ott, *Chaos in Dynamical System*. Cambridge, U.K.: Cambridge University Press, 1993.

[16] S. Hemmady, X. Zheng, T. M. Antonsen, E. Ott, and S. M. Anlage, "Universal statistics of the scattering coefficient of chaotic microwave cavities," *Phys. Rev. E*, vol. 71, no. 5, p. 056215, 2005.

[17] L. K. Warne and R. E. Jorgenson, "High-frequency electromagnetic scarring in three-dimensional axisymmetric convex cavities," *Electromagnetics*, vol. 36, no. 3, pp. 186–213, 2016.

[18] J. Song, C.-C. Lu, and W. C. Chew, "Multilevel fast multipole algorithm for electromagnetic scattering by large complex objects," *IEEE Transactions on Antennas and Propagation*, vol. 45, pp. 1488–1493, Oct. 1997.

[19] E. Wigner, "Random matrices in physics," *SIAM Review*, vol. 9, no. 1, pp. 1–23, 1967.

[20] A. F. Molisch, *Wireless Communications, 2nd Edition*. Wiley-IEEE Press, New York, 2011. ISBN: 978-0-470-74186-3.

Surface Integral Computation for the Higher Order Surface Integral Equation Method of Moments

Sanja B. Manić and Branislav M. Notaroš
Department of Electrical and Computer Engineering
Colorado State University
Fort Collins, Colorado, USA
smanic@colostate.edu, notaros@colostate.edu

***Abstract*—This paper presents extraction technique applied to the double higher order surface integral equation method of moments and discusses the numerical results compared with previously implemented extraction method and numerical Gauss-Legendre integration.**

Keywords*— *double higher order method of moments, integral accuracy, integration extraction technique, surface integral equation.

I. Introduction

This paper presents our ongoing study of convergence behavior of near-singular (potential) and near-hypersingual (field) integrals for double higher order large-domain surface integral equation method of moments (SIE-MoM). The fast and accurate integral computation that will effectively give the MoM matrix entries is essential in the computational electromagnetics (CEM). The main challenge arises with small source-to-field distances which often occur in microstrip and printed circuit design but are part of almost any model analysis. The technique for integral evaluation presented here uses the singularity extraction method. The analytically evaluated integral of the principal singular part is computed over a parallelogram which surface is defined to be similar to the surface of the generalized quadrilateral in the near area of the singular point. Numerical integrals over parallelogram and quadrilateral are using Gauss-Legendre quadrature formula.

II. The Method

A. 2D Double Higher Order Integrals

In the double higher order SIE-MoM the 2D surface integrals are defined on the Lagrange-type generalized curved parametric quadrilateral MoM-SIE surface elements (in Fig. 1) defined in the parametric u-v domain as [1]:

$$\mathbf{r}(u,v)=\sum_{k=0}^{K_u}\sum_{l=0}^{K_v}\mathbf{r}_{kl}u^k v^l\,,\quad \text{for } -1\le u,v\le 1\,, \tag{1}$$

where $\mathbf{r}_{kl}$ are vector coefficients and K_u and K_v are geometrical orders (K_u, $K_v \geq 1$). The current is approximated by higher order polynomial basis functions [1] leading to 2D integrals over the quadrilateral having the following form:

$$I_{ij}^{s}=\int_{-1}^{1}\int_{-1}^{1}\frac{u^i v^j e^{-\mathrm{j}\beta R}}{4\pi R}\mathrm{d}u\mathrm{d}v\,,\quad I_{ij}^{hs}=\int_{-1}^{1}\int_{-1}^{1}\frac{u^i v^j(1+\mathrm{j}\beta R)e^{-\mathrm{j}\beta R}}{4\pi R^3}\mathrm{d}u\mathrm{d}v\,, \tag{2}$$

where s and hs represent singular and hypersingular integrals respectively, i and j are arbitrary polynomial orders of the basis functions, $\beta=2\pi f\sqrt{\varepsilon\mu}$, f is the operating frequency, ε and μ are permittivity and permeability of the dielectric medium respectively and R is the distance of the source point from the field point.

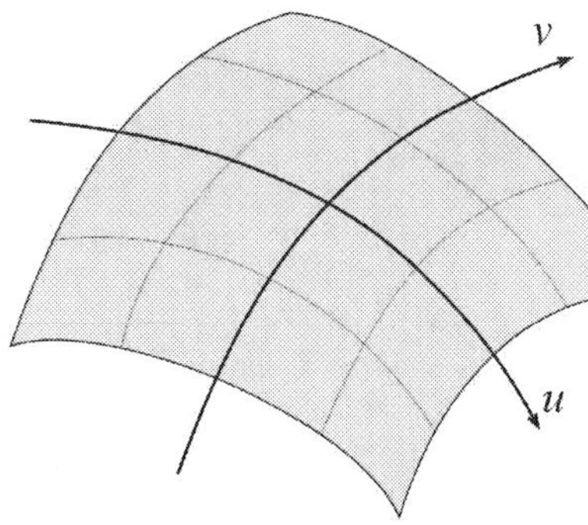

Fig. 1. Quadrilateral element.

B. Defining the Paralelogram for the Extraction Technique

The quadrilateral element and the parallelogram constructed at projection point (u_0, v_0) are shown in Fig. 2. The distance of the point on the parallelogram and singular point is defined as:

$$R_p^2=d^2+a_u^2\Delta u^2+a_v^2\Delta v^2+2a_u a_v\cos\alpha\Delta u\Delta v\,, \tag{3}$$

where a_u, a_v and cosα are computed to take into account the curvature of the quadrilateral element, $\Delta u=u-u_0$, $\Delta v=v-v_0$ and d is the distance between singular point and the close point projection on the quadrilateral element.

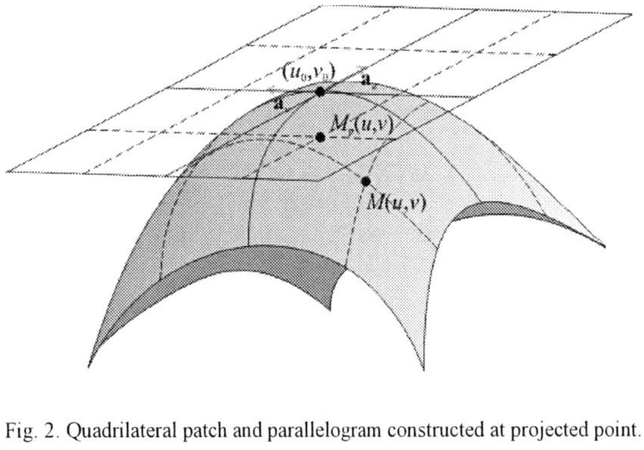

Fig. 2. Quadrilateral patch and parallelogram constructed at projected point.

C. Taylor's Expantion and Analytical Integration

The relation between quadrilateral and parallelogram parametric surfaces is given by:

$$R(u,v)^2 = R_P^2(u,v) + t(u,v)\,, \quad R(u,v) = R_P\sqrt{1+x(u,v)}\,, \qquad (4)$$

where $x(u,v) = t(u,v)/R_p^2(u,v)$. The singular and hypersingular parts of integrands for the integration over the parallelogram are represented through Taylor's expansion over x having in mind (4). Analytical integrals are computed by dividing parallelogram into triangles and using recursive formulas similarly to the procedure described in [2].

D. Projected Points Outside of the Patch

For the case of large and negative $2a_u a_v \cos\alpha\Delta u\Delta v$ contribution in (3), $|x(u,v)|$ becomes large because $R_p^2(u,v)$ is taking a small value. As a result, the Taylor's expansion over x does not approximate the (hyper) singular function well. In this situation, when the projection point is outside of the element domain, the parallelogram is constructed using parameters at the closest point, i.e. the most singular point on the quadrilateral. For the large values of $|x(u,v)|$, the patch is divided into four parts and the extraction method is applied to each part separately (example in Fig. 5).

III. Results

The results shown in this section are computed for second order curvilinear patch (one of the six patches modeling 1 m radius sphere) shown in Fig. 2. The integral convergence is obtained for d=5e-7 and β = 0.775462658083873 and results are compared to Gauss-Legendre numerical integration and previously implemented traditional (old) extraction technique.

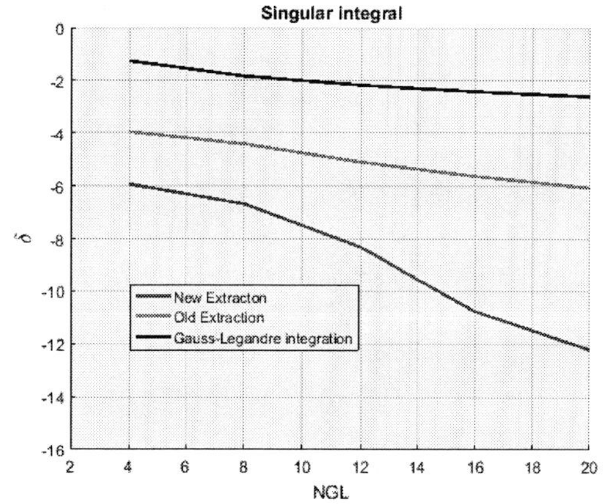

Fig. 3. Singular integral convergence for u_0 = 0.1, v_0=-0.1 (the projection point) and i=0, j=0 orders of the basis function.

The NGL label on the graphs represents the square root of the number of Gauss-Legendre points used for the numerical integration over quadrilateral or parallelogram. The relative convergence error is computed as $\delta = \log_{10}\left|I - \tilde{I}\right|/\left|\tilde{I}\right|$, where $\tilde{I}$ is the integral computed using described extraction method with high value of Gauss-Legendre points and I represents the integrals as function of NGL.

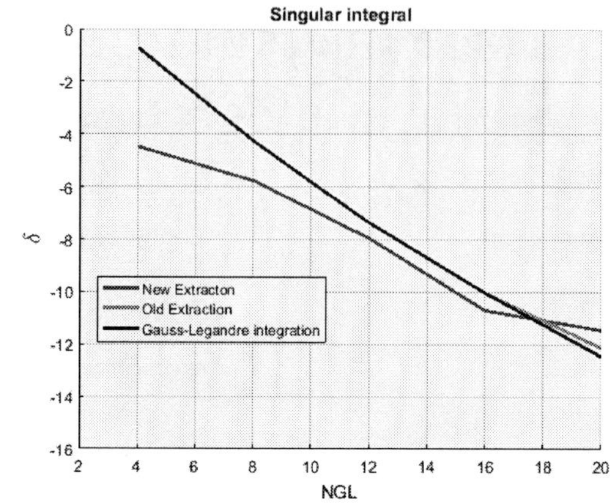

Fig. 4. Singular integral convergence for u_0 = 0.1, v_0=-0.1 (the projection point) and i=6, j=6 orders of the basis function.

Results in Fig. 5 are computed for the point described in part D of previous section and the improvement in convergence is shown for the divided patch method.

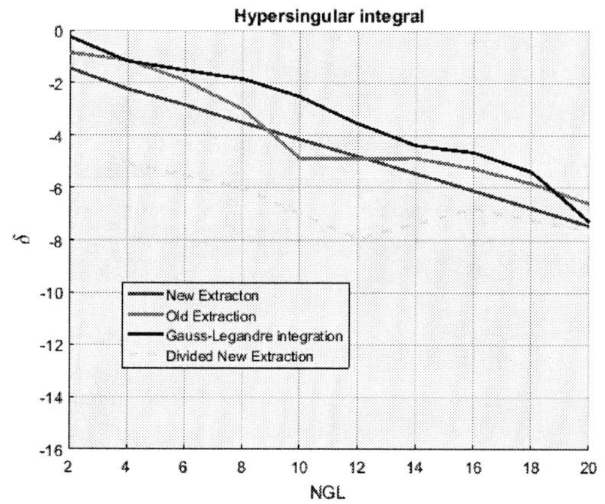

Fig. 5. Hypersingular integral convergence comparison for the projection point u_0 = 1.1, v_0=1.1 and i=0, j=0 orders of the basis function. Patch is divided at (0.8, 0.8) point in u-v domain.

IV. Conclusion

New extraction method is introduced and the method is verified with results. The convergence improvement is shown compared to the traditional extraction technique as well as further improvements achieved by dividing the patch. The convergence improvement is due the integral of the difference of the two functions defined over the constructed parallelogram and quadrilateral being accurately evaluated with small number of integration points.

References

[1] M. Djordjevic and B. M. Notaros, "Double higher order method of moments for surface integral equation modeling of metallic and dielectric antennas and scatterers," IEEE Transactions on Antennas and Propagation, vol. 52, no. 8, pp. 2118-2129, August 2004.

[2] S. Jarvenpaa, M. Taskinen, and P. Yla-Oijala, "Singularity subtraction technique for high-order polynomial vector basis functions on planar triangles," IEEE Transactions on Antennas and Propagation, vol. 54, no. 1, pp. 42-49, January 2006.

Vector Parabolic Equation Modeling of Wireless Propagation in Tunnels with Statistically Rough Surface Walls

Xingqi Zhang* and Costas D. Sarris
The Edward S. Rogers Sr. Department of Electrical and Computer Engineering
University of Toronto, Toronto, ON, Canada
xingqi.zhang@mail.utoronto.ca, costas.sarris@utoronto.ca

Abstract—**Vector parabolic equation (VPE) methods can be employed to model wave propagation in tunnel environments with high accuracy and computational efficiency. However, the relevant literature is rather limited in terms of modeling wall roughness, a statistical source of additional and often significant path loss. We present a comprehensive approach to embed wall roughness in VPE and demonstrate its validity through comparisons to experimental data.**

I. Introduction

The study of electromagnetic wave propagation in railway and mine tunnels is of great practical interest for the deployment of reliable wireless communication systems in such environments [1], [2]. Although it is often disregarded, surface roughness of tunnel walls can play an important role, as an additional source of path loss.

In [1], an analytical model is developed by Emslie et al. to estimate the excess loss caused by wall roughness. However, the analysis is limited to the dominant mode in canonical waveguides. In addition to waveguide models, the vector parabolic equation (VPE) [3], [4] has emerged as a more versatile propagation modeling technique, especially for tunnels. It is by far more efficient than ray or full-wave methods, while accounting for arbitrary tunnel cross-section and variations in ground elevation.

Research on modeling wall roughness with VPE has been limited so far to small scale roughness in canonical geometries [5]. This paper presents a new approach to incorporating roughness into VPE, which can be applied to arbitrary tunnel geometries and large-scale surface roughness. Validation is provided by comparisons with measured data in realistic guideway scenarios.

II. Statistical Modeling of Rough Surface Walls

A. Parametrization of Random Rough Surface

Surface roughness is the local variation of the tunnel wall relative to a mean surface level. Due to lack of complete knowledge of realistic rough surfaces, it is natural to adopt a probabilistic framework, where the height variation of the rough surface is modeled as a random process.

The Karhunen-Loève (KL) expansion is a widely-used technique to represent and parametrize random processes. Let $s(\xi,\omega)$ represent the random process characterizing the height variation of a rough surface:

$$s(\xi,\omega) = \overline{s}(\xi) + \sigma_s \sum_{m=1}^{\infty} \sqrt{\lambda_m} f_m(\xi) Y_m(\omega), \quad (1)$$

where $\overline{s}(\xi)$ is mean surface height and σ_s is the height deviation. For any fixed ω, $s(\xi,\cdot)$ is a deterministic function representing a realization of the surface geometry; $\omega \in \Omega$ indicates a realization in the probability space Ω; and at a given location ξ, $s(\cdot,\omega)$ is a random variable representing the uncertain height of the surface at this location. $Y_m(\omega)\,(m \geq 1)$ are independent random variables, and λ_m and $f_m(\xi)$ are eigenvalues and eigenfunctions of Fredholm equations:

$$\int_0^L \rho_s(\xi_1,\xi_2) f_m(\xi_2)\, \mathrm{d}\xi_2 = \lambda_m f_m(\xi_1), \quad (2)$$

where L is the total length of the rough surface and $\rho_s(\xi_1,\xi_2)$ is the correlation function.

B. Cross-Section Rough Surface Walls

First, a rough surface is generated according to Eqn. (1). Then, as shown in Fig. 1, the generated surface is mapped to the cross-section geometry of the tunnel, where ξ can be expressed as a function of angle θ_0. For every point near the wall, the normal angle and the distance to the wall are

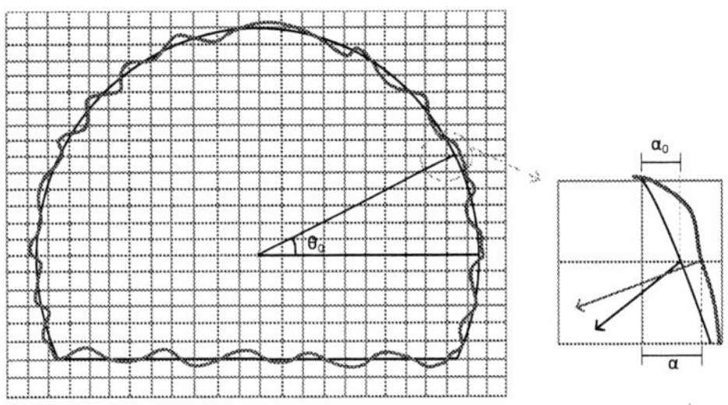

Fig. 1: Cross-section roughness.

considered as perturbations to values obtained from the case with smooth surface wall:

$$\theta = \pi/2 - \tan^{-1}\left(s'\left(\xi\left(\theta_0,\omega\right)\right)\right), \quad (3a)$$

$$\alpha = \alpha_0 + s\left(\xi\left(\theta_0,\omega\right)\right), \quad (3b)$$

θ_0 and θ are the normal angles correspond to a smooth surface and a rough surface, respectively; α_0 and α are the distances to the smooth and rough surface walls, respectively.

C. Longitudinal Rough Surface Walls

A two-dimensional cut of a tunnel with rough surface walls is shown in Fig. 2. First, the top and bottom rough surfaces are generated according to Eqn. (1). Then, their profiles are approximated using staircase fitting. Each gray bar in Fig. 2 represents one short tunnel section with a length equal to the mesh cell size ($\sim \lambda/10$) along the propagation direction. At the end of each short section, the fields generated on that plane are used as initial conditions for the next section.

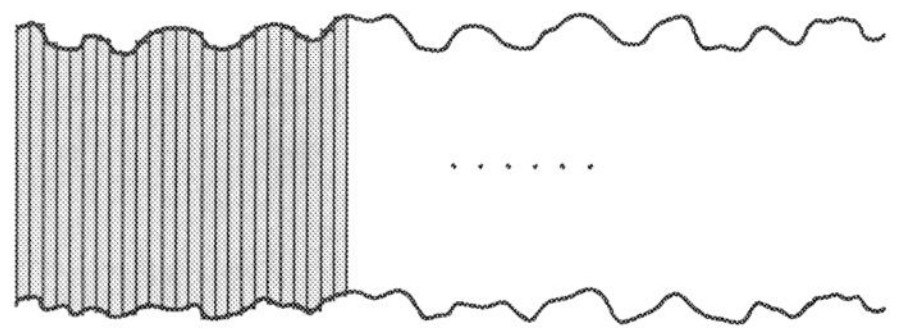

Fig. 2: Staircase fitting of the longitudinal rough surface profile.

III. Numerical Examples

In this section, first, the proposed approach is compared with known theoretical solutions and results in [5] for the case of a canonical waveguide. Then, a realistic mine tunnel geometry is considered.

A. Canonical Waveguide

The analytical expressions for the excess loss due to roughness can be found using ray tracing techniques, as outlined in Emslie et al. [1]. The excess loss (in dB) caused by surface roughness for a rectangular waveguide is:

$$L_{\text{rough}} = 4.343\pi^2{\sigma_s}^2\lambda\left(\frac{1}{d_1^4}+\frac{1}{d_2^4}\right)z, \tag{4}$$

where d_1 and d_2 are the width and height of the tunnel, respectively; z is the distance along the propagation direction; σ_s is the height deviation of the rough surface and λ is the free-space wavelength.

For verification, the cross-section dimensions of the tunnel are chosen to correspond with the coal mine tunnel studied in [1], where the width is $2.3\,\text{m}$ and the height is $2.1\,\text{m}$. The operating frequency is $1\,\text{GHz}$ and the fundamental mode, EH_{11}, with horizontal polarization is used as the initial field. Regarding the rough surface, the height deviation is $0.1\,\text{m}$ and the correlation length is $2.5\,\text{m}$. The electrical parameters of the surrounding walls are set to $\varepsilon_r = 12$ and $\sigma_0 = 0.02\,\text{S/m}$.

The attenuation factors obtained from the proposed approach, analytical solutions, and the method in [5], are summarized in Table I. It can be seen that the excess loss obtained from the proposed approach has a better agreement with the analytical result.

TABLE I: Comparison of the Attenuation Factors

Unit: dB/km	Smooth Surface	Rough Surface	Excess Loss
Analytical	31.0	38.0	7.0
Method in [5]	29.8	36.1	6.3
This work	30.0	37.0	7.0

B. Morina-Amerika Mine Tunnel

The tunnel under consideration here is a mine tunnel, which was previously studied in [6]. The cross-section dimensions are $2.3\,\text{m}\times 2.1\,\text{m}$. A vertically polarized omnidirectional monopole antenna operating at $860\,\text{MHz}$ is employed. The transmitter is mounted on an anchored wooden rod with a height of $1.2\,\text{m}$, as shown in Fig. 3. The receiving antenna is a vertically polarized half-wave dipole antenna placed at the center of the tunnel. Further details for the measurement setup can be found in [6].

The height deviation for the bilateral and top rough surface walls is chosen to be $0.4\,\text{m}$ and the correlation length is set to be $2.5\,\text{m}$. The ground is assumed to be smooth. A comparison of the received power is shown in Fig. 3. As can be seen, the obtained simulated results have a good agreement with the measured data.

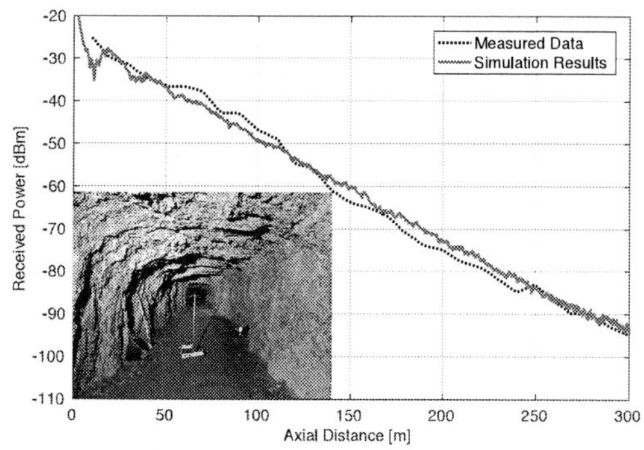

Fig. 3: Comparison between simulated received power and measured data. Source of on-site photo: [6].

References

[1] A. Emslie, R. Lagace, and P. Strong, "Theory of the propagation of UHF radio waves in coal mine tunnels," IEEE Trans. Antennas Propag., vol. 23, no. 2, pp. 192–205, Mar. 1975.

[2] X. Zhang, N. Sood, J. K. Siu, and C. D. Sarris, "A hybrid ray-tracing/vector parabolic equation method for propagation modeling in train communication channels," IEEE Trans. Antennas Propag., vol. 64, no. 5, pp. 1840–1849, May 2016.

[3] X. Zhang and C. D. Sarris, "Error analysis and comparative study of numerical methods for the parabolic equation applied to tunnel propagation modeling," IEEE Trans. Antennas Propag., vol. 63, no. 7, pp. 3025–3034, Jul. 2015.

[4] ——, "A Gaussian beam approximation approach for embedding antennas into vector parabolic equation based wireless channel propagation models," IEEE Trans. Antennas Propag., vol. 65, no. 2, pp. 1840–1849, Feb. 2017.

[5] R. Martelly and R. Janaswamy, "Modeling radio transmission loss in curved, branched and rough-walled tunnels with the ADI-PE method," IEEE Trans. Antennas Propag., vol. 58, no. 6, pp. 2037–2045, Jun. 2010.

[6] M. Rak and P. Pechac, "UHF propagation in caves and subterranean galleries," IEEE Trans. Antennas Propag., vol. 55, no. 4, pp. 1134–1138, Apr. 2007.

A DC to HF Volume PEEC Formulation Based on Hertz Potentials and the Cell Method

Riccardo Torchio, Piergiorgio Alotto, Paolo Bettini, Dimitri Voltolina, and Federico Moro
Dipartimento di Ingegneria Industriale
Università di Padova
Padova, Italy
riccardo.torchio@studenti.unipd.it

Abstract—**A new Partial Element Equivalent Circuit formulation based on Hertz potentials and the Cell Method is presented. Conductive, dielectric, and magnetic linear-homogeneous media are considered by means of conduction, polarization, and magnetization current densities. The use of edge unknowns leads to reduce system size with respect to typical face-based approaches.**

I. Introduction

A large body of literature shows that integral methods are particularly suited to the solution of high frequency electromagnetic problems (EM) involving large domains with the characteristics of vacuum. In particular, the Partial Element Equivalent Circuit (PEEC) method has been shown to be well suited for the analysis of electromagnetic devices, such as printed circuit boards and antennas. The aim of this work is to present a novel 3-D Hertz-PEEC formulation, including conductive, dielectric, and magnetic media. This approach is based on the theory of Hertz potentials [1] and magnetization currents for the magnetic media [2], [3], while in literature Amperian currents [4] or the magnetization [5] are applied. The discretization of the formulation is obtained by means of the Cell Method (CM) [6] and the current density vector, which is the only unknown, is expanded by Whitney face functions [7]. The proposed approach leads to a unified treatment of magnetic and dielectric media which can be handled with a single set of robust and efficient semi-analytical integration routines. The approach is thus capable of solving EM problems over a larger frequency range compared to extant PEEC approaches for magnetic media [5]. Furthermore, the formulation uses edge unknowns, leading to the reduction of the linear system size with respect to other approaches.

II. Integral Formulation

Conductive, dielectric, and magnetic domains Ω_c, Ω_d, and Ω_m (with boundaries Γ_c, Γ_d, and Γ_m, respectively) are considered in the formulation. The domains have no intersection and their disjoint union is $\Omega = \Omega_c \sqcup \Omega_d \sqcup \Omega_m$.

When conductive, dielectric and magnetic media are considered, the following constitutive relations can be introduced:

$$\mathbf{J}_f = \sigma \mathbf{E} \ in \ \Omega_c, \qquad \mathbf{D} = \varepsilon_0 \mathbf{E} + \mathbf{P} \ in \ \Omega_d, \qquad \mathbf{B} = \mu_0 \mathbf{H} + \mu_0 \mathbf{M} \ in \ \Omega_m, \tag{1}$$

where $\mathbf{J}_f$ is the conduction current density, $\mathbf{E}$ and $\mathbf{H}$ are the electric and the magnetic field, $\mathbf{D}$ is the electric displacement and $\mathbf{B}$ is the magnetic flux density, σ is the conductivity, ε_0 and μ_0 are the vacuum permittivity and permeability. The polarization $\mathbf{P}$ and the magnetization $\mathbf{M}$ are introduced as equivalent sources in vacuum, so the effects of dielectric and magnetic media are taken into account. With the introduction of (1), following the approach and notation of [8] (chap. 5, 7), Maxwell's equations in frequency domain can be re-written in a more symmetric form avoiding the use of $\mathbf{D}$ and $\mathbf{B}$:

$$\begin{aligned} \nabla \cdot \mathbf{E} &= \frac{\varrho_f + \varrho_p}{\varepsilon_0}, & -\nabla \times \mathbf{E} &= \mathbf{J}_{m^*} + i\omega\mu_0 \mathbf{H}, \\ \nabla \cdot \mathbf{H} &= \frac{\varrho_{m^*}}{\mu_0}, & \nabla \times \mathbf{H} &= \mathbf{J}_f + \mathbf{J}_p + i\omega\varepsilon_0 \mathbf{E}, \end{aligned} \tag{2}$$

where ϱ_f is the free electric charge density, $\mathbf{J}_p = i\omega \mathbf{P}$ and $\varrho_p = -\nabla \cdot \mathbf{P}$ are the polarization current and bound dielectric charge densities, $\mathbf{J}_{m^*} = i\omega\mu_0 \mathbf{M}$ is the magnetization current density and $\varrho_{m^*} = -\nabla \cdot \mu_0 \mathbf{M}$ is the bound magnetic charge density. As shown in [1] and [9], it is possible to write the electric field $\mathbf{E}$ and the magnetic field $\mathbf{H}$ as:

$$\begin{aligned} \mathbf{E} &= -(i\omega)^2 \mathbf{\Pi}_e - \nabla\varphi_e - \frac{1}{\varepsilon_0}\nabla \times (i\omega \mathbf{\Pi}_m) + \mathbf{E}_0, \\ \mathbf{H} &= -(i\omega)^2 \mathbf{\Pi}_m - \nabla\varphi_m + \frac{1}{\mu_0}\nabla \times (i\omega \mathbf{\Pi}_e) + \mathbf{H}_0, \end{aligned} \tag{3}$$

where $\mathbf{\Pi}_e$ and $\mathbf{\Pi}_m$ are the Hertz electric and magnetic vector potentials, φ_e and φ_m are electric and magnetic scalar potentials and $\mathbf{E}_0$ and $\mathbf{H}_0$ are imposed sources.

By defining $\mathbf{A}_e = i\omega\mathbf{\Pi}_e$, and $\mathbf{A}_m = i\omega\mathbf{\Pi}_m$ as "new" electric and magnetic vector potentials, applying Lorenz gauge, $\nabla \cdot \mathbf{A}_e = -i\omega\varepsilon_0\mu_0\varphi_e$, $\nabla \cdot \mathbf{A}_m = -i\omega\varepsilon_0\mu_0\varphi_m$, and letting (3) into (2), four partial differential equations can be obtained:

$$\begin{aligned} \Box \mathbf{A}_e &= \mu_0(\mathbf{J}_f + \mathbf{J}_p), & \Box \varphi_e &= \frac{\varrho_f + \varrho_p}{\varepsilon_0}, \\ \Box \mathbf{A}_m &= \varepsilon_0 \mathbf{J}_{m^*}, & \Box \varphi_m &= \frac{\varrho_{m^*}}{\mu_0}, \end{aligned} \tag{4}$$

where $\Box = (i\omega)^2 \frac{1}{c^2} - \nabla^2$ is the d'Alembert operator and c is the speed of light. The solution of the first equation of (4) is:

$$\mathbf{A}_e(\mathbf{r}_y) = \mu_0 \int_\Omega (\mathbf{J}_f(\mathbf{r}_x) + \mathbf{J}_p(\mathbf{r}_x)) g(\mathbf{r}_x, \mathbf{r}_y) dr_x, \tag{5}$$

where $\mathbf{r}_y$ is the field point, $\mathbf{r}_x$ is the integration point and $g(\mathbf{r}_x, \mathbf{r}_y) = \frac{e^{-i\omega c^{-1}|\mathbf{r}_y - \mathbf{r}_x|}}{|\mathbf{r}_y - \mathbf{r}_x|}$ is the scalar retarded free space Green function. The solution of the other three equations in (4) is obtained likewise (5).

III. Cell Method Discretization

The electric domains Ω_c and Ω_d are discretized into primal tetrahedral grids $\mathcal{G}_{\Omega_c}$ and $\mathcal{G}_{\Omega_d}$, consisting of n_c, n_d nodes, e_c, e_d edges, f_c, f_d faces, and v_c, v_d volumes. Then, dual grids $\tilde{\mathcal{G}}_{\Omega_c}$ and $\tilde{\mathcal{G}}_{\Omega_d}$ can be obtained by taking the barycentric subdivision of $\mathcal{G}_{\Omega_c}$ and $\mathcal{G}_{\Omega_d}$ [10]. The same approach can be applied to the magnetic domain Ω_m, but in this case $\tilde{\mathcal{G}}_{\Omega_m}$ is chosen to be made up of tetrahedral elements, while $\mathcal{G}_{\Omega_m}$ is obtained by its barycentric subdivision. The following incidence matrices can be obtained: $\mathbf{G}_{\Omega_\alpha}$ (edges to nodes), $\mathbf{C}_{\Omega_\alpha}$ (faces to edges), and $\mathbf{D}_{\Omega_\alpha}$ (volumes to faces), on $\mathcal{G}_{\Omega_\alpha}$, where $\alpha = c, d, m$ indicates the domain. Dual matrices can be obtained for $\tilde{\mathcal{G}}^a_{\Omega_\alpha}$, i.e., $\tilde{\mathbf{G}}^a_{\Omega_\alpha}$, $\tilde{\mathbf{C}}^a_{\Omega_\alpha}$, $\tilde{\mathbf{D}}^a_{\Omega_\alpha}$, where the superscript a indicates that the matrix is *augmented* [10]. To build the CM formulation, following arrays of degrees of freedom are introduced:

- $\mathbf{j_c} = (j_{c_i})$ on faces $f_i \in \mathcal{G}_{\Omega_c}$, $j_{c_i} = \int_{f_i} \mathbf{J}_c \cdot d\mathbf{S}$,
- $\mathbf{j_p} = (j_{p_i})$ on faces $f_i \in \mathcal{G}_{\Omega_p}$, $j_{p_i} = \int_{f_i} \mathbf{J}_p \cdot d\mathbf{S}$,
- $\tilde{\mathbf{j}}_{\mathbf{m}^*} = (\tilde{j}_{m^*_i})$ on faces $\tilde{f}_i \in \tilde{\mathcal{G}}_{\Omega_m}$, $\tilde{j}_{m^*_i} = \int_{\tilde{f}_i} \mathbf{J}_{m^*} \cdot d\mathbf{S}$,
- $\mathbf{h} = (h_i)$ on edges $e_i \in \mathcal{G}_{\Omega_m}$, $h_i = \int_{e_i} \mathbf{H} \cdot d\mathbf{l}$,
- $\tilde{\mathbf{e}} = (\tilde{e}_i)$ on edges $\tilde{e}_i \in \tilde{\mathcal{G}}_{\Omega_c \sqcup \Omega_d}$, $\tilde{e}_i = \int_{\tilde{e}_i} \mathbf{E} \cdot d\mathbf{l}$,
- $\mathbf{a}_m = (a_{m_i})$ on edges $e_i \in \mathcal{G}_{\Omega_m}$, $a_{m_i} = \int_{e_i} \mathbf{A}_m \cdot d\mathbf{l}$,
- $\tilde{\mathbf{a}}_e = (\tilde{a}_{e_i})$ on edges $\tilde{e}_i \in \tilde{\mathcal{G}}_{\Omega_c \sqcup \Omega_d}$, $\tilde{e}_i = \int_{\tilde{e}_i} \mathbf{A}_e \cdot d\mathbf{l}$,
- $\tilde{\boldsymbol{\phi}}_e = (\tilde{\phi}_{e_i})$ on nodes $\tilde{n}_i \in \tilde{\mathcal{G}}_{\Omega_c \sqcup \Omega_d}$, $\tilde{\phi}_{e_i} = \varphi_e(\mathbf{r}_{n_i})$,
- $\boldsymbol{\phi}_m = (\phi_{m_i})$ on nodes $n_i \in \mathcal{G}_{\Omega_m}$, $\phi_{m_i} = \varphi_m(\mathbf{r}_{n_i})$.

The coupling between the domains is enforced by weakly imposing (1):

$$\begin{aligned} &\int_{\Omega_c \sqcup \Omega_d} \mathbf{w}^f_i \cdot \big(\rho_e \mathbf{J}_e(\mathbf{r}) - \mathbf{E}(\mathbf{r})\big) d\mathbf{r} = 0, \\ &\int_{\Omega_m} \mathbf{w}^f_i \cdot \big(\rho_{m^*} \mathbf{J}_{m^*}(\mathbf{r}) - \mathbf{H}(\mathbf{r})\big) d\mathbf{r} = 0, \end{aligned} \tag{6}$$

where $\mathbf{J}_e$ is the electric current, equals to $\mathbf{J}_c$ in Ω_c and $\mathbf{J}_p$ in Ω_d, $\rho_e = (\sigma_c)^{-1}$ in Ω_c and $(i\omega\varepsilon_0(\varepsilon_r - 1))^{-1}$ in Ω_d. $\rho_{m^*} = (i\omega\mu_0(\mu_r - 1))^{-1}$ while $\mathbf{w}^f_i$ is the Whitney face basis function.

By expanding $\mathbf{J}_e$ and $\mathbf{J}_{m^*}$ with $\mathbf{w}^f_i$ and letting (3) into (6), the following system is obtained:

$$\begin{bmatrix} \mathbf{Z}_{11} & \mathbf{Z}_{12} \\ \mathbf{Z}_{21} & \mathbf{Z}_{22} \end{bmatrix} \begin{bmatrix} \mathbf{j}_e \\ \tilde{\mathbf{j}}_{m^*} \end{bmatrix} = \begin{bmatrix} \tilde{\mathbf{e}}_0 \\ \mathbf{h}_0 \end{bmatrix}, \tag{7}$$

where:

- $\mathbf{Z}_{11} = \mathbf{R}_e + i\omega\mathbf{L}_e - \frac{1}{i\omega}\tilde{\mathbf{G}}^a_{\Omega_c \sqcup \Omega_d} \mathbf{P}_e \mathbf{D}^a_{\Omega_c \sqcup \Omega_d}$,
- $\mathbf{Z}_{12} = \mathbf{M}_{1/\varepsilon_0} \mathbf{C}_{\Omega_c \sqcup \Omega_d} \mathbf{L_{em}}$,
- $\mathbf{Z}_{21} = -\mathbf{M}_{1/\mu_0} \tilde{\mathbf{C}}_{\Omega_m} \mathbf{L_{me}}$,
- $\mathbf{Z}_{22} = \mathbf{R}_m + i\omega\mathbf{L}_m - \frac{1}{i\omega}\tilde{\mathbf{G}}^a_{\Omega_m} \mathbf{P}_m \mathbf{D}^a_{\Omega_m}$.

R, **L**, and **P** are respectively the "traditional" PEEC resistance, inductance and potential matrices. The full paper will describe how to obtain the block matrices and how to solve the system applying a change of variables (from faces to edges of the mesh) and a projection into a reduced set of equations.

IV. Numerical Results

The 3-D Hertz-PEEC code has been developed with MATLAB® for the system assembly and data handling, while MEX-FORTRAN functions combined with OpenMP libraries have been adopted for the computation of the matrix coefficients and post-processing.

The code has been validated on several benchmarks, including the case, shown here, of two spheres with 1m radius, a dielectric one ($\varepsilon_r = 2$) and a magnetic one ($\mu_r = 10$) placed 3m apart on the y-axis and excited by a linearly polarized plane wave $\mathbf{E_0} = e^{-ik_0 x}\mathbf{u}_z$. Where $k_0 = 2\pi f\sqrt{\varepsilon_0\mu_0}$, $f = 30$MHz. The magnitude of the real and imaginary part of the scattered electric field has been compared with the Radio-Frequency module of COMSOL® with good agreement (Fig. 1). Small discrepancies are due to the sphere meshes required by PEEC and FEM, the intrinsic differences of the two approaches, and the numerical post processing adopted for PEEC. In the full paper a thorough discussion of the numerical results in terms of accuracy and computational cost will be presented.

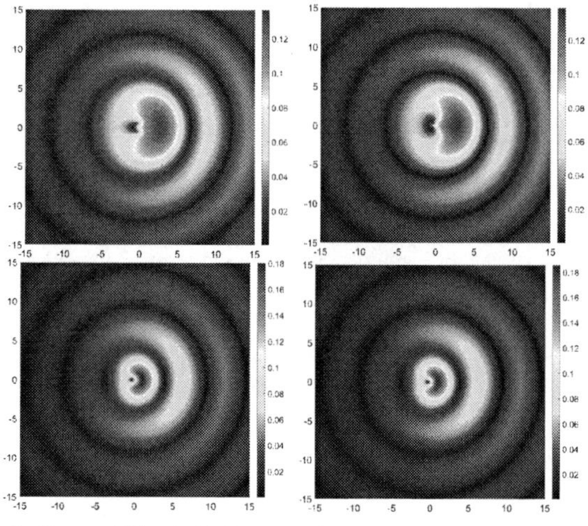

Fig. 1. Scattered Electric Field magnitude V/m, xz-plane, dimensions in m. Left: 3-D PEEC-Hertz. Right: COMSOL®. Top: $\Re$ part. Bottom: $\Im$ part.

References

[1] A. Nisbet, "Herzian electromagnetic potentials and associated gauge transformation," Proceedings of the Royal Society of London A: Mathematical, Physical and Engineering Sciences, 1955.

[2] A. G. Polimeridis, et al., "On the computation of power in volume integral equation formulations," in IEEE Trans. on Antennas and Propag., vol. 63, no. 2, pp. 611-620, Feb. 2015.

[3] J. Markkanen, et al., "Discretization of volume integral equation formulations for extremely anisotropic materials," in IEEE Trans. on Antennas and Propag, vol. 60, no. 11, pp. 5195-5202, Nov. 2012.

[4] R. Torchio, et al., "A 3D PEEC formulation based on the cell method for full wave analyses with conductive, dielectric, and magnetic media," in IEEE Trans. Magn., 2017.

[5] D. Romano and G. Antonini, "Quasi-static partial element equivalent circuit models of linear magnetic materials," in IEEE Trans. Magn., vol. 51, no. 7, pp. 1-15, July 2015.

[6] F. Freschi and M. Repetto, "A general framework for mixed structured/unstructured PEEC modelling," Applied Computational Electromagnetic Society Journal, vol. 23, no. 3, pp. 200-206, 2008.

[7] J. Siau, et al., "Volume integral formulation using face elements for electromagnetic problem considering conductors and dielectrics," in IEEE Trans. on Electromag. Compat., vol. 58, no. 5, pp. 1587-1594, Oct. 2016.

[8] R. M. Fano, L. J. Chu, and R. B. Adler, *Electromagnetic Fields, Energy, and Forces*. M.I.T. Press, 1960.

[9] J. A. Stratton, *Electromagnetic Theory*. M.I.T. Press, 1941.

[10] L. Codecasa, "Refoundation of the cell method using augmented dual grids," IEEE Trans. Magn., vol. 50, no. 2, Art. ID 7012204, Feb. 2014.

Recent Developments in the Application of Contactless Inductive Flow Tomography

Matthias Ratajczak
Helmholtz-Zentrum Dresden-Rossendorf
Institute of Fluid Dynamics
Dresden, Germany
m.ratajczak@hzdr.de

Thomas Wondrak
Helmholtz-Zentrum Dresden-Rossendorf
Institute of Fluid Dynamics
Dresden, Germany
t.wondrak@hzdr.de

Frank Stefani
Helmholtz-Zentrum Dresden-Rossendorf
Institute of Fluid Dynamics
Dresden, Germany
f.stefani@hzdr.de

Abstract—**In many industrial processes dealing with liquid metals or semiconductors, the quality of the resulting product is directly affected by the flow of the melt. These melts are often too hot or too aggressive for direct flow measurement with conventional techniques. One candidate for a feasible application to metallurgical processes is the contactless inductive flow tomography (CIFT), which works by exposing the melt to a magnetic excitation field, measuring the flow-induced perturbances to that field and solving the underlying inverse problem. This paper gives an overview about the theory of CIFT and its application in small-scale models of continuous casting under the influence of a strong static magnetic field.**

Index Terms—**tomography, continuous casting, inverse problems, magnetic field measurement**

I. Introduction

More than 95 % of today's steel is produced by means of continuous casting, making it the most relevant casting method. During this process liquid metal flows from a tundish through a submerged entry nozzle (SEN) into a mould, which consists of enclosing water-cooled copper walls. A solid steel shell is formed at the inside of the mould walls, and the resulting strand with the still molten core is pulled out at the bottom of the mould and solidifies completely. After complete solidification, the cast steel can be processed further.

Especially in the casting of slabs, only the so-called double roll flow structure is expected to yield optimum results, while other flow profiles (like the chaotic-unstable flow) are associated with various kinds of defects, like slag entrainment, segregation or pinholes [1]. In industry electromagnetic brakes (EMBr) are often used because it is expected that their strong DC magnetic flux has a stabilizing and decelerating effect on the flow, reducing the likelihood of defects. However, lab scale experiments [2] as well as simulations [3] suggest that the effect of an EMBr in continuous casting is more complex, and strongly dependent on electrical boundary conditions.

For operators of continuous casters, an immediate feedback from the flow would therefore be highly benefecial. Yet, today's market-ready flow measurement techniques fail when it comes to measuring the global flow structure in hot or chemically agressive melts. One promising candidate for such a scenario is the contactless inductive flow tomography (CIFT) [4], [5] which relies on contactless measurement of the flow-induced perturbances of an applied magnetic field, and solving the underlying inverse problem in order to infer the global flow structure in the mould.

In this paper we will first delineate the basic theory of CIFT. After that the paper is concerned with a cold lab-scale model of a casting mould under the influence of an EMBr. In contrast to previous experiments [6], the EMBr was positioned so that the maximum flux was applied just below the bottom of the nozzle outlet.

II. Theory

We start by assuming a non-magnetic fluid with constant electrical conductivity σ and velocity $\mathbf{v}$, located inside a non-conducting container. The fluid has a volume V and surface S, and is exposed to a magnetic field $\mathbf{B}$, which is either steady or has a very low frequency. Then, according to Ohm's law for moving conductors, currents are induced in the fluid, which give rise to a new magnetic field $\mathbf{b}$:

$$\begin{aligned}\mathbf{b}(\mathbf{r}) =& \frac{\mu_0\sigma}{4\pi}\iiint_V \frac{[\mathbf{v}(\mathbf{r}')\times\mathbf{B}(\mathbf{r}')]\times(\mathbf{r}-\mathbf{r}')}{|\mathbf{r}-\mathbf{r}'|^3}dV' \\ &-\frac{\mu_0\sigma}{4\pi}\oiint_S \varphi(\mathbf{s}')\frac{\mathbf{n}(\mathbf{s}')\times(\mathbf{r}-\mathbf{s}')}{|\mathbf{r}-\mathbf{s}'|^3}dS'\,.\end{aligned} \tag{1}$$

Here $\mathbf{r}$ describes a position in space, and $\mathbf{n}$ denotes a normal vector at position $\mathbf{s}$ on surface S. The surface potential is denoted by φ and can be described as follows:

$$\begin{aligned}\varphi(\mathbf{s}) =& \frac{1}{2\pi}\iiint_V \frac{[\mathbf{v}(\mathbf{r}')\times\mathbf{B}(\mathbf{r}')]\cdot(\mathbf{s}-\mathbf{r}')}{|\mathbf{s}-\mathbf{r}'|^3}dV' \\ &-\frac{1}{2\pi}\oiint_S \varphi(\mathbf{s}')\frac{\mathbf{n}(\mathbf{s}')\cdot(\mathbf{s}-\mathbf{s}')}{|\mathbf{s}-\mathbf{s}'|^3}dS'\,.\end{aligned} \tag{2}$$

In general, the magnetic field $\mathbf{B}$ is the sum of the induced magnetic field $\mathbf{b}$ and the excitation field $\mathbf{B}_0$. However, by calculating the magnetic Reynolds number Rm one can show that in continuous casting $\mathbf{b}$ is much smaller than $\mathbf{B}_0$, and can therefore be neglected in $\mathbf{B}$ [6], yielding a linear inverse problem. The intrinsic non-uniqueness is solved by jointly applying Tikhonov's regularization, penalizing high velocities in our case, and the L-curve method, where the residual is traced over the mean squared velocities for different values of the regularization parameter [7]. The optimal solution with a

Figure 1. The Mini-LIMMCAST mould (M) with the EMBr (E) and the CIFT excitation coil (X) and sensors (S)

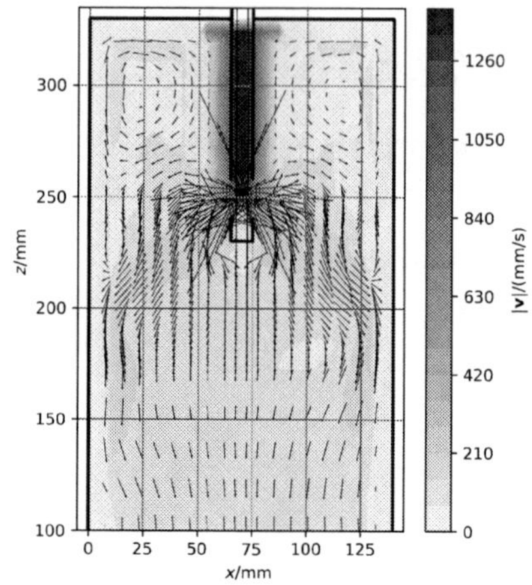

Figure 2. Typical reconstruction with the EMBr in low position, but switched off

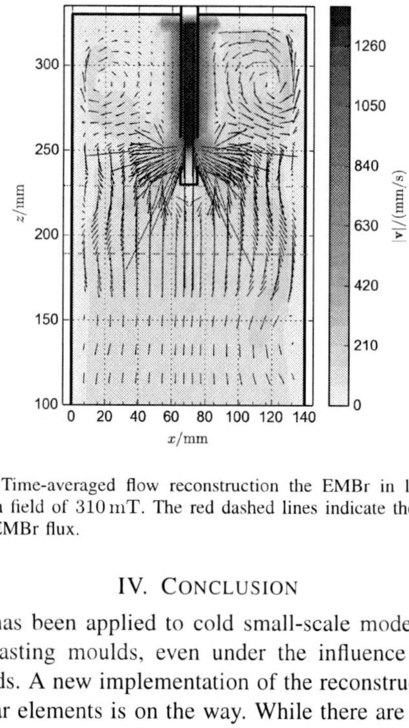

Figure 3. Time-averaged flow reconstruction the EMBr in low position, generating a field of $310\,\mathrm{mT}$. The red dashed lines indicate the area of the maximum EMBr flux.

small residual and sensible velocities can be found at the point of maximum curvature of the curve. The integral equation system is then solved by minimizing the quadratic functional

$$F[\mathbf{v}] = F_{B_0}[\mathbf{v}] + F_{\text{div}}[\mathbf{v}] + F_{\text{pen}}[\mathbf{v}] + F_{2D}[\mathbf{v}] + F_{\text{inlet}}[\mathbf{v}], \quad (3)$$

where the separate functionals (a) minimize the deviations between the modelled and measured fields, (b) ensure divergence-free flows, (c) apply the Tikhonov penalty function, (d) force a 2D-flow for slab casting and (e) set inlet velocities in the area of the entry nozzle. The basic coupled integral equation system (1) and (2) has been extended to account for conducting walls and AC excitation [8], as well as gradiometric sensors [6] (the latter two increasing robustness against noise). The accuracy and comparison of CIFT with the well-established ultrasonic doppler velocimetry technique is beyond the scope of this paper, but can be studied in [5] for the same mould but without the EMBr.

III. Experimental Results

Modelling experiments of the flow in a continuous casting mould can be conducted at the Mini-LIMMCAST facility [9]. We used an acrylic glass model of a slab mould with dimensions $(140 \times 35 \times 335)\,\mathrm{mm}^3$, filled with the eutectic alloy GaInSn, which is liquid at room temperature. The mould is surrounded by an EMBr which creates a maximum flux of $310\,\mathrm{mT}$ at an area just below the nozzle outlets (see Figure 1). It is important to note that the amplitude of the excitation field is minimal in the area of maximum EMBr flux, because of the high μ_r of the EMBr pole shoes. In this new, low EMBr position, the jet is located in an area with larger excitation field amplitude, which leads to different flow structures and simultaneously enhances reconstruction accuracy. An experimental run with the EMBr switched off resulted in a CIFT-reconstructed flow as depicted in Figure 2, where the diagonal jet from the nozzle and the upper rolls on both sides are clearly visible. As soon as we switch on the EMBr (Figure 3), changes in the average flow structure become apparent, with an intensified upper roll and a more vertically oriented jet. Additionally, regular superimposed flow oscillations occur.

IV. Conclusion

CIFT has been applied to cold small-scale models of continuous casting moulds, even under the influence of strong static fields. A new implementation of the reconstruction code with linear elements is on the way. While there are still many challenges to be overcome, it is expected that in the future CIFT will enable industrial operators to discern relevant flow structures in their processes in real-time.

References

[1] P. H. Dauby, Revue de Metallurgie, vol. 109, pp. 113–136, 2012.
[2] K. Timmel, et al., Met. Mat. Trans. B, vol. 42, pp. 68–80, 2011.
[3] R. Chaudhary, et al., Met. Mat. Trans. B, vol. 43, pp. 532–553, 2012.
[4] F. Stefani, et al., Phys. Rev. E, vol. 70, ID 056306, 2004.
[5] T. Wondrak, et al., Met. Mat. Trans. B, vol. 42, 1202–1210, 2011.
[6] M. Ratajczak, et al., Phil. Trans. Roy. Soc. A, vol. 374, ID 20150330, 2016.
[7] P. C. Hansen, SIAM Review, vol. 34, pp. 561–580, 1992.
[8] M. Ratajczak, et al., IEEE Sensors Conference, Busan, Republic of Corea, 2015.
[9] K. Timmel, et al., ISIJ Int., vol. 50, 1134–1141, 2010.

Parametric Models for Signature Prediction and Feature Extraction

(Invited Paper)

Julie Ann Jackson
Department of Electrical and Computer Engineering
Air Force Institute of Technology
Wright Patterson AFB, Ohio
julie.jackson@afit.edu

Abstract—**This paper compares and contrasts numerical electromagnetic (EM) prediction methods and parametric scattering models for radar signature prediction and feature extraction.**

I. Introduction

Both radar model validation and target recognition applications require accurate, and preferably fast, signature prediction methods, as illustrated in Fig. 1. Prediction methods are nonparametric (e.g., numerical electromagnetic prediction codes) and parametric (e.g., attributed scattering centers). Choice of method should be based on the trade space between model accuracy and computational efficiency. Computational efficiency includes not only the ability to quickly compute the prediction model (the forward problem) but also the complexity and feasibility to extract signatures from measured data (the inverse problem). Numerical electromagnetic (EM) prediction methods are geared toward the forward problem, while parametric models (PMs) have been developed with the inverse problem in mind. The complexity-accuracy trade space for each model type is qualitatively depicted in Fig. 2.

II. Signature Prediction

EM numerical prediction techniques include method of moments (MoM), differential techniques, integral equation solvers, shooting and bouncing rays (SBR) geometric/physical optics (GO/PO), and many other methods, discussed in [1]–[5]. Computation time varies with the electrical size of the target and is extended by the time it takes to draw/import and facetize/mesh a target model. A method to speed up the EM part of SBR is given in [6], and [7] provides a technique to extend single frequency computations over a band of frequencies. An attempt to speed the drawing portion is provided in [2], which converts a picture into a facet model. Alternatively, [2] lets users build simple targets by combining primitive shapes, which can be characterized by PMs.

PMs developed for signal processing tasks may also be used for signature prediction. The isotropic point model is characterized by scatterer position and radar cross section (RCS). The isotropic point model is a key assumption in radar

The views expressed in this article are those of the authors and do not reflect the official policy or position of the U.S. Air Force, Department of Defense, or the U.S. Government. Approved for public release #88ABW-2017-4831.

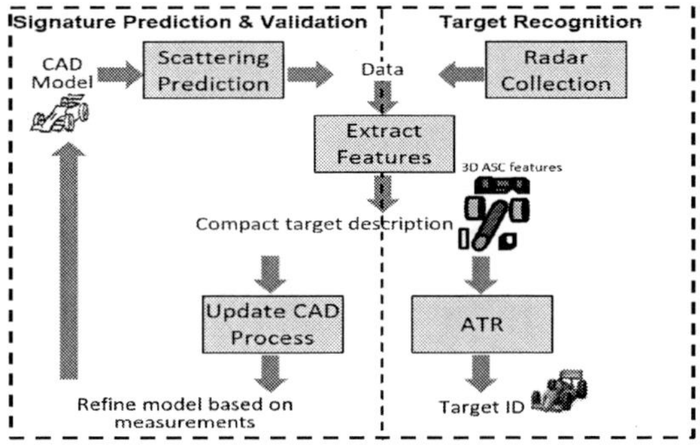

Fig. 1. Process flow diagram for signature prediction (forward problem) and signature extraction (inverse problem).

imaging; however, realistic scatterer persistence is typically less than 20° [8]. The monostatic 2D attributed scattering center (ASC) model [9] is parameterized by frequency, polarization, aspect (along the length of the target), and length. Other monostatic models include the Huynen and Cameron decompositions that break monostatic polarization responses into primary forms [10]–[12]. Bistatic canonical shape models parameterized by type, size, and orientation capture 3D physical geometry and model frequency, polarization, and azimuth and elevation aspect dependence [13]. The canonical models are built from products of planar solutions for strip, dihedral, and circular scattering mechanisms [14], [15] to approximate the 3D solution. A full analytic 3D GO/PO solution for bistatic scattering from a dihedral is given in [16]. EM predictions, PMs, and measurements of a dihedral are compared in [17]; PMs took milliseconds to compute, while MoM took hours.

PMs are extremely fast because the equations are written analytically and do not need a numerical solver like EM methods. However, accuracy is limited by underlying GO/PO and planar assumptions; edge diffraction, traveling waves, etc. are not included. Also, the dihedral and trihedral models are defined only within the interior of the corner, though plate models could be combined to model the back sides. Furthermore, PMs do not capture interactions between scatterers. Thus, a major challenge for using PMs for prediction is how to break a complex target into scattering primitives. For example, con-

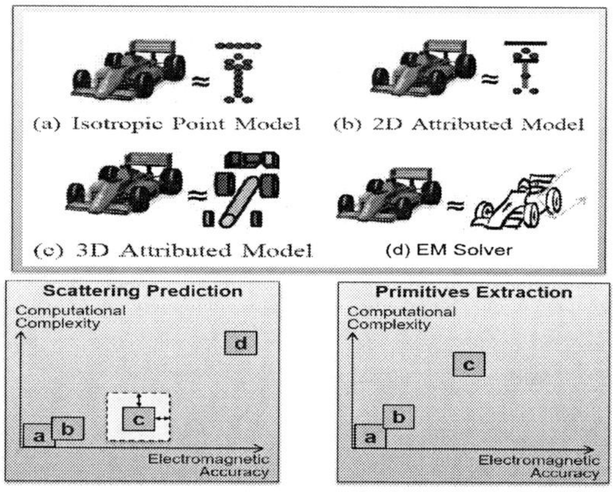

Fig. 2. Scattering models and notional complexity vs. accuracy trade space.

structing a vehicle's sides with plates neglects vehicle/ground interaction, which is better modeled with dihedrals.

III. Signature Extraction

Numerical EM techniques are not suited to signature extraction since each iteration in an optimization would require update to the facet model and re-run of computationally expensive prediction code. However, as shown in Fig. 1, other feature extraction methods can be used along with model refinement and EM predictions for RCS signature validation.

Parametric methods were developed with signal estimation techniques and target recognition applications in mind. Parameters may be estimated from measured data, though estimation complexity increases with model complexity. Isotropic points may be estimated using the CLEAN algorithm [18], [19]. Two-dimensional ASCs may be estimated using Prony's method or matrix pencil method [9]. Canonical shape primitives are more difficult to extract since shape selection and parameter estimation are coupled; however, an initial iterative approach is given in [20]. Other approaches to parametric model extraction include Expectation-Maximization [21], sparse dictionary techniques [22]–[24], and ray-tracing methods [19], [25]. Limited data from practical radar flight paths complicates the classification and estimation problem, as illustrated in [26], since objects may look similar for a narrow-angle data slice.

IV. Conclusion

We have provided an overview of numerical EM prediction versus PMs. While PMs are limited to simple scattering mechanisms, they are fast and well-suited to signature extraction. Numerical EM codes enable high fidelity prediction of complex targets; however, it is not computationally feasible to use EM methods for signature extraction. Thus, one should choose a signature prediction method depending on the application.

References

[1] C. Uluisik, et al., "Radar cross section (RCS) modeling and simulation, part 1: A tutorial review of definitions, strategies, and canonical examples," *IEEE Antennas Propag. Mag.*, vol. 50, no. 1, pp. 115–126, Feb. 2008.

[2] G. Cakir, M. Cakir, and L. Sevgi, "Radar cross section (RCS) modeling and simulation, part 2: A novel FDTD-based RCS prediction virtual tool for the resonance regime," *IEEE Antennas Propag. Mag.*, vol. 50, no. 2, pp. 81–94, Apr. 2008.

[3] A. K. Bhattacharyya and D. L. Sengupta, *Radar Cross Section Analysis and Control*. Boston: Artech House, 1991.

[4] W. C. Chew, et al., "Fast solution methods in electromagnetics," *IEEE Trans. on Antennas Propag.*, vol. 45, no. 3, pp. 533–543, Mar. 1997.

[5] J. Song, C.-C. Lu, and W. C. Chew, "Multilevel fast multipole algorithm for electromagnetic scattering by large complex objects," *IEEE Trans. on Antennas Propag.*, vol. 45, no. 10, pp. 1488–1493, Oct. 1997.

[6] R. Bhalla and H. Ling, "A fast algorithm for signature prediction and image formation using the shooting and bouncing ray technique," *IEEE Trans. on Antennas Propag.*, vol. 43, no. 7, pp. 727–731, Jul. 1995.

[7] C. J. Reddy, et al., "Fast RCS computation over a frequency band using method of moments in conjunction with asymptotic waveform evaluation technique," *IEEE Trans. on Antennas Propag.*, vol. 46, no. 8, pp. 1229–1233, Aug. 1998.

[8] D. E. Dudgeon, R. T. Lacoss, C. H. Lazott, and J. G. Verly, "Use of persistent scatterers for model-based recognition," in *Proc. SPIE*, vol. 2230, 1994, pp. 2230–2230–13.

[9] L. C. Potter and R. L. Moses, "Attributed scattering centers for SAR ATR," *IEEE Trans. Image Process.*, vol. 6, no. 1, pp. 79–91, Jan. 1997.

[10] J. R. Huynen, "Phenomenological theory of radar targets," in *Electromagnetic Scattering*, P. L. E. Uslenghi, Ed. Academic Press, 1978.

[11] W. L. Cameron, "Feature motivated polarization scattering matrix decomposition," in *Record of the IEEE 1990 Int'l Radar Conference*, May 1990, pp. 549–557.

[12] S. R. Cloude and E. Pottier, "A reveiw of target decomposition theorems in radar polarimetry," *IEEE Trans. Geosci. Remote Sens.*, vol. 34, no. 2, pp. 498–518, Mar. 1996.

[13] J. A. Jackson, B. D. Rigling, and R. L. Moses, "Canonical scattering feature models for 3D and bistatic SAR," *IEEE Trans. Aerosp. Electron. Syst.*, vol. 46, no. 2, pp. 525–541, Apr. 2010.

[14] M. Gerry, *Two-Dimensional Inverse Scattering Based on the GTD Model*. The Ohio State University: Ph.D. Disseration, 1997.

[15] N. Akhter, *Far Zone Electromagnetic Scattering From Complex Shapes Using Geometrical Theory of Diffraction*. The Ohio State University: Ph.D. Dissertation, 1993.

[16] J. A. Jackson, "Analytic physical optics solution for bistatic, 3D scattering from a dihedral corner reflector," *IEEE Trans. on Antennas Propag.*, vol. 60, no. 3, pp. 1486–1495, Mar. 2012.

[17] A. Tempelis, M. Jussaume, and J. Jackson, "Comparison of measured and predicted bistatic scattering from a right-angle dihedral," in *IEEE Radar Conference*, May 2011, pp. 135–140.

[18] J. A. Hogbom, "Aperture synthesis with a non-regular distribution of interferometer baselines," *Astronomy and Astrophysics Supplement Series (0365-0138)*, vol. 15, no. 3, pp. 417–426, 1974.

[19] R. Bhalla and H. Ling, "Three-dimensional scattering center extraction using the shooting and bouncing ray technique," *IEEE Trans. on Antennas Propag.*, vol. 44, no. 11, pp. 1445–1453, Nov. 1996.

[20] J. Jackson and R. Moses, "Synthetic aperture radar 3D feature extraction for arbitrary flight paths," *IEEE Trans. Aerosp. Electron. Syst.*, vol. 48, no. 3, pp. 2065–2084, Jul. 2012.

[21] J. A. Richards, A. S. Willsky, and J. W. Fisher III, "Expectation-maximization approach to target model generation from multiple synthetic aperture radar images," *Optical Engineering*, vol. 41, no. 1, pp. 150–166, Jan. 2002.

[22] K. R. Varshney, M. Cetin, J. W. Fisher, and A. S. Willsky, "Sparse representation in structured dictionaries with application to synthetic aperture radar," *IEEE Trans. Signal Process.*, vol. 56, no. 8, pp. 3548–3561, Aug. 2008.

[23] G. B. Hammond and J. A. Jackson, "Canonical feature extraction using molecule dictionaries," in *IEEE Radar Conference, Paper 5092, pp. 1-6*, 29 Apr-3 May 2013.

[24] H. Liu, et al., "Attributed scattering center extraction algorithm based on sparse representation with dictionary refinement," *IEEE Trans. on Antennas Propag.*, vol. 65, no. 5, pp. 2604–2614, May 2017.

[25] Y. He, et al., "A forward approach to establish parametric scattering center models for known complex radar targets applied to sar atr," *IEEE Trans. on Antennas Propag.*, vol. 62, no. 12, pp. 6192–6205, Dec. 2014.

[26] J. A. Jackson and R. L. Moses, "Identifiability of 3D attributed scattering features from sparse nonlinear apertures," in *Proc. SPIE*, vol. 6568, 2007, pp. 6568–6568–12.

Sparse Recovery Method for Order-of-Magnitude Reduction in RCS Measurments

Tayfun Özdemir, Kevin Bi and Santos Campos
Virtual EM, Inc., Ann Arbor, Michigan, USA,
tayfun@virtualem.com

Robert J. Burkholder
The Ohio State University, Columbus, Ohio, USA
burkholder.1@osu.edu

***Abstract*— There are two national facilities in the US that can meet the stringent RCS test requirements of the government for classification, size and fidelity of the data. Characterization of each object takes a long time and slows down research and development. Therefore, innovative methods are needed for reducing the time spent in the chamber without compromising the fidelity of the data. Presented here are direct and statistical methods to arrive at a solution. Direct methods such as spare recovery making use of the range-aspect profiles of the objects demonstrates potential to be useful but Machine Learning (ML) algorithms were also employed to provide relief. Optical measurements were used to augment the methods and the presented solution has high potential of success in reducing the chamber time by 90%.**

I. Introduction

RCS measurements can be sped up without compromising accuracy by exploiting the naturally sparse radar signature in the image domain and range-aspect domain (see Fig.1). Many researchers have used the inverse synthetic aperture (ISAR) image (Fig.1b) to develop sparse representations based on scattering center expansions. This is a very useful approach for compressing radar signature data [1], but it requires full angular and frequency sampling to obtain the expansion and therefore does not reduce the measurement time. Compressive sensing techniques attempt to obtain this sparse expansion using random sampling to reduce the data measurement requirement [2]. However, random sampling is problematic to implement in practice, and convergence can be slow and difficult to monitor.

Key to chamber time reduction is to reduce the number of angular samples without compromising critical features contained in the RCS profiles. Therefore, a non-uniform sampling is needed and one has to know when to sample high and low (i.e., the angular profile of minimum sampling rate is needed). A combination of direct and statistical methods are needed to reach the stated goal: (1) Main approach is to use the coarsely sampled range-aspect plots (see Fig.1c) to construct the fine-sampled patterns through amplitude and phase interpolation, (2) in order to prevent under-sampling of strong scattering profiles, optical images of the object will be used to indentify flash points (i.e., scattering centers), and (3) still to ensure that no other critical features are missed, Machine Learning (ML) will be employed to generate a sampling profile through simulation trials. What is presented here is a methodology that authors believe will lead to significant reductions in chamber time while maintaining accuracy. What will be presented at the conference is partial progress toward achieving this end goal.

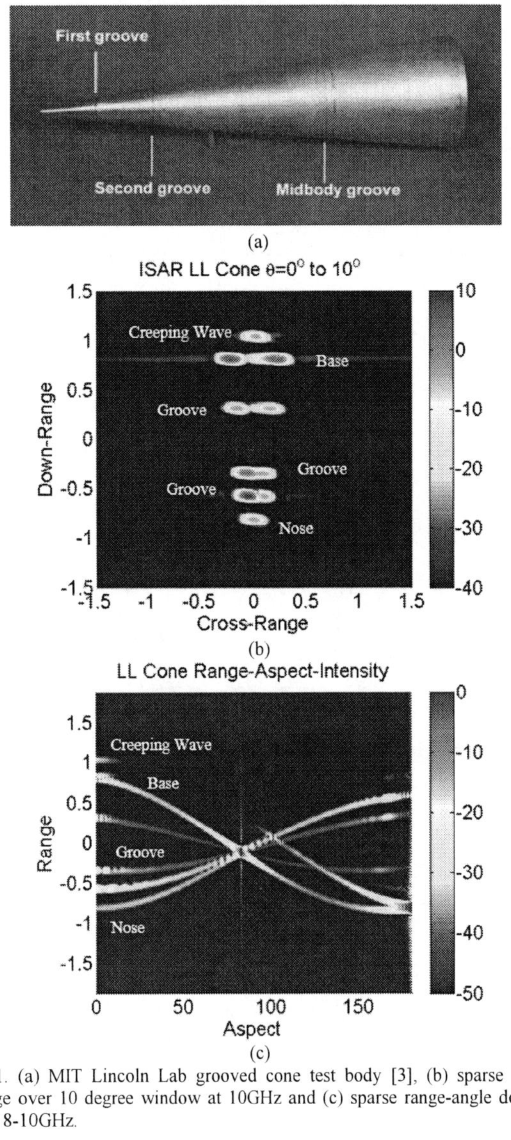

Fig.1. (a) MIT Lincoln Lab grooved cone test body [3], (b) sparse ISAR image over 10 degree window at 10GHz and (c) sparse range-angle domain over 8-10GHz.

II. COARSELY-SAMPLED RANGE-ASPECT PLOTS

The range-aspect domain (Fig.1c) was preferred choice because it is constructed angle-by-angle, whereas an ISAR image requires a range of angles to generate. The range-aspect plot is simply a sequence of downrange profiles computed at every angle, where strong scattering centers appear as smoothly continuous tracks. These tracks remain relatively smooth even with a coarse angular sampling. For example, it was possible to obtain the 0.25° sampled tracks (required to avoid aliasing in the ISAR domain) from those generated using 1.0° coarse sampling via interpolation. Because frequency scans in RCS measurement ranges are relatively fast compared to the angular sampling, the focus is on reducing the angular sampling requirement.

Naturally, interpolation in angle is challenging due to the fast phase variation of the radar signature with angle but the range-aspect domain provide great help as the scattering centers are separated out in downrange, allowing interpolation of the phase as well as the amplitude in each downrange bin. The particular phase interpolation method employed will be discussed in detail during the presentation.

III. LOCATING FLASH POINTS

In order to ensure strong scattering mechanisms such as flash points are not missed due to coarse angular sampling, some *a priori* knowledge of the target must be introduced by, for example, obtaining optical videos of the object under test through a fast pre-scan at a single frequency. Fig.2 depicts the measurement set up inside the RCS chamber and the placement of the optical video recording equipment with respect to the Tx/Rx antenna. Camera 1 is right next to the antenna and points to the objects for extracting flash points while Camera 2 is directly above the object to extract object outline. This information was used to detect and locate flash points as a function of aspect angle.

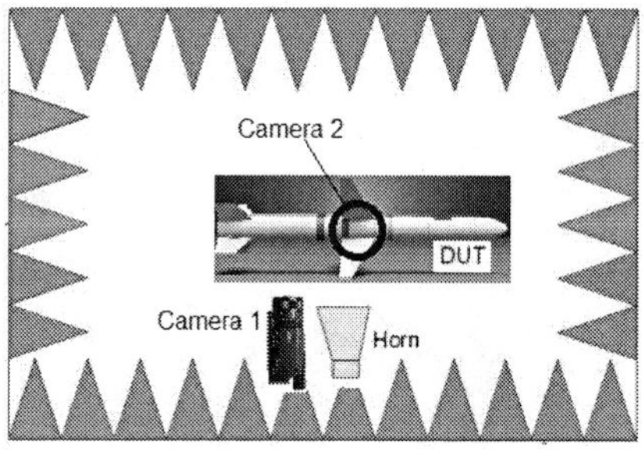

Fig.2. Optical video recording of the object under test.

IV. MACHINE LEARNING (ML)

The main direct method of using coarsely sampled range-aspect plots augmented with optical images presented above may or may not lead to significant reduction in chamber time while maintaining sufficient accuracy. There may still be a need for an independent statistical method to inject still further information regarding the target and this can ideally be done through ML. RCS of a variety of missiles are computed using their CAD models and Virtual EM's VirAntenn™ [4] software. On one hand, the minimum angular sampling rate (required to recover the RCS profile) as a function of aspect angle is computed from the RCS profiles and this is the desired output of the ML algorithms. On the other hand, geometrical details are extracted from the CAD models and, along with the frequency of excitation, comprise the input to the ML algorithms. ML algorithms are trained using the training data set as shown in Fig.3. An independent set of CAD models and associated sampling rate profiles are used to test the algorithms to ensure that the ML algorithms have been properly trained. ML approach works well when there is strong correlation between the input and the observation variables and this is certainly the case here because the RCS profile and therefore the sampling rate profile is a function of the geometrical features and the frequency. ML algorithms operate as neural networks (mimicking how human brain learns) and are excellent in establishing very accurate relationships between the input and the output data sets when the training data set is a good representation of the sampling space. Therefore, care must be taken to ensure the missile models used in training are balanced representation of the types to be encountered in the chamber.

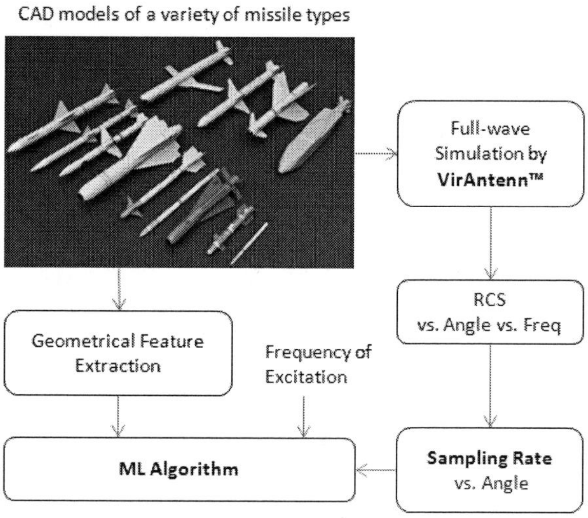

Fig.3. Training of the ML algorithms using simulated RCS of variety of missiles.

REFERENCES

[1] L.-C. T. Chang, I. J. Gupta, W. D. Burnside, and C.-L. Chang, "A Data Compression Technique for Scattered Fields from Complex Targets," *IEEE Trans. on Antennas and Propagation*, 45(8): 1245-1251, Aug. 1997.

[2] L. C. Potter, E. Ertin, J. T. Parker, and M. Certin "Sparsity and Compressed Sensing in Radar Imaging," *Proceedings of the IEEE*, vol. 98, Issue 6, pp. 1006-1020, 2010.

[3] K. M. Cuomo, J. E. Piou, and J. T. Mayhan, "Ultrawide-band coherent processing," *IEEE Trans. on Antennas and Propagation*, vol. 47, pp. 1094—1107, 1999.

[4] T. Özdemir, R. J. Burkholder, M. J. Miranda, and Y. M. Goykhman, "Multi-Core CPU and GPU Accelerated FMM-FFT Solver for Antenna Co-Site Interference Analysis on Large Platforms," *2014 IEEE Intl Symp. Antennas Propagat.*, Memphis, TN, USA, July 6-11, 2014.

Analytic Solutions for the Bistatic Radar Signature of a Dihedral Target of Arbitrary Angle

Robert J. Burkholder
The Ohio State University ElectroScience Lab
Dept. of Electrical and Computer Engineering
Columbus, U. S. A.
burkholder.1@osu.edu

***Abstract*—Closed-form high-frequency asymptotic solutions are developed for the double-bounce bistatic scattering from dihedral reflectors of arbitrary angle. It is shown that the scattering may be represented using an equivalent single plate model that is defined by considering the geometrical optics rays that illuminate the second plate after reflecting from the first plate. Then a closed-form physical optics solution gives the scattering from the single plate. Validation with an iterative physical optics reference solution shows very good agreement between bistatic scattering patterns. The approach may be extended to trihedral corner reflectors.**

Keywords*—bistatic radar cross-section, corner reflectors, geometrical optics, physical optics.

I. Introduction

Analytic solutions for computing the radar signature of canonical shapes are often needed for attributed scattering center characterization, feature extraction, and fast computation of synthetic aperture radar images [1-4]. Bistatic solutions have been presented in [3,4] for flat plates, 90° dihedral and trihedral corner reflections, cylinders, top hats, and spheres using high-frequency asymptotic approximations. In this paper we focus on 90° and non-90° dihedrals. The solution in [3,4] is for 90° only, and is somewhat cumbersome based on the 2D solution presented in [5]. The solution introduced here is based on a consideration of the double-bounce geometrical optics (GO) field reflected from the concave side of the dihedral. It is shown that the bistatic scattering can be represented by a single flat plate for the 90° dihedral, and by two flat plates for the non-90° dihedral. The solution is validated using iterative physical optics [6]. The single-plate equivalence approach is extended to the case of a 90° trihedral. These solutions have the advantage of speed, simplicity, and physical insight into the dominant multi-bounce scattering mechanism. In the following it is assumed that the geometries are constructed of perfect electrically conducting (PEC) flat plates.

II. 90° Dihedral Solution

Fig. 1 shows the geometry of a 90° dihedral corner reflector viewed from edge on. A plane wave is incident from the concave side of the dihedral. In Fig. 1 it is shown in the transverse plane, but could also be incident from an oblique angle. The sides are of length H and the length of the crease in the transverse direction is L. The incidence angle projected in the transverse plane is θ_t with respect to one of the sides of the dihedral.

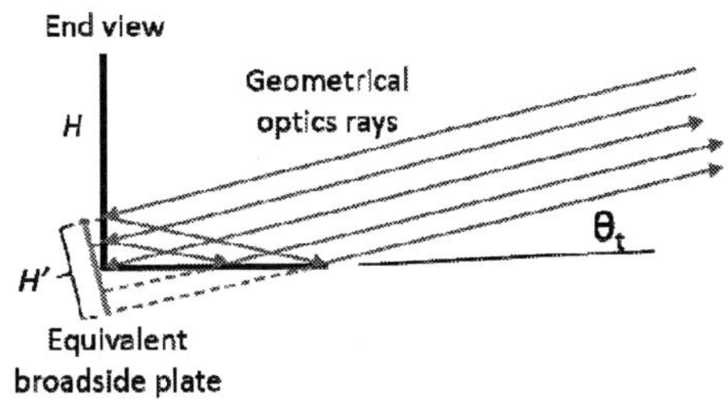

Fig. 1. Edge-on view of a 90° dihedral corner reflector illuminated by a plane wave incident on the concave side. The double-bounce geometrical optics rays are identical to a single bounce from an equivalent flat plate.

Consider the double-bounce GO rays shown in Fig. 1. It is clear that the rays remain in phase after two reflections, exactly the same as if they reflected from a flat plate of height H' and transverse length L. The equivalent plate is broadside to the incidence direction in the transverse plane and the height is given by,

$$H' = \begin{cases} 2H\sin\theta_t, & 0<\theta_t<45^\circ \\ 2H\cos\theta_t, & 45^\circ<\theta_t<90^\circ \end{cases}. \tag{1}$$

It follows that the physical optics bistatic scattering solution for the equivalent broadside plate may be used to characterize the 90° dihedral. Let $\hat{k}^i$ and $\hat{k}^s$ be the unit vectors in the incidence and scattering directions, respectively, $\hat{n}$ is the unit normal of the plate, and $\hat{l}$ is the unit vector along the dihedral crease, such that $\hat{h}' = \hat{l}\times\hat{n}$ is the unit vector along the orthogonal edge of the equivalent plate. Then,

$$\hat{n} = \frac{-\hat{k}^i + (\hat{l}\cdot\hat{k}^i)\hat{l}}{\left\| -\hat{k}^i + (\hat{l}\cdot\hat{k}^i)\hat{l} \right\|}. \tag{2}$$

Note that $\hat{n}$ is the negative of the projection of the incident unit vector in the transverse plane. The bistatic scattering solution is then similar to the expression in [4],

$$M_{\text{plate}}\left(\hat{k}^i,\hat{k}^s\right)=-\frac{jk}{\sqrt{\pi}}LH'\operatorname{sinc}\left[\frac{kL}{2}\left(\hat{k}^i+\hat{k}^s\right)\cdot\hat{l}\right] \cdot\operatorname{sinc}\left[\frac{kH'}{2}\left(\hat{k}^i+\hat{k}^s\right)\cdot\hat{h}'\right], \tag{3}$$

where $k=2\pi/\lambda$ and λ is the free space wavelength. Note that a minus sign is needed to account for the extra bounce of the GO rays for a dihedral.

III. Arbitrary Angle Dihedrals

Fig. 2 shows the geometry of a non-90° dihedral corner reflector viewed from edge on. The dihedral angle is α+90°. Notice that the GO rays are split into two directions. Fig. 2 shows the rays that reflect from the lower plate to the upper plate. Likewise, there is another set of rays that reflect from the upper plate to the lower plate. Both cases may be handled using the same approach by flipping the order of the plates, so here we consider only the case shown in Fig. 2.

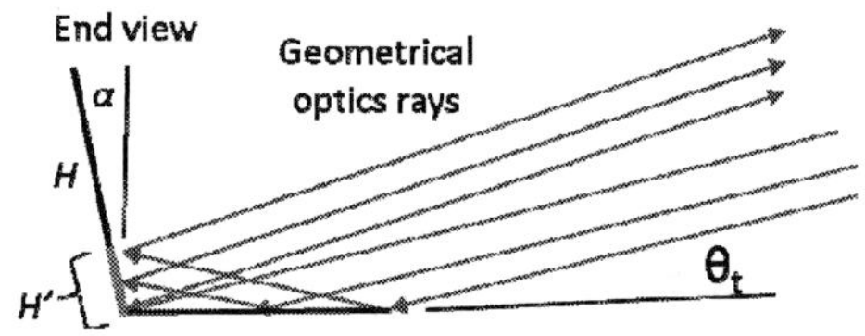

Fig. 2. Edge-on view of a non-90° dihedral corner reflector illuminated by a plane wave incident on the concave side. The dihedral angle is α+90°.

The equivalent plate shown in red in Fig. 2 is a shortened version of the upper plate. Its length is given by,

$$H'=\min\left[H,\frac{H\sin\theta_t}{\cos(\alpha-\theta_t)}\right],\ \theta_t\le 90^\circ-\alpha. \tag{4}$$

Note that the upper plate will not be illuminated by the reflection from the lower plate if $\theta_t>90^\circ-\alpha$. Also notice that there will be a certain incidence angle θ_t above which H' will be greater than H, so we always take the minimum to satisfy the physical constraint.

Since the reflection from the lower plate illuminates the upper plate, $\hat{k}^i$ is replaced by its reflection $\hat{k}^r$ in (3) where,

$$\hat{k}^r=\frac{\hat{k}^i-2\left(\hat{n}_{\text{lp}}\cdot\hat{k}^i\right)\hat{n}_{\text{lp}}}{\left\|\hat{k}^i-2\left(\hat{n}_{\text{lp}}\cdot\hat{k}^i\right)\hat{n}_{\text{lp}}\right\|}, \tag{5}$$

where $\hat{n}_{\text{lp}}$ is the upward pointing unit normal vector of the lower plate.

IV. Validation Results

Fig. 3 shows a comparison between the solution of [4], IPO, and the equivalent broadside plate model of Section II. Additional validation results will be presented at the conference.

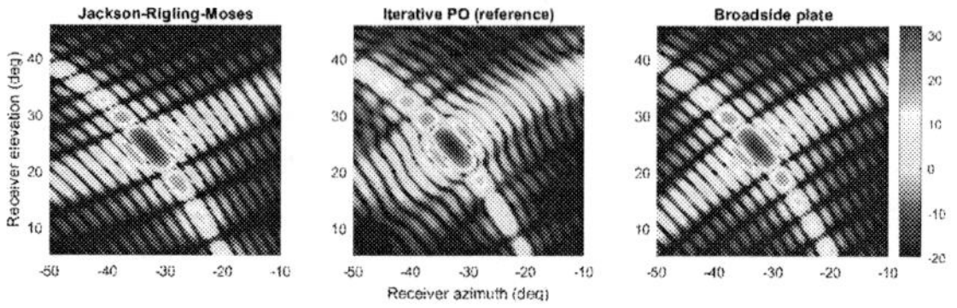

Fig. 3. Bistatic scattering patterns for a 90° dihedral with L=36" and H=12" tilted backward 25°. A plane wave is incident in the x-z plane with elevation 40° and the frequency is 10 GHz.

V. Conclusions

The closed form solutions introduced here for the scattering from dihedrals of arbitrary angle allow very fast computation of bistatic scattering patterns and yield physical insight into the scattering mechanisms. The solutions agree well with a reference solution, considering that only the GO double bounce mechanism is included. Additional validation results will be presented at the conference. The equivalent broadside plate model will also be extended to a 90° trihedral.

References

[1] L. C. Potter and R. L. Moses, "Attributed scattering centers for SAR ATR," *IEEE Trans. on Image Processing*, vol. 6, pp. 79–91, Jan. 1997.

[2] J. A. Jackson and R. L. Moses, "Feature extraction algorithm for 3D scene modeling and visualization using monostatic SAR," *Algorithms for Synthetic Aperture Radar Imagery XIII, Proc. of SPIE*, E. G. Zelnio and F. D. Garber, Eds. vol. 6237, 2006.

[3] J. A. Jackson, B. D. Rigling, and R. L. Moses, "Parametric Scattering Models for Bistatic Synthetic Aperture Radar," 2008 Radar Conference, pp. 1-5.

[4] J. A. Jackson, B. D. Rigling, and R. L. Moses, "Canonical scattering feature models for 3D and bistatic SAR," *IEEE Trans. on Aerospace and Electronic Systems*, vol. 46, no. 2, pp. 525-541, April 2010.

[5] N. Akhter, "*Far zone electromagnetic scattering from complex shapes using geometrical theory of diffraction*," Ph.D. dissertation, The Ohio State University, Columbus, OH, 1993.

[6] R. J. Burkholder, C. Tokgoz, C. J. Reddy, and W. O. Coburn, "Iterative physical optics for radar scattering predictions," *Applied Computational Electromagnetics Society Journal*, vol. 24, no. 2, pp. 241-258, April 2009.

GNSS AoA Estimation Based on Dual-frequency Joint Processing

Boyi Wang[1,2], Yafeng Li[3,1], Nagaraj Channarayapatna Shivaramaiah[1], Dennis M. Akos[1]
[1]Dept. of Aerospace Engineering Sciences, University of Colorado at Boulder, Boulder, CO 80309, USA
[2]School of EIC, Huazhong University of Science and Technology, Wuhan, 430074, China
[3]School of Automation, Beijing Institute of Technology, Beijing, 100081, China

***Abstract*—In this paper, we gave a brief introduction of AoA estimations of GPS signals. The preliminary work has been described, including data collection, software-defined receiver processing, and AoA estimation. Several interesting AoA related issues have been listed to conduct our experiments.**

Keywords—AoA; GNSS; GPS; Matlab; SDR; Array Signal

I. Introduction

With the development of Global Navigation Satellite Systems (GNSS), both high-accuracy and robust receivers are in high demand. To address the accuracy and reliability issue, sophisticated anti-multipath and high-sensitivity signal processing techniques are being incorporated into the receivers. One solution for the multipath and sensitivity problem is the angle of arrival (AoA) estimation of array GNSS signal. The AoA estimation is a fundamental problem of array signal processing as well as a critical task of radar, sonar and navigation systems. Several existing methods tackle the AoA estimation issue, including ARMA spectrum analyze, maximum likelihood estimation, and eigenvalue decomposition method [1]. This paper provides a review of AoA for GPS/GNSS, as well as how we initiate the AoA work for GPS array signal. Also several AoA related challenges and promising applications are presented, which act as guidelines for future experiments.

II. The Angle of Arrival for GNSS

A. Development and applications of GNSS

GNSS has developed for 60 years. On October 4th, 1957, the former Soviet Union successfully launched the first man-made satellite, which turned a brand new page in the human history of utilizing satellites for navigation and positioning [2]. Meanwhile, the rapid development of advanced computers, microprocessors, solid-state semiconductors, atomic clocks, signal processing and communications and other related fields provided a solid foundation for satellite positioning and navigation techniques.

Now, GNSS has been playing a critical role. First, benefit from the development of GNSS, the vehicle navigation system can provide accurate positions, velocity and directions for drivers' route instructions. Secondly, GNSS is widely used for marine including rescue, navigating and the port control, as well as aviation including communication, navigation and air traffic management systems. More importantly, Satellite navigation applications have brought a revolution to the world of surveying and mapping. Specifically, GNSS has been widely adopted for geodesy, resource exploration, crustal movement, cadastral surveying and engineering surveying. Moreover, satellite navigation technology is essential for digital map data collection, intelligent transportation, information management systems, and clock synchronization. In summary, GNSS has been necessary for people's daily life. Therefore, developing high-accuracy, high-reliability GNSS receivers is of critical demand.

Though GNSS receivers perform well in an unobstructed open sky environment, it still faces some challenges in many other situations. Concretely, in the presence of multipath and occlusion of the receiving environment, it is difficult for a GNSS receiver to receive a clean Line-of-Sight (LOS) signal which results in an erroneous solution and sometimes no solution.

B. AoA for GNSS

To address the low Carrier-to-Noise Ratio (CNR) and multipath issue, array signal processing technologies, including beamforming and AoA estimation, have been used for GNSS receivers. The principle of beamforming, also known as spatial filtering, is to weight each of the array elements while combining the signal. In this case, the desired signals will be enhanced, while other undesired signals will be suppressed. The AoA estimation is one of an essential approach to obtain the weighting coefficient of beamforming. Several AoA techniques have been proposed, including ARMA spectrum analysis, maximum likelihood estimation, and eigenvalue decomposition.

III. AoA Estimation for GPS Signals

In this research effort, it is planned to focus on the estimation of the AoA of GNSS signals based on dual-frequency joint processing. This task is divided into three parts: (1) GNSS signal data collection; (2) Obtaining the observations by processing the collected data into GNSS software-defined receiver (SDR); (3) Utilizing the Matlab toolbox to analyze the observations to estimate the AoA. As of now, step one and step two is complete. For step three, we provide a work plan and present the results at the conference.

A. GPS Data Collection

Multi-band RF transceivers for the L-band do exist, though limited, that help collect GNSS data. One such hardware is the Amungo board [3], as shown in Figure 1 (a). The Amungo board is equipped with NT1065 "Nomada" (as shown in Figure 1 (b)) [4], which is a four-channel radio frequency (RF) front-end for simultaneous reception of GPS, GLONASS, Galileo, Beidou, IRNSS, QZSS and SBAS signals of various frequency bands L1, L2, L3, L5, E1, E5a, E5b, E6, B1, B2, B3 [4].

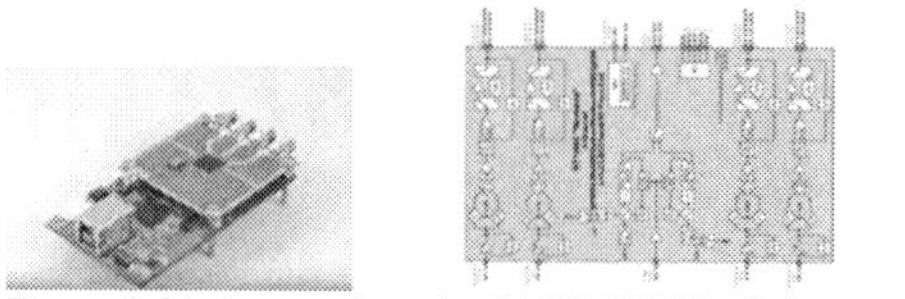

Figure 1 (a) Amungo board (b) NT1065 block diagram

Rooftop data was collected on September 29th, 2017, as shown in Figure 2 (a). To achieve the dual-frequency AoA estimation work, and four channels of NT1065 and two antennas were used with half-wavelength baseline at GPS L1 carrier 1575.42 MHz, ~= 9 cm. Two channels of NT1065 were configured to GNSS L1 band, the other two to GNSS L2 band. The selected data collection scenario is shown in Figure 2 (b).

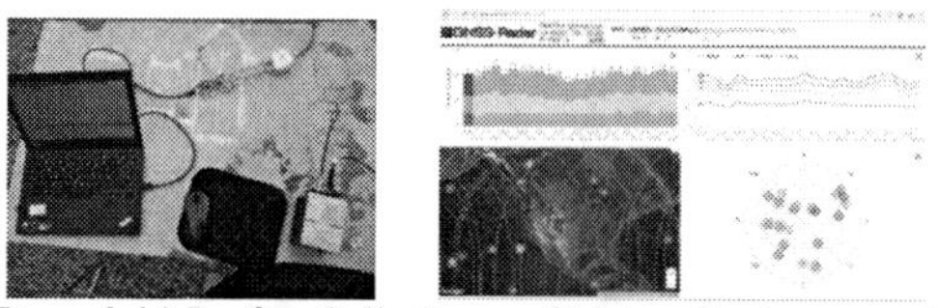

Figure 2 (a) Rooftop Collection (b)data collection scenario

B. GNSS Software-Defined receiver

To obtain the observations from raw data, GNSS SDR was used [5]. The correlator output and the carrier frequency of GPS L1 C/A PRN 18 are shown in Fig. 3 as an example. From the output of I/Q branches and carrier frequency, we can see that GPS signal has been correctly processed.

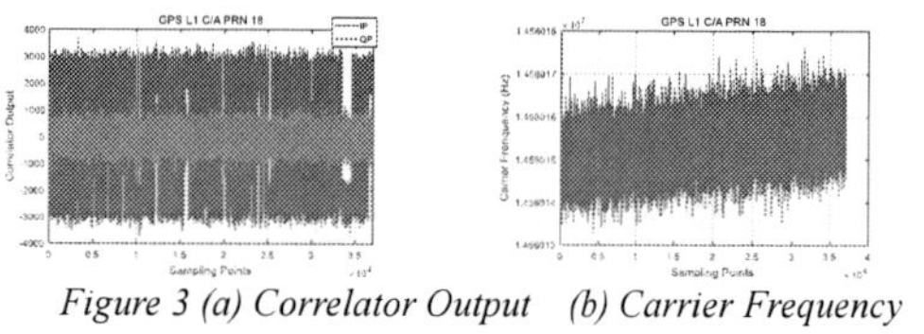

Figure 3 (a) Correlator Output (b) Carrier Frequency

C. AoA estimation method illustration

In this paper, we use the same local reference signal to despread two received signals. Figure 4 shows the sechematic diagram of AoA estimation method. Assuming we have two received signals, $r^1(t)$ and $r^2(t)$, from two antennas.

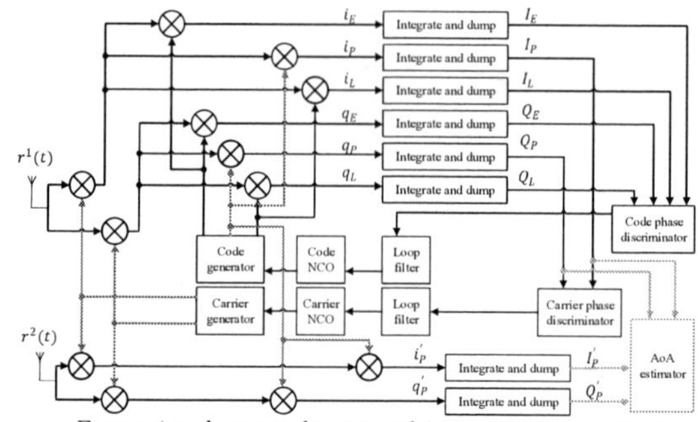

Figure 4 sechematic diagram of AoA estimation method

The received signal $r^1(t)$ is multiplied with locally generated carrier signal, $s_{carrier}(t)$, and then down converted to baseband in-phase (I) and quadrature-phase (Q). Down converted I and Q signals are multiplexed by locally generated signals, $s_{code}(t)$, which are genereated by code generators. The multiplexed results are resampled by integrate and dump (I&D) accumulators. The integration results are sent into code phase and carrier phase discriminator.

Another received signal, $r^2(t)$, is mutiplied by the carrier signal and code signal generated in the tracking process of $r^1(t)$ (shown as red line in Figure 4), then resampled by I&D as well.

After that, all the correlator outputs are sent into AoA estimator (shown as blue line in Figure 4). The correlator outputs can be written as

$$I_P(n) = aD(n)R(\tau)sinc(f_eT_{coh}) \cos \phi_e$$
$$Q_P(n) = aD(n)R(\tau)sinc(f_eT_{coh}) \sin \phi_e$$
$$I_P'(n) = aD(n)R(\tau)sinc(f_eT_{coh}) \cos(\phi_e + \theta_0)$$
$$Q_P'(n) = aD(n)R(\tau)sinc(f_eT_{coh}) \sin(\phi_e + \theta_0)$$

I_P and Q_P are the correlator outputs of received signal $r^1(t)$ and local signal $s_{code}(t)$, while I_p' and Q_p' are the correlator outputs of received signal $r^2(t)$ and the same local signal $s_{code}(t)$. Where a is signal amplitude, $D(n)$ is navigation bit, $R(\tau)$ is PRN auto correlation function, and τ is code phase error between local PRN and received PRN, f_e and ϕ_e is carrier frequency and carrier phase error respectively, θ_0 is the carrier phase difference between $r^1(t)$ and $r^2(t)$ signals.

Therefore we can combine the above four correlator outputs to calculate the carrier phase difference between the received $r^1(t)$ and $r^2(t)$ signals,

$$\theta_0\ (n) = \text{angle}\{\ (I_p + jQ_p) \times \text{conj}(I_p' + jQ_p')\ \}$$

Where "angle" is angle calculation operation, and "conj" is conjugate operation. Then the AoA can be written as

$$\theta_{AoA} = \arccos(\frac{\theta_0\lambda}{l})$$

Where λ is the wavelength of received GNSS signal, and l is the distance between two antennas.

D. Estimation results

Figure 5 shows the AoA estimation and elevation of GPS L1 C/A signal.

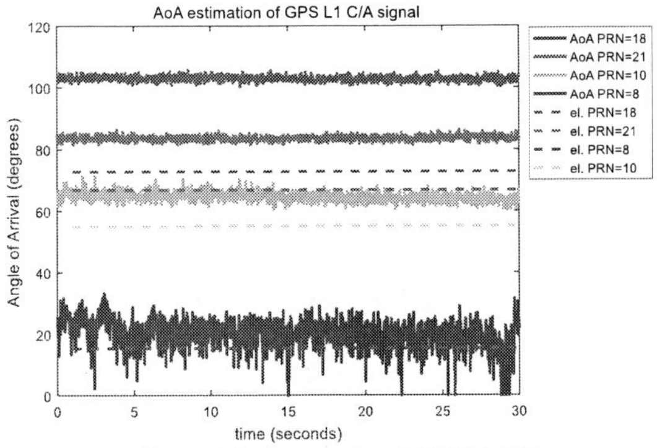

Figure 5 AoA estimation of GPS L1 C/A

IV. CHALLENGES AND APPLICATIONS OF GPS AOA ESTIMATIONS BASED ON DUAL-FREQUENCY JOINT PROCESSING

Nowadays, AoA estimation of GNSS still has several interesting issues to be explored. Specifically, the interests are in how the front-end, the antenna array, and multi-constellation affects the estimation of AoA.

A. The influence of front-end

As mentioned above, NT1065 was used for the data collection. NT1065 has two separate VCOs for the two sets of channels. So an interesting question is that whether the different VCOs that influence the signal combination will result in any carrier-phase measurement noise. To address this question, it is planned to use other front-ends which share the same PLL/VCO, for instance, ADI AD9364 or LimeMicro LM7002.

B. Antenna spacing with the multi-frequency receiver

As described in III.A, GNSS data was collected from both L1 and L2 bands. An impressive question would be how the antenna element spacing affects AoA estimation algorithm given the dual-frequency processing, i.e., what are the challenges due to the difference in half wavelength (3cm in the L1/L2 case)? Furthermore, it will be interesting to explore how the difference in half-wavelengths affect the multi-path performance.

C. Decision of multi-constellation

Though it is good to receive more signals from different constellations in most cases, some signals still need to be eliminated due to their residual errors. For example, suppose there is a good GPS satellite view (SV) and a bad GLONASS SV at about the same elevation and azimuth. Then the GPS SV might be eliminated if we want to include the GLONASS SV. So how to deal with this situation becomes a challenge. Consequently, one important thing is that how to decide to eliminate/include under the multi-constellation situation.

D. Applications of multi-frequency multi-constellation of AoA estimation

The multi-frequency multi-constellation AoA estimation can be applied in many different fields. Primarily, it is of greatest usefulness for high accuracy as the CNR can be improved by adopting the AoA estimation-based beamforming technique. Secondly, the multi-path mitigation is expected to improve as the AoA information helps distinguish LOS and reflected signals.

V. CONCLUSIONS

In this paper, we gave a brief introduction of AoA estimation of GNSS signals, as well as the preliminary work of our experiment. The guidelines of the next step have been given, and we will provide the whole experiments results at the conference.

REFERENCES

[1] Zhang, X. and R. Cao, Direction of Arrival Estimation: Introduction. 2017: John Wiley & Sons, Inc.

[2] Xie, G., Principles of GNSS : GPS, GLONASS, and Galileo. 2013: Publishing House of Electronics Industry.

[3] https://www.Amungo-navigation.com/nut4nt

[4] http://www.ntlab.com/IP/NT1065/NT1065_USB3_description_v1.03.pdf

[5] Kai, B., et al., A Software-Defined GPS and Galileo Receiver. 2007: Birkhäuser Boston. 1632-1637.

[6] https://www.mathworks.com/products/phased-array.htm

Design of Platform-Based HF Direction Finding Antennas Using the Characteristic Mode Theory

Ruyu Ma
Electrical and Computer Engineering
University of Wisconsin-Madison
Madison, WI
rma56@wisc.edu

Nader Behdad
Electrical and Computer Engineering
University of Wisconsin-Madison
Madison, WI
behdad@wisc.edu

***Abstract*—This paper presents a method for utilizing the platform as the antenna array for the on-board HF direction finding (DF) system. In the HF band, due to the large wavelength of electromagnetic waves, practical antennas deployed on the platforms are electrically small, limiting the DF accuracy. To address this issue in platform-based DF systems, the platforms that have dimensions comparable with the wavelength can be used as the antenna elements in a DF array themselves. However, due to the complex shape and radiation features of the platforms, it is challenging to use them efficiently. We present a characteristic mode (CM) based approach that allows for selecting the subset of the platform's CMs with the lowest Cramer Rao lower bound. This approach can achieve the lowest DF error and considers the field of view and polarization of impinging waves quantitatively. We apply this approach to design and simulate an HF DF antenna array for a midsize aircraft at 10 MHz. Our results demonstrate that the selected subset has significant advantage over the others.**

***Index Terms*—characteristic mode, direction finding, CRLB, platform-based antenna.**

I. Introduction

Direction finding (DF) systems are widely used at HF, VHF and UHF bands. Knowing the direction of an impinging wave in the HF band is necessary in many surveillance, electronic warfare support, navigation, and geolocation applications. However, due to the large wavelength of electromagnetic waves at this frequency band, it is impractical to deploy conventional DF arrays that are usually a few wavelengths long on the platforms. In order to alleviate the size requirements of platform-based HF DF antennas, using the metallic platform as the DF array is a promising substitution.

The concept of using the platform as the antenna itself has been examined before. In [1], radiating currents on a ship were excited to achieve certain radiation patterns. In [2] the platform was used to enhance the bandwidth of HF and VHF antennas. However, these papers did not investigate the use of such platform-based antennas for DF. In [3] and [4], employing multi-mode antennas for DF purposes was investigated, but the design of suitable multi-mode antennas was not investigated. Similarly, in [5], the strategic placement of monopoles on an airplane was investigated as a means of enhancing the DF accuracy. The DF accuracy improvements were attributed to the positive effects of the platform. However, efficiently exciting the platform as the antenna was not investigated. In addition, none of the above mentioned papers did consider the impact of the polarization of impinging waves and the field of view (FOV) of the DF system.

This work is supported by Office of Naval Research under ONR award No. N00014-11-1-0618. The authors are with the Department of Electrical and Computer Engineering, University of Wisconsin-Madison, Madison, WI 53706-1691 USA (e-mail: rma56@wisc.edu; and behdad@wisc.edu).

In this paper, we propose a systematic method for efficiently employing the platform as the DF antenna array. This method selects the subset of the platform's characteristic modes (CMs) that provides the lowest Cramer Rao lower bound (CRLB) by assuming that each CM is one element in the DF array. This CRLB considers the FOV and the polarization. In this way, the proposed method yields a design that approaches the optimal DF performance while considering the FOV and polarization quantitatively. We apply our approach to design and simulate a Boeing 737 airplane at 10 MHz. Our results demonstrate that the selected subset has significant advantage over others. In the following sections, we will formulate the CRLB, describe the modal selection procedure, and show the design example and simulation results.

II. CRLB of Diversely Polarized Antenna Arrays

In DF applications, CRLB provides a lower bound for angle-of-arrival (AoA) estimation error [6]. CRLB of an antenna array can be computed with the formulas proposed in [6]. However, this CRLB varies with the AoAs and the impinging waves' polarization, and is a matrix. Therefore, to be used a figure of merit, this CRLB is first averaged over the FOV and polarization. A weighted average may be more appropriate if the impinging wave is more likely to have a specific type of polarization. Then, the sum of this averaged CRLB matrix's azimuth and elevation AoA elements is used as a figure of merit. This idea is mathematically described as:

$$\mathbf{CRLB}_{avg} \triangleq \frac{\int p(\gamma,\eta)d\gamma d\eta \int_{\Omega} \mathbf{CRLB}(\theta,\phi,\gamma,\eta)\sin(\theta)d\theta d\phi}{\Omega}, \tag{1}$$

$$CRLB_{AoA} \triangleq \mathbf{CRLB}_{avg,\theta\theta} + \mathbf{CRLB}_{avg,\phi\phi}, \tag{2}$$

where $\mathbf{CRLB}_{avg}$ denotes weighted average CRLB matrix; $\mathbf{CRLB}(\theta,\phi,\gamma,\eta)$ is the CRLB matrix formulated in [6]; θ,ϕ

are the elevation and azimuth AoA respectively; γ and η are the tilt angle and phase difference of two polarization components of the impinging wave; $p(\gamma,\eta)$ is the probability distribution function (PDF) of polarization; Ω is the FOV; $CRLB_{AoA}$ is the scalar average CRLB; $\mathbf{CRLB}_{avg,\phi\phi}$ and $\mathbf{CRLB}_{avg,\theta\theta}$ are the ϕ and the θ components of $\mathbf{CRLB}_{avg}$ respectively. $p(\gamma,\eta)$ and Ω are assumed known.

III. Design of the Platform-Based Antenna Array

A. Mode Selection Procedure

The CM theory states that a plane wave impinging on a platform induces a superposition of CMs on it. The weights of these CMs depend on the AoA and polarization of the incident wave [7], [8]. As a result, by measuring these weights, the AoA and polarization can be estimated. However, it is more practical to measure a small subset of these CMs, rather than all of them. To achieve the lowest AoA estimation error, this subset should provide the lowest CRLB among all the subsets. This subset can be picked up with two steps. In the first step, the infinite set of the CMs is truncated to a finite set. All the CMs should be identified by CM analysis, and then the CMs with modal significance (MS) values smaller than a certain value are abandoned. In the CM theory, the CMs with smaller MS values contribute less to the overall induced currents.

It is a good practice to set this minimum MS as 0.7. On one hand, if this value were large, the AoA estimation accuracy of the design might be low. This is because the radiation patterns of higher order modes (usually with small MS) tend to change more rapidly with respect to AoA. On the other hand, if this value is small, it would be hard to excited the desired modes. Value 0.7 is a good balance; CMs with MS values less than 0.7 can be omitted in radiation pattern synthesis without introducing significant error [9].

In the second step, let us assume the number of receivers is smaller than the number of the CMs identified in the first step. The scalar average CRLB of each combination is computed with (1) and (2). The combination with the lowest CRLB will be picked up. After this, coupling elements for each of these CMs can be designed to interface with one receiver.

B. Platform-based Antenna Design on an Airplane

We used a simplified model of a Boeing 737-900 airplane of 42-meter long and 34-meter wide. We assume the DF system has four receivers working at 10 MHz. An impinging wave is supposed to randomly come from any possible direction and with random linear polarization, i.e., $p(\gamma,\eta)=1$ and the FOV is $\theta\in[0,\pi],\phi\in[0,2\pi]$.

CM analysis with FEKO 7.0 shows that this simplified model has six significant modes (MS>0.7). Selecting four modes out of these six modes may produce $\binom{6}{4}=15$ combinations. For these combinations, the scalar average CRLBs ($\sqrt{CRLB_{AoA}}$) formulated in (1) and (2) are computed and compared in Fig. 1. The signal-to-noise ratio (SNR) was assumed 25 dB. As can be seen, $\sqrt{CRLB_{AoA}}$ significantly varies with the combination. In fact, the largest value (9.9°) is more than twice of the smallest one (4.6°). In other words, an array design with a poorly selected combination (e.g., 11) may have more than twice of AoA estimation error, compared with a well-selected combination (e.g., 3). Small loops and patches conform to the airplane can then be used as the coupling elements for the selected modes.

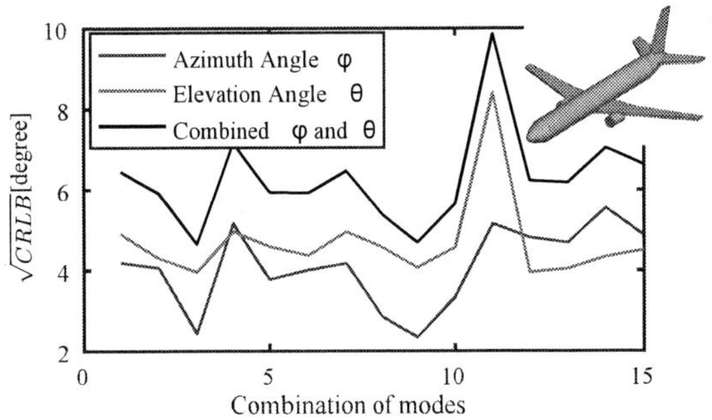

Fig. 1. Average CRLB of combinations of an Boeing 737 airplane's significant CMs (MS>0.7), assuming SNR=25 dB. Combination 3 may provide more AoA estimation accuracy than twice of that of combination 11.

IV. Conclusion

This paper proposed a CM theory-based method for efficiently utilizing the platform as the elements of a DF antenna array. This method selects the subset of CMs with the lowest CRLB. Simulation results demonstrate significant advantage of DF accuracy. At the conference, we will present the modal currents and radiation patterns of the airplane's CMs. Also, we will report a detailed design of the coupling elements based on the modal selection results. Besides, simulation and measurement results, numerical DF experiment results, and the DF performance throughout the whole HF band will be presented.

References

[1] Y. Chen and C.-F. Wang, "Hf band shipboard antenna design using characteristic modes," *IEEE Transactions on Antennas and Propagation*, vol. 63, no. 3, pp. 1004–1013, 2015.

[2] T.-Y. Shih and N. Behdad, "Bandwidth enhancement of platform-mounted hf antennas using the characteristic mode theory," *IEEE Transactions on Antennas and Propagation*, vol. 64, no. 7, pp. 2648–2659, 2016.

[3] T. Svantesson, "Multimode based direction finding," in *Signals, Systems and Computers, 2000. Conference Record of the Thirty-Fourth Asilomar Conference on*, vol. 1. IEEE, 2000, pp. 595–599.

[4] R. Pöhlmann, S. Zhang, T. Jost, and A. Dammann, "Power-based direction-of-arrival estimation using a single multi-mode antenna," *arXiv preprint arXiv:1706.09690*, 2017.

[5] C. F. Corbin, "High frequency direction finding using structurally integrated antennas on a large airborne platform," AIR FORCE INST OF TECH WRIGHT-PATTERSON AFB OH GRADUATE SCHOOL OF ENGINEERING AND MANAGEMENT, Tech. Rep., 2011.

[6] A. J. Weiss and B. Friedlander, "Performance analysis of diversely polarized antenna arrays," *IEEE Transactions on signal processing*, vol. 39, no. 7, pp. 1589–1603, 1991.

[7] M. Cabedo-Fabres, E. Antonino-Daviu, A. Valero-Nogueira, and M. F. Bataller, "The theory of characteristic modes revisited: A contribution to the design of antennas for modern applications," *IEEE Antennas and Propagation Magazine*, vol. 49, no. 5, pp. 52–68, 2007.

[8] R. Garbacz, "Modal expansions for resonance scattering phenomena," *Proceedings of the IEEE*, vol. 53, no. 8, pp. 856–864, 1965.

[9] Y. Chen and C.-F. Wang, *Characteristic Modes: Theory and Applications in Antenna Engineering*. John Wiley & Sons, 2015.

Impact of Flat Radomes on Amplitude-Only Direction Finding Performance

Muhannad A. Al-Tarifi and Dejan S. Filipovic
Department of Electrical, Computer, and Energy Engineering
University of Colorado Boulder
Boulder, CO USA
muhannad.altarifi@colorado.edu, dejan.filipovic@colorado.edu

***Abstract*—We investigate the impact of placing a thin flat radome in front of an amplitude-only direction finding (AODF) antenna system. The considered system consists of two identical Ka-band, air-filled horn antennas squinted off boresight by 30° for direction finding (DF) error within ±0.82 °/dB over a field-of-view (FoV) from -20° to +20°. Computational results with various radome materials, thicknesses, and placements indicate that it is possible to maintain excellent DF performance if radome is properly designed and located.**

Keywords—amplitude only direction finding, antenna radome, horn antennas, millimeter-wave antennas

I. Introduction

Radomes are often desired to provide mechanical and environmental protection of antenna front-ends in air-borne warfare, communication, and sensing applications. A properly-designed radome should provide the required protection with minimal influence on electrical performance [1]. The design challenge varies with the acceptable compromise between the level of protection and electrical transparency as allowed for a specific application. In amplitude-only direction finding (AODF) systems, any alteration of radiation performance is carried to the DF performance in terms of accuracy, field of view (FoV), and bandwidth. Therefore, a careful radome design is essential in order to avoid any degradation of radiation patterns, such as rippling and beamwidth instability.

In this paper we investigate the effect of thin, flat radomes on AODF antenna system operating in the Ka band (26.5–40 GHz). The system consists of two nearly-sectoral horn antennas squinted off in the H-plane to provide two differential beams suitable for low-error DF over -20°–20° FoV. The plane-wave analysis suggests that lower radome permittivity and thickness entails minimal degradation of radiation and, thus, DF performance. This is computationally validated by full-wave simulation in HFSS [2] with the radome placed flush over horn aperture. However, since the radome exists in the near field of the antenna, it is found that far-field performance can also be controlled by adjusting the separation between the radome and horn aperture. Subsequently, excellent DF performance can be maintained with thicker radome sheets.

II. Horn and System Configurations

Fig. 1 shows the configuration and far-field performance of a stand-alone, nearly H-sectoral horn antenna designed for smooth and stable H-plane patterns over the entire Ka band. By squinting two horns off in the H-plane, two distinctive beams suitable for DF scanning are produced. Fig. 2 shows an AODF front-end system with 30° squinted antennas. The direction finding function (DFF), in dB, is the difference between voltage amplitudes at antenna ports or, alternatively, the difference between realized gains of the generated beams. The quality of DFF is determined by its slope (dB/°), shown in Fig. 3, which is inversely proportional to DF errors (°/dB). As seen, the minimum slope is 0.61 dB/°, which corresponds to a maximum DF error of ±0.82 °/dB. The purpose is to maintain similar or close DF performance after radome is introduced.

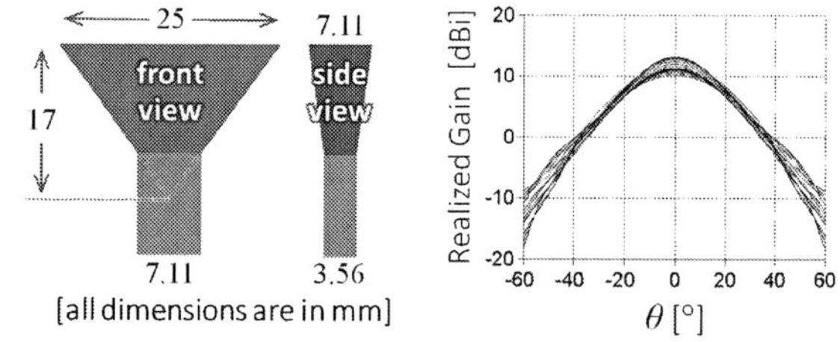

Fig. 1 Configuration of a stand-alone horn antenna (left) and its H-plane radiation patterns (right, 15 curves, 26–40 GHz, 1-GHz step).

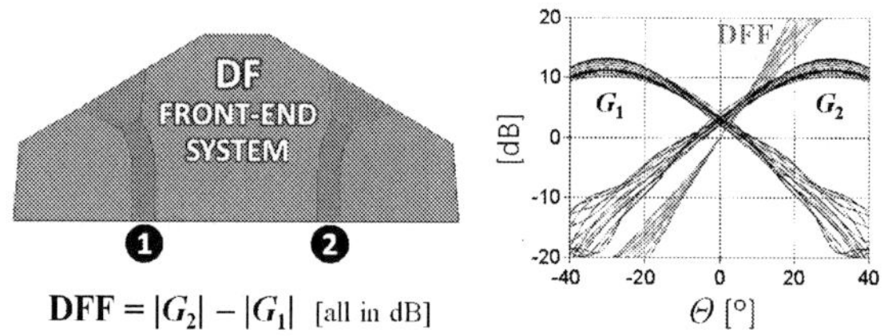

Fig. 2 AODF configuration (left) and DFF performance (right).

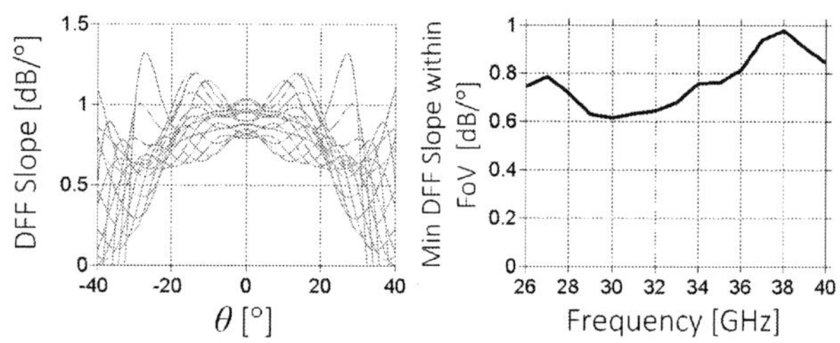

Fig. 3 DFF slope (left) and its minimum in -20°–20° FoV (right)

This research is supported by the Office of Naval Research (ONR) award # N00014-15-1-2111.

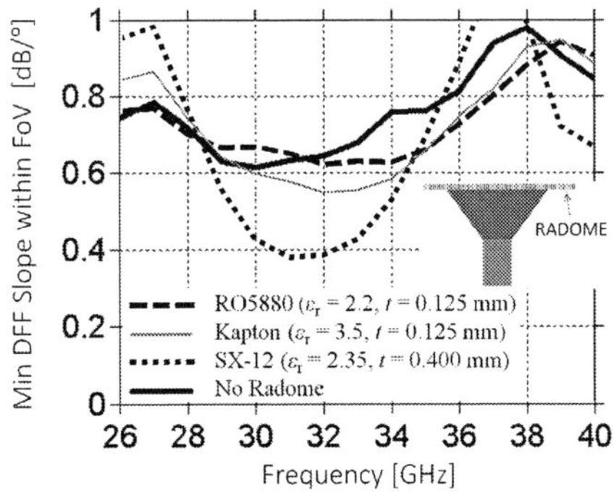

Fig. 4 Minimum DFF slope after applying various radome sheets flush to horn aperture.

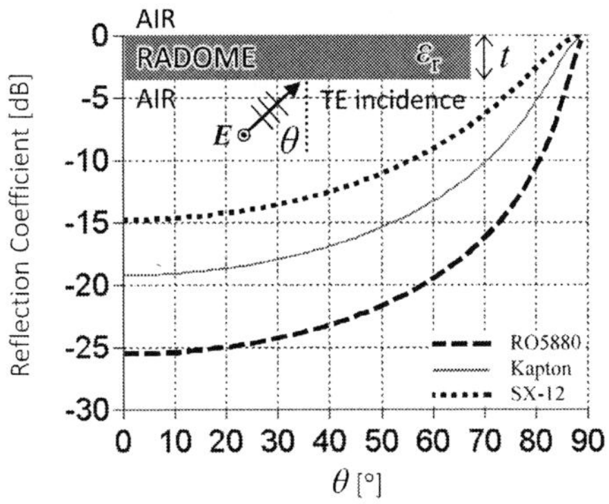

Fig. 5 Reflection coefficient amplitude of a TE plane wave impinging upon various radome sheets.

III. Radome Permittivity and Thickness

Initially, the permittivity and thickness of radome are investigated by means of full-wave simulations with various radome types. Specifically, three, commercially-available, dielectric sheets are considered: Rogers RO5880 (ε_r = 2.2) of 0.125-mm thickness, Kapton (ε_r = 3.5) of 0.125-mm thickness, and SHEERGARD™ SX-12 (ε_r = 2.35) of 0.4-mm thickness. All of these sheets are placed flush to the horn aperture, and computational results are presented in Fig. 4 as curves of minimum DFF slope. It is found that the RO5880 radome maintains the best DF performance compared to the higher permittivity Kapton sheet and to the thicker SX-12 composite. This result is expected because thinner and lower permittivity sheets correspond to lower reflection coefficients as analytically predicted by plane-wave analysis of the stand-alone radome [3]. Fig. 5 shows that the RO5880 sheet reflects much less energy compared to Kapton and SX-12; therefore, the total DF performance resembles more closely to the originally designed system with no radome.

It is worth to mention that the outcome from the preceding investigation is typically conflicting with mechanical durability that requires more dense radome material (i.e., higher ε_r), higher thickness, or both. Half-wavelength radomes and sandwich arrangements [4] are common choices to increase radome durability at the expense of limiting the bandwidth or field of view, especially for low-error DF applications. Nevertheless, designing radomes based solely on plane-wave analysis ignores the fact that the radome exists at the near field of the antenna and that there might be additional effects of the radome other than energy reflection. Thus, a computational study of radome location is essential in order to choose the best placement of a desired durable radome sheet (such as SX-12).

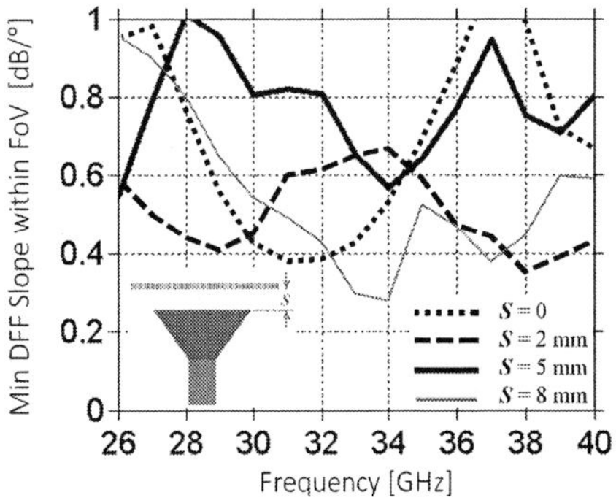

Fig. 6 Minimum DFF slope after applying SX-12 radome at a separation distance S from horn aperture.

IV. Radome Separation

Fig. 6 shows DF performance with an SX-12 radome placed at a separation distance S from the horn aperture. It is evident that performance varies significantly with S, which should not be the case if the plane-wave analysis is an accurate approximation of radome effect. The shown results demonstrate that it is possible to maintain a very high DF accuracy if the SX-12 sheet is placed 5mm away from horn aperture. Despite the added installation complexity (a foam sheet is needed for separation), this radome arrangement presents a more durable choice than a thinner RO5880 flush to the horn. Since radome placement primarily affects the near-field distribution, a new computational study is required when any modification is applied to antenna structure, radome material, or AODF geometry and performance requirement.

V. Conclusion

Impact of placing a flat radome in front of an amplitude-only direction finding system is investigated. While thinner, lower-permittivity radomes are preferred, it is still possible to maintain decent DF performance using thicker radomes if it is separated properly from the antenna aperture.

References

[1] D. J. Kozakoff, *Analysis of Radome-Enclosed Antennas*. Norwood, MA: Artech House, 1997.

[2] Ansoft Inc. *High Frequency Structure Simulation (HFSS)*. Accessed on Nov. 2017. [Online]. Available: http://www.ansys.com.

[3] W. C. Chew, *Waves and Fields in Inhomogeneous Media*. New York: Van Nostrand, 1990, pp. 49–53.

[4] G. A. E. Crone, A. W. Rudge, and G. N. Taylor, "Design and performance of airborne radomes: A review," *Proc. Inst. Elect. Eng.*, pt. F, vol. 128, pp. 451–463, Dec. 1981.

Directional of Arrival Tag Response for Reverse RFID Localization

Allee D. Zarrini
Department of Electrical Engineering
Colorado School of Mines
Golden, CO 80401 USA
adzarrini@mines.edu

Atef Elsherbeni
Department of Electrical Engineering
Colorado School of Mines
Golden, CO 80401 USA
aelsherb@mines.edu

Jürgen F. Brune
Mining Engineering Department
Colorado School of Mines
Golden, CO 80401 USA
jbrune@mines.edu

***Abstract*—A positioning system implemented with RFID technology is explored for a GPS-denied environment such as an underground mine or tunnel. A new method of two-dimensional localization is developed based on the angles of arrival of three tag's responses that are located at known positions. This method reduces the error when the localization process is based on the received signal strength from an RFID tag signal. Passive tags are placed in predefined locations with known information about their coordinates. An RFID reader attached to a robot with a directive antenna is used to get the AOA of the signals received from the tags. The AOA information is then used for triangulating the position of a reader's location (reverse localization).**

Keywords—Localization, RFID.

I. INTRODUCTION

Respirable dust is a known health hazard in underground mines and tunnels as well as in surface quarries and construction sites. To better track respirable dust exposure, a dust monitor with geolocating capabilities can be used to map dust exposure in spatial-temporal environment to improve engineering and management solutions for mines and industrial plant dust control.

For surface mines or other outdoor applications, the dust monitor can be equipped with a global positioning system (GPS). GPS is easily applicable, but it does not work in underground mine or tunnel environments. In such GPS-denied conditions, RFID locating technology can be used instead. RFID has been gaining popularity for its low cost compared to other locating methods. For this project, a systematic approach to locating an RFID reader using the signal strength and direction of three independent tags is developed.

II. LOCALIZATION USING DISTANCE APPROXIMATIONS

A. Mathematical Theory

The 2-D position of an unknown point can be discovered by knowing the position (x and y coordinates) of 3 different points and the distances to each of these points. Fig. 1 shows 3 circles whose radii correspond to the signal travel distance from the RFID tag to the unknown reader location. The intersections of any two circles determines the possible positions, usually 2, of the point with unknown coordinates. The intersection of all three circles then defines the exact coordinates of the unknown location. The x_1, y_1, x_2, y_2, x_3, y_3 are the known coordinates of points 1, 2, and 3 with r_1, r_2, and r_3 being the known distances away from point P with unknown coordinates x, y and z;

$$(x-x_1)^2+(y-y_1)^2=r_1^2,\quad (x-x_2)^2+(y-y_2)^2=r_2^2,\quad (x-x_3)^2+(y-y_3)^2=r_3^2.$$

As an example, consider the set of points P1, P2, P3 with coordinates (1,1), (6,3), (0,9) that are at distances of $r_1 = 7.2$, $r_2 = 4.1$, $r_3 = 5.4$ units away from the unknown point P. The unknown coordinates of point P can be found from the intersection of the circles as shown in Fig. 1 to be at location (5,7).

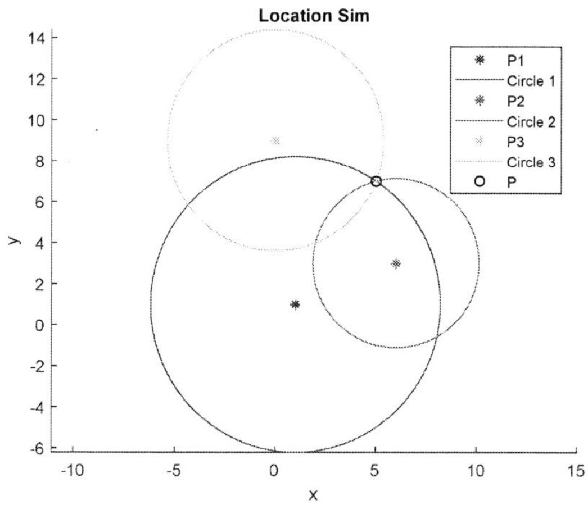

Fig. 1. A set of points P1, P2, P3 with known coordinates and the interesecting circles determining the coordinate of point P.

B. RFID Implementation

In this project, ultra-high frequency (UHF) passive RFID tags are placed at known locations as reference tags to locate the RFID reader position. The reader uses an omnidirectional antenna that will record the received signal from a tag in terms of the received signal strength (RSS). Distances between the reader and the tags can be calculated from RSS values via a generated empirical function. The reader will continuously scan all nearby tags for a predetermined amount of time. Multiple readings from each tag are averaged to reduce error from extraneous readings. If echoes from more than three tags are received, the three tags with the greatest signal strengths are chosen for the coordinate triangulation.

C. Errors and Limitations

As Fig. 2 shows, even in a clean laboratory environment the RSS-distance relation is not smooth and will produce calculation errors. Note that this data set will not result in a function because there exist many instances where a single RSS value corresponds to more than one distance.

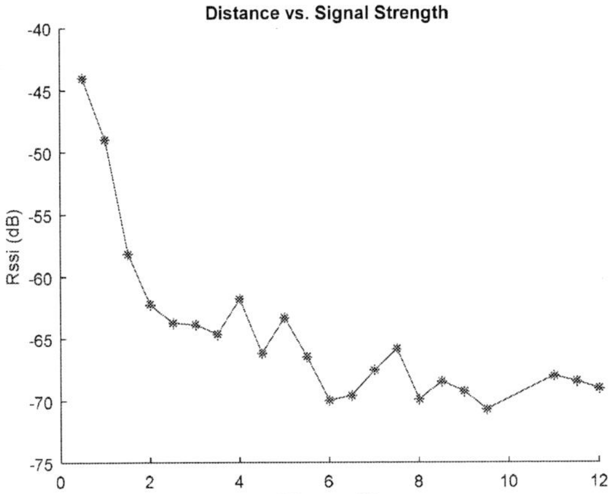

Fig. 2. Sample data showing how RSS varies greatly relative to distance.

In an underground mine environment, there may be metallic objects and electromagnetic noise that could create further interference and echoes that further distort the direct line of sight, RSS-distance relationship. Initial laboratory tests showed that location through RSS alone would not provide the desired level of accuracy. The authors decided to refine the triangulation algorithm and to improve its accuracy by recording the angle of arrival (AOA) of the received signal along with the RSS.

III. LOCALIZATION USING ANGLE OF ARRIVAL

A. Mathematial Theory

The directional algorithm similarly requires a minimum of 3 readings from the three known position tags to properly locate the unknown position of the reader. Instead of using the distance information, the reader records the AOA of the strongest signal from the known position tags. The reader must be equipped with a directional antenna which typically has a higher gain compared to the traditional omni-directional antennas, to improve the read range.

Fig. 3 illustrates the AOA from the three tags, the coordinates of the three tags and other parameters to use for solving for the unknown distances r_1, r_2, and r_3 using the following 9 equations:

$$\frac{d_{21}}{\sin(a_{21})}=\frac{r_1}{\sin(a_2)},\quad \frac{d_{21}}{\sin(a_{21})}=\frac{r_2}{\sin(a_1)},\quad \frac{d_{32}}{\sin(a_{32})}=\frac{r_2}{\sin(b_3)},$$

$$\frac{d_{32}}{\sin(a_{32})}=\frac{r_3}{\sin(b_2)},\quad \frac{d_{13}}{\sin(a_{13})}=\frac{r_3}{\sin(c_1)},\quad \frac{d_{13}}{\sin(a_{13})}=\frac{r_1}{\sin(c_3)},$$

$$d_{32}^2=d_{21}^2+d_{13}^2-2d_{21}d_{13}\cos(a_1+c_1),\quad d_{13}^2=d_{32}^2+d_{21}^2-2d_{32}d_{21}\cos(b_2+a_2),$$
$$d_{23}^2=d_{13}^2+d_{21}^2-2d_{13}d_{21}\cos(c_3+b_3).$$

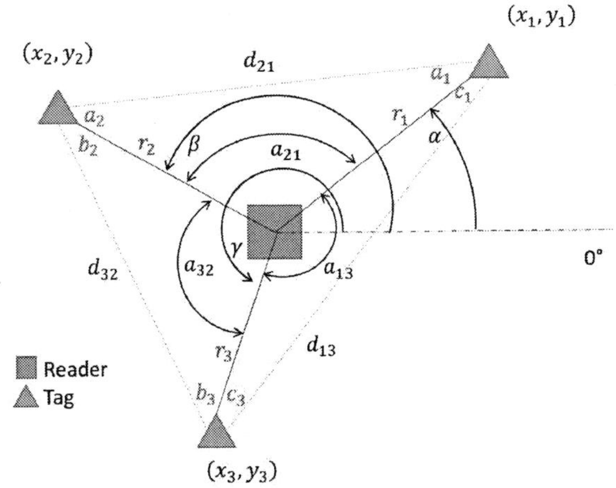

Fig. 3. The known variables in this system. α, β, γ are angles measured from the coordinate system zero axis represented by the dashed line.

Using r_1, r_2, and r_3 locating the unknown position of the reader can be achieved by the triangulation method described in section II. For example, given a set of points P1, P2, P3 with coordinates (3,0), (12,1), (5,8) that are at angle of α = 213°, β = 351°, γ = 99° , the unknown reader position can be found from the intersection of the circles to be at location (6,2).

B. Implementation

The algorithm based on the AOA estimation requires the use of a rotating directional antenna. The antenna will rotate 360 degrees at a fixed angular velocity while recording RSS values of all tags it finds. AOA values will be registered where the strongest signals (RSS values) are obtained along with the corresponding, calculated antenna direction. The triangulation algorithm will be applied to the three strongest readings to determine the reader location.

IV. CONCLUSION

This implementation will be less susceptible to RSS variability caused by signal reflections off surrounding objects. Even though the reader will continue to detect those readings, the maximum RSS will be obtained from a direct line of sight with the tag which will be the strongest signal reflected from the tag. Thus, the accuracy of determining the distances is greatly enhanced. Further advantage of this process is the use of a directive antenna which will have a much greater range than an omni-directional antenna. This will also minimize the number of tags that are required and maximize the area in which the reader can detect itself. The biggest limitation however for this algorithm is coordinates of the unknown reader position need to be within the triangle that is made by the three tags with known positions. However, for the localization of operators inside mines carrying a portable RFID reader, this special condition will not exist, hence this procedure would be applicable.

Modal Analysis of Stacked Gratings using B-splines Basis.

Gérard Granet
Université Clermont-Auvergne
CNRS, Institut Pascal
F-63000 Clermont-Ferrand, France
gerard.granet@uca.fr

***Abstract*—We analyse stacked rotated 1D gratings. Although the whole structure is bi-periodic, introducing non orthogonal coordinates allows to formulate the problem in each layer grating in terms of a sole 1D spectral problem. The numerical solution is then obtained by using the Galerkin method with B-splines basis.**

***Index Terms*—B-splines, gratings, modal method.**

I. Introduction

Stacking one-dimensional arrays of rods gives rise to very interesting structures such as woodpile crystals for instance. Generally, the axis of periodicity are orthogonal to each other. In the present paper, we add a supplementary degree of freedom by considering that this is not necessarily the case. However, we restrict our analysis to the case where only two 1D gratings are involved in the stack. Each layer may be separately considered as a 1D grating enlightened under properly chosen conical incidence angles. See Fig. 1 and Fig. 2. The bi-periodic nature of the problem is taken into account when writing the boundary conditions at the interfaces of the different layers. Now, it remains to solve efficiently the 1D layer problems. We face a standard grating problem whose solution should be chosen, in our opinion, in accordance with the grating's cross section. If the layers are piecewise translation invariant along the z axis, modal methods are very efficient since they avoid discretization in that direction. Among them, the Fourier modal method [1] is certainly the most popular and is present in many commercial codes. Its accuracy is linked with the number of spatial harmonics retained in the calculation. On the one hand, using periodic functions for analysing periodic structures seems an obvious choice, on the other hand it is well known that such functions are not well suited for representing discontinuous or highly spatially located fields. That is why it is worth looking for alternatives to the use of periodic functions in numerical modal methods. In this paper, we consider B-splines which have proven effective for one dimensional gratings [2], [3], [4].

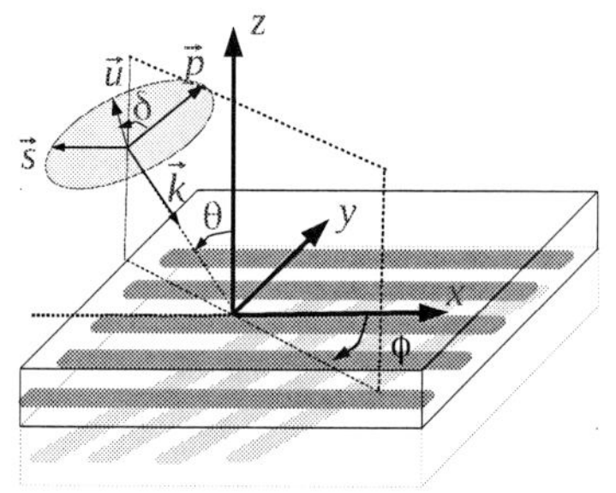

Fig. 1. Illustration of a two layers structure illuminated by a plane wave.

II. Theory

A. *Presentation of the Problem*

The structure consists of a stack of 1D gratings layers. Within the structure, the gratings may be aligned along two and only two different axis. We restrict our analysis to structures that incorporate different kinds of non magnetic linear materials characterized by their relative permittivity function which may be either real or complex. A typical structure includes four kinds of materials: the input medium with relative permittivity ϵ_1 (optical index ν_1), the output medium with relative permittivity ϵ_2 (optical index ν_2), the host medium with permittivity ϵ_a and lastly the rods with permittivity ϵ_b. For simplicity, we assume rods with rectangular cross sections. Hence, the stack is bi-periodic. We assume that one axis coincides with the x axis and the other one forms an angle ξ with respect to the y axis. It is illuminated from the vacuum by a linearly polarized monochromatic plane wave that has a vacuum wavelength λ and an angular frequency ω. The wave vector $\boldsymbol{k}$ forms an angle θ relative to the z axis, the angle between the x axis and the plane of incidence is denoted ϕ and δ represents the angle between the polarization vector $\hat{u}$ and the plane of incidence. The incident plane wave may therefore be expressed in the form:

$$\boldsymbol{E} = \hat{u}\exp(-j\boldsymbol{k}.\boldsymbol{r}), \tag{1}$$

where the incident wave vector has the expression:

$$\boldsymbol{k} = \alpha_x\hat{x} + \beta_y\hat{y} + \gamma_z\hat{z}, \tag{2}$$

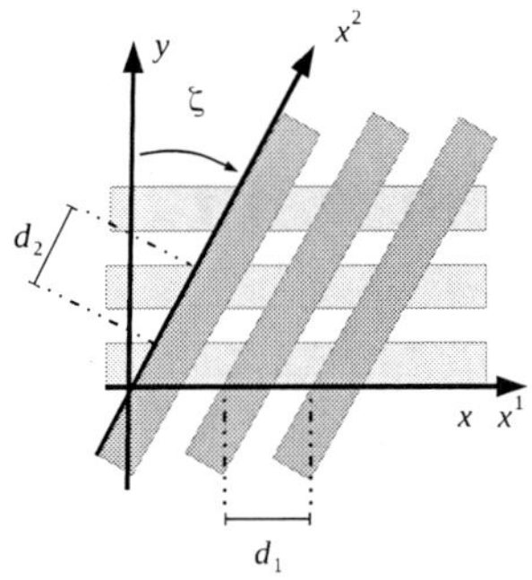

Fig. 2. Top view of a two layers structure and of coordinates x^1 and x^2.

with $\alpha_x = k\sin\theta\cos\phi$, $\beta_y = k\sin\theta\sin\phi$, $\gamma_z = -k\cos\theta$, $k = 2\pi/\lambda$.

B. New Coordinates

The structure as a whole is bi-periodic. However, each layer may be analysed separately as a 1D grating provided to carry out the following change of coordinates:

$$x = x^1 + \sin(\xi)x^2, \quad y = cos(\xi)x^2, \quad z = x^3. \tag{3}$$

Since the new coordinate system (x^1, x^2, x^3) is not orthogonal we write Maxwell's equations under the covariant form.

C. Modal Formulation

Now, all gratings are aligned along a coordinate axis and their permittivity function writes either $\epsilon(x^1)$ or $\epsilon(x^2)$. Hence, each layer may be considered as a 1d grating. Moreover, since the layers are translation invariant along x^3, the problem has the form of a spectral problem. In every layer, any component of the field writes:

$$\psi(x^1, x^2, x^3) = \Sigma_p {X_1}_p(x^1)\Sigma_q {X_2}_q(x^2)\exp(-j\gamma_{pq}x^3), \tag{4}$$

where function ${X_1}_p(x^1)$ and ${X_2}_q(x^2)$ are subject to pseudo periodicity conditions:

$$\begin{array}{l} {X_1}_p(x^1 + d_1) = \tau_1 {X_1}_p(x^1) \\ {X_2}_p(x^2 + d_2) = \tau_2 {X_2}_p(x^2), \end{array} \tag{5}$$

with $\tau_1 = k\sin(\theta)\cos(\phi)d_1$, and $\tau_2 = k\sin(\theta)\sin(\phi+\xi)d_2$. The problem is transformed into an algebraic eigenvalue problem thanks to the method of moments [5].

D. Numerical Solution

Numbers γ_{pq}, and functions ${X_1}_p(x^1)$ and ${X_2}_q(x^2)$ are the eigenvalues and the eigenvectors of a matrix obtained by using the method of moments. Instead of the usual Fourier basis as expansion and test functions, we introduce B-splines basis in order to avoid instability or convergence problems when dealing with metallic rods in the optical domain. The B splines are a family of splines defined piecewise by polynomials of the same degree on a mesh $u_0, u_1, \ldots, u_n$ where the points u_i are called knots [6]. The degree of the spline is the degree of the polynomial. The B-splines $B_{i,p}$ of order p are recursively defined as:

For $0 \le i \le n-1$

$$B_{i,0}(u) = 1 \text{ if } u_i < u < u_{i+1}, \quad B_{i,0}(u) = 0, \text{ else}, \tag{6}$$

and, for $p \ge 1$ and $0 \le i \le n-p-1$

$$B_{i,p}(u) = \frac{u-u_i}{u_{i+p}-u_i}B_{i,p-1} + \frac{u_{i+p+1}-u}{u_{i+p+1}-u_{i+1}}B_{i+1,p-1}, \tag{7}$$

We interpret the terms $\frac{u-u_i}{u_{i+p}-u_i}B_{i,p-1}$ and $\frac{u_{i+p+1}-u}{u_{i+p+1}-u_{i+1}}B_{i+1,p-1}$ as zero, respectively, whenever $u_{i+p}-u_i = 0$ and $u_{i+p+1}-u_{i+1} = 0$. This method permits an arbitrary knot spacing and the knots may coincide, which allows to approximate efficiently the various situations faced by the components of the field at the interface between two media. Fig. 3 illustrates the case where the first and the last knot at the boundary of two domains have multiplicity 3. Using such a discretization scheme within each piecewise homogeneous sub-domain allows to approximate effectively a continuous function with a discontinuous derivative. Lastly, the constant coefficients of the linear combination of eigenvectors are determined by matching the tangential components at the boundary of adjacent layers thanks to the S-matrix algorithm.

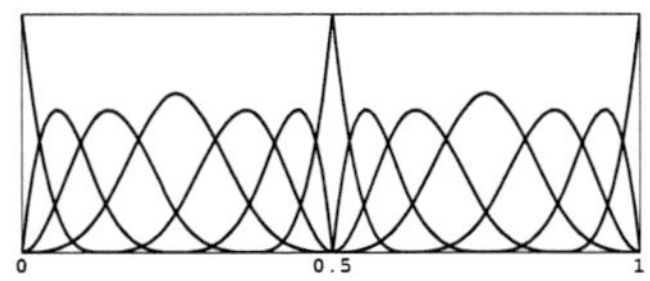

Fig. 3. Discretization scheme in which knots situated at $x = 0$, $x = .5$, $x = 1$ have multiplicity 3.

III. Conclusion

We developed a new numerical modal method for stacked 1D grating layers. The originality of the method lies in the use of a non orthogonal coordinate system and of B-splines basis as expansion and test functions in the Galerkin method. In the presentation, we will investigate how the rotation angle ξ affects the response of various multilayer structures and more specifically the polarization of diffracted waves.

References

[1] E. Noponen and J. Turunen, "Eigenmode method for electromagnetic synthesis of diffractive elements with three-dimensional profiles," J. Opt. Soc. Am. A, vol. 11, pp 2494–2502, 1994.
[2] K. Edee, P. Schiavone, and G. Granet, "Analysis of defect in extreme UV Lithography mask using a modal method based on nodal B-spline expansion," Japanese Journal of Applied Physics., vol. 44, pp. 6458–6462, 2005.
[3] A. M. Armeanu, K. Edee, G. Granet, and P. Schiavone, "Modal method based on spline expansion for the electromagnetic analysis of the lamellar grating, "PIER, vol. 106, pp. 243–261, 2010.
[4] G. Granet, "Efficient implementation of B-spline modal method for lamellar gratings," J. Opt. Soc. Am. A, vol. 31, pp. 332–337, 2014.
[5] R. Harrington, "Matrix methods for field problem," Proc. IEEE 55, pp. 136–149, 1967.
[6] M. G. Cox, "The numerical evaluation of B-splines," IMA J. Appl. Math. vol. 10, pp. 134–149, 1972.

Resonant Nanoantennas for Enhancing the Interaction of Terahertz Radiation with Nanomaterials

L. Razzari
Institut National de la Recherche Scientifique - Énergie, Matériaux et Télécommunications (INRS-EMT)
1650 Blvd Lionel Boulet, J3X 1S2 Varennes (Québec), Canada

***Abstract*— We present our investigation regarding the interaction of localized terahertz radiation with nanomaterials. Details about the design of metallic nanoantennas for THz field confinement will be given, together with some examples of applications.**

Keywords*— *Nanoantennas, Nanomaterials, Surface Enhancement, Terahertz Spectroscopy.

I. Introduction

During the last three decades, terahertz (THz) technology has been experiencing significant progress, especially through the development of time-domain spectroscopy (TDS), which retrieves the properties of a material using short pulses of THz radiation [1]. In particular, THz light can probe several elementary excitations in condensed matter, such as phonons, excitons, and magnons. However, its long wavelength (300 μm at 1 THz) severely hinders its interaction with nano-objects and molecules, practically limiting THz studies to macroscopic ensembles of these compounds.

In our investigation, we have exploited the electromagnetic properties of metallic nanostructures to engineer nanopatterned sensitive surfaces for enhanced THz radiation – nanomatter interaction.

II. Enhanced Terahertz Spectroscopy of Quantum Dots

Improving the sensitivity of THz spectroscopy deals with enhancing the interaction of THz radiation with the investigated specimen. Several strategies to implement this idea have been explored in the last years: waveguide-assisted THz sensing [2] takes advantage of an increase of the effective interaction length (up to several cm) in a guided geometry and has been employed for the investigation of thin layers (that however need to cover the whole length of the waveguide) of biomolecules, explosives and drugs, to name but a few examples. On the other hand, THz split-ring resonator arrays [3] have been proposed to sense thin (down to sub-μm) films of various compounds, by exploiting their narrowband resonance, whose spectral position is sensitive to small changes in the dielectric constant of the surrounding environment. However, such mechanism is not suitable for identifying the spectroscopic signatures of the investigated analyte. Recently, a new approach based on nano-apertures (slits) on a thin metallic layer was proposed [4]. The technique was able to identify the presence of small molecules within the slit (at the nanogram-level), making use of a significant field enhancement, but did not retrieve their THz absorption peak positions and bandwidths.

Optical dipole nanoantennas (NAs) are devices able to convert free-space radiation into nano-localized energy, thanks to the resonant coupling between the collective excitations (named "plasmons") of their conduction electrons and the incoming light. NAs guarantees deep sub-wavelength localization and strong enhancement of the electric field, which have been used, for example, to enhance Raman scattering and direct infrared absorption. In the past few years, we have investigated THz resonant dipole NAs [5,6], showing that they can confine THz radiation on a scale a thousand times smaller than the wavelength, with a field enhancement factor F (namely, the ratio of the local electric field to the illuminating field) of several hundreds at the NA extremities. This represents a promising feature for THz sensing, since the absorption of an object scales with F^2.

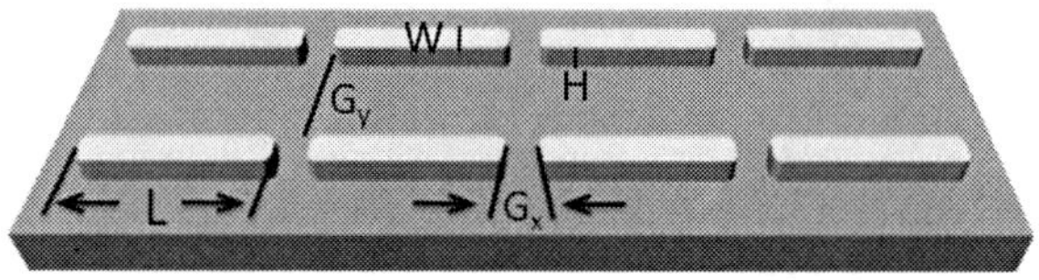

Fig. 1. Sketch of a portion of a THz NA array and definition of geometrical parameters.

By employing properly designed THz NAs, we demonstrated "NA Enhanced THz Spectroscopy" [7,8]. We prepared an array (5x5 mm^2) of gold NA chains (Fig. 1, L = 8 μm, W = 200 nm, H = 60 nm, G_y = 14 μm) coupled through nanogaps of width G_x = 20 nm, which guarantee an improved local field enhancement. The resonance of the NA array was tuned to match the phonon absorption band of Cadmium Selenide quantum dots (QDs) at 5.65 THz. A monolayer of QDs with a diameter of 5 nm was then spin-coated over the NA array and THz transmission spectroscopy was performed on the sample. When the THz polarization was set perpendicular to the long axis of the NAs (non-resonant illumination) the presence of the QDs could not be detected. Conversely, when the polarization was aligned to the NA long axis, a destructive interference peak centered at the QD phonon resonance appeared over the NA spectral response. We estimated that about half of the detected QD absorption signal resulted from the nano-objects located within the nanogaps, each of which contained roughly 150 QDs. This was made possible by a significant absorption enhancement within the gaps ($F^2 > 10^6$).

The proposed THz spectroscopic technique requires only a coarse alignment between the NA resonance and the sample absorption bands, which can be easily retrieved using a simple analytical model [7]. Novel improved NA designs for intensified THz radiation - matter interactions within nanoscale volumes will be discussed on site.

REFERENCES

[1] Terahertz Spectroscopy: Principles and Applications, ed. S. L. Dexheimer, *CRC Press*, (2007).

[2] G. Gallot, et al., *J. Opt. Soc. Am. B* **17**, 851 (2000).

[3] J. F. O'Hara, et al., *Opt. Express* **16**, 1786 (2008).

[4] H.-R. Park, et al., *Nano Lett.* **13**, 1782 (2013).

[5] L. Razzari, et al., *Opt. Express* **19**, 26088 (2011).

[6] L. Razzari, et al., *Plasmonics* **8**, 133 (2013).

[7] A. Toma, et al., *Nano Lett.* **15**, 386 (2015).

[8] R. Piccoli, et al., Terahertz Nanoantennas for Enhanced Spectroscopy, in Terahertz Spectroscopy - A Cutting Edge Technology, ed. J. Uddin, *InTech*, (2017).

L.R. is grateful for financial support from the Natural Sciences and Engineering Research Council of Canada (NSERC) and PRIMA Quebec.

Bi-Anisotropic Homogenization for Efficient Metasurface Design *(invited)*

Zhaxylyk A. Kudyshev
School of Electrical and Computer Engineering and Birck Nanotechnology Center
Purdue University
West Lafayette, USA
zkudyshev@purdue.edu

Ludmila J. Prokopeva
School of Electrical and Computer Engineering and Birck Nanotechnology Center
Purdue University
West Lafayette, USA
lprokop@purdue.edu

Maowen Song
School of Electrical and Computer Engineering and Birck Nanotechnology Center
Purdue University
West Lafayette, USA
song491@purdue.edu

Sajid Choudhury
School of Electrical and Computer Engineering and Birck Nanotechnology Center
Purdue University
West Lafayette, USA
sajidmc@purdue.edu

Alexander V. Kildishev
School of Electrical and Computer Engineering and Birck Nanotechnology Center
Purdue University
West Lafayette, USA
kildishev@purdue.edu

***Abstract*—In order to develop metasurfaces and fully analyze their functionalities, it is important to have an accurate and efficient model to describe a unit cell, as well as possibility to realize large scale device performance analysis. In this work we propose bi-anisotropic homogenization method suitable for large-scale simulations in frequency and time domains. First, the proposed method is probed with various types of metasurface designs at normal incidence in frequency domain. Then, we demonstrate its generalization for oblique incidence and extend this technique to time-domain simulations.**

Keywords— metamaterials, metasurfaces, bi-anisotropic homogenization

I. Introduction

Metamaterials, a class of engineered materials (En-Mats), have been used for manipulating light to achieve optical properties not existing in nature, including negative index of refraction, optical magnetism, and superlensing [1-3]. 2D variation of EnMats, so called metasurfaces, attracted significant interest due to their relatively simple fabrication, lack of propagation losses, and versatile ability to control the wavefront of light. Metasurfaces can already offer a line of prospective building blocks for a new generation of transformative on-chip applications [4], including nm-scale planar optics such as achromatic flat lenses, circular polarizers, half-wave and quarter wave plates [5,6], etc.

To design and optimize metasurfaces, it is important to have an accurate and efficient model describing the optical response of a unit cell. On the other hand to fully analyze their functionalities, it is vital to have a way to simulate a large scale device entirely. That becomes a problem for conventional full wave solvers due to their limitations in required computational resources. In this work we propose to use a multiscale approach, utilizing a bi-anisotropic (BA) homogenization technique to significantly improve computational efficiency of metasurface modeling, without sacrificing the predictive accuracy of numerical simulations.

The authors acknowledge the financial support by DARPA/DSO Extreme Optics and Imaging (EXTREME) Program, Award HR00111720032.

II. BA Homogenization

The electromagnetic waves propagating inside the BA structure satisfy the following material equation for the field components of a normally incident plane wave [7]:

$$\begin{pmatrix} \mathbf{D} \\ \mathbf{B} \end{pmatrix} = c^{-1} \begin{pmatrix} z_0 \boldsymbol{\varepsilon} & \mathbf{u} \\ \mathbf{v} & z_0^{-1} \boldsymbol{\mu} \end{pmatrix} \begin{pmatrix} \mathbf{E} \\ \mathbf{H} \end{pmatrix}$$

here $\boldsymbol{\varepsilon}, \boldsymbol{\mu}$ are the relative permittivity and permeability tensors, and $\mathbf{u}, \mathbf{v}$ are the bi-anisotropic tensors, z_0 is a free space impedance and c is a speed of light. The diagonal terms of $\mathbf{u}, \mathbf{v}$ model the mirror asymmetry effect (chirality) and their off-diagonal terms are responsible for breaking the directional symmetry of the propagating wave.

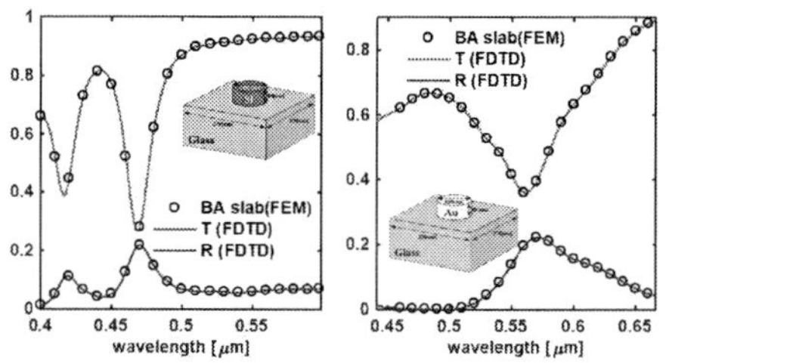

Fig.1. Results of BA homogenization applied to the resonant dielectric (right) and plasmonic (left) structures. Solid curves show the results of FDTD simulations of the full structure, dots depict the results obtained from the FEM model with the equivalent BA slab.

The core idea of this multiscale approach is to represent a nanostructure as a homogeneous slab with BA material properties. Governing equation which determines a relation between the complex reflection and transmission coefficients with effective material parameters can be formulated as follows [8]

$$\begin{pmatrix} z_0\varepsilon & \mathbf{u}' \\ \mathbf{v} & z_0^{-1}\boldsymbol{\mu} \end{pmatrix} = \frac{1}{ik_0 l}\mathbf{N}^{-1}\ln\left(\mathbf{V}_2\mathbf{V}_1^{-1}\right),$$

where all four illumination states are grouped together in $\mathbf{V}_1$ and $\mathbf{V}_2$ matrixes, l is a thickness of the metasurface, $\mathbf{N}$ is a unity tensor, k_0 is a free space wavevector.

Figure 1 shows the results of BA homogenization applied to resonant dielectric and plasmonic nano-antenna cases. Solid curves show the results of full wave simulations (FDTD) of the nanostructures, while dots depict the results obtained with a finite element method (FEM) with a homogenized BA slab using retrieved material parameters. Insets show the unit cell configurations. The comparison clearly indicates that the proposed method gives a very good agreement with full wave simulations, achieved through less expensive computational efforts.

III. LARGE SCALE SIMULATIONS

One of the problems that could be addressed with BA homogenization is full device simulation, which is very difficult, or even impossible with conventional full wave solvers.

This multiscale approach can be arranged in four main steps: (a) construct a library of the homogenized unit cells (BA tiles) with all possible BA parameters of a given metasurface; (b) reconstruct a desired metasurface based on the stored BA tiles; (c) determine the output near field distribution from the metasurface using the BA transfer matrix for each metasurface tile; (d) then, obtain far zone field distribution, by applying the computationally efficient Huygens–Fresnel principle as shown in Fig. 2.

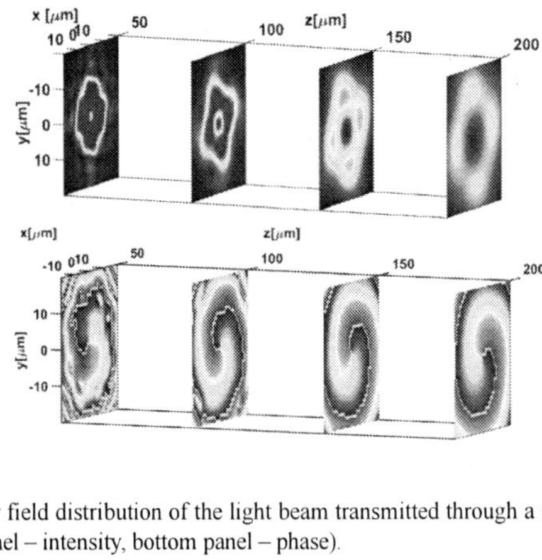

Fig. 2. Far field distribution of the light beam transmitted through a metasurface (upper panel – intensity, bottom panel – phase).

IV. GENERALIZED DISPERSIVE MATERIAL (GDM) MODEL FOR BA SLAB

Once the parameters of the equivalent BA slab for a given unit cell are calculated within a given frequency range, we can obtain a dispersion curve for each component of BA tensors that can be analytically approximated with a GDM model [9]. The approximated dispersion can be also linked to the geometrical and material parameters of the unit cell. Thus, we can control the dispersive features by tuning the unit cell parameters. Most importantly, the GDM model provides an efficient way to simulate the structure in the time domain [9].

Previously, analytical dispersion models for ideal cases (e.g. with PEC boundaries) were demonstrated (see, for example [10]). Here, we show that dispersive functions, consisting of several poles, can be derived for other cases of BA tiles.

V. CONCLUSION

We demonstrate that the multiscale approach with BA homogenization can be extremely useful for efficient design and optimization problems of optical metasurfaces. The proposed methodology opens up vast possibilities to realize large scale simulations of metasurface-based devices, which can bring us to more realistic and comprehensive problem solution. Generalization of the proposed method to the oblique incidence case combined with the GDM characterization of the retrieved dispersion, could lead to even more efficient analysis of the large scale EnMat design and optimization problems in time and frequency domains.

REFERENCES

[1] V. M. Shalaev, "Optical negative-index metamaterials," Nat. Photonics 1(1), 41–48, 2007.

[2] J. B. Pendry, "Negative refraction makes a perfect lens," Phys. Rev. Lett., 85(18), 3966–3969, 2000.

[3] D. Schurig, J. J. Mock, B. J. Justice, S. A. Cummer, J. B. Pendry, A. F. Starr, and D. R. Smith, "Metamaterial electromagnetic cloak at microwave frequencies," Science, 314(5801), 977–980, 2006.

[4] N. Engheta, "Antenna-guided light," Science, 334(6054), 317–318, 2011.

[5] X. Ni, N. K. Emani, A. V. Kildishev, A. Boltasseva, and V. M. Shalaev, "Broadband light bending with plasmonic nanoantennas," Science, 335(6067), 427–427, 2012.

[6] A. V. Kildishev, A. Boltasseva, and V. M. Shalaev, "Planar Photonics with Metasurfaces", Science, 339(6125), 1232009, 2013

[7] A. V. Kildishev, J. D. Borneman, X. Ni, V. M. Shalaev, and V. P. Drachev, "Bianisotropic effective parameters of optical metamagnetics and negative-index materials," Proc. IEEE 99(10), 1691–1700, 2011.

[8] A. Shaltout, V. M. Shalaev, and A. V. Kildishev, "Homogenization of bi-anisotropic metasurfaces", Opt. Exp. 21(19), 21941-21950, 2013.

[9] L. J. Prokopeva, J. D. Borneman, A. V. Kildishev, "Optical dispersion models for time-domain modeling of metal-dielectric nanostructures", IEEE Transactions on Magnetics, 47(5), 1150-1153, 2011.

[10] C. E. Kriegler, M. S. Rill, S. Linden, & M. Wegener, "Bianisotropic photonic metamaterials", IEEE J. Sel. Topics Quantum Electron., 16(2), 367-375, 2010.

The Constitutive Effective Parameters of Two-Dimensional Multilayered Dielectric Grating Slab

Quang Nguyen and Amir I. Zaghloul
US Army Research Laboratory,
Adelphi, MD, 20783
93nguyen@cua.edu, amir.i.zaghloul.civ@mail.mil

Mario J. Mencagli and Nader Engheta
Department of Electrical and Systems Engineering,
University of Pennsylvania,
Philadelphia, PA, 19104
mencagli@seas.upenn.edu, engheta@ee.upenn.edu

***Abstract*—The 2D regular lattice of multilayered dielectric resonant inclusions made from different dielectric and/or magnetic material embedded in the slab is considered in this paper. An equivalent magneto-dielectric slab is found using the first-principles homogeneous theory for extracting the effective permittivity and permeability. Example is presented to study the relationship between the physical parameters of multilayered dielectric inclusions arranged in 2D lattice and their effective parameters. This study can be used as a tool for designing metamaterials with negative permittivity and/or permeability using multilayered dielectric grating slab.**

***Index Terms*—Metamaterial, multilayered dielectric inclusion, negative permittivity, negative permeability.**

I. Introduction

MEDIUM with negative permittivity and/or permeability known as epsilon-negative (ENG) and/or mu-negative (MNG) metamaterials can be formed by regular lattice of metallic or dielectric resonant structures. The most metamaterials have been developed so far based on metallic resonant structures. Recently, many works have been reported the use of dielectric resonant inclusions [1], [2]. Furthermore, most of the previous works had been focused on magneto-dielectric spheres, cylinders or disks arranged in 3D lattice for designing metamaterials. In many practical cases, dielectric cube embedded in the slab are more appealing because of the simple fabrication. Additionally, having multilayered dielectric/magnetic cube can add more degree of freedom for designing metamaterials.

The use of effective constitutive parameters has been useful in describing and predicting the properties of waves in metamaterials, which can be used as the rule of thumb for designing materials. The most common techniques to retrieve those parameters are Nicolson-Ross-Weir (NRW) approaches which are based on inverting Fresnel equations of the equivalent slab [3]. However, these constitutive parameters retrieved by the NRW approaches for metamaterial medium may not satisfy some of the important conditions for permittivity and permeability, as extensively shown in [4].

In this paper, we analyze the metamaterial composed of multilayered dielectric cubes arranged in 2D lattice, as depicted in Fig. 1, to study the relationship between the physical parameters of dielectric cubic inclusions and their equivalent effective parameters. The constitutive effective parameters are obtained by using the first-principles homogeneous theory [4]. The S-parameters of the equivalent magneto-dielectric slab using the extracted permittivity and permeability are compared with the S-parameters obtained by full-waves electromagnetic (EM) simulation tool, FEKO.

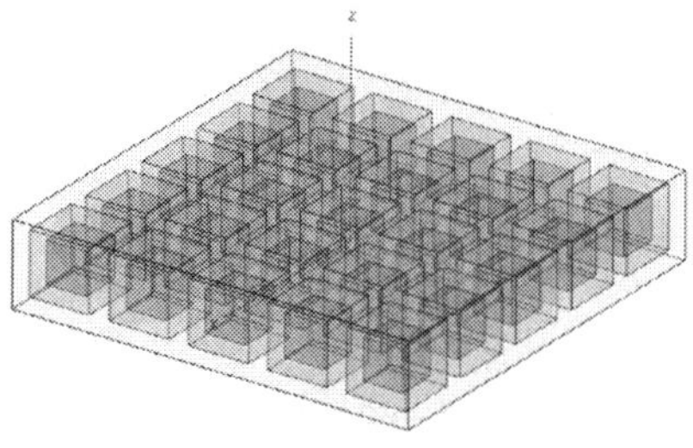

Fig. 1. Geometry of 2D multilayered dielectric grating slab.

II. The Frist-Principles Approach

In this section, we briefly discuss the first-principles homogeneous theory (FPHT), pioneered by Alu [4], which is used to extract the effective permittivity and permeability of dielectric grating slab here. This approach can be summarized in two steps as follows: (i) the electric and magnetic polarizabilities of the individual inclusion are calculated using either measured or simulated S-parameters of planar array of inclusions, and (ii) these polarizabilities are then substituted into the expressions obtained in [4] in order to find bulk the effective permittivity, ε_r, and effective permeability, μ_r. The complete discussion of FPHT can be found in [4].

Calculating the polarizabilities of the inclusion is essential in FPHT. Unlike existing schemes, we calculate the polarizabilities through S-parameters obtained from the EM simulation tool, FEKO [5]. This approach can be proven to be general.

III. ANALYSIS OF MULTILAYERED DIELECTRIC RESONANT INCLUSION

The geometry of single unit cell inclusion considered in this work is shown in Fig. 2. It is assumed that the unit cell is periodic in the x and y directions and has thickness a_1 in z direction. The unit cell inclusion is composed of two concentric cubes of side lengths a_1, a_2 with $a_1 > a_2$, surrounded by host material with permittivity ε_0 and μ_0. The concentric layers are assumed to be made of isotropic homogeneous materials, which have relative permittivity ε_1, ε_2, and permeabilities μ_1, μ_2, as indicated in the figure.

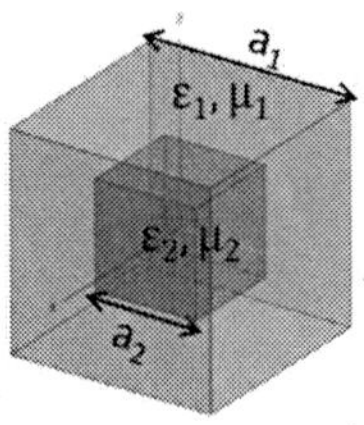

Fig. 2. Unit cell of a cubic resonator composed of two concentric layers.

TABLE I. THE PARAMETERS OF CUBIC RESONATOR

a_1	a_2	ε_1	ε_2	μ_1	μ_2
2.4mm	1.2mm	1	1000	5	1

The S-parameters (amplitude and phase) for cubic resonator arranged in 2D array, having parameters indicated in Table I, are computed using FEKO, assuming a plane wave that propagates along the z axis of the Cartesian coordinate system with its electric field directed along the x axis. As we can see in Fig. 3, there are two resonant regions, which correspond to the magnetic resonant (happened at lower frequency) and electric resonant (happened at higher frequency). These resonances will result in the peak in the effective permeability and permittivity, respectively.

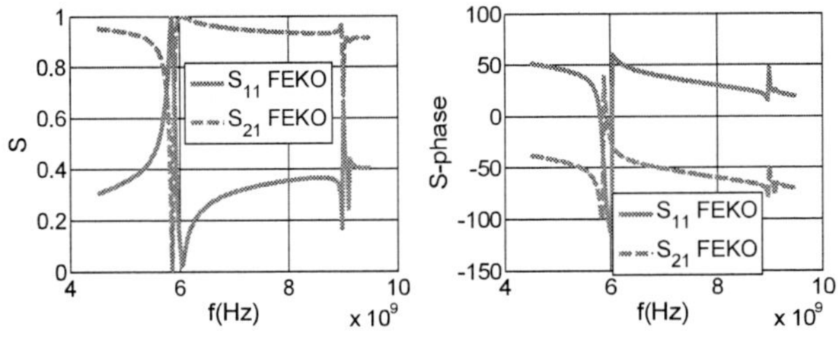

Fig. 3. Magnitude and phase of simulated S-parameters for cubic resonator.

Once we obtain S-parameters from FEKO, using the approach described in [5] we calculate the electric polarizability, α_{ee}, and magnetic polarizability, α_{mm}, as depicted in Fig. 4. The magneto-electric polarizability, α_{em}, term is ignored due to the symmetry of cubic resonator. The peak in α_{ee} and α_{mm} are corresponding to the peak in S-parameters which indicate electric and magnetic resonance. The effective permittivity, ε_r, and effective permeability, μ_r can be found by substituting α_{ee} and α_{mm} into the expressions in [4], as seen in Fig. 5. Fig. 6 shows the comparison between S-parameters from equivalent slab and S-parameters from FEKO. One can notice a good agreement between the two results.

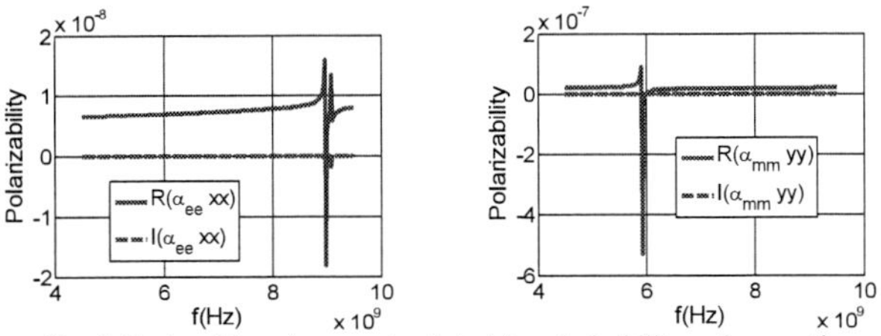

Fig. 4. Real and imaginary parts of electric polarizability and magnetic polarizability of cubic resonator as shown in Fig. 2.

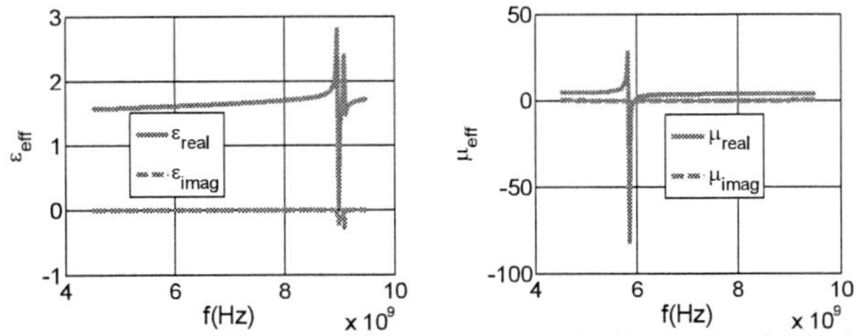

Fig. 5. Constitutive permittivity and permeability of cubic resonator in Fig. 2 using the FPHT [4].

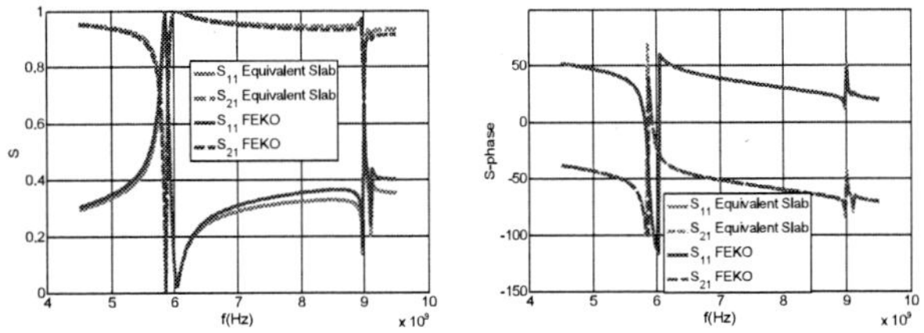

Fig. 6. Comparison between S-parameters from equivalent slab and S-parameters from FEKO.

IV. CONCLUSIONS

In this work, we study 2D regular lattice of multilayered dielectric resonant inclusions. S-parameters obtained from the equivalent slab using the extracted permittivity and permeability based on FPHT [4]. The resulting S-parameters agree well with numerical results obtained by FEKO.

REFERENCES

[1] P. Moitra, B. A. Slovick, Z. G. Yu, S. Krishnamurthy, and J. Valentine, "Experimental demonstration of a broadband all-dielectric metamaterial perfect reflector," *Applied Physics Letters*, vol. 104, no. 17, p. 171102, 2014.

[2] I. Staude, A. E. Miroshnichenko, M. Decker, N. T. Fofang, S. Liu, E. Gonzales, J. Dominguez, T. S. Luk, D. N. Neshev, I. Brener, and Y. Kivshar, "Tailoring directional scattering through magnetic and electric resonances in subwavelength silicon nanodisks," *ACS Nano*, vol. 7, no. 9, pp. 7824-7832, 2013.

[3] A. M. Nicolson and G. F. Ross, "Measurement of the intrinsic properties of materials by time domain techniques," *IEEE Trans. Instrum. Meas.*, vol. IM-17, pp. 395-402, Dec. 1968.

[4] A. Alu, "First-principles homogenization theory for periodic metamaterials," *Physical Review B*, vol. 84, no. 7, 2011.

[5] T. D. Karamanos, S. D. Assimonis, A. I. Dimitriadis, and N. V. Kantartzis. "Robust technique for the polarisability matrix retrieval of bianisotropic scatterers via their reflection and transmission coefficients," *IET Microwaves, Antennas & Propagation*, vol. 8, no. 15, pp. 1398-1407, 2014.

Optimization of Plasmonic Metasurfaces for Subtractive Color Filtering

Walied Sabra
School of Electrical and Computer Engineering and Birck Nanotechnology Center
Purdue University
West Lafayette, USA
Physics Department, Faculty of Sciences,
Beni-Suef University,
Beni-Suef, Egypt
wabdelha@purdue.edu

Maowen Song
School of Electrical and Computer Engineering and Birck Nanotechnology Center
Purdue University
West Lafayette, USA
Key Lab of Optoelectronic Technology and Systems of Education Ministry of China
Chongqing University
Chongqing 400044, China

Shaimaa I. Azzam
School of Electrical and Computer Engineering and Birck Nanotechnology Center
Purdue University
West Lafayette, USA
sazzam@purdue.edu

Arafa H. Aly
Physics Department, Faculty of Sciences,
Beni-Suef University,
Beni-Suef, Egypt
arafaaly@aucegept.edu

Alexander V. Kildishev
School of Electrical and Computer Engineering and Birck Nanotechnology Center
Purdue University
West Lafayette, USA
kildishev@purdue.edu

***Abstract*—We demonstrate an optimization process to obtain subtractive reflective color filters based on plasmonic metasurface arranged of silver cylindrical nanoantennas. In our study, colors are produced by absorbing light of specific wavelengths and reflecting the remaining spectrum. Accordingly, we can get different subtractive color filters from the reflected spectrum such as yellow, magenta, and cyan. Our results show that we obtain higher absorption resonance peaks (reflection dips) which give good performance for the proposed devices.**

Keywords—plasmonic metasurface, subtractive color filter, reflectance spectra, objective function

I. Introduction

Subtractive color filters can be produced by absorbing certain wavelengths of the white light while the combination of the reflected spectrum gives rise to other colors such as yellow, magenta, and cyan. This process can be achieved by using plasmonic metasurfaces where the interaction between the light and the surface plasmons results in resonant absorption due to either localized surface plasmons (LSPs) or surface plasmon polaritons (SPPs), or both of them depending on the proposed plasmonic structure as reported in the literature [1-4]. In our work, we report numerical results of subtractive color filters (SCFs) based on plasmonic metasurfaces by using an optimization process. The problem here is to find the values of the design parameters that yield the best SCF performance. Accordingly, we compute the target reflectance spectra for each SCF depending on the specific band for the primary color (blue, green, and red) in the visible range. Then, by using a commercial solver built on the finite element method in the frequency domain (COMSOL Multiphysics, Wave Optics Module), we obtain simulated results of SCFs close to the target cases.

The authors acknowledge the financial support by DARPA Extreme Optics and Imaging (EXTREME) Program.

II. Numerical Results

In our optimization model, we consider the objective function to be the root mean square deviation (RMSD) that gives the measure of differences between the target reflectance spectra and the simulated one. In other words, our objective function gives the equivalent error between the target and simulated results. The target subtractive color filters are computed based on specific ranges of the primary colors blue, green, and red in the visible spectrum. The selected ranges are (420 - 490 nm), (495 - 570 nm), and (580 - 660 nm) for blue, green, and red colors, respectively [5]. The proposed objective function in our optimization set up is given by Eq. 1:

$$Objective = \sqrt{\sum_{\lambda_i}^{\lambda_f} (R_T - R_S)^2 / N}, \quad (1)$$

where λ_i and λ_f are the initial and final wavelengths values of the visible spectrum range, respectively ($\lambda_i = 400$ and $\lambda_f = 750$ nm); the scalar quantities R_T and R_S are representing the target and simulated reflectance spectra, respectively. N is the number of points for the wavelength range of the visible spectrum.

The proposed unit cell of the plasmonic metasurface structure is shown in Fig. 1. It is arranged of a periodic array of silver cylindrical nanoantennas on top of a dielectric spacer made of silicon dioxide (SiO2) with thicknesses of 30 nm, 45 nm, and 80 nm for cyan, magenta, and yellow SCFs, respectively. A back-reflector of silver with a thickness of 100 nm on top of a SiO2 substrate is used to ensure that the metasurface works in the reflection mode. The period of the square unit cell is P = 150 nm, 200 nm, and 270 nm for yellow, magenta, and cyan SCFs, respectively. The permittivity data for silver is taken from Ref [6]. The normal incident plane wave comes from the top in the negative direction of z-axis and we applied periodic boundary condition for x and y directions. The simulated results of yellow, magenta, and cyan SCFs obtained by the proposed optimization process compared to the target color filters are shown in Fig. 2. Each color filter is obtained for different dimensions of the plasmonic cylindrical nanoantenna as shown in Fig. 2, where these parameters are considered as design (control) variables in our optimization process. All these results are obtained based on the Nelder-Mead optimization algorithm that supports variations in the geometry of the structure [7-8]. From these results, yellow filter in Fig. 2 (a) is obtained due to the combination of the reflected green and red colors where the absorption peak resonance is obtained at a wavelength of 450 nm. Magenta filter in Fig. 2 (b), is obtained due to a combination of the reflected blue and red colors where the absorption peak resonance is obtained at a wavelength of 534 nm. In Fig. 2 (c), the reflected blue and green colors give a cyan filter at a resonance wavelength of 628 nm. Based on these results, we get higher absorption resonance peaks (approximately perfectly absorption peaks) that give a good saturation for the proposed subtractive colors as shown in the insets of Fig. 2 corresponding to each subtractive color filter.

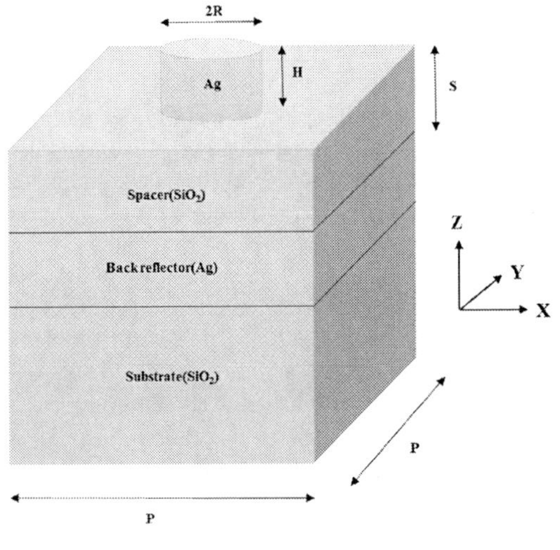

Fig. 1. Schematic diagram of the unit cell of the proposed plasmonic metasurface structure where 2R and H are respectively the diameter and height of the silver cylindrical nanoantenna. S is the dielectric spacer thickness.

III. V. CONCLUSION

The proposed optimization process is a straightforward process that generates subtractive reflective color filters based on plasmonic metasurfaces. The numerical results show that higher absorption peaks resonance (reflection dips) can be obtained at visible wavelengths. These absorption peaks are obtained by the contribution of both localized surface plasmon resonance (LSPR) and surface plasmon polariton resonance (SPPR). This leads to producing colors by absorbing light of specific wavelengths and reflecting the remaining bands. In this case we can have different subtractive color filters from the reflected spectrum. This approach can be used in color printing and other related applications.

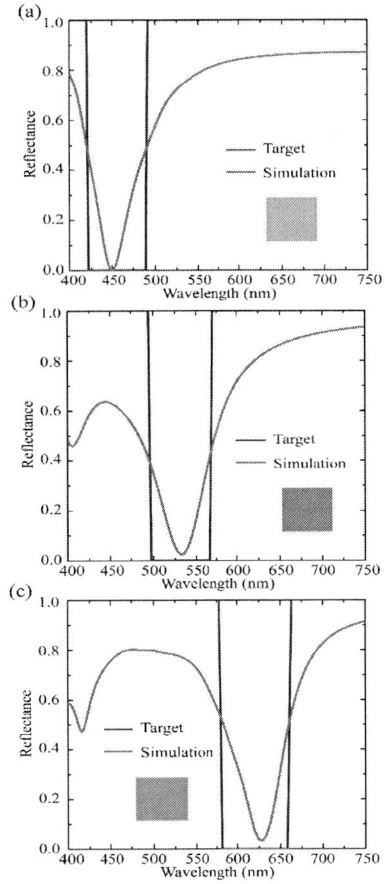

Fig. 2. Simulated reflectance compared to the target spectra. (a) Yellow filter is obtained at (R = 49.456 nm and H = 40.353 nm). (b) Magenta filter is obtained at (R = 30.307 nm and H = 20 nm). (c) Cyan filter is obtained at (R = 38.938 nm and H = 20.979 nm).

REFERENCES

[1] K. Kumar, H. Duan, R. S. Hegde, S. C. W. Koh, J. N. Wei, and J. K. W. Yang, "Printing colour at the optical diffraction limit," Nature Nanotechnology, 7, pp. 557–561, 2012.

[2] A. S. Roberts, A. Pors, O. Albrektsen, and S. I. Bozhevolnyi, "Subwavelength plasmonic color printing protected for ambient use," Nano Lett., 14 (2), pp. 783–787, 2014.

[3] V. R. Shrestha, S.-S. Lee, E.-S. Kim, and D.-Y. Choi, "Aluminum plasmonics based highly transmissive polarization-independent subtractive color filters exploiting a nanopatch array," Nano Lett., 14 (11), pp. 6672–6678, 2014.

[4] M. Miyata, H. Hatada, and J. Takahara, "Full-color subwavelength printing with gap-plasmonic optical antennas," Nano Lett., 16 (5), pp. 3166-72, 2016.

[5] T. J. Bruno and P. D. N. Svoronos, "CRC Handbook of fundamental spectroscopic correlation charts," CRC Press, ISBN 9780849332500, 2005.

[6] A. D. Rakic, A. B. Djurisic, J. M. Elazar, and M. L. Majewski, "Optical properties of metallic films for vertical-cavity optoelectronic devices," Applied Optics, 37 (22), pp. 5271-5283, 1998.

[7] A. R. Conn, K. Scheinberg, and L. N. Vicente, "Introduction to derivative-free optimization, MPS-SIAM series on optimization," SIAM, 2009.

[8] D. Lee and M. Wiswall, "A parallel implementation of the simplex function minimization routine," Computational Economics, 30 (2), pp. 171–187, 2007.

Millimeter-Wave Electromagnetic Metasurfaces based on Perforated Dielectrics

Naquash A. Sheikh, Khaled Madhoun, Sonya Stuhec-Leonard and Shulabh Gupta
Department of Electronics, Carleton University, Ottawa, Ontario,
Canada, scottstewart@cmail.carleton.ca

***Abstract*—A Huygens' unit cell configuration based on perforated dielectrics is proposed and demonstrated using full-wave simulations. The proposed unit cell consists of a high permittivity dielectric resonator surrounded by a honey-comb lattice. The Honey comb structure provides mechanical integrity to the unit cell, thereby enabling the unit cell scaling to mm-wave frequency bands. Two different designs are shown to demonstrate diversity of transmission characteristics achievable through the proposed cells.**

I. Introduction

Metasurfaces are two dimensional arrays of sub-wavelength electromagnetic (EM) scatterers, which are the dimensional reduction of more general volumetric metamaterial structures [1] and functional extensions of Frequency Selective Surfaces (FSSs). By engineering the electromagnetic properties of the scattering particles, the metasurface can be used to manipulate and engineer the spatial wavefronts of the incident waves. In this way, they provide a powerful tool to transform incident fields into specified transmitted and reflected fields [2][3].

An attractive class of metasurfaces is a *Huygens' metasurface*, which is constructed using a 2D array of electrically small Huygen's sources, which provide perfect impedance matching to free-space, due to an optimal interaction of the electric and magnetic dipole moments ($\mathbf{p}$ and $\mathbf{m}$) constituting the metasurface [4]. An efficient implementation of Huygens' metasurfaces is using all-dielectric resonators [5]. They are ideal for providing wave-shaping, particularly in transmission, due to their zero reflection response. The wave-shaping operation to transform input wavefronts into specified output wavefronts, typically requires a complete control of the transmission magnitude and phase response of the metasurface, *independently*, i.e. a full phase coverage of 2π radians and a transmission magnitude between $[0-1]$, for a passive structure.

In this paper, a new Huygens' unit cell configuration is proposed, which is suitable for mm-wave implementations, due to its simple configuration, ease of fabrication and compatibility to standard printed circuit board (PCB) implementation, while maintaining good electromagnetic performances.

II. Proposed MM-Wave Metasurface

A. Conventional Huygen's Unit Cells

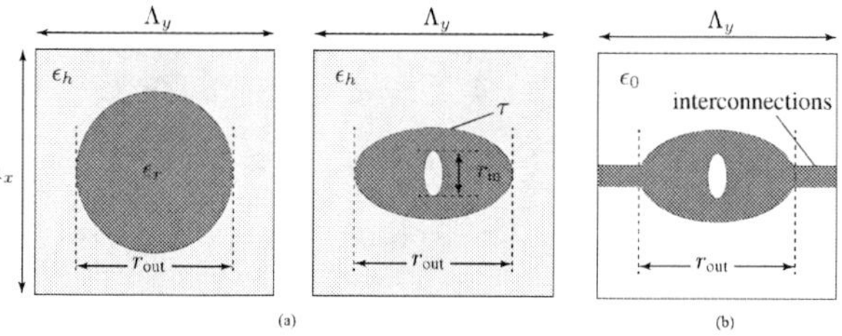

Fig. 1. Various all-dielectric unit cells for wave-shaping applications. a) cylindrical and elliptical ($\tau = r_{\text{in}}/r_{\text{out}}$) unit cells for transmission phase control maintaining full transmission. b) Elliptical-Cylindrical unit cell for phase control.

Figure 1Various all-dielectric unit cells for wave-shaping applications. a) cylindrical and elliptical ($\tau = r_{\text{in}}/r_{\text{out}}$) unit cells for transmission phase control maintaining full transmission. b) Elliptical-Cylindrical unit cell for phase controlfigure.1(a) shows a conventional all-dielectric metasurface unit cell structure, which is typically repeated along two dimensions to construct the entire metasurface. Unit cell comprises of a dielectric resonator (ϵ_r) surrounded by a low permittivity host medium (ϵ_h). Upon incidence of an input plane wave, the electric and magnetic dipole responses of the dielectric resonators are excited. If the coupled dielectric resonators are designed such that the induced electric dipoles $\mathbf{p}$ and magnetic dipoles $\mathbf{m}$ occur at the same frequency and have the same quality factor, it ensures backscattering and thereby full-transmission in the forward direction. By modifying the shape of the resonator, such as using an elliptical shape, a wide coverage of resonant frequencies can be achieved, while maintaining good transmission characteristics.

At microwave frequencies, interconnections are typically used to provide mechanical support for the dielectric resonators [6], as shown in Fig. 1Various all-dielectric unit cells for wave-shaping applications. a) cylindrical and elliptical ($\tau = r_{\text{in}}/r_{\text{out}}$) unit cells for transmission phase control maintaining full transmission. b) Elliptical-Cylindrical unit cell for phase controlfigure.1(b). They do not have any electromagnetic role, but are purely required for physical realizations of the device. When excited with a wave polarized perpendicular to the interconnections, a good transmission characteristics can be easily achieved. However, these interconnections cause poor performance for the other orthogonally polarized wave, and thus are not ideal when operating the metasurface for dual polarization. Furthermore, as frequency is increased, these interconnections become physically thin, thereby risking the mechanical integrity of the metasurface structure.

B. Proposed Structure

Considering the limitation of the frequency scaling of the unit cell structure with single interconnections, a new unit cell is proposed, as shown in Fig. 2Proposed all-dielectric Huygens' unit cell based on perforated dielectricsfigure.2. It consists of a single high permittivity dielectric material, which is perforated to expose a central dielectric region, which acts as a dielectric resonator of arbitrary shape.

The perforations in the dielectric layer lead to reduction of the permittivity, as required resulting in an effective permittivity, much lower than the original value. A honeycomb perforation structure is an optimal choice for this, as it provides an ideal material to air ratio, in a tight lattice space. A honeycomb shaped interconnection, in addition, provides a strong background mechanical support, for a given interconnection thickness $\Delta\ell$. The proposed honeycomb interconnection provide the required mechanical support to hold the dielectric resonators together and the structure is easily fabricated using standard laser drilling processes.

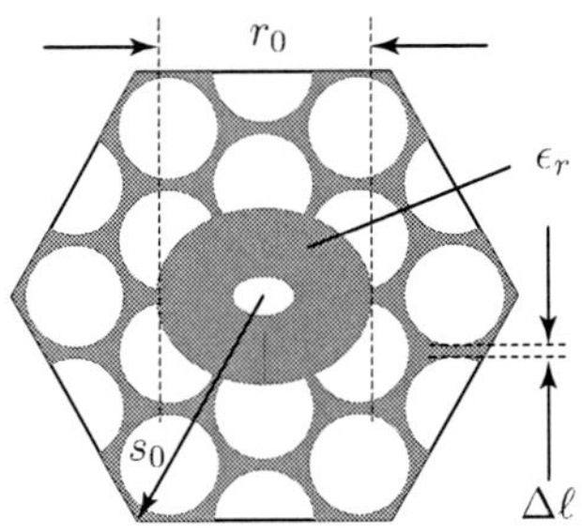

Fig. 2. Proposed all-dielectric Huygens' unit cell based on perforated dielectrics.

III. Results

The FEM-HFSS results of the proposed hexagonal unit cell are shown in Fig. 3FEM-HFSS simulated transmission, reflection and dispersion response of the proposed unit cell based on RO 3006 ($\epsilon_r = 6.15$) with interconnection width of 10 mils, exhibiting different responses for each wave polarization. Each side of the unit cell is 6.6 mmfigure.3. The material is 150 mils thick Rogers RO3006, with a relative permittivity of 6.15. The interconnection thickness $\Delta\ell = 10$ mils and the puck ellipticity is 0.75. The periodicity is modelled using Floquet (periodic) boundary conditions in HFSS. The unit cell is excited with a uniform plane wave normally incident on the metasurface, with two orthogonal polarizations E_x and E_y.

The full-wave S-parameters of Fig. 3FEM-HFSS simulated transmission, reflection and dispersion response of the proposed unit cell based on RO 3006 ($\epsilon_r = 6.15$) with interconnection width of 10 mils, exhibiting different responses for each wave polarization. Each side of the unit cell is 6.6 mmfigure.3 shows that both the polarizations are well matched, with good transmission in a wide frequency band. Furthermore, its dispersion (group delay) response is different for both polarizations as expected due to elliptic shape, with different group delay maxima. Therefore, the cell provides good electromagnetic performance for both polarizations. Since, both polarizations are well matched, but exhibit different dispersion profiles, it can be easily used as a linear-to-circular polarization convertor at two specific frequencies.

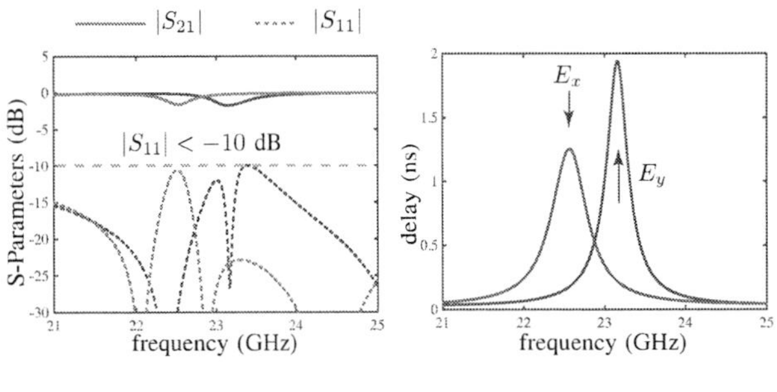

Fig. 3. FEM-HFSS simulated transmission, reflection and dispersion response of the proposed unit cell based on RO 3006 ($\epsilon_r = 6.15$) with interconnection width of 10 mils, exhibiting different responses for each wave polarization. Each side of the unit cell is 6.6 mm.

Finally Fig. 4FEM-HFSS simulated transmission, reflection and dispersion response of the proposed unit cell based on RO 3010 ($\epsilon_r = 10.2$) with interconnection width of 5 mils, exhibiting identical responses for both polarizations. Each side of the unit cell is 5.53 mmfigure.4 shows another unit cell design, made of RO 3010 dielectric of permittivity 10.2. The dielectric puck in this case is cylindrical with unity ellipticity. Due to structure symmetry, both polarizations exhibit identical responses, as also shown in Fig. 4FEM-HFSS simulated transmission, reflection and dispersion response of the proposed unit cell based on RO 3010 ($\epsilon_r = 10.2$) with interconnection width of 5 mils, exhibiting identical responses for both polarizations. Each side of the unit cell is 5.53 mmfigure.4.

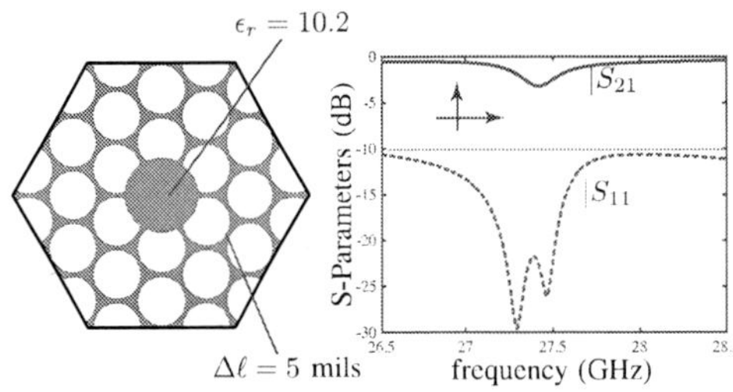

Fig. 4. FEM-HFSS simulated transmission, reflection and dispersion response of the proposed unit cell based on RO 3010 ($\epsilon_r = 10.2$) with interconnection width of 5 mils, exhibiting identical responses for both polarizations. Each side of the unit cell is 5.53 mm.

IV. Conclusions

A Huygens' unit cell configuration based on perforated dielectrics has been proposed and demonstrated using full-wave simulations. The proposed unit cell consists of a high permittivity dielectric resonator surrounded by a honey-comb lattice. By controlling the material filling factor, a lower effective permittivity is obtained around the resonator, required for constructing it as a Huygens' source. The Honey comb structure, in addition, provides mechanical integrity to the unit cell, thereby enabling the unit cell scaling for mm-wave bands. Finally, two different designs have been shown to provide either same or different electromagnetics responses for two orthogonal polarizations, demonstrating the diversity of transmission characteristics achievable through the proposed cells.

REFERENCES

[1] C. Holloway, E. F. Kuester, J. Gordon, J. O'Hara, J. Booth, and D. Smith, "An overview of the theory and applications of metasurfaces: The two-dimensional equivalents of metamaterials," *IEEE Antennas Propag. Mag.*, vol. 54, no. 2, pp. 10–35, April 2012.

[2] V. S. Asadchy, I. A. Faniayeu, Y. Ra'di, S. A. Khakhomov, I. V. Semchenko, and S. A. Tretyakov, "Broadband reflectionless metasheets: Frequency-selective transmission and perfect absorption," *Phys. Rev. X*, vol. 5, p. 031005, Jul 2015.

[3] C. Pfeiffer and A. Grbic, "Metamaterial huygens' surfaces: Tailoring wave fronts with reflectionless sheets," *Phys. Rev. Lett.*, vol. 110, p. 197401, May 2013.

[4] E. Saenz, I. Semchenko, S. Khakhomov, K. Guven, R. Gonzalo, E. Ozbay, and S. Tretyakov, "Modeling of spirals with equal dielectric, magnetic, and chiral susceptibilities," *Electromagnetics*, vol. 28, no. 7, pp. 476–493, 2008.

[5] S. Jahani and Z. Jacob, "All-dielectric metamaterials," *Nature Nanotechnology*, vol. 2, no. 11, pp. 23–36, Jan 2016.

[6] K. Achouri, A. Yahyaoui, S. Gupta, H. Rmili, and C. Caloz, "Dielectric resonator metasurface for dispersion engineering," *IEEE Transactions on Antennas and Propagation*, vol. 65, no. 2, pp. 673–680, Feb 2017.

Implicit and Explicit FDTD Methods for Modelling EM Metasurfaces

Tom J. Smy, Scott A. Stewart and Shulabh Gupta
Department of Electronics, Carleton University, Ottawa, Ontario,
Canada, scottstewart@cmail.carleton.ca

***Abstract*—A numerical comparison between the explicit and implicit finite difference time-domain (FDTD) methods is presented for simulating broadband and dispersive metasurfaces. It has been found that, while the implicit method is rigorous in computing the scattered fields in both reflection and transmission region of the metasurface, care must be taken using the explicit method, which is applicable under paraxial wave propagation conditions only.**

I. Introduction

Two finite difference time-domain (FDTD) methods - Explicit [1] and Implicit [2] - have been recently proposed, to simulate broadband and dispersive electromagnetic metasurfaces, for specified constitutive parameters of the metasurface. While the explicit method is developed for paraxial wave propagation cases, the implicit method rigorously models the metasurface without making any approximations. In this work, these two methods are discussed and compared, highlighting their benefits and drawbacks, along with quantifying the errors involved in explicit due to the paraxial approximations.

A zero thickness metasurface is a space-discontinuity and can be modelled using Generalized Sheet Transition Conditions (GSTCs) that were developed by Idemen, and were later applied to metasurface problems in [3]. The modified Maxwell-Faraday and Maxwell-Ampere equations can be written in the time-domain for a uniaxial metasurface, for instance, as,

$$\hat{z} \times \Delta\mathbf{H} = \frac{d\mathbf{P}_{||}}{dt}, \quad \Delta\mathbf{E} \times \hat{z} = \mu_0 \frac{d\mathbf{M}_{||}}{dt} \tag{1}$$

where $\Delta\psi$ represents the differences between the fields on the two sides of the metasurface for all the vector component of the field ψ, which could be either the $\mathbf{H}$ or $\mathbf{E}$ fields. The other terms $\mathbf{P}_{||}$ and $\mathbf{M}_{||}$ represent the electric and magnetic surface susceptibility densities, *in the plane of the metasurface*, which depend on the total average fields at the metasurface [4].

The FDTD method proposed in [1], simulates the time-domain scattered fields from a broadband metasurface, for frequency dispersive surface susceptibilities ($\tilde{\chi}_{\text{ee}}$ and $\tilde{\chi}_{\text{mm}}$). The susceptibilities in this method are expressed as series expansions in terms of Lorentzian contributions, given by

$$\tilde{\chi}(\omega) = \sum_{i=1}^{N} \frac{\omega_{p,i}^2}{(\omega_{0,i}^2 - \omega^2) + i\alpha_i\omega} \tag{2}$$

where ω_p, ω_0 and α are the plasma frequency, resonant frequency and the loss-factor of the oscillator, respectively. This Lorentzian model not only presents a causal model of the metasurface, it can be easily described in time-domain using a second-order differential equation relating the polarizations with their respective field excitations. Moreover, by varying the various parameters of the Lorentzian contributions, a general space-time modulated metasurface can be naturally modelled.

II. Explicit vs Implicit Method

The explicit method of [1], solves (1) and (2) for a given input field, to compute the time-domain scattered fields (transmitted and reflected fields). In this method, the transmission and reflection regions are considered separately, and the field relations between the two are enforced using the GSTCs. The explicit method, thus treats metasurface as a boundary of each transmission and reflection regions. This explicit method further assumes *paraxial wave conditions*, where the scattered fields from the metasurface are treated as plane-waves, with small diverging angles, as is typically done in optics [5]. For example, if the metasurface lies in the $x - y$ plane, then the GSTCs of (1) can be expressed in simpler form as

$$\mu_0\frac{dM_t}{dt} - \mu_0\frac{dM_r}{dt} + \mu_0\frac{dM_0}{dt} = 2(E_0 + E_r - E_t) \tag{3a}$$

$$\frac{dP_t}{dt} + \epsilon_0\frac{dP_r}{dt} + \epsilon_0\frac{dP_0}{dt} = 2c(E_0 - E_t - E_r), \tag{3b}$$

where $c = 1/\sqrt{\mu_0\epsilon_0}$ is the speed of light in vacuum and $|H(z = 0_\pm)| = |E(z = 0_\pm)|/\eta$, with η being the free-space impedance, following the plane-wave approximation. The paraxial approximation thus lead to scalar field equations (to be solved for E-fields only), are valid for small variations of surface susceptibilities along the metasurface (or weakly diffracting aperatures) [5].

While the explicit method is simple to implement and applicable to modelling of large classes of optical metasurfaces, it is limited by the paraxial approximation. A rigorous numerical model shouldn't make this approximation and should solve the full vectorial E- and H-fields taking GSTCs into account. This method has been presented in [2], where the GSTCs were directly integrated in an FDTD Yee-Cell, along with the broadband and dispersive Lorentzian models of the surface susceptibilities (2). This method thus computes the total scattered field for arbitrary field excitations, and treats metasurface as a scattering devices, as opposed to boundaries as in explicit method. The drawback of implicit method is increased computational speed and resources compared to explicit method.

III. Method Comparison

To judge the accuracy and validity of the explicit method, let us consider a simple of case of wave refraction, where a normally incident plane-wave is converted into an oblique outgoing wave, using an uniaxial metasurface.

For the explicit method, let us further assume the metasurface to be *locally* matched (valid only for normal plane-waves), so that $\chi_{ee}(x) = \chi_{mm}(x)$, for a given frequency, ω_0 (2D problem considered here for simplicity). Next, by spatial modulation of the resonant frequencies of the Lorentzians, a linear phase gradient is created across the metasurface to a produce the wave refraction on the transmission side. Under paraxial approximations, the explicit method is restricted to small refraction angles only.

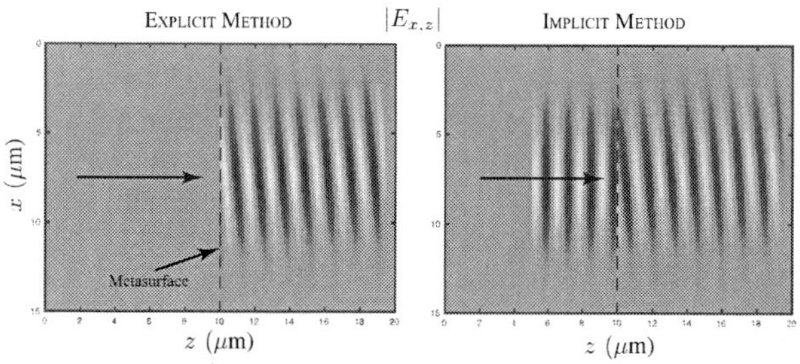

Fig. 1. Computed steady-state scattered fields from a linear phase gradient metasurface, excited with a normally incident Gaussian wave using a) explicit method, and b) implicit method. Fields are normalized and shown in linear scale. The phase gradient along x is $2\pi/15$ μm and the excitation wavelength is 1.3 μm.

Figure 1(a) shows the scattered fields computed using the explicit method. As expected, there are no reflections, and the transmitted fields are refracted following the linear phase gradient profile of the metasurface. The implicit method is next applied to this metasurface, and the corresponding total scattered fields are also shown in Fig. 1(a). A close agreement is seen between the two, suggesting that the explicit method is able to produce the transmitted fields correctly. Implicit method naturally has the incident fields on the reflection side.

Before making the conclusions on the accuracy of the explicit method with respect to the implicit method, let us consider the exact form of susceptibilities required to achieve wave refraction with zero reflection from the metasurface, given by [4]

$$\chi_{mm}(x) = \frac{2}{jk_0}\left(\frac{1-e^{-jk_0\sin\theta_0 x}}{1+\cos\theta_0 e^{-jk_0\sin\theta_0 x}}\right) \tag{4a}$$

$$\chi_{ee}(x) = \frac{2}{jk_0}\left(\frac{1-\cos\theta_0 e^{-jk_0\sin\theta_0 x}}{1+e^{-jk_0\sin\theta_0 x}}\right). \tag{4b}$$

Clearly, a perfect refractive metasurface with zero reflections, must exhibit *unequal* susceptibilities. In other words, if the two susceptibilities are assumed to be equal, as in Fig. 1, there must be non-zero reflections from the metasurface. Therefore, while the explicit method produced correct refraction angles of the transmission fields, zero reflection field is a consequence of the paraxial approximation made in this method, and is not correct rigorously.

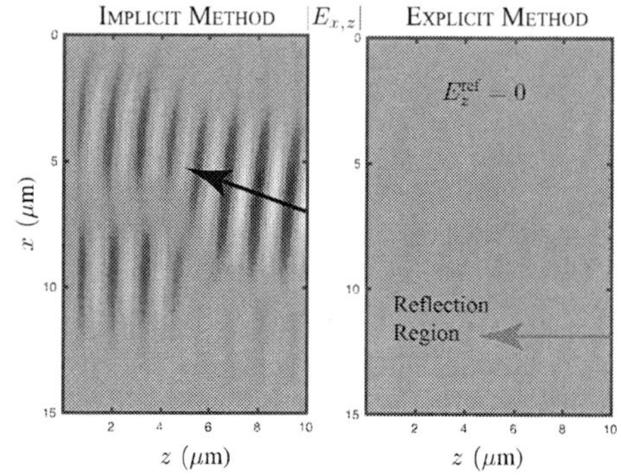

Fig. 2. Computed scattered fields in the reflection region only for the cases of implicit and explicit methods, for the example of Fig. 1.

The implicit method on the other hand, doesn't involve any approximations, and must produce finite reflection fields for the case of Fig. 1. Fig. 2 confirms this predictions, whereby the scattered fields in the reflection region only are shown using the two method. Finite reflection fields ($\approx 4\%$) are clearly seen in the implicit case, as opposed to zero fields in explicit, as expected.

IV. Conclusions

A numerical comparison between the explicit and implicit FDTD methods has been presented for simulating broadband and dispersive metasurfaces. It has been found that, while the implicit method is rigorous in computing the scattered fields in both reflection and transmission region of the metasurface, care must be taken using the explicit method, which assumes paraxial wave propagation conditions. A generalized refracting metasurface with zero reflections has been taken as an example to demonstrate and study the numerical error in field computations using the explicit method. An error of $\approx 4\%$ in field amplitudes has been found for the case considered.

References

[1] T. J. Smy and S. Gupta, "Finite-difference modeling of broadband huygens' metasurfaces based on generalized sheet transition conditions," *IEEE Transactions on Antennas and Propagation*, vol. 65, no. 5, pp. 2566–2577, May 2017.

[2] T. J. Smy, S. Stewart, and S. Gupta, "Integrated Generalized Sheet Transition Conditions (GSTCs) in a Yee-Cell based Finite-Difference Time-Domain (FDTD) Simulation of Electromagnetic Metasurfaces," *ArXiv e-prints*, Jun. 2017.

[3] E. F. Kuester, M. A. Mohamed, M. Piket-May, and C. L. Holloway, "Averaged transition conditions for electromagnetic fields at a metafilm," *IEEE Transactions on Antennas and Propagation*, vol. 51, no. 10, pp. 2641–2651, Oct 2003.

[4] K. Achouri, M. Salem, and C. Caloz, "General metasurface synthesis based on susceptibility tensors," *IEEE Trans. Antennas Propag.*, vol. 63, no. 7, pp. 2977–2991, July 2015.

[5] J. Goodman, *Introduction to Fourier Optics*. Roberts and Company Publishers; 3rd Edition edition, 2004.

28 GHz Propagation Channel Measurements for 5G Microcellular Environments

C.Umit Bas*, Rui Wang*, Seun Sangodoyin* , Sooyoung Hur†, Kuyeon Whang†,
Jeongho Park†, Jianzhong Zhang‡, Andreas F. Molisch*
*University of Southern California, Los Angeles, CA, USA
†Samsung Electronics, Suwon, Korea
‡Samsung Research America, Richardson, TX, USA

***Abstract*—This paper presents results from several 28 GHz propagation channel measurement campaigns performed with a real-time channel sounder that is capable of performing directionally-resolved channel measurements in dynamic environments. We summarize the key results from three measurement campaigns; microcellular in a residential environment, stationarity region, and dynamic scatterers measurements in urban environments.**

I. Introduction

The design and deployment of any wireless system requires a thorough understanding of the wireless propagation channel. Specifically for millimeter-wave (mm-wave) frequencies, due to the higher path- and penetration losses, any system operating over distances larger than a few meters will have to utilize beamforming antenna arrays [1], [2]. The statistics of the angular spectrum and their temporal variations should be taken into account when designing a system with such beamforming capabilities. However, almost all of the directional outdoor measurements for mm-wave frequencies were performed with rotating horn antenna channel sounders, which can no measure in real-time and thus are not suitable for dynamic channels [3].

In this paper, we summarize results from our recent channel sounding campaigns performed with a one-of-its-kind real-time mm-wave channel sounder [4], [5] which is described in Section II. Section III summarizes the results obtained in three measurement campaigns performed to investigate the different aspects of the microcellular environment at 28 GHz.

II. Measurement Setup

The channel sounder used in these measurements is a real-time mm-wave channel sounder [4], [5]. By using beamforming arrays, it can perform 90° sweeps in the azimuth at the RX and the TX. Furthermore, TX and RX are synchronized by using GPS-disciplined Rubidium frequency references without requiring a physical connection.

Table I. Sounder Parameters Used In Measurements

Parameters	Microcell [6]	Stationarity [7]	Dynamic [8]
Frequency	27.85 GHz		
Bandwidth	400 MHz		
Array size	8 by 2		
Beam steering	-45° to 45°		
3dB beam width	12°		
Steering steps	5°		10°
Switching speed	$2\mu s$		
TX EIRP	57 dBm		
RX noise figure	≤ 5 dB		
SISO duration	$2\ \mu s$		
SISO repetition	10	10	1
Total sweep time	14.44 ms	14.44ms	0.4 ms

Thanks to the flexible design, the operation parameters of the channel sounder can be modified on a per campaign basis. Table I summarizes the parameters used in the three measurement campaigns. For the residential microcell and stationarity region measurements, we employed SISO repetition to improve RX SNR by averaging. For the dynamic measurements, we only measured a subset of available azimuth beams to increase the MIMO repetition frequency to measure higher Doppler frequencies.

III. Measurement Campaigns

A. *Residential Microcell*

In [6], we investigated pathloss and delay spread in a suburban residential environment for a microcell and the impact that beamforming has on it. The obtained results also include the effect of the foliage, which is typical to a suburban street. The measurements were taken in two scenarios; first when the RX on the same street with the TX (denoted as line-of-sight (LOS), although most of the time the direct path was blocked by foliage), and when the RX is on a crossing street and the direct path is blocked by buildings.

The estimated parameters for the path loss model are summarized in Table II. The directional pathloss is calculated by using the power of the best TX-RX beam pair as the received power, while for the omnidirectional pathloss, we combine the power received via all TX-RX beams. The TX-RX distances for LOS measurements vary from 36 m to 400 m, and from 130 m to 273 m for the NLOS. Hence the provided pathloss model is only applicable within these ranges. Furthermore, the median root mean square delay spreads (RMS-DS) for the omnidirectional power delay profiles were estimated as 25.63 ns and 67.18 ns for LOS and NLOS respectively.

B. *Dynamic Environment*

In [8], we presented the first *dynamic* double directional measurements for a microcell scenario. A sample measurement location is shown in Fig. 1. During this measurement, both the

Table II. Parameters of the Path Loss Models

	Data	n	P_0	χ_σ σ	χ_σ P-Value
Omni	LoS - ABG Model	2.82	63.47	6.44	0.975
Omni	LoS- CI Model	2.92	61.34	6.45	0.978
Omni	NLoS - ABG Model	4.97	29.53	2.58	0.745
Omni	NLoS - CI Model	3.58	61.34	3.06	0.706
Directional	LoS - ABG Model	3.17	58.01	7.75	0.840
Directional	LoS - CI Model	3.15	61.34	7.76	0.928
Directional	NLoS - ABG Model	5.85	18.12	4.53	0.856
Directional	NLoS - CI Model	3.96	61.34	5.06	0.958

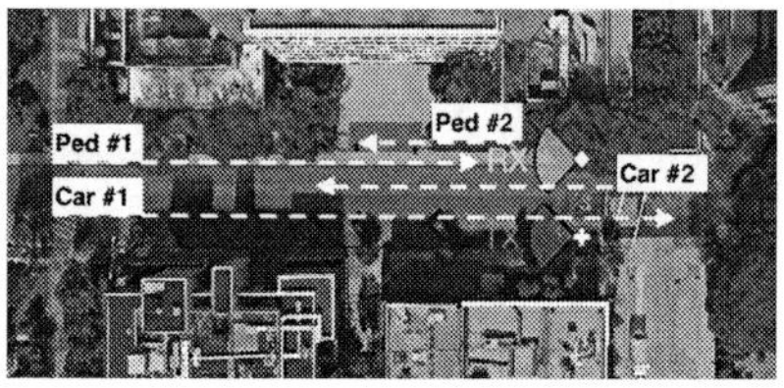

Fig 1. Environment for dynamic measurements.

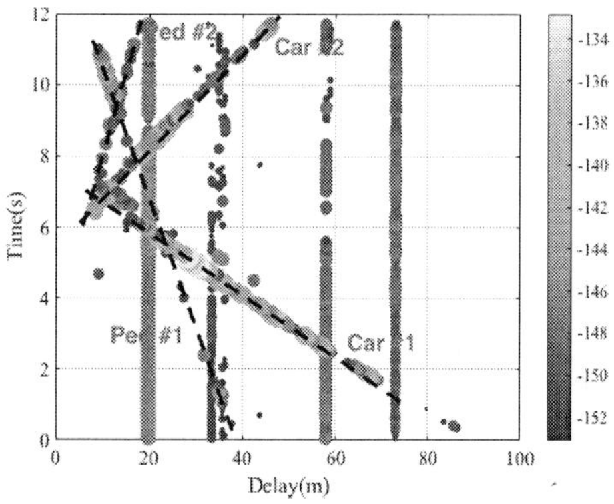

Fig 2. Temporal evolution of the power delay profile (dB).

RX and TX are placed parallel to the road facing the same direction and perform 90° scans in the azimuth. The TX is placed at 4 m height, while the RX is at 1.8 m. Along with some fixed objects, there are four moving objects; two cars and two pedestrians as indicated in Fig. 1.

Fig. 2 shows the power of the multipath components and their evolution over time. The multipath components for the four moving objects are clearly visible and their routes are marked in Fig. 2.

C. Stationarity Region

In a third campaign, we investigated the stationarity region of MIMO mm-wave channels at 28 GHz based on an outdoor measurement campaign. We analyzed results in an urban microcell LoS and LoS to NLoS transition region scenario, for the stationarity region of shadowing, power delay profile and the angular power spectrum [7].

We have found that the foliage effect can significantly alter the PL exponent even in the LoS scenario, which leads to the channel nonstationarity captured by our proposed dual-slope PL model. The propagation loss increases rapidly, about 30 dB, during the transition from LoS to NLoS. We propose to model it with a street-by-street PL model, similar to the method in [9]. More results related to the PL fitting can be found in Fig. 3. The autocorrelation distance of shadowing is 1.2 m in the LoS route, although this value might be affected by the signal variation observed in the two-path channel. It increases up to 4.8 m for the LoS to NLoS transition route. The average correlation distance as computed based on the similarity of PDP, is 0.9 m for the LoS route. It can become as high as 4 m at the beginning section of the transition route and drops to about 1.26 m afterward. The analysis based on the correlation of shadowing and PDP has suggested that mm-wave channels

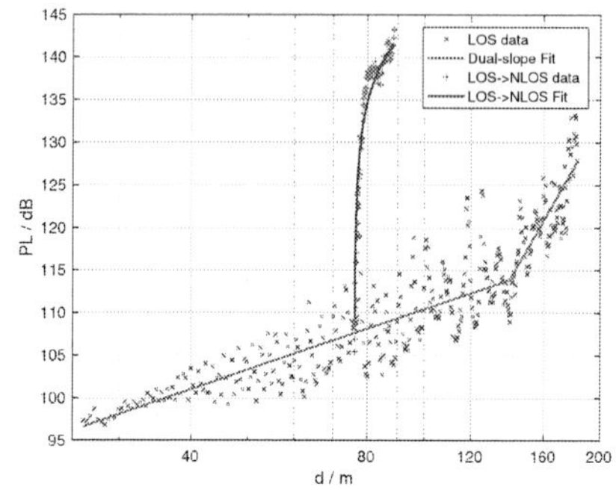

Fig 3. The pathloss data fitting for the microcell LoS and LoS to NLoS transition region scenarios.

exhibit a smaller stationarity region compared with cm-wave channels.

IV. Conclusions

This paper discusses results from various 28 GHz propagation channel measurements performed with a real-time double-directional channel sounder for three different investigations. Through extensive measurements allowed by the nature of the used channel sounder, we were able to propose statistical models for path loss, shadowing, RMS-DS and the stationarity region. Furthermore, we presented results from the first dynamic double directional measurement campaign for microcell environment at mm-wave frequencies.

Acknowledgements

Part of this work was supported by grants from the National Science Foundation and National Institute of Standards and Technology.

References

[1] F. Boccardi, R. W. Heath, A. Lozano, T. L. Marzetta, and P. Popovski, "Five disruptive technology directions for 5G," *IEEE Communications Magazine*, vol. 52, no. 2, pp. 74–80, February 2014.

[2] A. F. Molisch, A. Karttunen, R. Wang, C. U. Bas, S. Hur, J. Park, and J. Zhang, "Millimeter-wave channels in urban environments," in *2016 10th European Conference on Antennas and Propagation (EuCAP)*, April 2016, pp. 1–5.

[3] T. S. Rappaport, G. R. Maccartney, M. K. Samimi, and S. Sun, "Wideband millimeter-wave propagation measurements and channel models for future wireless communication system design," *Communications, IEEE Transactions on*, vol. 63, no. 9, pp. 3029–3056, September 2015.

[4] C. U. Bas, R. Wang, D. Psychoudakis, T. Henige, R. Monroe, J. Park, J. Zhang, and A. F. Molisch, "A real-time millimeter-wave phased array MIMO channel sounder," in *Vehicular Technology Conference, 2017. VTC 2017-Fall. IEEE*, September 2017.

[5] C. U. Bas, R. Wang, S. Sangodoyin, D. Psychoudakis, T. Henige, R. Monroe, J. Park, J. Zhang, and A. F. Molisch, "Real-time millimeter-wave MIMO channel sounder for dynamic directional measurements," submitted.

[6] C. U. Bas, R. Wang, S. Sangodoyin, S. Hur, K. Whang, J. Park, J. Zhang, and A. F. Molisch, "28 GHz microcell measurement campaign for residential environment ," in *2017 IEEE Global Communications Conference (GLOBECOM)*, December 2017.

[7] R. Wang, C. U. Bas, S. Sangodoyin, S. Hur, K. Whang, J. Park, J. Zhang, and A. F. Molisch, "Stationarity region of mm-wave channel based on outdoor microcellular measurements at 28 GHz," in *Military Communications Conference, MILCOM 2017- 2017 IEEE*, October 2017.

[8] C. U. Bas, R. Wang, S. Sangodoyin, S. Hur, K. Whang, J. Park, J. Zhang, and A. F. Molisch, "Dynamic double directional propagation channel measurements at 28 GHz," submitted.

[9] A. F. Molisch, A. Karttunen, S. Hur, J. Park, and J. Zhang, "Spatially consistent pathloss modeling for millimeter-wave channels in urban environments," in *2016 10th European Conference on Antennas and Propagation (EuCAP)*, April 2016, pp. 1–5.

Improving Millimeter-Wave Channel Models for Suburban Environments with Site-Specific Geometric Features

Yaguang Zhang, David J. Love,
Nicolo Michelusi, and James V. Krogmeier
School of Electrical and Computer Engineering
Purdue University
West Lafayette, IN 47907, USA
{ygzhang, djlove, michelus, jvk}@purdue.edu

Soumya Jyoti and Alex Sprintson
Department of Electrical
and Computer Engineering
Texas A&M University
College Station, TX 77843, USA
{soumyajyoti.jh, spalex}@tamu.edu

Christopher R. Anderson
Department of Electrical
and Computer Engineering
United States Naval Academy
Annapolis, MD 21402, USA
canderso@usna.edu

***Abstract*—This paper proposes simple procedures to improve traditional statistical millimeter-wave channel models for suburban environments with site-specific geometric features. Blockages by buildings and vegetation were considered and existing models were verified with measurement data for an emulated microcell deployment. The results indicate that a holistic, network-level approach for channel modeling will help deal with the high dependence of millimeter waves on site-specific features.**

***Index Terms*—channel modeling, millimeter wave, site-specific geometric features, suburban environments.**

I. Introduction

Millimeter wave (mm-wave) bands have become the most promising candidate for enlarging the usable radio spectrum in future wireless networks such as 5G [1]. Since frequent and location-specific blockages are expected at mm-waves, the challenge is understanding the propagation characteristics of mm-wave signals and accordingly predicting the channel state information as needed, so that the high mobility requirements of these wireless networks can be addressed in real-time.

The majority of current research has focused on urban areas with high population densities [1]–[3]. Very few measurement campaigns have been performed in suburban and rural environments. Moreover, statistical models for point-to-point links have received significant attention, but this approach ignores all or most of site-specific geometric features, which mm-waves are sensitive to due to blockages. In this paper, we explore this research gap by focusing on suburban environments and improving standard 5G channel models with site-specific geometric features.

II. Mm-Wave Propagation Measurements for Suburban Environments

An outdoor propagation measurement campaign was carried out at the United States Naval Academy (USNA) in Annapolis, Maryland. The transmitter (TX) was temporarily installed on the Mahan Hall clock tower to emulate a typical 5G suburban microcell deployment. A custom-designed broadband sliding correlator channel sounder was used as the receiver (RX) and moved around the campus to obtain path loss measurements. More details for the measurement setup can be found in [4].

Sponsorship for this work was provided by NSF under grant CNS-1642982.

III. Building Blockage Analysis

One approximately 200-m-long straight track was chosen for a continuous signal recording, to investigate the shadowing effect of buildings on a moving user. The resulting basic transmission losses are shown in Fig. 1 (a). The dotted lines illustrate the boundaries between the line-of-sight (LoS) area and the none-line-of-sight (NLoS) area due to blockages. As we can see, the most significant blockage was from Michelson Hall, which obstructed the southern half of the track. Rickover Hall partially blocked the track at the north end.

To estimate the path loss caused by building blockages, the knife-edge diffraction (KDE) model [3] was utilized. In our case, the Universal Transverse Mercator (UTM) coordinate system was extended with height to form a 3-dimensional (3D) space for computing the effective height of the obstructing screen, as well as the distances between the TX, the RX, and the screen. Note that the path obstruction may occur either on a horizontal roof edge or a vertical side edge of the building. Finally, the screen height was computed as the distance between the obstruction point and the direct Euclidean path between the TX and the RX. The resulting diffraction losses were used to shift the large-scale path loss predictions from the International Telecommunication Union (ITU) site-general model for propagations over rooftops [5]:

$$PL(d, f) = 10 \cdot \alpha \cdot \log_{10}(d) + \beta + 10 \cdot \gamma \cdot \log_{10}(f) + N(0, \sigma), \quad (1)$$

where d is the 3D direct distance between the TX and the RX in meters and f is the operating frequency in GHz. In our case, $f = 28$ GHz. The parameter values $\alpha = 2.29$, $\beta = 28.6$, $\gamma = 1.96$, and $\sigma = 3.48$, were chosen for the LoS propagation in a suburban environment [5], which are recommended by ITU for distances from 55 m to 1200 m at 2.2–73 GHz frequency.

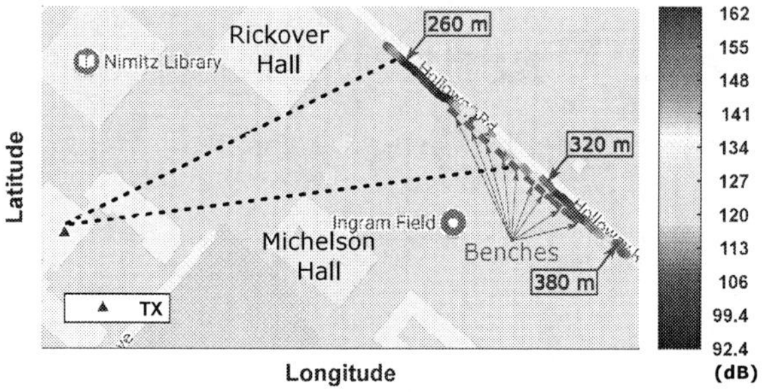

(a) Track with Basic Transmission Losses on Holloway Road

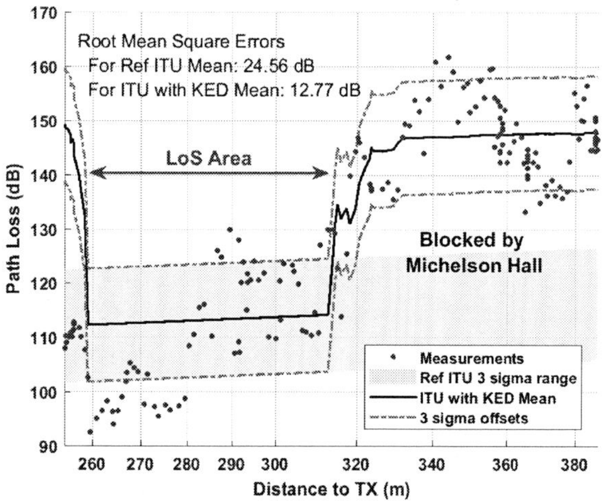

(b) Path Loss for the Modified ITU Model

Fig. 1. Considering building blockages to improve a statistical channel model. (a) Path losses on Holloway road illustrate the shadowing effect of buildings. The numbers in the boxes are distances to the TX. (b) After being shifted by diffraction losses, the ITU model closely follows the measurement results.

Fig. 1 (b) shows the final results. The ITU model provides path loss predictions in the form of Gaussian variables. Accordingly, 3-sigma ranges for both the original and shifted ITU models are shown and root mean square errors (RMSEs) are computed separately according to the mean of each model. As we can see, the modified ITU predictions follow the measurement data much better than the original ones, providing a RMSE improvement of 11.79 dB. Another observation is, for distances below 280 m, the original ITU model overestimated the path loss by around 20 dB. This may be caused by some strong reflection path(s). Also, the KED model overestimated the attenuation caused by Rickover Hall. This was probably because the blockage happened at the southern vertical edge of the building, which corresponds to a very short obstructing screen, whereas the KED model applies for a screen with infinite height. Still, the KED model helped identify the path loss peak below 260 m.

IV. Foliage Analysis

The effect of foliage for modeling mm-wave channel is a vital consideration for suburban environments as scattering and absorption at these frequencies can significantly attenuate

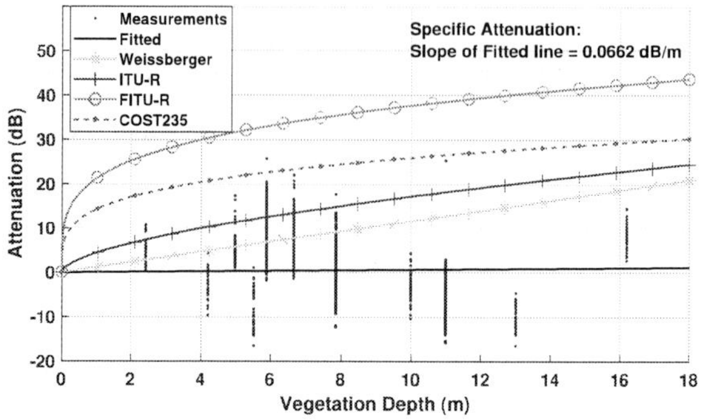

Fig. 2. Comparison of computed and measured path loss at 28 GHz.

the signal. In our measurement campaign, eleven sites had partial or total obstruction of the LoS signal from foliage, ranging from a single tree to a small grove of trees. Our measurement results were compared against four well known empirical models [6] that are valid in this frequency range: COST235, Weissberger, ITU-R and FITU-R models.

Fig. 2 illustrates our measured *excess* vegetation attenuation versus vegetation depth as well as existing model predictions. We can see that the mean measured value of foliage attenuation (0.07 dB/m) is significantly less than those of model-predicted values. In fact, our measurements demonstrate a significant amount of multipath energy arriving at the receiver, likely being scattered from other objects in the environment. As a result, we recorded a greater signal strength than what would be predicted by these simple single-path attenuation models.

V. Conclusion

In this paper, we illustrate two measurement- and geometry-based techniques for improving existing statistical mm-wave channel models. Our approach is suitable for a holistic, network-level model that utilizes side information and the results could be updated in real-time. Our techniques demonstrate a modest, but significant, overall improvement in propagation modeling accuracy.

References

[1] T. S. Rappaport, *et al.*, "Millimeter wave mobile communications for 5g cellular: It will work!," *IEEE Access*, vol. 1, pp. 335–349, 2013.

[2] G. R. MacCartney and T. S. Rappaport, "73 ghz millimeter wave propagation measurements for outdoor urban mobile and backhaul communications in new york city," in *IEEE International Conference on Communications (ICC), 2014*. IEEE, 2014, pp. 4862–4867.

[3] T. S. Rappaport, G. R. MacCartney, S. Sun, H. Yan, and S. Deng, "Small-scale, local area, and transitional millimeter wave propagation for 5g communications," *IEEE Transactions on Antennas and Propagation*, vol. 65, no. 12, pp. 6474–6490, 2017.

[4] Y. Zhang, *et al.*, "28-ghz channel measurements and modeling for suburban environments," in *IEEE International Conference on Communications (ICC), 2018*. IEEE, May 2018, to be published.

[5] ITU, "Propagation data and prediction methods for the planning of short-range outdoor radiocommunication systems and radio local area networks in the frequency range 300mhz and 100ghz," Tech. Rep., June 2017. [Online]. Available: https://www.itu.int/rec/R-REC-P.1411-9-201706-I/en

[6] H. M. Rahim, C. Y. Leow, and T. A. Rahman, "Millimeter wave propagation through foliage: Comparison of models," in *2015 IEEE 12th Malaysia International Conference on Communications (MICC)*, Nov 2015, pp. 236–240.

Analysis of Radar Altimeter Interference due to Wireless Avionics Intra-Communication Systems by Using Large-Scale FDTD Method

- Investigation on Airbus A320 Class Passenger Aircraft-

Shunichi Futatsumori, Kazuyuki Morioka, Akiko Kohmura, and Naruto Yonemoto
Surveillance and Communications Department, Electronic Navigation Research Institute
National Institute of Maritime, Port and Aviation Technology
Chofu, Tokyo, Japan
futatsumori@mpat.go.jp

Takashi Hikage, Tetsuya Sekiguchi, Manabu Yamamoto, and Toshio Nojima
Graduate School of Information Science and Technology
Hokkaido University
Sapporo, Hokkaido, Japan
hikage@wtemc.ist.hokudai.ac.jp

***Abstract*—Radio altimeters and wireless avionics intra-communication (WAIC) systems are both operated at the frequency band 4,200 MHz–4,400 MHz. Hence, a detailed analysis is required for spectrum sharing in the same band. Firstly, a large-scale finite-difference time-domain analysis is performed to obtain the detailed characteristics of the electromagnetic field (EMF) around the three-dimensional Airbus A320 aircraft model, which assumes that a WAIC device is located inside the cabin. Then, the 4-GHz EMF propagation characteristics are evaluated based on the analyzed results. Finally, the methodology of the interference analysis is discussed based on the obtained EMF characteristics.**

Keywords—aircraft, interference, large-scale finite-difference time-domain method, radio altimeter, wireless avionics intra-communication.

I. Introduction

Wireless avionics intra-communication (WAIC) systems are employed for wireless communications among sensors in an aircraft for monitoring and telemetry applications [1]. The usage scenario and the standardization of the WAIC systems have been widely studied in recent years. On the other hand, the electromagnetic compatibility (EMC) between the WAIC systems and the existing avionics systems requires to be investigated for further implementation. For WAIC systems, the frequency band 4,200–4,400 MHz is allocated. Radio altimeters are operated in the same frequency band as the WAIC systems. To investigate the EMC issues of the WAIC systems, the electromagnetic field (EMF) estimation method has been developed based on the large-scale finite-difference time-domain (FDTD) analysis [2], [3].

In this paper, the feasibility of the 4-GHz band radio altimeter interference investigation, which is due to WAIC systems, based on the large-scale FDTD method is discussed. The 4-GHz EMF propagation characteristics around the three-dimensional (3D) model of an Airbus A320 passenger aircraft are obtained by the FDTD analysis. In addition, the desensitization criteria of the radio altimeter are discussed and the EMF distributions are analyzed.

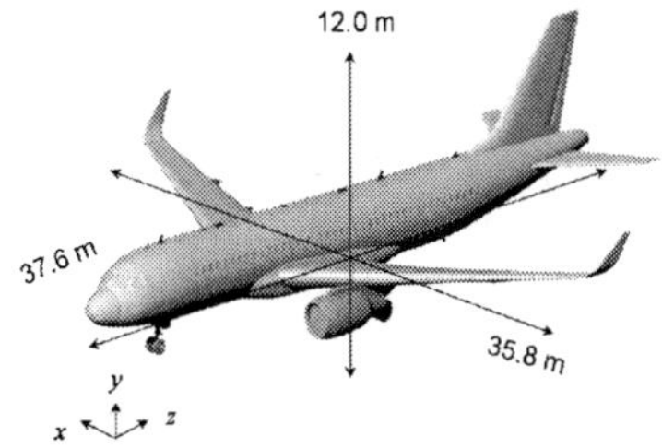

Fig. 1. Three-dimensional aircraft model based on Airbus A320-200.

II. Large-Scale FDTD Analysis at 4 GHz

The detailed distributions of the EMF that radiates from the WAIC device is estimated by using the FDTD analysis. The FDTD method is employed for the analysis because it is suitable to simulate complicated 3D models with various material constants. Fig. 1 and Fig. 2 show the overview of the 3D model based on Airbus A320-200 developed for analysis purposes and the cabin configurations, respectively. This model is developed based on a commercially available 3D aircraft model [3]. In addition, an in-house FDTD program is used for the analysis. As shown in the figures, the outlines and the internal structure of the model are designed to have the dimensions of the actual aircraft.

The aircraft structures such as the body, cabin partition, lavatory, galley, and ceiling luggage rack consist of a perfect electric conductor. On the other hand, some structures such as the seat ($\varepsilon_r = 2.0$, $\sigma = 3.02 \times 10^{-3}$ S/m), the cabin floor and the inside panel wall ($\varepsilon_r = 3.5$, $\sigma = 1.51$ S/m), and the windows ($\varepsilon_r = 2.25$, $\sigma = 8.34 \times 10^{-4}$ S/m) have limited electric conductivity [3]. This is because some materials used inside the aircraft cabin are nonflammable and have electromagnetic lossy characteristics. No passengers are modeled in the aircraft cabin to obtain the

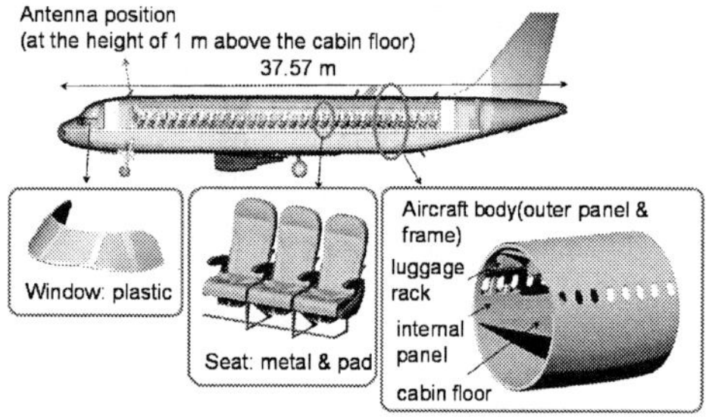

Fig. 2. Cabin configurations of the aircraft model.

TABLE I. PARAMETERS OF FDTD ANALYSIS

Problem Space (mm^3)	18,125 × 12,245 × 37,625
Cell size (mm)	5
Number of cells	3,625 × 2,449 × 7,525
Frequency (GHz)	4.4
A. B. C.	CPML (10 layers)
Number of nodes	40
Required memory	6,400 GB
Antenna	1/2 dipole (0.1 W input power)

fundamental characteristics of the EMF propagation around the aircraft. The transmitting antenna is located at 1 m above the cabin floor as shown in Fig. 2. As this analysis is a feasibility investigation, parameters such as the antenna type, height, and input power will be varied in the future.

III. ELECTROMAGNETIC FIELD CHARACTERISTICS

Table I shows the parameters used in the FDTD analysis. Uniform 5-mm cubic cells are used for the analysis. In addition, to reduce the size of the memory required for the analysis, a perfect magnetic conductor is modeled at the center of the aircraft. The numbers of cells including the 10-layer convolutional perfectly matched layer (CPML) absorbing boundary condition (ABC.) were 3,625 × 2,449 × 7,525. Assuming that the WAIC system operates at the 4-GHz band, the transmitting frequency is set as 4.4 GHz. A HITACHI SR16000 M-1 supercomputer is employed for the analysis. The number of analysis nodes and required memory are 40 nodes and 6,400 GB, respectively. Fig. 3 and Fig. 4 show the typical analyzed two-dimensional electric-field (E-field) strength distributions at the *xy*-plane and *yz*-plane, respectively. As shown in the figure, detailed EMF distributions are obtained both inside and outside the aircraft.

The desensitization criteria of the radio altimeter are defined as follows [4]:

$$N = -114dBm + 10\log(B_{R,IF}) + N_F, \tag{1}$$

$$I_{T,IF} \geq N - 6dB, \tag{2}$$

where $B_{R,IF}$ is the IF bandwidth of the radio altimeter in MHz and N_F is the noise figure at the receiver input in dB, respectively. In addition, $I_{T,IF}$ is the interference power threshold at which the radio altimeter performance starts to degrade. Radio altimeter characteristics such as $B_{R,IF}$ and N_F are described in the [4]. The interference power can be directly calculated from the para-

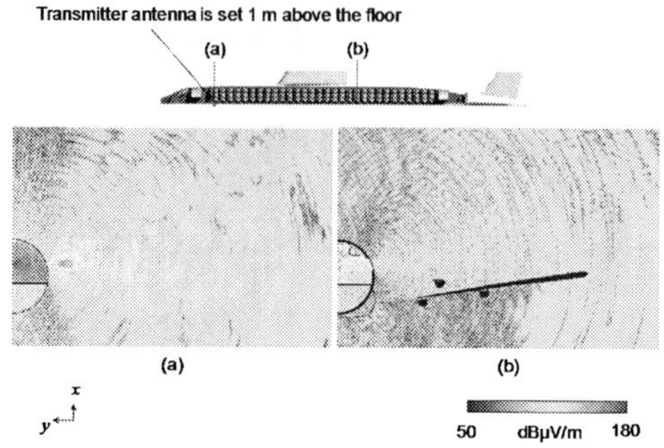

Fig. 3. Typical analyzed two-dimensional E-field strength distributions at the *xy*-plane. (a) E-field strength at the location of the antenna. (b) E-field strength at the middle of the aircraft body.

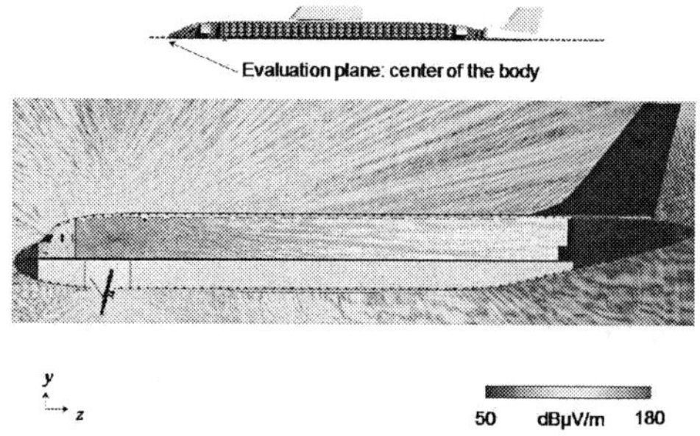

Fig. 4. Typical analyzed two-dimensional E-field strength distributions at the *yz*-plane.

meters of the radio altimeter antenna.

IV. CONCLUSIONS

The feasibility of radio altimeter interference investigation using the FDTD method were discussed. The detailed EMF propagation characteristics around the A320 class passenger aircraft at 4 GHz were obtained for analyzing the interference due to the WAIC systems. In addition, the desensitization criteria of the radio altimeter were defined for the future interference assessments based on the large-scale FDTD analysis. The sensitivity degradation of the radio altimeter by the WAIC devices will be analyzed and investigated in the future.

REFERENCES

[1] International Telecommunication Union, "Technical characteristics and operational objectives for wireless avionics intra-communications (WAIC)," Report M.2197-0, Nov. 2011.

[2] T. Hikage, K. Yahagi, M. Shirafune, T. Nojima, S. Futatsumori, A. Kohmura, and N. Yonemoto, "Numerical estimation of WAIC-band propagation characteristics in aircraft cabin using large-scale FDTD analysis," Proceedings of the 2016 IEEE International Symposium on Antennas and Propagation and USNC-URSI National Radio Science Meeting, TH-UB.5P.6, June 2016.

[3] K. Yahagi, M. Shirafune, T. Hikage, M. Yamamoto, T. Nojima, S. Narahashi, S. Futatsumori, A. Kohmura, and N. Yonemoto, "Large-scale FDTD analysis of 4.4 GHz-band propagation characteristics in aircraft cabin," Proceedings of the 2016 International Symposium on Antennas and Propagation, 3B1-3, pp. 566-567, Oct. 2016.

[4] International Telecommunication Union, "Operational and technical characteristics and protection criteria of radio altimeters utilizing the band 4 200-4 400 MHz," Report M.2059-0, Feb. 2014.

Recent Advances in Spatiotemporally-Modulated (STM) Magnetless Circulators

Dimitrios L. Sounas, Ahmed Kord, and Andrea Alù

Department of Electrical and Computer Engineering
The University of Texas at Austin
Austin, U.S.A.
dimitrios.sounas@utexas.edu, ahmed.kord@gmail.com, alu@mail.utexas.edu

***Abstract*—We present our recent advances on the design of spatiotemporally modulated (STM) magnetless circulators based on angular-momentum biasing. We show the two main topologies that can be used to design such devices, in particular wye with series *LC* resonators and delta with parallel *LC* resonators, and discuss their respective advantages. We show how we can reduce insertion loss by cancelling the additional harmonics resulting from modulation through the use of a differential topology. We also show how we can extend the bandwidth by adding passive matching circuits at the ports of the circulator. Finally, we discuss the implementation of such devices in an integrated circuit.**

Keywords*— *angular-momentum biasing, magnetless circulators, nonreciprocity, spatiotemporal modulation.

I. Introduction

Circulators are nonreciprocal elements with three or more ports, which support unidirectional signal transmission between the ports, e.g., from ports 1, 2, 3 to 2, 3, 1 in a three-port circulator [1]. Circulators are necessary for the design of full-duplex systems, since they allow to connect a receiver and a transmitter operating over the same channel to the same antenna, while at the same time they provide the isolation between them that is necessary in order to prevent saturation of the sensitive receiver circuits from the strong transmitter signal [2]. Conventionally, circulators are based on magnetic materials biased with a static magnetic field, but this approach is not very attractive for integration due to the large cost of such materials related to their scarcity in nature, their incompatibility with integrated circuit technology and the limitation imposed on the minimum size by the biasing magnets. For this reason, the design of magnetless circulators has recently received a lot of attention. Different approaches have been investigated towards this end. One interesting possibility is to use transistor-based circuits by using the inherent nonreciprocal properties of transistors when operated as active elements [3]-[8]. However, this approach is subject to limitations in terms of power handling and noise performance. Another option is to use time variant circuits, exploiting the fact that the reciprocity theorem is derived under the assumption of linear, time-invariant materials [9]-[24]. This approach does not require the use of active elements and as a result it can lead to better power and noise performance than active circulators.

One important type of STM circulators that we have developed in our group is based on the concept of angular momentum biasing [20]-[25]. In particular, starting from a more general form of the reciprocity theorem, according to which reciprocity can be broken through biasing with any quantity that is asymmetric under time reversal, we have shown the possibility of designing devices with giant nonreciprocity through biasing with the angular momentum vector. In the case of circuits, angular momentum biasing can be obtained by modulating the circuit in space and time so that we make it look rotating in a particular direction. In this direction, an appealing approach is to use a symmetric loop of three resonators modulated by signals of the same frequency, the same amplitude and a phase of 0, 120 and 240 deg. Modulation can be implemented either through varactors or switches, with the latter approach being very attractive for integrated circuits. During the past years, we have shown how this concept can be used to design circulators with very large isolation, however with suboptimal performance in other metrics, such as insertion loss, bandwidth, power handling and intermodulation products.

During this talk, we will present our latest developments in the area of angular-momentum STM circulators, showing that these devices can be designed to exhibit exceptional performance in all the metrics that are important for deployment in practical communication systems. We will first present the two main topologies that can be used, in particular a wye topology with series *LC* resonators and a delta topology with parallel *LC* resonators, and discuss their respective advantages. We will discuss the advantages of the parallel-delta topology in terms of power handling, stemming from the fact that a parallel *LC* resonator amplifies the current, but not the voltage, which is responsible for the nonlinear effects. Another important issue in STM circulators are the intermodulation products, which increase insertion loss and create interference problems. We show how we can eliminate these products by using a differential connection of two circulators with a phase difference of 180 deg for their modulation signals. Finally, we will cover the issue of designing broadband circulators and show how it can be addressed by adding passive matching circuits at the circulator ports. In this context, we will present an analytical theory for determining the required impedance in order to achieve a desired bandwidth which can be combined with filter-synthesis techniques to obtain the required matching networks. Our results will demonstrate that STM circulators can already meet many of the specifications required in the implementation of the next generation of full-duplex systems and therefore consist a viable option for the design of such systems.

ACKNOWLEDGMENT

This work was supported by a Qualcomm Innovation Fellowship, the Air Force Office of Scientific Research, the Defense Advanced Research Projects Agency, Silicon Audio, the Simons Foundation, and the National Science Foundation.

REFERENCES

[1] D. M. Pozar, Microwave engineering. John Wiley & Sons, 2009.

[2] D. Bharadia, E. McMilin, and S. Katti, "Full duplex radios," *ACM SIGCOMM Computer Comm. Rev.*, vol. 43, no. 4, pp. 375-386, 2013.

[3] S. Tanaka, N. Shimomura, and K. Ohtake, "Active circulators: The realization of circulators using transistors," *Proc. IEE*E, vol. 53, no. 3, pp. 260-267, 1965.

[4] Y. Ayasli, "Field effect transistor circulators," *IEEE Trans. on Magnetics*, vol. 25, no. 5, pp. 3243-3247, 1989.

[5] G. Carchon and B. Nanwelaers, "Power and noise limitations of active circulators," *IEEE Trans. on Microw. Theory and Techn.*, vol. 48, no. 2, pp. 316-319, 2000.

[6] C.-H. Chang, Y.-T. Lo, and J.-F. Kiang, "A 30 GHz active quasi-circulator with current-reuse technique in CMOS technology," *IEEE Microw. Components Lett.*, vol. 20, no. 12, pp. 693-695, 2010.

[7] T. Kodera, D. L. Sounas, and C. Caloz, "Artificial Faraday rotation using a ring metamaterial structure without static magnetic field," *Appl. Phys. Lett.*, vol. 99, p. 03114, July 2011.

[8] T. Kodera, D. L. Sounas, and C. Caloz, "Magnetless nonreciprocal metamaterial (MNM) technology: Application to microwave components," *IEEE Trans. Microw. Theory and Techn.*, vol. 61, no. 3, pp. 1030-1042, Mar. 2013.

[9] S. Qin, Q. Xu, and Y. E. Wang, "Nonreciprocal components with distributedly modulated capacitors," *IEEE Trans. Microw. Theory and Techn.*, vol. 62, no. 10, pp. 2260-2272, Oct. 2014.

[10] S. Qin and Y. E. Wang, "Broadband parametric circulator with balanced monolithic integrated distributedly modulated capacitors (DMC)," Proc. IEEE MTT-S Int. Microw. Symp. Dig., San Francisco, CA, USA, May 2016.

[11] N. Reiskarimian and H. Krishnaswamy, "Magnetic-free non-reciprocity based on staggered commutation," *Nature comm.*, vol. 7, no. 4, 2016.

[12] J. Zhou, N. Reiskarimian, and H. Krishnaswamy, "Receiver with integrated magnetic-free N-path-filter-based non-reciprocal circulator and baseband self-interference cancellation for full-duplex wireless," *IEEE ISSCC Dig. Techn. Papers*, pp. 178-180, Jan. 2016.

[13] M. M. Biedka, R. Zhu, Q. M. Xu, and Y. E. Wang, "Ultra-wide band non-reciprocity through sequentially-switched delay lines," *Sci. Rep.*, vol. 7, p. 40014, Jan. 2017.

[14] J. Kerckhoff, K. Lalumière, B. J. Chapman, A. Blais, and K. W. Lehnert, "On-Chip Superconducting microwave circulator from synthetic rotation," *Phys. Rev. Appl.*, vol. 4, no. 3, Sept. 2015.

[15] F. Lecocq, et al., "Nonreciprocal microwave signal processing with a field-programmable Josephson amplifier," *Phys. Rev. Appl.*, vol. 7, no. 2, Feb. 2017.

[16] K. M. Sliwa et al., "Reconfigurable Josephson circulator/directional amplifier," *Phys. Rev. X*, vol. 5, no. 4, Nov. 2015.

[17] H. Lira, Z. Yu, S. Fan, and M. Lipson, "Electrically driven Nonreciprocity induced by interband photonic transition on a silicon chip," *Phys. Rev. Lett.*, vol. 109, no. 3, Jul. 2012.

[18] E. Schwartz, "Broadband mathcing of resonant circuits and circulators," *IEEE Trans. Microw. Theory Techn.*, vol. 16, no. 3, pp. 158–165, 1968.

[19] K. Buisman, L. C. N. de Vreede, L. E. Larson, M. Spirito, A. Akhnoukh, T. L. M. Scholtes, and L. K. Nanver, "Distortion-free varactor diode topologies for RF adaptivity," Proc. IEEE MTT-S Int. Microw. Symp. Dig., Long Beach, CA, USA, June, 2005.

[20] D. L. Sounas, C. Caloz, and A. Alù, "Giant non-reciprocity at the subwavelength scale using angular momentum-biased metamaterials," *Nat. Commun.*, vol. 4, p. 2407, Sept. 2013.

[21] N. A. Estep, et al. "Magnetic-free non-reciprocity and isolation based on parametrically modulated coupled-resonator loops," *Nature Physics*, vol. 10, no. 12, pp. 923-927, 2014.

[22] N. A. Estep, D. L. Sounas, and A. Alù, "Magnetless microwave circulators based on spatiotemporally modulated rings of coupled resonators," *IEEE Trans. Microw. Theory Techn.*, vol. 64, no. 2, pp. 502-518, 2016.

[23] A. Kord, D. L. Sounas, and A. Alù, "Magnet-less circulators based on spatiotemporal modulation of bandstop filters in a Delta topology," *IEEE Trans. Microw. Theory Techn.*, to be published.

[24] A. Kord, D. L. Sounas, and A. Alù, "Pseudo-linear-time-invariant magnet-less circulators based on differential spatio-temporal modulation of resonant junctions," under review.

[25] R. Fleury, D. L. Sounas, C. F. Sieck, M. R. Haberman, and A. Alù, "Sound isolation and giant linear nonreciprocity in a compact acoustic circulator," *Science*, vol. 343, pp. 516-519, Jan. 2014.

Millimeter-wave Frequency FDTD Simulation for Error Vector Magnitude of Modulated Signals*

Joseph Elliott Diener
Colorado School of Mines
Golden, USA
jdiener@mines.edu

Jeanne Quimby
National Institute of Standards and Technology
Boulder, USA
jeanne.quimby@nist.gov

Kate A. Remley
National Institute of Standards and Technology
Boulder, USA
kate.remley@nist.gov

Atef Z. Elsherbeni
Colorado School of Mines
Golden, USA
aelsherb@mines.edu

***Abstract*— At millimeter-wave frequencies, a simulation of propagating complex modulated signals through an environmental channel can be computationally prohibitive using the finite difference time domain (FDTD) method. The "grid impulse response" method uses a delta-function as a source signal to solve for the transfer function of the finite difference time domain grid. Once the transfer function of the channel is known, any number of source signals of differing lengths, such as those involving M-ary quadrature amplitude modulation may be used to estimate the propagation of a complex modulated signal through the environmental channel. Numerical investigations show that the maximum error between the two approaches can be very small. Simple environmental channels are used to present the error vector magnitude at mmWave frequencies obtained from the grid impulse response method.**

Keywords*— *EVM, FDTD, QAM.

I. Introduction

Modern millimeter-wave communication systems have complex hardware and modulation schemes that can be modeled with finite difference time domain directly by propagating the source signal through a simulated channel. Use of the full FDTD approach can be a computationally-demanding task for dense FDTD grids propagating long-duration signals due to the gridding requirements based on the very small wavelengths found at millimeter-wave frequencies. Authors in [1-2] show that transfer functions derived from the system response to a delta-function source signal can be used to predict the response of a 1D FDTD grid for an arbitrary input. Perrin *et al.* use a similar technique to predict the grid response in 3D [3]. We extend this previous work to millimeter-wave frequencies and show numerically that a delta-function excitation of the grid can be used to obtain the transfer function of the FDTD grid. Once obtained, the transfer function can be used to solve for the signal received at any grid point when the source is excited by an arbitrary source signal. This approach is known as the grid impulse response (GIR) method. We will discuss the use of the GIR method to calculate the distortion of a modulated signal using error-vector-magnitude as the metric of distortion.

II. The Transfer Function and Grid Impulse Response

We define the transfer function of the FDTD grid as:

$$T(\omega) = \frac{F(\,RX(t)\,)}{F(\,TX(t)\,)}\,, \tag{1}$$

where F is the fast Fourier transform, RX is the time-domain sampled signal at a point of interest in the FDTD grid, TX is the source signal used to excite the FDTD grid, and $T(\omega)$ is the transfer function. Working with the time domain representation of the transfer function, the grid impulse response (GIR) is given by:

$$GIR(t) = F^{-1}(T\,(\omega)\,)\,. \tag{2}$$

Note that for a delta-function source signal incident on the FDTD grid, the GIR is directly obtained by sampling the grid, $GIR(t) = RX(t)$. Once the GIR is found, any signal of interest can be solved at the RX sampling point by convolution, and is given by:

$$RX_{calculated}(t) = GIR(t) * TX_{arbitrary}(t)\,, \tag{3}$$

where * indicates convolution and $RX_{calculated}$ is the predicted signal obtained from the arbitrary signal source $TX_{arbitrary}$. This formulation is most useful in solving for signals where the number of time steps needed to inject the signal into the grid is much larger than the number of time steps needed for the GIR to converge.

III. Numerical Demonstration of Accuracy

We used an M-ary quadrature-amplitude modulation (M-QAM) signal to examine the accuracy of the GIR method. The FDTD code from [5] is used for all simulations, run in single precision. A source transmitting an M-QAM signal is placed in free-space and terminated in either convolutional perfectly-matched layer (CPML) [6] or perfect electrical conductor (PEC) boundaries. The signal is 16-QAM modulation, 10 GSym/s, with five symbol durations. The CPML is eight-cells thick. We compare a simulation using the full FDTD approach and another using the GIR method. The signals at a given point of interest in space as a function of time-step are recorded for both methods. The received signal from the full-length simulation RX_{full} is compared with the predicted signal from the GIR method. The signals are compared with an error metric defined by:

$$Error = \left|RX_{full} - RX_{GIR}\right|\,. \tag{4}$$

* Work partially supported by US government not protected by US copyright.

RX_{full} has its maximum amplitude normalized to 1 and RX_{GIR} is normalized with the same normalization constant. The free-space propagation case is shown in the solid line in Fig. 1. At 500 time steps, the jump in the figure is due to the transmitted signal arriving at the receiver. The signal variation previous to this time step is due to numeric noise. The GIR determination uses 1816 time steps. Through time step 1816, the error is less than 10^{-6}. At time step 1817, the error increases by ~10x, with a maximum error of approximately 10^{-3} from time step 1888 and beyond. Thus, for time steps less than or equal to the number of time steps used in the full FDTD simulation, the GIR method will capture the grid response with the error of a predicted signal $< 10^{-6}$. For time steps after this point, the error will reflect the degree to which the long-term GIR has been captured. When the GIR has begun to converge, the error for future time steps is relatively low ($\sim 10^{-3}$), and will be reduced further when the grid is sampled for more time steps. When the long-term GIR has not been captured, the error for future time steps will be large. This is shown in the dashed line in Fig. 1, where the convolutional perfectly matched layer (CPML) boundaries are replaced with PEC walls to simulate a metal enclosure shown by the box results. Through the time step of the GIR simulation, the response of the grid is captured well ($< 10^{-6}$ error). The maximum error very quickly approaches 0.5 for time steps after this point, corresponding to essentially no agreement between predicted and actual signals. This is due to the resonant nature of the box, and shows that the transfer function method can fail when used inappropriately.

IV. Error Vector Magnitude Calculation

The GIR method is an excellent compromise between accuracy and computational expense for determining distortion in a modulated signal from a channel. By creating a modulated signal and convolving with the GIR, the effects of the channel will be seen on the received signal. This can show channel effects such as path loss, power delay profile, and the error vector magnitude (EVM) [4] introduced by the channel. Application of the technique to an EVM calculation is shown for two identical dipole antennas operating at 90 GHz as a TX/RX pair in a free-space channel and in a channel with an infinite ground plane below the antennas. The distance between the two antennas is swept through 0.12 m, as seen in Fig. 2. A 1000 symbol, duration 16-QAM signal is the excitation and the signal is post-processed to yield the EVM. The mean EVM is shown in Fig. 2. The ground-bounce case shows significantly increased distortion resulting from the reflected signal, with two distinct peaks appearing. These peaks are not present in the free-space case, and so are solely attributable to the reflected signal from the ground-plane.

V. Conclusion

We have shown that the use of transfer functions in the full 3D FDTD grid can give long-term grid responses with error less than $< 10^{-6}$. An understanding of the error in such an approach has been introduced, showing clear cases where the GIR is not satisfactory. Through the use of the transfer function of the grid, simulations of the modulated signals can be solved rapidly, and channel effects on the EVM of the signal derived directly. Further investigation of the computational speedup is warranted.

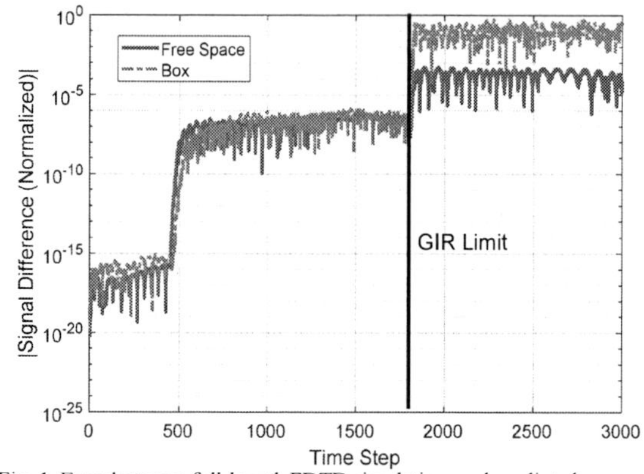

Fig. 1. Error between full-length FDTD simulation, and predicted response using the GIR method. Dashed line shows the PEC box case, while the solid line shows the free-space case. Truncated at 3000 timesteps for clarity.

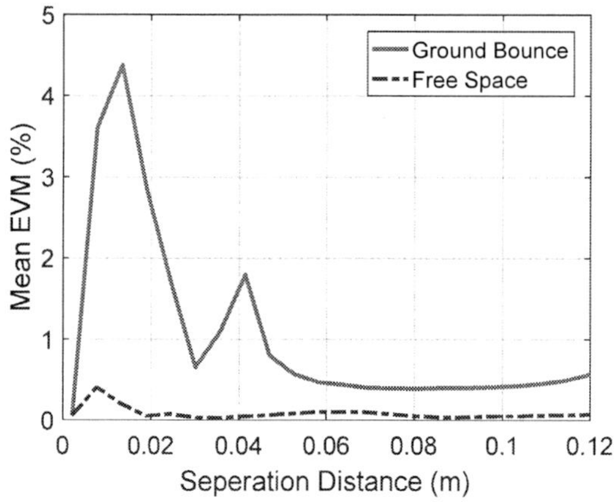

Fig. 2. EVM for a dipole-dipole case using 16-QAM signal, with results calculated by the GIR. Distinct peaks are seen from ground-bounce effects.

References

[1] J. B. Schneider and C. L. Wagner, "FDTD dispersion revisited: Faster-than-light propagation," in *IEEE Microwave and Guided Wave Letters*, vol. 9, no. 2, pp. 54-56, Feb. 1999.

[2] J. P. Bérenger, "Propagation and aliasing of high frequencies in the FDTD grid," in *IEEE Transactions on Electromagnetic Compatibility*, vol. 58, no. 1, pp. 117-124, Feb. 2016.

[3] E. Perrin, C. Guiffaut, A. Reineix, and F. Tristant, "Using transfer function calculation and extrapolation to improve the efficiency of the finite-difference time-domain method at low frequencies," in *IEEE Transactions on Electromagnetic Compatibility*, vol. 52, no. 1, pp. 173-178, Feb. 2010.

[4] M. Mckinley, K. A. Remley, M. Mylinshi, and J. S. Kenney, "EVM Calculation for Broadband Modulated Signals," in ARFTG Microwave Measurement Conference, Orlando, FL, 2004.

[5] A. Z. Elsherbeni and V. Demir, *The Finite Difference Time Domain Method for Electromagentics with MATLAB Simulations*, second edition, ACES series on Computational Electromagnetics and Engineering, SciTech Publishing, an Imprint of IET, Edison, NJ, 2015.

[6] J. A. Roden and S. D. Gedney, "Convolutional PML (CPML): An efficient FDTD implementation of the CFS-PML for arbitrary media," *Microw. Opt. Technol. Lett.*, vol. 27, pp. 334-339, 2000.

Near-Field Far-Field Transformations for Automobile Antenna Measurements

Thomas F. Eibert and Raimud A.M. Mauermayer
Chair of High-Frequency Engineering
Department of Electrical and Computer Engineering
Technical University of Munich
80290 Munich, Germany
hft@ei.tum.de

Abstract—**Automobile antenna measurements become more and more important and especially near-field measurements are very attractive in terms of accuracy, reliability and usefulness. Since automobiles are commonly used on streets within cities or over land, the question of the most appropriate measurement environment for antennas on automobiles is very interesting and there is a need for appropriate near-field far-field transformation approaches. Several measurement approaches for automobile antennas are discussed, where the focus is on an integral equation based near-field far-field transformation technique, which has great flexibility and can be adapted to various measurement environments by working with appropriate Green's functions. Simulation results are shown to highlight some of the capabilities of this method.**

Keywords—antenna measurement, automobile antenna, near-field far-field transformation.

I. Introduction

Traditionally, automobile antenna measurements were performed in open test sites with the measurement probe in a relatively large distance to the device under test (DUT) (possibly in the far-field). Such measurements were commonly restricted to just one horizontal cut around the DUT, i.e., for one fixed height of the probe antenna. Also, these measurements were heavily influenced by environmental conditions and by the particular properties of the ground at the test site. Closed-room antenna measurement systems for automobiles have become popular more recently and rely commonly on near-field measurements with a subsequent near-field far-field transformation. Two examples of automobile antenna measurement systems are found in [1] and [2]. The approach in [1] tries to measure the radiation of the DUT only or of the DUT on a relatively small support structure, whereas the approach in [2] measures the DUT radiation when the DUT is placed on a large metallic ground plane. In both cases, the measurement surface is more or less a hemisphere above the DUT. In [2], the measurement surfaces is restricted by the metallic ground plane, whereas in [1] such a restriction is not given and free-space like measurements can also be collected below the DUT, if the DUT is lifted up. In the case of [1], it is obvious that a common free-space near-field far-field transformation [3] is the method of choice to transform the measured near-field into the far-field. However, in the case of [2] a near-field far-field transformation may be chosen, which is able to transform the near-field into the far-field with appropriate consideration of the influence of the metallic ground plane [4],[5].

In view of the ever increasing requirements for improved performance of automobile radio services and the increasing number of antennas on automobiles, one may ask which antenna measurement technique is most appropriate for automobile antennas? Is it a free-space measurement technique? Is it a measurement technique with a metallic ground plane or is it a measurement technique which works with a ground; which is as realistic as possible? No matter what technique is used it is desirable to work with an appropriate near-field far-field transformation and it may also be an attractive option to extract equivalent radiation sources on the DUT, which can be used to perform radiation simulations in varying environments. In what follows, some issues related to automobile antenna measurements are addressed and illustrated by simulation results.

II. Automobile Antenna Measurements and Field Transformations

A. Equivalent Radiation Model of a DUT Above Ground

A DUT above planar ground together with equivalent surface current densities representing the relevant radiation mechanisms is illustrated in Fig. 1. The antenna on the DUT is excited by a voltage U_0 and on the DUT primary surface current densities (subscript *pr*) together with secondary surface current densities (subscript *se*) due to the influence of the ground interaction are induced. After removing the DUT, the overall radiation can be represented by equivalent electric $\vec{J}_{A,gr}$ and $\vec{J}_{A,se}$ as well as magnetic $\vec{M}_{A,pr}$ and $\vec{M}_{A,se}$ surface current densities on the DUT together with equivalent electric $\vec{J}_{A,gr}$ and magnetic $\vec{M}_{A,gr}$ surface current densities on the ground interface. From this consideration, it is clear that the secondary source on the DUT as well as the sources in the ground interface depend on the chosen ground material, whereas the primary sources are those which represent the free-space radiation of the DUT. If we interpret a near-field far-field transformation approach in a way that it determines equivalent radiation sources, which reproduce the measured near-fields, then it is immediately clear that any near-field far-field transformation can follow one out of two options. First, it can try to determine equivalent sources, which are equivalent to the primary plus the secondary sources on the DUT under the presence of the sources on the ground interface. Second, it can try to determine the primary plus the secondary sources on the DUT without the presence of the ground interface sources, i.e., as if the primary plus the secondary sources on the DUT were radiating in free space. In the latter case, these sources can be utilized to perform radiation simulations of these sources in different environments, where it should, however, be clear that the secondary equivalent sources on the DUT might not be correct for this environment.

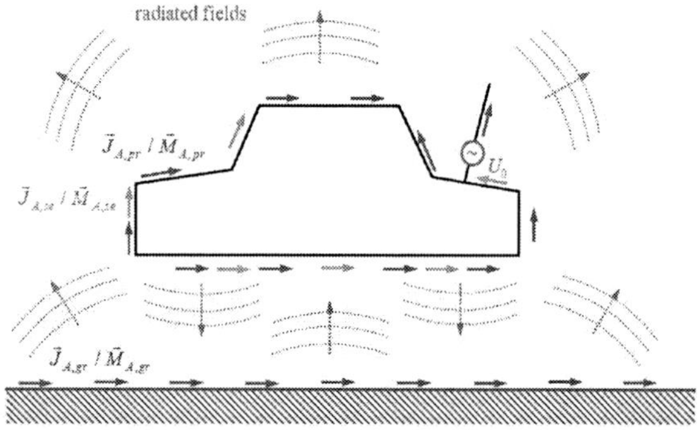

Fig. 1. Antenna in radiation mode on a car above a material interface: The antenna is excited by a voltage U_0 and in addition to the primary electric and magnetic surface currents also secondary electric and magnetic surface currents are induced on the antenna and the car, together with surface currents on the material interface.

B. *Transformation Results Above Metallic Ground*

In order to illustrate some capabilities of hemispherical near-field measurements above infinite metallic (perfect electrically conducting (PEC)) ground and of the so-called fast irregular antenna field transformation algorithm (FIAFTA) [5],[6] with PEC half-space Green's function, the measurement configuration in Fig. 2 is considered and simulated with the Altair FEKO integral equation solver.

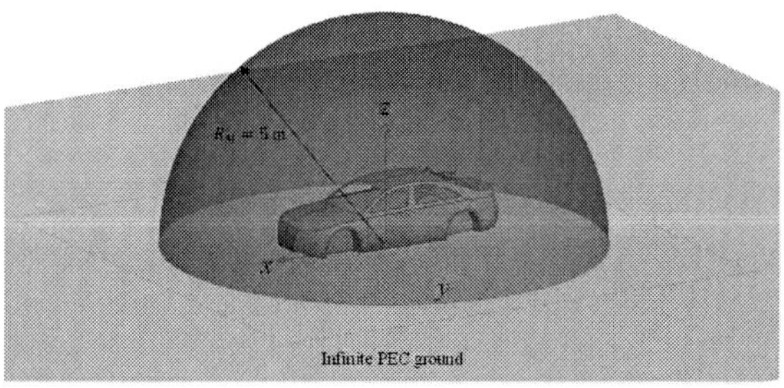

Fig. 2. Hemispherical near-field measurement setup and FEKO model.

Near-field samples have been simulated on the shown hemisphere and transformed into the far-field by FIAFTA [5],[6]. The obtained far-fields above infinite metallic ground and in free space according to the primary plus the secondary souces on the DUT only are shown in Fig. 3 and Fig. 4, respectively. As expected, in Fig. 3 the agreement with the reference is very good. In Fig. 4, for the extracted free-space far-field larger but still not too bad errors have been found for the employed model.

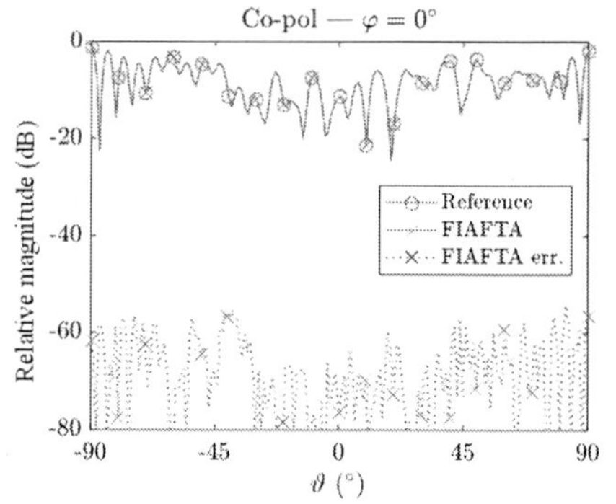

Fig. 3. Far-field above infinite metallic ground.

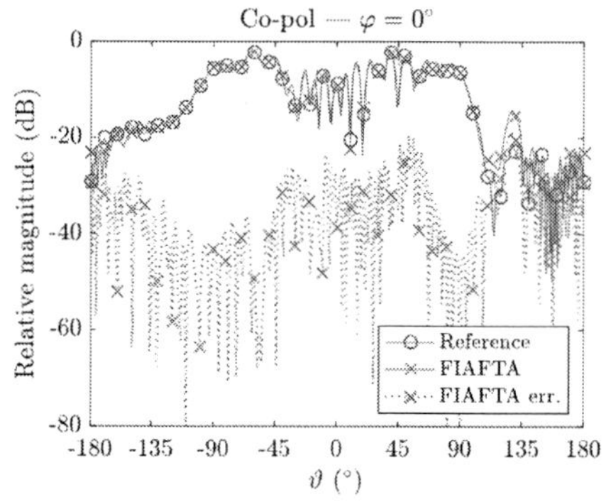

Fig. 4. Far-field of the reonstructed sources on the car when radiating in free space, i.e., with the ground not present anymore.

III. Conclusions

Some issues related to near-field antenna measurements of antennas on automobiles and the corresponding near-field far-field transformations have been discussed. It was shown that equivalent sources based near-field far-field transformations with appropriate Green's functions provide good flexibility for various measurement configurations.

References

[1] L. Le Danvic, M. Huard, E. Lardjane, P. Besnier, and M. Drissi, "Experimentation and validation of spherical near-field techniques for vehicle-mounted antenna measurements," *European Conference on Antennas and Propagation*, Edinburgh, UK, Nov. 2007.

[2] P. N. Betjes, D. Pototzki, and D. J. van Rensburg, "A hemi-spherical near-field system for automotive antenna testing," *Annual Symposium of the Antenna Measurement Techniques Association*, Newport, Rhode Island, Nov. 2005.

[3] A. D. Yaghjian, "An overview of near-field antenna measurements," *IEEE Transactions on Antennas and Propagation*, vol. 34, no. 1, pp. 30-45, Jan. 1986.

[4] R. A. M. Mauermayer and T. F. Eibert, "Spherical field transformation for hemispherical antenna measurements above perfectly conducting ground planes," *Annual Symposium of the Antenna Measurement Techniques Association*, Austin, TX, 2016.

[5] R. A. M. Mauermayer and T. F. Eibert, "Fast irregular antenna field transformation above perfectly conducting ground planes," *European Conference on Antennas and Propagation*, Davos, 2016.

[6] T. F. Eibert, E. Kilic, C. Lopez, R. A. M. Mauermayer, O. Neitz and G. Schnattinger, "Electromagnetic field transformations for measurements and simulations (Invited Paper)," *Progress in Electromagnetics Research*, vol. 151, pp. 127-150, 2015.

Hierarchical Universal Matrices for Sensitivity Analysis by Curvilinear Finite Elements

László Levente Tóth
Chair for Electromagnetic Theory
Saarland University
D-66123 Saarbrücken, Germany
l.toth@lte.uni-saarland.de

Romanus Dyczij-Edlinger
Chair for Electromagnetic Theory
Saarland University
D-66123 Saarbrücken, Germany
edlinger@lte.uni-saarland.de

***Abstract*—A new method for calculating the geometric sensitivities of curvilinear finite elements is presented. Approximating the relevant metric tensors by hierarchical orthogonal polynomials enables the sensitivity matrices to be integrated analytically. The resulting numerical method is based on pre-calculated universal matrices and achieves significant savings in computer runtime over conventional techniques based on numerical integration. Moreover, there exists a representation limit for the geometry, i.e., the degree of basis functions fully determines a critical order of the geometry expansion, beyond which the derivatives of the finite-element matrices will remain constant. To validate the suggested approach, a numerical example is presented.**

***Keywords*—curvilinear, eigenvalues, finite elements, hierarchical, sensitivity, universal matrix.**

I. Introduction

Higher-order finite elements (FEs) are attractive because they yield exponential convergence in case of smooth fields. However, to harvest their full potential, curvilinear boundaries must be taken into account. Typically, the resulting metric terms do not admit analytical integration of the FE matrices. Numerical integration is possible, though computationally expensive. An alternative is polynomial interpolation or approximation of the metric terms followed by exact integration. The resulting algorithms [1], [2] achieve significant savings in computer runtime, by utilizing pre-calculated universal matrices (UMs).

Applications such as sensitivity analysis and gradient-based optimization require not only the FE matrices but also their derivatives with respect to the parameters. This paper presents an efficient procedure for computing such derivatives in the curvilinear case. The method will be demonstrated for the $\boldsymbol{H}$(curl) shape functions of [3], using hierarchical UMs.

II. Model Problem

Consider a cavity resonator Ω whose boundary Γ_E is a perfect electric conductor (PEC). Maxwell's equations lead to the following eigenvalue problem (EVP) for the modal electric field $\boldsymbol{E}$ and the corresponding wavenumber k:

$$\nabla \times \left(\boldsymbol{\mu}_r^{-1} \nabla \times \boldsymbol{E}\right) - k^2 \boldsymbol{\varepsilon}_r \boldsymbol{E} = \boldsymbol{0} \quad \text{in } \Omega, \tag{1}$$

$$\hat{\boldsymbol{n}} \times \boldsymbol{E} = \boldsymbol{0} \quad \text{in } \Gamma_E. \tag{2}$$

Herein μ_r and ε_r denote the relative magnetic permeability and electric permittivity, respectively. FE discretization using a set of $\boldsymbol{H}$(curl) basis functions $\boldsymbol{w}_i^m$, where $(\cdot)^m$ indicates the polynomial degree, leads to the algebraic EVP:

$$\left(\boldsymbol{S} - k^2 \boldsymbol{T}\right) \boldsymbol{v} = \boldsymbol{0}, \tag{3}$$

with eigenvector $\boldsymbol{v}$. Herein the stiffness matrix $\boldsymbol{S}$ and the mass matrix $\boldsymbol{T}$ are given by:

$$[\boldsymbol{S}^{mn}]_{ij} = \int_\Omega \nabla \times \boldsymbol{w}_i^m \cdot \boldsymbol{\mu}_r^{-1} \nabla \times \boldsymbol{w}_j^n \, \mathrm{d}\boldsymbol{x}, \tag{4a}$$

$$[\boldsymbol{T}^{mn}]_{ij} = \int_\Omega \boldsymbol{w}_i^m \cdot \boldsymbol{\varepsilon}_r \boldsymbol{w}_j^n \, \mathrm{d}\boldsymbol{x}. \tag{4b}$$

According to [4], the sensitivity of the eigenvalue k_i^2 with respect to a parameter τ is given by:

$$\frac{\partial}{\partial \tau} k_i^2 = \boldsymbol{v}_i^T \left(\frac{\partial}{\partial \tau} \boldsymbol{S} - k_i^2 \frac{\partial}{\partial \tau} \boldsymbol{T} \right) \boldsymbol{v}_i. \tag{5}$$

Thus, sensitivity analysis requires the considered eigenpair $(k_i^2, \boldsymbol{v}_i)$ as well as the matrix derivatives $\frac{\partial}{\partial \tau}\boldsymbol{S}$ and $\frac{\partial}{\partial \tau}\boldsymbol{T}$.

III. Hierarchical Universal Matrices

In an unstructured mesh, FEs of different sizes and shapes are present. It is customary to compute the contributions of a single FE Ω_e, the element matrices $\boldsymbol{S}_e$ and $\boldsymbol{T}_e$, from a reference domain $\widehat{\Omega}_e$ equipped with local coordinates $\boldsymbol{\varphi}$. Let $\widehat{\boldsymbol{w}}_i^m(\boldsymbol{\varphi})$ denote the basis functions on $\widehat{\Omega}_e$ and $\boldsymbol{J}(\boldsymbol{\varphi})$ the Jacobian of the geometry mapping. By means of the metric tensors $\widehat{\boldsymbol{\Lambda}}^1(\boldsymbol{\varphi})$ and $\widehat{\boldsymbol{\Lambda}}^2(\boldsymbol{\varphi})$ defined by:

$$\widehat{\boldsymbol{\Lambda}}^1 = |\boldsymbol{J}| \boldsymbol{J}^{-T} \boldsymbol{\varepsilon}_r \boldsymbol{J}^{-1}, \tag{6a}$$

$$\widehat{\boldsymbol{\Lambda}}^2 = |\boldsymbol{J}|^{-1} \boldsymbol{J} \boldsymbol{\mu}_r^{-1} \boldsymbol{J}^T, \tag{6b}$$

the element matrices $\boldsymbol{S}_e$ and $\boldsymbol{T}_e$ take the form:

$$[\boldsymbol{S}_e^{mn}]_{ij} = \int_{\widehat{\Omega}_e} \nabla_\varphi \times \widehat{\boldsymbol{w}}_i^m \cdot \widehat{\boldsymbol{\Lambda}}^2 \nabla_\varphi \times \widehat{\boldsymbol{w}}_j^n \, \mathrm{d}\boldsymbol{\varphi}, \tag{7a}$$

$$[\boldsymbol{T}_e^{mn}]_{ij} = \int_{\widehat{\Omega}_e} \widehat{\boldsymbol{w}}_i^m \cdot \widehat{\boldsymbol{\Lambda}}^1 \widehat{\boldsymbol{w}}_j^n \, \mathrm{d}\boldsymbol{\varphi}. \tag{7b}$$

In [5] a hierarchical basis of scalar polynomials $b_l^k(\boldsymbol{\varphi})$ which are pairwise orthogonal on $\widehat{\Omega}_e$ was introduced:

$$\int_{\widehat{\Omega}_e} b_l^k(\boldsymbol{\varphi}) b_n^m(\boldsymbol{\varphi}) \, \mathrm{d}\boldsymbol{\varphi} = \begin{cases} 1 & \text{for } (k,l) = (m,n), \\ 0 & \text{else.} \end{cases} \tag{8}$$

Here $(\cdot)^k$ gives the polynomial order, and $(\cdot)_l$ denotes functions of same order. Expanding $\widehat{\mathbf{\Lambda}}^{(\cdot)}$ in that basis leads to:

$$\widehat{\mathbf{\Lambda}}^{(\cdot)}(\varphi) = \sum_{k=0}^{\infty} \sum_{l=1}^{L(k)} \widehat{\mathbf{\Lambda}}_{kl}^{(\cdot)} b_l^k(\varphi), \qquad \varphi \in \widehat{\Omega}, \tag{9}$$

with constant matrix-valued coefficients $\widehat{\mathbf{\Lambda}}_{kl}$. Eq. (9) yields a polynomial representation for (7), which hereby becomes accessible to analytical integration. We thus have:

$$\boldsymbol{S}^{mn} = \sum_{k=0}^{m+n-2} \sum_{l=1}^{L(k)} \sum_{i,j} \left[\widehat{\mathbf{\Lambda}}_{kl}^{2}\right]_{ij} \boldsymbol{S}_{ijl}^{mnk}, \tag{10a}$$

$$\boldsymbol{T}^{mn} = \sum_{k=0}^{m+n} \sum_{l=1}^{L(k)} \sum_{i,j} \left[\widehat{\mathbf{\Lambda}}_{kl}^{1}\right]_{ij} \boldsymbol{T}_{ijl}^{mnk}, \tag{10b}$$

wherein $\boldsymbol{S}_{ijl}^{mnk}$ and $\boldsymbol{T}_{ijl}^{mnk}$ are metric-independent UMs, which are computed only once. The UMs inherit the hierarchical structure of the basis functions [3]. Thanks to orthogonality, the results of the truncated sums in (10) are exact; see [5].

IV. Universal Matrices for Sensitivity Analysis

When the geometry is parameterized by τ, the Jacobian $\boldsymbol{J}$ and, in consequence, the metric tensors $\mathbf{\Lambda}^{(\cdot)}$ become τ dependent, whereas the $\widehat{w}_i^m(\varphi)$ remain unchanged. In view of (6) and (7), the derivatives of the element matrices read:

$$\frac{\partial}{\partial \tau}[\boldsymbol{S}_e^{mn}]_{ij} = \int_{\widehat{\Omega}_e} \nabla_\varphi \times \widehat{\boldsymbol{w}}_i^m \cdot \frac{\partial}{\partial \tau}\widehat{\mathbf{\Lambda}}^2 \nabla_\varphi \times \widehat{\boldsymbol{w}}_j^n \,\mathrm{d}\varphi, \tag{11a}$$

$$\frac{\partial}{\partial \tau}[\boldsymbol{T}_e^{mn}]_{ij} = \int_{\widehat{\Omega}_e} \widehat{\boldsymbol{w}}_i^m \cdot \frac{\partial}{\partial \tau}\widehat{\mathbf{\Lambda}}^1 \widehat{\boldsymbol{w}}_j^n \,\mathrm{d}\varphi. \tag{11b}$$

The structure of (11) implies that $\frac{\partial}{\partial \tau}\boldsymbol{S}$ and $\frac{\partial}{\partial \tau}\boldsymbol{T}$ may be constructed from UMs too, by a method similar to Section III: The polynomial expansions of $\frac{\partial}{\partial \tau}\mathbf{\Lambda}^{(\cdot)}$ in terms of b_l^k read:

$$\frac{\partial}{\partial \tau}\widehat{\mathbf{\Lambda}}^{(\cdot)}(\varphi) = \sum_{k=0}^{\infty} \sum_{l=1}^{L(k)} \frac{\partial}{\partial \tau}\widehat{\mathbf{\Lambda}}_{kl}^{(\cdot)} b_l^k(\varphi), \qquad \varphi \in \widehat{\Omega}. \tag{12}$$

Substituting the series expansion (12) for the derivatives of the metric tensors in (11) leads to polynomial representations which, again, allow for analytical integration. We arrive at:

$$\frac{\partial}{\partial \tau}\boldsymbol{S}^{mn} = \sum_{k=0}^{m+n-2} \sum_{l=1}^{L(k)} \sum_{i,j} \left[\frac{\partial}{\partial \tau}\widehat{\mathbf{\Lambda}}_{kl}^{2}\right]_{ij} \boldsymbol{S}_{ijl}^{mnk}, \tag{13a}$$

$$\frac{\partial}{\partial \tau}\boldsymbol{T}^{mn} = \sum_{k=0}^{m+n} \sum_{l=1}^{L(k)} \sum_{i,j} \left[\frac{\partial}{\partial \tau}\widehat{\mathbf{\Lambda}}_{kl}^{1}\right]_{ij} \boldsymbol{T}_{ijl}^{mnk}. \tag{13b}$$

Eq. (13) provides an efficient proceduce for assembling the matrix derivatives, based on the same UMs as (10). Again, it can be shown that metric expansions of order $m+n-2$ and $m+n$, respectively, yield exact results.

V. Numerical Example

We consider a spherical resonator of nominal radius r_0 = 1 m, with the material properties of free space and a PEC boundary. The structure is discretized into 256 tetrahedra, using piecewise 3rd order polynomials for the geometry. For sensitivity analysis, the radius is parameterized by:

$$r(\tau) = (1+\tau)r_0. \tag{14}$$

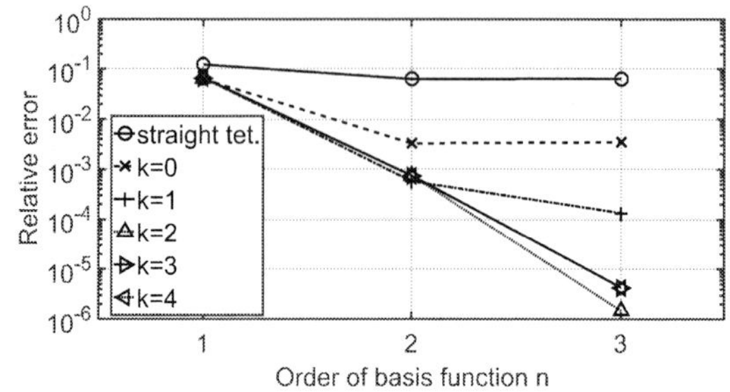

Fig. 1. Relative error in sensitivity of dominant eigenvalue k^2 versus order of FE basis. Parameter: order of metric approximation.

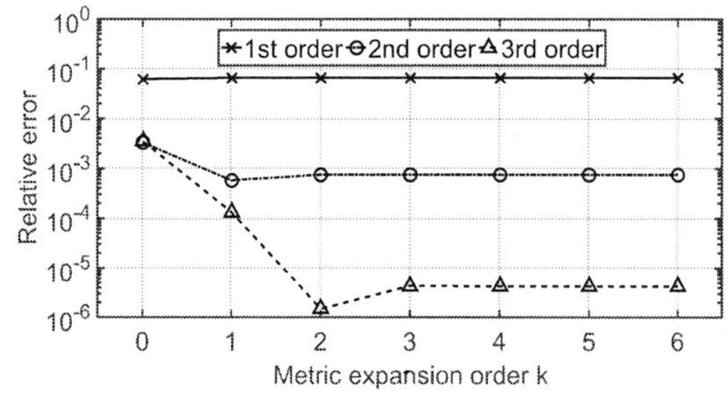

Fig. 2. Relative error in sensitivity of dominant eigenvalue k^2 versus order of metric approximation. Parameter: order of FE basis.

Fig. 1 presents the relative error in the first nonzero eigenvalue: High-order FEs yield fast convergence provided that the curvilinear boundary is approximated well enough. Moreover, approximation by constant metrics ($k = 0$) yields significantly better results than interpolating the sphere by conventional straight-sided tetrahedra.

Fig. 2 demonstrates that increasing the metric approximation beyond a FE-order specific limit does not improve the solution, because the FE matrices are sharp. Beyond this point, the error is due to the approximation properties of the FE basis.

References

[1] D. Villeneuve and J. P. Webb, "Hierarchical universal matrices for triangular finite elements with varying material properties and curved boundaries," International Journal for Numerical Methods in Engineering, vol. 44, no. 2, pp. 215–228, 1999.

[2] D. A. O. Beig, J. Wang, Z. Peng, and J. F. Lee, "A universal array approach for finite elements with continuously inhomogeneous material properties and curved boundaries," IEEE Transactions on Antennas and Propagation, vol. 60, no. 10, pp. 4745–4756, Oct. 2012.

[3] P. Ingelstrom, "A new set of h(curl)-conforming hierarchical basis functions for tetrahedral meshes," IEEE Transactions on Microwave Theory and Techniques, vol. 54, no. 1, pp. 106–114, Jan. 2006.

[4] R. B. Nelson, "Simplified calculation of eigenvector derivatives," AIAA Journal, vol. 14, no. 9, pp. 1201–1205, 1976.

[5] L. L. Toth and R. Dyczij-Edlinger, "Universal finite-element matrices for curvilinear tetrahedra with continuously varying material properties," in Kleinheubacher Tagung, 2017, p. 32. [Online]. Available: https://www.kh2017.de/KH2017 book of abstracts.pdf.

Embedding the Shooting and Bouncing Rays Method in a Hybrid Solver Framework

Benjamin Motz
CST – Computer Simulation Technology GmbH
64289 Darmstadt, Germany
Benjamin.Motz@3ds.com

Thomas Weiland
Institut für Theorie Elektromagnetischer Felder
Technische Universität Darmstadt
64289 Darmstadt, Germany

***Abstract*—This contribution discusses aspects of the simulation of the radar cross section (RCS) for electrically large scatterers. Such simulations are needed in the development of automotive radar systems or aerospace applications. Simulating the RCS of large scatterers is typically very demanding in terms of computer runtime and memory if performed by a full wave simulation method. An asymptotic method is much less affected by these restrictions and therefore a good choice for this kind of simulation. On the other hand, asymptotic simulations are limited to structures of moderate geometrical complexity, i.e., features with sizes much larger than the simulated wavelength. In this work a hybrid domain decomposition framework is therefore used with an asymptotic method and a full wave simulation method to leverage the advantages of both simulation types.**

I. Introduction

Specific coupling formulations of an asymptotic method with other simulation methods have been described in the past [1]. In this work, however, we strive for an abstract coupling formulation of both methods. By employing a general domain decomposition framework, the simulation methods for the domains may be easily replaced. We implement the Shooting and Bouncing Rays (SBR) method to simulate the scattering effects of the large structure. The influence of complex parts of the structure is treated by full wave methods. These methods are chosen depending on the features encountered in the geometrically complex parts of the structure and may comprise both frequency- and time-domain simulations.

We will shortly introduce the used hybrid framework, before discussing the implementation of the asymptotic simulation. A focus of this work is on accurate modeling of the domain interfaces. Verification examples are shown, in order to illustrate the accuracy of the method.

II. Hybrid Domain Decomposition Framework

We assume a scattering problem which can not be solved by a single simulation method due to limitations of accuracy or efficiency. To facilitate the solution a black box domain decomposition approach will be applied as described in [2]. A decomposed system with two subdomains can be described by the system matrix:

$$\begin{bmatrix} \mathbb{1} & \mathbf{R}_1\mathbf{A}_1^{-1}\mathbf{C}_{12}^S \\ \mathbf{R}_2\mathbf{A}_2^{-1}\mathbf{C}_{21}^S & \mathbb{1} \end{bmatrix} \begin{bmatrix} x_1^S \\ x_2^S \end{bmatrix} = \begin{bmatrix} b_1^S \\ b_2^S \end{bmatrix}, \quad (1)$$

where $x_i^S = [H_i^S, E_i^S]^T$ are the equivalent surface fields for the coupled system on a surface enclosing subdomain i. b_i^S is the surface field solution for the uncoupled domains. For RCS computations b_1^S is obtained by evaluating plane wave scattering on S for domain Ω_1, and $b_2^S = 0$. The coupling operator $\mathbf{C}_{ij}$ transforms surface fields into surface currents. $\mathbf{A}_i$ denotes the system operator of subdomain i. Application of $\mathbf{A}_i^{-1}$ corresponds to finding the solution for that subdomain. The operator $\mathbf{R}_i$ records the field solution on the coupling surface. The entire system can be solved iteratively by a GMRES solver to obtain the solution on surface S. From this, the final solution in the individual subdomains can be derived. The procedure is shown schematically in Fig. 1.

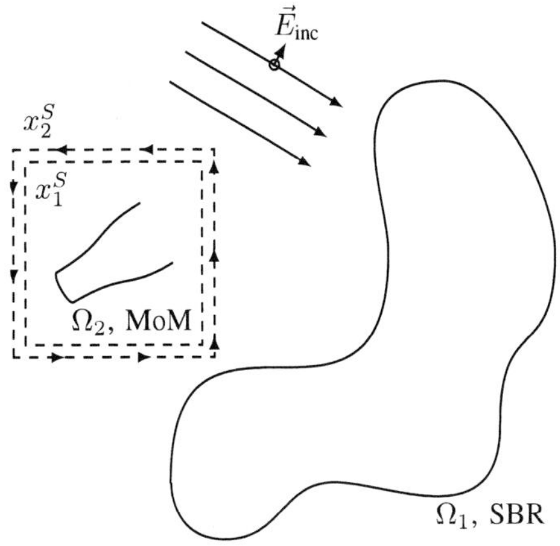

Fig. 1. Schematic sketch of the setup for the separate simulation of the individual domains. Ω_1 is a domain containing an electrically large structure. Ω_2 is a smaller, more complex domain. x_i^S denote field solutions on a boundary interface.

The used domain decomposition framework has the advantage of being modular, i.e., the framework is agnostic to the simulation methods used for the subdomains. The simulation methods need to implement the current source imprint from huygens sources, as well as the field monitoring on the domain interface. The following section discusses these implementations for the Shooting and Bouncing Rays method.

III. Shooting and Bouncing Rays

The Shooting and Bouncing Rays [3] method is used for the simulation of the domain containing the electrically large part of the structure. Rays are launched from a point source and their paths are traced as they bounce back and forth across the structure. Geometrical Optics is used to determine the incident fields on the structure. Finally, Physical Optics (PO) integration of the incident fields is used to determine the scattered fields. Edge diffraction effects are accounted for by an equivalent edge current model.

Imprint of the equivalent surface currents is implemented by hierarchical subdivision of the currents [4]. The currents are aggregated into current groups of different sizes. Based on a far field criterion involving the sizes of the groups and the distance to the scatterer, the current groups used for illuminating the structure are chosen. By superimposing the contributions of several source groups, the incident field of the entire current distribution is obtained.

The near field calculation, which corresponds to operator $\mathbf{R}_i$ at the domain interfaces, is realized by a modified PO integration [5]. This implemenation uses the same fast and robust integral evaluation techniques as already developed for the far field PO integration [3]. It leads to accurate results in the transition near field of the scattering structure.

IV. Verification

The hybrid algorithm is verified by investigating the radar cross section (RCS) of a simple model as shown in Fig. 2. The scattered far field result will then be used to determine the quality of the obtained results.

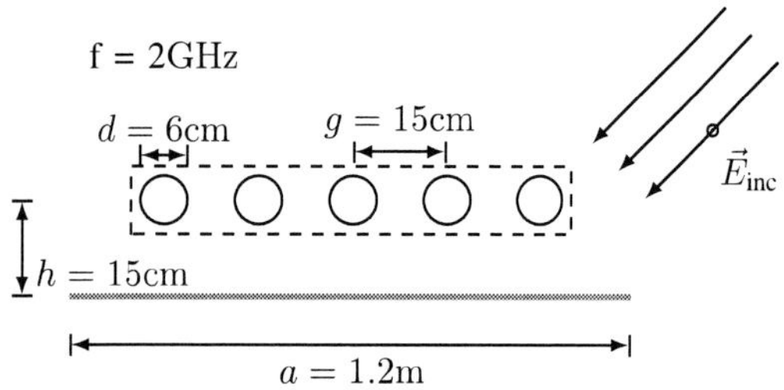

Fig. 2. Verification scenario: 5 solid cylinders over a quadratic plate made of perfect electric conducting material. The structure is illuminated by a plane wave with incidence angle $\theta = 45°$.

The solution obtained by the hybrid simulation, consisting of an SBR domain and a method of moments (MoM) domain, is compared to the solution obtained by SBR alone. As a reference, MoM is used to simulate the entire domain.

SBR is not capable of capturing the interference effects between the cylinders. Therefore a significant improvement of the Hybrid simulation compared to SBR only simulation is observed (see Figs. 3 and 4). The Hybrid simulation converges within 6 iterations to a residual of the system matrix of 0.01.

V. Conclusion

The inclusion of the SBR method into a general hybrid domain decomposition framework has been implemented. The results of the hybrid method were shown to improve significantly for an RCS simulation compared to the SBR simulation. Application examples will be demonstrated in the talk.

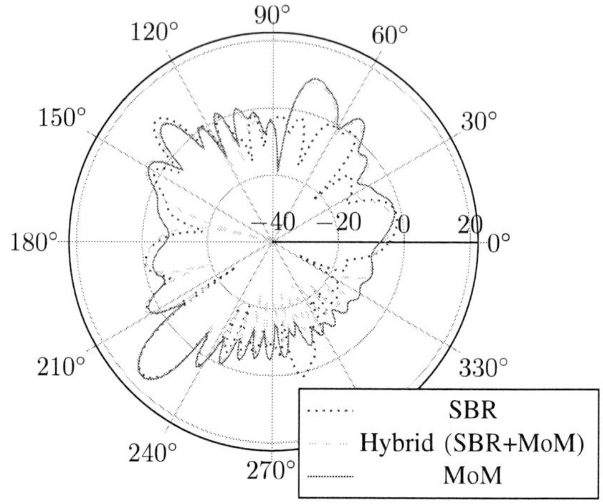

Fig. 3. Bistatic RCS [dBV/m]: cut along θ-direction.

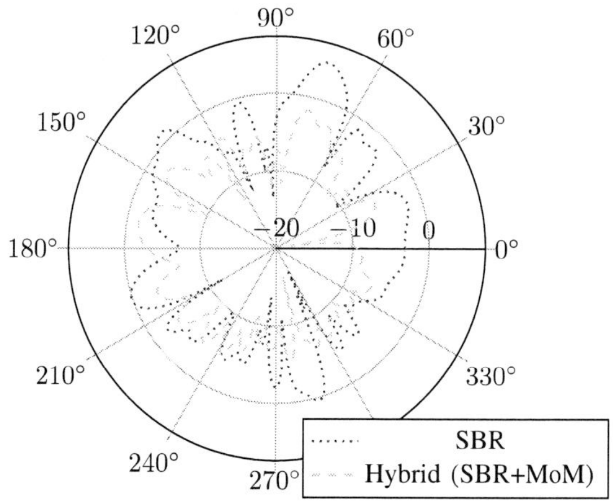

Fig. 4. Relative error [dB] on a cut along θ-direction as given by $\epsilon(\theta) = |\vec{E}_{\text{test}}(\theta) - \vec{E}_{\text{ref}}(\theta)|/|\vec{E}_{\text{inc}}|$, with $\vec{E}_{\text{ref}}$ being the MoM-solution of the full model.

References

[1] R. J. Burkholder, P. H. Pathak, K. Sertel, R. J. Marhefka, J. L. Volakis, and R. W. Kindt, "A hybrid framework for antenna/platform analysis," *Applied Computational Electromagnetics Society Journal*, vol. 21, no. 3, pp. 177–192, 2006.

[2] F. Muth, H. Schneider, and T. Euler, "From surface equivalence principle to modular domain decomposition," *Lecture Notes in Computational Science and Engineering*, vol. 116, pp. 245–252, 2017.

[3] H. Ling, R.-C. Chou, and S.-W. Lee, "Shooting and bouncing rays: calculating the RCS of an arbitrarily shaped cavity," *IEEE Transactions on Antennas and Propagation*, vol. 37, no. 2, pp. 194–205, 1989.

[4] R. Brem and T. F. Eibert, "Multi-radiation center transmitter models for ray tracing," *IEEE Transactions on Antennas and Propagation*, vol. 60, no. 7, pp. 3382–3388, 2012.

[5] B. Motz, A. Langwost, H. Krüger, and T. Weiland, "Physical optics near field calculations on electrically large platforms," in *2015 International Conference on Electromagnetics in Advanced Applications (ICEAA)*, Turin, 2015, pp. 602–605.

Mode Tracking for Parametrized Eigenvalue Problems in Computational Electromagnetics

Philipp Jorkowski
FG Theoretische Elektrotechnik
Technische Universität Berlin
Berlin, Germany
philipp.jorkowski@tu-berlin.de

Rolf Schuhmann
FG Theoretische Elektrotechnik
Technische Universität Berlin
Berlin, Germany
rolf.schuhmann@tu-berlin.de

***Abstract*—An algorithm to perform a mode tracking for parameter dependent eigenvalue problems is presented. By computing the eigenvalue and eigenvector derivatives a Taylor expansion can be used to efficiently calculate the Brillouin diagram for periodic structures. Furthermore, the derivatives allow distinguishing intersection and touching points in the diagram. The discrete model with periodic boundaries is described using the Finite Integration Technique.**

***Keywords*—eigenvalue derivative, finite integration technique, parametrized eigenvalue problem, periodic structures.**

I. Introduction

Since many years, a number of efficient algorithms for the solution of eigenvalue problems (EVP) in electromagnetic field simulation have been proposed. A special class are EVPs with a dependency of a parameter, e.g., material constants, geometric properties, or the phase shift of Floquet modes [1]. In this paper, we present a mode tracking algorithm for EVPs with a parameter dependency, in our case the phase shift. We use the sensitivity of eigenvalues which is described by their derivatives. A first efficient method for the calculation of eigenvalue and eigenvector derivatives has been published by Nelson in 1976 [2] and was extended for non-simple eigenvalues by Dailey in 1989 [3]. In [4] we have shown how to extend this method for higher-order derivatives and applied it to periodic structures. Now the mode tracking is added, which is based on a point by point sampling of the dispersion diagram by using Taylor expansions. In Sect. 2 a very short overview of the basic formulas is given followed by the introduction of the mode tracking algorithm in Sect. 3. Finally in Sect. 4 we discuss the numerical results and present an outlook for further improvements in Sect. 5.

II. Eigenvalue Derivatives

We start with the left and right EVP $\mathbf{y}^H(\mathbf{A}-\lambda\mathbf{I})=0$ and $(\mathbf{A}-\lambda\mathbf{I})\mathbf{x}=0$, where the matrix $\mathbf{A}$ as well as the eigensolution $\{\mathbf{x},\mathbf{y}^H,\lambda\}$ depend on the parameter p. Differentiating n times w.r.t. the parameter p yields the n-th order eigenvalue derivative [4]:

$$\lambda^{(n)} = \mathbf{y}^H\mathbf{A}^{(n)}\mathbf{x} + \sum_{k=1}^{n-1}\binom{n}{k}\mathbf{y}^H\left(\mathbf{A}^{(n-k)} - \lambda^{(n-k)}\mathbf{I}\right)\mathbf{x}^{(k)}. \tag{1}$$

Note, that for the n-th order derivative in (1) all previous derivatives of the eigenvalue, eigenvector and system matrix are required. With this information, the derivative is calculated with less effort, just by matrix vector multiplications. The n-th order eigenvector derivative can be calculated similarly by:

$$(\mathbf{A}-\lambda\mathbf{I})\,\mathbf{x}^{(n)} = -\sum_{k=0}^{n-1}\binom{n}{k}\left(\mathbf{A}^{(n-k)} - \lambda^{(n-k)}\mathbf{I}\right)\mathbf{x}^{(k)}. \tag{2}$$

Thereby a linear system with rank defect has to be solved. Methods are given for example in [2], [3]. Since the right hand side of (2) remains the same for each n, a matrix decomposition technique is efficient if higher orders are desired.

III. Mode Tracking Algorithm

The mode tracking algorithm can best be explained by Fig. 1. First a starting point is chosen at an arbitary $p \in [p_{min}, p_{max}]$, the EVP is solved, and the derivatives $\mathbf{A}^{(i)}$, $\lambda^{(i)}$, $\mathbf{x}^{(i)}$ of the system matrix, the eigenvalue and the eigenvector are calculated, respectively. Next, the approximated eigenvector for the new value $p+\Delta p$ is calculated using a Taylor expansion by:

$$\mathbf{x}_{approx} = f\left(p, \mathbf{x}, ..., \frac{\partial^n}{\partial p^n}\mathbf{x}\right). \tag{3}$$

The approximated eigenvalue is calculated accordingly. In the next step the derivatives are calculated from the approximated values and a backward check is performed [5]. Since we do not use a corrector equation, an EVP needs to be solved every couple of steps to eliminate divergence errors. Therefore a correlation factor is introduced

$$\rho_i = \frac{\mathbf{x}_i^H\mathbf{x}_{approx}}{||\mathbf{x}_i||\,||\mathbf{x}_{approx}||}, \tag{4}$$

to identify the right eigenpair at intersection or touching points when the EVP is recalculated. At these points, the eigenvectors of nearby modes are highly changing which aggravates the proper assignment of the eigenpair. With the approximated eigenvector, we have an indicator which is close to the true one, and therefore the correlation shows good results.

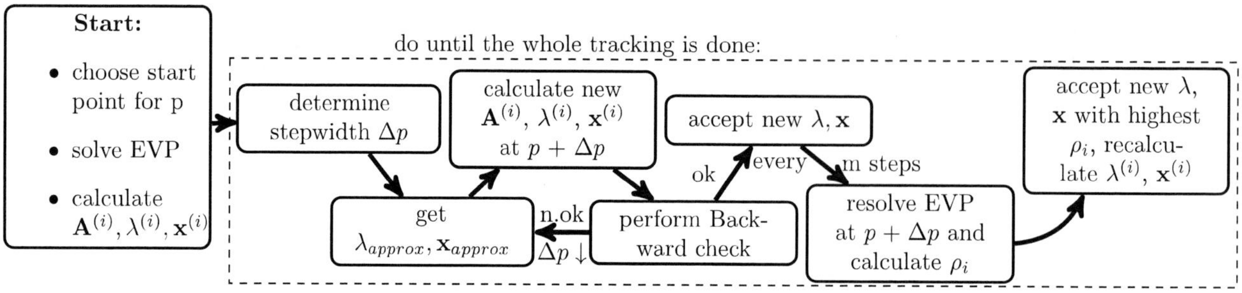

Fig. 1: Flowchart of the mode tracking algorithm.

IV. Numerical results

To test the algorithm, an electrodynamic periodic model from the CST-library [6], as shown in Fig. 2, is considered. The model is discretized by the Finite Integration Technique [1] and the resulting EVP reads:

$$\left(\mathbf{A}_{cc,\varphi} - \omega^2 \mathbf{I}\right) \widehat{\mathbf{e}} = 0. \tag{5}$$

Where $\mathbf{A}_{cc,\varphi}$ is the system matrix, ω the angular frequency and $\widehat{\mathbf{e}}$ the electric grid voltage, respectively. Equation (5) can be interpreted as discrete representation of the continuous curl-curl-equation $\text{curl}(\frac{1}{\mu}\text{curl}(\mathbf{E})) - \omega^2 \varepsilon \mathbf{E} = 0$ of the electric field $\mathbf{E}$. The periodic phase shift between the front and the back plane is described by the Floquet condition which maps the electric field from one boundary to the other, multiplied by the phase shift $\widehat{\mathbf{e}}_1 = \widehat{\mathbf{e}}_2 \exp(j\varphi)$. Thereby j is the complex unit, and $\widehat{\mathbf{e}}_1$ and $\widehat{\mathbf{e}}_2$ are the electric grid voltages at the front and back plane, respectively. The phase shift can be interpreted as a parametric dependency of the EVP since it appears in $\mathbf{A}_{cc,\varphi}$.

The simulation results are shown in Fig. 3. A mode in the middle of the spectrum is chosen for the mode tracking algorithm. A zoom of an interesting section of the dispersion diagram is shown in Fig. 3 in the right bottom corner. The algorithm detects an intersection and a touching point and tracks the eigenvalue in a proper way. The reference, which originates from multiply solved EVPs, fails to distinguish between these intersection or touching points.

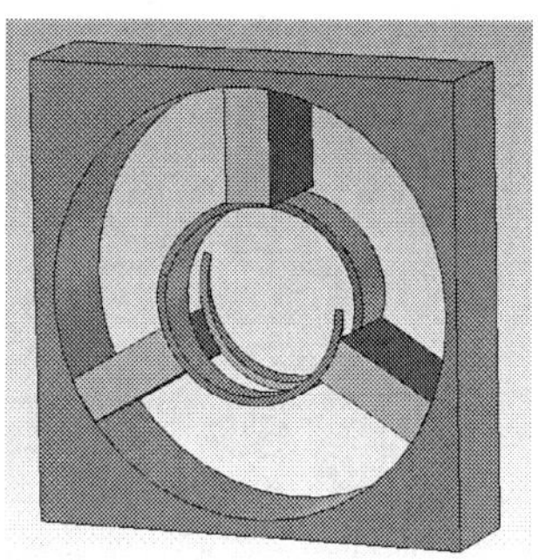

Fig. 2: Simulation setup with periodic boundaries at the front and back plane.

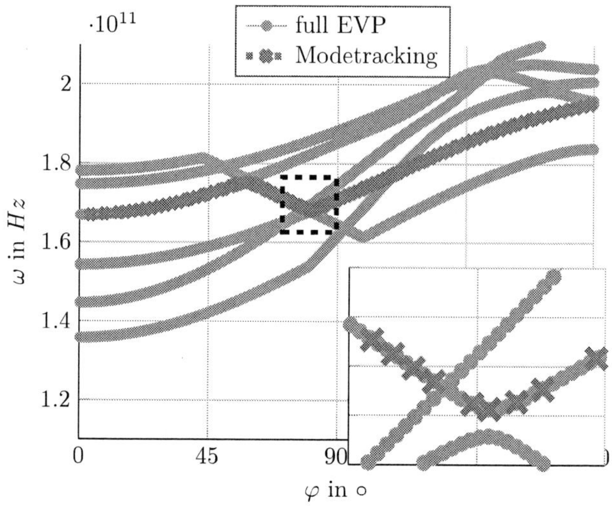

Fig. 3: Modetracking of a chosen mode within the spectrum with zoom on the black marked section of interest.

V. Conclusion and Outlook

The major advantage of the new algorithm is the detection of intersection and touching points without any additional post-processing, which is often necessary for comparable approaches. Furthermore, the presented algorithm is not limited to periodic structures and has been successfully tested with other parameter dependent problems. Since the formulation is for linear EVPs the next step is to extend the algorithm to nonlinear EVPs with other parameter dependencies.

References

[1] T. Weiland, "Modes in infinitely repeating structures of cylindrical symmetry," 1986.
[2] R. B. Nelson, "Simplified calculation of eigenvector derivatives," AIAA Journal, vol. 14, no. 9, pp. 1201-1205, 1976.
[3] R. L. Dailey, "Eigenvector derivatives with repeated eigenvalues," AIAA Journal, vol. 27, no. 4, pp. 486-491, 1989.
[4] P. Jorkowski and R. Schuhmann, "Higher-order sensitivity analysis of periodic 3-D eigenvalue problems for electromagnetic field calculations," Adv. Radio Sci., 15, 215-221, doi:10.5194/ars-15-215-2017, 2017.
[5] D. Klindworth and K. Schmidt, "An efficient calculation of photonic crystal band structures using Taylor expansions," Commun. Comput. Phys., 16(5): 13551388, 2014.
[6] CST, CST Studio Suite, www.cst.com, latest access: 15.11.2017.

Estimation of Mutual Coupling in Irregular Planar Arrays

Andrej Konforta, Thomas Bertuch and Peter Knott
Antenna Technology and Electromagnetic Modeling
Fraunhofer FHR
Fraunhofer Str. 20, 53343 Wachtberg, Germany
andrej.konforta@fhr.fraunhofer.de

***Abstract*—An efficient method for estimating the mutual coupling is reviewed specifically with regard to irregular planar arrays. A peculiarity of the method is its flexibility. It can be used in conjunction with arbitrarily inclined and arbitrarily distributed radiators of any shape. Full-wave simulations of the entire array model are avoided by only considering the first order radiator interaction. Results for an array that consists of inclined apertures are shown and compared to a reference solution.**

I. Introduction

The design of array antennas requires a detailed analysis of the mutual coupling because interactions between the radiators can cause performance degradation over frequency and scan angle [1]. Usually, full-wave simulations are performed to obtain a measure for the element interaction. However, having a large number of broadband radiators, full-domain simulations can become time and memory-demanding, which limits the array optimization to a small number of iterations.

Periodic structures can be efficiently investigated by Floquet modal analysis [2]. For large finite regular arrays this method typically leads to acceptable accuracy within short time, except for radiators located near the aperture outer edges. However, the Floquet modal approach cannot be applied on arrays that consist of irregularly placed and irregularly oriented radiators due to the absence of periodicity. Nevertheless, irregular arrays, for example conformal arrays [3] or thinned planar arrays [4], are of great practical importance. An efficient generalized unit-cell-like approach is therefore highly desirable.

Recently, a method has been proposed which allows estimating the mutual coupling by utilizing the fields of an isolated radiator by exploiting surface equivalence in conjunction with the reciprocity theorem [5]. Results have been shown for two elements. However, no statement was given concerning larger arrays.

In this paper, investigations are presented with focus on the methods performance if it is applied on inclined radiators. Results are shown for an exemplary array that consists of nine individually inclined waveguide apertures.

II. Test Case

A. *Waveguide Aperture*

A plain waveguide aperture is used as an exemplary radiator. The waveguide has the dimensions 22.86 mm x 10.16 mm (WR-90) and is excited by a coaxial-probe. The fields are solved using the CST MWS® F-Solver and sampled on a box-shaped Huygens surface (Fig. 1, a). The ground plane size is equal to $10\lambda_u \times 10\lambda_u$, where $\lambda_u = 29.98$ mm is the wavelength at the upper frequency limit. With the aid of the free space dyadic Green's Function $\overline{\overline{G}}_{FS}$ the field outside the box can be maintained considering only the equivalent currents J_s, M_s and the tangential currents flowing in the xy-plane (Fig. 1, b). To further simplify the field calculation the dyadic Green's Function $\overline{\overline{G}}_{HS}$, obtained by Image Theory and valid for a half-space with vacuum ($z \geq 0$) over perfect electric conducting material, is used here (Fig. 1, c). To account for the individual inclination angle the source distribution is reoriented numerically within the used coupling algorithm.

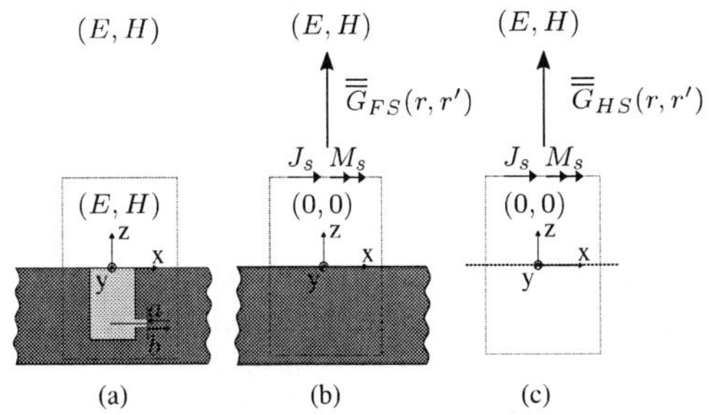

Fig. 1. Equivalent sources of plain waveguide aperture.

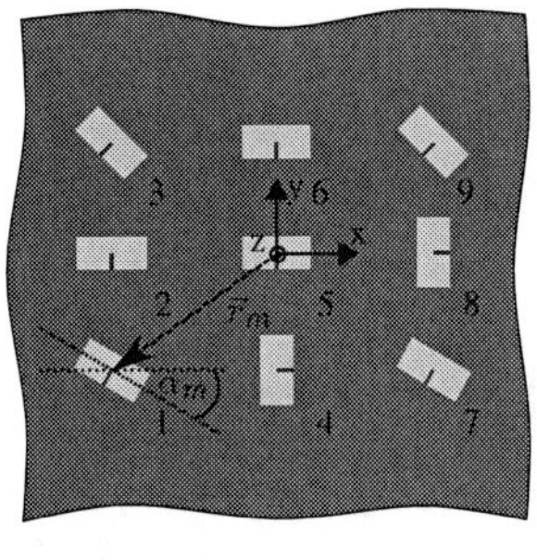

Fig. 2. Array test case.

TABLE I. Array configuration.

Index m	$\vec{r}_m/\lambda_u$ (1)	α_m (rad)
1	$\{-1,-1,0\}$	$-\pi/6$
2	$\{-1,0,0\}$	0
3	$\{-1,1,0\}$	$-\pi/4$
4	$\{0,-1,0\}$	$\pi/2$
5	$\{0,0,0\}$	0
6	$\{0,1,0\}$	0
7	$\{1,-1,0\}$	$-\pi/6$
8	$\{1,0,0\}$	$\pi/2$
9	$\{1,1,0\}$	$-\pi/4$

B. *3x3 Planar Array*

The simulated structure is depicted in Fig. 2. The placement and orientation of each radiator is given in Table I.

The full-wave full-domain solution computation time is equal to 5h, 34min and 19 seconds (4 cores @3.6GHz). Execution of the estimate (non-optimized code) takes about 27 seconds on a single CPU core running at 2.40GHz, assuming that the equivalent sources of an isolated radiator are provided.

III. Simulation Results and Discussion

The scattering parameters are shown in Fig. 3. Reference results directly obtained by the CST MWS® F-Solver (full-domain) are shown as dashed lines.

Due to the method's principle, the estimate indicates no impact on the self-coupling S_{ii} through neighboring radiators. This is true only for the asymptotic case when the distance between all elements gets electrically very large. The maximum error in self-coupling occurs for the radiator in the center (e_{55}=0.8dB).

The maximum absolute error in coupling for directly neighboring radiators stays below 2dB (S_{32}, S_{74}). For greater distances, the quality of estimation is poor due to neglect of the perturbation through surrounding radiators. Depending on the radiator position the correlation between estimate and full-domain solution is hardly observable for coupling values below -30dB. On the other hand, the overall impact on the active impedance due to radiators which are located electrically far away is probable weak. The estimate may therefore deliver a better quality of performance prediction in comparison to design methodologies where mutual coupling is simply neglected. If desired, a better accuracy can possibly be achieved by using iterative techniques to calculate higher order interactions between the radiators. However, at the expense of being bound to specialized toolsets.

IV. Conclusion

An existing method for efficient estimation of the mutual coupling has been evaluated in conjunction with an irregular planar array. The error of estimation is about 2dB over 22.2% of fractional bandwidth in coupling between directly neighboring radiators. For greater distances the error becomes relatively large. Once the near field of a single element is obtained, the overall computation time is relatively small in comparison to a full-wave full-domain simulation.

References

[1] D. M. Pozar, "A relation between the active input impedance and the active element pattern of a phased array," in IEEE Transactions on Antennas and Propagation, vol. 51, no. 9, pp. 2486-2489, Sep. 2003.

[2] A. K. Bhattacharyya, Phased Array Antennas: Floquet Analysis, Synthesis, BFNs and Active Array Systems. Hoboken, N.J: Wiley-Interscience, 2006.

[3] L. Josefsson, P. Persson, Conformal Array Antenna Theory and Design. Hoboken, N.J: Wiley-Interscience, 2006.

[4] R. L. Haupt, "Thinned arrays using genetic algorithms," in IEEE Transactions on Antennas and Propagation, vol. 42, no. 7, pp. 993-999, July 1994.

[5] M. Kragalott, M. S. Kluskens, D. A. Zolnick, W. M. Dorsey, and J. A. Valenzi, "A toolset independent hybrid method for calculating antenna coupling," in IEEE Transactions on Antennas and Propagation, vol. 59, no. 2, pp. 443-451, Feb. 2011.

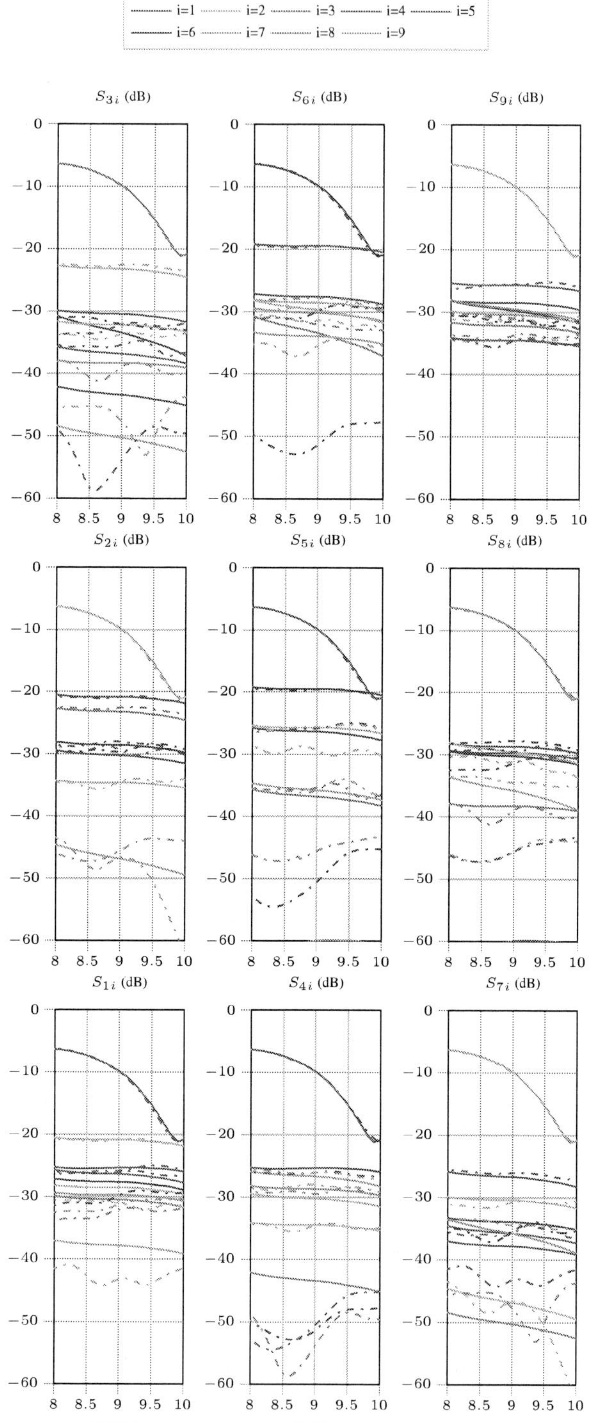

Fig. 3. Scattering parameters. Full-domain results are shown as dashed lines.

Effects of Internal Reflections on The Performance of Lens-Integrated mmW and THz Antennas

Burak Ozbey and Kubilay Sertel
ElectroScience Laboratory, Ohio State University, Columbus, OH 43212
ozbey.2@osu.edu, sertel.1@osu.edu

Abstract—**Multiple reflections from electrically large hemispherical lens surfaces of lens-integrated antennas are investigated using an iterative Huygens' integral approach. In particular for mmW- and THz-band applications, double-slot antennas on extended hemispherical high-resistivity Silicon lenses have been widely used due to the high Gaussisicity of their radiation/reception patterns. Previous studies assumed an electrically-large lens and evaluated the antenna pattern using first-order physical optics approximation. Although this approach is fairly accurate for estimating the radiation pattern of such antennas, the reception pattern and the associated performance of receiving sensors need a more careful consideration due to the relatively large level of internal reflections from the concave boundary of the high index lens. Here, we present an iterative method to compute and study the effects of multiple refections inside electrically large lenses. The rich nature of quasi-optical wave behavior is demonstrated through several examples corresponding to individual bounces of the incident, reflected, and transmitted waves from a double slot antenna.**

I. Introduction

Lens-integrated antennas have been very popular for mmW and THz sensor applications due to key advantages that allow efficient coupling to quasi-optical systems. Most importantly, the high Gaussicity and absence of spherical aberrations, coupled with high directivity make such sensors the preferred choice for various sensing and imaging applications [1]–[4]. Although the ideal lens shape is elliptical, hyperhemispherical and extended hemispherical lenses perform equally well in terms of quasi-optical coupling performance. Typically, an electrically large lens is used to collimate slot antenna radiation (typically 30λ in diameter), making their computational analysis quite challenging. To address this, a ray-optics/field integration approach was employed by Filipovic et al. in [1] and [2] to find the radiation patterns at the boundary and outside the lens. However, this approach ignores the effect of multiple reflections inside the lens. Although internal reflections in the lens do not significantly impact the radiation pattern of a transmitting antenna, in receiving mode the internal bounces degrade the signal quality and deserve a more accurate analysis. Internally-reflected power can be quite significant, particularly for high dielectric constant materials such as high-resistivity Silicon. In this paper, we study the effects of such multiple reflections within an extended hemispherical lens, integrated with a double-slot antenna. Multiple internal reflections from the lens-air interface, as well as the cylindrical extension section and the ground plane are taken into account, and their effects on the lens performance are examined.

II. Analysis of Multiple Internal Reflections in Lens-Integrated Antennas

The geometry of the extended hemispherical lens considered here is shown in Fig. 1. The aperture fields (viz. magnetic currents) of the double-slot antenna with a slot length $0.28\lambda_{air}$ and a spacing of $0.16\lambda_{air}$ inside a high-resistivity Silicon ($\epsilon_r = 11.7$) lens are used to calculate the radiation pattern, assuming radiation into the material half space and a first-order Fresnel transmission through the lens-air boundary [1], [2]. For a representative frequency of 246 GHz, an extension length of $L = 7.3\lambda_d$, and a $19\lambda_d$ radius lens result in a physically-compact 13.7 mm diameter lens (λ_d is the wavelength inside the lens). The antenna is located at the center of the xy-plane, and the slots are along the y-direction.

The radiated fields inside and outside the lens are shown in Fig. 2, by including the multiple paths shown in Fig. 1. That is, although a sizable portion of the radiated field ($E_{i,1}$) is transmitted through the lens ($E_{t,1}$), a significant amount is also reflected back at the air-lens boundary (E_r). This reflected field converges to a "conjugate" focal point inside the Silicon lens and subsequently impinges on the antenna ground plane (i.e., the original focal plane of the extended hemispherical lens), before reflecting back to the lens-air boundary one more time ($E_{i,2}$). E_r can be calculated by finding the equivalent current densities using the reflected fields on the lens-air boundary, and then radiating them back into the lens using Huygens' integrals. For evaluating the integrals, Stratton-Chu formulation is preferred since the gradient of Green's function is defined at the source region and hence it is easier to perform. For completeness, it is given here in the form [5]:

$$\mathbf{E}(\mathbf{r}) = \oiint_{S'} \{-j\omega\mu[\hat{n} \times \mathbf{H}(\mathbf{r}')]g(\mathbf{r},\mathbf{r}') + [\hat{n}\cdot\mathbf{E}(\mathbf{r}')]\nabla' g(\mathbf{r},\mathbf{r}') + [\hat{n}\times\mathbf{E}(\mathbf{r}')]\times\nabla' g(\mathbf{r},\mathbf{r}')\}dS'. \quad (1)$$

We also note that the wave reflected from the ground plane ($E_{i,2}$) can also be computed using image theory. The conventional, first-order transmitted field outside the lens from a radiating double slot antenna is shown in Fig.2 (a), with the inset on the right illustrating instantaneous field distribution inside the extended hemispherical lens. As seen, the first-order transmitted wave has a fairly collimated Gaussian beam profile with its waist occurring at about $25\lambda_0$ away from the lens surface.

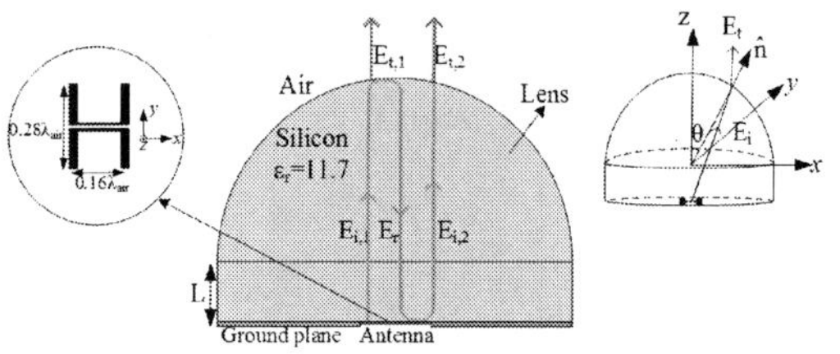

Fig. 1. Geometry of a typical lens-integrated antenna, illustrating the multiple reflection and transmission paths internal to the lens. A 3-d view is shown in the bottom left inset.

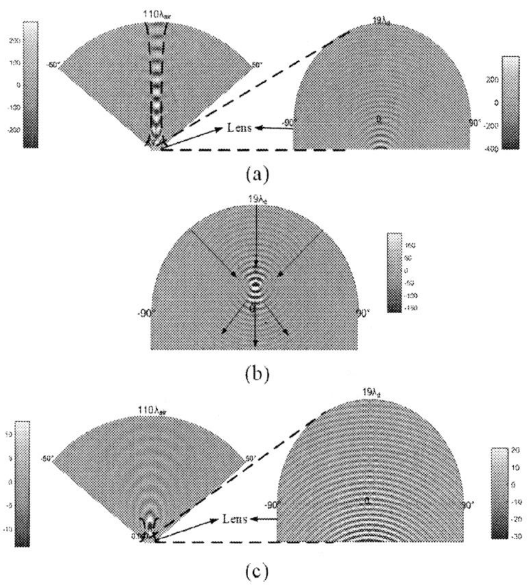

Fig. 2. Incident and transmitted instantaneous fields computed inside and outside the extended hemispherical lens. (a) $E_{i,1}$ and $E_{t,1}$: x-component of the first-order incident (right) and transmitted (left) electric fields on E-plane at a time instant, $t = 0$; (b) E_r: x-component of the first-order reflected electric field on E-plane at a time instant, $t = 0$; (c) $E_{i,2}$ and $E_{t,2}$: x-component of the second-order incident electric field (right) and the second-order transmitted (left) electric field on E-plane at a time instant, $t = 0$.

The instantaneous E-field reflected back into the lens is depicted in Fig. 2 (b). As seen, the reflected beam first focuses back to the conjugate focal point of the ellipse that is approximated by the extended hemispherical geometry, before it diverges and reflects from the ground plane on the original focal plane. Fig. 2 (c) illustrates the Gaussian beam nature of the second-order transmitted E-field ($E_{t,2}$). It is interesting to note here that the beam waist and focal point of this second-order field is completely different from the first-order transmitted wave $E_{t,1}$, in that the beam waist of $E_{t,2}$ is much narrower and the focal point for $E_{t,2}$ occurs very close to the lens surface, at about $5\lambda_0$ away. The antenna radiation pattern is shown in Fig. 3. As seen, the side lobes are more prominent when the second-order reflection contributions are included in the calculation. Furthermore, it is observed that the Stratton-Chu formulation yields a much shallower first null, as

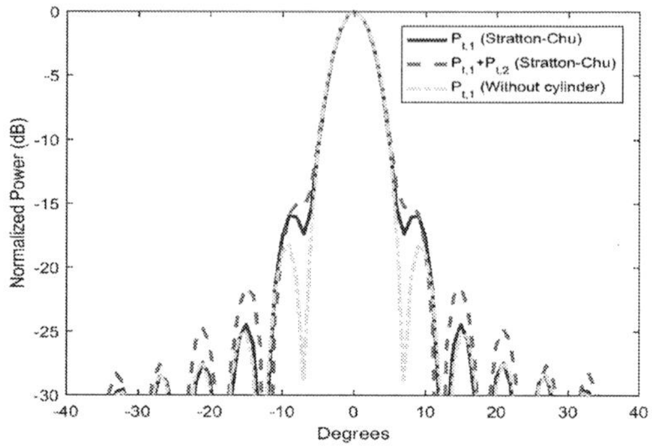

Fig. 3. Computed E-plane radiation pattern for the first-order transmitted wave (solid) compared to the computed pattern after multiple reflections inside the lens using Stratton-Chu evaluation of equivalent sources on the lens boundary (dashed), and pattern calculated using far-field approximation (dash-dotted).

well as a higher side lobe level, as compared to the far-field approximation used in [1], [2]. Finally, the far-field patterns obtained from Stratton-Chu formulation agrees better with the experiment results given in [1].

III. Conclusion

In this paper, the effects of multiple reflections within a lens-integrated double-slot antenna are investigated. The fields incident on the lens-air boundary are evaluated using the radiation pattern of a double-slot antenna on a dielectric interface. Subsequently, utilizing Huygens' principle, the fields reflected from the boundary are calculated by employing the equivalent current densities within the Stratton-Chu framework. Image theory is also utilized to find the fields that reflect back from the ground plane, which are subsequently transmitted through the lens boundary as a second-order radiation effect. It is shown that the contributions from multiple reflections yield higher side-lobe levels, and should be considered for a more accurate characterization of lens-integrated antenna structures.

Acknowledgment

The authors would like to thank the Turkish Fulbright Commission for their support under the Postdoctoral Program Grant.

References

[1] D. F. Filipovic, et al., "Double slot antennas on extended hemispherical and elliptical silicon dielectric lenses," IEEE Trans. Microw. Theory Techn., vol. 41, no. 10, pp. 1738–1749, Oct. 1993.
[2] D. F. Filipovic, et al., "Off-axis properties of silicon and quartz dielectric lens antennas," IEEE Trans. Microw. Theory Techn., vol. 45, no. 5, pp. 760–766, May 1997.
[3] G. C. Trichopoulos, et al., "A novel approach for improving off-axis pixel performance of terahertz focal plane arrays," IEEE Trans. Microw. Theory Techn., vol. 58, no. 7, pp. 2014-2021, Jul. 2010.
[4] G. C. Trichopoulos, et al., "A broadband focal plane array camera for real-time THz imaging applications," IEEE Trans. Antennas Propag., vol. 61, no. 4, pp. 1733-1740, Apr. 2013.
[5] J. A. Kong, Electromagnetic Wave Theory, John Wiley & Sons, 1986.

Ray Tracing Using Shooting-Bouncing Technique to Model Mine Tunnels: Theory and Verification for a PEC Waveguide

Blake Troksa, Cam Key, Forest Kunkel, Slobodan V. Savić, Milan M. Ilić, and Branislav M. Notaroš
Colorado State University, Electrical & Computer Engineering Department, Fort Collins, CO
notaros@colostate.edu

***Abstract*—We present a shooting-bouncing approach to ray-tracing as applied to signal propagation modeling in electrically large waveguides, such as underground mine tunnels at wireless communication frequencies. The method is verified for a dominant-mode rectangular metallic waveguide excited by a dipole antenna.**

Keywords—communications, computational electromagnetics, high-frequency, microwave, ray tracing, signal propagation, waveguide.

I. Introduction

This paper addresses application of computational electromagnetics (CEM) to signal propagation modeling in underground mines. One of our main approaches to the wireless propagation analysis of underground mines, which is an extremely challenging CEM problem, relies primarily on shooting-bouncing rays (SBR) ray-tracing (RT).

Using traditional full-wave EM solvers for microwave frequencies in an underground mine may prove impractical in many cases due to computation run time required, as well as memory requirements, depending on the particular technique employed. Ray-tracing provides a significant decrease in computational run time for these electrically large structures. Ray-tracing methods enable propagation modeling in very complicated scenarios such as railway stations, and they can provide useful prediction of signal loss characteristics [1,4].

II. Ray Tracing Theory

The shooting-bouncing rays approach in RT involves launching a set of test rays in all directions in which propagation from the source can be expected. These rays are then traced through the scene, and their intersections with objects in the scene recorded. This method is described in detail in [1]. The electric field at a desired location in the scene is then found by employing an ideal plane wave approximation for each ray. Then, using the reflection coefficients based on surface parameters for each reflection, the final electric field at the desired observation point can be approximated due to each ray path between the source and observation point [3]. This process may be repeated for several observation points to produce a 2D or 3D field profile at a desired location in the scene.

When a 2D field profile is desired, we discretize the plane of the desired field profile into a grid of uniform pixels or grid blocks. The complex-valued field vectors of all rays intersecting a given block are added to approximate the total field at that block due to the given source and scene geometry. This process naturally approximates interference. While this introduces phase and magnitude error, the error can be minimized by ensuring the grid blocks are small relatively to the wavelength, and that a large number of rays are used, such that each block has a sufficiently high sample density to accurately approximate the field.

The shooting-bouncing approach to ray-tracing is advantageous because it is conveniently parallelizable which allows for efficient and expeditious computations. This is essential because it enables analysis of problems that require very high ray counts to achieve sufficient sample density for field convergence. Another benefit to the acceleration (by parallelization) of ray-tracing is that larger structures can be evaluated for signal propagation characteristics more easily and more quickly. This technique may be further accelerated by reducing the total cost of ray to facet (environment objects) intersection tests. The rays that propagate in this model interact with environment objects that cause the rays to be reflected. These interactions with the environment can be optimized using space-partitioning trees that efficiently store and access obstacles located in the environment (similar to a binary search tree) [1,2].

III. Results and Discussion

Testing of the ray-tracing method we developed was conducted on a perfect electric conductor (PEC) rectangular waveguide. This scene was chosen because of the ability to compare with an analytic solution for verification. The waveguide dimensions are chosen to be 0.5842 m × 0.2921 m, and the waveguide was excited with a Hertzian dipole antenna of unit peak field magnitude and frequency 350 MHz. The observation plane was placed 50 cm from the source. Operation frequency was chosen to only propagate the dominant TE_{10} mode in this waveguide.

This waveguide embodies a very challenging case for ray-tracing, as it is PEC, so all reflections must be considered (this is a completely convex scene), and it is not electrically very large, as convenient in ray-tracing technique.

This work was supported by the National Science Foundation under grant ECCS-1646562.

The analytical solution for the dominant mode in the rectangular PEC waveguide states that the electric field should be uniform in the direction parallel to the short axis of the waveguide, and vary with a half-cosine in the axis parallel with the long axis of the waveguide. Fig. 1 shows the result of the ray-tracing method on this scene.

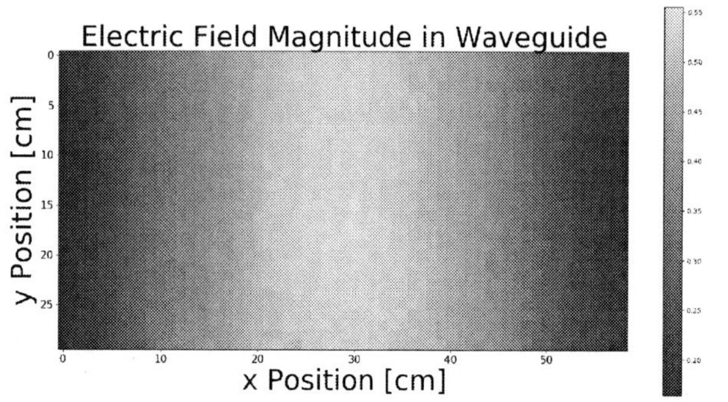

Fig. 1. Magnitude of the electric field for the waveguide excited with a Hertzian dipole at 350 MHz. The cutoff frequency for the waveguide is 256 MHz, which only allows propagation of the TE_{10} mode.

We observe in Fig. 1 the expected trends along both axes. The magnitude varies only slightly along y for any x coordinate in the waveguide, and the magnitude is peaked in x at the center of the waveguide, and is relatively symmetrical about the center of the waveguide.

The final electric field is found by summing a discrete number of uniform plane waves at the observation plane. The number of rays that intersect the observation plane determines the number of plane waves. The solution generated by a ray-tracing method should converge to the analytical solution as the number of rays increases. Fig. 2 shows the electric field magnitudes for a cross section of the waveguide for varying numbers of rays.

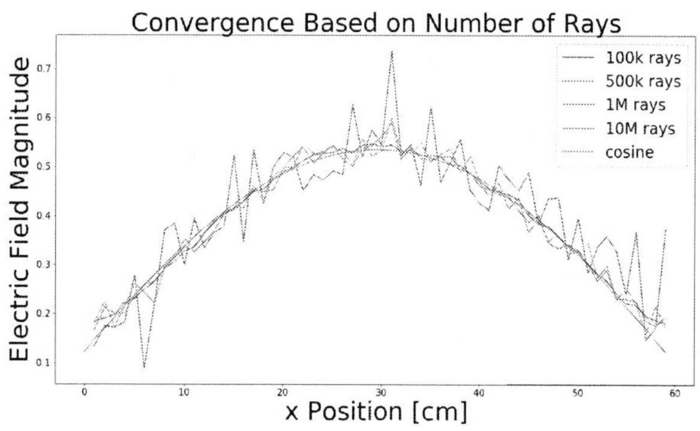

Fig. 2. Electric field magnitude in the cross section of the waveguide, with the waveguide parameters and excitation frequency remaining identical to Fig. 1. The number of rays was varied from 100 thousand rays to 10 million rays.

We observe from Fig. 2 the expected convergence of the ray tracing results with increasing the number of rays in the simulation. As the number of rays increases, the cross-section magnitude begins to smoothen to a cosine. The analytical solution states the electric field should be zero at the walls of the waveguide. The ray-tracing method results in a symmetrical offset of approximately 0.2 units on the edges. The offset is a result of the loss of accuracy from sending a finite number of rays resulting in a finite sampling density.

Each ray is terminated after a given number of reflections; if it did not reach the observation plane within the reflection limit, it will not contribute to a field at observation location. The solution should converge as the number of permissible reflections increases, as each additional ray that intersects the observation plane increases the sampling density. Fig. 3 shows the cross-sectional magnitude for varying number of reflections.

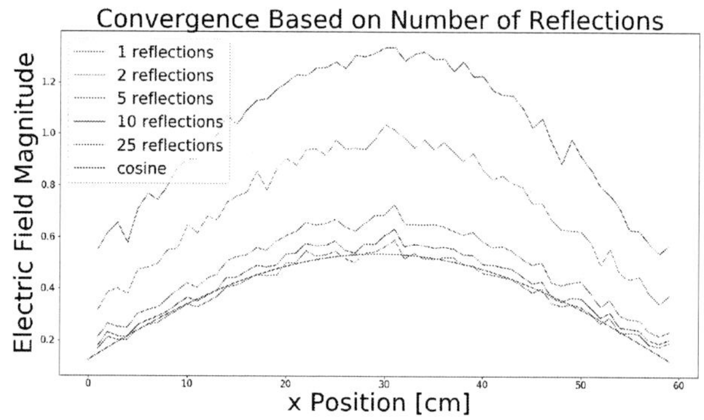

Fig. 3. Electric field magnitude based on the reflection order. The waveguide parameters remain identical to Fig. 1. The reflection order allowed varied from 1 to 25.

We observe from Fig. 3 a good convergence of the ray tracing results to the offset cosine as reflection order increases. The error is worst for low reflection order, and best for high reflection order, as expected.

REFERENCES

[1] M. F. Cátedra and J. Perez, Cell Planning for Wireless Communications. Norwood, MA, USA: Artech House, 1999.

[2] T. S. Rappaport, S. Y. Seidel, and K. R. Schaubach, "Site-specific propagation for PCS system design," in *Wireless Personal Communications*, M. J. Feuerstein, T. S. Rappaport, eds., Boston: Kluwer Academic Publishers, 1993, pp. 281-315.

[3] B. M. Notaros, *Electromagnetics*, New Jersey: PEARSON Prentice Hall; 2010.

[4] X. Zhang, N. Sood, J. Siu, and C. D. Sarris, "A hybrid ray-tracing/vector parabolic equation method for propagation modeling in train communication channels," in IEEE Transactions On Antennas And Propagation, vol. 64, no. 5, May 2016.

Integral Accuracy and Experimental Evidence for the Stability of Time Domain Integral Equations

Jielin Li and Daniel S. Weile
Department of Electrical and Computer Engineering
University of Delaware
Newark, DE 19711, USA
weile@udel.edu

David A. Hopkins
RDRL-WMM-B
Army Research Laboratory, APG
Aberdeen, MD 21005, USA
david.a.hopkins.civ@mail.mil

Abstract—**In the analysis of time domain integral equations for the solution of electromagnetic problems, experience is the primary guide to choosing simulation parameters (such as integration rules and orders for the computation of kernel elements) that ensure stability. To improve this state of affairs, previous work examined the effects of integration orders on stability. In this work, adaptive quadrature will be used so that impact of integration accuracy on stability can be more finely assessed. Numerical results show that numerical integrals are not as reliable as practitioners often assume, and that high accuracy in the near field integration must be employed to achieve stability.**

I. Introduction

Due to the complicated nature of numerical simulation of electromagnetic phenomena, researchers implementing time domain integral equations (TDIEs) have had difficulty locating the precise causes of their instability. Causes of these difficulties abound; for instance analytical proofs of the stability always assume the integrations are performed exactly. Similarly, numerical integrals can be computed on flat patches through series expansion, yet the truncation of the series makes the approximation numerical approximation. In short, the accuracy of the spatial overlap integral computations affect their stability properties, mixing space and time in a confusing way making it hard to predict stability based on the quantification of error.

In our previous work [1], we examined the nature of this relationship using the convolution quadrature (CQ) approach of [2]. The results of that study demonstrated that the stability of the method is not necessarily improved by increasing the order of the integrals involved, and that in many cases stability hinges on using different integration orders for the near field and the far field basis function integration. To further demonstrate this effect, in this paper, we will use adaptive quadrature to compute the near field integrals. Numerical results will demonstrate we cannot simply assume the integrations are exact, but that more accurate setting in the near field integrations can ensure stability.

II. Convolution Quadrature

Let S be the surface of a perfect electrical conductor (PEC) in free space, and let the permittivity and permeability of free space be ϵ_0 and μ_0, respectively. Let S be illuminated by a incident electric field which can be written in the Laplace domain as $\tilde{\mathbf{E}}^{\text{inc}}(\mathbf{r}, s)$. By applying the the PEC boundary condition to the equivalent current on S, we derive the Laplace domain electric field integral equation:

$$s\tilde{\mathbf{E}}^{\text{inc}}(\mathbf{r}, s) = \frac{s^2\mu_0}{4\pi} \iint\limits_S \tilde{\mathbf{J}}(\mathbf{r}', s)\frac{e^{-\frac{s|\mathbf{r}-\mathbf{r}'|}{c}}}{|\mathbf{r}-\mathbf{r}'|}d\mathbf{r}' - \frac{1}{4\pi\epsilon_0} \iint\limits_S \nabla' \cdot \tilde{\mathbf{J}}(\mathbf{r}', s)\frac{e^{-\frac{s|\mathbf{r}-\mathbf{r}'|}{c}}}{|\mathbf{r}-\mathbf{r}'|}d\mathbf{r}'. \quad (1)$$

Spatial discretization can be accomplished by approximating the current with the series:

$$\tilde{\mathbf{J}}(\mathbf{r}, s) = \sum_{n=0}^{N_s} \tilde{I}_n(s)\mathbf{S}_n(\mathbf{r}), \quad (2)$$

where the $\mathbf{S}_n(\mathbf{r})$ are a set of suitable spatial basis functions. The result of this operation is then multiplied by the $\mathbf{S}_m(\mathbf{r})$, for $m = 1, \ldots, N_s$, and integrated over S, resulting in a spatially discretized equation.

Discretization in time is accomplished with CQ [2] with time step Δt. CQ is motivated by the two observations: In the Laplace domain, multiplication by s corresponds to temporal differentiation, and in the $\mathcal{Z}$-domain (its discrete analog) multiplication by z^{-1} indicates a Δt delay. We thus approximate s by the second order backward difference formula in z^{-1},

$$s = \frac{3 - 4z^{-1} + z^{-2}}{2\Delta t}, \quad (3)$$

and compute the inverse $\mathcal{Z}$ transform. This directly leads to a set of equations for $\mathbf{I}_i$, the set of unknown currents at time $i\Delta t$, of the form:

$$\mathbf{Z}_0\mathbf{I}_i = \mathbf{V}_i - \sum_{j=0}^{i-1} \mathbf{Z}_{i-j}\mathbf{I}_j, \quad (4)$$

which we can solve iteratively by marching on in time. The elements of the vectors $\mathbf{V}_i$ are given by:

$$[\mathbf{V}_i]_n = \iint\limits_S \dot{\mathbf{E}}^{\text{inc}}(\mathbf{r}, i\Delta t) \cdot \mathbf{S}_n(\mathbf{r})d\mathbf{r}, \quad (5)$$

where $\dot{\mathbf{E}}^{\text{inc}}(\mathbf{r}, t)$ is the derivative of the time domain incident field, and the elements of the matrices $\mathbf{Z}_k$ are given by:

$$[\mathbf{Z}_k]_{mn} = \iint\limits_S \iint\limits_S \frac{\mu_0 \mathbf{S}_m(\mathbf{r}) \cdot \mathbf{S}_n(\mathbf{r}')}{4\pi |\mathbf{r} - \mathbf{r}'|} \beta_k (|\mathbf{r} - \mathbf{r}'|) \, d\mathbf{r}' d\mathbf{r} - \iint\limits_S \iint\limits_S \frac{\nabla \cdot \mathbf{S}_m(\mathbf{r}) \nabla' \cdot \mathbf{S}_n(\mathbf{r}')}{4\pi \epsilon_0 |\mathbf{r} - \mathbf{r}'|} \alpha_k (|\mathbf{r} - \mathbf{r}'|) \, d\mathbf{r}' d\mathbf{r}. \quad (6)$$

In this equation,

$$\alpha_k(t) = \frac{1}{k!} \left(\frac{t}{2}\right)^{\frac{k}{2}} e^{-\frac{3}{2}t} H_k\left(\sqrt{2t}\right), \quad (7)$$

for $k \geq 0$, $\alpha_k = 0$ for $k < 0$, $H_k(\cdot)$ is the kth order Hermite polynomial, and

$$\beta_k(t) = \frac{\alpha_{k-4} - 8\alpha_{k-3} + 22\alpha_{k-2} - 24\alpha_{k-1} + 3\alpha_k}{4(\Delta t)^2}. \quad (8)$$

Since our concern is the dependence of the stability of the algorithm the numerical approximation accuracy the integrals of (6) for different distances, we use adaptive quadrature method to allow precise accuracy control of the integrals.

III. Adaptive Quadrature

Adaptive quadrature works by prescribing a relative error goal, and approximating the desired integral as a sum over smaller and smaller intervals until the desired error is achieved [3]. More specifically, a numerical approximation $Q[a, b]$ to the integral of $f(x)$ over the interval $[a, b]$ is computed first, followed by the approximation over two subintervals. An error estimate ϵ thus presents itself:

$$\epsilon = \frac{\left|\left(Q[a, \frac{a+b}{2}] + Q[\frac{a+b}{2}, b]\right) - Q[a, b]\right|}{\left|\left(Q[a, \frac{a+b}{2}] + Q[\frac{a+b}{2}, b]\right)\right|}. \quad (9)$$

If the estimated error is larger than the input tolerance τ, the intervals are subdivided again, and the process is repeated on each half. The subdivision continues until the error is less than τ on every interval.

IV. Numerical Results

To examine the dependence of TDIE stability on integration accuracy, consider a 264 flat-patch approximation to the NASA almond excited by a plane wave with x-polarized electric field:

$$E_x^{\text{inc}}(\mathbf{r}, t) = \exp\left[\frac{(t - t_0 - z/c)^2}{2\sigma^2}\right] \cos(3 \times 10^9 \pi t). \quad (10)$$

Here, $\sigma = \pi/3B$, with $B = 1$ GHz. The number of time steps is 5000 and each step has length $\Delta t = 1 \times 10^{-9}$ s. The longest dimension of the almond is 25.8 cm and lays on the x-axis, and its thinnest dimension is 3.2 cm and lays on the z-axis. We call a simulation stable if all the currents at the end of the simulation are less than 1 fA/m^2.

The integral equation we use is the combined field integral equation with equal electric and magnetic field parts. The self integration rules described in [4] are used when a basis patch and a test patch overlap. The underlying basis and

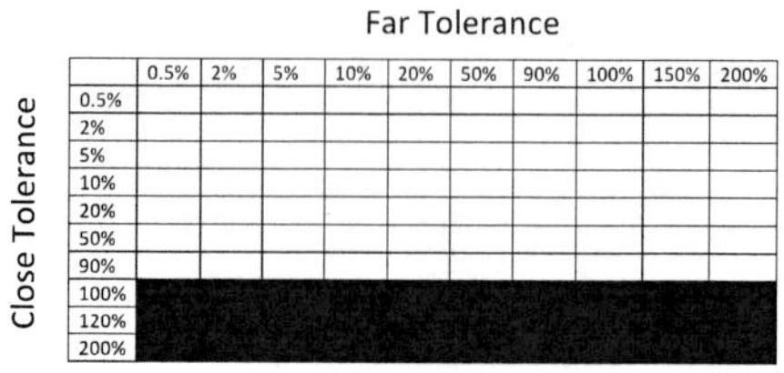

Fig. 1. Stability of the simulation versus integration rules; black squares mark unstable computations, white squares mark stable ones.

testing integration rules are Dunavant rules described in [5]. We define basis integrations to be close when their centroids are separated by less than 3 cm. The close integration rule and the far integration rule are Dunavant rules with up to 6 levels of adaptive refinement. For the testing integration, static Dunavant rules are applied. Numerical results were obtained for different values of the error allowed by the adaptive integrator.

Fig. 1 shows the result of the experiment obtained when the base order of all of the integration rules is 5. Because the figure was made using adaptive quadrature rules based on standard rules, tt shows the integration which we often assume nearly exact could be in error by more than 100%. It also shows by improving the accuracy of the near field integration, the simulation can be made stable even when the far integration is much less accurate.

V. Conclusions

TDIE stability can be improved by increasing the accuracy of the near field integration. Numerical integrations cannot always be assumed exact, and research presented in the talk will show that increasing integration order does not always increase accuracy. More results will be presented in the talk to further demonstrate these claims.

References

[1] D. S. Weile, I. Uluer, J. Li, and D.A. Hopkins, "Integration rules and experimental evidences for the stability of time domain integral equations," 2017 International Applied Computational Electromagnetics Society Symposium(ACES), pp. 1–2, 2017.

[2] X. B. Wang, R. A. Wildman, D. S. Weile, and P. Monk, "A finite difference delay modeling approach to the discretization of the time domain integral equations of electromagnetics," IEEE Transactions on Antennas and Propagation, vol. 56, no. 8, pp. 2442–2452, 2008.

[3] W. H. Press, S. A. Teukolsky, W. T. Vetterling, and B. P. Flannery, "Section 4.7. Adaptive Quadarature," Numerical Recipes: The Art of Scientific Computing, 3rd ed., New York: Cambridge University Press, pp. 194–195, 2007.

[4] D. S. Weile and X. B. Wang, "Strong singularity reduction for curved patches for the integral equations of electromagnetics," IEEE Antennas and Wireless Propagation Letters, pp. 1370–1373, 2009

[5] D. A. Dunavant, "High degree efficient symmetrical Gaussian quadrature rules for the triangle," International Journal for Numerical Methods in Engineering, vol.21, pp. 1129–1148, 1985.

A Novel Port Extraction Technique for Coupling Circuits with Full Wave Time Domain Integral Equation Solvers

S. O'Connor, S. Hughey, and B. Shanker
Dept. of Electrical and Computer Engineering, Michigan State University, East Lansing, MI 48824
bshanker@egr.msu.edu

***Abstract*—Fully coupled transient analysis of electromagnetic-circuit systems is highly desirable for a number of applications. Over the last decade or so, there have been several papers that present effective solutions to this problem within the context of full-wave differential or integral equation solvers. The method typically espoused is as follows: discretize the underlying electromagnetic (EM) system, couple with the circuit subsystem self-consistently, and then solve the coupled system. Within this framework, non-linearities are easily accounted for in the solution process. This is in direct contrast to frequency domain analysis, wherein one defines ports that couple the electromagnetic and circuit subsystems, i.e., representation of the EM system using an effective impedance. This approach permits: (a) solution only at the circuit level, and (b) one can readily incorporate different circuits without having to solve the coupled system repeatedly. In this paper, we present a technique that helps realize the same efficiency in the time domain. We will prescribe the means to effectively represent the EM subsystem in terms of a transient admittance, thus facilitating a solution to the coupled system via a circuit-level solve. Several results are presented that serve to validate the proposed approach and demonstrate its effectiveness.**

Keywords–harmonic balance, TDIE.

I. Introduction

The co-simulation of circuits together with full-wave electromagnetics is of paramount importance to radio frequency (RF) device design, understanding and mitigation of electromagnetic interference, signal integrity, and so on. The approach that one takes is to develop modeling tools that permit both a lumped element representation for circuits and distributed element representation for the fields, and solve for the mutual coupling self consistently. To a large extent, this problem has been visited several times in the recent past. An extensive body of work exists in both frequency and time domain analysis; see for example [1], [2] and references therein. In the frequency domain, the analysis of coupled circuit-electromagnetic (CKT-EM) analysis is relatively straightforward. The incorporation of non-linearities is effected via combining with harmonic balance (HB) [1], [3].

Given the extent of the literature, it is natural to question the nature of open problems that this paper seeks to address. Typical approaches follow a self-consistent solution methodology with tight coupling between the linear and nonlinear system. However, this approach is not necessarily the one adopted in frequency domain analysis; one often uses a Schur complement approach to obtain an equivalent port impedance as seen by the circuit system. The benefit of such an approach is that it becomes circuit agnostic. Unlike frequency domain, developing a similar approach in time calls for obtaining a transient impulse response; a challenging and unstable endeavor. This paper presents a solution to this problem, validates and demonstrates its efficiency.

II. Formulation of the Coupled EM-CKT System

To set the stage for the analysis, assume that a perfectly conducting object occupies a domain D_- residing in $\mathbb{R}^3$. Henceforth, this object is called the EM system. Attached to the EM system are N_p ports, each of which contain circuit sub-systems. With no loss of generality, assume that that the CKT-EM system is excited by a field $\mathbf{E}^{EM,i}(\mathbf{r},t) = \mathbf{E}^i(\mathbf{r},t) + \mathbf{E}^c(\mathbf{r},t)$ where $\mathbf{E}^i(\mathbf{r},t)$ denotes the contribution due to an incident electromagnetic field and $\mathbf{E}^c(\mathbf{r},t)$ denotes contributions due to coupling with source currents at the ports. Furthermore, it is assumed that the excitation is temporally band-limited to f_{max} and is identically zero for $t < 0$. To analyze this problem, we will assume the excitations induce voltages in the circuit system and an electric current density $\mathbf{J}(\mathbf{r},t)$ in the EM system. These currents in turn radiate electric and magnetic fields $\{\mathbf{E}^s(\mathbf{r},t), \mathbf{H}^s(\mathbf{r},t)\}$.

A. TDIE Solver

The total electric field comprises a superposition of incident ($\mathbf{E}^i(\mathbf{r},t)$) and scattered fields ($\mathbf{E}^s(\mathbf{r},t)$), respectively. Casting $\mathbf{E}^s(\mathbf{r},t)$ in terms of $\mathbf{J}(\mathbf{r},t)$ yields the time-domain electric field integral equation (TD-EFIE):

$$\hat{n}\times\hat{n}\times\mathbf{E}^{EM,i}(\mathbf{r},t) = \mathcal{L}_T\{\mathbf{J}(\mathbf{r},t)\}, \tag{1}$$

where

$$\mathcal{L}_T\{\mathbf{J}(\mathbf{r},t)\} = \hat{n}\times\hat{n}\times\left\{\frac{\mu_0\partial_t}{4\pi}\int_{D_-} d\mathbf{r}'\frac{\delta(t-R/c)}{R} *_t \mathbf{J}(\mathbf{r}',t) - \frac{\nabla}{4\pi\varepsilon_0}\int_{D_-} d\mathbf{r}'\frac{\delta(t-R/c)}{R} *_t \int_0^t dt'\nabla'\cdot\mathbf{J}(\mathbf{r}',t')\right\}. \tag{2}$$

Detail on the TDIE solver used in this work, specifically development of the discrete system, can be obtained from [4], [5]. Here, $*_t$ denotes the convolution operation in time

t, $R = |\mathbf{r} - \mathbf{r}'|$, ∇' denotes that the derivatives are taken with respect to $\mathbf{r}'$, c is the speed of light in free space, and ε_0 and μ_0 are the permittivity and permeability of free space, respectively. The solution to the above equation is obtained by the following discretization scheme.

B. Circuit System

Next, we briefly describe a circuit system solver that will be used in the analysis. As is typically done, the analysis of each of the sub-systems is performed using a SPICE-like framework that can incorporate an arbitrary network of linear and non-linear elements [6]. In general, the system of equations representing the circuit physics can be written as:

$$Y^{CKT}(t) *_t e^{CKT}(t) + i^{CKT,nl}\left(e^{CKT}(t)\right) = i^{CKT,i}(t), \quad (3)$$

where Y^{CKT} denotes the linear modified nodal admittance matrix (MNA), e^{CKT} represents the circuit unknowns, $i^{CKT,nl}$ denotes branch currents of non-linear elements, and $i^{CKT,i}(t) = i^{c,i}(t) + i^{EM,i}(t)$ denotes the system excitation due to current sources $i^{c,i}(t)$ and the external electromagnetic fields $i^{EM}(t)$.

C. Coupling the EM-CKT System and Port Extraction

Coupling between the two systems is implied in above equations, and involves specifying $i^{EM,i}(t)$ and/or $\mathbf{E}^c(\mathbf{r}, t)$. Again, the means of defining these so as to couple both system is well known. To obtain a port response, we use the fact that the transient response can be constructed in terms of circuit basis functions. Using a temporal basis function for the circuit system such that it has a non-trivial right hand side for multiple time steps.

III. Numerical Results

In this section, we present a result that demonstrates the validity of the proposed method. We demonstrate the application of port extraction to analyze a non-linear system comprising a bowtie antenna coupled to a diode mixer. We compare the transient port voltage at steady state with an inverse Fourier-transform of the harmonic balance (HB) solution. The bowtie antenna is discretized using 7767 unknowns to capture frequencies up to 1.85 GHz, allowing for proper capture of several harmonics. The circuit design mixes two signals, the RF and local oscillator (LO) input, so that the output V_{port} contains integer multiples of RF and LO signal frequencies. We set the RF source to 900 MHz, the LO to 800 MHz, and the time step to 27.777 ps to properly capture frequencies supported by the mesh. Setting V_{bias} to 0.7V turns on the diode. The RF and LO amplitudes are set to 0.4V. As seen in Fig. 1, there is agreement with the time harmonic result.

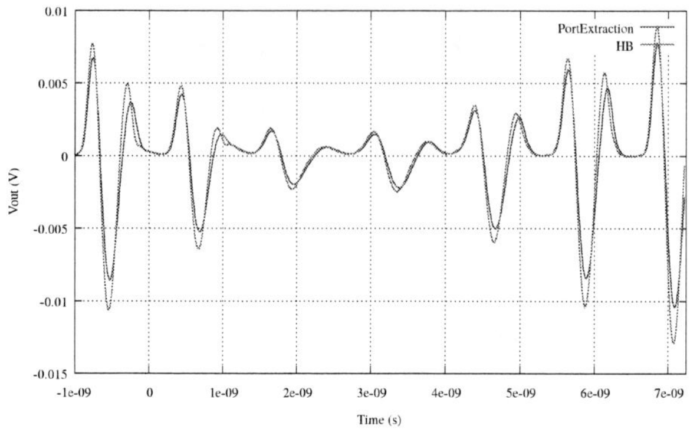

Fig. 1: Port voltages at the bowtie antenna input due to the diode attenuator circuit obtained via the TD port extraction method. The solution is compared with a Harmonic Balance (HB) solution using 45 harmonics.

IV. Summary

In this paper, we have presented a method to perform port extraction in the time domain for efficient analysis of coupled EM-CKT systems. The approach relies on three aspects: (a) the use of an highly stable transient integral equation analysis methodology, (b) using a transient CKT basis function to excite the system, and (c) using temporal Galerkin testing that couples CKTs to the EM system. As is evident from the result, as is to be expected, the port extracted system produces equivalent admittances that are stable, results that are identical to the fully coupled system, and sufficiently captures higher order non-linearities. Several results are presented that validate the presented approach. Extension of this approach to more complex TDIE system involving composite objects is currently under study as is coupling with finite element solvers; these will be published in subsequent papers.

V. Acknowledgement

This work was supported in part by HPCC facility at Michigan State University under Grant NSF ECCS-1408115, and in part by the Department of Defense High Performance Computing and Modernization Program.

References

[1] Y. Wang, D. Gope, V. Jandhyala, and C.-J. Shi, "Generalized Kirchoff's current and voltage law formulation for coupled circuit-electromagnetic simulation with surface integral equations," *IEEE Transactions on Microwave Theory and Techniques*, vol. 52, no. 7, pp. 1673–1682, 2004.

[2] K. Aygun, B. C. Fischer, J. Meng, B. Shanker, and E. Michielssen, "A fast hybrid field-circuit simulator for transient analysis of microwave circuits," *IEEE Transactions on Microwave Theory and Techniques*, vol. 52, no. 2, pp. 573–583, 2004.

[3] S. A. Maas, *Nonlinear Microwave and RF Circuits*. Artech House, 2003.

[4] A. J. Pray, N. V. Nair, and B. Shanker, "Stability properties of the time domain electric field integral equation using a separable approximation for the convolution with the retarded potential," *IEEE Transactions on Antennas and Propagation*, vol. 60, no. 8, pp. 3772–3781, 2012.

[5] A. J. Pray, Y. Beghein, N. V. Nair, K. Cools, H. Bağcı, and B. Shanker, "A higher order space-time galerkin scheme for time domain integral equations," *IEEE Transactions on Antennas and Propagation*, vol. 62, no. 12, pp. 6183–6191, 2014.

[6] C.-W. Ho, A. Ruehli, and P. Brennan, "The modified nodal approach to network analysis," *IEEE Transactions on circuits and systéms*, vol. 22, no. 6, pp. 504–509, 1975.

A Modified Streamline Upwind/Petrov-Galerkin Stabilization Matrix for Time-Domain FEM

Srijith Rajamohan
Advanced Research Computing
Virginia Tech
Blacksburg, USA
srijithr@vt.edu

William Kyle Anderson
NASA
Langley, USA
william.k.anderson@nasa.gov

***Abstract*—While both discontinuous-Galerkin (DG) and Petrov-Galerkin (PG) methods are used for solving electromagnetic problems, it has been shown in that on a given mesh the approximate degrees of freedom for a DG scheme is about 24 times for a linear element and about 7 times for a quadratic element compared to the PG scheme. The stabilization matrix, often simply referred to as $[\tau]$, in the Streamline Upwind/Petrov-Galerkin (SUPG) scheme is computed from the flux Jacobians. Computing $[\tau]$ is an expensive process, therefore in this work $[\tau]$ is approximated by a diagonal matrix which renders its computation trivial. The proposed formulation is verified by the computation of Radar Cross Sections (RCS) for canonical spheres made up of Perfectly Electric Conducting (PEC).**

***Index Terms*—FEM, Petrov-Galerkin, Radar Cross Section**

I. Introduction

While both DG and PG methods are used for solving electromagnetic problems, it has been shown in [1] that on a given mesh the approximate degrees of freedom for a DG scheme is about 24 times for a linear element and about 7 times for a quadratic element compared to the PG scheme. The PG method has a computational cost advantage when the fields are represented using cubic elements or less [1]. For this reason the Stabilized Petrov-Galerkin method is utilized in this work.

In most implementations the Maxwell's equations are posed as a single second-order wave equation in one of the field variables while the secondary variable is obtained during post processing [4]. However, this method suffers from the limitation that the order of accuracy of the secondary variable is one order less than the primary variable [1]. In the present work Maxwell's curl equations are expressed in conservation form and solved in the time domain resulting in a system of six equations at each node of a discretized element. Because Maxwell's equations represent wave propagation or convection, unstabilized Galerkin methods fail to damp out numerical oscillations for these types of problems [2], [?] . In this work the Streamline Upwind/Petrov-Galerkin (SUPG) scheme [2] is used, which provides stabilization along the direction of wave propagation. The stabilization matrix, often simply referred to as $[\tau]$, is computed from the flux Jacobians [1], [3]. The computation of this matrix is often expensive and involves matrix multiplication and inversion.

II. Methodology

A. Full Stabilization Matrix

As shown in [1], the inverse of the stabilization matrix $[\tau]$ is computed as:

$$[\tau]^{-1} = \sum_{k=1}^{n} \left| \frac{\partial N_k}{\partial x}[A] + \frac{\partial N_k}{\partial y}[B] + \frac{\partial N_k}{\partial z}[C] \right|, \tag{1}$$

where *n* is the number of node points in the element, a matrix $[\bar{A}]_k$ can be written as:

$$[\bar{A}]_k = \frac{\partial N_k}{\partial x}[A]_k + \frac{\partial N_k}{\partial y}[B]_k + \frac{\partial N_k}{\partial z}[C]_k, \tag{2}$$

and $[\tau]^{-1}$ can be written from (1) as:

$$[\tau]^{-1} = \sum_{k=1}^{n} \left|[\bar{A}]_k\right|, \tag{3}$$

$[\bar{A}]_k$ can be diagonalized and $\left|[\bar{A}]_k\right|$ can be written as:

$$\left|[\bar{A}]_k\right| = [T]\left|[\Lambda]\right|[T]^{-1}. \tag{4}$$

In (4) above, $[\Lambda]$ is a diagonal matrix of eigenvalues and $[T]$ and $[T]^{-1}$ are the matrices of right and left eigenvectors for $[\bar{A}]_k$. Assuming an isotropic material characterized by permittivity ϵ and permeability μ, the non-zero eigenvalues have a magnitude of $\sqrt{\dfrac{k_x^2+k_y^2+k_z^2}{\epsilon\mu}}$ where k_x, k_y, k_z are given by $\dfrac{\partial N_k}{\partial x}$, $\dfrac{\partial N_k}{\partial y}$ and $\dfrac{\partial N_k}{\partial z}$ respectively [1], [4].

Similarly, the eigenvectors are computed as shown in [4]. An exact computation of $[\tau]$ requires matrix inversion and in the case of dispersive or frequency dependent material models, where additional equations for the polarization terms need to be solved, a singular value decomposition (SVD) needs to be performed to compute the pseudoinverse of $[\tau]^{-1}$.

B. Approximate Stabilization Matrix

Because the Jacobian-based stabilization matrix is expensive to implement, an approximate $[\tau]$ matrix inspired by the Lax Friedrich flux [5] is proposed. This formulation is designed with speed and scalability in mind for problems that are computationally demanding such as the simulation of multipole dispersive models. The proposed form of the approximate diagonal matrix $[\tau]$ for a region in vacuum can be written from (3) using a modified matrix $[\bar{A}]_k$ as:

$$[\bar{A}]_k = [T][\Lambda_{diag}][T^{-1}]. \quad (5)$$

In the above equation, $[\Lambda_{diag}]$ has the absolute value of the non-zero eigenvalue from (4) on all diagonal terms. This ensures optimal damping for all wave components. $[\bar{A}]_k$ can be simplified to give a diagonal matrix of dimension 6 $\text{diag}(\sqrt{\frac{L_k}{\epsilon\mu}}, \sqrt{\frac{L_k}{\epsilon\mu}}, \sqrt{\frac{L_k}{\epsilon\mu}}, \sqrt{\frac{L_k}{\epsilon\mu}}, \sqrt{\frac{L_k}{\epsilon\mu}}, \sqrt{\frac{L_k}{\epsilon\mu}})$. Here the term $\sqrt{\frac{L_k}{\epsilon\mu}}$ is the maximum eigenvalue of the term $[T][|\Lambda|][T^{-1}]$, given in (4). Hence, the inverse of the stabilization matrix is obtained by summing up the principal submatrix of $[\bar{A}]_k$ of size 6, over the nodes. The resultant diagonal matrix is then trivially inverted to obtain the 6x6 stabilization matrix $[\tau]$ for all material models.

III. Results

A. *Runtime Comparisons of Diagonal Stabilization Matrix and Jacobian-based Stabilization Matrix*

The benefits of the approximate diagonal stabilization matrix, from the perspective of computational time, was investigated using a PEC sphere which has 6 equations per node and a Debye sphere which has 9 equations per node. The code was run for 2 time-steps using a single processor and it was profiled using the GNU profiler gprof. The time spent in the subroutines for the computation of the stabilization term was noted. Table I compares this time for the Jacobian based stabilization matrix with the diagonal stabilization matrix.

TABLE I
Time Taken (s) for Stabilization Matrix Computation with Jacobian Based $[\tau]$ and Diagonal $[\tau]$

Material	Jacobian Based τ (Total Time)	Approximate τ(Total Time)
Debye	213.09s (1041.59s)	27.90s (479.85s)
PEC	70.69s (323.99s)	10.12s (147.04s)

B. *Comparison of Bistatic RCS for PEC Sphere*

Bistatic RCS of a PEC sphere of radius 0.6m was computed by propagating a Gaussian wave of 150Mhz and a bandwidth of 100Mhz, with E_x and B_y components, in the z direction. The mesh was discretized using 54996 tetrahedral elements and 10846 node points. Fig. 1 illustrates the variation of the bistatic RCS, for a fixed ϕ corresponding to 36, 45 and 90 degrees, over θ which ranges from 0 to 180 degrees. The obtained solutions are compared against the solutions from HFSS [6], a frequency-domain solver for electromagnetic problems. A time-step of 0.01s with a second-order BDF2 temporal scheme was used for marching this wave in time. This time-step was chosen to accurately resolve the frequency content of the source wave, while ensuring that the temporal truncation error does not corrupt the solution. Quadratic or P2 elements were used for the computation of the bistatic RCS, which results in a solution accuracy of order 3. The solution regions were terminated with Perfectly Matched Layers (PMLs) [1], [4] for damping.

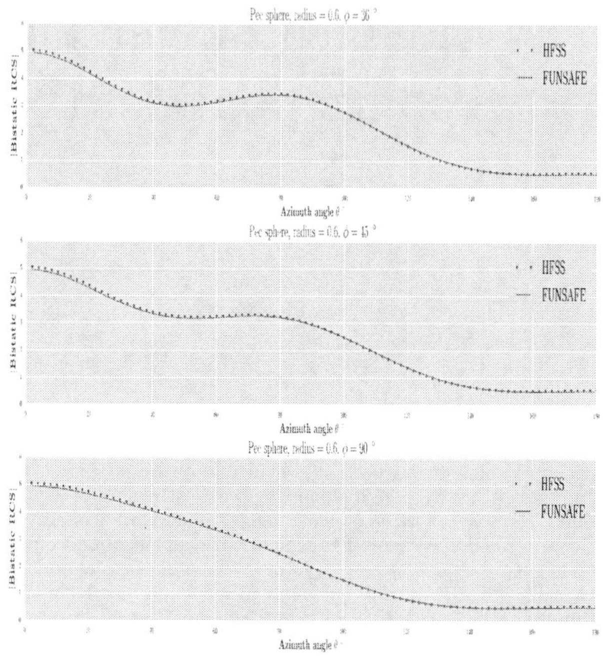

Fig. 1. Simulation of a PEC sphere using P2 elements with a Gaussian pulse source of 150 Mhz and 100Mz bandwidth.

IV. Conclusion

An approximate diagonal-based stabilization scheme was proposed for the SUPG formulation and this was verified and tested by computing the bistatic RCS using a PEC sphere and comparing the results with those obtained from HFSS. The speed improvements with the new stabilization scheme was also compared with the full Jacobian-based stabilization matrix for a PEC sphere and a sphere characterized by a single pole diagonally-anisotropic Debye model.

References

[1] W. Anderson, L. Wang, S. Kapadia, and B. Hilbert, "Petrov-Galerkin and Discontinuous Galerkin methods for time domain and frequency domain electromagnetic simulations," *Journal of Computational Physics*, vol. 230, no. 23, pp. 8360–8385, 2011.

[2] A. Brooks and T. Hughes, "Streamline Upwind/Petrov-Galerkin formulations for convection dominated flows with particular emphasis on the incompressible Navier-Stokes equations," *Comp. Methods Appl. Mech. Eng*, vol. 32, no. 1-3, pp. 199–259, 1982.

[3] T. Barth, *Numerical Methods for Gasdynamic Systems on Unstructured Meshes, an Introduction to Recent Developments in Theory and Numerics for Conservation Laws*. New York: Springer, 1998.

[4] S. Rajamohan, "A Streamline Upwind/Petrov-Galerkin FEM based time-accurate solution of 3d time-domain Maxwell's equations for dispersive materials," Ph.D. dissertation, University of Tennessee, Chattanooga, Aug. 2014. [Online]. Available: https://scholar.utc.edu/theses/134/

[5] R. Leveque, *Finite Volume Methods for Hyperbolic Problems*. Cambridge University Press, 2002.

[6] Hfss. [Online]. Available: www.ansys.com

Using an Approximate Streamline Upwind/Petrov-Galerkin Stabilization Matrix for the Solution of Maxwell's Equations in Dispersive Materials

Srijith Rajamohan
Advanced Research Computing
Virginia Tech
Blacksburg, USA
srijithr@vt.edu

William Kyle Anderson
NASA
Langley, USA
william.k.anderson@nasa.gov

***Abstract*—The use of a full stabilization matrix in a Streamline Upwind Petrov Galerkin for the solution of Maxwell's equations when applied to dispersive materials tends to be an expensive computation. Here, an approximate diagonal-based stabilization matrix is used for dispersive material models and their solution is verified by comparing the Radar Cross Sections for two-pole Debye and Lorentz materials.**

***Index Terms*—FEM, Petrov-Galerkin, Radar Cross Section**

I. Introduction

In the Streamline Upwind Petrov Galerkin (SUPG) formulation, the cost associated with the computation of the stability matrix $[\tau]$, for a nodal element corresponding to a dispersive region, can be significant [1]. This term involves an eigen-decomposition followed by a Singular Value Decomposition (SVD) to compute a pseudoinverse because the intermediate matrix is rank deficient when polarization terms are included. Also, for matrices of dimension greater than 12, which is common when dispersive materials are involved, it is quite difficult to obtain symbolic eigendecompositions or when possible quite cumbersome to incorporate into a code framework. To circumvent these issues an alternative diagonal formulation for the stabilization matrix is proposed that eliminates the eigendecomposition and renders the matrix inversion trivial. In many implementations for solving Maxwell's equations, the frequency dependence of the material parameters can be ignored and constant parameters are assumed [2]. However this is an inaccurate model for many materials such as biological tissues, where large multipole model are required, and must be properly accounted for in simulations that compute broadband frequency responses. Incorporating the frequency dependence into the curl equations involves modifying the constitutive equations, however this modification can be absorbed into the permittivity tensor [1]. In this work an isotropic diagonal permittivity tensor is used, although the approach used poses no such restrictions and is suited for solving problems that involve fully-anisotropic material models. An auxiliary differential equation (ADE) [1] approach is used to incorporate the polarization terms for a particular model.

II. Methodology

A. Dispersive Material Model

The assumption material properties, such as permittivity ϵ and permeability μ, being independent of frequency is no longer valid in many broadband applications where these parameters vary significantly over the frequency range of interest. Here we consider a diagonally anisotropic susceptibility matrix given as:

$$\begin{bmatrix} \tilde{P}_x \\ \tilde{P}_y \\ \tilde{P}_z \end{bmatrix} = \begin{bmatrix} \tilde{\chi}_x & 0 & 0 \\ 0 & \tilde{\chi}_y & 0 \\ 0 & 0 & \tilde{\chi}_z \end{bmatrix} \begin{bmatrix} \tilde{E}_x \\ \tilde{E}_y \\ \tilde{E}_z \end{bmatrix}. \tag{1}$$

Below, two such models [3] for frequency dependence, Debye and Lorentz, are considered.

B. Approximate Diagonal Stabilization Matrix

As shown in the [3], an exact computation of the full stabilization matrix $[\tau]$ requires matrix inversion and in the case of dispersive or frequency dependent material models, where additional equations for the polarization terms need to be solved, a singular value decomposition (SVD) needs to be performed to compute the pseudoinverse of $[\tau]$. This is necessitated due to the fact that the resulting matrix for $[\tau]^{-1}$ is rank deficient. Evaluation of SVD is a computationally expensive process, being almost five times as slow as a matrix inversion [4]. It must also be pointed out that this cost increases with the number of poles that are incorporated in the model since the size of the block that is subject to an SVD is equal to the number of equations to be solved for that model. Because the Jacobian-based stabilization matrix is expensive to implement, an approximate $[\tau]$ matrix inspired by the Lax

Friedrich flux [5] is proposed. For a dispersive material, this can be formulated as shown below:

$$[\tau] = \left[\sum_{k=1}^{nnodes} [\bar{A}]_k \right]^{-1}, \tag{2}$$

where $[\bar{A}]_k$ now takes the form:

$$[\bar{A}]_k = [T][\Lambda_{diag}][T^{-1}]. \tag{3}$$

$[\bar{A}]_k$ can be simplified, for a diagonally anisotropic mode, to give a diagonal matrix of dimension $6 + npoles * 3$ where $npoles$ is the number of poles in the dispersive model. For a single pole model, this matrix is then given by diag($\sqrt{\frac{L_k}{\epsilon\mu}}$,$\sqrt{\frac{L_k}{\epsilon\mu}}$,$\sqrt{\frac{L_k}{\epsilon\mu}}$,$\sqrt{\frac{L_k}{\epsilon\mu}}$,$\sqrt{\frac{L_k}{\epsilon\mu}}$,$\sqrt{\frac{L_k}{\epsilon\mu}}$,0,0,0). Here the term $\sqrt{\frac{L_k}{\epsilon\mu}}$ is the maximum eigenvalue of the full stabilization matrix term $[\bar{A}]_k$, given in [3], [6]. The stabilization matrix is then obtained by summing up the principal submatrix of $[\bar{A}]_k$ of size 6, over the nodes. The resultant diagonal matrix is then inverted by taking the inverse of the non-zero diagonal entries to obtain the stabilization matrix $[\tau]$ for all material models.

III. Results

Scattering is performed from a sphere of radius 0.6m, with frequency-dependent dielectric properties modeled using an the following material properties. The bistatic RCS at 150 Mhz is computed, using a mesh with 13597 nodes and 72480 tetrahedral elements, and plotted at 150 Mhz, using two pole models.

A. Bistatic Radar Cross Section Plots for Debye Sphere

Table I illustrates the material properties associated with this model. The Bistatic RCS results are shown in Fig. 1a. These results are compared with the solution obtained from HFSS. Both the computed solutions are found to be in good agreement with the corresponding solutions obtained from HFSS.

TABLE I
Material Properties for the Debye Model Listed by Pole Number (Non-Dimensionalized)

Pole Number	ϵ_∞	$\Delta\epsilon$	τ_d
1	2.88	2.0	0.1194
2	2.88	2.5	0.3

B. Bistatic Radar Cross Section Plots for Lorentz Sphere

Table II illustrates the material properties associated with this Lorentz model. The results of Bistatic RCS are shown in Fig. 1b. The mesh used for this simulation consists of 13597 nodes and 72480 tetrahedral elements. These results are compared with the solution obtained from HFSS and are found to be in good agreement.

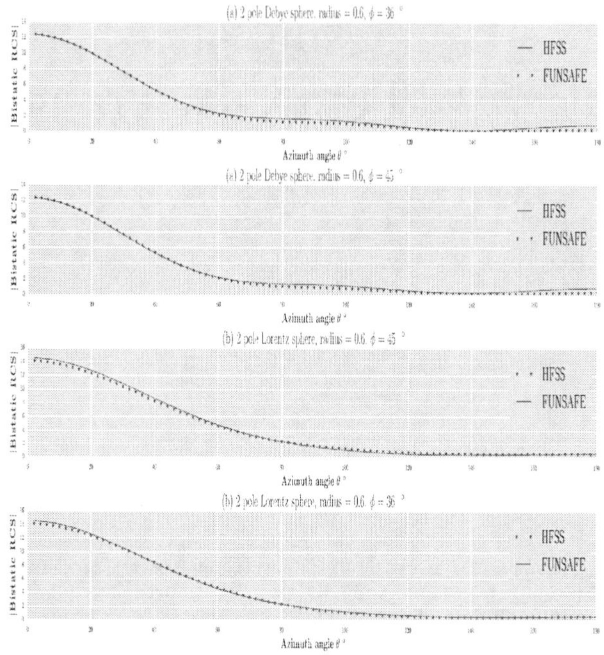

Fig. 1. Simulation results for: (a) 2 pole Debye dielectric sphere, (b) 2 pole Lorentz dielectric sphere.

TABLE II
Material Properties for the Lorentz Model Listed by Pole Number (Non-Dimensionalized)

Pole Number	ϵ_∞	δ_p	Δ_{ϵ_p}	ω_p
1	2.88	2.0	2.5	0.1194
2	2.88	2.0	2.5	0.1194

IV. Conclusion

The solution of Maxwell's equations with dispersive materials was obtained with a faster diagonal-based stabilization scheme for SUPG. Bistatic RCS was obtained and compared for two-pole Debye and Lorentz models with Ansys HFSS. Work is proposed, in the future, to generalize this to other multipole material models.

References

[1] W. Anderson, L. Wang, J. Newman, and S.Kapadia, "Extension of the petrov-galerkin time-domain algorithm for dispersive media," *Microwave and Wireless Components Letters*, vol. 23, no. 5, pp. 234–236, 2013.

[2] J. Schneider. (2010) Understanding the FDTD Method. [Online]. Available: www.eecs.wsu.edu/ schneidj/ufdtd

[3] S. Rajamohan, "A Streamline Upwind/Petrov-Galerkin FEM based time-accurate solution of 3d time-domain Maxwell's equations for dispersive materials," Ph.D. dissertation, University of Tennessee, Chattanooga, Aug. 2014. [Online]. Available: https://scholar.utc.edu/theses/134/

[4] E. Anderson, Z. Bai, and C. Bischof. (1999) LAPACK Users' Guide: Third Edition. [Online]. Available: http://www.netlib.org/lapack/lug/

[5] R. Leveque, *Finite Volume Methods for Hyperbolic Problems*. Cambridge University Press, 2002.

[6] W. Anderson, L. Wang, S. Kapadia, and B. Hilbert, "Petrov-Galerkin and Discontinuous Galerkin methods for time domain and frequency domain electromagnetic simulations," *Journal of Computational Physics*, vol. 230, no. 23, pp. 8360–8385, 2011.

Analysis of Transient Scattering from Impedance Surfaces using Physical Optics Approximation

Hüseyin A. Serim
Informatics and Information Security Research Center
The Scientific and Technological Research Council of Turkey
Kocaeli, 41470, Turkey
huseyin.serim@tubitak.gov.tr

H. Arda Ülkü
Department of Electronics Engineering
Gebze Technical University
Kocaeli, 41400, Turkey
haulku@gtu.edu.tr

***Abstract*—The physical optics approximation is widely used for electromagnetic scattering analysis due to the fast calculation of the fields. In this work, the scattering from impedance surfaces is analyzed in the time domain using the physical optics approximation. The resulting time dependent radiation integrals are determined in closed-form. A numerical example that demonstrates the accuracy and validity of the scheme is presented.**

***Index Terms*—coated body, impedance surface, physical optics, time domain analysis**

I. Introduction

The physical optics (PO) approximation has a common usage, e.g., in analyzing antenna radiation [1] or scattering from electrically large structures [2]. The main interest of the PO approximation is the accurate evaluation of highly oscillatory radiation integral, which is called PO integral, over the scatterer surface [2], [3]. In [3], analytical expressions of the PO integral for perfect electrically conducting (PEC) surfaces modelled with planar triangular patches is introduced in both the frequency and time domains. As a result, the accuracy of the PO integral, does not depend on the frequency or size of the triangles.

In this work, the scheme introduced in [3] is extended to analysis of transient scattering from impedance surfaces [4]. The time domain PO approximation [5] of scattered fields for an impedance boundary condition is formulated using the electric and magnetic equivalent currents. In particular, the surface of the scatterer is modelled with planar triangular patches, and the electric and magnetic equivalent currents on the triangular patches are determined using the PO approximation. The resulting radiation integrals are interpreted as a planar Radon transform [3], [6] and determined as the intersection of the triangular patches and the plane formed by the propagation direction of the incident field and the observation direction. Numerical results show the accuracy and validity of the presented scheme.

II. Formulation

Let S denote the surface of a scatterer with the impedance boundary condition and the scatterer is discretized with the planar triangular patches $S \simeq \bigcup_n S_n$. An incident plane wave with a time signature $G(t)$ excites the scatterer. The electric and magnetic field components of the incident plane wave are given as:

$$\mathbf{E}_{\text{inc}}(\mathbf{r},t) = \hat{\mathbf{p}}G(t - \hat{\mathbf{k}}_i \cdot \mathbf{r}/c) = \hat{\mathbf{p}}G(t) * \delta(t - \hat{\mathbf{k}}_i \cdot \mathbf{r}/c), \quad (1)$$

$$\begin{aligned}\mathbf{H}_{\text{inc}}(\mathbf{r},t) &= \eta_0^{-1}(\hat{\mathbf{k}}_i \times \hat{\mathbf{p}})G(t - \hat{\mathbf{k}}_i \cdot \mathbf{r}/c) \\ &= \eta_0^{-1}(\hat{\mathbf{k}}_i \times \hat{\mathbf{p}})G(t) * \delta(t - \hat{\mathbf{k}}_i \cdot \mathbf{r}/c),\end{aligned} \quad (2)$$

where $\hat{\mathbf{p}}$ is the polarization, $\hat{\mathbf{k}}_i$ is the propagation direction of the plane wave, c is the propagation speed, and $*$ denotes temporal convolution.

The impedance boundary condition on S is given as:

$$-\hat{\mathbf{n}}(\mathbf{r}) \times \hat{\mathbf{n}}(\mathbf{r}) \times \mathbf{E}_{\text{tot}}(\mathbf{r},t) = Z(t) * \hat{\mathbf{n}}(\mathbf{r}) \times \mathbf{H}_{\text{tot}}(\mathbf{r},t), \quad (3)$$

where $\mathbf{E}_{\text{tot}}(\mathbf{r},t)$ and $\mathbf{H}_{\text{tot}}(\mathbf{r},t)$ are the total electric and magnetic field intensities, $\hat{\mathbf{n}}(\mathbf{r})$ is the unit normal vector directed to outward of S, and $Z(t)$ is the time dependent surface impedance [4]. In this work, the surface impedance is assumed to be constant ($Z(t) = Z$) for simplicity. Using (3), the electric and magnetic currents can be defined in terms of the total magnetic field intensity as:

$$\mathbf{J}(\mathbf{r},t) = \hat{\mathbf{n}}(\mathbf{r}) \times \mathbf{H}_{\text{tot}}(\mathbf{r},t), \quad (4)$$

$$\mathbf{M}(\mathbf{r},t) = -Z\hat{\mathbf{n}}(\mathbf{r}) \times \hat{\mathbf{n}}(\mathbf{r}) \times \mathbf{H}_{\text{tot}}(\mathbf{r},t), \quad (5)$$

The PO approximation of the total magnetic field intensity [4] is given as:

$$\mathbf{H}_{\text{tot}}(\mathbf{r},t) = \eta_0^{-1}G(t) * \delta(t - \hat{\mathbf{k}}_i \cdot \mathbf{r}/c)\mathbf{u}(\mathbf{r}), \quad (6)$$

where η_0 is the intrinsic impedance. Here the vector $\mathbf{u}(\mathbf{r})$ is defined as:

$$\begin{aligned}\mathbf{u}(\mathbf{r}) = &(1 - R_{\parallel})\left(\left(\hat{\mathbf{k}}_i \times \hat{\mathbf{p}}\right) \cdot \hat{\mathbf{e}}_{\parallel}\right)\hat{\mathbf{e}}_{\parallel} \\ &+ (1 - R_{\perp})\left(\left(\hat{\mathbf{k}}_i \times \hat{\mathbf{p}}\right) \cdot \hat{\mathbf{e}}_{\perp}\right)\hat{\mathbf{e}}_{\perp},\end{aligned} \quad (7)$$

where $\hat{\mathbf{e}}_{\parallel}$ and $\hat{\mathbf{e}}_{\perp}$ are the orthogonal unit vectors to $\hat{\mathbf{k}}_i$. The parallel and perpendicular reflection coefficients [4] are given as:

$$R_{\parallel} = \frac{Z/\eta_0 - \cos\theta_i}{Z/\eta_0 + \cos\theta_i}, \quad R_{\perp} = \frac{Z/\eta_0 - \sec\theta_i}{Z/\eta_0 + \sec\theta_i}, \quad (8)$$

where θ_i is the narrow angle between the propagation direction of the plane wave and the surface normal $\hat{\mathbf{n}}(\mathbf{r})$ [4]. Note that

$R_{\|}$, $R_{\perp}$, $\hat{\mathbf{e}}_{\|}$ and $\hat{\mathbf{e}}_{\perp}$ are functions of $\mathbf{r}$ and/or $\hat{\mathbf{k}}_i$, however on a triangular patch S_n, they are constant. For brevity their dependence is not shown explicitly.

Once the currents are known using the PO approximation, for an observation direction $\hat{\mathbf{k}}_s$ the scattered electric field at the far field can be found as:

$$\mathbf{E}_{\text{sca}}(\mathbf{r},t) = -\frac{1}{4\pi c}\frac{G'(t-r/c)}{r} * \left\{ \hat{\mathbf{k}}_s \times \hat{\mathbf{k}}_s \times \sum_n \mathbf{u}_n \times \hat{\mathbf{n}}_n h_n(t) + \frac{Z}{\eta_0}\hat{\mathbf{k}}_s \times \sum_n \hat{\mathbf{n}}_n \times (\hat{\mathbf{n}}_n \times \mathbf{u}_n) h_n(t) \right\}, \quad (9)$$

where $G'(t)$ denotes the derivative of $G(t)$, $\hat{\mathbf{n}}_n$ and $\mathbf{u}_n$ denote $\hat{\mathbf{n}}(\mathbf{r})$ and $\mathbf{u}(\mathbf{r})$ for the surface patch S_n. $h_n(t)$ is defined as:

$$h_n(t) = \int_{S_n} \delta\left(t - \frac{2}{c}\mathbf{k}_r \cdot \mathbf{r}'\right) d\mathbf{r}', \quad (10)$$

where $\mathbf{k}_r = (\hat{\mathbf{k}}_i - \hat{\mathbf{k}}_s)/2$ and analytical expression of $h_n(t)$ is presented in [3].

Once the temporal samples of the expression in the brackets in (9) are determined, it can be convolved with the derivative of a given time signature of the incident wave to calculate the scattered electric field.

III. Numerical Results

To demonstrate the accuracy and validity of the proposed scheme, a unit square plate located on $x-y$ plane in free space is analyzed for a modulated Gaussian signature $G(t) = \cos(2\pi f_0 t) \times \exp(-t^2/(2\sigma^2))$, where the center frequency $f_0 = 700$ MHz, the effective bandwidth $f_{\text{bw}} = 300$ MHz and the duration $\sigma = 2.5/(2\pi f_{\text{bw}})$. Two values of surface impedance are used: $Z = 0$, which is also called the PEC case, and $Z = 0.6\eta_0$.

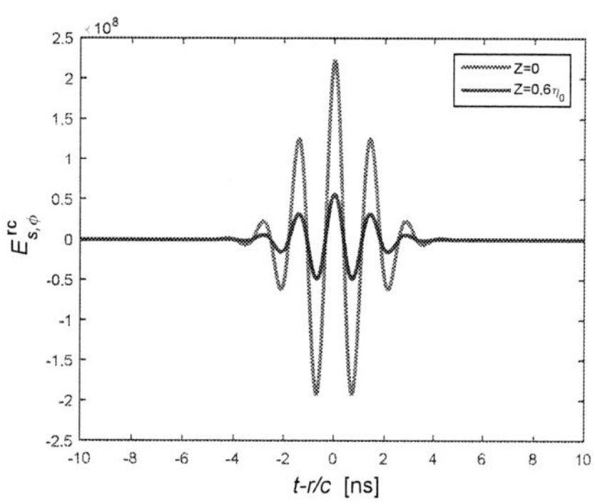

Fig. 1. The time domain response from the plate.

The polarization is chosen in ϕ direction, i.e., horizontal polarization ($\hat{\mathbf{p}} = \hat{\phi}$ in (1)) and the backscattered ($\hat{\mathbf{k}}_i = -\hat{\mathbf{k}}_s$) electric field is analyzed for $\theta \in [0, 90]^\circ$ and $\phi = 0^\circ$. Fig. 1 plots time response of the backscattered range corrected electric field [6] for the aspect angle $\theta = 5^\circ$. The generated time domain results are transformed into the frequency domain and monostatic RCS values are determined. In Fig. 2, the RCS values at 700 MHz obtained by the proposed scheme are compared with the RCS results in [4]. To show the polarization dependence of the scattered field, tests are repeated for vertical polarization ($\hat{\mathbf{p}} = \hat{\theta}$). It can be seen from Fig. 3 that the monostatic RCS results for vertical polarization are different than the horizontal ones given in Fig. 2. In addition, the results plotted in Figs. 2 and 3 are in good agreement with the results given in the reference [4].

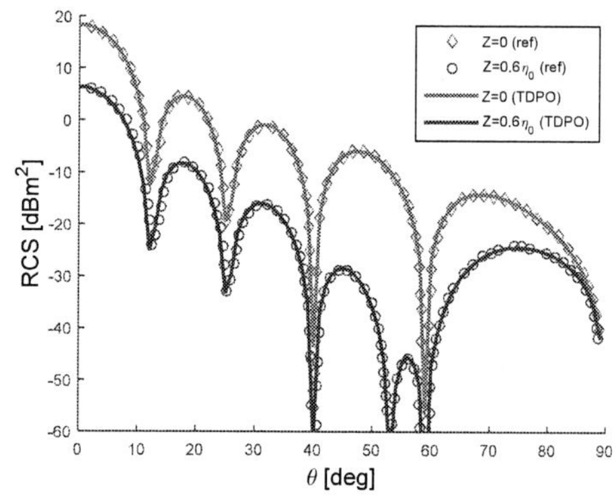

Fig. 2. Monostatic RCS - horizontal polarization.

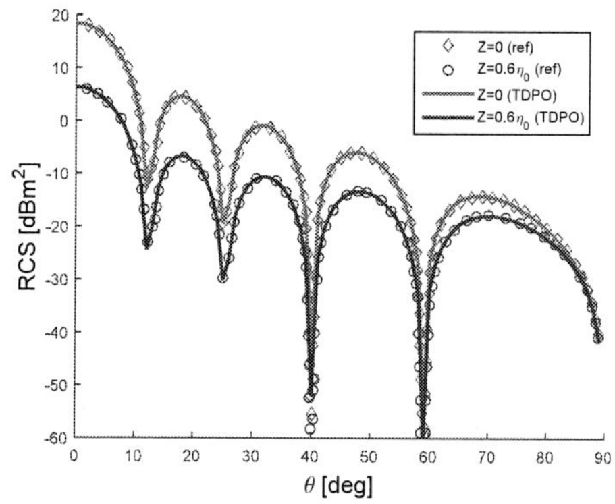

Fig. 3. Monostatic RCS - vertical polarization.

References

[1] F. Obelleiro, J. M. Taboada, L. Landesa, and I. T. Castro, "Synthesis of array antennas onboard complex platforms considering coupling effects by means of a hybrid MM-PO technique," *Microw. Opt. Technol. Lett.*, vol. 33, no. 3, pp. 207–212, 2002.

[2] W. Gordon, "Far-field approximations to the Kirchoff-Helmholtz representations of scattered fields," *IEEE Trans. Antennas Propag.*, vol. 23, pp. 590–592, July 1975.

[3] D. Bölükbaş and A. A. Ergin, "A Radon transform interpretation of the physical optics integral," *Microw. Opt. Technol. Lett.*, vol. 44, no. 3, pp. 284–288, 2005.

[4] D. W. Hill and C. C. Cha, "Physical optics approximation of the RCS of an impedance surface," in *1988 IEEE AP-S. International Symposium, Antennas and Propagation*, pp. 416–419, vol. 1, June 1988.

[5] E.-Y. Sun and W. V. T. Rusch, "Time-domain physical-optics," *IEEE Trans. Antennas Propag.*, vol. 42, no. 1, pp. 9–15, Jan. 1994.

[6] H. A. Serim and A. A. Ergin, "Computation of the physical optics integral on NURBS surfaces using a Radon transform interpretation," *IEEE Antennas Wireless Propag. Lett.*, vol. 7, pp. 70–73, 2008.

Physiologically Inspired Model of the Skin for Use in Electrical Impedance Tomography

Michelle M. Mellenthin
Department of Bioengineering
University of Colorado Denver
Aurora, Colorado 80045
michelle.mellenthin@ucdenver.edu

Jennifer L. Mueller
Department of Mathematics
School of Biomedical Engineering
Colorado State University
Fort Collins, Colorado 80523
mueller@math.colostate.edu

***Abstract*—A new model for the skin-electrode interface in electrical impedance tomography (EIT) is presented in which electric current is transmitted through sub-macroscopic skin features. The results of a FEM implementation are compared to measured EIT voltages collected on a human volunteer.**

I. Introduction

Electrical impedance tomography (EIT) is a medical imaging technique in which low amplitude AC currents are applied on surface electrodes on the body. The resulting voltages are measured on the electrodes, and the distribution of conductivity and/or permittivity is reconstructed inside the domain. For thoracic imaging, plotting these reconstructed values for each frame results in functional images of ventilation and perfusion.

To obtain absolute images, it is necessary to model the contact impedance that occurs at the interface of the electrodes and skin [1]. Typically the Complete Electrode Model (CEM) [1] is used to model this impedance and the resulting nonuniform current distribution. It includes a Robin boundary condition with a parameter specifiying the contact impedance on each electrode, which is either an estimate of a single or electrode-dependent contact impedance or is recovered in the inverse problem [2].

In this work, an anatomical model describing current flow through human skin for the EIT forward problem is implemented instead of adopting the CEM. Individual variations in the physical properties of the epidermis skin layer across human subjects leads to differences in the electrode-skin contact impedance [3]. Factors altering the impedance at the electrode-gel-skin interface include: temperature, humidity, and thickness of the stratum corneum (outermost layer of skin), and pore thickness [4].

The objective of this work was to determine if the EIT measured voltages on human subjects could be readily be predicted by considering current flow at the sub-macroscopic level with an anatomical model.

II. Methods

A. EIT Forward Problem

In EIT the electric potential $u(x, y)$ in a 2-D bounded domain Ω is modeled by the generalized Laplace equation:

$$\nabla \cdot (\sigma(x,y)\nabla u(x,y)) = 0, \quad (x,y) \text{ in } \Omega, \qquad (1)$$

where $\sigma(x, y)$ is the conductivity to be reconstructed. The boundary conditions for the CEM are:

$$\begin{aligned} \int_{e_\ell} \sigma \frac{\partial u}{\partial \nu} dS &= I_\ell, \quad \text{on } e_\ell, \ \ell = 1, \dots, L, \\ \sigma \frac{\partial u}{\partial \nu} &= 0, \quad \text{off } \bigcup_{\ell=1}^{L} e_\ell, \\ u + z_\ell \sigma \frac{\partial u}{\partial \nu} &= U_\ell, \quad \text{on } e_\ell, \ \ell = 1, \dots, L, \end{aligned}$$

where e_ℓ is the spatial area of electrode ℓ, L is the number of electrodes, I_ℓ is the applied current, U_ℓ is the constant voltage on electrode ℓ, and $\partial/\partial\nu$ refers to the outward normal derivative. For existence and uniqueness of the solution of the forward problem, charge is conserved and a ground is imposed:

$$\sum_{\ell=1}^{L} I_\ell = 0, \qquad \sum_{\ell=1}^{L} U_\ell = 0.$$

The boundary conditions are modified for the proposed anatomical model.

B. Anatomical Model

In the model [5], the travel of current J through a single skin pore with cross sectional area A_{cs} depends on the conductivity of gel filling the pore σ_r and change in voltage ϕ along the pore with length x. Assumptions include: (1) the epidermis layer acts as a perfect insulator with thickness h, (2) current travels down pores with a mean radius r, and (3) each pore can reasonably be represented as a semi-infinite tube. Additional parameters include: specific pore wall capacitance C_w, pore wall conductance G_w, and a known pore density n. Together, this gives [5]:

$$C_w \frac{\partial \phi}{\partial t} = \frac{\sigma_r}{2} \frac{\partial^2 \phi}{\partial x^2} - G_w \phi, \text{ where } x > -h, \, t > 0, \qquad (2)$$

$$\phi(\infty, t) = 0, \text{ where } t > 0, \qquad (3)$$

$$-A_{cs}\sigma_r \left.\frac{\partial \phi}{\partial x}\right|_{x=-h} = J. \qquad (4)$$

Use of AC current results in harmonic voltages ($\phi = \widetilde{\phi} e^{i\omega t}$) and currents ($J = \widetilde{J} e^{i\omega t}$) inside the pores. Solutions to the equations (2) - (4), were modified to be used with with the forward problem EIT finite element code. These new boundary conditions are given by:

$$\tilde{\phi}(x) = \underbrace{\left(\frac{\tilde{J}}{\sqrt{\tilde{b}}A_{cs}\sigma_r}\right)}_{C} e^{-\sqrt{\tilde{b}x}}, \tag{5}$$

$$\text{where: } \tilde{b} = \frac{2G_w}{\sigma_r}\left(\frac{C_w}{G_w}i\omega + 1\right), \tag{6}$$

$$\frac{\partial\tilde{\phi}}{\partial x} = -C\sqrt{\tilde{b}}e^{-\sqrt{\tilde{b}x}}, \tag{7}$$

$$\tilde{J}_{pore}(x) = \frac{-\tilde{J}}{A_{cs}}e^{-x\sqrt{\tilde{b}}}. \tag{8}$$

The solution gives nodal voltages V_n at $x = h$. To recover electrode potentials V_ℓ on the electrode nodes, potentials are summed for all nodes M under electrode ℓ:

$$V_\ell = \sum_{m=1}^{M} V_n(m)e^{-x\sqrt{\tilde{b}}}. \tag{9}$$

To preserve directionality, on injecting electrode nodes $x = -h$ in equation (9) and for non-injecting electrodes $x = h$.

III. Results and Discussion

A finite element mesh was constructed using Gmsh 2.4.8 software with 33564 triangular elements (Fig. 1) for the chest shape of a healthy human volunteer imaged in an IRB approved study at Colorado State University with the ACE1 EIT system [6] using the Skip 0 current patterns. Organ boundaries were approximated by those typically seen on a CT scan. Anatomical parameters were selected empirically: $\sigma_r = 0.525$ mS/cm, $C_w = 0.075$ μF/cm, $G_w = 0.01$ mS/cm, $h = 10$ μm, and pore radius 20 μm.

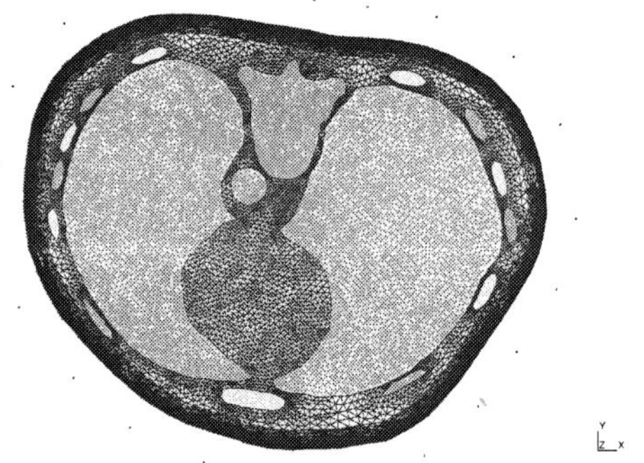

Fig. 1. This triangular element mesh used was used to compare models. The mesh elements are more refined at the boundary.

In this initial work, a single empirically determined contact impedance z in the CEM was used for all electrodes. The error shown in Fig. 2 is the difference between the measured voltages and those computed from equation (9) or the CEM for current pattern 5. For this current pattern and others, we found that when the CEM model overpredicts the measured voltages, the anatomically inspired model underpredicts.

For both models, for any given current pattern the error depends on the proximity to the injecting electrodes. The percent error, relative to the measured voltages, for all current patterns for injecting electrodes was: 2.6 % ± 3.1 % for the CEM and 2.6 % ± 3.8 % for the anatomical model. On the three electrodes adjacent to the injecting ones, the relative error was 331 % ± 1055 % for the CEM and 305 % ± 1158 % for the anatomical model.

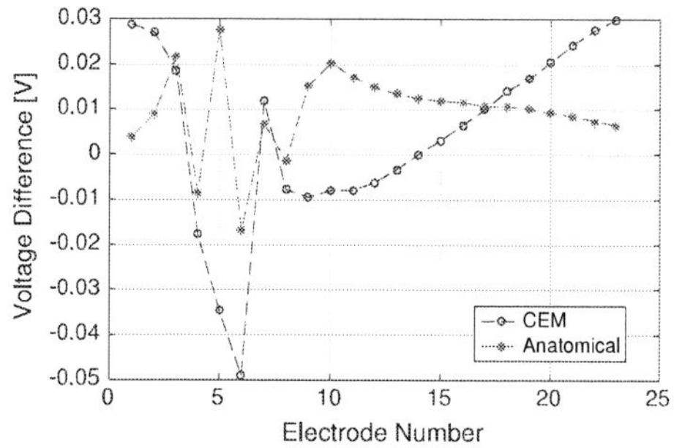

Fig. 2. Comparison of voltage difference between model and measured for current pattern 5 for the CEM and the anatomical model. Electrodes 5 and 6 are the injecting electrodes.

IV. Conclusion

The anatomical model may predict voltages with comparable accuracy for injecting and near injecting electrodes. However, the anatomical model is less accurate than the CEM when further from the injecting electrodes. Future work is needed to refine this model. However, combining it with the CEM may be promising.

Acknowledgment

This project was supported by award 1R21EB016869-01 from the NIBIB. The content is solely the responsibility of the authors and does not necessarily represent the official view of the NIBIB or NIH.

References

[1] K.-S. Cheng, D. Isaacson, J. C. Newell, and D. G. Gisser, "Electrode models fo electric current computed tomography," *IEEE Transactions on Biomedical Engineering*, vol. 36, pp. 918–924, September 1989.

[2] G. Boverman, D. Isaacson, G. J. Saulnier, and J. C. Newell, "Methods for compensating for variable electrode contact in eit," *IEEE Transactions on Bioemdical Engineering*, vol. 56, no. 12, pp. 2762–2772, 2009.

[3] J. G. Webster, *Medical Instrumentation: Application and Design*. John Wiley & Sons, Inc., 4th ed., 2010.

[4] E. McAdams, J. Jossinet, A. Lackermeier, and F. Risacher, "Factors affecting electrode-gel-skin interface impedance in electrical impedance tomography," *Medical & Biological Engineering & Computing*, vol. 34, pp. 397–408, 1996.

[5] Y. A. Chizmadzhev, P. I. Kuzmin, J. C. Weaver, and R. O. Potts, "Skin appendageal macropores as a possible pathway for electrical current," *The Journal of Investigative Dermatology Symposium Proceedings*, vol. 3, no. 2, pp. 148–152, 1998.

[6] M. Mellenthin, J. Mueller, E. Dario León Bueno de Camargo, F. Silva de Moura, S. J. Hamilton, and R. Gonzalez Lima, "The ACE1 thoracic electrical impedance tomography system for ventilation and perfusion," in *37th Annual International Conference of the IEEE Engineering in Medicine and Biology Society*, (Milan, Itlay), August 2015.

Reconstruction of Complex Conductivities by Calderón's Method on Subject-Specific Domains

Peter Muller
Department of Mathematics & Statistics
Villanova University
Philadelphia, Pennsylvania 19085
peter.muller@villanova.edu

Jennifer L. Mueller
Department of Mathematics
School of Biomedical Engineering
Colorado State University
Fort Collins, Colorado 80523
mueller@math.colostate.edu

***Abstract*—Calderón's method is a direct linearization-based method for the inverse conductivity problem in electrical impedance tomography (EIT) data. It has the advantage of being able to simultaneously reconstruct the real and imaginary parts of the admittivity (conductivity and susceptivity) at a fixed frequency. In this work, the method is implemented to produce real-time reconstructions of both conductivity and susceptivity on subject-specific domains. The method's effectiveness is demonstrated with reconstructions of changes due to ventilation in a human subject thorax.**

I. Introduction

Electrical impedance tomography (EIT) is a non-ionizing functional imaging modality with medical applications in the monitoring and diagnosis of pulmonary function. Typically, a band of electrodes is placed on the skin around the circumference of the chest, low amplitude, low frequency (LF) current patterns are applied on the electrodes, and the resulting voltages are measured. From this data, a nonlinear inverse problem is solved to dynamically image changes in the electrical properties of the tissues in the body in the plane of the electrodes.

The electromagnetic field induced by the applied currents is governed by Maxwell's equations, but the LF current, and small magnetic permeability of human tissue allow these to be simplified to the generalized Laplace equation:

$$\nabla \cdot (\gamma \nabla u) = 0 \quad \text{in} \quad \Omega, \tag{1}$$

where $\gamma = \sigma + i\omega\epsilon$ is the admittivity, σ is the conductivity, ϵ is the permittivity, and ω is the angular frequency of the applied currents. It is also assumed that the applied current satisfies Kirchhoff's Law, and the measured voltage distribution on the boundary corresponds to the Dirichlet boundary condition $u|_{\partial\Omega} = f$. The data for the inverse problem of determining γ is the voltage-to-current density, or Dirichlet-to-Neumann (DN) map Λ_γ defined by $\Lambda_\gamma : u|_{\partial\Omega} \to \sigma \frac{\partial u}{\partial \nu}|_{\partial\Omega}$.

Calderón was the first to address the mathematical questions of whether γ can be uniquely determined from the DN map, and if so, how to reconstruct γ [1]. He proved injectivity of the linearized DN map, answering the question of unique determination for the linearized problem and presented a direct method of reconstruction for that case. In [2], a real-time implementation of Calderón's linearization method was provided for subject-specific domains, and difference images of conductivity were presented for experimental data sets, including human subject volunteers. Here, we present difference images of conductivity and permittivity computed by the real-time implementation of Calderon's method on subject-specific domain. Functional images of permittivity changes may have important clinical applications for pulmonary imaging, such as distinguishing between a pneumothorax and hyperinflation in real time.

II. Methods

Define the Fourier transform of a function f by:

$$\hat{f}(\mathbf{z}) := \int_{\mathbb{R}^n} f(\mathbf{x}) e^{2\pi i(\mathbf{z}\cdot\mathbf{x})} d\mathbf{x}.$$

Calderón introduces two special harmonic functions u_1 and u_2 defined by:

$$u_1(\mathbf{x}) = e^{\pi i(\mathbf{z}\cdot\mathbf{x}) + \pi(\mathbf{a}\cdot\mathbf{x})}, \tag{2}$$
$$u_2(\mathbf{x}) = e^{\pi i(\mathbf{z}\cdot\mathbf{x}) - \pi(\mathbf{a}\cdot\mathbf{x})}, \tag{3}$$

where $\mathbf{z}, \mathbf{a} \in \mathbb{R}^n, \mathbf{z}| = |\mathbf{a}|$ and $\mathbf{a} \cdot \mathbf{z} = 0$. Here $n = 2$, since we are reconstructing a 2-D slice of the chest.

Calderón's method relates the DN map to the Fourier transform of γ through the special functions u_1 and u_2 under the assumption that γ is a small perturbation from a known constant:

$$\hat{\gamma}(\mathbf{z}) \approx -\frac{1}{2\pi^2|\mathbf{z}|^2} \int_{\partial\Omega} u_1 \Lambda_\gamma u_2 dS(\mathbf{x}) =: \hat{F}(\mathbf{z}). \tag{4}$$

To reconstruct $\gamma(\mathbf{x})$, one must construct the function $\hat{F}(\mathbf{z})$ from the measured data and compute the inverse Fourier transform.

In practice, a discrete matrix approximation to the DN map is computed from the measured data, and (4) is discretized. Denote the discrete approximation to the Neumann-to-Dirichlet (ND) map by $\mathbf{R}_\gamma$ and the discrete approximation to the DN map by $\mathbf{L}_\gamma = \mathbf{R}_\gamma^{-1}$. Since currents are applied, and voltages measured, we compute the ND map from the data, and then take $\mathbf{L}_\gamma = \mathbf{R}_\gamma^{-1}$.

Let $\mathbf{T}^k$ be the vector of current amplitudes applied on the L electrodes for the kth current pattern with entries T_ℓ^k. The trigonometric current patterns with current amplitude M are defined by:

$$T_\ell^k = M\begin{cases} \cos(k\theta_\ell), & k = 1, ..., \frac{L}{2} \\ \sin\left((k - \frac{L}{2})\theta_\ell\right), & k = \frac{L}{2}+1, ..., L-1. \end{cases} \tag{5}$$

These patterns can be synthesized from any linearly independent set of $L-1$ current patterns. Here k denotes the pattern and ℓ the electrode located at angular position θ_ℓ. To compute $\mathbf{L}_\gamma$ the current patterns are normalized so that $\mathbf{t}^k \equiv \mathbf{T}^k/||\mathbf{T}^k||_2$, and the corresponding vectors of measured voltages, $\mathbf{V}^k$, are also normalized so that $\mathbf{v}^k \equiv \mathbf{V}^k/||\mathbf{T}^k||_2$ (see also [?]). The m,nth entry of the discrete ND map is given by $R_\gamma^{m,n} = (\mathbf{t}^m/A, \mathbf{v}^n)_L$, where A is the area of an electrode and $(u(\cdot), v(\cdot))_L \equiv \sum_{\ell=1}^{L} \bar{u}(\theta_\ell)v(\theta_\ell)$.

Parameterizing the boundary of the domain Ω by $r(\theta)$, and defining arclength function $s(\theta) := \sqrt{r^2(\theta)+(r'(\theta))^2}$, the integral (4) can be discretized as:

$$\hat{F}(\mathbf{z}) = -\frac{\Delta\theta}{2A\pi^2|\mathbf{z}|^2}\times \tag{6}$$

$$\sum_{j,k=0}^{\infty} \tilde{a}_j\tilde{b}_k \left(s(\theta)r^j(\theta)\mathrm{e}^{\mathrm{i}j\theta}, (R_\gamma/A)^{-1}\left(r^k(\theta)\mathrm{e}^{\mathrm{i}k\theta}\right)\right)_L,$$

where A is the area of an electrode, and $\Delta\theta$ is the (equal) electrode spacing, and,

$$\tilde{a}_j(\mathbf{z}) = \frac{(|\mathbf{z}|\mathrm{i}\pi\mathrm{e}^{\mathrm{i}\phi})^j}{j!} \quad \text{and} \quad \tilde{b}_k(\mathbf{z}) = \frac{(|\mathbf{z}|\mathrm{i}\pi\mathrm{e}^{-\mathrm{i}\phi})^k}{k!}. \tag{7}$$

The complex conductivity is computed by taking the Fourier inverse of $\hat{F}(\mathbf{z})$, which is done in polar coordinates:

$$\begin{aligned} \gamma(\mathbf{x}) &\approx \mathcal{F}^{-1}(\hat{\gamma}(\mathbf{z})) = \int_{-\infty}^{\infty}\int_{-\infty}^{\infty} \hat{F}(\mathbf{z})\mathrm{e}^{-2\pi\mathrm{i}(\mathbf{x}\cdot\mathbf{z})}\mathrm{d}z_1\mathrm{d}z_2 \\ &= \int_0^{\infty}\int_0^{2\pi} |\mathbf{z}|\hat{F}(|\mathbf{z}|,\phi)\mathrm{e}^{-2\pi\mathrm{i}(\mathbf{x}\cdot\mathbf{z})}\mathrm{d}\phi\mathrm{d}|\mathbf{z}| \\ &\approx \int_0^{T_z}\int_0^{2\pi} |\mathbf{z}|\hat{F}(|\mathbf{z}|,\phi)\mathrm{e}^{-2\pi\mathrm{i}(\mathbf{x}\cdot\mathbf{z})}\mathrm{d}\phi\mathrm{d}|\mathbf{z}|. \end{aligned} \tag{8}$$

By truncating the $|\mathbf{z}|$ integration, the regularization variable T_z is introduced, as explained in [4]. Integration is performed using a 2-D Simpson's Rule for fast implementation, $O(M^2)$ compared to FFT's $O(M^2\log(M))$. See [2] for further details.

III. Results and Discussion

This data was collected as part of a larger study conducted in accordance with the amended Declaration of Helsinki. Data were collected at Children's Hospital Colorado (CHCO), Aurora, CO under the approval of the Colorado Multiple Institutional Review Board (COMIRB) (approval number is COMIRB 14-0652) with CHCO and the University of Colorado Denver and the institutional review board (IRB) of Colorado State University (CSU). Informed written parental consent and children's informed assent was obtained from the subject.

The results shown in Figs. 1 and 2 are from a tidal breathing dataset taken with the ACE1 system [5]. The reference frame for these difference images was midway between the subject's full exhalation and full inhalation. In the images, red indicates a higher conductivity/permittivity than the reference frame and blue indicates a lower conductivity/permittivity than the reference frame. This means that the subject was at full exhalation at frame 36 followed by inhalation through maximum inhalation at frame 72 and then exhalation. Fig. 1 shows this ventilatory sequence in conductivity. Fig. 2 shows this sequence in permittivity.

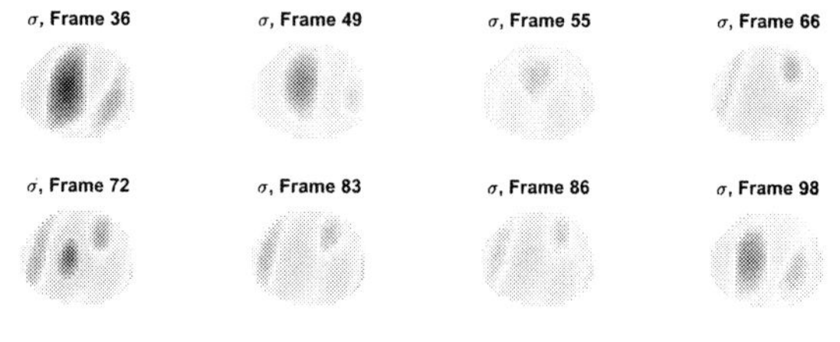

Fig. 1 Time snapshots in the ventilatory sequence for conductivity.

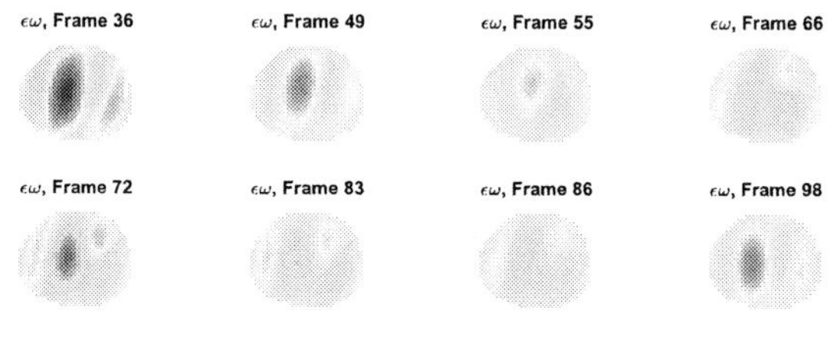

Fig. 2 Time snapshots in the ventilatory sequence for susceptivity.

IV. Conclusion

Calderón's method provides a linearized, real-time, subject-specific reconstruction method for EIT. The ability to reconstruct both the conductivity and permittivity is desirable in clinical applications.

Acknowledgment

This project was supported by award 1R21EB016869-01 from the NIBIB. The content is solely the responsibility of the authors and does not necessarily represent the official view of the NIBIB or NIH.

References

[1] A. P. Calderón, "On an inverse boundary value problem," Comp. Appl. Math., vol. 25, pp. 133–138, Oct. 2006.

[2] P. A. Muller, J. L. Mueller, and M. M. Mellenthin, "Real-time implementation of Calderón's method on subject-specific domain," IEEE Trans. Med. Imaging, vol. 36, pp. 1868–1875, Sep. 2017.

[3] D. Isaacson, J. Mueller, J. Newell, and S. Siltanen, "Reconstructions of chest phantoms by the D-bar method for electrical impedance tomography," IEEE Trans. Med. Imaging, vol. 23, pp. 821–8, 2004.

[4] J. Bikowski, and J. L. Mueller, "2D EIT reconstructions using Calderón's method," Inv. Problems and Imag., vol. 2, pp. 43–61, Feb. 2008.

[5] M. M. Mellenthin, J. L. Mueller, E. D. L. B. de Camargo, F. S. de Moura, S. J. Hamilton, and R. G. Lima, "The ACE1 thoracic electrical impedance tomography system for ventilation and perfusion," in 37th Annual International Conference of the IEEE Engineering in Medicine and Biology Society (EMBC). IEEE, 2015.

Spatial Priors in the D-bar Method for Human Thoracic Electrical Impedance Tomography Data

Melody Alsaker
Department of Mathematics
Gonzaga University
Spokane, Washington 92258
alsaker@gonzaga.edu

Jennifer L. Mueller
Department of Mathematics
School of Biomedical Engineering
Colorado State University
Fort Collins, Colorado 80523
mueller@math.colostate.edu

***Abstract*—The inclusion of a spatial prior in the high-frequency regime of the scattering transform for the 2-D D-bar method for electrical impedance tomography is studied for use with human subject data. Preliminary results on data from a human volunteer reveal improved spatial resolution when compared to a CT scan.**

I. Introduction

The inverse problem of electrical impedance tomography (EIT) is modeled by the generalized Laplace equation:

$$\nabla \cdot (\sigma(x,y)\nabla u(x,y)) = 0, \quad (x,y) \text{ in } \Omega, \tag{1}$$

where $\sigma(x,y)$ is the conductivity distribution to be reconstructed from boundary data represented by the Dirichlet-to-Neumann (DN) map:

$$\Lambda_\sigma : u|_{\partial\Omega} \mapsto \sigma\frac{\partial u}{\partial \nu}|_{\partial\Omega}, \tag{2}$$

which physically takes boundary voltages to current densities on the boundary. It was established in [1] that for $\sigma \in C^2(\Omega)$, the DN map Λ_σ uniquely determines σ.

The inverse problem is severely ill-posted, and hence highly sensitive to measurement noise and modeling errors. As a result, EIT reconstructions tend to suffer from low spatial resolution. The use of prior information in the reconstruction process is a classic approach in inverse problems to regularize and improve spatial resolution.

D-bar reconstruction methods are based on special functions known as complex geometrical optics (CGO) solutions, which satisfy a direct relationship to the unknown conductivity, and through the computation of the CGO solutions from measured EIT data, the inverse problem can be solved directly (non-iteratively). A method for including a spatial prior in the D-bar reconstruction algorithm was first proposed in [2] and tested on simulated data. In [3] a method for optimizing the spatial prior was presented for use with experimental tank data. In this work we demonstrate the effectiveness of that method on data collected on a human subject during tidal breathing.

II. Methods

A. Outline of the D-bar Method (No Priors)

The D-bar method applied here is based on the global uniqueness proof for the 2-D inverse conductivity problem [1] and subsequent implementation and development (see [4] and the references therein). The CGO solutions are defined by $\psi(z,k)$ and $\mu \equiv e^{ikz}\psi(z,k)$ where z is the spatial point (x,y) identified with a point in the complex plane $z = x+iy$, and k is a non-physical complex frequency.

The CGO solution $\psi(z,k)$ is related to the DN map, and hence the measured data, through the boundary integral equation:

$$\psi(z,k)|_{\partial\Omega} = e^{ikz}|_{\partial\Omega} - \int_{\partial\Omega} G_k(z-\zeta)(\Lambda_\sigma - \Lambda_1)\psi(\cdot,k)ds,$$

where G_k is the Faddeev's Green's function for the Laplacian operator, and Λ_1 denotes the DN map corresponding to $\sigma \equiv 1$ in Ω. The conductivity can be directly computed from knowledge of $\mu(z,k)$ in the interior of Ω through:

$$\sigma(z) = \mu^2(z,0).$$

To compute μ in the interior, the scattering transform $\mathbf{t}(k)$ of the conductivity is needed, and an integral equation is solved for μ:

$$\mu(z,k) = 1 + \frac{1}{(2\pi)^2}\int_{\mathbb{R}^2} \frac{\mathbf{t}(k')}{\overline{k'}(k-k')} e^{-i(kz+\bar{k}\bar{z})}\overline{\mu(z,k')}dk',$$

where the scattering transform is computed from:

$$\mathbf{t}(k) = \int_{\partial\Omega} e^{i\bar{k}\bar{z}}(\Lambda_\sigma - \Lambda_1)\psi(z,k)ds. \tag{3}$$

B. Outline of the D-bar Method with Spatial Priors

Since the computation of the scattering transform blows up in the presence of noise outside $|k| \le R_1$ for some R_1, as in [2] the scattering transform is extended to a larger k disk by computing it for the noise-free case of a known conductivity and by using the definition of the scattering transform, rather than the equation utilizing the data (3); this scattering transform is denoted $\mathbf{t}_{\rm pr}$. This leads to a piecewise-defined scattering transform $\mathbf{t}_{\rm pw}$, where the prior information is encoded in the method in the high-frequency components of the scattering transform through $\mathbf{t}_{\rm pr}$:

$$\mathbf{t}_{\rm pw}(k) := \begin{cases} \mathbf{t}(k), & |k| \le R_1 \\ \mathbf{t}_{\rm pr}(k), & R_1 < |k| \le R_2 \\ 0, & |k| > R_2 \end{cases}. \tag{4}$$

The prior information is included in a second location in the computations as well. Denoting the CGO solution computed for the noise-free case of a known conductivity by:

$$\mu_{\mathrm{int}}(z) := \frac{1}{\pi R_2^2} \int_{|k|\le R_2} \mu_{\mathrm{pr}}(z,k)dk, \qquad (5)$$

we solve a modified integral equation:

$$\mu_{R_2,\alpha}(z,k) = \alpha + (1-\alpha)\mu_{\mathrm{int}}(z) + \frac{1}{(2\pi)^2}\int_{|k|\le R_2} \frac{\mathbf{t}_{\mathrm{pw}}(k')}{\bar{k}'(k-k')} e_{-k'} \overline{\mu_{R_2,\alpha}(z,k')}\, dk', \qquad (6)$$

where the weighting parameter α is used to control the influence of the term μ_{int} upon the resulting reconstruction.

C. *Construction of the Spatial Prior*

The prior consists of a simple phantom representative of known features of the true conductivity distribution with assigned conductivity values. Denoting the vector of conductivity values in each of the regions by $\mathbf{c}$, we seek to find a $\mathbf{c}$ that minimizes the difference between the scattering transform computed from the measured data $\mathbf{t}^{\mathrm{vec}}$ and the scattering transform computed from the prior $\mathbf{t}^{\mathrm{vec}}_{\mathrm{pr}}$. We define the objective function:

$$J(\mathbf{c}) := \|\mathbf{t}^{\mathrm{vec}}_{\mathrm{pr}}(\mathbf{c}) - \mathbf{t}^{\mathrm{vec}}\|_2^2, \qquad (7)$$

and solve the constrained minimization problem:

$$\underset{\mathbf{c}\in\mathbb{R}^n}{\mathrm{minimize}}\ J(\mathbf{c}) \quad \text{subject to } \ell \le \mathbf{c} \le u, \qquad (8)$$

where ℓ and u are n-vectors of lower and upper bounds.

III. Results and Discussion

This data was collected as part of a larger study conducted in accordance with the amended Declaration of Helsinki. Data were collected at Children's Hospital Colorado, Aurora, CO under the approval of the Colorado Multiple Institutional Review Board (COMIRB) (approval number COMIRB 14-0652). Informed written parental consent and children's informed assent was obtained from the subject. The CT scan was performed as part of the subject's standard care.

Approximate organ boundaries and the outer boundary were visually extracted from the CT scan, and the domain was divided into four regions: background, heart, left lung, and right lung. Initial guesses for the conductivity in each of the four regions were chosen from a preliminary reconstruction, and the constrained optimization problem (8) was solved to obtain values for the prior in each of the four regions. The scattering transform $\mathbf{t}_{\mathrm{pr}}$ was then computed, and the scattering transform (4) was used for the final reconstruction.

Results on a 10-year old human male subject are shown in Fig. 1 and can be compared to the CT scan. Regions of high relative conductivity are shown in red, and regions of low relative conductivity are plotted in blue. It is evident that the use of the spatial prior results in better resolution of the lung shape, but the heart appears smaller. This apparent artifact may, however, be an accurate representation of the fact that the reconstructions are difference images from a reference frame in which the voltage on each electrode was averaged over all of the frames in the data collection sequence.

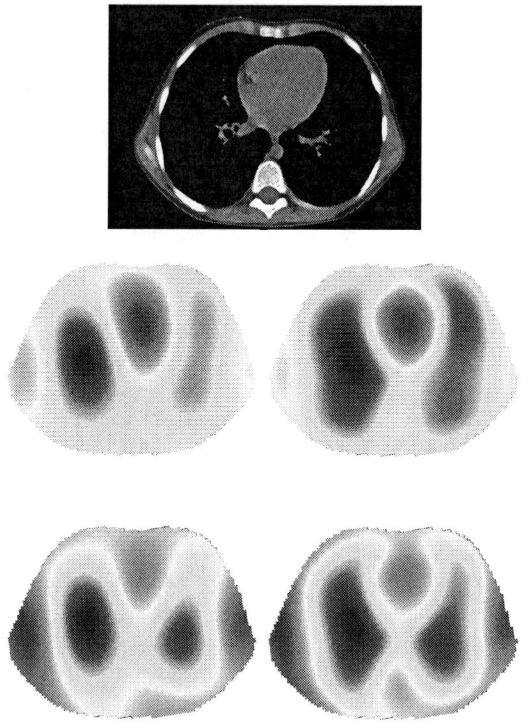

Fig. 1. Top: Inspiratory CT of subject in the plane of most electodes. Bottom: D-bar reconstructions at two time snapshots in a sequence of tidal breathing. Left column: Standard D-bar reconstruction. Right Column: Reconstruction with optimized prior.

IV. Conclusion

Spatial resolution of the EIT images reconstructed by the D-bar method is improved through the use of simple spatial priors. Further research is needed to determine their clinical value and whether they aid in detecting pathologies.

Acknowledgment

This project was supported by award 1R21EB016869-01 from the NIBIB. The content is solely the responsibility of the authors and does not necessarily represent the official view of the NIBIB or NIH.

References

[1] A. I. Nachman, "Global uniqueness for a two-dimensional inverse boundary value problem," *Ann. Math.*, vol. 143, no. 1, pp. 71–96, 1996.
[2] M. Alsaker and J. Mueller, "A D-bar algorithm with a priori information for 2-dimensional electrical impedance tomography," *SIAM J. Imaging Sci.*, vol. 9, no. 4, pp. 1619–1654, 2016.
[3] M. Alsaker and J. L. Mueller, "Use of an optimized spatial prior in d-bar reconstructions of EIT tank data," *In review*, 2017.
[4] J. L. Mueller and S. Siltanen, *Linear and Nonlinear Inverse Problems with Practical Applications*. Philadelphia, PA: SIAM, 2012.

An experimental study of the human scapula movement for the development of an anatomical atlas for Electrical Impedance Tomography

1st Tayran M. M. Olegário
Department of Mechanical Engineering
University of São Paulo
São Paulo, Brazil
tayranmila@usp.br

2nd Erick L. B. de Camargo
(CECS)
Federal University of ABC
São Bernardo, Brazil
erick.leon@ufabc.edu.br

3rd Marcelo B. P. Amato
Faculty of Medicine
University of São Paulo
São Paulo, Brazil
amato.marcelo.bp@gmail.com

4th Raul Gonzalez Lima
Department of Mechanical Engineering
University of São Paulo
São Paulo, Brazil
rauglima@usp.br

***Abstract*—The solution of Bayesian Inverse Problem for Electrical Impedance Tomography (EIT) requires the prior knowledge of the probability density function (PDF) of impeditivity. One method to estimate the PDF for EIT applications is using CT-scan images. The collection of images should be acquired under similar EIT acquisition conditions and should reflect the correct frequency of significant physical conditions. CT-scans usually are acquired with *over the head* arms while EIT images are acquired with *below the head* arms. The present work constitutes an experimental study of the human scapula and ribcage positions after the displacement of the arms. Six CT-Scans of the human thorax were segmented and 3D models of the thorax bones were computed. A description of main morphological variations due to the scapula and ribcage displacement is presented.**

***Index Terms*—prior, Bayes, inference, electrical impedance, anatomy**

I. Introduction

Electrical Impedance Tomography (EIT) estimates the distribution of impeditivity inside a domain given the measures of current injection and potential at its boundary [1]. This estimation requires the solution of an ill-posed inverse problem that involves regularization. Some researchers [2], [3] suggest the use of Bayes theorem to address this inverse problem. This approach, the Bayesian solution of inversion problems, requires the estimation of the Probability Density Function (PDF) of the sought property, oftentimes called *prior information*, sometimes called anatomical atlas.

An anathomical atlas can be computed by a collection of samples [2]. In lung applications of EIT these samples are frequently CT-scan images of the human chest. Ideally, this collection should be large, should be acquired under similar EIT acquisition conditions, for instance, the scapula should be in the same position. Implementing such a sample collection that satisfies all requirements would be highly demanding in terms of time, costs and risks due to unnecessary exposure to ionizing radiation.

Normally, hospitals maintain a large collection of CT-scan exams. These images are obtained following a protocol, patients are asked to have their arms *over the head* [4]. The direct use of such collections could introduce some artifacts and couldn't reflect usual EIT acquisition conditions. EIT exams are acquired with arms *bellow the head.*

The present work aims to describe morphological variations in CT chest images due to the *over the head* arms compared to EIT condition, *bellow the head* arms. If there is large morphological variations, they should be *corrected* before they can be used for estimating an anatomical atlas of the human thorax. The use of historical data may turn feasible the building of an anatomical atlas of the human thorax.

A. Objectives

The objective of the present work is describe main morphological variations of the human chest when the arms change from *over the head* position to *bellow the head* position, like in ICU conditions.

II. Methodology

Ideally, in the long period of time, we plan to develop eight anatomical atlases, depending on age, BMC (body mass index) and gender. The development of an anatomical atlas for a subgroup of the human population leads to a more effective regularization of the EIT inverse problem. Since the variability of our initial subgroup is small, meaning, they are all adults, healthy volunteers and medium to low body mass index, we consider the number of samples, $N = 6$, sufficient to detect main morphological variations of the human thorax when the arms go from *over the head* to *bellow the head* position.

The CT-Scans used in the present work were collected under an Ethical Committee approval number FINEP 01.14.0089.00. Six volunteers were asked to remain in a specific condition, either arms *over the head* or arms *bellow the head.* A pair of images belonging to a volunteer was then segmented through a threshold method. The tissues identified were: ribs, spine, scapula, humerus and clavicles. Each tissue was then transformed into a surface model. These surface models were then imported into Blender^{TM} animation software.

Finep project number 01.14.0089.00

Once in Blender™ environment, the surface models were then manually aligned. This alignment was performed taking the position of spine as reference: the spine of an *over the head* arm image was aligned to the spine of a *below the head* arm image. Differences of the aligned images were used in the analysis of the scapula and ribcage movements.

III. Results

A. Data of the volunteers

Tables I shows the Anterior-Posterior (A-P) distance and the Right-Left (R-L) distance measured near the T8 vertebra height. These distances were measured for the *below the head* and for the *over the head* arms positions, they are presented in the Below and Over columns, respectively. As can be noticed for the relative difference presented in the [(B-O)/O] columns, the relative difference between the arms *over the head* and the *below the head* arms positions is not significant. EIT tomography in ICU conditions is performed regularly with up to 10% variations in boundary description in polar coordinates. The radius representing the position of the boundary can be modified 10% when the patient is receiving intravenous fluids. A variation of the ribcage of the order of 1.3% is not significant.

TABLE I: Anterior-Posterior and Right-Left distances measured near the T8 vertebra.

Vol.	A-P (mm)			R-L (mm)		
—	Below	Over	(B-O)/O	Below	Over	(B-O)/O
A	190.4	182.4	4.4%	265.7	255.2	4.12%
B	175.5	179.8	-2.4%	252.1	249.2	1.16%
C	161.0	168.3	-4.3%	232.7	230.7	0.89%
D	181.6	183.6	-1.1%	289.1	290.0	-0.34%
E	175.8	178.4	-1.4%	227.5	231.4	-1.69%
F	181.6	186.9	-2.8%	250.0	261.5	-4.39%
Mean	—	—	**-1.3%**	—	—	**-0.04%**
STDV	—	—	**3.0%**	—	—	**2.87%**

B. Anatomical results

Fig. 1 shows the scapula during a *bellow the head* (in green) and an *over the head* (in red) arm positions. There is a difference between the scapula position inside the electrode belt region. Let us imagine a 3D domain defined inside the boundary surface that is the belt of electrodes. We will denote this domain by the Greek letter Σ. The intersection of the green scapula and the domain Σ occurs in the lower third of the scapula in green when the volunteer is female, see fig. 1a. The intersection of the red scapula and the domain Σ occurs in the central third of the scapula in red, see fig. 1a. Additionally, the intersection of the green scapula and the domain Σ is closer to the posterior portion of the belt of electrodes than the intersection of the red scapula and the domain Σ. The intersection of the red scapula and the domain Σ occurs close to the lower tip of the scapula in red, when the volunteer is male, see fig. 1b. There is no intersection of the scapula in green and the domain Σ, see fig. 1b.

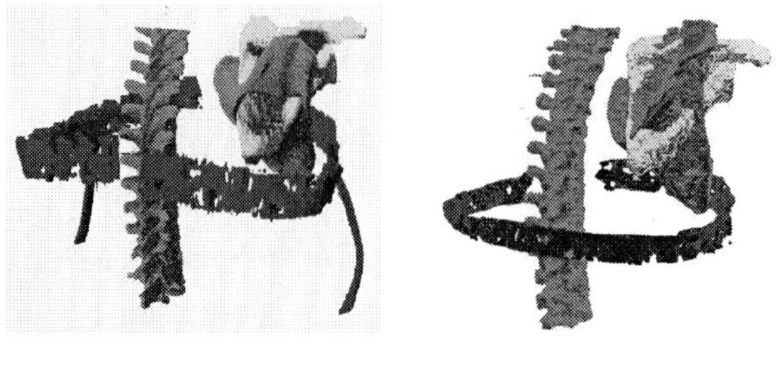

(a) (b)

Fig. 1: Position of scapula relative to the position of the electrode belt.

IV. Discussion

The A-P distance of the ribcage when arms are *below the head* is in average 1.3% smaller than the A-P distance when arms are *over the head*. The R-L distance of both positions presents no significant variation. Therefore, the geometrical variation of the ribcage may not be significant for the building of an anatomical atlas with *below the head* arms when the CT-scans were obtained when the arms were *over the head*. It is important for the development of an anatomical atlas to consider the position of the scapula. Before the use of CT-scans with the *over the head* arms, the CT-scans must be modified to take into consideration the new position of the scapula, specially for female patients.

V. Conclusions

The presented results show that CT-scans from individuals with *over the head* arms, standard exam conditions, cannot be used without modification of the position of the scapula. Since most hospitals around the world keep a large collection of those CT-scans and it is expensive to collect a large number of CT-scans with *below the head* arms, non-standard exam condition, we conclude that a repositioning of the scapula may transform CT-scans collected with *over the head* arms into useful CT-scans to develop an anatomical atlas for human individuals with *below the head* arms, the normal ICU condition of the patients. Future work comprehends the development of a CAD/CAE procedure to reposition the scapula so that CT-scans performed under standard exam conditions become useful for the development of a human thorax EIT anatomical atlas.

References

[1] D. S. Holder, "Electrical Impedance Tomography," Institute of Physics Publishing, 1st edition, 2005.

[2] J. Kaipio and E. Somersalo, "Statistical and Computational Inverse Problems," Applied Mathematical Sciences.

[3] D. Calvetti and E. Somersalo, An Introduction to Bayesian Scientific Computing, 1st, 2007, Springer-Verlag New York.

[4] H. Liu, Y. Gao, A. Ding, P. Caracappa, and G. Xu, "The profound effects of patient arm positioning on organ doses from CT procedures calculated using Monte Carlo simulations and deformable phantoms", 2014, Radiation protection dosimetry.

Introduction of statistical priors into the D-bar method for electrical impedance tomography

Talles B. R. Santos
Escola Politécnica
Universidade de São Paulo
São Paulo, Brazil
tallesrattis@usp.com

Erick L. B. de Camargo
CECS
Universidade Federal do ABC
São Bernardo, Brazil
erick.leon@ufabc.edu.br

Jennifer L. Mueller
Department of Mathematics & SBME
Colorado State University
Fort Collins, United States
mueller@math.colostate.edu

Raul Gonzalez Lima
Escola Politécnica
Universidade de São Paulo
São Paulo, Brazil
lima.raul@gmail.com

***Abstract*—The D-bar method is a direct (noniterative) reconstruction method for 2-D electrical impedance tomography that solves the full nonlinear inverse conductivity problem. However, the idealized model underlying the method is an obstacle to the computation of absolute images by the D-bar method. In this work, a method of correcting the data based on Bayesian techniques to better fit the idealized assumptions is proposed. Preliminary results are shown on experimental tank data.**

***Index Terms*—D-bar, Bayesian Inference, Approximation Error Theory, Anatomical Atlas**

I. Introduction

Electrical impedance tomography (EIT) is a non-invasive imaging technique with a variety of clinical applications, including pulmonary imaging. In EIT, current is applied on electrodes on the body, the voltage is measured, and an inverse problem is solved numerically to estimate the conductivity distribution in the interior. While there are numerous approaches to the reconstruction problem, D-bar methods are the only noniterative technique proven to converge, effective on real data, and providing real-time reconstructions [1]. However, the assumption of knowledge of the Dirichlet-to-Neumann, or voltage-to-current map, in the D-bar method makes it difficult to include information about hardware and environmental noise in the reconstruction algorithm, which can result in severe artefacts in absolute images.

In this work, a method of correcting the data based on Bayesian techniques to better fit the idealized assumptions is proposed, and statistical priors are included in the D-bar reconstruction algorithm. The construction and application of prior probability density functions has been successful [2] for solving a variety of inverse problems by Bayesian statistical theory. Furthermore, Camargo [3] has shown that the use of an anatomical atlas, which for medical imaging applications describes prior information based on samples containing anatomical and physiological information [2], and the Approximation Error Method [2] improves the spatial resolution of chest images using the Gauss-Newton method.

Objective

The development and evaluation of a method to incorporate a prior probability density function of the conductivity distribution of a population into the D-bar method is proposed.

II. Methodology

To introduce prior information and minimize the modeling simplifications implicit in the D-bar method, the Approximation Error Method and Bayesian inference are employed. The presented method consists of correcting the inverse problem formulation to take into account the simplified model implicitly used in the D-bar method and prior information.

The D-Bar method implicit model is simplified by stating that the domain is 2D and by adopting an electrode model that does not reflect electrical reality. The correction term suggested by the Approximation Error Method is computed with the aid of the prior information, by the minimization of an objective function that considers modeling errors and the prior information in the space of the measurement vectors. The objective function is a consequence of Bayes' Theorem as developed in the sequel.

A normal distribution is assumed for the electrical potential vector. This distribution can be computed by the forward model and samples of the normal distribution of the conductivities, e.g. the anatomical atlas, and it is represented by

$$y \sim N(y_0, \Gamma_{pr_y}), \tag{1}$$

where y_0 is the expected value of the vector of voltages y and Γ_{pr_y} is the covariance matrix of the vector of voltages y.

The vector of measurements is denoted by y_m. Bayes' theorem can be stated in terms of y and y_m,

$$\pi(y|y_m) = \frac{\pi(y_m|y)\pi(y)}{\pi(y_m)}, \tag{2}$$

where $\pi(y_m|y)$ is the likelihood function, $\pi(y)$ the prior probability density function of y and $\pi(y_m)$ the marginal likelihood of the vector of measurements y_m.

From Bayes' Theorem, (2), and the Approximation Error Method, an objective function can be written,

$$r(y) = \| y_m - y - \tilde{e}_0 \|_{\tilde{\Gamma}_n^{-1}} + \beta^2 \| y - \tilde{y}_0 \|_{\tilde{\Gamma}_{pr_y}^{-1}}, \tag{3}$$

where $\tilde{y}_0$ is the expected vector of measurements, $\tilde{\Gamma}_{pr_y}$ is its covariance matrix, $\tilde{e}_0$ is the expected vector of the approximation error vector and $\tilde{\Gamma}_n$ is its covariance matrix.

After the objective function (3) is minimized for a given voltage measurements y_m, the adjusted voltage vector y is used to reconstruct the image by the D-bar method.

In this work the objective function (3) is minimized for several values of β, and two sets of adjusted voltages are computed. The first set of adjusted voltage data set was formed by y from (3) when $\tilde{e}_0$ is the Approximation Error correction vector from simulated voltages. A second set of adjusted voltages was formed by y from (3) when $\tilde{e}_0$ is the difference between voltage measurements of a basal data set and numerically simulated voltages of the basal case. We will refer to these as Approach 1 and Approach 2.

III. Results

Three experimental phantoms were used, Fig 1. Electric potentials were measured when the tank (150 mm radius) was filled with a saline solution (basal) and when cucumbers slices (50 mm radius) were positioned in two different arrangements, *aligned* and in a *triangular arrangement*. The ACE1 hardware [4] was used with a bipolar current source with excitation amplitude of 3.35 mA and frequency of 125 kHz for the data collection.

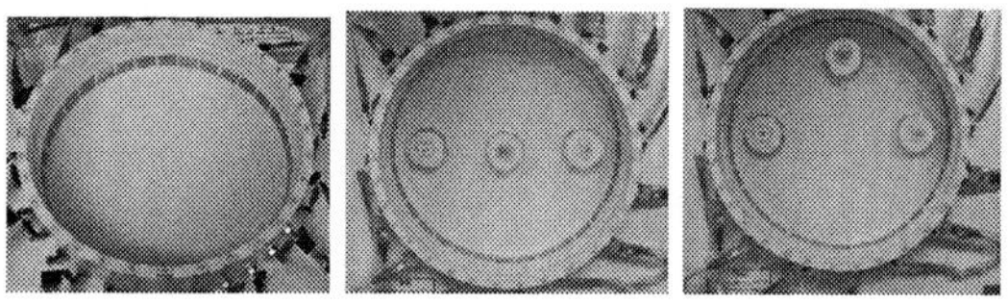

(a) Basal (b) Aligned (c) Triangular

Fig. 1. Experimental phantoms

The prior distribution was computed from a set of simulated samples. 200,000 samples were generated representing a homogeneous tank with one cylindrical object with random position and random diameter between 40 and 60 mm. From each sample measured voltages were simulated using a *simplified* forward problem model closer to the assumptions of the D-bar method. Finally, the expected value $\tilde{y}_0$ and the covariance matrix $\tilde{\Gamma}_{pr_y}$ of the electric potential measurements were computed.

The images of the experimental phantoms were reconstructed for the different data sets; figures 2 and 3 represent the results. In the first row of images the cucumber slices are *aligned*. In the second row of images the cucumber slices are in the *triangular arrangement*. In the figures, subfigures (a) and (e) show the images when no prior was used. The subfigures (b), (c), (d), (f), (g) and (h) show the result of using different values of β in (3).

IV. Discussion

Although the reconstructed images still include artifacts and distortion of the cucumber positions, the quality of the images is improved by using the methods presented. Approach 2 consistently presented better results due to use the basal measurements, which reduces the error caused by the modeling error and the measurement noise.

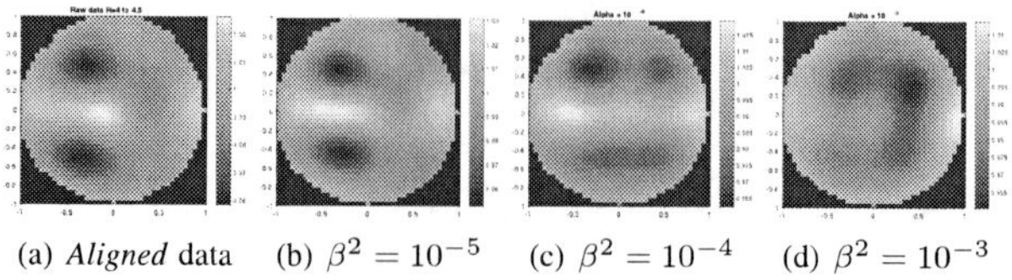

(a) *Aligned* data (b) $\beta^2 = 10^{-5}$ (c) $\beta^2 = 10^{-4}$ (d) $\beta^2 = 10^{-3}$

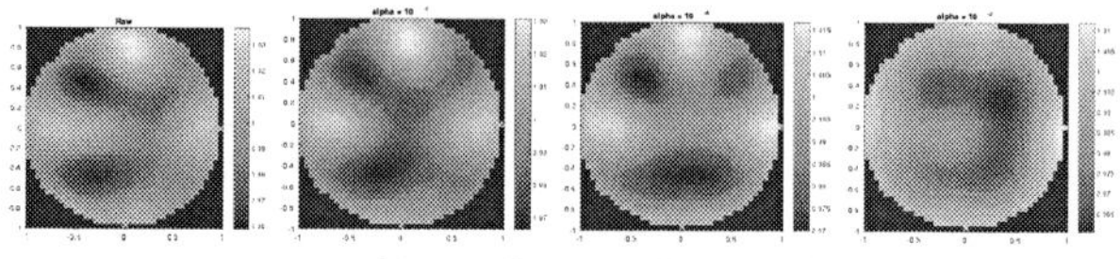

(e) *Tri. arr.* data (f) $\beta^2 = 10^{-5}$ (g) $\beta^2 = 10^{-4}$ (h) $\beta^2 = 10^{-3}$

Fig. 2. Results of Approach 1. Top row: Aligned Bottom row: Triangular

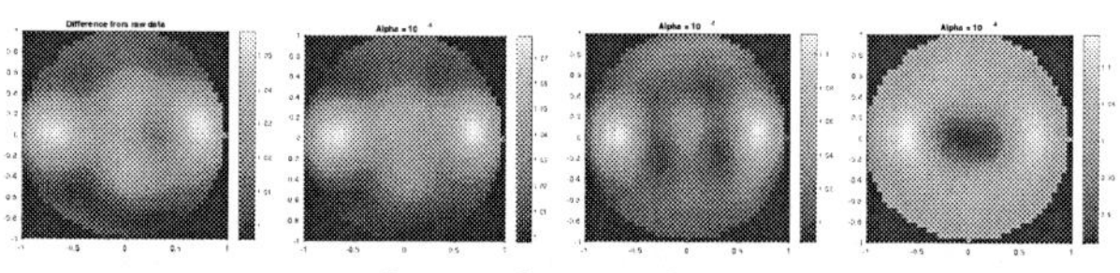

(a) *Aligned* data (b) $\beta^2 = 10^{-6}$ (c) $\beta^2 = 10^{-5}$ (d) $\beta^2 = 10^{-4}$

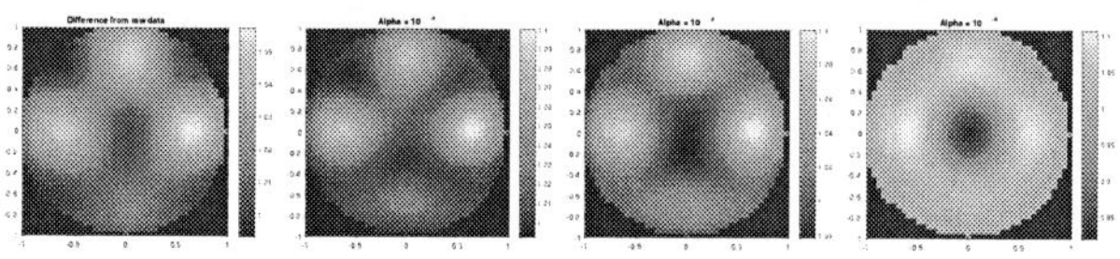

(e) *Tri. arr.* data (f) $\beta^2 = 10^{-6}$ (g) $\beta^2 = 10^{-5}$ (h) $\beta^2 = 10^{-4}$

Fig. 3. Results of Approach 2. Top row: Aligned Bottom row: Triangular

V. Conclusions

The results show that the method is a feasible approach for obtaining improved images by the D-bar method. More refined evaluation could be performed by studying phantoms with targets of different conductivities, sizes, shapes and arrangements.

Acknowledgment

We thank the research development agency CAPES, University of São Paulo and Colorado State University for supporting and founding this research.

References

[1] M. Dodd and J.L. Mueller, " A real-time D-bar algorithm for 2-D electrical impedance tomography data," Inverse Probl. Imag., 8(4):1013–1031, 2014..

[2] Jari Kaipio and Erkki Somersalo, " Statistical and computational inverse problems, " Springer, 2005..

[3] Erick Darío León Bueno Camargo, "Desenvolvimento de algoritmo de imagens absolutas de Tomografia por Impedância Elétrica para uso clínico," PhD thesis, Universidade de São Paulo, 2013..

[4] Michelle M. Mellenthin, " The active complex electrode (ACE1) electrical impedance tomography system and anatomically inspired modeling of electrode skin contact impedance." PhD thesis, School of Biomedical Engineering of Colorado State University, Fort Collins, EUA, 2016..

Wideband GCPW-Fed Dielectric Resonator Antenna for WLAN Applications

Wei-Chung Weng
Department of Electrical Engineering
National Chi Nan University
301, University Rd., Puli, Nantou 54561, Taiwan
E-mail: wcweng@ncnu.edu.tw

Min-Chi Chang and Min-Sian Chen
R&D Department
Master Wave Technology Co., Ltd.
309, Sec. 1, Fuxing E. Rd., Zhubei City, 302, Taiwan
Email: minsian.chen@masterwave.com.tw

***Abstract*—A dielectric resonator antenna is designed for WLAN 5.5 GHz band applications in this study. The dielectric resonator antenna is fabricated on a cheap FR4 substrate with grounded CPW structure. Results of the designed dielectric resonator antenna show that good agreement between simulated and measured reflection coefficients, radiations, and antenna gains is observed. The measured -10 dB bandwidth of the proposed dielectric resonator antenna is 1.6 GHz (28.6 %, 4.8 – 6.4 GHz), which covers the WLAN 5.5 GHz band.**

***Keywords*—dielectric resonator; DRA; GCPW; wideband; WLAN**

I. Introduction

Dielectric resonators [1] have the advantages of no conductor loss, low quality factor, and high dielectric constant; hence, they are widely used for designing dielectric resonator antennas (DRAs). DRAs have many advantages such as compact size, wideband, and high efficiency. DRAs also can be fed by coplanar waveguide (CPW) lines [2]–[3]. However, CPW fed structure without a ground plane on the backside has a drawback that decreases the antenna gain and efficiency due to backside radiations. To overcome this drawback, a grounded CPW (GCPW) structure can be used. The GCPW structure has a ground plane on the bottom layer of the substrate to block the backside radiations. Also, the ground plane can create an additional image radiator to improve the gain of the DRA.

In this study, a wideband DRA with a GCPW structure is proposed. The designed DRA operates at the WLAN 5.5 GHz (5.15 – 5.85 GHz) band. The proposed DRA has characteristics of wideband, high gain, and wide beamwidth. Details of the proposed DRA design are described, and results of the prototype are presented and discussed.

II. Antenna Design

Fig. 1 shows the geometry of the proposed wideband DRA. The proposed antenna is fabricated on an FR4 substrate with a thickness (h) of 0.8 mm, dielectric constant of 4.4, and loss tangent of 0.02. The size of the DRA is 60.0 mm by 60.0 mm. The cylindrical dielectric resonator used is a 4.2 mm height (Hd) with a radius (Rd) of 14.9 mm, dielectric constant of 9.8, and loss tangent of 0.01. The GCPW fed line becomes a closed circular loop line in the end. The closed circular loop GCPW line consists of a circular patch and a circular slot. They are concentric. The radii of the outer and inner edge of the circular slot are R1 and R2, respectively. This closed circular loop GCPW slot line excites a ring of magnetic current, which is equivalent an electric dipole source normal to the plane of the fed line [2]. By properly adjusting the orientation of the cylindrical dielectric resonator and dimensions of the closed circular loop GCPW slot line structure, the desired mode can be excited and wideband impedance matching of the DRA can be obtained. The distance from the center of the dielectric resonator to the center of the circular patch is d. Wf is the width of the center fed line. g is the gap between the edge of the center fed line and the edge of the ground plane on the top layer of the FR4 substrate. Detailed dimensions of the proposed wideband DRA are listed in Table I.

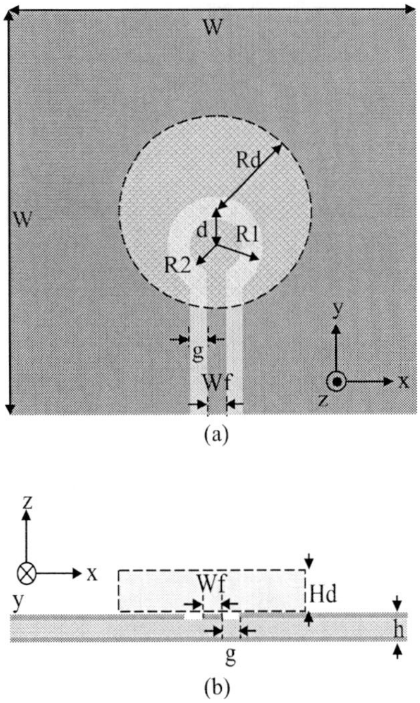

Fig. 1. The geometry of proposed wideband GCPW fed DRA, (a) top view and (b) side view.

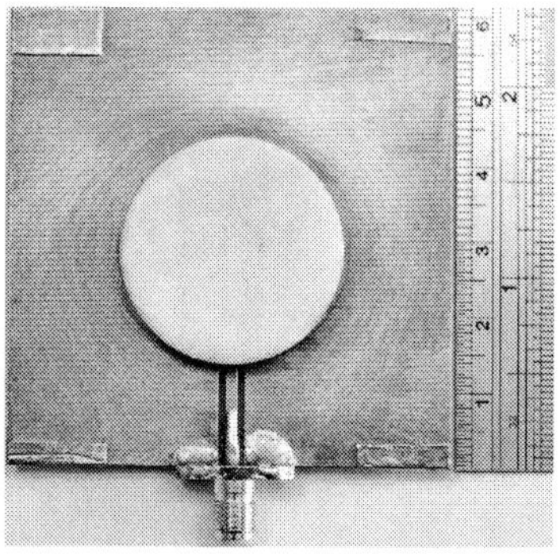

Fig. 2. The picture of the proposed wideband DRA.

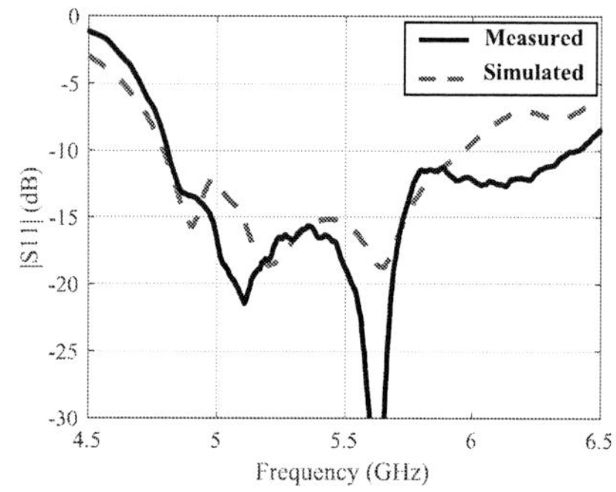

Fig. 3. The reflection coefficients of the proposed DRA.

TABLE I
DIMENSIONS OF THE PROPOSED
DIELECTRIC RESONATOR ANTENNA (UNIT: mm)

Parameter	Size	Parameter	Size
W	60.0	R1	10.0
Wf	2.52	R2	6.5
g	1.0	d	4.0
h	0.8	Rd	14.9
Hd	4.2		

Fig. 2 shows the picture of the fabricated wideband DRA. The magnitude of reflection coefficients (|S11|) of the proposed DRA is shown in Fig. 3. The simulated |S11| reasonably agrees with the measured one. The measured -10 dB bandwidth is 1.6 GHz (28.6 %, 4.8-6.4 GHz), which covers the WLAN 5.5 GHzband. Fig. 4 reveals the radiation patterns of the proposed DRA at 5.5 GHz. The DRA has a broadside radiation. Good agreement between simulated and measured radiation patterns is seen, which shows the validity of the simulation. The measured 3 dB beamwidth is around 55 degrees in the x-z plane. Fig. 5 shows the measured peak gain of the proposed DRA. The measured peak gain is 5.2 dBi at 5.5 GHz and 7.3 dBi at 5.75 GHz. Based on the results of reflection coefficients and radiation properties, the proposed DRA has good performance and is suitable for operating at the WLAN 5.5 GHz band.

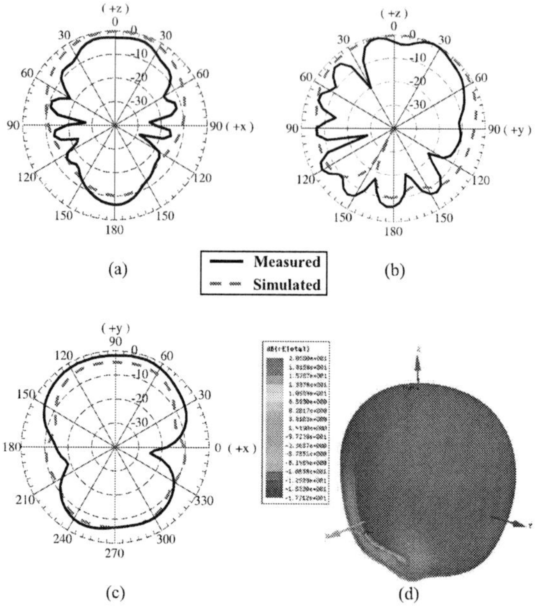

Fig. 4. The radiation patterns (normalized) of the proposed DRA at 5.5 GHz (a) in the x-z plane, (b) in the y-z plane, (c) in the x-y plane, and (d) simulated 3D pattern.

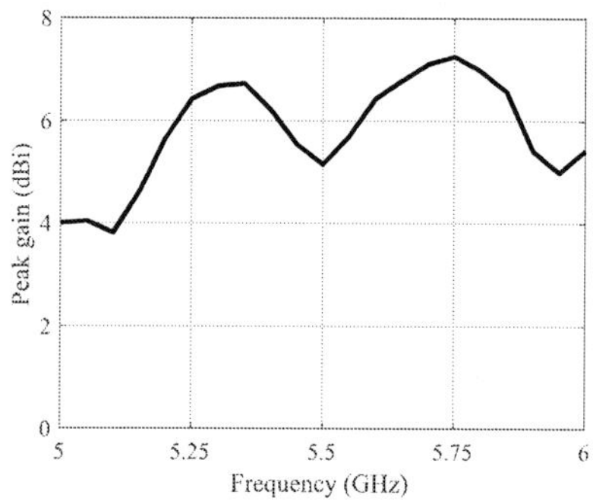

Fig. 5. The measured peak gain of the proposed antenna.

REFERENCES

[1] S. A. Long, M. W. McAllister, and L. C. Shen,"The resonant cylindrical dielectric cavity antenna," *IEEE Trans. Antennas Propag.* vol. 31, pp. 406–412, May 1983.

[2] R. A. Kranenburg, S. A. Long, and J. T. Williams,"Coplanar Waveguide Excitation of Dielectric Resonator Antennas," *IEEE Trans. Antennas Propag.* vol. 39, pp. 119–122, Jan. 1991.

[3] Y. Gao, Z. Feng, and L. Zhang, "Compact CPW-Fed Dielectric Resonator Antenna With Dual Polarization," *IEEE Antennas and Wireless Propagation Letters*, vol. 10, pp. 544–547, May 2011.

Design of Broadband Luneburg Lens Feed Manifold

Maxim Ignatenko, Carlos A. Mulero Hernandez, and Dejan Filipovic
Department of Electrical, Computer, and Energy Engineering
University of Colorado, Boulder
Boulder, Colorado, USA, 80309
{Maxim.Ignatenko, Carlos.Mulerohernandez, Dejan.Filipovic}@colorado.edu

***Abstract*—Design of broadband feed manifolds for Luneburg lenses requires intensive numerical calculations that can be time and memory consuming. This paper presents a simple and fast numerical procedure for the estimation of the field of view (FOV) coverage by a lens antenna. Details of the routine are described and the example of the lens having at least 12 dBi directivity within the FOV from 18 to 45 GHz is shown. The lens is fed by a 6x6 feed manifold made of phase center stabilized horns.**

Keywords*—*feed manifold, Luneburg lens, method of moments.

I. Introduction

The Luneburg lens (LL) is a spherical radially stratified dielectric lens. The radial profile of refractive index overcomes spherical aberrations intrinsic for monolithic spherical lenses. When fed by a feed manifold, the LL enables radiation of multiple beams, where beam scanning is achieved by switching on and off the predefined discrete beams. In contrast to phase arrays, there is no beam degradation due to scanning; however, lens bulkiness reduces its attraction at frequencies lower than approximately X-band.

Discrete nature of the LL antenna poses a significant challenge for broadband designs - the lens is getting more directive at higher frequency end, therefore deeper gain drops within the field of view may not allow for a continuous coverage at all frequencies. In contrast to narrowband designs, where high aperture efficiency is one of the design priorities, wideband systems may need to sacrifice aperture efficiency for the better FOV coverage. We found that broadband LL feed manifold designs are heavily underreported in open literature and present herein a simple and fast approach for coverage estimations. The paper describes the details of the approach and shows an example of the LL with feed manifold operating from 18 to 45 GHz. The lens system demonstrates more than 12 dBi directivity within the FOV. The manifold consists of phase center stabilized horns shown in Fig. 1 [1].

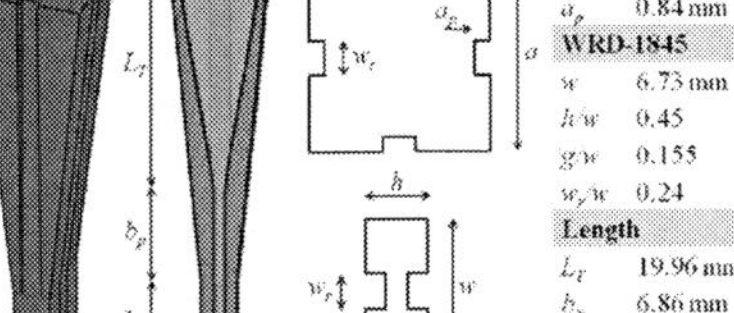

Fig. 1. Stabilized phase center horn antenna operating from 18 to 45 GHz.

This work was supported by the Office of Naval Research under grant #N00014-15-1-2125.

II. Numerical Approach

Geometry of the problem is shown in Fig. 2. Instead of working with a feed manifold, a single feed is considered aiming to improve directivity at a triple crossover point. The projection of the feeder apertures and LL beams on the far field sphere is shown in Fig. 2 (right). The triple crossover point is equally distant from centers of three adjacent beams, and thus LL directivity is therein minimal. For the shown manifold geometry, triple crossover full angle θ_3 relates to the feeder angular width θ_s as:

$$\theta_3 = 1.25\theta_s. \tag{1}$$

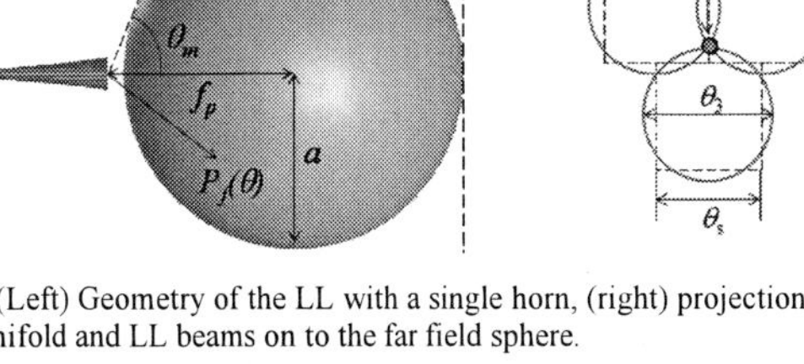

Fig. 2. (Left) Geometry of the LL with a single horn, (right) projection of the feed manifold and LL beams on to the far field sphere.

Due to large electrical size of the problem, using full wave numerical methods for intensive estimation and optimizations can be time consuming. The numerical routine described herein relies on analytical Geometrical Optics (GO) expressions and uses a few assumptions. First, it is assumed that the GO approximation is valid even though the lens is placed in the near-field of the feeder. The validity of this assumption is proved by good agreement between GO and full wave results. Second, the feeder beam is considered to be axially symmetric.

The numerical routine consists of a few steps:

1. The calculation starts from the full wave evaluation of the feeder linear pattern P_f. The pattern is calculated only once, and then it is used for all parametric sweeps.

2. Then, the lens spillover efficiency is calculated as:

$$\eta_{spill} = \frac{\int_0^{\theta_m} P_f(\theta)\sin\theta d\theta}{\int_0^{\pi} P_f(\theta)\sin\theta d\theta}, \tag{2}$$

where, $\theta_m = \mathrm{asin}(1/f_p)$ is the lens half-subtended angle, with f_p is the focal distance normalized by the lens radius.

3. Power distribution P_a in the lens aperture is determined by means of the GO lens transformation [2]:

$$P_a(r) = \frac{P_f\left(\operatorname{asin}\left(\frac{r}{f_p}\right)\right)}{f_p\sqrt{f_p^2 - r^2}}, \tag{3}$$

where, radius r is normalized by the lens radius a. The radius varies from 0 to 1, since the aperture is given by the lens cross-section.

4. Field at the lens aperture is transformed into linear directivity D_{LL} as [3]:

$$D_{LL}(\theta) = \frac{k^2|SF(\theta)|^2\eta_{spill}}{8\pi^2 a^2 \int_0^1 P_a(r)rdr}, \tag{4}$$

here, space factor SF given by:

$$SF(\theta) = 4\pi a^2 \int_0^1 \sqrt{P_a(r)}J_0(kar\sin\theta)rdr, \tag{5}$$

where, J_0 is the Bessel function of first kind. No phase distribution is taken into account; since an ideal LL transforms a spherical wave into a plane wave.

Fig. 3 shows results of calculations with the LL of 35.56 mm radius and 71.12 mm focal distance performed by means of the presented routing and full wave ANSYS HFSS package as well. The HFSS model approximates continuous radial profile of refractive index by 10 discrete layers. The lens is illuminated by a uniform aperture of 10 mm size located at the focal surface (feed is offset by 35.56 mm from the lens surface). As seen, there is excellent agreement between GO and FEM results in terms of broadside directivity; however, agreement is poor for the side lobe level (SLL). This can be partially explained by the fact that a point source approximation may not be very accurate for SLL calculations; moreover, the spillover field is ignored in the code. Demonstrated accuracy of the presented routine for directivity calculations makes it particularly suitable for the estimations of coverage.

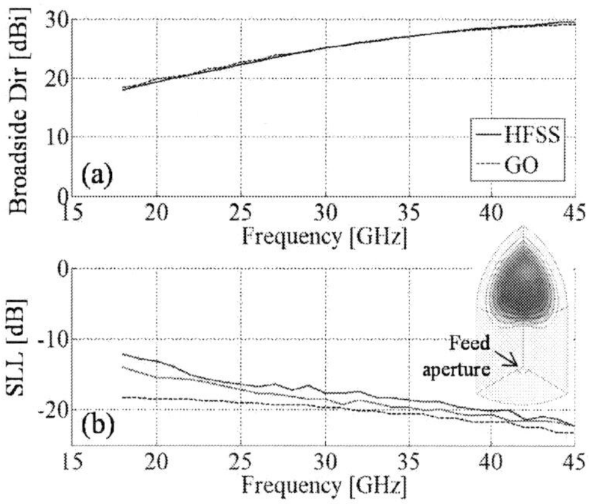

Fig. 3. (a) Broadside directivity and (b) side lobe level calculated by means of the GO code and FEM solver of HFSS. Dashed lines correspond to GO results, solid lines – FEM results in E- and H-plane. Geometry of the HFSS setup is shown in inset with symmetry planes used to reduce computation time.

III. Example Design

The design procedure accepts minimum directivity D_{min} within FOV as a design parameter. Lens radius and focal distance are varied and figure of merit is evaluated. Horn is always placed at the focal point. Figure of merit is given by the ratio between the LL beamwidth at D_{min} and triple point half-angle. For having continuous coverage, the figure of merit should be more than 1. When the lens parameters are identified, the result is confirmed in HFSS and a full manifold is modeled.

As an example, condition D_{min} = 12 dBi is considered. GO estimations identify the lens with 35 mm radius and 60 mm focal point as a good candidate. Fig. 4 shows HFSS results for broadside and triple crossover point directivity. As seen, GO estimations are confirmed. SLL not shown here is better than -15 dB. Superposition of beam patterns for a 6x6 feed manifold shown in Fig. 5 confirms that the design goal is achieved.

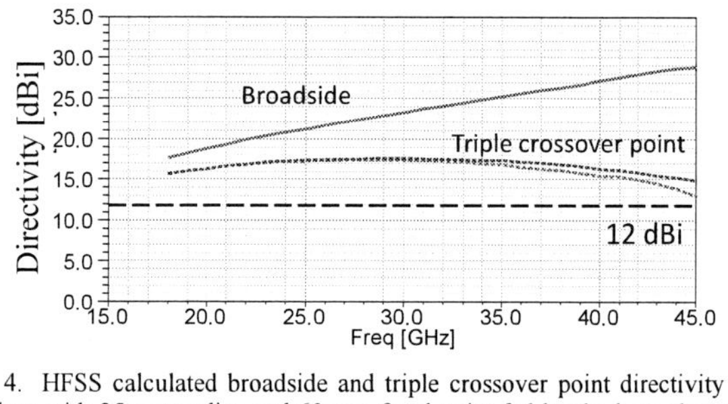

Fig. 4. HFSS calculated broadside and triple crossover point directivity for the lens with 35 mm radius and 60 mm focal point fed by the horn shown in Fig. 1. Result for the triple crossover point is shown in E- and H-planes.

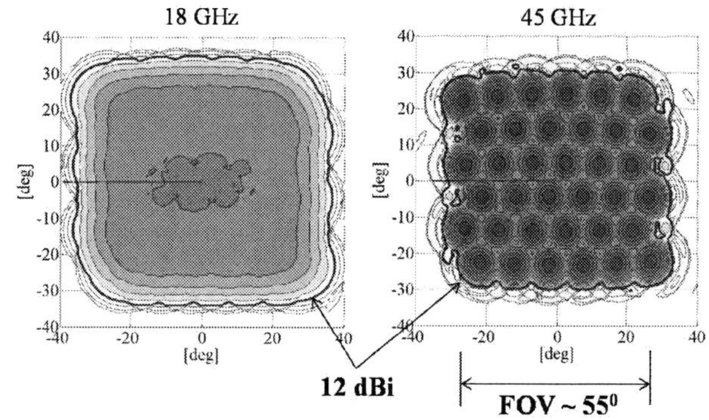

Fig. 5. Field of view coverage of the LL antenna with at least 12 dBi directivity in field of view. The lens is fed by the 6x6 feed manifold.

References

[1] M. Ignatenko, B. Simakauskas, M. Notaros, and D. Filipovic, "A phase center-stabilized K/Ka/V-band linearly polarized horn for Luneburg lens," IEEE Antennas Wireless Propag. Lett., vol. 16, pp. 2726-2729, 2017.

[2] S. P. Morgan, "General solution of the Luneberg lens," J. Appl. Phys., vol. 29, pp. 1358-1368, 1958

[3] C. A. Balanis, Antenna Theory: Analysis and Design, 2nd ed., Hoboken, NJ, USA: Wiley, 1997.

Multioctave Antenna Array for Simultaneous Transmit and Receive Applications

Mohamed A. Elmansouri, Jaegeun Ha, and Dejan Filipovic
Department of Electrical, Computer, and Energy Engineering
University of Colorado, Boulder
Boulder, Colorado, USA, 80309
{Mohamed.Elmansouri, Jaegeun.Ha, and Dejan.Filipovic}@colorado.edu

***Abstract*—This paper presents the design and performance of a high-isolation, wideband, and monostatic simultaneous transmit and receive (STAR) antenna system. The proposed configuration is composed of four dual-polarized conical sinuous antennas sequentially rotated and fed using two 2×4 Butler matrix beamforming networks; one for transmitting (TX) and the other for receiving (RX). Due to the applied phase progression and the symmetry of the proposed configuration, the coupled TX signals are fully cancelled at the RX port leading to theoretically infinite isolation. Numerical modelling conducted using method of moments (MoM) and finite element method (FEM) solvers is used to demonstrate the performance of the proposed configuration over 8:1 bandwidth.**

Keywords— Conical sinuous, Isolation, STAR.

I. Introduction

Self-interference (SI) is the chief challenge encountered in the practical implementation of simultaneous transmit and receive (STAR) systems [1]. Isolation in the order of 120-140 dB is typically required to cancel SI and restore the receiving operation. 30% and more of the desired isolation level can be achieved at the antenna layer without the use of conventional circulators by considering the use of antenna separation, polarization diversity, antenna geometrical symmetry and excitation, near-field cancelation, and modes multiplexing [2]. Efficiency, size, bandwidth, and dissimilarity between TX and RX patterns are some issues of the previously-proposed STAR antenna approaches [2]-[3]. Recently, we proposed a monostatic co-polarized STAR antenna array that can operate with high efficiency and isolation [3]. Therein, the antenna system utilizes a sequential rotation array (SRA) of four dual-polarized elements and two modified Butler matrix beamforming networks (BFN) (Fig. 1) to cancel the coupled TX signals at the RX port. Co-polarized TX/RX left- or right-hand circular polarization (LHCP or RHCP) patterns can be radiated by exciting appropriate port of the input TX/RX 90° hybrids. The principle of operation is experimentally validated using SRA of dual-polarized patch antennas and extending the bandwidth up to 2:1 is also discussed by considering a quad-ridge horn as an array's element [3]. In this paper, the bandwidth is extended further by utilizing the quasi frequency-independent conical sinuous antenna. The performance of the array is computationally studied using the commercial MoM (Altair FEKO) and FEM (Ansys HFSS) solvers. The isolation and radiation performances are analyzed in the context of the obtained numerical results. Also, the computational settings and brief comparison between the two solvers are discussed.

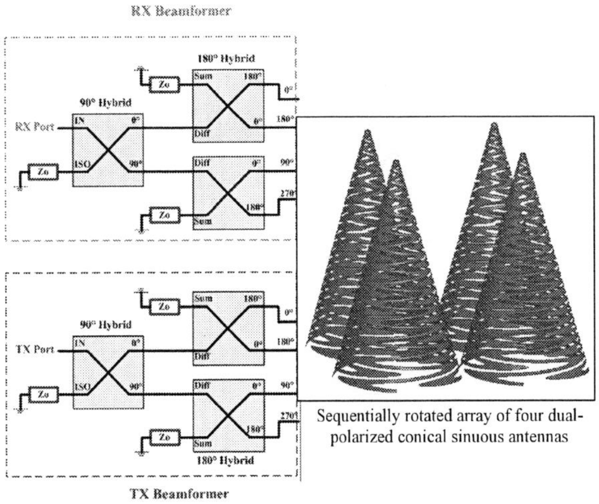

Fig. 1. Proposed STAR antenna system composed of four-element conical sinuous SRA and TX and RX Butler matrix BFNs.

II. Array Element

The planar four-arm sinuous antenna can provide multioctave dual-polarization operation with excellent radiation characteristics and smaller size than the log-periodic antenna [4]. To eliminate the backward radiation of planar topology, an absorptive backing is typically used at the expense of 50% or less radiation efficiency which is undesired for the intended applications. The conical structure is inherently unidirectional and it is chosen herein to achieve efficient and consistent operation over a wide bandwidth. The outer diameter of the antenna is chosen to have turn-on frequency around 500MHz while the height is tuned to achieve front-to-back ratio (F/B) > 10dB at the low end. The impact of growth rate (τ), number of cells (P), and angular width (α) on the antenna performance are studied and it is found that having variable τ and α along the cells (as shown in the inset of Fig. 2) leads to consistent gain, stable impedance match, high F/B, and low cross polarization. The geometrical parameters of the designed antenna are shown in Fig. 2 (a). Each two opposite arms are excited 180° out of phase to obtain orthogonal linear polarizations. As seen from Fig. 2, the antenna has good

This work is supported by the Office of Naval Research (ONR) # N00173-15-C-2021.

impedance match (VSWR<1.5) with respect to the nominal impedance (133Ω from the arm to the ground). Also, consistent linearly-polarized gain > 8dBi is obtained from 0.5 to 4GHz. Excellent quality radiation patterns (not shown) are obtained.

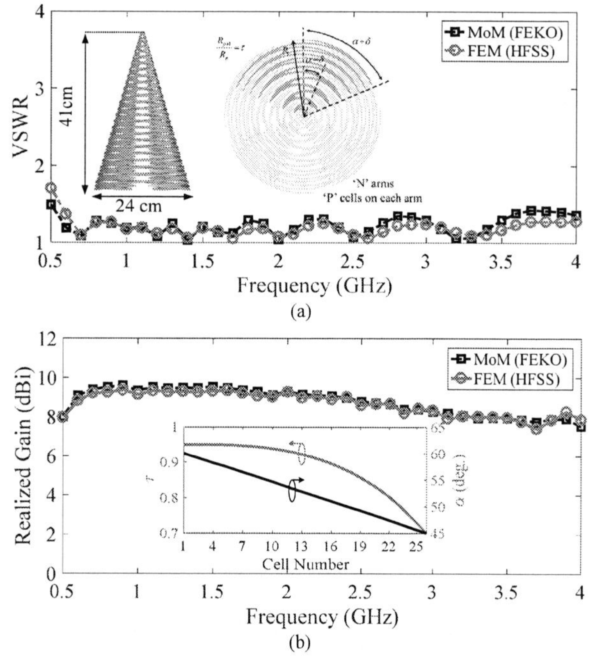

Fig. 2. Simulated (a) VSWR (w.r.t nominal impedance) and (b) realized gain of the designed conical sinuous antenna. Gometerial parameters are shown in the inset.

III. STAR Array Performance

Four conical sinuous antennas arranged in SRA fashion are modeled and the S-parameters obtained from the full-wave simulation are exported to AWR circuit simulator to estimate the system isolation. Each antenna contains TX and RX ports corresponding to orthogonal polarizations. Each set of TX and RX ports is excited with 90° phase progression by using TX/RX 2×4 Butler matrix BFNs as shown in Fig. 1. Any coupled TX signal will be canceled at the RX port leading to theoretically infinite isolation in imbalances-free configuration [3]. In simulation, the isolation is limited by the symmetry of the meshing and the numerical noise floor. Some coupled signals are terminated at the BFN loads and is accounted as a power loss.

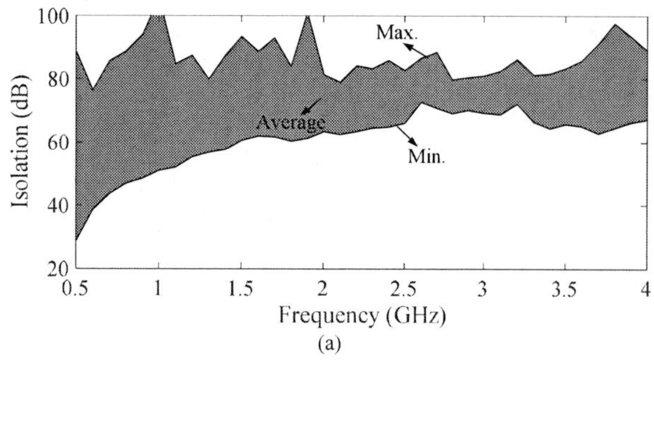

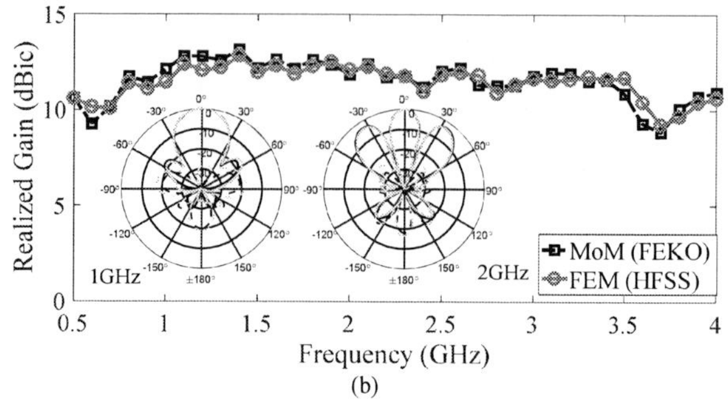

Fig. 3. Simulated (a) isolation and (b) realized gain of the porposed STAR antenna configuration (Fig. 1). FEKO (dark-color) and HFSS (light-color) RHCP (solid line) and LHCP (dashed line) paterns are shown in the inset.

As shown in Fig. 3 (a), the maximum obtained isolation (in FEKO) is >79dB assuming ideal BFN. If the imbalances are introduced the isolation degrades as shown by the shaded area for phase imbalances up to 5°. However, the isolation stays > 50dB over most of the band. Power loss in the loads of BFN is < 3.65% over most of the band. The array's far-field performance is shown in Fig. 3 (b). CP gain > 9.8dBic and low axial ratio are obtained over the band. As expected, side lobe level (SLL) increases as the frequency increases. Reasonable SLL < -10dB is achieved up to 3:1 bandwidth. Miniaturizing the antenna, use of tilted conical to reduce the electrical spacing, and the practical realization are part of future work.

Excellent agreement is observed between FEKO and HFSS in all cases. A brief comparison between the two solvers is shown in Table I. The antenna is meshed at 4GHz and modeled as PEC sheets. Also, the meshing of single antenna is rotated in FEKO to enforce the symmetry. As seen, FEKO outperforms HFSS in terms of memory for this setup. Multiprocessing options in FEKO and HFSS helps to keep the simulation time to be considerable for multiple frequency points.

TABLE I. Comparsion between FEKO and HFSS array simulation

Parameter	FEKO	HFSS
Memory	3.63GB	47.1GB
Meshing Elements	21640 triangular	742913 tetrahedral
Basis Function	RWG	Mixed order
Boundary Condition	Green's function	FEBI

References

[1] D. Bharadia, E. McMilin, and S. Katti, "Full duplex radios," in Proc. SIGCOMM'13 Conf., China, 2013, pp. 375–386.

[2] E. A. Etellisi, M. A. Elmansouri, and D. S. Filipovic, "Antenna systems for simultaneous transmit and receive (STAR) applications," in Proc. Int. Symp. on Microelectronics, Raleigh, NC, Oct. 2016, pp. 590–594.

[3] J. Ha, M. A. Elmansouri, and D. S. Filipovic, "Monostatic co-polarized full-duplex antenna with left- or right-hand circular polarization," IEEE Trans. Antennas and Propag., vol. 65, no. 10, Oct. 2017, pp. 5103–5111.

[4] D. S. Filipovic and T. P. Cencich Sr., Frequency Independent Antennas, in *Antenna Engineering Handbook*, 4th ed., New York: Mc-Graw Hill, 2007, ch. 13.

Wideband, Scanning Array for Simultaneous Transmit and Receive

Alexander Hovsepian, Satheesh Bojja Venkatakrishnan, Elias A. Alwan, and John L. Volakis
Department of Computer and Electrical Eningeering
Florida International University
Miami, FL, USA
{ahovsepi, sbojjave, ealwan, jvolakis)@fiu.edu

***Abstract*—We present a low profile wideband spiral antenna array with high transmit/receive (Tx/Rx) isolation and beam steering capability for simultaneous transmit and receive (STAR) systems. STAR increases a channel's spectral efficiency by transmitting and receiving across the full bandwidth of a channel. To our knowledge, this is the first wideband STAR spiral array with scanning. Each 4-arm spiral element consists of two arms for Tx and two more for Rx. To suppress grating lobes, the element spacing is kept at $\lambda_{HIGH}/2$. Full wave infinite array simulations show the port-to-port Tx/Rx isolation is >40dB at boresight across a 3 GHz bandwidth from 2-5GHz (2.5:1). This level of port-to-port isolation reduces to about 30dB when scanning down to 30°. In addition, VSWR is < 2 and axial ratio < 3dB. A 3×3 array was fabricated and showed an average Tx/Rx isolation of 36dB with VSWR < 2.4.**

Keywords—Antenna, beam steering, full duplex, simultaneous transmit and receive

I. Introduction

The radio frequency (RF) spectrum's congestion has spurred interest in spectrally efficient techniques such as Simultaneous Transmit and Receive (STAR). STAR allows systems to concurrently transmit as well as receive across the entire channel's bandwidth and therefore double data capacity [1]. Alternatively, the bandwidth can be reduced by half while maintaining the same data rate.

A key challenge with STAR is suppressing transmit/receive (Tx/Rx) coupling that interferes with the receiver. As expected, Tx/Rx coupling lowers the signal-to-noise plus interference ratio (SINR), reducing communication reliability. Time and frequency division duplexing (TDD/FDD) avoid self-interference (SI) by partitioning Tx and Rx across time and frequency respectively at the expense of spectral efficiency. Thus, STAR allows for double the data capacity compared to TDD/FDD. Therefore, we must always maintain high isolation between the Tx/Rx paths to suppress self-interference (SI).

STAR systems overcome SI through the following techniques: (1) high isolation Tx/Rx antennas, (2) RF/analog filters, and (3) digital filters [2]. The antenna stage isolation is critical, particularly as transmit power increases. Analog and digital filtering can cancel the remaining SI as the antenna reduces the interference's dynamic range to an acceptable level for analog to digital converters (ADC) [3]. We aim to produce high Tx/Rx port-to-port isolation across wide bandwidth (>1GHz) with a scanning array of collocated Tx/Rx elements (See Fig. 1).

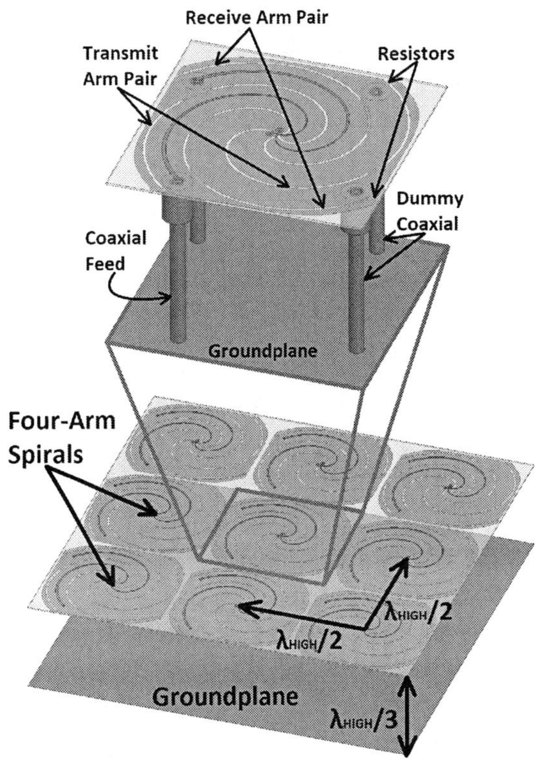

Fig. 1. The 3×3 STAR spiral array exhibiting high Tx/Rx isolation is shown with an enlarged unit cell.

This work was supported by ONR grant # N00014-16-1-2253 and a DAGSI fellowship with AFRL.

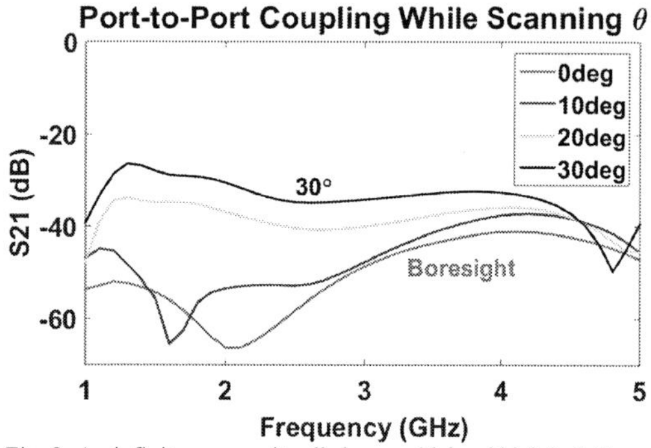

Fig. 2. An infinite array unit cell shows wideband high isolation, even when scanning down to 30°.

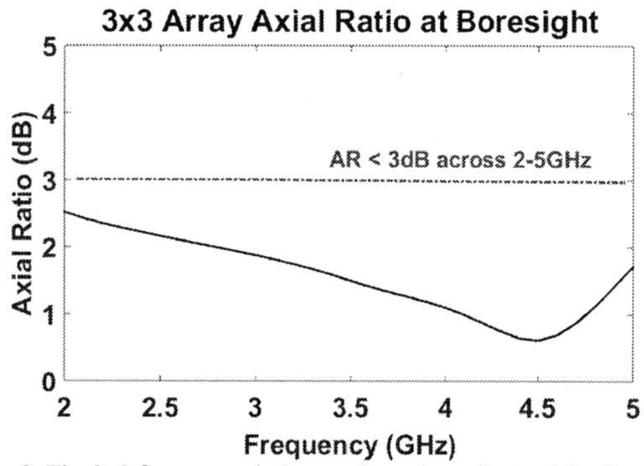

Fig. 3. The 3×3 four-arm spiral array showed excellent axial ratio across the 2-5GHz bandwidth.

We propose an array of miniaturized four-arm slot spirals to achieve wideband, high isolation, even while scanning. In order to design and fabricate such an array, we must overcome several challenges that limit the array's bandwidth. First, to place the four-arm spiral antennas into a $\lambda/2$-spaced array, we must miniaturize the spiral elements. Second, we must maintain symmetry in the spiral arms, baluns, and feeds to ensure high Tx/Rx isolation. Third, we must ensure balanced feeding during fabrication and assembly.

To our knowledge, this is the first low profile, wideband, beam steering array of spirals for STAR. As compared with other works, this array achieves a high port-to-port isolation across GHz bandwidths, also when scanning (26× greater bandwidth compared to previous efforts). Others have demonstrated STAR, but scanning was only achieved across very narrow bandwidths on the order of 100MHz or less. For example, a 2×2 patch antenna array in [4] used narrowband filters to cancel coupling between adjacent elements across a 110MHz bandwidth while scanning (30dB isolation at boresight). A linear array of dipoles in [5] employed digital beamforming to reduce Tx/Rx coupling across 100 MHz. In addition, wideband STAR was demonstrated from 0.6-2.5GHz, but only for a single element four-arm spiral antenna [6]. However, this approach did not consider scanning.

II. STAR Spiral Array

We introduce a low profile array of four-arm slot spiral antennas for STAR systems. As depicted in Fig. 1, each spiral element contains two arms for transmission and another two for reception. Spiral antennas were selected for their excellent circularly polarized (CP) radiation and inherent wideband performance. Our miniaturized array element is based upon a previously developed single element two-arm square spiral [7]. A single termination resistor placed at the end of each slot arm reduces reflections, which radiate the opposite polarization sense, increasing cross-polarization, axial ratio, and VSWR. A balun transformed the 50Ω coaxial input to a balanced 120 Ω feed. No external balun was needed. In addition to the Tx and Rx coaxial cable feeds, dummy coax feeds were added to maintain symmetry, and therefore high isolation (See Fig. 1). Frequency independent isolation is achieved through geometrical symmetry and the orthogonality of the Tx/Rx polarizations [6].

Full wave simulations of an infinite array confirmed that the spirals achieved a high port-to-port isolation of >40 dB across 1-5 GHz at boresight, as shown in Fig. 2. When scanning down to 30°, the isolation remained >30dB across 2-5GHz (2.5:1 bandwidth). The active VSWR was < 2 with a corresponding axial ratio of < 3dB across the entire bandwidth (2-5GHz), even when scanning. A 3×3 finite array simulation produced similar results with excellent matching and axial ratio < 3dB (See Fig. 3). The port-to-port isolation was 40dB. Sweeps of manufacturing tolerances (±10%) showed that excellent isolation performance was possible with standard printed circuit board (PCB) fabrication. A prototype was fabricated and measurements will be shown at the conference.

References

[1] D. Bharadia, E. McMilin, S. Katti, "Full Duplex Radios," in Proceedings of the ACM SIGCOMM 2013 conference on SIGCOMM, Hong Kong, China, 2013, p.375

[2] K. L. Scherer et al., "Simultaneous transmit and receive system architecture with four stages of cancellation," 2015 IEEE International Symposium on Antennas and Propagation & USNC/URSI National Radio Science Meeting, Vancouver, BC, 2015, pp. 520-521.

[3] A. Sabharwal, P. Schniter, D. Guo, D. W. Bliss, S. Rangarajan and R. Wichman, "In-Band Full-Duplex Wireless: Challenges and Opportunities," in IEEE Journal on Selected Areas in Communications, vol. 32, no. 9, pp. 1637-1652, Sept. 2014.

[4] A. T. Wegener, "Broadband near-field filters for Simultaneous Transmit and Receive in a small two-dimensional array," 2014 IEEE MTT-S International Microwave Symposium (IMS2014), Tampa, FL, 2014, pp. 1-3.

[5] J. P. Doane, K. E. Kolodziej and B. T. Perry, "Simultaneous transmit and receive performance of an 8-channel digital phased array," 2017 IEEE International Symposium on Antennas and Propagation & USNC/URSI National Radio Science Meeting, San Diego, CA, 2017, pp. 1043-1044.

[6] E. A. Etellisi, M. A. Elmansouri and D. S. Filipovic, "Wideband Monostatic Simultaneous Transmit and Receive (STAR) Antenna," in IEEE Transactions on Antennas and Propagation, vol. 64, no. 1, pp. 6-15, Jan. 2016.

[7] B. A. Kramer, Ming Lee, Chi-Chih Chen and J. L. Volakis, "Design and performance of an ultrawide-band ceramic-loaded slot spiral," in IEEE Transactions on Antennas and Propagation, vol. 53, no. 7, pp. 2193-2199, July 2005.

Hexagonal Waveguides: New Class of Waveguides for mm-wave Circulaly Polarized Horns

Shubhendu Bhardwaj
Electrical and Computer Engineering
Florida International University
10555, W. Flagler Street, Miami, FL, USA
sbhardwa@fiu.edu

John Volakis
College of Engineering,
Florida International University
10555, W. Flagler Street, Miami, FL, USA
jvolakis@fiu.edu

***Abstract*—In this work, we develop a class of broadband circularly polarized (CP) horn antennas that are realizable at sub-mm-wave and terahertz frequencies. Here, the underlying technology is a hexagonal waveguide that act as linear to circular polarizer enabling the generation circularly polarized (CP) wave in a waveguide environment. We have developed analytical models to characterize these waveguides and thus optimize the designs of CP horns. The optimized designs have shown 3dB axial-ratio bandwidths upto 30-40% with 18-21 dBi gain in WR-8 band.**

Keywords—CP horn, EDM, fabrication, pattern measurements, sub-mm-wave, terahertz, WR-8.

I. Introduction

There has been strong recent interest in sub-mm-wave and terahertz communication and radar applications [1]. For these, antennas with low loss, high gain have been important. These characteristics can be realized in waveguide based antennas [2], but usually antenna-structures become complex for high gain applications. Therefore, horn antennas present themselves as attractive alternatives due to ease of design and fabrication. Having said that, generation of CP wave in horns still requires waveguide partitions (or septum-based designs) [3, 4], which are quite difficult to fabricate in sub-mm-wave waveguides.

We use hexagonal waveguide sections that act as linear to circular polarizer to solve these issues. Such waveguides carry orthogonal modes with varying dispersion constants, creating phase lag between the modes. This phase lag can be optimized to 90° by optimizing the length of the waveguide. Nevertheless, design and modeling of such waveguide leading to CP-horns becomes rather rigorous task. In this work we present analysis of hexagonal waveguides and a formal design procedure for CP horns based on these waveguides. The design procedure is verified by developing CP horns that are verified via simulation.

II. Theory of Hexagonal Waveguide based Propagation

A. Modes in a Hexagonal Section

Fig. 1 (a) shows the possible modes in such a waveguide. As shown, two orthogonal modes, with E-field aligned with the two diagonals, exist in such waveguides. Since the two diagonals have different dimension, the modes have different prop

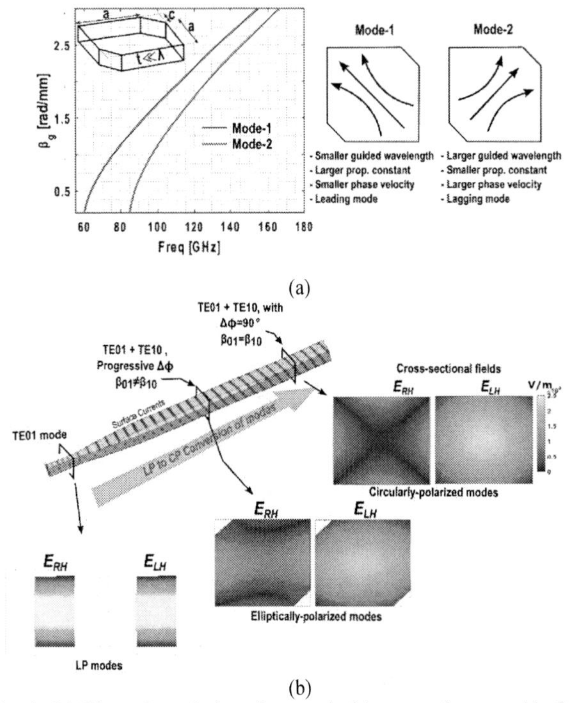

Fig. 1. (a) Dispersion relations for a typical hexagonal waveguide for WR-8 band. Chosen dimensions were a=2.032 mm, c=0.5 mm. (b) Surface currents and cross-sectional fields in the waveguide.

constant. Thus, the excited modes can develop phase-lag, leading to linear to elliptical and then to circular polarization.

A practical waveguide design can be achieved based on this basic theory. This is shown in Fig. 1 (b). As shown, TE_{01} mode is excited in a rectangular waveguide, which was transitioned into a square section waveguide and then to a hexagonal section waveguide. The length of the waveguide was optimized for polarization pure left-hand CP generation. Towards the end, the waveguide was transitioned back into a square section to preserve the polarization of the obtained CP wave.

As shown in Fig. 2, the polarization of the wave changes from linear to elliptical and then to circular near the end of hexagonal section. Polarization purity of around 40 dB is achieved at the end of the waveguide. This illustrates the operation of LP to CP polarizer using hexagonal waveguide.

B. *Tapered Waveguide Sections for Efficient Horn Design*

Since the waveguide length depends on a specific frequency operation, the bandwidth of the LP to CP polarizer needs to be justified. Our analysis shows that a tapered hexagonal section (as shown in Fig. 2) allows enhancement of the axial ratio bandwidth of the waveguide. That is, the dispersion characteristics within the waveguide vary rather slowly across the band for a tapered waveguide section. This aids to our designs since the tapered sections simultaneously provide the gain within the waveguides, leading to compact and wideband polarizer-horns.

III. Design Optimization of CP Horn

A. *Design of Hexagonal Waveguide based CP Horn*

We developed analysis and procedural step for optimizing the horn based on hexagonal waveguide concept. One such optimized CP-horn is shown in Fig. 2, left. The detailed dimensions will be presented in the conference, but here we briefly discuss the design procedure and horn performance.

The simulation based optimization for such a horn is a time and memory consuming task. In order for an efficient design to take place, semi-analytical methods were developed for this modeling. Note that to predict the axial-ratio related performance of the structure, we must identify the phase-lag between the modes propagating in the horn. It can be done if the propagation constants of the modes are known. However, these propagation constants are varying along the length of the horn due to non-uniform cross-section.

Therefore, we generate a data base of propagation constants for different cross-sectional dimensions using eigen-mode solver in HFSS. Thus, knowing the propagation constant $\beta_1(z_i,f)$ and $\beta_2(z_i,f)$ for an ith discretized section along the horn, we write phase lag at the end of a waveguide of length L as:

$$\Delta\phi(f) = \sum_{i=1}^{i=L/\delta z} [\beta_2(z_i,f) - \beta_1(z_i,f)]\delta z. \quad (1)$$

Here, δz (=1 μm) is the step-size used for the discretization. Thus, using the phase lag, we can calculate the axial ratio performance of the horn antenna. Using on-time generated database, the above calculation-methods provide axial-ratio predictions for for any tapering and transitioning waveguide assembly.

B. *Gain Prediction for the Developed Horn*

To analytically predict and optimize the gain, we pursue an analysis similar to [5] for E/H sectorial linearly polarized horn antennas. We begin by writing the fields in the aperture. Here, two orthogonal modal fields exist. Using model field data,

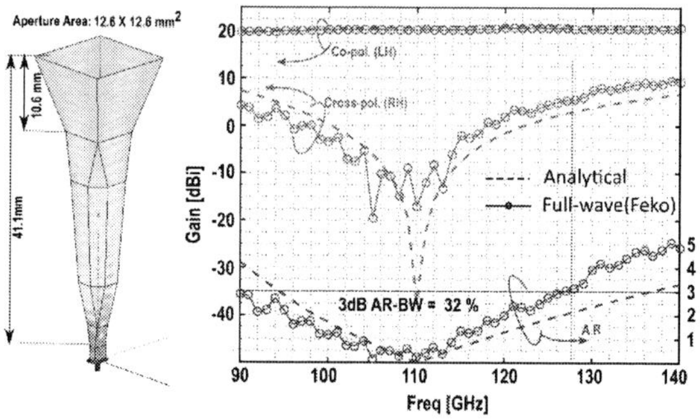

Fig. 2. Designed horn antenna and its performance at sub-mm-wave frequencies. 32% axial ratio bandwidth and 20 dBi gain was shown using analysis and simulation.

equivalent current calculation and near-zone to far-zone transformation can be done. Using these models, we predict the directivity of the antenna for an efficient optimization. Using the analysis similar to linear polarized horns, we also develop relation between the horn aperture size and ρ (the distance between the phase-center and aperture). We find that for maximum gain scenario, aperture size a_l is related to ρ as $a_1 = \sqrt{2.4\rho\lambda}$.

Thus, by using the axial ratio prediction as well as directivity prediction, complete analytical modeling of the CP horn is presented.

IV. Conclusions

We have proposed a new class of horn antennas that provide circular polarization by using properties of hexagonal waveguides. Formal analytical design procedure and equations are developed for a fast design process. Optimized design performance is compared with simulation data and agreement was found between the two (Fig. 2, right). The developed design shows 32% 3dB axial-ratio bandwidth and 20 dBi gain in a design optimized for WR-8 band operation. Due to hollow nature of the waveguide, the horns can be fabricated at sub-mm-wave and terahertz frequencies, which is not possible via traditional partition/septum based designs.

References

[1] T. Schneider, A. Wiatrek, S. Preussler, M. Grigat, and R. P. Braun, "Link budget analysis for terahertz fixed wireless links," IEEE Transactions on Terahertz Science and Technology, vol. 2, pp. 250–256, March 2012.

[2] J. Hirokawa, D. Kim, M. Ando, T. Nagatsuma, J. Takeuchi, and A. Hirata, "Wideband waveguide slot array antennas with corporatefeed in 120 GHz and 350 GHz bands," in 2013 International Symposium on Electromagnetic Theory, pp. 866–867, May 2013.

[3] D. Davis, O. Digiondomenico, and J. Kempic, "A new type of circularly polarized antenna element," in 1967 Antennas and Propagation Society International Symposium, vol. 5, pp. 26–33, Oct. 1967.

[4] M. J. Franco, "A high-performance dual-mode feed horn for parabolic reflectors with a stepped-septum polarizer in a circular waveguide [Antenna Designer's Notebook]," IEEE Antennas and Propagation Magazine, vol. 53, pp. 142–146, June 2011.

[5] C. A. Balanis, Antenna theory: Analysis and Design. John Wiley & Sons 2016.

Size-Reduced Patch-Antenna Feedpoint Parametric Study

Randall L. Musselman
Dep. of Electrical and Computer Engineering
US Air Force Academy, CO, USA
randall.musselman@usafa.edu

James L. Vedral
Draper Laboratory, Cambridge, MA, USA
jvedral@draper.com

Abstract — **Size-reduction techniques are applied to a circular UHF patch antenna, by introducing slits into the patch structure. The optimum slit dimensions are determined to maximize the amount of antenna-size reduction. A parametric study of the probe-feed location versus slit dimensions determines the optimum location for the probe feed location, in order to achieve matched input impedance for different slit lengths.**

Index Terms – antenna size reduction, patch antenna slits, probe fed antenna, slotted UHF antenna.

I. Introduction

We have previously reported on size-reduction techniques for circular patch antennas, using slits [1], including design rules for optimizing the dimensions of those slits [2]. As stated in previous work, changing the slit dimensions W and L in Fig. 1 also changes the input impedance, which requires new feed-point locations in order to maintain a desired input-impedance match. Previously, finding these new probe-feed locations was mostly an iterative process. This paper extends the previously reported size-reduction design rules, by presenting the results of a new parametric study for locating the optimum probe-feed location, as the slit dimensions vary.

II. Patch Size Reduction

Patch antennas typically resonate with dimensions that are near one-half of a wavelength [3], which can be cumbersomely large at UHF frequencies. This large size is reduced by a factor of approximately $1/\sqrt{\varepsilon_r}$ by using higher permittivity ($\varepsilon = \varepsilon_0 \varepsilon_r$) dielectric material. However, the decreased bandwidth caused by higher permittivity can make this approach unattractive. In an attempt to focus on size-reduction techniques rather than exotic materials, we used common FR4 printed circuit-board material for our UHF patch-antenna size-reduction analysis. The dielectric constant of 4.5, at UHF, provides nearly 50% size reduction, even before any other size-reduction techniques are used.

The addition of slits in a circular patch antenna has proven to reduce the patch radius by nearly an additional 50%, beyond the effects of permittivity alone [4,5]. The parametric study in [2] demonstrated that the maximum size reduction can be obtained by maximizing the length of the slits, without bisecting the patch (approximately 95% of the radius). Further size reduction can be achieved by increasing the width of the slits. However, diminishing returns limits the effectiveness of increasing the width to approximately 3% of the slit length.

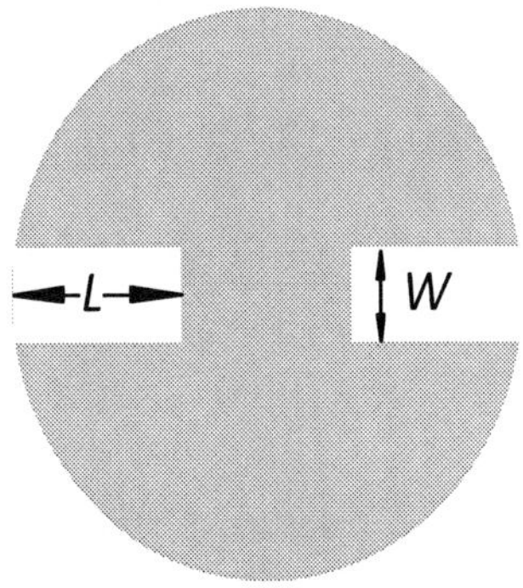

Fig. 1. Two-slit patch with varying dimensions: slit length, L and slit width, W.

Therefore, by setting the slit lengths to 95% of the radius and the widths to 3% of the radius, the patch size can be minimized. Further increasing the width provides minimal effectiveness while making the probe-feed location more difficult to obtain. As shown in [2], circular polarization is possible using this size-reduction technique, by introducing orthogonal slits, as illustrated in Fig. 2, and feeding the patch accordingly. The same guidelines apply to both orthogonal pairs of slits, and no significant coupling effects were observed from one pair of orthogonal slits on the other. Incidentally, the two pairs of slits can be adjusted to different lengths, if a dual-band is desired. Of course, the polarization of the two bands would be orthogonal as well.

III. Feed Location

A desired input-impedance match can be found for each slit-length/width combination by relocating the probe feed-point location [2]. To find a trend in the feed location that would aid in the design of circular patches with slits, we explored the optimum feed-point location as a percentage of patch radius, for successively longer slits. The circular patch antenna in Fig. 2 had a radius of 14.6*mm* and was modeled using HFSS, while treating the feed location as a variable parameter. The slit width, W of the circular patch was set to 0.2*mm*, i.e., the slit width was set to a constant 1.37% of the patch radius. By treating the location of the probe-feed location as a variable parameter, the input impedance was determined for the different feed locations. Therefore, the feed point location was determined that provided the desired impedance.

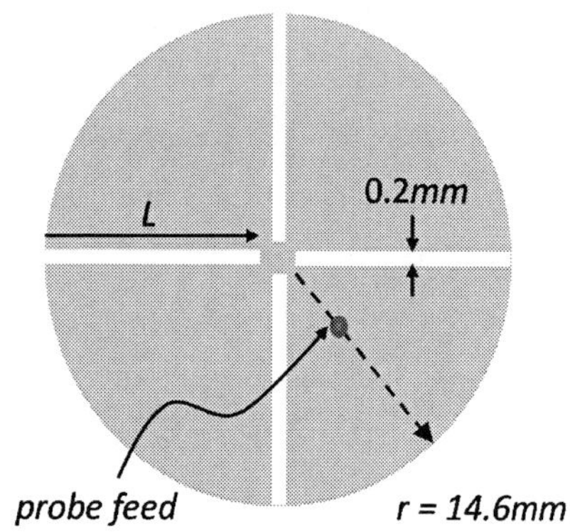

Fig. 2. Probe feed relocated along the dashed radial line, in order to match the input impedance to 50Ω, for each successively longer length, *L* for a fixed width, *W* = 1.37% of the radius.

The antenna feed point was relocated along the dashed radial line in Fig 2, for successively longer slit lengths, *L* in order to achieve a matched input impedance of 50Ω. Fig. 3 plots the relationship between the probe-feed location and the slit length, *L*, while maintaining a 50Ω input impedance. The feed-point distance from the center, along the dashed line in Fig. 3, as well as the length, *L* are both normalized to the patch radius.

It is clear by the trend shown in Fig. 3 that the probe feed must be relocated closer to the center of the patch, as the slit length increases, i.e., for the length that provides the maximum size reduction. If the slit length is 95% of the radius, i.e., 13.9*mm* in this example, the probe feed should be located at 14.5% of the radius from the center of the patch, which is 2.12*mm* in this case. Therefore, since physically smaller antennas are typically desired, a good starting point would be to set the slit lengths to 95% of the radius and to locate the probe feed to 14% of the radius from the center of the circular patch. These guidelines should minimize the overall size of a circular patch antenna at resonance.

IV. Conclusion

A parametric study was conducted, in order to find the optimum probe-feed location for various slit lengths that reduced the size of a circular patch antenna. The slit width was set to 1.4% of the radius, while the slit length was varied. The almost linear trend showed that for increasing slit lengths, the optimum feed point should be located closer to the center of the patch, in order to achieve a matched 50Ω input impedance.

Summarizing the results of this and previous parametric studies, the best results for reducing the physical size of circular patch antennas can be obtained by (1) making the slit lengths as long as physically possible, without bisecting the patch (i.e., 95% of the radius); (2) setting the slit widths to 3% of the radius (increasing the slit width any further provides diminishing returns and makes impedance matching more difficult); and (3) locating the probe feed at approximately 14% of the radius, from the center of the patch.

By following these simple design guidelines, the radius of a circular patch antenna was reduced to half of the radius of a similar patch, without the slits, while maintaining a 50Ω input impedance. If linear polarization is desired, only one pair of slits is required. If circular polarization is desired, simply create the two orthogonal pairs of these slits that are shown in Fig. 2, with equal dimensions, and feed the patch using typical circular-polarization techniques. If dual-mode resonances are desired, the orthogonal pairs of slits can be set to different lengths.

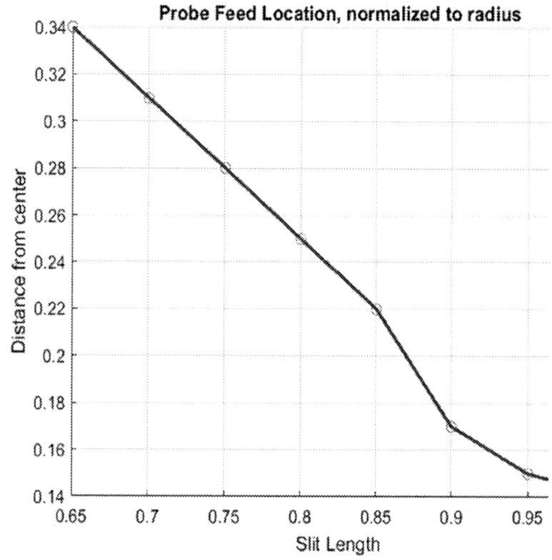

Fig. 3. Probe-feed location vs. slit length, normalized to the patch radius.

References

[1] R. L. Musselman and J. L. Vedral, "Circular patch antenna size-reduction technique" 17th Biennial IEEE Confr. on Electromagnetic Field Computation, Miami, 2016.

[2] R. L. Musselman and J. L. Vedral, "Patch antenna size-reduction parametric study," *International Applied Computational Electromagnetics Society (ACES) Symposium*, Firenze, Italy, March 2017.

[3] C. A. Balanis, *Antenna Theory Analysis and Design*, New York, Harper & Row, 1982.

[4] R. L. Musselman, et al., "Adaptive null-steered interference-rejection for a mobile satellite receiver," IEEE Int'l Symp. on Phased Array Syst. and Tech., Boston, Oct. 2010.

[5] R. L. Musselman, et al., "Circular array for satcom interference rejection," IEEE Int'l Conf. on Wireless Inf. Tech. and Syst., Maui, Nov. 2012.

Multiband Antenna for Wireless Applications Including GSM/UMTS/LTE and 5G Bands

Amirreza Jalali Khalilabadi, Student Member IEEE, and Ata Zadehgol, Sr. Member IEEE
Department of Electrical and Computer Engineering
University of Idaho, Moscow, ID, USA
Emails: jala9498@vandals.uidaho.edu, and Ata.Zadehgol@gmail.com

***Abstract*—A simple ultra thin multiband antenna is introduced. The proposed antenna with four bands covers many wireless applications. The proposed antenna has simple configuration including two open L-shaped slots to create resonat mode at GSM and GPS bands and also two rectangular slots on the radiating element for creating multi resonant modes to meet the specifications of mentioned frequency bands. According to the simple, small and planar configuration, the proposed antenna design is inexpensive and can easily be integrated with the other microwave circuit boards. The proposed antenna has the small size of 10 mm and the total size of 120 mm × 60 mm × 0.5 mm, promising to be used widely in compact and ultra slim handsets.**

***Index Terms*—Multiband antenna, wireless handset, wireless applications, planar configuration**

I. Introduction

Owing to development of mobile communication systems, the design of modern antennas with compact size, multiband operation, and integrability with other microwave circuits has attracted much attention. As a result, various types of multiband antennas have been reported [1]–[3]; however, by having two or three bands, most existing antennas are unable to cover more bands with one structure.

In this paper, we introduce a four–band slot antenna for the GSM (890–960 MHz), Galileo (1563–1591 MHz), GPS (1575.42 ± 5 MHz), Glonass (1602–1615.5 MHz), DCS (1710–1880 MHz), PCS (1850–1990 MHz), UMTS (1920–2170 MHz), LTE2300 (2305–2400 MHz)/LTE2500 (2500–2690 MHz), WLAN (2.4–2.484/5.15–5.35/5.7–5.8 GHz), and WiMAX (2.5–2.7/3.4–3.7/5.2–5.8 GHz) applications. Also the proposed antenna is able to cover some suggested bands of 5G systems including 3.3–3.8 GHz, 4.8–4.99 GHz, 5.150–5.925 GHz, 5.925–7.025 GHz, 7.235–7.25 GHz, and 7.750–8.025 frequency ranges [4]. The proposed antenna covers several applications which are narrowband and also provides the essential bandwidth for higher data rate applications.

II. Antenna configuration

Fig. 1 shows the structure of the proposed antenna. The antenna is fabricated on a low-loss FR-4 substrate with dielectric constant of 4.3, thickness of 0.5 mm and loss tangent of 0.02. The antenna with a simple structure consists of a rectangular radiation patch, an open L-shaped slot for 900 MHz band, a horizontal open slot for GPS band and two rectangular slots for generating multi resonant modes to meet the specifications of desirable frequency bands. It is notable that an open-end slot can generate a quarter-wavelength resonant mode. Also, a wide slot can create several resonance modes, and by merging nearby resonance modes a wider bandwidth can achieved. The proposed antenna occupies an area of 10 mm × 60 mm, while the ground plane has an area of 110 mm × 60 mm which is a typical system board of mobile devices. A comparison between usage of lumped elements, structure, antenna size and

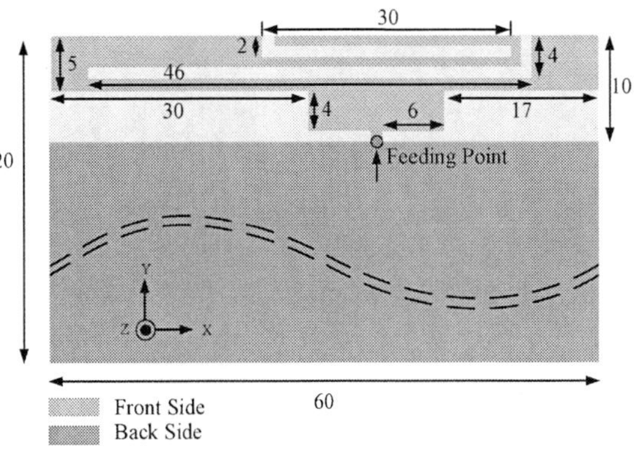

Fig. 1. Configuration of the proposed antenna (unit: mm)

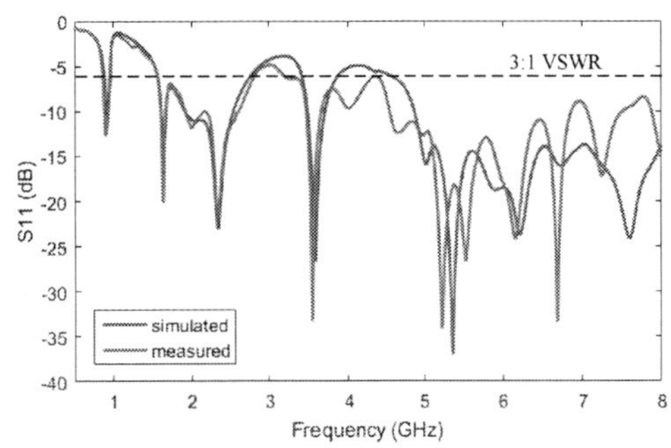

Fig. 2. Comparison between the HFSS (version 15) simulated and measured result of reflection coefficient

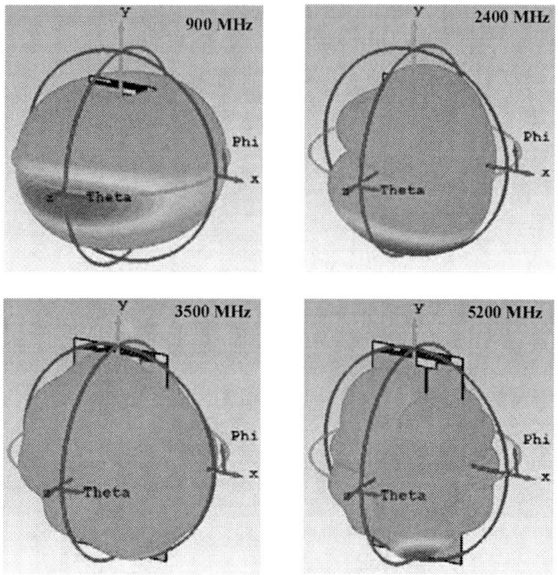

Fig. 3. Radiation patterns of the proposed antenna at different frequencies simulated by CST STUDIO SUITE 2017 Software

TABLE I
COMPARISON OF THE PROPOSED ANTENNA WITH RECENT WORKS

[Ref] (year)	[1] (2013)	[2] (2014)	[3] (2015)	Proposed
Lumped Element	No	No	Yes	No
Structure	Planar	Planar	3D	Planar
Antenna size (mm×mm×mm)	78×0.6 ×18	115×0.5 ×15	120×0.8 ×8	120×0.5 ×10
-6 dB bandwidth (MHz)	890–960 1570–2500 ——— ———	790–1061 1650–2775 3132–6382 ———	800–1150 1700–2580 ——— ———	860-970 1560–2820 3180–4350 4400–8000

bandwidth of the proposed antenna with some recent studies is illustrated in Table I. It is notable that simultaneously covering all mentioned frequency bands with one structure is difficult, somehow none of the antenna in [1]–[3] can achieve this goal.

III. Results and Discussions

To validate the simulation results, the designed antenna is fabricated and tested. The measured reflection coefficient S_{11} is compared to the simulated result in Fig 2. It is seen that the bandwidths for $|S_{11}| < -6$ dB (or VSWR > 3) are 12.02% (860-970 MHz) for the 900-MHz band, 57.53% (1.56-2.82 GHz) for the 2-GHz band, 31.07% (3.18-4.35 GHz) for the 3.5-GHz band, and 58.06% (4.4-8 GHz) for the 5.5-GHz band. Note that the $|S_{11}| < -6$ dB as the specification of the impedance matching bandwidth is widely acceptable for practical internal antennas [1], [3], [5], [6].

TABLE II
SIMULATED GAIN AND RADIATION EFFICIENCY RESULTS

Frequency [MHz]	CST [Gain (dB)–Efficiency (%)]	HFSS [Gain (dB)–Efficiency (%)]
900	0.8–69.18	-0.7–76
2400	3.64–61.65	4.08–77
3500	1.14–45.7	0.99–49
5200	3.79–46.7	2.86–55

The simulated peak gain and radiation efficiency values of the proposed antenna at different frequencies are presented at Table II. The results which have been obtained from the HFSS and CST softwares are almost close together and acceptable for mobile devices.

Fig. 3. demonstrates the simulated radiation patterns of the proposed antenna at 900 MHz, 2.4 GHz, 3.5 GHz, and 5.2 GHz. It can be observed that the radiation pattern of the proposed antenna at 900 MHz is dipole-like radiation pattern which shows that the radiation characteristic is stable at lower frequency [5]. Moreover, the simulated radiation patterns are almost omni-directional in the X-Z plane (with respect to position of the proposed antenna in the Cartesian coordinate) which are desired for the practical communication applications [1].

IV. Conclusion

In this paper, a simple planar multiband antenna for GSM, Galileo, GPS, Glonass, DCS, PCS, UMTS, LTE2300/LTE2500, WLAN (2.4–5.2–5.8 GHz), WiMAX (2.5–3.5–5.5 GHz) and 5G applications is presented and discussed. The antenna has small, ultra thin, and simple structure. We show that by inserting different slots with proper size in the truncated radiation patch, good multiband features can be achieved. It is also shown that the suggested antenna has good radiation characteristics such as stable radiation patterns, high radiation efficiency, and also acceptable gain values.

References

[1] K. C. Lin, C. H. Lin, and Y. C. Lin, "Simple printed multiband antenna with novel parasitic-element design for multistandard mobile phone applications," *IEEE Trans. Antennas propag*, vol. 61, no. 1, pp. 488–491, Jan. 2013.

[2] Z. Liang, Y. Li, and Y. Long, "Multiband monopole mobile phone antenna with circular polarization for GNSS application," *IEEE Trans. Antennas propag*, vol. 62, no. 4, pp. 1910–1917, Jan. 2014.

[3] D. Wu, S. W. Cheung, and T. I. Yuk, "A compact and low-profile loop antenna with multiband operation for ultra-thin smartphones," *IEEE Trans. Antennas propag*, vol. 63, no. 6, pp. 2745–2750, Jun. 2015.

[4] *5G Spectrum Recommendations*, 5G Americas, Seattle, WA, USA, 2017. [Online]. Available: http://www.5gamericas.org/files/9114/9324/1786/5GA_5G_Spectrum_Recommendations_2017_FINAL.pdf

[5] Y. L. Ban, J. H. Chen, S. Yang, J. Li, and Y. J. Wu, "Low-profile printed octa-band LTE/WWAN mobile phone antenna using embedded parallel resonant structure," *IEEE Trans. Antennas propag*, vol. 61, no. 7, pp. 3889–3894, Apr. 2013.

[6] Y. L. Ban, Y. F. Qiang, Z. Chen, K. Kang, and J. H. Guo, "A dual-loop antenna design for hepta-band WWAN/LTE metal-rimmed smartphone applications," *IEEE Trans. Antennas propag*, vol. 63, no. 1, pp. 48–58, Jan. 2015.

2 to 18 GHz Ultra-Wideband Dual-Linear Polarized Phased Array with 60° Scanning

Jingni Zhong, Elias A. Alwan, and John L. Volakis
Dept. of Electrical and Computer Engineering, College of Engineering and Computing
Florida International University
Miami, FL 33174, USA.
{jizhong, ealwan, jvolakis}@fiu.edu

***Abstract*— In this paper, we present for the first time a novel dual-linear polarized phase array based on tightly coupled dipole topology. The array operates across an impressive 9:1 impedance bandwidth spanning 2-18GHz with scanning capability down to 60° from boresight. Importantly, the array is extremely low profile, with a total height less than 12mm ($\lambda_{low}/10$). The overall geometry consists of cross-located tightly coupled dipoles integrated with a folded Marchand balun that serves as an impedance transformer and a feeding network. The traditional dielectric superstrate is replaced with double layers of frequency selective surfaces (FSS) to enable scanning down to 60° in both E and H plan across the entire band. Notably, the polarization and port-to-port isolations are kept at least 40dB at broadside and 30dB with scanning cases. Such high isolation makes this array great candidate for Simultaneous Transmit and Receive (STAR) systems.**

Keywords—Tightly coupled dipole array, ultra-wideband, wide scanning, STAR system.

I. Introduction

Modern wireless systems require large bandwidths for high data rates. Targeted bands include S (2-4GHz), C (4-8GHz), X (8-12GHz), and Ku (12-18GHz). In addition, modern platforms are becoming smaller in size such as small satellites, unmanned aerial vehicles, and cars. Therefore, there is a strong need for ultra-wideband (UWB) phased array that are concurrently small to allow inconspicuous integration on such platforms.

Existing UWB arrays include Vivaldi array [1] and Planar UWB Modular Antenna (PUMA) array [2]. However, these arrays are associated with either large profile or limited bandwidth. Comparing with those two UWB arrays, tightly coupled dipole arrays (TCDA) [3-7] exhibit superior features of wide bandwidth and wide scanning angle, together with compact antenna size. These arrays consist of capacitively coupled dipoles to realize Wheeler's current sheet concepts [3]. TCDAs are integrated with a folded Marchand balun to provide balanced feeding and impedance matching. As much as 7:1 bandwidth has been achieved in previous work [5].

Besides wide operational bandwidth and wide scanning angle, high polarization isolation is essential to realize full-duplex or simultaneous transmit and receive (STAR) systems. In our previous work [7]-[8], we showed that as much as 30dB isolation can be achieved using two orthogonal radiators. However, the major drawback is the existence of in-band

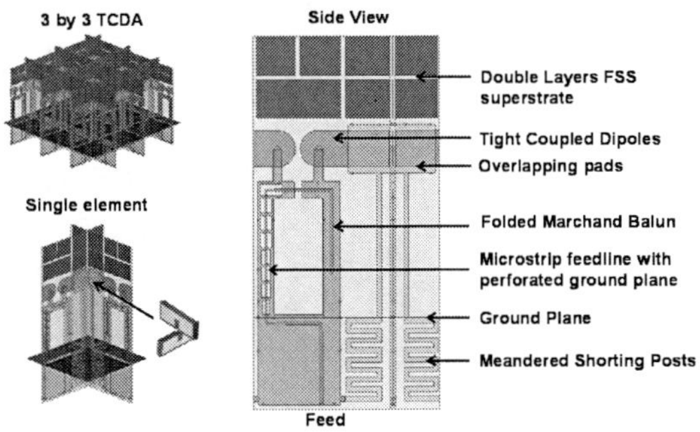

Fig. 1. Proposed dual-linear polarized TCDA.

resonance while scanning into E plane down to 60°, which greatly reduces the impedance bandwidth.

In this paper, we present an improved version of UWB dual-linear polarized phased array for STAR systems. We tackle the abovementioned problems by introducing three new structures to the TCDA: (1) Meandered shorting posts to remove the unwanted in-band resonance, (2) double layers of FSS superstrate with varied FSS width to improve matching the array across the entire bandwidth, (3) tapered stripline matching network to match the input impedance to 50Ω. The resulting array operates from 2GHz to 18GHz (9:1 bandwidth) with port-to-port isolation of at least 45dB at broadside. It scans down to 60° in both E and H planes across the entire bandwidth with the port-to-port isolation kept at least 30dB to meet the requirement of STAR system. To our knowledge, this is so far the most suitable high isolation array for STAR applications that can achieve 9:1 bandwidth with scanning down to 60°.

II. 2 to 18GHz UWB TCDA Design Concept

The proposed UWB dual-linear polarized tightly coupled dipole array is depicted in Fig. 1. The tightly coupled dipole is integrated with the folded Marchand balun serving as the feed and matching network. Meandered shorting posts are applied to remove in-band resonances created while scanning [6]. To enhance scanning performance, periodic repeated metallic squares, forming a double layer FSS structure are placed on top of the array [5]. The operational frequency of these FSS structures are determined by metallic square's width and height. In our design, each of the double layer FSS contains metallic squares with very small width and height. This is to ensure good performance at high frequencies. At low frequencies, since the wavelength becomes significantly larger, the closely placed two-layer FSS can be treated as one layer FSS with double the height. Therefore, the double layer FSS helps with matching at low frequencies as well.

III. Simulated Array Performance

The dual-linear polarized TCDA was simulated using the commercial finite element solver High Frequency Structural Simulator (HFSS). The voltage standing wave ratio (VSWR) of the TCDA while scanning for both E and H planes down to 60° is shown in Fig. 2. As seen, the dual-linear polarized TCDA operates from 2GHz to 18GHz with VSWR<5 at broadside and scanning down to 30° in both E and H plane. The array exhibits a VSWR<6 while scanning down to 60° in E and H plane. In general, the array is well matched across the entire 2 to 18GHz both in broadside and scanning cases, with an average VSWR of around 2.5.

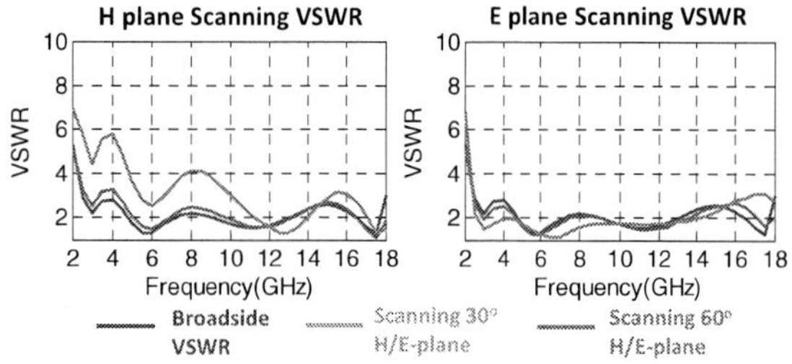

Fig. 2. VSWR of the designed dual-linear polarized TCDA while scanning in the H (left) and E planes (right).

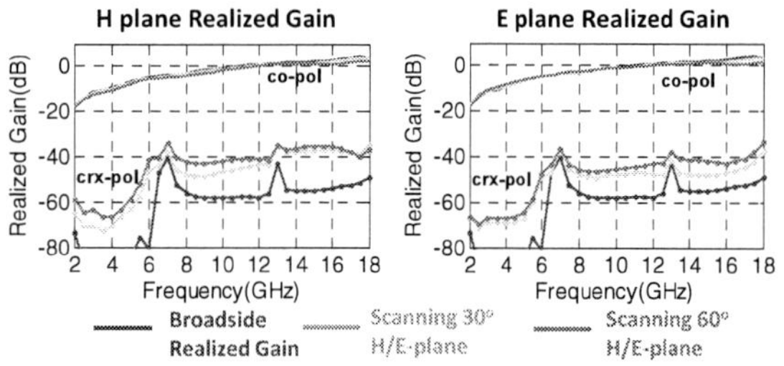

Fig. 3. Co-polarized and cross-polarized realized gain of the designed dual-linear polarized TCDA while scanning in the H (left) and E planes (right).

The cross-pol isolation was also calculated and depicted in Fig. 3. At broadside, the array has a polarization isolation of at least 40dB across the entire bandwidth, and 35 dB in scanning cases. The port-to-port isolation (S_{21}) curved are plotted in Fig. 4. Where at broadside the array achieved a port-to-port isolation of S21 < -35dB. When scanning into H plane and E plane down to 60°, the port-to-port isolation is kept at least 30dB. These levels of polarization isolation and port-to-port isolation make the proposed array very attractive for various STAR applications. More results including finite array simulation, radiation patterns together with detailed array structure will be discussed during the conference.

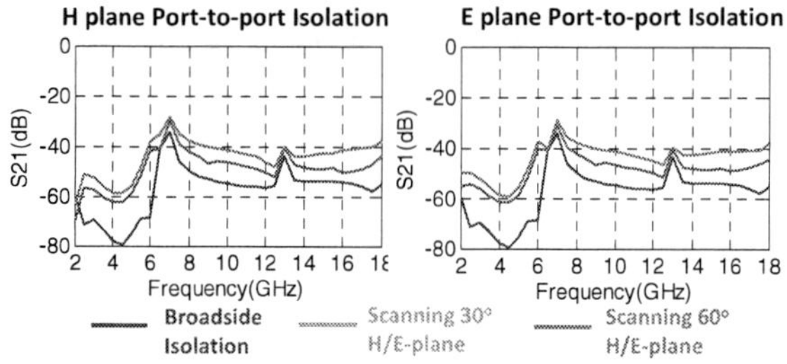

Fig. 4. Port-to-port isolation of proposed dual-linear polarized TCDA when scanning in H plane (left) and E plane (right).

IV. Conclusoin

We presented a new UWB dual-linear polarized TCDA that operates from 2 to18 GHz. The array was based on our previous work on TCDA for STAR applications. We improved the performance by introducing new array structures including double layers FSS and meandered shorting posts. The proposed TCDA has scanning capability down to 60° in both E and H plane. Further, the array exhibits polarization isolation of 40dB at broadside and 35dB with scanning, along with port-to-port isolation of at least 35dB at broadside and 30dB while scanning, across the entire 2 to 18GHz bandwidth. Such performance makes our TCDA an excellent candidate for wideband STAR systems.

References

[1] J. B. Yan, S. Gogineni, B. Camps-Raga, et al., "A dual-polarized 2–18-GHz Vivaldi array for airborne radar measurements of snow," IEEE Trans on Antennas and Propag. vol. 64, no. 2, pp. 781–785, Feb. 2016.

[2] S. S. Holland and M. N. Vouvakis, "The planar ultra-wideband modular antenna (PUMA) array," IEEE Trans. on Antennas and Propag., vol. 60, no. 1, pp. 130-140, Jan. 2012.

[3] J. P. Doane, K. Sertel, and J. L. Volakis, "A wideband, wide scanning tightly coupled dipole array with integrated balun (TCDA-IB)," IEEE Trans. Antennas Propag., vol. 61, no. 9, pp. 4538–4548, Sep. 2013.

[4] W. F. Moulder, K. Sertel, and J. L. Volakis, "Ultrawideband superstrate-enhanced substrate-loaded array with integrated feed," IEEE Trans. Antennas Propag., vol. 61, no. 11, pp. 5802–5807, Nov. 2013.

[5] E. Yetisir, N. Ghalichechian, and J. L. Volakis, "Ultrawideband array with 70° scanning using FSS superstrate," IEEE Trans. Antennas Propag., vol. 64, no. 10, pp. 4258–4265, Jul. 2016

[6] J. Zhong, E. A. Alwan, and J. L. Volakis, "7.2 to 1 ultra-wideband dual-linear polarized phased array with 60° scanning," IEEE International Symposium on Antennas and Propagation, 2017.

[7] J. Zhong, E. A. Alwan, and J. L. Volakis, "Ultra-wideband dual-linear polarized phased array with 60° scanning for simultaneous transmit and receive systems," International Workshop on Antenna Technology, 2017.

[8] S. Bojja-Venkatakrishnan, E. Alwan, and J. L. Volakis, "Wideband RF and analog self-interference cancellation filter for simultaneous transmit and receive system," IEEE International Symposium on Antennas and Propagation, 2017.

Biomedical Magnetic Induction Tomography: An Inhomogeneous Green's Function Approach

Philippe De Tillieux
Dept. of Electrical Engineering
Polytechnique Montreal
Montreal, Canada
louis-philippe.de-tillieux@polymtl.ca

Yves Goussard
Dept. of Electrical Engineering
Polytechnique Montreal
Montreal, Canada
yves.goussard@polymtl.ca

***Abstract*—Magnetic induction tomography aims to reconstruct the passive electric properties of an object by measuring its scattered magnetic field. Current state-of-the-art numerical techniques are based on differential formulations such as the finite element method. A formulation based on volume integral equations has not yet been applied to its biomedical field and could improve the reconstruction speed by reducing the number of unknowns. This paper investigates salient characteristics of the approach and offers a solution based on inhomogeneous Green's functions.**

***Keywords*—Biomedical, Magnetic Induction, Volume Integral.**

I. Introduction

Biomedical magnetic induction tomography (MIT) is a novel imaging technique with applications to stroke detection, inductive measurement of wound conductivity and lung imaging [1]. Its main benefits are a very low operating and construction cost, non-ionizing interactions with matter and contactless operation. A low frequency field (in the kHz to the MHz range) is used to induce eddy currents inside an object of interest. The eddy currents depend on the passive electric properties (PEP) of the object and these in turn induce a secondary magnetic field, which can be measured at sensors outside the volume of interest. Computation of the scattered magnetic field is done through the forward model. Current state-of-the-art forward models are based on approximate, differential or surface integral equations. Here, the main challenge is to obtain accurate results while maintaining a low computation cost. The forward model may be formulated as a large linear system, which needs to be solved iteratively. While a finer discretization may yield more accurate results, it also leads to a more computationaly burdensome model. For imaging purposes, the PEP of the domain of interest must be reconstructed from the known incident and scattered fields, which is refered to as the inverse problem. The inverse problem is solved iteratively by minimizing the differences between the measured scattered magnetic field and the forward model evaluation for estimated values of the PEP to which a penalty term may be added. For each iteration of the inverse solver, the forward problem must be solved, so an efficient forward model is critical. Biological tissues in the MIT frequency range may be considered as penetrable objects and volume integral equations (VIEs) can adequatly model the problem. VIEs offer several advantages such as the need to discretize a much smaller domain than differential methods, a better accuracy than approximate methods and a wider range of applicability than surface integral methods. Although VIEs are commonly used in a higher frequency range (e.g., microwave tomography) and for non-destructive evaluation (NDE), specific issues plague their application to biomedical MIT. Since both permittivity and conductivity are being reconstructed (as opposed to only conductivity for NDE) and because at these frequencies biological tissues have very high dielectric properties [2], conditioning issues arise. For large domains requiring the implementation of iterative solvers, this yields a slow convergence of both the forward and the inverse solvers [1]. This paper presents and validates a model that tackles this conditioning issue arising from the high contrasts in biomedical MIT by using Green's function theory.

II. Problem Formulation

A. *Volume Integral Equation based Model*

The standard VIE is obtained by using Green's function and the volume equivalence principle to solve the wave equation [3]. Discretization is performed by the method of moments with Dirac basis functions. The scattered magnetic field at the sensors is obtained through $\boldsymbol{h}^{scat}(\boldsymbol{x}) = -\tilde{\sigma}_b \boldsymbol{X} \boldsymbol{G}^R \boldsymbol{\mathcal{L}}^{-1} \boldsymbol{e}^0$ with $\boldsymbol{\mathcal{L}}^{-1} = (\boldsymbol{I} - k_b^2 \boldsymbol{G}\boldsymbol{X})^{-1}$ the scattering operator, $\boldsymbol{X}$ a diagonal matrix containing the electric contrast values $X(\boldsymbol{r}) = \tilde{\sigma}(\boldsymbol{r})/\tilde{\sigma}_b - 1$, with $\tilde{\sigma}_b = \sigma - j\omega\epsilon_r\epsilon_0$ the background complex conductivity, $\boldsymbol{G} = \Delta V(\boldsymbol{I} + \nabla\nabla/k_b^2)g$ the dyadic Green's function, $g(\boldsymbol{r}, \boldsymbol{r}') = e^{jk_b|\boldsymbol{r}-\boldsymbol{r}'|}/4\pi|\boldsymbol{r} - \boldsymbol{r}'|$ denotes the scalar Green's function, ΔV the discretization volume and $\boldsymbol{e}^0$ is the incident electric field. The matrix $\boldsymbol{G}^R = \xi\nabla g$ is defined through the Levi-Civita tensor and represents the cross product of the gradient and the scalar Green's function.

The selected criterion is the L_2 norm of the differences between the measurements and the forward model evaluation. To deal with the ill-posedness of the problem, an additive regularization term is added to include *a priori* information about the domain to reconstruct. An L_2L_1 penalization term on the first differences of the contrast is chosen in order to preserve the object edges. The function $R(\boldsymbol{X}) = \lambda\sqrt{\delta^2 + t(\boldsymbol{X})^2}$ is well adapted, where t is the sum of contrast variations along each axis, δ is a hyperparameter that defines the transition between the quadratic and linear behaviors of the penalty function and λ is the regularization parameter. The cost functional to minimize is therefore: $F(\boldsymbol{X}) = \|y - f(\boldsymbol{X})\|_2^2 + \lambda R(\boldsymbol{X})$. To minimize this cost functional, the L-BFGS algorithm is chosen. This quasi-Newton method offers a lower computation cost per iteration than a Newton method, while converging faster than a gradient method. The gradient of the cost functional is obtained by computing its Fréchet derivative. Straightforward computations yield $\nabla F = \boldsymbol{J}^{\dagger}(y - f) + \lambda R'_{HS}$ where Jacobian $\boldsymbol{J}$ can be expressed as $\boldsymbol{J} = \boldsymbol{G}^R(\boldsymbol{I} - \boldsymbol{G}\boldsymbol{X})^{-\intercal} \operatorname{diag}\{e\}$.

The issue with the VIE model is that the scattering operator $\mathcal{L}$ is ill-conditioned due to the high contrast values of biological tissues in this low frequency range. This implies a very slow convergence of the forward model. The poor conditioning of the forward model also results in a slow convergence of the inverse solver. This yields a very high computation cost, which makes the model impractical for realistic applications.

B. Inhomogeneous Green's Function based Model

A solution to the problem's poor conditioning and slow convergence is to perform a change of variables to a new contrast value $\boldsymbol{X}_2$, which is defined as a perturbation in an otherwise healthy tissue. Since in biomedical imaging the goal is to identify a small perturbation in a known background, this healthy tissue can be included into the background propagation medium. Two approaches may be considered. The first one is the linear embedding via Green's operator (LEGO), which makes use of the port theory to include the mutual scattering events between the background and the perturbation domain [4], but is computationally burdensome. The second one is based on the Green's function theory [5]. If one considers an inhomogeneous propagation medium including the healthy tissue, an inhomogeneous Green's function (IG) can be computed by solving $\boldsymbol{G}^{in} = \boldsymbol{\mathcal{L}}_1^{-1}\boldsymbol{G}_{12}$. Domains 1 and 2 respectively denote the inhomogeneous propagation medium and the volume of interest, which contains the contrast values $\boldsymbol{X}_2$ that are to be determined. After discretization, the forward model is given by $\boldsymbol{h}^{scat}(\boldsymbol{X}_2) = \boldsymbol{G}^R\boldsymbol{X}_1(\boldsymbol{e}_1 + \boldsymbol{G}^{in}\boldsymbol{X}_2\boldsymbol{e}_2)$. Here, $\boldsymbol{e}_2 = \boldsymbol{\mathcal{L}}_2^{-1}\boldsymbol{e}_{1|2}$ and $\boldsymbol{e}_1 = \boldsymbol{\mathcal{L}}_1^{-1}\boldsymbol{e}_1$ are the total fields in each domain and $\boldsymbol{e}_{1|2}$ is the total field in Domain 2 due to the inhomogeneous Domain 1. Matrices involving $\boldsymbol{X}_1$ may be computed only once so that only $\boldsymbol{e}_2$ needs to be computed at each iteration of the inverse solver. The new scattering operator $\boldsymbol{\mathcal{L}}_2^{-1}$ has a much better conditioning and convergence of both the forward and inverse problems are greatly improved. The new Jacobian is given by $\boldsymbol{J} = \boldsymbol{G}^R\boldsymbol{X}_1\boldsymbol{G}^{in}(\boldsymbol{I}_2 + \boldsymbol{X}_2\boldsymbol{\mathcal{L}}_2^{-1}\boldsymbol{G}_{22}) \operatorname{diag}\{\boldsymbol{\mathcal{L}}_2^{-1}\boldsymbol{e}_{1|2}\}$.

III. Results

The LEGO and IG models were compared to the standard VIE for a dielectric sphere emulating white matter with a layer of cerebrospinal fluid and a small blood perturbation as seen in Fig. 1 (a). The left pane of Fig. 1 (c) shows good agreement between the scattered magnetic field for the three models and the right pane shows improvement in the convergence of the inverse solver for the LEGO and IG models. In Fig 1 (b) the reconstructed domain using the IG model is presented. The data were generated using the VIE model with 80 dB of added gaussian noise in order to avoid the inverse crime. We notice that, although the boundaries of the pertubation are properly identified, the conductivity values are slightly underestimated, which seems to be an effect of the regularization.

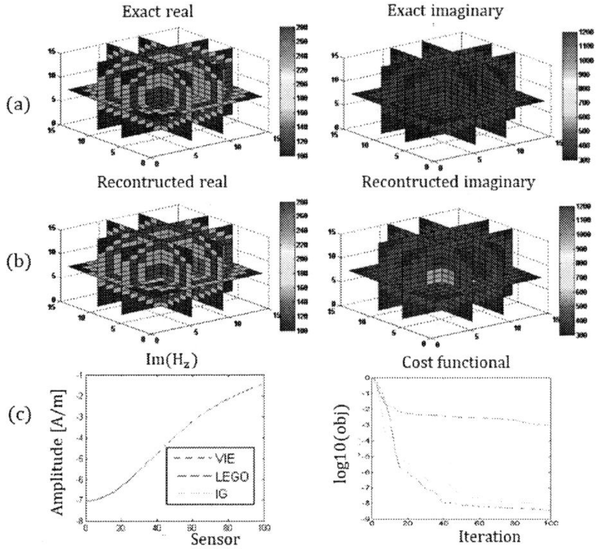

Fig. 1. (a) Exact and (b) reconstructed domains, (c) Im(H_z) component of the scattered magnetic field and convergence of the cost functional for each model. The simulation domain is a cube with 20 cm edges, discretized onto a 15 X 15 X 15 cartesian grid. It is illuminates by 15 sources (z oriented magnetic dipoles of unit amplitude) and 15 detectors are placed circularly (r = 16 cm) on three planes (z = 2:5; 0; 2:5 cm).

IV. Discussion

These results indicate that, although the standard VIE model is not suitable for MIT, the alternate IG model offers considerable improvements regarding convergence of both the foward and inverse solvers. Although the proposed method shows some advantages over state-of-the-art numerical methods such as fewer unknows and a structure well suited to parallelization, further work is required in order to reconstruct images with a lower SNR and to reduce computational cost through numerical methods such as Block algorithms and preconditioning.

References

[1] P. De Tillieux and Y. Goussard, "A volumetric integral equation formulation for magnetic induction tomography," Antenna Measurements & Applications (CAMA), 2016 IEEE Conference, pp. 1-4, 2016.

[2] S. Gabriel, R. W. Lau, and C. Gabriel, "The dielectric properties of biological tissues: II. Measurements in the frequency range 10 Hz to 20 GHz," Physics in Medicine and Biology, 41(11), 1996.

[3] M. Pastorino, Microwave Imaging, vol. 208. John Wiley & Sons, 2010.

[4] V. Lancelloti, B. P. de Hon, and A. G. Tijhuis, "Scattering from large 3-D piecewise homogeneous bodies through linear embedding via Green's operators and Arnoldi basis functions," Progress in Electromagnetics Research, 103, pp. 305-322, 2010.

[5] C. T. Tai, "Dyadic Green functions in electromagnetic theory," Institute of Electrical & Electronics Engineers (IEEE), 1994.

Approaches for Magnetic Sources Reconstruction in Controlled Thermo-Nuclear Fusion Technology

A. G. Chiariello, A. Formisano, R. Martone
Dept. of Ind. and Inform. Engineering
Univ. della Campania "L. Vanvitelli", Aversa (CE), Italy
Raffaele.Martone@unicampania.it

JET Contributors
See the author list of "X. Litaudon et al *2017* Nucl. Fusion *57 102001. EUROfusion Consortium, JET, Culham Science Centre, Abingdon, Oxfordshire, OX14 3DB, UK*

***Abstract*—The estimation of the unknown magnetic sources in Fusion devices by external measurements is a critical task due to its impact on several actions, including the assessment of the magnetic diagnostic system. Suitably treating the modelling of ferromagnetic materials, a linear model can be used also in presence of iron, based on the use of equivalent magnetizing currents. The several available numerical approaches provide quite different solutions while all preserving a good representation capability**

Keywords*—*inverse problems, fusion technology, magnetic sources identification.

I. Introduction

The magnetic diagnostic is called to play a critical role in all the systems where the control of operation is based on a suitable knowledge of the magnetic field distribution. In these cases, the correct functioning of the system depends on the accuracy and resolution of the measurements. The fusion technology [1], a challenging scientific research for the energy of the future, presents a typical example. As a matter of fact, in the Tokamak [1], the most promising device for the commercial reactors, the feedback plasma shape and position control is based on a magnetic monitoring; in addition, also the counteraction of possible instabilities is performed taking benefit of a suitable magnetic detection of precursors.

In order to guarantee the required standard, the diagnostic system should be frequently assessed, possibly on line, with the aim to detect the failure probes and, possibly, to provide each of them with a suitable confidence qualification. Several assessments procedures have been proposed. A classical and reliable approach is based on the comparison, probe by probe, of the actual measurements (field components, magnetic fluxes linked with a closed line, or related quantities) with the evaluation of the same quantities from the numerical elaboration of the magnetic sources, including free currents and the current possibly modelling the effect of ferromagnetic materials. If the discrepancy between the measured and calculate quantity related to a probe overcame its error bar (depending on the noise and, in addition, on the modelling uncertainties and computation approximation), the probe should be included in the list of suspected to be wrong and, additional investigation to assess its actual performances are recommended. Unfortunately, in several cases, the sources (or part of them) are not known; but when the number of probes are high enough and their distribution is suitable, an estimation of the sources can be effectively performed, taking advantage of the system's own measuring. In the general frame of fusion technology, this is the case of the Tokamak; in fact, the plasma current profile is not known because the position and shape can be estimated only in a rough way by specific diagnostics; a possible solution is based on the equivalent plasma current approach [2]. In addition, in case of iron presence treated by means of magnetizing currents, also the equivalent iron currents can be suitably included in the list of unknown sources.

In any case, the assessment of the diagnostic system is articulated in two stages: (i) a preliminary step aimed to estimate the unknown (free and magnetizing) currents; (ii) the comparison between calculated and measured quantities, aimed to assess the performance of each probe. The first step falls in the class of inverse problems because it should identify the sources of a magnetic field starting from its effect on a sampled domain; its solution can be found in the general approaches based on the minimization of a suitable error function or, in the case of linear behaviour, can benefit from the well assessed approaches of the matrix algebra.

This paper is focused on the first step of the procedure, with the specific application to the diagnostic systems of the JET [1] a Tokamak presently operating in U.K., that includes a ferromagnetic core in the magnetic poloidal system in order to drive the toroidal loop voltage. Several approaches to estimate the unknown are considered and the results are compared in terms of both identified currents and their impact on the reconstructed magnetic field.

II. Mathematical Model

The magnetic field is modelled as the superposition of the effects of the active poloidal currents and the iron equivalent currents [3]; in addition, in the limit of high permeability in the external arms of the iron core, a vanishing tangential component of the magnetic field is supposed to affect the external iron surface (see [4] for more details):

$$\underline{\underline{G_i}}\ \underline{s_i} + \underline{\underline{G_a}}\ \underline{s_a} = \underline{n}\,, \qquad (1)$$

where $\underline{s_a}$ and $\underline{s_i}$ represent the active and equivalent magnetizing currents, respectively; $\underline{n} = [\mathrm{n}_m \quad \mathrm{n}_c]^{\mathrm{T}}$ collects the actual n_m measurements and the $\mathrm{n}_c$constraints on the vanishing tangential field imposed by the iron, respectively; finally, $\underline{\underline{G_i}}$ and $\underline{\underline{G_a}}$ are the matrixes of coefficients. It should be noticed that the $\underline{s_i}$ equivalent sources are not aimed to provide a realistic map of the actual iron magnetization, but just to assess the impact of iron on probes response. Here a vacuum pulse is considered (dry run) and, in addition, the eddy currents are supposed negligible; therefore, just the iron equivalent currents are unknown in a linear algebraic model. The active currents $\underline{s_a}$ are supposed known; therefore the N_i iron currents in $\underline{s_i}$ can estimated by suitably treating the N_n linear equations in (1). Among the different alternatives, here the following approaches [5] are considered and the results compared.

Single Values decomposition (SVD). The "inverse" matrix $\underline{\underline{G_i^\dagger}}$ is assumed in the form $\underline{\underline{G_i^\dagger}} = \sum_{k=1}^{r} \frac{1}{\sigma_k} \mathbf{v}_k \mathbf{u}_k^T$ where σ_k, $\mathbf{v}_k$ and $\mathbf{u}_k$ are singular values, right and left singular vectors, respectively and r is the rank of $\underline{\underline{G_i}}$. The solution corresponds to the minimization of the quadratic norm of the residuals of the N_n equations (pseudoinversion). The SVD is very effective because provides the contribution of each singular vector; unfortunately it presents a poor regularization of the ill-conditioned problems due to the relevant effect of the small singular value; the most effective measures to mitigate such difficulties are based on the introduction of a suitable weighting function in the inverse matrix $\underline{\underline{G_i^\dagger}} = \sum_{k=1}^{r} \frac{W_\mu(\sigma_k)}{\sigma_k} \mathbf{v}_k \mathbf{u}_k^T$ [4].

Truncated SVD (TSVD). The weighting function $W_\mu(\sigma_k)$ is assumed vanishing when $\sigma_k^2 < \mu$, the unit otherwise, where μ is a suitable threshold. It should be noticed that the effect of the weighting function is to remove a suitable number of singular vectors from the reconstruction process.

Tichonov regularization (TichR). The weighting function is assumed $W_\mu(\sigma_k) = \sigma_k^2/(\sigma_k^2 + \mu)$ where μ is a regularization parameter. It can be shown that this approach minimizes the sum of the quadratic norm of the residuals of the N_n equations, and μ times the quadratic norm of unknown. An optimal value μ_{opt} is suggested by the L curve method, to suitably balance the norms of the solution and the residual error [5].

III. Numerical Results

The procedure has been assessed versus the experimental data of the dry run #86570 at t=52s operated by JET. Here the axi-symmetry assumption is done but the fully 3D extension can be easily provided. The list of probes considered 18x4 pick-up coils, 14x4 saddle loops and 6 flux loops [1]; all the signals have been elaborated according the standard JET procedure and normalized on the number of probes of each class. A set of $N_i = 62$ unknown equivalent currents have been introduced to model the iron in (1). Apart from the 134 actual measurements, the set of available equations includes also vanishing tangential field constraints in 148 points. More details in [3]. The calculation of the unknown iron currents has been performed with the mentioned approaches, calibrating the parameters when the case. To effectively perform the diagnostic system assessment, the procedure should guarantee a suitable "generalization" capability; this ability has been checked by using just 60 (over 72) pickup coils in (1) for the reconstruction and the remaining 12 for the cross-check. For each approach, the following data have been collected (Table I): the norm of the evaluated sources S_N and the normalized norm of the residuals on the pickup coils measurements used for the inverse $R_I = \left\| \underline{n_p} - \underline{n_p^{inv}} \right\| / \left\| n_p \right\|$ where $\underline{n_p^{inv}}$ are the measurement estimated by S_N. In addition, to evaluate the "generalization" capability. The same norm has been evaluated for just the cross-check probes confirms a good generalization capability.

Table I Comparison among the performance of inversion procedures

Approach	Regularization Parameter μ	S_N	R_I %
TichR	0.1*μ_{opt}	7.98e+06	3.0
	μ_{opt} = 1.1e-10	4.68e+06	3.3
	10*μ_{opt}	3.92e+06	10
	15*μ_{opt}	3.40e+06	17
TSVD	14e-10	4.54e+06	7.2
	9.5e-10	4.60e+06	4.5
	4.7e-10	4.62e+06	4.0

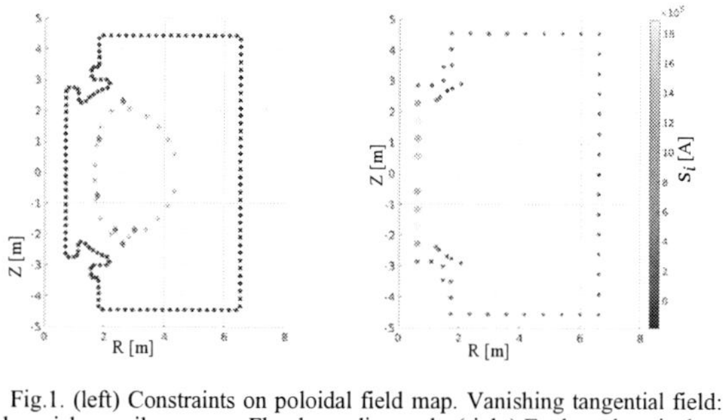

Fig.1. (left) Constraints on poloidal field map. Vanishing tangential field: circles; pickup coils: crosses. Flux loop: diamonds. (right) Evaluated equivalent currents by TichR approach with μ_{opt} = 1.1e-10.

Acknowledgment

This work has been partly supported by ENEA/Euratom/CREATE association. This work has been carried out within the framework of the EUROfusion Consortium and has received funding from the Euratom research and training programme 2014-2018 under grant agreement No 633053. The views and opinions expressed herein do not necessarily reflect those of the European Commission. The authors are thankful to the fruitful discussions held with Dr. F. Rimini (EURATOM-CCFE Fusion Association) and Dr. A. Murari (EUROfusion Consortium, JET).

. References

[1] P. H. Rebut, R. J. Bickerton and B. E. Keen, "The Joint European Torus: installation, first results and prospects," Nucl. Fusion, vol. 25, n. 9, 1985.

[2] P. Bettini, et al., "Identification of the plasma magnetic contour from external magnetic measurements by means of equivalent currents, " EUR. Phys. J-Appl. Phys., vol. 13, n. 1, pp. 51-57, 2001.

[3] A .G. Chiariello, A. Fomisano, F. Ledda, R. Martone and F. Pizzo, "A Fast Reconstruction Approach for the Assessment of Magnetic Diagnostic Systems in Nuclear Fusion Devices," IEEE Tr MAG 10.1109/TMAG.2017.2771753.

[4] A. G. Chiariello, F. Ledda, R. Martone, A. Murari, F. Pizzo and F. Rimini, "A 3D electromagnetic model of the iron core in JET," Fusion Engineering and Design, vol. 123, pp. 527-531, 201 , doi: 10.1016/j.fusengdes.2017.05.109.

[5] P. C. Hansen, Rank-Deficient and Discrete Ill-Posed Problems. SIAM, 1998

Resolution Limits of Near-Field Electromagnetic Imaging

Vijay Harid
Electrical Engineering
University of Colorado Denver
Denver, USA
vijay.harid@ucdenver.edu

Abstract—**Low frequency electromagnetic tomography is a non-destructive imaging technique that utilizes low frequency ($<$ 100 kHz) signals to image objects based on observed sensor data at a standoff distance. However, given the several kilometer wavelengths associated with low frequency signals, sensors are typically in the near-field region of the object being imaged. From a measurement point of view, near-field imaging inherently results in very similar measurements across sensors. This blurring effect determines the maximum possible resolution of a given near-field imaging system. In this work, we describe how to determine this resolution limit by replacing the object being imaged with an equivalent array of infinitesimal dipoles. Using this formalism, the scattered fields can be modeled by a matrix vector product; we then use a numerical rank analysis to determine the maximum resolution for which the dipole array can be inverted. Using this approach, we demonstrate how the resolution limit of near-field imaging systems can be determined based on sensor geometry, dyadic Green's functions, and other a-priori information.**

Index Terms—**Near-field Imaging, Computational Electromagnetics, Low Frequency, Tomography.**

I. Introduction

Electromagnetic tomography (ET) has truly revolutionized modern society with technologies such as X-ray Tomography, Ground Penetrating Radar (GPR), Magnetic Induction Tomography (MIT), Electroencephalography (EEG), Magnetotetullruics and several others [1]–[4]. ET is a non-destructive imaging modality that utilizes electromagnetic signals to image objects with arbitrary passive electrical properties [1], [5]–[7]. Despite many advances in ET, the ability to image through barriers that are made of electrically conductive materials remains a challenging front. Applications include underwater wreckage detection, identifying defects in industrial manufacturing, imaging through biological tissue, imaging the Earth's deep layers, detection of underground tunnels, and countless others.

When considering objects composed of conductive materials, low frequency signals ($<$ 100 kHz) are necessary to achieve appreciable levels of depth penetration. Although low frequency signals can penetrate conductive barriers, the corresponding wavelengths are typically orders of magnitude greater than the object being imaged. Sensors that are part of a low frequency imaging system are typically close to the object being imaged; this constraint ensures that low frequency electromagnetic tomography (LFET) is necessarily in the near-field regime. The localization of the near-fields results in spatial correlation across sensors and imposes a physical limit on the possible imaging resolution.

In order to determine the resolution limit of near-field imaging systems, we consider a rank analysis of matrices that model electromagnetic scattering. This novel method utilizes a computational electromagnetic approach to obtain resolution limits of near-field imaging.

II. Model and Simulations

For the specific problem of a known transmitted signal that is incident upon an object of arbitrary material properties, Maxwell's equations can be written in integral equation form by using the volume equivalence principle. For simplicity of analysis, magnetic materials are not considered even though the final result will be structurally identical. Under these considerations, the scattered electric field is given by the electric field integral equation:

$$\mathbf{E}^s(\mathbf{r}) = \int_{\mathbf{r}' \in V'} \hat{\mathbf{G}}^{(e)}(\mathbf{r}, \mathbf{r}')\mathbf{J}_{eq}(\mathbf{r}')dV', \tag{1}$$

where the operator $\hat{\mathbf{G}}^{(e)}$ is the dyadic electric Green's function [8], [9] and represents the fields generated by a point electric dipole located at position $\mathbf{r}'$ (i.e the spatial impulse response). Although quasi-static approximations may be utiilized by modifying the Green's function, doing so does not measurably change the results of this work and hence the general propagating Green's function is considered. The quantity $\mathbf{J}_{eq}$ represents the volume equivalent electric current density $(\frac{A}{m^2})$, and is given by $\mathbf{J}_{eq}(\mathbf{r}') = j\omega\left[\epsilon(\mathbf{r}') - \epsilon_0\right]\mathbf{E}(\mathbf{r}')$. The quantity ω is the angular frequency, $\epsilon(\mathbf{r})$ represents the permittivity profile of the object, and ϵ_0 is the permittivity of free space.

In order to solve (1), a method of moments (or similar) technique is typically employed and the integral equation is transformed into a linear system of equations [10]. In order to then determine the scattered fields outside the object being imaged, the linear system is given by:

$$\mathbf{E}^{(s)} = \hat{\mathbf{P}}\mathbf{J}_{V'}, \tag{2}$$

where $\mathbf{E}^{(s)}$ is a vector of $3N_r$ elements and each consecutive three elements represents the scattered electric field at the N_r receiver locations. The matrix $\hat{\mathbf{P}}$ contains $3N_r \times 3N$ elements and maps the equivalent currents $\mathbf{J}_{V'}$ to the scattered fields at locations $\mathbf{r}_n$. Each 3×3 block in $\hat{\mathbf{P}}$ corresponds to the dyadic Green's function for each pair of dipole-receiver locations.

In order to determine the resolution of a near-field electromagnetic imaging system, the scenarios under which the equivalent currents can be perfectly extracted based on receiver measurements must be considered. This equivalent current description is a good proxy for the material distribution given the problem is linear and time-invariant. To illustrate the basic procedure, the model problem of imaging a thin rod is considered.

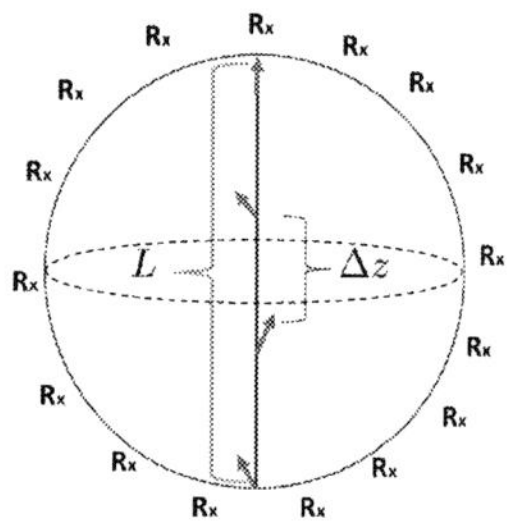

Fig. 1. N dipoles are placed Δz apart on a line of length L. Receivers are placed on a spherical surface of radius $L/2$.

The rod can be replaced by an array of N infinitesimal dipole antennas each with dipole moment $\mathbf{J}_n$, equally spaced along a line of length L as in Fig. 1. N_r hypothetical receivers (sensors) are uniformly distributed placed on spherical surface of radius $\frac{L}{2}$ directly around the center of the dipole array. The quantity Δz is the distance between consecutive dipoles and can be thought of as the size of a "pixel" in the final image. If the dipole moments are stacked into a single column vector $\mathbf{J}$, the electric field at the receiver locations are then given by

$$\mathbf{E} = \hat{\mathbf{P}}\mathbf{J}, \tag{3}$$

where the matrix $\hat{\mathbf{P}}$ is identical to the one in (2), which shows the connection of this hypothetical example to the scattering problem. To see whether or not the dipole moments can be extracted based on receiver measurements (*i.e.* imaging), rank $\left[\hat{\mathbf{P}}\right]$ must be considered. In order to examine the maximum resolution for inversion, the case of a large (approaching infinity) number of receivers can be considered, such that $\hat{\mathbf{P}}$ is a skinny matrix and the rank always reaches its maximum attainable value. Since $\hat{\mathbf{P}}$ is a skinny matrix, the maximum possible rank is simply given by the number of columns. This rank-based approach to inversion is a useful complement to typical singular value decomposition (SVD) analysis. Fig. 2 shows the rank (normalized to the number of columns) as a function of the number of dipoles $\frac{L}{\Delta z}$ for two wavelengths ($\lambda = L$, and $\lambda = 1000L$). As shown, the normalized rank for both wavelengths is unity until the number of dipoles is increased past a threshold value of (shown by the black dashed line). Past this threshold value, the matrix is not full rank and cannot be inverted without additional information. This result demonstrates the resolution limits of near-field imaging when constrained to a specific receiver geometry.

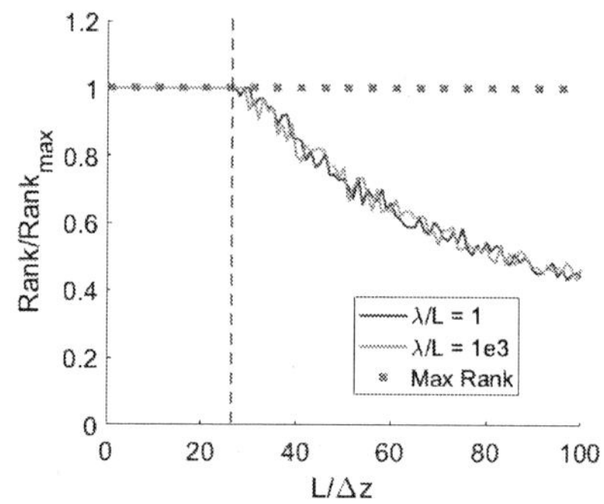

Fig. 2. The rank of of $\hat{\mathbf{P}}$ as a function of the number of dipoles for two wavelengths. Imaging resolution is shown by the vertical dashed line.

III. Conclusions

Imaging objects using low frequency electromagnetic signals is inherently in the near-field regime. Near-field signals result in spatially correlated observations which thus limits the maximum possible imaging resolution. In order to determine the resolution limit, the object being imaged is replaced by an array of equivalent dipoles. The smallest resolvable distance between adjacent dipoles then determines the resolution limit. This resolution limit is determined by numerically computing the rank of the matrix associated with the dipole array and sensor locations. This procedure is quite general and can be utilized to determine the resolution limit of any imaging system that relies on near-field measurements.

References

[1] M. Soleimani, "Computational aspects of low frequency electrical and electromagnetic tomography: A review study," *International Journal of Numerical Analysis and Modeling*, vol. 5, no. 3, pp. 407–440, 2008.

[2] A. P. Annan, "Ground-penetrating radar," in *Near-surface geophysics*, pp. 357–438, Society of Exploration Geophysicists, 2005.

[3] M. Broxton, L. Grosenick, S. Yang, N. Cohen, A. Andalman, K. Deisseroth, and M. Levoy, "Wave optics theory and 3-D deconvolution for the light field microscope," *Optics express*, vol. 21, no. 21, pp. 25418–25439, 2013.

[4] Y. Sasaki, "Full 3-D inversion of electromagnetic data on PC," *Journal of Applied Geophysics*, vol. 46, no. 1, pp. 45–54, 2001.

[5] J. Salach and R. Szewczyk, "High resolution eddy current tomography system for nondestructive testing," *Acta Physica Polonica A*, vol. 126, no. 1, pp. 402–403, 2014.

[6] L. Borcea, J. G. Berryman, and G. C. Papanicolaou, "High-contrast impedance tomography," *Inverse problems*, vol. 12, no. 6, p. 835, 1996.

[7] J. R. Wait, "Theory of magnetotelluric fields," *Journal of Research of the National Bureau of Standards-D*, vol. 66, no. 5, pp. 509–541, 1962.

[8] L. Li, P. Kooi, M. Leong, and T. Yee, "Electromagnetic dyadic Green's function in spherically multilayered media," *IEEE Transactions on Microwave Theory and Techniques*, vol. 42, no. 12, pp. 2302–2310, 1994.

[9] C. Tai, *Dyadic Green functions in electromagnetic theory*. Institute of Electrical & Electronics Engineers (IEEE), 1994.

[10] W. C. Gibson, *The method of moments in electromagnetics*. CRC press, 2014.

Perturbation Approach to Shape Reconstruction in a Rectangular Waveguide using Experimental Data

Martin Norgren
School of Electrical Engineering
KTH Royal Institute of Technology
Stockholm, Sweden
mnorgren@kth.se

Irene Ortiz de Saracho
School of Electrical Engineering
KTH Royal Institute of Technology
Stockholm, Sweden
iodsp@kth.se

Mariana Dalarsson
Faculty of Technology
Linnæus University
Växjö, Sweden
mariana.dalarsson@lnu.se

***Abstract*—We consider the inverse problem of reconstructing the shape of a deformation in one of the broad walls of a rectangular waveguide. Assuming a small deformation, resulting in weak scattering, the direct problem is solved using a first order perturbation approach. Hence, the inverse problem becomes linear and is formulated as an equation system for a set of expansion coefficients. The illposedness of the inverse problem is handled with regularization, by adding a penalty term which weight is determined by the L-curve method. The theory is tested on experimental reflection data, using the dominant mode of the waveguide. The reconstructed shape is in qualitative agreement with the true shape, but a detailed resolution cannot be obtained due to insufficient quality of the experimental data. Extensions and improvements of the method are discussed.**

I. Introduction and Problem Formulation

Shape reconstruction of perfectly conducting objects is a class of inverse problems that has been studied from the open region and the guided wave perspectives [1]–[3]. Applications are e.g. detecting and diagnosing adverse structural changes in various component and devices. For closed structures, the theory of boundary deformations in waveguides becomes a pertinent tool of analysis. For rectangular and coaxial waveguides, a perturbation approach applicable to weak scattering situations has been presented in [4] together with results from numerical simulations. In this paper, we supplement a part of the study in [4] with experimental results. We consider

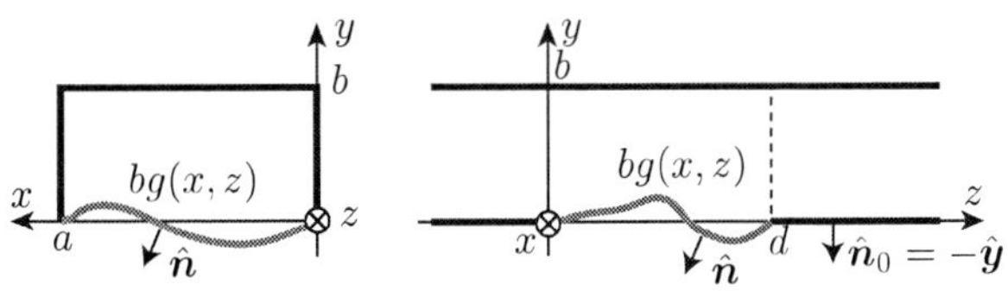

Fig. 1. Rectangular waveguide with localised shape deformation $y = bg(x, z)$ in the lower broad wall.

a rectangular waveguide of cross-section $a \times b$ ($a > b$), in which there is a localized shape deformation in the lower broad wall within the section $0 < z < d$ along the waveguide; see Fig. 1. The inverse problem is to reconstruct the shape function $g(x, z)$ from measured scattering (S-)parameters of the waveguide modes. Due to practical difficulties in exciting and detecting multiple modes, this work is restricted to using only the dominant mode TE_{10}.

II. First Order Scattering Theory

We utilize the perturbation approach in [4], where results for the first order S-parameters between all TE_{m0}-modes can be found. Restricting to the frequency interval where only the dominant TE_{10}-mode propagates, we obtain the following reflection coefficient from the left:

$$S_{11} = \frac{\mathrm{j}}{ak_z} \int_0^a \mathrm{d}x \int_0^d \mathrm{d}z \; g(x,z) \mathrm{e}^{-\mathrm{j}2k_z z} \left[k^2 \cos(2k_x x) - k_z^2\right], \quad (1)$$

where $k_x = \pi/a$ and $k_z = \sqrt{k^2 - k_x^2}$, and where the wavenumber $k = \omega/c$. (1) refers to $z = 0$ as the plane where the reflection occurs. Transferring S_{22}, the reflection coefficient from the right, to the same plane, the first order theory implies:

$$S_{22} = -S_{11}^*, \quad (2)$$

which copes with that reciprocity and negligible losses imply:

$$|S_{22}| = |S_{11}|. \quad (3)$$

III. The Inverse Problem

The shape $g(x, z)$ is expanded into a Fourier-sine series:

$$g(x,z) = \sum_{p=0}^{p_{\max}} \sum_{q=0}^{q_{\max}} g_{pq} \sin\left(\frac{p\pi x}{a}\right) \sin\left(\frac{q\pi z}{d}\right). \quad (4)$$

Hence, the inverse problem is to find the expansion coefficients g_{pq}, which are collected into a vector $\boldsymbol{g}$. Similarly, S_{11} and S_{22}, measured at multiple frequencies, are collected into another vector $\boldsymbol{S}$. The expansions coefficients are found from the regularized problem:

$$\min_{\boldsymbol{g}} \left\{ \|\boldsymbol{A}\boldsymbol{g} - \boldsymbol{S}\|^2 + \lambda^2 \|\nabla g\|^2 \right\}, \quad (5)$$

where the elements of the matrix $\boldsymbol{A}$ are found explicitly by insertion of (4) into (1). The norm of the shape gradient:

$$\|\nabla g\| = \left(\int_0^a \mathrm{d}x \int_0^d \mathrm{d}z \; |\nabla g(x,z)|^2 \right)^{1/2} = \|\boldsymbol{L}\boldsymbol{g}\|, \quad (6)$$

where the diagonal matrix $\boldsymbol{L}$ puts the penalty weight,

$$\frac{\pi}{2}\sqrt{\frac{d}{a}p^2 + \frac{a}{d}q^2},$$

on each g_{pq}, hence suppressing rapid variations in the shape. In (5), the optimal value of the regularization parameter λ is determined using the L-curve method [5].

IV. Experimental Results

We have performed measurements using a 560 mm long waveguide WR284, with cross-section $a = 72.14$ mm, $b = 34.04$ mm. The waveguide was terminated with two waveguide to coaxial cable transitions connected to a network analyzer. An SSST calibration procedure was performed prior to every measurement campaign. To mimic an intrusion in the lower broad wall, a facetted block of aluminum, with a flat bottom surface, was placed inside the waveguide; see Fig. 2. The aluminum block was positioned symmetrically inside the

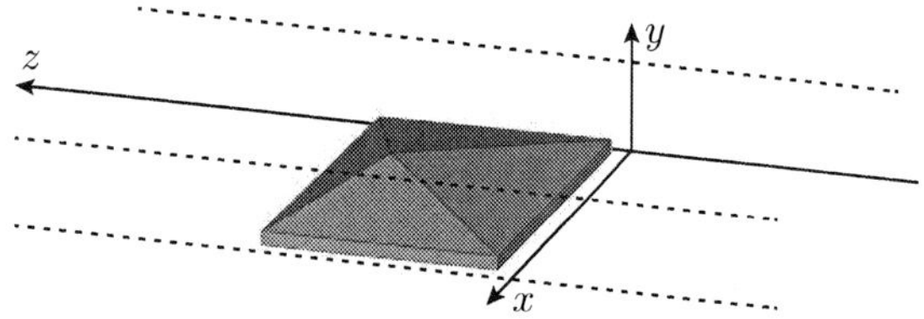

Fig. 2. Aluminum block inserted into a waveguide. The lower part of the block has dimensions 70 x 70 x 5 mm^3. The tip of the block is 10 mm above its bottom surface and off-centered 14 mm towards one of its sides.

waveguide; see Fig. 2. S_{11} and S_{22} of the dominant mode TE_{10} were measured at 384 evenly spaced frequencies in the interval 2.3-3.8 GHz. To evaluate the quality of the data, the conditions (2) and (3) were checked. The results, depicted in Fig. 3, exhibit clear deviations, which are expected to deteriorate the reconstruction results.

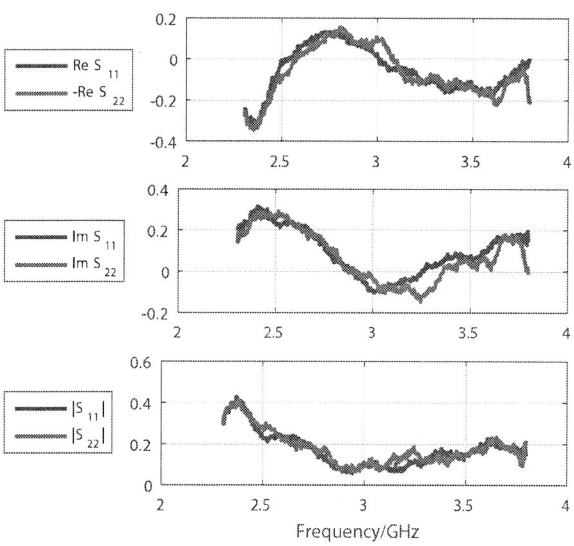

Fig. 3. The fulfillment by the measured S_{11} and S_{22} of the first order condition (2) (top and middle) and the sharper condition (3) (bottom).

The reconstructed shape shown in Fig. 4 is correct as far as it is predominantly an intrusion, with small extruding parts near the boundaries of the estimation domain. Furthermore, its main peak is located near the tip of the true shape. However, the 30 mm height of the main peak exceeds considerably the true 10 mm height of the tip, but the reconstructed shape

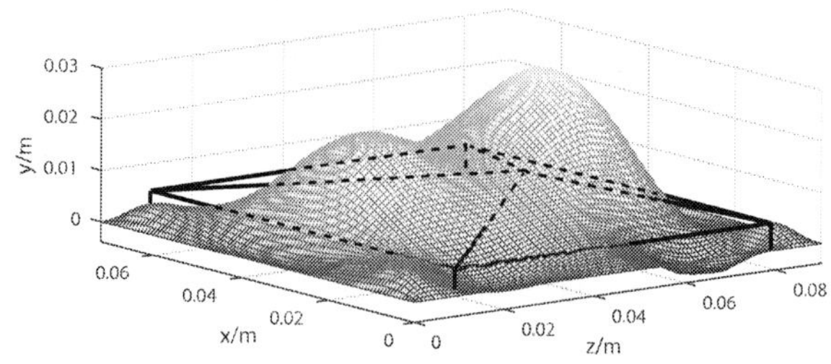

Fig. 4. Reconstructed shape of the aluminum block depicted in Fig. 2, with the true edges superimposed. The estimation domain occupies the entire waveguide width $a = 72.14$ mm and $d = 90$ mm along the mid-part, extending 10 mm outside the block in both directions.

attains values below the true shape elsewhere. From (1), it follows that an extrusion and an intrusion only differ in the sign of the reflection coefficient (in the first order setting). Defining the effective volume as the integral over the shape function, the reconstructed volume exceeds the true volume with about 15 %. Apart from theses observations, no additional features can be clearly seen. Reconstructions using only S_{11} or S_{22} were of similar quality, i.e. the use of double-sided data gave no apparent improvement. In addition to insufficient calibration over the frequency range used, another possible source of error is the galvanic contact between the test sample and the waveguide wall.

V. Conclusion and Future Work

Qualitatively, the experimental results verify the earlier theoretical work. However, for quantitative reconstructions it is clear that more accurate measurement are needed, by using extended calibration covering different parts of the frequency band. A more fundamental limitation is that using only the TE_{10}-mode, one can only reconstruct shapes that are symmetric with respect to the waveguide symmetry plane $x = a/2$, as shown in Figs. 2 and 4. Reconstructing the antisymmetric part of a shape requires cross-scattering data between TE_{m0}-modes which m-index differ by an odd number [4]. Future work thus concerns extended measurements, by exciting and detecting multiple waveguide modes. On the theoretical side, it is of interest to consider strong scatterers, possibly by extension to a second order perturbation approach.

References

[1] M. Cayören, I. Akduman, A. Yapar and L. Crocco, "A new algorithm for the shape reconstruction of perfectly conducting objects," Inverse Problems vol. 23, no. 3, 2007.

[2] D. Rovetta, A.V. Bosisio, G. Bernasconi and G. Drufuca, "Detection of anomalies inside hollow metal cylindrical structures," Inverse Probl. Sci. Eng. vol. 18, no. 5, pp. 613634, 2010.

[3] M. Dalarsson, "Perturbation approach to reconstructions of boundary deformations in waveguide structures," Ph.D. thesis, KTH Royal Institute of Technology, Stockholm, Sweden, Feb. 2016.

[4] M. Dalarsson and M. Norgren, "Two-dimensional boundary shape reconstructions in rectangular and coaxial waveguides," Wave Motion, vol. 66, pp. 10–20, 2016.

[5] P. C. Hansen, "Analysis of discrete ll-posed problems by means of the L-curve," SIAM Review, vol. 34, no. 4, pp. 561–580, Dec. 1992.

High-Order Moment-Matching MOR with Impedance Boundaries for Signal Integrity Analysis

Matthew B. Stephanson
ANSYS, Inc.
San Jose, California
matt.stephanson@ansys.com

Abstract—**This paper presents an extension of high-order moment-matching model order reduction to frequency-dependent impedance boundary conditions. Such boundary conditions are essential for accurately and efficiently modeling conductors at high frequency, where skin effect is significant. These boundary conditions involve complicated transcendental functions, whereas previous MOR methods assume polynomial dependence. Automatic differentiation is used to easily and accurately calculate the higher derivatives of such functions. Substantial improvement is shown, not only compared to discrete frequency sweeps, but also compared to non-moment-matching S matrix interpolation.**

I. Introduction

Model order reduction (MOR) is a frequently-used technique to develop efficient approximations to discretizations of Maxwell's equations that depend on one or more parameters (e.g., frequency or material properties). Although there are many methods to accomplish this, they can broadly be classified according to how well the reduced-order solution matches the full-order solution (order) and how many points in parameter space the two solutions match (single- vs. multi-point). High-order methods, in which not only the value but also the derivatives of the solutions are equal, can be efficient for systems with smooth parameter dependence because the incremental cost of each order is a matrix forward-backward substitution, rather than a factorization [1]. The disadvantage is that the derivatives of the system matrix with respect to the parameters must be known.

For signal integrity (SI) analysis of electronic packages and circuit boards, this presents a problem. Modeling of high-speed interconnects requires analysis up to tens of gigahertz, where losses from skin effect significantly affect performance. One approach to capture this effect is to model the volume inside the conductors with a mesh fine enough to resolve the decaying field. The system matrix entries are then second-order polynomials of frequency and the derivatives are easily calculated. Alternatively, an impedance boundary condition (IBC) can be used, but the matrix entries are no longer polynomials.

This work shows that the accuracy of an IBC can be achieved with the ease-of-implementation of a polynomial formulation by using automatic differentiation to calculate the higher-order derivatives of the surface impedance. This is a method for transforming the computer code of a function so that it not only calculates the value of the function, but also the derivatives with respect to the inputs. In contrast to finite difference methods, there is no discretization error, only round-off error. There are also advantages compared to symbolic differentiation, e.g., it is unnecessary to translate the computer code into a single mathematical expression.

II. Background

A. Finite Element Modeling of SI Problems

The finite element method is used to discretize Maxwell's equations, as applied to the problem geometry. For non-dispersive materials and ohmic conductors, this results in a matrix equation of the form

$$A(s)\mathbf{E} = \left(S + sY + s^2M\right)\mathbf{E} = \mathbf{J}(s), \tag{1}$$

where $s = j\omega$ is the complex frequency, and $\mathbf{J}$ and $\mathbf{E}$ are the current excitation and electric field solution vectors. The matrices S, Y, and M are the stiffness, admittance, and mass matrices, and depend, respectively, on the materials' permeability μ, conductivity σ, and permittivity ε. Inside good conductors, the fields decay exponentially on a length scale given by the skin depth $\delta = \sqrt{2/\omega\mu\sigma}$ (e.g., about $0.3\,\mu\text{m}$ for copper at $40\,\text{GHz}$). With trace cross sections on the order of tens of microns or more, this requires an extremely dense mesh to accurately resolve.

Because the traces and ground planes are typically wide compared to their thickness, it is common to model them with a layered media impedance boundary [2]. For a single layer, this has the form

$$Z_{IBC} = Z_0\frac{1 + \Gamma e^{-2\gamma T}}{1 - \Gamma e^{-2\gamma T}}, \tag{2}$$

where $Z_0 = \sqrt{\mu/\varepsilon}$ is the intrinsic impedance, Γ is the reflection coefficient from the surrounding dielectric, $\gamma = j\omega\sqrt{\varepsilon\mu}$ is the propagation constant, and T is the metal thickness. For good conductors, $\Gamma \approx 1$, $\gamma \approx (1+j)/\delta$, and $Z_0 \approx \gamma/\sigma$, leading to a rather complicated expression. It is this expression (actually, its inverse) that the matrix entries now depend on and which must be differentiated for moment-matching.

B. Projection-Based Model Order Reduction

A projection-based reduced order model is obtained by Galerkin-testing the $N \times N$ system matrix A with the $N \times M$ reduced-order basis vectors V:

$$\widehat{A}(s) = V^H A(s) V. \tag{3}$$

The reduced-order matrix equation is then

$$\widehat{A}(s)\widehat{\mathbf{E}} = V^H\mathbf{J}, \tag{4}$$

$$\mathbf{E} \approx V\widehat{\mathbf{E}}. \tag{5}$$

Because $M \ll N$, this equation can be solved much more rapidly than the original. In order for $\widehat{\mathbf{E}}$ and $\mathbf{E}$ to match up to the p-th order at frequency s_0, it can be shown that it is sufficient that the column space of V equal $\text{span}(\mathbf{E}|_{s_0}, \mathbf{E}'|_{s_0}, \ldots, \mathbf{E}^{(p)}|_{s_0})$ [3]. Applying the product rule to $A\mathbf{E} = \mathbf{J}$ shows that these are given by

$$\mathbf{E}^{(p)} = A^{-1}\left[\mathbf{J}^{(p)} - \sum_{k=1}^{p}\binom{p}{k}A^{(k)}\mathbf{E}^{(p-k)}\right]. \tag{6}$$

C. Automatic Differentiation

Automatic differentiation consists of analyzing each line of code that involves the dependent variable and augmenting it with a line that calculates the derivative as well [4]. Thus, for example, calculation of δ would include

$$\frac{d\delta}{df} = \left(\frac{1}{f\pi\mu\sigma}\right)^{-1/2} \cdot \frac{-1}{f^2\pi\mu\sigma}. \tag{7}$$

The power of automatic differentiation is that this augmentation can be done automatically, either by source code translation or operator overloading. Furthermore, the process can be applied recursively to obtain arbitrarily high orders.

Because many of the system matrix entries have the same frequency dependence, up to a multiplicative constant, it would be inefficient to calculate them entry-by-entry. Rather, the matrix is decomposed into a linear combination of scalar functions and constant matrices:

$$A(s) = \sum_i \phi_i(s)A_i. \tag{8}$$

The number of functions is typically less than a few dozen, e.g., one IBC-related function for each unique pair (T, σ). The derivatives $\phi_i^{(p)}$ can therefore be rapidly calculated, at which point evaluating $A^{(p)}(s)$ becomes trivial. Furthermore, this decomposition permits rapid online computation of the reduced-order matrix $\widehat{A}$, by precomputing each $V^H A_i V$.

III. Results and Conclusions

To demonstrate the benefit of MOR with IBCs, a simple test project consisting of a very long trace, as might be found on a PCB, is used. The trace is 127 µm wide, 48 µm thick, and 30 cm long. The ground plane underneath is 33 µm thick, separated by 69 µm-thick FR4 ($\varepsilon_r = 4.4$, $\tan\delta = 0.02$). The S parameters are extracted to 40 GHz using the Sentinel-PSI solver in ANSYS SIwave, which uses a 5th-order moment matching algorithm.

Four different analysis methods are considered. The first is using IBC on both the trace and ground plane and using the MOR with automatic differentiation described above. Second, MOR is also used, but with the simplest conductor modeling that gives a polynomial system matrix and a similar number of unknowns. In particular, the trace is modeled as a volume

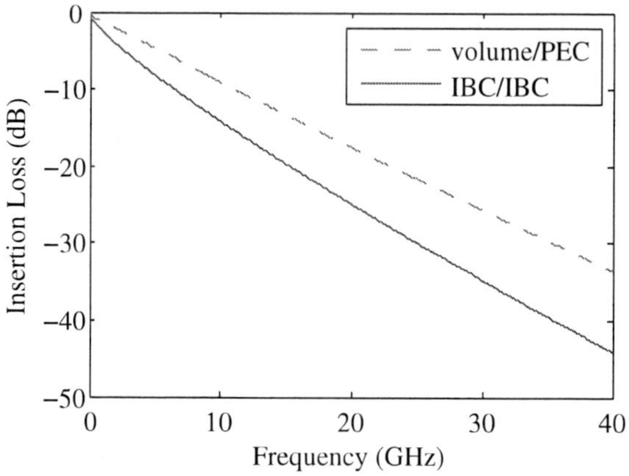

Fig. 1. Insertion loss for two different conductor models: (dashed red) volume conductor for traces, PEC for ground (solid blue) IBC for both.

TABLE I. Performance Results

Model	Sweep Method	Freq. Samples	Time (min.)	Memory (GB)	% Error RMS/Peak
IBC	MOR	33	33.9	9.00	0.06/0.48
σ/PEC	MOR	31	27.6	8.50	65/105
IBC	S interp.	262	112.3	3.93	3.6/18.5
IBC	none	800	344.9	3.95	—/—

conductor and the ground plane is PEC; note that the mesh is not heavily refined, so this is expected to result in less loss. Third, IBCs are again used on all metals, but S matrix interpolation is used for the frequency sweep. Finally, for reference, the IBC results are calculated without any fast-sweep algorithm.

The resulting insertion loss is shown in Fig. 1. As expected, the model using volume conductivity and PEC shows significantly less loss at high frequency, up to 10 dB at 40 GHz. The performance measurements are shown in Table I. The error is defined as $||S - S_{ref}||_F / ||S_{ref}||_F$. Two conclusions can be drawn. First, for a problem with a given number of unknowns, the addition of IBCs has no significant impact on the runtime of the MOR algorithm, compared to the polynomial case. Second, the use of higher-order moment matching allows for a significantly reduced number of frequency samples compared to S matrix interpolation.

References

[1] R. D. Slone, R. Lee, and J.-F. Lee, "Multipoint Galerkin asymptotic waveform evaluation for model order reduction of frequency domain FEM electromagnetic radiation problems," IEEE Transactions on Antennas and Propagation, vol. 49, no. 10, pp. 1504–1513, Oct. 2001.

[2] HFSS Online Help, ANSYS, Inc., Canonsburg, PA, "Finite conductivity boundaries", release 19.0.

[3] O. Farle and R. Dyczij-Edlinger, "Numerically stable moment matching for linear systems parameterized by polynomials in multiple variables with applications to finite element models of microwave structures," IEEE Trans. Antennas Propag., vol. 58, no. 11, pp. 3675–3684, Nov. 2010.

[4] M. Bartholomew-Biggs, S. Brown, B. Christianson, and L. Dixon, "Automatic differentiation of algorithms," J. Comput. and Appl. Math., vol. 124, no. 1, pp. 171–190, 2000.

Circuit-Based Model Order Reduction for EM-CAD

Valentín de la Rubia and Sofía Tinoco-Galafate
Departamento de Matemática Aplicada a las TIC. ETSI de Telecomunicación. Universidad Politécnica de Madrid
Avda. Complutense 30, 28040 Madrid, Spain, e-mails: valentin.delarubia@upm.es, s.tinoco@alumnos.upm.es

Abstract—**In this work, we focus on obtaining an accurate and reliable physical-based description of the Electromagnetics we are dealing with in order to carry out a fast and accurate computer-aided design. Appropriate Finite Element solution to time-harmonic Maxwell's equations in the frequency band of interest is involved and a reliable reduced-order model is obtained. Then, the electromagnetic behavior in the microwave device is rearranged and described in terms of circuit theory, giving rise to the coupling matrix representation of the original Maxwell problem.**

Index Terms—**Circuit theory, computer aided engineering, error analysis, finite element methods, Galerkin method, reduced basis methods, reduced order systems.**

I. Introduction

In this work, we focus on a rapid and reliable frequency-parameter sweep in microwave circuits based on the reduced-basis method [1], [2] and we place especial attention in getting valuable circuit theory information out of the reliable reduced-order model. The proposed model order reduction is based upon the following observation: should the field solution of the original system be considered as a function of frequency, the field solution itself does not arbitrarily vary as frequency changes, but it varies smoothly with frequency, i.e., the field solution resides on a very low dimensional subspace induced by the frequency variation. The reduced-basis method focuses on approximating the evolution of the electromagnetic field as a function of frequency, rather than approximating the electromagnetic field itself as the FEM does. We propose a model order reduction approach where field solutions at different frequencies are used as new basis functions to capture the dynamics of the electromagnetic field as frequency changes. Galerkin projection is applied to reduce the original FEM system into a small system detailing the frequency behavior of the original Maxwell problem.

II. Problem Statement

Throughout this work, we deliberately refer to the wavenumber k as frequency for convenience. Thus, given a frequency band of interest, namely, $[k_{\min}, k_{\max}]$, the FEM problem we aim at solving results in the following linear system of equations after discretization:

$$\begin{array}{c}\text{Find } \mathbf{x}(k) \text{ such that:}\\ \mathbf{A}(k)\mathbf{x}(k) = \mathbf{b}(k)\end{array} \quad \text{for } k \in [k_{\min}, k_{\max}], \tag{1}$$

where $\mathbf{A}(k)$ is a $\mathcal{N}\times\mathcal{N}$ matrix operator, $\mathbf{x}(k)$ and $\mathbf{b}(k)$ are the field solution and forcing term vectors, respectively. Making explicit the frequency dependence in the matrix operator and the right hand side, the following structure arises whenever homogeneous waveguide ports are taken into account:

$$\begin{array}{c}\mathbf{A}(k) = \mathbf{S} - k^2\mathbf{T}\\ \mathbf{b}(k) = f(k)\mathbf{b},\end{array} \tag{2}$$

where $\mathbf{S}$ and $\mathbf{T}$ are the stiffness and mass matrices and $f(k)$ is an analytic function of frequency [1].

A. Model Order Reduction

The reduced-order model that we propose draws upon using field solutions at specific frequencies as basis functions to represent the evolution of the electromagnetic field as a function of frequency. Thus, we carry out Galerkin projection onto the space $\mathcal{W}^N = span\{\zeta_1 \equiv \mathbf{x}(k_1), \dots, \zeta_\mathbf{N} \equiv \mathbf{x}(k_N)\}$, where $k_1, \dots, k_N \in [k_{\min}, k_{\max}]$, to obtain the following reduced system:

$$\begin{array}{c}\text{Find } \widetilde{\mathbf{x}}(k) \text{ such that:}\\ \widetilde{\mathbf{A}}(k)\widetilde{\mathbf{x}}(k) = \widetilde{\mathbf{b}}(k)\end{array} \quad \text{for } k \in [k_{\min}, k_{\max}], \tag{3}$$

where $\widetilde{\mathbf{A}}(k)$ is the reduced $N \times N$ matrix operator ($N \ll \mathcal{N}$), $\widetilde{\mathbf{x}}(k)$ is the reduced solution coefficient vector and $\widetilde{\mathbf{b}}(k)$ is the reduced forcing term. So far,

$$\begin{array}{c}\widetilde{\mathbf{A}}(k) = \widetilde{\mathbf{S}} - k^2\widetilde{\mathbf{T}}\\ \widetilde{\mathbf{b}}(k) = f(k)\widetilde{\mathbf{b}},\end{array} \tag{4}$$

where $\widetilde{\mathbf{S}} = \mathbf{P}^T\mathbf{S}\mathbf{P}$, $\widetilde{\mathbf{T}} = \mathbf{P}^T\mathbf{T}\mathbf{P}$ and $\widetilde{\mathbf{b}} = \mathbf{P}^T\mathbf{b}$, $\mathbf{P} = cols\{\zeta_1, \dots, \zeta_\mathbf{N}\}$. Finally, the field solution is obtained with ease as $\mathbf{x}(k) \simeq \mathbf{P}\widetilde{\mathbf{x}}(k) = \sum_{n=1}^{N} \widetilde{x}_n(k)\zeta_\mathbf{n}$.

We refer to [1] for a detailed explanation on the actual automatic adaptive selection of the frequency samples $k_1, \dots, k_N \in [k_{\min}, k_{\max}]$ while certifying the accuracy of the reduced order model. As a result, a fully automatic and reliable model order reduction is carried out.

B. Circuit Theory Representation in Electromagnetics

In the reduced-order model (3), an eigendecomposition is carried out to write down the reduced-order electromagnetic problem in terms of global eigenresonances or eigenmodes. Thus, (3) reads

$$\begin{array}{c}\text{Find } \widetilde{\mathbf{x}}(k) \text{ such that:}\\ (\mathbf{\Lambda} - k^2\mathbf{I})\mathbf{V}\widetilde{\mathbf{x}}(k) = f(k)\mathbf{V}\widetilde{\mathbf{T}}^{-1}\widetilde{\mathbf{b}}\end{array} \quad \text{for } k \in [k_{\min}, k_{\max}], \tag{5}$$

where $\widetilde{\mathbf{T}}^{-1}\widetilde{\mathbf{S}} = \mathbf{V}^{-1}\mathbf{\Lambda}\mathbf{V}$, $\mathbf{\Lambda}$ is a diagonal matrix and $\mathbf{I}$ is the identity matrix. It should be noted that a change of basis has been applied. This matrix representation gives rise to a coupling matrix in transversal topology introduced

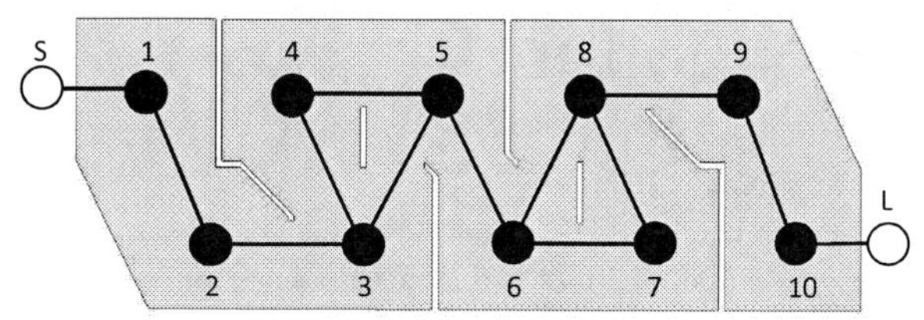

Fig. 1. 10th order 1800MHz ceramic TM mode filter. Intended coupling topology.

by Cameron in microwave filters [3] once the Generalized Admittance Matrix is computed in this problem, cf. [1]. As a result, we have a circuit representation of the electromagnetic behavior by means of a rigorous solution of the Maxwell problem (1). In order to obtain further physical insight of the microwave device, a coupling matrix representation of the Electromagnetics for the actual coupling topology in the microwave device layout is obtained by applying the technique proposed in [4]. This serves for electromagnetic design and diagnosis purposes since all electromagnetic phenomena are taking into account.

III. Numerical Results

In this section, we apply the proposed reliable circuit model for electromagnetic diagnosis in a 10th order 1800MHz ceramic TM mode filter with two transmission zeros. See Fig. 1, where the intended coupling topology is highlighted. The purpose in here is to understand the actual electromagnetic coupling behavior among the different resonators in the structure. The 1.6-1.9 GHz band is taken into account, which give rise to a reduced-order model of dimension 14, namely 14 eigenmodes are present. Among these 14 eigenmodes described in the reduced-order model, 10 correspond to dominant global resonances (the order of the filter), whereas the remaining 4 stand for parasitics behavior in electromagnetics. The latter will be taken into account as a direct source to load coupling in the coupling matrix representation. Once this technique is applied to this filter, the coupling matrix described in equation (6) is obtained. This coupling matrix reveals that leakage couplings are present between resonators 1 and 3, and between resonators 8 and 10. See Fig. 2. These additional couplings are the result of Electromagnetics. However, not only this technique is able to predict the existence of additional unwanted couplings, but also their actual location within the circuit layout and their corresponding coupling values. This information is extremely helpful not only for diagnosis but also in the design process. Having a reliable circuit representation of electromagnetic behavior allows a better understanding of the physics in microwave engineering.

IV. Conclusion

A reduced-order model in FEM analysis has been detailed. Special emphasis has been placed in determining a circuit theory representation within the reduced-order model in FEM analysis. The proposed technique has been applied for electromagnetic diagnosis in microwave devices. A coupling matrix representation, namely, a circuit theory representation, of electromagnetic phenomena has given rise to a better understanding for CAD in Maxwell problems.

$$\begin{pmatrix} 0 & 1.03 & 0 & 0 & 0 & 0 & 0 & 0 & 0 & 0 & 0 & 0 \\ 1.03 & -0.53 & 0.82 & 0.01 & 0 & 0 & 0 & 0 & 0 & 0 & 0 & 0 \\ 0 & 0.82 & 0.01 & 0.63 & 0 & 0 & 0 & 0 & 0 & 0 & 0 & 0 \\ 0 & 0.01 & 0.63 & 0.02 & 0.56 & 0.24 & 0 & 0 & 0 & 0 & 0 & 0 \\ 0 & 0 & 0 & 0.56 & -0.41 & 0.53 & 0 & 0 & 0 & 0 & 0 & 0 \\ 0 & 0 & 0 & 0.24 & 0.53 & 0.02 & 0.52 & 0 & 0 & 0 & 0 & 0 \\ 0 & 0 & 0 & 0 & 0 & 0.52 & 0.03 & 0.55 & 0.20 & 0 & 0 & 0 \\ 0 & 0 & 0 & 0 & 0 & 0 & 0.55 & -0.51 & 0.54 & 0 & 0 & 0 \\ 0 & 0 & 0 & 0 & 0 & 0 & 0.20 & 0.54 & 0.02 & 0.65 & 0.01 & 0 \\ 0 & 0 & 0 & 0 & 0 & 0 & 0 & 0 & 0.65 & 0.21 & 0.83 & 0 \\ 0 & 0 & 0 & 0 & 0 & 0 & 0 & 0 & 0.01 & 0.83 & -0.39 & 1.03 \\ 0 & 0 & 0 & 0 & 0 & 0 & 0 & 0 & 0 & 0 & 1.03 & 0 \end{pmatrix}. \tag{6}$$

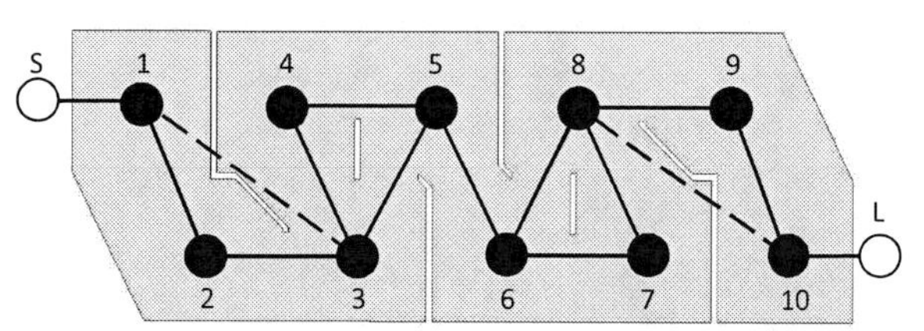

Fig. 2. 10th order 1800MHz ceramic TM mode filter. Actual coupling topology.

References

[1] V. de la Rubia, U. Razafison, and Y. Maday, "Reliable fast frequency sweep for microwave devices via the reduced-basis method," *IEEE Trans. Microwave Theory Tech.*, vol. 57, no. 12, pp. 2923–2937, Dec. 2009.

[2] A. Quarteroni, A. Manzoni, and F. Negri, *Reduced Basis Methods for Partial Differential Equations: An Introduction.* Springer, 2016, vol. 92.

[3] R. J. Cameron, "Advanced coupling matrix synthesis techniques for microwave filters," *IEEE Trans. Microwave Theory Tech.*, vol. 51, no. 1, pp. 1–10, Jan. 2003.

[4] P. Kozakowski and M. Mrozowski, "Quadratic programming approach to coupled resonator filter cad," *IEEE Trans. Microwave Theory Tech.*, vol. 54, no. 11, pp. 3906–3913, Nov. 2006.

Necessary Conditions for the Diagonalizability of Maxwell's Equations in Inhomogeneous and Fully Bi-anisotropic Media

A. R. Baghai-Wadji
University of Cape Town & Xi'an University of Science and Technology

***Abstract*— Considering inhomogeneous and fully bi-anisotropic media necessary conditions have been identified for the diagonalizability of Maxwell's electrodynamic equations. The same conditions also permit the construction of a system of equations supplementing the diagonalized ($\mathcal{D}$) equations. The combined $\mathcal{D}-$ and the associated supplementary ($\mathcal{S}$) equations are sharply equivalent with the originating Maxwell's equations, a fact which ascertains the internal consistency of the derived $\mathcal{D}-$ and $\mathcal{S}$ forms.**

I. Introduction

Modeling and simulation of miniaturized electronic, plasmonic and photonic devices require numerical calculation of electromagnetic (EM) fields in complex media characterized by inhomogeneous and/or fully bi-anisotropic material parameters. Irrespective of the nature and properties of commonly used computational techniques; i.e., the boundary element method, the finite difference method, and the finite element method, fundamental equations in mathematical physics can be written in diagonalized ($\mathcal{D}$) form, [1]. The $\mathcal{D}-$ forms possess distinctively favorable properties. In particular they transform to eigenvalue equations in spectral domain. This property is the genesis of a myriad of theoretical, numerical, and computational advantages. In addition, it can be shown that there is a set of equations supplementary ($\mathcal{S}$) to the $\mathcal{D}-$form. The $\mathcal{D}-$ and $\mathcal{S}$ forms are sharply and consistently equivalent with the originating governing and constitutive sets of equations (Refer to [2] for the analysis of the thermo-elasto-electro-magnetic coupled fields in the quasi static limit; i.e., thermo-piezoelectric fields.). This paper focuses on Maxwell's equations in their most general form. In an accompanying paper in this proceedings the procedure for the inclusion of thermal effects has been discussed.

II. $z-$Diagonalization of Maxwell's Electrodynamic Equations

Assuming a harmonic time-dependence according to $\exp(-j\omega t)$ Maxwell's electrodynamic equations in (x, y, z) Cartesian coordinates are as follows

$$
\begin{aligned}
-\partial_{\tilde{z}} H_2 + \partial_{\tilde{y}} H_3 &= -D_1 + \tilde{J}_1, && \text{(1a)}\\
\partial_{\tilde{z}} H_1 - \partial_{\tilde{x}} H_3 &= -D_2 + \tilde{J}_2, && \text{(1b)}\\
-\partial_{\tilde{y}} H_1 + \partial_{\tilde{x}} H_2 &= -D_3 + \tilde{J}_3, && \text{(1c)}\\
-\partial_{\tilde{z}} E_2 + \partial_{\tilde{y}} E_3 &= B_1, && \text{(1d)}\\
\partial_{\tilde{z}} E_1 - \partial_{\tilde{x}} E_3 &= B_2, && \text{(1e)}\\
-\partial_{\tilde{y}} E_1 + \partial_{\tilde{x}} E_2 &= B_3, && \text{(1f)}
\end{aligned}
$$

with $\partial_{\tilde{x}} = \partial_x/j\omega$, $\partial_{\tilde{y}} = \partial_y/j\omega$, $\partial_{\tilde{z}} = \partial_z/j\omega$, and $\tilde{\mathbf{J}} = \mathbf{J}/j\omega$. The constitutive equations in inhomogeneous and fully bi-anisotropic (complex) media are

$$
\begin{aligned}
\mathbf{D} &= \boldsymbol{\varepsilon}^{3\times3}(x,y,z)\mathbf{E} + \boldsymbol{\xi}^{3\times3}(x,y,z)\mathbf{H}, && \text{(2a)}\\
\mathbf{B} &= \boldsymbol{\zeta}^{3\times3}(x,y,z)\mathbf{E} + \boldsymbol{\mu}^{3\times3}(x,y,z)\mathbf{H}. && \text{(2b)}
\end{aligned}
$$

The superscript 3×3 emphasizes the fact that the inhomogeneous (position dependent) material tensors $\boldsymbol{\varepsilon}$, $\boldsymbol{\xi}$, $\boldsymbol{\zeta}$, and $\boldsymbol{\mu}$ are characterized by 3×3 matrices.

For the diagonalization with respect to $\tilde{z}$, field variables accompanied by $\partial_{\tilde{z}}$ (hereafter referred to as the "essential" field variables) must be identified first. It is easily seen that these are E_1, E_2, H_1, and H_2, constituting the hybrid vector $\boldsymbol{\Psi} = [E_1, E_2, H_1, H_2]^T$. The superscript T denotes transposition. Considering Eqs. (1e), (1d), (1b), and (1a), and slightly rearranging

$$
\begin{aligned}
\partial_{\tilde{x}} E_3 + B_2 &= \partial_{\tilde{z}} E_1, && \text{(3a)}\\
\partial_{\tilde{y}} E_3 - B_1 &= \partial_{\tilde{z}} E_2, && \text{(3b)}\\
\partial_{\tilde{x}} H_3 - D_2 &= \partial_{\tilde{z}} H_1 - \tilde{J}_2, && \text{(3c)}\\
\partial_{\tilde{y}} H_3 + D_1 &= \partial_{\tilde{z}} H_2 + \tilde{J}_1. && \text{(3d)}
\end{aligned}
$$

Equations (1c) and (1f), grouped together, are

$$
\begin{aligned}
-\partial_{\tilde{y}} H_1 + \partial_{\tilde{x}} H_2 &= -D_3 + \tilde{J}_3, && \text{(4a)}\\
-\partial_{\tilde{y}} E_1 + \partial_{\tilde{x}} E_2 &= B_3. && \text{(4b)}
\end{aligned}
$$

To obtain the desired $z-$diagonalized ($\mathcal{D}_z$) form the "non-essential," "auxiliary" field variables appearing at the LHS of (3) must be expressed in terms of the "essential" field components of $\boldsymbol{\Psi}$. Employing Eqs. (2) the components of $\mathbf{D}$ and $\mathbf{B}$ can be expressed in terms of $\mathbf{\Psi}$, and E_3 and H_3. Let the latter field components constitute the hybrid vector $\mathbf{\Phi} = [E_3, H_3]^T$. Using $\mathbf{\Psi}$ and $\mathbf{\Phi}$ Eqs. (2) are $(i = 1, 2, 3)$

$$D_i = [\varepsilon_{i1} \quad \varepsilon_{i2} \quad \xi_{i1} \quad \xi_{i2}]\mathbf{\Psi} + [\varepsilon_{i3} \quad \xi_{i3}]\mathbf{\Phi}, \quad (5a)$$

$$B_i = [\zeta_{i1} \quad \zeta_{i2} \quad \mu_{i1} \quad \mu_{i2}]\mathbf{\Psi} + [\zeta_{i3} \quad \mu_{i3}]\mathbf{\Phi}. \quad (5b)$$

Using (5) and substituting for D_1, D_2, B_1, and B_2 at the LHS of (3) we obtain

$$\mathbf{A\Psi} + \mathbf{P\Phi} + \begin{bmatrix} 0 & 0 & \tilde{J}_2 & -\tilde{J}_1 \end{bmatrix}^T = \partial_{\tilde{z}}\mathbf{\Psi}, \quad (6)$$

$$\mathbf{A} = \begin{bmatrix} \zeta_{21} & \zeta_{22} & \mu_{21} & \mu_{22} \\ -\zeta_{11} & -\zeta_{12} & -\mu_{11} & -\mu_{12} \\ -\varepsilon_{21} & -\varepsilon_{22} & -\xi_{21} & -\xi_{22} \\ \varepsilon_{11} & \varepsilon_{12} & \xi_{11} & \xi_{12} \end{bmatrix}, \quad (7)$$

$$\mathbf{P} = \begin{bmatrix} \zeta_{23} + \partial\tilde{x} & \mu_{23} \\ -\zeta_{13} + \partial\tilde{y} & -\mu_{13} \\ -\varepsilon_{23} & -\xi_{23} + \partial\tilde{x} \\ \varepsilon_{13} & \xi_{13} + \partial\tilde{y} \end{bmatrix}. \quad (8)$$

Employing (5) and substituting for D_3 and B_3 at the RHS of (4) result in

$$\mathbf{Q\Psi} + \begin{bmatrix} 0 & \tilde{J}_3 \end{bmatrix}^T = \mathbf{M}_c\mathbf{\Phi}, \quad (9)$$

$$\mathbf{Q} = -\begin{bmatrix} \varepsilon_{31} & \varepsilon_{32} & \xi_{31} - \partial\tilde{y} & \xi_{32} + \partial\tilde{x} \\ \zeta_{31} + \partial\tilde{y} & \zeta_{32} - \partial\tilde{x} & \mu_{31} & \mu_{32} \end{bmatrix}, \quad (10)$$

$$\mathbf{M}_c = \begin{bmatrix} \varepsilon_{33} & \xi_{33} \\ \zeta_{33} & \mu_{33} \end{bmatrix}. \quad (11)$$

A. *Supplementary System of Equations*

Multiplying both sides of (9) by $\mathbf{M}_c^{-1}$

$$\mathbf{\Phi} = \mathbf{M}_c^{-1}\mathbf{Q\Psi} + \mathbf{M}_c^{-1}\begin{bmatrix} 0 & \tilde{J}_3 \end{bmatrix}^T. \quad (12)$$

This equation is referred to as the "supplementary" $\mathcal{S}_z-$form: once $\mathbf{\Psi}$ is known, $\mathbf{\Phi}$ can be determined.

B. *z−Diagonalized System of Equations*

Substituting (12) into (6)

$$\left[\mathbf{A} + \mathbf{PM}_c^{-1}\mathbf{Q}\right]\mathbf{\Psi} + \mathbf{PM}_c^{-1}\begin{bmatrix} 0 & \tilde{J}_3 \end{bmatrix}^T + \begin{bmatrix} 0 & 0 & \tilde{J}_2 & -\tilde{J}_1 \end{bmatrix}^T = \partial_{\tilde{z}}\mathbf{\Psi}. \quad (13)$$

In source-free regions (13) assumes the form

$$\left[\mathbf{A} + \mathbf{PM}_c^{-1}\mathbf{Q}\right]\mathbf{\Psi} = \partial_{\tilde{z}}\mathbf{\Psi}, \quad (14)$$

which explicates the motivation for referring to (13) as the $\mathcal{D}_z-$form. It is immediate that Eq. (14) in spectral domain transforms to an eigenvalue equation.

III. Interpretation of the Results

Consistency and Completeness of the $\mathcal{D}_z-$ and $\mathcal{S}_z$ forms: Considering the $\mathcal{D}_z-$ and $\mathcal{S}_z$ forms in Eqs. (13) and (12), respectively, and arguing conversely, Maxwell's equations can be recovered, a fact which shows the internal consistency and the completeness of the $\mathcal{D}_z-$ and $\mathcal{S}_z$ forms, and demonstrates their sharp equivalence with Maxwell's electrodynamic equations.

Necessary Conditions: For obtaining the $\mathcal{D}_z-$ and $\mathcal{S}_z$ forms, the only condition required was the existence of the inverse $\mathbf{M}_c^{-1}$. Similarly, the $x-$ and $y-$diagonalization would require the existence of $\mathbf{M}_a^{-1}$ and $\mathbf{M}_b^{-1}$, *mutatis mutandis*. Consequently, conditions necessary for carrying out the diagonalization and supplementation of Maxwell's EM equations are merely the existence of $\mathbf{M}_a^{-1}$, $\mathbf{M}_b^{-1}$, and $\mathbf{M}_c^{-1}$; i.e., non-vanishing determinants of $\mathbf{M}_a$, $\mathbf{M}_b$, and $\mathbf{M}_c$ $(i = 1, 2, 3)$

$$\varepsilon_{ii}(x, y, z)\mu_{ii}(x, y, z) - \xi_{ii}(x, y, z)\zeta_{ii}(x, y, z) \neq 0 \quad (15)$$

at every point (x, y, z) in the medium.

IV. Conclusions

Considering inhomogeneous and fully bi-anisotropic media diagonalization and the corresponding supplementation of Maxwell's EM equations in complex media are shown. The resulting $\mathcal{D}-$ and $\mathcal{S}$ forms possess unique properties which are significant in theoretical and computational electromagnetics when dealing with modeling and simulation of electronic, plasmonic and photonic devices. The paper extends author's earlier work by considering inhomogeneity, constructing supplementary equations, and alluding to the internal consistency and completeness of the formulation.

ACKNOWLEDGMENTS

Support and generous hospitality by Professor Tao Zhang and his research group at Xi'an University of Science and Technology (XUST), and partial support from University of Cape Town are gratefully acknowledged. The author is currently on sabbatical with XUST.

References

[1] A. R. Baghai-Wadji, *A Symbolic Procedure for the Diagonalization of Linear PDEs in Accelerated Computational Engineering*, Symbolic and Numerical Scientific Computing, pp. 347-360, Franz Winkler and Ulrich Langer (Eds.), Springer- Verlag Heidelberg, LNCS 2630, 2003.

[2] A. R. Baghai-Wadji, *3D Diagonalization and Supplementation in Thermo-Elasto-Electro-Magnetics: Proof of Existence by Construction & Validation of Relative Consistency*, in the proceedings ICEAA, Verona, 2017.

Diagonalizability of Thermo Electromagnetic Equations in Inhomogeneous and Fully Tri-anisotropic Media

A. R. Baghai-Wadji
University of Cape Town & Xi'an University of Science and Technology

Abstract— **Considering inhomogeneous and fully tri-anisotropic media the coupled system of thermo electromagnetic equations have been diagonalized ($\mathcal{D}$-form). In addition a system of supplementary equations ($\mathcal{S}$-form) has been constructed. The combined $\mathcal{D}$- and $\mathcal{S}$ forms are sharply equivalent with the originating coupled thermal and electrodynamic equations. The $\mathcal{D}$- and $\mathcal{S}$ forms provide a plethora of theoretical and computational advantages. The generality of the underlying assumptions renders this work by far the most comprehensive investigation of the coupled thermo electromagnetic equations.**

I. Introduction

Extreme miniaturization of electronic, plasmonic, and photonic devices requires the inclusion of thermal phenomena in modeling and simulation processes. This work extends the scope of an accompanying paper in this proceedings by accounting for the coupled thermo-electromagnetic phenomena in inhomogeneous and fully tri-anisotropic media. The essence of the work is the diagonalization and the associated supplementation of the underlying governing and constitutive equations (for complementary considerations and the treatment of thermo-piezoelectric coupling refer to [1], [2]).

II. $z-$Diagonalization of Thermo Electromagnetic Equations

Assuming a harmonic time dependence according to $\exp(-j\omega t)$ the coupled system of thermo-electromagnetics can be written as follows (the current density vector $\mathbf{J}$ has been omitted for notational simplicity)

$$\tilde{\nabla} \times \mathbf{H} = -\mathbf{D}, \tag{1a}$$

$$\tilde{\nabla} \times \mathbf{E} = \mathbf{B}. \tag{1b}$$

Here, $\tilde{\nabla}\times = \nabla\times/j\omega$; i.e., $\partial_{\tilde{x}} = \partial_x/j\omega$, $\partial_{\tilde{y}} = \partial_y/j\omega$, and $\partial_{\tilde{z}} = \partial_z/j\omega$ have been introduced. Adopting (x, y, z) Cartesian coordinates, the constitutive equations in inhomogeneous and fully tri-anisotropic media are

$$\mathbf{D} = \boldsymbol{\varepsilon}^{3\times3}(\mathbf{x})\mathbf{E} + \boldsymbol{\xi}^{3\times3}(\mathbf{x})\mathbf{H} + \boldsymbol{\alpha}^{3\times1}(\mathbf{x})\theta, \tag{2a}$$

$$\mathbf{B} = \boldsymbol{\zeta}^{3\times3}(\mathbf{x})\mathbf{E} + \boldsymbol{\mu}^{3\times3}(\mathbf{x})\mathbf{H} + \boldsymbol{\beta}^{3\times1}(\mathbf{x})\theta. \tag{2b}$$

The superscripts 3×3 and 3×1 indicate that position dependent ($\mathbf{x} = (x, y, z)$) material tensors $\boldsymbol{\varepsilon}$, $\boldsymbol{\xi}$, $\boldsymbol{\zeta}$, $\boldsymbol{\mu}$, $\boldsymbol{\alpha}$, and $\boldsymbol{\beta}$ can be expressed by 3×3 and 3×1 matrices, accordingly. Furthermore, θ refers to the temperature T with respect to the reference temperature T_0.

The equations for the entropy η, its time variation $\partial\eta/\partial t$, and the heat flux vector $\mathbf{q}$ are, respectively,

$$\eta = \boldsymbol{\alpha}^T\mathbf{E} + \boldsymbol{\beta}^T\mathbf{H} + \gamma\theta, \tag{3a}$$

$$T_0\frac{\partial\eta}{\partial t} + \nabla^T\mathbf{q} = 0, \tag{3b}$$

$$\mathbf{q} + \tau_0\frac{\partial\mathbf{q}}{\partial t} = -\boldsymbol{\kappa}\nabla\theta. \tag{3c}$$

The superscript T signifies transposition.

On the construction of an equation for $\partial_{\tilde{z}}q_3$: Substituting (3a) into (3b), replacing the time derivative by $-j\omega$, dividing through by $j\omega$, and employing $\partial_{\tilde{x}}$, $\partial_{\tilde{y}}$, and $\partial_{\tilde{z}}$

$$-T_0[\alpha_1E_1 + \alpha_2E_2 + \alpha_3E_3 + \beta_1H_1 + \beta_2H_2 + \beta_3H_3 + \gamma\theta] + \partial_{\tilde{x}}q_1 + \partial_{\tilde{y}}q_2 + \partial_{\tilde{z}}q_3 = 0. \tag{4}$$

Bringing $\partial_{\tilde{z}}q_3$ to the RHS and introducing the hybrid vectors $\boldsymbol{\Psi} = [E_1, E_2, H_1, H_2]^T$ and $\boldsymbol{\Phi} = [E_3, H_3]^T$

$$[T_0\alpha_1 \;\; T_0\alpha_2 \;\; T_0\beta_1 \;\; T_0\beta_2]\boldsymbol{\Psi} + [T_0\alpha_3 \;\; T_0\beta_3]\boldsymbol{\Phi} \\ T_0\gamma\theta - \partial_{\tilde{x}}q_1 - \partial_{\tilde{y}}q_2 = \partial_{\tilde{z}}q_3. \tag{5}$$

On the construction of an equation for $\partial_{\tilde{z}}\theta$: Consider Eq. (3c) component-wise

$$\left[\frac{1}{j\omega} - \tau_0\right]q_1 = -\kappa_{11}\partial_{\tilde{x}}\theta - \kappa_{12}\partial_{\tilde{y}}\theta - \kappa_{13}\partial_{\tilde{z}}\theta, \tag{6a}$$

$$\left[\frac{1}{j\omega} - \tau_0\right]q_2 = -\kappa_{21}\partial_{\tilde{x}}\theta - \kappa_{22}\partial_{\tilde{y}}\theta - \kappa_{23}\partial_{\tilde{z}}\theta, \tag{6b}$$

$$\left[\frac{1}{j\omega} - \tau_0\right]q_3 = -\kappa_{31}\partial_{\tilde{x}}\theta - \kappa_{32}\partial_{\tilde{y}}\theta - \kappa_{33}\partial_{\tilde{z}}\theta. \tag{6c}$$

Dividing both sides of (6c) by κ_{33} and rearranging

$$-\left(\frac{\kappa_{31}}{\kappa_{33}}\partial_{\tilde{x}} + \frac{\kappa_{32}}{\kappa_{33}}\partial_{\tilde{y}}\right)\theta - \frac{1}{\kappa_{33}}\left[\frac{1}{j\omega} - \tau_0\right]q_3 = \partial_{\tilde{z}}\theta, \tag{7}$$

which for brevity is written in the form

$$\mathcal{L}_{\theta,\theta}\theta + \mathcal{L}_{q_3,\theta}q_3 = \partial_{\tilde{z}}\theta, \tag{8}$$

with obvious definitions of the operators $\mathcal{L}_{\theta,\theta}$, $\mathcal{L}_{q_3,\theta}$.

This is the desired equation for $\partial_{\tilde{z}}\theta$. Using (7) and eliminating $\partial_{\tilde{z}}\theta$ from (6a) and (6b) and rearranging give

$$\begin{aligned} q_1 &= \frac{j\omega}{1-j\omega\tau_0}\left(\left[-\kappa_{11}+\frac{\kappa_{13}\kappa_{31}}{\kappa_{33}}\right]\partial_{\tilde{x}}\right. \\ &\quad \left.+\left[-\kappa_{12}+\frac{\kappa_{13}\kappa_{32}}{\kappa_{33}}\right]\partial_{\tilde{y}}\right)\theta+\frac{\kappa_{13}}{\kappa_{33}}q_3, \end{aligned} \tag{9a}$$

$$\begin{aligned} q_2 &= \frac{j\omega}{1-j\omega\tau_0}\left(\left[-\kappa_{21}+\frac{\kappa_{23}\kappa_{31}}{\kappa_{33}}\right]\partial_{\tilde{x}}\right. \\ &\quad \left.+\left[-\kappa_{22}+\frac{\kappa_{23}\kappa_{32}}{\kappa_{33}}\right]\partial_{\tilde{y}}\right)\theta+\frac{\kappa_{23}}{\kappa_{33}}q_3. \end{aligned} \tag{9b}$$

For brevity Eqs. (9) are written compactly

$$q_1 = \mathcal{A}_{q_1,\theta}\theta + \mathcal{A}_{q_1,q_3}q_3, \tag{10a}$$

$$q_2 = \mathcal{A}_{q_2,\theta}\theta + \mathcal{A}_{q_2,q_3}q_3. \tag{10b}$$

Eqs. (10) are parts of the $\mathcal{S}-$form. Using (10) in (5)

$$\begin{aligned} &[T_0\alpha_1\ \ T_0\alpha_2\ \ T_0\beta_1\ \ T_0\beta_2]\mathbf{\Psi} + [T_0\alpha_3\ \ T_0\beta_3]\mathbf{\Phi} \\ &(T_0\gamma - \partial_{\tilde{x}}\mathcal{A}_{q_1,\theta} - \partial_{\tilde{y}}\mathcal{A}_{q_2,\theta})\,\theta \\ &+(-\partial_{\tilde{x}}\mathcal{A}_{q_1,q_3} - \partial_{\tilde{y}}\mathcal{A}_{q_2,q_3})\,q_3 = \partial_{\tilde{z}}q_3. \end{aligned} \tag{11}$$

On the construction of an equation for $\partial_{\tilde{z}}\mathbf{\Psi}$: Writing (1) in component form the six equations split into the two systems. Firstly,

$$\mathbf{A}\left[\begin{array}{cc}\mathbf{\Psi} & \theta\end{array}\right]^T + \mathbf{P}\mathbf{\Phi} = \partial_{\tilde{z}}\mathbf{\Psi}, \tag{12}$$

$$\mathbf{A} = \left[\begin{array}{ccccc} \zeta_{21} & \zeta_{22} & \mu_{21} & \mu_{22} & \beta_2 \\ -\zeta_{11} & -\zeta_{12} & -\mu_{11} & -\mu_{12} & -\beta_1 \\ -\varepsilon_{21} & -\varepsilon_{22} & -\xi_{21} & -\xi_{22} & -\alpha_2 \\ \varepsilon_{11} & \varepsilon_{12} & \xi_{11} & \xi_{12} & \alpha_1 \end{array}\right], \tag{13}$$

$$\mathbf{P} = \left[\begin{array}{cc} \zeta_{23}+\partial\tilde{x} & \mu_{23} \\ -\zeta_{13}+\partial\tilde{y} & -\mu_{13} \\ -\varepsilon_{23} & -\xi_{23}+\partial\tilde{x} \\ \varepsilon_{13} & \xi_{13}+\partial\tilde{y} \end{array}\right], \tag{14}$$

and secondly,

$$\mathbf{Q}\left[\begin{array}{cc}\mathbf{\Psi} & \theta\end{array}\right]^T = \mathbf{M}\mathbf{\Phi}, \tag{15}$$

$$\mathbf{Q} = -\left[\begin{array}{ccccc} \varepsilon_{31} & \varepsilon_{32} & \xi_{31}-\partial\tilde{y} & \xi_{32}+\partial\tilde{x} & \alpha_3 \\ \zeta_{31}+\partial\tilde{y} & \zeta_{32}-\partial\tilde{x} & \mu_{31} & -\mu_{32} & \beta_3 \end{array}\right] \tag{16}$$

$$\mathbf{M} = \left[\begin{array}{cc} \varepsilon_{33} & \xi_{33} \\ \zeta_{33} & \mu_{33} \end{array}\right]. \tag{17}$$

Multiplying both sides of (15) by $\mathbf{M}^{-1}$

$$\mathbf{\Phi} = \mathbf{M}^{-1}\mathbf{Q}\left[\begin{array}{cc}\mathbf{\Psi} & \theta\end{array}\right]^T. \tag{18}$$

Substituting (18) into (12) with the null vector $\mathbf{0}^{4\times1}$

$$\left[\begin{array}{cc}\mathbf{A}+\mathbf{P}\mathbf{M}^{-1}\mathbf{Q} & \mathbf{0}^{4\times1}\end{array}\right]\left[\begin{array}{ccc}\mathbf{\Psi} & \theta & q_3\end{array}\right]^T = \partial_{\tilde{z}}\mathbf{\Psi}. \tag{19}$$

Considering Eqs. (11) and (18)

$$\left[\begin{array}{ccc}\mathcal{L}_{\mathbf{\Psi},q_3} & \mathcal{L}_{\theta,q_3} & \mathcal{L}_{q_3,q_3}\end{array}\right]\left[\begin{array}{ccc}\mathbf{\Psi} & \theta & q_3\end{array}\right]^T = \partial_{\tilde{z}}q_3. \tag{20}$$

Equations (19), (8), and (20) can be cast into the desired diagonalized equation (the $\mathcal{D}-$form)

$$\mathcal{L}\left[\begin{array}{ccc}\mathbf{\Psi} & \theta & q_3\end{array}\right]^T = \partial_{\tilde{z}}\left[\begin{array}{ccc}\mathbf{\Psi} & \theta & q_3\end{array}\right]^T. \tag{21}$$

Next consider (18) which expresses $\mathbf{\Phi}$ in terms of $\mathbf{\Psi}$ and θ. Furthermore, consider (10) which expresses q_1 and q_2 in terms of θ and q_3. Combining (18) with (10) the supplementary equation (the $\mathcal{S}-$form)

$$\left[\begin{array}{ccc}\mathbf{\Phi} & q_1 & q_2\end{array}\right]^T = \mathcal{A}\left[\begin{array}{ccc}\mathbf{\Psi} & \theta & q_3\end{array}\right], \tag{22}$$

associated with the diagonalized form, Eq. (21), can be obtained.

III. Conclusions

For obtaining the $\mathcal{D}-$ and the associated $\mathcal{S}$ forms in inhomogeneous and fully tri-anisotropic media the only conditions required were the existence of the inverse $\mathbf{M}^{-1}$; i.e., the conditions $\varepsilon_{ii}\mu_{ii} - \xi_{ii}\zeta_{ii} \neq 0$, in addition to the conditions $\kappa_{ii} \neq 0$ $(i = 1,2,3)$. The latter conditions are trivially satisfied in virtue of the positive definiteness property of $\boldsymbol{\kappa}^{3\times3}$.

Acknowledgments

Support and generous hospitality by Professor Tao Zhang and his research group at Xi'an University of Science and Technology (XUST), and partial support from University of Cape Town are gratefully acknowledged. The Author is currently on sabbatical with XUST.

References

[1] A. R. Baghai-Wadji, *A Symbolic Procedure for the Diagonalization of Linear PDEs in Accelerated Computational Engineering*, Symbolic and Numerical Scientific Computing, pp. 347-360, Franz Winkler and Ulrich Langer (Eds.), Springer- Verlag Heidelberg, LNCS 2630, 2003.

[2] A. R. Baghai-Wadji, *3D Diagonalization and Supplementation in Thermo-Elasto-Electro-Magnetics: Proof of Existence by Construction & Validation of Relative Consistency*, in the proceedings ICEAA, Verona, 2017.

A Study of SAR on Child Passengers and Driver Due to Cellphone Connectivity Within Vehicle

M. Lyell
Graduate Student, ECE Dept.
Oakland University
Rochester, MI USA
mjlyell@oakland.edu

Daniel Aloi
Professor and Chair, ECE Dept.
Oakland University
Rochester, MI USA
aloi@oakland.edu

***Abstract*—In this work, SAR values in passenger head and body regions due to the presence of one or more cellphones were determined via simulation for the situation in which all vehicle passengers are children. Additionally, the adult driver has access to a hands free cellphone as part of increased in-vehicle connectivity.**

Keywords—cellphones, In-vehicle connectivity, RF, SAR

I. Introduction

Potential adverse impacts to health due to tissue heating [1] can result from radio frequency (RF) emissions. Such emissions are becoming more ubiquitous, due to the prevalence of cellphones, connected devices and increased expectations of connectivity, e.g., within a vehicle. SAR is defined as:

$$\mathrm{SAR} = (\sigma / \rho)\,|E|^2, \qquad (1)$$

where σ is the tissue conductivity (S/m), ρ is the tissue mass density (Kg/m^3) and E is the (rms) Electric field (v) in the tissue. Limits on the SAR values (in W/kg) allowable have been set by various jurisdictions; e.g., in the United States, this limit is 1.6 W/kg. A standard SAR value of interest is the spatial peak SAR averaged over 1 gram of tissue.

It is known that SAR values for the same level of RF can be larger in a child's brain tissue (due to increased conductivity in the brain tissue) as contrasted with that of an adult [2, 3]. Gender differences also exist; this work utilizes a male child model at ten years old, in the fiftieth percentile of growth.

An initial study [4] on the level of SAR in a vehicle from cellphones involved a driver and adult passengers; a subset of whom utilized a cellphone at frequency 900 MHz. This study was extended [5] to higher frequencies. ***Our work considers*** an in-vehicle scenario in which a*ll passengers are children*, each with a cellphone, and the *adult driver has the option of using a 'hands-free' cellphone*.

The paper is organized as follows. Section II presents relevant models used in the FEKO simulation environment with the Method of Moments (MOM) technique. Section III provides (spatial) peak SAR results (head and body) of vehicle occupants for different cases of passenger loading. Conclusions are noted in Section IV.

II. Model Development

A. Adult 'Driver' Model and Child 'Passenger' Models

The shape properties for the adult driver model are (1) a sphere for the head and (2) parallelepipeds for the torso, right and left lap and right and left legs. The adult model, shown in Fig. 1, utilizes dimensions from [4, 5]. Adult dimensions include: brain radius, 0.1 m and height from bottom of leg to center of head, 0.94 m. Neither brain nor body are modeled with any internal structure, following [4, 5].

Ibrani et al. [3] state that a child's head size phantom is eighty percent of an adult phantom, for children between seven and ten years old. Child body height is approximately seventy percent of an adult's height [2]. The ten year old male child's dimensions are: brain radius, 0.08 m and height from bottom of the leg to center of brain, 0.668 m.

Permittivity(ε_r) and conductivity (σ) values differ between adult and child models and are frequency dependent. Our simulations use 900 MHz frequency. For adult brain tissue, ε_r = 45.81 and σ = 0.77 S/m. For adult muscle tissue, ε_r = 55.96 and σ = 0.97 S/m. In child brain tissue, ε_r = 56.01 and σ = 1.00 S/m. In child muscle tissue, ε_r = 58.01 and σ = 0.99 S/m.

B. Cellphone Model

The cellphone model used is that of a (λ/4) monopole antenna radiating at frequency 900 MHz, also used in [4], [5]. The S1,1 parameter value, with resonant frequency at 900

MHz, is less than -25 dB. Antenna length is 108.3 mm. Antenna ground plane is 40 mm length and 20 mm width.

C. Vehicle Model

Fig. 2 shows the vehicle structure used in [4], modified for use in this work. Red lines show the modifications; these make the vehicle much boxier. The windscreen is now flat above the metal front bottom. Side windows are rectangular; additional roof surface adjacent to side windows is now glass. This results in 1 m^2 more glass instead of metal in the front part of the roof. Note coordinate directions in Fig. 2. Vehicle components are aluminum and untreated glass. Permittivity and conductivity values are found in [4].

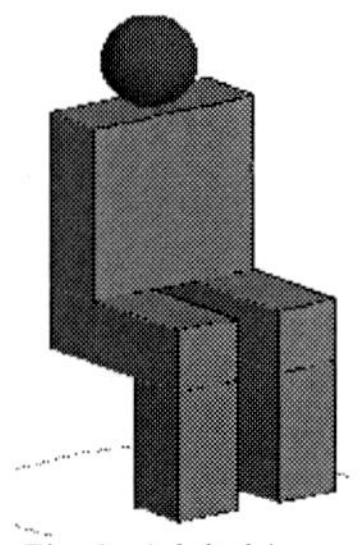

Fig. 1. Adult driver model.

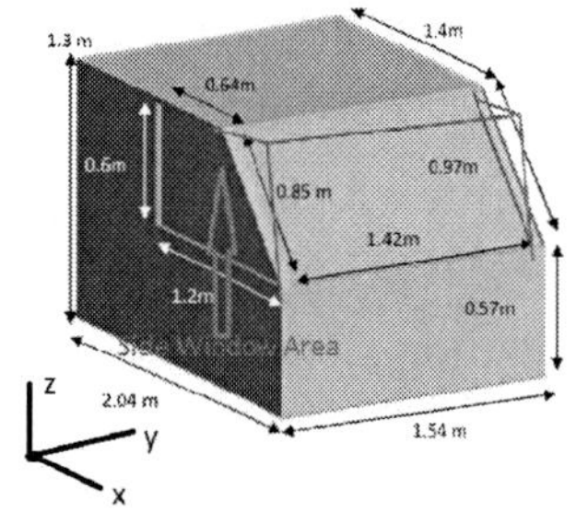

Fig. 2 Boxy vehicle superimposed on vehicle from [4]. Red lines show shape used in current study.

D. Passengers, Driver and Cellphones Placed in Vehicle

Fig. 3(a) shows passenger layout (as in [4]). Rear seat passengers (with cellphones) have their torsos' back edge at x=0.167 m; front seat passenger's and driver's are at x=0.883 m. Fig. 3(b) shows driver; the front windscreen is x=0.75m beyond the driver's front edge. Note the hands free antenna.

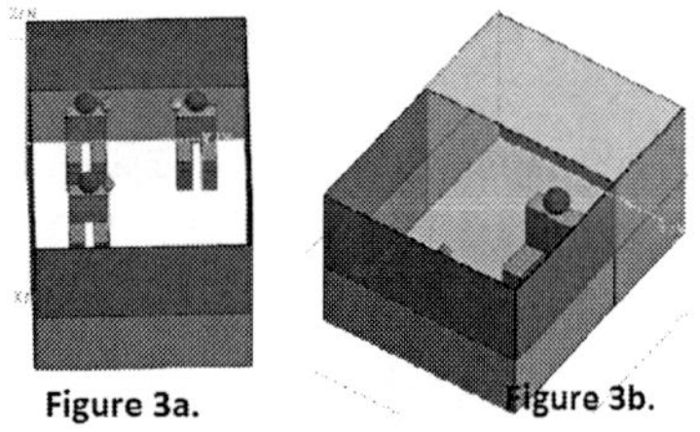

Fig. 3. In 3(a), Three child passengers, each with cellphone (monopole). In 3(b), Adult driver and hands free antenna (red dot).

III. Simulation Results: Spatial Peak SAR Values

Peak spatial SAR results for eleven different simulations are given in Table 1. Total power in each sim run is 1.6 W. In understanding these results, note that Case 1 has one cellphone using 1.6W power; all SAR is due to one high powered phone.

Note that RF reflection occurs off the vehicle's metal panels and that rear seat children's bodies are close to the vehicle's rear metal panels. When passenger loading includes children in the rear seat, such children usually have the larger body SAR and that their body SAR is greater than the head SAR.

TABLE I. SAR Simulation Results

KEY: D= Driver, RF= Right Front Child, RB= Right Back Child, LB= Left Back Child, MHS = Max Head SAR (W/Kg), MBS = Max Body SAR (W/Kg), WHS=Person with Max Head SAR, WBS =Person with Max Body SAR.
Hands free cellphone is *not* used in cases 1, 2, 9 and 11.

	D	RF	RB	LB	MHS	WHS	MBS	WBS
1		X			0.845	RF	1.728	RF
2				X	0.914	LB	1.170	LB
3	X				0.015	DR	0.105	DR
4	X			X	0.596	LB	0.165	LB
5	X		X	X	0.32	LB, RB	0.573	LB
6	X		X		0.607	RB	0.843	RB
7	X	X		X	0.337	RF	0.563	LB
8	X	X			1.012	RF	1.272	RF
9	X	X		X	0.471	RB	0.755	RF
10	X	X	X		0.377	RB	0.622	RB
11				X	0.900	LB	1.148	LB

Note that driver's head SAR is roughly an order of magnitude less than body SAR. In Sim4 (hands-free antenna), body SAR is 0.105 W/kg and head SAR is 0.014 W/kg.

IV. Conclusions

This work, part of a larger effort investigating SAR in vehicle occupants when devices are in use, provides SAR results for child (and driver) head and body regions. The hands free option offers *increased in-vehicle connectivity.* Physical reflection also contributes to SAR; as metal surface area was decreased by 1 m^2 relative to [4], reflections will be reduced.

References

[1] Specific Absorption Rate for Cellular Telephones, US Federal Communications Agency, https://www.fcc.gov/general/specific-absorption-rate-sar-cellular-telephones. [Accessed 10-11-17].

[2] M. Ibrani, L. Ahma, E. Hamiti, and J. Haxhibeqiri, "Derivation of electromagnetic properties of child biological tissues at radio frequencies", Prog. Electromagnetics Research Letters, vol. 25, pp. 87 - 100, 2011.

[3] M. Ibrani, L. Ahma and E. Hamiti, "Comparative SAR assessment in adults and children exposed to electromagnetic fields of radio frequency devices", WSEAS Trans. on Communications, Issue 2, Vol. 9, 2010.

[4] K.H. Chan, S. W. Leung, Y.M. Siu, "Specific Absorption Rate Evaluation for People Using Wireless Communication Device in Vehicle", IEEE Paper 978-1-4244-6307-7, 2010.

[5] Y. Diao, W.N. Sun, K.H. Chan, S.W. Leung, Y.M. Siu, "Specific Absorption Rate for People using Wireless Communication Devices in Vehicle", Proceedings of the 2013 International Symposium on Electromagnetic Theory, IEICE.

Reduction of Coupling between Flush-Mounted Antennas

Prathap Valale Prasannakumar, Mohamed A. Elmansouri, Maxim Ignatenko, and Dejan Filipovic
Department of Electrical, Computer, and Energy Engineering
University of Colorado, Boulder
Boulder, Colorado, USA, 80309
{Prathap.Valaleprasannakumar, Mohamed.Elmansouri, Maxim.Ignatenko, and Dejan.Filipovic}@colorado.edu

***Abstract*—This paper discusses some numerical aspects of the coupling study between two flush-mounted antennas. It is shown that a bed of nails embedded between flush-mounted quad-ridge horns separated by 20 cm ($4\lambda_{6\ GHz}$) edge-to-edge greatly reduces coupling by about 17 dB at lower frequency end, where the electrical distance between antennas is the shortest. The considered antenna system operates from 6-19 GHz and has $|S_{11}|$ < -10 dB, and coupling < -60 dB. The numerical modelling is carried out using MoM and FEM solvers. The computed results are in good agreement with measurements.**

Keywords*—*Bed of nails, coupling, method of moments.

I. Introduction

Coupling between antennas sharing common platform is a critical parameter in the design of in-band full duplex systems. Often, coupling < -60 dB (or isolation > 60 dB) is desired from the antenna layer itself to achieve total system isolation in the order of 110-140 dB [1]. Minimizing the coupling for an electrically-short separation between transmitter (TX) and receiver (RX) is a challenging task. Various techniques to improve the antenna layer isolation are considered in open literature including recessing the RX antenna in absorber, the use of band-gap structures, and the implementation of high impedance surfaces (HIS) [2,3]. High impedance surfaces (capacitive or inductive) can be implemented over an octave bandwidth by means of a bed of nails [4,5]. The practical realization and fabrication of these structures are relatively easy and cost effective. However, numerical modelling and solving of the bed of nails (312 nails/unit cells in this paper) requires intricate meshing and thereby, considerable computational resources. Moreover, computation of the expected low level of coupling can be challenging because of high required accuracy. Further, the reflections from absorbing/radiation boundaries could influence the calculation of low level of coupling, when finite element method (FEM) solvers are used. In this work, coupling between two quad-ridge horns operating in 6-19 GHz is considered using commercially available method of moment (MoM) solver – Altair FEKO. In spite of numerical challenges, good agreement between measurements and simulated results is achieved. It is demonstrated that 17 dB reduction in coupling can be obtained by embedding bed of nails between the antennas separated 20 cm edge-to-edge.

This work is supported by the Office of Naval Research (ONR) # N00173-15-C-2021.

II. Antennas Coupling Mechanism

Radiation is the main path of coupling between two co-located antennas in free space. Hence, the coupling is proportional to the gain in the direction between the antennas. When the antennas are flush mounted on a metallic ground plane, surface currents provide an additional path for coupling. Specifically, when two WR90 (X-band) open-ended waveguides (OWG) oriented in **E**-plane are flush mounted on a metallic ground plane, the coupling due to surface currents alone is approximately 10% of the total coupling at 8 GHz, as shown in the Fig. 1. This coupling is calculated in FEKO using currents on the ground plane as a source of the received power at the RX aperture. Suppressing these currents will reduce coupling. It should be noted that manipulating the surface currents will also affect the electromagnetic waves above the surface, and thus much stronger than 10% impact on coupling is expected.

The predominant E_z amplitude at the surface in the E-plane of the antennas (x-axis in Fig. 2) is in accordance with the study in [3] that TM waves are supported over a metal with finite conductivity. TM surface waves have capacitive wave impedance, and hence a capacitive surface will inhibit its propagation. Desired capacitive impedance is realized by using $\lambda/4$ (at 8 GHz) grounded metallic nails arranged in double-periodic structure [4]. To reduce computational requirements, pins are modeled as wire segments of radius 1 mm in FEKO. As seen in Fig. 2 (d), the bed of nails reduces E_z at the RX aperture by 18 dB. This clearly demonstrates that the bed of nails can be effectively used to reduce coupling between flush-mounted antennas, as further discussed in Section III. The CAD model of the bed of nails consisting of 0.93cm ($\lambda_{8\ GHz}/4$) long metallic pins is shown in Fig. 2 (b).

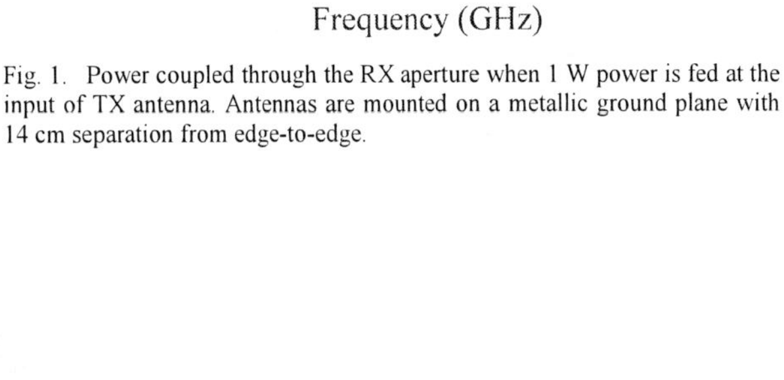

Fig. 1. Power coupled through the RX aperture when 1 W power is fed at the input of TX antenna. Antennas are mounted on a metallic ground plane with 14 cm separation from edge-to-edge.

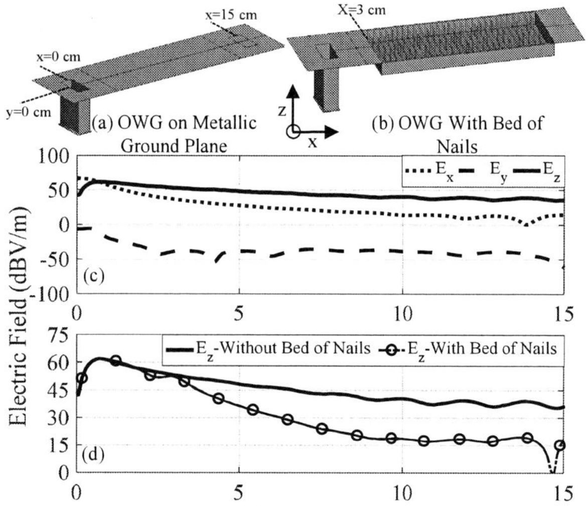

Fig. 2. CAD model of open ended waveguide flush mounted on: (a) metallic ground plane, and (b) with bed of nails. Magnitude of electric field components over the ground plane: (c) without, and (d) with bed of nails at 8 GHz.

III. Flush-Mounted Quad-Ridge Horns

The considered quad-ridge horn (QRH) antenna supports dual-polarization operation, and can handle high power [5]. Impedance match of the antenna is a crucial parameter for high power applications. Therefore, to reduce the reflections from the aperture, the ridges of the horn are shaped as a Klopfenstein taper. Moreover, the edges of the horn aperture and the ridges are rolled into semielliptical shape to reduce the reflections resulting from the edge diffraction. The designed horn is 8cm long and has an aperture of 3 cm × 3 cm. FEM and MoM hybridization supported by FEKO is used in order to excite quad-ridge waveguide cross-section. Adaptive mesh shown by green bubbles in the inset of Fig. 3 was found to be critical for achieving good accuracy. The antenna has reflection coefficient ($|S_{11}|$) < -10 dB (< -20 dB for 94% of the bandwidth) when fed at the quad ridge section (see Fig. 3 (a)). The designed quad-ridge to double-ridge transition used in measurements has $|S_{11}|$ < -10 dB over 98% of bandwidth. Good agreement between simulation and measurement is observed.

The QRHs are flush mounted on a metallic ground plane of size 13 cm × 38 cm (Fig. 4 (a)), which corresponds to 8 λ_{19GHz} × 24 λ_{19GHz}. Also, QRH with the transition is about 10λ_{19GHz} in z-axis which results in a computationally-large problem. The system has coupling < -40 dB at 6 GHz over a metallic ground plane and < -60 dB when the proposed bed of nails is embedded between the antennas oriented 45° to each other, as seen from Figs. 4 (b) and (c). Good agreement between the measured and simulated results highlights the ability and accuracy of numerical solvers in handling complex and electrically-large problems. The model solved using MoM in FEKO, meshed at 19 GHz, has 51,616 triangles, 758 FEM surface triangles, 624 metallic segments, and 28,658 tetrahedral.

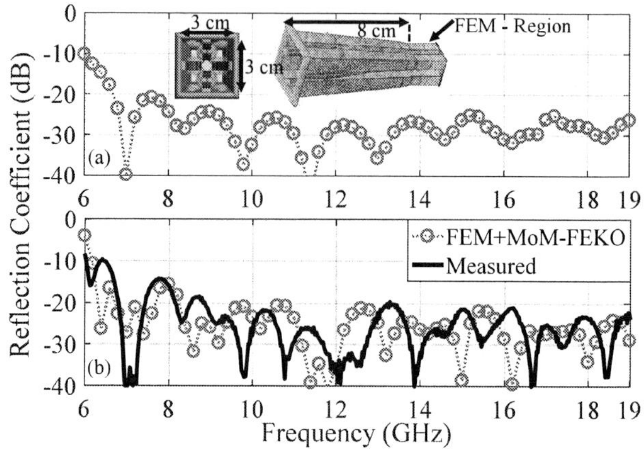

Fig. 3. Reflection coefficient of quad-ridge horn: (a) fed at the input of quad-ridge section (simulated results), and (b) fed using quad ridge to double ridge section (FEKO, and measured results).

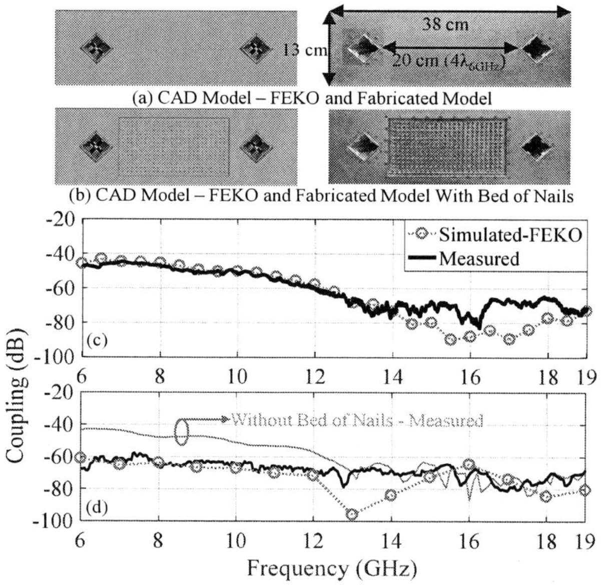

Fig. 4. CAD and fabricated models of QRH over metallic ground plane: (a) without and (b) with bed of nails. Simulated and measured coupling: (c) without and (d) with bed of nails.

References

[1] D. Bharadia, E. McMilin, and S. Katti, "Full duplex radios," Proc. SIGCOMM'13 Conf., China, pp. 375-386, 2013.

[2] J. A. M. Lyon, C. J. Digenis, W. W. Parker, and M. A. H. Ibrahim, "Electromagnetic coupling reduction techniques," The University of Michigan, Ann Arbor, MI, USA, AFAL-TR-68-132, June 1968. Available: https://deepblue.lib.umich.edu/handle/2027.42/6402

[3] D. Sievenpiper, "High-impedance electromagnetic surfaces," Ph.D. dissertation, Dept. Elect. Eng., Uni. California, Los Angeles, CA, 1999.

[4] R. J. King and K. S. Park, "Synthesis of surface reactances using grounded pin bed structure," in Electronics Letters, vol. 17, no. 1, pp. 52-53, Jan. 1981.

[5] P. Valale Prasannakumar, M. A. Elmansouri, and D. S. Filipovic, "Wideband decoupling techniques for dual-polarized bi-static simultaneous transmit and receive antenna subsystem," in IEEE Trans. Antennas and Propag., vol. 65, no. 10, pp. 4991-5001, Oct. 2017.

Review of Selected New Features in FEKO 2018

Ulrich Jakobus, Andrés Aguilar, and Elia Attardo
Altair Engineering GmbH
Böblingen, Germany
jakobus@altair.com, aguilar@altair.de,
attardo@altair.de

Marlize Schoeman and Johann van Tonder
Altair Development S.A. (Pty) Ltd
Stellenbosch, South Africa
schoeman@altair.co.za,
jvtonder@altair.co.za

Kitty Longtin
Altair Engineering, Inc.
Hampton, VA, USA
klongtin@altair.com

***Abstract*—This paper describes new features to the electromagnetic simulation software FEKO as introduced in the FEKO 2018 version. These include the GPU support for the RL-GO (ray launching geometrical optics) solver, a direct solver for ACA (adaptive cross approximation), and various cable modeling extensions.**

***Keywords*—ACA, cable harness, FEKO, GPU, RL-GO.**

I. Introduction

For many years, FEKO [1] has been a popular CEM code widely used for academic research and commercial applications. Its applicability and efficiency are continuously being extended through annual major releases with quarterly feature updates in-between. Here in this paper we review some selected new features of the CEM solver in the FEKO 2018 release.

II. GPU-based Acceleration of RL-GO

RL-GO (sometimes also referred to as SBR = shooting and bouncing rays) is an asymptotic high frequency technique very suitable for electrically large PEC and dielectric objects with multiple reflections. In general, ray tracing techniques perfectly fit the requirements of exploiting a high degree of parallelism. For that reason, GPUs are the best candidate in addressing that challenge and provide significant acceleration over the sequential implementation of the RL-GO method.

The ray-geometry intersection test is the most computationally demanding phase of the RL-GO algorithm. In this paper we present preliminary results on the GPU acceleration of these ray-geometry intersection tests. The model under test is depicted in Fig. 1. A linearly polarized plane wave is used as an excitation. The ship is discretized into 6 000 flat triangles, and for the speed test, 100 million rays have been created. The information relative to the rays (origins, and directions) jointly with the geometry description of the model (vertices of the triangles, and normal to each triangle) are transferred from CPU to the GPU device. The ray-geometry test consists of determining if a ray hits the geometry or not. For comparison, the test is performed on both CPU and GPU. On the GPU, CUDA kernels have been designed to fully exploit the parallelism of the device for the ray-geometry intersection tests. The time for the ray geometry intersection tests is 6 844 msec on an Intel E5-2650 2 GHz CPU, while on an NVIDIA K20 GPU this can be reduced to 923 msec (speedup factor 7.4).

Accelerating the remaining RL-GO solution phases beyond the ray-geometry intersection tests is planned for the future. This will further increase the solution speed on GPU.

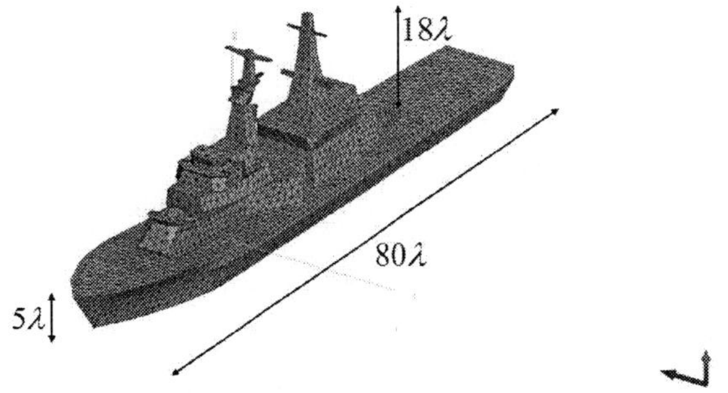

Fig. 1. Ship model used in the ray-geometry intersection tests of RL-GO. The ship is discretized with 6 000 flat triangles.

III. Direct ACA Matrix Solver

The ACA available in FEKO is a well-known technique for approximating a large dense matrix, such as a Method of Moments (MoM) matrix, with a so-called H-matrix. The H-matrix represents low-rank blocks of size N x M of the original matrix as products of two matrices, one of size N x k and one of size k x M, where k is the rank of the original block. When k is small this representation dramatically reduces the memory required to store the approximation to the original matrix.

The resulting H-matrix approximation of the original matrix, however, cannot be solved with the direct methods generally used with MoM matrices. In the final paper we will present results for the memory usage and speed for a direct ACA solver, based on [2], complementing FEKO's iterative ACA solver (final optimizations in progress at the time of the submission). A benefit of the direct ACA solver compared with iterative methods is that the direct solver does not require a preconditioner and so uses approximately as much memory as is required by the H-matrix to be solved, since the solution is done "in place", and that it offers superior efficiency when multiple right-hand sides must be solved for, e.g., for monostatic RCS problems or S-parameter calculations.

IV. Cable Harness Modeling

FEKO supports the solution of coupled EM field / cable harness problems, where the cable harness solver is based on MTL (Multiconductor Transmission Line) theory for both radiation and irradiation problems. Cables play such a dominant role in modern systems that the FEKO cable harness solver is being improved continuously. In the following sections three extensions are discussed.

A. Speed Improvements

Two of the dominant phases in the cable harness calculation were optimized:

- An efficient dense to sparse matrix conversion and solution of the associated linear system with a multifrontal direct solver was applied to the 2D FEM Laplace solver for calculating the cable per-unit-length parameters.
- FEKO now use Altair's superfast HyperSpice circuit solver. Table I illustrates the speedup obtained for solving the MTL circuit of three typical cable cross sections using HyperSpice as compared to ngspice.

TABLE I. HyperSpice Speedup Factor Solving Three MTL Models Compared to ngspice

	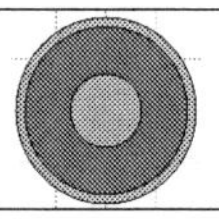	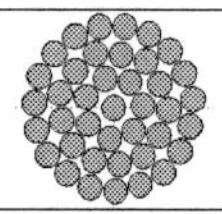	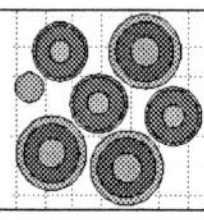
No. of segments	485	151	500
No. of nodes	7 277	30 252	52 027
No. of components	13 591	395 833	152 535
Speedup factor	1 666	62	1 985

B. Irradiation Coupling with Finite Difference Time Domain

The ability to compute electromagnetic fields is one of the key aspects in modeling irradiation coupling into cables in a complex environment. In FEKO this is described by the Taylor approach [3]. The cable harness solver was traditionally hybridized only with the MoM, but has been extended to FDTD (Finite Difference Time Domain). The benefit of using the FDTD as field solver is illustrated for a typical broadband EMC problem from the automotive industry.

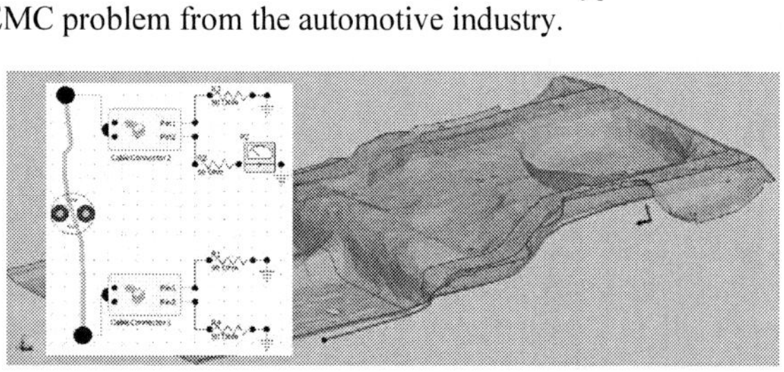

Fig. 2. PEC ground plane with harness routed along the bottom of chassis.

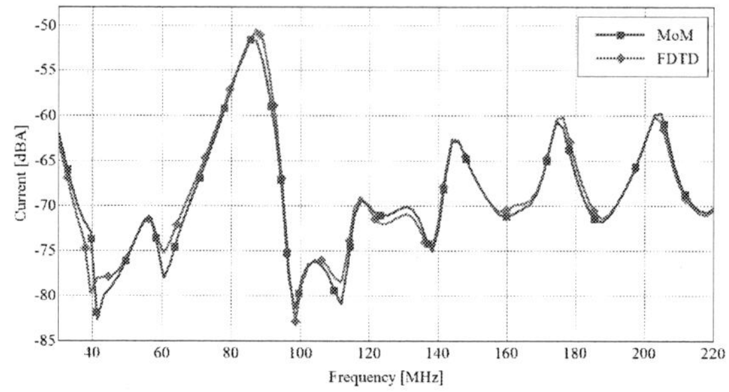

Fig. 3. Comparison of MoM and FDTD irradiating coupling responses.

In Fig. 2 a PEC ground plane with a twisted wire pair routed along the bottom of a car chassis is excited by a plane wave. In Fig. 3 the current measured through a terminating load is compared using either the MoM or the FDTD as field solvers. For 101 frequency samples evaluated between 30 MHz and 220 MHz, the MoM solution needed 10 parallel processes to complete within one hour, while the FDTD solution ran sequentially on a GPU in only half an hour.

C. MTL Current Return Reference Conductor

The currents that are modeled by the MTL equations are assumed to be differential mode or transmission line currents. This means that currents always need to return on a reference conductor, which implies that the harness must be installed nearby to a conducting surface that could act as such a return reference. In practice, harnesses do not always run close to a conducting surface. FEKO introduced earlier the Combined MoM/MTL method to relax this condition, and this was now further relaxed for cross sections consisting of multiple (unshielded) conductors. In Fig. 4 a two-wire cable is excited by a plane wave. The full MoM solution is compared to the MTL solution showing good agreement.

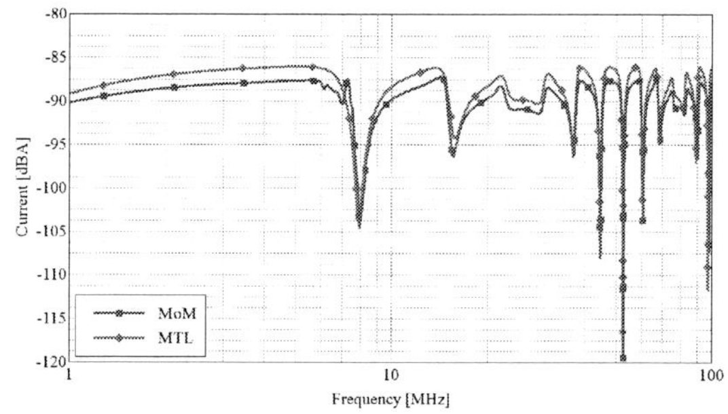

Fig. 4. Comparison of MoM and MTL responses without nearby ground.

References

[1] FEKO, Altair Engineering, Inc., www.hyperworks.com/feko

[2] S. Borm, L. Grasedyck. and W. Hackbusch, Hierarchical Matrices, Max-Planck-Institut fuer Mathematik in den Naturwissenschaften, Leipzig, Germany, 2003.

[3] C. D. Taylor, R. S. Satterwhite, and C. W. Harrison, Jr., "The response of a terminated two-wire transmission line excited by a nonuniform electromagnetic field," IEEE Transactions on Antennas and Propagation, vol. AP-13, no. 6, pp. 987-989, Nov. 1965

FEKO™ Modeling Study of Passive UHF RFID Tags Embedded in Pavement

Sourabh R. Walvekar and Robert J. Burkholder
The Ohio State University ElectroScience Lab
Dept. of Electrical and Computer Engineering
Columbus, U. S. A.
sourabh.w@somaiya.edu, burkholder.1@osu.edu

***Abstract*—Radio frequency identification (RFID) is investigated as a technology that may be useful for smart cars and autonomous vehicles to read information about local road conditions and geographic location. Passive UHF RFID tags can transmit this data wirelessly to an RFID reader mounted on the vehicle. Coupling between a tag that is on or embedded in pavement, and the reader antenna mounted on the vehicles, is investigated by simulating the tag antenna, reader antenna and local environment in FEKO™. Preliminary simulation results show that it is feasible to implement such a system such that a vehicle traveling up to 200 km/hr. can read the tags as it passes over them.**

Keywords* — *antennas, autonomous cars, navigation, propagation, RFID.

I. Introduction

We are close to the days when our cars will become completely autonomous and will not require human input for navigation. GPS is used to get geographical co-ordinates of the current location, and is the primary navigational guidance system for autonomous or self-driving cars, aided by local visual cues and vehicular radar. However, it is difficult to receive GPS signals in tunnels or in "urban canyons" surrounded by high-rises and construction [1]. The vehicle not knowing its precise geographical location and direction of travel for a brief moment of time can be dangerous. During these times RFID tags embedded into the road can provide the vehicle with specific data about the location. Another problem autonomous cars have to deal with is the presence of temporary construction sites on roads. Signs are sufficient for a human driver to take a different path to avoid the area, but may not be sufficient for autonomous cars to make a navigation decision. Even though these cars can recognize road signs using various sensors, any distortion of the signs caused by weather, wear-and-tear, tampering, etc., can put these cars into confusion. Human intervention is still required to maneuver the car in such situations.

Existing RFID technology can help vehicles obtain more information about the local environment. RFID tags can be embedded on the surface of the road or under the first layer of pavement, and the vehicles passing above them with an RFID reader can interrogate the tags and download the information embedded on the tag or associated with the tag ID number. Certain information can be stored directly in the RFID tag's chip, but as discussed in [1], if this is not enough we can rely on a database system where the data can be retrieved via cellular communication from a database which will have a list of tag IDs and their corresponding data. The advantage of this system is that the data may be updated as road conditions or construction areas change.

The two key issues to be investigated to make a passive UHF RFID system for roads feasible are: 1) read range, and 2) time to read the tag. RFID chips take time to communicate with the reader and this puts a constraint on the speed of the vehicle trying to read the information from the tag. The read range is important because a longer read range means the reader will have more time to communicate with a given tag. These two interdependent issues are investigated here using Altair's FEKO™ computational electromagnetics simulation software.

Section II describes the simulation setup and assumptions made, including information on the reader antenna, the tag antenna, their orientation, and the electrical characteristics of the materials used for simulating the pavement. Section III presents the results obtained from the simulation study and Section IV discusses conclusions on the feasibility of and RFID road system. It also discusses the limitations of the current simulations and proposes future work for improving the simulations and implementation of the system.

II. Simulation Setup

Fig. 1 shows the geometry of a linearly polarized rectangular patch antenna for 915 MHz used as the reader antenna. It is excited by a wire port in FEKO. Most commercially available UHF passive RFID tag antennas have a dipole-like structure and a dipole like gain pattern, hence a small wire dipole antenna matched at 915 MHz is used in the simulations to represent an RFID tag. A single layer 22 cm thick dielectric is used to model the road. Concrete and asphalt roads are chosen for the simulations. The concrete is chosen from the media library of FEKO. The electrical characteristics of asphalt are chosen as follows: permittivity = 6, conductivity = 10^{-4} S/m, and mass density = 2322 kg/m^3 [2]. These parameters represent dry asphalt. The reader antenna facing downward is kept 35 cm above the road. Simulations were performed for tags on the surface and embedded 3 cm into the road. The dipole antenna is oriented to match the polarization of the patch antenna (X-polarized in Fig. 1). Each antenna has a port assigned. The patch antenna is the active port with 1 W of radiated power.

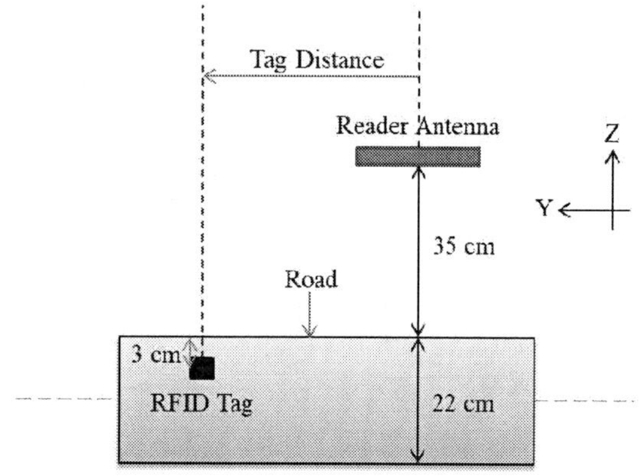

Fig. 1. Side view of the simulation setup. The pavement is infinite in the X and Y directions. The RFID tag antenna and reader antenna are linearly polarized in the X direction.

III. RESULTS

For successful communication between the tag and the reader, a certain amount of RF power must be delivered to the passive RFID tag by the reader antenna. The threshold power for activating the chip is usually specified in the data sheet. For the Impinj Monza 2 RFID chip it is -11.5 dBm (decibels relative to a mW). 1 W of power is fed into the reader antenna, hence the S_{21} between the two ports of the antennas, the wire dipole and the patch antenna, tells us the amount of power received by the wire dipole representing the RFID tag. It is noted that normally the tag antenna is matched to the impedance of the RFID chip, but that is not necessary for the power transfer computations presented here. The tag is moved horizontally away from the reader antenna along the Y-axis in steps of 10 cm. The corresponding S_{21} is computed. The distance where the power reaching the tag falls below the -11.5 dBm threshold is important because this is where the chip will not be activated. Multiplying this distance by two (symmetry on both sides of the Z-axis) gives us the total length of the zone over which the reader can successfully communicate with the tag (because in this zone it is able to deliver sufficient power to the chip for communication). The power delivered to the tag as a function of the Y-distance is plotted in Fig. 2.

According to Chon et al. [1], for successful communication between a tag and a reader, 18 ms are required for transferring 128 bits of data (such as the tag ID number). So the tag and the reader have to be in communication range for at least 18 ms. If we consider a vehicle travelling at 200 km/hr., then in 18 ms it travels 1 m. So the range over which the reader transfers threshold power to the tag should be at least 1 m. We can calculate the communication range for each scenario plotted in Fig. 2 by multiplying by two the distance where the power reaching the tag goes below -11.5 dBm. For example, the communication zone for a tag embedded 3 cm below the concrete pavement is 2 times 50.76, or 101.52 cm. Since this is more than 1 m, all the vehicles travelling at speeds up to 200 km/hr. should be able to successfully communicate with the tags on the road. The communication ranges for the other cases are higher than the one we considered above since the threshold power reaching the tag goes below -11.5 dBm over a greater distance than 50.76 cm. Hence, vehicles travelling at speeds up to 200 km/hr. will certainly be able to communicate with the tags embedded in the roads under the assumed conditions.

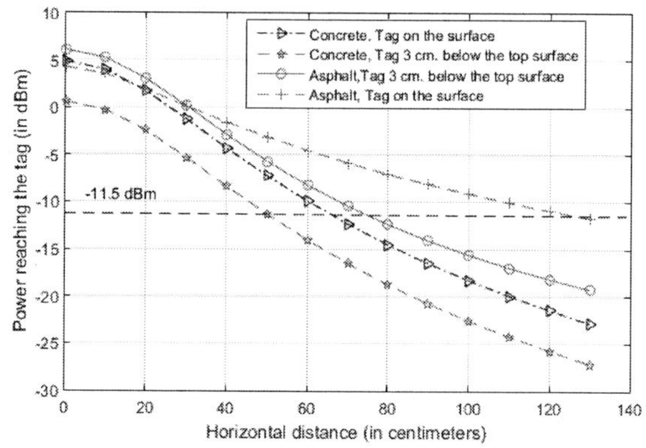

Fig. 2. Power received by the tag antenna as a function of the horizontal distance from the reader antenna for tags on or inside concrete and asphalt pavement. The threshold power of -11.5 dBm is required to activate the RFID chip.

IV. CONCLUSION

Preliminary simulations show that implementing a passive UHF RFID system for concrete or dry asphalt pavement is feasible. The vehicle will not always travel directly over the tag, so more than one reader antenna should be used to make sure that the reader doesn't miss any. Multiple reader antennas are typically connected to a single reader to provide spatial diversity in UHF RFID systems. Placement of these extra antennas will be investigated in the future, as well as various positions and orientations of the tags on the roads. Most importantly, rain, ice and snow will most certainly affect the communication range of the tag and the reader. Therefore, these conditions should be carefully studied in future simulations and experiments.

REFERENCES

[1] H. Chon, S. Jun, H. Jung, and S. An, "Using RFID for accurate positioning," Journal of Global Positioning Systems, vol. 3, no. 1-2, pp. 32-39, 2004.

[2] O. Franek, P. Kyritsi, and G. F. Pedersen, "RFID on the road – some considerations about passive tag antennas," in Proc. 5th EuCAP, Rome, Italy, pp. 1203–1207, Apr. 2011.

The Application of Design of Experiments to RF Systems

Scott Burnside
Northrop Grumman Mission Systems
Sacramento, United States
s.burnside@ieee.org

Abstract— **Design of Experiments (DOE) provides a methodical, consistent framework to execute design optimization and to determine which parameters have the most impact on system performance. The process performs multiple computations using a stepped-sampling of the selected parameters to perform a sensitivity analysis for each parameter. The DOE process can yield a parameter sensitivity ranking and a surrogate model of the design. In this article, the DOE approach is applied to a simple antenna design as an example. By using the approach of Design of Experiments, the designer can specify appropriate production tolerances or limits to achieve best performance at lowest cost.**

Keywords*— *antennas, computational electromagnetics, design of experiments, optimization

I. Introduction

THE Design of Experiments (DOE) approach provides a robust framework for the study of RF systems and antennas. It is a tool for data analysis or process analysis when the data or process is complex, non-linear and/or multivariate. In the field of Computational Electromagnetics (CEM) and non-linear RF system design, the problem being studied is often too complex for a basic regression analysis, and full-wave analysis is cumbersome to repeat. This is the kind of analysis for which Design of Experiments is a great tool.

The Design of Experiments started in agriculture with the work of Sir Ronald Fisher [1]. Current numerical tools have once again renewed interest in using DOE to improve analytical efficiency [2-6].

II. Overview of Design of Experiments

Design of Experiments presents a tool for multi-variable and multi-objective characterization and optimization. This is particularly useful for problems which are either stochastic (random processes), require complex or lengthy calculations, or data which is poorly understood or noisy. With DOE, we cast these problems into an algebraic problem by representing the response with a function. The function can take numerous inputs and provide an estimate of the response. This function is often thought of as a multi-dimensional surface function.

With the so-called surrogate function defined, determining an optimum value for the various input values is a much simpler and faster task. It can be carried out quickly using basic optimization techniques.

Design of Experiments comprises two categories: classical DOE, which is applied to stochastic data and processes; and modern DOE, which is applied to deterministic data and processes [6]. Stochastic processes have random variability in the outcome. In Deterministic processes, given a set of inputs, the response will be repeated. These are the problems of interest to us in RF and antenna analyses.

DOE reduces our complex analytic response to a calculation in the form of a polynomial. This polynomial can be a simple linear combination, a quadratic or higher order such as a cubic, and can include cross-variable coefficients, if needed. The order of the function is determined by the range of the input variables as well as the complexity of the response. Recall the concept of a multi-dimensional surface. With this in mind, if the surface is very complex with multiple ripples, as opposed to a simple surface, higher order coefficients will be required.

Using the DOE approach, this response surface is now characterized by a function which can be quickly optimized and calculated. In addition, the surrogate function can also provide a good intuitive understanding of the system behavior. Finally, the same function can be used to determine sensitivities to process and fabrication variations for the system, enabling the study of process yields and product quality.

III. Basic Approach to Design of Experiments

DOE for CEM begins with the model; the user identifies the design variables, and sets limits for each variable, based on the geometry of the design. Then a variable sampling approach is selected and sensitivity of output response to each of the variables is calculated. Variables that don't have a large impact on the response are dropped from further study.

Next, the 'fit' approach is selected, and the surrogate model is created. With the surrogate model, the engineer is able to optimize performance and to test production yield and sensitivities. These steps are well covered in the Altair Hyperstudy documentation [8].

For the engineer who would like to perform model design manually, or with personal code, the reader is referred to Lorenzen [2]. Lorenzen presents several algorithms for extracting Orthogonal Main Effect Designs for simple linear designs, interactive models (with cross-terms), as well as quadratic and higher-order polynomials.

IV. Example of DOE in CEM

An example is presented to illustrate the approach. It is a simple patch antenna with a tuning notch. Figure 1 shows the geometry of the layout for the patch antenna, including the mesh for the initial layout as entered into CEM software, FEKO™ [7].

For the example, the author picked some fairly generic

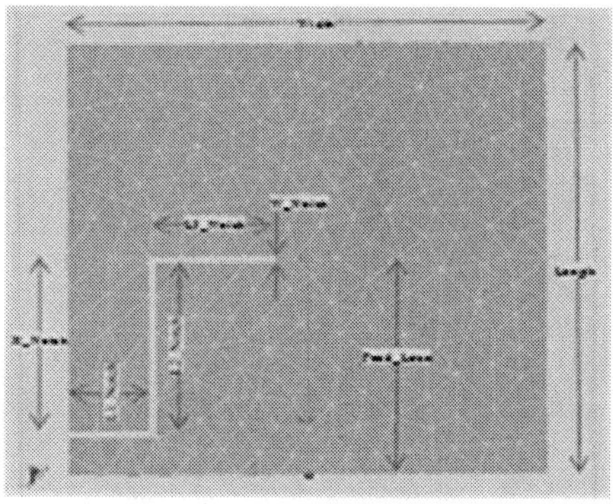

Figure 2 Example Patch Antenna

dimensions as a starting point, shown in Table I. As stated earlier, each dimension (variable), has a minimum value, an initial value, and a maximum value.

TABLE I. PATCH ANTENNA DESIGN VARIABLES

Factor	Var	Min (mm)	Initial (mm)	Max (mm)
Feed_Locn	dv_1	10.800	12.000	13.200
L1_notch	dv_2	5.000	14.000	38.000
L2_notch	dv_3	5.000	30.000	33.000
L3_notch	dv_4	5.000	20.000	35.000
W_notch	dv_5	0.9144	1.0160	2.0000
Width	dv_6	40.0000	60.000	81.400
X_notch	dv_7	9.1440	10.160	11.176
freq_hi	dv_8	2.70e+09	3.00e+09	3.30e+09
freq_lo	dv_9	1.80e+09	2.00e+09	2.20e+09
height	dv_10	1.37160	1.5240	1.6764
lambda	dv_11	89.9377	99.9308	109.923
length	dv_12	40.0000	80.000	88.000

Once the factor space is probed with DOE, we determine the sensitivity of the response to each of the factors. There are two graphical ways to present this result in a very concise way. Parametric sensitivity graphs and Pareto charts each provide a clear graphical understanding of variable sensitivity. Figure 2 is a parametric sensitivity graph for the example problem. For each factor, the extracted response sensitivity is plotted, showing the range of response values that result from the spread of factor values analyzed, with the slope of each line giving an indication of sensitivity of response to each a factors. The factors with the steepest slopes have the most impact on response.

Using the sensitivity information for each of the factors allows the engineer to know which factors should be kept in the further analysis, and which factors can be held constant. It may be judicious to assign those values according to manufacturability concerns and tolerances. Once those values are assigned and fixed, the DOE should be re-run with those values assigned. That should ensure the best model fit with the CEM analysis.

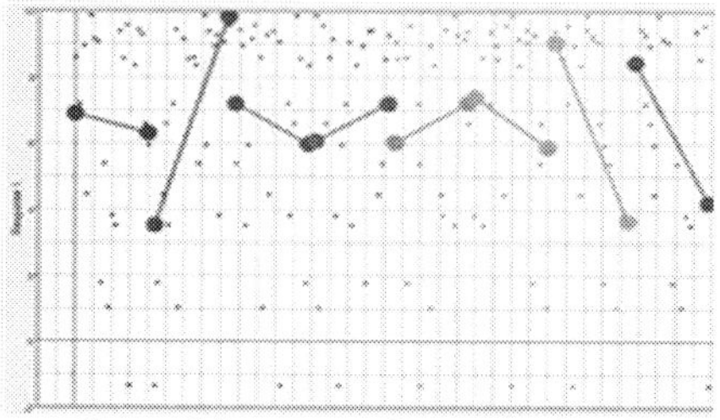

Figure 1 Parametric Sensitivity Graph

The next step in the DOE process is to perform the fit and check how check its quality against the CEM response. For the present example, Figure 3 shows a plot of DOE model response (vertical axis) to CEM analysis response (horizontal axis). Each point on the graph represents the response to a combination of the factors for each of the response approaches.

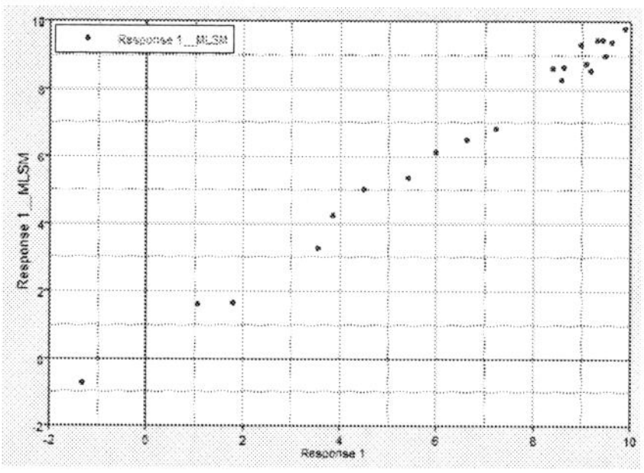

Figure 3 Correlation CEM to DOE Model

Finally, the surrogate model is optimized for performance; the optimum was found after 21 iterations, in only fractions of a second. CEM optimization took 294 calls and 106 minutes.

V. Conclusion

Design of Experiments offers a proven method for creating a surrogate mathematic model for a variety of applications. The method provides a powerful tool for characterization, understanding and optimization.

References

[1] R. A. Fisher, "The correlation between relatives on the supposition of Mendelian inheritance," in Transactions of the Royal Society of Edinburgh, 1918, pp. 399-433.

[2] T. J. Lorenzen, Design of experiments, a no-name approach. New York: Marcel Dekker, Inc., 1993.

[3] Y. Mack, T. Goel, W Shyy, and R. Haftka, "Surrogate model-based optimization framework: a case study in aerospace design," in Studies in Computational Intelligence, Heidelberg: Springer-Verlag, 2007.

[4] M. Cavazzuti, Design of experiments, in Optimization Methods: From Theory to Design. Heidelberg: Springer-Verlag, 2013.

[5] K. L. Virga and R. J. Engelhardt, Jr., Efficient statistical analysis of microwave circuit performance using design of experiments, in Dig. IEEE MTT-S, 1993, pp. 123-126.

[6] A. Giunta, S. Wojtkiewicz Jr., and M. Eldred, "Overview of modern design of experiments methods for computational simulations," in Digest of 41st Aerospace Sciences Meeting and Exhibit, 2003.

[7] FEKO, ver. 14, Altair Engineering, 2016.

[8] Altair Hyperworks software, ver. 14, Altair Engineering, 2016.

System Modeling of a Quad-band Antenna Using the Singularity Expansion Method

Sajjad Ur Rehman and Majeed A. S. Alkanhal
Department of Electrical Engineering, King Saud University, Riyadh, Saudi Arabia
srehman@ksu.edu.sa, majeed@ksu.edu.sa

***Abstract*—This paper presents system modeling of a quad-band antenna using the singularity expansion method (SEM). To discriminate between the physical complex poles and the non-physical poles with their corresponding residues for the quad band antenna, a matrix pencil method based on poles energy has been applied to the bore sight impulse response of the antenna. This method determines the model order of the matrix pencil (MP) method based on the pole energies. This improves the performance of the MP method to extract the genuine physical poles and eliminate the nonphysical poles. The proposed scheme is applied to the far field impulse response of a quad band antenna. The poles extracted by the proposed scheme are positioned accurately within the four bands of the tested antenna.**

Keywords—Singularity expansion method, matrix pencil method, quad band antenna, poles energy.

I. INTRODUCTION

Since the introduction of SEM by Baum [1], it has been widely used for radar signal detection and recognition. The SEM allows modeling the time response of a system as a decay exponentials sum using the complex poles and residues of the system. More recently SEM has been successfully applied to characterize ultra wide band (UWB) antennas in both time and frequency domain [2, 3]. To develop the SEM model, a numerical scheme is required for the physical poles extraction. There are different methods like Prony's, Cauchy's and Matrix Pencil Methods, that are used for pole extraction. Amongst these methods, the Matrix Pencil (MP) method is proven to be more precise and efficient [4].

The SEM with the MP method is used accurately to extract the physical poles of a dipole antenna in [4]. A comparison between two main methods, Cauchy's and MP Method is presented therein. The MP method is proven to be immune to noise and computationally more efficient as compared to Cauchy's method [4]. The SEM has been applied successfully in both time and frequency domains to model UWB antenna's effective height in order to fully describe the antenna radiation patterns, directivity, and gain [3]. The sensitivity of the SEM to identify antenna is examined in [5]. A dipole antenna is considered and it is shown that the variations in length, diameter and load impedance of the dipole antenna produce variations of the poles in the complex plane.

In reality, the number of physical poles enclosed in an antenna's far field radiated response are unknown. Most of the times the model order is typically overestimated by the MP method which results in the extraction of numerical/non-physical poles alongside the physical ones. In order to use the physical poles to model the antennas, there is a need for a scheme that can discriminate between the physical and non-physical poles. Previously, the window moving technique and the window increasing technique are used to eliminate the non-physical poles of resonant dipole antennas [6]. However, both techniques are limited to the prior knowledge of the model order.

In this paper, we propose a new method for accurate model order estimation for the MP method. The proposed method, with pole energy based matrix pencil (PEMP) scheme, can accurately extract the physical poles of multiband antennas. The model order of the antenna is determined based on the energies of the extracted poles. The PEMP scheme is applied to a quad band antenna. The four pairs of physical poles of the quad band antenna are extracted using the proposed scheme.

II. SINGULARITY EXPANSION METHOD (SEM)

The SEM allows modeling the time response of a systems as a decay exponential sum by using the physical poles and residues:

$$h(t) = \sum_{i=1}^{M} R_i e^{s_i t} \tag{1}$$

$$H(S) = \sum_{i=1}^{M} \frac{R_i}{s - s_i} \tag{2}$$

where $h(t)$ is the far field impulse response, $s_i=\sigma_i+j\omega_i$ represents the complex poles, σ_i is the damping factor, ω_i are the angular frequencies, R_i are the residues, and M is the total number of complex poles (model order). It is apparent from equations (1) and (2) that SEM needs extraction of complex physical poles and corresponding residues in order to model the antenna in time and frequency domains.

A. Pole Energy Based Matrix Pencil (PEMP) Method

The MP method is implemented in this paper with an additional phase to estimate the model order of the scheme based on the energy (E) of the extracted poles. The model order estimation, based on E of the poles, improves the performance of the MP method to extract the physical poles of multi band antennas. The E of the pole pair is proportional to the square of the magnitude of the corresponding residues and inversely proportional to the damping factor:

$$|E| = \frac{|R|^2}{\sigma} \tag{3}$$

where R is the residue and σ is the damping factor of the pole.

III. CHARATERIZATION OF MULTIBAND ANTENNA

Fig. 1 (a) shows the geometry of the tested microstrip quad band antenna. The parameters are L= 37.2mm, W= 48.6mm,

w_1=20mm, w_2=2mm and l_1=24mm with dielectric constant of 4.3 and substrate height of 0.78mm. The antenna operates at 1.1GHz, 1.2GHz, 1.9GHz and 2.3GHz. The simulated S_{11} of the antenna is shown in Fig. 1 (b).

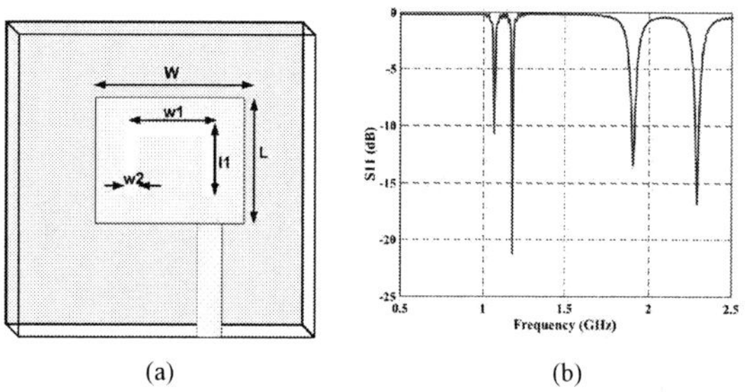

Fig. 1. (a) Schematics of the quadband antenna, and (b) S_{11} of the antenna.

The far field impulse response of the antenna is shown in Fig. 2 (a). The late time impulse response of the antenna is directly applied to the code developed to implement the classical MP method. Fig. 2 (b) shows the extracted pairs of poles using classical MP method. It can be seen from Fig. 2 (b) that there are several pairs of poles located at different frequencies.

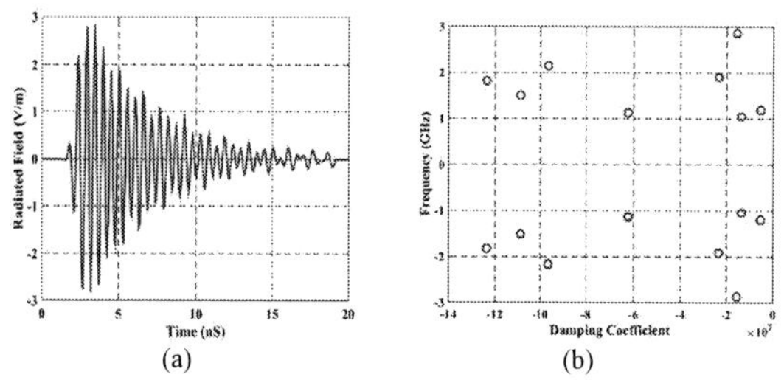

Fig. 2. (a) Simulated boresight far field impulse response of the antenna, and (b) Location of poles with damping factor using classical MP method.

In the proposed PEMP scheme, an additional step is added to the MP method to evaluate the E levels of the poles. The E of each extracted pair of pole is calculated using equation (3). The normalized E levels of the extrated poles are shown in Fig. 3 (a). It can be seen from Fig. 3 (a) that four pairs of poles located at resonance bands of the antenna has high E level as compared to the others. The high E level poles are considered as the physical poles of the antenna and the model order for MP scheme is selected as four. The late time impulse response of the antenna is applied to the developed code for the PEMP scheme. The poles as a function of the damping factor is plotted in Fig. 3 (b). The result in Fig. 3 (b) shows that all of the low E non-physical poles in the antenna response are eliminated. There are only four pairs of physical poles located at resonance bands of the antenna. To validate the extracted poles, the impulse response of the antenna is reconstructed using SEM equation (1). Comparison of the original and the reconstructed response is shown in Fig. 4.

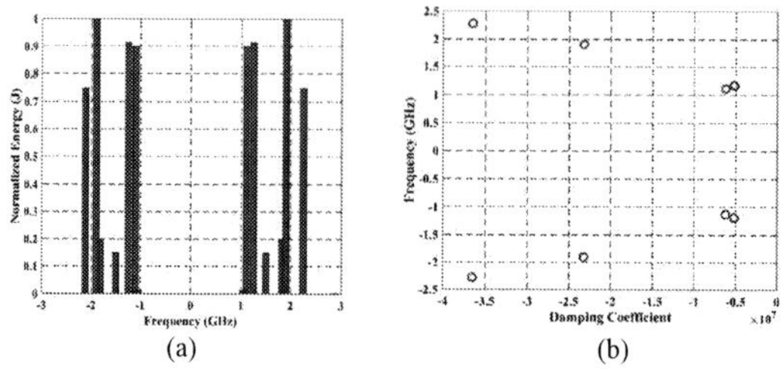

Fig. 3. (a) Normalized E of the extracted poles, and (b) Location of poles with damping factor using proposed PEMP method.

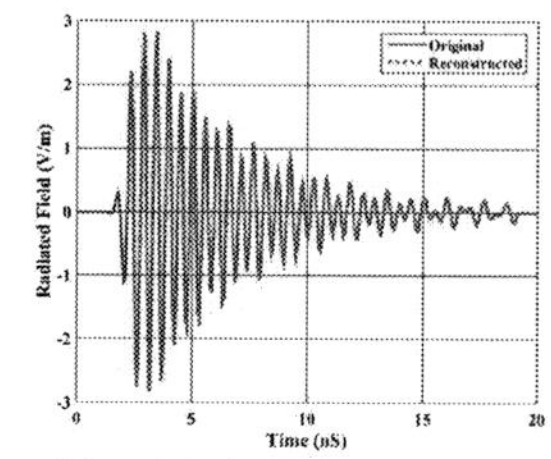

Fig. 4. Comparison of the original and reconstructed impulse responses.

IV. Conclusion

The paper presents transfer function system modeling of a quad band antenna using the SEM. To obtain the accurate model order, a pole energy based matrix pencil method has been proposed and applied to the far field impulse response of the tested quad band antenna. Additional phase of evaluating the energy levels (E) of each extracted pair of poles is added to the MP scheme to discriminate between physical and non-physical poles of the quad band antenna. The poles extracted by the proposed method are located accurately within the four bands of the antenna. The extracted physical poles are validated further by reconstructing the far field impulse response of the quad band antenna using the SEM based model.

References

[1] C. E. Baum, E. J. Rothwell, K.-M. Chen, and D. P. Nyquist, "The singularity expansion method and its application to target identification," *IEEE Proceedings*, vol. 79, pp. 1481-1492, 1991.

[2] S. U. Rehman and M. A. Alkanhal, "Characterization of Ultra-wide band diamond shaped monopole using singularity expansion method," *Progress in Electromagnetic Research Symposium (PIERS)*, 2016, pp. 431-434.

[3] S. Licul and W. A. Davis, "Unified frequency and time-domain antenna modeling and characterization," *IEEE Transactions on Antennas and Propagation*, vol. 53, pp. 2882-2888, 2005.

[4] F. Sarrazin, J. Chauveau, P. Pouliguen, P. Potier, and A. Sharaiha, "Accuracy of singularity expansion method in time and frequency domains to characterize antennas in presence of noise," *IEEE Transactions on Antennas and Propagation*, vol. 62, pp. 1261-1269, 2014.

[5] F. Sarrazin, A. Sharaiha, P. Pouliguen, J. Chauveau, and P. Potier, "Sensitivity of the singularity expansion method applied on dipole antenna backscattering," *16th International Symposium on Antenna Technology and Applied Electromagnetics (ANTEM)*, 2014, pp. 1-2.

[6] F. Sarrazin, P. Pouliguen, A. Sharaiha, P. Potier, and J. Chauveau, "Window increasing technique to discriminate mathematical and physical resonant poles extracted from antenna response," *Electronics Letters*, vol. 50, pp. 343-344, 2014.

Inverted P-Shaped UWB Antenna with Dual/Tri-Band-Notch Characteristics

Asim Quddus
Department of Electrical Engineering
University of Engineering and Technology (UET)
Taxila, Pakistan
asim.quddus@uettaxila.edu.pk

Rashid Saleem
Department of Telecommunication Engineering,
University of Engineering and Technology (UET)
Taxila, Pakistan

M. Farhan Shafique
Center for Advanced Studies in Telecommunication
COMSATS Institute of Information Technology
Islamabad, Pakistan

Sabih ur Rehman
School of Computing and Mathematics
Charles Sturt University (CSU)
Australia

***Abstract*—A miniaturized tri-band-notch ultrawideband (UWB) antenna is presented. The antenna element consists of a P-shaped patch with a truncated ground plane. The band-notch function is achieved by introducing three distinct L-shaped slots in the main radiator. Three notches are achieved for frequency bands, i.e., WiMAX (3.1-3.8), WLAN (5.5-6.1 GHz), and downlink X-band (7.25-7.75 GHz). The antenna system is realized on Rogers Duroid 5880 having compact dimensions of 20 x 20 mm^2. Moreover, the simulated as well as measured results are in good agreement.**

***Keywords*—band-notch; EESS; Ultrawideband (UWB); WLAN; X-band.**

I. Introduction

In general, wireless technologies have gained significant attention over last few decades. The main focus of wireless technologies is to utilize minimum resources, achieve high data rate and cause minimum interference to other wireless standards. The US Federal Communication Commission (FCC) has assigned license free frequency band of 3.1 to 10.6 GHz for UWB. The frequency spectra allowed for UWB communication contain other high-power narrow and wide band wireless standards. These wireless standards contain WiMAX (3.1-3.8 GHz), WLAN (5.5-6.1 GHz), and downlink X-band satellite (7.25-7.75 GHz) [1] etc. among others.

UWB antenna designing is becoming ever popular and challenging with increase in use of UWB wireless technology [2-3]. In general, requirement is to design a low-cost antenna with minimum interference from nearby communication systems. The interference mitigation can be achieved by implementing band notching directly in UWB. However, an appropriate placement of these notching structure in ground and radiator is challenging as compare to traditional RF techniques. Various techniques have been reported for band notching. These techniques include but are not limited to slots, parasitic structures, fractals and defected ground structures [3-5]. In this work, an inverted P-shape UWB antenna with tri band notch is presented as shown in Fig. 1. Finite Element Method (FEM) based simulations in Ansys High Frequency Structural Simulator (HFSS) are employed for the proposed design.

(a) (b) (c)

Fig. 1. Fabricated design of proposed tri-band-notch antenna: (a) Dual-band-notch antenna, (b) Tri-band-notch antenna, and (c) Back view.

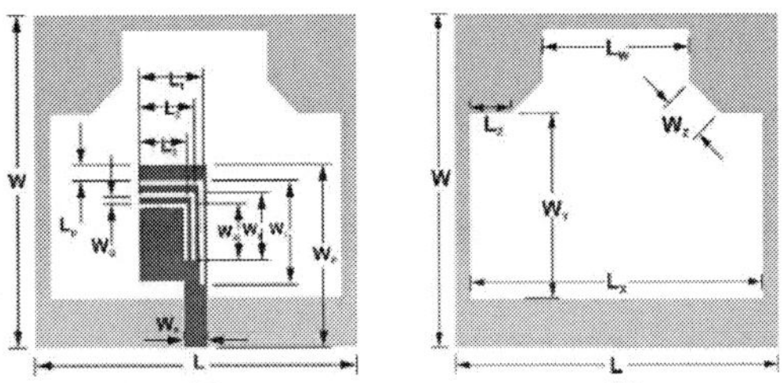

(a) (b)

Fig. 2. Geometric structure of proposed tri-band-notch antenna: (a) Front view and (b) Back view

II. Antenna Design and Configuration

A. Antenna Structure

An inverted P-shape patch antenna is shown in Fig. 1. The radiating patch and truncated ground planes are etched on the front and rear side of substrate respectively, as shown in Fig. 2. The antenna is printed on Rogers Duroid 5880 with thickness 0.8 mm, relative permittivity $\varepsilon_r = 2.2$ and an overall size of 20 mm × 20 mm. Three inverted L-shaped slots are introduced in the main P-shape radiator to obtain tri-band-notch characteristics. The notching structures length at desired frequency bands can be obtained using equation 1. The parameters of the proposed antenna are given in Table I. The L_x

and L_y slots provide band notch characteristics for WiMAX 3.5 GHz, and WLAN 5.7 GHz, respectively. The downlink X-band 7.5 GHz is filtered by adding L_z slot:

$$f_{r_x}=\frac{c}{4L_x\sqrt{\varepsilon_{eff}}}\ ,\ f_{r_y}=\frac{c}{4L_y\sqrt{\varepsilon_{eff}}}\ ,\ f_{r_z}=\frac{c}{4L_z\sqrt{\varepsilon_{eff}}}\ , \qquad (1)$$

and,

$$L_x=L_1+W_1\ ,\ L_y=L_2+W_2\ ,L_z=L_3+W_3\ .$$

TABLE I.
Optimized Values of Proposed Dual/Tri-Band-Notch Antenna

Parameter	Lx	Lw	Lz	WY	WZ	WG	WP	WF
Value(mm)	18	9	2.5	11	2	0.5	11	1.5
Parameter	W1	W2	W3	L1	L2	L3	Lp	_
Value(mm)	6	3.8	3.1	4	3.5	3	1	_

III. Results and Discussions

A. VSWR Performance of Dual/Tri-Band-Notch Antenna

The dual-band notch antenna, shown in Fig. 1 (a) provides interference mitigation to/from WiMAX (3.1-3.8) and WLAN (5.5-6.1 GHz). An impedance match for 3.1-10.6 GHz, except the two intended bands, is depicted in Fig. 3 (a). For the tri-band configuration the slots filter out WiMAX, WLAN, and downlink X-band. The impedance match of tri-band-notch antenna is shown in Fig. 3 (b). The simulated results are in good agreement with the measured results.

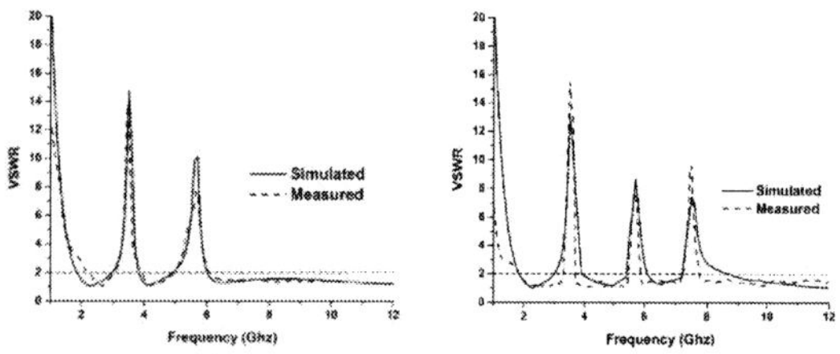

(a) (b)

Fig. 3. VSWR Performance of dual/tri-band-notch antenna: (a) Dual-band-notch antenna, and (b) Tri-band-notch antenna

B. Surface Current Density (J-surf)

Surface current distribution for the tri-band design is shown in Fig. 4. It can be seen that at notch frequencies the concentration of current is high, resulting in band reject.

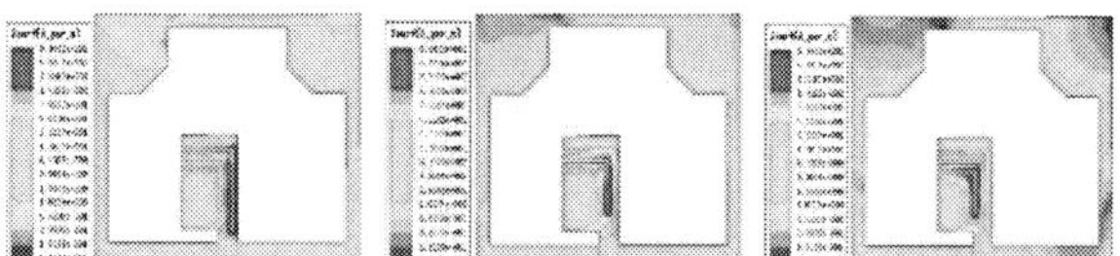

(a) (b) (c)

Fig. 4. Surface current distribution for tri-band-notch antenna: (a) WiMAX (3.1-3.8), (b) WLAN (5.5-6.1 GHz), and (c) Downlink X-band (7.25-7.75 GHz).

C. Gain and Efficiency Performance of Tri-band Design

It is desirable to have minimum gain and efficiency at notching frequencies. The simulated gain and efficiency results are shown in Fig. 5. The gain varies from 5.5 to 8.5 dBi with gain values of around -2dBi, -3.5dBi and -7.2dBi at respective notch frequencies. The efficiency at these notched bands drops down to relatively lower values as well i.e. 0.32, 0.43 and 0.37.

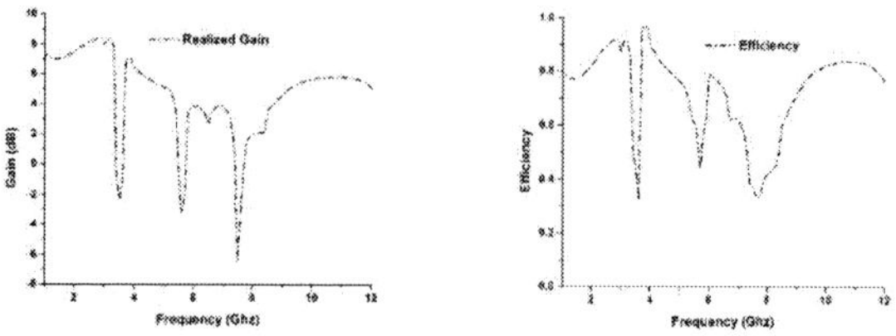

(a) (b)

Fig. 5. Simulated gain and Efficiency of tri-band-notch antenna.

D. Radiation Characteristics

The E-plane and H-plane radiation patterns of proposed antenna at 3 GHz, 7 GHz and 9 GHz are shown in Fig. 6. The radiation patterns are omnidirectional in H-plane and directional in E-plane over the UWB frequency band, within the allowable limits.

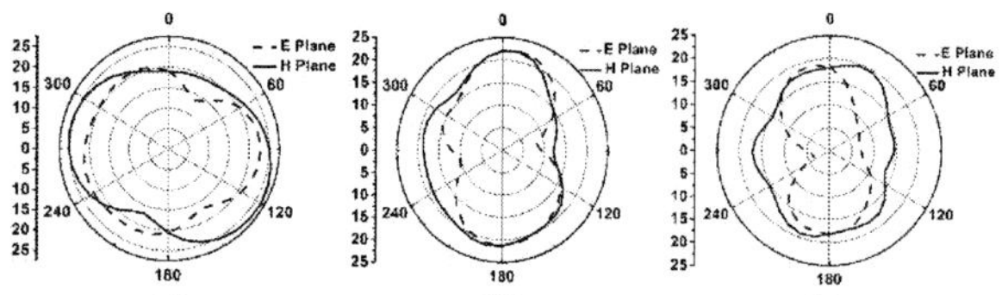

(a) (b) (c)

Fig. 6. Radiation patterns in E-Plane and H-Plane at: (a) 3 GHz, (b) 7 GHz, and (c) 9 GHz.

IV. Conclusion

A miniaturized UWB antenna with tri-band-notch characteristics is proposed. The notching characteristics are achieved by etching L-shaped slots of desired lengths in the main radiator. These notching structures are tuned to mitigate the interference in WiMAX (3.1-3.9 GHz); WLAN, upper frequency ranges (5.5-6.1 GHz) and downlink X-band (7.25-7.75 GHz) overlapping with the UWB band. More importantly simulated as well as measured results are in good agreement, indicating that the proposed antenna design is suitable candidate for UWB applications.

REFERENCES

[1] N. Ojaroudi, M. Ojaroudi, and N. Ghadimi, "Dual band-notched small monopole antenna with novel W-shaped conductor backed-plane and novel T-shaped slot for UWB applications," *IET Microwaves, Antennas & Propagation*, vol. 7, pp. 8-14, Jan. 2013.

[2] J. J. Liu, K. P. Esselle, S. G. Hay, and S. S. Zhong, "Planar ultra-wideband antenna with five notched stop bands," *Electronics Letters*, vol. 49, pp. 579-580, April. 2013.

[3] N. Ojaroudi, and N. Ghadimi, "UWB small slot antenna with WLAN frequency band-stop function," *Electronics Letters*, vol. 49, pp. 1317-1318, Jan. 2013.

[4] Y. Z. Cai, H. C. Yang and L. Y. Cai, "Wideband monopole antenna with three band-notched characteristics," *IEEE Antennas and Wireless Propagation Letters*, vol. 13, pp. 607-610, 2014.

[5] R. Karimian, H. Oraizi, and S. Fakhte, "Design of a compact ultra-wide-band monopole antenna with band rejection characteristics," *IET Microwaves, Antennas & Propagation*, vol. 8, pp. 604-610, Feb. 2014.

Printed Cross-Slot Wideband Conformal Antenna for GPS Application

Ratikanta Sahoo
Dept. of ECE
National Institute of Technology
Warangal, India
ratikanta.sahoo15@gmail.com

D. Vakula
Dept. of ECE
National Institute of Technology
Warangal, India
vakula@nitw.ac.in

NVSN Sarma
Dept. of ECE
National Institute of Technology
Warangal, India
sarma@nitw.ac.in

***Abstract*—A novel cross-slot printed wideband conformal antenna is proposed for GPS application. The combination of partial ground plane and cross-slot on the patch are used for bandwidth enhancement. The proposed conformal antenna exhibits a fractional bandwidth(for the definition of -10dB) of 79.28% operating from 1091 to 2524 MHz. The radiation pattern exhibits an omnidirectional pattern and gain of the proposed conformal antenna is 2.37 to 5.33dBi within operating frequency range.**

Keywords—conformal antenna; wideband antenna; printed antenna; GPS application

I. Introduction

Global Positioning System(GPS) requires a wideband antenna for receivers installed on moving vehicles, missiles, and handheld devices. The platform for mounting the antenna is not always flat. Some cases, it is recommended to make the antenna conformal to the device to reduce aerodynamic drag and less visible to the human eye and omnidirectional coverage for example on missile or aircraft [1].

There are some recent studies on GPS antenna on a flat surface only for the L1 single band [2-4] with narrow bandwidth. Although a wideband GPS Antenna has been reported [5], but that is designed on a flat surface. In [6], two elements conformal antenna has been designed for a multi-GNSS reception with narrow bandwidth. A proximity coupled fed circular patch with a cross-slot on the Patch has been demonstrated on the flat surface in [7] with less bandwidth. So with the rapid development of wireless communication systems and increase in their applications, wideband antenna design has become a challenging topic.

In this paper, a novel high performance cross-slot wideband conformal antenna is proposed. The proposed conformal antenna exhibits wideband bandwidth. The simulation results show that the proposed GPS antenna offers overall good performance.

II. Design of a Cross-Slot Wideband Cylindrical Conformal Antenna

For designing this antenna, flexible and thermally stable substrate like Rogers RT/duroid 5880 of permittivity (ε_r) 2.2 and thickness of 0.787 mm with microstrip line feed for 50 Ohm impedance matching are used. The dimension of the substrate is $100\times110\times0.787$ mm^3 and dimension of the patch is 50×50 mm^2.The geometry of the proposed planar antenna is shown in Fig. 1.

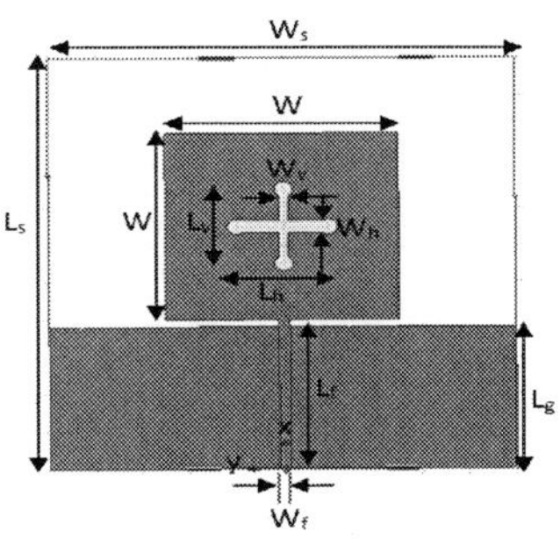

Fig. 1. Geometry of planar antenna: L_s=110 mm, W_s=100 mm, W=50 mm, L_g=38 mm, L_f=40 mm, W_f=2.4 mm, L_h=20 mm, W_h=3 mm, L_v=20 mm, W_v=2 mm, Radius=2 mm.

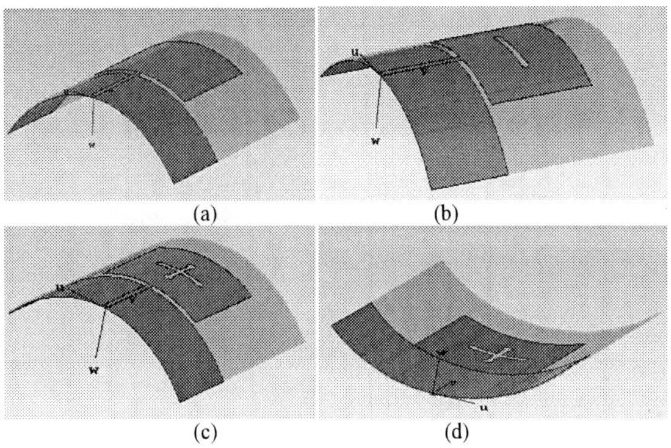

Fig. 2. Conformal Antenna Model (a) Top view of the conformal antenna without a slot. (b) Top view of conformal antenna with horizontal slot (c) Top view of conformal antenna with cross-slot (d) Bottom view of conformal antenna

The antenna used in this paper employs a cross dumbbell shape slot on the patch feed to excite the partial ground plane.

The use of circle on the cross-slot end is the best case among the other geometries. It is because that the circle makes the fields on the slots more uniform than the other cases. The concept of the partial ground plane is reported in this paper. The bandwidth is increased because of suppression of surface wave propagation. The cylindrical conformal antenna with 60 mm radius of curvature is shown in Fig. 2, which is obtained by the transformation of the planar antenna.

III. RESULTS AND DISCUSSION

The proposed antenna is designed and simulated using CST STUDIO SUITE 2016. The simulated return loss of proposed conformal antenna with a 60mm radius of curvature compared in Fig. 3. The proposed cylindrical antenna achieves -10dB impedance bandwidth of 1433 MHz, covering the frequency range 1.09-2.524 GHz with 79.28% fractional bandwidth indicating wideband bandwidth.

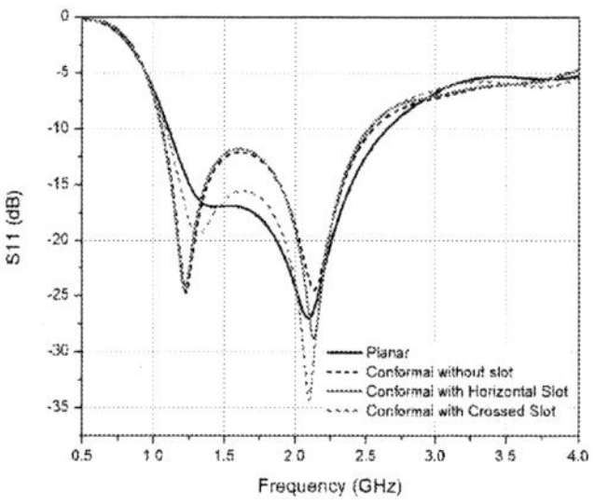

Fig. 3. The return loss of the planar and conformal antenna.

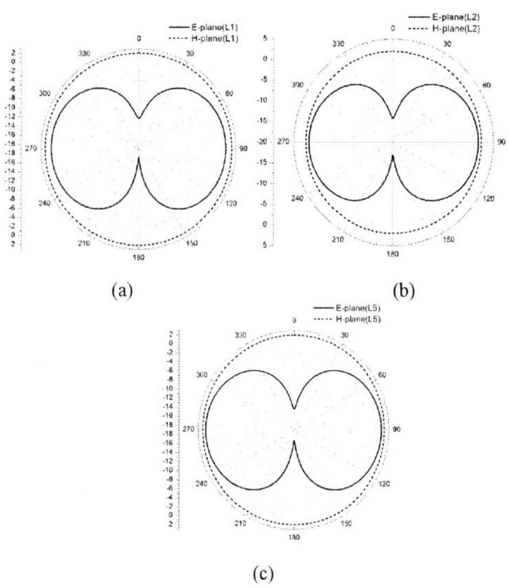

(a) (b) (c)

Fig. 4. Radiation pattern of proposed cylindrical conformal antenna at (a) L1 band (1.57542 GHz) (b) L2 band (1.2276 GHz) (c) L5 band (1.17645 GHz).

There is a slight change in resonant frequency from planar to cylindrical conformal antenna because of increasing the effective resonant length due to bending. Also, there is a change in return loss between conformal antenna without any slot, with only horizontal dumbbell shape slot and cross dumbbell shape slot. This is because of the resonant frequency also depends on slot's length.

The comparison between the 2-D radiation pattern(E-plane and H-plane) of the cylindrical conformal antenna with a 60mm radius of curvature at different GPS bands like L1, L2, and L5 is shown in Fig. 4. In H-plane, the designed antenna is giving an omnidirectional pattern.

The peak gain of the cylindrical conformal antenna with 60 mm radius of curvature and the planar one are compared and shown in Fig. 5. The curved patches of the cylindrical antenna distracted the radiation wave for which differences in the gain values between conformal and planar one.

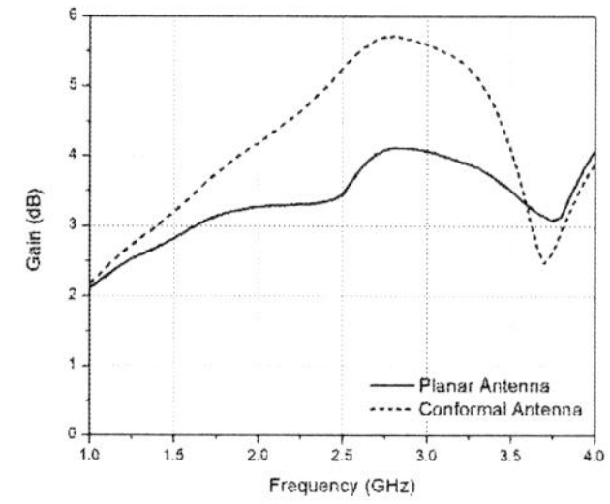

Fig. 5. The gain of the planar and conformal antenna.

IV. CONCLUSION

This paper presents the design of cross-slot wideband cylindrical conformal antenna with 60 mm radius of curvature. The designed cylindrical conformal antenna offers a good wideband fractional bandwidth of about 79.28% and covering the bandwidth requirements of the modernized GPS application which can be used to guide the anti-tank guided missile (ATGM). Furthermore, the antenna has an omnidirectional radiation pattern in H-plane with a gain of about 2.37 to 5.33 dB within the operating frequency range of 1.09 to 2.525 GHz.

REFERENCES

[1] L. Josefsson, and P. Persson, Conformal Array Antenna Theory, and Design, IEEE Press, 2006.

[2] Hua-Ming Chen, Yi-Fang Lin, Chen-Hung Chen, Chen-Yuan Pan, and You-Shiang Cai, "Miniature folded patch GPS antenna for vehicle communication devices" IEEE Trans. on Antennas and Propagation, Vol. 63, No. 5, pp.1891-1898, May 2015.

[3] M.M. Bilgic and K. Yegin, "Modified annular ring antenna for GPS and SDARS automotive applications" IEEE Antenna and Wireless Propagation Letters, Vol. 15, pp.1442-1445, 2016.

[4] Encheng Wang and Qiuping Liu, "GPS patch antenna loaded with fractal EBG structure using organic magnetic substrate" Progress in Electromagnetics Research Letters, Vol. 58,pp. 23-28, 2016.

[5] Francesca Scire-Scappuzzo and Sergey N. Makarove, "A low-multipath wideband GPS antenna with cutoff or non-cutoff corrugated ground plane" IEEE Trans. on Antennas and Propagation, Vol. 57, No.1, pp.33-46, January 2009.

[6] Jae-Hoon Bang, Wan-Joo Kim, and Bierng-Chearl Ahn, "Two-Element Conformal Antenna for Multi-GNSS Reception," IEEE Antenna and Wireless Propagation Letters, Vol. 16, 2017.

[7] Albooyeh, Mohammad, N. Kamjani, and Mojtaba Shobeyri. "A novel cross-slot geometry to improve impedance bandwidth of microstrip antennas." Progress In Electromagnetics Research Letters 4,pp.63-72 2008.

A Volume Integral Equation Solver for Quantum-Corrected Transient Analysis of Scattering from Plasmonic Nanostructures

Sadeed B. Sayed, Ismail Enes Uysal, and Hakan Bagci
Computer, Electrical and Mathematical Sciences and Engineering,
King Abdullah University of Science and Technology (KAUST),
Thuwal, 23955-6900, Saudi Arabia
Email: {sadeed.sayed, ismail.uysal, hakan.bagci}@kaust.edu.sa

H. Arda Ulku
Department of Electronics Engineering,
Gebze Technical University,
Kocaeli, 41400, Turkey
Email: haulku@gtu.edu.tr

Abstract—**Quantum tunneling is observed between two nanostructures that are separated by a sub-nanometer gap. Electrons "jumping" from one structure to another create an additional current path. An auxiliary tunnel is introduced between the two structures as a support for this so that a classical electromagnetic solver can account for the effects of quantum tunneling. The dispersive permittivity of the tunnel is represented by a Drude model, whose parameters are obtained from the electron tunneling probability. The transient scattering from the connected nanostructures (i.e., nanostructures plus auxiliary tunnel) is analyzed using a time domain volume integral equation solver. Numerical results demonstrating the effect of quantum tunneling on the scattered fields are provided.**

I. Introduction

Recent advances in the fabrication of nanoparticles have paved the way to miniature electromagnetic devices to nanoscale. To accurately analyze electromagnetic scattering from such devices, quantum tunneling effects be accounted for. Quantum tunneling is observed between two structures when the gap between them is less than a nanometer. Electrons tunneled from one structure to the other one generate an additional current path that cannot be modeled by classical electromagnetic solvers. This results in errors in scattered field computations. In such cases, one could use a "full" quantum mechanical solver to obtain accurate results, but computational requirements of this solver would be prohibitively high. To alleviate this problem, one can use a (one dimensional) quantum mechanical solver for only the gap and obtain an effective permittivity for an auxiliary tunnel supporting the current generated by tunneled electrons [1]. Then, one can use a classical electromagnetic solver to compute scattered fields from the combined structure (nanostructures plus auxiliary tunnel).

Among several types of classical electromagnetic solvers, time domain volume integral equation (TD-VIE) solvers offer several advantages over their differential equation counterparts [2]. In this work, a time domain-electric field volume integral equation (TD-EFVIE) is developed for transient quantum-corrected analysis of scattering from plasmonic nanostructures. The dispersive permittivity of the auxiliary tunnel, which is introduced to support the currents generated by tunneled electrons, is represented by a Drude model whose parameters are computed from electron tunneling probability as described in [1]. The unknown electric flux density, field intensity and polarization density induced inside the nanostructures and the auxiliary tunnel are expanded in terms of full and half Schaubert-Wilton-Glisson (SWG) functions in space [3], [4] and approximate prolate spherical wave (APSW) functions [5] in time. These expansions are inserted into the TD-EFVIE and the constitutive relation (obtained by inverse Fourier transforming the Drude model) and the resulting coupled system of equations is Galerkin-tested in space. The final semi-discrete matrix system is cast in the form of an ordinary differential equation and integrated in time using a PE(CE)^m type linear multistep scheme [6] to yield the coefficients of the unknown expansions.

II. Formulation

Let V denote the volume of the combined structure (the plasmonic nanostructures plus the auxiliary tunnel) residing in an unbounded background medium with permittivity ε_0 and permeability μ_0. The combined structure is excited by band-limited electric field intensity $\mathbf{E}^{\text{inc}}(\mathbf{r}, t)$. Upon excitation, flux density $\mathbf{D}(\mathbf{r}, t)$ and field intensity $\mathbf{E}(\mathbf{r}, t)$ induced in V satisfy:

$$\mathbf{D}(\mathbf{r}, t) = \varepsilon_0 \varepsilon_\infty(\mathbf{r}) \mathbf{E}(\mathbf{r}, t) + \mathbf{P}(\mathbf{r}, t), \quad (1)$$

$$\partial_t \mathbf{E}^{\text{inc}}(\mathbf{r}, t) = \partial_t \mathbf{E}(\mathbf{r}, t) + \mathcal{L}\{\mathbf{E}(\mathbf{r}, t)\} - \mathcal{L}\{\varepsilon_0^{-1} \mathbf{D}(\mathbf{r}, t)\}, \quad (2)$$

for $\mathbf{r} \in V$. Here, the $\varepsilon_\infty(\mathbf{r})$ is the relative permittivity at infinite frequency, $\mathbf{P}(\mathbf{r}, t)$ is the polarization density, and the integral operator $\mathcal{L}\{\cdot\}$ is:

$$\mathcal{L}\{\mathbf{X}(\mathbf{r}, t)\} = -\frac{\varepsilon_0 \mu_0}{4\pi} \int_V \frac{1}{R} \partial_{t'}^3 \mathbf{X}(\mathbf{r}', t')\big|_{t'=t-R/c_0} d\mathbf{r}' + \frac{1}{4\pi} \nabla \int_V \frac{1}{R} [\nabla' \cdot \partial_{t'} \mathbf{X}(\mathbf{r}', t')]_{t'=t-R/c_0} d\mathbf{r}', \quad (3)$$

where $R = |\mathbf{r} - \mathbf{r}'|$ is the distance between source and observation points, $\mathbf{r}'$ and $\mathbf{r}$, and $c_0 = 1/\sqrt{\varepsilon_0 \mu_0}$ is the speed of light in the background medium. When the permittivity in

V is represented using a Drude model [1], the $\mathbf{P}(\mathbf{r},t)$ satisfies:

$$\partial_t \mathbf{P}(\mathbf{r},t) = \hat{\mathbf{P}}(\mathbf{r},t),$$
$$\partial_t \hat{\mathbf{P}}(\mathbf{r},t) = -\gamma_{\mathrm{p}}(\mathbf{r})\mathbf{P}(\mathbf{r},t) + \varepsilon_0(\omega_{\mathrm{p}}(\mathbf{r}))^2\mathbf{E}(\mathbf{r},t), \quad (4)$$

where $\hat{\mathbf{P}}(\mathbf{r},t)$ is an intermediate variable, $\gamma_{\mathrm{p}}(\mathbf{r})$ is the damping factor, and $\omega_{\mathrm{p}}(\mathbf{r})$ is the plasmon frequency. To numerically solve the coupled equations (1), (2), and (4), V is discretized into tetrahedrons and unknowns $\mathbf{D}(\mathbf{r},t)$, $\mathbf{E}(\mathbf{r},t)$, $\mathbf{P}(\mathbf{r},t)$, and $\hat{\mathbf{P}}(\mathbf{r},t)$ are expanded:

$$\mathbf{D}(\mathbf{r},t) = \sum_{i=0}^{N_t}\sum_{n=1}^{N_{\mathrm{F}}} I_{n,i}^{\mathrm{D}} T_i(t)\mathbf{f}_n^{\mathrm{F}}(\mathbf{r}),$$
$$\mathbf{U}(\mathbf{r},t) = \sum_{i=0}^{N_t}\sum_{n=1}^{N_{\mathrm{H}}} I_{n,i}^{\mathrm{U}} T_i(t)\mathbf{f}_n^{\mathrm{H}}(\mathbf{r}), \mathrm{U} \in \{\mathrm{E,P,\hat{P}}\}. \quad (5)$$

Here, $\{\mathbf{f}_n^{\mathrm{F}}(\mathbf{r}), \mathbf{f}_n^{\mathrm{H}}(\mathbf{r})\}$ are the full and half SWG functions respectively [3], [4], $T_i(t) = T(t - i\Delta t)$, where $T(t)$ is the APSW function [5] and Δt is the time step, and $I_{n,i}^{\mathrm{K}}$, $\mathrm{K} \in \{\mathrm{E,D,P,\hat{P}}\}$ are unknown expansion coefficients. Inserting (5) into (1) and spatially testing the resulting equation with $\mathbf{f}_n^{\mathrm{F}}(\mathbf{r})$, $m = 1 : N_{\mathrm{F}}$, yields a matrix system at time step j:

$$\mathbf{G}^{\mathrm{FF}}\mathbf{I}_j^{\mathrm{D}} = \mathbf{G}^{\mathrm{FH}}\left(\varepsilon_0\varepsilon_\infty \mathbf{I}_j^{\mathrm{E}} + \mathbf{I}_j^{\mathrm{P}}\right). \quad (6)$$

Here, $\{\mathbf{I}_j^{\mathrm{K}}\}_n = I_{n,j}^{\mathrm{K}}$ and the elements of the $\mathbf{G}^{\mathrm{AB}}$, $\mathrm{A} \in \{\mathrm{F,H}\}$, $\mathrm{B} \in \{\mathrm{F,H}\}$:

$$\{\mathbf{G}^{\mathrm{AB}}\}_{m,n} = \int_{V_m} \mathbf{f}_m^{\mathrm{A}}(\mathbf{r}) \cdot \mathbf{f}_n^{\mathrm{B}}(\mathbf{r}) d\mathbf{r}. \quad (7)$$

Similarly, inserting (5) into (2), and (4) and testing the resulting equations with $\mathbf{f}_n^{\mathrm{H}}(\mathbf{r})$, $m = 1 : N_{\mathrm{H}}$, yield three coupled matrix systems at j:

$$\partial_t \mathbf{I}_j^{\mathrm{P}} = \mathbf{I}_j^{\hat{\mathrm{P}}}, \ \partial_t \mathbf{I}_j^{\hat{\mathrm{P}}} = -\gamma_{\mathrm{p}}\mathbf{I}_j^{\hat{\mathrm{P}}} + \varepsilon_0\omega_{\mathrm{p}}^2 \mathbf{I}_j^{\mathrm{E}}, \quad (8)$$
$$\mathbf{G}^{\mathrm{HH}}\partial_t \mathbf{I}_j^{\mathrm{E}} = \mathbf{V}_j^{\mathrm{inc}} - \mathbf{Z}_0^{\mathrm{HH}}\mathbf{I}_j^{\mathrm{E}} - \sum_{i=0}^{j-1}\mathbf{Z}_{j-i}^{\mathrm{HH}}\mathbf{I}_i^{\mathrm{E}} +$$
$$\varepsilon_0^{-1}\mathbf{Z}_0^{\mathrm{HF}}\mathbf{I}_j^{\mathrm{D}} + \varepsilon_0^{-1}\sum_{i=0}^{j-1}\mathbf{Z}_{j-i}^{\mathrm{HF}}\mathbf{I}_i^{\mathrm{D}}, \quad (9)$$

where $\{\mathbf{Z}_{j-i}^{\mathrm{AB}}\}_{m,n} = \int_{V_m} \mathbf{f}_m^{\mathrm{A}}(\mathbf{r}) \cdot \mathcal{L}\{\mathbf{f}_m^{\mathrm{B}}(\mathbf{r})T_i(t)\}\big|_{t=j\Delta t} d\mathbf{r}$. Coupled system of equations (6), (8) and (9) are integrated in time using a linear k-step PE(CE)^{m} scheme [6] to yield the unknown expansion coefficients $\mathbf{I}_j^{\mathrm{K}}$ for $j = 1 : N_t$.

III. Numerical Results

The proposed solver is used for analyzing scattering from a sodium dimer consisting of spheres with radius 2.17 nm. The separation between the spheres is 0.265 nm. The auxiliary tunnel is modeled using four concentric cylinders. The outer radius of the outermost shell is 0.8 nm. The Drude model parameters for the sodium and the tunnel are same as the ones in [1]. The dimer is excited using a plane wave with $\mathbf{E}^{\mathrm{inc}}(\mathbf{r},t) = \hat{\mathbf{x}}\cos[2\pi f_0(t - t_0 - \mathbf{r}\cdot\hat{\mathbf{z}}/c_0)]e^{-(t-t_0-\mathbf{r}\cdot\hat{\mathbf{z}}/c_0)^2/2\sigma^2}$, where $f_0 = 1200$ THz, $\sigma = 3.6/(2\pi f_0)$, and $t_0 = 6\sigma$. Discretization parameters $N^{\mathrm{F}} = 5330$, $N^{\mathrm{H}} = 10196$, $\Delta t = 0.01$ fs, and $N_t = 4000$. The predictor-corrector coefficients used for the PE(CE)^{m} scheme are the sixth order Adams-Bashforth and backward difference formula (BDF6) coefficients. For comparison, scattering from the dimer without the auxiliary tunnel is also studied under the same excitation.

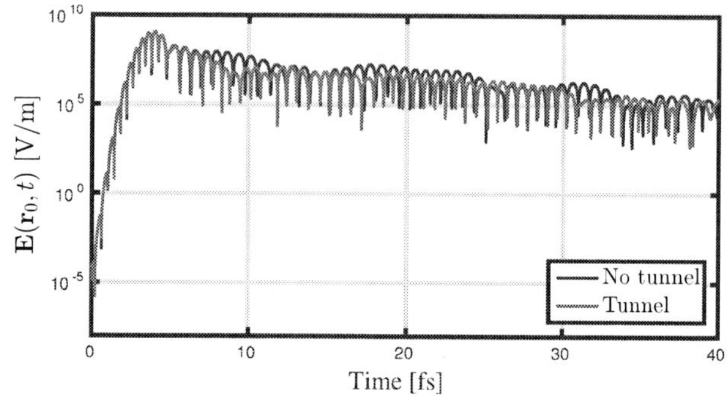

Fig. 1. $\mathbf{E}(\mathbf{r}_0,t)$ at $\mathbf{r}_0 = (2.3, 0.0, 0.0)$ nm.

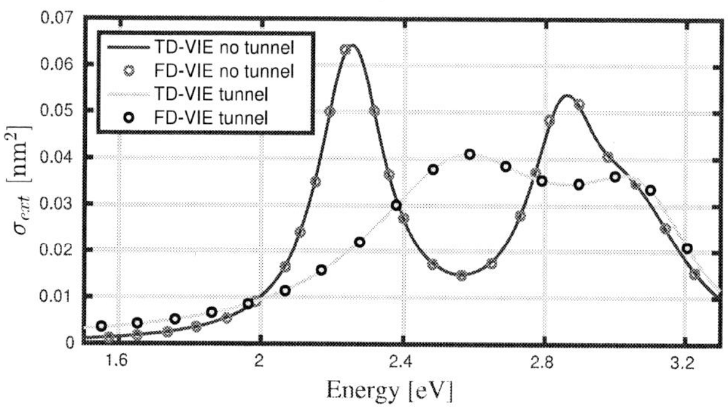

Fig. 2. Extinction cross section of the sodium dimer.

Fig. 1 compares $\mathbf{E}(\mathbf{r}_0,t)$ for $\mathbf{r}_0 = (2.3, 0.0, 0.0)$ nm computed for the dimers with and without the auxiliary tunnel. The result clearly shows that the solver provides stable results for both the cases. In Fig. 2, the extinction cross section of the dimers obtained by Fourier transforming the time domain solution is compared to that obtained directly by a frequency domain VIE solver. The results agree well. The figure also shows that introducing an auxiliary tunnel significantly changes the computed radiation pattern of the dimer.

References

[1] R. Esteban, A. G. Borisov, P. Nordlander, and J. Aizpurua, "Bridging quantum and classical plasmonics with a quantum-corrected model," Nat. Comm., vol. 3, 825, 2012.

[2] S. B. Sayed, H. A. Ulku, and H. Bagci, "A stable marching on-in-time scheme for solving the time domain electric field volume integral equation on high-contrast scatterers," IEEE Trans. Antennas Propag., vol. 63, no. 7, pp. 3098–3110, July 2015.

[3] D. H. Schaubert, R. W. Donald, and W. G. Allen, "A tetrahedral modeling method for electromagnetic scattering by arbitrarily shaped inhomogeneous dielectric bodies," IEEE Trans. Antennas Propag., vol. 32, no. 1, pp. 77–85, Jan. 1984.

[4] G. Kobidze, J. Gao, S. Balasubramaniam, and E. Michielssen, "A fast time domain integral equation based scheme for analyzing scattering from dispersive objects," IEEE Trans. Antennas Propag., vol. 53, no. 3, pp. 1215–1226, Mar. 2005.

[5] R. Wildman, G. Pisharody, D. S. Weile, S. Balasubramaniam, and E. Michielssen, "An accurate scheme for the solution of the time-domain integral equations of electromagnetics using higher order vector bases and bandlimited extrapolation," IEEE Trans. Antennas Propag., vol. 52, no. 11, pp. 2973–2984, Nov. 2004.

[6] H. A. Ulku, H. Bagci, and E. Michielssen, "Marching on-in-time solution of the time domain magnetic field integral equation using a predictor-corrector scheme," IEEE Trans. Antennas Propag., vol. 61, no. 8, pp. 4120–4131, Aug. 2013.

Mixed Finite Element Methods for the Maxwell's Equations with Matrix Parameters

Asad Anees
Institute of Mathematics
Clausthal University of Technology
Clausthal-Zellerfeld, Germany, D-38678
asad.anees@tu-clausthal.de

Lutz Angermann
Institute of Mathematics
Clausthal University of Technology
Clausthal-Zellerfeld, Germany, D-38678
lutz.angermann@tu-clausthal.de

***Abstract*—In this paper we investigate mixed finite element methods for solving decoupled time-dependent Maxwell's equations with matrix-valued parameters as functions of space. The equations are discretized in space by Nédeléc conforming elements on simplicial meshes, then semidiscrete the problem is converted into an operator form. We demonstrate error estimates for the semidiscrete problem.**

***Index Terms*—Mixed finite element methods, matrix parameters, error estimate**

I. Introduction

Previous investigations and numerical methods such as FDTD and TDFE methods for Maxwell's equations were mostly devoted to the situation where the electrical permittivity $\varepsilon = \varepsilon(\mathbf{x})$, the magnetic permeability $\mu = \mu(\mathbf{x})$ and the conductivity $\sigma = \sigma(\mathbf{x})$ are constant scalar functions. Because of the difficulty of dealing with the case of matrix-valued, space-dependent parameters, there is little rigorous analysis of finite element methods available for the Maxwell's equations. To overcome this difficulty, in the paper [1] we have proposed a splitting approach such that the original system splits into two uncoupled systems. Moreover, the method proposed in [1] is stable, convergent and easy to implement. Let $\Omega \subset \mathbb{R}^3$ be a smooth, simply connected domain with boundary Γ and unit outward normal $\mathbf{n}$. Let $\mathbf{E} = \mathbf{E}(\mathbf{x}, t)$ and $\mathbf{H} = \mathbf{H}(\mathbf{x}, t)$ denote the electric and magnetic field intensities respectively, where the time-variable t belongs to some interval $(0, T)$, $T > 0$. Given a function $\mathbf{J} = \mathbf{J}(\mathbf{x}, t)$ specifying the applied current, Maxwell's equations state that:

$$\varepsilon\mathbf{E}_t + \sigma\mathbf{E} - \nabla \times \mathbf{H} = \mathbf{J} \quad \text{in } \Omega \times (0, T), \tag{1}$$

$$\mu\mathbf{H}_t + \nabla \times \mathbf{E} = 0 \quad \text{in } \Omega \times (0, T). \tag{2}$$

The system (1) and (2) can be decomposed into two uncoupled systems (3)-(4) and (5)-(6), for details see [1]:

$$\varepsilon\mathbf{E}_{1,t} + \sigma\mathbf{E}_1 - \nabla \times \mathbf{H} = \mathbf{J}_1, \tag{3}$$

$$\mu\mathbf{H}_t + \nabla \times \mathbf{E}_1 = 0. \tag{4}$$

We shall assume a perfect conducting boundary condition on Ω, that is:

$$\mathbf{n} \times \mathbf{E}_1 = 0 \quad \text{on } \Gamma \times (0, T).$$

The authors would like to thank the DAAD to provide the research grant 91564387 within the funding program 57129429.

In addition, initial conditions have to be specified so that:

$$\mathbf{E}_1(\mathbf{x}, 0) = \mathbf{E}_{1,0}(\mathbf{x}) \text{ and } \mathbf{H}(\mathbf{x}, 0) = \mathbf{H}_0(\mathbf{x}) \text{ for all } \mathbf{x} \in \Omega,$$

where $\mathbf{E}_{1,0}$ and $\mathbf{H}_0$ are given functions and $\mathbf{H}_0$ satisfies

$$\nabla \cdot (\mu\mathbf{H}_0) = 0 \quad \text{in } \Omega, \quad \mathbf{H}_0 \cdot \mathbf{n} = 0 \quad \text{on } \Gamma.$$

The second problem reads as:

$$\varepsilon\mathbf{E}_{2,t} + \sigma\mathbf{E}_2 = \mathbf{J}_2, \tag{5}$$

$$\nabla \times \mathbf{E}_2 = 0, \tag{6}$$

with initial condition,

$$\mathbf{E}_2(\mathbf{x}, 0) = \mathbf{E}_{2,0}(\mathbf{x}) \quad \text{for all } \mathbf{x} \in \Omega.$$

We consider ε, μ and σ as symmetric, uniformly positive definite, $\mathbb{R}^{3,3}$-valued functions being sufficiently smooth on Ω. To shorten the presentation, we assume $\sigma = 0$ in what follows. Now, we shall obtain an appropriate operator form of the system (3) and (4).

II. Weak Formulation

The weak solution $(\mathbf{E}_1, \mathbf{H})$ of the system (3)-(4) satisfies:

$$(\varepsilon\mathbf{E}_{1,t}, \mathbf{\Phi}) - (\nabla \times \mathbf{H}, \mathbf{\Phi}) = (\mathbf{J}_1, \mathbf{\Phi}) \quad \forall \mathbf{\Phi} \in \mathbf{L}^2(\Omega), \tag{7}$$

$$(\mu\mathbf{H}_t, \mathbf{\Psi}) + (\mathbf{E}_1, \nabla \times \mathbf{\Psi}) = 0 \quad \forall \mathbf{\Psi} \in \mathbf{H}(\mathrm{curl}; \Omega), \tag{8}$$

for $t \in (0, T)$ with the initial conditions,

$$\mathbf{E}_1(0) = \mathbf{E}_{1,0} \quad \text{and} \quad \mathbf{H}(0) = \mathbf{H}_0.$$

The weak solution $\mathbf{E}_2$ of the equation (5) satisfies:

$$(\varepsilon\mathbf{E}_{2,t}, \mathbf{\Phi}) = (\mathbf{J}_2, \mathbf{\Phi}) \quad \forall \mathbf{\Phi} \in \mathbf{L}^2(\Omega), \tag{9}$$

for $t \in (0, T)$ with the initial condition,

$$\mathbf{E}_2(0) = \mathbf{E}_{2,0}.$$

It also holds that $\mathbf{E}_0 = \mathbf{E}_{1,0} + \mathbf{E}_{2,0}$. Next we shall convert the equations (3) and (4) into the operator form.

III. Operator Form

The discrete operators $\mathbf{G}$ and $\tilde{\mathbf{G}}$ are used to convert the system of Maxwell's equations into an operator form. Let $\mathbf{G} : \mathbf{V} \to \mathbf{U}_h$ be defined as follows: For $\mathbf{v} \in \mathbf{V}$, the element $\mathbf{G}\mathbf{v} \in \mathbf{U}_h$ is the solution of the variational problem,

$$(\mathbf{G}\mathbf{v}, \mathbf{\Phi}^h) = (\nabla \times \mathbf{v}, \mathbf{\Phi}^h) \quad \forall \mathbf{\Phi}^h \in \mathbf{U}_h, \tag{10}$$

(the operator $\mathbf{G}$ is similar to the operator defined in [7]). Since $\nabla \times \mathbf{V}_h \subset \mathbf{U}_h$, we may conclude that,

$$\mathbf{G}\mathbf{v}^h = \nabla \times \mathbf{v}^h \quad \forall \mathbf{v}^h \in \mathbf{V}_h. \tag{11}$$

Now, we define an operator $\tilde{\mathbf{G}} : \mathbf{L}^2(\Omega) \to \mathbf{V}_h$ as follows: Given $\mathbf{u} \in \mathbf{L}^2(\Omega)$, the element $\tilde{\mathbf{G}}\mathbf{u} \in \mathbf{V}_h$ is the solution of the variational problem,

$$(\tilde{\mathbf{G}}\mathbf{u}, \mathbf{\Psi}^h) = (\mathbf{u}, \nabla \times \mathbf{\Psi}^h) \quad \forall \mathbf{\Psi}^h \in \mathbf{V}_h. \tag{12}$$

Furthermore, the system (3)-(4) can be written in the operator form,

$$\frac{\partial}{\partial t}\begin{pmatrix}\mathbf{E}_1^h \\ \mathbf{H}^h\end{pmatrix} - \mathcal{F}(\varepsilon)\begin{pmatrix}\mathbf{E}_1^h \\ \mathbf{H}^h\end{pmatrix} = \begin{pmatrix}(\varepsilon)^{-1}\mathbf{J}_1^h \\ 0\end{pmatrix}, \tag{13}$$

with the operator matrix,

$$\mathcal{F}(\varepsilon) = \begin{pmatrix} 0 & (\varepsilon)^{-1}\mathbf{G} \\ -\tilde{\mathbf{G}} & 0\end{pmatrix}. \tag{14}$$

Now we define the inner product on the vector functions $\mathbf{u}_1 = (\mathbf{E}_1^h, \mathbf{H}_1^h)^T$ and $\mathbf{u}_2 = (\mathbf{E}_2^h, \mathbf{H}_2^h)^T$ for all $\mathbf{u}_1, \mathbf{u}_2 \in \mathbf{L}_\varepsilon^2(\Omega) \times \mathbf{L}_\mu^2(\Omega)$:

$$\left(\begin{pmatrix}\mathbf{E}_1^h \\ \mathbf{H}_1^h\end{pmatrix}, \begin{pmatrix}\mathbf{E}_2^h \\ \mathbf{H}_2^h\end{pmatrix}\right) = (\mathbf{E}_1^h, \mathbf{E}_2^h)_\varepsilon + (\mathbf{H}_1^h, \mathbf{H}_2^h)_\mu. \tag{15}$$

The associated norm is:

$$\left|\left|\left|\begin{pmatrix}\mathbf{E}_1^h \\ \mathbf{H}^h\end{pmatrix}\right|\right|\right| = \left(\begin{pmatrix}\mathbf{E}_1^h \\ \mathbf{H}^h\end{pmatrix}, \begin{pmatrix}\mathbf{E}_1^h \\ \mathbf{H}^h\end{pmatrix}\right)^{1/2}. \tag{16}$$

The pair (ξ, ζ) is defined by:

$$\begin{pmatrix}\xi(t) \\ \zeta(t)\end{pmatrix} = \begin{pmatrix}\mathbf{P}_h\mathbf{E}_1(t) \\ \Pi_h\mathbf{H}(t)\end{pmatrix}, \tag{17}$$

where $\mathbf{P}_h$ and Π_h are certain projection operators for the electric $(\mathbf{E}_1)$ and magnetic field intensities, respectively (cf. [1], [4], [5], [7], [8]).

IV. Results

(a) Let $(\mathbf{E}_1, \mathbf{H})$ be the weak solution of (7)-(8), and $(\mathbf{E}_1^h, \mathbf{H}^h)$ be a finite element approximation resulting from the application of Nédeléc curl- and div-conforming elements. Then the pair (ξ, ζ) satisfies:

$$\frac{\partial}{\partial t}\begin{pmatrix}\xi \\ \zeta\end{pmatrix} - \mathcal{F}(\varepsilon)\begin{pmatrix}\xi \\ \zeta\end{pmatrix} = \begin{pmatrix}(\varepsilon)^{-1}\mathbf{J}_{1,h} \\ 0\end{pmatrix}. \tag{18}$$

(b) Let $(\mathbf{E}_1, \mathbf{H})$ and $\mathbf{E}_2$ be the weak solution of (7)-(8) and (9) respectively. Let $(\mathbf{E}_1^h, \mathbf{H}^h)$ and $\mathbf{E}_2^h$ be a finite element approximation resulting from the application of Nédeléc curl- and div-conforming elements. Then there exists a constant C independent of h and t such that:

$$\begin{aligned} &\|\mathbf{E}-\mathbf{E}^h\|_{\mathbf{L}_\varepsilon^2(\Omega)} + \|\mathbf{H} - \mathbf{H}^h\|_{\mathbf{L}_\mu^2(\Omega)} \\ &\quad \leq C\Big(\|(\mathbf{E}_1 - \mathbf{P}_h\mathbf{E}_1)(t)\|_{\mathbf{L}_\varepsilon^2(\Omega)} + \|(\mathbf{H} - \Pi_h\mathbf{H})(t)\|_{\mathbf{L}_\mu^2(\Omega)} \\ &\quad + \|(\mathbf{E}_1^h - \mathbf{P}_h\mathbf{E}_1)(0)\|_{\mathbf{L}_\varepsilon^2(\Omega)} + \|(\mathbf{H}^h - \Pi_h\mathbf{H})(0)\|_{\mathbf{L}_\mu^2(\Omega)} \\ &\quad + \|\mathbf{P}_h^\perp\mathbf{E}_{2,0} - \mathbf{E}_{2,0}\|_{\mathbf{L}_\varepsilon^2(\Omega)} + \|\mathbf{E}_{2,0} - \mathbf{E}_{2,0}^h\|_{\mathbf{L}_\varepsilon^2(\Omega)} \\ &\quad + \|(\mathbf{E}_2 - \mathbf{P}_h^\perp\mathbf{E}_2)(t)\|_{\mathbf{L}_\varepsilon^2(\Omega)} \\ &\quad + \int_0^t \|\mathbf{P}_h^\perp\mathbf{E}_{2,t} - \mathbf{E}_{2,t}\|_{\mathbf{L}_\varepsilon^2(\Omega)} d\tau \Big), \end{aligned}$$

where $\mathbf{P}_h^\perp$ is a certain projection operator for the electric field intensity $\mathbf{E}_2$.

V. Conclusion

Progress in the advancement of mixed finite element methods for solving the three-dimensional Maxwell's equations is presented for the case when the permittivity ϵ and the permeability μ are matrix-valued functions of space. Error estimates for the the time-dependent Maxwell's equations are obtained if Nédeléc's conforming finite element on tetrahedra are used. In addition, the method allows a stability and convergence analysis. The operator form of the problem is easy to implement.

In the ongoing work we extend the above time-dependent Maxwell's equations to a nonlinear situation, the publication is in preparation. Numerical results are also obtained for several other problems. Updated numerical results for linear and nonlinear problems can be obtained from [10].

References

[1] A. Anees and L. Angermann, "A mixed finite element method approximation for the Maxwell's equations in Electromagnetics," in the processing IEEE International Conference on Wireless Information Technology and Systems (ICWITS) and Applied Computational Electromagnetics (ACES), 2016, 179-180.

[2] A. Anees and L. Angermann, "Time domain finite element methods for Maxwell's equations in three dimensions," in the processing IEEE International Conference and Applied Computational Electromagnetics Society (ACES) Symposium, in press.

[3] L. Angermann and V. V. Yatsyk, "Numerical simulation of the diffraction of weak electromagnetic waves by a Kerr-type nonlinear dielectric layer," Int. J. Electromagnetic Waves and Electronic Systems, vol. 13, pp. 15-30, 2008.

[4] P. Monk, "An analysis of Nédélec's method for the spatial discretization of Maxwell's equations," J. Comput. Appl., Math., vol. 47, pp. 101-121, 1993.

[5] P. Monk, "A mixed method for approximating Maxwell's equations," SIAM J. Numer. Anal., vol. 28, pp. 1610-1634, 1991.

[6] P. Monk, "Analysis of a finite element method for Maxwell's equations," SIAM J. Numer. Anal., vol. 29, pp. 714-729, 1992.

[7] C. G. Makridakis and P. Monk, "Time discrete finite element scheme for Maxwell's equations," Mathematical Modelling and Numerical Analysis, vol. 29, pp. 171-197, 1995.

[8] J. C. Nédélec, "Mixed finite element method in $\mathbb{R}^3$," Numer. Math., vol. 35, pp. 315-341, 1980.

[9] J. C. Nédélec, "A new family of mixed finite element method in $\mathbb{R}^3$," Numer. Math., vol. 50, pp. 57-81, 1986.

[10] https://github.com/Asadanees

Time-Domain Magnetic Shielding Effectiveness of Planar Stratified Shields

R. Araneo, G. Lovat, and S. Celozzi
DIAEE - EE Division
Sapienza University of Rome
Rome, Italy
rodolfo.araneo, giampiero.lovat, salvatore.celozzi@uniroma1.it

P. Burghignoli
D.I.E.T.
Sapienza University of Rome
Rome, Italy
burghignoli@diet.uniroma1.it

***Abstract*—The shielding effectiveness of a planar multilayered screen is computed in the time domain in the presence of near-field magnetic sources. The proposed numerical method involves the efficient evaluation of classical Sommerfeld integrals and the inverse-Fourier transform through double-exponential formulas. For sufficiently thin screens with highly-conductive properties, an analytical method, based on a modified Cagniard-de Hoop approach, is also presented to validate the results.**

I. Introduction

Recently, shielding of typical transient sources [1]–[4] has been the subject of time-domain (TD) numerical and analytical studies [5], [6] aimed at assessing the relevant theoretical electromagnetic (EM) phenomena. In the literature, relatively few papers [7], [8] have tried to address the problem of evaluating the transient EM field due to a pulsed source in the presence of general planar multilayered structures. In particular cases, when the screen is thin and the sources are pulsed lines or pulsed vertical dipoles, the solution can be obtained in analytical or semi-analytical form through modified Cagniard-de Hoop approaches [5], [9]–[11]. In more general cases and when the shield is thick and/or multilayered, the numerical approach is often the only possible way.

Recently, the TD potential Green's function in planar multilayered structures has been derived through a generalized ray theory, based on the Cagniard-de Hoop approach [12] originally proposed in [13] for non-dispersive and lossless media. Other approaches [14] are also available, but their applicability remains limited.

In this paper we consider the evaluation of the TD shielding effectiveness (SE) of a planar multilayered shield excited by a pulsed magnetic vertical dipole through a conventional two-steps procedure: at first we obtain the frequency-domain (FD) solution via a spatial-wavenumber synthesis through the inverse Fourier-Bessel transform; then we compute the TD solution via the inverse Fourier transform (IFT). Usually, such an approach can be computationally intensive since the evaluation of oscillatory infinite integrals is required. However, by using efficient techniques based on the double-exponential formulas, the numerical burden is drastically reduced, thus allowing for a rapid solution of the problem.

With a practical engineering approach, the methodology is applied to compute new figures of merit proposed directly in the time domain [4] in order to carry out predictive results allowing deeper insights into the behaviour of metal shielding.

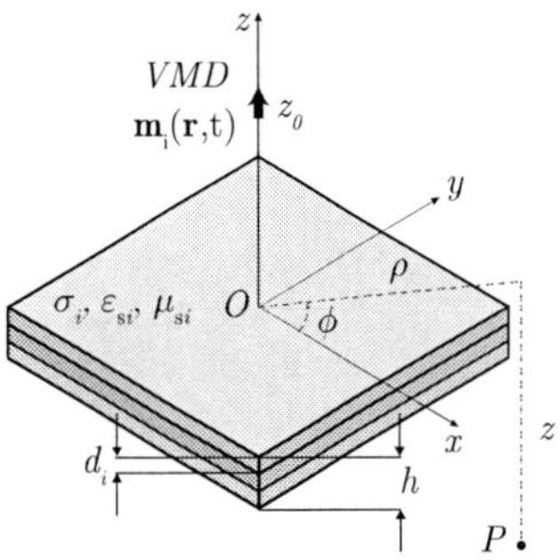

Fig. 1. The configuration under analysis with the relevant reference system and physical parameters.

II. The Problem and its Numerical Solution

Figure 1 shows the configuration under analysis: it consists of an infinite planar screen of total thickness h constituted by N layers. Each layer is characterized by its thickness d_i, electric permittivity $\varepsilon_{si} = \varepsilon_0\varepsilon_{sri}$, magnetic permeability $\mu_{si} = \mu_0\mu_{sri}$, and conductivity σ_i ($i = 1, \ldots, N$); two non-conductive half-spaces $z > 0$ and $z < -h$ with electric permittivity ε_0 and magnetic permeability μ_0 are assumed above and below the shield; the shield is excited by a vertical magnetic dipole source $\mathbf{m} = \mu_0 i(t)S\mathbf{u}_z$ at $z = z_0 > 0$ in air.

In the FD domain, due to the axial symmetry of the configuration, the solution can be obtained through a spectral-domain approach, where, according to [15], the structure is represented with a cascade of equivalent transmission lines.

Since we are interested in computing only the field in the shielded region (for $z < 0$), we compute the generalized transmission coefficient T [15], [16] at the shield-air interface. In the FD the expressions of the field components radiated by a VMD in the shielded region are:

$$E_\phi(\rho, z) = \frac{\omega m(\omega)}{4\pi} \int_0^\infty T^{\mathrm{TE}} \frac{k_\rho^2}{k_{z,0}} \mathrm{e}^{-jk_{z,0}|\Delta z|} \mathrm{J}_1(k_\rho\rho)\, \mathrm{d}k_\rho\,, \tag{1}$$

$$H_\rho(\rho, z) = -\frac{m(\omega)}{4\pi\mu_0}\int_0^\infty T^{\mathrm{TE}} k_\rho^2 \mathrm{e}^{-jk_{z,0}|\Delta z|} \mathrm{J}_1(k_\rho \rho)\, \mathrm{d}k_\rho\,, \tag{2}$$

$$H_z(\rho, z) = \frac{-jm(\omega)}{4\pi\mu 0}\int_0^\infty T^{\mathrm{TE}} \frac{k_\rho^3}{k_{z,0}} \mathrm{e}^{-jk_{z,0}|\Delta z|} \mathrm{J}_0(k_\rho \rho)\, \mathrm{d}k_\rho\,, \tag{3}$$

where $\mathrm{J}_{0,1}(\cdot)$ are the Bessel functions of the first kind, of order 0 and 1, respectively, and T^{TE} is the generalized TE transmission coefficient of the multilayer. Finally, the TD expressions of the EM field can be computed performing the inverse Fourier transform as:

$$f(t) = \frac{1}{\pi}\int_0^\infty \left[\Re(F)\cos(\omega t) - \Im(F)\sin(\omega t)\right] \mathrm{d}\omega\,, \tag{4}$$

where F is the generic FD field component. All the relevant integrations, both in the spectral and the frequency domain, have been performed with efficient double-exponential formulas [17].

Figures 2 show the peak-reduction (PR) efficiency and the derivative-reduction (DR) efficiency [4] of a double-layer aluminum-iron shield ($\sigma_1 = 37.7$ MS/m and $\sigma_2 = 1$ MS/m; note that the layers are considered of equal thickness $h/2$) as a function of the total thickness h considering a current waveform in the $m(t)$ the first time derivative of a power exponential pulse (DPEP - with parameters $I_0 = 1$ A, $T_c = 10$ ms, and $n = 16$) [5].

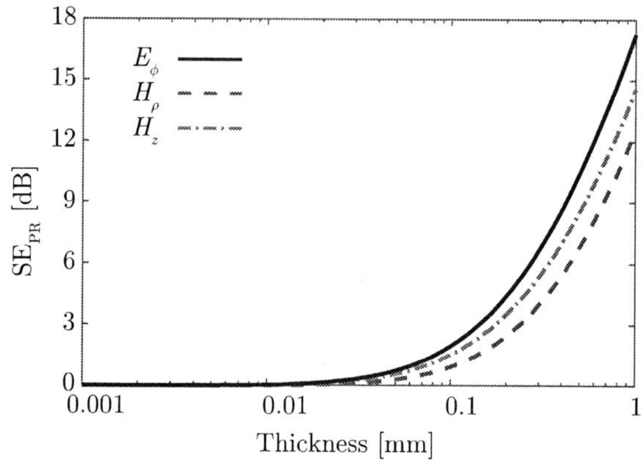

(a)

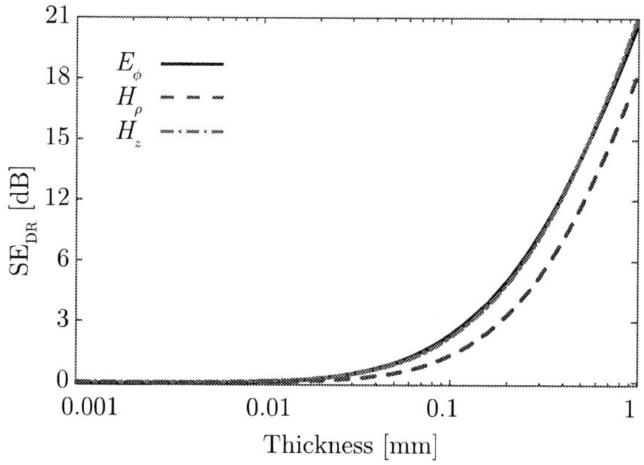

(b)

Fig. 2. Peak-reduction efficiency $\mathrm{SE}_{\mathrm{PR}}$ (a) and derivative-reduction efficiency $\mathrm{SE}_{\mathrm{DR}}$ (b) of a double layer aluminum-iron shield ($\sigma_1 = 37.7$ MS/m and $\sigma_2 = 1$ MS/m) with respect to the total thickness h.

REFERENCES

[1] W. A. Radasky and M. Wik, "Overview of the threat of intentional electromagnetic interference (IEMI)," in *Proc. IEEE Electromagn. Compat. Symp.*, vol. 2, 2003, pp. 1024–1027.

[2] R. Araneo, S. Celozzi, A. Tatematsu, and F. Rachidi, "Time-domain analysis of building shielding against lightning electromagnetic fields," *IEEE Trans. Electromagn. Compat.*, vol. 57, no. 3, pp. 397–404, Jun. 2015.

[3] R. Araneo and S. Celozzi, "TD-Shielding effectiveness of enclosures in presence of ESD," in *Proc. EMC Europe Symp.*, Brugge (NL), 2-6 Sep. 2013, pp. 541–544.

[4] S. Celozzi and R. Araneo, "Alternative definitions for the time-domain shielding effectiveness of enclosures," *IEEE Trans. Electromagn. Compat.*, vol. 56, no. 2, pp. 482–485, Apr. 2014.

[5] P. Burghignoli, G. Lovat, R. Araneo, and S. Celozzi, "Time-domain shielding of a thin conductive sheet in the presence of pulsed vertical dipoles," *IEEE Trans. Electromagn. Compat.*, vol. 60, no. 1, pp. 157–165, Feb. 2018.

[6] R. Araneo, G. Lovat, S. Celozzi, and P. Burghignoli, "Time domain magnetic shielding performance of thin shields," in *2017 17th Int. Conf. Environ. and Electr. Eng. and 1st Ind. and Com. Power Systems Europe*, Milan, Italy, 6-9 Jun. 2017, pp. 1–5.

[7] M. R. Cabello, L. D. Angulo, J. Alvarez, I. D. Flintoft, S. Bourke, J. F. Dawson, R. G. Martín, and S. G. Garcia, "A hybrid Crank-Nicolson FDTD subgridding boundary condition for lossy thin-layer modeling," *IEEE Trans. Microw. Theory Techn.*, vol. 65, no. 5, pp. 1397–1406, May 2017.

[8] M.-L. Zhai, H.-L. Peng, D.-M. Li, D.-W. Wang, H. Xie, and W.-Y. Yin, "Characterization of tunable graphene metasurfaces over an ultrawide terahertz band using a 1-step leapfrog hybrid implicit-explicit FDTD method," *Int. J. Numer. Modell. Electron. Networks Devices Fields*, vol. 30, no. 6, 2017.

[9] A. T. D. Hoop, M. Stumpf, and I. E. Lager, "Pulsed electromagnetic field radiation from a wide slot antenna with a dielectric layer," *IEEE Trans. Antennas Propag.*, vol. 59, no. 8, pp. 2789–2798, Aug. 2011.

[10] G. Lovat, R. Araneo, and S. Celozzi, "Near-field time-domain shielding effectiveness of thin conductive screens," *Progr. Electromag. Res.*, vol. 146, pp. 47–56, 2014.

[11] G. Lovat and R. Araneo, "Semi-analytical representation of the two-dimensional time-domain Green's function of a graphene sheet in the intraband regime," *IEEE Trans. Nanotech.*, vol. 14, no. 4, pp. 681–688, Jul. 2015.

[12] M. Štumpf, A. T. D. Hoop, and G. A. E. Vandenbosch, "Generalized ray theory for time-domain electromagnetic fields in horizontally layered media," *IEEE Trans. Antennas Propag.*, vol. 61, no. 5, pp. 2676–2687, May 2013.

[13] R. Dai and C. T. Young, "Transient fields of a horizontal electric dipole on a multilayered dielectric medium," *IEEE Trans. Antennas Propag.*, vol. 45, no. 6, pp. 1023–1031, Jun. 1997.

[14] G. W. Hanson, A. B. Yakovlev, and J. Hao, "Leaky-wave analysis of transient fields due to sources in planarly layered media," *IEEE Trans. Antennas Propag.*, vol. 51, no. 2, pp. 146–159, Feb. 2003.

[15] K. A. Michalski and J. R. Mosig, "Multilayered media Green's functions in integral equation formulations," *IEEE Trans. Antennas Propag.*, vol. 45, no. 3, pp. 508–519, Mar. 1997.

[16] W. C. Chew, *Waves and Fields in Inhomogenous Media*. Piscataway, NJ: IEEE Press, 1999.

[17] A. G. Polimeridis and J. R. Mosig, "Fast computation of Sommerfeld integral tails via direct integration based on double exponential-type quadrature formulas," *IEEE Trans. Antennas Propag.*, vol. 59, no. 2, pp. 694–699, Feb. 2011.

Modeling Time Domain Multiphysics of Reverse Saturable Absorption

Shaimaa I. Azzam and Alexander V. Kildishev
School of Electrical and Computer Engineering and Birck Nanotechnology Center
Purdue University
West Lafayette, IN 47907, USA
kildishev@purdue.edu

***Abstract*— In this work, a time domain model that can accurately describe the dynamics of materials exhibiting reverse saturable absorption is proposed and validated. A set of rate equations is used to describe the atomic transitions between different singlet ant triplet states which is then coupled to the finite difference time domain method through a Lorentzian equation. The results of our model match the experimental measurements and we believe it will enable accurate design and optimization of optical limiting devices.**

Keywords*— *Finite difference time domain; rate equations; reverse saturable absorption; optical limiters.

I. Intoduction

There has been a growing need in the optical community to protect optical sensors and more importantly human eyes from accidental or intentional harm caused by high intensity optical sources. This is accomplished by an optical limiter, which should have a low linear absorption at low intensities and high absorption at higher intensities. This is the characteristic of some nonlinear materials that exhibit reverse saturable absorption (RSA). Surprisingly there have been few efforts to develop complete multiphysics models of optical devices that can act as, or perhaps more importantly, enhance the RSA behavior of optical limiting devices. We believe that one critical factor that is hindering the ability to optimize and enhance optical limiting devices is the lack of material models that account for the quantum mechanical origin of RSA and its relevant representation in the time domain. RSA is a resonant nonlinear absorption effect that takes place when the absorption is more efficient in the excited states than it is in the ground states. Stated more rigorously, RSA occurs when the absorption cross-section of the excited states is much larger than the absorption cross-section of the ground states ($\sigma_{ex} \gg \sigma_g$). RSA also requires the lifetime of the triplet state to be relatively long.

In this work, we propose what is to our knowledge a novel time domain approach based on the finite difference time domain method which models the RSA as an atomic four level system, Fig. 1. Using this model, we can not only model the different transitions taking place in the material and how it affects its nonlinear optical response, but we can also use it to help understand the chemical decomposition effects on the efficiency of the RSA.

The authors acknowledge the financial support by DARPA/DSO Extreme Optics and Imaging (EXTREME) Program, Award HR00111720032.

II. Atomic Model for RSA

The atom or molecule of the absorbing material is modeled by an atomic 4-level system with the Jablonski diagram shown in Fig. 1. The atom is excited from the ground singlet state S0 to the first singlet state S1 by absorbing a photon of incident light. The excited molecule at S1 can then return to S0 by radiating the same photon again or can exhibit an intersystem crossing (ISC) relaxation to the first triplet state T1. The atom at T1 can either relax to S0 or can be promoted to the second triplet state T2 by absorbing a second photon. For the RSA to be efficient, two important conditions should be satisfied. First, sufficient population of molecules should be transferred to T1, which requires efficient ISC and long triplet state lifetime. Second, the absorption cross section of the excited triplet states must be larger than that of the ground singlet state $\sigma_{ex} \gg \sigma_g$.

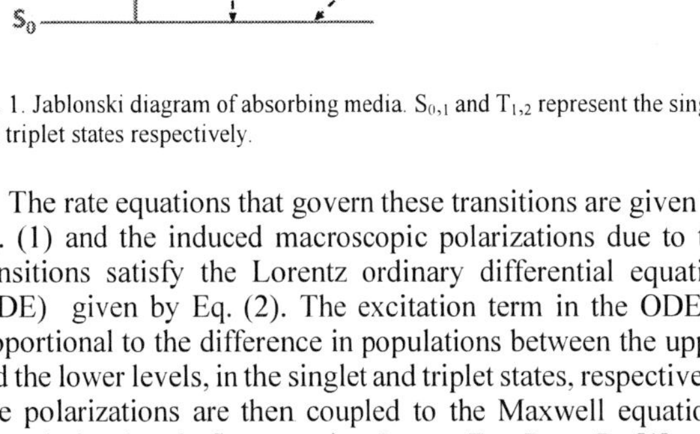

Fig. 1. Jablonski diagram of absorbing media. $S_{0,1}$ and $T_{1,2}$ represent the singlet and triplet states respectively.

The rate equations that govern these transitions are given by Eq. (1) and the induced macroscopic polarizations due to the transitions satisfy the Lorentz ordinary differential equation (ODE) given by Eq. (2). The excitation term in the ODE is proportional to the difference in populations between the upper and the lower levels, in the singlet and triplet states, respectively. The polarizations are then coupled to the Maxwell equations through the electric flux equation $\boldsymbol{D} = \epsilon_0 \boldsymbol{E} + \boldsymbol{P}_T + \boldsymbol{P}_S$ [1].

$$\frac{\partial N_{S1}}{\partial t} = -\frac{N_{S1}}{\tau_{S10}} - \frac{N_{S1}}{\tau_{ISC}} + \frac{1}{\hbar\omega_0}\boldsymbol{E}\cdot\frac{\partial \boldsymbol{P}_s}{\partial t},$$
$$\frac{\partial N_{S0}}{\partial t} = \frac{N_{S1}}{\tau_{S10}} + \frac{N_{T1}}{\tau_{T10}} - \frac{1}{\hbar\omega_0}\boldsymbol{E}\cdot\frac{\partial \boldsymbol{P}_s}{\partial t}, \quad (1)$$
$$\frac{\partial N_{T2}}{\partial t} = -\frac{N_{T2}}{\tau_{T21}} + \frac{1}{\hbar\omega_0}\boldsymbol{E}\cdot\frac{\partial \boldsymbol{P}_T}{\partial t},$$
$$\frac{\partial N_{T1}}{\partial t} = \frac{N_{S1}}{\tau_{ISC}} + \frac{N_{T2}}{\tau_{T21}} - \frac{N_{T1}}{\tau_{T10}} - \frac{1}{\hbar\omega_0}\boldsymbol{E}\cdot\frac{\partial \boldsymbol{P}_T}{\partial t}.$$

$$\frac{\partial^2 \boldsymbol{P}_i}{\partial t^2} + \Delta\omega_{ij}\frac{\partial \boldsymbol{P}_i}{\partial t} + \omega_0^2 \boldsymbol{P}_i = k_i(N_l - N_u)\boldsymbol{E}, \quad (2)$$
$$i \in \{S, T\}.$$

The coupling coefficients k_i define the strength of the coupling of each oscillator to the light.

III. Results and Discussions

We use a thin film of 100 μm of the organic material Zinc 5,10,15,20-tetra(4-pyridyl)-porphyrin (ZnTPyP) as an example to test our model [2]. Life times and absorption cross sections are fitted from the experiment [2]. A 10-ps plane wave laser pulse centered at 532 nm is normally incident on the film and the transmittance is recorded as shown in Fig. 2 (a). As expected, the transmittance drops with increasing the incident energy of the input beam. A sample of one of the numerous time dynamics records available from our model is the kinetics of molecule population densities at different singlet and triplet states at Energy = 0.1 mJ can be seen in Fig. 2 (b). A more detailed analysis illustrated with a gallery of 'snapshots' capturing the evolution of diverse physics will be addressed in our presentation.

IV. Conclusion

In conclusion, a numerical model for reverse saturable absorption based on rate equations has been presented and validated. The suggested model is reproducing behavior similar to reported experiments. We are very optimistic that the proposed model can open up new opportunities for optimizing and enhancing optical limiting devices and for significantly improving the predictive power of our multiphysics design tools.

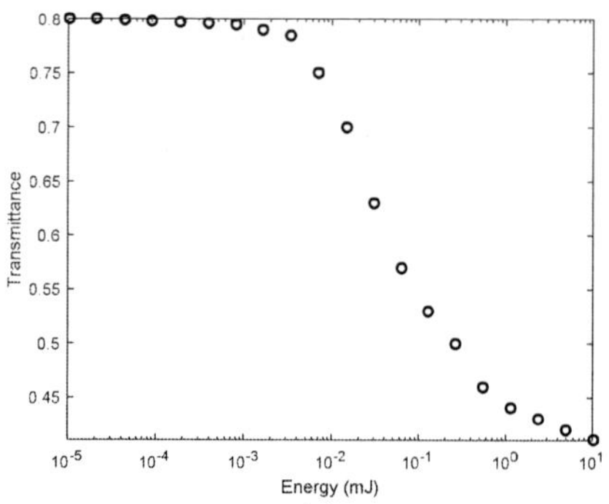

(a)

V.

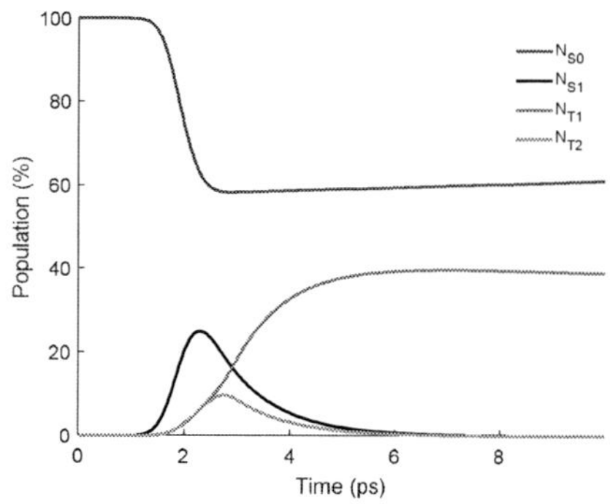

(b)

Fig. 2. (a) Transmittance of a thin film of ZnTPyP versus incident energy. (b) Molecule population densities at different singlet and triplet states at Energy = 0.1 mJ.

References

[1] A. Taflove and S. C. Hagness, Computational electrodynamics: The Finite-Difference Time-Domain Method, Artech House, 2005.

[2] N. M. Barbosa Neto, S. L. Oliveira, I. Guedes, L. R. Dinelli, L. Misoguti, C. R. Mendonça, A. A. Batista, and S. C. Zílio, "Reverse saturable absorption in 5, 10, 15, 20-Tetra (4-pyridyl)-21H, 23H-porphyrin with ruthenium outlying complexes," Journal of the Brazilian Chemical Society, vol. 17, pp. 1377-1782, 2006.

Time Domain Finite Element Methods for Maxwell's Equations in Three Dimensions

Asad Anees
Institute of Mathematics
Clausthal University of Technology
Clausthal-Zellerfeld, Germany, D-38678
asad.anees@tu-clausthal.de

Lutz Angermann
Institute of Mathematics
Clausthal University of Technology
Clausthal-Zellerfeld, Germany, D-38678
lutz.angermann@tu-clausthal.de

***Abstract*—In this paper, time-domain finite element simulations for Maxwells equations in bounded three-dimensional domains are presented. We describe fully discrete time-domain methods and provide some numerical results. The obtained fields are visualized on tetrahedral meshes. The proposed methods are accurate in time up to order 4, in case of symplectic time integration they are conditionally stable.**

***Index Terms*—Maxwell's equations, time domain finite element methods, visualization, absolute error.**

I. Introduction

Let Ω be a smooth, simply connected domain in $\mathbb{R}^3$ with boundary Γ and unit outward normal $\mathbf{n}$. Let $\mathbf{E} = \mathbf{E}(\mathbf{x}, t)$ and $\mathbf{H} = \mathbf{H}(\mathbf{x}, t)$ denote the electric and magnetic field intensities respectively, where the time variable t belongs to some interval $(0, T)$, $T > 0$. Given a current density function $\mathbf{J} = \mathbf{J}(\mathbf{x}, t)$, specifying the applied current, Maxwell's equations state that

$$\varepsilon \mathbf{E}_t + \sigma \mathbf{E} - \nabla \times \mathbf{H} = \mathbf{J} \quad \text{in } \Omega \times (0, T), \tag{1}$$

$$\mu \mathbf{H}_t + \nabla \times \mathbf{E} = 0 \quad \text{in } \Omega \times (0, T). \tag{2}$$

We shall assume a perfect conducting boundary condition on Ω, that is,

$$\mathbf{n} \times \mathbf{E} = 0 \quad \text{on } \Gamma \times (0, T).$$

In addition, initial conditions have to be specified so that

$$\mathbf{E}(\mathbf{x}, 0) = \mathbf{E}_0(\mathbf{x}) \text{ and } \mathbf{H}(\mathbf{x}, 0) = \mathbf{H}_0(\mathbf{x}) \text{ for all } \mathbf{x} \in \Omega,$$

where $\mathbf{E}_0$ and $\mathbf{H}_0$ are given functions and $\mathbf{H}_0$ satisfies:

$$\nabla \cdot (\mu \mathbf{H}_0) = 0 \quad \text{in } \Omega, \quad \mathbf{H}_0 \cdot \mathbf{n} = 0 \quad \text{on } \Gamma.$$

We consider time-independent dielectric permittivity ε, magnetic permeability μ and electric conductivity σ. Basis functions of arbitrary order are constructed for all the fields in (1)-(2). Based on [3] and [4], 1-form basis functions are constructed for $\mathbf{E}$ and $\mathbf{J}$ with order p. Similarly p-order 2-form basis function are constructed for $\mathbf{H}$.

The authors would like to thank the DAAD to provide the Research-Grant (91564387) within funding program 57129429. .

II. Weak Formulation

The weak solution $(\mathbf{E}, \mathbf{H})$ of the system (1)-(2) satisfies

$$(\varepsilon \mathbf{E}_t, \mathbf{\Phi}) - (\mathbf{H}, \nabla \times \mathbf{\Phi}) = (\mathbf{J}, \mathbf{\Phi}) \forall \mathbf{\Phi} \in \mathbf{H}(\text{curl}; \Omega), \tag{3}$$

$$(\mu \mathbf{H}_t, \mathbf{\Psi}) + (\nabla \times \mathbf{E}, \mathbf{\Psi}) = 0 \quad \forall \mathbf{\Psi} \in \mathbf{H}(\text{div}; \Omega) \tag{4}$$

for $t \in (0, T)$ with the initial conditions,

$$\mathbf{E}(0) = \mathbf{E}_0 \quad \text{and} \quad \mathbf{H}(0) = \mathbf{H}_0.$$

The method uses edge finite elements as a basis for the electric field and face finite elements for the magnetic flux density. The edge elements have tangential continuity whereas the face elements have normal continuity across interfaces. This leads to the following semi-discrete matrix equations

$$\mathbf{M}_\varepsilon^{(1)} \mathbf{e}_t + \mathbf{M}_\sigma^{(1)} \mathbf{e} = \left(\mathbf{G}^{(12)}\right)^\top \mathbf{h} + \mathbf{J}^{(1)}, \tag{5}$$

$$\mathbf{M}_\mu^{(2)} \mathbf{h}_t = -\mathbf{G}^{(12)} \mathbf{e}, \tag{6}$$

where $\mathbf{M}^{(1)}$ and $\mathbf{M}^{(2)}$ are the first 1-form and 2-form mass matrices respectively. The matrix $\mathbf{G}^{(12)}$ is a discrete representation of the curl operator. $\mathbf{e}$ and $\mathbf{h}$ are the vectors of electric fields and magnetic fields degrees of freedom. $\mathbf{J}^{(1)}$ is a discrete current source. Since the vectors $\mathbf{e}$ and $\mathbf{h}$ have different dimensions, $\mathbf{G}^{(12)}$ is rectangular.

III. Time Discretization

For brevity, a first order symplectic method for the system (3)-(4) is given here as an example:

$$\mathbf{nstep} = \frac{t_{final} - t_0}{\Delta t}$$

Set the initial conditions

$\mathbf{e}_1 \leftarrow \mathbf{e}_{Initial}, \mathbf{h}_1 \leftarrow \mathbf{h}_{Initial}$

loop over time steps.

for i=1 to nstep do

begin integration method update

$\mathbf{e}_{in} \leftarrow \mathbf{e}_i$,

$\mathbf{h}_{in} \leftarrow \mathbf{h}_i$

update the field values

$$\mathbf{e}_{out} \leftarrow \mathbf{e}_{in} + \Delta t (\mathbf{M}_\varepsilon^{(1)})^{-1} \left(\left(\mathbf{G}^{(12)}\right)^\top \mathbf{h}_{in} - \mathbf{M}_\sigma^{(1)} \mathbf{e}_{in} + \mathbf{J}^{(1)} \right)$$

$$\mathbf{h}_{out} \leftarrow \mathbf{h}_{in} + \Delta t (\mathbf{M}_\mu^{(2)})^{-1} (\mathbf{G}^{(12)}) \mathbf{e}_{out}$$

Update field value for this time step

$\mathbf{e}_{i+1} \leftarrow \mathbf{e}_{out}$;

$\mathbf{h}_{i+1} \leftarrow \mathbf{h}_{out}$

end for

$\mathbf{e}_{final} \leftarrow \mathbf{e}_{nstep+1}$;

$\mathbf{h}_{final} \leftarrow \mathbf{h}_{nstep+1}$.

IV. Simulation Results and Validations

Numerical experiment are performed for the fully discretized Maxwell's equations to check the stability and convergence properties, where the frequency $f = \frac{\sqrt{3}}{2}c_0$ Hz and c_0 is the speed of light in vacuum. $\varepsilon = \varepsilon_0$ and $\mu = \mu_0$ are the vacuum permittivity and permeability respectively. The angular frequency is $\omega = 2\pi f\,(\text{rad}\cdot\text{s}^{-1})$. The exact electric and magnetic fields are taken from [5]:

$$\begin{aligned}
\mathbf{E}_1(t) &= -\cos(\pi x)\sin(\pi y)\sin(\pi z)\cos(\omega t),\\
\mathbf{E}_2(t) &= 0.0,\\
\mathbf{E}_3(t) &= \sin(\pi x)\sin(\pi y)\cos(\pi z)\cos(\omega t),\\
\mathbf{H}_1(t) &= -\frac{\pi}{\omega}\sin(\pi x)\cos(\pi y)\cos(\pi z)\sin(\omega t),\\
\mathbf{H}_2(t) &= \frac{2\pi}{\omega}\cos(\pi x)\sin(\pi y)\cos(\pi z)\sin(\omega t),\\
\mathbf{H}_3(t) &= -\frac{\pi}{\omega}\cos(\pi x)\cos(\pi y)\sin(\pi z)\sin(\omega t).
\end{aligned}$$

For this method we have to ensure a stable time step Δt. The CFL stability condition for symplectic integration method is

$$\Delta t \leq \frac{2}{\sqrt{\rho((\mathbf{M}_\varepsilon^{(1)})^{-1}((\mathbf{G}^{(12)})^\top \mathbf{M}_\mu^{(2)} \mathbf{G}^{(12)})}},$$

where ρ denotes the spectral radius. In Table 1, we summarize the results of the absolute errors $Err(\mathbf{E}) = \|\mathbf{E}(t^n) - \mathbf{E}_h^n\|_{\mathbf{L}^2_\varepsilon(\Omega)}$ and $Err(\mathbf{H}) = \|\mathbf{H}(t^n) - \mathbf{H}_h^n\|_{\mathbf{L}^2_\mu(\Omega)}$ for the fourth order symplectic integration method. We have also

TABLE I:
Absolute Error

Refinement level	Electric and magnetic fields		
	$Err(\mathbf{E})$	$Err(\mathbf{B})$	*stable time step* Δt
l=2	2.786666	1.17524e-08	0.282302ns
l=3	0.733713	2.2434e-09	0.140619ns

tested the convergence for the L-stable backward Euler and for the A-stable implicit midpoint method. Krylov solvers are used for inverting the 1-form (curl-conforming) and 2-form (div-conforming) mass matrices. A conjugate gradient preconditioned linear solver is also implemented in these simulations. Indeed, uniform mesh refinement and several time steps suggested that the methods analyzed in this paper possess good accuracy. Updated simulation results for linear and nonlinear electromagnetic problems can be obtained from [6].

Figs. 1 and 2 represent the relative error of electric and magnetic fields on Esher and beam tetrahedron meshes respectively for the backward Euler method.

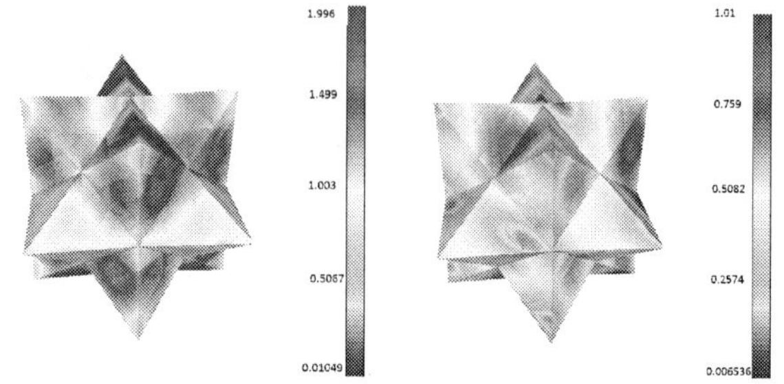

(a) Electric field (b) Magnetic field

Fig. 1: Escher meshes

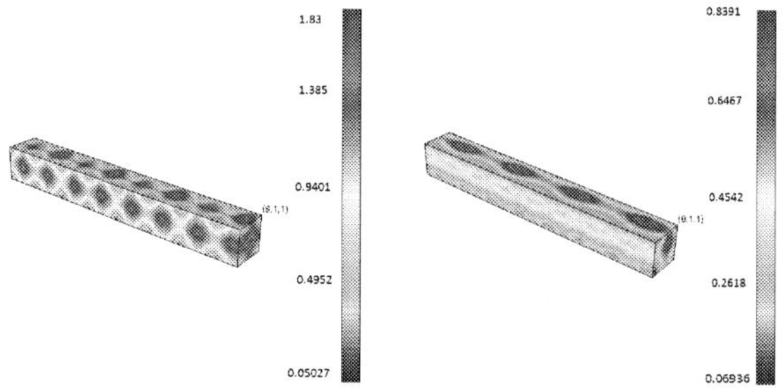

(a) Electric field (b) Magnetic field

Fig. 2: Beam tetrahedron meshes

V. Conclusion

In this paper, Maxwell's equations simulations using finite elements of curl-conforming and div-conforming families have been presented. The simulations have been performed on 3D tetrahedral meshes using time-domain finite element methods. These are direct simulations of Maxwell's equations. The presented time-domain finite element methods are conditionally stable and convergent, they are accurate in time up to order 4.

References

[1] A. Anees and L. Angermann, "A mixed finite element method approximation for the Maxwell's equations in Electromagnetics," in Proceedings of IEEE International Conference on Wireless Information Technology and Systems (ICWITS) and Applied Computational Electromagnetics (ACES), 2016, 179-180.

[2] A. Anees and L. Angermann, "Mixed finite element methods for the Maxwells Equations with matrix parameters," in Proceedings of IEEE international conference and Applied Computational Electromagnetics Society (ACES) Symposium, in press.

[3] A. C Fisher, D. A White, and G. H Rodrigue, "An efficient vector finite element method for nonlinear Electromagnetic modeling," Journal of Computational Physics, June 29, 2006.

[4] G. Rodrigue and D. White, "A vector finite element time-domain method for solving Maxwell's equations on unstructured hexeahedral grids," SIAM J. Sci. Comp., vol. 23, pp. 683-706, 2001.

[5] A. Christophe, S. Descombes, and S. Lanteri, "An implicit hybridized discontinuous Galerkin method for the 3D time-domain Maxwell equations," Applied Mathematics and Computations, in press.

[6] https://github.com/Asadanees

[7] http://mfem.org/

Numerical Simulation of EMP Environment Radiated by X-rays inside a High-Power Laser Facility

Zhiqian Xu
The Department of Engineering Physics
Tsinghua University
Beijing, China

Cui Meng
The Department of Engineering Physics
Tsinghua University
Beijing, China

***Abstract*—In high-power laser facility, X-rays could generate very strong system-generated electromagnetic pulse (SGEMP). There are two types of SGEMP response and they are both studied through the numerical simulation.**

***Keywords*—Finite-difference time-domain method, Monte Carlo method, PIC particle simulation, SGEMP, X-rays.**

I. INTRODUCTION

Researchers in the National Ignition Facility (NIF), which is a high-power laser facility, estimated that the X-rays and electromagnetic pulse (EMP) inside a target chamber would be significant after the laser shooting [1], [2]. To shield against the EMP, a metal shell is essential for the electronic equipment. However, it does not work for the system-generated electromagnetic pulse (SGEMP) caused by X-rays. When X-rays irradiate the metal shielding, a large number of photoelectrons would be emitted toward the internal area. The movement of these high-speed electronics could form a strong transient EM field, or induce a current response on the conductor of cables. As shown in Fig. 1, there are two types of SGEMP, the cavity SGEMP and the cable SGEMP. The SGEMP interference, which is generated by the system's own electrons, could cause severe impact on experiments. Scholars have developed a lot of models and corresponding software, such as ABORC, CEPTRE and CABANA, to predict the SGEMP caused by nuclear explosion and explore the effects of some parameters like the energy and fluence of X-rays [3]-[5].

II. CALCULATION MODEL

In the article, efforts are made to calculate the two SGEMP responses with the cavity model and cable model.

A. Cavity Model

Fig. 2 (a) is the model of a cylindrical metal cavity outside diagnostics. X-rays uniformly irradiate along the direction of the axis. After complex interactions such as photoelectric affect, electrons are emitted with the same speed and orientation, which would excite a strong EM field.

B. Cable Model

Fig. 2 (b) is the model of a coaxial cable consisting of three layers. From inner to outside, each layer's radius is respectively 0.1 mm, 0.5 mm, and 0.7 mm. The X-ray generates electrons inside the cable, which would excite EM field and finally couple current on the center conductor.

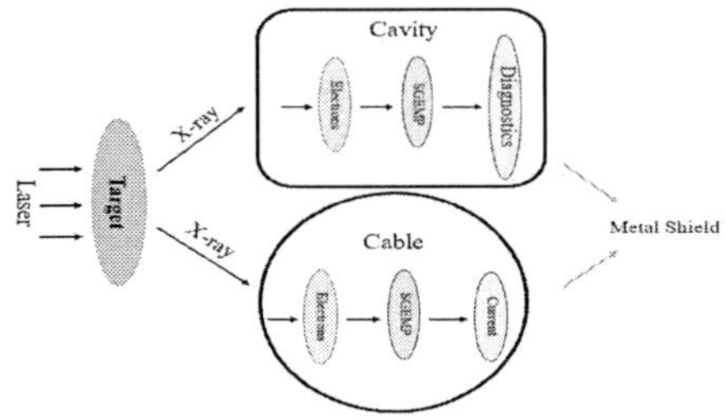

Fig. 1. Two types of SGEMP in ICF chamber.

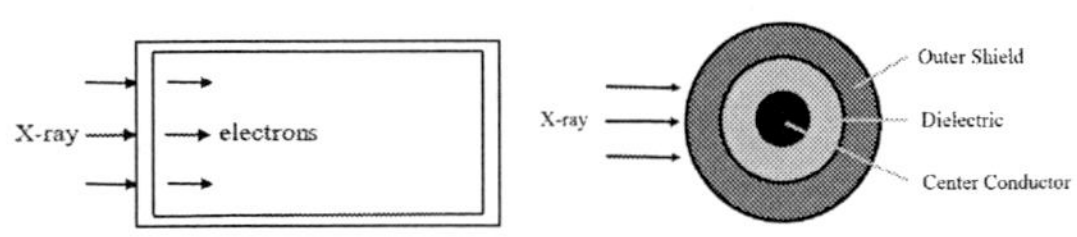

(a) Cavity model (b) Cable model

Fig. 2. Model of the metal shield cavity and the cable.

III. METHODS

Due to the symmetry of models, simulations can be simplified into the two-dimensional coordinate system. Three methods are combined to accomplish the simulation.

A. PIC Particle Simulation

The particle-in-cell (PIC) method is applied to solve the motion of numerous electrons by classifying particles with similar characteristics as a particle cloud. Therefore, the movement of different particles can be represented by that of a particle cloud. The motion equation of particle clouds, as in (1), where γ is the Lorentz factor, is solved by the EM field where they are, which can be calculated by interpolation for the proportion of a particle cloud in grids. Meanwhile, the Boris method is introduced to calculate the velocity since it is close to the speed of light, in which the effect of the EM field is equivalent to the accelerations and the rotation [6];

$$\frac{d(\gamma m v)}{dt} = q(\boldsymbol{E} + v \times \boldsymbol{B}). \tag{1}$$

B. FDTD Method

The finite-difference time-domain (FDTD) method is commonly used to calculate the time-domain EM field. The Maxwell equation was transformed into the central difference schemes. The space and time interval should satisfy Courant stability condition to ensure convergence. Therefore, the EM field at any moment can be solved by repeated iterations, while the current density dispersed to the grid node is known [6]. However, the discrete process will generate high-frequency noise in the results. The time-biased algorithm is added [7], in which the magnetic field at three consecutive moments and a relaxation iteration approach are used. Here, the equation of the EM field becomes (2), where α_1, α_2, and α_3 are the time bias factors and $\tau_i (i = 1, 2, \cdots, I)$ is the relaxation factor;

$$\boldsymbol{E}^{n+1,i} = (1-\tau_i)\boldsymbol{E}^{n+1,i-1} + \tau_i \boldsymbol{E}^{n+1,I} + \frac{\tau_i \Delta t}{\varepsilon}[\nabla \times (\alpha_1 \boldsymbol{H}^{n+\frac{3}{2},i-1} + \alpha_2 \boldsymbol{H}^{n+\frac{1}{2},I} + \alpha_3 \boldsymbol{H}^{n-\frac{1}{2},I}) - \boldsymbol{J}^{n+\frac{1}{2}}]. \quad (2)$$

Because of the restraint of models, the EM field should satisfy certain boundary conditions. In general, it satisfies the ideal conductor boundary condition where the tangential component of electric field is 0. At both ends of the cable, the absorbing boundary condition is applied. The propagation of the EM wave satisfies the unidirectional wave equation, which is equivalent to impedance matching [6].

C. Monte Carlo Method

The Monte Carlo method is an important numerical method for the computer to solve randomness problems. Based on the theory of possibility and statistics, a random number is generated to simulate many physical processes. It is commonly applied in the problem of particle transport and the Monte Carlo N-Particle Code (MCNP) is a software package designed for this. If the energy and fluence of X-rays are known, the emitted electrons can be calculated by the MCNP.

IV. Calculation Results

A program is written to conduct the calculations and the EM field or current response at the sampling point is obtained.

A. Cavity SGEMP

Fig. 3 shows the waveform and frequency spectrum of the cavity SGEMP, which is excited inside the shielding cavity of an equipment. The peak value of the electric field strength is approximately 1.5 MV/m and the frequencies of the SGEMP are mainly distributed in the range of less than 1 GHz, indicating the high-frequency noise has been filtered by the time-biased algorithm.

B. Cable SGEMP

The cable SGEMP would generate current response in the center conductor, which can be calculated by Ampere's circuit law. Fig. 4 is the waveform of the current. The peak current response on the cable with a length of 1 m is approximately 0.25 A with a frequency range of 0 - 1 GHz.

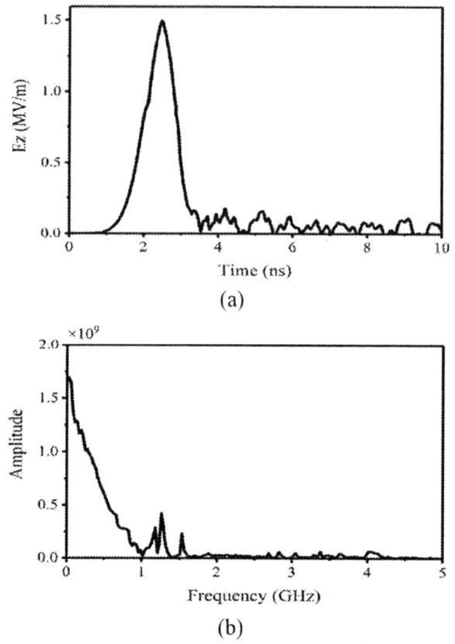

Fig. 3. Waveform and frequency spectra of the electric field.

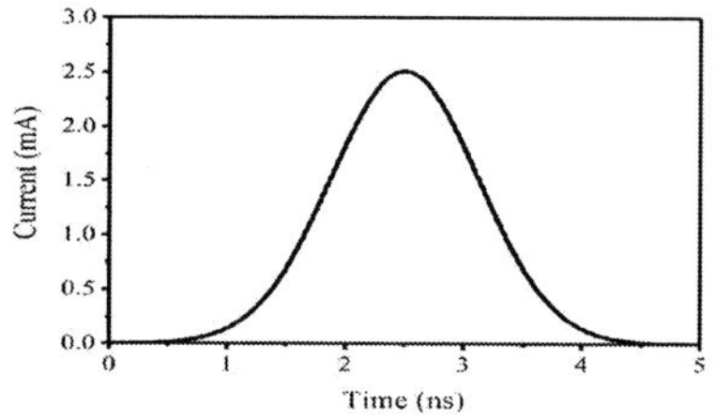

Fig. 4. Waveform of the current response on the conductor.

References

[1] C. G. Brown, E. Bond, T. Clancy, S. Dangi, D. C. Eder, and W. Ferguson, et al., "Assessment and mitigation of electromagnetic pulse (EMP) impacts at short-pulse laser facilities," Lawrence Livemore National Laboratory (LLNL), Livemore, CA, vol. 244, pp. 032001, 2010.

[2] M. J. May, K. B. Fournier, J. D. Colvin, M. A. Barrios, E. L. Dewald, and M. Hohenberger, "Bright X-ray stainless steel K-shell source development at the National Ignition Facility," Physics of Plasmas, vol. 22, pp. 275003-3771, 2015.

[3] E. P. Wenaas, S. C. Rogers, and A. J. Woods, "Sensitivity of SGEMP response to input parameters," IEEE Trans. Nucl. Sci., vol. NS-22, no. 6, pp. 2362-2367, Dec. 1975.

[4] W. L. Chadsey, B. L. Beers, V. W. Pine, and C. W. Wilson, "Radiation-induced signals in cables," IEEE Trans. Nucl. Sci., vol. 23, pp. 1933-1941, 1976.

[5] D. F. Higgins, "Time-domain calculation of the leakage of SGEMP transients through braided cable shields," IEEE Trans. Nucl. Sci., vol. 36, pp. 2042-2049, 1989.

[6] D. Ge and Y. Yan, *FDTD Methods in Electromagnetics*. Xi'an: Xidian University Press, pp. 1-9, 32-35, 2005.

[7] J. Zhou, D. Zhu, D. Liu, and S. Liu, "Time-biased FDTD method for particle-in-cell simulation," Computational Physics, vol. 05, pp. 566-572, 2007.

A Multiphysics Time-Dependent Model of Dielectric Breakdown in Solids

Raymond A. Wildman
RDRL-WMM-B
US Army Research Laboratory
Aberdeen Proving Ground, USA
raymond.a.wildman.civ@mail.mil

George A. Gazonas
RDRL-WMM-B
US Army Research Laboratory
Aberdeen Proving Ground, USA
george.a.gazonas.civ@mail.mil

***Abstract*—A time-dependent model of dielectric breakdown in solids is presented wherein electro-quasi-statics, adiabatic heating, and peridynamics are coupled. First, the time dependent electro-quasi-static approximation is used to solve for the electrostatic potential and a nonlinear, electric-field- and temperature-dependent conductivity is used. The electric field is coupled to both the temperature (through Joule heating) and the mechanical displacement (through the Lorentz and Kelvin forces). Fracture and failure of the material are modeled using peridynamics, a non-local formulation of solid mechanics, and failure of the material may occur due to both high temperatures and high mechanical strain induced by thermal expansion. Results demonstrate several features of dielectric breakdown that are consistent with experiments.**

Keywords—electro-quasi-statics, nonlinear, peridynamics.

I. Introduction

Dielectric breakdown occurs in a material when an applied electric field exceeds the magnitude necessary to strip electrons away from their nuclei in that material. These newly freed electrons may impact nearby atoms, resulting in an avalanching process and runaway breakdown. The effect involves several fields of physics as high temperatures, light, and sound emission are observed. Further, in solids, high temperatures result in large strains due to thermal expansion, and may result in secondary fracture and failure of a material.

We attempt to model this process by coupling a nonlinear, electro-quasi-static approximation with adiabatic heating and peridynamics, a nonlocal approximation of solid mechanics that is useful for fracture modeling. These field equations model the electrostatic potential, temperature, and mechanical displacements and are coupled together in several ways. The discretization uses a standard finite element formulation for the electro-quasi-static problem and a collocation method for the peridynamics for spatial discretizations. For the temporal discretizations, backward Euler is used along with a linearization scheme for the nonlinear electro-quasi-static-problem and velocity Verlet is used for peridynamics.

II. Model Formulation

A. Field Equations

First, the electo-quasi-static approximation has the form:

$$\nabla \cdot (\sigma(T, |\mathbf{E}|)\nabla\Phi) + \frac{\partial}{\partial t}\nabla \cdot (\epsilon\nabla\Phi) = 0, \tag{1}$$

where $\mathbf{E}$ is the electric field, Φ is the electrostatic potential, T is temperature, σ is conductivity, and ϵ is permittivity. Next, the temperature dependence is defined as:

$$\frac{\partial}{\partial t}T = \frac{1}{c_p\rho}Q - \beta\delta(T - T_c), \tag{2}$$

where $\delta(\cdot)$ is the Dirac delta function, ρ is the mass density, c_p is the heat capacity, T_c is a phase change temperature, β is related to the energy required for the phase change, and Q is a heat source term, which will be defined in Section 2.2.

Finally, peridynamics will be used to model the effects of thermal expansion and electrostatic (Lorentz and Kelvin) forces on the solid body. Peridynamics is a nonlocal formulation of elastodynamics that naturally incorporates discontinuities that arise from fracture [1], [2], and is defined as:

$$\rho\frac{\partial^2}{\partial t^2}\mathbf{u} = c\int_{\mathcal{H}_\mathbf{x}} h(t,\boldsymbol{\eta},\boldsymbol{\xi})\left[s(t,\boldsymbol{\eta},\boldsymbol{\xi}) - \alpha\Delta T\right]\frac{\boldsymbol{\eta}+\boldsymbol{\xi}}{|\boldsymbol{\eta}+\boldsymbol{\xi}|}dV', \tag{3}$$

where $\mathcal{H}_\mathbf{x}$ is the nonlocal neighborhood, usually defined as a sphere with radius δ (called the horizon), constant c is a constitutive parameter related to Young's modulus and the horizon, ΔT is the temperature difference relative to ambient T_{amb}, and α is the isotropic thermal expansion coefficient. Further, the peridynamic stretch s is defined as:

$$s(t,\boldsymbol{\eta},\boldsymbol{\xi}) = \frac{|\boldsymbol{\eta}(t)+\boldsymbol{\xi}| - |\boldsymbol{\xi}|}{|\boldsymbol{\xi}|}, \tag{4}$$

where $\boldsymbol{\xi} = \mathbf{x}' - \mathbf{x}$, $\boldsymbol{\eta}(t) = \mathbf{u}'(t) - \mathbf{u}(t)$. Damage is modeled in bond-based peridynamics with a bond-breaking scheme, wherein the microforce is set to zero if a pair of points has ever had a stretch or average temperature that exceed given critical values. The health h of a given bond may be expressed as:

$$h(t,\boldsymbol{\xi},\boldsymbol{\eta}) = \begin{cases} 1 & \text{if } s(t',\boldsymbol{\eta},\boldsymbol{\xi}) - \alpha\Delta T(t') < s_0 \text{ and} \\ & T_{avg}(t',\boldsymbol{\xi}) < T_c \text{ for all } 0 < t' < t \\ 0 & \text{otherwise} \end{cases}, \tag{5}$$

and the critical stretch s_0 is related to the fracture energy and T_c is a given critical temperature.

Finally, peridynamic damage is defined as the ratio:

$$d = 1 - \frac{\int_{\mathcal{H}_\mathbf{x}} h\, dV'}{\int_{\mathcal{H}_\mathbf{x}} dV'}. \tag{6}$$

This value is useful for postprocessing and will also be used in a modified permittivity as described in the next section.

B. Coupling

The main field equations [(1), (2), and (3)] are coupled together in several ways. First, electrostatic forces couple the electric field to the displacement, the first of which is the Lorentz force, defined as:

$$\mathbf{F}_{\mathrm{L}} = q\mathbf{E} = \nabla \cdot (\epsilon \mathbf{E})\, \mathbf{E}, \tag{7}$$

where q is the charge density. This force acts on free charges in the material in areas of high conductivity. The second force is the Kelvin force, or the force on a dielectric, defined as:

$$\mathbf{F}_{\mathrm{K}} = \mathbf{P} \cdot \nabla \mathbf{E} = (\epsilon - \epsilon_0)\, \mathbf{E} \cdot \nabla \mathbf{E}, \tag{8}$$

where $\mathbf{P}$ is the polarization. The equation of motion is then modified to:

$$\rho \frac{\partial^2}{\partial t^2} \mathbf{u} = \mathbf{F}_{\mathrm{PD}} + \mathbf{F}_{\mathrm{L}} + \mathbf{F}_{\mathrm{K}}, \tag{9}$$

where $\mathbf{F}_{\mathrm{PD}}$ is the peridynamic force defined on the right-handside of (3).

The peridynamic damage is used to modify the permittivity as:

$$\epsilon = \epsilon_0 \left[\epsilon_r (1 - d) + d \right]. \tag{10}$$

The intent is to model the effect of damage in a material as the formation of voids so that a fully damaged material point (with $d = 1$) acts as free space.

The heat source term Q in (2) is derived from Joule heating, or the heat generated from current flowing through a dissipative material, and is given by:

$$Q = \mathbf{J} \cdot \mathbf{E} = \sigma \left| \mathbf{E} \right|^2. \tag{11}$$

As mentioned above, the conductivity is dependent on both the electric field $\mathbf{E}$ and the temperature T and is given by:

$$\sigma(T, |\mathbf{E}|) = \sigma_0 f(T) e^{\gamma |\mathbf{E}|}, \tag{12}$$

where σ_0 is a base conductivity with zero applied field [3], and f is a function describing the temperature dependence as the two-phase Arrhenius model:

$$f(T) = \begin{cases} A_1 e^{-B_1/T} & T < T_{\mathrm{c}} \\ A_2 e^{-B_2/T} & T \geq T_{\mathrm{c}} \end{cases}, \tag{13}$$

where the A_i and B_i are constants of the model [4]. The constants A_1 and B_1 are associated with the weakly conductive phase and A_2 and B_2 are associated with the highly conductive phase, meaning that $A_1 \ll A_2$.

III. Results

The material properties of the model strongly influence the results and both channel-like and tree-like breakdown patterns are achievable. For example, a 2D, point-plane geometry was used with two different sets of parameters. The first had an initial relative permittivity of $\epsilon_r = 20$, an initial conductivity of $\sigma_0 = 10^{-19}$ S/m, an initial temperature of $T_{\mathrm{amb}} = 300$ K, a transition temperature of $T_{\mathrm{c}} = 1000$ K, a maximum voltage of $V_0 = 3$ MV, and a conductivity-electric field coupling value of $\gamma = 5 \times 10^{-8}$ m/V. The remaining parameters and discretization details may be found in [5]. The peridynamic damage at 5.5 μs is shown in Fig. 1, which demonstrates a channel-like pattern of breakdown from the probe to the ground plane and perpendicular fractures due to thermal expansion in the channel.

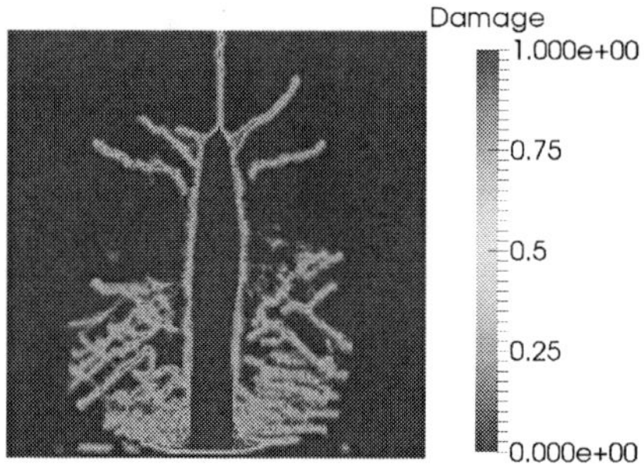

Fig. 1: Channel-like breakdown pattern.

Next, the following parameters were adjusted to generate the result shown in Fig. 2, which gives the peridynamic damage at 1.76 μs: $\gamma = 0$, $T_{\mathrm{amb}} = 670$ K, $\sigma_0 = 1$ S/m, and $V_0 = 50$ kV. In other words, the initial conductivity and temperature were raised significantly and the nonlinearity was removed. The resulting figure is strikingly different than before, displaying a tree-like breakdown pattern.

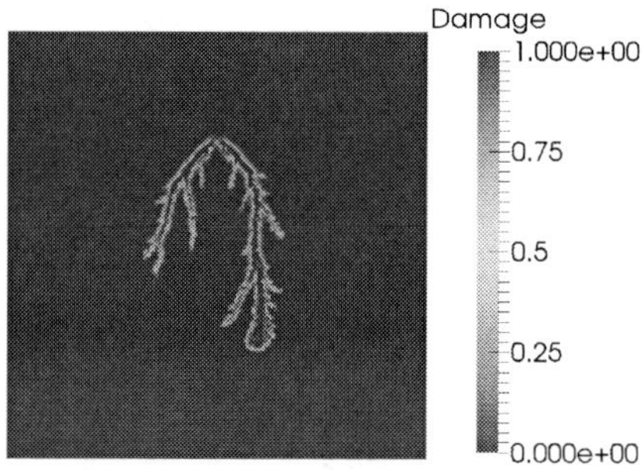

Fig. 2: Tree-like breakdown pattern.

References

[1] S. Silling, "Reformulation of elasticity theory for discontinuities and long-range forces," J. Mech. Phy. Sol., vol. 48, no. 1, pp. 175–209, 2000.

[2] S. Silling and E. Askari, "A meshfree method based on the peridynamic model of solid mechanics," Comp. Struc., vol. 83, no. 17-18, pp. 1526–1535, 2005.

[3] P. T. Flynn, "Field-dependent conductivity in non-uniform fields and its relation to electrical breakdown," Proc IEE–Part C: Mono., vol. 102, no. 2, pp. 264–269, 1955.

[4] M. Noskov, V. Lopatin, A. Cheglokov, and A. Shapovalov, "Computer simulation of discharge channel propagation in solid dielectric," in Proc IEEE 7th Int Conf Solid Dielec. IEEE, pp. 465–468, 2001.

[5] R. A. Wildman and G. A. Gazonas, "A multiphysics finite element and peridynamics model of dielectric breakdown," US Army Research Laboratory, Tech. Rep. ARL-TR-8128, 2017.

Massive MIMO – Beyond 4G and a Basis for 5G

Gopinath Gampala and C. J. Reddy
Altair Engineering, Inc.
Hampton, USA
gopi@altair.com, cjreddy@altair.com

***Abstract*—Massive Multiple-Input Multiple-Output (MIMO) is the most compelling wireless technology and a key component of fifth generation (5G) systems. This paper discusses the technology and its objectives in detail. The paper also discusses the complete design process of a 5G antenna system.**

***Keywords*—5G, FEKO, Massive MIMO, WinProp.**

I. INTRODUCTION

Starting from the first generation of mobile network standards, a new standard comes along every 10 years or so. A new technology has evolved with each new standard to meet its specifications, starting from analog communications to the existing Long Term Evolution (LTE). The antenna technology for the mobile handheld devices also advanced with each technology, starting from simple monopoles to the complex MIMO antennas [1]. However, the existing technologies will not sustain the exponential growth in demand for the network capacity. We need new technologies that can sustain the future demand and also lay the foundation for the next set of standards, namely 5G. The 3rd Generation Partnership Project (3GPP) is on the fast track of standardizing the requirements for 5G to meet these growing network demands [2].

II. MASSIVE MIMO

The technology being investigated to meet the high data rate demands of 5G is massive MIMO.

A. Concept

Massive MIMO is a multi-user MIMO system that serves multiple users through spatial multiplexing over a channel with favorable propagation [3, 4], where the channel vectors between the base station and user terminal are nearly orthogonal. The main concept of massive MIMO is to use large antenna arrays at M base stations to simultaneously serve K autonomous terminals or users, where $M \gg K$.

B. Benefits

Massive MIMO offers two key benefits [5]:

- Excellent spectral efficiency.
- Superior energy efficiency.

The key technological characteristics of massive MIMO that are aiding the above benefits are [6]: digital processing, reciprocity of propagation and Time Division Duplexing (TDD) operation, computationally inexpensive precoding/decoding, array gain, channel hardening, good quality of service to all terminals in a cell, autonomous operation of the base stations and the possibility to reduce accuracy and resolution of transceiver frontends.

III. 5G ANTENNA SYSTEM DESIGN PROCESS

A 5G antenna system consists of antenna arrays at both the mobile handset and the base station, to cater for massive MIMO. The following steps constitutes the complete design process of a 5G antenna system:

- Antenna array design for the mobile handset.
- Base station antenna array design.
- Coverage analysis of base station.
- Channel capacity between the base station and terminal.

The following subsections describe each stage of the design process. The process is explained for the 29 GHz 5G frequency band that is recently standardized by FCC, but can be adapted for any other frequency band. Simulation results presented in this paper are computed using Altair's 3D computational electromagnetic simulation software, FEKO [7] and radio propagation and network planning tool, WinProp [7].

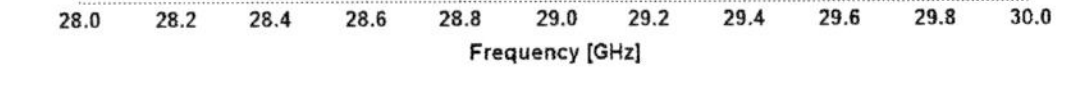

Fig. 1. Reflection coefficient of the rectangular patch.

A. Mobile Handset

To showcase the 5G antenna system design process, a 2×2 patch antenna array is designed for the mobile handset. Array consists of 4.1×3.08725 mm rectangular patches on a metal backed dielectric substrate with a permittivity 2.2, as shown in Fig. 1. The 2×2 antenna arrays are then integrated into the mobile handset at the four corners, as shown in Fig. 2. The antenna arrays are placed orthogonal to each other on the adjacent corners to provide polarization and spatial diversity.

B. Base Station

To support massive MIMO, a 240-element reflector backed dipole array is designed. It is possible to generate several pointed beams in various directions through different combinations of array elements, serving different mobile handsets. One such configuration is illustrated in Fig. 3.

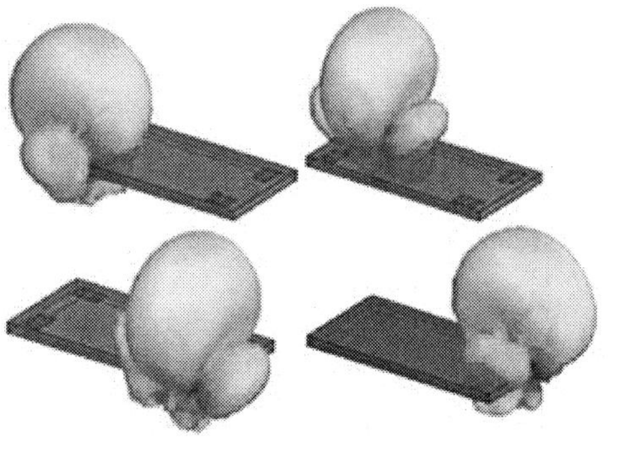

Fig. 2. 2x2 antenna arrays placed at the four corners of the mobile handset.

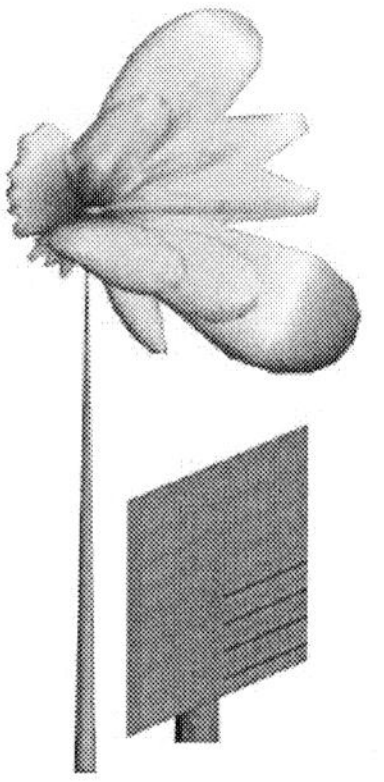

Fig. 3. Base station with a sub-section of the array excited to point a beam in a particular direction.

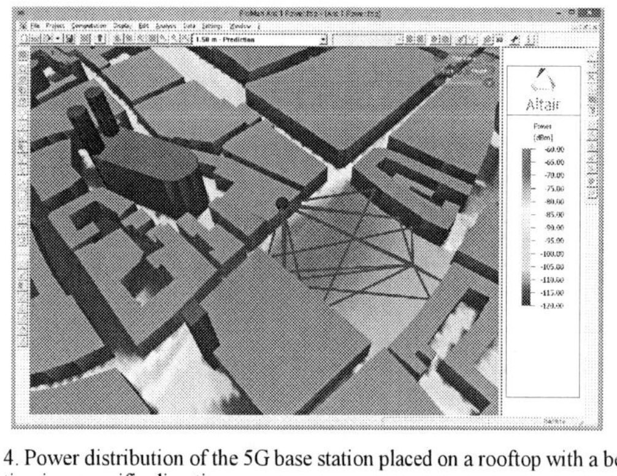

Fig. 4. Power distribution of the 5G base station placed on a rooftop with a beam pointing in a specific direction.

C. Coverage and Channel Capacity

A 5G antenna system design is not complete without verifying the channel capacity (bits/s/Hz) it offers. This is performed by placing the base station antenna on a roof top in an urban scenario while the mobile handset is moving along a pre-defined path. Power distribution calculations shown in Fig. 4 confirms that the highest power densities are in the areas where the array beam is pointing. Fig. 5 illustrates the channel capacity when transmitting 4 data streams from the base station with 4 receivers on four corners of the mobile handset, as in a 4x4 MIMO.

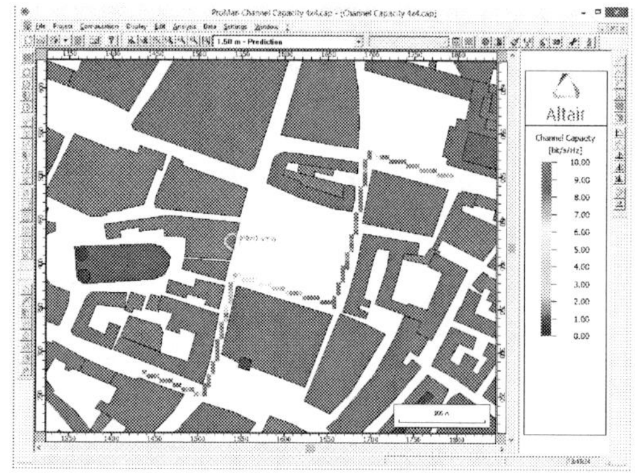

Fig. 5. Channel capacity of a 4x4 MIMO configuration computed along a path in an Urban environment.

IV. Conclusion

Massive MIMO offers both the efficiency and scalability required to meet the demands of 5G and is becoming more matured for practical implementation. This paper discussed the complete design process of a massive MIMO enabled 5G antenna system that includes the design of the base station and mobile handset antenna arrays and simulation of channel capacity in an urban environment.

References

[1] J. Anguera, A. Andújar, M. C. Huynh, C. Orlenius, C. Picher, and C. Puente, "Advances in antenna technology for wireless handheld devices," Int. Jour. Ant. and Prop, vol. 2013, 2013.

[2] 3rd Generation Partnership Project: http://www.3gpp.org/news-events.

[3] T. L. Marzetta, E. G. Larsson, H. Yang, and H. Q. Ngo, Fundamentals of Massive MIMO, Cambridge University Press, 2016.

[4] H. Q. Ngo, E. G. Larsson, and T. L. Marzetta, "Aspects of favorable propagation in Massive MIMO," European Signal Processing Conference (EUSIPCO), Lisbon, Portugal, Sept. 2014.

[5] H. Q. Ngo, E. G. Larsson, and T. L. Marzetta, "Energy and spectral efficiency of very large multiuser MIMO systems," IEEE Trans. Commun., vol. 61, no. 4, Apr. 2013.

[6] E. G. Larsson and L. V. der Perre, "Massive MIMO for 5G", IEEE 5G Tech Focus, vol. 1, number1, Mar. 2017.

[7] Altair Engineering, Inc., FEKO Suite 2017 and WinProp Suite 14.5 (http://www.altairhyperworks.com/product/FEKO).

Ultra-Wideband Antenna Performance Comparison

William Coburn and Seth McCormick
US Army Research Laboratory
Adelphi, USA
william.o.coburn.civ@mail.mil, seth.a.mccormick.civ@mail.mil

***Abstract*—For ground penetrating radar applications antennas with bandwidth typically 3-to-1 or greater are required. Many designs can be found in the literature but performance tends to suffer when extending the bandwidth to lower frequencies. Here the nominal frequency range is 0.3–2.3 GHz (154%) and the TEM horn is used as a reference for performance comparisons. Planar antenna designs have many advantages such as low-profile, light-weight, and ease of fabrication and integration. Various planar monopole and a slot-type antennas are compared where the results show that increasing the size can extend the bandwidth to lower frequencies but introduce radiation pattern instability at high frequency. This paper summarizes a numerical investigation using FEKO to provide antenna alternatives for multistatic radar systems. The results serve to guide the selection of broadband antenna elements for ground penetrating radar system developers.**

Keywords*—*monopole antenna, planar antennas, slot antenna, TEM horn, ultra-wideband, Vivaldi antennas.

I. Introduction

This paper presents a numerical analysis of Ultra-Wideband (UWB) antennas using FEKO (www.feko.info) software using the Method of Moments. The TEM horn [1] is used as a 3D reference antenna for comparing various designs as it exceeds the impedance bandwidth (IBW) requirement. UWB antennas are often compared according to the electrical size at some frequency and performance such as peak gain, fractional IBW, etc. The performance vs. frequency can be shown but a combined figure-of-merit (FOM) is more desirable as a performance comparison and can be tabulated at critical frequencies. Here we choose a FOM based on the gain, G, normalized to the antenna VSWR and electrical size, L, at each frequency. So FOM = G/(VSWR x L) is used to compare performance as a function of frequency. The largest antenna dimension, D, is used to calculate the electrical size, $L = D/\lambda$ at each frequency. The linear gain in the desired direction is used in the FOM for antennas radiating in both endfire and. other directions. The antenna width in the operational configuration may be more important since it determines how many transmit/receive (TX/RX) pairs can be used in the cross-range direction. The objective is to improve the low frequency performance compared to existing alternatives to allow ground penetrating radar (GPR) system developers to conduct trade studies on size, weight, and power plus cost (SWAP-C) vs. performance for downward-looking multistatic GPR systems in the frequency range 0.3–2.3 GHz (154% fractional IBW). Various antenna simulation and measured results will be compared using this frequency dependent FOM.

The planar antennas are microstrip or coplanar waveguide fed on Rogers low-loss substrates having ε_r = 2.33 or 3.5 and FR4 having ε_r = 4.4 and tanδ = .02 with maximum thickness 1.574 mm (62-mils). In some cases microwave absorber loading is used to extend the IBW to lower frequencies [2]. A metal ground plane can also be used to increase directivity, but the height must be larger than about 0.2 wavelengths and causes variations in the gain vs. frequency. For downward-looking GPR applications many TX/RX pairs of small antennas are often used such as the cavity backed spiral or planar slot antennas [3]. Here the objective is to increase the boresight (i.e., at nadir) gain at low frequency in the most compact size possible without reducing the high frequency performance. For multistatic radar systems it may be possible to reduce the number of TX/RX pairs by using larger elements having improved gain without sacrificing the overall system performance. The results show that increasing the antenna size can extend the IBW but at high frequency transitions to a traveling wave type antenna with poor pattern stability in the desired direction.

II. Antenna Alternatives

A planar antipodal Vivaldi antenna can be obtained by careful design of the tapered slot with a common implementation shown in Fig. 1 (left) [4]. A TEM horn is used as a 3D performance references for the IBW and pattern stability in a relatively large size as shown in Fig. 1 (right). A Vivaldi monopole radiating at 54° above the ground plane is also used as a performance reference. Planar antenna alternatives radiating at broadside are compared to these reference antennas. The antennas were simulated with FEKO over the desired frequency range where the FOM is reduced by the VSWR and if the boresight gain does not increase as expected with increasing electrical size. At low frequency (LF) the realized gain at 0.3 GHz or the frequency where VSWR = 3 is used in the FOM_{LF}. The mid-band performance at 1 GHz, FOM_{MF}, and the high-band, FOM_{HF}, are also summarized. The numerical results have similar frequency dependence with most designs exhibiting the onset of beam tilting or splitting at high frequency. Those designs that have sufficient IBW are normalized to the antenna electrical size and VSWR to provide a frequency dependent FOM. In this summary the FOM_{LF}, FOM_{MF}, and FOM_{HF} are tabulated for comparison. An analysis of antenna alternatives is done primarily by simulation with the

GPR system developers down selecting the antenna options based on the overall system performance and SWAP-C considerations.

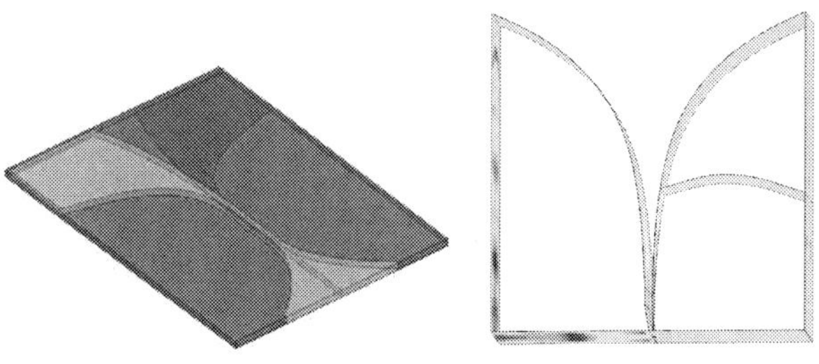

Fig. 1. Endfire antennas: (left) antipodal Vivaldi and (right) TEM horn.

III. RESULTS

The simulated radiation pattern for the Vivaldi monopole is shown in Fig. 2 at 1 and 2 GHz where the pattern is stable vs. frequency so the antenna would be installed at the appropriate angle to obtain the required coverage. For planar antenna designs radiating at broadside the peak gain often tilts from zenith at higher frequencies which is captured in the FOM. An example is shown in Fig. 3 (left) at 2 GHz for a planar sleeve monopole and in Fig. 3 (right) for a planar slot with additional resonant slots to better control this beam tilt. Additional results for planar antenna designs with the available measured data will be included in the presentation.

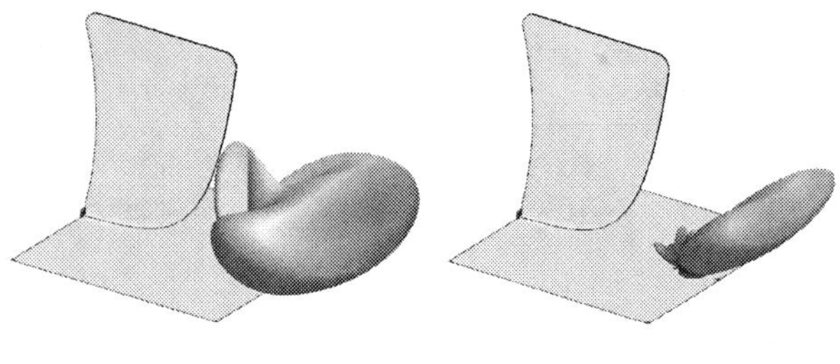

Fig. 2. A 305 mm (12-inch) tall Vivaldi monopole radiation pattern at: (left) 1 GHz and (right) 2 GHz.

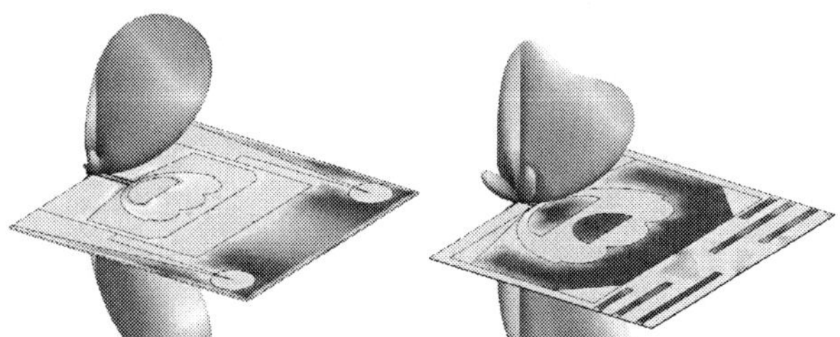

Fig. 3. Bulbous sleeve monopole: (left) and slotted planar slot antenna (right).

The results indicate that for planar antennas the slot-type antenna is better matched at low frequency. The antenna transient excitation and radiated field indicate some late time ringing which can be mitigated by absorber loading. This loading requires a tradeoff between impedance matching at low frequencies and antenna efficiency and should be measured to determine adequate radar performance [2]. An example is shown in Fig. 4 (left) at 2 GHz for an absorber loaded asymmetric hourglass monopole and in Fig. 4 (right) for a planar dual slot antenna both with a one-inch air gap. A summary of the FOM calculated at three frequencies is shown in Table I.

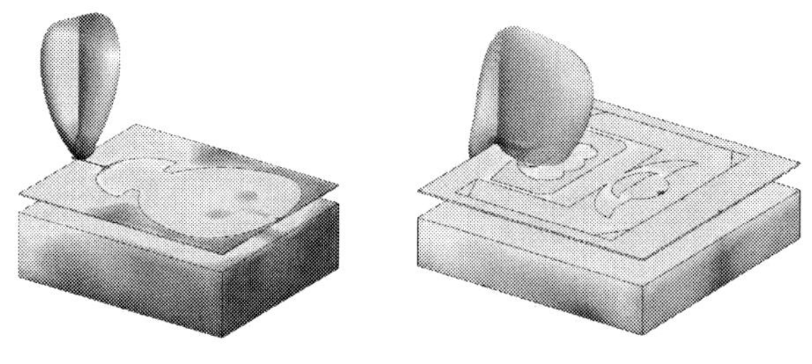

Fig. 4. Absorber loaded antennas: (left) hourglass monopole and (right) dual slot radiation patterns at 2 GHz.

TABLE I. FOM AT THREE FREQUENCIES FOR VARIOUS ANTENNAS

Antenna Type	D (mm)	LF (GHz)	FOM_{LF}	FOM_{MF}	FOM_{HF}
TEM Horn	590	0.3	3.2	4.1	2.3
Antipodal Vivaldi	437	0.67	0.48	1.1	2.6
Vivaldi Blade	254	0.3	1.7	4.3	3
Vivaldi Blade	305	0.3	2.1	2.7	3.4
Asymmetric Hourglass	254	0.34	1.4	1.3	0.9
Asymmetric Hourglass (w/ABS)	254	0.3	1	0.7	1.2
Asymmetric Hourglass	305	0.3	2.2	1.2	1.1
Asymmetric Hourglass (w/ABS)	305	0.3	0.8	0.9	1.4
Sleeve Monopole (FR4)	263	0.6	1.52	1.16	0.56
Sleeve Monopole (Duroid)	300	0.4	0.42	1.36	0.31
Planar Dual Slot	254	0.4	1.03	0.66	0.77
Planar Dual Slot (w/ABS)	254	0.37	1.14	1.37	0.58
Slotted Planar Slot	200	0.45	1.56	2.46	1.07
Slotted Planar Slot	300	0.33	1.2	1.2	0.46
Large Planar Slot	300	0.46	1.5	0.64	0.5
Large Planar Slot (w/ABS)	300	0.43	0.64	0.6	0.66

IV. CONCLUSION

The objective to improve the low frequency gain requires larger antennas with some trade-offs in performance. A frequency dependent FOM is proposed that captures these trade-offs and allows a comparison of alternatives based on size and performance. Various antennas will be compared using this FOM for both simulated and measured results.

REFERENCES

[1] C. Grosvenor, et al., "TEM Horn Antenna Design Principles," Nat. Inst. of Stand. and Tech., NIST TN-1544, January 2007.

[2] W. Coburn, "An ultra-wideband absorber backed planar slot antenna," App. Comp. Electro. Express Journal, vol. 1, no. 1, January 2016.

[3] C. Ly, et al., "Detection of Buried IEDs Using a Novel Planar Slot Antenna Array for Downward-Looking Radar," Proc. Tri-Service Radar Symposium, Springfield VA, July 2017.

[4] S. McCormick, "Modeling, Simulation, and Measurement of Balanced Antipodal Vivaldi Antennas," US Army Research Lab., ARL-TR-8111, August 2017.

A DC to HF Volume PEEC Formulation Based on Hertz Potentials and the Cell Method

Riccardo Torchio, Piergiorgio Alotto, Paolo Bettini, Dimitri Voltolina, and Federico Moro
Dipartimento di Ingegneria Industriale
Università di Padova
Padova, Italy
riccardo.torchio@studenti.unipd.it

Abstract—**A new Partial Element Equivalent Circuit formulation based on Hertz potentials and the Cell Method is presented. Conductive, dielectric, and magnetic linear-homogeneous media are considered by means of conduction, polarization, and magnetization current densities. The use of edge unknowns leads to reduce system size with respect to typical face-based approaches.**

I. Introduction

A large body of literature shows that integral methods are particularly suited to the solution of high frequency electromagnetic problems (EM) involving large domains with the characteristics of vacuum. In particular, the Partial Element Equivalent Circuit (PEEC) method has been shown to be well suited for the analysis of electromagnetic devices, such as printed circuit boards and antennas. The aim of this work is to present a novel 3-D Hertz-PEEC formulation, including conductive, dielectric, and magnetic media. This approach is based on the theory of Hertz potentials [1] and magnetization currents for the magnetic media [2], [3], while in literature Amperian currents [4] or the magnetization [5] are applied. The discretization of the formulation is obtained by means of the Cell Method (CM) [6] and the current density vector, which is the only unknown, is expanded by Whitney face functions [7]. The proposed approach leads to a unified treatment of magnetic and dielectric media which can be handled with a single set of robust and efficient semi-analytical integration routines. The approach is thus capable of solving EM problems over a larger frequency range compared to extant PEEC approaches for magnetic media [5]. Furthermore, the formulation uses edge unknowns, leading to the reduction of the linear system size with respect to other approaches.

II. Integral Formulation

Conductive, dielectric, and magnetic domains Ω_c, Ω_d, and Ω_m (with boundaries Γ_c, Γ_d, and Γ_m, respectively) are considered in the formulation. The domains have no intersection and their disjoint union is $\Omega = \Omega_c \sqcup \Omega_d \sqcup \Omega_m$.

When conductive, dielectric and magnetic media are considered, the following constitutive relations can be introduced:

$$\mathbf{J}_f = \sigma\mathbf{E} \ in \ \Omega_c, \qquad \mathbf{D} = \varepsilon_0\mathbf{E} + \mathbf{P} \ in \ \Omega_d, \qquad \mathbf{B} = \mu_0\mathbf{H} + \mu_0\mathbf{M} \ in \ \Omega_m, \tag{1}$$

where $\mathbf{J}_f$ is the conduction current density, $\mathbf{E}$ and $\mathbf{H}$ are the electric and the magnetic field, $\mathbf{D}$ is the electric displacement and $\mathbf{B}$ is the magnetic flux density, σ is the conductivity, ε_0 and μ_0 are the vacuum permittivity and permeability. The polarization $\mathbf{P}$ and the magnetization $\mathbf{M}$ are introduced as equivalent sources in vacuum, so the effects of dielectric and magnetic media are taken into account. With the introduction of (1), following the approach and notation of [8] (chap. 5, 7), Maxwell's equations in frequency domain can be re-written in a more symmetric form avoiding the use of $\mathbf{D}$ and $\mathbf{B}$:

$$\begin{aligned} \nabla\cdot\mathbf{E} &= \frac{\varrho_f + \varrho_p}{\varepsilon_0}, & -\nabla\times\mathbf{E} &= \mathbf{J}_{m^*} + i\omega\mu_0\mathbf{H}, \\ \nabla\cdot\mathbf{H} &= \frac{\varrho_{m^*}}{\mu_0}, & \nabla\times\mathbf{H} &= \mathbf{J}_f + \mathbf{J}_p + i\omega\varepsilon_0\mathbf{E}, \end{aligned} \tag{2}$$

where ϱ_f is the free electric charge density, $\mathbf{J}_p = i\omega\mathbf{P}$ and $\varrho_p = -\nabla\cdot\mathbf{P}$ are the polarization current and bound dielectric charge densities, $\mathbf{J}_{m^*} = i\omega\mu_0\mathbf{M}$ is the magnetization current density and $\varrho_{m^*} = -\nabla\cdot\mu_0\mathbf{M}$ is the bound magnetic charge density. As shown in [1] and [9], it is possible to write the electric field $\mathbf{E}$ and the magnetic field $\mathbf{H}$ as:

$$\begin{aligned} \mathbf{E} &= -(i\omega)^2\mathbf{\Pi}_e - \nabla\varphi_e - \frac{1}{\varepsilon_0}\nabla\times(i\omega\mathbf{\Pi}_m) + \mathbf{E}_0, \\ \mathbf{H} &= -(i\omega)^2\mathbf{\Pi}_m - \nabla\varphi_m + \frac{1}{\mu_0}\nabla\times(i\omega\mathbf{\Pi}_e) + \mathbf{H}_0, \end{aligned} \tag{3}$$

where $\mathbf{\Pi}_e$ and $\mathbf{\Pi}_m$ are the Hertz electric and magnetic vector potentials, φ_e and φ_m are electric and magnetic scalar potentials and $\mathbf{E}_0$ and $\mathbf{H}_0$ are imposed sources.

By defining $\mathbf{A}_e = i\omega\mathbf{\Pi}_e$, and $\mathbf{A}_m = i\omega\mathbf{\Pi}_m$ as "new" electric and magnetic vector potentials, applying Lorenz gauge, $\nabla\cdot\mathbf{A}_e = -i\omega\varepsilon_0\mu_0\varphi_e$, $\nabla\cdot\mathbf{A}_m = -i\omega\varepsilon_0\mu_0\varphi_m$, and letting (3) into (2), four partial differential equations can be obtained:

$$\begin{aligned} \Box\mathbf{A}_e &= \mu_0(\mathbf{J}_f + \mathbf{J}_p), & \Box\varphi_e &= \frac{\varrho_f + \varrho_p}{\varepsilon_0}, \\ \Box\mathbf{A}_m &= \varepsilon_0\mathbf{J}_{m^*}, & \Box\varphi_m &= \frac{\varrho_{m^*}}{\mu_0}, \end{aligned} \tag{4}$$

where $\Box = (i\omega)^2\frac{1}{c^2} - \nabla^2$ is the d'Alembert operator and c is the speed of light. The solution of the first equation of (4) is:

$$\mathbf{A}_e(\mathbf{r}_y) = \mu_0\int_\Omega(\mathbf{J}_f(\mathbf{r}_x) + \mathbf{J}_p(\mathbf{r}_x))g(\mathbf{r}_x, \mathbf{r}_y)dr_x, \tag{5}$$

where $\mathbf{r}_y$ is the field point, $\mathbf{r}_x$ is the integration point and $g(\mathbf{r}_x, \mathbf{r}_y) = \frac{e^{-i\omega c^{-1}|\mathbf{r}_y - \mathbf{r}_x|}}{|\mathbf{r}_y - \mathbf{r}_x|}$ is the scalar retarded free space Green function. The solution of the other three equations in (4) is obtained likewise (5).

III. Cell Method Discretization

The electric domains Ω_c and Ω_d are discretized into primal tetrahedral grids $\mathcal{G}_{\Omega_c}$ and $\mathcal{G}_{\Omega_d}$, consisting of n_c, n_d nodes, e_c, e_d edges, f_c, f_d faces, and v_c, v_d volumes. Then, dual grids $\tilde{\mathcal{G}}_{\Omega_c}$ and $\tilde{\mathcal{G}}_{\Omega_d}$ can be obtained by taking the barycentric subdivision of $\mathcal{G}_{\Omega_c}$ and $\mathcal{G}_{\Omega_d}$ [10]. The same approach can be applied to the magnetic domain Ω_m, but in this case $\tilde{\mathcal{G}}_{\Omega_m}$ is chosen to be made up of tetrahedral elements, while $\mathcal{G}_{\Omega_m}$ is obtained by its barycentric subdivision. The following incidence matrices can be obtained: $\mathbf{G}_{\Omega_\alpha}$ (edges to nodes), $\mathbf{C}_{\Omega_\alpha}$ (faces to edges), and $\mathbf{D}_{\Omega_\alpha}$ (volumes to faces), on $\mathcal{G}_{\Omega_\alpha}$, where $\alpha = c, d, m$ indicates the domain. Dual matrices can be obtained for $\tilde{\mathcal{G}}^a_{\Omega_\alpha}$, i.e., $\tilde{\mathbf{G}}^a_{\Omega_\alpha}$, $\tilde{\mathbf{C}}^a_{\Omega_\alpha}$, $\tilde{\mathbf{D}}^a_{\Omega_\alpha}$, where the superscript a indicates that the matrix is *augmented* [10]. To build the CM formulation, following arrays of degrees of freedom are introduced:

- $\mathbf{j_c} = (j_{c_i})$ on faces $f_i \in \mathcal{G}_{\Omega_c}$, $j_{c_i} = \int_{f_i} \mathbf{J}_c \cdot d\mathbf{S}$,
- $\mathbf{j_p} = (j_{p_i})$ on faces $f_i \in \mathcal{G}_{\Omega_p}$, $j_{p_i} = \int_{f_i} \mathbf{J}_p \cdot d\mathbf{S}$,
- $\tilde{\mathbf{j}}_{\mathbf{m}^*} = (\tilde{j}_{m_i^*})$ on faces $\tilde{f}_i \in \tilde{\mathcal{G}}_{\Omega_m}$, $\tilde{j}_{m_i^*} = \int_{\tilde{f}_i} \mathbf{J}_{m^*} \cdot d\mathbf{S}$,
- $\mathbf{h} = (h_i)$ on edges $e_i \in \mathcal{G}_{\Omega_m}$, $h_i = \int_{e_i} \mathbf{H} \cdot d\mathbf{l}$,
- $\tilde{\mathbf{e}} = (\tilde{e}_i)$ on edges $\tilde{e}_i \in \tilde{\mathcal{G}}_{\Omega_c \sqcup \Omega_d}$, $\tilde{e}_i = \int_{\tilde{e}_i} \mathbf{E} \cdot d\mathbf{l}$,
- $\mathbf{a}_m = (a_{m_i})$ on edges $e_i \in \mathcal{G}_{\Omega_m}$, $a_{m_i} = \int_{e_i} \mathbf{A}_m \cdot d\mathbf{l}$,
- $\tilde{\mathbf{a}}_e = (\tilde{a}_{e_i})$ on edges $\tilde{e}_i \in \tilde{\mathcal{G}}_{\Omega_c \sqcup \Omega_d}$, $\tilde{e}_i = \int_{\tilde{e}_i} \mathbf{A}_e \cdot d\mathbf{l}$,
- $\tilde{\boldsymbol{\phi}}_e = (\tilde{\phi}_{e_i})$ on nodes $\tilde{n}_i \in \tilde{\mathcal{G}}_{\Omega_c \sqcup \Omega_d}$, $\tilde{\phi}_{e_i} = \varphi_e(\mathbf{r}_{n_i})$,
- $\boldsymbol{\phi}_m = (\phi_{m_i})$ on nodes $n_i \in \mathcal{G}_{\Omega_m}$, $\phi_{m_i} = \varphi_m(\mathbf{r}_{n_i})$.

The coupling between the domains is enforced by weakly imposing (1):

$$\begin{aligned} &\int_{\Omega_c \sqcup \Omega_d} \mathbf{w}_i^f \cdot \big(\rho_e \mathbf{J}_e(\mathbf{r}) - \mathbf{E}(\mathbf{r})\big) d\mathbf{r} = 0, \\ &\int_{\Omega_m} \mathbf{w}_i^f \cdot \big(\rho_{m^*} \mathbf{J}_{m^*}(\mathbf{r}) - \mathbf{H}(\mathbf{r})\big) d\mathbf{r} = 0, \end{aligned} \tag{6}$$

where $\mathbf{J}_e$ is the electric current, equals to $\mathbf{J}_c$ in Ω_c and $\mathbf{J}_p$ in Ω_d, $\rho_e = (\sigma_c)^{-1}$ in Ω_c and $(i\omega\varepsilon_0(\varepsilon_r - 1))^{-1}$ in Ω_d. $\rho_{m^*} = (i\omega\mu_0(\mu_r - 1))^{-1}$ while $\mathbf{w}_i^f$ is the Whitney face basis function.

By expanding $\mathbf{J}_e$ and $\mathbf{J}_{m^*}$ with $\mathbf{w}_i^f$ and letting (3) into (6), the following system is obtained:

$$\begin{bmatrix} \mathbf{Z}_{11} & \mathbf{Z}_{12} \\ \mathbf{Z}_{21} & \mathbf{Z}_{22} \end{bmatrix} \begin{bmatrix} \mathbf{j}_e \\ \tilde{\mathbf{j}}_{m^*} \end{bmatrix} = \begin{bmatrix} \tilde{\mathbf{e}}_0 \\ \mathbf{h}_0 \end{bmatrix}, \tag{7}$$

where:

- $\mathbf{Z}_{11} = \mathbf{R}_e + i\omega\mathbf{L}_e - \frac{1}{i\omega}\tilde{\mathbf{G}}^a_{\Omega_c \sqcup \Omega_d} \mathbf{P}_e \mathbf{D}^a_{\Omega_c \sqcup \Omega_d}$,
- $\mathbf{Z}_{12} = \mathbf{M}_{1/\varepsilon_0} \mathbf{C}_{\Omega_c \sqcup \Omega_d} \mathbf{L_{em}}$,
- $\mathbf{Z}_{21} = -\mathbf{M}_{1/\mu_0} \tilde{\mathbf{C}}_{\Omega_m} \mathbf{L_{me}}$,
- $\mathbf{Z}_{22} = \mathbf{R}_m + i\omega\mathbf{L}_m - \frac{1}{i\omega}\tilde{\mathbf{G}}^a_{\Omega_m} \mathbf{P}_m \mathbf{D}^a_{\Omega_m}$.

R, **L**, and **P** are respectively the "traditional" PEEC resistance, inductance and potential matrices. The full paper will describe how to obtain the block matrices and how to solve the system applying a change of variables (from faces to edges of the mesh) and a projection into a reduced set of equations.

IV. Numerical Results

The 3-D Hertz-PEEC code has been developed with MATLAB® for the system assembly and data handling, while MEX-FORTRAN functions combined with OpenMP libraries have been adopted for the computation of the matrix coefficients and post-processing.

The code has been validated on several benchmarks, including the case, shown here, of two spheres with 1m radius, a dielectric one ($\varepsilon_r = 2$) and a magnetic one ($\mu_r = 10$) placed 3m apart on the y-axis and excited by a linearly polarized plane wave $\mathbf{E_0} = e^{-ik_0x}\mathbf{u}_z$. Where $k_0 = 2\pi f\sqrt{\varepsilon_0\mu_0}$, $f = 30$MHz. The magnitude of the real and imaginary part of the scattered electric field has been compared with the Radio-Frequency module of COMSOL® with good agreement (Fig. 1). Small discrepancies are due to the sphere meshes required by PEEC and FEM, the intrinsic differences of the two approaches, and the numerical post processing adopted for PEEC. In the full paper a thorough discussion of the numerical results in terms of accuracy and computational cost will be presented.

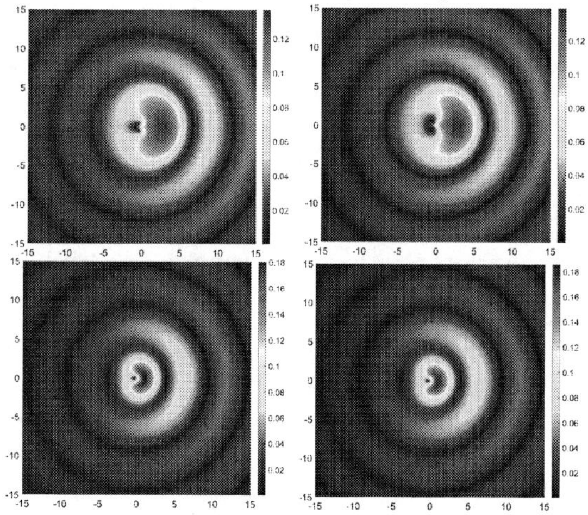

Fig. 1. Scattered Electric Field magnitude V/m, xz-plane, dimensions in m. Left: 3-D PEEC-Hertz. Right: COMSOL®. Top: $\Re$ part. Bottom: $\Im$ part.

References

[1] A. Nisbet, "Herzian electromagnetic potentials and associated gauge transformation," Proceedings of the Royal Society of London A: Mathematical, Physical and Engineering Sciences, 1955.

[2] A. G. Polimeridis, et al., "On the computation of power in volume integral equation formulations," in IEEE Trans. on Antennas and Propag., vol. 63, no. 2, pp. 611-620, Feb. 2015.

[3] J. Markkanen, et al., "Discretization of volume integral equation formulations for extremely anisotropic materials," in IEEE Trans. on Antennas and Propag, vol. 60, no. 11, pp. 5195-5202, Nov. 2012.

[4] R. Torchio, et al., "A 3D PEEC formulation based on the cell method for full wave analyses with conductive, dielectric, and magnetic media," in IEEE Trans. Magn., 2017.

[5] D. Romano and G. Antonini, "Quasi-static partial element equivalent circuit models of linear magnetic materials," in IEEE Trans. Magn., vol. 51, no. 7, pp. 1-15, July 2015.

[6] F. Freschi and M. Repetto, "A general framework for mixed structured/unstructured PEEC modelling," Applied Computational Electromagnetic Society Journal, vol. 23, no. 3, pp. 200-206, 2008.

[7] J. Siau, et al., "Volume integral formulation using face elements for electromagnetic problem considering conductors and dielectrics," in IEEE Trans. on Electromag. Compat., vol. 58, no. 5, pp. 1587-1594, Oct. 2016.

[8] R. M. Fano, L. J. Chu, and R. B. Adler, *Electromagnetic Fields, Energy, and Forces*. M.I.T. Press, 1960.

[9] J. A. Stratton, *Electromagnetic Theory*. M.I.T. Press, 1941.

[10] L. Codecasa, "Refoundation of the cell method using augmented dual grids," IEEE Trans. Magn., vol. 50, no. 2, Art. ID 7012204, Feb. 2014.

Decoupled Potential Integral Equations for Electromagnetic Scattering*

J. Li
Department of Electrical and Computer Engineering
Michigan State University
East Lansing, USA
jieli@egr.msu.edu

B. Shanker
Department of Electrical and Computer Engineering
Department of Computational Mathematics, Science and Engineering
Michigan State University
East Lansing, USA
bshanker@egr.msu.edu

***Abstract*—In this paper, an integral equation formulation will be presented in terms of decoupled scalar and vector potentials to model electromagnetic scattering from dielectric objects. The formulation can lead to several sets of integral equations with different properties; one of the sets is a second kind integral equation that doesn't result in low-frequency breakdown or dense mesh breakdown.**

***Index Terms*—electromagnetic scattering, second kind integral equation, low-frequency breakdown**

I. Introduction

Recently, the decoupled potential based approach [1], [2] was introduced in part to overcome low-frequency breakdown of standard integral equations. To date, only scattering from perfect electrically conducting (PEC) bodies has been discussed. In [2], using an indirect approach, a second kind integral equation (IE) is constructed using nonphysical unknowns. The resulting IE is well-conditioned so that it does not suffer from either the low-frequency or dense mesh breakdown. In contrast, [1] construct an IE that bears a strong resemblance to the augmented electric field integral equation (AEFIE). While it does take a direct approach, it is not a second kind IE.

II. Decoupled Boundary Conditions

Consider a dielectric object whose surface is denoted by Ω, whose permittivity is denoted by ε_2. This object is illuminated by an incident electromagnetic field. We start the discussion with the well-known representation of the electromagnetic (EM) fields in terms of the vector and scalar potentials, viz., $\mathbf{E}_i = -j\omega\mathbf{A}_i - \nabla\Phi_i$ and $\mathbf{H}_i = \frac{1}{\mu_i}\nabla\times\mathbf{A}_i$, where the subscript denotes either the exterior ($i = 1$) or interior($i = 2$) domain.

The scalar potential satisfies the scalar Helmholtz equation, whereas the vector potential satisfies the vector Helmholtz equation (rather than the curl-curl equation).

This work was supported in part by HPCC facility at Michigan State University under Grant NSF CMMI- 1250261, and Grant NSF ECCS-1408115.

From the Green's identity and the governing Helmholtz equation, the scattered potential (denoted with superscript "s") can be written in terms of potentials on S as:

$$\begin{aligned}\Phi^s(\mathbf{r}) &= \int_S \left[-G(\mathbf{r},\mathbf{r}')\frac{\partial\Phi(\mathbf{r}')}{\partial n'} + \Phi(\mathbf{r}')\frac{G(\mathbf{r},\mathbf{r}')}{\partial n'}\right] dS' \\ &= -\mathcal{S}_k\left[\frac{\partial\Phi(\mathbf{r}')}{\partial n'}\right] + \mathcal{D}_k\left[\Phi(\mathbf{r}')\right]\end{aligned}, \quad (1)$$

where, as in the acoustics, the single and double layer potential operators are defined as:

$$\mathcal{S}_k[x](\mathbf{r}) = \int_S G(\mathbf{r},\mathbf{r}')x(\mathbf{r}')dS', \quad (2a)$$

$$\mathcal{D}_k[x](\mathbf{r}) = \int_S \frac{\partial G(\mathbf{r},\mathbf{r}')}{\partial n'}x(\mathbf{r}')dS'. \quad (2b)$$

It can be derived, using the dyadic Green's function for the vector Helmholtz equation, that $\mathbf{A}^s(\mathbf{r})$ has the following representation [3]:

$$\begin{aligned}\mathbf{A}^s(\mathbf{r}) =& \mathcal{S}_k[\mathbf{n}'\times\nabla'\times\mathbf{A}(\mathbf{r}')] + \nabla\times\mathcal{S}_k[\mathbf{n}'\times\mathbf{A}(\mathbf{r}')] \\ &- \nabla\mathcal{S}_k[\mathbf{n}'\cdot\mathbf{A}(\mathbf{r}')] - \mathcal{S}_k[\mathbf{n}'\nabla'\cdot\mathbf{A}(\mathbf{r}')].\end{aligned} \quad (3)$$

As is evident from the above representation, there are four types of surface *sources*, associated with the total vector potential $\mathbf{A} = \mathbf{A}^i + \mathbf{A}^s$, to represent the scattered vector potential. For notational simplicity, the following are used to denote surface sources that will be the unknown quantities in the integral equations derived later;

$$\mathbf{a}(\mathbf{r}) = \mathbf{n}\times\nabla\times\mathbf{A}(\mathbf{r}), \quad (4a)$$

$$\mathbf{b}(\mathbf{r}) = \mathbf{n}\times\mathbf{n}\times\mathbf{A}(\mathbf{r}), \quad (4b)$$

$$\gamma(\mathbf{r}) = \mathbf{n}\cdot\mathbf{A}(\mathbf{r}), \quad (4c)$$

$$\sigma(\mathbf{r}) = \nabla\cdot\mathbf{A}(\mathbf{r}). \quad (4d)$$

where ∇ is the 3D volume gradient operator. Using this notation, the representation for vector potential can be rewritten as:

$$\mathbf{A}^s = \mathcal{S}_k[\mathbf{a}] - \nabla\times\mathcal{S}_k[\mathbf{n}'\times\mathbf{b}(\mathbf{r}')] - \nabla\mathcal{S}_k[\gamma] - \mathcal{S}_k[\mathbf{n}'\sigma]. \quad (5)$$

To formulate the integral equation, one needs to set up the boundary conditions for different trace data as in regular current-based formulations. Using $\mathbf{A}-\Phi$ representation in the boundary conditions for the EM fields, one gets

$$\mathbf{n}\times(-j\omega\mathbf{A}_1-\nabla\Phi_1)=\mathbf{n}\times(-j\omega\mathbf{A}_2-\nabla\Phi_2), \tag{6a}$$

$$\frac{1}{\mu_1}\,\mathbf{n}\times\nabla\times\mathbf{A}_1=\frac{1}{\mu_2}\,\mathbf{n}\times\nabla\times\mathbf{A}_2, \tag{6b}$$

$$\epsilon_1\mathbf{n}\cdot(-j\omega\mathbf{A}_1-\nabla\Phi_1)=\epsilon_2\mathbf{n}\cdot(-j\omega\mathbf{A}_2-\nabla\Phi_2), \tag{6c}$$

$$\mathbf{n}\cdot\nabla\times\mathbf{A}_1=\mathbf{n}\cdot\nabla\times\mathbf{A}_2. \tag{6d}$$

After some algebra, one gets the following two decoupled sets of boundary conditions; the first set is only in terms of scalar potential whereas the second in terms of the vector potential. Specifically,

$$\Phi_1=\Phi_2, \tag{7a}$$

$$\epsilon_1\mathbf{n}\cdot\nabla\Phi_1=\epsilon_2\mathbf{n}\cdot\nabla\Phi_2, \tag{7b}$$

$$\int_S\frac{\partial\Phi_1}{\partial n}dS'=0. \tag{7c}$$

$$\mathbf{n}\times\mathbf{A}_1=\mathbf{n}\times(\mathbf{A}_2), \tag{8a}$$

$$\frac{1}{\mu_1}\mathbf{n}\times\nabla\times\mathbf{A}_1=\frac{1}{\mu_2}\mathbf{n}\times\nabla\times\mathbf{A}_2, \tag{8b}$$

$$\epsilon_1\mathbf{n}\cdot\mathbf{A}_1=\epsilon_2\mathbf{n}\cdot\mathbf{A}_2, \tag{8c}$$

$$\epsilon_1\nabla\cdot\mathbf{A}_1=\epsilon_2\nabla\cdot\mathbf{A}_2, \tag{8d}$$

$$\int\mathbf{n}\cdot\mathbf{A}_1dS'=0. \tag{8e}$$

III. Decoupled Potential Integral Equation

The integral equation associated with scalar potential can be constructed in the same way as the integral equation for acoustic transmission problem [4]. Only the vector potential integral equation is given here. For exterior domain, the integral equation can be set up involving the unknown Cauchy data as:

$$\begin{pmatrix}\mathbf{a}_1\\ \mathbf{b}_1\\ \gamma_1\\ \sigma_1\end{pmatrix}=\begin{pmatrix}\mathbf{a}^i\\ \mathbf{b}^i\\ \gamma^i\\ \sigma^i\end{pmatrix}+\mathcal{Z}\begin{pmatrix}\mathbf{a}_1\\ \mathbf{b}_1\\ \gamma_1\\ \sigma_1\end{pmatrix}, \tag{9}$$

where

$$\mathcal{Z}=\begin{pmatrix}\mathcal{K}_{k_1} & -\mathcal{T}_{k_1} & 0 & -\mathcal{Q}^1_{k_1}\\ \mathcal{S}^t_{k_1} & -\mathcal{K}'_{k_1} & -\mathcal{P}^2_{k_1} & -\mathcal{Q}^2_{k_1}\\ \mathcal{S}^r_{k_1} & -\mathcal{M}^3_{k_1} & -\mathcal{D}'_{k_1} & -\mathcal{Q}^3_{k_1}\\ \nabla\cdot\mathcal{S}_{k_1} & 0 & k_1^2\mathcal{S}_{k_1} & \mathcal{D}_{k_1}\end{pmatrix}. \tag{10}$$

The operators $\mathcal{T}$, $\mathcal{K}$, and $\mathcal{K}'$ are the hyper-singular EFIE operator, the MFIE operator and its adjoint operator, respectively. $\mathcal{D}$ and $\mathcal{D}'$ are scalar double layer potential operator and its adjoint operator. The other operators are less well-known and their explicit expressions are as follows:

$$\mathcal{M}^3_k[\mathbf{b}]=\mathbf{n}\cdot\nabla\times\mathcal{S}_k[\mathbf{n}'\times\mathbf{b}], \tag{11a}$$

$$\mathcal{P}^2_k[\gamma]=\mathbf{n}\times\mathbf{n}\times\nabla\mathcal{S}_k[\gamma], \tag{11b}$$

$$\mathcal{Q}^1_k[\sigma]=\mathbf{n}\times\nabla\times\mathcal{S}_k[\mathbf{n}'\sigma], \tag{11c}$$

$$\mathcal{Q}^2_k[\sigma]=\mathbf{n}\times\mathbf{n}\times\mathcal{S}_k[\mathbf{n}'\sigma], \tag{11d}$$

$$\mathcal{Q}^3_k[\sigma]=\mathbf{n}\cdot\mathcal{S}_k[\mathbf{n}'\sigma]. \tag{11e}$$

In the operator system, non-compact operators, besides the hyper-singular one at the first row and the second column, only exist in the skew diagonal.

Similarly, the integral equation for the interior domain can be written as follows:

$$\begin{pmatrix}\mathbf{a}_2\\ \mathbf{b}_2\\ \gamma_2\\ \sigma_2\end{pmatrix}=-\begin{pmatrix}\mathcal{K}_{k_2} & -\mathcal{T}_{k_2} & 0 & -\mathcal{Q}^1_{k_2}\\ \mathcal{S}^t_{k_2} & -\mathcal{K}'_{k_2} & -\mathcal{P}^2_{k_2} & -\mathcal{Q}^2_{k_2}\\ \mathcal{S}^r_{k_2} & -\mathcal{M}^3_{k_2} & -\mathcal{D}'_{k_2} & -\mathcal{Q}^3_{k_2}\\ \nabla\cdot\mathcal{S}_{k_2} & 0 & k_2^2\mathcal{S}_{k_2} & \mathcal{D}_{k_2}\end{pmatrix}\begin{pmatrix}\mathbf{a}_2\\ \mathbf{b}_2\\ \gamma_2\\ \sigma_2\end{pmatrix}. \tag{12}$$

After applying the boundary conditions for the vector potential and linearly combing the two sets of integral equations, one can get one set of four equations for the four unknowns on the interface. There are many possible choices to formulate the final integral equation. However, to get a second kind integral equation, off-diagonal non-compact operators have to be regularized to construct the diagonal-dominant integral equation.

The second kind integral equation for the vector potential will be free from low-frequency breakdown and dense mesh breakdown due to the diagonal dominance of the well-conditioned system. Other choices of combining schemes might lead to EFIE-like system that can be easily tested using Galerkin approach without using any dual-space basis functions.

Another point worth that is worth to be noted here is that one can formulate similar systems for either the electric or the magnetic field, all based on boundary conditions on the electric field or magnetic field. Hence it will be a single-field based formulation. Such integral equation would be also immune from low frequency breakdown and dense mesh breakdown , if set up and scaled correctly. The $A-\Phi$ based system derived in this communication will be more suitable to situations that need explicit scalar and/or vector potentials for multi-physics simulations.

IV. Conclusion

In this communication, the decoupled potential based boundary value description of the electromagnetic transmission problem is discussed and used to formulate potential based formulation to have some stability properties. Details about the formulation and in-depth discussions on this type of formulations will be provided at the conference.

References

[1] Q. S. Liu, S. Sun, and W. C. Chew, "An Integral Equation Method based on Vector And Scalar Potential Formulations," in *2015 IEEE International Symposium on Antennas and Propagation & USNC/URSI National Radio Science Meeting*. IEEE, Jul. 2015, pp. 744–745.

[2] F. Vico, M. Ferrando, L. Greengard, and Z. Gimbutas, "The Decoupled Potential Integral Equation for Time-Harmonic Electromagnetic Scattering," *Communications on Pure and Applied Mathematics*, vol. 69, no. 4, pp. 771–812, Apr. 2016.

[3] W. C. Chew, "Vector Potential Electromagnetics with Generalized Gauge for Inhomogeneous Media: Formulation," *Progress In Electromagnetics Research*, vol. 149, pp. 69–84, 2014.

[4] D. Colton and R. Kress, *Integral Equation Methods in Scattering Theory*. New York: John Wiley & Sons, 1983.

A Lagrange Multiplier Approach to Constraining Electromagnetic Surface Integral Equations

Daniel L. Dault and Andrew J. Pray
Air Force Research Laboratory
Wright Patterson AFB, OH

Abstract—**Enforcement of current continuity at material junctions in surface integral equation (SIE) formulations for composite objects has generally relied on somewhat intrusive constraint procedures that complicate system assembly and preconditioning, especially in the context of low rank solvers. The method proposed alleviates these problems by enforcing constraints in a manner equivalent to earlier approaches, but with a less invasive implementation. In addition to solving these challenges, the method is sufficiently general to handle other types of constraints, e.g., unknowns in symmetry planes.**

Keywords— Composite Domains, Moment Method, Symmetry.

I. Introduction

Electromagnetic analysis of composite structures, i.e., those with piecewise homogeneous constitutive parameters, can be efficiently analyzed using surface integral equations (SIEs). This is effected by bounding each region of constant (ε,μ) with equivalent sources. In comparison to volumetric full-wave methods, SIEs can be a more efficient approach as the unknowns can be restricted to a surface discretization. It is, however, very challenging to develop SIE solvers that can analyze arbitrary composite geometries. A general SIE needs to support many different operators, boundary conditions and formulations of the equations at each boundary, e.g., PMCHWT vs. N-Muller.

An arguably greater challenge is to develop a general approach for handling junction contours, where 2 or more boundaries meet. Historically, the approach has been to introduce new degrees of freedom around the junction to ensure current continuity. The linear dependence in the resulting currents is handled by either explicitly removing degrees of freedom, or through an SVD-based approach. The former can only be done for relatively simple junction configurations. While the latter is more general, both methods rely on degrees of freedom that span multiple boundaries. This restricts the choice of formulations as incompatible formulations meeting at a junction can lead to challenging line integrals. Coupling between different boundaries also poses challenges to the maintainability of the EM software. Careful implementation of such junctioning schemes in the context of iterative solvers can sidestep some of these complications, but implementation in direct solvers and preconditioners remains a challenge.

This paper presents a novel method for handling current distributions at junctions, using Lagrange multipliers. This allows for mixing arbitrary formulations and boundary conditions to at a junction without the need to introduce degrees of freedom across the junction contour. A small modification of the method can also handle problems with unknowns spanning one or more planes of symmetry. Lagrange multipliers are also used to represent these unknowns, making extension to junctions lying in one or two planes of symmetry straightforward.

II. Problem Statement

A. Currents at Junctions

We seek to enforce relations between moment method (MoM) degrees of freedom that enforce physical continuities at material junctions. Fig. 1 shows a junction with multiple incident fins, each with a different boundary condition. The *i*th fin (denoted by F_i) carries two currents that may be dependent based on the fin's boundary condition, and fins are separated by sectors S_i that may represent different material regions or sectors in free space. Several procedures for enforcing physical continuity of the currents have been proposed [1], [2].

These approaches all replace the original set of unknowns that do not appropriately enforce continuity conditions with another set of unknowns that enforce continuity by construction. Usually this involves transforming the original MoM system as

$$(R^T Z R)I = R^T V, \tag{1}$$

with Z, V, and I the unconstrained MoM impedance matrix, forcing vector, and solution respectively. The matrix R contains constraints obtained by satisfying KCL-like constraints between currents on adjacent fins. R has dimensions N_s x N_c, with N_s the total number of degrees of freedom in the un-transformed MoM impedance matrix and N_c the number of constraints. The transformation of Z by R can be simply effected in iterative solvers via cascaded multiplication. If direct solution of portions of Z is required, e.g., in a direct solver or for preconditioning,

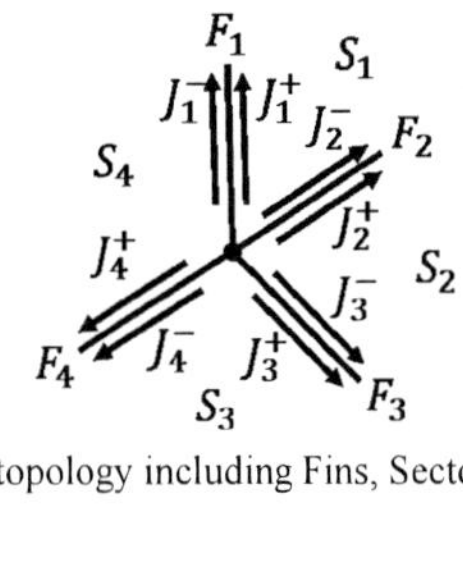

Fig 1. Junction topology including Fins, Sectors, and currents J.

application of R can lead to higher assembly and storage cost, especially if Z is stored in compressed format.

III. Formulation

We propose a different strategy in which constraints are imposed not by taking linear combinations of unknowns incident on the junction, but by enforcing the equivalent linear combinations through a Lagrange multiplier approach. To assemble the forward junction constraints, we first enforce the condition that two fin currents sharing a sector must be continuous. Second, for each fin we apply the appropriate constraint that relates fin currents on either side of a fin, e.g., for penetrable/transparent boundaries the constraint is $J^+ = J^-$ for the electric current, with an equivalent constraint for the magnetic current M. Finally, all of these constraints are assembled into a table. In many cases the rows of this table are linearly dependent and a low fill-in rank-revealing factorization is employed to obtain a linearly independent system. We denote the resulting constraint table as the "forward" constraint, and the corresponding prolongation onto the MoM basis set as C.

It can be verified that the row space of the R matrices in eq. (1) is equivalent to the nullspace of C; a standard procedure for finding R consists of using an algorithm like the SVD to build a basis for $N(C)$ [1]. Instead, we form the system,

$$\begin{bmatrix} Z & C^T \\ C & 0 \end{bmatrix} \begin{bmatrix} I \\ \lambda \end{bmatrix} = \begin{bmatrix} V \\ 0 \end{bmatrix}, \quad (2)$$

where the vector λ contains a set of auxiliary unknowns which may be identified as Lagrange multipliers. Due to the small number of unknowns incident upon junctions in typical practical MoM systems, C generally has $O(1)$ rows. The solution I in eq. (2) is precisely the same as that in eq. (1).

Several advantages accrue from using the Lagrange multiplier approach. First, the extra step of finding the null space of the forward constraint is avoided. Second, the entries of Z are unchanged, permitting the easy use of different formulations within the same system. Third, because the row dimension of C is usually $O(1)$ for practical problems, the system in eq. 2 can be directly factored at little additional cost. Fourth, the assembly of eq. 2 is easy to implement in a maintainable way in production level codes. Fifth, eigendecomposition of the augmented operator in eq. 2 exposes structure that can be exploited to construct effective

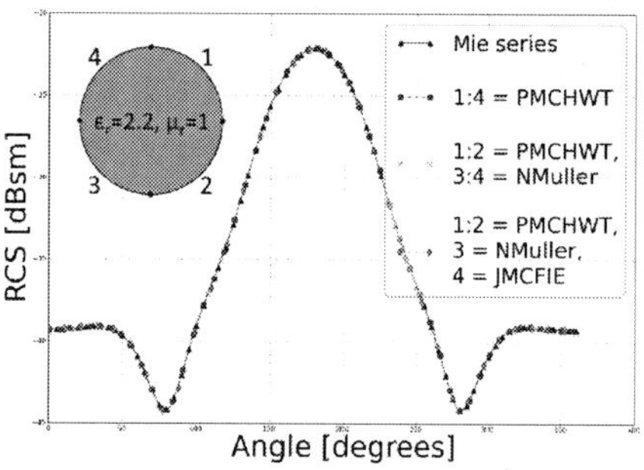

Fig 2. Scattering from dielectric sphere, mixed formulations.

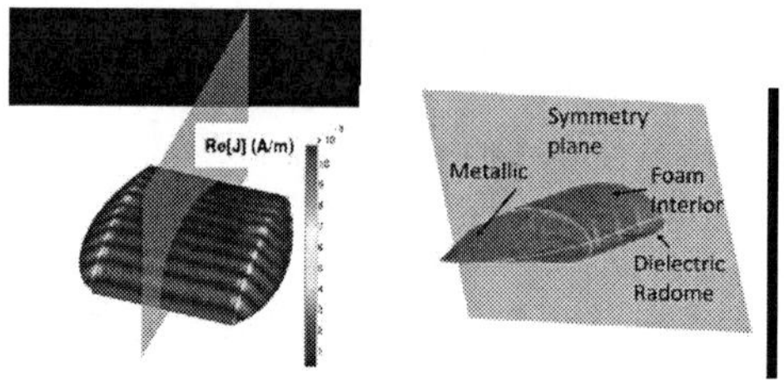

Fig 3. NACA airfoil. Left: surface currents, Right: geometry.

reconditioners for junctioned systems. Sixth, the introduction of traditional junction constraints can pollute low rank representations of matrix blocks, leading to higher rank and fillin in the final operators. By segregating the constraints from the unperturbed Z, eq. 2 retains the same compressibility as the original moment method system. Finally, the structure in eq. 2 is very general, permitting simple enforcement of other types of constraints, e.g., symmetry or waveport constraints. We note in passing that the structure of eq. 2 is similar to that used in [3] to treat non-conformal PEC junctions; although the present work is restricted to conformal junctions, initial tests have shown that it also generalizes readily to nonconformal junctions if the approximations inherent in such discretizations are accepted.

IV. Results

The first result demonstrates the mixing of several penetrable formulations objects including "N" and "T" type formulations [4]. A dielectric sphere is partitioned into four quadrants and excited with an incident plane wave. Different surfaces on the sphere are assigned different traces; the resulting problem is assembled and solved using the formulation of equation 2. The result using the mixed traces agrees well both with a pure PMCHWT approach and the analytical Mie Series result. The second result shows the mixing of material junction and symmetry constraints. Again, the system is structured using eq. 2 (with the size of Z reduced through symmetry exploitation [5]). Fig. 3 shows the result both with and without symmetry.

References

[1] E. Yip, and B. Dembart, "Matrix assembly in FMM-MOM codes," ISS Tech97-001, 1997.

[2] P. Yla-Oijala, M. Taskinen, and J. Sarvas, "Surface integral equation method for general composite metallic and dielectric structures with junctions," *Progress In Electromagnetics Research*, vol. 52, pp. 81-108, 2005.

[3] K. Cools, "A Mortar Element Method for the Electric Field Integral Equation on Sheets and Junctions," in *Computational Electromagnetics—Retrospective and Outlook*, Singapore, 2015.

[4] X. Q. Sheng, J. M. Jin, J. Song, W. C. Chew, and C. C. Lu, "Solution of combined-field integral equation using multilevel fast multipole algorithm for scattering by homogeneous bodies," *IEEE Transactions on Antennas and Propagation*, vol. 46, no. 11, pp. 1718-1726, 1998.

[5] L. N. Medgyesi-Mitschang, J. M. Putnam, and M. B. Gedera, "Generalized method of moments for three-dimensional penetrable scatterers," *JOSA A*, vol. 11.4, pp. 1383-1398, 1994.

Sparse Direct Matrix Solvers of Finite Element Discretizations in Electromagnetics

Marinos N. Vouvakis
Electrical and Computer Engineering
University of Massachusetts Amherst
Amherst, MA, USA
vouvakis@ecs.umass.edu

Javad Moshfegh
Electrical and Computer Engineering
University of Massachusetts Amherst
Amherst, MA, USA
jmoshfegh@umass.edu

***Abstract*—The paper outlines some direct solution strategies for sparse matrices arising from the finite element (FE) discretization of electromagnetic (EM) models, and explores whether the conventional thinking followed by highly optimized direct method tools for sparse matrices is indeed the best available option for directly solving FEM problems in EM. Factorization memory and time, solution time, parallelization potential, and error will be considered in the comparisons between approaches. Drawing from advances in the area of integral equation (IE) methods that rely on relatively small but dense matrices, we will conjecture that direct solvers that minimize factorization fill-in while maintaining sparsity may not lead to the best overall strategy after all. We present an direct solution algorithm for FEM, based on domain decomposition that generates and operates on a lesser sparse matrix with block-wise sparse pattern, thus bridging the gap between the two extreme matrix structures, (a large fully sparse encountered in FEM and a smaller fully dense encountered in IE methods). Early results on 3D arbitrary tetrahedron meshes and arbitrary volumetric geometries suggest that the proposed approach significantly outperform state-of-the-art sparse matrix direct solvers in terms of memory while maintaining competitive run times for serial implementations.**

***Index Terms*—Numerical Linear Algebra, Sparse Matrix Direct Methods, Finite Element Methods**

I. Introduction

Finite Element Method (FEM) based computational electromagnetic models result in very large but sparse linear systems that are often solved iteratively in lieu of direct factorization methods that tend to use more memory and have higher computational complexity. When these models have near-resonant and/or multi-wavelength structures or involve many independent excitations, even the most advanced preconditioned iterative method will lose its effectiveness and resilience. This problematic behavior, coupled with the proliferation of RAM and cores in modern computing platforms has lead to a recent resurgence of direct solution methods as serious contenders to their iterative counterparts. Efficient computer implementations of classical sparse Cholesky, LDL^T or LU factorization relay on advanced cache-aware algorithms such as multifrontal methods [1] or the super-nodal methods [2] to speed-up computations. When coupled with powerful fill-reducing matrix reordering schemes such as nested dissection [3] and its variants they can lead to very impressive performances in terms of memory and time.

This paper will outline this conventional direct solution to sparse matrices arising from FEM electromagnetic models, and explore he conventional thinking followed by highly optimized direct method tools for sparse matrices is indeed the best available option for directly solving FEM problems in EM. Factorization memory and time, solution time, parallelization potential, and error will be considered in the comparisons between approaches. Drawing from advances in the area of integral equation (IE) methods that rely on relatively small but dense matrices, we will conjecture that direct solvers that minimize factorization fill-in while maintaining sparsity may not lead to the best overall strategy after all. We present an direct solution algorithm for FEM, based on domain decomposition that generates and operates on a lesser sparse matrix with block-wise sparse pattern, thus bridging the gap between the two extreme matrix structures, (a large fully sparse encountered in FEM and a smaller fully dense encountered in IE methods). Early results on 3D arbitrary tetrahedron meshes and arbitrary volumetric geometries suggest that the proposed approach significantly outperform state-of-the-art sparse matrix direct solvers in terms of memory while maintaining competitive run times for serial implementations.

II. Approach

Unlike conventional direct sparse matrix solvers that are extremely general and opaque to the underlying computational or data science problem that produced the sparse matrix, the proposed approach is tailored to matrices resulting from the finite element discretization of second order nonelliptic differential equations (lead to a non-positive definite often symmetric matrices that do not have zeroes in the diagonal). It is based on a domain decomposition (DD) strategy and aims at recovering a *numerical exact* factorization of the FEM matrix. This direct DD strategy relies on a judicious re-formulation of the boundary value problem (BVP) as a decomposed BVP on a collection of domains. It is noted that the method is not restricted to Maxwell equations or electromagnetics (EM), but is simply presented in that context. It is paramount that the decomposed BVP and its subsequent mixed/hybrid variational formulation are such that all domains are always regular while the overall problem remains symmetric (self-adjoint). Next a process akin to the finite element tearing and interconnecting

(FETI) reduction in iterative domain decomposition methods, a reduced (auxiliary) problem is produced with the aid of he discrete Dirichlet-to-Neumann (DtN) operation of each domain. This reduced problem is then used to facilitate a very efficient direct factorization.

The resultant auxiliary matrix is symmetric but orders of magnitude smaller than the original one, and is block-wise sparse (sparse collection of dense blocks), something computational very appealing because it enables the use the blazing fast level 3 basic linear algebra subroutines (BLAS). This matrix is LDL^T re-ordered and symbolically factorized with aid of clique graphs, followed by a custom block LDL^T with restricted (within the blocks) Bunch-Kaufman pivoting. Once the the auxiliary problem has been efficiently factorized, the solution of all or a subset of primal unknowns are recovered in an embarrassingly parallel manner via many smaller size sparse forward backward substitutions.

III. NUMERICAL COMPARISONS

A set of moderate complexity unstructured FEM models are used as test cases to compare the proposed method with MUMPS 5.0.2 [1], and PARDISO-MKL11.1 [2] state-of-the-art 'black-box' direct sparse matrix solvers where METIS 5.1.0 reordering has been used for all methods. The FEM model corresponds to a dielectric ($\epsilon_r = 3$) sphere of progressively larger sizes, (domain increases in three dimensions) and excited with 200 independent RHS (plane wave) excitations. In all cases, the discretization is maintained to approximately $h = \lambda/12$ using second order tangential vector finite elements (20 degrees-of-freedom per tetrahedron). The memory, factorization time and forward/backward substitution times of those test cases are presented in Figs 1. The proposed direct DD method shows a clear edge in memory requirements, which is a major improvement on a key direct method weakness. For a comparison, the plot includes the memory requirement of a stat-of-the-art preconditioned iterative method, showing that the proposed method now rivals the memory of iterative methods. Both factorization and forward backward substitution times of the proposed method are on par or slightly slower that the state-of-the-art. It is noted that the accuracy (based on the relative residual of the linear equation) for all the methods approximately 10^{-12}.

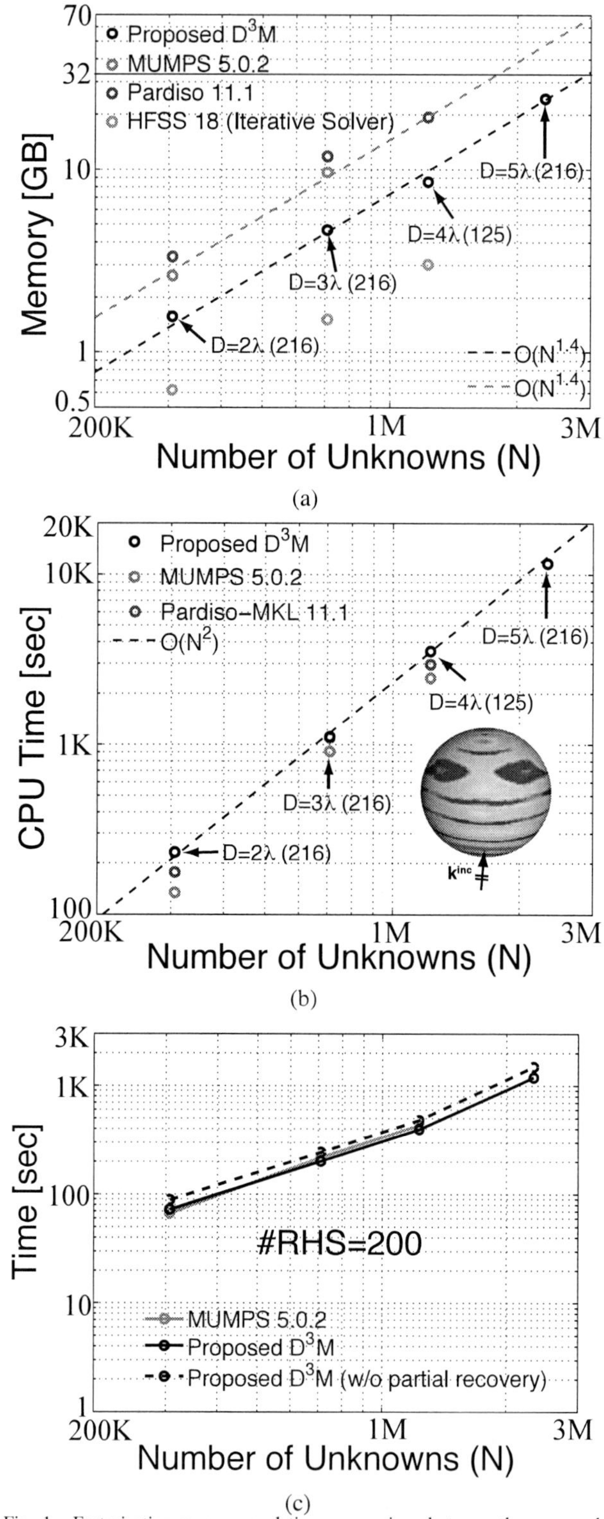

Fig. 1. Factorization memory and time comparison between the proposed direct DD approach and state-of-the-art direct solvers on progressively electrically larger dielectric spheres (serial runs, i.e. 1 core). (a) Memory; (b) CPU time (serial run); (c) forward/backward substitution time for 200 excitations.

REFERENCES

[1] P. R. Amestoy, I. S. Duff, J. Koster, and J.-Y. L'Excellent, "A fully asynchronous multifrontal solver using distributed dynamic scheduling," *SIAM Journal on Matrix Analysis and Applications*, vol. 23, no. 1, pp. 15–41, 2001.

[2] Intel, "Intel math kernel library ver. 11.1," Intel Corporation, Santa Clara, CA, USA, 2009.

[3] G. Karypis, "MeTiS: A software package for partitioning unstructured graphs, partitioning meshes, and computing fill-reducing orderings of sparse matrices - version 5.1.0," Mar. 2013.

Fast Integral Equation Solvers based on the Randomized Cross Approximation

Constantinos L. Zekios
Electrical and Computer Engineering
University of Massachusetts Amherst
Amherst, MA, USA
kzekios@umass.edu

Marinos N. Vouvakis
Electrical and Computer Engineering
University of Massachusetts Amherst
Amherst, MA, USA
vouvakis@ecs.umass.edu

***Abstract*—This paper outlines a fast and fully algebraic integral equation method for the solution of electromagnetic scattering and radiation of perfect electric conducting structures via the Rao-Wilton-Glisson (RWG) Boundary Element Method (BEM) discretization of the Electric Field Integral Equation (EFIE). The present single-level grouping implementation accelerates computations by exploiting the well documented rank deficiency of non-neighboring group BEM interactions. The rank-revealing computational kernel of the proposed method resembles that of the popular Adaptive Cross Approximation (ACA), but bypasses altogether the time-consuming adaptive partial-pivoting of rows and columns using a much simpler randomized scheme for selecting crosses, i.e. row and column pivots, and leveraging blocked linear-algebra operations. More importantly, the method borrows an essential, yet often understated, ingredient from the Fast Multiple Method (FMM), i.e. working with the Green's function instead of the fully assembled BEM matrix, thus strives to numerically factorize the integral equation kernel (Green's function). As a result, the proposed Randomized Cross Approximation (RCA) method delivers considerably lower ranks than ACA, and same memory and set-up time and matrix-vector multiplication time complexities as the single-level FMM while avoiding the low-frequency breakdown of FMM.**

***Index Terms*—Method of Moments, Boundary Element Methods, Fast Integral Equations. Adaptive Cross Approximation**

I. Introduction

Fast integral equation (IE) methods such as the Multi-level Fast Multiple Algorithm (MLFMA) [1] are among the most powerful computational electromagnetic methods for iteratively solving scattering problems from electrically large structures, or radiation of antennas near large platforms (where MLFMA is often coupled with differential equation methods). More recently, ideas and algorithms from fast integral equations have evolved to the area of fast (approximate) direct solvers for Boundary Element Methods (BEM), and Nystrom discretization of IEs. Algebraic methods such as the ACA [2], $\mathcal{H}^2$-matrix methods [3] and the Multilevel Matrix Decomposition (MLMDA)/Butterfly Algorithm [4], although less efficient than MLFMA, have found a new niche in (approximate) direct solvers and are becoming increasingly important.

The goal of this paper is to develop a simple yet improved version of the ACA [2] by integrating some randomized linear algebra ideas, with some key ideas from the FMM theory [5]. Randomization is an effective vehicle for developing amazingly simple and reliable algorithms, whereas FMM ideas lead to nearly optimal complexity algorithms by leveraging the a-priori knowledge of the integral kernel i.e. Green's function. The proposed work, at its present stage, only deals with single-level groupings of the scatterer and seeks to achieve very low memory usage and complexities that rival those of the single level FMM for both high-and low-frequency problems, while maintaining tight error control and numerical stability. For the sake of simplicity and brevity, the work is confined to the RWG-BEM solution of the electric field integral equation (EFIE). The proposed method is termed Randomized Cross Approximation (RCA).

II. Approach

This paper outlines a fast and fully algebraic integral equation method for the solution of electromagnetic scattering and radiation of perfect electric conducting structures via the Rao-Wilton-Glisson (RWG) Boundary Element Method (BEM) discretization of the Electric Field Integral Equation (EFIE). The present single-level grouping implementation accelerates computations by exploiting the well documented rank deficiency of non-neighboring group BEM interactions. The rank-revealing computational kernel of the proposed method resembles that of the popular Adaptive Cross Approximation (ACA), but bypasses altogether the time-consuming adaptive partial-pivoting of rows and columns using a much simpler randomized scheme for selecting crosses, i.e. row and column pivots, and leveraging blocked linear-algebra operations. More importantly, the method borrows an essential, yet often understated, ingredient from the Fast Multiple Method (FMM), i.e. working with the Green's function instead of the fully assembled BEM matrix, thus strives to numerically factorize the integral equation kernel (Green's function). As a result, the proposed Randomized Cross Approximation (RCA) method delivers considerably lower ranks than ACA, and same memory and set-up time and matrix-vector multiplication time complexities as the single-level FMM while avoiding the low-frequency breakdown of FMM's translator operator associated with the analytic plane-wave factorization. A complete mathematical presentation and algorithmic prescription of the proposed RCA will be presented in the oral talk.

III. PRELIMINARY RESULTS

The commonly used PEC sphere benchmark is used to study memory, speed and error performance of the proposed RCA method. The computational complexity is obtained by progressively increasing sphere unknowns in two distinct fashions: a) by maintaining the same frequency but increasing the discretization density (constant frequency regime), and b) by maintaining the same discretization density per wavelength, in our case $h = \lambda/15$, but increasing the frequency (constant discretization density regime). These two cases are known to give different complexities, with the latter been the more challenging for algebraic approaches as it amount to solving electrically larger problems. Conversely, depending on the frequency the former regime could be more challenging for analytic factorization methods such as the plane-wave FMM. The results of this study are summarized in Fig. 1 that show the the memory, set-up time and Frobenius error norm of the BEM or Method of Moments (MoM) impedance matrix. The resulting memory complexities agree with the theoretically predicted complexities, of $O(N^{3/2})$ for constant frequency regime and $O(N^{7/4})$ for constant discretization regime, and the $O(N^{7/4})$ complexity in time for both cases. It is noted that the error is approximately constant with increasing size and hovers around the predefined numerical tolerance $\texttt{tol} = 10^{-3}$. When this single-level RCA is used in conjunction with iterative solvers, the matrix-vector multiplication time complexity scales as $O(N^3/2)$, which is same as the single-level FMM. It should be noted that this FMM-like complexity of the RCA is not expected to hold in multilevel settings. Larger problem will be presented in the oral talk.

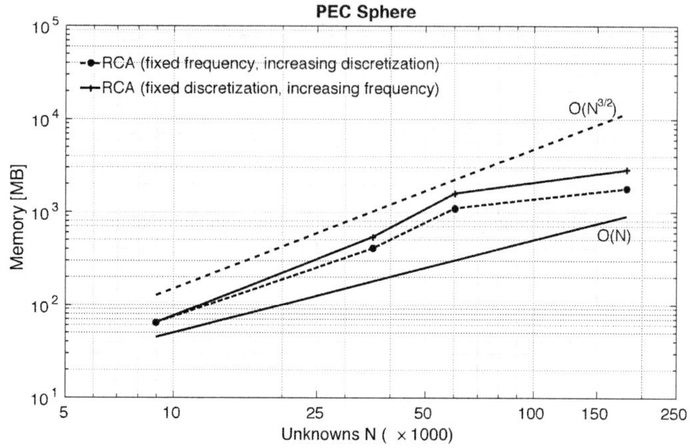

(a)

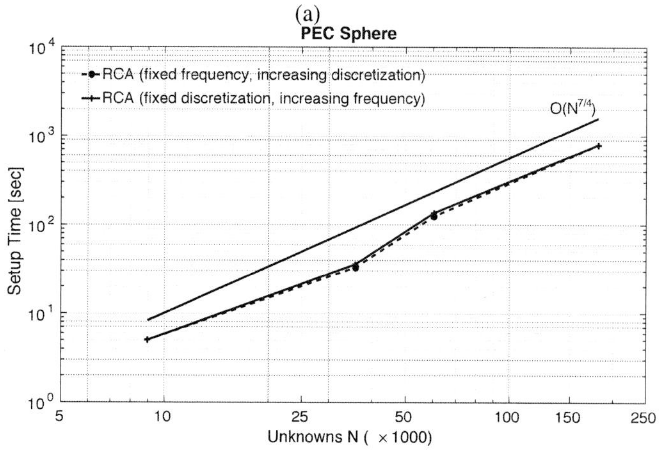

(b)

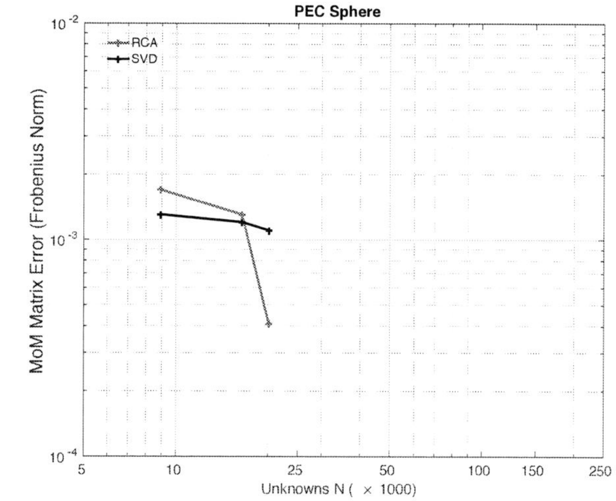

(c)

Fig. 1. Computational scaling and error of the proposed RCA approach on progressively larger spheres (constant frequency regime and constant discretization density regime). (a) Memory of non-near interactions only; (b) Set-up CPU time of non-near interactions only; (c) MoM matrix error (Forbinius norm).

REFERENCES

[1] W. C. Chew, J.-M. Jin, E. Michielssen, and J. Song, *Fast and Efficient Algorithms in Computational Electromagnetics*. Boston MA: Artech House, 2001.

[2] K. Zhao, M. N. Vouvakis, and J.-F. Lee, "The adaptive cross approximation algorithm for accelerated method of moments computations of EMC problems," *IEEE Trans. Electromagnetic Compatibility*, vol. 47, no. 4, pp. 763–773, 2005.

[3] W. Hackbusch and S. Börm, "Data-sparse approximation by adaptive $\mathcal{H}2$-matrices," *Computing*, vol. 69, no. 1, pp. 1–35, Sep 2002.

[4] H. Guo, J. Hu, and E. Michielssen, "On MLMDA/Butterfly compressibility of inverse integral operators," *IEEE Antennas and Wireless Propagation Letters*, vol. 12, pp. 31–34, 2013.

[5] R. Coifman, V. Rokhlin, and S. Wandzura, "The fast multipole method for the wave equation: a pedestrian prescription," *IEEE Ant. Propag. Mag.*, vol. 35, no. 3, pp. 7–12, Jun. 1993.

Adjoint Methods for Uncertainty Quantification in Applied Computational Electromagnetics: FEM Scattering Examples

Cam Key, Aaron Smull, Branislav M. Notaroš
Electrical & Computer Engineering Dept.
Colorado State University
Fort Collins, CO, USA
notaros@colostate.edu

Donald Estep
Department of Statistics
Colorado State University
Fort Collins, CO, USA

Troy Butler
Department of Mathematical and Statistical Sciences
University of Colorado Denver
Denver, CO, USA

***Abstract*— We present methods for quantifying uncertainty and discretization error of numerical electromagnetics solvers based on adjoint operators and duality. We briefly introduce the concept of the adjoint operator and describe applications of adjoint solutions for predicting and analyzing numerical error and approximating sensitivity of a given quantity of interest to a given parameter. Forward solutions are based on the higher order finite element method (FEM).**

Keywords*— *adjoint methods; computational electromagnetics; finite element method; radar; scattering; sensitivity analysis; uncertainty quantification.

I. Introduction

Computational error estimation, model sensitivity prediction, and optimization are growing areas of interest in the field of computational electromagnetics. While full wave numerical methods using the finite element method (FEM) are ubiquitous in the field, analyzing solutions from these methods is challenging due to geometric discretization error, field order expansion error, and lengthy computation times. Problems requiring numerical methods typically lack analytical solutions, making computational error difficult to discern from measurement error when comparing model results to real-world data where error analysis is desired. Meanwhile, prohibitive computation times make techniques like Monte-Carlo simulation computationally untenable where model sensitivity analysis and optimization are desired.

This summary paper focuses on an application of adjoint methods toward sensitivity analysis for computational electromagnetics problems. Specifically, it presents an example of an application of an adjoint operator to quantify sensitivity of a quantity of interest (QoI) to perturbations in an input parameter. We use the sensitivity information to predict the QoI over the parameter domain. The computational modeling, both for forward and reverse solutions, in the given example was performed using a double-higher-order FEM solver [1].

II. The Adjoint Solution and its Applications

To define the adjoint operator for a given problem, we first put the problem in variational form. If the problem is nonlinear, we use the integral Mean Value Theorem to write the problem in linear form. For the illustrative dielectric scatterer problem, we consider the solution of the Dirichlet boundary value problem:

Find $\mathbf{E}^{sc} \in H^1$ (the space of L^2 functions with L^2 first derivatives) such that the variational formulation of the following equations hold:

$$\nabla\times\overline{\overline{\mu}}_r^{-1}\nabla\times \mathrm{E}^{sc} - k_0^2\overline{\overline{\varepsilon}}_r \mathrm{E}^{sc} = -\nabla\times\overline{\overline{\mu}}_r^{-1}\nabla\times \mathrm{E}^{inc} + k_0^2\overline{\overline{\varepsilon}}_r \mathrm{E}^{inc}, \quad (1a)$$

$$n\times \mathrm{E}^{sc} = 0, \quad (1b)$$

where the former equation holds through the volume of the domain and the latter holds on the boundary of the domain. This may be stated in linear operator form as:

$$L\mathbf{v} = \mathbf{f}, \quad (2)$$

The adjoint operator of L is then the operator L^* which satisfies

$$\langle \mathbf{u}, L\mathbf{v}\rangle = \langle L^*\mathbf{u}, \mathbf{v}\rangle, \quad (3)$$

with angle brackets denoting the L^2 inner product between two

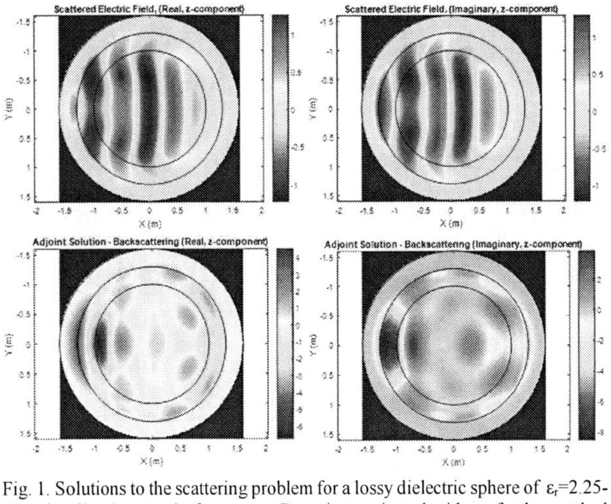

Fig. 1. Solutions to the scattering problem for a lossy dielectric sphere of ε_r=2.25-1i and radius 1 meter in free space. Domain terminated with perfectly matched layer with perfect electric conductor (PEC) exterior boundary. Incident wave was chosen to arrive from θ = 90°, ϕ = 0° and θ-polarized at 300 MHz with unit electric field amplitude. Solutions to the adjoint problem are given below the corresponding forward solution.

vectors. The adjoint problem may then be formulated as:

This work was supported by the US Air Force Research Laboratory, CREATE SENTRi, Riverside Research Institute, under contract FA8650-14-D-1725(6F1957).

$$\mathcal{L}^{*}\mathbf{v} = \mathbf{p}, \tag{4}$$

where **p** denotes a vector representation of a linear functional defining a QoI <**u**,**p**>. A solution for one such adjoint problem is presented in Fig. 1 for scattering from a 1m-radius lossy dielectric sphere with relative permittivity ε_r=2.25-1i. Here, the incident wave was chosen to arrive from $\theta = 90°$, $\phi = 0°$ and was modeled to be θ-polarized at 300 MHz with unit electric field amplitude. Fig. 2 shows the magnitude of the adjoint solution.

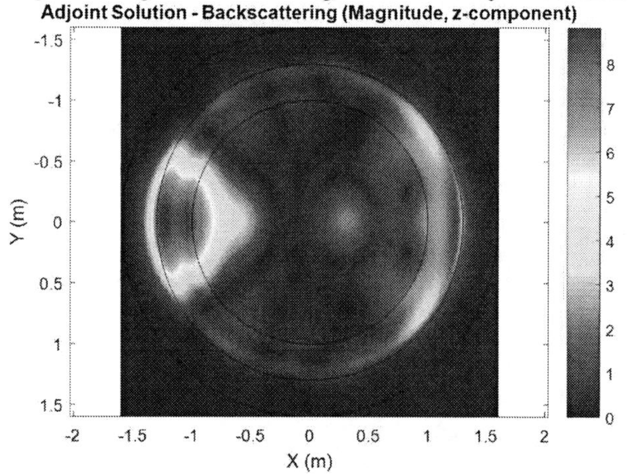

Fig. 2. Magnitude of the z-component of the adjoint solution for the problem described in Fig. 1. The areas most affecting the backscattered field lie in the region facing the radar receiver and the Arago spot. Z = 0 cross section is given.

III. Further Results and Discussion

Given the forward and adjoint solutions at a nominal value of a parameter, values of a desired QoI may be approximated linearly around this parameter value using the adjoint to estimate the derivative of the QoI at the parameter.

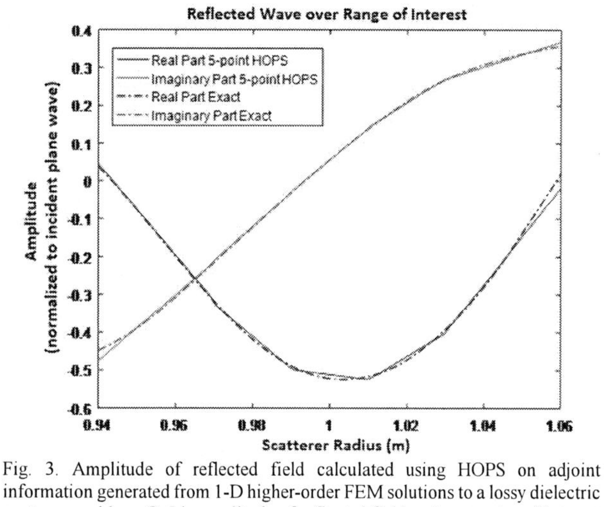

Fig. 3. Amplitude of reflected field calculated using HOPS on adjoint information generated from 1-D higher-order FEM solutions to a lossy dielectric scatterer problem. QoI is amplitude of reflected field and parameter of interest is dielectric scatterer radius.

In [2], this approach is used to construct piecewise linear approximations to the QoI response over the parameter domain in the higher-order parameter sampling method (HOPS). In Fig. 3, we show HOPS results for a 1D analogue of the problem described in Fig. 1. Here, the QoI is the amplitude of the reflected field, and the parameter is the radius of the dielectric scatterer.

Fig. 4 gives another illustrative example for the same QoI, in this case with respect to the parameter of scatterer conductivity. In both Figs. 3 and 4, we also plot the exact QoI response for which HOPS exhibits excellent agreement. For multiple parameters, we can similarly reconstruct gradient information about the QoI using adjoint solutions. This gradient information allows for faster optimization methods to be employed to optimize a QoI with respect to a set of input parameters. Such information can also be used to reconstruct the underlying relationship between the desired QoI and the given set of input parameters, as shown in Fig. 3 and Fig. 4. An adjoint solution, as given in Fig. 2, may also be used directly to determine areas in the computational domain most affecting some QoI. As expected, for the spherical lossy dielectric scatterer in Fig. 1 the magnitude of the adjoint solution is highest in the region facing the radar receiver and the so-called "Arago Spot" at the center of the opposite face. Further work will concern utilizing such information for targeted mesh refinement and higher field-order expansion to improve forward solutions.

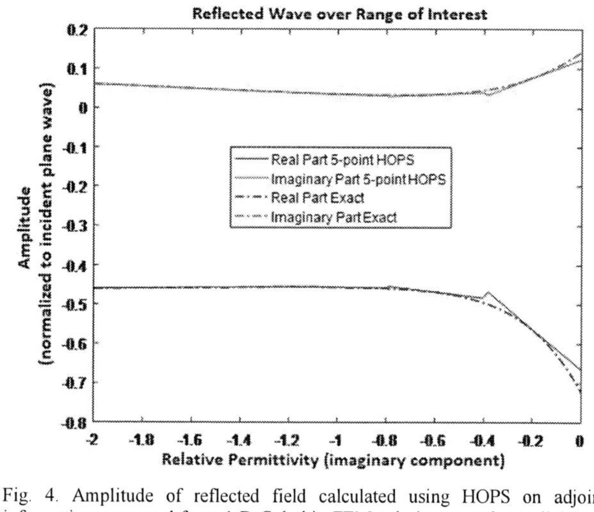

Fig. 4. Amplitude of reflected field calculated using HOPS on adjoint information generated from 1-D Galerkin FEM solutions to a lossy dielectric scatterer problem. QoI is chosen as the magnitude of the reflected field. This is shown with respect to changes in conductivity of the lossy scatterer.

References

[1] B. Notaros and M. Ilic, (2003). "Higher order hierarchical curved hexahedral vector finite elements for electromagnetic modeling," *IEEE Transactions on Microwave Theory and Techniques*, *51*(3), 1026-1033.

[2] D. Estep and D. Neckels, (2006). "Fast and reliable methods for determining the evolution of uncertain parameters in differential equations," *Journal of Computational Physics*, *213*(2), 530-556.

Numerical Validation of a Boundary Element Method With $\boldsymbol{E}$ and $\frac{\partial \boldsymbol{E}}{\partial N}$ as the Boundary Unknowns

Johannes Markkanen
Department of Physics
University of Helsinki
P.O. Box 64, FI-00014, Finland
johannes.markkanen@helsinki.fi

Alex J. Yuffa, Joshua A. Gordon
National Institute of Standards and Technology
Boulder, Colorado 80305, USA
{alex.yuffa, josh.gordon}@nist.gov

***Abstract*—We recently developed a surface integral equation method where the electric field and its normal derivative are chosen as the boundary unknowns. After reviewing this formulation, we present preliminary numerical calculations that show good agreement with the known results. These calculations are encouraging and invite the further development of the numerical solution.**

I. Introduction

We have recently formulated a frequency domain surface integral equation method [1] that is applicable to penetrable closed surface scatterers. The method has several unique applications and advantages over the standard Stratton–Chu formulation as discussed in [1]. In our formulation, we choose the electric field (E-field) and its normal derivative as the boundary unknowns. This choice leads to 12 scalar unknowns on the surface of the scatterer; for each homogeneous region we have three scalar unknowns associated with the E-field and three scalar unknowns associated with its normal derivative. Similar to a typical surface integral equation formulation, our formulation is also based on the Green's theorem (Green's second identity). This formulation leads to *six* scalar equations, and thus it must be supplemented with *six* additional constraints in order to have the same number of equations as unknowns. Three of these constraints come from the well-known continuity condition of the E-field across an interface and the other three come from the recently derived continuity condition for the normal derivative of the E-field [1]–[3].

In this paper, we numerically solve the above discussed equations for spherical scatterers and compare the results to the well-known Mie series solution. We also comment on the choice of the basis functions in the Galerkin's method and its effects on numerical convergence.

II. Formulation Review

Consider a scatterer with permittivity $\overset{2}{\epsilon}$ and permeability $\overset{2}{\mu}$. The space surrounding the scatterer is assumed to be lossless with permittivity $\overset{1}{\epsilon}$ and permeability $\overset{1}{\mu}$, i.e., $\{\overset{1}{\epsilon}, \overset{1}{\mu}\} \in \mathbb{R}$. If we apply the Green's second identity to the scatterer and the surrounding space, then, after setting the observation point on the surface of the scatterer, we obtain:

$$\overset{\text{inc}}{\boldsymbol{E}}(\widetilde{S}) - \fint_{\Sigma} \left[\overset{1}{G} \frac{\partial \overset{1}{\boldsymbol{E}}}{\partial N} - \overset{1}{\boldsymbol{E}} \frac{\partial \overset{1}{G}}{\partial N} \right] \mathrm{d}S = \frac{1}{2} \overset{1}{\boldsymbol{E}}(\widetilde{S}), \tag{1a}$$

and

$$\fint_{\Sigma} \left[\overset{2}{G} \frac{\partial \overset{2}{\boldsymbol{E}}}{\partial N} - \overset{2}{\boldsymbol{E}} \frac{\partial \overset{2}{G}}{\partial N} \right] \mathrm{d}S = \frac{1}{2} \overset{2}{\boldsymbol{E}}(\widetilde{S}), \tag{1b}$$

where $\overset{\text{inc}}{\boldsymbol{E}}$ is the incident E-field, $\fint$ denotes the Cauchy principal value integral, Σ denotes the surface of the scatterer, $\frac{\partial}{\partial N}$ denotes the normal derivative, G is the free-space Green's function, and $\widetilde{S}$ is the observation point on Σ. In (1), the overset digit indicates if the quantity is associated with the scatterer or the surrounding space, e.g., $\overset{2}{\boldsymbol{E}}$ is the E-field just inside the scatterer. In the Gaussian unit system, the continuity condition for the E-field across an interface can be written as [1]:

$$\overset{2}{\boldsymbol{E}} = \overset{r}{\epsilon}^{-1} \left(\boldsymbol{N} \cdot \overset{1}{\boldsymbol{E}} \right) \boldsymbol{N} + \left(\boldsymbol{S}^{\alpha} \cdot \overset{1}{\boldsymbol{E}} \right) \boldsymbol{S}_{\alpha}, \tag{2a}$$

and the continuity condition for its normal derivative as [1]:

$$\begin{aligned} \frac{\partial \overset{2}{\boldsymbol{E}}}{\partial N} = \overset{r}{\mu} \left(\frac{\partial \overset{1}{\boldsymbol{E}}}{\partial N} - \nabla^{\alpha} \left[\left(\boldsymbol{N} \cdot \overset{1}{\boldsymbol{E}} \right) \boldsymbol{S}_{\alpha} - \left(\boldsymbol{S}_{\alpha} \cdot \overset{1}{\boldsymbol{E}} \right) \boldsymbol{N} \right] \right) \\ + \nabla^{\alpha} \left[\left(\boldsymbol{N} \cdot \overset{2}{\boldsymbol{E}} \right) \boldsymbol{S}_{\alpha} - \left(\boldsymbol{S}_{\alpha} \cdot \overset{2}{\boldsymbol{E}} \right) \boldsymbol{N} \right], \end{aligned} \tag{2b}$$

where $\overset{r}{\mu} = \overset{2}{\mu} / \overset{1}{\mu}$, $\overset{r}{\epsilon} = \overset{2}{\epsilon} / \overset{1}{\epsilon}$, $\boldsymbol{N}$ is the unit-normal pointing out of the scatterer, $\boldsymbol{S}_{\alpha}$ is the surface covariant basis [4], and ∇^{α} is the contravariant surface derivative [4]. Notice that (2) is written in the Einstein summation convention where the Greek indices range from 1 to 2. Substituting (2) into (1b) and using Gauss's theorem in two dimensions yields [1]:

$$\begin{aligned} \frac{1}{2} \overset{2}{\boldsymbol{E}}(\widetilde{S}) = & \fint_{\Sigma} \left[\overset{r}{\mu} \overset{2}{G} \frac{\partial \overset{1}{\boldsymbol{E}}}{\partial N} - \overset{1}{\boldsymbol{E}} \frac{\partial \overset{2}{G}}{\partial N} \right] \mathrm{d}S \\ & + \left(\overset{r}{\mu} - \overset{r}{\epsilon}^{-1} \right) \fint_{\Sigma} \left(\boldsymbol{N} \cdot \overset{1}{\boldsymbol{E}} \right) \boldsymbol{\nabla} \overset{2}{G} \, \mathrm{d}S \\ & + \left(1 - \overset{r}{\mu} \right) \fint_{\Sigma} \left(\overset{1}{\boldsymbol{E}} \cdot \boldsymbol{\nabla} \overset{2}{G} \right) \boldsymbol{N} \, \mathrm{d}S, \end{aligned} \tag{3a}$$

where

$$\overset{2}{\boldsymbol{E}} = \overset{1}{\boldsymbol{E}} + \left(\overset{r}{\epsilon}^{-1} - 1 \right) \left(\boldsymbol{N} \cdot \overset{1}{\boldsymbol{E}} \right) \boldsymbol{N}. \tag{3b}$$

This work was partially supported by U.S. government, not protected by U.S. copyright.

Equation (3) and (1a) form a set of *six* scalar integral equations with *six* scalar unknowns, namely, $\overset{1}{\boldsymbol{E}}$ and $\frac{\partial}{\partial N}\overset{1}{\boldsymbol{E}}$. This is the set of the integral equations that we numerically solve in the next section.

III. Numerical Calculations

We discretize the spherical scatterer with flat triangular elements and construct a basis for the E-field and its normal derivative. We use piecewise constant basis functions for each component associated with the triangle surfaces. Thus, the number of unknowns is six times the number of the triangular elements. Furthermore, we use Galerkin's method to discretize the equations. In other words, the test and basis functions are identical. It is worth noting that the basis functions *do not* enforce any continuity conditions for the E-field or its normal derivative along the surface. Hence, it is clear that we cannot obtain an optimal convergence rate. Moreover, we anticipate that the sharp wedges may also cause some difficulties. Finding a better set of basis functions is an interesting question for future research.

The integral equation set given by (3) and (1a) contains strongly singular integrals. The gradient of the Green's function has the strongest singularity and we decompose it into the normal and surface derivative parts. With the help of integration by parts, the latter one reduces to an integral over a triangle surface and a closed integral over the triangle's edges. We evaluate these integrals using the standard singularity extraction technique [5] in which the singular part is calculated analytically and the remaining part is calculated numerically.

To assess the method, we compare the radar cross section (RCS) of a sphere in free-space meshed by 940 flat triangular patches with the Mie series solution. Fig. 1 shows the RCS of a dielectric sphere with $\overset{1}{k}\rho = 1$, $\overset{2}{\epsilon} = 4$, and $\overset{2}{\mu} = 1$, where ρ is the radius of the sphere and Fig. 2 shows the RCS of a lossy sphere with $\overset{1}{k}\rho = 4$, $\overset{2}{\epsilon} = -2 + \mathrm{i}$, and $\overset{2}{\mu} = 1$. From the figures, we see that our solution agrees well with the Mie series solution in both the dielectric case and the lossy case. More specifically, the L^2-norm relative error of the far-field $\|\boldsymbol{E}\|^2$ integrated over a solid angle is 4.832×10^{-3} for Fig. 1 and 9.360×10^{-3} for Fig. 2.

IV. Conclusions

We numerically tested a recently formulated surface integral equation method where the electric field and its normal derivative are chosen as the boundary unknowns. The preliminary results presented here are in agreement with the Mie series solution for both dielectric and lossy spheres. Furthermore, the method seems to be viable for numerical computations and may be further improved if we employ basis functions that enforce the continuity conditions.

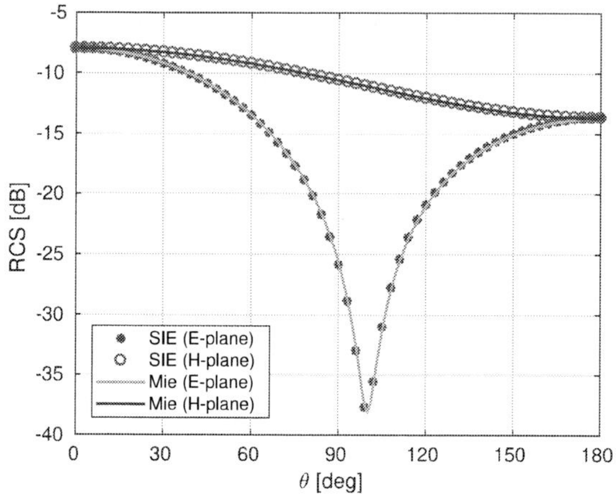

Fig. 1. (Color online) Comparison of the dielectric sphere's RCS as a function of the scattering angle θ computed via the surface integral equation (SIE) method with the Mie series solution.

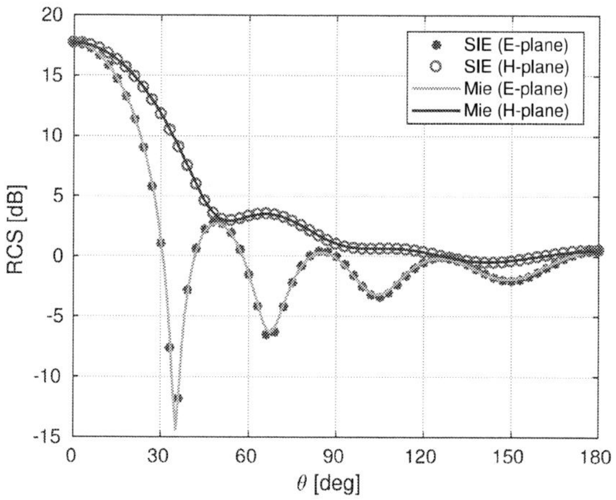

Fig. 2. (Color online) Comparison of the lossy sphere's RCS as a function of the scattering angle θ computed via the surface integral equation (SIE) method with the Mie series solution.

References

[1] A. J. Yuffa and J. Markkanen, "A 3D tensorial integral formulation of scattering containing intriguing relations," submitted for publication.

[2] J. DeSanto and A. Yuffa, "A new integral equation method for direct electromagnetic scattering in homogeneous media and its numerical confirmation," *Waves in Random and Complex Media*, vol. 16, no. 4, pp. 397–408, Nov. 2006. [Online]. Available: http://dx.doi.org/10.1080/17455030500486742

[3] J. A. DeSanto, "A new formulation of electromagnetic scattering from rough dielectric interfaces," *Journal of Electromagnetic Waves and Applications*, vol. 7, no. 10, pp. 1293–1306, Jan. 1993. [Online]. Available: http://dx.doi.org/10.1163/156939393X00480

[4] P. Grinfeld, *Introduction to Tensor Analysis and the Calculus of Moving Surfaces*. Springer, 2013.

[5] S. Järvenpää, M. Taskinen, and P. Ylä-Oijala, "Singularity subtraction technique for high-order polynomial vector basis functions on planar triangles," *IEEE Trans. Antennas Propag.*, vol. 54, no. 1, pp. 42–49, 2006.

Locally Corrected Nyström Discretization for Impressed Current Cathodic Protection Systems

John C. Young
Depatrment of Electrical & Computer Engineering
University of Kentucky
Lexington, KY USA
john.c.young@uky.edu

Robert Pfeiffer
Depatrment of Electrical & Computer Engineering
University of Kentucky
Lexington, KY USA
robert.pfeiffer@uky.edu

Robert J. Adams
Depatrment of Electrical & Computer Engineering
University of Kentucky
Lexington, KY USA
robert.adams@uky.edu

Stephen D. Gedney
Department of Electrical Engineering
University of Colorado-Denver
Denver, CO USA
stephen.gedney@ucdenver.edu

***Abstract*—A high-order locally corrected Nyström discretization for analyzing impressed current cathodic protection systems is presented. Non-linear polarization curves are incorporated using a Newton-Raphson scheme. A Schur complement scheme is introduced to handle large domains with small electrodes. The scheme is validated by comparing to the analytic solution for a sphere.**

Keywords*—*impressed current cathodic protection systems, integral equations, locally corrected Nyström method.

I. Introduction

Hull corrosion of ocean-going vessels has been an area of much interest since hulls began to be constructed using metal. Various methods are used to mitigate hull corrosion including hull painting and cathodic protection systems. Cathodic protection systems are primarily classified as either sacrificial or impressed current. In a sacrificial system, a more easily corroded metal is used to inject electrons into the electrolyte, whereas in an impressed current system electrons are injected directly using a battery or generator. Cathodic protection system electrodes often exhibit non-linear behavior which can be approximately modeled using polarization curves.

In this paper, an overview of the integral formulation [1-4] for the analysis of an impressed current cathodic protection (ICCP) system is presented. The equation is discretized using the arbitrary-order locally corrected Nyström (LCN) method. The Newton-Raphson method is used to handle non-linear polarization curves. A Schur complement-based method is discussed to reduce the computational complexity of the Newton-Raphson iteration when the boundary conditions are mostly constant. Validation and convergence of the method is investigated using a sphere with non-constant boundary conditions.

II. Theory

A. Formulation

Consider a region V bound by a surface S with inward surface normal $\hat{\mathbf{n}}_i$. The region may represent either an internal or an external region, and, if the region is external, part of S recedes to infinity. Furthermore, let the region be filled with an electrolyte of conductivity σ. Green's second identity relates the electric potential Φ in the electrolyte to the boundary potential Φ and its normal derivative $\hat{\mathbf{n}}_i \cdot \nabla\Phi$ as:

$$\Phi(\mathbf{r}) + \oint_S \Phi' \nabla' G \cdot \hat{\mathbf{n}}_i' ds' - \Phi^{\infty} - \oint_S G \nabla' \Phi' \cdot \hat{\mathbf{n}}_i' ds' = 0, \quad \mathbf{r} \in V \quad (1)$$

where the additional unknown Φ^{∞} is only included for an external problem. For both the interior and exterior problems, a meaningful solution exists only if the total flux over the boundary S is zero [5]:

$$\oint_S \nabla\Phi \cdot \hat{\mathbf{n}}_i dS = 0 \ . \quad (2)$$

Furthermore, for the linear interior Neumann problem [5], the additional constraint :

$$\oint_S \Phi dS = C \ , \quad (3)$$

with constant C (usually zero) is applied. Enforcement of (1) on S produces the integral equation:

$$\frac{1}{2}\Phi(\mathbf{r}) - \text{P.V.}\oint_S \Phi' \nabla' G(\mathbf{r},\mathbf{r}') \cdot \hat{\mathbf{n}}_i' ds' - \Phi^{\infty} + \oint_S G \nabla' \Phi' \cdot \hat{\mathbf{n}}_i' ds' = 0, \quad \mathbf{r} \in S \ . \quad (4)$$

The hull surface may be split up into three parts: an insulating part S^i in which $\nabla'\Phi' \cdot \hat{\mathbf{n}}_i' = 0$, electrodes S^p in on which the potential Φ is known, and electrodes S^f on which the normal derivative (flux) is known $\nabla'\Phi' \cdot \hat{\mathbf{n}}_i'$. Often electrodes S^f are polarized and are specified using a polarization curve P such that:

$$\hat{\mathbf{n}}_i \cdot \nabla\Phi = P(\Phi) \ . \quad (5)$$

B. Locally Corrected Nyström Discretization

This work was supported in part by Office of Naval Research Grant N00014-16-1-3066.

The integral equation (4) with the conditions (as necessary) (2) and (3) is discretized using an arbitrary-order locally corrected Nyström (LCN) method where the surface is meshed with either triangle or quadrilateral elements of arbitrary order. As an example, the discretization of (2) and (4) for the exterior Neumann problem with polarized electrodes is:

$$\left[H^e\right]\begin{bmatrix}\Phi^f\\ \Phi^i\\ \Phi^\infty\end{bmatrix}=\begin{bmatrix}H^{ff} & H^{fi} & -1\\ H^{if} & H^{ii} & -1\\ 0 & 0 & 0\end{bmatrix}\begin{bmatrix}\Phi^f\\ \Phi^i\\ \Phi^\infty\end{bmatrix}$$
$$=\begin{bmatrix}G^{ff} & G^{fi} & 0\\ G^{if} & G^{ii} & 0\\ S^f & S^i & 0\end{bmatrix}\begin{bmatrix}P\left(\Phi^f\right)\\ 0\\ 0\end{bmatrix}=\left[G^e\right]\begin{bmatrix}P\left(\Phi^f\right)\\ 0\\ 0\end{bmatrix}, \quad (6)$$

where the matrix definitions are determined by comparing (6) to (2) and (4). Note that the additional zero column in the G^e matrix is added so that H^e and G^e are of the same dimensions. Also, the S^x entries are related to the surface areas of the elements and are used to enforce (2).

C. Newton-Raphson Method

For a non-constant polarization curve $P(\Phi)$, the Newton-Raphson method [3] is applied with the iterative update $\Phi^{k+1}=\Phi^k+\delta\Phi^k$ where $\left[\delta\Phi^k\right]=-\left[J\left(\Phi^k\right)\right]^{-1}\left[P\left(\Phi^{f,k}\right)\right]$ and the Jacobian matrix is:

$$[J]=\left[\frac{\partial P}{\partial\Phi^k}\right]=\left[G^e\right]\cdot\operatorname{diag}\left(\begin{bmatrix}P'\left(\Phi^{f,k}\right)\\ 0\\ 1\end{bmatrix}\right)-\left[H^e\right]. \quad (7)$$

For large problems in which the electrodes only cover a small portion of the surface, the Schur complement can be applied to avoid factoring a full Jacobian matrix at each iteration. A partitioning of the Jacobian matrix amenable to the Schur complement is:

$$[J]=\begin{bmatrix}G^{nc,nc}\cdot\operatorname{diag}\left(P'\left(\Phi^{nc}\right)\right)-H^{nc,nc} & -H^{nc,co}\\ G^{co,nc}\cdot\operatorname{diag}\left(P'\left(\Phi^{nc}\right)\right)-H^{co,nc} & -H^{co,co}\end{bmatrix} \quad (8)$$

where the superscripts *nc* and *co* indicate those portions of the matrix corresponding to non-constant and constant boundary conditions, respectively. Before the Newton-Raphson iteration begins, the matrix $H^{co,co}$ is pre-factored and stored. Then, at each Newton-Raphson step, a matrix is only factored that has the dimensions of the degrees-of-freedom associated with the electrodes having non-constant polarization curves. The above Schur complement form is also amenable for use in fast-direct solvers.

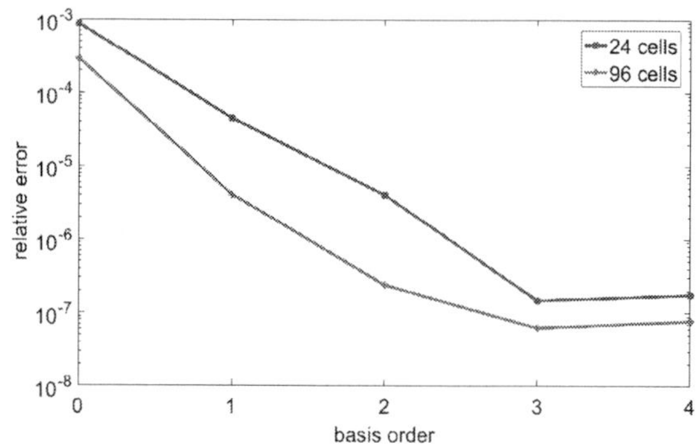

Fig. 1. Relative RMS error between computed and analytic solutions versus basis order for 10th order spherical mesh. Blue line is for a 24-quadrilateral cell mesh and red line is for a 96-quadrilateral cell mesh.

III. Results

As validation, an exterior Neumann problem comprising a one meter sphere with boundary condition [2]:

$$P^f(\Phi)=\frac{\partial\Phi}{\partial n'}=\Phi+\cos\theta+3, \quad 0\le\theta\le\pi \quad (9)$$

representing a cathodic surface was analyzed. The analytic solution is $\Phi=-3-\cos\theta/\left(3r^2\right)$ and $\Phi^\infty=-3$. The discretization in (7) was used and the Newton-Raphson iteration converged in one step. The sphere was discretized with 10th order quadrilateral elements and two meshes of 24 cells and 96 cells were analyzed for various LCN basis orders. The RMS relative error versus basis order is plotted in Fig. 1. The relative error decreases as the basis order increases and stagnates around the square root of machine precision 10^{-7}. It is believed the stagnation is due to the integration of the normal derivative $\nabla' G(\mathbf{r},\mathbf{r}')\cdot\hat{\mathbf{n}}_i'$ in the self-term on curved surfaces [6].

References

[1] J. M. Chuang, N. G. Zamani, and C. C. Hsuing, "Some computational aspects of BEM simulation of cathodic protection systems," Applied Mathematical Modelling, vol. 11, pp. 371-379, October 1987.

[2] N. G. Zamani, J. M. Chuang, and J. F. Porter, "BEM simulation of cathodic protection systems employed in infinite electrolytes," International Journal for Numerical Methods in Engineering, vol. 45, pp. 605-620, 1987.

[3] J. F. Yan, S. N. R. Pakalapati, T. V. Nguyen, R. E. White, and R. B. Griffin, "Mathematical modeling of cathodic protection using the boundary element method with a nonlinear polarization curve," Journal of The Electrochemical Society, vol. 139, pp. 1932-1936, July 1, 1992.

[4] W. Sun, G. Yuan, and Y. Ren, "Iterative algorithms for impressed cathodic protection systems," International Journal for Numerical Methods in Engineering, vol. 49, pp. 751-768, 2000.

[5] G. C. Hsiao and W. L. Wendland, Boundary Integral Equations, vol. 164. Berlin: Springer-Verlag, 2008.

[6] R. Pfeiffer, J. C. Young, and R. J. Adams, "Numerical characterization of divergence-conforming constrained basis functions for surface integral equations," IEEE Transactions on Antennas and Propagation, vol. 65, pp. 1867-1874, 2017.

A Huygens Surface Source Model for Field Prediction Valid from sub-ELF to High Frequencies

Nastaran Hendijani and Stephen D. Gedney
Dept. of Electrical Engineering
University of Colorado-Denver
Denver, CO USA
nastaran.hendijani@ucdenver.edu, stephen.gedney@ucdenver.edu

John C. Young and Robert J. Adams
Dept. of Electrical & Computer Engineering
University of Kentucky
Lexington, KY USA
john.c.young@uky.edu, robert.adams@uky.edu

***Abstract*— A broad-band Huygens surface method to predict fields having knowledge of only the near magnetic field (no derivatives) on an arbitrary shaped closed boundary is presented. The proposed approach applies an augmented-integral equation formulation to calculate the electric field on the Huygens surface. The method is accurate and stable down to DC for arbitrary shaped Huygens surfaces. The proposed formulation is discretized using a locally corrected Nyström (LCN) method.**

Keywords—Huygens surface, locally corrected Nyström method surface integral equations.

I. Introduction

Predicting radiated emissions by electric machinery has been an area of much interest in electromagnetic compatibility (EMC) community. Radiated emissions by motors can impact the magnetic signature of naval vessels which increases the possibility of reconnaissance by hostile magnetic sensors. The broad-band nature of radiated emissions makes it challenging to mitigate them by shielding methods. As a consequence, having accurate approximations of the motor radiated fields over a broad spectrum is very useful in prototyping shielding methods.

Different strategies have been used to approximate motor fields including single dipole source models [1], equivalent source models [2], and methods applying the equivalence principle (Green's theorem) [3, 4]. Based on the equivalence principle the electric and magnetic fields exterior to a closed surface can be computed having only knowledge of the fields on the surface. The reported methods mostly rely on filling the volume inside the hypothetical closed surface by perfect electric conductors or perfect magnetic conductors shorting out one field [3]. In this work, a more accurate and practical approach is proposed by which one can measure one of the fields on an arbitrarily shaped, closed Huygens surface. An augmented form of the integral equation is developed that computes the dual field on the Huygens surface. The measured field and the computed dual field are then used to compute the near or far fields outside the Huygens surface. The proposed method is referred to as the Huygens surface source model (HSSM) and is accurate and well-posed over a wide frequency range including extremely low frequencies [5].

II. The HSSM

The electromagnetic fields are assumed to be radiated by a set of sources located in a volume V_1 bound by an imaginary Huygens surface $S_{1,2}$. The volume V_2 exterior to $S_{1,2}$ is assumed to be free-space, however it is not restricted to this. Equivalent magnetic ($\vec{M}$) and electric currents ($\vec{J}$) are introduced on $S_{1,2}$ [6]:

$$\vec{M} = \vec{E}_2 \times \hat{n}\Big|_{S_{1,2}}, \; \vec{J} = \hat{n} \times \vec{H}_2\Big|_{S_{1,2}}, \tag{1}$$

where $\vec{E}_2$ and $\vec{H}_2$ are the electric and magnetic fields on $S_{1,2}$ just inside V_2 that are radiated by the sources in V_1, and $\hat{n}$ is unit vector normal to $S_{1,2}$ directed into V_2. An augmented form of the magnetic field integral equation can be formed:

$$\begin{aligned}\vec{H}(\vec{r}) = &\oint\!\!\oint_{S_{1,2}} \nabla G(\vec{r},\vec{r}') \times \vec{J}(\vec{r}') ds' \\ &- j\omega\varepsilon \oint\!\!\oint_{S_{1,2}} \vec{M}(\vec{r}') G(\vec{r},\vec{r}') ds' - \oint\!\!\oint_{S_{1,2}} \nabla G(\vec{r},\vec{r}') \rho_m(\vec{r}') ds',\end{aligned} \tag{2}$$

where ρ_m is the scaled magnetic surface charge density on $S_{1,2}$ which satisfies the boundary condition:

$$\rho_m = \hat{n} \cdot \vec{H}_2\Big|_{S_{1,2}}, \tag{3}$$

and magnetic continuity equation:

$$\nabla' \cdot \vec{M}(\vec{r}') = -j\omega\mu\rho_m. \tag{4}$$

By duality, the augmented form of the EFIE is expressed as:

$$\begin{aligned}\vec{E}(\vec{r}) = &-\oint\!\!\oint_{S_{1,2}} \nabla G(\vec{r},\vec{r}') \times \vec{M}(\vec{r}') ds' \\ &- j\omega\mu \oint\!\!\oint_{S_{1,2}} \vec{J}(\vec{r}') G(\vec{r},\vec{r}') ds' - \oint\!\!\oint_{S_{1,2}} \nabla G(\vec{r},\vec{r}') \rho_e(\vec{r}') ds',\end{aligned} \tag{5}$$

with scaled surface electric charge density $\rho_e = \hat{n} \cdot \vec{E}_2\Big|_{S_{1,2}}$.

It is assumed that the vector magnetic field is known on $S_{1,2}$. Consequently, from (1) and (3), the equivalent sources $\vec{J}$ and ρ_m are known. Testing (2) with a test vector $\vec{T}(\vec{r})$

This work was supported in part by Office of Naval Research Grant N00014-15-1-2258.

tangential to $S_{1,2}$ and using (1), one can show:

$$\oiint_{S_{1,2}} \vec{T}(\vec{r})\cdot \vec{\underset{\sim}{M}}(\vec{r}')G(\vec{r},\vec{r}')ds' =$$

$$\frac{1}{2}\vec{T}\cdot\left(\hat{n}\times\vec{J}(\vec{r})\right)-\oiint_{S_{1,2}}\vec{T}(\vec{r})\cdot\vec{J}(\vec{r}')\times\nabla G(\vec{r},\vec{r}')ds' \tag{6}$$

$$-\oiint_{S_{1,2}}\vec{T}(\vec{r})\cdot\nabla G(\vec{r},\vec{r}')\rho_m(\vec{r}')ds',$$

where $\vec{\underset{\sim}{M}} = j\omega\varepsilon\vec{M}$ is the scaled magnetic current density. Testing (5) with a test vector $\hat{n}(\vec{r})$ normal to $S_{1,2}$, we obtain:

$$\frac{\underset{\sim}{\rho_e}(\vec{r})}{2}+\oiint_{S_{1,2}}\hat{n}(\vec{r})\cdot\nabla G(\vec{r},\vec{r}')\underset{\sim}{\rho_e}(\vec{r}')ds'$$

$$+\oiint_{S_{1,2}}\hat{n}(\vec{r})\cdot\nabla G(\vec{r},\vec{r}')\times\vec{\underset{\sim}{M}}(\vec{r}')ds' \tag{7}$$

$$=k_0^2\oiint_{S_{1,2}}\hat{n}(\vec{r})\cdot\vec{J}(\vec{r}')G(\vec{r},\vec{r}')ds'.$$

The HSSM linear system of equations is obtained by combining (6) and (7) to solve for $\vec{\underset{\sim}{M}}$ and $\underset{\sim}{\rho_e}$. Having $\vec{\underset{\sim}{M}}$ and $\underset{\sim}{\rho_e}$, (2) and (5) are used to calculate the vector magnetic and electric fields outside the Huygens surface.

III. Numerical Results

To validate the HSSM, consider an array of 18 linear electric dipoles parallel to the z-axis, uniformly spaced around a cylinder of radius 0.1016 m and two magnetic point dipoles located on the z-axis at $z = \pm 0.0509$m. Each electric dipole has length 0.1016 m and a complex current amplitude that is a function of the operating frequency. The Huygens surface surrounding the dipole array is a cylinder of radius 0.1648m and length 0.3048 m centered about the dipole array. The cylinder surface is meshed by fourth order quadrilateral cells.

The vector magnetic field due to the dipole array is calculated analytically on the nodes of the Huygens surface curvilinear mesh as input to the HSSM. The complex vector magnetic and electric fields radiated by the equivalent sources on the Huygens surface are calculated by the HSSM on the semi-circle having radius 0.2794 m in the $\theta = 90^{\circ}$ plane. Fig. 1 represents the root-mean-square (RMS) errors in the complex vector magnetic and electric fields of the dipole array source model at DC and 205.0 Hz computed using the HSSM on the semi-circle with radius 0.2794 m in the $\theta = 90^{\circ}$ plane. The errors are plotted versus the LCN basis orders $p = 0,1,2$ for a mesh consisting of 112 fourth order quadrilateral cells. The reference solution is the fields radiated from dipole array computed analytically on the semicircle. The solution from HSSM demonstrates convergence by increasing the LCN basis order. Fig. 2 illustrates the condition number of the system matrix used to compute the dual field as a function of discretization density and basis order, showing that the formulation is very well conditioned, even at ELF.

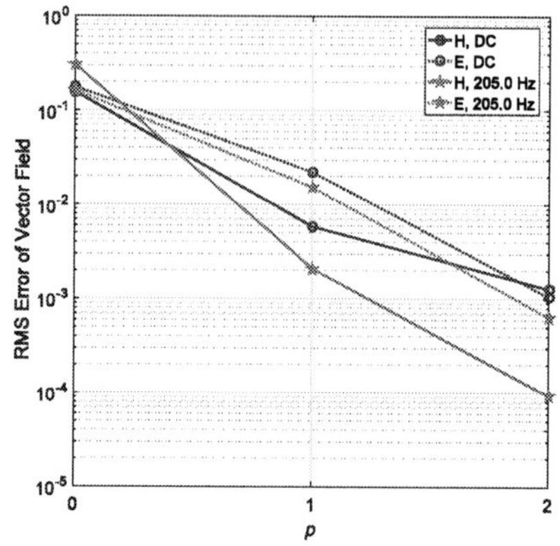

Fig. 1. The RMS error of vector magnetic (H) and electric (E) fields from HSSM vs. LCN order p on the semicircle.

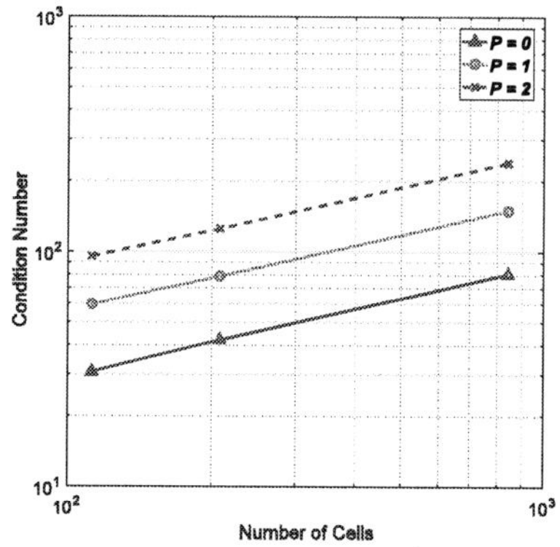

Fig. 2. The condition number of the Huygens matrix.

References

[1] R. Forrester, M. S. Huq, M. Ahmadi, and P. Straznicky, "Magnetic Signature Attenuation of an Unmanned Aircraft System for Aeromagnetic Survey," IEEE - ASME Transactions on Mechatronics, vol. 19, pp. 1436-1446, Aug 2014.

[2] M. R. Barzegaran and O. A. Mohammed, "A Generalized equivalent source model of AC electric machines for numerical electromagnetic field signature studies," IEEE Transactions on Magnetics, vol. 48, pp. 4440-4443, Nov 2012.

[3] X. Gao, J. Fan, Y. J. Zhang, H. Kajbaf, and D. Pommerenke, "Far-Field Prediction Using Only Magnetic Near-Field Scanning for EMI Test," IEEE Transactions on Electromagnetic Compatibility, vol. 56, pp. 1335-1343, Dec 2014.

[4] Y. Alvarez, F. Las-Heras, and M. R. Pino, "Reconstruction of Equivalent Currents Distribution Over Arbitrary Three-Dimensional Surfaces Based on Integral Equation Algorithms," IEEE Transactions on Antennas and Propagation, vol. 55, pp. 3460-3468, Dec. 2007 2007.

[5] N. Hendijani, S. D. Gedney, R. McConnell, M. J. Roberts, J. C. Young, and R. J. Adams, "A Broad-band Huygens surface source model for near-field to near-field transformations," IEEE Transactions on Electromagnetic Compatibility, vol. 60, no. 4, April 2018.

[6] C. A. Balanis, Advanced Engineering Electromagnetics. New York: Wiley, 1989.

Micromagnetic Model Simulation of Spin-Torque Oscillator and Write Head for Microwave-Assisted Magnetic Recording – Spin Injection Layer with In-Plane Anisotropy –

Yasushi KANAI and Ryo ITAGAKI
Department of Information and Electronics Engineering
Niigata Institute of Technology
Kashiwazaki, Japan
kanai@iee.niit.ac.jp, r_itagaki@cc.niit.ac.jp

Simon GREAVES and Hiroaki MURAOKA
Research Institute of Electrical Communication (RIEC)
Tohoku University
Sendai, Japan
{simon, muraoka}@riec.tohoku.ac.jp

***Abstract*— Micromagnetic simulations were carried out to obtain stable oscillation of a spin transfer torque oscillator (STO) inserted into the gap between the main pole and trailing shield of a write head. We assumed a spin injection layer with in-plane anisotropy. Results show that reducing the magnetostatic interaction between the write head and the STO is the key to obtaining stable STO oscillation.**

Keywords*— *micromagnetic simulations, microwave-assisted magnetic recording, spin-torque oscillator, write head.

I. Introduction

Microwave-assisted magnetic recording (MAMR) [1] is one candidate for next-generation perpendicular magnetic recording [2]. Stable oscillation is one of the most important factors for spin-torque oscillators (STO) used in a MAMR system. We performed micromagnetic simulations and found that the oscillation states of the isolated (without write head), and integrated (with write head), STO models were different, i.e., stable STO oscillations were hard to obtain primarily due to the magnetostatic interactions between the STO and write head [3].

In this paper, we investigate STOs utilizing a spin injection layer (SIL) with in-plane anisotropy [4]. We also introduce a STO tilted with respect to the medium plane, along with a tilted main pole – trailing shield gap (tilted STO) to reduce the magnetostatic interactions between the STO and write head. Results show that the SIL with in-plane anisotropy worked well when the STO was isolated. Whilst the integrated STO only worked when the tilted STO was used.

II. Calculation Model

A micromagnetic model analysis was carried out considering a STO utilizing transmission spin torque . We used the commercial micromagnetic software (Fujitsu, EXAMAG v.2.1, http://www.fujitsu.com/global/about/resources/ news/press-releases/2015/0324-01.html).

In Fig. 1, the isolated STO, without write head, used for the calculations is shown. A double-layered STO was used, with a non-magnetic interlayer (IL) placed between the field generation layer (FGL) and SIL. Table I lists the main parameters of the FGL and SIL that were used unless stated otherwise in sections III and IV. We modelled both soft and hard, in-plane magnetic SILs. A uniform external field and uniform injected current were assumed along the z-axis over the STO volume. The STO was divided into cubes with 2.5 nm sides. Note that we modeled an STO with 20 nm × 20 nm area as it rotated stably with low injected current density, J, and low external field.

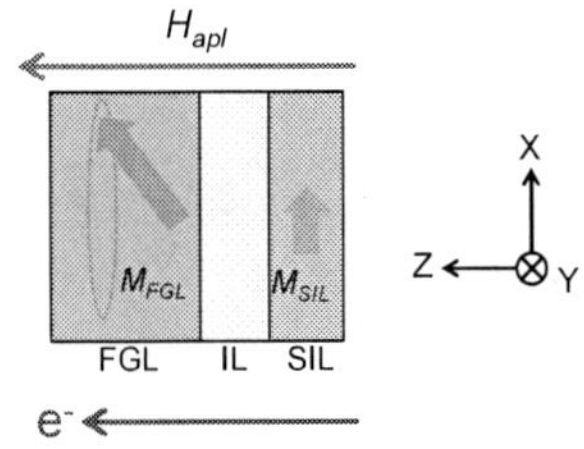

Fig. 1. STO model used for the calculations. Double-layered STO with transmission spin torque utilized.

TABLE I. Main Parameters of FGL and SIL Used in the Calculations

	FGL	SIL
$4\pi M_s$	20 kG	6 kG
H_k (*) in-plane	31.4 Oe	31.4 Oe, 20 kOe
α	0.02	0.02
Exchange, A	2.5×10^{-6} erg/cm	0.75×10^{-6} erg/cm
Thickness	10 nm	2 nm
P_o = 0.5, Width × height = 20 nm × 20 nm, Inter layer = 2 nm		

* H_k: anisotropy field

The authors acknowledge the financial support from JSPS Kaken-hi (16K06321) and Advance Storage Research Consortium (ASRC); software support from JSOL, Japan.

III. Results – Isolated STO –

In Fig. 2, FGL rotations under a 1 GHz, external field are shown for soft and hard SILs, where the horizontal axis is the time. The results are shown from t = 0, initial state. The left vertical axis shows M/M_s for the in-plane (M_y) and perpendicular-to-the-plane (M_z) components of the FGL magnetization averaged over the FGL volume, i.e., the FGL magnetization rotated perfectly in the x-y plane when M_y/M_s = 1. As can be seen, the FGL rotated well for both soft (H_k = 31.4 Oe) and hard (H_k = 20 kOe) SIL materials with in-plane anisotropy, which was quite different from STOs utilizing SILs with perpendicular anisotropy [3].

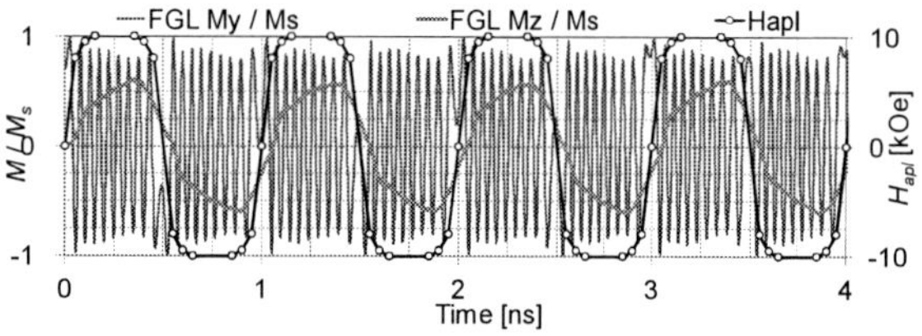

(a) SIL H_k = 31.4 Oe (in-plane)

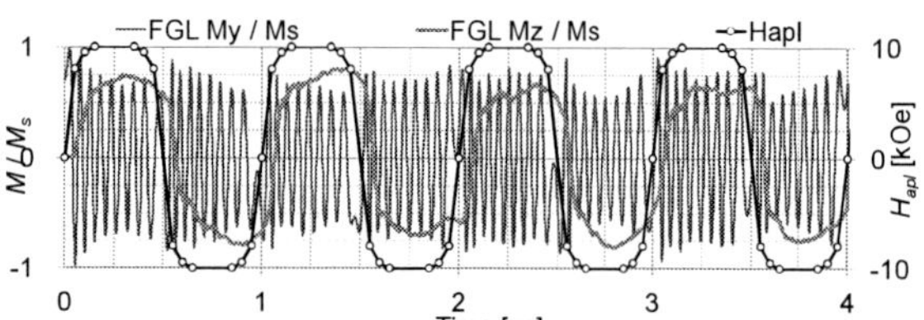

(b) SIL H_k =20 kOe (in-plane)

Fig. 2. FGL rotations vs. time for soft and hard SILs. $J = 3.0\times10^8$ A/cm^2.

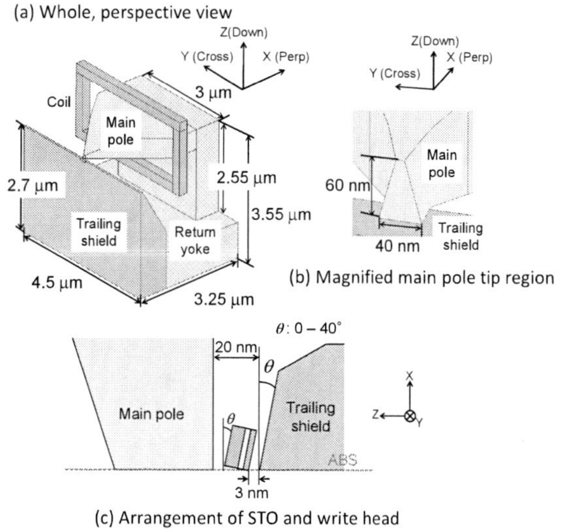

Fig. 3. Schematics of write head and STO integrated into the tilted MP–TS gap used in the calculations.

IV. Results – Integrated STO –

In Fig. 3, the STO was integrated into the main pole and trailing shield (MP–TS) gap of the write head. We considered both perpendicular STOs (STO perpendicular to the medium plane (parallel to ABS)), and tilted STOs (STO tilted to the medium plane). In the tilted STO, the magnetostatic interactions between the STO and the write head were smaller than the perpendicular STO. The STOs had the same parameters shown in Table I.

In Fig. 4, FGL rotations vs. time are shown for the perpendicular and tilted STOs when a 1 GHz coil current was applied. It is seen that the perpendicular STO did not rotate stably, while the tilted STO worked quite well. It is also seen that the oscillation state of the integrated STO was quite different from isolated one. This shows that an integrated STO utilizing an SIL with in-plane anisotropy works only when used in a tilted MP-TS gap.

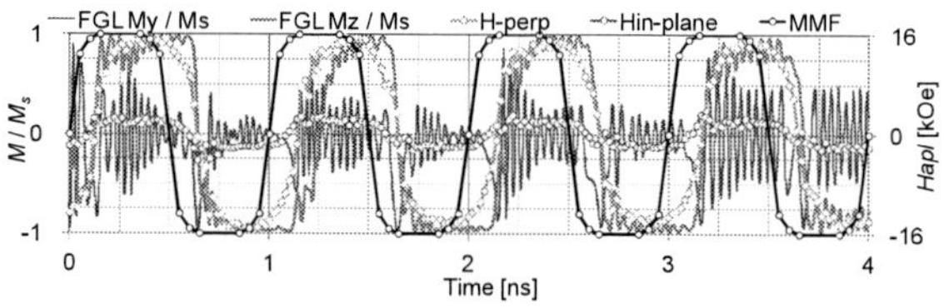

(a) Perpendicular STO: θ = 0°

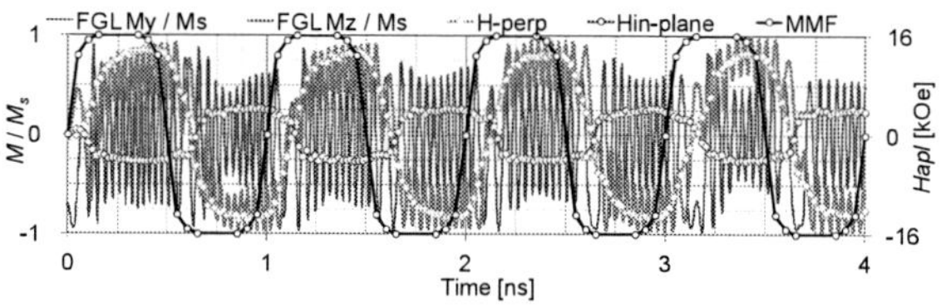

(b) Tilted STO: θ = 40°

Fig. 4. FGL rotations vs. time. Integrated perpendicular and tilted STO models. Applied MP-TS gap fields to FGL are also shown. $J = 3.0\times10^8$ A/cm^2, SIL H_k = 20 kOe (in-plane).

References

[1] J.-G. Zhu, X. Zhu, and Y. Tang, "Microwave assisted magnetic recording," *IEEE Trans. on Magn.*, vol. 44, no. 1, pp. 125-131, Jan. 2008.

[2] Energy-assisted Recording Technology, [Online.] Available: https://play.vidyard.com/ JZLozr2ujb2jR964BaFNPW

[3] Y. Kanai, R. Itagaki, S. Greaves, and H. Muraoka, "Micromagnetic model analysis of various spin torque oscillators with write head for microwave-assisted magnetic recording," *IEEE Trans. on Magn.*, vol. 53, no. 11, Nov. 2017. Art. no. 3001105.

[4] H. Sepeheri-Amin, S. Bosu, C. Abert, Y. Sakuraba, S. Kasai, M. Hayashi, D. Suess, and K. Hono, "Design and development of spin-torque-oscillator for microwave assisted magnetic recording," *The Magnetic Recording Conference*, E2, Tsukuba, Japan, Aug. 2017.

A Finite-Difference Frequency Domain Solver for Quasi-TEM Applications

J. Patrick Donohoe
Department of Electrical and Computer Engineering
Mississippi State University
Mississippi State, MS 39762
donohoe@ece.msstate.edu

Abstract — **A finite-difference frequency-domain (FDFD) solver applicable to quasi-TEM applications is defined. The FDFD solver is applicable to a wide variety of transmission line structures where the cross-sectional dimensions govern the frequency range over which the quasi-TEM approximation is valid. The quasi-TEM FDFD solver provides an efficient solution for conductor current distributions involving both skin effect and proximity effect. Simulation results obtained using the quasi-TEM FDFD solver are compared to measurements and other numerical methods.**

Keywords* — *finite-difference time-domain, quasi-TEM approximation.

I. Introduction

Low-frequency electromagnetic simulation presents a variety of computational challenges, irrespective of the general solution technique employed. The accuracy of low-frequency solutions using the method of moments (MOM), the finite-element method (FEM) and the finite-difference time-domain (FDTD) technique all suffer due to ill-conditioned matrices for the frequency-domain schemes, and the exorbitant number of time-steps required for time-domain schemes.

A transmission line structure, operating under the quasi-TEM approximation, generates small longitudinal fields internal and external to the transmission line conductors. Under the quasi-TEM approximation, these longitudinal fields are assumed to be negligible in comparison to the transverse fields, such that the transverse fields are accurately approximated by the true TEM fields of the corresponding static problem. A low-frequency FDFD scheme which exploits the quasi-TEM approximation and avoids the numerical pitfalls described above is defined in the next section.

II. Quasi-TEM FDFD Solver

A simple transmission line model is used to demonstrate the formulation of the quasi-TEM FDFD scheme. Non-ideal ($\sigma_c < \infty$) and nonmagnetic ($\mu_c = \mu_o$) transmission line conductors are assumed along with an ideal (μ_i, ϵ_i, $\sigma_i = 0$) insulating medium. Under quasi-TEM operation, the displacement current is assumed to be negligible relative to the conduction current, and the fields are assumed to be invariant in the direction of wave propagation (the transmission line is assumed to be short relative to wavelength).

The transmission line structure carries a true TEM mode only if the conductors are assumed to be ideal. The transverse fields of the true TEM mode are identical to the static fields for the given conductor configuration. Low-level longitudinal fields are present throughout the system when realistic conductors are assumed, leading to a quasi-TEM mode (designated here as qTEM). According to the quasi-TEM approximation, the qTEM transverse fields are essentially identical to those of the corresponding static fields. Both electrostatic and magnetostatic solutions are not required to determine the complete qTEM transverse fields, however, since the transverse electric and magnetic fields of a TEM mode are related by a simple cross-product relationship. Thus, the electrostatic problem can be solved to determine the transverse electric field, and the resulting transverse magnetic field is found by implementing the TEM cross-product relationship. The qTEM transverse magnetic field on the surface of the non-ideal conductors is equated to the TEM transverse magnetic field on the surface of the ideal conductors, based on the quasi-TEM approximation [1]. One can then determine the surface qTEM electric field on the surface of the non-ideal conductors using Maxwell's equations, and solve the governing differential equation for the electric field internal to each non-ideal conductor. The basic steps of the FDFD scheme based on the quasi-TEM approximation are summarized as follows. All parameters designated with a tilde represent phasor quantities.

Step 1. Solve for the quasi-TEM electric field surrounding the given conductor configuration according to:

$$\nabla^2 \tilde{V}_{qTEM} = 0, \tag{1}$$

$$\tilde{\boldsymbol{E}}_{qTEM} = -\nabla \tilde{V}_{qTEM}, \tag{2}$$

where $\tilde{V}_{qTEM}$ and $\tilde{\boldsymbol{E}}_{qTEM}$ are the phasor potential and electric field, respectively, surrounding the conductors. The finite-difference solution for the quasi-TEM electric field is fundamentally equivalent to an electrostatic solution.

Step 2. Determine the quasi-TEM magnetic field surrounding the conductors ($\tilde{\boldsymbol{H}}_{qTEM}$) according to [1]:

$$\tilde{\boldsymbol{H}}_{qTEM} = \frac{1}{\eta_i}\hat{z} \times \tilde{\boldsymbol{E}}_{qTEM}, \tag{3}$$

where η_i is the wave impedance of the insulating medium surrounding the conductors and $\hat{z}$ is the unit normal to the transverse plane.

Step 3. Use the quasi-TEM magnetic field surface boundary condition to solve the governing magnetic field PDE internal to each non-ideal conductor via FDFD as given by:

$$\nabla^2 \tilde{\boldsymbol{H}}_{qTEM} - \gamma_c^2 \tilde{\boldsymbol{H}}_{qTEM} = 0\,, \tag{4}$$

$$\gamma_c^2 = j\omega\mu_o(\sigma_c + j\omega\epsilon_c) \approx j\omega\mu_o\sigma_c\,, \tag{5}$$

where γ_c is the propagation constant of the respective conductor.

The aforementioned scheme accounts for both proximity effect and skin effects. The transverse components of the qTEM magnetic field in step 2 account for the proximity effects for the conductor configuration. These transverse qTEM fields are large in regions where the currents tend to crowd on the surface of the transmission line conductors. The governing PDE of the non-ideal conductor accounts for the skin effect within the conductor at the given frequency of operation, based on the proximity effect embedded in the surface field boundary conditions.

III. Results

The qTEM FDFD technique is applied to an isolated square copper conductor of 2.54cm×2.54cm cross-section, in order to compare results with measured values (skin effect only). The ratio of the AC resistance (R_{ac}) to DC resistance (R_{dc}) is computed and compared to results obtained using the method of moments [2] where the qTEM FDFD AC resistance is computed based on the conductor current distribution and given by:

$$R_{ac} = \frac{1}{\sigma_c}\frac{\iint\left|\tilde{J}_{qTEM}\right|^2 dxdy}{\left|\iint \tilde{J}_{qTEM}\, dxdy\right|^2}\,. \tag{6}$$

The qTEM FDFD results are found to agree favorably, as shown in the axial electric field comparison of Fig. 1, even though the FDFD model actually includes a conductor within a large enclosure (side length = 25.4 cm) as opposed to an isolated conductor.

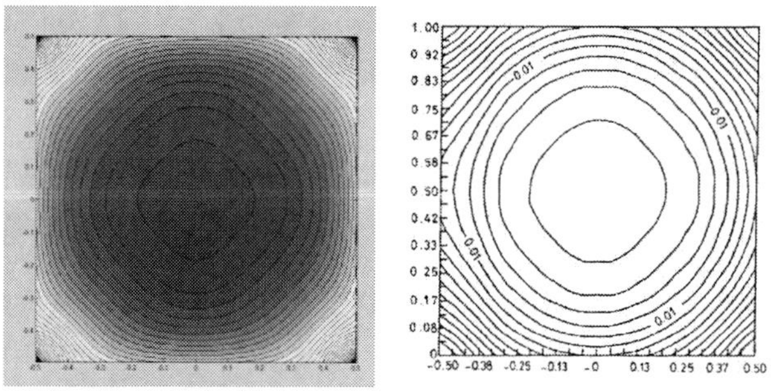

(a) (b)

Fig. 1. Comparison of the axial electric field for a 2.54×2.54cm copper conductor using (a) qTEM FDTD (R_{ac}/R_{dc} = 1.72), and (b) method of moments [2]. The measured value of R_{ac}/R_{dc} = 1.75.

The qTEM FDTD solver is used to compare two diverse applications that have similar skin effect and proximity effect characteristics. As shown in Fig. 2, the current distribution of a bus conductor in proximity to an enclosure (low frequency) is compared to that of a microstrip conductor in proximity to its ground plane (high frequency). Note that the conductor dimensions are quite different, but the conductor shape, aspect ratio and spacing exhibit the "principle of similitude" [3] where a conductor, or a combination of conductors, having a certain proportionate shape will have the same value for the R_{ac}/R_{dc} ratio. The current distributions and conductor resistance ratios R_{ac}/R_{dc} are shown to agree well for the large bus conductor at low frequency and the small microstrip conductor at high frequency.

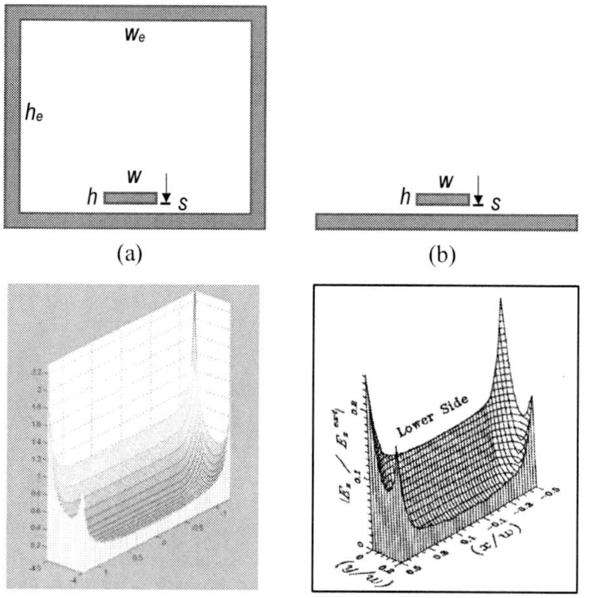

(c) (d)

Fig. 2. (a) Bus conductor in proximity to an enclosure, copper conductors, h = 1.27cm, $w/h = w/s = 5$, f = 689 Hz, (b) microstrip conductor in proximity to its ground plane, gold conductors, h = 4μm, $w/h = w/s = 5$, f = 9.83 GHz, (c) bus conductor axial electric field [qTEM FDTD, (R_{ac}/R_{dc} = 3.05)], and (d) microstrip conductor axial electric field [method of moments [4], (R_{ac}/R_{dc} = 2.95)].

References

[1] R. E. Collin, Field Theory of Guided Waves, 2nd Ed, IEEE Press, Piscataway, NJ, 1991, p. 253.

[2] R. Faraji-Dana and L. Chow, "Edge condition of the field and AC resistance of a rectangular strip," IEE Proc., Apr. 1990, vol. 137, Pt. H, no. 2, pp. 133-140.

[3] S. J. Haefner, "Alternating current resistance of rectangular conductors," Proc. IRE, 1937, 25, pp. 434-447.

[4] R. Faraji-Dana and Y. L. Chow, "The current distribution and AC resistance of a microstrip structure," IEEE Trans. MTT, Sept. 1990, vol. 38, no. 9, pp. 1268-1277.

SAR and Temperature Rise Distributions in a Human Head Due to a Multi-Frequency Antenna Source

Fatih Kaburcuk
Electrical and Electronic Engineering Deparment
Erzurum Technical University
Erzurum, Turkey
fatih.kaburcuk@erzurum.edu.tr

Atef Z. Elsherbeni
Electrical Engineering Department
Colorado School of Mines
Golden, CO, USA
aelsherb@mines.edu

***Abstract*—Temperature rise and specific absorption rate (SAR) distribution in a human head due to an antenna are evaluated at multiple frequencies in a single simulation. An algorithm is developed by integrating the Debye model of head tissues parameters into the finite-difference time-domain (FDTD) method by using the auxiliary differential equation (ADE) approach along with the use of bioheat equation for SAR and temperature computations. The tissue EM parameters are used from the available three-term Debye coefficients from 500 MHz to 20 GHz.**

Keywords—Dispersive, FDTD method, SAR, Temperature rise

I. Introduction

Many researchers have studied the temperature rise and specific absorption rate (SAR) distribution in the human head due to cellular phones with different types of antennas [1-3] using the traditional finite-difference time-domain (FDTD) method. In the majority of the previous work [1-3], the SAR computations for a human head was conducted at only one frequency of interest in a single simulation because the depressiveness properties of the biological tissue. A dispersive algorithm is developed to obtain SAR and temperature distributions at multiple frequencies of interest from a single FDTD simulation. The dispersive algorithm is based on the integration of Debye model into FDTD method based on the ADE as presented in [4] with the Pennes bioheat equation from [5]. The head tissue parameters for a wide range of frequencies (500 MHz to 20 GHz) used in this investigation are based on the three-term Debye coefficients calculated and tabulated in [6]. To prove the validity of the developed algorithm, the radiation from an antenna is evaluated in the presence of a head model obtained from [7]. The temperature rise and SAR distributions at multiple frequencies centered around 900 MHz and 1.5 GHz are obtained using multiple simulations using the traditional FDTD method and a single simulation using the developed algorithm.

II. Dispersive Head Model and Methods

The head model consists of 8 tissues (skin, muscle, bone, blood, fat, lens, grey and white matter). The EM parameters of these tissues are dispersive and frequency dependent. Thus, a solution at only one frequency can be obtained in a single simulation. A numerical procedure developed in [6] provides three-term Debye coefficients to accurately fit the experimental data from [8] for the frequency range 500 MHz to 20 GHz. The antenna is placed 24 mm away from the left ear of the head and excited by a voltage source with a Gaussian waveform containing the frequencies of interest. The cell size is 2 mm in the three Cartesian directions.

A. SAR Calculation in the Head

The SAR at each frequency of interest is considered the EM heating source and is defined at a given location as:

$$SAR(i,j,k) = \frac{\sigma(i,j,k)}{2\rho(i,j,k)}|E|^2 = \frac{\sigma(i,j,k)}{2\rho(i,j,k)}\left(|E_x|^2 + |E_y|^2 + |E_z|^2\right), \quad (1)$$

where $\sigma(i,j,k)$ and $\rho(i,j,k)$ are the electric conductivity and mass density [kg/m^3] of the tissue, respectively, and E is the enduced electric field in the tissue.

B. Temperature Rise Calculation in the Head

The temperature simulation is performed by solving the bioheat equation [5]. After the initial temperature distribution in the head is calculated by using the bioheat equation without EM power (SAR=0), the final temperature distribution is calculated by replacing the SAR distribution into the bioheat equation. The temperature rise distribution is achieved by taking the difference between final and initial temperature distributions. The bioheat equation is given by,

$$\rho \cdot C \cdot \frac{\partial T}{\partial t} = K \cdot \nabla^2 T + \rho \cdot SAR - B \cdot (T - T_b), \quad (2)$$

where T is the temperature of a tissue [°C] at time t, C is the specific heat of a tissue [J/(kg · °C)], K is the thermal conductivity of a tissue [J/(m·°C)], B is the blood perfusion rate [W/(m^3.°C)], and T_b is the blood temperature. The boundary condition between the skin surface and air for equation (2) is expressed as:

$$K \cdot \frac{\partial T}{\partial n} = -h \cdot (T - T_a), \quad (3)$$

where T_a is the air temperature, n is the normal vector to the skin surface, and h is the convection heat transfer coefficient [W/(m^2·°C)]. The derivative of T in (3) is with respect to the normal direction to the skin surface. The convection heat transfer coefficients (h) is set to 10.5 from the skin surface to air. In order to avoid the numerical instability, the temperature time-step must satisfy the criterion of $\delta t \leq \frac{2\rho C d^2}{12K + Bd^2}$. Table I gives the mass density (ρ) and thermal parameters of the head tissues [2].

Table I. Mass Density and Thermal Parameters of the Head Tissues.

Type of Tissue	ρ [kg/m^3]	C [J/(kg.°C)]	K [W/(m.°C)]	B [W/(m^3.°C)]
Skin	1125	3600	0.42	9100
Fat	916	3000	0.25	1700
Bone	1810	1300	0.40	1000
Blood	1058	3900	0.56	0
Muscle	1047	3800	0.50	2700
Lens	1100	3000	0.40	0
White Matter	1038	3500	0.50	40000
Grey Matter	1038	3800	0.57	40000
Air (internal)	1.2	1000	0.03	0

III. NUMERICAL RESULTS

In this section, the temperature rise and SAR distributions are obtained using the developed dispersive algorithm at frequencies of interest in a single simulation and using the traditional FDTD algorithm by performing multiple simulations, each at a single frequency. The output power of the antenna was set to 0.6 W for 900 MHz and 0.27 W for 1.5 GHz. The air temperature (T_a) and initial head temperature (T_b) in the simulations were set to 20 °C and 37 °C, respectively.

In order to obtain solutions at multiple frequencies, the antenna should have at least two frequency bands. Thus, two passive wires are replaced 4 mm away at the two sides of the 156 mm dipole antenna with the diameter of 0.74 mm. The length and diameter of the passive wires are 1.56 mm and 88 mm, respectively. The center operating frequencies of this dipole antenna loaded with passive wires are 900 MHz and 1.5 GHz. The input reflection coefficient of the antenna is shown in Fig. 1.

The temperature rise and SAR distributions of the head due to the antenna are calculated at three frequencies centered at 900 MHz and three frequencies centered at 1.5 GHz using a single simulation. The maximum 1 gram averaged SAR value in the head is 1.63 Watt/kg at 900 MHz and 1.06 Watt/kg at 1.5 GHz. Fig. 2 shows the 1 gram averaged SAR distribution at 900 MHz and 1.5 GHz in the *xy* cross section of the head model. Fig. 3 shows the resulting temperature rise distribution at 900 MHz and 1.5 GHz in the *xy* cross section of the head model. The maximum temperature rise in the head is 0.28 °C at 900 MHz and 0.15 °C at 1.5 GHz. The maximum temperature variation in the head as a function of time is shown in Fig. 4.(a) at 870, 900, 930 MHz and 1.46, 1.50, 1.54 GHz. The SAR and temperature rise distributions obtained using the dispersive algorithm agree very well with the results obtained the traditional FDTD algorithm. To show the efficiency of the proposed dispersive algorithm, the computation time of both algorithms is recorded for results at six frequencies and shown in Fig. 4.(b). As shown, when the number of frequencies of interest is increased the dispersive algorithm is more efficient than the traditional FDTD algorithm while producing the same results.

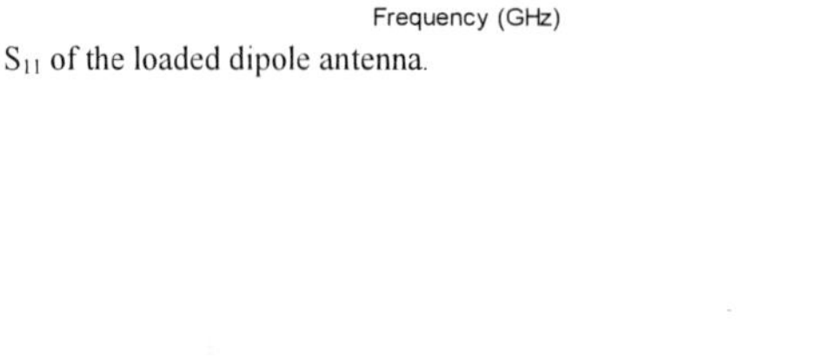

Fig. 1. S_{11} of the loaded dipole antenna.

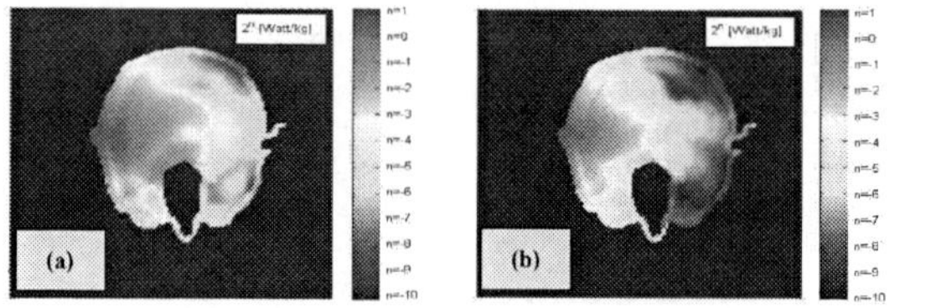

Fig. 2. 1 gram averaged SAR distribution at (a) 900 MHz and (b) 1.5 GHz.

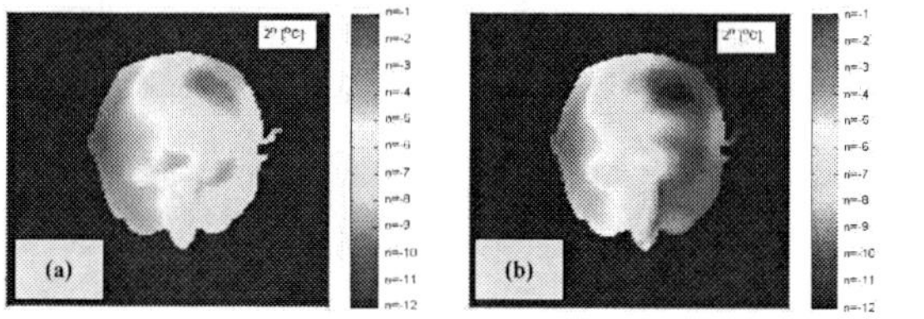

Fig. 3. Temperature rise distribution at (a) 900 MHz and (b) 1.5 GHz.

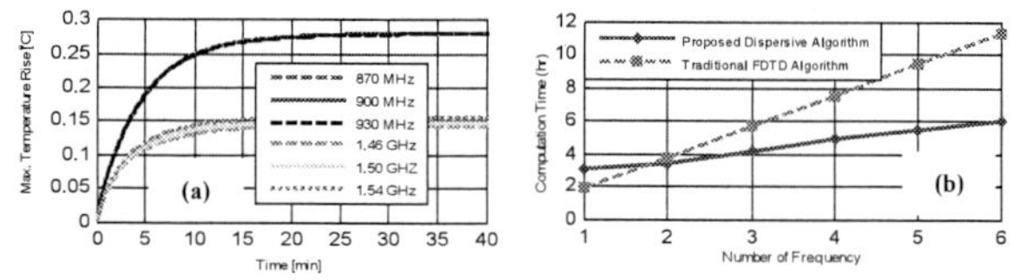

Fig. 4. (a) Max. temperature rise vs. time at frequencies of interest, and (b) Computation time of both algorithms vs. number of frequency.

IV. CONCLUSION

An efficient algorithm is developed for the computation the temperature rise and SAR distributions in a human head model due to the radiation from a nearby antenna at several frequencies. The proposed dispersive algorithm provides the temperature rise and SAR distributions at all frequencies of interest using a single simulation. Remarkable saving in computation time is achieved when the analysis is performed at more than one frequency.

REFERENCES

[1] J. Wang and O. Fujiwara, "FDTD computation of temperature rise in the human head for portable telephones," *IEEE Trans. Microwave Theory Tech.*, vol. 47, pp. 1528-1534, Aug. 1999.

[2] P. Bernardi, M. Cavagnaro, S. Pisa, and E. Piuzzi, "Specific absorption rate and temperature increases in the head of a cellular-phone user," *IEEE Trans. Microwave Theory Tech.*, vol. 48, pp. 1118-1126, July 2000.

[3] A. Hirata, M. Morita, and T. Shiozawa, "Temperature increase in the human head due to a dipole antenna at microwave frequencies," *IEEE Trans. Electromag. Compat.*, vol. 45, no. 1, pp. 109-116, Feb. 2003.

[4] A. Z. Elsherbeni and V. Demir, *The Finite-Difference Time-Domain Method for Electromagnetics with MATLAB Simulations*, second edition, ACES Series on Computational Electromagnetics and Engineering, SciTech Publishing, an Imprint of IET, Edison, NJ, 2016.

[5] H. H. Pennes, "Analysis of tissue and arterial blood temperature in resting forearm," *J. Appl. Physiol.*, vol. 1, pp. 93–122, 1948.

[6] M. A. Eleiwa and A. Z. Elsherbeni, "Debye constants for biological tissues from 30 Hz to 20 GHz," *ACES Journal*, vol. 16, no. 3, Nov. 2001.

[7] Online website. http://noodle.med.yale.edu/zubal/

[8] S. Gabriel, R. W. Lau, and C. Gabriel, "The dielectric properties of biological tissues: III. Parametric models for the dielectric spectrum of tissues," *Phys. Med. Biol.*, 41, pp. 2271–2293, 1996.

Provably Stable Local Application of Crank-Nicolson Time Integration to the FDTD Method with Nonuniform Gridding and Subgridding

A. Van Londersele, D. De Zutter, and D. Vande Ginste
Department of Information Technology (INTEC)
Electromagnetics (EM) Group
Ghent University/imec/IDLab, Belgium
arne.vanlondersele@ugent.be, daniel.dezutter@ugent.be, dries.vandeginste@ugent.be

***Abstract*—This contribution removes some doubts about the stability issues associated with the local and anisotropic use of Crank-Nicolson (CN) time integration in Finite-Difference Time-Domain (FDTD) simulations with spatial irregularities such as nonuniformity and subgridding. Due to the lack of space, only the most significant steps in the stability analysis are treated here. Intermediate steps as well as numerical examples and implementation details will be provided during the presentation.**

I. Introduction

To tackle the present-day multiscale electromagnetic problems, Finite-Difference Time-Domain (FDTD) solvers must provide a minimum degree of spatial flexibility, which is typically offered by nonuniform gridding and subgridding techniques. Both techniques allow varying cell sizes that are needed to efficiently resolve the multiscale geometry, but the former preserves the overall tensor-product structure of the grid, whereas the latter supports edge termination as to yield nested tensor-product grids. Although subgridding definitely uses less memory, the more intricate memory organization can cause it to be actually less efficient than nonuniform grids in terms of CPU time depending on the type of problem. Apart from reducing the number of spatial samples, the FDTD algorithm can be further optimized by reducing the number of time samples. However, the time step cannot exceed a certain stability upper bound, better known as the Courant limit, which is proportional to the smallest cell size occurring inside the grid. Conventional subgridding techniques typically assign a local time step, matching the local stability constraint, to each subgrid. This approach virtually always suffers from late-time instability and, although being explicit, the high number of iterations inside each subgrid can be less efficient than applying a (partially) implicit method, such as the Crank-Nicolson (CN) scheme and its Hybrid Implicit-Explicit (HIE) derivatives. Despite some interesting research on this topic, e.g., [1,2], no rigorous stability analysis has been proposed, until the recent publishing of [3], where the local and anisotropic application of CN, Newmark-beta and leapfrog alternating-direction implicit (ADI) schemes to nonuniform grids are thoroughly discussed in terms of stability. Here, we first summarize the key findings of [3] and then extend the stability analysis to a very general class of subgridding schemes. This should provide the reader with the necessary insights on how to combine explicit leapfrog and implicit CN FDTD methods in a stable way, not merely based on intuition.

II. Nonuniform Gridding

With the notations copied from [3, eqns. (2)-(15)], the hybrid explicit-leapfrog implicit-CN FDTD update equation for a general lossless inhomogeneous medium discretized on a nonuniform tensor-product grid is,

$$\begin{bmatrix} \frac{1}{\Delta t} D_\varepsilon & -\frac{1}{2}(I+\mathcal{P})\,\hat{\mathcal{V}}\,\mathcal{C}\,\hat{\mathcal{W}} \\ \frac{1}{2}\mathcal{V}\,\mathcal{C}^T\mathcal{W}\,(I-\mathcal{P}) & \frac{1}{\Delta t} D_\mu \end{bmatrix} x|^{n+1} = \begin{bmatrix} \frac{1}{\Delta t} D_\varepsilon & \frac{1}{2}(I-\mathcal{P})\,\hat{\mathcal{V}}\,\mathcal{C}\,\hat{\mathcal{W}} \\ -\frac{1}{2}\mathcal{V}\,\mathcal{C}^T\mathcal{W}\,(I+\mathcal{P}) & \frac{1}{\Delta t} D_\mu \end{bmatrix} x|^{n} + s|^{n}\,, \tag{1}$$

with s the source vector and x the field vector,

$$x|^{n} = \begin{bmatrix} \mathcal{P}\,e(n\,\Delta t) + (I-\mathcal{P})\,e((n-0.5)\,\Delta t) \\ h((n-0.5)\Delta t) \end{bmatrix}\,, \tag{2}$$

and $\mathcal{P}$ the diagonal matrix with elements,

$$[\mathcal{P}]_{i,i} = \begin{cases} 1 & \text{if } e_i \text{ is updated explicitly} \\ 0 & \text{if } e_i \text{ is updated implicitly} \end{cases}\,. \tag{3}$$

The FDTD system is exponentially stable if the poles of the z-domain transfer matrix are not located outside the unit disk. Besides, it is also polynomially stable if the repeated poles on the unit circle have linearly independent eigenvectors. An appropriate change of basis shows that the inverse of the transfer matrix belonging to (1) is algebraically similar to,

$$T(z) = \begin{bmatrix} (z-1)I & -z\,\mathcal{I}_2\,\tilde{\mathcal{C}} \\ \tilde{\mathcal{C}}^T\mathcal{I}_1 & (z-1)I \end{bmatrix}\,, \tag{4}$$

with *implicitization operators*,

$$[\mathcal{I}_1]_{i,i} = \begin{cases} 1 & \text{if } e_i \text{ is updated explicitly} \\ (z+1)/2 & \text{if } e_i \text{ is updated implicitly} \end{cases}\,, \tag{5}$$

$$[\mathcal{I}_2]_{i,i} = \begin{cases} 1 & \text{if } e_i \text{ is updated explicitly} \\ (1+z^{-1})/2 & \text{if } e_i \text{ is updated implicitly} \end{cases}\,, \tag{6}$$

and modifield curl,

$$\tilde{\mathcal{C}} = \Delta t \left(D_\varepsilon^{-1}\hat{\mathcal{V}}\,\mathcal{W}\right)^{1/2} \mathcal{C} \left(D_\mu^{-1}\,\mathcal{V}\,\hat{\mathcal{W}}\right)^{1/2} . \tag{7}$$

Hence, the FDTD system is exponentially stable if the roots of the characteristic equation $\det(T(z)) = 0$ satisfy $|z| \leq 1$. A separate treatment of static and dynamic solutions together with a partitioned-matrix rule translates the characterstic equation to,

$$\det\left(z^{-1}(z-1)^2 I_{n_h} + \tilde{\mathcal{C}}^T \mathcal{I}_1 \mathcal{I}_2 \tilde{\mathcal{C}}\right) = 0 \,. \tag{8}$$

Note that this is the wave equation in the z-space. Now, substitution of the bilinear transformation $z = (\zeta-1)/(\zeta+1)$ allows to interpret (8) as a linear eigenvalue problem. More specifically,

$$\zeta^2\, \tilde{\mathcal{C}}^T \tilde{\mathcal{C}}\, v = \left(\tilde{\mathcal{C}}^T \mathcal{P} \tilde{\mathcal{C}} - 4 I_{n_h}\right) v \,. \tag{9}$$

Left-multiplying (9) by the hermitian transpose of v and subsequently subtracting/adding the hermitian-transposed equation, yields respectively,

$$\mathrm{Im}(\zeta^2)\, \|\tilde{\mathcal{C}}\, v\|_2^2 = 0 \,, \tag{10}$$

$$\mathrm{Re}(\zeta^2)\, \|\tilde{\mathcal{C}}\, v\|_2^2 = \|\mathcal{P}\,\tilde{\mathcal{C}}\, v\|_2^2 - 4\|v\|_2^2 \,. \tag{11}$$

As (10) and (11) should hold for any non-zero vector v, the condition $|z| \leq 1$, which is equivalent to $\mathrm{Re}(\zeta) \geq 0$, is satisfied if and only if $\mathrm{Re}(\zeta^2) \leq 0$. A more careful analysis shows that this can only occur for ζ lying on the imaginary axis or, equivelantly, z lying on the unit circle. In other words, the FDTD system has been proven to be stable if $\mathrm{Re}(\zeta^2) \leq 0$, which upon inspection of (11) yields,

$$\|\mathcal{P}\,\tilde{\mathcal{C}}\|_2 = \max_{v \neq 0} \frac{\|\mathcal{P}\,\tilde{\mathcal{C}}\, v\|_2}{\|v\|_2} \leq 2 \,. \tag{12}$$

As shown in [3], the limit on Δt imposed by (12) is the exact Courant limit, but in order to avoid polynomial growth the strict inequality should hold. It is clear from (12), that the operator $\mathcal{P}$ can be tuned as to eliminate the smallest cell sizes from the stability limit at the cost of implicit CN computations.

III. Subgridding

Consider a nonuniform coarse grid that is locally overlapped by a nonuniform subgrid, whose outer edges coincide with coarse primary edges. If the overlapped coarse part would be filled with perfect magnetic conductors, which cannot reduce the time step limit for trivial reasons, the resulting scheme is equivalent to a conventional grid stitching scheme without overlap. Hence, stability with overlap is a sufficient condition for stability without overlap. This insight allows us to detach coarse curl $\mathcal{C}_\mathrm{c}$, fine curl $\mathcal{C}_\mathrm{f}$ and coupling operator $\mathcal{S}$ from each other, such that, for the subgridding scheme with overlap, (4) translates to,

$$T(z) = \begin{bmatrix} (z-1)I & -z\,\tilde{\mathcal{C}}_\mathrm{c} & & -s\,z\,\mathcal{I}_{2,\mathrm{s}}\,\tilde{\mathcal{S}}^T \\ \tilde{\mathcal{C}}_\mathrm{c}^T & (z-1)I & & \\ & & (z-1)I & -z\,\mathcal{I}_{2,\mathrm{f}}\,\tilde{\mathcal{C}}_\mathrm{f} \\ \tilde{\mathcal{S}}\,\mathcal{I}_{1,\mathrm{s}} & & \tilde{\mathcal{C}}_\mathrm{f}^T \mathcal{I}_{1,\mathrm{f}} & (z-1)I \end{bmatrix} , \tag{13}$$

where implicitization operators of the form (5)–(6) were added to the subgrid and the coupling. Note that the construction of (13) requires some symmetry relation between the coarse-to-fine and fine-to-coarse coupling operators as well as some nonuniformity rescaling. Also, the scalar s is a normalization factor. More details will be given during the presentation. Following the same procedure as for the nonuniform gridding, we end up with a quadratic eigenvalue problem $(\zeta^2 A + \zeta\, B + C)\, v = 0$, with

$$A = A^T = \begin{bmatrix} \frac{1}{4}\tilde{\mathcal{C}}_\mathrm{c}\,\tilde{\mathcal{C}}_\mathrm{c}^T & 0 \\ 0 & \frac{1}{4}\tilde{\mathcal{C}}_\mathrm{f}^T\,\tilde{\mathcal{C}}_\mathrm{f} \end{bmatrix} , \tag{14}$$

$$B = -B^T = \begin{bmatrix} 0 & -\frac{\sqrt{s}}{2}\,\tilde{\mathcal{S}}_i^T \\ \frac{\sqrt{s}}{2}\,\tilde{\mathcal{S}}_i & 0 \end{bmatrix} , \tag{15}$$

$$C = C^T = \begin{bmatrix} I - \frac{1}{4}\tilde{\mathcal{C}}_\mathrm{c}\,\tilde{\mathcal{C}}_\mathrm{c}^T & \frac{\sqrt{s}}{2}\,\mathcal{P}_\mathrm{s}\,\tilde{\mathcal{S}}_i^T \\ \frac{\sqrt{s}}{2}\,\tilde{\mathcal{S}}_i\,\mathcal{P}_\mathrm{s} & I - \frac{1}{4}\tilde{\mathcal{C}}_\mathrm{f}^T\,\mathcal{P}_\mathrm{f}\,\tilde{\mathcal{C}}_\mathrm{f} \end{bmatrix} . \tag{16}$$

An eigenvalue problem with this particular symmetry and with $A \succeq 0$ has roots ζ in the right half-plane if and only if $C \succeq 0$. With the decomposition $C = I - D$, the required positive semi-definiteness gives rise to the condition $\lambda_{\max}(D) \leq 1$. Separating on-diagonal from off-diagonal blocks by means of the triangle inequality finally yields,

$$\frac{1}{4} \max\left(\|\tilde{\mathcal{C}}_\mathrm{c}\|_2^2 \,,\, \|\mathcal{P}_\mathrm{f}\,\tilde{\mathcal{C}}_\mathrm{f}\|_2^2 \right) + \frac{\sqrt{s}}{2} \|\tilde{\mathcal{S}}_i\,\mathcal{P}_\mathrm{s}\|_2^2 \leq 1 \,. \tag{17}$$

By updating the subgrid and the coupling updates implicitly, the coarse-grid Courant limit is retrieved.

IV. Conclusion

The exact time step limit is provided for nonuniform grids with local and anistropic application of CN time integration. A similar limit is shown to exist for general subgridding schemes. However, this limit is a sufficient but not a necessary upper bound for Δt. The concept of a z-domain implicitization operator in combination with the bilinear transformation can be extended to other stability proofs. For example, a spatial analog may be used to find the exact stability condition for the hybrid staggered-collocated methods proposed in [4,5], which apply the CN scheme both in space and time.

References

[1] Z. Huang, G. G. Pan, and K. S. Chen, "A synchronized multigrid time domain method via Huygens subgridding and implicit algorithms," *IEEE Transactions on Antennas and Propagation*, vol. 61, no. 5, pp. 2605–2614, May 2013.

[2] M. R. Cabello, L. D. Angulo, J. Alvarez, I. D. Flintoft, S. Bourke, J. F. Dawson, R. G. Martn, and S. G. Garcia, "A hybrid Crank-Nicolson FDTD subgridding boundary condition for lossy thin-layer modeling," *IEEE Transactions on Microwave Theory and Techniques*, vol. 65, no. 5, pp. 1397–1406, May 2017.

[3] A. Van Londersele, D. De Zutter, and D. Vande Ginste, "An in-depth stability analysis of nonuniform FDTD combined with novel local implicitization techniques," *Journal of Computational Physics*, vol. 342, no. Supplement C, pp. 177 – 193, 2017.

[4] ——, "A new hybrid implicit-explicit FDTD method for local subgridding in multiscale 2-D TE scattering problems," *IEEE Transactions on Antennas and Propagation*, vol. 64, no. 8, pp. 3509–3520, Aug 2016.

[5] ——, "A collocated 3-D HIE-FDTD scheme with PML," *IEEE Microwave and Wireless Components Letters*, vol. 27, no. 7, pp. 609–611, July 2017.

Model Order Reduction for Finite Difference Modeling of Cardiac Propagation using DMD Modes

Riasat Khan
Department of Electrical and Computer Engineering
New Mexico State University
Las Cruces, NM, USA
rkhan@nmsu.edu

Kwong T. Ng
Department of Electrical and Computer Engineering
New Mexico State University
Las Cruces, NM, USA
ngnsr@nmsu.edu

***Abstract*—Numerical simulations of cardiac electrophysiology are now considered a valuable tool for medical research. To study and explore the cardiac electrical propagation, it is essential to develop and study techniques that allow efficient simulation as well as retain accuracy. The finite difference method has been a popular method for solving the governing equation in the monodomain model of cardiac propagation due to its simplicity and low computational overhead. The inhomogeneous and anisotropic conductive anatomy of the three-dimensional cardiac tissue represents a complex system which involves spatial and temporal derivatives as well as a nonlinear ionic current term. This makes the simulation computationally intensive, and consequently, the development of an efficient computational technique is required to improve the accuracy and efficiency of the simulations. In this paper, a model order reduction technique has been developed which provides low-dimensional approximations for the full-dimensional cardiac monodomain system by using dynamic mode decomposition method. Numerical results show that the reduced order approximations reduce the CPU time by a factor of 5.9, while its RMS difference with original model is 0.9443 mV.**

***Index Terms*—Dynamic Mode Decomposition, Monodomain Model, Transmembrane Potential, Finite Difference Method, Model Order Reduction.**

I. Introduction

Numerical demonstration of cardiac electrical activity now plays an important role in the study of specific medications intended to treat different heart diseases. During electrical stimulation of the cardiac tissue, an action potential is generated, which creates an electric field on the surface of the human body. Monodomain modeling of cardiac tissue, which is a simplified representation of the bidomain model, provides important information about various complex activities. The governing monodomain equation involves temporal derivative term, diffusion or Laplacian term, and a nonlinear ionic current term. The semi-implicit method has been utilized to discretize the monodomain equation in time. The analytical solution of the complex monodomain equation is only possible for simple and unrealistic cardiac tissue, and that's why its numerical solution is generally preferred. In this paper, the most common finite difference method has been used to solve the monodomain equation numerically. A three-dimensional cube of a cardiac tissue has been considered where the conductivity has a discrete change on every finite element node as well as with the change of fiber angle.

Due to the involvement of an extensive range of spatial and temporal scales, as well as due to the inhomogeneous and anisotropic conductivity and nonlinear ionic current, the solution of the cardiac monodomain system is computationally intensive. Therefore, a model order reduction method has been implemented on the monodomain equation which reduces the computational complexity as well as preserves almost the same accuracy. The reduced order dynamic mode decomposition basis functions are generated from the snapshot matrix, which is obtained from the simulations of the original full order solution [1]. The reduced order model is then obtained by Galerkin projection of the full order solution onto the reduced order basis functions. The reduced order solution has significantly fewer unknowns and hence requires lower solution time than the original full order solution. The performance of the model order reduction technique has been presented in terms of the root-mean-square (RMS) error potential between the original and reduced order model and the computational time.

II. Full-order Cardiac Monodomain Model

The monodomain model is considered one of the most comprehensive models for simulating cardiac tissue behavior. The nonlinear parabolic form of the monodomain equation can be derived from the continuity of transmembrane potential, intracellular and interstitial currents which is given by:

$$\frac{\delta V_m}{\delta t} = \frac{1}{C_m}\left\{\frac{1}{\beta}\left[\nabla.(\bar{\bar{\sigma}}_i \nabla V_m) + I_{si}\right] - \sum I_{ion}\right\} \quad (1)$$

Here β is the total membrane surface area per unit volume, C_m is the capacitance per unit area, $\sum I_{ion}$ is the total ionic current per unit area, and V_m is the transmembrane potential, i.e., the difference between the intracellular and interstitial potentials. $\bar{\bar{\sigma}}_i$ is the intracellular conductivity tensor, which is assumed to be inhomogeneous and anisotropic. Semi-implicit temporal discretization and higher order finite difference approximations for the spatial derivatives are considered to solve the monodomain equation [2]. The Luo-Rudy model is used to represent the ionic current and the derivatives of the conductivities are evaluated analytically.

III. Dynamic Mode Decomposition Method

A. Construction of the DMD Basis Function

The reduced order basis functions are generated from the snapshots, which are obtained from the simulation of the original full order system at certain discrete time instances, $t_1, t_2, ..., t_m$. Snapshot matrix $x(t_i)$ is of dimension NXM, where M is the number of snapshots and N is the number of state variables, and generally $N > M$. Next, two data matrices X_1 and X_2 are obtained from the snapshot matrix:

$$X_1 = [x(t_1), x(t_2), .., x(t_{M-1})]; X_2 = [x(t_2), x(t_3), .., x(t_M)] \quad (2)$$

Next, the QR decomposition of the X_1 matrix is obtained. A matrix S is calculated which is given by:

$$S = R^{-1}Q^H X_2 \quad (3)$$

The eigen-decomposition of the S matrix is required to obtain the DMD basis functions. The dynamic mode decomposition (DMD) modes are finally obtained from the truncated eigenvectors of the S matrix corresponding to the largest eigenvalues. As the S matrix has complex eigenvalues, the norm of the eigenvalues is considered. If w is the eigenvectors of the S matrix, then the DMD basis functions are given by:

$$\phi = X_1 w \quad (4)$$

The DMD basis matrix ϕ contains l columns and $l < M$.

B. Model Order Reduction by DMD-Galerkin Technique

The DMD basis functions are now used to find the reduced order model by using Galerkin projection. The reduced state variables z is related to the full order state variables as follows:

$$x = \phi z \quad (5)$$

If $\frac{dx}{dt} = f(x; t)$ is a full order model, which is a nonlinear ODE, (6) is its exact same form according to DMD-Galerkin method:

$$\frac{dz}{dt} = f(x; t) \quad (6)$$

The DMD-Galerkin method has been implemented on the cardiac monodomain equation (1), where the dimension of the unknown transmembrane potential V_m is reduced from N to l.

IV. Results and Discussion

In this section, numerical results are presented for the implementation of the DMD-Galerkin based model order reduction method on the cardiac monodomain equation. The conductivity $\bar{\bar{\sigma}}_i$ is assumed to be anisotropic and inhomogeneous, i.e., it changes with respect to the tissue position as well as with the rotation of the fiber angle. The tissue is excited with a constant magnitude current I_{si}, located at the origin of the coordinate system and has a duration of 1 ms. For the full order model, (1) is approximated with semi-implicit scheme ($\theta = 0.5$) with 36X36X36 nodes. The snapshot matrix $x(t_i)$ is constructed from the full order model, which has $36^3 = 46,656$ unknowns or state variables. The reduced order DMD basis matrix ϕ is obtained from the snapshot matrix and the largest 3,060 eigenvectors of the S matrix. Then the original full order model is projected onto the DMD basis matrix ϕ, which gives the expected reduced order model. The reduced order model is then solved with the same iterative conjugate gradient method, as of the full order system. The benefits of the MOR method is achieved as the number of unknowns reduced by ~15, i.e., from 46,656 to 3,060. The RMS deviation or error between the full model and reduced model of 0.9443 mV indicates the reduced model approximates the full model satisfactorily. Fig. 1 shows the distortion of the transmembrane potential obtained from the original full order and reduced order models.

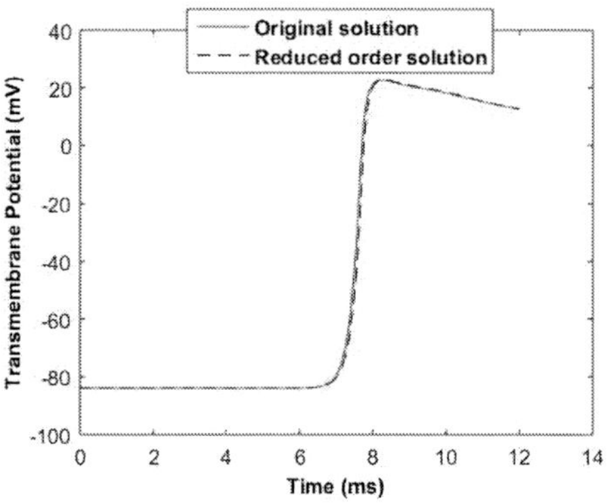

Fig. 1. Transmembrane potential for original and DMD reduced order solution.

V. Conclusion

Model order reduction has been implemented for the finite-difference monodomain model of cardiac tissue with an inhomogeneous and anisotropic medium. The reduced order basis has been constructed from the dynamic mode decomposition method, and then the original full order system is projected onto it according to Galerkin approximation. The proposed method reduces the order of the system by a factor of ~15 and the solution time by a factor of ~5.9. The RMS error between the original and reduced order solution is 0.9443 mV, which indicates the accuracy is still maintained in the model order reduction method. Prospective future studies can consist of implementation of different model order reduction methods and compare their performance.

References

[1] P. J. Schmid, L. Li, M. P. Juniper, and O. Pust, "Applications of the dynamic mode decomposition," *Theoretical and Computational Fluid Dynamics*, vol. 25, no. 1, pp. 249–259, Jun 2011.

[2] R. Khan and K. T. Ng, "Higher order finite difference modeling of cardiac propagation," in *2017 IEEE International Conference on Bioinformatics and Biomedicine (BIBM)*. Nov 2017, pp. 1945–1951.

Numerical Dispersion Analysis for Spherical FDTD

Ravi C. Bollimuntha
Dept. of ECEE
University of Colorado Boulder
Boulder, USA
ravi.bollimuntha@colorado.edu

Mohammed F. Hadi
EE Dept.
Colorado School of Mines
Golden, USA
mhadi@mines.edu

Melinda J. Piket-May
Dept. of ECEE
University of Colorado Boulder
Boulder, USA
mjp@colorado.edu

Atef Z. Elsherbeni
EE Dept.
Colorado School of Mines
Golden, USA
aelsherb@mines.edu

***Abstract*—Analyses of spherical functions-based numerical dispersion relation are performed for the finite-difference time-domain method in spherical coordinates. Errors in the numerically rendered wavenumber due to finite mesh densities are analyzed as a function of absolute position within the spherical mesh, solutions mode orders and mesh density. Solution singularities near the origin and the z-axis are properly tracked and fully quantified for the different spherical solution modes.**

***Keywords*—numerical dispersion, numerical wave number, spherical coordinates, spherical FDTD.**

I. Introduction

Wave propagation within finite-difference time-domain (FDTD) meshes deviate from continuous space predictions due to the discrete nature of the underlying update equations. For any given FDTD variant, a numerical dispersion relation can be derived through populating its update equations with the corresponding set of elemental harmonic functions. The resulting relation, which approaches the continuous space at the limit ($\omega^2\mu\epsilon = \beta^2$ in a lossless medium) faithfully predicts numerical wavenumber solutions. Armed with such knowledge, an optimal selection of mesh and update equations parameters can be ascertained from the outset, with total control of incurred simulation errors. For the standard Cartesian FDTD, the numerical dispersion relation is obtained by substituting plane wave solutions in the discretized Maxwell's equations [1] to produce:

$$\mu\epsilon D_t^2 = D_x^2 + D_y^2 + D_z^2, \tag{1}$$

where $D_t = j\frac{\sin\omega\Delta t/2}{\Delta t/2}$, $D_\zeta = j\frac{\sin\tilde{\beta}_\zeta\Delta\zeta/2}{\Delta\zeta/2}$, $\zeta \to x, y, z$, where Δx, Δy, Δz and Δt are spatial and temporal discretization steps respectively, and $\tilde{\beta}$ is the numerical wave number. This relation can be solved for $\tilde{\beta}$ for any given set of frequency, intrinsic parameters and discrete step values. Spherical FDTD is interesting in the context of modeling conical and spherical structures, and earth-ionosphere system [2], when compared to Cartesian FDTD. The numerical dispersion relation for spherical FDTD is dealt with in the rest of the paper.

II. Numerical Dispersion Relation for Spherical FDTD

The spherical FDTD update equations, given in [2], [3], are used to obtain the numerical dispersion relation. The TE^r wave solutions for the Helmholtz equation in spherical coordinate system are given by [4]:

$$F = \beta r h_n^{(2)}(\beta r) P_n^m(\cos\theta) e^{-j(m\phi-\omega t)}, \tag{2}$$

where $h_n^{(2)}(\beta r)$ is the outgoing spherical Hankel function, $P_n^m(\cos\theta)$ is the associated Legendre function, and $m \le n$ are solution mode numbers.

When the spherical wave solutions (2) are substituted in the Spherical FDTD update equations in a similar procedure [5], we obtain the spherical FDTD numerical dispersion relation:

$$\mu\epsilon D_t^2 = D_r^E D_r^H + D_\theta^E D_\theta^H + D_\phi^E D_\phi^H, \tag{3}$$

where

$$D_r^E = \frac{\tilde{\beta}(r+\Delta r)h_n^{(2)}[\tilde{\beta}(r+\Delta r)] - \tilde{\beta} r h_n^{(2)}(\tilde{\beta} r)}{\Delta r\left(h_n^{(2)}(\tilde{\beta} r^+) + \tilde{\beta} r^+ h_n^{\prime(2)}(\tilde{\beta} r^+)\right)}, \tag{4}$$

$$D_r^H = \frac{N^+ - N^-}{\tilde{\beta} r \Delta r h_n^{(2)}(\tilde{\beta} r)}, \tag{5}$$

$$D_\theta^E = \frac{\Delta\theta/2}{\sin\Delta\theta/2} \cdot \frac{\sin^2(\theta+\Delta\theta)P_n^{\prime m}[\cos(\theta+\Delta\theta)] - \sin^2\theta P_n^{\prime m}(\cos\theta)}{r\sin\theta^+\Delta\theta P_n^m(\cos\theta^+)}, \tag{6}$$

$$D_\theta^H = \frac{P_n^m(\cos\theta^+) - P_n^m(\cos\theta^-)}{r\sin\theta\Delta\theta P_n^{\prime m}(\cos\theta)}, \tag{7}$$

$$D_\phi^E = -j\frac{\sin m\Delta\phi/2}{\Delta\phi/2}\frac{\Delta\theta/2}{\sin\Delta\theta/2}\frac{1}{r^2\sin^2\theta^+}, \tag{8}$$

$$D_\phi^H = -j\frac{\sin m\Delta\phi/2}{\Delta\phi/2}, \tag{9}$$

and

$$N^\pm = h_n^{(2)}(\tilde{\beta} r^\pm) + \tilde{\beta} r^\pm h_n^{('2)}(\tilde{\beta} r^\pm), \tag{10}$$

with $r^\pm = r \pm \Delta r/2$, $\theta^\pm = \theta \pm \Delta\theta/2$.

This numerical dispersion relation is a function of absolute position along r and θ directions, an anticipated dependence since mesh cell sizes in spherical FDTD vary with radius and elevation angle, (r, θ).

III. Numerical Wave Number Sensitivity Analysis

Equation (3) is solved for the numerical wavenumber $\tilde{\beta}$ using `fsolve` function in MATLAB. The chosen time step Δt is stable expression from [2];

$$\Delta t \le \left[c\sqrt{l_r^{-2} + l_\theta^{-2} + l_\phi^{-2}}\right]^{-1}. \tag{11}$$

The resulting numerical wave number is typically complex-valued, especially near the origin, which is a departure from the continuous space β quantity. This behavior is further studied for different radii, mesh resolutions, elevation angles, and mode numbers.

A. Sensitivity to Mesh Resolution

The numerical dispersion relation (3) is solved for different mesh resolutions $\Delta r = \lambda_0/R$ where $R = 10, 20, 40$ free-space cells per wavelength at a frequency of 1 GHz, $\Delta\theta = \frac{\pi}{20}$, and $\Delta\phi = \frac{2\pi}{40}$. The time step Δt is chosen as maximum value of (11), where $l_r = \Delta r$, $l_\theta = \Delta r\Delta\theta$ and $l_\phi = \Delta r\Delta\phi\sin(\Delta\theta)$. The elevation angle θ is chosen as $\Delta\theta$.

The normalized real and imaginary parts of the numerical wave number with respect to normalized distance from the origin are shown in Fig. 1 for different mesh resolutions. As we move towards the origin, $Re(\tilde{\beta}/\beta_0)$ increases beyond unity. The $Im(\tilde{\beta}/\beta_0)$ quantity is totally a spurious error and causes either solution attenuation or growth near the origin, depending on its sign. As we approach origin, the wave is initially attenuated and then amplified in close proximity to the origin. Also, as one would expect, Fig. 1 shows that the higher mesh resolutions simulate wave propagation better near the origin.

B. Sensitivity to Mode Numbers

Next, the mode numbers n or m are varied while keeping the other integer constant. Solutions for higher n modes get affected more as we move towards the origin for a fixed m as shown in Fig. 2. The increased sensitivity with increasing n can be attributed to the fact that higher order Legendre functions vary rapidly with θ, and become sparsely sampled. For example, when $m = 0$, $P_n^m(\cos\theta)$ for $n = 1, 2, 3$ are $\cos\theta, \frac{1}{2}(3\cos^2\theta - 1), \frac{1}{2}\cos\theta(5\cos^2\theta - 3)$. It is also observed that the effect of changing m for a fixed n is minimal on the behavior of numerical wave number (not shown).

C. Sensitivity to Elevation Angle

Figure 3 shows wave number sensitivity to different elevation angles, which is relatively minimal compared to radial distance.

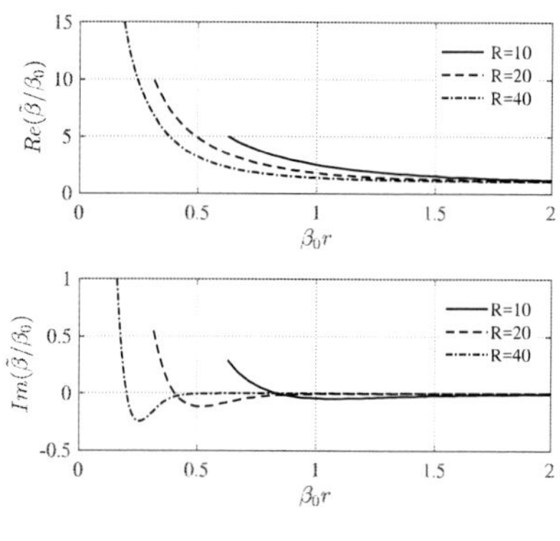

Fig. 1. Real and imaginary parts of wave number vs. normalized distance from origin at different resolutions ($\theta = \Delta\theta$, $n = 3$, and $m = 0$).

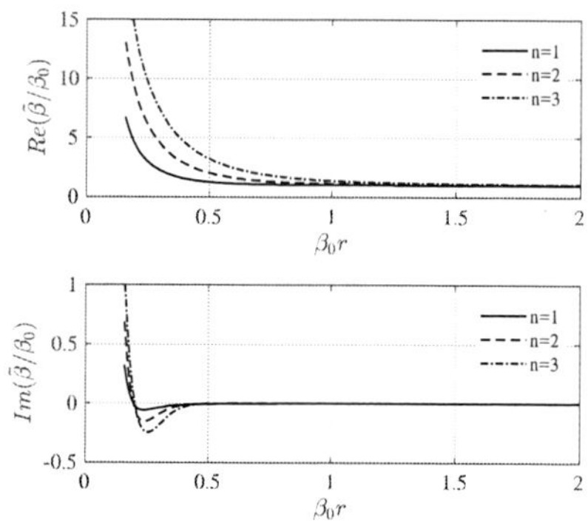

Fig. 2. Real and imaginary parts of wave number vs. normalized distance from origin for different mode numbers ($\theta = \Delta\theta$, R= 40, and $m = 0$).

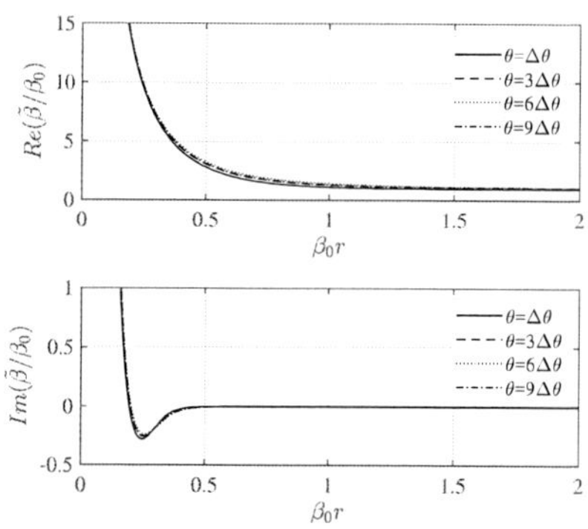

Fig. 3. Real and imaginary parts of wave number vs. normalized distance from origin at different elevation angles ($R = 40$, $n = 3$, and $m = 1$).

IV. Conclusion

The numerical dispersion relation for spherical FDTD derived based on wave solutions native to the spherical coordinate system is presented. The sensitivity of numerical wave number to mesh resolution, mode numbers, and elevation angle is analyzed. This analysis will help us understand the errors in wave propagation within spherical FDTD and select better simulation parameters with appropriate error control.

References

[1] A. Z. Elsherbeni and V. Demir, The Finite-Difference Time-Domain Method for electromagnetics with MATLAB Simulations. Raleigh, NC: SciTech Publishing, 2009.

[2] O. Franek, G. F. Pedersen, and J. B. Andersen, "Numerical modeling of a spherical array of monopoles using FDTD method," IEEE Transactions on Antennas and Propagation, vol. 54, no. 7, pp. 1952–1963, Jul. 2006.

[3] R. Holland, "THREDS: A finite-difference time-domain EMP code in 3D spherical coordinates," IEEE Transactions on Nuclear Science, vol. NS-30, no. 6, pp. 4592–4595, Dec. 1983.

[4] R. F. Harrington, Time-Harmonic Electromagnetic Fields. New York, NY: McGraw-Hill, 1961.

[5] M. F. Hadi, A. Z. Elsherbeni, M. J. Piket-May, and S. F. Mahmoud, "Radial waves based dispersion analysis of the body-of-revolution FDTD method," IEEE Transactions on Antennas and Propagation, vol. 65, no. 2, pp. 721–729, Feb. 2017.

Improved FDTD Method around Dielectric and PEC Interfaces using RBF-FD Techniques

Brad Martin
Department of Applied Mathematics and Statistics
Colorado School of Mines
Golden, CO 80401 USA
bmartin@mines.edu

Atef Elsherbeni
Department of Electrical Engineering
Colorado School of Mines
Golden, CO 80401 USA
aelsherb@mines.edu

Gregory E. Fasshauer
Department of Applied Mathematics and Statistics
Colorado School of Mines
Golden, CO 80401 USA
fasshauer@mines.edu

Mohammed Hadi
Department of Electrical Engineering
Colorado School of Mines
Golden, CO 80401 USA
mhadi@mines.edu

***Abstract*—A high-order, radial basis function-generated finite difference (RBF-FD) method is prepared for simulation of electromagnetic (EM) wave propagation near dielectric and perfectly conducting (PEC) interfaces. The method uses piecewise polynomial support along with RBFs to form explicit, FDTD-like updating equations that uphold high-order accuracy even when applied across a dielectric interface or near a PEC boundary. The method is tested on two 2D problems involving EM wave propagation around PEC and dielectric cylinders.**

***Keywords*—2D, FDTD, high order, interfaces, RBF-FD.**

I. INTRODUCTION

The finite difference time domain (FDTD) method has been and remains a popular and powerful computational tool for solving Maxwell's equations which dictate how electromagnetic (EM) waves move through space [1]. The method is often used to simulate EM wave propagation around conductors and dielectric materials, though sophisticated augmentations are required for FDTD to maintain high (order) accuracy with such material interfaces present [2].

To achieve high accuracy in numerical EM wave propagation around dielectric and conducting materials, we adapt previous work with radial basis function-generated finite differences (RBF-FD) to solve heat- and seismic propagation problems near analogous interfaces [3]. Significant interest has recently been directed toward local and global RBF-based methods for EM wave modeling [4]. The main novelty we offer here is in the high-order handling of jump conditions in fields and derivatives: interface accommodation is elevated from the 1st or 2nd-order treatment in [5] to an arbitrary order of accuracy.

II. METHODOLOGY

We direct our presentation of the method toward numerically solving problems with a simplified, isotropic version of the 2D transverse electric (TE_z) Maxwell equations from (1.32) in [1] (omitting impressed electric and magnetic currents):

$$\begin{cases} \varepsilon(\partial E_x/\partial t) = (\partial H_z/\partial y) - \sigma^e E_x \\ \varepsilon(\partial E_y/\partial t) = -(\partial H_z/\partial x) - \sigma^e E_y \\ \mu(\partial H_z/\partial t) = (\partial E_x/\partial y) - (\partial E_y/\partial x) - \sigma^m H_z . \end{cases} \tag{1}$$

E and H are local electric and magnetic field strengths, respectively; the parameter ε holds a value of free space permittivity ε_0 everywhere except within the dielectric cylinder model (where its value is $4\varepsilon_0$); σ^e is electrical conductivity (set to 10^{10} within the PEC model for FDTD testing and zero in all other models and locations); the parameter μ holds a value of free space permeability μ_0 everywhere in our test models; and the magnetic conductivity parameter σ^m is unused here (set to zero everywhere). The square domain employed for all testing is shown with RBF-FD nodes in Fig. 1. Electric and magnetic field values on the boundary of the square are obtained from an appropriate linear combination of analytical solutions from [6].

Enforcement of proper jump conditions in E and H (for RBF-FD stencils near the cylinder in Fig. 1) assures the accuracy of the RBF-FD method. In the present work and in its past application in [3], the method receives significant heritage from [7]. The novelty here is in proper use of the divergence-free requirement of EM wave physics along with the continuity conditions present at dielectric interfaces and PEC boundaries. Updating equations are formed across interfaces on a mesh-free grid – to a theoretically arbitrary order of accuracy – while avoiding the use of extrapolated or fictitious data as in [2].

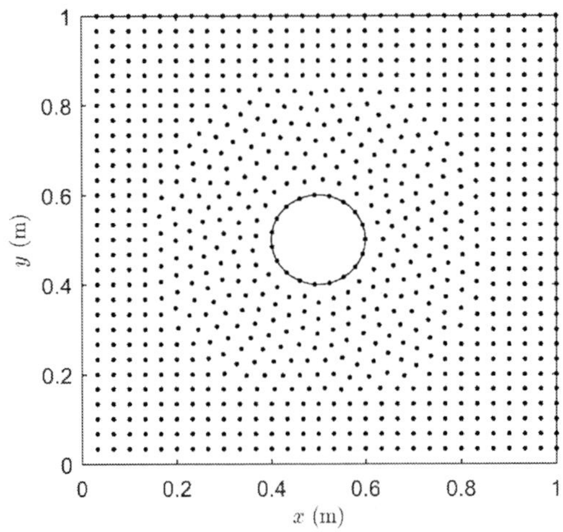

Fig. 1. An unstructured cloud of RBF-FD data nodes surrounds a 0.1m-radius PEC cylindrical cross section in the middle of the unit square (1m on each side). Elsewhere, a computationally efficient Cartesian mesh is used.

III. NUMERICAL TEST CASES

Both our RBF-FD method and the Yee cell-based FDTD method from [1] are used to solve two particular problems in the 1m-square domain shown in Fig. 1. The area within the cylindrical cross-section (circle) is considered a PEC region in the first test case and a dielectric region in the second test case, with parameter values as described in the methodology section. The RBF-FD method employs fourth-order Runge-Kutta time integration. Both the RBF-FD and FDTD methods are run with a discrete time step near the maximum stable time interval at a given resolution, determined by the Courant-Friedrichs-Lewy (CFL) condition.

In both cases, a Gaussian-shaped incident plane wave begins at the bottom of the domain ($y = 0$m) and moves upward beginning at $t = 0$ ns. The incident wave encounters the cylinder at about 1.33 ns, when that wave is then scattered (or scattered and refracted, in the dielectric case) by the cylinder. An example snapshot of the resulting magnetic field from the PEC test case is shown in Fig. 2. A time series of H_z data at (0.5m,0.2m) is shown in Fig. 3.

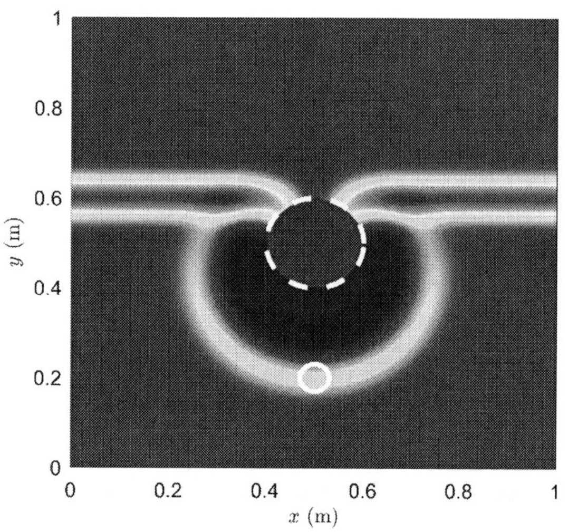

Fig. 2. A colormap (at $t = 2$ ns) of z-oriented magnetic field values (H_z) after a plane wave traveling upwards (red beam) encounters a PEC cylinder (dashed white line). Error assessment occurs at (0.5m,0.2m) (solid, small white circle).

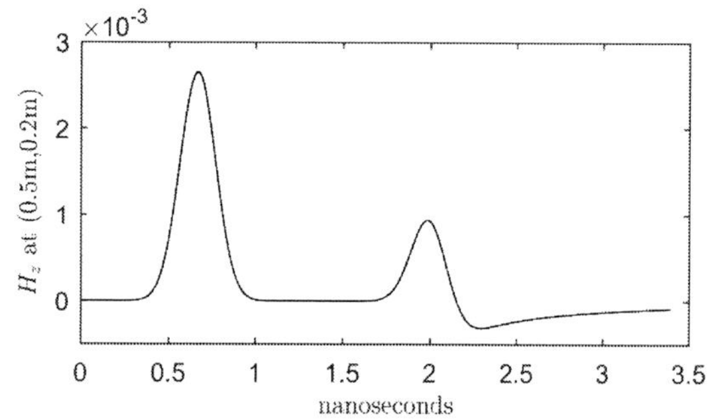

Fig. 3. Time series for H_z at (0.5m,0.2m) as measured for the PEC test case. Errors in the reflected wave (the peak seen near 2 ns) are shown in Table 1. The percent errors shown in Table 1 are calculated by dividing max norm error in replicating the time series by the reflected wave magnitude (about 1E-3 A/m).

IV. RESULTS

Error is assessed in H_z at the point (0.5m,0.2m). In the PEC test case, the incident waveform is expressed as a Fourier series. Error is then determined via a linear combination of analytical solutions for each frequency as outlined in [6]. Computational effort required to achieve various error thresholds are shown in Table 1. Results from the dielectric test case are similar.

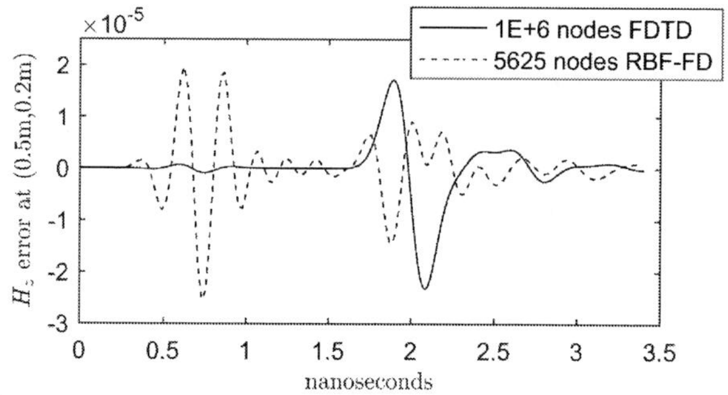

Fig. 4. Errors in H_z. Far fewer nodes (lower resolution; less computational effort) are needed with RBF-FD to obtain the errors above.

TABLE I. COMPUTATIONAL TIME AND MEMORY REQUIRED*, PEC CASE

Error	*Time (FDTD)*	*Memory (FDTD)*	*Time (RBF)*	*Mem. (RBF)*
10%	0.98 sec	0.9 MB	1.7 sec	4.0 MB
5.0%	10.6 sec	3.8 MB	2.1 sec	4.6 MB
2.5%	140 sec	15.1 MB	2.5 sec	5.1 MB
1.0%	3128 sec	69.0 MB	3.0 sec	5.8 MB

**Matlab implementation; double precision; Core i7-6700k CPU at 4.3 GHz. Refinement (more nodes) is needed to reach a given error threshold.*

CONCLUSION

The accuracy provided by RBF-FD method can dramatically increase efficiency in EM wave simulation across and near smooth interfaces and boundaries, particularly when very low error is desired. Future work will involve 3D simulations and GPU implementation of the RBF-FD process.

REFERENCES

[1] A. Z. Elsherbeni and V. Demir, The Finite Difference Time Domain Method for Electromagnetics with MATLAB Simulations (2nd ed.), New Jersey: SciTech Publishing, 2016.

[2] S. Zhao and G. W. Wei, "High-order FDTD methods via derivative matching for Maxwell's equations with material interfaces," J. Comput. Phys., vol. 200, pp. 60–103, 2004.

[3] B. Martin and B. Fornberg, "Seismic modeling with radial basis function-generated finite differences (RBF-FD) – a simplified treatment of interfaces," J. Comput. Phys., vol. 335, pp. 828–845, April 2017.

[4] T. Kaufmann, Y. Yu, C. Engstrom, Z. Chen and C. Fumeaux, "Recent developments of the meshless radial point interpolation method for time-domain electromagnetics," Int. J. Numer. Model., vol. 25, pp. 468–489, 2012.

[5] Y. Yu and Z. Chen, "Implementation of material interface conditions in the radial point interpolation meshless method," IEEE Trans. Antennas Propag., vol. 59, pp. 2916–2923, 2011.

[6] C. A. Balanis, Advanced Engineering Electromagnetics (2nd ed.), New Jersey: John Wiley & Sons, Inc., 2012.

[7] R. J. Leveque and Z. Li, "The immersed interface method for elliptic equations with discontinuous coefficients and singular sources," SIAM J. Numer. Anal., pp. 1019–1044, 1994.

GA-MoM Optimization of Slot Arrays

Sembiam R. Rengarajan
Department of Electrical and Computer Engineering
California State University
Northridge, CA 91330
srengarajan@csun.edu

***Abstract*— A review of the genetic algorithm (GA) optimization of slot arrays in rectangular waveguides using a method-of-moments (MoM) analysis engine is presented. Examples of design of waveguide power divider/combiner for distributed amplifier applications and linear and planar slot array antenna designs are discussed. An initial design using the circuit model is carried out prior to GA optimization. Rapid evaluation of the MoM analysis in the GA optimization is carried out.**

Keywords—genetic algorithm, method-of-moments, power divider/combiner, slot arrays

I. Introduction

The genetic algorithm (GA), a powerful global optimization technique, has been employed in numerous electromagnetics applications [1, 2]. The GA in conjunction with a full wave electromagnetic analysis, e.g., MoM, can provide accurate and optimum designs. In GA, we used a population size of 10, a mutation probability of 0.1, a crossover probability of 0.5 with uniform crossover, 7 bits per variable, and tournament selection. The best individual was replicated into the next generation. In this paper, we provide a brief review of some examples of GA-MoM optimizations of waveguide power dividers and slot array antennas. Further details will be discussed in the conference.

II. Power Divider

A one to 25 way waveguide power divider shown in Fig. 1, used as a power combiner also, is employed in distributed power amplifiers. Using the scattering wave representation of each coupler an initial design was carried out.

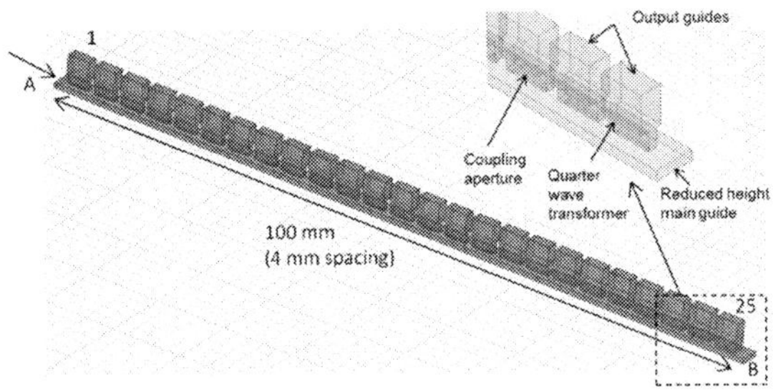

Fig. 1. Geometry of the 1 to 25 way power divider (reproduced from [3]).

A MoM analysis of the entire power divider so designed showed excellent characteristics over the frequency range of 71-77 GHz. The return loss was better than 30 dB, the load power was less than 7%, and the efficiency of a back to back connected power divider/combiner was better than 86%. The coupling phase was nearly linear while the coupling amplitude varied between +1.5 dB and -4.5 dB from the ideal uniform distribution. A GA optimization exercise in conjunction with the full wave moment method analysis of the power divider helped reduce the amplitude variation substantially as shown in Fig. 2 [3]. The load power and the divider/combiner efficiency of the GA design are shown in Figs. 3 and 4 respectively. Excellent agreement between results computed by MoM and the commercial code HFSS is noted.

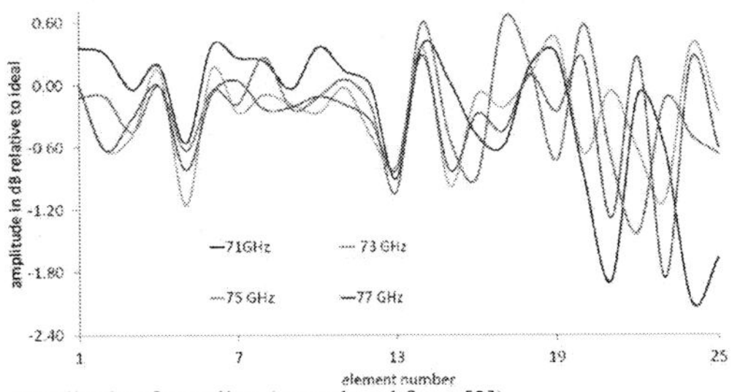

Fig. 2. Amplitude of coupling (reproduced from [3]).

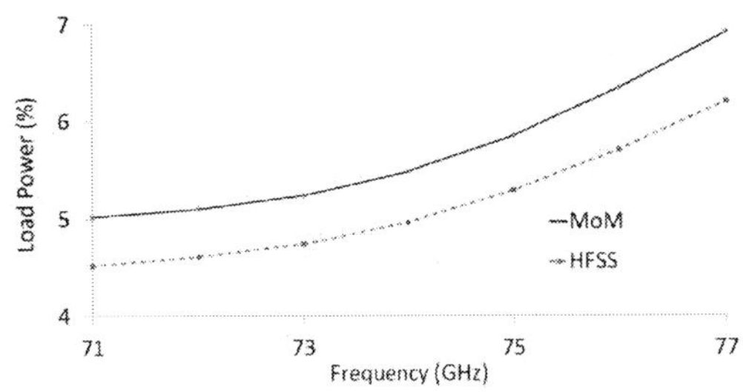

Fig. 3. Load power versus frequency (reproduced from [3]).

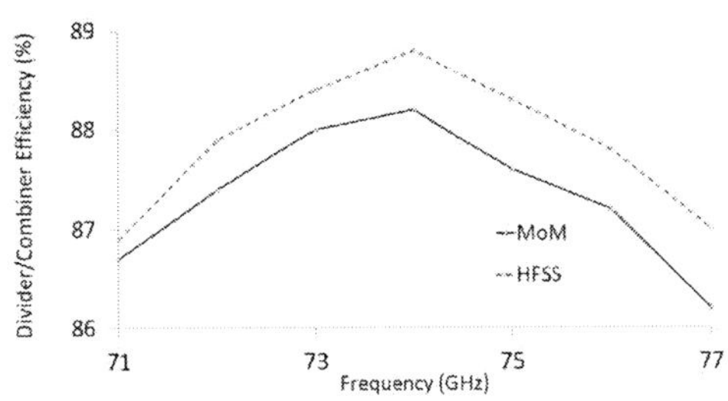

Fig. 4. Efficiency of the power divider/combiner (reproduced from [3]).

III. A TRAVELING WAVE LINEAR ARRAY

Fig. 5 shows a linear array of slots, all cut on one side of the centerline of a broad wall of a rectangular waveguide. The radiated beam of this array points at an angle θ_0 from the waveguide axis given by (1).

$$\theta_0 = \cos^{-1}(\beta / k_0), \tag{1}$$

where β / k_0 is the phase constant of the TE_{10} mode in the waveguide normalized to the free space wavenumber. A 21-element array was designed to have a 30-dB Chebyshev aperture distribution using the scattering wave model for each radiating slot. While the radiation characteristics and the return loss of the array were excellent, the power dissipated in the load became substantial especially away from the design frequency. The GA-MoM optimization improved the performance of the array by reducing the power dissipated in the load [4]. Fig. 6 shows the power dissipated in the load in the original design and the GA optimized design (denoted as GA3). In the MoM analysis only one basis function is used instead of nine and equivalence between the two models allows accurate design optimization [5]. Fig. 7 shows the H-plane pattern of the original design using the scattering matrix representation of each slot and the GA optimized design. GA design produces lower sidelobes.

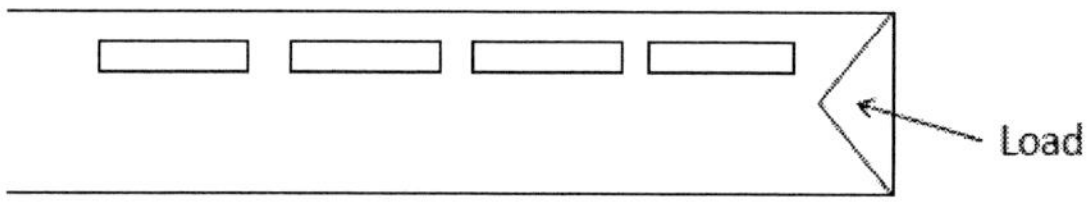

Fig. 5. A linear array of traveling wave slot array.

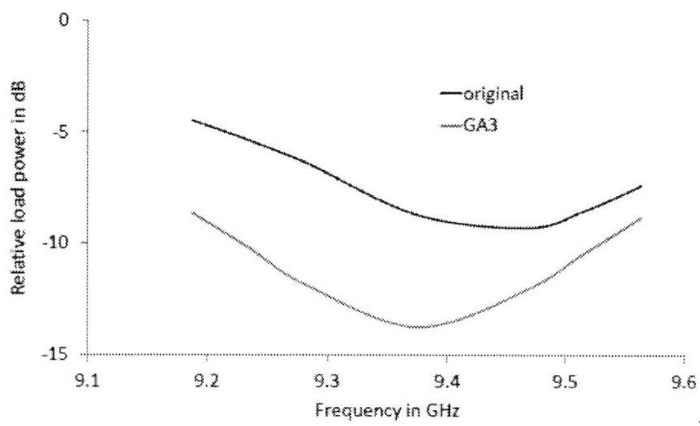

Fig. 6. Power dissipated in the load relative to the incident wave power.

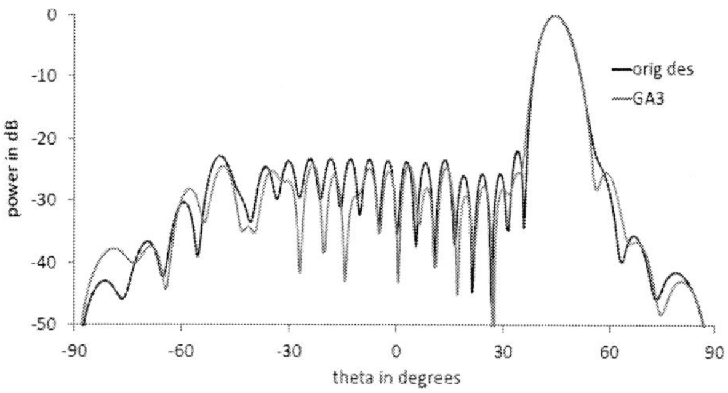

Fig. 7. H-plane pattern of a 21-element array.

IV. OPTIMIZATION OF A PLANAR SLOT ARRAY

A planar standing wave array consisting of 8x10 slots (8 radiating waveguides, each containing ten radiating slots) was first designed by the Elliott's method [6]. Subsequently a GA-MoM optimization technique was used to maximize the gain of the array over a 5% bandwidth as seen in Fig. 8. GA optimization was used in conjunction with the mode matching technique to achieve a good return loss. Such an exercise produced better than -15 dB reflection coefficient over 7% bandwidth as seen in Fig. 9. The MoM analysis used in the GA optimization employed only one basis function and accurate design results were obtained by using equivalence between models using a single basis function and multiple basis functions as mentioned in Section III [5].

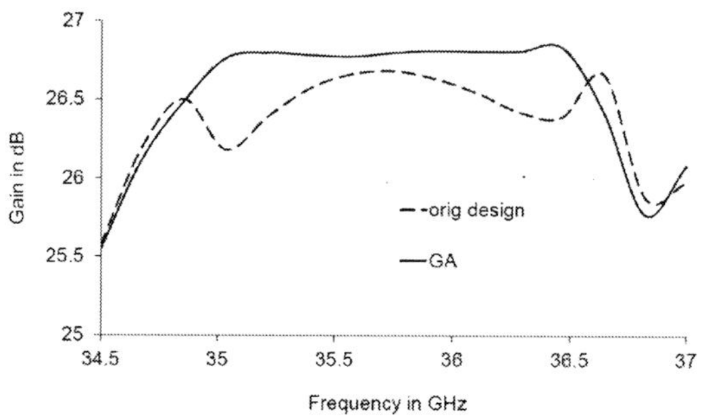

Fig. 8. Computed gain versus frequency for the original design and GA-MoM design (reproduced from [5]).

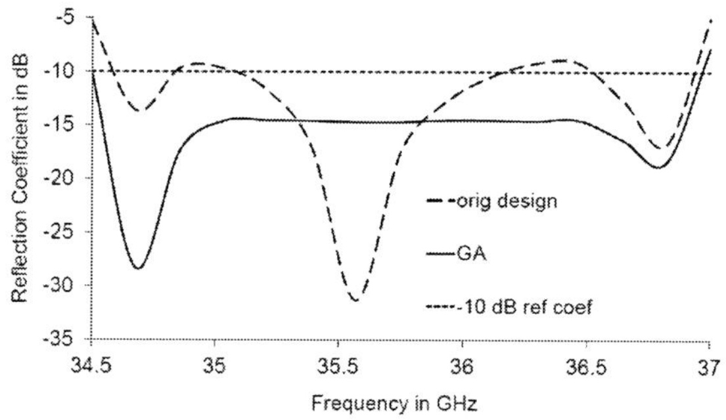

Fig. 9. Computed reflection coefficient versus frequency for the original design and GA-MoM design (reproduced from [5]).

REFERENCES

[1] D. Goldberg, Genetic Algorithms in Search, Optimization and Machine Learning, Reading, MA, Addison-Wesley, 1989.

[2] R. Haupt, and D. H. Werner, Genetic Algorithms in Electromagnetics, Hoboken, NJ: Wiley-IEEE Press; 2007.

[3] S. R. Rengarajan and J. J. Lynch, "Design of high efficiency traveling wave power combiners," IEEE Trans. Micowave Theory Tech., vol. 63, pp. 3981-87, Dec. 2015.

[4] S. R. Rengarajan, "Genetic algorithm optimization of traveling wave slot arrays using full wave method of moments analysis," URSI General Assembly and Scientific Symposium, Montreal, Canada, Aug. 2017.

[5] S. R. Rengarajan, "Genetic algorithm optimization of a planar slot array using full wave method of moments analysis," International Journal of Computer Aided RF and Microwave Engineering, vol. 23, Issue 4, pp. 430-436, July 2013.

[6] R. S. Elliott, The Design of Waveguide-Fed Slot Arrays Chapter 12, Antenna Handbook, (Y. T. Lo and S. W. Lee, Eds.), Van Nostrand Reinhold, New York, 1988.

Uniform Sampling Procedure for Constrained Surrogate Modeling of Antenna Structures

Slawomir Koziel[1,2] and Ari T. Sigurðsson[1]

[1] School of Science and Engineering, Reykjavik University, Reykjavik, Iceland, koziel@ru.is, arisl4@ru.is
[2] Faculty of Electronics, Telecommunications and Informatics, Gdansk University of Technology, 80-233 Gdansk, Poland

***Abstract*—A procedure for uniform sampling in constrained domains is proposed. It is used to generate training data for construction of fast surrogate models of antenna structures with the region of interest defined by a set of reference designs optimized w.r.t. selected figures of interest. To set up the domain, the reference designs are triangulated and the resulting simplexes are extended in orthogonal directions. We demonstrate that the proposed technique provides significantly more uniform sample distribution than rudimentary random sampling, which leads to improved predictive power of the surrogate model. Our considerations are illustrated using a uniplanar dual-band dipole antenna.**

Keywords — antenna design, EM-driven design, constrained domain, surrogate modeling, uniform sampling.

I. Introduction

Fast surrogate models are indispensable in reducing the cost of simulation-driven design of antenna structures. Construction of such models is typically based on approximating sampled EM simulation data using kriging [1], neural networks [2], support vector regression [3], etc. Due to curse of dimensionality, practical use of such techniques is limited to design spaces with a few independent parameters and limited parameter ranges [2]-[4].

As indicated in [5], focusing the modeling process on a vicinity of a reference set consisting of designs optimized with respect to selected figures of interest (e.g., operating frequencies, material parameters of the substrate, etc.) allows for significant reduction of the model domain volume. Consequently, the surrogate model can be established even for higher-dimensional spaces and for wider ranges of parameter variation [5]. A practical problem is allocation of the training samples. In [5], this was done by generating samples within the hypercube containing the model domain and accepting those that are in the domain. Clearly, this results in a rather non-uniform sample distribution.

In this paper, a generalized version of constrained modeling is discussed along with a sampling procedure that allows for obtaining uniform allocation of the training data. As demonstrated using a dual-band dipole antenna example, this leads to improved predictive power of the surrogate as compared to the rudimentary random sampling of [5].

II. Performance-Driven Surrogate Modeling

We denote by F_k, $k = 1, \ldots, N$, the performance figures of interest considered for a given structure (e.g., operating frequencies). In the first step, p reference designs are found, $\boldsymbol{x}^{(j)}$, $j = 1, \ldots, p$, by optimizing the antenna for selected values $\boldsymbol{F}^{(j)} = [F_1^{(j)} \ldots F_N^{(j)}]$. Then, Delaunay triangulation [6] is used to create simplexes $S^{(k)} = \{\boldsymbol{x}^{(k.1)},\ldots, \boldsymbol{x}^{(k.N+1)}\}$, $k = 1, \ldots, N_S$, where $\boldsymbol{x}^{(k.j)} \in \{\boldsymbol{x}^{(1)}, \ldots, \boldsymbol{x}^{(N)}\}$, $j = 1, \ldots, N + 1$, are vertices (cf. Fig. 1).

Let M be a manifold defined as:

$$M = \bigcup_k \{y = \sum_{j=1}^{N+1} \alpha_j \boldsymbol{x}^{(k.j)} : 0 \le \alpha_j \le 1, \sum_{j=1}^{N+1} \alpha_j = 1\}\cdot \qquad (1)$$

Consider an arbitrary point z and its projection $P_k(z)$ onto the hyper-plane H_k containing the simplex $S^{(k)}$. Let $\boldsymbol{x}^{(0)} = \boldsymbol{x}^{(k.1)}$ and $\boldsymbol{v}^{(j)} = \boldsymbol{x}^{(k.j+1)} - \boldsymbol{x}^{(0)}$, $j = 1, \ldots, N$. The projection $P_k(z)$ is determined by expansion coefficients $\bar{\alpha}^{(j)}$ obtained by solving:

$$\arg \min_{[\bar{\alpha}^{(1)},\ldots,\bar{\alpha}^{(N)}]} \left\| z - \left[\boldsymbol{x}^{(0)} + \sum_{j=1}^{N} \bar{\alpha}^{(j)} \bar{\boldsymbol{v}}^{(j)}\right] \right\|^2 \cdot \qquad (2)$$

Vectors $\bar{\boldsymbol{v}}^{(j)}$ are obtained by orthogonalization: $\bar{\boldsymbol{v}}^{(1)} = \boldsymbol{v}^{(1)}$, $\bar{\boldsymbol{v}}^{(2)} = \boldsymbol{v}^{(2)} - a_{12}\boldsymbol{v}^{(1)}$ where $a_{12} = \boldsymbol{v}^{(1)T}\boldsymbol{v}^{(2)}/(\boldsymbol{v}^{(1)T}\boldsymbol{v}^{(1)})$, etc. We have:

$$\bar{\boldsymbol{V}} = \left[\bar{\boldsymbol{v}}^{(1)}\ \bar{\boldsymbol{v}}^{(2)}\ \ldots \bar{\boldsymbol{v}}^{(N)}\right] = \left[\boldsymbol{v}^{(1)}\ \boldsymbol{v}^{(2)}\ \ldots \boldsymbol{v}^{(N)}\right]\boldsymbol{A}, \qquad (3)$$

where $\boldsymbol{A}$ is an upper-triangular matrix. We also have

$$\left[\bar{\alpha}^{(1)} \ldots \bar{\alpha}^{(N)}\right]^T = (\bar{\boldsymbol{V}}^T\bar{\boldsymbol{V}})^{-1}\bar{\boldsymbol{V}}(z - \boldsymbol{x}^{(0)}), \qquad (4)$$

whereas the expansion coefficients $\alpha^{(j)}$ of z w.r.t. $\boldsymbol{v}^{(j)}$ are:

$$\left[\alpha^{(1)} \ldots \alpha^{(N)}\right]^T = \boldsymbol{A}\left[\bar{\alpha}^{(1)} \ldots \bar{\alpha}^{(N)}\right]^T \qquad (5)$$

Clearly, $P_k(z) \in S^{(k)}$ if and only if $\alpha^{(j)} \ge 0$ for $j = 1, \ldots, N$, and $\alpha^{(1)} + \ldots + \alpha^{(N)} \le 1$. Let $\boldsymbol{x}_{\max} = \max\{\boldsymbol{x}^{(k)}, k = 1, \ldots, p\}$ and $\boldsymbol{x}_{\min} = \min\{\boldsymbol{x}^{(k)}, k = 1, \ldots, p\}$; the vector $\boldsymbol{dx} = \boldsymbol{x}_{\max} - \boldsymbol{x}_{\min}$ determines the range of variation of the antenna parameters within M.

The surrogate model domain X_S is defined as follows: given a user-defined parameter $d_{\max}$, a point $\boldsymbol{y} \in X_S$ if and only if,

1. Set $K(y) = \{k \in \{1, \ldots, N_S\} : P_k(y) \in S^{(k)}\} \neq \varnothing$;
2. $\min\{\|y - P_k(y)\|/\|\boldsymbol{dx}\| : k \in K(y)\} \le d_{\max}$, where // denotes component-wise division.

In other words, $\boldsymbol{y}$ has to be "within" the manifold M the "tangential" sense, and it has to be close to M in the "orthogonal" sense (measured in relation to $\boldsymbol{dx}$).

It should be noted that the volume of X_S is significantly smaller than the volume of the interval $[\boldsymbol{x}_{\min}, \boldsymbol{x}_{\max}]$ so that building the surrogate in X_S will require less data samples. At the same time, the designs of interest (i.e., optimal w.r.t. the selected figures of interest) will be either in X_S or close to it.

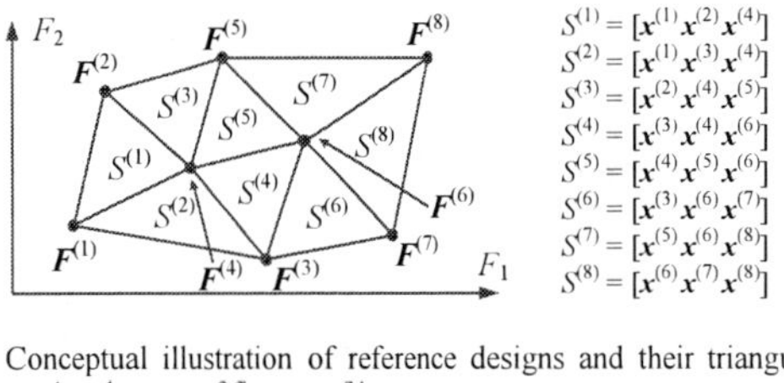

Fig. 1. Conceptual illustration of reference designs and their triangulation in two-dimensional space of figures of interest.

III. Uniform Sampling in Constrained Domain

The surrogate is constructed in the domain X_S. The simplest design of experiments method (cf. [5]) is pure random sampling in the interval $[\boldsymbol{x}_{\min}, \boldsymbol{x}_{\max}]$, accepting the samples that are within X_S, and continuing the process until the required number of samples, say, K, has been found. Here, an improved procedure is proposed that works as follows:

1. Calculate the volumes V_k of simplexes $S^{(k)}$;
2. Set $K_k = \lceil KV_k/\sum_j V_j \rceil$;
3. For each $k = 1, \ldots, N_S$:
   - Allocate mK_k LHS samples in a unit hypercube $[0, 1]^N$ and choose samples lying in the unit N-simplex;
   - Map the samples selected in the previous step onto convex hull of simplex $S^{(k)}$ as follows: $\boldsymbol{x} \rightarrow \boldsymbol{x}^{(0)} + \sum_j x_j \boldsymbol{v}^{(j)}$, where $\boldsymbol{x}^{(0)}$ and $\boldsymbol{v}^{(j)}$ are defined under (1), and $\boldsymbol{x} = [x_1 \ldots x_n]^T$;
   - Perturb the mapped samples by adding vectors $\boldsymbol{x}_d = \boldsymbol{r} - P_k(\boldsymbol{r})$, where $\boldsymbol{r}$ is a random vector in the interval $[-\boldsymbol{dx}, \boldsymbol{dx}]$, and $P_k(\boldsymbol{r})$ is a projection of $\boldsymbol{r}$ onto $S^{(k)}$ (cf. Section II).

Steps 1 and 2 of the above procedure aim at allocating the number of samples to particular simplexes according to their sizes. In Step 3, we first get the uniform sets of samples within unit simplexes (m is the volume ratio of the unit hypercube and simplex of appropriate dimension), then use the affine transformation to obtain uniform distributions on the simplexes. Finally, the samples are perturbed in orthogonal directions (w.r.t. the simplex spanning hyperplanes H_k) in order to fill in the domain X_S. Clearly, due to using a ceiling function in Step 2 as well as quasi-uniform distribution obtained by LHS, the actual (total) number of samples will be slightly different than the required number K but this can be easily corrected by adding/removing individual samples where necessary. Fig. 2 shows an example distribution obtained using the reference and the proposed sampling technique. For visualization, a low-dimensional example is illustrated.

IV. Case Study and Results

Consider a dual-band uniplanar dipole antenna shown in Fig. 3 [7], implemented on Taconic RF-35 ($\varepsilon_r = 3.5$, $h = 0.762$ mm). The structure consists of two ground plane slits interconnected through a thick slot. It is fed by a 50 Ohm CPW. The variables are: $\boldsymbol{x} = [l_1\ l_2\ l_3\ w_1\ w_2\ w_3]^T$, whereas $l_0 = 30$, $w_0 = 3$, $s_0 = 0.15$ and $o = 5$ are fixed (all dimensions in mm). The EM antenna model $\boldsymbol{R}$ is simulated in CST.

The goal is to model the antenna for the following ranges of operating frequencies 2.0 GHz $\leq f_1 \leq$ 4.0 GHz (lower band), and 4.5 GHz $\leq f_2 \leq$ 6.5 GHz (upper band). We choose 12 reference designs, optimized for the operating frequencies $\{f_1,f_2\}$ [GHz]: {2.0,4.6}, {2.1,5.9}, {2.2,6.2}, {2.4,5.0}, {2.8,4.6}, {2.8,5.4}, {3.0,6.0}, {3.1,6.5}, {3.4,4.8}, {3.8,5.4}, {3.9,5.8}, {4.0,6.4}. The lower and upper bounds for design variables were set using the reference designs as $\boldsymbol{l} = [25.0\ 6.0\ 14.0\ 0.2\ 1.6\ 0.5]^T$, and $\boldsymbol{u} = [35.0\ 15.0\ 21.0\ 0.55\ 4.0\ 2.0]^T$. The surrogate model has been constructed using 100, 200, and 500 training samples, using constrained surrogate of Section II with random sampling and then with uniform sampling of Section III. Unconstrained sampling in the interval $[\boldsymbol{x}_{\min}, \boldsymbol{x}_{\max}]$ has also been carried out for comparison. Table I gathers the modeling errors (average RMS error estimated using 30-fold cross-validation).

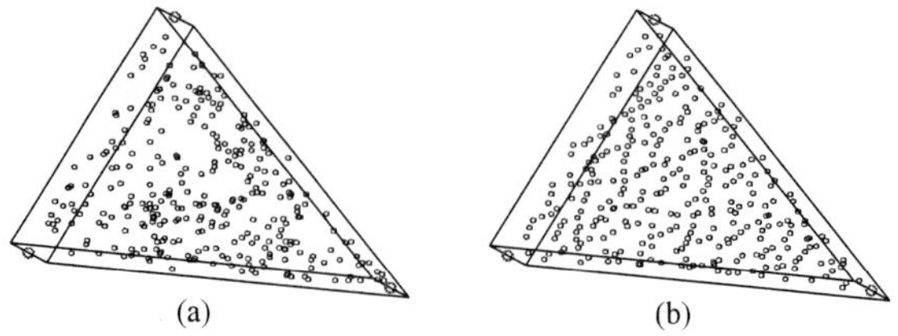

Fig. 2. Sampling on constrained domain spanned by a set of reference designs: (a) random sampling, and (b) proposed uniform sampling.

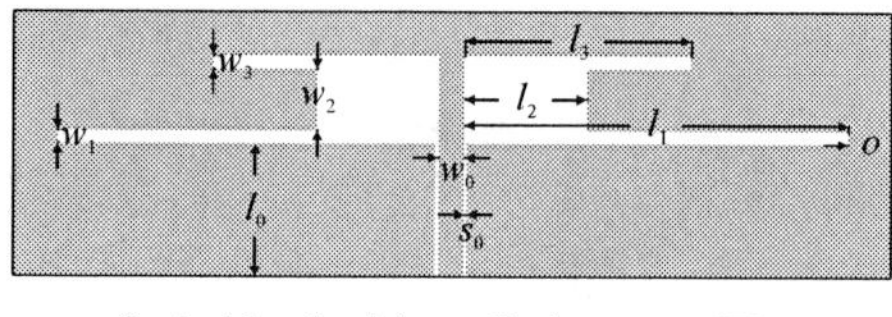

Fig. 3. Geometry of a dual-band uniplanar dipole antenna [7].

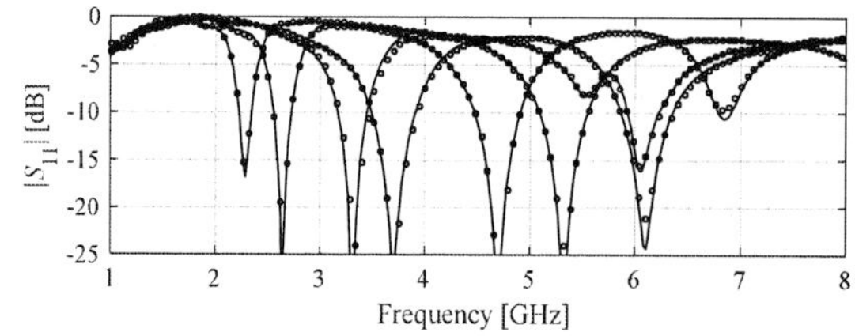

Fig. 4. Responses of the antenna of Fig. 3 at the selected test designs for N = 500: high-fidelity EM model (—), constrained surrogate with uniform sampling (o).

TABLE I. Surrogate Model Accuracy

Number of Training Samples	Average RMS Error		
	Unconstrained Surrogate	Constrained Surrogate (Random Sampling)	Constrained Surrogate (Uniform Sampling)
100	15.6 %	7.7 %	4.8 %
200	11.7 %	4.6 %	3.7 %
500	7.8 %	3.2 %	2.5 %

It can be observed that utilization of the proposed uniform sampling results in significant accuracy improvement, particularly for small number of training samples. Fig. 4 shows the surrogate model responses at the selected test designs.

Acknowledgment

This work is partially supported by the Icelandic Centre for Research (RANNIS) Grant 163299051 and by National Science Centre of Poland Grant 2015/17/B/ST6/01857.

References

[1] N. V. Queipo, R. T. Haftka, W. Shyy, T. Goel, R. Vaidynathan, and P. K. Tucker, "Surrogate-based analysis and optimization," *Progress in Aerospace Sciences*, vol. 41, no. 1, pp. 1-28, Jan. 2005.

[2] G. Gosal, E. Almajali, D. McNamara, and M. Yagoub, "Transmitarray antenna design using forward and inverse neural network modeling," *IEEE Ant. Wireless Prop. Lett.*, vol. 15, no. 1, pp. 1483-1486, 2016.

[3] J. P. Jacobs, S. Koziel, and S. Ogurtsov, "Computationally efficient multi-fidelity Bayesian support vector regression modeling of planar antenna input characteristics," *IEEE Trans. Ant. Prop.*, vol. 61, no. 2, pp. 980-984, 2013.

[4] S. Ulaganathan, S. Koziel, A. Bekasiewicz, I. Couckuyt, E. Laermans, and T. Dhaene, "Cost-efficient modeling of antenna structures using gradient-enhanced kriging," *Loughborough Ant. Prop. Conf. (LAPC)*, pp. 1-5, 2015.

[5] S. Koziel, "Low-cost data-driven surrogate modeling of antenna structures by constrained sampling," *IEEE Ant. Wireless Prop. Lett.*, vol. 16, pp. 461-464, 2017.

[6] H. Borouchaki, P. L. George, and S. H. Lo, "Optimal Delaunay point insertion," *Int. J. Num. Methods in Eng.*, vol. 39, no. 20, pp. 3407-3437, 1996.

[7] Y.-C. Chen, S.-Y. Chen, and P. Hsu, "Dual-band slot dipole antenna fed by a coplanar waveguide," *IEEE Int. Symp. Ant. Prop.*, pp. 3589-3592, 2006.

Novel Structure and EM-Driven Design of Miniaturized Microstrip Rat-Race Coupler

Adrian Bekasiewicz[1,2] and Slawomir Koziel[1,2]

[1] School of Science and Engineering, Reykjavik University, Reykjavik, Iceland
bekasiewicz@ru.is, koziel@ru.is

[2] Faculty of Electronics, Telecommunications and Informatics, Gdansk University of Technology, 80-233 Gdansk, Poland

***Abstract*—In this paper, a novel structure and design procedure of a miniaturized microstrip rat-race coupler (RRC) is described. Small size of the RRC is achieved by folding the transmission lines of the conventional circuit into its interior, as well as by implementation of the structure on three layers. The final size of the coupler realized for the operating frequency of 1 GHz is only 220 mm^2, which gives over 95% footprint reduction w.r.t. a reference RRC. At the same time, rigorous optimization of coupler dimensions using variable-fidelity EM models permits rapid EM-driven design closure with the final design featuring 240 MHz bandwidth, equal power split, and obtained at the computational cost corresponding to only 12 simulations of the circuit at the high-fidelity level.**

Keywords—compact couplers, design optimization, EM-driven design, rat-race couplers.

I. Introduction

Rat-race couplers (RRCs) are important components of many microwave systems. Conventional RRCs, implemented in microstrip technology, are characterized by large footprints which limit their usefulness for modern applications such as portable or wearable devices. At the same time, size reduction of couplers is a challenging task, because small dimensions stay in conflict with maintaining required circuit performance [1]-[4]. Size reduction is often achieved through topological modifications of the coupler structure. Popular approaches include replacing transmission line sections by compact microstrip resonant cells or defected ground structures [4], [5]. Alternatively, the footprint can be reduced by folding transmission lines to the interior of the RRC [6]. Such geometrical changes allow for obtaining small dimensions along with acceptable performance. However, the resulting structures have complex geometries with multiple cross-couplings. Therefore, electromagnetic (EM) simulations are required for reliable evaluation of their performance.

In this work, a novel topology of a miniaturized RRC has been proposed. Small footprint of the circuit have been achieved by folding its transmission lines. Further size reduction has been obtained by implementing its 180 degree section on a separate layer connected to the remaining part of the circuit through viaholes. The final design is eleven times smaller compared to the conventional RRC structure and around 50% smaller compared to a single-layer compact design. At the same time, the structure features 24% bandwidth and equal power-split for the center frequency of 1 GHz. Low RRC design cost, corresponding to only to about 12 simulations of the high-fidelity model, has been achieved using variable-fidelity EM simulation models.

II. Proposed RRC Structure

Consider a hybrid RRC shown in Fig. 1. The circuit is implemented on a Taconic RF-35 dielectric substrate ($\varepsilon_r = 3.5$, $h = 0.762$ mm, $\tan\delta = 0.018$). Compact structure dimensions are achieved by folding its 70.7-ohm sections to the interior (cf. Fig. 1 (a)). For further size reduction, its 180 degree section has been implemented on a separate layer and connected to the remaining part of the circuit through viaholes (cf. Fig. 1 (b)). This modification allows for reducing size by about 50% compared to the planar implementation of the RRC. The design parameters of the three-layer circuit are: $\boldsymbol{x} = [l_1, l_2, l_3, d, w]^T$, whereas dimensions $r = 0.3$ (diameter of the viaholes) and $w_0 = 1.7$ (width of the input ports) remain fixed. The unit for all parameters is mm. The operating frequency is set to 1 GHz. The lower and upper bounds are set to $\boldsymbol{l} = [2, 2, 6, 0.2, 0.3]^T$ and $\boldsymbol{u} = [10, 15, 20, 1, 1.2]^T$.

The high-fidelity model $\boldsymbol{R}_f$ of the three-layer coupler (cf. Fig. 1 (b)) consists of ~200,000 tetrahedral mesh cells and its typical evaluation time on a dual Intel Xeon E5540 machine is 10 min. The coarsely-discretized planar realization of the structure (cf. Fig. 1 (a)) is used in the design process as the low-fidelity model $\boldsymbol{R}_c$ (~20,000 tetrahedrons; simulation time: 130 s). Both models are implemented in CST Microwave Studio and evaluated using its FEM solver.

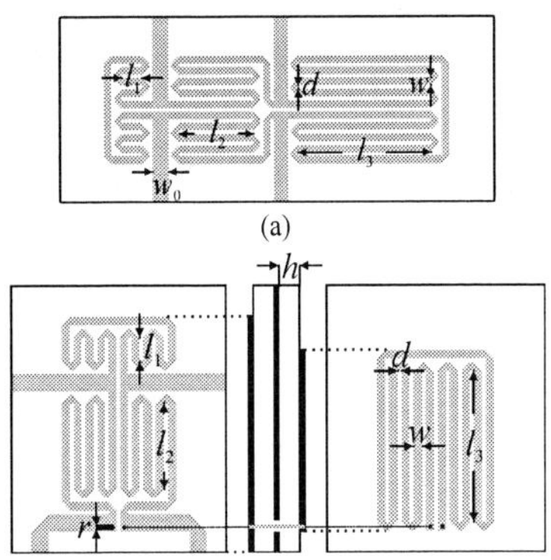

Fig. 1. Topology evolution of the proposed RRC: (a) folded structure and (b) three-layer implementation of the coupler. Viaholes are marked using black circles.

III. Design Optimization Methodology

Design closure of the proposed RRC is conducted with the aim of obtaining the best possible electrical performance parameters, in particular (here, S_{11}, S_{21}, S_{31} and S_{41} stands for matching, transmission, coupling and isolation, respectively; f_0 is the operating frequency; $\boldsymbol{x}$ is a vector of geometry parameters of the RRC):

- Minimization of $S_{max} = \max(\min\{S_{11}(\boldsymbol{x}),S_{41}(\boldsymbol{x})\})$ at f_0;
- Obtaining equal power split at f_0, $d_S = |S_{21}(\boldsymbol{x}) - S_{31}(\boldsymbol{x})| = 0$;
- Ensuring that $f_{S11}(\boldsymbol{x})$ and $f_{S41}(\boldsymbol{x})$, i.e., the frequencies realizing minimum of $S_{11}(\boldsymbol{x})$ and $S_{41}(\boldsymbol{x})$, respectively, are as close to f_0 as possible.

In order to take into account all of these goals the following objective function is minimized:

$$U(\boldsymbol{x}) = \max(\min\{S_{11}(\boldsymbol{x}),S_{41}(\boldsymbol{x})\}) + \beta_1\left(\max\{(d_S-\varepsilon)/\varepsilon,0\}\right)^2 + \beta_{f1}\left|(f_{S_{11,f}}(\boldsymbol{x})-f_0)/f_0\right|^2 + \beta_{f2}\left|(f_{S_{41,f}}(\boldsymbol{x})-f_0)/f_0\right|^2 \quad (1)$$

Obtaining possibly equal power split, as well as allocating the minima of return loss and isolation characteristics at the operating frequencies are enforced by the appropriate penalty terms. The coefficients β_1, β_{f1}, and β_{f2} are all set to 10^3.

The objective function (1) is minimized using a trust-region gradient search [7] of the form:

$$\boldsymbol{x}^{(i+1)} = \arg \max_{\boldsymbol{x},\,||\boldsymbol{x}-\boldsymbol{x}^{(i)}||\le\delta^{(i)}} L^{(i)}(\boldsymbol{x}), \quad (2)$$

where $\boldsymbol{x}^{(i)}$, i = 0, 1, …, is a sequence approximating the optimum design $\boldsymbol{x}^*$, whereas $L^{(i)}$ is an auxiliary objective function at iteration i, with high-fidelity-simulated S-parameters replaced by their local linear approximation models (first-order Taylor expansions). In order to reduce the CPU cost of the optimization process, S-parameter Jacobians are estimated using low-fidelity EM coupler model, which is a circuit of Fig. 1 (a) with coarser discretization.

IV. Results

The initial design of the coupler of Fig. 1 (b) is set to $\boldsymbol{x}_0$=[4.2, 4.5, 16.9, 0.2, 0.6]^T. The final design $\boldsymbol{x}^*$ = [2.7, 8.75, 14.2, 0.45, 0.8]^T has been obtained after only a few iterations of (2). The size of the optimized structure is 11.7 × 18.8 = 220 mm^2 which is over 11-fold smaller compared to conventional RRC design implemented at RF-35 substrate (47.5 × 95.5 = 4536 mm^2) [2]. Fig. 2 shows response characteristics of the RRC at the initial and final designs. The detailed performance figures of the proposed coupler are shown in Table I. For the optimized design, the bandwidth BW_1, defined as the frequency range where both $|S_{11}|$ and $|S_{41}|$ are below –20 dB, is 24%. At the same time bandwidth BW_2, defined as a range where $d_S \le 0.2$ dB, is 20%.

The proposed structure has been compared with other state-of-the-art RRC structures in terms of the bandwidth BW_1 and size reduction (expressed in terms of the guided wavelength λ_g defined for the center frequency and the given substrate properties). The results shown in Table II indicate that the proposed structure provides the highest miniaturization rate while ensuring competitive bandwidth compared to remaining RRCs.

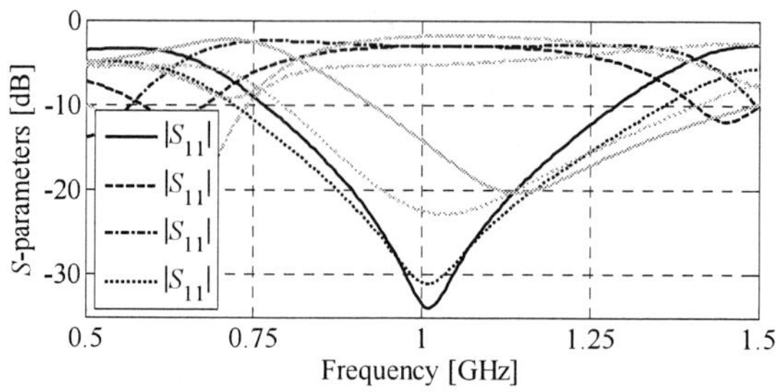

Fig. 2. S-parameter responses of the proposed RRC at the initial (gray) and final (black) designs.

TABLE I. Performance Figures of the Proposed RRC

Obtained w.r.t. f_0							
$\lvert S_{11}\rvert$ [dB]	$\lvert S_{21}\rvert$ [dB]	$\lvert S_{31}\rvert$ [dB]	$\lvert S_{41}\rvert$ [dB]	d_S [dB]	BW_1 [MHz]	BW_2 [MHz]	$\angle(S_{21} - S_{31})$ [°]
–33.4	–3.01	–3.07	–31.0	0.06	240	200	0

TABLE II. Comparison with State-of-the-Art RRCs

Coupler	Bandwidth [%]	Dimensions [mm × mm]	Effective λ_g	Size reduction [%]*
Design [1]	16.8	22.4 × 22.4	0.14 × 0.14	85.8
Design [2]	20.2	22.8 × 17.0	0.13 × 0.09	91.5
Design [3]	15.1	6.67 × 52.5	0.04 × 0.28	92.2
Design [4]	25.6	14.9 × 26.3	0.07 × 0.13	93.4
This work	24.0	11.7 × 18.8	0.06 × 0.10	95.2

* w.r.t. conventional RRC (effective λ_g: 0.26 × 0.53, size: 4536 mm^2) [2].

The computational cost of the design optimization corresponds to 12.3 simulations of the high-fidelity model $\boldsymbol{R}_f$ (~2 hours) and includes 43 evaluations of the low-fidelity model $\boldsymbol{R}_c$ and 3 $\boldsymbol{R}_f$ model simulations. For the sake of comparison, a high-fidelity model of the RRC of Fig. 1 (b) has been directly optimized using algorithm of [7]. The final design has been obtained after 26 model evaluations, over 50 percent more compared to optimization using procedure of Section III.

Acknowledgment

This work is partially supported by the Icelandic Centre for Research (RANNIS) Grant 163299051 and by National Science Centre of Poland Grant 2014/15/B/ST7/04683.

References

[1] J. Wang, B.-Z. Wang, Y. X. Guo, L. C. Ong, and S. Xiao, "Compact slow-wave microstrip rat-race ring coupler," El. Lett., vol. 43, no. 2, pp. 111-113, 2007.
[2] A. Bekasiewicz and P. Kurgan, "A compact microstrip rat-race coupler constituted by nonuniform transmission lines," Microwave Opt. Tech. Lett., vol. 56, no. 4, pp. 970-974, 2014.
[3] S. Koziel, A. Bekasiewicz, and P. Kurgan, "Rapid multi-objective simulation-driven design of compact microwave circuits," IEEE Microwave Wireless Comp. Lett., vol. 25, no. 5, pp. 277-279, 2015.
[4] C. H. Tseng and C. L. Chang, "A rigorous design methodology for compact planar branch-line and rat-race couplers with asymmetrical T-structures," *IEEE Trans. Microwave Theory Techn.*, vol. 60, no. 7, pp. 2085-2092, July 2012.
[5] W. Song, H. Deguchi, and M. Tsuji, "A novel heptagonal microstrip rat-race hybrid coupler with harmonic suppression and size reduction," IEEE Int. Symp. Ant. Prop., pp. 1-2, 2012.
[6] A. Bekasiewicz and S. Koziel, "Miniaturised dual-band branch-line coupler," Electronics Lett., vol. 51, no. 10, pp. 769-771, 2015.
[7] S. Koziel and A. Bekasiewicz, "Expedited simulation-driven design optimization of UWB antennas by means of response features," Int. J. RF Microwave CAE, vol. 27, no. 6, pp. 1-8, 2017.

Coplanar Waveguide-based Lowpass Filters with Non-uniform Signal Trace and Ground Planes

Qizhen Li and Khair Al Shamaileh
Electrical and Computer Engineering Department
Purdue University Northwest
Hammond 46323, IN, USA
li2234@pnw.edu

Vijay Devabhaktuni
Electrical Engineering and Computer Science Department
The University of Toledo
Toledo 43606, OH, USA
Vijay.Devabhaktuni@utoledo.edu

***Abstract*—In this paper, we propose a new and systematic methodology for the design of a coplanar waveguide (CPW) low pass filter (LPF). The widths of the signal trace and adjacent ground planes are continuously varied based on an optimization process to obtain predefined electrical characteristics taking into account physical constraints. A non-uniform CPW LPF with a 3.5 GHz cutoff frequency is designed, analytically verified, and simulated. Simulation results show input port matching, S_{11}, better than –10 dB and transmission parameter, S_{21}, in the order of –0.2 dB in the passband.**

Keywords—coplanar waveguide (CPW), low pass filter (LPF), non-uniform.

I. INTRODUCTION

Coplanar waveguide (CPW) technology, introduced in [1], has many advantages over other wave-carrying media (e.g., microstrip lines), such as the low transmission losses and the convenient series and parallel mounting of passive and active devices without substrate drilling [2, 3]. As a result, the design of CPW-based front-ends such as lowpass filters (LPF) has been widely addressed in recent research. In [4], a CPW LPF was designed based on cascading asymmetric LPF unit cells and dumbbell defected ground structures. The resulting design was compact with an extended stopband to seven times the cutoff frequency. In [5], a CPW LPF was obtained by incorporating open stubs. The resulting design exhibited passband ripple in the range of 1.5 dB and a stopband rejection better than 45 dB. In [6], stepped impedance resonators etched on the bottom of the substrate were used to design a LPF. The measured stopband rejection was better than 30 dB up to 6.4 GHz, and a narrow transition band was obtained. However, substrate etching could cause more losses.

In this paper, a design of a CPW LPF is proposed by modulating the width profiles of the center conductor and the adjacent ground planes. The width of the signal trace is expressed as a truncated Fourier series expansion, and the series coefficients are determined based on an optimization-driven procedure, where optimum frequency matching at the passband, end terminations (i.e., impedance matching), and the minimum-maximum signal trace widths are addressed in the optimization process.

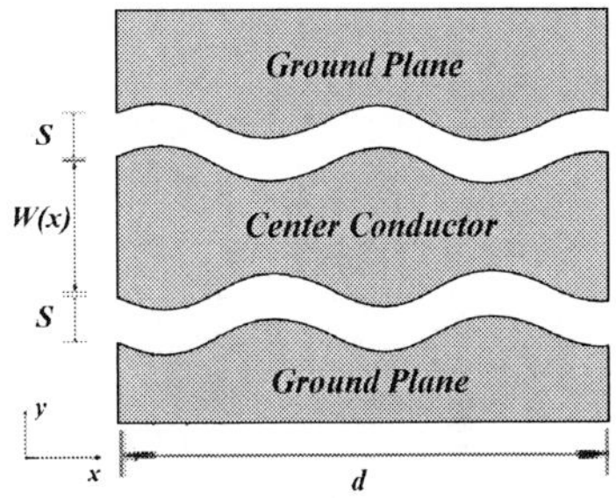

Fig. 1. Top view of the proposed CPW LPF.

II. DESIGN PROCEDURE

Fig. 1 shows a schematic diagram of the proposed CPW LPF. The non-uniform center conductor is subdivided into M short segments, each of a length Δx, and the $ABCD$ parameters of the ith (i=1, 2, ... M) segment is given as [7]:

$$\begin{bmatrix} A & B \\ C & D \end{bmatrix}_i = \begin{bmatrix} \cos\theta_i & jZ_i\sin\theta_i \\ (j/Z_i)\sin\theta_i & \cos\theta_i \end{bmatrix}, \tag{1}$$

where Z_i is the impedance of each segment, given as [2]:

$$Z_i = \frac{30\pi}{\sqrt{\varepsilon_{eff}}}\frac{K(k')}{K(k)}, \tag{2}$$

where $K(\cdot)$ is the complete elliptic integral of the first kind, $k'=(1-k^2)^{0.5}$, and ε_{eff} is the effective permittivity of the ith segment, which can be expressed as follows:

$$\varepsilon_{eff} = 1 + \frac{\varepsilon_r - 1}{2}\frac{K(k_1)}{K(k_1')}\frac{K(k')}{K(k)}, \tag{3}$$

where ε_r is the relative substrate permittivity. The parameters k and k_1 can be given as [2]:

$$k = \frac{W(x)}{W(x)+2S}, \tag{4a}$$

$$k_1 = \frac{\sinh\left[\pi W(x)/4h\right]}{\sinh\left\{\pi\left[W(x)+2S\right]/4h\right\}}, \tag{4b}$$

In (4), S represents the gap between the signal trace and adjacent ground planes, and h is the substrate thickness.

The electrical length of the ith segment, θ_i, is expressed as:

$$\theta_i = 2\pi\left(f\sqrt{\varepsilon_{eff}}/c\right)\Delta x, \quad (5)$$

The non-uniform width, $W(x)$ is expressed in terms of a truncated Fourier series expansion as follows:

$$W(x) = w_{ref}\exp\left\{c_0 + \sum_{n=0}^{N}\left[a_n\cos\left(\frac{2\pi nx}{d}\right) + b_n\sin\left(\frac{2\pi nx}{d}\right)\right]\right\}, \quad (6)$$

where w_{ref}, is a reference width, and d is the length of the transmission line. The N series coefficients, c_0, a_n, and b_n are set as optimization variables. The *ABCD* matrix of entire structure can be obtained by multiplying the *ABCD* matrices of all M segments. Then, the scattering parameters can be expressed in terms of the overall *ABCD* matrix as follows [7]:

$$S_{11} = \frac{A + B/Z_0 - CZ_0 - D}{A + B/Z_0 + CZ_0 + D}, \quad (7a)$$

$$S_{21} = \frac{2}{A + B/Z_0 + CZ_0 + D}, \quad (7b)$$

where Z_0 is the characteristic impedance of the input/output ports (set to 50-Ω to match the impedance of the end-termination connectors). In order for the CPW line to function as a LPF, the following error function is considered at each frequency stepsize, Δf=0.2GHz, in a frequency range $[0, f_{max}]$:

$$error = \begin{cases} \sqrt{|S_{11}|^2 + (|S_{21}| - 1)^2} & 0 \le f \le f_{cutoff} \\ \sqrt{(|S_{11}| - 1)^2 + |S_{21}|^2} & f_{cutoff} \le f \le f_{max} \end{cases} \quad (8)$$

where f_{cuoff} is the cutoff frequency of the designed LPF. Finally the summation of the errors at all frequencies is minimized subject to the following constraints that ensure physical matching and realization of practical widths:

$$W_{min} \le W(x) \le W_{max} \quad (9a)$$

$$W(0) = W(d) = W_{ref} \quad (9b)$$

To minimize this constrained non-linear optimization problem sequential quadrature programming is adopted.

III. Analytical and Simulated Results

A non-uniform CPW LPF is designed considering a 0.813 mm-thick RO4003C substrate with a dielectric constant of 3.55. The length of the LPF is set to 100mm; whereas the reference and gap widths are set to W_{ref}=2 mm and S=0.2 mm, respectively. The minimum and maximum widths are set to 10 mm and 0.2 mm, respectively. Fig. 2 shows the resulting optimized width profile of the non-uniform trace, which is in a good agreement with the predefined constraints. Analytical and simulated results of the *S*-parameters are shown in Fig. 3. Within the passband, the input port matching parameter, S_{11}, is below −10 dB, and the transmission parameter, S_{21}, is around –0.2 dB. At the predefined cutoff frequency (3.5 GHz), S_{21} gradually decreases to almost –20 dB. The discrepancies between the analytical and simulated results are due to different types of losses, (e.g., conductor, dielectric, and radiation losses).

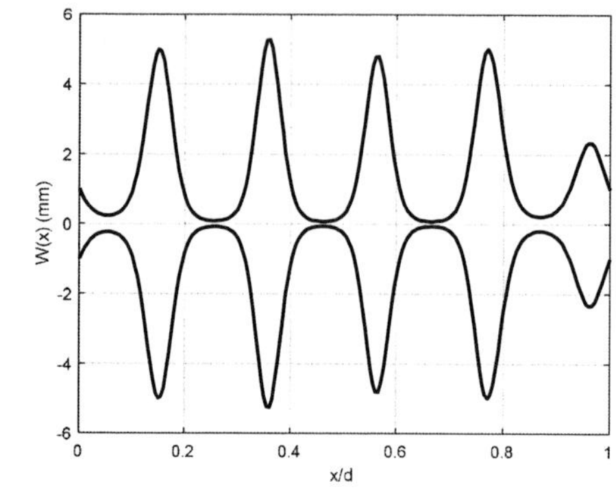

Fig. 2. Resulting optimized CPW LPF width profile.

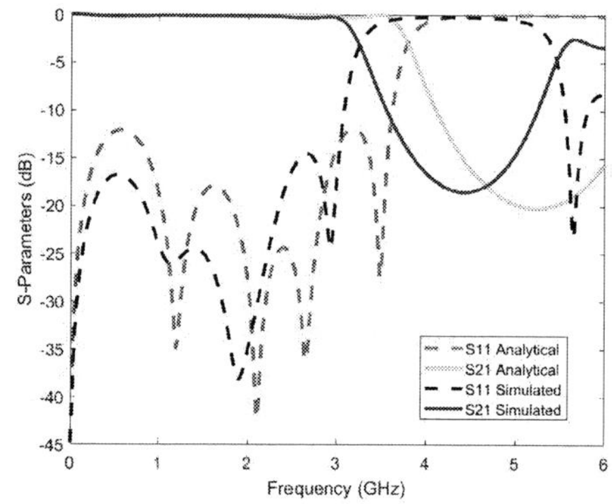

Fig. 3. *S*-parameters analytical and simulated results.

IV. Conclusion

A CPW LPF with non-uniform metallic traces is presented. Mathematical and theoretical analysis is established, optimized, and the resulting filter is simulated. Simulation results show input port matching better than −10 dB and transmission parameter in the order of –0.2 dB in the passband. This ongoing research aims to further enhance the electrical response at the stopband by applying different optimization techniques to tackle the high nonlinearity degree of the CPW structures resulting from the complete elliptic integral and its approximations.

References

[1] C. P. Wen, "Coplanar waveguide: A surface strip transmission line suitable for nonreciprocal gyromagnetic device applications," IEEE Trans. Microw. Theory Techn., vol. 17, no. 12, pp. 1087-1090, 1969.

[2] R. Simons, Coplanar Waveguide Circuits Components and Systems, Wiley, 2001.

[3] G. Ghione and C. Naldi, "Analytical formulas for coplanar line in hybrid and monolithic MICs," Electronics Letters, vol. 20, no. 4, pp. 179-181, February 1984.

[4] J. W. No and H. H.-Yong, "A design of cascaded CPW low-pass filter with broad stopband," IEEE Microw. Wireless Compon. Letters, vol. 17, no. 6, pp 427-429, 2007.

[5] S. Kanamaluru, L. M. Yi, and C. Kai, "Coplanar waveguide low-pass filter using open circuit stubs," Microw. Opt. Technol. Letters, vol. 6, no. 12, pp. 715-717, 1993.

[6] D. S. Miguel, B. Jordi, and M. Ferran, "Compact elliptic-function coplanar waveguide low-Pass filters using backside metallic patterns," IEEE Microw. Wireless Compon. Letters, vol. 20, no. 11, pp 601-603, 2010.

[7] D. Pozar, Microwave Engineering, 4th ed., Wiley, 2011.

Nonlinear Neural Network Equalizer for Metro Optical Fiber Communication Systems

Mahmoud M.T. Maghrabi, Shiva Kumar, and Mohamed H. Bakr

Department of Electrical and Computer Engineering
McMaster University, Hamilton, Ontario, L8S 4K1, Canada
maghrabm@mcmaster.ca, kumars@mcmaster.ca, mbakr@mcmaster.ca

Abstract —We present a neural network-based nonlinear electronic feed-forward equalizer. It compensates for the chromatic dispersion (CD) distortions in fiber optic communication systems with direct photo-detection. The proposed equalizer achieves bit error rate (BER) performance comparable to the maximum-likelihood sequence estimator (MLSE), with significantly lower computational cost. The complexity of the introduced equalizer scales linearly with the length of the inter-symbol interference (ISI) as opposed to exponential growth the MLSE complexity.

I. INTRODUCTION

Direct detected fiber-optic communication systems operating at 10 $Gbps$ and beyond suffer from severe ISI caused by CD [1]. Electronic dispersion compensation (EDC) techniques have been identified as cost-effective solutions to combat ISI and to guarantee speed, robustness, stability and adaptability [1]. Feed-forward equalizer (FFE) [1], decision feedback equalizer (DFE) [2] and MLSE [3] are most common amongst EDC techniques. Although the CD causes linear distortions to the received optical signal, they turn into nonlinear impairments in the electrical domain, due to the square law detection. As a result, linear equalizers, e.g. FFEs and DFEs, fail to compensate for these nonlinear distortions. Only nonlinear equalizers, e.g. MLSEs, can effectively mitigate these nonlinear impairments [4]. However, the MLSE suffers from its intensive computational cost that grows exponentially with the length of ISI span.

In this paper, we introduce a nonlinear FFE that is capable of compensating for the nonlinear distortions, with computational cost growing linearly with the ISI span. The proposed equalizer consists of single artificial neural network (NN) layer [5]. At first, the parameters of the NN are optimized using extensive training process considering all possible data combinations that will be transmitted through the optical channel. Then, this trained NN acts as a nonlinear filter whose impulse response inverts the nonlinear response of the optical communication channel.

II. CHANNEL and EQUALIZER MODELS

The received optical field $r(t)$ of a metro fiber-optic communication channel is related to the transmitted optical modulated signal $x(t)$ as [1]:

$$r(t)=\left(x(t)*h_f(t)\right)*h_o(t), \tag{1}$$

where the operation $*$ denotes convolution and $h_f(t)$ and $h_o(t)$ are the impulse responses of the fiber and the optical filter, respectively. $x(t)$ is the input optical field consisting of binary sequence $\{a_k\}$. The received optical field $r(t)$ is passed through a photo-detector, electrical low pass filter (LPF) and analog-to-digital converter with $1/T_s$ oversampling rate. The output electrical current at each sampled time $y_k = y(kT_s)$ is then given by

$$y(kT_s)=\left(\left|r(kT_s)\right|^2+n_e(kT_s)\right)*h_e(kT_s), \tag{2}$$

where $h_e(t)$ is the impulse response of the electrical LPF and $n_e(t)$ denotes to the receiver noise. Due to linear distortions imposed by the channel $h_f(t)$ and the square-law detection, nonlinear ISI is introduced at the output signal $y(t)$. Therefore, a nonlinear equalizer is necessary to compensate for these nonlinear impairments and to recover the transmitted data effectively.

The model of the introduced nonlinear NN equalizer is shown in Fig. 1. Given an input kth vector $\boldsymbol{y}_k$ that contains n-samples corresponding to the current symbol and its interfering neighbors, kth output $\hat{X}_k$ of the equalizer is given as

$$\hat{X}_k=\sum_{j=1}^{m} w_j^o f_h\left(\sum_{l=1}^{n} w_{jl}^h y_l\right), \tag{3}$$

where n and m are the numbers of equalizer taps and hidden neural layer nodes, respectively. $f_h(\cdot)$ is the nonlinear activation function, w_{jl}^h is the weight assigned to the connection between lth input and jth node of the hidden layer, and w_j^o is the weight assigned to the connection between jth node of the hidden layer and the output layer node. These NN weights are optimized

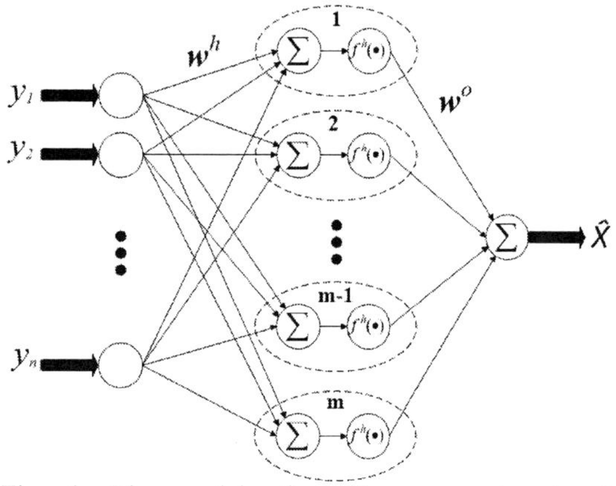

Fig. 1. The model of nonlinear neural network equalizer.

in the training process in order to minimize the difference between the equalizer output $\hat{X}_k$ and the transmitted data X_k.

III. RESULTS

To evaluate the performance of the introduced equalizer, we consider a metro fiber-optic communication systems operating at $10\,Gbps$. The optical carrier is modulated by raised-cosine non-return to zero (NRZ) on-off keying (OOK). A single-mode fiber with dispersion coefficient of $17\,ps/nm/km$ is used in the system. The bandwidth of the optical and electrical filters are set as $50\,GHz$ and $7\,GHz$, respectively. In the Monte-Carlo simulation, pseudorandom binary sequence (PRBS) of length $2^{10}-1$ is used to estimate BER. Total number of bits simulated $= 2^{14}$ bits. The parameters of equalizers are set as: $n = 7$, $m = 6$, and $f_h(\cdot) = \tanh(\cdot)$. Figure 2 shows the optical signal to noise ratio (OSNR) required to achieve a BER of 10^{-3} (sufficient for error-free operation with an advanced forward error correction) versus swept fiber-optic lengths. As can be seen, without equalization the maximum feasible transmission distance is limited to about $100\,km$. However, using the NN-equalizer this feasible distance is extended up to $200\,km$. Furthermore, in Fig. 2, we compare the performance of our NN-equalizer to the performance obtained using FFE, DFE and MLSE. It is clear that the linear equalizers (FFE and DFE) do not provide performance benefit since the channel (fiber channel + detection) is nonlinear. Although the MLSE slightly outperforms the NN-equalizer, it requires $128-$multiplication operations per bit. In contrast, our NN-equalizer needs only $42-$multiplication operations per bit. Hence, the NN-equalizer provides a better trade-off between performance and computational complexity.

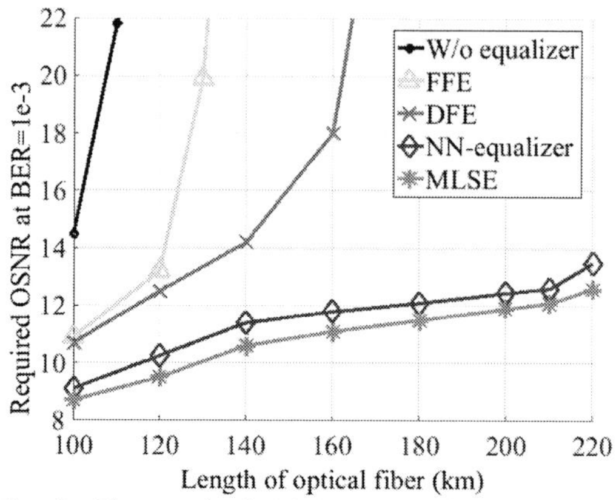

Fig. 2. The required OSNR at received $BER = 1 \times 10^{-3}$ versus fiber optic length. The performance without equalization is compared to the performance obtained using NN-equalizer with $n = 7$ and $m = 6$, FFE with 7-taps, DFE with 4-forward-taps and 3-backward-taps, and MLSE with 7-memory-size.

IV. CONCLUSION

A nonlinear feed forward equalizer exploiting neural networks has been proposed to mitigate chromatic dispersion impairments of fiber-optic communication systems with direct detection. We show that the introduced equalizer extends the feasible transmission distance up to 200 km, whereas the distance is limited to about $100\,km$ in the case of no equalizer used. The introduced equalizer is shown to have performance comparable to performance achieved by MLSE, with much lower computational cost.

REFERENCES

[1] S. Kumar and M.J. Deen, *Fiber Optic Communications: Fundamentals and Applications*, John Wiley & Sons, 2014.

[2] G. Katz, D. Sadot, "A nonlinear electrical equalizer with decision feedback for OOK optical communication systems," *IEEE Trans. Commun*, vol. 56, no. 12, pp.2002-2006, 2008.

[3] M. Bohn, C. Xia, "Electrical and optical equalizeation strategies in direct detected high speed transmission systems," *AEU-Int. J. Electron. Commun*, vol. 63, no. 7, pp.526-532, 2009.

[4] T. Foggi, E. Forestieri, G. Colavolpe, and G. Prati, "Maximum-likelihood sequence detection with closed-form metrics in OOK optical systems impaired by GVD and PMD," *J. Lightwave Technol.*, vol. 24, no. 8, pp. 3073-3087, 2006.

[5] M. Bakr, *Nonlinear Optimization in Electrical Engineering with Applications in Matlab*, The Institution of Engineering and Technology, London, 2013.

Towards Batteryless Wearables and Implants

Wei-Chuan Chen, Brock DeLong, Ramandeep Vilkhu, and Asimina Kiourti
Dept. of Electrical and Computer Engineering
The Ohio State University
Columbus, OH, USA
{chen.5825, delong.178, vilkhu.2, kiourti.1}@osu.edu

***Abstract*—Powering of wearables and implants is a critical challenge. Conventional batteries are rigid and require frequent recharging and/or replacement, making their use cumbersome and obtrusive for body-area applications. Instead, this paper discusses three novel technologies that we have recently explored towards batteryless wearables and implants, viz. a) DC power generation using fabric electrochemistry, b) RF power harvesting, and c) fully-passive RF backscattering. Notably, the proposed technologies bring forward transformational possibilities in batteryless sensing and stimulation.**

Keywords—batteryless, wireless powering, power harvesting, RF backscattering, wearables, implants, electrochemistry.

I. Introduction

Wearable and implanted electronics are recently gaining significant attention for a wide range of applications (medical, sports, tracking, consumer electronics, etc.) [1],[2]. Such devices may operate as sensors of human vitals (temperature, glucose levels, brain signals, etc.), or as stimulators of the central or peripheral nervous system. In either case, powering of wearables and implants is a critical challenge. The conventional way of powering such devices entails use of batteries. Expectedly, batteries are typically bulky and rigid, and require frequent recharging and/or replacement. As such, they are cumbersome, obtrusive, and thus, undesirable for body-area applications.

With these in mind, this paper discusses three novel technologies that we have recently explored towards batteryless wearables and implants, viz. a) DC power generation using fabric electrochemistry, b) RF power harvesting, and c) fully-passive RF backscattering. Notably, the proposed technologies bring forward transformational possibilities in batteryless sensing and stimulation.

II. DC Power Generation Using Fabric Electrochemistry

We have recently introduced a new class of electrochemical fabrics which, when moistened by a conductive liquid, generate DC power capable of powering wearable electronics [3]. Contrary to conventional rigid power generation techniques (batteries), the proposed electrochemical fabrics are fully-flexible, feel and behave like regular clothing, do not include any heavy or rigid components, and provide DC power via moistening by readily available conductive liquids. Generation of DC power is achieved via a redox reaction, which occurs between the Zinc to Silver Oxide-printed electrodes (anodes and cathodes), facilitated by a conductive liquid that enables electron movement. These anodes and cathodes are 'printed' onto the flexible fabrics with the use of polyvinyl binders, and can further be inter-connected via conductive E-threads to boost the generated voltage/current.

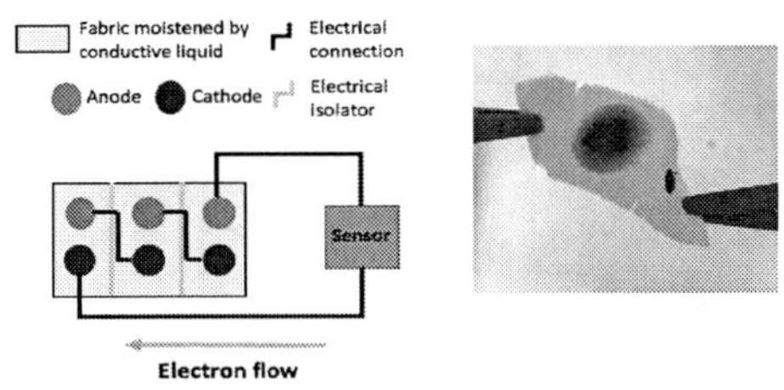

(a) (b)

Fig. 1. (a) Proposed concept of 'printed' battery cells wired in series on a fabric connected to a sensor, and (b) a single 'printed' battery cell deposited on a fabric as a proof-of-concept.

Fig. 1 (a) shows the proposed concept of inter-connecting multiple 'printed' batteries on flexible fabrics, while Fig. 1 (b) shows a single 'printed' battery cell created as a proof-of-concept. Notably, the latter single cell has been demonstrated to generate voltage and current levels as high as 1.4 V and 100 μA, respectively. Higher voltage and current levels can be achieved in future via the inter-connections mentioned above.

III. RF Power Harvesting

Wireless activation of implanted stimulators/actuators can significantly improve their practicality and unobtrusiveness while dissolving critical concerns associated with patient safety. As an example, Fig. 2 shows an implanted and wirelesss actuator placed right under the skin, and incorporating a miniaturized implanted antenna and a rectifier (rectenna). The first is responsible for capturing the Radio Frequency (RF) waves transmitted by an exterior antenna placed in close proximity, and the latter converts the RF energy to DC. This DC power may then be either stored in a low-leakage capacitor as in [4], or used in real-time for medical device actuation. The external transmitter can be placed in very close proximity to the implant and fabricated on e-textiles for unobtrusive integration into shirts, wrap-around garments, etc.

A proof-of-concept implanted and batteryless actuator has already been demonstrated. At this stage, it occupies a 15 mm x 25 mm footprint, and can be encapsulated into polymers for biocompatibility and improved matching. We have also demonstrated low power rectifiers with conversion efficiency above 70% [5]. In this particular case, the RF device operated at 2.4GHz.

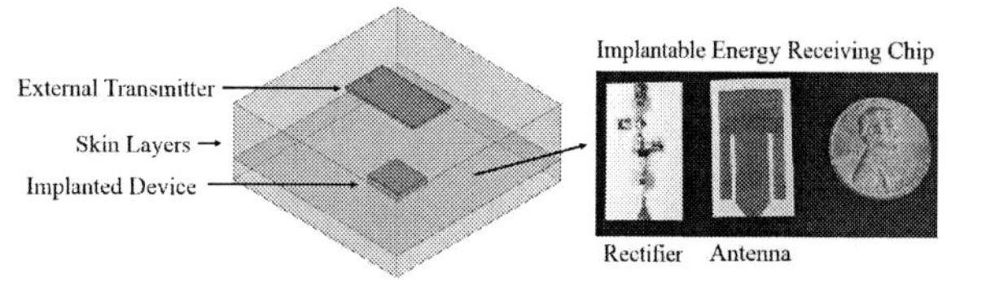

Fig. 2. RF power harvesting technology used to activate a batteryless device implanted inside the human body.

IV. Fully-Passive RF Backscattering

Fully-passive RF backscattering is recently gaining significant attention in the area of batteryless brain implants. The conventional way of detecting deep brain signals relies on integrated circuits (IC) chips [6]. However, the latter consist of a multitude of power-hungry components (pre-amplifier, multiplexer, analog-digital converters etc.), that require batteries and generate excessive amounts of heat in the surrounding tissues. As an alternative, we recently proposed batteryless and wireless brain implants that rely on fully-passive RF backscattering for signal acquisition [7]-[9].

The block diagram of our proposed neuropotential monitoring system is depicted in Fig. 3. The system is comprised of two sub-systems: the brain implant and the exterior interrogator. The interrogator sends a carrier (2.4GHz) to activate the implant. That, in return, detects the neural signals (f_{neuro}). To receive these signals at the interrogator, they are first mixed with the carrier at the implant prior to transmission. To do so, we employed an anti-parallel diode pair (APDP) mixer within the implant. The latter captures both positive and negative legs of the 2.4GHz carrier, allowing for high-efficiency harmonic mixing at 4.8GHz. We note that the latter is a unique aspect of our design. Subsequently, the mixed (4.8GHz$\pm f_{neuro}$) signal is transmitted to the exterior interrogator. The ~2X difference in frequency between the transmitted (2.4GHz) and received (4.8GHz$\pm f_{neuro}$) signals is used for isolation. For wireless communication, a dual-band (2.4/4.8GHz) patch antenna is employed both in the implanted device and interrogator. The designated geometry of the patch antenna and the matching circuit between the APDP and antenna further reduce the transmission loss and mismatch loss respectively. The reduced system loss enhances the sensitivty to 20μV_{pp}, implying detection of almost neural signal generated by human body. The received signal on the interrogator can eventually be viewed on a spectrum analyzer (frequency domain) or on a oscilloscope (after demodulating in time domain).

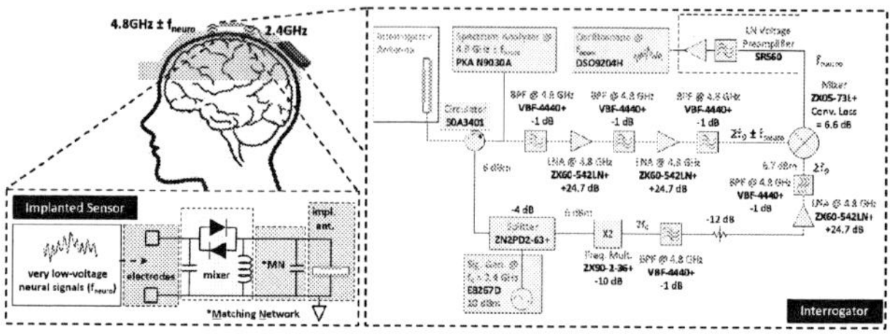

Fig. 3. Fully-passive RF backscattering technology used to collect deep-brain signals via a batteryless implant.

V. Conclusion

This paper discussed three novel technologies used for unobtrusively powering wearables and implants, viz. a) DC power generation via fabric electrochemistry, b) RF power harvesting, and c) fully-passive RF backscattering. At the conference, we will show experimental proof-of-concept results for each of these methods. Overall, the proposed technologies are expected to be of utmost significance for powering electronics in several military, healthcare (e.g., electroceutical), entertainment, arts, sports, and emergency applications, among others.

References

[1] S. C. Mukhopadhyay, "Wearable sensors for human activity monitoring: A review," IEEE Sensors J., vol. 15, no. 3, pp. 1321-1330, 2015.

[2] J. Li et al., "Characterization of in-body radio channels for wireless implants," IEEE Sensors J., vol. 17, no. 5, pp. 1528-1537, 2017.

[3] R. Vilkhu, et al., "Power harvesting for wearable electronics using fabric electrochemistry," 2017 IEEE Int. Symp. Antennas Propog., San Diego, CA, 2017.

[4] B. DeLong, C. C. Chen, and J. L. Volakis, "Wireless energy harvesting for medical applications," 2015 IEEE Int. Symp. Antennas Propag., Vancouver, BC, 2015.

[5] B. DeLong, A. Kiourti, and J. L. Volakis, "A 2.4-GHz wireless sensor network using single diode rectennas," 2016 IEEE Int. Symp. Antennas Propag., Fajardo, Puerto Rico, 2016.

[6] R. R. Harrison, "The design of integrated circuits to observe brain activity," Proc. IEEE, vol. 96, no. 7, pp. 12031216, Jul. 2008.

[7] C. W. L. Lee, A. Kiourti, J. Chae, and J. L. Volakis, "A high-sensitivity fully-passive neurosensing system for wireless brain signal monitoring," IEEE Trans. Microw. Theory Techn., vol. 63, no. 6, pp. 2060-2068, Jun. 2015.

[8] A. Kiourti, C. W. L. Lee, J. Chae, and J. L. Volakis, "A wireless fully-passive neural recording device for unobtrusive neuropotential Monitoring," IEEE Trans. Biomed. Eng., *vol. 63*, no. 1, pp. 131-137, Jan. 2016.

[9] C. W. L. Lee, A. Kiourti, and J. L. Volakis, "Miniaturized fully-passive brain implant for wireless neuropotential acquisition," IEEE Antennas and Wireless Propag. Lett., vol. 16, pp. 645648, 2017.

Optimizing Scattering Coefficients of Disordered Metamaterials Using the Finite-Difference Time-Domain Method

Adam Mock and Sheldon Hewlett
School of Engineering and Technology
Science of Advanced Materials Program
Central Michigan University
Mount Pleasant, Michigan 48859
mock1ap@cmich.edu

Abstract—**A technique based on the finite-difference time-domain method is presented for calculating optical transmission and reflection of disordered nanoparticle stacks. The approach is used to optimize a nanoparticle stack exhibiting greater than 98% average absorption over the visible spectrum.**

I. Introduction

Most electromagnetic metamaterials consist of a repeating unit cell with sub-wavelength features designed to impart a specific scattering response in a particular frequency range [1]. Metamaterials can be designed to achieve permittivities and permeabilities not found in natural materials, and these exotic material parameters can then be used to design metalenses, cloaks, mirrors and absorbers. For the case of highly absorbing metamaterials, many applications require low reflection and transmission over a broad wavelength range and over a wide range of incident angles. However, ordered metamaterials typically provide high absorption over only a limited wavelength range and over a limited range of incident angles. Alternatively, the use of disordered metamateirals has become an interesting alternative for achieving high absorption over extremely large bandwidths and incident angles [2]. However, the lack of long range order makes their analysis and design more challenging. In this work we describe our progress on obtaining reflection and transmission coefficients in disordered metamaterials consisting of dense agglomerations of gold nanoparticles using the finite-difference time-domain method (FDTD) [3], [4].

II. Dense Nanoparticle Stacks

In addition to impressive absorption, disordered metamaterials are amenable to low-cost solution-based fabrication techniques. Our approach begins with synthesis of gold nanoparticles in solution using the Turkevitch method in which nanoparticle size is controllable. In our work diameters between 5 nm and 45 nm are used. A single drop of the nanoparticle solution is deposited in a glass well using a micropipette and allowed to dry. Then a second drop is applied and allowed to dry, and this process is repeated until an opaque layer is formed, which typically requires 15-20 drops. This process is schematically

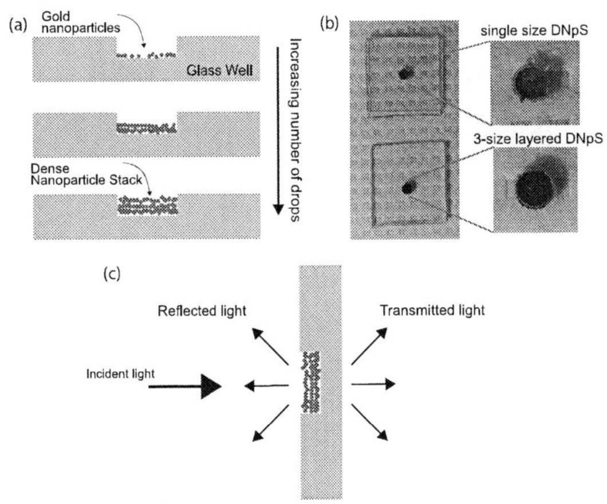

Fig. 1. (a) Experimental process for fabricating layer-by-layer dense nanoparticle stacks. The substrate is borosilicate glass, and the red spheres represent gold nanoparticles. (b) Photographs of fabricated samples. Single size DNpS indicates that nanoparticles of only a single size were used (diameter = 18 nm); whereas 3-size DNpS indicates that nanoparticles of three different sizes were used to construct the DNpS (diameters = 12, 18 and 48 nm). (c) Experimental arrangement for measuring reflection and transmission.

shown in Fig. 1 (a), and fabricated samples are shown in Fig. 1 (b). After each drop, the reflection and absorption is measured using the configuration shown in Fig. 1 (c).

III. Numerical Approach

To gain further insight into the electromagnetics of our metamaterials, the reflection and transmission coefficients were determined numerically using FDTD. If the nanoparticles had been placed in an ordered arrangement, then a minimum-sized repeating unit cell can be employed to minimize computational demands. However, in our disordered materials, this approach cannot be applied directly. Therefore, we defined a unit cell that contained a large set of randomly distributed particles, and then applied periodic boundary conditions on this disordered supercell. The scheme is depicted in Figs. 2 (a)-(b).

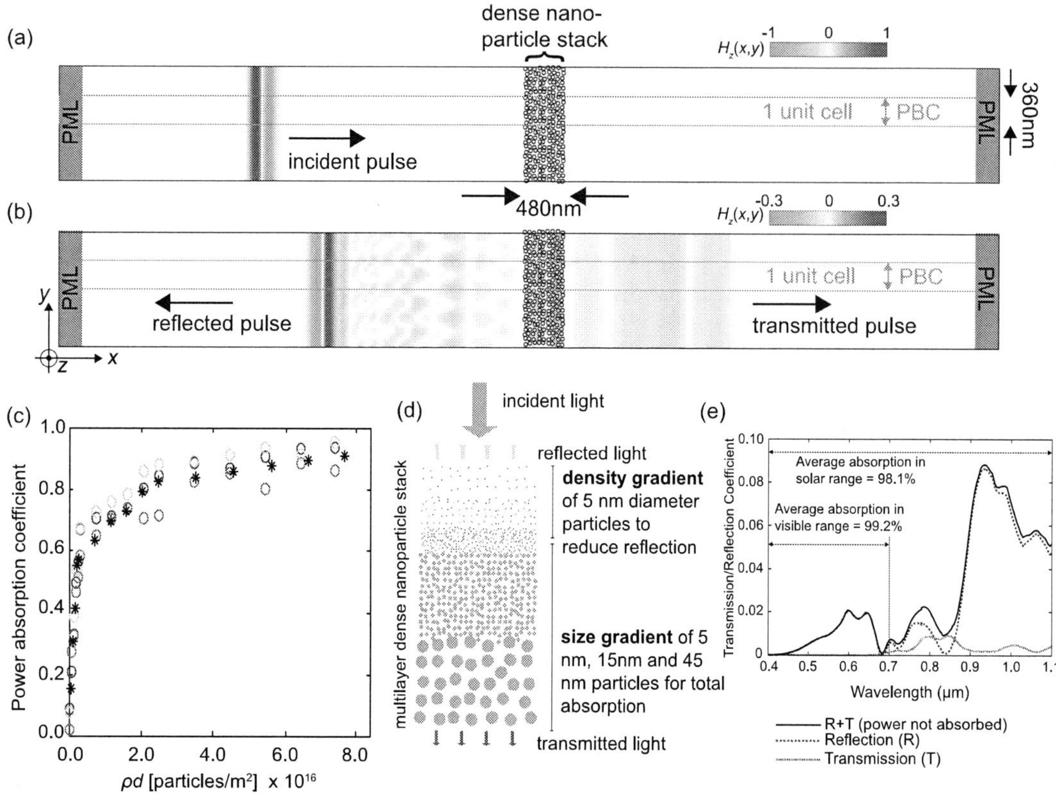

Fig. 2. (a) Computational domain depicting incident pulse on a dense nanoparticle stack. Periodic boundary conditions (PBC) are implemented along the y-direction. Four unit cells are depicted concatenated along y. The boundaries along the x-direction are terminated with perfectly matched layer (PML) absorbing boundary conditions. (b) Same as (a) but at a later time when the pulse has scattered from the dense nanoparticle stack. Reflected and transmitted field is visible. (c) Comparison between numerically calculated and experimentally measured absorption as a function of ρd where ρ is particle density and d is sample thickness. (d) Particle arrangement for structure optimized for greater than 98% absorption. (e) Numerically calculated scattering spectra for optimized structure. Coefficients in (c) and (e) are unitless power coefficients. (c)-(e) reproduced from [4], with the permission of AIP publishing.

A two-dimensional implementation of FDTD was used, so the gold nanoparticles are actually infinitely long cylinders. We deliberately used the TM_z polarization, so that the electric field would be perpendicular to the axis of the cylinder. In this sense, one can consider a cylindrical scattering cross section σ_c per unit length of cylinder along z. Then in order to obtain the approximate scattering cross section for a cylinder of finite length l, multiply σ_c by l. In order to compare the 2D FDTD results to the three-dimensional experimental results, we assume $\sigma_s \approx \sigma_c 2r\delta$ where σ_s is the spherical cross section of the nanoparticles, r is their radius, and δ is an empirical fitting factor. Fig. 2 (c) shows a comparison between the absorption measured experimentally and calculated using our 2D approach with a fitting factor of $\delta = 0.29$. The agreement is very good.

The data shown in Fig. 2 (c) corresponds to a sample with engineered disorder. We intentionally deposited nanoparticles of three different sizes with the largest particles at the exit side of the sample, and the smallest particles on the incident side. Intuitively, the small nanoparticles scatter less, so small particles on the front of the sample will reduce reflection while larger particles at the back will reduce transmission. The photograph in Fig. 1 (b) shows that the 3-size layered DNpS is indeed darker to the naked eye than the single size DNpS.

This gradient approach was further explored using our numerical approach in which we incorporate both a density gradient and a size gradient as depicted in Fig. 2 (d). Our optimized structure exhibits better than 98% absorption averaged over the entire visible spectrum as shown in Fig. 2 (e).

References

[1] N. I. Landy, S. Sajuyigbe, J. J. Mock, D. R. Smith, and W. J. Padilla, "Perfect metamaterial absorber," Physical Review Letters, vol. 100, no. 20, p. 207402, 2008.

[2] M. K. Hedayati, F. Faupel, and M. Elbahri, "Review of plasmonic nanocomposite metamaterial absorber," Materials, vol. 7, pp. 1221–1248, 2014.

[3] S. Hewlett and A. Mock, "Plasmonic metamaterial absorbers from dense gold nanoparticle stacks," Plasmonics, vol. 12, no. 2, pp. 419–425, 2016.

[4] ——, "Engineering metamaterial absorbers from dense gold nanoparticle stacks," Journal of Applied Physics, vol. 122, no. 9, p. 093103, 2017.

Dual-Band (2.4 / 4.8 GHz) Implantable Antenna for Biomedical Telemetry Applications

John Blauert
Electrical and Computer Engineering
The Ohio State University
Columbus Ohio
blauert.1@osu.edu

Asimina Kiourti
Electrical and Computer Engineering
The Ohio State University
Columbus Ohio
kiourti.1@osu.edu

***Abstract*—We present a novel 12 mm x 12 mm dual-band implantable patch antenna with resonances at 2.4 GHz and 4.8 GHz. The antenna exhibits a simulated maximum realized gain of -26.5 dB and -13.5 dB at these frequencies, respectively. Concurrently, it is coated with a thin polymer layer to ensure biocompatibility. In this paper, we present the antenna design and Finite Element (FE) simulations of its reflection coefficient, realized gain, and Specific Absorption Rate (SAR) performance. Overall, the proposed design brings forward transformational possibilities for wireless implants that utilize mixing technologies to backscatter in the second harmonic of the received signal, among others.**

Keywords—Backscattering, biomedical telemetry, dual-band, implantable antenna.

I. Introduction

Implantable antennas are an area of significant scientific interest [1], [2] due to their prevalence in emerging medical implant technologies, such as wireless sensors, stimulators, and energy harvesters [3]-[5]. Design of implantable antennas is associated with several limiting factors [6], which include, but are not limited to, miniaturization, transmission path loss through the human body, conformance to Specific Absorption Rate (SAR) guidelines [7], and biocompatibility.

In this paper, we introduce a novel miniaturized (12 mm x 12 mm) E-shaped patch antenna for implantable biomedical telemetry applications at the 2.4 GHz and 4.8 GHz bands. Specifically, the first resonance (2.4 GHz) lies in the Industrial, Scientific and Medical applications band, which has long been used for wireless implant communications [8]. Since several recent implantable technologies utilize mixing technologies to transmit in the second harmonic of the received signal [3], [9], the antenna is designed to also operate at 4.8 GHz. Alternatively, the second resonance may be used for sending a "wake-up" signal towards the implant as a way of preserving battery life. The antenna is also designed to be biocompatible and conform to Federal Communication Commission (FCC) SAR guidelines [7], while still maintaining a miniature footprint. Hereafter, we present the design of the proposed dual-band 2.4/4.8 GHz implantable antenna, along with Finite Element (FE) simulations of its reflection coefficient, realized gain, and SAR performance.

II. Antenna Design

The proposed patch antenna layout is shown in Fig. 1 (a) with design parameters given in Table I. It exhibits an E-shaped patch, where the currents flow in the center rectangle for the 4.8 GHz resonance, and around the arms for the 2.4 GHz resonance. For miniaturization, a high-permittivity substrate was selected, viz. Rogers 3010 ($\varepsilon_r = 10.2$ and $\tan(\delta) = 0.0035$). The substrate was 635 μm thick, and the copper layers on the ground plane and conducting plane were 35 μm thick, each. To ensure biocompatibility, the antenna was coated with a 700 μm-thick layer of Polydimethylsiloxane (PDMS) polymer ($\varepsilon_r = 2.8$ and $\tan(\delta) = 0.001$). As shown in Fig. 1 (a), excitation occurs via a 50 Ω microstrip line. Coupling slots line the microstrip feed and allow for adequate matching between the microstrip feed and the interior patch. All antenna dimensions were optimized for a low reflection coefficient at the desired 2.4 GHz and 4.8 GHz frequency bands using an in-house genetic algorithm.

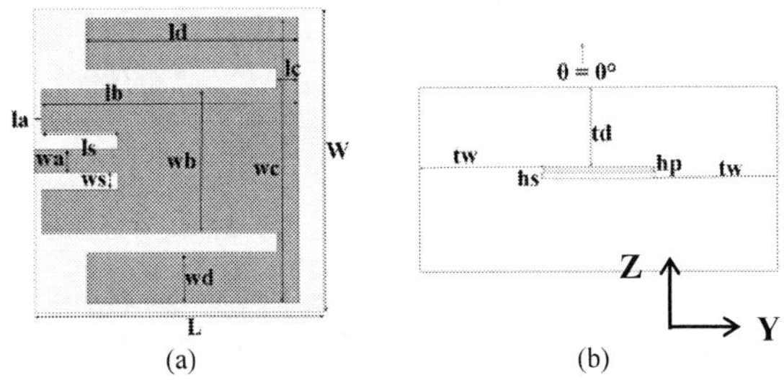

Fig. 1. (a) Dual-band implantable antenna design. (b) Simulation model showing the antenna surrounded by a tissue-emulating box

Table I. Dimensions of 2.4 / 4.8 GHz Implantable Antenna

Parameter	Value	Parameter	Value
L	12 mm	W	12 mm
la	0.275 mm	wa	0.874 mm
lb	9.85 mm	wb	5.65 mm
lc	0.881 mm	wc	11.2 mm
ld	8.03 mm	wd	1.97 mm
ls	3.15 mm	ws	0.714 mm
td	8 mm	hp	0.7 mm
tw	14 mm	hs	0.635 mm

III. ANTENNA PERFORMANCE

FE simulations for the dual-band implantable antenna were performed in Ansys HFSS. As shown in Fig. 1 (b), the antenna was placed 8 mm deep inside a dielectric box (40 mm x 40 mm x 20 mm in size) that represented the average electrical properties of human tissues.

Numerical results of the implantable antenna performance are shown in Figs. 2 to 4. Specifically, Fig. 2 shows the antenna reflection coefficient as a function of frequency. As seen, good matching was achieved at both 2.4 and 4.8 GHz. The realized gain radiation patterns for both bands are shown in Fig. 3, indicating maximum values of -26.5 dB (at 2.4 GHz) and -13.5 dB (at 4.8 GHz) in the $\theta=0°$ direction (see Fig. 1 (b)). The antenna performance was further analyzed as a function of depth within the tissue-emulating box of Fig. 1 (b). As shown in Fig. 4, the average realized gain was found to peak at a depth of 3.8 mm from the outer tissue surface. Expectedly, antenna matching deteriorates as the antenna gets closer to the surface, thus lowering the realized gain. SAR simulations were also performed. It was found that input power levels as high as 3.18 mW guarantee conformance with FCC guidelines (i.e., $SAR_{1g} \leq$ 1.6 W/kg [7]) for both 2.4 and 4.8 GHz frequency bands.

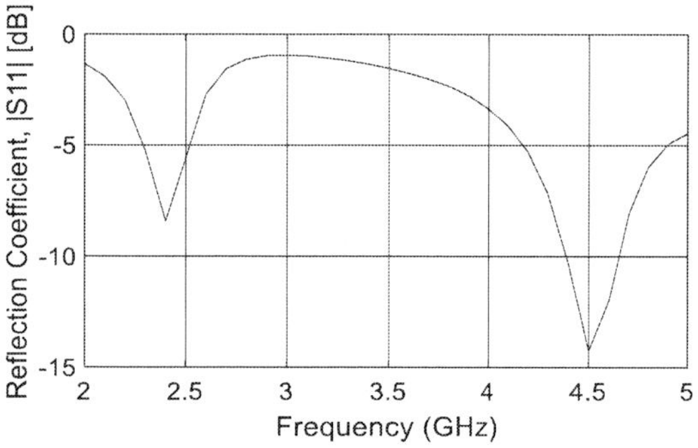

Fig. 2. Antenna reflection coefficient ($|S_{11}|$).

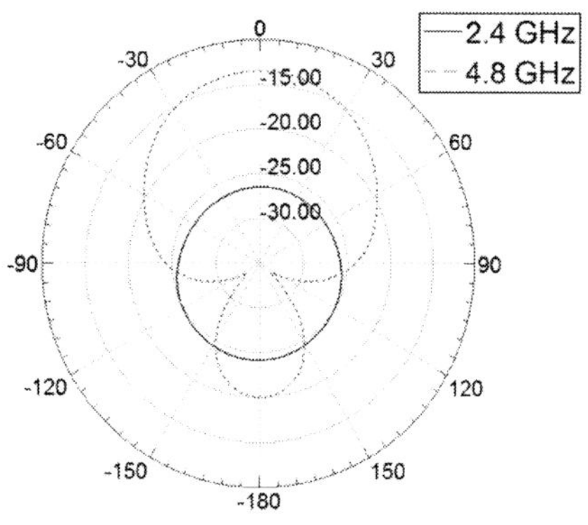

Fig. 3. Antenna realized gain (dB) in the yz-plane shown in Fig. 1 (b).

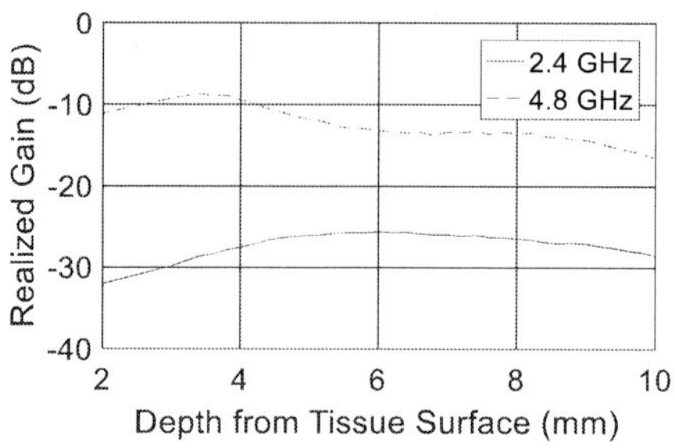

Fig. 4. Maximum realized gain vs. antenna depth within the tissue-emulating box of Fig. 1 (b).

IV. CONCLUSIONS

In this paper, we presented a novel 12 mm x 12 mm dual-band implantable patch antenna with resonances at 2.4 GHz (max. realized gain of -26.5 dB) and 4.8 GHz (max. realized gain of -13.5 dB). The antenna was coated with a thin polymer layer to ensure biocompatibility, and was found to conform with FCC SAR standards for input power levels < 3.18 mW. Notably, the proposed antenna is bringing forward new opportunities for implants that utilize mixing technologies to backscatter in the second harmonic of the received signal, among others.

REFERENCES

[1] Y. Liu, Y. Chen, H. Lin, and F. Juwono, "A novel differentially fed compact dual-band implantable antenna for biotelemetry applications," IEEE Antennas and Wireless Propagation Letters, vol. 15, pp. 1791-1794, Mar. 2016.

[2] Y. Cho and H. Yoo, "Miniaturized dual-band implantable antenna for wireless biotelemetry," Electronics Letters, vol. 52, iss. 12, pp. 1005-1007, Jun. 2016.

[3] C. W. L. Lee, A. Kiourti, and J. Volakis, "Miniaturized fully passive brain implant for wireless neuropotential acquisition," IEEE Antennas and Wireless Propagation Letters, vol. 16, pp. 645-648, Jul. 2016.

[4] V. Ranganathan, et al, "A high-voltage compliant neural simulator with HF wireless power and UHF backscatter communication," Wireless Power Transfer Conference, May 2016.

[5] P. Anacleto, P. M. Mendes, E. Gultepe, and D. H. Gracias, "3D small antenna for energy harvesting applications on implantable micro-devices," 2012 Loughborough Antennas & Propagaion Conference, Nov. 2012.

[6] A. Kiourti and K. S. Nikita, "A review of implantable patch antennas for biomedical telemetry: Challenges and solutions," IEEE Antennas and Propagation Magazine, vol. 54, no. 3, pp. 210-228, Jun. 2012.

[7] "Evaluating compliance with FCC guidelines for human exposure to radio frequency electromagnetic fields," FCC, Washington, DC, USA.

[8] OET Bulletin.65, 1997. "ITU-R Radio Regulations section 5.138 and 5.150," Int. Telecommun. Union-Radiocommun., Geneva, Switzerland.

[9] H. N. Schwerdt, et al, "A fully passive wireless microsystem for recording of neuropotentials using RF backscattering methods," Journal of Microelectromechanical Systems, vol. 20, no. 5, pp. 1119-1130, Oct. 2011.

An RF-Driven Lightweight Implantable Insulin Pump

Bingxi Yan
Department of Electrical and Computer Engineering
The Ohio State University
Columbus, USA

Brock DeLong
Department of Electrical and Computer Engineering
The Ohio State University
Columbus, USA

Duo An
Department of Biological and Environmental Engineering
Cornell University
Ithaca, USA

Asimina Kiourti
Department of Electrical and Computer Engineering
The Ohio State University
Columbus, USA

Kathleen Dungan
Department of Internal Medicine
Division of Endocrinology, Diabetes and Metabolism
The Ohio State University
Columbus, USA

John Volakis
Department of Electrical and Computer Engineering
Florida International University
Miami, USA

Minglin Ma*
Department of Biological and Environmental Engineering
Cornell University
Ithaca, USA
mm826@cornell.edu

Liang Guo*
Department of Electrical and Computer Engineering
Department of Neuroscience
The Ohio State University
Columbus, USA
guo.725@osu.edu

***Abstract*—Lightweight wireless implantable insulin pumps are highly desired by Type 1 Diabetes patients. This study reports the development of a polypyrrole-electroactuated micropump equipped with a non-fouling catheter tip. It can generate a consistent volumetric output of 16 μL at an RF power of 1.2 mW, supplied by an integrated wireless harvester. This motor-and- battery-free design significantly improves the pump's adoptability and biocompatibility.**

Keywords—battery-free, electroactuator, implantable, insulin pump, wireless.

I. Introduction

Patients with Type 1 Diabetes (T1D) rely on exogenous insulin therapy for survival. Traditionally, patients with T1D use insulin subcutaneously, either as multiple daily injections or as continuous subcutaneous insulin infusion [1-2]. Comparing to subcutaneous injections, advantages of continuous intraperitoneal insulin infusion (CIPII) using an implanted insulin pump include improved glycaemic regulation and decreased frequency of hypoglycaemia, as well as improved quality of life and treatment satisfaction [3]. However, most implantable pumps require a sizable piston-plunger motor and a bulky battery. To substitute the motor with a lightweight actuator, existing pumps primarily rely on piezoelectric actuators operating at a high voltage around 100 V [4], whereas piezoelectric materials for these actuators are inherently cytotoxic. In contrast, biocompatible electroactive polymers like polypyrrole (PPy) can operate at a much lower voltage around 1–2 V [5]. We have shown that a pair of PPy electroactuators only required 2–3 mW to operate [6], making the implementation of a battery-free micropump possible by using transcutaneous wireless power transfer for electroactuation. The current study describes such a motor-and-battery-free design for an RF-driven implantable insulin pump.

This research was supported by the Juvenile Diabetes Research Foundation (JDRF) through the Award No. 2-SRA-2016-237-Q-R and the 2016-2017 OSU IMR Facility Grant through the Award No. IMR-FG0183.

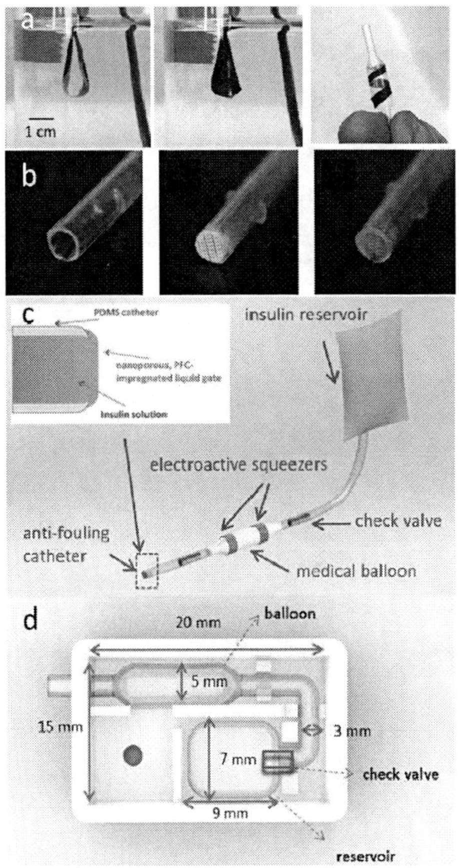

Fig. 1. Illustration of the prototype pump, including a PPy-driven balloon squeezer (a), a non-fouling catheter tip comprising a porous membrane (b), and other parts before (c) and after (d) being integrated into a case.

II. Results and Discussions

The micropump shown in Fig. 1 has three prominent features: a PPy-driven balloon serving as the pumping component, a polydimethylsiloxane (PDMS) catheter tip accommodating a nanoporous polytetrafluoroethylene (PTFE) membrane (Fig. 1(b)), and a wireless powering unit as demonstrated in Fig. 2(e). The PPy electroactuator (Fig. 1(a)) can reversibly generate large strains in phosphate buffered saline (PBS) under ± 1 V stimulation. The design employs a PPy-driven balloon squeezer as the pumping component to draw insulin solution in the reservoir toward the catheter tip. Unidirectional regulation of the flow is achieved by a pair of miniature check valves (Fig. 1(c)). The nanoporous membrane filled with perfluorocarbon (PFC) only allows liquid to pass through when a critical pressure is reached [7]. A preliminary subcutaneous implantation of the liquid-gating membrane showed excellent biocompatibility (Fig. 2(a–d)); number of cells attached onto it after 4 days in culture, as seen in Fig. 2(c), was much smaller than that observed on a contral polystyrene substrate (Fig. 2(b)). In parallel, a smaller harvester (Fig. 2(f)) was recently achieved and readily integrated on the back of a pump case (Fig. 1(d)). A comparison of transmitting efficiency in Fig. 2(g) suggested that the smaller harvester featured higher transmitting efficiency than the larger one. The maximum efficiency of 60% was achieved at 10 dB; and the maximum power output recorded was 1.2 mW (0.8 mA at 1.5 V), which drove the PPy electroactuator through a full squeeze-recover actuation cycle within 40 s (data not shown).

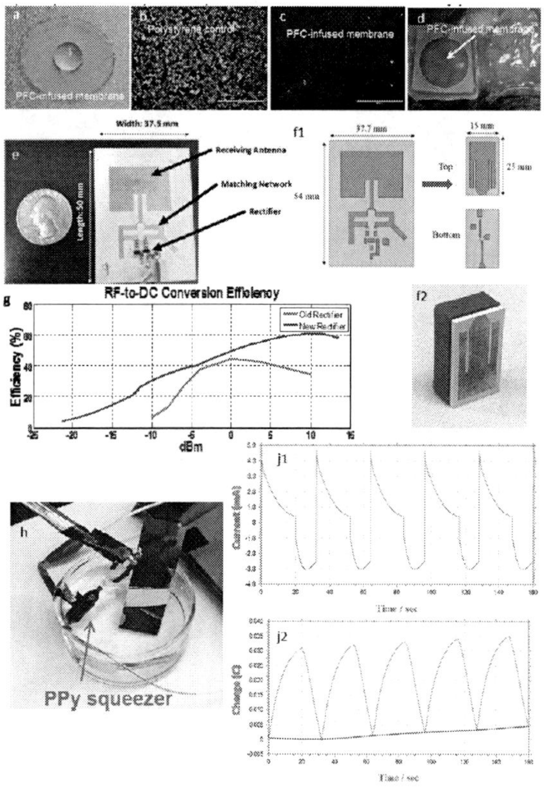

Fig. 2. Characterization on biocompatibility of the nanoporous liquid-gating membrane for a non-fouling catheter tip (a–d), power transmitting efficiency of two harvesters (e–g), and actuation power of the PPy-driven squeezer operating in PBS (h–j). Methylene blue was used to visualize solution flow in the capillary tube.

The output capacity and flow rate were controlled by the stimulation voltage's amplitude and duration. Specifically, the squeezing PPy electroactuators biased at -1.3 V produced an output capacity of 14 μL solution in 20 s and then gradually recovered to their original state during the following oxidation half-cycle at 0.5 V. Current feedback throughout five cycles is shown in Fig. 2(j1), from which the average power consumption for the reduction and oxidization half-cycle was calculated to be 2.0 mW and 1.3 mW, respectively. Although a similar output capacity could have been achieved by combining a higher voltage and a shorter actuation time, the power plan adopted in Fig. 2(j1) achieved the minimum charge accumulation of 1 mC/cycle (Fig. 2(j2)) in the electroactuator, preventing rapid strain degradation of the PPy [8]. *In vivo* studies are underway to identify the optimal stimulation protocol for insulin delivery.

To conclude, PPy electroactuators operating at a small RF power of 1–2 mW succeeded in driving a prototype micropump. A consistent output capacity of 16 μL was achieved at a flow rate of 0.8 μL/s. The integration of a non-fouling catheter tip based on a nanoporous liquid-gating membrane further improved its biocompatibility for long-term subcutaneous implantation.

References

[1] A. Mahnama, A. Nourbakhsh, and G. Ghorbaniasl, "A survey on the applications of implantable micropump systems in drug delivery," Curr. Drug Deliv., vol. 11, pp. 123–131, 2014.

[2] K. M. Bratlie, R. L. York, M. A. Invernale, R. Langer, and D. G. Anderson, "Materials for diabetes therapeutics," Adv. Healthcare Mater., vol. 1, pp. 267–284, 2012.

[3] C. K. Wan, A. Giacca, M. Matsuhisa, B. El-Bahrani, L. Lam, C. Rodgers, and Z. Q. Shi, "Increased responses of glucagon and glucose production to hypoglycemia with intraperitoneal versus subcutaneous insulin treatment," Metabolism, vol. 49, pp. 984–989, August 2000.

[4] P. Woias, "Micropumps—past, progress and future prospects," Sens. Actuators, B, vol. 105, pp. 28–38, 2005.

[5] B. Yan, Y. Wu, and L. Guo, "Recent advances on polypyrrole electroactuators," Polymers, vol. 9, p. 446, 2017.

[6] B. Yan, B. Li, F. Kunecke, Z. Gu, and L. Guo, "Polypyrrole-based implantable electroactive pump for controlled drug microinjection," ACS Appl. Mater. Interfaces, vol. 7, pp. 14563–14568, 2015.

[7] X. Hou, Y. Hu, A. Grinthal, M. Khan, and J. Aizenberg, "Liquid-based gating mechanism with tunable multiphase selectivity and antifouling behaviour," Nature, vol. 519, pp. 70–73, March 2015.

[8] L. Valero, J. G. Martinez, and T. F. Otero, "Creeping and structural effects in faradaic artificial muscles," J. Solid State Electrochem., vol. 19, pp. 2683–2689, 2015.

Miniature Implantable Antenna Design for Blood Glucose Monitoring

1st Ayesha Ahmed
School of Comp. Science & Tech.
University of Bedfordshire
Luton LU1 3JU, United Kingdom
ayesha.ahmed@study.beds.ac.uk

2nd Masood Ur-Rehman
School of Comp. Science & Tech.
University of Bedfordshire
Luton LU1 3JU, United Kingdom
masood.urrehman@beds.ac.uk

3rd Qammer Hussain Abbasi
School of Engineering
University of Glasgow
Glasgow G12 8QQ, United Kingdom
qammer.abbasi@glasgow.ac.uk

***Abstract*—In this paper, a miniaturised implantable antenna with the dimensions of $8\times8\times1$ mm^3 has been studied for continuous monitoring of Blood Glucose Levels (BGL). The antenna performance is analysed numerically for both free space and implanted operation. It has the lowest resonant frequency of 3.58 GHz in free space with a gain 1.18 GHz while operates at 2.58 GHz with a gain of 4.18 dBi when implanted. Good performance and small size make it a good for implantable glucose monitoring devices.**

***Index Terms*—Implanatable antennas, Glucose monitoring.**

I. Introduction

Diabetes, the most worried threat to the modern people, has brought about substantial economic loss not only to people with them but also to the public health system and national economy system [1]. According to [2], effective diabetes management could reduce the risk of the complications associated with the disease; therefore, real time monitoring techniques are indispensable. Among these techniques, implanted glucose sensors attract a lot of interest [3] and various implanted antenna are designed [4]–[6], where the miniaturization of the antenna with high performances is still a great challenge. To realise such antennas, several methods like high-permittivity substrates, fractal structures, shorting pins loading and *etc.* have been studied [7]. The high permittivity method and split-ring resonator (SRR) is more commonly used techniques. In [5], the miniaturization was completed realising an antenna size of $8.5\times8.5\times1.27$ mm^3 by loading C-shaped slots and Complimentary Split-Ring Resonator (CSRR) on the radiation patch. However, there is a need to further decrease the size of the antenna to meet the requirements of continually miniaturizing implantable devices.

In this paper, following the work in [5], efforts are made to further reduce the antenna size. A smaller implantable antenna size is realised for glucose monitoring located in subcutaneous layer of the human tissues with the techniques of the CSRR and high permittivity substrates. The antenna performance is studied through numerical modelling and analysis. The paper is organized as follows: Section II presents the configuration of the proposed implantable antenna and the numerical model of the human body phantom with antenna injected in the subcutaneous layers.

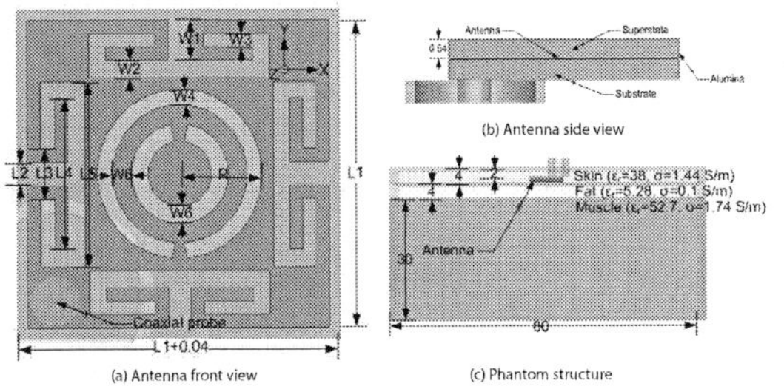

Fig. 1. Schematics of the antenna and three-layer phantom with implanted antenna.

Section III gives the analysis of the antenna performance in terms of numerical results. Conclusions are drawn in Section IV.

II. Antenna Design and Discussion

A. Antenna design

The structure of the proposed antenna is shown in Fig. 1(a-b) while the corresponding geometrical parameters are given in Table I. The antenna is modelled and simulated using Computer Simulation Technology (CST) Microwave Studio package. The substrate and superstate used are the lossy Rogers TMM 13i ($\epsilon_r = 12.85, tan\delta = 0.0019$) with a height of 0.5 mm. The patch and ground are all considered as Perfect Electric Conductors (PEC) for simplification having the length and width of same size as the substrate and thickness of 35 μm. The antenna is fed through a 50 ohm coaxial probe. The SMA connector is also modelled as shown in Fig. 1(b). To alleviate the effects of the human tissues, the antenna is covered in a film made of Alumina with $\epsilon_r = 9.2$, $tan\delta = 0.008$ and a thickness of 0.02 mm.

B. Numerical Phantom Model

The in-body antenna performance is tested using a three-layer numerical phantom of size $80\times80\times38$ mm^3 and implanting it 2 mm in the skin. The phantom consists of three layers, i.e., skin, fat, and muscle. The configuration of the phantom with electrical parameters (the relative permittivity and the conductivity [8]) in the ISM band is shown in Fig. 1(c).

TABLE I
STRUCTURAL PARAMETERS OF THE PROPOSED ANTENNA

Ant. Para.	Value(mm)	Ant. Para.	Value(mm)
W_1	1.05	L_1	8.0
W_2	0.45	L_2	0.6
W_3	0.35	L_3	1.3
W_4	0.4	L_4	3.9
W_5	0.5	L_5	4.8
W_6	0.45	R	2.2

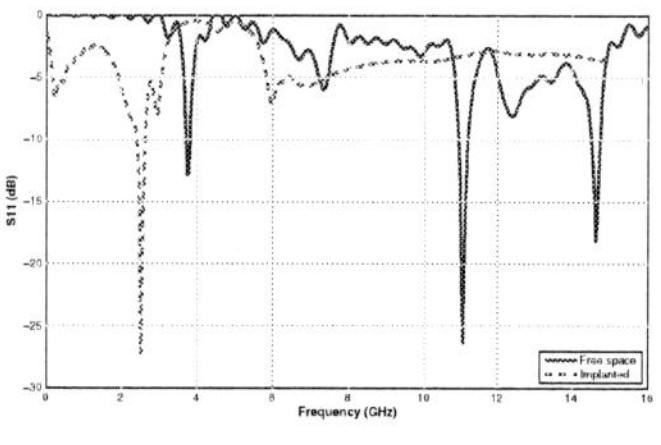

Fig. 2. S11 response of the antenna in free space and implanted configurations.

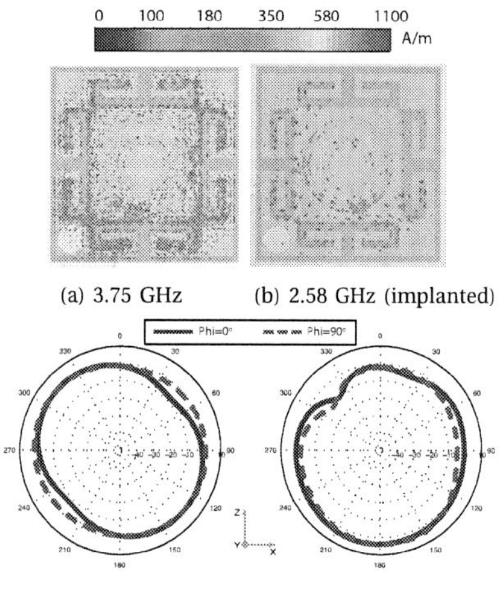

Fig. 3. Surface current distribution and radiation patterns for proposed antenna's operation in free space at 3.75 GHz and in implantable condition at 2.58 GHz.

III. NUMERICAL RESULTS AND ANALYSIS

The antenna performance is analysed in terms of surface current distribution, reflection coefficient, radiation pattern and gain in free space and implanted configurations. The reflection coefficient (S_{11}) response of the proposed antenna in free space and in the phantom are shown in Fig. 2. It can be seen that the resonance frequency changes from 3.75 GHz in free space to 2.58 GHz with excellent impedance matching for the antenna in implanted condition. For the free space case, the antenna has various parasitic resonances in the higher frequency band but it has limited effect on the antenna performance when the antenna is implanted in human body.

Fig. 3(a-b) shows the current distribution on the antenna surface for the two operational conditions at free space frequencies of 3.75 GHz and implanted frequency of 2.58 GHz. It shows that the current path has increased with the introduction of the slots and CSRR in the patch thus lowering the resonant frequency. The radiation patterns are observed at 3.75 GHz for the free space operation while at 2.58 GHz for the implanted scenario as illustrated in Fig. 3(c-d). These results indicate that the antenna has good radiation coverage in both $\phi = 0^o$ and $\phi = 90^o$ planes with nearly omni-directional far-field at all the observed frequencies. More tellingly, the antenna successfully maintains the pattern shape and coverage in both the planes when implanted into the skin tissues as evident from Fig. 3(d). The near-omnidirectionallty helps the antenna to send and receive the signal/information in all directions, hence mitigating possible body posture and shape implications. The simulated peak gain of the proposed antenna in free space is noted to be 1.8 dBi, 4.0 dBi and 5,4 dBi at 3.75 GHz, 11 GHz and 14 GHz. In implanted scenario, the gain is observed to be 4.18 dBi at 2.58 GHz. It is evident that the proposed antenna offers a good gain performance in all working conditions.

IV. CONCLUSION

A miniaturized implantable antenna has been studied for the free space and implanted conditions for continuous blood sugar monitoring. The antenna performance is analysed numerically using a three-layer human body phantom. The results have shown that good radiation coverage and a peak gain of 4.18 dBi could be obtained despite the small size of the antenna at 2.58 GHz when implanted in body. Small size, good gain and resilience to the human body effects makes the antenna a good candidate for tele-health monitoring systems.

REFERENCES

[1] World Health Organization et al. *Global report on diabetes.* World Health Organization, 2016.
[2] Horizon Scanning Research and Intelligence Centre. *New and emerging non-invasive glucose monitoring.* Horizon Scanning Research and Intelligence Centre, 2016.
[3] P. S. Hall and Y. Hao. *Antennas and Propagation for Body-Centric Wireless Communications.* Artech House, 2012.
[4] Y Cho and H Yoo. Miniaturised dual-band implantable antenna for wireless biotelemetry. *Electronics Letters*, 52(12):1005–1007, 2016.
[5] Xiong Ying Liu, Ze Tao Wu, Yi Fan, and Emmanouil M Tentzeris. A miniaturized csrr loaded wide-beamwidth circularly polarized implantable antenna for subcutaneous real-time glucose monitoring. *IEEE Antennas and Wireless Propagation Letters*, 16:577–580, 2017.
[6] Tuba Yilmaz, Robert Foster, and Yang Hao. Broadband tissue mimicking phantoms and a patch resonator for evaluating noninvasive monitoring of blood glucose levels. *IEEE Transactions on Antennas and Propagation*, 62(6):3064–3075, 2014.
[7] Hua Li, Yong-Xin Guo, Changrong Liu, Shaoqiu Xiao, and Lin Li. A miniature-implantable antenna for medradio-band biomedical telemetry. *IEEE Antennas and Wireless Propagation Letters*, 14:1176–1179, 2015.
[8] S. Gabriel, R. W. Lau, and C. Gabriel. The dielectric properties of biological tissues: II. measurements in the frequency range 10 Hz to 20 GHz. *Physics in Medicine and Biology*, 41(11):2251–2269, 1996.

Field-Plate Length Variation on GaN Devices for BV and On-Resistance Characterization

Christopher R. Lashway, Alberto Berzoy, *Student Members, ACES & IEEE*
Osama Mohammed, *ACES, Fellow, IEEE*

Energy Systems Research Laboratory, 10555 West Flagler St, Engineering Center 3983, Miami, FL, 33174

***Abstract*— Field plate (FP) inclusion is the most attractive technique for improving the breakdown voltage mechanism on single heterojunction field effect transistors (SHFETs). Furthermore, the most typical SHFET is the GaN device. For these reasons, in this article, a comprehensive physics-based model of a depletion-mode GaN-FET with a gate FP is conducted. Variations are made in the FP length and are evaluated in a progression toward the optimal configuration. Additionally, the on-resistance is studied for some of the simulated cases to observe its trend. The electric field distribution across the source, gate, and drain is analyzed, as well as their I-V curves until the breakdown voltage (BV).**

***Index Terms*—GaN, SHFETs, physics-based modeling, finite element analysis, wide band-gap devices.**

I. INTRODUCTION

SHFETs have gathered great attention due to the fact that they can operate higher in temperature, switching frequencies, and voltage, within minimum volumetric dimensions. This miniaturization is enabled by their wide band-gap characteristic, and by higher performance and a lower figure of merit $(FOM = R_{ds(on)} x Q_G)$ [1]. The most famous single heterojunction is the AlGaN/GaN, which renders a two-dimensional electron gas (2DEG) layer [2] with very low on-resistance $(R_{ds(on)})$ as compared to silicon. However, GaN devices have to overcome some hurdles before they can completely replace silicon including: cost-reduction in their fabrication, their susceptibility to the surface breakdown, their scalability to higher power and their reliability.

Therefore, there is a necessity to investigate strategies to improve the performance of GaN SHFET by increasing its BV, reducing the FOM and augmenting its reliability. Three solutions have been suggested in literature in an effort to improve the these characteristics and mainly the BV: 1) a variation of the passivation material, 2) changing the substrate material, and 3) the application of a FP on either the source or gate [3]. The purpose of this work is to investigate a FP inclusion on the gate conductor. A variation of the FP length is performed to determine the optimum length, as well as to study its on-resistance.

This work was partially supported by grants for the Office of Naval Research. The authors are with the Energy Systems Research Laboratory, Department of Electrical and Computer Engineering, Florida International University, Miami, FL 33174 (e-mail: mohammed@fiu.edu).

In this work, a depletion-mode device is used because of its simplicity and the findings for this type of transistor can be extended to the enhancement-mode device without major complications. The dimensions and material properties used are provided in Table I [4], [5]. The device simulation is performed using commercial Silvaco software for the Finite Element Analysis. The structure schematic is shown in Fig. 1(a).

TABLE I. GAN-FET DESIGN PARAMETERS AND CASES OF STUDY

Name	Value	Name	Value
Source – to – Gate Distance	1.70 μm	Si Substrate Thickness	2.98 μm
Gate – to – Drain Distance	6.60 μm	GaN Layer Thickness	1.00 μm
Source/Drain Length	1.00 μm	AlGaN Layer Thickness	0.02 μm
Gate Width	3.00 μm	AlGaN Composition	$x = 20\%$

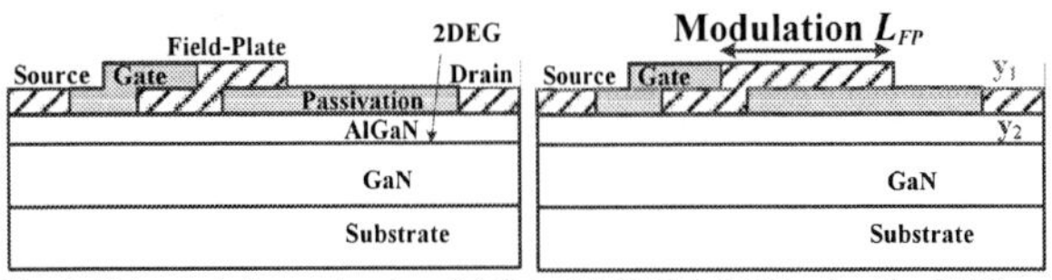

Fig. 1: Schematic layer structure (a) Gate FP (G-FP) (b) Varying the G-FP.

II. ANALYSIS OF FP LENGTH ON GAN PERFORMANCE

The FP is placed directly atop of the gate, stretching toward the drain with a length of 0.6 μm, beginning from the center of the gate. The length is then increased in 0.5 μm steps until it approaches closer to the drain. For each step, the GaN device is swept in off-state ($v_g = -2$V), where the I-V characteristic curve for each case is shown in Fig. 2. Fig. 2 suggests the FP length modulation has only a minor impact on the BV. However, to more clearly demonstrate the progression of the BV versus the FP width, the BV is calculated by pinpointing the voltage, where the I-V slope is at its maximum. Fig. 3 reveals that despite the fact all I-V curves appear similar, there are minute differences in where the breakdown occurs. Initially, an increase in the FP length results in an increase of the BV, approaching a maximum value at 3.1 μm. Following this point, the BV slowly begins to fall, until a drop of 20 V occurs after the length exceeds 4 μm. Some fluctuations occur past this point, until a collapse occurs following 5 μm, as only a small isolation gap remains between the FP and drain contacts after this point.

To gain a better insight into the performance associated with each case, an electric field (E_f) analysis was conducted at two important heights across the length of the structure. y_1 corresponds to the surface of the device (0.721 μm) and y_2 corresponds to the 2DEG channel (1.020 μm) as shown in Fig.

1(b). For each case, the maximum E_f at each height is summarized in Table II. Table II reveals a desirable range for the device operation, where the FP length is between 1.1 μm to 3.1 μm. The lowest E_f peaks are observed in y_2. This is particularly of interest, because the breakdown typically occurs near or along the 2DEG. As the FP width increases, initially $E_{fmax\,y_1}$ and $E_{fmax\,y_2}$ are inversely correlated until 4.1 μm, where both peaks rapidly increase. Based on our definition, the best BV occurs with a FP width of 3.1 μm.

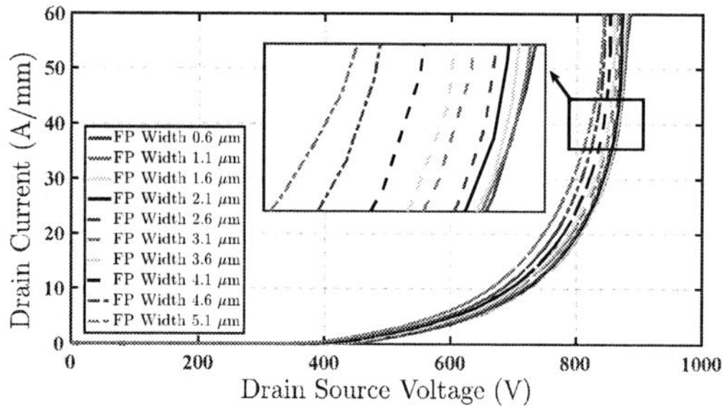

Fig. 2: I-V Characteristic Curves for all Cases.

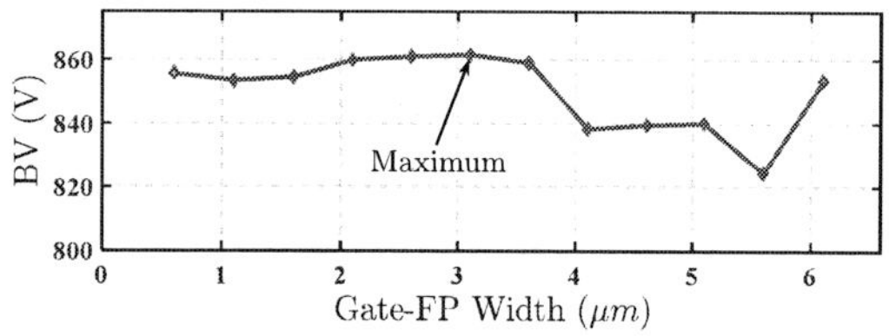

Fig. 3: Breakdown Voltage versus the Gate-FP Width.

TABLE II. BV AND MAXIMUM E FIELD FOR ALL CASES AT 2 HEIGHTS

L_{FP} (μm)	0.6	1.1	1.6	2.1	2.6	3.1	3.6	4.1	4.6	5.1
BV (V)	855.6	853.4	854.5	859.9	861.0	861.5	858.9	838.3	839.6	840.1
$E_{fmax\,y_1}$ (MV/cm)	13.07	15.36	14.03	12.96	9.83	8.22	8.91	9.88	10.78	21.31
$E_{fmax\,y_2}$ (MV/cm)	12.20	9.89	9.79	9.93	10.04	10.74	12.18	13.87	15.77	21.54
$R_{ds(on)}$ (μΩ/cm^2)	22.17	-	-	-	-	22.34	-	-	-	22.33

III. CLOSER ANALYSIS OF THREE CASES

A deeper analysis has been conducted for three important cases in particular: the shortest (0.6 μm), optimal (3.1 μm), and longest (5.1 μm) FP width. For these cases, new I-V characteristic curves were generated with the device under on-state ($v_g = 0$ V) with a drain voltage of 10 V, where the $R_{ds(on)}$ of the device was taken. An area factor (AF) was used to generate a normalized resistance based on the area of the device. As can be seen from Table II, all three values produce similar performance. The electric field distribution across each of the three structures is shown in Fig. 4 and as a 2D map in Fig. 5. In the 0.6 μm case, the FP width is too small, thus the peak is not well-distributed, resulting in concentrations at the edge of the gate facing the drain. Once the FP width increases to 3.1 μm, the peak field is distributed and a wide isolation to the drain results in the lowest value. For the final case of 5.1 μm, although the peak is widely distributed, its proximity to the drain results in a higher bias across most of the device as well as significant increases in the peaks along both y_1 and y_2.

IV. CONCLUSION

FP modulation has only a small effect on the BV and $R_{ds(on)}$, but the E_f stress can be reduced with the optimal selection of the FP length.

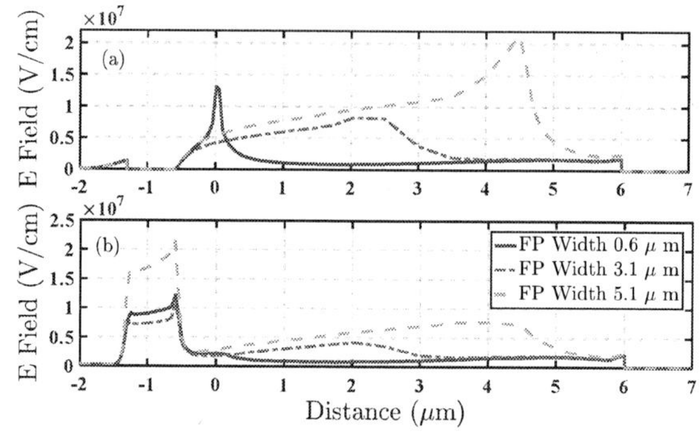

Fig. 4: E_f distribution along the x axis at 2 y distances for the FP case. Simulation performed at $V_{ds} = 853V$.

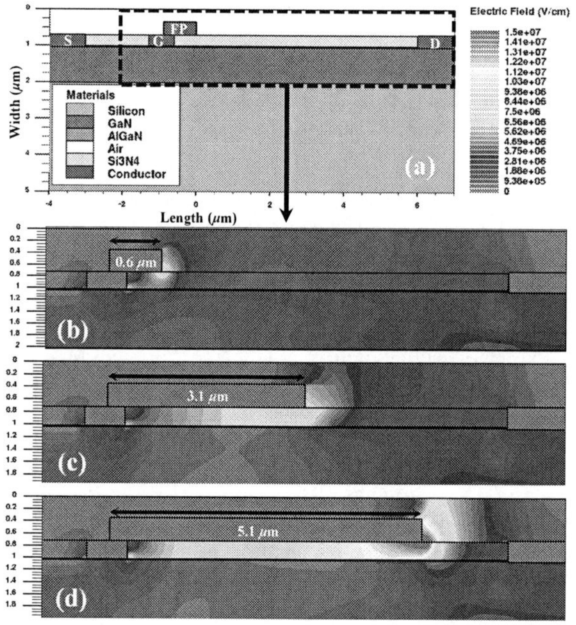

Fig. 2: 2D E_f Distribution at $V_{ds} = 853V$ (a) schematic (b) shortest $L_{FP} =$ 0.6 μm (c) optimal $L_{FP} = 3.1$ μm (d) longest $L_{FP} = 5.1$ μm.

REFERENCES

[1] Andrew Binder and Jiann-Shiun Yuan, "Optimization of an Enhancement-mode AlGaN/GaN/AlGaN DHFET towards a High Breakdown Voltage and Low Figure of Merit," presented at the Workshop on Wide Bandgap Power Devices and Applications, New Mexico, USA, 2017.

[2] K. Shenai, "Switching Megawatts with Power Transistors," *Electrochem. Soc. Interface*, vol. 22, no. 1, pp. 47–53, Jan. 2013.

[3] W. Saito *et al.*, "Field-Plate Structure Dependence of Current Collapse Phenomena in High-Voltage GaN-HEMTs," *IEEE Electron Device Lett.*, vol. 31, no. 7, pp. 659–661, Jul. 2010.

[4] Alberto Berzoy, Christopher R. Lashway, and Osama Mohammed, "Breakdown Voltage Improvement and Analysis of GaN HEMTs through Field Plate Inclusion and Substrate Removal," presented at the Workshop on Wide Bandgap Power Devices and Applications, New Mexico, USA, 2017.

[5] C. R. Lashway, A. Berzoy, N. Elsayad, and O. Mohammed, "Breakdown voltage assessment of GaN HEMT devices through physics-based modeling," in *2017 International Applied Computational Electromagnetics Society Symposium - Italy (ACES)*, 2017, pp. 1–2.

Numerical Analysis of Mutual Transient Voltages in Grounding Systems of Offshore Wind Farms

R. Araneo, G. Lovat, and S. Celozzi
DIAEE - EE Division
Sapienza University of Rome
Rome, Italy
rodolfo.araneo, giampiero.lovat, salvatore.celozzi@uniroma1.it

P. Burghignoli
D.I.E.T.
Sapienza University of Rome
Rome, Italy
burghignoli@diet.uniroma1.it

Abstract—**The paper illustrates a numerical procedure for the computation of mutual transient overvoltages transferred among typical grounding systems of wind turbines belonging to the same wind farm. We use a hybrid approach based on the circuit theory and the Method of Moments in the frequency domain. The transient response is obtained by means of the Inverse Fourier Transform efficiently computed trough a double-exponential formula.**

I. Introduction

In recent years, wind turbine (WT) installations have been boosted by environmental concerns correlated with conventional energy supply [1], [2]. Looking for increasing renewable energy supplies, wind towers have been installed also in those regions where lightning activity is significantly more intense [3]. Being tall, isolated towers composed of sensitive electronics, and often placed at higher altitudes where the isokeraunic level is high, wind turbines are persistently treated by lightning. Relevant statistics indicates that fatal damages in blades, generators, and specially in control circuits are caused either by direct lightning strokes to wind turbines or transferred overvoltages from nearby fault locations [4].

A lightning protection system (LPS) connected to a properly designed ground system (GS) is consequently mandatory in order to intercept the lightning and effectively and safely conduct it to the earth without risking physical damages [5], [6]. The GS is aimed at preventing against excessive overvoltages and potential gradients that could damage parts of the WT and at reducing human hazards [7], [8]. The design of the GS calls for several issues that must properly be addressed, e.g., the poor grounding conditions of the locations where the WTs are installed, the electrical interconnection of wind farms, the limited physical dimensions of the GS, the lightning protection level (LPL) of the WT.

In this paper, we focus on the mutual transient overvoltages [9] transferred among typical GSs of WT of the same wind farm. A transient analysis [10] is useful because it is able to assess the ground potential rise (GPR) during the transient injection of high impulse currents into the GS which can occur in a danger to humans, apparatus, and systems. The analysis is performed in the frequency domain (FD) by means of a hybrid approach [11]–[13] based on the circuit theory and the Method of Moments (MoM) that is able to account for resistive, inductive, and capacitive couplings. The corresponding transient response is obtained by means of the Inverse Fourier Transform (IFT) efficiently computed trough a double-exponential formula [14].

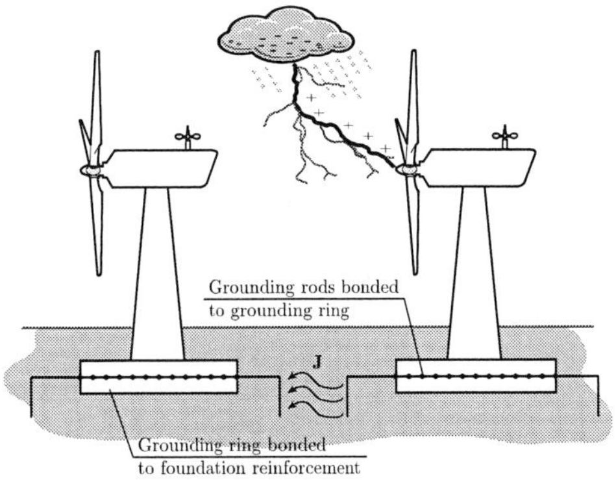

Fig. 1. Representation of typical GSs for WTs.

II. The Problem and its Numerical Solution

Figure 1 shows the problem under analysis: the GSs of adjacent WTs are buried below the ground and one is subjected to a transient current generated by a lighting strike. Typically, GSs are arranged in a ring shape around the tower's base and are connected with the tower itself through its foundation.

The conductors are completely buried in the earth that is considered stratified in $N_{\rm S}$ planar layers, each characterized by a complex conductivity $\overline{\sigma}_i = \sigma_i + j\omega\varepsilon_0\varepsilon_{{\rm r},i}$ (with $i = 1, \ldots, N_{\rm S}$) and permeability μ_0.

The hybrid method [11], [12] works in the frequency domain to obtain an equivalent electric circuit of the GS accounting for all the inductive, capacitive, and conductive couplings among different conductors. The network is composed of $N_{\rm B}$ branches and $N_{\rm N}$ nodes. Each conductor k carries a uniform longitudinal current $I_{{\rm LO},k}$ and each node has a scalar electric potential (SEP) V_i defined with respect to the infinite remote earth assumed to zero potential. In addition, each branch drains a uniform leakage current $I_{{\rm LE},k}$ to the surrounding earth. The grounding system is energized by the injection of single-frequency sinusoidal source currents F_m at M nodes.

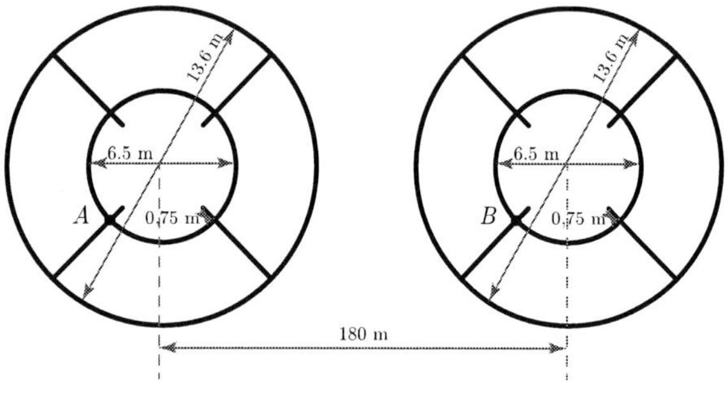

Fig. 2. Typical wind turbine grounding system arrangement.

Under these assumptions, after some manipulations, a network equation is readily obtained in a matrix form for the unknown nodal voltages $\mathbf{V}$ as:

$$\mathbf{F} = \left(\overline{\mathbf{K}}^t \cdot \overline{\mathbf{Y}}_{\mathrm{GC}} \cdot \overline{\mathbf{K}} + \overline{\mathbf{A}} \cdot \overline{\mathbf{Y}}_{\mathrm{RL}} \cdot \overline{\mathbf{A}}^t\right) \cdot \mathbf{V}\,, \qquad (1)$$

where $\mathbf{F}$ is the vector of nodal impressed currents, $\overline{\mathbf{K}}$ and $\overline{\mathbf{A}}$ are topological branch-to-node incidence matrices [11], [12], $\overline{\mathbf{Y}}_{\mathrm{GC}}$ is the admittance matrix accounting for conductive and capacitive couplings among the discretized segments, and $\overline{\mathbf{Y}}_{\mathrm{RL}}$ is the admittance matrix accounting for the internal impedance of the branches and the magnetic coupling among them. Both these matrices are obtained through the Galerkin's MoM which requires the computation of dyadic magnetic $\overline{\mathbf{G}}_{\mathrm{A}}(\mathbf{r},\mathbf{r}')$ and scalar electric $G_{\varphi}(\mathbf{r},\mathbf{r}')$ Green's functions for the stratified earth [15]. The Green's functions are computed in the spectral domain where the expressions for the elements of the Green's functions can be recast by using the transmission-line (TL) analogy described in [16]. The computation of the Sommerfeld integrals is performed with the double exponential-type quadrature formulas recently proposed in [17].

The proposed methodology has been used to study the mutual induced overvoltages among two WTs belonging to an off-shore windfarm. The GS is shown in Fig. 2: it is buried at a depth of 0.8 m below the seabed surface in a homogenous soil of relatively low resistivity, $\rho = 25\ \Omega\mathrm{m}$, which is a realistic scenario for off-shore wind farms and the relative permittivity is $\varepsilon_{\mathrm{r}} = 9$. The conductors of the grounding system have a transversal section equal to 35 mm^2 and to be made of galvanized steel. We assume that the current of the first subsequent lightning strike [18] is injected into the point A of Fig. 2 and the mutual induced voltage is computed in the point B.

Figure 3 shows the voltage waveforms computed at both points A and B. The final paper will present a full discussion of the obtained results, will provide more insight on the nature of the early-time transient response of GSs, and will draw up useful design guidelines.

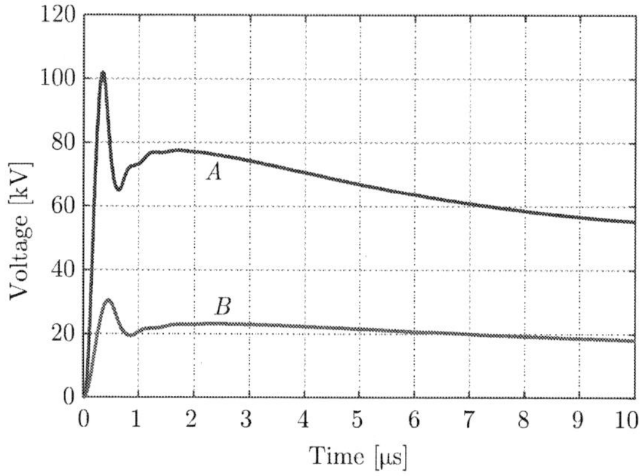

Fig. 3. Induced transient voltages at points A and B of the GS depicted in Fig. 2.

REFERENCES

[1] R. Araneo, S. Celozzi, and C. Vergine, "Eco-sustainable routing of power lines for the connection of renewable energy plants to the Italian high-voltage grid," *Int. J. Energy Environ. Eng.*, vol. 6, no. 1, pp. 9–19, 2014.

[2] E. Lucchetti, J. Barbier, and R. Araneo, "Assessment of the technical usable potential of the TUM Shaft Hydro Power plant on the Aurino River, Italy," *Renew. Energy*, vol. 60, pp. 648–654, Dec. 2013.

[3] D. Cavka, D. Poljak, V. Doric, and R. Goic, "Transient analysis of grounding systems for wind turbines," *Renew. Energy*, vol. 43, pp. 284–291, 2012.

[4] R. Rodrigues, V. Mendes, and J. Catalão, "Protection of wind energy systems against the indirect effects of lightning," *Renew. Energy*, vol. 36, no. 11, pp. 2888–2896, Nov. 2011.

[5] R. Araneo and S. Celozzi, "Transient behavior of wind towers grounding systems under lightning strikes," *Int. J. Energy Environ. Eng.*, vol. 7, no. 2, pp. 235–247, 2016.

[6] R. Araneo, G. Lovat, and S. Celozzi, "Transient response of grounding systems of wind turbines under lightning strikes," in *Proc. EMC Europe Int. Symp.*, Sep. 2014, pp. 1080–1085.

[7] G. Parise, L. Martirano, L. Parise, S. Celozzi, and R. Araneo, "Safety criteria for testing ground systems within their influence zone," in *2014 14th Int. Conf. Environ. and Electr. Eng.*, 2014, pp. 301–306.

[8] ——, "Simplified conservative testing method of touch and step voltages by multiple auxiliary electrodes at reduced distance," *IEEE Trans. Ind. Appl.*, vol. 51, no. 6, pp. 4987–4993, Nov. 2015.

[9] R. Araneo and S. Celozzi, "Direct time-domain analysis of transmission lines above a lossy ground," *IEE Proceedings - Science, Measurement and Technology*, vol. 148, no. 2, pp. 73–79, Mar. 2001.

[10] L. Grcev, "Time- and frequency-dependent lightning surge characteristics of grounding electrodes," *IEEE Trans. Power Delivery*, vol. 24, no. 4, pp. 2186–2196, Oct. 2009.

[11] Z.-X. Li, Y. Yin, C.-X. Zhang, and L.-C. Zhang, "A mathematical model for the transient lightning response from grounding systems," *Progr. Electromag. Res. B*, vol. 57, pp. 47–61, 2014.

[12] Z. Li and J. Fan, "Numerical calculation of grounding system in low frequency domain based on the boundary element method," *Int. J. Numer. Methods Engrg.*, vol. 73, pp. 685–705, May 2008.

[13] R. Araneo, M. Maccioni, S. Lauria, A. Geri, F. Gatta, and S. Celozzi, "Hybrid and pi-circuit approaches for grounding system lightning response," in *Proc. IEEE PowerTech*, Jun. 2015, pp. 1–6.

[14] M. Mori and M. Sugihara, "The double-exponential transformation in numerical analysis," *J. Comput. Appl. Math.*, vol. 127, no. 12, pp. 287–296, Jan. 2001.

[15] V. Kourkoulos and A. C. Cangellaris, "Accurate approximation of Green's functions in planar stratified media in terms of a finite sum of spherical and cylindrical waves," *IEEE Trans. Antennas Propagat.*, vol. 54, no. 5, pp. 1568–1576, May 2006.

[16] K. A. Michalski and J. R. Mosig, "Multilayered media Green's functions in integral equation formulations," *IEEE Trans. Antennas Propagat.*, vol. 45, no. 3, pp. 508–519, Mar. 1997.

[17] A. G. Polimeridis and J. R. Mosig, "Fast computation of Sommerfeld integral tails via direct integration based on double exponential-type quadrature formulas," *IEEE Trans. Antennas Propagat.*, vol. 59, no. 2, pp. 694–699, Feb. 2011.

[18] R. Araneo, S. Celozzi, A. Tatematsu, and F. Rachidi, "Time-domain analysis of building shielding against lightning electromagnetic fields," *IEEE Trans. Electromagn. Compat.*, vol. 57, no. 3, pp. 397–404, Jun. 2015.

Shielding Effectiveness of Finite Width Shields Against Low-impedance Magnetic Near-field Sources

R. Araneo, G. Lovat, and S. Celozzi
DIAEE - EE Division
Sapienza University of Rome
Rome, Italy
rodolfo.araneo, giampiero.lovat, salvatore.celozzi@uniroma1.it

P. Burghignoli
D.I.E.T.
Sapienza University of Rome
Rome, Italy
burghignoli@diet.uniroma1.it

Abstract—**The preformance of finite size planar shields usually adopted in EMC practice against near field extremely low-frequency magnetic sources magnetic sources are here investigated. The analysis is performed numerically with frequency-domain techniques and it is aimed at assessing the influence of shield constitutive parameters and of the source distance on the shielding parameters.**

I. Introduction

In industrial and electronic applications, the electromagnetic interference (EMI) problem is today frequent, because of the existence of a large number of natural and man-made sources, and may represent a serious issue, since it slowly degrades equipments inducing failure in their operation and is even able to create irreparable damages [1]. When studying the functional safety of a product, several EMI factors must be taken into account from three main viewpoints: characterization of generation sources (emission), effectiveness on victim components (susceptibility), and safekeeping methods. One of the prevalent methods for safekeeping against EMI is shielding [2]–[5]. However, if higher frequency EMI is normally shielded by thin electrically metal layers (e.g., copper, aluminum), the shielding of extremely low-frequency (ELF) magnetic fields is more challenging due to the inefficiency of classical conductive materials when the penetration effect is considerable [6]–[8].

The design of shields against near ELF magnetic field sources is made particulary tricky by the fact that shielding is strongly dependent on the location and orientation of sources, on the physical parameters of the conductive and magnetic material of the shield, and on the geometrical configuration of the shield that often requires complex numerical approaches [9]. From a physical point of view, when dealing with finite size shields [10]–[12], the shielding effectiveness (SE) [13] of the shield depends on the combined effects [1] of the EM penetration (or better diffusion) in the shield and the EM leakage in the air around the shield edges. These two effects must be properly assessed to draw practical guidelines for the optimum design of shields.

The goal of this paper is to investigate the magnetic shielding effetiveness $\mathrm{SE_H}$ of conductive shields of finite size against ELF magnetic fields generated by near field sources (e.g., magnetic loops) in order to assess the influence of several key parameters on the shielding configuration, e.g., transverse dimensions, thickness and material of the shield, position and operative frequency of the source. The goal is accomplished by using a Finite Element Method (FEM) [14], [15] and spectral domain approaches [16].

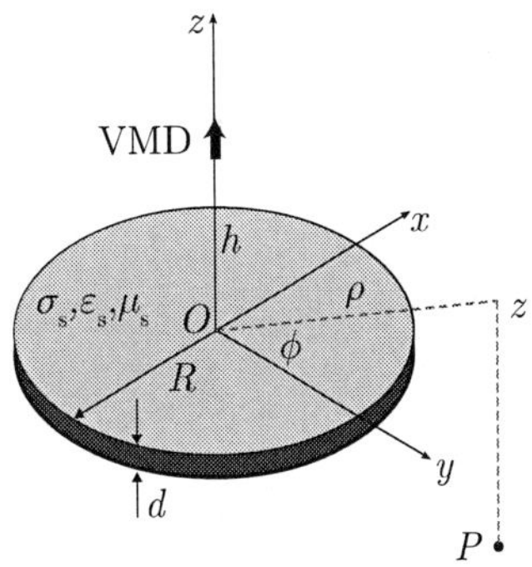

Fig. 1. The configuration under analysis with the relevant reference system and physical parameters.

II. The Problem and its Numerical Solution

The geometry of the problem is reported in Fig. 1. Referring to a cylindrical coordinate system (ρ, ϕ, z), a vertical magnetic dipole (VMD) source $m_z \mathbf{u}_z$ is placed at the source point $(0, 0, h)$ in air, i.e., a lossless medium with dielectric permittivity ε_0 and magnetic permeability μ_0. The source radiates above a finite size circular conductive sheet with thickness d, radius R and constitutive parameters ε_s, μ_s and σ_s. The observation point P is assumed placed below the sheet at coordinates (ρ, ϕ, z). The problem geometry refers to the co-axial loop configuration proposed by the Standards MIL-STD-285 and NSA 65-6.

The problem of the finite-shield size is solved in the frequency domain though a two dimensional (2-D) axial symmetric FEM (through the commercial software Comsol) using only the magnetic potential component A_ϕ to describe the magnetic field [14] in the quasi-stationary limit where displacement currents $\partial D/\partial t$ are neglected. Third-order lagrangian elements are used and infinite elements are introduced to truncate the computational domain [17]. When the shield is considered of radial infinite

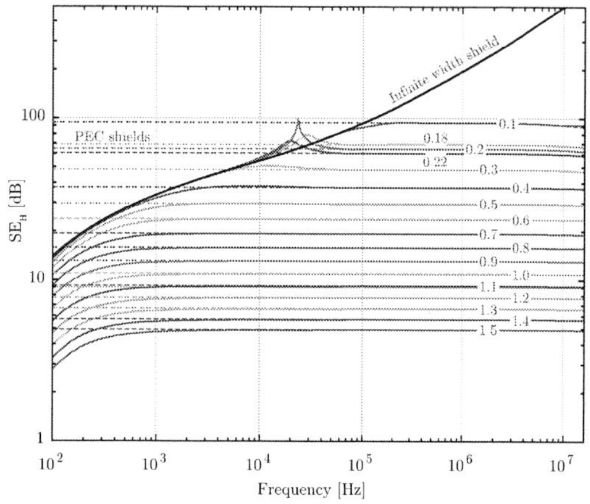

Fig. 2. $\mathrm{SE_H}$ for various h/R ratios of a copper shield compared to a PEC shield of the same size and a copper shield of infinite size.

extent, the spectral domain formulation proposed in [16] and recently applied by the authors in [18], [19]is used.

Figure 2 shows the $\mathrm{SE_H} = 20\log_{10}\left[\frac{H_{\text{incident}}(P)}{H_{\text{shielded}}(P)}\right]$ computed at $P = (0, 0, -h)$ in the frequency range from 100 Hz ro 16 MHz for different h/R ratios (in the simulations h is always kept fixed and equal to 30 cm while R is changed accordingly to the h/R ratio) for a copper shield with thickness $d = 1$ mm and conductivity $\sigma = 57$ MS/m. The SE of the PEC shields and the SE of the copper shield of infinite extent are also reported for comparison purposes. It should be observed that, by increasing the shield radius R, the shielding phenomenon is more distinctly dominated by the diffusion of the EM field in the shield at low frequencies (infinite extent behaviour) while it is dominated by the EM leakage around the shield edges at high frequencies (PEC behaviour). In the middle range there is transition region where resonances can occur for particular h/R ratios.

Figures 3 show two magnetic field maps computed at 100 kHz for two different h/R ratios, specifically 0.3 in Fig. 3(a) and 1 in Fig. 3(b). From the two figures it is evident that by increasing the radius R with respect to the height h (i.e., at lower h/R ratios) the leakage effect at the border of the circular shield increases and affects the measuring point placed at $z = (0, 0, -h)$.

Further discussions on the effect of shield thickness d and on the behaviour of different materials (e.g., steel and aluminum) will be provided in the final presentation.

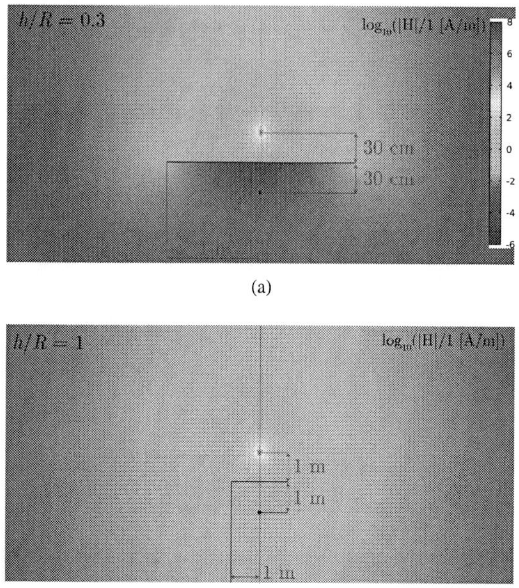

(a)

(b)

Fig. 3. Magnetic field maps at 100 kHz for two different h/R ratios.

REFERENCES

[1] S. Celozzi, R. Araneo, and G. Lovat, *Electromagnetic Shielding*. Hoboken: Wiley-IEEE, 2008.

[2] R. B. Schulz, V. C. Plantz, and D. R. Brush, "Shielding theory and practice," *IEEE Trans. Electromagn. Compat.*, vol. 30, no. 3, pp. 187–201, Aug. 1988.

[3] G. Lovat, R. Araneo, and S. Celozzi, "Electromagnetic shielding of resonant frequency-selective surfaces in presence of dipole sources," *ACES Journal*, vol. 29, no. 7, pp. 442–450, Jul. 2014.

[4] R. Araneo, G. Lovat, and S. Celozzi, "Shielding effectiveness of periodic screens against finite high-impedance near-field sources," *IEEE Trans. Electromagn. Compat.*, vol. 53, no. 3, pp. 706–716, Aug. 2011.

[5] R. Araneo, S. Celozzi, and G. Lovat, "Shielding effectiveness of artificial magnetic screens in the VHF band," in *Proc. IEEE Electromagn. Compat. Symp.*, 17-21 Aug. 2009, pp. 72–77.

[6] J. R. Moser, "Low-frequency low-impedance electromagnetic shielding," *IEEE Trans. Electromagn. Compat.*, vol. 30, no. 3, pp. 202–210, Aug. 1988.

[7] R. Araneo and S. Celozzi, "Analysis of the shielding performance of ferromagnetic screens," *IEEE Trans. Magn.*, vol. 39, no. 2, pp. 1046–1052, Mar. 2003.

[8] ——, "Exact solution of the low-frequency coplanar loops shielding configuration," *IEE Proc. Science, Meas. and Tech.*, vol. 149, no. 1, pp. 37–44, Jan. 2002.

[9] R. G. Olsen and P. Moreno, "Some observations about shielding extremely low-frequency magnetic fields by finite width shields," *IEEE Trans. Electromagn. Compat.*, vol. 38, no. 3, pp. 460–468, Aug. 1996.

[10] P. Moreno and R. G. Olsen, "A simple theory for optimizing finite width elf magnetic field shields for minimum dependence on source orientation," *IEEE Trans. Electromagn. Compat.*, vol. 39, no. 4, pp. 340–348, Nov. 1997.

[11] M. Istenic and R. G. Olsen, "A simple hybrid method for ELF shielding by imperfect finite planar shields," *IEEE Trans. Electromagn. Compat.*, vol. 46, no. 2, pp. 199–207, May 2004.

[12] S. Kong, Y. Du, and J. Bunnett, "Experiment on finite-width planar sheets for elf magnetic field shielding," in *Proc. IEEE Electromagn. Compat. Symp.*, 1999, pp. 524–527.

[13] S. Celozzi and R. Araneo, "Alternative definitions for the time-domain shielding effectiveness of enclosures," *IEEE Trans. Electromagn. Compat.*, vol. 56, no. 2, pp. 482–485, Apr. 2014.

[14] O. Biro, K. Preis, and K. R. Richter, "On the use of the magnetic vector potential in the nodal and edge finite element analysis of 3d magnetostatic problems," *IEEE Trans. Magn.*, vol. 32, no. 3, pp. 651–654, May 1996.

[15] E. Silva and R. Mesquita, "Three dimensional magnetostatics using the magnetic vector potential with nodal and edge finite elements," *ACES Journal*, vol. 12, pp. 153–156, Mar. 1997.

[16] C. Scott, *The Spectral Domain Method in Electromagnetics*, A. House, Ed., 1989.

[17] J.-M. Jin, *The Finite Element Method in Electromagnetics*. Wiley-IEEE Press, 2014.

[18] P. Burghignoli, G. Lovat, R. Araneo, and S. Celozzi, "Time-domain shielding of a thin conductive sheet in the presence of pulsed vertical dipoles," *IEEE Trans. Electromagn. Compat.*, vol. 60, no. 1, pp. 157–165, Feb. 2018.

[19] R. Araneo, G. Lovat, S. Celozzi, and P. Burghignoli, "Time domain magnetic shielding performance of thin shields," in *2017 17th Int. Conf. Environ. and Electr. Eng. and 1st Ind. and Com. Power Systems Europe*, Milan, Italy, 6-9 Jun. 2017, pp. 1–5.

CT Eccentricity Error Evaluation Model Based on the Actual Magnetization Curve

Hao Zhang, Zeyao Huang, Xiao Zhang

China University of Mining and Technology, Xuzhou, China

Abd A. Arkadan, IEEE&ACES Fellow

Colorado School of Mines, Golden, CO. USA

Abstract—In view of the importance of the accuracy of current transformers (CTs) for monitoring and protection, a mathematical model based on actual magnetization curve is presented to predict the error caused by the eccentricity of the primary conductor. It is shown that the eccentricity will result in asymmetric magnetic field distribution and causes an error in the measurement result. In addition, the model predicted results are compared to corresponding two-dimensional transient finite element model results for verification.

Keywords—current transformer, magnetization curve, error, eccentricity, finite element

I. INTRODUCTION

Ideally, a bus bar should be positioned right at the center of a CT to get proper reading of the measured current. However, in most cases, a bus bar is generally positioned off center of a CT, which causes an asymmetric distribution of the magnetic field and increases the error in the measurement [1]. In this paper, a model is developed to estimate the eccentricity error and its results are verified by comparison to corresponding finite element analysis results. As such, this model could be used in the development of manufacturing methods of CTs.

II. ECCENTRICITY ERROR MODEL AND APPLICATION

In this work, an ideal condition is defined as when the location of the primary conductor is at the center of a CT and the resulting measured induced current is considered as the ideal value, with minimum error [2]. That is to say, the eccentricity error in this paper refers to the relative error between the induced current when the bus bar is at the center and when it is off center. In the remainder of this paper, the model used to predict the error will be presented and the results will be verified by comparison to corresponding 2D transient finite element model results.

A. CT Eccentricity Error Evaluation Model

In most cases, CTs have their magnetization curve given by manufacturers. By applying curve fitting to a curve's data, the relationship between B and H can be found and represented by B(H). When the magnetic filed is asymmetrically distributed, the net magnetic field intensity and the relative permeability at a specific location is defined as $H_{(i)}$ and $\mu_{r(i)}$ respectively. So the relative permeability can be expressed with the function (1), where $B'(H)$ is the derivative of the function $B(H)$

$$\mu_{r(i)} = B'(H_{(i)})/\mu_0 = f(H_{(i)}) \tag{1}$$

The net magnetic field intensity is the vector sum of the magnetic field intensity generated by the primary conductor and by the secondary winding, which is given by

$$\mu_{r(i)} = f(H_{(i)}) = f\left(\left|\vec{H}_{1(i)} - \vec{H}_{2(i)}\right|\right) \tag{2}$$

As shown in figure 1, the parameters of the CT are defined as follows: The radius ratio is R=b/a; The number of turns of the secondary winding is N. Also, i_1 and i_2 refer to the current of primary and secondary sides respectively. The bus bar is shifted to the right with a distance of λ. The eccentricity is defined as $\sigma = \lambda/a$. Further, ρ and k are the distance between OP and O'P respectively. The flux density perpendicular to OP is defined as $B_p(\lambda,t)$. As noted above, $i_2(0,t,\mu_r)$ (when at center) is taken as the reference. The eccentricity error is defined as

$$\delta(\sigma,t) = \left|i_2(0,t,\mu_{r(i)}) - i_2(\sigma,t,\mu_r)\right| / i_2(0,t,\mu_r) \tag{3}$$

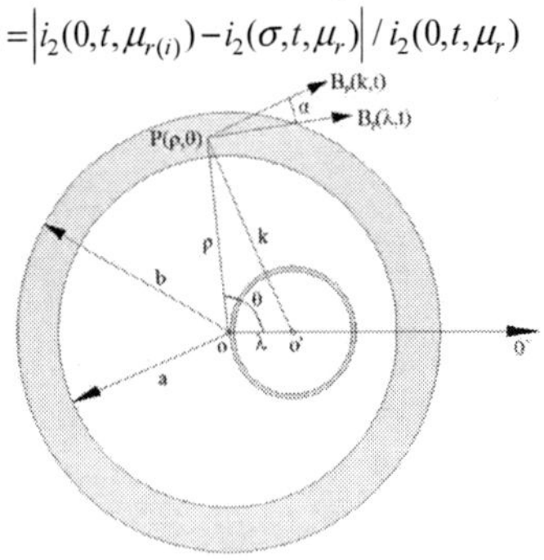

Fig. 1. Primary Conductor is Eccentric with a Distance of λ

For a specific position P, from the Biot-Savart law

$$B_P(\lambda,t,\mu_{r(p)}) = \frac{\mu_0\mu_{r(p)}}{2\pi k} i_1(t)\cos\alpha = \frac{\mu_0\mu_{r(p)}(\rho - \lambda\cos\theta)}{2\pi(\rho^2 + \lambda^2 - 2\rho\lambda\cos\theta)} i_1(t) \tag{4}$$

The induced electromotive force in each turn is given by

$$\varepsilon_P(\theta,\lambda,t,\mu_{r(p)}) = -\frac{\mu_0\mu_{r(p)}}{2\pi}\frac{di_1(t)}{dt}\int_{-h/2}^{h/2}\int_a^b \frac{(\rho - \lambda\cos\theta)d\rho dh}{\rho^2 + \lambda^2 - 2\rho\lambda\cos\theta}$$
$$= -\frac{\mu_0\mu_{r(p)}}{4\pi}\ln\left(\frac{k^2 + \sigma^2 - 2k\sigma\cos\theta}{1 + \sigma^2 - 2\sigma\cos\theta}\right)\frac{di_1(t)}{dt} \tag{5}$$

The induced electromotive force in the whole winding is

$$\varepsilon(\sigma,t,\mu_{r(i)}) = \sum_{i,n=0}^{N-1} \varepsilon_i(2\pi\frac{n}{N},\lambda,t,\mu_{r(i)}) \tag{6}$$

This work was supported by the National Undergraduate Innovation Training Program (201610290077) and the National Program on Key Research Project (2016YFC0600804)

$$= \sum_{n=0}^{N-1} -\frac{\mu_0 \mu_{r(i)}}{4\pi} \ln\left(\frac{k^2 + \sigma^2 - 2k\sigma\cos(2\pi n / N)}{1+\sigma^2 - 2\sigma\cos(2\pi n / N)} \right) \frac{di_1(t)}{dt}$$

The magnetic field intensity at position P generated by primary conductor is given by

$$H_{1(p)}(k,t,i_1(t)) = \frac{i_1(t)}{2\pi\rho}\cos\alpha = \frac{i_1(t)(\rho - \lambda\cos\theta)}{2\pi(\rho^2 + \lambda^2 - 2\rho\lambda\cos\theta)} \quad (7)$$

The magnetic field intensity at position P generated by the secondary winding is given by

$$H_{2(p)}(k,t,i_2(t)) = \frac{Ni_2(t)}{2\pi\rho} = \frac{i_1(t)(1-\delta(\sigma))}{2\pi\rho} \quad (8)$$

The relative permeability at position P is given by

$$\mu_{r(p)} = f\left(\frac{i_1(t)(\rho - \lambda\cos\theta)}{2\pi(\rho^2 + \lambda^2 - 2\rho\lambda\cos\theta)} - \frac{i_1(t)(1-\delta(\sigma))}{2\pi\rho} \right) \quad (9)$$

The error of the CT caused by the eccentricity is

$$\delta(\sigma,t) = 1 - \frac{1}{2N\mu_r \ln R}\left(\sum_{n=0}^{N-1} \mu_{r(i)} \ln\left(\frac{R^2 + \sigma^2 - 2R\sigma\cos(2\pi n / N)}{1+\sigma^2 - 2\sigma\cos(2\pi n / N)} \right) \right) \quad (10)$$

B. Application of the Eccentricity Error Evaluation Model

The core material of the CT used in this work is 23ZH90, as shown in figure 2. The parameters are as follows: $\sigma = \lambda/a$ = 0.3125; N=8000; λ=50mm; R=200mm/160mm=1.25; Primary nominal current is 8000A. For this model, the maximum error can be considered as 0.05% without eccentricity [2].

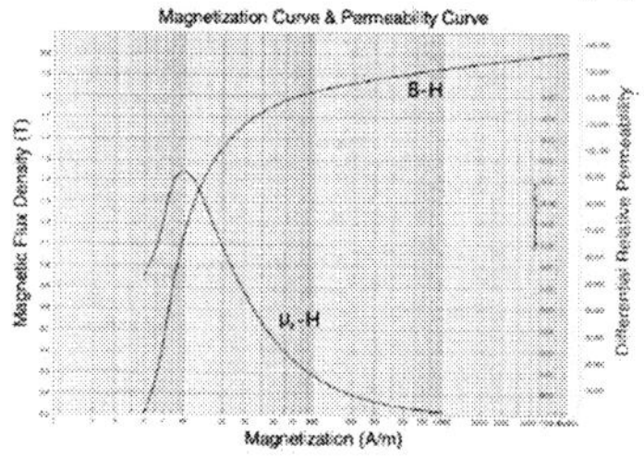

Fig. 2. Magnetization Curve and Permeability Curve of 23ZH90

The curve fitting result is given by B(H)=2.6arctan(0.009H -0.18)+0.44 arctan(0.216H-2.18). The relative permeability is

$$\mu_{r(i)} \approx \frac{1.862\times10^4}{\left(90\delta(\sigma)+102\frac{7.29-10.32\cos(2\pi n/N)}{1.52-0.86\cos(2\pi n/N)}\right)^2+1} + \frac{7.563\times10^4}{\left(2160\delta(\sigma)+2443\frac{7.29-10.32\cos(2\pi n/N)}{1.52-0.86\cos(2\pi n/N)}\right)^2+1} \quad (11)$$

Using the expression of (10) and (11), the CT eccentricity error can be estimated at any given current value. Consider a sinusoidal current excitation for the bus bar, a sample error value at σ = 0.3125 corresponding to a current at t=5ms is obtained as $\delta(0.3125, 0.005s) = 0.262\%$ relative to the induced current when the bus bar is at center. Additional results are presented and verified in the following section.

III. Model Verification

A two-dimensional finite element model with the corresponding dimensions and a position-variable bus bar was developed and applied to evaluate the error, figure 3. The value of the induced current as obtained from this model is shown in figure 4. Using these results, the sample error value at $\sigma = \lambda/a$ =0.3125 corresponding to a current at t=5ms is obtained as $\delta(0.3125, 0.005s) = 0.286\%$ relative to the induced current when the bus bar is at center.

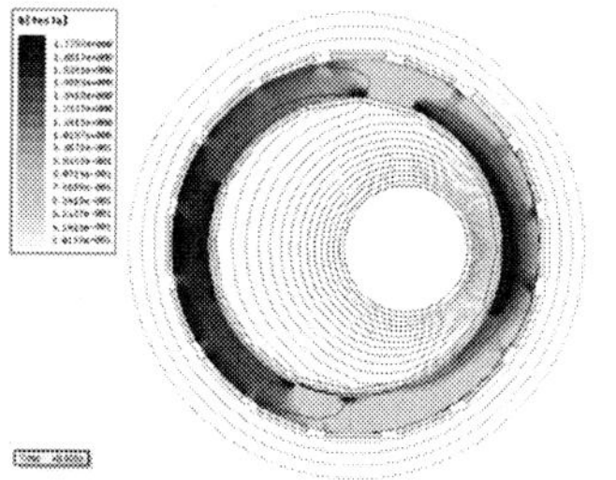

Fig. 3. Simulation Result of the Flux Density Distribution

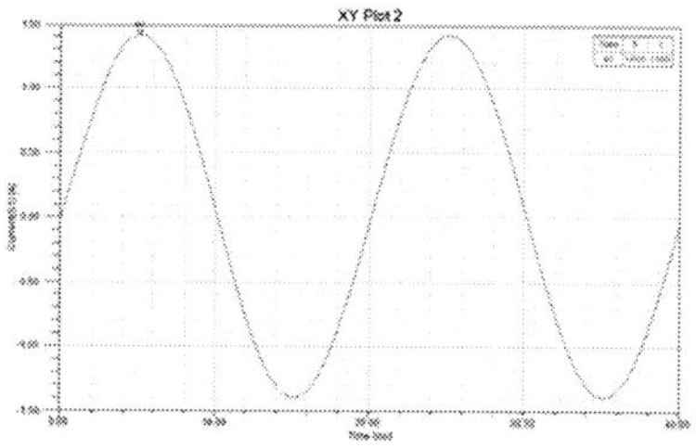

Fig. 4. Simulation Result of the Induced Current

In addition, the maximum and average errors obtained from the mathematical model are compared with the corresponding errors from the finite element model and are given in Table 1.

TABLE I. Verification of the Calculation

Error \ Model	Math Model	FE Model	Difference
Maximum Error	0.262%	0.286%	8.39%
Average Error	0.065%	0.071%	9.16%

IV. Conclusion

Based on the actual magnetization curve of a CT, an eccentricity error evaluation model is proposed. Also, a 2D transient finite element model is implemented for verification.

References

[1] H. Givi, J. S. Moghani, Z. M. A. Vakilian and M. A. Noroozi, "Three dimensional finite element modeling of a current transformer and analyzing its operation under normal condition," 2013 21st Iranian Conference on Electrical Engineering (ICEE), Mashhad, 2013, pp. 1-4.

[2] G. F. Freeman, "The predetermination of current transformer errors," Journal of the Institution of Electrical Engineers - Part II: Power Engineering, vol. 92, no. 27, pp. 190-193, June 1945.

Field Analysis of a Moving Current-Carrying Coil in OMOP Kibble Balances

S. Li, M. Stock, F. Biesla, A. Kiss and H. Fang
Bureau international des poids et mesures (BIPM), F-92312 Sèvres, France
leeshisong@sina.com; fang@bipm.org

***Abstract*—The Kibble balance will be one of the major instruments in the future for realizing the unit of mass, kilogram, in the new international system of units (SI). A recent experimental study at the Kibble balance group at the Bureau international des poids et mesures (BIPM) showed that the magnetic profile measured in weighing and velocity phases is sloped differently due to the movement of the current-carrying coil. This phenomenon has been explained by an analysis of the coil inductance energy (weighing) and self-induction (velocity). In this paper, the magnetic field change at the coil position due to the current is analyzed, in which the slope difference can be well integrated.**

I. Introduction

The Kibble balance, formally known as the watt balance [1], is a precision instrument for measuring the Planck constant and in the future will be employed for mass realizations at different levels in a revised SI. The Kibble balance can be operated in different ways, e.g., two-mode two-phase (TMTP), one-mode one-phase (OMOP), etc [2]. A TMTP Kibble balance contains two separated measurement phases: in the weighing phase, a current-carrying coil is placed in a radial magnetic field B, and the magnetic force generated is balanced by the weight of a test mass m, i.e., $(Bl)_w I = mg$, where l is the wire length, I the coil current and g the local gravitational acceleration. In the velocity phase, the coil is moved along the vertical direction with a velocity $\mathcal{V}$, and the induced voltage $\mathcal{E}$ is measured, i.e., $(Bl)_v\mathcal{V} = \mathcal{E}$. It is assumed that $(Bl)_w = (Bl)_v = Bl$, and by eliminating the same geometrical factor Bl in both measurement phases, a link between the test mass m and the Planck constant can be established [2]. However, a Bl difference between the weighing phase and the velocity phase should be taken into account in the measurement when the coil flux is considered, i.e.,

$$(Bl)_w \approx (Bl)_v(1 + \alpha I + \beta I^2), \tag{1}$$

where α and β are linear and nonlinear coefficients. Note that both theoretical analysis and experimental measurement showed the nonlinear term is negligibly small ($< 2 \times 10^{-9}$) when a BIPM-type magnet is employed [3], [4]. It is shown in [5] and clarified in [6] that a linear current dependence of Bl exists in all air-gapped Kibble balance magnets. More specially, in the OMOP scheme, which runs simultaneously the weighing and the velocity measurements and aims to keep the same conditions for both measurements [7], the magnetic profile change due to the coil flux in the velocity measurement is twice the change determined by the weighing measurement.

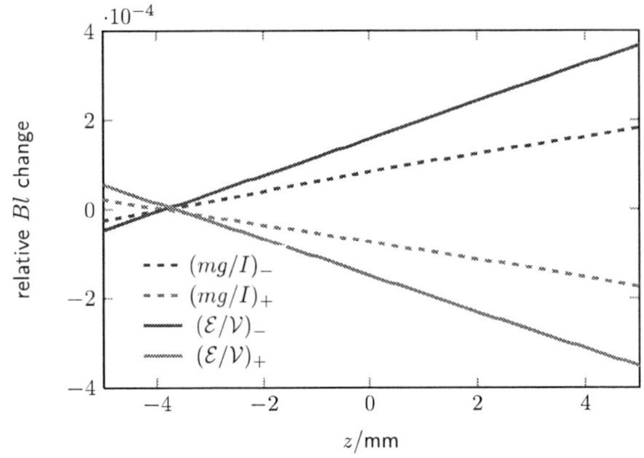

Fig. 1. Measurement results of the profile change due to the coil current in the BIPM Kibble balance. The measurement was carried out with a simultaneous measurement. The currents used are $I_+ = 13.33\,\mathrm{mA}$, $I_- = -13.33\,\mathrm{mA}$, which can respectively generate a 4.9 N (500 g mass) magnetic force in upward and downward directions.

As shown in Fig. 1, two different geometrical factors, mg/I and $\mathcal{E}/\mathcal{V}$, are obtained from the weighing and velocity measurements, and one question we need to answer is: which profile is the true field change at the coil position due to the coil current? To give a certain answer to this question, in this paper we present an understanding of the measurement result by analyzing the magnetic field change at the coil position.

II. Magnetic Field Center

One important conclusion obtained from this measurement result in Fig. 1 is that $\Delta(Bl)_v = 2\Delta(Bl)_w$, where $\Delta(Bl)_v$, $\Delta(Bl)_w$ denote the magnetic profile change in a fixed vertical interval. Before starting to discuss the field created by the coil, the position of the magnetic field center, or the zero-crossing point in Fig. 1 is explained. The magnet used in the measurement is a half-closed magnet, details can be found in [5]. It is assumed that the magnetic field center of the magnet, where the inductance of the coil L has a maximum value, is at $z = z_0$. Since the coil flux mainly stays in the air gap, the following equation can be obtained by Hopkinson's law, i.e.,

$$NI = \phi(R_1 + R_2), \tag{2}$$

where N is the total number of coil turns, R_1, R_2 respectively the magnetic reluctance of the upper portion of the air gap

($z > z_0$) and the lower portion of the air gap ($z < z_0$). Based on an equivalent electrical circuit, R_1 and R_2 can be written as:

$$R_1 = \frac{R_{a1}(R_m + R_g)}{R_{a1} + R_m + R_g}, \quad R_2 = \frac{R_{a2}R_m}{R_{a1} + R_m}, \tag{3}$$

where R_{a1} and R_{a2} denote respectively the magnetic reluctance of the upper air gap (from z to upper end) and the lower air gap (from z to lower end). R_m is the magnetic reluctance of each permanent magnet while R_g is the magnetic reluctance of the open air gap of the half closed magnetic circuit [5]. The inductance of the coil can be written as:

$$L = \frac{N\phi}{I} = \frac{N^2}{R_1 + R_2}. \tag{4}$$

Since $R_1 > 0$, $R_2 > 0$, we have $R_1 + R_2 \geq 2\sqrt{R_1R_2}$, and hence L should be $L \leq N^2/(2\sqrt{R_1R_2})$. As is shown, the coil inductance L has a maximum value with $R_1 = R_2$, which gives:

$$R_{a1} - R_{2a} = -\frac{R_{a1}R_{a2}R_g}{R_m(R_m + R_g)} < 0. \tag{5}$$

Since $R_{a1} < R_{a2}$, $R_{a1} \propto 1/(H - z_0)$, and $R_{a2} \propto 1/(H + z_0)$ where H is the half-height of the air gap, therefore we can obtain $z_0 < 0$. This conclusion explains why the zero-crossing point in Fig. 1 is below zero at $z_0 = -3.7$ mm.

III. Magnetic Field Change at Coil Position

The majority of the coil flux will go through the air gap, and the direction of the coil flux is approximately horizontal. Based on Ampere's law, the magnetic flux density generated by the coil, ΔB_r, would be a step function along the vertical direction: above or below the coil, the magnetic flux density is constant due to a fixed number of coil ampere-turns, NI; in the coil range, the magnetic flux density is a linear function of z because the ampere-turns is proportional to z. This statement is verified by the finite element analysis (FEA) based on the BIPM Kibble balance magnet design, shown in Fig. 2.

Fig. 2 also presents the magnetic field in the air gap when the coil is at different vertical positions. The integral (mean) of the coil section gives a sloped ΔB_r curve when the coil current is fixed. The slopes of $I = \pm 13.33$ mA agree with the measurement result of mg/I ratio in Fig. 1. Therefore, the magnetic profile obtained by the mg/I measurement presents the averaged magnetic field at the coil position, which can be expressed as $\Delta B_w = k(z - z_0)$.

Next, we give a field understanding of why the slope of the magnetic profile measured by $\mathcal{E}/\mathcal{V}$ is twice the slope of mg/I measurement. By Faraday's law of induction, the induction due to the coil magnetic field in the Kibble balance system can be written as:

$$\Delta\mathcal{E} = N\frac{\partial(\Delta B_r S)}{\partial z}\frac{\partial z}{\partial t} = N\mathcal{V}\left(\Delta B_r\frac{\partial S}{\partial z} + S\frac{\partial \Delta B_r}{\partial z}\right), \tag{6}$$

where $S = 2\pi r_c(z - z_0)$ is the flux area at mean coil radius plane $r = r_c$. Substituting $\Delta B_r = k(z - z_0)$ into (6) yields an equivalent (not real) magnetic field change,

$$\Delta B_v = \frac{\Delta\mathcal{E}}{2\pi r_c N\mathcal{V}} = 2k(z - z_0) = 2\Delta B_w. \tag{7}$$

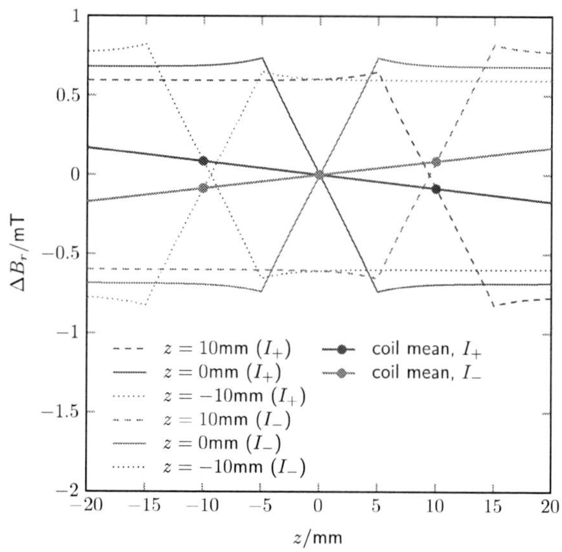

Fig. 2. The magnetic flux density distribution along z direction in the air gap when the current is running through the coil. Three coil positions, $z = -10$ mm, $z = 0$ mm, $z = 10$ mm, are chosen, and the currents used are $I_+ = 13.33$ mA, $I_- = -13.33$ mA.

This conclusion well explains the measurement result in Fig. 1. With more general words, it can be seen as that the moving current-carrying coil introduces a time varying magnetic field at the coil position, which contributes the same amount of self-induction as the movement.

IV. Conclusion

In an OMOP Kibble balance, the slope of the magnetic profile measured by $\mathcal{E}/\mathcal{V}$ has twice the slope determined by mg/I. The zero-profile change point is shown as a symmetry point of upper/lower magnetic reluctances. The analysis confirmed the mg/I profile presents the real field change in the air gap while the slope difference is explained by an additional induction caused by a time-varying field at the coil position. Note that these conclusions also hold for the one-mode two-phase (OMTP, with current in two separated measurement phases) Kibble balance scheme.

References

[1] B. P. Kibble, "A measurement of the gyromagnetic ratio of the proton by the strong field method," *Atomic Masses and Fundamental Constants 5*, pp. 545-551, Springer US, 1976.

[2] I. A. Robinson and S. Schlamminger, "The watt or Kibble balance: a technique for implementing the new SI definition of the unit of mass," *Metrologia*, vol. 53, no. 5, pp. A46-A74, 2016.

[3] S. Li, *et al.*, "Nonlinear magnetic error evaluation of a two-mode watt balance experiment," *Metrologia*, vol. 50, no. 5, pp. 482-489, 2013.

[4] D. Haddad, *et al.*, "Measurement of the Planck constant at the National Institute of Standards and Technology from 2015 to 2017," *Metrologia*, vol. 54, no. 5, pp. 633-641, 2017.

[5] S. Li, *et al.*, "A permanent magnet system for Kibble balances." *Metrologia*, vol. 54, no. 5, pp. 775-783, 2017.

[6] S. Li, *et al.*, "Coil-current effect in Kibble balances: Analysis, measurement, and optimization," *Metrologia*, vol. 55, no. 1, pp. 75-83, 2018.

[7] H. Fang, *et al.*, "A watt balance based on a simultaneous measurement scheme," *Metrologia*, vol. 51, no. 2, pp. S80-S87, 2014.

Roger Harrington and Shielded Planar Microwave Electromagnetic Analysis

James C. Rautio
Sonnet Software, Inc.
North Syracuse, NY USA
rautio@sonnetsoftware.com

Abstract—**Roger Harrington had major influence in many areas of electromagnetics with his formalization of the method of moments. This paper describes his influence in the early application of the method of moments to analysis of shielded planar microwave circuits. This narrative is based on the author's personal experience starting as a graduate student under Roger Harrington in developing and then commercializing method of moments over a period of 35 years.**

Keywords—electromagnetic analysis, history, method of moments, microwave, planar shielded circuits.

I. Introduction

I first met Roger Harrington in 1982. I had just transferred from GE Space Systems, Valley Forge, PA to GE Electronics Laboratory, Syracuse, NY. Having completed a BSEE at Cornell and a MS Systems Engineering at University of Pennsylvania, I was looking for an interesting topic and a good advisor for my doctorate. At the Electronics Laboratory, I was designing some of the first GaAs MMICs (monolithic microwave integrated circuits). I noticed that some designs at the Laboratory would require five or six iterations at US$50 000 and six months per iteration. I discovered that Prof. Harrington was working on numerical electromagnetic (EM) analysis using something called method of moments (MoM) [1], [2] and felt this might be a good match for my interests, and might actually result in something useful. I obtained funding from GE, David Sarnoff Research Laboratories, and HP to seek a numerical EM solution for spiral inductors on GaAs and proceeded.

II. Initial Impressions

At the time, I did not know Prof. Harrington was so well known. The first hint that this was going to be something very special came in 1983 when I attended the International Microwave Symposium (IMS, then called MTT-S) with Syracuse University on my name badge. People kept asking me if I knew Roger Harrington.

Fig. 1 shows Roger Harrington in his office in the spring of 1985. His office and desk was always full of papers and books and would have been cluttered…except that he kept everything so neat. Occasionally, I might find a small error in his Time Harmonic book [3], and I would come into his office to point it out. He would pull his copy off the book shelf up and to his right and make a note for a correction in the next printing. I spent hours reading and working homework problems. I found his writing style to be extremely concise, which means I had to slowly read, and often re-read, passages and consider them carefully. All the needed information was there, and when a new concept came together into full understanding, it was a most rewarding feeling. His style of writing, combined with a strong dose of Strunk and White from Cornell, substantially influenced my own writing.

Fig. 1. Prof. Harrington in his office, Spring 1985.

I found Prof. Harrington to be thoughtful and soft spoken. However, I quickly learned that his, "I think this might be the way to go," is best given much greater weight than assertive, even bombastic statements others might make. He had a very special insight into problems, intuitively knowing the right direction to proceed. For example, I was using roof-top basis functions [4] combined with a spectral domain Green's function [5] to solve the shielded planar circuit problem. It was easiest to write the software with both *x*- and *y*-directed basis functions sharing the same centers. It would not work. I checked everything very carefully, the Green's function was correct and the MoM matrix was being filled correctly. I was up against a wall. I described the problem to Prof. Harrington and he suggested that I should offset the centers of the *x*-directed basis functions with respect to the *y*-directed basis functions, as in [4]. It was a big re-write of the software, but when completed, it worked beautifully! I still remember that first successful MoM matrix solve.

III. COMPUTING HARDWARE

My office was also a small storage room, directly across the hall from Prof. Harrington. One of the items stored there was a large electromechanical calculator, a little smaller than a typical dorm room refrigerator. Prof. Harrington told me that he used that machine to do all the calculations for his books in the late 1960's. I never did think to take a picture of it.

Prof. Harrington also related to me some stories about his first publications, some of which were rejected. He described how one reviewer commented something like, "All your numerical EM work is useless because it has been proven that it is impossible for a computer to invert even a 100×100 matrix…because the magnetic tape will wear out going back and forth." Undoubtedly true, at the time.

My involvement in this field coincided with the introduction of the IBM-PC. Prof. Harrington got one for me, and I also got one for home use. It was amazing with a clock rate of 4.77 MHz (not a typo: MEGA Hertz!). That was a higher frequency than my first ham radio contact. It really was amazing. And 640 kB (not a typo: KILO Bytes) of RAM. For the day, that was huge! Oh, and no hard drive (too expensive). But it had dual 5.25-inch floppy drives (google it, kids).

My first MoM software was developed on that machine. The CPU was the Intel 8088 with a separate 8087 coprocessor, about US$2000. Using Turbo Pascal (US$50 for the entire compiler and documentation, compared to US$400 for IBM FORTRAN), I was able to program the inner loop of the matrix solve in assembly language and run it directly on the coprocessor. I was able to invert a 100×100 matrix in about one hour. Prof. Harrington was most pleased.

Even with this incredible computing ability now on our desktops, we still had a problem when it came to commercialization. Let's go with a burst of wild imagination. Let's pretend that someday, computer clock speed might get to, say, 50 MHz. That is VHF. Would that ever even be possible? And if it were possible, because matrix solve is an n^3 operation, we might then be able to invert a 200×200 matrix, only two times bigger. Would that be big enough to have even a tiny chance of successfully commercializing software? Probably not. I was even told by a famous microwave engineer, whom I held in the very highest regard, that all my numerical EM ivory tower stuff was totally useless. What hurt, was that he was 100% correct…at that time.

I remember considering this problem, realizing the hopelessness of the situation, even if I were to blindly wish for a wildly optimistic future. And then I continued on to commercialization anyway. I still do not know why I made that very foolish decision.

Today, my most recent high-end benchmark was done in 2013 using an IBM-PC at 2.4 GHz, 12 cores and 96 GB of RAM, about US$3000. I do a direct matrix solve of a 100 000×100 000 matrix in about two hours. Given matrix solve is an n^3 operation, computing hardware and software for this problem has improved over 500 million times. A 100×100 matrix is milliseconds. Who could have imagined?

IV. EPILOG

While I was working on my degree, I had also founded what was basically a hobby company, Sonnet Software, to sell antenna analysis software to amateur radio operators. It was very successful, selling over 500 copies. But at US$50 per copy, selling software into a narrow technical niche was fun, but it was also definitely a 'keep the day job' situation. By the time I completed my degree [6], [7], I taught for two years, and then took Sonnet, in 1988, to become a full time company to develop, support, and sell MoM software to microwave circuit designers. Plugging in numbers, it looked like I could quit the day job if I could sell software into this very narrow technical niche market for US$25 000 per copy. But, at that price, would anyone buy this 'useless ivory tower' stuff?

It worked. In fact, in 1995, Sonnet was listed on the Inc. 500 list of fastest growing US companies, the first and only microwave software company ever so listed. While there are many companies today that sell MoM software, I also had the pleasure to be the first, and as best as I know, the only Harrington student to take MoM full time commercial. It is not a 'keep the day job' situation. It *is* my day job, and my total professional focus now for 35 years. It has been an amazing ride. Thank you, Prof. Harrington.

REFERENCES

[1] R. F. Harrington, "Matrix methods for field problems," Proc. IEEE, vol. 55, pp. 136–149, 1967.

[2] R. F. Harrington, Field Computation by Moment Methods, New York: Macmillan, 1968.

[3] R. F. Harrington, Time-Harmonic Electromagnetic Fields, New York: McGraw-Hill, 1961.

[4] A. W. Glisson and D. R. Wilton, "Simple and efficient numercial methods for problems of electromagnetic radiation and scattering from surfaces," IEEE Trans. Antennas Propagat., vol. AP-28, pp. 593–603, Sept. 1980.

[5] R. H. Jansen, "The spectral-domain approach for microwave integrated circuits," IEEE Trans. Microwave Theory Tech., vol. MTT-33, pp. 1043–1056, 1985.

[6] J. C. Rautio, "A time-harmonic electromagnetic analysis of shielded microstrip circuits," Ph.D. dissertation, Syracuse University, Syracuse, NY, 1986.

[7] J. C. Rautio and R. F. Harrington, "An electromagnetic time-harmonic analysis of shielded microstrip circuits," IEEE Trans. Microwave Theory Tech., vol. MTT-35, pp. 726–730, Aug. 1987.

HODLR Direct MOM Solver

John Shaeffer
Matrix Compression Technologies, LLC
Marietta, Georgia
john@shaeffer.com

Abstract—**This note outlines the theory and initial testing of recently developed methods to hierarchically factor low rank Method of Moments system matrices. This method is unique in that it is specific to low rank MOM formulations and is a direct solver which takes significant advantage of the low rank formulation. This direct solver factors a matrix Z into a product of low rank easily invertible matrices using the Sherman Morrison Woodbury formula for low rank updates to a matrix inverse. The factorization phase is much faster than LU and once the system matrix is factored, the solution x = Z^{-1} b is much faster and requires much less memory than ordinary LU factor back solve.**

Keywords—Direct Factor Method of Moments, electromagnetic scattering.

I. Background

Full wave solvers for Maxwell's integral equations are the much-preferred approach when they can be implemented. And direct factor rather than iterative solutions avoids the well-known failures of the latter. However, the direct factor computational cost for N unknowns is immense: N^3 for matrix LU factorization and N^2 for each RHS solution.

Researchers in the last 20-30 years have improved on this situation by recognizing that MOM system matrices, when unknowns are spatially grouped, lead to low rank blocks within the overall system matrix. Early researchers developed iterative solvers based on analytic Green's Function expansions (FMM and MLFMM). While these approaches significantly increased problem sizes they suffered from several problems: 1) They required special development of analytical Green's functions; 2) They were not well adapted for multiple RHS problems where the iterative scheme has to restart fresh for each new RHS vector. This limits FMM and MLFMM usefulness for backscatter problems with many RHS's; 3) They often have slow and no convergence for the iterative solution for problems involving significant interactions; and 4) They often require matrix preconditioners.

More recently the development of the Adaptive Cross Approximation (ACA) for computing the low rank UV approximation to system matrix blocks, based on spatial grouping of unknowns, has spawned whole new approaches to solving MOM system matrices including this author's development in 2006 of the first MOM code (Mercury MOM) to LU factor a problem with one million unknowns [4,6].

Significant advantages over the early FMM / MLFMM approaches are: 1) There is no need for analytic Green's function formulations; 2) The ACA does not require computation of a full matrix block before obtaining its UV Rk approximation. Only specific rows and columns of a block need computation; 3) The ACA low rank blocks of a system matrix can be used for iterative as well as direct LU factorizations.

While a number of researchers in the last ten years have reported on direct LU solutions, few if any have reported doing problem sizes much larger than one million unknowns. Mercury MOM has pushed to five million unknowns [5], but further progress in problem size with many RHS forcing functions has been limited. This lack of progress is due partly to the lack of adaptation of multi-level techniques in the case of Mercury MOM and to lack of direct factor approaches keyed directly to low rank formulations. In Mercury MOM with its low rank block formulation, the diagonal blocks are typically composed of 2000 to 10,000 unknowns. The LU factorization of these blocks and their use in D^{-1} operations in LU factorization and back solve is a significant time and memory limitation.

More recently there have been several papers showing how to direct factor a Hierarchically Off Diagonal Low Rank (HODLR) system matrix formulation [1-3]. This development is the subject of this note. Of interest is whether or not this rather new approach can be incorporated into Mercury MOM so as to increase the maximum problem size or to solve existing problems in less time, memory and IO requirements.

II. Hierarchical Off Diagonal Low Rank (HODLR) Factorization

HODLR factorization [1-2] is the first specific factorization that I know of which is directly applicable to low rank matrices. The binary hierarchical factorization is:

$$Z\,x = D_L\,D_{L-1}\,...\,D_l\,...\,D_1\,D_0\,x = b \qquad (1)$$

where l is the level index and L is the total number of binary hierarchical levels. Each factor is composed of diagonal block

Funded by a retirement account

groups and each D_l except D_L is a low rank update of the identity matrix which is inverted using the Sherman Morrision Woodbury (SMW) formula. Each D_l matrix is composed of $2^{**l} = 1, 2, 4, 8, \ldots$ diagonal low rank groups (blocks) where l is the level. D_L is a diagonal block matrix of 2^{**L} small independent blocks.

The solution is:

$$x = Z^{-1}\, b = D_0^{-1}\, D_1^{-1} \ldots D_l^{-1} \ldots D_{L-1}^{-1}\, D_L^{-1}\, b\,. \quad (2)$$

The Fig. 1 from [3] shows the factorization for L = 3.

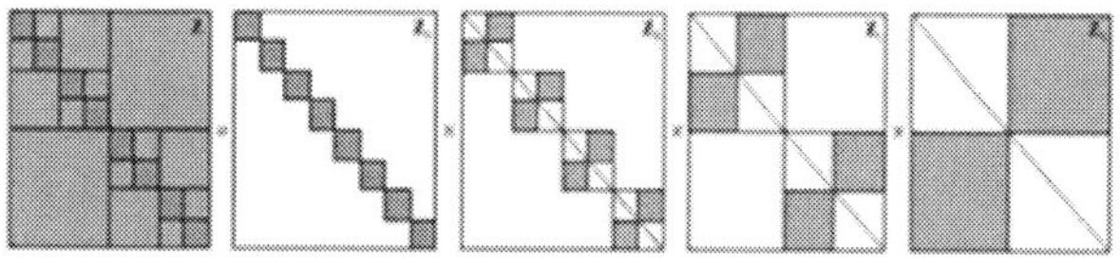

Fig. 1. Hierarchically factored matrix for L = 3

The light shaded green blocks are low rank R_k matrices expressed in UV product form while the diagonal lined white blocks are identity matrices. The blue blocks are the small full rank (dense) matrices at the highest level.

Unknown blocks must be hierarchically grouped so as to obtain spatial locality required for R_k interaction blocks. The first spatial group is splitting all the unknowns in half (right most block in above figure). Then each of those two groupings are split again by half. This continues down to the leaf level which would have $2^L = 2, 4, 8, 16 \ldots$ smaller full dense self-matrix blocks. The cobblestone grouping approach of [4] is used.

III. Initial Results

The test case is a right angle circular cone PEC corner reflector, Fig. 2, with a height and radius of 6.67 λ, resulting in 58,396 unknowns with an average edge length of 0.11 λ. The θ-θ monostatic return is shown in Fig. 3. This test case stresses EM codes in that there are multiple bounces between curved right-angle surface segments and, at each bounce, an incident wave reflects as a concave spherical wave. This geometry is not one likely to be solved using shooting bouncing ray or MOM iterative methods. The right-hand side used 3001 incident angles for θ and φ polarizations for a total rhs count of 6002. ACA tolerance was 10^{-3} for Z fill and the maximum level was L = 4 resulting in 16 leaf blocks each of approximate size 3649.

Fig. 2. Right angle circular cone corner reflector

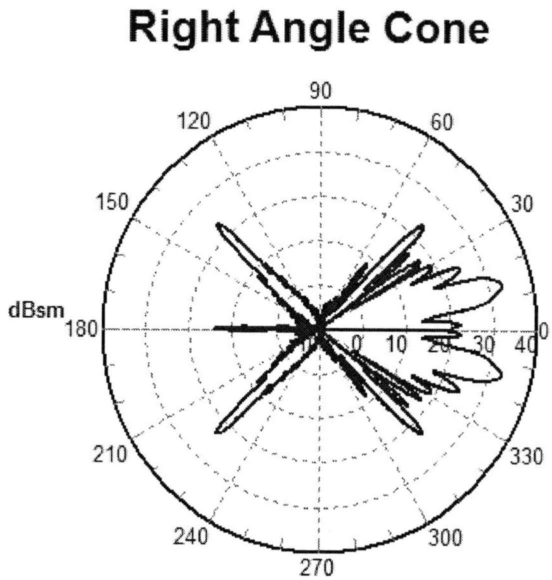

Fig. 3. Right angle cone θ-θ monostatic scattering

References

[1] S. Ambikasaran, "Fast algorithms for dense numerical linear algebra and applications," Ph.D. Dissertation, Stanford University, Aug. 2013.

[2] S. Ambikasaran, E. Darve, "An O(N log N) fast direct solver for partial hierarchically semi-separable matrices", J. Sci. Comput., 2013, 57:477-501, Springer.

[3] X. Chen, C. Gu, Z. Li, and Z. Niu, "Accelerated direct solution of electromagnetic scattering via characteristic basis function method with sherman-morrison-woodbury formula-based algorithm," IEEE Trans. Antennas Propag., vol. 64, no. 10, pp. 4482-4486, Oct. 2016.

[4] J. Shaeffer, "Direct solve of electrically large integral equations for problem sizes to 1 M unknowns," IEEE Trans. Antennas Propag., vol. 56, no. 8, pp. 2306-2313, Aug. 2008.

[5] J. Shaeffer, "Five million unknown MOM LU factorization on a PC workstation," Antenna Measurement Techniques Association Meeting, Long Beach, CA, Oct. 11-16, 2015.

[6] J. Shaeffer, "Direct solve of electrically large integral equations for problem Sizes to 1M unknowns," NASA/CR-2008-215353, Sept. 2008.

History of Developments Leading to the Method of Moments

Donald R. Wilton
Dept. of Electrical and Computer Engineering
University of Houston
Houston, TX, U.S.A.
wilton@uh.edu

***Abstract*— The method of moments, originated by R.F. Harrington a half-century ago, remains one of the most common methods used today for solving electromagnetic boundary value problems. Here we summarize the history, principal methods, and insights that led to the recognition of its unifying principles and approach.**

Keywords*— *Method of Moments, numerical methods.

I. Introduction

The Method of Moments (MoM) [1],[2], as conceived by Roger Harrington, is a general method for solving any linear operator equation. Broadly speaking, it therefore incorporates, for example, finite difference, finite element, and boundary element (integral equation) methods. More particularly, the MoM can in principle be used to solve any linear electromagnetic boundary value problem arising from Maxwell's equations. It is interesting to explore the history of related methods that eventually led to recognition of the unifying approach that MoM provides. The method is now a standard approach used throughout applied mathematics and engineering, though, depending on the application area, it often goes by a different name, such as the projection method. In this work, we explore the history and background of numerical treatments and developments that preceded and led to the development of the MoM.

II. Developments Preceding the Moment Method

The use of variational methods [3],[4],[5], integral equations [6], finite differences [7], and finite element methods [5],[8] to provide numerical solutions for electromagnetic and related boundary value problems dates back to at least the end of the nineteenth and beginning of the twentieth centuries. Some of the earliest formulations, employing both manual and computer-aided computations, treated simple wire-dipole antennas [9],[10],[11], often employing what came to be called entire domain bases, such as sinusoidal or Fourier series, to approximate the axial wire current component. Both finite difference and integral equation formulations were used in electrostatics and the latter formulations were among the earliest applications employing subdomain bases in integral equations [12],[13]. Early electrodynamics applications employing subdomain bases in integral equations were primarily scattering or antenna problems, either with unknown quantities defined on one-dimensional domains or reduceable to a series of such problems. They included cylinders [14],[15] bodies of revolution [16], and wire [17] geometries. The geometry restrictions were mainly due to limitations in both the speed and memory of early computers. Even as computer capabilities expanded, conducting bodies were initially modeled as a grid of wires [18] for simplicity.

One of the more serious efforts toward applying computational methods using integral equation capabilities to the calculation of radar cross sections for practical structures was undertaken in the mid-1960s in a series of Northrop corporation studies [19],[20],[21]. These studies were remarkable in anticipating tools and trends ultimately needed and used in computational electromagnetics, including the following:

- Use of symmetries to reduce the number of unknowns.
- Need for combined field formulations to eliminate internal resonances (probably inspired by similar approaches used in acoustic problems).
- The use of subdomain bases in surface integral equation formulations.
- Applications of the Maue integral equation [22].
- The use of Calderon identities.

In addition to introducing these ideas, a number of very simple electrostatics and scattering problems using subdomain bases were solved numerically to demonstrate the feasibility of modeling conducting scatterers.

III. Insights Leading to the Moment Method

During and following World War II, many practical electromagnetics problems in microwaves were also solved using the variational methods originally pioneered by Schwinger and others [23]. This work, which generally employed Galerkin methods [24], was well known to Roger Harrington [25]. He also realized the method was formally equivalent to both the Rayleigh-Ritz variational method [3],[4] and to Rumsey's reaction concept [26], and was also related to similar linear and Hilbert space ideas being used in quantum mechanics. Until the arrival of high speed computers to perform the tedious calculations required, however, such methods were generally considered impractical [25].

In 1965, during a sabbatical year at Berkeley on leave from Syracuse University, Harrington became interested in the recent work of K. K. Mei and J. Van Bladel and others using subdomain-based numerical methods to solve integral equations. He also formed an idea. In his own words [25],

> "The accuracy obtained from these numerical solutions was impressive, but, being brought up on variational solutions, I thought that even greater accuracy could be obtained by the latter method. I had been taught that 'a parameter could be calculated correct to the second order if a function correct to the first order is used in a stationary formula.' Hence, if I used a numerical solution for the current in a stationary formula for a scattered field, I should get an order-of-magnitude higher accuracy for it than obtainable from a numerical solution. Or so I thought. I tried it for the simple case of scattering from a cylinder, and, to my surprise, I got exactly the same answer as obtained from the numerical solution. Something was wrong in my reasoning."

Harrington knew the methods in use were not true Galerkin methods, but wondered if they remained variational, nonetheless. He was then able to prove this to be the case, not only unifying many disparate numerical approaches, but also implying that expansion and testing functions could be chosen independently—and merely for their convenience properties—with the resulting formulation still guaranteed to be variational. In very short order, the approach gained a name, the advantages and power of the MoM approach began to become apparent and further developed, and it began to be applied to a wide variety of practical problems. A publication summarizing the MoM and its application to a number of examples (including both integral and differential equations) was submitted to the IEEE Trans. on Antennas and Propagation, but was rejected. It was then resubmitted and finally published in the IEEE Proceedings [1]. Among reviewer objections to the original submission were the following:

- "It is impossible to represent continuous quantities, such as current [on a wire], using discontinuous quantities."
- "It is not possible for a computer to invert a 100 x 100 matrix because the magnetic tape [unit] will wear out going back and forth."

While such concerns seem quaint today, they can be seen as legitimate concerns of the day. A short time later, Harrington published his well-known monograph [2] on the MoM with further details and examples. It also outlined MoM treatments for problems in electrostatics, two-dimensional scatterers, wire antennas and scatterers, introduced the generalized network concept and its application to multiport systems, discussed eigenvalue problems and their application to waveguides and cavity resonator problems, and treated optimization problems. The book, currently approaching 10,000 citations, remains the fundamental exposition of the MoM.

REFERENCES

[1] R. F. Harrington, "Matrix methods for field problems," Proc. IEEE, vol. 55, no. 2, pp. 136–149, 1967.

[2] R.F. Harrington, Field Computation by Moment Methods, New York: Macmillan, 1968. (reprinted Wiley-IEEE Press, 1993).

[3] Lord Rayleigh, Theory of Sound, Vols. I, II., London: Macmillan, 1894, 1896.

[4] W. Ritz, "Über eine neue Methode zur Lösung gewisser Variationsprobleme der mathematischen Physik," J. Reine, Angew. Math., 135, pp. 1-61, 1909.

[5] R. Courant, "Variational methods for the solution of problems of equilibrium and vibrations," Bull. Amer. Math. Soc., 49, pp. 1-23, 1943.

[6] H.C. Pocklington, "Electrical oscillations in wires," Proc. Cambridge Phil. Soc., London, 9, pp. 324-332, Oct. 1897.

[7] R. Courant, K.O. Friedrichs and H. Lewy, "On the partial difference equations of mathematical physics," (with commentaries by P.B. Lax, O.B. Widlund, S.V. Parter), IBM J. Res. Develop., 11, pp. 215-234, Mar. 1967. [R. Courant, K.O. Friedrichs, and H. Lewy, "Über die partiellen Differenzengleichungen der Mathematischen Physik," Math. Ann. 100, pp. 32-74, 1928.]

[8] R.W. Clough, "The finite element method in plane stress analysis," Proc. 2nd ASCE Conference on Electron. Comp., vol. 8, Pittsburg, Pennsylvania, pp. 345-378, 1960.

[9] E. Hallen, "Theoretical investigation into the transmitting and receiving qualities of antennae," Nova Acta Soc. Sci. Upsal., pp. 1-44, 1938.

[10] R.W.P. King and T.T. Wu, "Currents, charges, and near fields of cylindrical antennas," Rad. Sci., vol. 69D, 3, Mar. 1965.

[11] R.H. Duncan and F.A. Hinchey, "Cylindrical antenna theory," J. of Research of NBS, Vol. 64D, No. 5, pp. 569-584, Sept.-Oct. 1960.

[12] D.K. Reitan and T.J. Higgins, "Calculation of the electrical capacitance of a cube," J. Appl. Phys., 22, pp. 223-226, 1951.

[13] J. Van Bladel and K.K. Mei, "On the capacitance of a cube," Appl. Sci. Res., B9, pp. 267-270, 1961.

[14] K.K. Mei and J. Van Bladel, "Scattering by perfectly-conducting rectangular cylinders," IEEE Trans. Antennas Propagat., AP-11, pp. 185-193, Mar. 1963.

[15] M.G. Andreasen, "Scattering from parallel metallic cylinders with arbitrary cross sections," IEEE Trans. Antennas Propagat., AP-12, pp. 746-754, Nov. 1964.

[16] M.G. Andreasen, "Scattering from bodies of revolution," IEEE Trans. Antennas Propagat., AP-13, no. 2, pp. 303-310, Mar. 1965.

[17] J.H. Richmond, "Digital computer solutions of the rigorous equations for scattering problems," Proc. IEEE, 53, pp. 796-804, Aug. 1965.

[18] J.H. Richmond, "A wire-grid model for scattering by conducting bodies," IEEE Trans. Antennas Propagat., AP-14, pp. 782-786, Nov. 1966.

[19] F.K. Oshiro and R.C. Cross, "A source distribution technique for the solution of two dimensional scattering problems," Phase III Report, Northrop Corporation Report No. NOR-66-74, Mar. 1966.

[20] F.K. Oshiro, K.M. Mitzner, et al., "Calculation of radar cross section," Northrop Corporation Report No. NOR-67-31, Jan. 1967.

[21] F. Oshiro and K.M. Mitzner, "Digital computer solution of three-dimensional scattering problems," 1967 Antennas and Propagation Society International Symposium, Oct. 1967.

[22] A.W. Maue, "Toward formulation of a general diffraction problem via an integral equation," Z. Phys., 126, no. 7, pp. 601-618, 1949.

[23] N. Marcuvitz, Waveguide Handbook, Rad. Lab. Ser., vol. 10, New York: McGraw-Hill, 1951.

[24] B.G. Galerkin, "Rods and plates. Series occurring in various questions concerning the elastic equilibrium of rods and plates," Vestnik Insz., 19, pp. 897-908, 1915.

[25] R.F. Harrington, "Origin and development of the method of moments for field computation," IEEE Antennas Propagat. Mag., pp. 31-36, Jun. 1990.

[26] V.H. Rurmsey, "Reaction concept in electromagnetic theory," Phys. Rev., 17, pp. 952-956, 1954.

A Novel Stochastic Integral Equation Method for Wireless Communication in Diffuse Multipath Environments

Shen Lin and Zhen Peng
Electrical and Computer Engineering Department, University of New Mexico, Albuquerque, U.S.A.
shenlin@unm.edu, pengz@unm.edu

***Abstract*—This paper investigates a novel stochastic integral equation method for the statistical characterization of wave propagation within diffuse multipath environments. The stochastic integral equation rigorously integrates coherent and incoherent propagations within a compact form, which does not appear to be available in the literature. Furthermore, it quantitatively describes universal statistical properties of the environment through random matrix theory. The theoretical research is evaluated and validated through semi-empirical statistical fading models.**

***Index Terms*—diffuse multipath, Green's function, integral equation, propagation, statistical analysis.**

I. Introduction

Transmission of information through complicated diffuse mulitpath environments is a topic of both fundamental and practical importance to wireless communication. Representative applications include indoor communications [1], [2], communications in metropolitan areas [3], transmission through diffusive random media [4], [5], etc. The complexity of the scattering environment creates an extremely large number of multiple paths between transmitters and receivers. Attributed to the distinguished characteristics and unique behaviors, applied scientists and engineers has found diverse applications, including multiple-input and multiple-output (MIMO) communications [6], [7], time-reversal systems [8], [9], wavefront shaping and focusing [10], [11], sensing and targeting [12], [13], et al. Yet, much potential is not fully exploited due to a lack of rigorous and versatile mathematical models.

II. Methodology

A. Stochastic Green's Function

We propose a novel theoretical solution to Maxwell's Equations in the diffuse multipath media, leveraging wave chaos theory and random statistical analysis [14]–[16]. The resulting stochastic Green's function (SGF), G_S, can be written as a sum of a correlated component, G_co, and an uncorrelated component, G_uc. We obtain:

$$G_\mathrm{S}(\mathbf{r},\mathbf{r}') = \underbrace{\frac{1}{\pi}\sum_i \frac{\omega_i^2}{k^2-k_i^2}\frac{k\Delta}{k_i}\frac{\sin k_i|\mathbf{r}'-\mathbf{r}|}{4\pi|\mathbf{r}'-\mathbf{r}|}}_{\text{correlated, } G_\mathrm{co}} + \underbrace{\sum_i \frac{\omega_i\omega_i'}{k^2-k_i^2}\frac{k\Delta}{4\pi^2}\frac{\sin k_i|\mathbf{r}'-\mathbf{r}_0'|}{k_i|\mathbf{r}'-\mathbf{r}_0'|}\frac{\sin k_i|\mathbf{r}-\mathbf{r}_0|}{k_i|\mathbf{r}-\mathbf{r}_0|}}_{\text{uncorrelated, } G_\mathrm{uc}}. \quad (1)$$

In Eq. 1, ω_i and ω_i' are taken to be two independent Gaussian random variables with zero mean and unit variance. The eigenvalues k_i obey locally repulsion laws, which are distributed according to the random matrix hypotheses of Wigner. The $\mathbf{r}_0$ and $\mathbf{r}_0'$ are local expansion centers with respect to the source point, $\mathbf{r}$, and the receiving point $\mathbf{r}'$. In addition, Δ is the mean-spacing between adjacent eigenvalues of the Helmholtz operator predicted by Weyl Formula [15], [17].

B. Stochastic Integral Equation

Consider a Tx antenna array and a Rx antenna array in the chaotic environment. Each array contains three antenna elements. The exterior surfaces of the Tx and Rx antenna elements are denoted by $S_m^T, m=1,2,3$ and $S_n^R, n=1,2,3$, respectively, The basis and testing functions are introduced on the surfaces of the antennas, defined as λ_m^t on S_m^T and λ_n^r on S_n^R. We propose a new stochastic integral equation method using the SGF (SIE-SGF):

$$Z^\mathrm{RT} = \sum_{n=1}^{3}\sum_{m=1}^{3}\int_{S_n^R}\int_{S_m^T}\lambda_n^r\cdot\mathcal{F}(G_\mathrm{S})\cdot\lambda_m^t dS_n^R dS_m^T. \quad (2)$$

In Eq. 2, the $\mathcal{F}$ is defined as a general differential operator on the proposed SGF. Taking the electric field integral operator as an example, $\mathcal{F}=\left(\bar{\bar{\mathbf{I}}}-\frac{\nabla\nabla}{k^2}\right)$ for vector EM fields.

In analogy to the standard fast multipole method [18], the discrete matrix of SIE-SGF can be decomposed as:

$$\mathbf{Z}^\mathrm{RT} = \mathrm{Re}\left[\mathbf{Z}_0^\mathrm{RT}\right] + j\mathbf{D}_0^\mathrm{R}\cdot\underbrace{\left[\mathbf{T}_0^\mathrm{RT}\mathbf{g}_\mathrm{co}+\mathbf{g}_\mathrm{uc}\right]}_{\text{Translation}}\cdot\mathbf{A}_0^\mathrm{T}. \quad (3)$$

where $\mathbf{Z}_0^{**}$, $\mathbf{A}_0^*$, $\mathbf{D}_0^*$ are the impedance matrix, aggregation matrix, and disaggregation matrix using free-space Green's function, respectively. The $\mathbf{T}_0^{**}$ is the free-space translation matrix, which corresponds to the direct trajectory contributions between the source and receiver. The $\mathbf{g}_{**}$ represents the effects of multipath chaotic rays with random phases, whose statistics are obtained from random matrix theory [19].

III. Experimental Verfication

We begin with the verification of the work with semi-empirical Rayleigh fading model, which is introduced for extremely multipath environments [20]. In the experimental verification, we consider two monopole antennas as transmitting (Tx) and receiving (Rx) inside the complex multipath environment. The two antennas are separated by $L = 20\lambda$. The SIE-SGF is employed at the exterior surfaces of two antennas, and the finite element method is used for the modeling of volume domain of antennas. The probability distribution function (PDF) of the normalized S-parameter of the Rx antenna is depicted in Fig. 1 (a). Since the Tx and Rx are well-separated, the SGF is dominated by the uncorrelated component, G_{uc}, which corresponds to the diffuse multipath propagator. The PDF indeed follows the Rayleigh distribution.

Next, we calculate the PDF of the channel capacity with respect to Signal-to-Noise ratio: $\rho = 2$ in Fig. 1 (b). We notice that the results are consistent with the expression given in the literature for the single-input single-output case (SISO) in presence of Rayleigh fading [20]. Nevertheless, there are no fitting parameters needed in the proposed work.

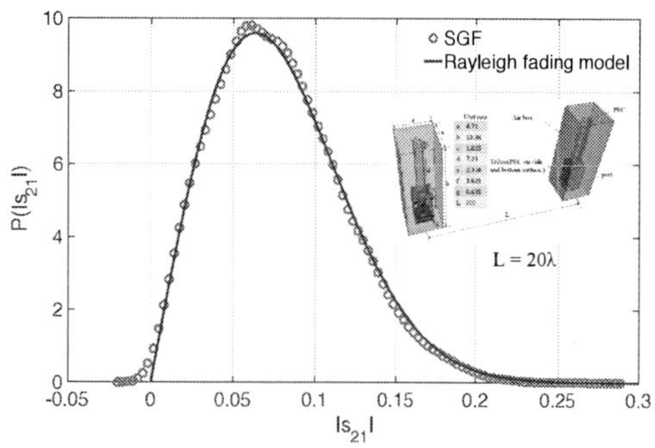

(a) Normalized S_{12} parameter

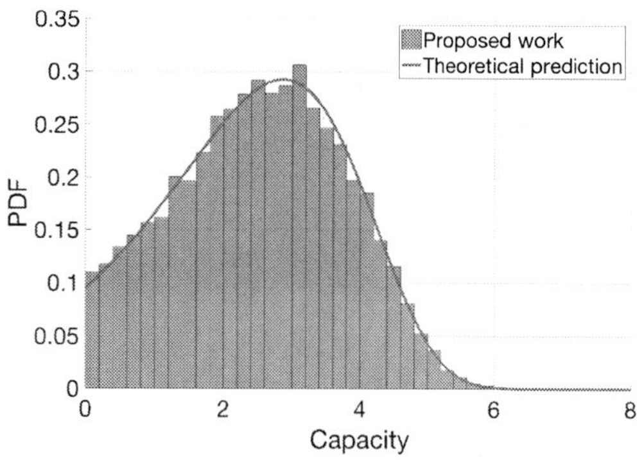

(b) Channel capacity

Fig. 1: Probability distribution functions

IV. Conclusion

The results verify that the proposed work leads to a competent statistical model for predicting the performance of wireless antennas in the multipath environment. The SGF statistically replicates the propagation phenomena that includes both direct orbits and uniform, isotropic multipath fading. Moreover, the computational costs are comparable to the free-space environment, since the SIE-SGF are placed only at the exterior surface of antennas. The advancements have diverse applications to wireless experimentation, time-reversal experiments, wavefront shaping, and sensing and targeting.

References

[1] A. O. Kaya, L. J. Greenstein, and W. Trappe, "Characterizing indoor wireless channels via ray tracing combined with stochastic modeling," *IEEE Transactions on Wireless Communications*, vol. 8, pp. 4165–4175, Aug. 2009.

[2] D. Micheli, M. Barazzetta, F. Moglie, and V. M. Primiani, "Power boosting and compensation during OTA testing of a real 4G LTE base station in reverberation chamber," *IEEE Transactions on Electromagnetic Compatibility*, vol. 57, pp. 623–634, Aug. 2015.

[3] P. Kyösti, J. Meinilä, L. Hentilä, X. Zhao, T. Jämsä, C. Schneider, M. Narandžić, M. Milojević, A. Hong, J. Ylitalo, M. A. V.-M. Holappa, R. Bultitude, Y. de Jong, and T. Rautiainen, "WINNER II channel models," tech. rep., European Commission, IST-WINNER, Technical Report D1.1.2, 2007.

[4] Z. Q. Zhang, I. P. Jones, H. P. Schriemer, J. H. Page, D. A. Weitz, and P. Sheng, "Wave transport in random media: The ballistic to diffusive transition," *Phys. Rev. E*, vol. 60, pp. 4843–4850, Oct. 1999.

[5] C. Jin, R. R. Nadakuditi, E. Michielssen, and S. C. Rand, "Iterative, backscatter-analysis algorithms for increasing transmission and focusing light through highly scattering random media," *J. Opt. Soc. Am. A*, vol. 30, pp. 1592–1602, Aug. 2013.

[6] S. H. Simon, A. L. Moustakas, M. Stoytchev, and H. Safar, "Communication in a disordered world," *Physics Today*, vol. 54, no. 9, pp. 38–43, 2001.

[7] A. L. Moustakas, H. U. Baranger, L. Balents, A. M. Sengupta, and S. H. Simon, "Communication through a diffusive medium: Coherence and capacity," *Science*, vol. 287, no. 5451, pp. 287–290, 2000.

[8] G. Lerosey, J. de Rosny, A. Tourin, A. Derode, G. Montaldo, and M. Fink, "Time reversal of electromagnetic waves," *Phys. Rev. Lett.*, vol. 92, p. 193904, May 2004.

[9] M. Frazier, B. Taddese, T. Antonsen, and S. M. Anlage, "Nonlinear time reversal in a wave chaotic system," *Phys. Rev. Lett.*, vol. 110, p. 063902, Feb. 2013.

[10] C. W. Hsu, S. F. Liew, A. Goetschy, H. Cao, and A. Douglas Stone, "Correlation-enhanced control of wave focusing in disordered media," *Nature Physics*, vol. 13, pp. 497–502, 2017.

[11] P. Ambichl, A. Brandstttter, J. Bhm, M. Khmayer, U. Kuhl, and S. Rotter, "Focusing inside disordered media with the generalized Wigner-Smith operator," *Phys. Rev. Lett.*, vol. 119, p. 033903, 2017.

[12] L. Carin, D. Liu, W. Lin, and B. Guo, "Compressive sensing for multi-static scattering analysis," *Journal of Computational Physics*, vol. 228, no. 9, pp. 3464 – 3477, 2009.

[13] S. D. Cohen, H. L. D. de S. Cavalcante, and D. J. Gauthier, "Subwavelength position sensing using nonlinear feedback and wave chaos," *Phys. Rev. Lett.*, vol. 107, p. 254103, Dec. 2011.

[14] M. V. Berry, "Regular and irregular semiclassical wavefunctions," *Journal of Physics A: Mathematical and General*, vol. 10, no. 12, p. 2083, 1977.

[15] E. Ott, *Chaos in Dynamical System*. Cambridge, U.K.: Cambridge University Press, 1993.

[16] S. Hemmady, X. Zheng, T. M. Antonsen, E. Ott, and S. M. Anlage, "Universal statistics of the scattering coefficient of chaotic microwave cavities," *Phys. Rev. E*, vol. 71, no. 5, p. 056215, 2005.

[17] L. K. Warne and R. E. Jorgenson, "High-frequency electromagnetic scarring in three-dimensional axisymmetric convex cavities," *Electromagnetics*, vol. 36, no. 3, pp. 186–213, 2016.

[18] J. Song, C.-C. Lu, and W. C. Chew, "Multilevel fast multipole algorithm for electromagnetic scattering by large complex objects," *IEEE Transactions on Antennas and Propagation*, vol. 45, pp. 1488–1493, Oct. 1997.

[19] E. Wigner, "Random matrices in physics," *SIAM Review*, vol. 9, no. 1, pp. 1–23, 1967.

[20] A. F. Molisch, *Wireless Communications, 2nd Edition*. Wiley-IEEE Press, New York, 2011. ISBN: 978-0-470-74186-3.

Spectral Element Boundary Integral Method for Rapid and Accurate Simulations of Inhomogeneous Objects in Layered Media in Nanophotonics

Yiqian Mao
Dept. of Electrical & Computer Engineering
Duke University
Durham, NC 27708, USA
yiqian.mao@duke.edu

Jun Niu
Dept. of Electrical & Computer Engineering
Duke University
Durham, NC 27708, USA
jun.niu@duke.edu

Qing Huo Liu*
Dept. of Electrical & Computer Engineering
Duke University
Durham, NC 27708, USA
qhliu@duke.edu

***Abstract*— We recently developed an efficient numerical solver, the spectral element boundary integral (SEBI) method with the periodic layered medium dyadic Green's functions, to perform rapid and accurate simulations in nanophotonic applications. The problem is Bloch (Floquet) periodic in the lateral directions but has a multilayer background medium in the vertical direction, and arbitrary objects are embedded in the layered medium. We employ the periodic layered medium dyadic Green's function, and the surface integral equations as the radiation boundary condition to truncate the top and bottom computation boundaries of the interior domain that is simulated by the spectral element method. Therefore, all multiple scatterings within the top and bottom layered media have been analytically accounted for in the radiation boundary condition, and the computational domain is only limited to the inhomogeneous objects embedded in the layered medium. Consequently, this SEBI solver can be much more efficient than conventional methods. We demonstrate the accuracy and efficiency of this solver for several typical nanophotonic applications.**

Keywords*— dyadic Green's functions, layered media, nanophotonics, spectral element method, spectral element boundary integral (SEBI) method.

I. Introduction

Many nanophotonic applications involve periodic structures in a layered medium background medium [1-8]. For example, in the extreme ultraviolet (EUV) lithography, the number of layers below a mask can be more than 80, thus creating a huge computational burden to numerical methods [8]. Such a problem is difficult to solve by using any single methodology such as the finite element method, finite difference method, or integral equation method with a homogeneous background medium.

With the philosophy used in the finite element - boundary integral (FEBI) method [9, 10, 11], the spectral element boundary integral (SEBI) method has been recently developed as one of the most promising methods for electromagnetic scattering analyses of such complex and multiscale problems [12-14]. This computational method incorporates the exact radiation boundary condition for the spectral element method (SEM) [15], thus it is able to solve electrically large problems.

Previously, the SEBI method uses the homogeneous background medium Green's function in the radiation boundary condition. Thus, the SEM needs to discretize the objects and all the layers up to the first and last layer interfaces. More recently, we have developed the SEBI method with layered medium Green's function for the radiation boundary condition [16]. Therefore, the computational domain only involves the inhomogeneous objects embedded in the layered medium, and there is no need to discretize other regions in the layered medium.

In this contribution, we first summarize the formulation of this SEBI method. Then we present some recent improvements of the method to speed up the surface integral equation solution and to allow curved geometries to be modeled for complex objects. We will compare our numerical solutions with reference finite element method.

II. Description of the SEBI Method

A. Periodic Layered Medium Dyadic Green's Functions

First, the dyadic Green's functions for a layered medium with lateral Bloch (Floquet) periodic boundary conditions are used to formulate the surface integral equations for the background medium [17, 18]. This allows the multiple reflections within the layered medium background to be rigorously included, thus avoiding the discretization of the SEM in the layered medium background.

B. Surface Integral Equations as Exact Radiation Boundary Conditions

We formulate the surface integral equations at two interfaces, one above and one below the embedded objects in the layered medium. Thus, there are two sets of dyadic Green's functions, i.e., one for the layers above the objects, and the other for the layers below the objects. When the two interfaces are complete interfaces covering one whole period, there are no communications between these two sets of Green's functions except through their coupling to the SEM unknowns, thus greatly simplifying the formulation.

C. The Spectral Element Method (SEM) for Objects Embedded in a Layered Medium

For the layers with objects, the SEM [15] is used to discretize the inhomogeneous medium up to the SIE interfaces. The use of SEM allows a much smaller number of unknowns than the finite element, especially for electrically large objects. We have made this SEM capable of handling complicated curved objects.

D. Non-Conformal Meshes Coupling Between Different Subdomains

We have improved our SEBI method further by making the SEM and BI meshes to be completely non-conformal to each other, thus allowing the SEM and BI subdomains to be meshed independently and more acceleration methods can be applied to these subdomains.

III. Validation and Examples

We first compare the accuracy and efficiency of the SEBI method with the finite element method. We found that our solver, at better accuracy, is at least one order of magnitude more efficient than the FEM as implemented in a commercial software package, COMSOL.

We then show several typical applications in nanophotonics, especially in extreme ultraviolet lithography, where the computational challenges remain severe for most conventional numerical methods. Figure 1 shows a model with normal incident plane wave with wavelength of 33.5 nm. Result is compared with reference result, in Figure 2.

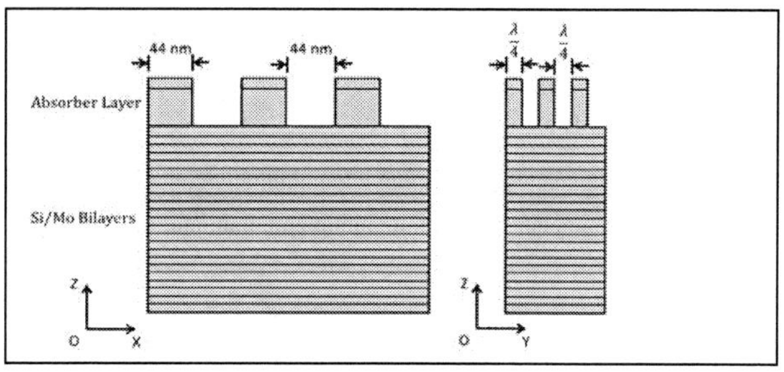

Fig. 1. The xz and yz cross sections of a 3D mask on 20 layers.

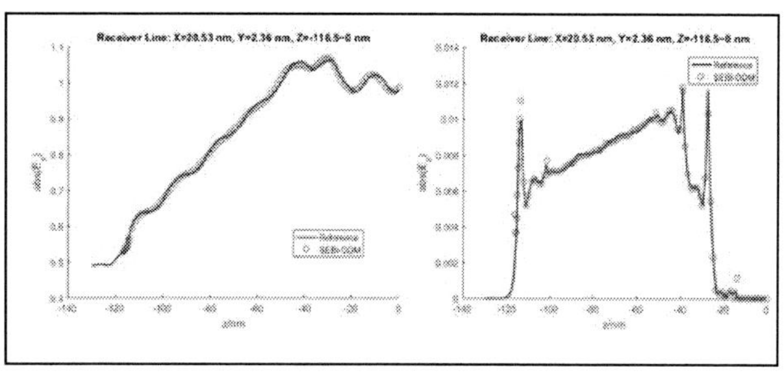

Fig. 2. Magnitude of Ey and Ez along the z direction at (x,y)=(20.53, 2.36) nm when the TE_z plane was is incident from the top.

References

[1] B. Wu and A. Kumar, "Extreme ultraviolet lithography: A review," Journal of Vacuum Science & Technology B: Microelectronics and Nanometer Structures Processing, Measurement, and Phenomena 25, 1743–1761 (2007).

[2] A. Vakil and N. Engheta, "Transformation optics using graphene," Science 332, 1291–1294 (2011).

[3] J. Pomplun, S. Burger, L. Zschiedrich, and F. Schmidt, "Adaptive finite element method for simulation of optical nano structures," Physica Status Solidi (b) 244, 3419–3434 (2007).

[4] H. Lin, M. F. Pantoja, L. D. Angulo, J. Alvarez, R. G. Martin, and S. G. Garcia, "Fdtd modeling of graphene devices using complex conjugate dispersion material model," IEEE Microwave and Wireless Components Letters 22, 612–614 (2012).

[5] I. Ahmed, E. H. Khoo, and E. Li, "Efficient modeling and simulation of graphene devices with the LOD-FDTD method," IEEE Microwave and Wireless Components Letters 23, 306–308 (2013).

[6] N. Stefanou, V. Yannopapas, and A. Modinos, "Heterostructures of photonic crystals: Frequency bands and transmission coefficients," Computer Physics Communications 113, 49–77 (1998).

[7] K. Saitoh and M. Koshiba, "Full-vectorial finite element beam propagation method with perfectly matched layers for anisotropic optical waveguides," J. Lightwave Technol. 19, 405 (2001).

[8] J. Niu, M. Luo, Y. Fang, and Q. H. Liu, "Boundary integral spectral element method analyses of extreme ultraviolet multilayer defects," J. Opt. Soc. Am. A 31, 2203–2209 (2014).

[9] J. Jin, The Finite Element Method in Electromagnetics. 3rd ed., Wiley-IEEE (2014).

[10] J. D. Collins, J. M. Jin, and J. L. Volakis, "Eliminating interior resonances in finite element-boundary integral methods for scattering," IEEE Transactions on Antennas and Propagation 40, 1583–1585 (1992).

[11] A. Nicolet, S. Guenneau, C. Geuzaine, and F. Zolla, "Modelling of electromagnetic waves in periodic media with finite elements," Journal of Computational and Applied Mathematics 168, 321–329 (2004).

[12] M. Luo, Y. Lin, and Q. H. Liu, "Spectral methods and domain decomposition for nanophotonic applications," Proceedings of the IEEE 101, 473–483 (2013).

[13] J. Niu, M. Luo, J. Zhu, and Q. H. Liu, "Enhanced plasmonic light absorption engineering of graphene: Simulation by boundary-integral spectral element method," Opt. Express 23, 4539–4551 (2015).

[14] J. Niu, M. Luo, and Q. H. Liu, "Enhancement of graphene's third-harmonic generation with localized surface plasmon resonance under optical/electro-optic kerr effects," J. Opt. Soc. Am. B 33, 615–621 (2016).

[15] J.-H. Lee, T. Xiao, and Q. H. Liu, "A 3-D spectral-element method using mixed-order curl conforming vector basis functions for electromagnetic fields," IEEE Transactions on Microwave Theory and Techniques 54, 437–444 (2006).

[16] J. Niu, Y. Ren, and Q. H. Liu, "Spectral element boundary integral method with periodic layered medium dyadic Green's function for multiscale nano-optical scattering analysis," Opt. Express, vol. 25, no. 20, pp. 24199-24214, Oct. 2017.

[17] W. C. Chew, J. L. Xiong, and M. A. Saville, "A matrix-friendly formulation of layered medium Green's function," IEEE Antennas and Wireless Propagation Letters 5, 490–494 (2006).

[18] K. Chen, J. Song, and T. Kamgaing, "Accurate and efficient computation of layered medium doubly periodic Green's function in matrix-friendly formulation," IEEE Transactions on Antennas and Propagation 63, 809–813 (2015).

Robust Feed Modeling of the Asymmetric Planar Mesh Dipole-Type Antenna

Jennifer Rayno and Derek S. Linden
AWR Group, NI
El Segundo, CA 90245
jennifer.rayno@ni.com, derek.linden@ni.com

***Abstract*— This paper explores the feed method for the asymmetric planar XY-mesh dipole-type antenna and the modifications needed to prevent its exploitation by automated genetic algorithm (GA) optimization for the application of RFID tag antennas, where the antenna is optimized to the conjugate of the chip impedance. By removing certain feed parameters from the GA optimization and instead making them wavelength dependent, the goal of creating robust models which achieve accurate and matching results between various electromagnetic (EM) simulators, with a focus on the WIPL-D and Axiem EM simulators, was achieved.**

Keywords—antenna synthesis, antenna modeling, genetic algorithm.

I. Introduction

In automated antenna synthesis using genetic algorithms (GA), the antenna model needs to be created such that it is robust to the multitude of various designs that can be created and not easily exploitable with unrealistic designs. The antenna feed can be a particularly sensitive component of the model. Most antennas are initially designed using an ideal feed, since this is the fastest and simplest way. These ideal feeds should not be a key component in achieving the desired antenna performance, as they are expected to be replaced with a real feed. The purpose of the ideal feed is to provide excitation of the antenna structure and the expected port impedance. In addition, since the feed methods vary with electromagnetic (EM) simulator, setting up the feed model is very important in achieving matching results between the different EM simulators. The primary focus in this paper is achieving matching results between WIPL-D and NI AWR Axiem. Both are full-wave 3D electromagnetics solvers using the Method of Moments, however WIPL-D [1] allows arbitrary 3D modeling with finite dielectric regions, whereas Axiem [2] uses stacked planar structures and vias with infinite dielectric substrate sheets. Although the feeding methods for WIPL-D and Axiem are both gap voltage sources, in WIPL-D the feed is assigned to a wire, which must be completely inside or outside of a dielectric region, whereas in Axiem the feed is assigned to the edge of a planar conductor on the surface of a dielectric substrate sheet or in air.

This paper explores the feed method for the asymmetric planar xy-mesh dipole-type antenna and modifications needed to prevent its exploitation when used for the automated design of RFID tag antennas with an atypical desired input impedance (e.g., Z_{in} = 16 + j148Ω rather than the more typical 50Ω).

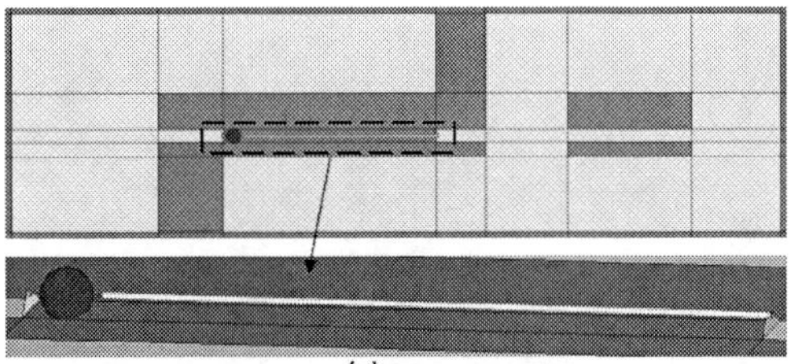

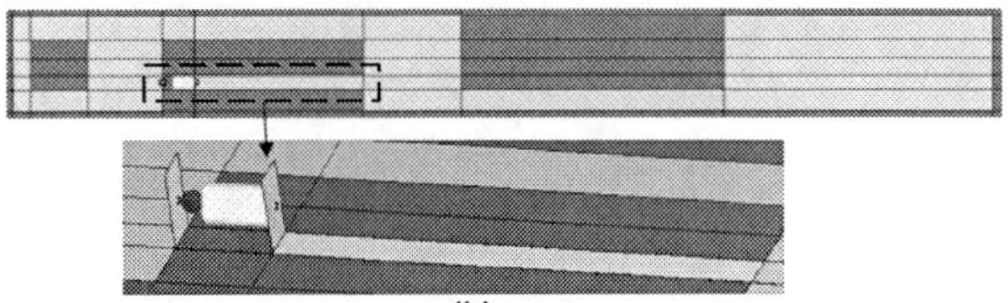

Fig. 1. Examples of WIPL-D feed models: (a) original wire and (b) final wire plus planar conducting strip.

Although the initial WIPL-D model exploited the feed wire length and diameter to meet the specifications [3], the final more robust model was also easily able to meet the specifications without needing to resort to such exploitation [4].

II. Challenges in Feed Modeling

The asymmetric planar XY-mesh dipole-type antenna in NI AWR AntSyn, a software for automated antenna synthesis, was created for use on fixed-size dielectric substrates which can simulate an environment (enviro-mesh antenna), and the capability to optimize the antenna on multiple substrates simultaneously makes it good for RFID tag applications. For RFID tag antennas, the antenna is optimized to the conjugate of the chip impedance, and a typical chip impedance value is 16 - j148Ω. This means the antenna impedance would need to have a really high inductance of j148Ω. In the initial enviro-mesh antenna WIPL-D model, the GA optimizer was easily able to exploit the feed wire to get the high inductance needed by making the feed wire really long and skinny (see Fig. 1(a)). This did come up with a working antenna [3], however it made getting matching results in the exported Axiem model problematic, as Axiem does not use a wire feed. Fabrication would have also been more difficult. Note that other EM simulators which are able to simulate the long, skinny wire did come up with reasonably well matching results.

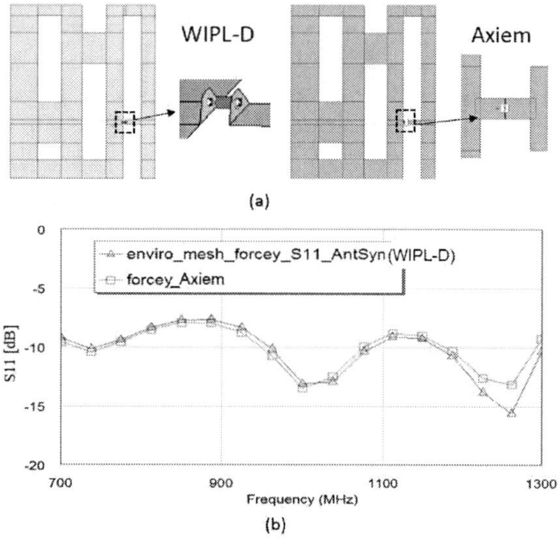

Fig. 2. Comparison of WIPL-D and Axiem for example 1 (no substrate): (a) antenna models and (b) return loss.

Several variations of feed methods in both WIPL-D and Axiem were investigated to see which would give accurate and reasonably well matching results, where an additional EM simulator was used as a tie breaker if necessary. The feed method which ended up working best utilizes a fixed, wavelength-dependent length/diameter for the feed wire in WIPL-D and an internal port with corresponding dimensions in Axiem, and the rest of the original feed was replaced by a planar conductor on the surface of the substrate, where the width is independent of the feed wire (see Fig. 1(b)). In WIPL-D, for the most accurate results with a cylindrical wire feed, the length to radius ratio should be greater than 30 [1]. Since the feed wire needs to be kept very short, this would require a much thinner wire than can be accurately represented in Axiem, as it is very hard to replicate the behavior of very thin feed wires in Axiem. The internal port in Axiem is assigned to the edge between two touching or electrically close planar conductors, and the smallest edge the mesh must represent is specified [2]. Once the internal port conductors are smaller than a certain amount, the port characteristics do not change as significantly as they would for the actual wire, and the very small edge needed to represent the very thin port conductor can significantly increase meshing time or cause errors depending on the antenna model. A tradeoff is made that achieves reasonably well matching results among the various simulators for a variety of cases. With this new WIPL-D model, the GA optimizer is not able to exploit the feed method to achieve the desired specifications but must instead work harder on the antenna design to meet tighter specifications. This new method was also able to come up with a working antenna [4].

III. Results

For comparison of the WIPL-D and Axiem results using the new feed modeling method, two enviro-mesh design examples are shown—the first without substrate and the second with various substrates. Since the purpose was to achieve matching results between the two simulators, the two antennas were not fully optimized and a 50Ω port impedance was used. Fig. 2 shows the design 1 models and return loss, whereas Fig. 3 shows the same for design 2. Both models show reasonably well matching return loss over the entire band. The design 2 results were compared on various substrate dielectrics (ε_r = 2, 4, and 8), and Fig. 3 shows the ε_r = 2 results. Reasonably well matching return loss was also achieved for the other two dielectrics with design 2. Also, the gain vs. frequency results were compared, and both design 1 and design 2 showed excellent matching between the two simulators.

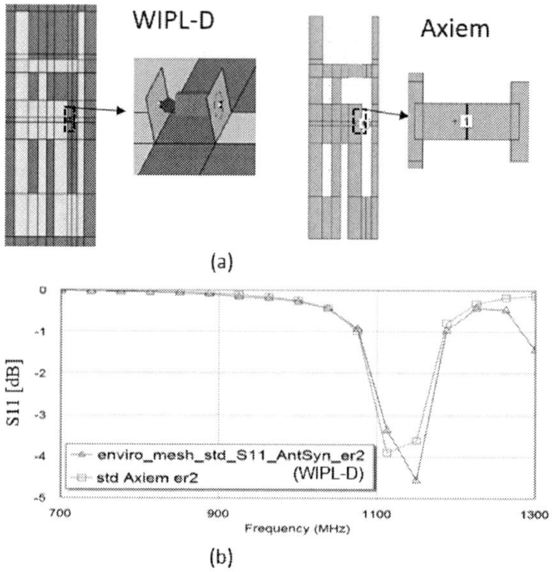

Fig. 3. Comparison of WIPL-D and Axiem for example 2 (has substrate): (a) antenna models and (b) return loss.

IV. Conclusions

The original enviro-mesh antenna model worked well and was robust for more typical 50Ω antenna impedance, however it was discovered to be easily exploitable when used with the complex impedances necessary for RFID tag antenna designs. By removing certain feed parameters from the GA optimization and instead making them wavelength dependent in addition to converting the rest of the original feed wire into a planar conducting strip, the goal of creating robust models which achieve accurate and matching results between various EM simulators, with a focus on the WIPL-D and Axiem EM simulators was achieved.

References

[1] WIPL-D Pro v11.0, Software and User's Manual, WIPL-D d.o.o., Belgrade, 2014.

[2] "Simulation and Analysis Guide," NI AWR Design Environment v13.02 Edition, 2017.

[3] D. S. Linden and J. Rayno, "Synthesis of robust UHF RFID antennas on dielectric substrates," Antenna Systems and Technology, Fall 2016, pp. 6-10.

[4] D. S. Linden and J. Rayno, "Create robust UHF RFID tag antennas on dielectric substrates," Microwaves and RF, March 2017.

Modeling and Validation of a mm-Wave Shaped Dielectric Lens Antenna

David C. Mooradd
MIT Lincoln Laboratory
Lexington, Massachusetts, USA
mooradd@LL.MIT.EDU

Alan J. Fenn
MIT Lincoln Laboratory
Lexington, Massachusetts, USA
ajf@LL.MIT.EDU

Peter T. Hurst
MIT Lincoln Laboratory
Lexington, Massachusetts, USA
hurst@LL.MIT.EDU

***Abstract*— The modeling and validation of a 33 GHz shaped dielectric antenna design is investigated. The electromagnetic modeling was performed in both WIPL-D and FEKO, and was used to validate the antenna design prior to fabrication of the lens. It is shown that both WIPL-D and FEKO yield similarly accurate results as compared to measured far-field gain radiation patterns.**

Keywords—antennas, FEKO, measurement, millimeter wave, shaped dielectric lens, simulations, WIPL-D..

I. Introduction

A 33 GHz uniquely shaped 50 cm diameter dielectric lens antenna has recently been developed, and it has been modeled in both WIPL-D and FEKO. The electromagnetic modeling effort was undertaken to validate the lens design prior to manufacturing. It will be shown that both models yielded similarly accurate results as compared to the final measured gain radiation patterns. The modeled antenna system shown in Fig. 1 is comprised of a Rexolite dielectric lens illuminated by a corrugated conical horn. The antenna design required dual linear polarization, an azimuth beamwidth of 1.2°, and an elevation beamwidth of 12° with a prescribed elevation beam response as shown in Fig. 2.

II. Dielectric Lens

The dielectric lens shown in Fig. 1 is a composite surface design. First, using the design equations in [1], a conventional rotationally-symmetric convex-plano lens design was used to produce a 1.2° conical beam. The next step was to shape the exiting surface of the lens in the elevation plane to achieve the desired elevation beam shape. The phase distortion required to achieve the desired elevation beam shape was derived numerically from which the required dielectric lens shape was derived.

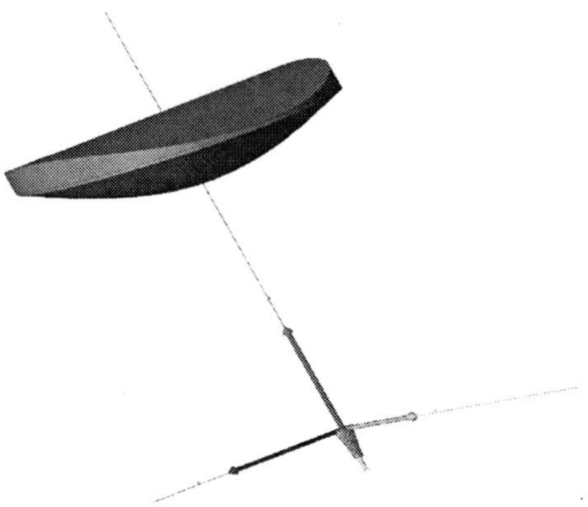

Fig. 1. Ka band corrugated horn and shaped dielectric lens as modeled in WIPL-D ProCAD.

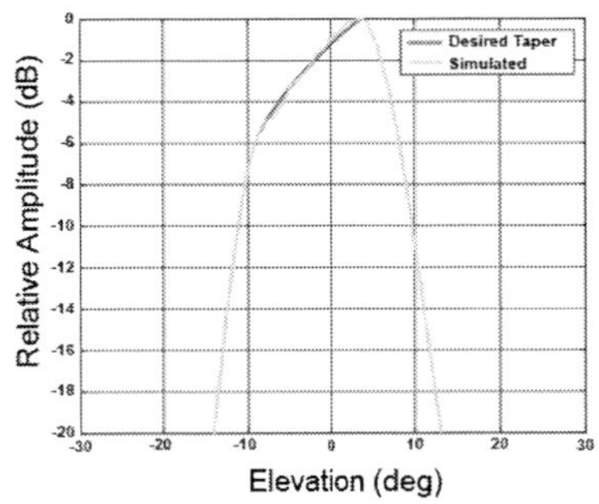

Fig. 2. Prescribed shaped beam elevation pattern.

III. Modeling, Simulation, and Measurements

The above antenna design was modeled in both FEKO and WIPL-D. The FEKO simulation used ray launching geometrical optics to solve the full antenna system, using a spherical mode expansion of the moment method modeled corrugated horn as the illumination source of the lens. WIPL-D performed the entire simulation with the method of moments (MoM), using one symmetry plane to reduce the size of the problem. Both simulation tools yielded similar results, thus validating the antenna system design. While the modeling steps are similar in both tools, the following modeling and simulation steps are specific to WIPL-D ProCAD 2017.

A. Corrugated Horn Model & Simulation

The profile of the corrugated horn was generated in Matlab, based on designs in [2], and imported into WIPL-D as a polyline. The sweep tool was used to generate the cylindrical horn, and a waveguide port was added as the excitation source. The input impedance and far-field radiation patterns were calculated, and the phase center of the horn was determined. The horn was translated to place the phase center at the center of the global coordinate system.

Approved for public release: distribution unlimited.
This material is based upon work supported under Air Force Contract No. FA8721-05-C-0002 and/or FA8702-15-D-0001. Any opinions, findings, conclusions or recommendations expressed in this material are those of the author(s) and do not necessarily reflect the views of the U.S. Air Force.

B. Dielectric Lens Model

Both surface profiles of the dielectric lens were generated in Matlab and imported into WIPL-D ProCAD as polylines. The inner surface is rotationally symmetric about the central axis and was created by sweeping the polynomial about a circle. The outer surface is shaped only in the vertical (elevation) axis, and it is constant along the horizontal axis. The outer surface was created by extruding the polynomial along a horizontal line. To merge the two surfaces and create the solid lens volume, a 50 cm diameter cylinder was generated along the central axis that encapsulated the two surfaces. The three bodies (inner surface, outer surface, and cylinder) were then merged using "Boolean/Intersect" and the unwanted portions of the structure deleted. The lens was translated along the lens axis by 50 cm to place it at the correct focal position relative to the feed. The final step was to define a dielectric domain with a relative permittivity, $\varepsilon_r = 2.54$, and assign it to the Rexolite dielectric lens structure.

C. Simulating the Full Antenna System

The WIPL-D and FEKO simulations were performed on different computers so a direct comparison of computational speed is not possible. The computational details of each simulation are as follows.

The WIPL-D simulations were performed on a desktop computer with two Xeon E5-2643V2 3.50 GHz processors, 64 GB RAM, a Tesla K20c GPU and six 2.65 TB solid state hard drives in RAID0 configuration for high speed scratch space. With one symmetry plane enabled, the total number of unknowns in the WIPL-D simulation was 304,240 (156,754 electric currents and 147,486 magnetic currents). Simulation time for one frequency and one polarization took 37 hours with the GPU Solver enabled.

The FEKO simulations were performed on a machine with two E5-2699 V3 2.30 GHz processors and 512 GB RAM. Approximately 91,000 moment method basis functions were used to compute the Ka-band corrugated horn spherical mode expansion functions used to illuminate the shaped lens. 65953 curvilinear triangles were used to mesh the shaped lens, which was solved for the far-field gain patterns using ray-launching geometrical optics. Total CPU time utilizing 36 cores on two CPUs was 21 hours.

The results of the FEKO and WIPL-D gain radiation pattern simulations are shown overlaid in Fig. 3. As can be seen the two simulations yield very similar results, thus validating the antenna design.

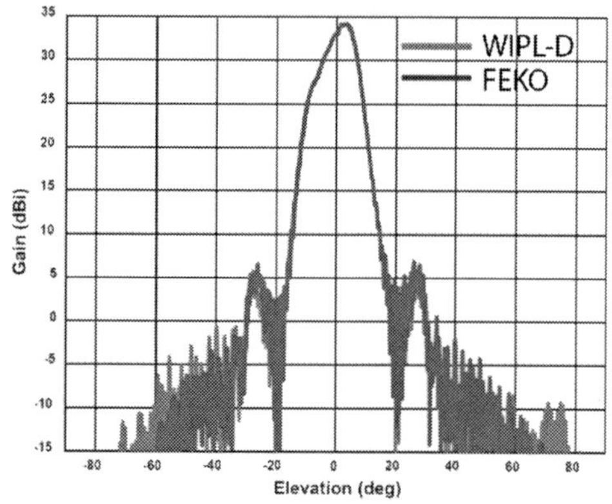

Fig. 3. Comparison of simulated elevation gain patterns for the shaped

D. Comparison of Simulations and Measurements

Gain and radiation pattern measurements of the shaped lens antenna system were performed in a compact range anechoic chamber. The final validation is given in Fig. 4 where the WIPL-D simulated and measured antenna elevation gain radiation patterns show good agreement.

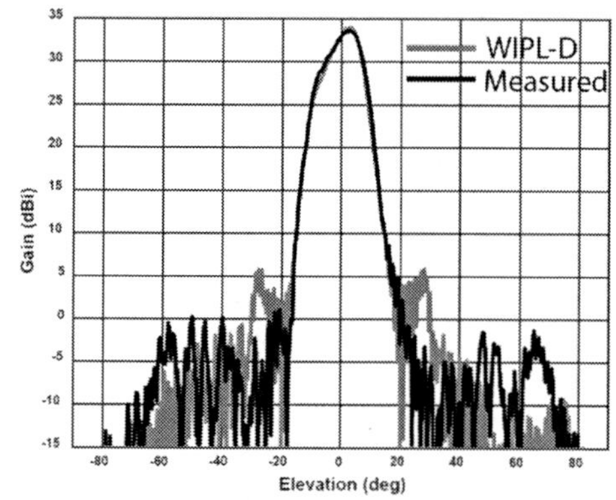

Fig. 4. Comparison of measured and WIPL-D simulated elevation gain patterns for the shaped lens antenna.

IV. Summary

A 50 cm diameter, 33 GHz, shaped beam dielectric lens antenna design was modeled in WIPL-D and FEKO. The two simulations yielded very similar results, validating design of the antenna prior to manufacturing of the lens. The simulated antenna far-field gain radiation patterns of the shaped lens antenna system also had good agreement with measured data.

References

[1] Y. T. Lo and S. W. Lee, Antenna Handbook, Van Nostrand Reinhold Co., New York, Chapter 16.

[2] T. A. Milligan, Modern Antenna Design, McGraw-Hill, New York, 1985.

Higher Order Mode Analysis in WIPL-D
A Tutorial

J. Lyn Alford
Alford Microwave Design Consultants, LLC
Somerset, NJ USA
lyn@alfordmicrowave.com

Milos S. Pavlovic
WIPL-D d.o.o.
Belgrade, Serbia

***Abstract*— WIPL-D Pro 3D EM Solver, method of moments (MoM) based EM analysis, and optimization tools with a reputation for efficient simulation of electrically large structures, can also be used to analyze the transmission of higher order propagation modes in waveguide filters. This paper describes a method that uses a co-simulation strategy, easily implemented with WIPL-D EM tools, to rapidly obtain accurate S parameter response data for higher order mode excitation of waveguide filter structures.**

Keywords—Co-simulation, Higher Order Modes, Waveguide Filters, WIPL-D.

I. Background Information

WIPL-D pioneered the use of higher order basis functions on larger structural elements with a MoM based solution engine, bringing the computation resource demands of larger structures within the capability of widely available low cost personal computers and work stations [1]. Recently WIPL-D further increased the value of its 3D EM tool by incorporating NVIDIA CUDA GPU technology, allowing reduction of large problem solution times by factors of 25-30, or more. This major speed increase may be achieved via the addition of attractively priced, high performance video cards to any PC that currently runs WIPL-D software tools.

Small, complex structures like electronic circuits and cavity filters have traditionally been simulated with volume discretization methods because the accurate modeling of such structures requires structural elements that are often much smaller than a wavelength and naturally consistent with very simple basis functions. However, sometimes the complexity and/or physical size and shape of the device causes the same computation resource problems presented by large structures.

WIPL-D offers a suite of EM analysis tools that can be used with a co-simulation strategy to accurately excite with, and analyze the response of, waveguide filters to higher order modes. The transmission of first higher order modes (TE_{01} and TM_{11} in rectangular waveguides, for example) are simple to excite and analyze with regular wire-based ports in WIPL-D. Excitation and transmission analysis of higher order modes in rectangular waveguides that have E field patterns with reversed polarity across the waveguide cross section are more difficult. The following sections of this paper describe a procedure to excite and analyze transmission of TM_{21} mode in a symmetric rectangular waveguide diplexer.

II. Higher Order Mode Excitation

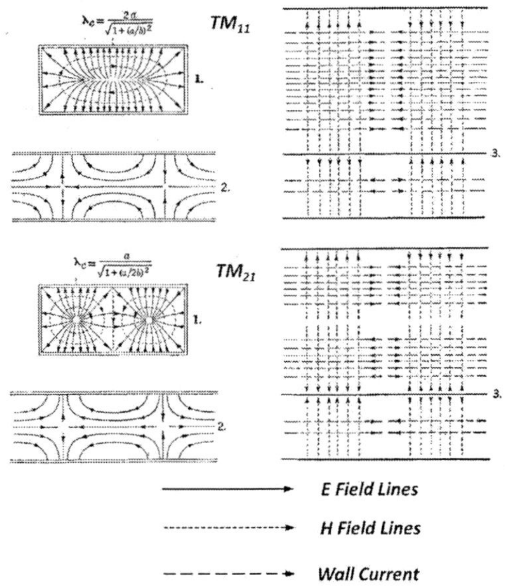

Fig.1 TM_{11} and TM_{21} EM field and wall current patterns [3]

$TE_{m,n}$ designates a waveguide mode with electric field components perpendicular to propagation direction; $TM_{m,n}$ modes have magnetic field components perpendicular to propagation direction. The m,n subscripts are integers indicating half-wave field variations across the width and height of the waveguide cross section. Fig. 1 shows the EM field patterns for TM_{11} and TM_{21} modes in rectangular waveguide.

When operated in the "all generators" antenna mode, higher order modes may be excited in WIPL-D with simple wire ports driven with the proper amplitude and phase for each generator, and properly positioned in the WIPL-D model. The "all generators" operating mode cannot be used when the desired solution data must include the transmission parameters between multiple ports. The "one generator at a time" operation mode must be used to obtain transmission parameters between the various ports of a multiport WIPL-D model. The repeating field patterns in Fig. 1 indicate a "work around" for this impasse.

Notice in Fig. 1 that the TM_{21} field components are simple side-by-side repeats, with opposite polarity, of the TM_{11} field components. Therefore, two square waveguides each excited by a TM_{11} wire port, positioned side-by-side and transitioned into a single rectangular waveguide, will produce the TM_{21} mode field components in the rectangular waveguide, if the generators in the individual square waveguides are the same amplitude, but opposite polarities (180 degrees out of phase). Such excitation is a simple generator voltage change when WIPL-D is operating in the "all generators" antenna mode; however, we must operate WIPL-D in the "one generator at a time" antenna mode if the transmission parameters between different ports are required. Transmission parameters between different ports can be derived from an analysis of a WIPL-D Microwave Pro circuit model consisting of a "black box" multi-port circuit element containing analysis data of the proper WIPL-D Pro model operating in the "one generator at a time" antenna mode, driven and loaded by ideal power splitting and phasing elements from the WIPL-D Microwave Pro "ideal" elements. [2] See Fig. 2 below.

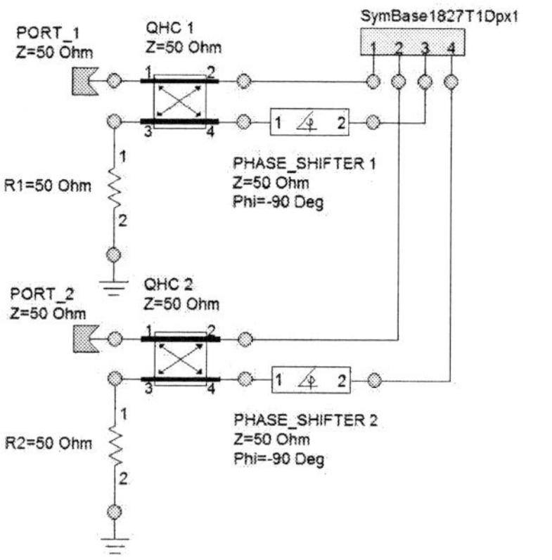

Fig. 2. WIPL-D Microwave Pro Circuit.

III. Symmetric Diplexer Example

Modern communications and sensing systems are utilizing much of the known electromagnetic spectrum. It is important that these various systems do not interfere with each other. A major source of interference between these systems is spurious output in the form of harmonics and noise. A special diplexer that separates a desired fundamental signal from undesired spurious harmonics and noise is a useful piece of test equipment to measure the levels of the undesirable output signals.

Fig. 3 (next column) shows the WIPL-D model of a diplexer as described in the previous paragraph. Figure 3 also shows the response to TM_{21} excitation analyzed using a WIPL-D Microwave Pro circuit similar to the one shown in Fig. 2; over the 18-40 GHz range.

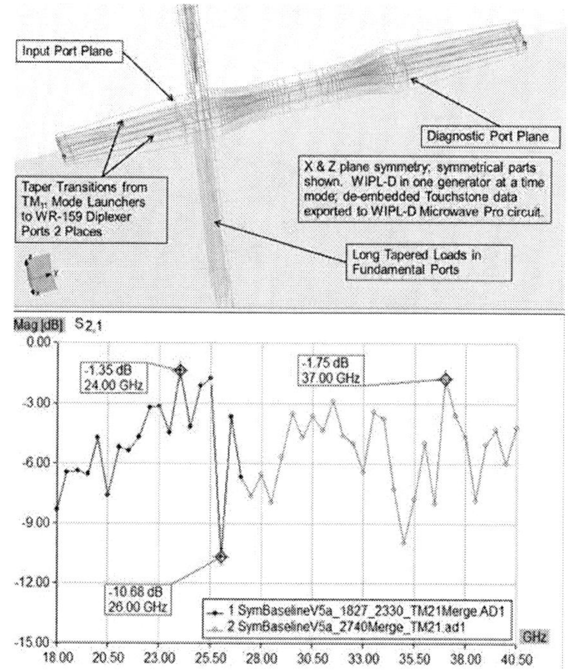

Fig. 3. WIPL-D Pro Diplexer Model & TM_{21} Response.

IV. Summary & Conclusions

This paper describes a method that may be used to obtain transmission data between the various ports of a multi-port device for higher order (description index >1) mode excitations. The described method uses a co-simulation strategy using WIPL-D Pro and WIPL-D Microwave Pro to derive the desired response data from a dominant mode, multi-port (>2) analysis of the device in WIPL-D Pro. The multi-port analysis is used to describe a multi-port "black box" element in a WIPL-D Microwave Pro circuit that excites the dominant mode ports of the "black box" element with generator voltages of the proper amplitude and phase.

References

[1] B. Kolundzija, "Electromagnetic modeling of composite metallic and dielectric structures,"IEEE Transactions on Microwave Theory and Techniques, vol. 47, Issue 7, July 1999.

[2] WIPL-D Microwave Pro v 4.0, Software and User's Manual, WIPL-D d.o.o., Belgrade, 2015.

[3] N. Marcuvitz, "Waveguide Handbook", 1986 edition.

Full-Wave Modeling of RF Exciters Using WIPL-D: Road to Real-Time Simulation and Optimization

Pranav S. Athalye, Branislav M. Notaroš
Electrical & Computer Engineering Department
Colorado State University
Fort Collins, CO, USA
athalye@rams.colostate.edu, notaros@colostate.edu

Milan M. Ilić
School of Electrical Engineering
University of Belgrade
Belgrade, Serbia
milanilic@etf.bg.ac.rs

***Abstract*—Computational tools for full-wave three-dimensional (3-D) simulations of linear passive electromagnetic (EM) components have reached a point where they became both practical and necessary in computer aided design (CAD) of RF devices. Although circuit-based solvers still offer unprecedented speed and true real-time tuning, full-wave software tools, which take into account almost all physical EM phenomena, rapidly approach similar efficiency and applicability. This, however, is not possible by just using modern hardware environment, but it also requires the numerical method of choice, encapsulated within a software tool, to be extremely precise and conservative in consumption of computer resources, i.e., CPU and memory. We here report a case study which demonstrates highly efficient utilization of higher order large-domain method of moments (MoM) modeling and optimization using WIPL-D. The example includes an RF exciter, based on axial-mode helical antennas mounted on a dielectric support, designed for utilization in the state-of-the-art pre-clinical magnetic resonance imaging (MRI) scanners.**

***Keywords*—7-T, computational electromagnetics, helical antenna, high-frequency, microwave, resonance imaging, RF coil.**

I. Introduction

Magnetic resonance imaging (MRI) is an important non-invasive diagnostic technique that is still being explored to its full potential. The radio frequency (RF) coil is a crucial element in any MRI system that is used to excite the water molecules inside the sample being imaged. This paper addresses application of computational electromagnetics (CEM) to the modeling and full-wave analysis of MRI RF coils for ultra-high field magnetic resonance imaging. Modeling of RF coil is generally performed using the finite difference-time domain (FD-TD) methods [1]. In this study we explore the possibility of using the method of moments (MoM) in the frequency domain to perform the same analysis.

We here compare the results obtained from the rigorous full-wave near field computational analysis in the frequency domain based on the MoM using the commercially available software WIPL-D [2] and the finite element method (FEM) using the commercially available software ANSYS HFSS, in the ANSYS Electronics Desktop [3].

II. FEM and MoM Modeling

For our simulation models we consider a 7-T MRI system. The MRI bore contains a quadrifilar helical antenna RF coil [4] as the RF exciter with a phantom, as shown in Fig. 1.

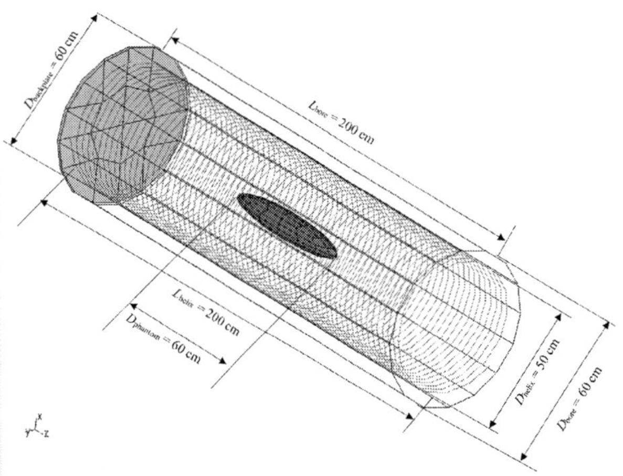

Fig. 1. WIPL-D model of the quadrifilar helical antenna RF coil with an ellipsoid phantom inside it.

The Larmor frequency for 7-T is 300 MHz. The diameter of the bore considered here is 60 cm and length is 200 cm. A helical antenna is a metallic wire antenna wound periodically with N wire turns and a pitch P about an imaginary (or dielectric) cylinder of diameter D_{helix} and length $L_{\text{helix}} = NP$ [5]. The pitch P relates to the pitch angle, α, as $P = C_{\text{helix}} \tan\alpha$, where $C_{\text{helix}} = \pi D_{\text{helix}}$ is the helix circumference. The antenna is fed at one wire end against a circular back plate, acting as a ground plane, i.e., the input power is supplied at a lumped excitation port between the wire end and the plate. A quadrifilar helical antenna is an array of four helical antennas connected to the same circular backplate and fed separately. The four helices (channels) are fed in proper phases in order to generate right handed circularly polarized magnetic field along the axis of the helices inside the coil.

The phantom used is a saline-water ($\varepsilon_r = 81$, $\sigma = 0.6$ S/m) filled ellipsoid. Ellipsoid longer axis is 60 cm long and aligned along the axis of the helix and the bore. It is rotationally symmetric and its shorter axis is 10 cm long.

In order to reduce complexity, the four "wire" helices were modeled in ANSYS-HFSS as a thin strips. The width of the strip is chosen as $a = 4r$, where $r = 1$ mm is the radius of the wire in the WIPL-D thin-wire model.

III. Results and Discussion

In the results we plot and compare $\boldsymbol{H}_{\mathrm{rcp}}$, i.e., the right handed circularly polarized magnetic field and $\boldsymbol{H}_{\mathrm{lcp}}$, i.e., the left handed circularly polarized magnetic field inside the phantom. The aim of the RF coil is to maximize the right handed circularly polarized component of the magnetic field and to minimize the left handed circularly polarized component. Therefore $\boldsymbol{H}_{\mathrm{rcp}}$ should be as high as possible and relatively uniform throughout the phantom, whereas $\boldsymbol{H}_{\mathrm{lcp}}$ should be minimized and almost 0 on the longer axis of the phantom.

In order to equalize the feed powers in both models the excitation voltage of delta-type generators in the WIPL-D model is scaled to match that of the lumped excitation ports in the ANSYS-HFSS model such that:

$$V_x = \sqrt{\frac{P_{\mathrm{incx}}\left(1-|S_{xx}|^2\right)}{\mathrm{Re}\{Y_{xx}\}}}, \quad (1)$$

where Y_{xx} is input admittance and S_{xx} is the corresponding *S*-parameter for each of the individual helices.

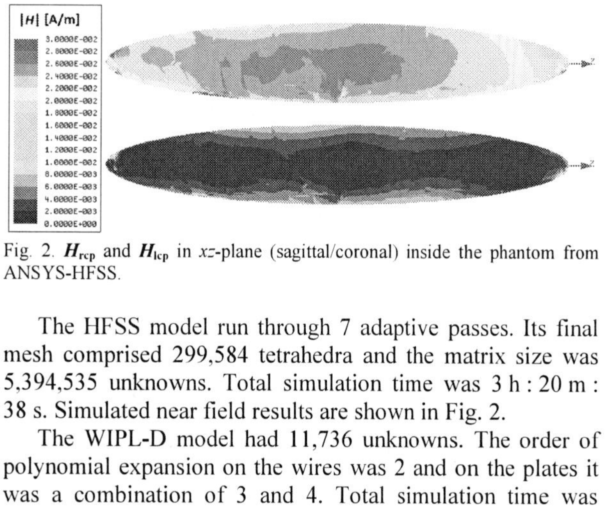

Fig. 2. $\boldsymbol{H}_{\mathrm{rcp}}$ and $\boldsymbol{H}_{\mathrm{lcp}}$ in *xz*-plane (sagittal/coronal) inside the phantom from ANSYS-HFSS.

The HFSS model run through 7 adaptive passes. Its final mesh comprised 299,584 tetrahedra and the matrix size was 5,394,535 unknowns. Total simulation time was 3 h : 20 m : 38 s. Simulated near field results are shown in Fig. 2.

The WIPL-D model had 11,736 unknowns. The order of polynomial expansion on the wires was 2 and on the plates it was a combination of 3 and 4. Total simulation time was 4 m : 24 s. Simulated near field results are shown in Fig. 3.

A comparison of $\boldsymbol{H}_{\mathrm{rcp}}$ and $\boldsymbol{H}_{\mathrm{lcp}}$ on the longer axis of the phantom, i.e., along the *z*-axis computed by ANSYS-HFSS and WIPL-D is shown in Fig. 4. We can conclude from Figs. 2-4 that the results are in a very good agreement.

Acknowledgement

This work was supported by the National Science Foundation under grant ECCS-1307863 and by the Serbian Ministry of Education, Science, and Technological Development under grant TR-32005.

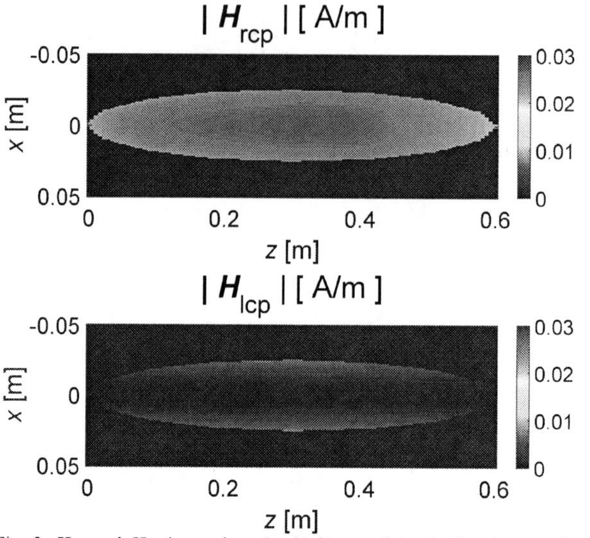

Fig. 3. $\boldsymbol{H}_{\mathrm{rcp}}$ and $\boldsymbol{H}_{\mathrm{lcp}}$ in *xz*-plane (sagittal/coronal) inside the phantom from WIPL-D. (Plotted using MATLAB).

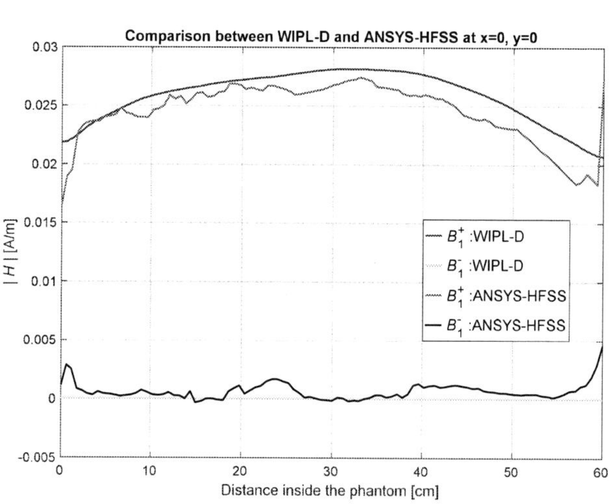

Fig. 4. Comparison of WIPL-D and ANSYS-HFSS results for $\boldsymbol{H}_{\mathrm{rcp}}$ and $\boldsymbol{H}_{\mathrm{lcp}}$ along the *z*-axis inside the phantom.

References

[1] H. Yoo, A. Gopinath, and J. T. Vaughan, "A method to localize RF B_1 field in high-field magnetic resonance imaging systems," *IEEE Trans. on Biomedical Engineering*, vol. 59, Dec. 2012, pp. 3365-3371.

[2] WIPL-D Pro v11. WIPL-D d.o.o. ed2014.

[3] HFSS, ANSYS®. Electromagnetics Suite 17.1.0, ed: ANSYS, Inc.

[4] B. M. Notaros, M. M. Ilic, A. A. Tonyushkin, N. J. Sekeljic, and P. Athalye, "Quadrifilar Helical Antenna as a Whole-Body Traveling-Wave RF Coil for 3T and 7T MRI," *Proceedings of the 23th Scientific Meeting of the International Society for Magnetic Resonance in Medicine, ISMRM 2015*, 30 May–5 June, 2015, Toronto, Ontario, Canada, pp. 1825.

[5] A. R. Djordjevic, A. G. Zajic, M. M. Ilic, and G. L. Stuber, "Optimization of helical antennas," *IEEE Antennas and Propagation Magazine*, vol. 48, no. 6, 2006, pp. 107-115.

Efficient Modeling of Towel Bar Antennas Using Model of Distributed Loading Along Wires

Milos M. Jovicic
Application/Technical Support
WIPL-D d.o.o.
Belgrade, Serbia
milos.jovicic@wipl-d.com

Saad N. Tabet
NAVAIR
Patuxent River, MD, USA
saad.tabet@navy.mil

Branko M. Kolundzija
Chair of General Electrical Engineering
School of Electrical Engineering,
Belgrade, Serbia
kol@etf.bg.ac.rs

***Abstract*—This paper presents an efficient technique to determine equivalents of towel bar antenna dielectric standoffs in the form of wires with distributed loadings using WIPL-D Pro (3-D EM solver) software. Benefits of this technique are simplicity of modeling and fast, but still accurate, simulations.**

***Keywords*—antenna modeling, dielectric standoff, distributed loading, WIPL-D Pro.**

I. Introduction

Let us consider a simple towel bar antenna, mounted above a Perfect Electric Conductor (PEC) ground plane using dielectric standoffs, as shown in Fig. 1. The antenna is excited on one end and short-circuited to the PEC ground on the other. Hence, the antenna uses the PEC ground to operate as a loop antenna. In general, the larger the conductivity of the ground below the antenna tube is, the better the antenna efficiency will be [1].

The antenna tube is capacitively coupled to the ground. The capacitive coupling along the parts of the tube containing standoffs is different from those without standoffs. The influence of each dielectric standoff can be emulated by an equivalent distributively loaded wire, whose radius is properly determined. The equivalent radius and distributed loading are determined by the cross-sectional dimensions of the dielectric standoff and its electrical properties (i.e., relative dielectric constant).

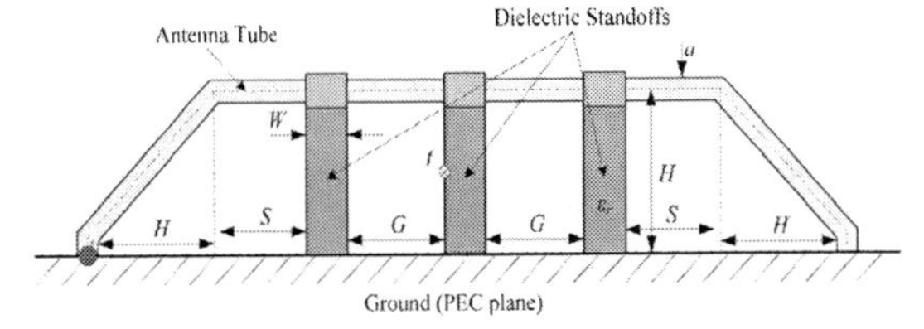

Fig. 1. Towel bar antenna mounted above a PEC ground plane.

II. Models of a Towel Bar Antenna in WIPL-D Pro

A. Metal-Dielectric Model of A Towel Bar Antenna

A full three-dimensional (3-D) metal-dielectric (M-D) model of a towel bar antenna in WIPL-D Pro is shown in Fig. 2. In order to reduce required number of unknowns and simulation time in WIPL-D, two symmetry planes are used; PEC in $x0y$ plane and symmetry in $y0z$ plane.

The dimensions of the model and the electrical properties of the dielectric standoffs are provided in Table I.

TABLE I. Dimensions of the Model and Electrical Properties of Dielectric Standoffs

Parameter [unit]	*Value*
a [mm]	12.7
H [mm]	609.6
S [mm]	750
W [mm]	150
t [mm]	12.7
G [mm]	800
ε_r	16

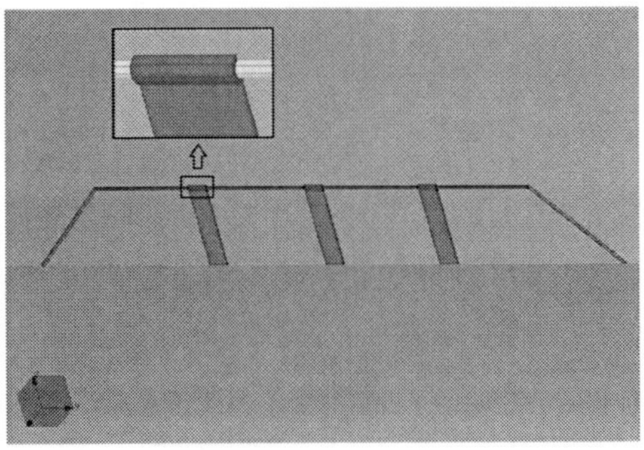

Fig. 2. Metal-Dielectric model of a towel bar antenna in WIPL-D Pro.

B. Equivalent Wire Model of a Towel Bar Antenna

An equivalent wire model of an M-D towel bar antenna, in WIPL-D Pro, is shown in Fig. 3. In this model, only a PEC in the $x0y$ plane is applied.

As a rule of thumb, the surface area of the cross-section of the dielectric standoff must be equal to the surface area of the cross-section of its equivalent wire. Therefore,

$$R_{equivalent} = \sqrt{\frac{W \cdot t}{\pi}}. \quad (1)$$

Also, the surface capacitance of the equivalent wire is related to the standoff's relative dielectric constant as shown in (2) below [2]:

$$C_{S,equivalent} = \frac{\varepsilon_0(\varepsilon_r - 1)R_{equivalent}}{2}. \quad (2)$$

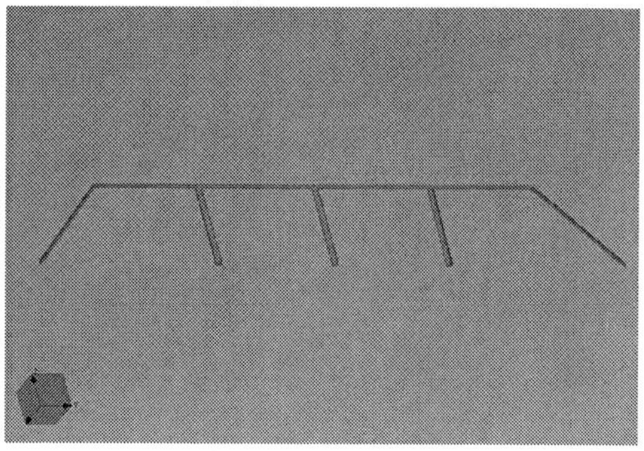

Fig. 3. Equivalent wire model of a towel bar antenna in WIPL-D Pro.

III. RESULTS

The values of the equivalent radius obtained from (1) and the surface capacitance obtained from (2), respectively, are provided in Table II. All other dimensions remained the same as those of the M-D model. It is to be noted that the equivalent wires are placed along the center of the standoffs. A comparison of the real and imaginary components of the reflection coefficient, for the models in Figs. 2 and 3, is shown in Fig. 4.

TABLE II. EQUIVALENT RADIUS AND SURFACE CAPACITANCE

***Parameter* [unit]**	***Value***
$R_{equivalent}$ [mm]	24.625
$C_{S,equivalent}$ [pF]	1.634

Furthermore, the surface capacitance in the equivalent wire model can be manually tuned to achieve better matching to the results of the M-D model. Figs. 5 and 6 show results for the reflection coefficient and radiation pattern comparisons, respectively, for the M-D model and the equivalent wire model with $C_{S,equivalent} = 2.452$ pF.

IV. SUMMARY AND CONCLUSIONS

The simulations of the M-D and equivalent wire models, as obtained through the provided equations, yielded very similar results. Moreover, tuning the equivalent capacitance of the equivalent wire model led to a near identical reflection coefficient and radiation pattern results when compared to those of the M-D model.

The mounting of a wire on an arbitrary platform does not require adapting the mesh of the platform, as is the case for the full 3-D M-D model. In WIPL-D Pro, the only requirement for connecting wires to a 3-D surface mesh of a platform is to properly position the wires and ensuring their connectivity to the 3-D surface mesh using non-trivial junctions at the connection points.

Moreover, the M-D model required a much larger number of unknowns, to estimate the currents over the elements, than the equivalent wire model did to approximate the axial currents along the wires. Hence, the M-D model simulation runtime far exceeded that of the equivalent wire model.

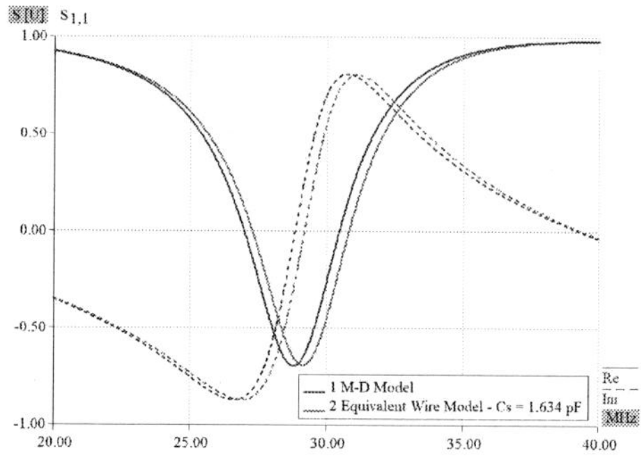

Fig. 4. Comparison of real and imaginary components of the reflection coefficient of the M-D and equivalent wire models, $C_{S,equivalent} = 1.634$ pF.

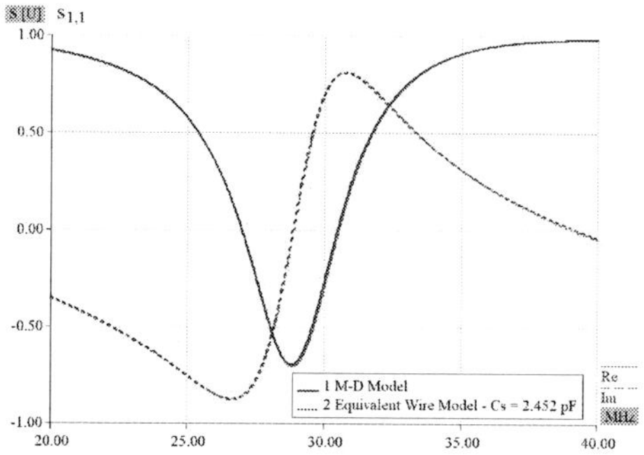

Fig. 5. Comparison of real and imaginary components of the reflection coefficient of the M-D and equivalent wire models, $C_{S,equivalent} = 2.452$ pF.

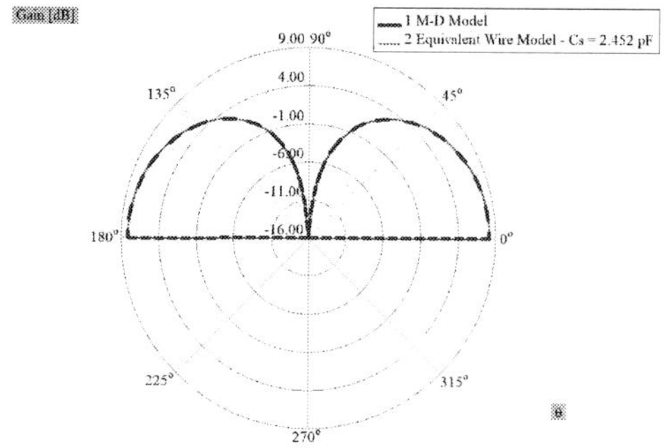

Fig. 6. Comparison of radiation pattern of the M-D and equivalent wire models, $C_{S,equivalent} = 2.452$ pF.

REFERENCES

[1] Towel Rail Antenna Arrays, Cobham Antenna System, 2011.

[2] WIPL-D Pro v14, Software and User's Manual, WIPL-D d.o.o., Belgrade, 2017.

Whistler Mode Wave Numerical Raytracing in a Finite Temperature Anisotropic Plasma Medium

Marek Gołkowski
Department of Electrical Engineering
University of Colorado Denver
Denver, CO USA
mark.golkowski@ucdenver.edu

Ashanthi Maxworth
Department of Electrical Engineering
University of Colorado Denver
Denver, CO USA
ashanthi.maxworth@ucdenver.edu

***Abstract*—Whistler mode waves, which exist in a magnetized plasma, are prevalent in the Earth's magnetosphere in the extremely low frequency (ELF) and very low frequency (VLF) bands (100 Hz - 30 kHz). Due to the impact of whistler mode waves on space weather processes, it is important to accurately predict the propagation trajectory of these waves. Numerical raytracing determines the power flow path of the whistler mode waves in the anisotropic medium of the magnetosphere. In the majority of previous work, magnetospheric raytracing has been implemented assuming a cold background plasma (0 K). However, a more accurate description of the magnetospheric plasma includes a background temperature of about 1 eV (11600 K). We present raytracing solutions which include the effects of finite electron and ion temperatures on the wave refractive index. The finite temperature effects are also introduced into the formulations for linear cyclotron resonance wave growth and Landau damping, which are the primary mechanisms for whistler mode amplification and attenuation in the magnetosphere. Finite temperature effects of the background plasma are shown to be most significant for highly oblique wave normal angles where the refractive index is bounded to smaller values than in the ideal cold plasma approximation.**

Keywords—***whistler mode, raytracing, radiation belts, warm plasma.***

I. Introduction

Whistler mode waves are electromagnetic plasma waves that exists in a magnetized plasma, typically with plasma frequency much greater than electron cyclotron frequency. They are characterized by group and phase velocities much less than the speed of light with significant dispersion and a polarization that is generally right hand elliptically polarized [1]. Whistler mode waves are prominent in certain laboratory plasma applications and also play a key role in the energy dynamics of the near-Earth space environment, which we focus on here. Due to the plasma medium therein and the dominant effect of the geomagnetic field, this region is termed the magnetosphere and hosts a variety of whistler mode waves from diverse sources including manmade transmitters, atmospheric lightning, and local plasma instabilities. The medium is highly anisotropic making the prediction of wave trajectories analytically intractable outside of special cases. The power flow path of whistler mode waves can be determined using numerical raytracing. The magnetosphere contains two distinct populations of plasma, the background low temperature plasma with densities of 10 - 5000 cm^{-3} and a much smaller population of hot plasma with densities well below 1 cm^{-3} but energies in the 10 keV – 1 MeV range. (The hot plasma population is often called the radiation belts.) The hot plasma drives instabilities, but the background low temperature plasma determines the propagation characteristics of waves. The majority of the previous work on magnetospheric raytracing was performed assuming an ideally cold background plasma. However, observations show that the magnetospheric background exhibits finite temperatures of around 1 eV or greater [2]. In this work we show results of raytracing with the inclusion of finite background temperature to electrons and ions. Additionally, the effect of finite temperature on the damping of wave power due to parallel interactions with the energetic electron distributions (Landau damping) and linear cyclotron wave growth for whistler mode waves are also explored. Finite temperature effects become important for highly oblique whistler mode waves.

II. Raytracing Model

A. Refractive Index Surfaces

Numerical ray tracing is the process of determining the power flow path of a whistler wave by solving the Haselgrove equations [3] under a WKB assumption. The medium properties enter the formulation through the refractive index, μ, which is a strong function of wave normal angle θ, which is the angle between the wave normal vector and the geomagnetic field. Under the ideal cold plasma assumption the dispersion relation is fourth order in μ:

$$A_0\mu^4 + B_0\mu^2 + C_0 = 0, \qquad (1)$$

where the parameters A_0, B_0, and C_0 are cold plasma Stix parameters (see [4,5]). With the inclusion of finite temperature, the dispersion relation becomes sixth order:

$$q^T A_1\, \mu^6 (A_0 + q^T B_1)\mu^4 + (B_0 + q^T C_1)\mu^2 + C_0 = 0, \qquad (2)$$

where temperature T_s of each plasma species, s, is captured in:

$$q^T = \frac{k_B T_s}{m_s c^2}. \qquad (3)$$

Details of derivation of (1), (2) and (3) and the parameters therein are provided in [4, 5]. Since in most cases $q^T A_1 << A_0$, the first term in (2) only becomes significant in cases where μ is large. This occurs for highly oblique wave normal angles near the so called resonance cone for which the cold plasma assumption yields $\mu \rightarrow \infty$. Fig. 1 shows the refractive index surface for an example case of 3 kHz wave at the geomagnetic equator two Earth radii from the surface (L = 2) for various electron and ion temperatures as well as the cold plasma case. It is seen that the finite temperature effects cause the refractive index surface to deviate from the cold plasma value only for highly oblique angles near the resonance cone. The magnitude of refractive index is seen to decrease with temperature.

There has recently been interest in estimating the refractive index for highly oblique whistler mode waves where cold plasma theory is inadequate. Ma *et al.* have employed a quasi-electrostatic assumption and shown reasonable agreement with spacecraft observations [6]. While the quasi-electrostatic assumption can provide reasonable results inside the plasmasphere, the model loses accuracy for lower background densities. The warm plasma theory presented here is more accurate in such cases. Fig.2 shows the refractive index surface values near the resonance cone calculated with the quasi-electrostatic approach and the warm plasma approach.

B. Landau Damping and Cyclotron Resonant Growth

In addition to propagation trajectory, the refractive index determines resonance conditions with the hot plasma particles of the radiation belts. Two important resonances are the parallel Landau resonance, which leads to wave damping and is accurately treated using linear theory. Cyclotron resonance, on the other hand, can lead to wave growth and is treated with linear and also nonlinear approaches. Finite temperature effects increase Landau damping rates for frequencies close to the lower hybrid resonance. Simulations with a large number of rays show that finite temperature inclusion leads to wave power concentration near the plasmapause boundary as is seen in spacecraft observations [7].

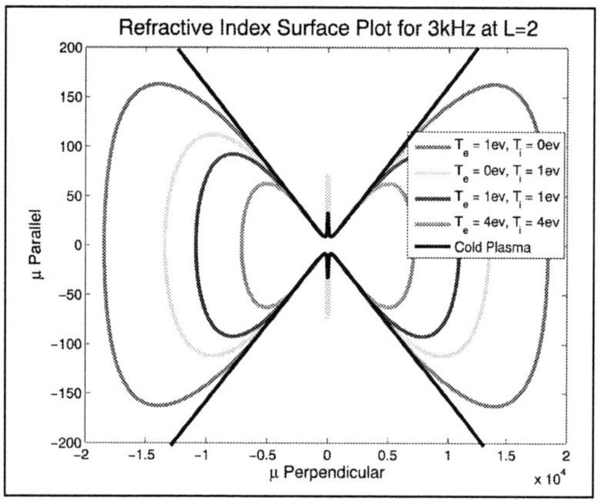

Fig. 1. Refractive index surfaces at the magnetic equator for the cold plasma and finite temperatures for ions and electrons. The refractive indeex is "open" under the cold plasma assumption but closed surfaces when temperature effects are included [5]. Note the disparate scale of the vertical and horizontal axes. The resonance cone angle is 89.1°.

Work was supported by the National Science Foundation grants AGS 1254365 and AGS 1451210 to University of Colorado Denver.

III. Conclusions

Inclusion of finite temperature of the background plasma changes the refractive index for highly oblique whistler waves. Recent spacecraft observations show a significant presence of such highly oblique whistler mode waves and their role in radiation belt dynamics are still being assessed. A primary effort in space weather research is modeling energetic particle populations using quasi-linear diffusion codes. The upper limit of the refractive index surface has been identified as an important parameter [8]. So even if inclusion of finite temperature does not significantly change a typical whistler wave trajectory from that predicted by cold plasms theory, the implications of refractive index change at oblique wave normal angles can have far reaching effects. The warm plasma theory discussed here allows for calculation of the maximum refractive index outside the resonance cone.

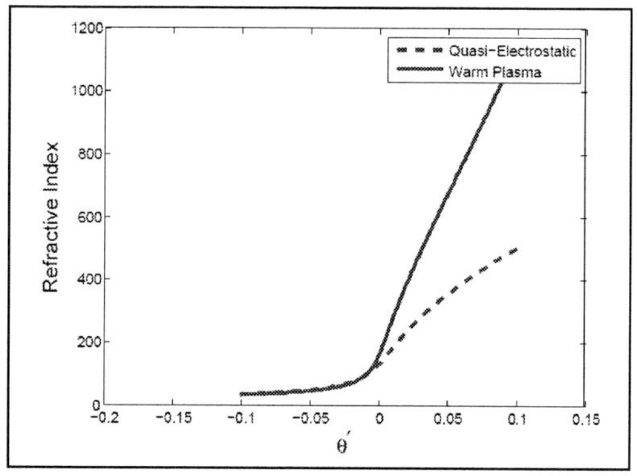

Fig. 2. Comparison of refractive index calculated with quasi-electrostatic and warm plasma models near the resonance cone (θ' = 0) for L = 6.

References

[1] U. S. Inan, Umran S., and M. Gołkowski, *Principles of Plasma Physics for Engineers and Scientists*. Cambridge University Press, 2010.

[2] P. M. E Decreau,., C. Beghin, and M. Parret, "Global characteristics of the cold plasma in the equatorial plasmasphere region as deduced from the GEOS 1 mutial impedance probe, " *J. Geophys. Res A87*, 695, 1982.

[3] J. Haselgrove, "Ray Theory and a New Method for Ray Tracing," in Physics of the Ionosphere, Physics of the Ionosphere Conference, Cambridge, London, 355-364, 1954.

[4] P. Kulkarni, M. Gołkowski, U.S. Inan, and T.F. Bell, "The effect of electron and ion temperature on the refractive index surface of 1-10 kHz whistler mode waves in the inner magnetosphere," *J. Geophys. Res. Space Physics, 120*, 1, 581-591, 2015.

[5] A. S. Maxworth and M. Gołkowski, "Magnetospheric whistler mode raytracing in a warm background plasma with finite electron and ion temperature, " *J. Geophys. Res. Space Physics, 122*, 7, 7323–7335,2017.

[6] Q. Ma et al., "Very Oblique Whistler Mode Propagation in the Radiation Belts: Effects of Hot Plasma and Landau Damping," *Geophys. Res. Lett.*., 2017.

[7] D. M Malaspina et al., "The distribution of plasmaspheric hiss wave power with respect to plasmapause location," *Geophys. Res. Lett., 43*, 15, 7878-7886, 2016.

[8] J. M Albert, "Quasi-linear diffusion coefficients for highly oblique whistler mode wave," *J. Geophys. Res., 122*, 5, 5339-5354, 2017.

Spatial Distributions of Magnetospheric Radio Energy due to Lightning

Austin P. Sousa
Smead Aerospace Engineering Sciences
University of Colorado Boulder
austin.sousa@colorado.edu

Robert A. Marshall
Smead Aerospace Engineering Sciences
University of Colorado Boulder
robert.marshall@colorado.edu

***Abstract*—We provide an improved model of the Whistler-mode radio energy generated by a terrestrial lightning flash, as a function of latitude and magnetic local time. We use a three-dimensional, cold plasma raytracing code to examine typical energy densities in J/m^3 in the magnetosphere. The results presented here are intended to guide future in-situ studies of lightning-induced electron precipitation from the radiation belts.**

I. Introduction

Terrestrial lightning flashes generate impulsive radio noise in the VLF band ($\sim$ 300 Hz – 30 kHz). The majority of radio emissions are guided by the Earth-Ionosphere waveguide, and can propagate large distances. However a small fraction of radiated energy may propagate upward through the ionosphere, and propagate in the Whistler mode throughought the near-Earth plasmasphere. Under certain circumstances, Magnetospherically-Reflecting (MR) Whistlers experience very little attenuation, and can persist from a few seconds, to two or more minutes.

MR Whistlers are coherent wave packets which can resonantly interact with trapped particle populations through pitch-angle scattering, and are thought to be an important loss mechanism for high-energy radiation belt electrons. MR Whistlers have also been theorized to contribute to incoherent VLF radio noise (chorus, hiss) as the packet reflects and disperses. VLF waves are thought to contribute to the slot region, a depletion of high-energy electrons between the inner and outer radiation belts. More recently, it has been suggested that resonant interactions with VLF waves, either from lightning or by terrestrial radio transmitters, may be responsible for the so-called "impenetrable barrier" as measured by [1].

Within this work, we seek to provide average distributions of VLF energy as a function of location and time, in order to locate regions of high activity, and to infer locations (L-shell and time) where the effects of pitch-angle scattering may be most relevant.

II. Radio Energy from a Single Lightning Flash

The MR Whistler generation process is divided into three steps: 1) illumination of the ionosphere by a terrestrial lightning flash; 2) propagation and attenuation through the ionosphere; and 3) reflection and attenuation throughout the plasmasphere.

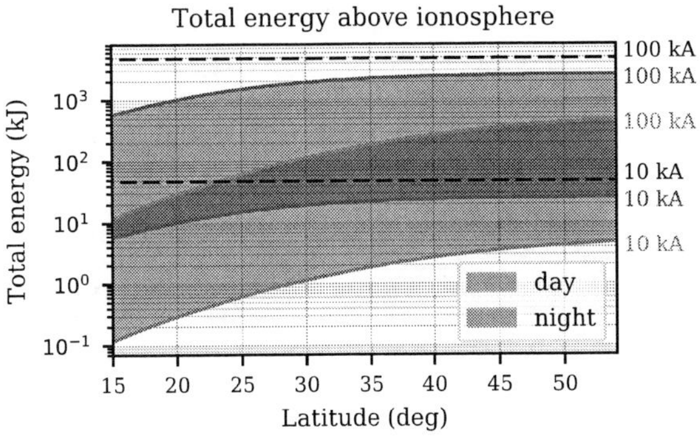

Fig. 1. Total energy above the ionosphere, integrated over area, time, and frequency, resulting from a single flash, for dayside and nightside ionospheres. 10kA represents a typical flash; 100kA is a strong, but not uncommon flash. Dashed lines indicate total radiated power before ionospheric attenuation.

A. Illumination

We consider only cloud-to-ground lightning, which can be modeled as a single, vertical current pulse. We use a double-exponential current function $I(t) = I_0(e^{-at} - e^{-bt})$ as in [2]–[4] and subsequent work, resulting radially-symmetric pattern peaked at approximately 4kHz. We consider illumination within a 1000 km radius.

B. Trans-Ionosphere Attenuation

The ionosphere is a substantial attenuator in the VLF band. In order to generalize to a wide set of lightning flashes, we treat the ionosphere as an attenuating slab from 100 km to 1000 km altitude. We assume VLF waves propagate directly upward, normal to the Earth's surface.

Numerous researchers have used the classic Helliwell curves [5], which are derived from sounding rocket measurements in the early 1960s. We use an updated model from [6], which reports attenuation curves at 2kHz and 20kHz, for day and night, as derived from extensive full-wave simulations. Studies of lightning-generated emissions often assume lightning from the dayside and from lower latitudes is of minimal importance; however the updated *Graf* curves show markedly less attenuation than the Helliwell curves, especially at equatorial ($< 20°$) latitudes, and for the dayside.

Fig. 1 shows the combined model of incident power after trans-ionospheric attenuation.

C. Magnetospheric Propagation

Magnetospheric propagation is determined using a three-dimensional, cold plasma raytracing code, as in [7]. Attenuation is computed due to Landau damping, using $\pm$ 5 modes. Rays are computed for 20 seconds, after which significant energy still remains. However, geometric spreading of the rays suggests that the energy is greatly dispersed.

We model the ambient medium as a four-component cold plasma using a simplified version of the Global Core Plasmasphere Model (GCPM) [8]. For computational efficiency and generalization to different longitudes, we use the equatorial electron density model alone, and ignore density enhancements at the polar cap and cusp region. Constituent ratios vary along each field line in the same manner as the full GCPM model.

For the Landau damping computation, we model the temperature profile using the hybrid model described in [7], which smoothly blends between a cooler distribution inside the plasmapause and a warmer distribution outside the plasmapause.

Rather than perform an interpolation and crossing-detection scheme as in [3], we adopt a "guide ray" approach. We compute ray tracing for all latitudes and longitudes within 1000 km from the incident flash, in 1° increments, for 33 log-spaced frequencies between 200 Hz and 30 kHz. We then analyze each set of guide rays, at adjacent latitudes, longitudes, and frequencies. We assert that the total illuminated energy between the initial corners is always bounded by these rays; therefore at each timestep along the ray, we can define a bounding box, between $(t_n, t_{n+1}), (f_1, f_2), (\mathrm{lat}_1,\mathrm{lat}_2), (\mathrm{lon}_1,\mathrm{lon}_2)$. We can then interpolate onto a regularized output grid by simply checking whether or not a point is within this bounding box; if so we assign it the average energy density. This approach is advantageous in that it allows us to undersample the geographic space, thus reducing the number of rays required, while still accounting for all incident energy.

Fig. 2 shows the time-averaged energy density in the meridional plane due to a 10kA nightside flash, for a variety of latitudes and K_p indices.

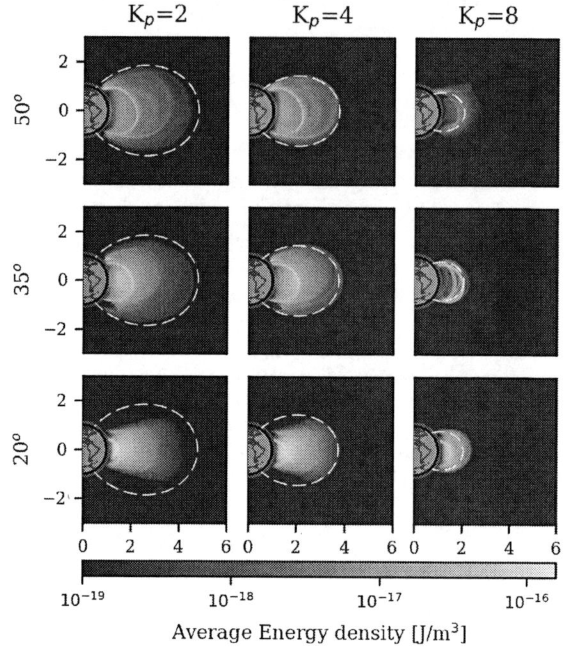

Fig. 2. Average energy density in the meridional plane above a 10kA flash on the nightside, originating at 20°, 35°, and 50°, for K_p= 2, 4, and 8. Dashed white lines denote the plasmapause location.

III. Conclusions

Two trends are apparent in Fig. 2. First, the plasmapause location effectively contains VLF energy within the plasmasphere; however the constraint only becomes relevant at higher values of K_p.

Second, energy imparted by lower-latitude flashes is more-dispersed along L-shell, but is more-constrained in latitude extent. Higher-latitude flashes impart energy over a wider spatial extent; however the initial first reflection is more-coherent, exhibiting a more "duct-like" behavior.

References

[1] D. N. Baker, A. N. Jaynes, V. C. Hoxie, R. M. Thorne, J. C. Foster, X. Li, J. F. Fennell, J. R. Wygant, S. G. Kanekal, P. J. Erickson, W. Kurth, W. Li, Q. Ma, Q. Schiller, L. Blum, D. M. Malaspina, A. Gerrard, and L. J. Lanzerotti, "An impenetrable barrier to ultrarelativistic electrons in the Van Allen radiation belts," *Nature*, vol. 515, no. 7528, pp. 531–534, 2014. [Online]. Available: http://www.nature.com/doifinder/10.1038/nature13956

[2] D. Lauben, "Precipitation of radiation belt Electrons by obliquely-propagating lightning-generated whistler waves," Ph.D. dissertation, Stanford University, 1998.

[3] J. Bortnik, "Precipitation of radiation belt electrons by lightning-generated magnetospherically reflecting whistlers," Ph.D. dissertation, Stanford University, 2005. [Online]. Available: http://vlf.stanford.edu/sites/default/files/publications/bortnik_thesis.pdf

[4] V. A. Rakov and M. A. Uman, *Lightning: Physics and Effects*. Cambridge University Press, 2003.

[5] R. A. Helliwell, *Whistlers and Related Ionospheric Phenomena*. Stanford University Press, 1965.

[6] K. L. Graf, N. G. Lehtinen, M. Spasojevic, M. B. Cohen, R. A. Marshall, and U. S. Inan, "Analysis of experimentally validated trans-ionospheric attenuation estimates of VLF signals," *Journal of Geophysical Research: Space Physics*, vol. 118, no. 5, pp. 2708–2720, 2013.

[7] D. I. Golden, M. Spasojevic, F. R. Foust, N. G. Lehtinen, N. P. Meredith, and U. S. Inan, "Role of the plasmapause in dictating the ground accessibility of ELF/VLF chorus," *Journal of Geophysical Research: Space Physics*, vol. 115, no. 11, pp. 1–15, 2010.

[8] D. L. Gallagher, P. D. Craven, and R. H. Comfort, "Global Core Plasma Model," *Journal of Geophysical Research: Space Physics*, vol. 105, no. A8, pp. 18 819–18 833, 1999.

FD-PIC Simulation of Broadband Whistler Mode Wave Interactions with Energetic Electrons in the Earth's Radiation Belts

Poorya Hosseini
Department of Electrical Engineering
Univrsity of Colorado Denver
Denver, CO, USA
Poorya.Hosseini@ucdenver.edu

Mark Golkowski
Department of Electrical Engineering
Univrsity of Colorado Denver
Denver, CO, USA
Mark.Golkowski@ucdenver.edu

Vijay Harid
Department of Electrical Engineering
Univrsity of Colorado Denver
Denver, CO, USA
Vijay.Harid@ucdenver.edu

I. INTRODUCTION

The distribution of energetic particles that form the Earth's radiation belts is extremely variable, with the trapped flux changing by several orders of magnitude on timescales of a few hours to days. These energetic particles pose a significant hazard to satellites and astronauts in the near-Earth space environment. Additionally, the Earth's magnetosphere hosts a large number of wave modes, which interact with the high energy particles. Here we focus on the whistler mode which exists for frequencies lower than the electron cyclotron frequency. The particles in the near-Earth space environment can be classified into two major "cold" and "hot" plasma populations. The cold plasma is more dense and therefore defines the background medium determining wave propagation and dispersion. Hot plasma particles, on the other hand, drive nonlinear interactions and resonances with the waves. These interactions can lead to wave growth or damping and also to pitch-angle scattering of these energetic particles where a portion of the particles would fall into the loss cone lowering the altitude of their mirror point to a level where they are absorbed by the atmosphere. Accurately modeling of waves in the Earth's radiation belts requires numerical approaches that can capture both the cold and hot plasma effects.

II. THEORY

A. Whistler Mode Waves in the Magnetosphere

Whistler mode wave are a type of electromagnetic wave that exists only in a magnetized plasma. The dispersion relation of whistler modes waves is determined by the plasma density and the strength and direction of the background static magnetic field. In the near-Earth space environment, known as the magnetosphere, the geomagnetic field is slowly changing and can be approximated as a magnetic dipole. Although in the general case, whistler mode waves can propagate at oblique angles to the geomagnetic field, field aligned propagation, as is shown at Fig. 1 (a), is associated with the greatest growth rates and minimal wave damping. Moreover, ground based observation of these emissions are believed to be dominant by the field aligned propagation [1]. Therefore, accurate modeling of field aligned propagated waves and coexistence of multiple particle species, is a key research area.

Whistler mode waves are circularly polarized EM waves in the ELF/VLF bands. Chorus and hiss emissions are among two of the most intense naturally occurring broadband whistler mode waves in this region. The exact generation processes of these emissions are not well understood but are known to involve wave-particle interactions [2]. Wave-particle interaction mechanisms have also been studied in the context of VLF triggered emissions, a closely related process where magnetospheric wave growth is excited by a coherent input wave [3]. VLF radiation from atmospheric lightning discharges is also known to be a key natural source of wave energy in the inner magnetosphere.

Applying a spatial-temporal Fourier transform on Maxwell's equations leads to whistler mode dispersion relation in a cold plasma. While propagation in the background cold plasma is analytically tractable, hot particle resonance interactions make the problem inherently nonlinear requiring numerical modeling.

B. Single Particle Motion in the Presence of a Wave

The Lorentz force governs motion of a single particle in presence of electromagnetic forces. In the absence of waves, the in-homogenous geomagnetic field leads to an unperturbed (adiabatic) magnetic mirroring motion, which is based on the following parallel velocity and perpendicular velocity spatial derivative equations:

$$\left(\frac{dv_\perp}{dz}\right)_U = \frac{v_\perp}{2\omega_c}\frac{d\omega_c}{dz}, \qquad (1\text{-a})$$

$$\left(\frac{dv_\parallel}{dz}\right)_U = \frac{-v_\perp^2}{2\omega_c v_\parallel}\frac{d\omega_c}{dz}, \qquad (1\text{-b})$$

where ω_c is cyclotron frequency, $v_\perp$ and $v_\parallel$ are particle velocities in the direction perpendicular and parallel to the geomagnetic field, respectively, and z is the direction along the magnetic field line. Fig. 1 (b) shows the field aligned coordinate system.

Once the whistler mode wave is introduced to the Lorentz force formula, Eqs. (1-a) and (1-b) will have one more wave-term besides the adiabatic-term:

$$\frac{d\vec{v}}{dt} = \left(\frac{d\vec{v}}{dt}\right)_{Wave} + \left(\frac{d\vec{v}}{dt}\right)_{Unpurturbed}. \quad (2)$$

Single particle motion (with charge of q and mass of m) in the presence of whistler wave in cylindrical coordinates, suggest a resonance condition ($v_{res} = \frac{\omega_c - \omega}{k}$) between the circularly polarized wave (ω) with wave number k, and the particle (ω_c) around the Earth's in-homogenous geomagnetic field.

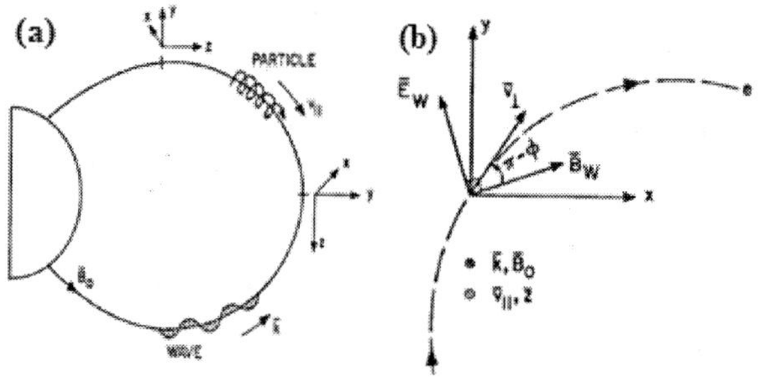

Fig. 1. Single particle motion at the presence of wave for (a) field-aligned propagation, and (b) cylindrical coordinates [4].

For the purpose of broadband wave-particle interaction, (2) is derived in Cartesian coordinates as time-derivative of particle's velocities in x, y, and z axis (v_x, v_y, v_z):

$$\frac{dv_x}{dt} = \frac{q}{m}\left[E_x - v_z B_y - v_y B_0\right] + \frac{v_x v_z}{2\omega_c}\frac{\partial \omega_c}{\partial z}, \quad (3\text{-a})$$

$$\frac{dv_y}{dt} = \frac{q}{m}\left[E_y + v_z B_x - v_x B_0\right] + \frac{v_x v_z}{2\omega_c}\frac{\partial \omega_c}{\partial z}, \quad (3\text{-b})$$

$$\frac{dv_z}{dt} = \left[v_x B_y - v_y B_x\right] - \frac{(v_x^2 + v_y^2)}{2\omega_c}\frac{\partial \omega_c}{\partial z}, \quad (3\text{-c})$$

where B_0 is geomagnetic field, (B_x, B_y) and (E_x, E_y) are wave magnetic and electric fields.

III. WAVE-PARTICLE INTERACTION

Further mathematical derivations on (3) lead to gyro-phase forced pendulum equation, which implies a threshold for the wave amplitude to keep the particle in resonance, a phenomena which is called phase-trapping:

$$B_{tr} = \frac{m}{qkv_\perp}\left[\frac{3}{2}v_{res} + \frac{kv_\perp^2}{2\omega_c}\right]\left|\frac{\partial \omega_c}{\partial z}\right|. \quad (4)$$

For $B_w < B_{tr}$ there is no phase-trapping, and the linear theory approximation is valid for the wave growth. However, for $B_w > B_{tr}$ is trapping or nonlinear region, and numerical simulation is the only method that can provide a self-consistent solution.

IV. FD-PIC HYBRID SIMULATION

A 1-dimensional fully broadband finite difference numerical simulation has been developed to investigate whistler mode wave propagation in the magnetosphere. The model is based on fundamental fluid equations for cold plasma solved simultaneously with full Maxwell's equations. Nonlinear hot plasma feedback is included via a particle-in-cell hybrid simulation to make the model self-consistent as is illustrated in Fig. 2 (a). Fig. 2 (b) shows simulation results in agreement with theoretical cold plasma dispersion relations.

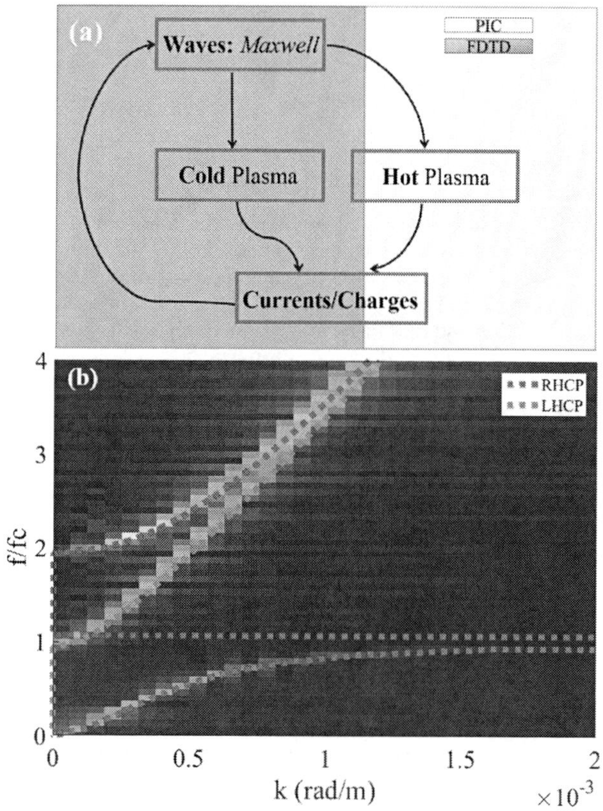

Fig. 2. (a) Schematic of FD-PIC hybric plasma simualtion, (b) Preliminary simulation results with right-hand circularly polarized (RHCP) whistler mode wave's desperion relation.

REFERENCES

[1] P. Hosseini, M. Golkowski, and D. L. Turner "Unique concurrent observations of whistler mode hiss, chorus, and triggered emissions" *Journal of Geophysical Research: Space Physics*, 2017.

[2] M. Gołkowski and U. S. Inan "Multistation observations of ELF/VLF whistler mode chorus" *Journal of Geophysical Research: Space Physics*, *113*(A8), 2008.

[3] V. Harid, M. Gołkowski, T. Bell, and U. S. Inan "Theoretical and numerical analysis of radiation belt electron precipitation by coherent whistler mode waves" *Journal of Geophysical Research: Space Physics*, *119*(6), 4370-4388, 2014.

[4] U. S. Inan "Non-linear gyroresonant interactions of energetic particles and coherent VLF waves in the magnetosphere" Doctoral dissertation, Stanford University, 1977.

Particle-In-Cell methods for modeling electromagnetic propagation in plasmas

John R. Cary[1,2].
[1]Tech-X Corporation, Boulder, CO 80303, USA, cary@txcorp.com
[2]Center for Integrated Plasma Studies, Department of Physics, University of Colorado, Boulder, CO 80309, USA

Abstract—**Because plasmas are a nonlinear medium, electromagnetic wave propagation in plasmas can lead to a variety of effects, including absorption, conversion, scattering, and wave decay. These different effects result from particle-wave interactions that arise due to the kinetic nature of collisionless plasmas, namely that the existence of certain plasma waves depends on the distribution of velocities in the plasma, not just the bulk quantities, like density, temperature, and velocity. This presentation will concentrate on the modeling of electromagnetic waves in plasmas using kinetic methods, in particular, particle-in-cell (PIC) methods and various refinements. The basics of PIC methods will be introduced, some results from using these methods will be discussed, and recent advances will be outlined.**

Index Terms—**electromagnetics, plasma, propagation.**

I. Introduction

Electromagnetic wave propagation in plasmas is complicated by the fact that the plasma creates currents in response to the electromagnetic field, thereby being a source that can modify the wave or create new waves. This also happens within dielectrics due to the polarizability, but there is a difference. In the typical dielectrics, the polarizability can often be modeled assuming the polarizable object, e.g., a atom or defect, is small compared with the wavelength of the propagating medium, with the consequence that the polarization depends on frequency only. However, in a plasma, in particular a collisionless kinetic plasma, a disturbance generated by the electric and magnetic fields can propagate, thus creating a current that is far from the original disturbance. This causes the polarization, χ, to be a function of the wavenumber **k** and frequency independently.

Modeling electromagnetic wave propagation must be able to take these many effects into account. There are several methods for doing so, including linear fluid models of plasma, kinetic models, and fully nonlinear models. In this paper, we will review the particle-in-cell (PIC) methods for fully kinetic modeling of electromagnetic wave propagation in plasmas. We will begin by discussing the basic algorithm, and then we will continue by showing the results of the basic propagation of waves in plasmas, electrostatic and electromagnetic, as well as magnetized and unmagnetized.

II. Vlasov-Maxwell equations

In the collisionless limit, the dynamics of plasmas is governed by the Vlasov-Maxwell equations. The particle dynamics for species (e.g., electrons or ions) s is given by the Vlasov equation,

$$\begin{aligned}\partial_t f_s(\vec{x},\vec{v},t) + \nabla_x \cdot [\vec{v} f_s(\vec{x},\vec{v},t)] \\ + \nabla_v \cdot [\vec{a}_s(\vec{x},\vec{v},t) f_s(\vec{x},\vec{v},t)] = 0,\end{aligned} \tag{1}$$

where $\vec{a}_s(\vec{x},\vec{v},t)$ is acceleration due to whatever forces act on a particle located at x with velocity v at time t. In the presence of an electromagnetic field, the acceleration is given by the Lorentz force,

$$\vec{a} = \frac{q_s}{m_s}\left(\vec{E} + v \times \vec{B}\right). \tag{2}$$

A closed system of equations is found by use of Faradays law,

$$\partial_t \vec{B} = -\nabla \times \vec{E} \tag{3}$$

and Ampere's law,

$$\partial_t\left(\epsilon_0 \vec{E}\right) = -\vec{J} + \nabla \times \vec{B}/\mu_0, \tag{4}$$

in which the current comes from summing the currents of all the species,

$$\vec{J} = \sum_s \vec{J}_s, \tag{5}$$

with the current of each species given by

$$\vec{J}_s = q_s \int d^3v \vec{v} f_s(\vec{x},\vec{v},t). \tag{6}$$

The Vlasov-Maxwell equations are a set of integro-differential equations with six independent variables. Consequently, the general solution cannot be found, and numerical approaches can be difficult. There are extensive textbooks [1], [2] on solving these equations in various limits, e.g., for linear homogeneous theory, or for single mode theory.

III. Solving the Vlasov-Maxwell equations using the Electromagnetic Particle-In-Cell (EMPIC) method

A standard way of solving partial differential and integro-differential equations is to discretize them using, e.g., finite element or finite difference methods. Indeed, this is the standard way of solving the Maxwell part of the Vlasov-Maxwell equations. Most common is to use the Finite-Difference, Time-Domain formulation [3], in which the electric and magnetic fields are considered offset in time and advanced by the leap-frog method.

$$\begin{aligned}\epsilon_0 \vec{E}^n &= \epsilon_0 \vec{E}^{n-1} \\ &+ \left(-\vec{J}^{n+1/2} + \nabla \times \vec{B}^{n+1/2}/\mu_0\right)\Delta t, \end{aligned} \tag{7}$$

$$\vec{B}^{n+1/2} = \vec{B}^{n-1/2} - \nabla \times \vec{E}^{n-1/2}\Delta t. \tag{8}$$

It remains to find the plasma current that is in Eq. (7).

The plasma current comes from a solution of the Vlasov Eq. 1. Here again, a standard procedure would be to discretize these equations in now the six-dimensional position-velocity space. However, that tends to be memory prohibitive, even on today's supercomputers. So instead the common method is to use the method of characteristics. This method gives the solution as a sum over particles (or trajectories),

$$f(x, v, t) = \sum_p w_p \delta(x - x_p(t))\delta(v - v_p(t)), \tag{9}$$

where x_p and v_p are particle trajectories, and w_p is a weight representing the number of real particles in macroparticle p. Thus, these variables satisfy

$$\dot{x}_p = v_p, \tag{10}$$

$$\dot{v}_p = a(x_p, v_p, t). \tag{11}$$

Until recently, the *de-facto* method of advancing particles has been the Boris push [4].

This is the basis of EMPIC simulation [5], [6], which has the following elements;

- Gather: interpolation the electromagnetic fields to the particle from the values on the grid,
- Accelerate: change the velocity of the particles according to the Lorentz force,
- Move: Move the particles according to their new velocities,
- Scatter: Distribute the current of the particle to the grid points;

for solving for the particle currents, which for the current deposition has been one of [7]–[9] for lower-order deposition, with a more general framework given in [10]. This is then coupled with FDTD-EM to obtain the evolution of the plasma system numerically. EMPIC methods have application far beyond plasma modeling, to areas including computational accelerator physics [11].

IV. Setting up plasma simulation in VSim

There are any number of EMPIC computational applications available today (with a listing given at [12]), ranging over open-source and closed-source, academic to commercial. With the advent of commercial EMPIC computational applications has come ease of use and run-time flexibility. Given our familiarity with VSim, we will describe that code here.

VSim is an electrostatic or electromagnetic particle-in-cell simulation package with two components. The computational engine, Vorpal, has been in existence [13] for more than a decade, with continuous improvement and advancing to modern processors and GPUs. Vorpal has a flexible input file format that allows knowledgeable users to code up the desired equations and choose the particle dynamics at run time. Vorpal was instrumental [14] in determining the dynamics underlying the generation of quality beams through laser-plasma interaction. The front end, VSimComposer, provides a point-and-click interface for setting up simulations. This interface is shown in Fig. 1. VSim runs on Linux, Windows, and MacOS.

The tree-based interface reffig:empicsetup provides the user with an easy interface for adding simulation components, including fields with specified dynamics, such as electrostatic or electromagnetic, particles of given dynamics, and reactions between particles or between particles and fluids (collisions), and reactions between fields and particles, e.g., field ionization. The purpose of such an interface in these modern codes it to limit the vast array of choices provided by the

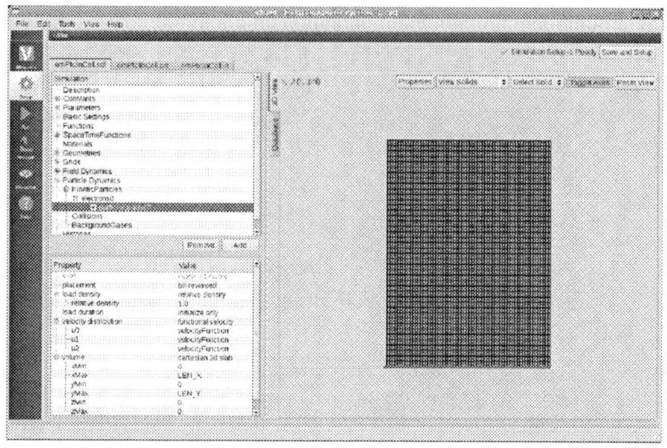

Fig. 1: Setting up an electromagnetic particle-in-cell simulation in VSim

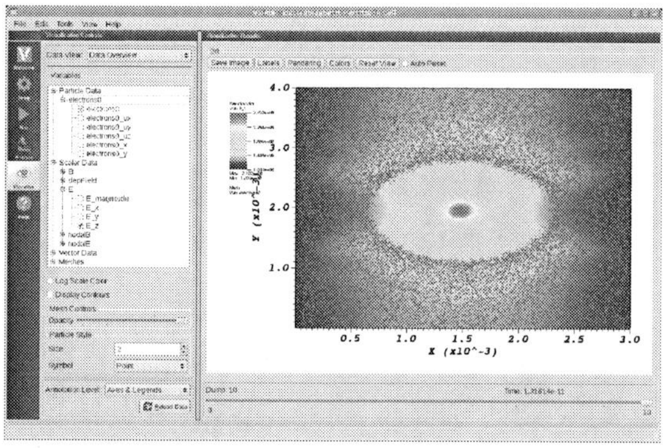

Fig. 2: Particles and fields in electromagnetic particle-in-cell simulation in VSim after strong fields from the central antenna have pushed the particles away.

computational engine to the most common choices that make sense. However, the user is still able to drop into text setup and create exotic simulations.

An easy-to-use front end also allows the user to get to results more quickly. For example, one can easily load the generated data into VSimComposer to visualize the fields or particles. For example, Fig. 2 comes up directly in the front-end visualization panel. The user need not manually extract the data with scripts that ultimately write out the images. Once again, if the user needs some custom visualizations, the user can write scripts to extract data. This is aided by the fact that all data is in HDF5 files following the open VizSchema [15], [16] standard for metadata.

V. Nonlinear EM pulse propagation

Particle-in-cell methods were instrumental in helping discover [17] and advance the generation of quality beams [14], [18], [19] from laser-plasma interaction, which has since generated [20] GeV beams from a single laser-plasma interaction. The simulations showed that during propagation, the laser pulse underwent a nonlinear modulation that made it optimal for generating a strong plasma wake for accelerating particles. Secondly, the evolution of the laser pulse during propagation allowed for the trapping of particles, which cannot occur in a pulse that does just moves at the group velocity. The evolved

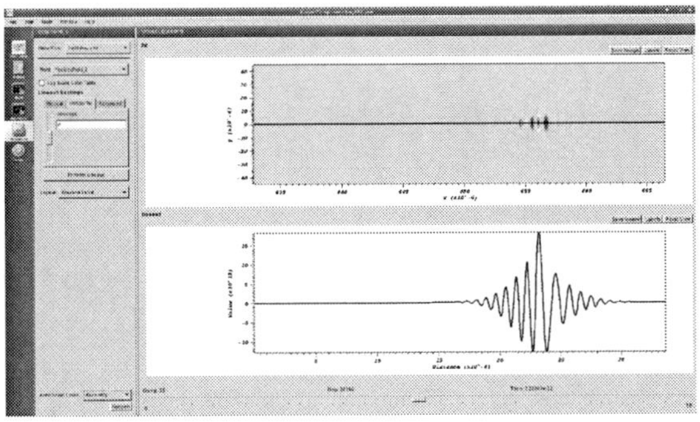

Fig. 3: Intense laser pulse after propagating some distance in a plasma

pulse is shown in Fig. 3. Simulations [21] have accurately predicted beam charges in the 10 pC range.

The field of laser-plasma acceleration of particles has developed rapidly over the last decade due to simulations. Simulations have shown [22] how to inject particles with a density downramp, the origin of beam emittance from this interaction, and how [23] one can modify the focusing using multiple laser modes to obtain a particle beam that can be more easily matched into conventional accelerator optics.

VI. New directions in modeling EM propagation in plasma

The EMPIC method is constantly being improved. For example, there are new electromagnetic solvers [24], [25] for eliminating the numerical Cerenkov instability [26]. New approaches [27], [28] to implicit solvers (which have been under exploration for many years [29]), have been developed to remove numerical instabilities [30]. Finite element approaches [31] may allow effective use of electromagnetic particle-in-cell on unstructured meshes. New particle movers (discussed below) are coming on line.

One example of an improvement to EMPIC modeling is controlled dispersion [24]. This line of research is aimed at minimized the numerical Cerenkov instability, which arises because the numerical phase velocity of light waves in FDTD-EM is less than actual speed of light. Hence, particles can resonate with the numerical waves, and this leads to energy emission, much like physical Cerenkov radiation.

In addition, there have been multiple improvements in particle movers. As noted above, for the longest time, the particle mover of choice was the Boris push [4]. However, Vay noted [32] that the Boris push did not have a stationary ($\vec{E} \times \vec{B}$) velocity in crossed electric and magnetic fields. Higuera and Cary [33] then noted that a further improvement to obtain phase-space volume preservation was possible. The Higuera-Cary push, which is showing up in new EMPIC codes [31], is now rapidly becoming the standard, as a detailed study [34] has shown that it has the best accuracy across most cases.

VII. Conclusion

Propagation of electromagnetic waves in collisionless, kinetic plasma is governed by the Vlasov-Maxwell equations. These are practically modeled using the electromagnetic particle-in-cell (EMPIC) method, which involves a cycle of FDTD-EM coupled with particle updates. This modeling method has been used to make discoveries in laser-plasma interactions, propagation of modes into plasmas for heating purposes, and many other areas. The field continues to evolve with developments of better algorithms for particle integration and wave-particle interactions.

Acknowledgment

The author would like to thank the Vorpal and Composer-Toolkit teams for results generation and implementations and Tech-X Corporation for its support.

References

[1] S. Ichimaru, "Basic principles of plasma physics: a statistical approach," 1973.

[2] D. R. Nicholson and D. R. Nicholson, *Introduction to plasma theory*. Wiley New York, 1983.

[3] K. S. Yee, "Numerical solution of initial boundary value problems involving Maxwell's equations in isotropic media," *IEEE Trans. Antennas Propag*, vol. 14, no. 3, pp. 302–307, 1966.

[4] J. Boris, *Proceedings of the Fourth Conference on Numerical Simulation of Plasmas, J.P. Boris, R.A. Shanny (Eds.), Naval Research Laboratory, Washington, DC*, p. 367, 1970.

[5] C. K. Birdsall and A. B. Langdon, *Plasma Physics via Computer Simulation*. CRC Press, 2014.

[6] R. W. Hockney and J. W. Eastwood, *Computer Simulation Using Particles*. CRC Press, 1988.

[7] R. Morse and C. Nielson, "Numerical simulation of the weibel instability in one and two dimensions," *The Physics of Fluids*, vol. 14, no. 4, pp. 830–840, 1971.

[8] J. Villasenor and O. Buneman, "Rigorous charge conservation for local electromagnetic field solvers," *Computer Physics Communications*, vol. 69, no. 2-3, pp. 306–316, 1992.

[9] T. Umeda, Y. Omura, T. Tominaga, and H. Matsumoto, "A new charge conservation method in electromagnetic particle-in-cell simulations," *Computer Physics Communications*, vol. 156, no. 1, pp. 73–85, 2003.

[10] T. Z. Esirkepov, "Exact charge conservation scheme for particle-in-cell simulation with an arbitrary form-factor," *Computer Physics Communications*, vol. 135, no. 2, pp. 144–153, 2001.

[11] J. R. Cary, D. T. Abell, G. I. Bell, B. M. Cowan, J. R. King, D. Meiser, I. V. Pogorelov, and G. R. Werner, "Select advances in computational accelerator physics," *IEEE Transactions on Nuclear Science*, vol. 63, no. 2, pp. 823–841, 2016.

[12] "Wikipedia Particle-In-Cell," http://en.wikipedia.org/wiki/Particle-in-cell.

[13] C. Nieter and J. R. Cary, "Vorpal: a versatile plasma simulation code," *Journal of Computational Physics*, vol. 196, no. 2, pp. 448–473, 2004.

[14] C. G. R. Geddes, C. Toth, J. van Tilborg, E. Esarey, C. B. Schroeder, D. L. Bruhwiler, C. Nieter, J. R. Cary, and W. Leemans, "High-quality electron beams from a laser wakefield accelerator using plasma-channel guiding," *Nature*, vol. 431, pp. 538–541, 2004.

[15] S. Shasharina, J. R. Cary, S. Veitzer, P. Hamill, S. Kruger, M. Durant, and D. A. Alexander, "Vizschema–visualization interface for scientific data," in *IADIS International Conference, Computer Graphics, Visualization, Computer Vision and Image Processing*, 2009, p. 49.

[16] "VizSchema homepage," https://ice.txcorp.com/trac/vizschema.

[17] A. Pukhov and J. Meyer-ter-Vehn, "Laser wake field acceleration: the highly non-linear broken-wave regime," *Appl. Phys. B*, vol. 74, pp. 355–361, 2002.

[18] J. Faure, Y. Glinec, A. Pukhov, S. Kiselev, S. Gordienko, E. Lefebvre, J.-P. Rousseau, F. Burgy, and V. Malka, "A laser-plasma accelerator producing monoenergetic electron beams," *Nature*, vol. 431, pp. 541–544, 2004.

[19] S. P. D. Mangles, C. D. Murphy, Z. Najmudin, A. G. R. Thomas, J. L. Collier, A. E. Dangor, E. J. Divall, P. S. Foster, J. G. Gallacher, C. J. Hooker, D. A. Jaroszynski, A. J. Langley, W. B. Mori, P. A. Norreys, F. S. Tsung, R. Viskup, B. R. Walton, and K. Krushelnick, "Monoenergetic beams of relativistic electrons from intense laser-plasma interactions," *Nature*, vol. 431, pp. 535–538, 2004.

[20] N. A. Hafz, T. M. Jeong, I. W. Choi, S. K. Lee, K. H. Pae, V. V. Kulagin, J. H. Sung, T. J. Yu, K.-H. Hong, T. Hosokai *et al.*, "Stable generation of gev-class electron beams from self-guided laser–plasma channels," *Nature Photonics*, vol. 2, no. 9, pp. 571–577, 2008.

[21] J. R. Cary, R. Giacone, C. Nieter, and D. Bruhwiler, "Clean beams from laser wake-field accelerators via optical injection with a cleanup pulse a," *Physics of plasmas*, vol. 12, no. 5, p. 056704, 2005.
[22] C. G. R. Geddes, K. Nakamura, G. R. Plateau, C. Toth, E. Cormier-Michel, E. Esarey, C. B. Schroeder, J. R. Cary, and W. P. Leemans, "Plasma-density-gradient injection of low absolute-momentum-spread electron bunches," *Phys. Rev. Lett.*, vol. 100, no. 21, p. 215004, 2008.
[23] E. Cormier-Michel, E. Esarey, C. Geddes, C. Schroeder, K. Paul, P. Mullowney, J. Cary, and W. Leemans, "Control of focusing fields in laser-plasma accelerators using higher-order modes," *Physical Review Special Topics-Accelerators and Beams*, vol. 14, no. 3, p. 031303, 2011.
[24] B. M. Cowan, D. L. Bruhwiler, J. R. Cary, E. Cormier-Michel, and C. G. R. Geddes, "Generalized algorithm for control of numerical dispersion in explicit time-domain electromagnetic simulations," *Phys. Rev. ST Accel. Beams*, vol. 16, p. 041303, Apr 2013.
[25] B. B. Godfrey, J.-L. Vay, and I. Haber, "Numerical stability analysis of the pseudo-spectral analytical time-domain pic algorithm," *Journal of Computational Physics*, vol. 258, pp. 689–704, 2014.
[26] B. B. Godfrey, "Numerical cherenkov instabilities in electromagnetic particle codes," *Journal of Computational Physics*, vol. 15, no. 4, pp. 504–521, 1974.
[27] S. Markidis, G. Lapenta *et al.*, "Multi-scale simulations of plasma with ipic3d," *Mathematics and Computers in Simulation*, vol. 80, no. 7, pp. 1509–1519, 2010.
[28] L. Chacón, G. Chen, and D. Barnes, "A charge-and energy-conserving implicit, electrostatic particle-in-cell algorithm on mapped computational meshes," *Journal of Computational Physics*, vol. 233, pp. 1–9, 2013.
[29] D. W. Hewett and A. B. Langdon, "Electromagnetic direct implicit plasma simulation," *Journal of Computational Physics*, vol. 72, no. 1, pp. 121–155, 1987.
[30] S. Markidis and G. Lapenta, "The energy conserving particle-in-cell method," *Journal of Computational Physics*, vol. 230, no. 18, pp. 7037–7052, 2011.
[31] D.-Y. Na, H. Moon, Y. A. Omelchenko, and F. L. Teixeira, "Conservative finite element time-domain pic algorithm for relativistic maxwell-vlasov equations on irregular meshes," *arXiv preprint arXiv:1707.04333*, 2017.
[32] J.-L. Vay, "Simulation of beams or plasmas crossing at relativistic velocity," *Physics of Plasmas (1994-present)*, vol. 15, no. 5, p. 056701, 2008.
[33] A. V. Higuera and J. R. Cary, "Structure-preserving second-order integration of relativistic charged particle trajectories in electromagnetic fields," *Physics of Plasmas*, vol. 24, no. 5, p. 052104, 2017.
[34] B. Ripperda, F. Bacchini, J. Teunissen, C. Xia, O. Porth, L. Sironi, G. Lapenta, and R. Keppens, "Comprehensive comparison of relativistic particle integrators," *arXiv preprint arXiv:1710.09164*, 2017.

Late-time Instability in Finite Difference Modeling of Very-Low-Frequency Propagation in the Earth-Ionosphere Waveguide

Robert A. Marshall
Smead Aerospace Engineering Sciences
University of Colorado Boulder
Boulder, CO, USA
robert.marshall@colorado.edu

Wei Xu
Smead Aerospace Engineering Sciences
University of Colorado Boulder
Boulder, CO, USA
wei.xu@colorado.edu

Austin P. Sousa
Smead Aerospace Engineering Sciences
University of Colorado Boulder
Boulder, CO, USA
austin.sousa@colorado.edu

***Abstract*—Finite-difference time-domain (FDTD) modeling is used to simulate electromagnetic wave propagation for frequencies up to 500 kHz in the waveguide formed by the Earth and lower ionosphere. Methods to solve Maxwell's equations in the magnetized plasma of the lower ionosphere are investigated and compared for their accuracy and stability. In particular, two methods are compared for long distance propagation (2000 km or longer), assessing accuracy and stability; we denote these the Lee & Kalluri method and the Boris method. The methods are compared in the presence of an absorbing boundary condition (ABC) just above the lower ionosphere. We find that both methods show late-time instabilities for certain magnetic field configurations when the ABC is used. Overall the Boris method is modestly more stable than the Lee & Kalluri method, though the two show similar stability characteristics.**

***Keywords*—FDTD, plasma, stability, waveguide**

I. Introduction

Very-low-frequency (VLF) and low-frequency (LF) electromagnetic waves, from hundreds of Hz to hundreds of kHz, propagate efficiently in the waveguide formed by the Earth and the lower ionosphere. These waves are produced by lightning and by VLF and LF transmitters used for long-range communications.

Thanks to the wavelengths of interest (hundreds of meters to hundreds of km) and the spatial scale of the Earth-ionosphere waveguide ($\sim$100 km by hundreds to thousands of km), the propagation channel is well-suited to modeling using Finite Difference (FD) methods, including both Finite-Difference Time Domain (FDTD) and Frequency Domain (FDFD). FDTD models are well suited for impulsive sources such as lightning, and can be used to extract narrowband propagation characteristics; FDFD models are valuable when only a single frequency is required.

However, both methods suffer from numerical dispersion, and from difficulties using FDTD methods in the presence of the ionospheric plasma. In this paper, we investigate different solutions to the auxiliary plasma equation (APE) that is solved together with Maxwell's equations for a cold, collisional, magnetized plasma:

$$\frac{\partial \mathbf{J}_n}{\partial t} + \nu_n \mathbf{J}_n = \vec{\omega}_{c,n} \times \mathbf{J}_n + \omega_{p,n}^2 \epsilon_0 \mathbf{E} \ , \quad (1)$$

where $\mathbf{J}_n$ is the current associated with species n (electrons or ions); ν_n is the electron-neutral collision frequency; $\vec{\omega}_{c,n} = q_n \vec{B}_0 / m_n$ is the particle gyrofrequency, related to the background magnetic field $\vec{B}_0$; and $\omega_{p,n}$ is the particle plasma frequency. Note that equation (1) is not easily solved in the time domain, due to the current terms on the right-hand-side of the equation. In this work, we use the model of [1] to compare the Lee & Kalluri [2] method, hereafter L&K, and the so-called Boris method [3], [4]. Both methods solve the APE in time-domain, and show comparable performance in terms of computational speed. The L&K method solves equation (1) through a convolutional update equation, using an auxiliary field that depends on all previous time steps. The Boris method instead solves equation (1) by applying the electric and magnetic terms on the right-hand-side in half-time-step iterations.

Fig. 1 shows a snapshot of a simulation using the L&K method. An impulsive source is injected at the lower left corner, and allowed to propagate and reflect from the ionospheric plasma. When single-frequency (i.e., narrowband) results are required, a running Discrete Fourier Transform (DFT) is computed at locations of interest in the simulation space (i.e., at a desired receiver location).

Some recent work [5] has used the argument that because the ionosphere is good reflector, very little energy reaches the upper simulation boundary, and therefore an Absorbing Boundary Condition (ABC) is not necessary. In our work, we compare simulation results with and without the ABC enabled, both in terms of accuracy and stability. We find that the difference between the observed signal amplitude and phase with and without the ABC is appreciable, and thus the ABC is likely required for applications where accuracy is important. However, for perturbation analysis (i.e., the difference between two simulations with different ionospheres), the perturbation is consistent with and without the ABC; in those cases, the ABC can be turned off.

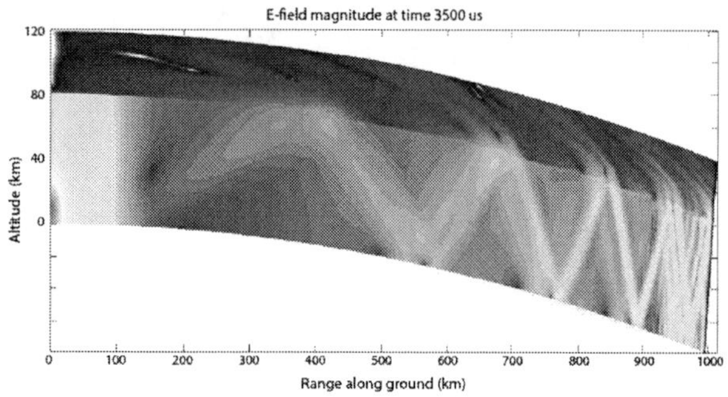

Fig. 1. Example simulation of propagation in the Earth-ionosphere waveguide. An impulsive source is used and allowed to propagate and reflect from the ionosphere. Amplitude and phase of narrowband signals are extracted along the ground using running Discrete Fourier Transforms.

Simulations without the ABC are generally stable, but simulations with the ABC result in a late-time instability for both the L&K and Boris methods; this instability begins to appear and corrupt the solution after some tens of thousands of time steps. We investigate both the Convolutional Perfectly Matched Layer (CPML) [6] and the second-order Mur absorbing boundary conditions [7], and both result in instabilities. In most applications, this instability is beyond the time range of interest; however for our long-distance simulations, in some cases over 100,000 time steps are required and the instability becomes important.

The circumstances under which the instability appears in these simulations depends on the maximum altitude of the simulation, the peak electron density, and the magnitude and direction of the background magnetic field. In this paper, we investigate the late-time instability that arises in these simulations, and the parameter dependence of this instability, using the two plasma methods and two ABC methods described above. As an example, Fig. 2 shows amplitude and phase at 16 kHz along the ground for daytime and nighttime ionospheres, with the vertical magnetic field amplitude varied between 10 and 50 μT, using the L&K method with the CPML. In both cases, the simulation becomes unstable for $B_0 = 10\ \mu$T, and the daytime simulation is also unstable for 20 μT. Higher values of the magnetic field remain stable over a 3500 km simulation path. In general, the lower magnetic field value becomes unstable earlier in the simulation, thus preventing longer simulations.

The exception is when the magnetic field is off-vertical at the source. Our simulations use cylindrically symmetric coordinate systems with the source on the axis of symmetry; thus, a non-vertical B_0 on this axis violates Gauss' Law. In these cases an instability grows very quickly with or without the ABC. A possible method to overcome this fundamental issue is to quickly vary the magnetic field from vertical on the axis to off-vertical a short distance away.

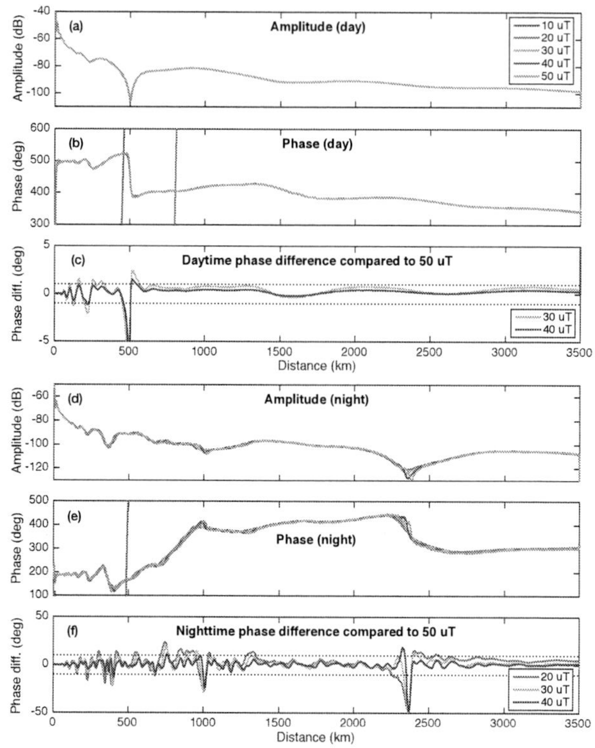

Fig. 2. (a) Amplitude and (b) phase (daytime; $h' = 73$ km, $\beta = 0.35$) simulated using the FDTD model at 16 kHz for different magnetic field magnitudes. The FDTD model is observed to go unstable in the PML boundary for $B_0 < 25\ \mu$T. (c) Variation in phase for different magnetic field magnitudes, compared to the 50 μT case. The dashed lines mark a 1 degree variation. (d) Amplitude and (e) phase (nighttime; $h' = 85$ km, $\beta = 0.5$); and (f) variation in phase for different magnetic field magnitudes, compared to the 50 μT case. The dashed lines mark a 10 degree variation.

REFERENCES

[1] R. A. Marshall, "An improved model of the lightning electromagnetic field interaction with the D-region ionosphere," J. Geophys Res., vol. 117, no. A03316, 2012.
[2] J. H. Lee and D. Kalluri, "Three-dimensional FDTD simulation of electromagnetic wave transformation in a dynamic inhomogeneous magnetized plasma," IEEE Trans. Ant. Prop., vol. 47, no. 7, pp. 1146–1151, 1999.
[3] J. J. Simpson, "Current and future applications of full-vector 3-D Maxwell's equations FDTD global earth-ionosphere waveguide models," Surv. Geophys., vol. 30, no. 2, pp. 105–130, 2009.
[4] A. Samimi and J. J. Simpson, "An efficient 3-D FDTD model of electromagnetic wave propagation in the magnetized plasma," IEEE Trans. Ant. Prop., vol. 63, no. 1, pp. 269–279, 2015.
[5] J.-P. Bérenger, "An implicit FDTD scheme for the propagation of VLF–LF radio waves in the earth–ionosphere waveguide," Comptes Rendus Physique, vol. 15, no. 5, pp. 393–402, 2014.
[6] J. A. Roden and S. D. Gedney, "Convolution PML (CPML): An efficient FDTD implementation of the CFS-PML for arbitrary media," Micro. and Opt. Tech. Lett., vol. 27, no. 5, pp. 334–339, 2000.
[7] G. Mur, "Absorbing boundary conditions for the finite-difference approximation of the time-domain electromagnetic field equations," IEEE Trans. Electromagnetic Compatibility, vol. 23, pp. 377–382, 1981.

Simplified FDTD Model of Electromagnetic Wave Propagation in Magnetized Plasma

Santosh Pokhrel
Department of Electrical and Computer Engineering
University of Utah
Salt Lake City, Utah, USA
santosh.pokhrel@utah.edu

Varun Shankar
Department of Mathematics
University of Utah
Salt Lake City, Utah, USA
vshankar@math.utah.edu

Jamesina J. Simpson
Department of Electrical and Computer Engineering
University of Utah
Salt Lake City, Utah, USA
jamesina.simpson@utah.edu

***Abstract*—A new finite-difference time-domain (FDTD) model of electromagnetic wave propagation in magnetized ionospheric plasma is presented that is simple to implement. This new anisotropic model permits the use of two time steps, one for Maxwell's equations and the second for the Lorentz equation of motion. This is particularly useful for scenarios in which a high collision frequency or a high background magnetic field intensity is present, in which case the Lorentz equation of motion may require a significantly smaller time step than Maxwell's equations. A major advantage of this algorithm is its ability to update the current density equation with a single update even when the current density time step increment is smaller than the time step increment for Maxwell's equations.**

***Keywords*—Current density, Electromagnetic wave propagation, FDTD, Plasma.**

I. INTRODUCTION

Electromagnetic (EM) wave propagation in anisotropic ionospheric plasma is important for many applications, such as communications, remote-sensing, geolocation, avionics control, etc. The finite-difference time-domain (FDTD) method [1, 2] is useful for modeling EM wave propagation in both nonmagnetized (isotropic) and magnetized (anisotropic) plasmas because of its ability to account for inhomogeneities within the plasma in three-dimensions in a straight-forward manner [3]-[6]. This is particularly useful for modeling EM wave propagation in the ionosphere, since the ionosphere is highly inhomogeneous, depending on the time of day, latitude, longitude, time of year, and any space weather events.

At sufficiently low frequencies, such as below about 1 kHz, the ionospheric may be approximated as an isotropic plasma. At very low frequencies (VLF: 3 – 30 kHz) and higher, the anisotropy of the plasma may no longer be ignored. Specifically, the effect of the Earth's magnetic field on the ionosphere must be included. This is accommodated by coupling Maxwell's equations to the Lorentz equation of motion.

Several approaches for modeling EM wave propagation in anisotropic plasma using FDTD have been published (e.g., [3-6]). Here, we present a formulation that is relatively simple to implement, offers about the same or better memory requirements as previous approaches, and also permits the use of two time step increments (one for Maxwell's equations, Δt, and one for the Lorentz equation of motion, Δt_c) as suggested in [5]. The electric field vectors and magnetic field vectors are spatially staggered in the Yee cell [2], and current density vectors are collocated with electric field components. Spatial averaging of current density vectors is performed using four nearest neighbors to find the current density at the location of interest. All the equations are solved in a leap frog manner. A major unique advantage of the new algorithm over all previous approaches is that only one update is needed for the Lorentz equation of motion even when Δt_c is smaller than Δt. The new algorithm is validated against analytical plasma theory results.

II. GOVERNING EQUATIONS

The governing Maxwell's equations are as follows:

$$\nabla \times E = -\frac{\partial B}{\partial t} \text{ (Faraday's Law)}, \quad (1)$$

$$\Delta \times H = \frac{\partial D}{\partial t} + \Sigma(J_j + J_{s)} \text{ (Ampere's Law)}, \quad (2)$$

$$\frac{\partial \vec{J_j}}{\partial t} + v_j\vec{J_j} = \varepsilon w_{pj}^2 \vec{E} - \overrightarrow{w_{cj}} \times \vec{J_j} \text{ (Lorentz Equation of Motion)}. \quad (3)$$

In Ampere's Law, J_j represents the plasma current density due to each j-species (the subscript j represents electrons, positive ions, etc.). In expression (3), v_j represents the collision frequency, ε is the electrical permittivity of the medium, w_{pj} is the angular frequency of plasma, and w_{pj} is the cyclotron frequency. These three equations are discretized and solved to model EM wave propagation in 3-D anisotropic plasma.

III. UPDATE EQUATIONS

Equation (3) is discretized to obtain update equations for the current density vector components (J_x, J_y and J_z). The resulting update equations are as follows:

$$\begin{bmatrix} J_x \\ J_y \\ J_z \end{bmatrix}^{n+\frac{1}{2}} = \varepsilon \Delta t_c w_{pj}^2 [A^{-1}]_{3\times3} \cdot \begin{bmatrix} E_x \\ E_y \\ E_z \end{bmatrix}^{n} [A^{-1}]_{3\times3}$$

$$\cdot [B]_{3\times3} \cdot \begin{bmatrix} J_x \\ J_y \\ J_z \end{bmatrix}^{n-\frac{1}{2}} , \qquad (4)$$

where matrices A & B are given by:

$$A = \begin{bmatrix} \mathrm{a} & -\frac{\Delta t_c}{2}\omega_z & \frac{\Delta t_c}{2}\omega_y \\ \frac{\Delta t_c}{2}\omega_z & \mathrm{a} & -\frac{\Delta t_c}{2}\omega_x \\ -\frac{\Delta t_c}{2}\omega_y & \frac{\Delta t_c}{2}\omega_x & \mathrm{a} \end{bmatrix},$$

$$B = \begin{bmatrix} \mathrm{b} & \frac{\Delta t_c}{2}\omega_z & -\frac{\Delta t_c}{2}\omega_y \\ -\frac{\Delta t_c}{2}\omega_z & \mathrm{b} & \frac{\Delta t_c}{2}\omega_x \\ \frac{\Delta t_c}{2}\omega_y & -\frac{\Delta t_c}{2}\omega_x & \mathrm{b} \end{bmatrix},$$

$$\mathrm{a} = \left(1 + \frac{v_j \Delta t_c}{2}\right) \text{and } \mathrm{b} = \left(1 - \frac{v_j \Delta t_c}{2}\right).$$

Equations (1) and (2) are discretized using central difference approximations to both time and space derivatives as for regular FDTD [2]. Putting all of this together, the nine resulting update equations (three electric field components, three magnetic field components, and three current density components) are solved in a leapfrog manner: the electric field vector components are solved at a given instant in time, and then the magnetic field components and current density components are solved one half-time step later.

IV. NUMERICAL STABILITY AND VALIDATION

Equations (1) and (2) are stable at and below the Courant limit (i.e., the CFL condition) given by:

$\Delta t < \frac{1}{c}\frac{1}{\sqrt{\frac{1}{\Delta x^2}+\frac{1}{\Delta y^2}+\frac{1}{\Delta z^2}}}$ (where Δx, Δy and Δz are the spatial grid cell dimensions in each Cartesian direction). The stability of Equation (3) is checked by Eigenvalue stability analysis. The growth factor (G) of each Fourier mode is evaluated, and the appropriate time step can be calculated by assuming the growth factor to be less than or equal to unity. If the time step is very small, two different time step values, Δt for Equations (1) and (2) and Δt_c for Equation (3) can be used. Furthermore, if Δt_c is smaller than Δt, then the coefficient matrices may be re-derived to permit the current density vector components to updated using a single update. For example, if $\Delta t_c = \Delta t/100$, the new A and B coefficient matrices are used once to update the current density components rather than 100 times for every electric and magnetic field update.

This new model has also been validated with several analytical plasma theory such as low frequency whistle mode propagation in magnetized plasma, excitations of R-wave (right hand circularly polarized wave) and L-wave (left hand circularly polarized wave), and Faraday rotation effect.

V. CONCLUSION

A new FDTD method has been proposed to model EM wave propagation in an anisotropic magnetized plasma. The advantages of this model are:

1) This method is very easy to implement and it is not memory intensive, especially compared to the approach presented in [6].
2) Two different time step increments may be chosen; however, even when the two increments are different, only a single update for Equations (1) – (3) are needed.

This proposed model has been validated against analytical plasma theory results.

ACKNOWLEDGMENT

The authors would like to thank the Extreme Science and Engineering Discovery Environment (XSEDE) for providing supercomputing resources (EAR140019) as well as the University of Utah's Center for High Performance Computing (CHPC).

REFERENCES

[1] K. S. Yee, "Numerical solution of initial boundary value problems involving Maxwell's equations in isotropic media," IEEE Trans. Antennas Propagat., vol. AP-14, pp. 302-307, 1966.

[2] A. Taflove and S. C. Hagness, Computational Electrodynamics: The Finite-Difference Time-Domain Method, 3rd ed., Norwood, MA: Artech House, 2005.

[3] Y. Yu and J. Simpson, "An E-J collocated 3-D FDTD model of electromagnetic wave propagation in magnetized cold plasma," IEEE Trans. Antennas Propagat., vol. 58, no. 2, pp. 469-478, Feb. 2010.

[4] A. Samimi and J. Simpson, "An efficient 3-D FDTD model of electromagnetic wave propagation in magnetized plasma," IEEE Trans. Antennas Propagat., vol. 63, no. 1, 2015.

[5] S. A. Cummer, "An analysis of new and existing FDTD methods for isotropic cold plasma and a method for improving their accuracy," IEEE Trans. Antennas Propagat., vol. 45, pp. 392-400, 1997.

[6] E. Gamliel, "Direct Integration 3-D FDTD method for single-species cold magnetized plasma", IEEE Trans. Antennas Propagat., vol. 65, no. 1, 2017.

Nonlinear FDTD Modeling of Ionospheric Cross-Modulation Experiments

Robert C. Moore
Department of Electrical and Computer Engineering
University of Florida
Gainesville, FL, USA
moore@ece.ufl.edu

Anthony J. Erdman
Department of Electrical and Computer Engineering
University of Florida
Gainesville, FL, USA
ajerdman@ufl.edu

Abstract—**In this paper, we discuss the details of a new plasma finite difference time domain (FDTD) model and demonstrate its performance characteristics. As opposed to recursive convolution or Z-transform methods, the presented method uses a direct integration method, and additionally applies the bilinear transform in the time-domain to ensure stability. The FDTD is expanded to include nonlinear terms so that the model can be used to analyze ionospheric HF heating experiments performed at the High-frequency Active Auroral Research Program (HAARP) Observatory. We present our initial results.**

Keywords—HF Heating, ionosphere, Nonlinear FDTD, Plasma..

I. Introduction

Radio wave propagation through the plasma of the lower ionosphere is one of the more complicated propagation environments in electromagnetics. In the linear case, the medium is dispersive and anisotropic. In the nonlinear case, the absorption of radio wave energy affects the way the radio wave propagates through the medium by changing the electrical properties of the medium itself. This paper focuses on so-called high-frequency (HF, 3-30 MHz) heating of the lower ionosphere (<100 km altitude) [1]. Such ionospheric heating can be used to quantify ionospheric characteristics [2] or to generate extremely low frequency radio waves (ELF, 3-3000 Hz) for communications purposes, for example [3,4]. They can also be used to simply study complicated interactions that occur in the ionosphere [5]. Until recently, numerical modeling of such an environment and at such high frequencies consisted of ray tracing tools [6]. This paper applies modern numerical methods to the high frequency ionospheric heating problem.

Finite difference time domain (FDTD) methods have been used for over 50 years to handle radio wave propagation through simple media, such as free space [7]. FDTD algorithms for anisotropic and dispersive media were subsequently developed in the 1980's and 1990's. Two main methods have emerged: Recursive Convolution methods (RC) [8] and Direct Integration methods [9]. There are a number of other methods in use, and each have definitive relevance and importance, but this paper will focus on the direct integration method.

II. Linear Plasma Modeling

The lower ionosphere at 50-100 km altitude is a highly collisional magnetized plasma. The plasma consists of a weakly-ionized atmosphere, so that the plasma response is dominated by the reaction of electrons to the radio wave. This plasma consists of an electron density that can vary with altitude (or with space in general), an electron-neutral collision frequency that can also vary with altitude (or with space in general), and a static magnetic field, the Earth's magnetic field. The basic equations describing radio wave propagation through such a medium form the basis of magneto-ionic theory [10]. These equations consist of Maxwell's equations plus the first-order moment of the Boltzmann equation, which describes momentum transfer between the electromagnetic wave and the plasma.

A number of techniques have been used to discretize these equations, and each different discretization results in a different stability factor. This work implements a second-order accurate discretization of these equations, and also applies the bilinear or Mobius transform [11]. Applying the bilinear transform has the effect of stabilizing the numerical implementation so that it performs as expected for a free-space (or simple medium) simulation. For example, high order differentials require more terms to evaluate with second-order accuracy; the bilinear transform effectively spreads the lower order differentials over the same total amount of time as the higher order differentials and has a stabilizing effect [11].

With this code in hand, one of the most telling examples of success is analysis of Faraday rotation. Fig. 1 (top) shows an example of Faraday rotation as the electric field rotates as the wave propagates through the plasma. In this case, there are no collisions. In the bottom panel of Fig. 1, collisions are now included so that components of the radio wave attenuate as they propagate through the plasma as well. Due to the anisotropy, however, different field components attenuate at different rates, and the field becomes elliptical as it propagates through the plasma. This effect is well demonstrated in the bottom panel of Fig. 1. In both the collisional and non-collisional cases, the wave polarization nearly exactly matches the analytical solutions, which are overlaid on each plot.

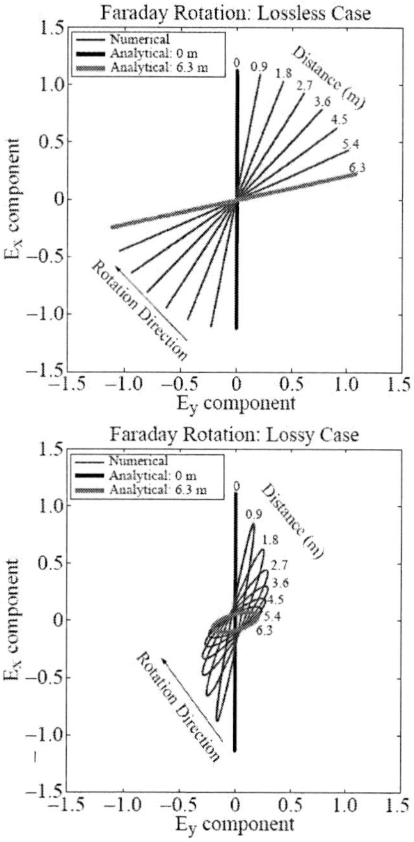

Fig. 1. (Top) Faraday rotation without collisions included, and (bottom) Faraday rotation with collisions included.

III. NONLINEAR PLASMA EXPERIMENTS

Fig. 2 presents the experimental results of [12]. It compares sinusoidal AM heating and square-wave AM heating at peak HF power levels of 10% and 100%. The ratio of the 10% power trace to the 100% power trace is not constant as a function of time; during both square-wave and sinusoidal AM heating, the ratio decreases during periods within the modulation cycle with higher HF power, consistent with the saturation effect first observed by [13] during ELF/VLF wave generation experiments. The saturation of the conductivity/temperature relationship may also indicate the end of Maxwellian electron energy distributions.

We will present the initial results of numerical modeling of these specific HF heating results. The nonlinear FDTD that has been developed is based on the linear FDTD described above, but also accounts for the second order moment of the Boltzmann Equation. The nonlinear FDTD has been employed to analyze each of these effects.

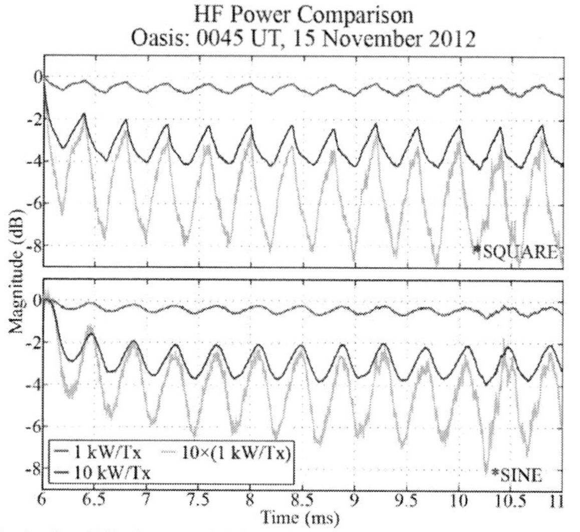

Fig. 2. See [12]. Cross-modulation (dB) at 10% (red) and 100% (blue) HF power for (top) square-wave and (bot) sine AM. Pink traces are 10% HF power traces multiplied by 10.

REFERENCES

[1] C. G. Getmantsev et al., "Combination frequencies in the interaction between high-power short-wave radiation and ionospheric plasma," JETP Lett., vol. 20, pp. 101–102, 1974.

[2] A. Senior, M. T. Rietveld, M. J. Kosch, and W. Singer, "Diagnosing radio plasma heating in the polar summer mesosphere using cross modulation: Theory and observations," J. Geophys. Res., vol. 115, A09318, 2010, doi:10.1029/2010JA015379.

[3] R. Barr and P. Stubbe, Radio Sci., vol. 19, p. 1111, 1984.

[4] M. T. Rietveld, H. Kopka, and P. Stubbe, J. Atmos. Terr. Phys., vol. 48, p. 311, 1986.

[5] R. C. Moore, S. Fujimaru, D. A. Kotovsky, and M. Golkowski, "Observations of ionospheric ELF and VLF wave generation by excitation of the thermal cubic nonlinearity," Phys. Rev. Lett., vol. 111, 235007, doi:10.1103/PhysRevLett.111.235007.

[6] R. C. Moore (2007), "ELF/VLF wave generation by modulated HF heating of the auroral electrojet," Ph.D. thesis, Stanford University, Stanford, California.

[7] K. Yee, "A numerical solution of initial boundary value problems involving Maxwell's equations in isotropic media," IEEE Trans. Antennas Propag., vol. 14, pp. 302-307, 1966.

[8] F. Hunsberger, R. Luebbers, and K. Kunz, "Finite-difference time-domain analysis of gyrotropic media-I: magnetized plasma," IEEE Trans. Antennas Propag., vol. 40, no. 12, pp.1489-1495, 1992.

[9] D. F. Kelley and R. J. Luebbers, "Piecewise linear recursive convolution for dispersive media using FDTD," IEEE Trans. Antennas Propag., vol. 44, pp. 792-797, 1996.

[10] J. A. Ratcliffe, The Magneto-Ionic Theory and Its Application to the Ionosphere, Cambridge, U.K.: Cambridge Univ. Press, 1959.

[11] J. A. Pereda, A. Vegas, and A. Prieto, "FDTD modeling of wave propagation in dispersive media by using the mobius transformation technique," IEEE Trans. Microw Theory Tech., vol. 50, pp. 1689-1695, 2002.

[12] J. Langston, and R. C. Moore, "High time resolution observations of HF cross-modulation within the *D*-region ionosphere," Geophys. Res. Lett., vol. 40, pp. 1912-1916, 2013, doi:10.1002/grl.50391.

[13] R. C. Moore, U. S. Inan, and T. F. Bell, Geophys. Res. Lett., vol. 33, L12106, 2006, doi:10.1029/2006GL025934.

Monostatic RCS for General Aviation Aircraft

Dennis W. Richardson
NAWCAD
Radar and Antenna Systems
Engineering Division
Patuxent River, MD, USA
dennis.w.richardson@navy.mil

Ruben P. Ortega
NAWCAD
Radar and Antenna Systems
Engineering Division
Patuxent River, MD, USA
ruben.ortega1@navy.mil

Saad N. Tabet
NAWCAD
Radar and Antenna Systems
Engineering Division
Patuxent River, MD, USA
saad.tabet@navy.mil

Abstract—**Proliferation of High Performance Computing (HPC) has significantly furthered the ability of Computational Electromagnetics (CEM) codes to solve Radar Cross Section (RCS) problems at higher frequencies, finer angular resolutions and greater accuracy. Typically, platforms become very large electrically with increase in frequency and are nearly impossible to solve using full wave methods. Asymptotic codes that incorporate various advanced scattering mechanisms/features are required to best predict complex field contributions. In this study, Signa (an advanced asymptotic monostatic RCS code) is compared to the proven and highly accurate full wave Method of Moments (MoM) code, WIPL-D. The monostatic RCS at the horizon of a small commercial aircraft (Beechcraft Bonanza) is chosen for Signa to WIPL-D comparisons at L, S and C bands. In general, Signa and WIPL-D comparisons were very favorable, barring a small sector response in the tail region of the aircraft.**

Keywords—Asymptotic, Full Wave, High Frequency, Method of Moments, Monostatic, Radar Cross Section, Signa, WIPL-D.

I. INTRODUCTION

As HPC platforms become more powerful, CEM has achieved a dramatic surge in capability. Anually, the latest methods allow RF engineers to solve problems involving larger platforms, higher frequencies and at a fraction of previous run times. Full wave solvers benefit significantly from the ability of HPCs to utilize multi-core processors and Graphical Processing Units (GPUs) to parallel partition/solve very large systems of linear equations. This provides dramatic reduction in run times and enables broader areas of research to be undertaken. Applications wise, the Naval Air Warfare Center Aircraft Division (NAWCAD) benefits greatly from those advanced technologies. Very costly in-flight measurements are reduced to spot checking results achieved through high fidelity CEM modeling, at a small fraction of the cost.

A main area of interest to NAWCAD is the accuracy of various methods in determining the monostatic RCS response (RCS from hereon) of small commercial aircraft. High fidelity RCS is required in Air Traffic Control (ATC), range clearing missions, and maritime drug interdiction applications. A full wave solution is always preferred over asymptotic solvers. However, for electrically large platforms, hardware/software limitations and extended run times are still a major obstacle to overcome. Hence, there continues to be significant room for the development and use of more advanced high frequency asymptotic codes. One such code is Signa [1]. Signa is based on the Shooting and Bouncing Rays (SBR) technique, with a large number of controls and advanced features to improve results and/or overcome asymptotic methods' limitations. Signa is designed to take advantage of multi-core CPUs and GPUs on Windows workstations and Linux clusters.

In this study, the RCS at the horizon of a single-engine propeller Beechcraft Bonanza aircraft is studied. A comparison of Signa to WIPL-D [2] is conducted at L (1 GHz), S (2 GHz) and C (5 GHz) bands to assess the accuracy that can be achieved with Signa. HH and VV RCS performances are compared at each frequency under study. This assessment is of critical importance, especially when assessing the RCS at frequencies that cannot be accomplished with a full wave solver. Comparisons of the computational complexity, run time, and RCS accuracy are provided.

II. CEM MODELING EFFORT

A. WIPL-D and Signa Model Setup

A Beechcraft Bonanza CAD model was prepared for CEM and assumed to be a Perfect Electric Conductor (PEC) to be used in WIPL-D and Signa simulations. As required by WIPL-D, a quadrilateral mesh was prepared. For Signa, a triangular facet mesh was prepared. This allows the Curvature extraction feature in Signa to be employed. Fig. 1 shows WIPL-D and Signa CEM models.

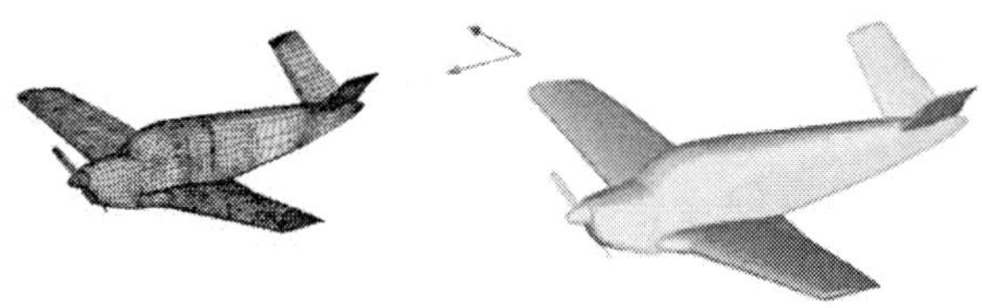

Fig 1. Beachcraft Bonanza CEM Models: WIPL-D (Left); Signa (Right).

In order to generate HH and VV RCS polarizations, and at every frequency under study, WIPL-D requires a separate run for each. However, Signa automatically provides both

HH and VV polarizations in a single run, as well as, HV and VH polarizations. All models were run to generate the principal Azimuth RCS (Elevation = 0 degrees) cut, in 0.5-degree increments.

Signa requires adjusting certain advanced features to improve its performance. The following summarizes the final advanced features used for the comparisons:

Ray Density = 20 per wavelength
Max Number of Bounces = 20
Creeping Waves = OFF
GO blockage = OFF

B. Signa Versus WIPL-D Performance Comparison

All WIPL-D and Signa simulations were performed using a Windows workstation with Dual 16-Core Xeon processors and 3 K-40 GPUs. Table I highlights the sizing and timing results for each of the runs for the HH polarization case. The VV polarization case results are very similar. For WIPL-D, the relevant sizing parameter is the number of unknowns (NUN), and for Signa the number of rays launched.

TABLE I. Sizing and Timing Results.

Frequency (GHz)	WIPL-D NUN	Signa Rays (Millions)	WIPL-D Time (Sec)	Signa Time (Sec)
1	70,141	35.5	8,345	81
2	155,617	103.8	10,394	253
5	692,038	478.3	308,923	1,266

Table I clearly shows impressive WIPL-D run times for 1 and 2 GHz. However, there is a substantial increase in NUN and run time at 5 GHz. As expected, Signa run times are a fraction of WIPL-D's, especially when you factor in Signa's solutions provide all RCS polarization components in the same run.

C. Model Accuracy Comparison

Figs. 2-4 provide WIPL-D and Signa HH and VV RCS comparisons, at the aforementioned frequencies.

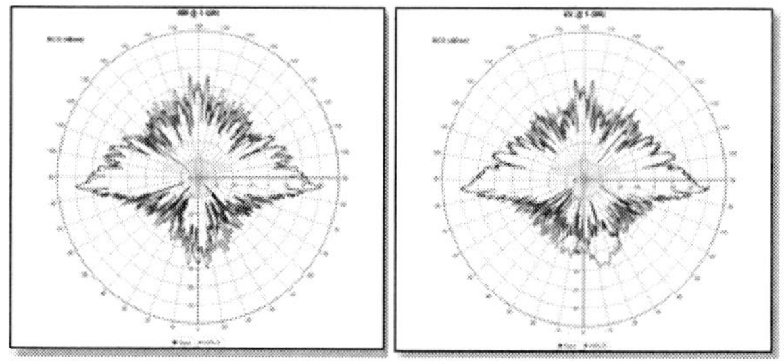

Fig. 2. WIPL-D Vs. Signa HH and VV Comparison at 1 GHz.

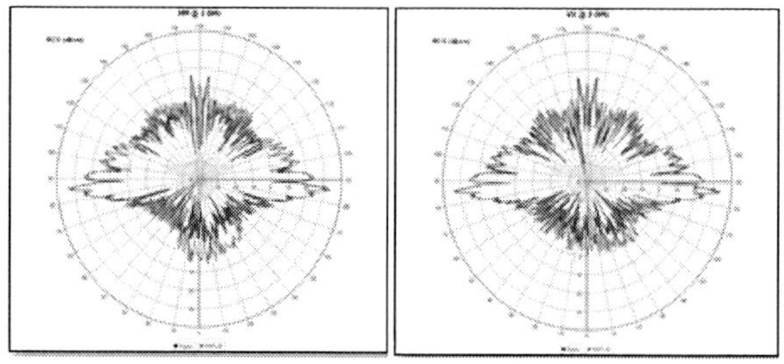

Fig. 3. WIPL-D Vs. Signa HH and VV Comparison at 2 GHz.

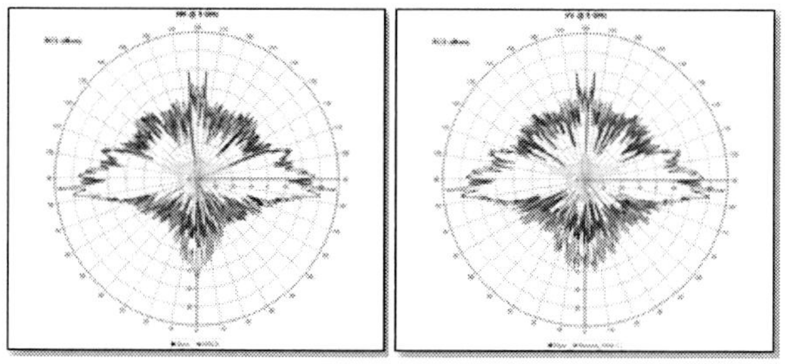

Fig. 4. WIPL-D Vs. Signa HH and VV Comparison at 5 GHz.

It is to be noted that, for every frequency compared, there is a very good correlation between WIPL-D and Signa. However, there is as much as 10 dB difference in RCS response in the tail region. One possible explanation for this discrepancy is the potential that some of the launched rays in Signa are getting trapped and eventually released to the far-field without accounting for their contributions. A potential mitigation for this issue is to include the Geometric Optics (GO) Blockage advanced feature in Signa. However, this comes at the expense of significant increase in run time.

REFERENCES

[1] D. L. Setterdahl, R. A. Kipp, M. C. Miller, "Signa: A Radar Signature Prediction Tool for Electrically Large Targets," IEEE Radar Conference, 2014.

[2] WIPL-D Pro v14, Software and User's Manual, WIPL-D d.o.o., Belgrade, 2017.

Comparison of Commercial Simulation Performance for Efficient RCS Analysis

*Note: Sub-titles are not captured in Xplore and should not be used

Dongeun Lee
Moasoft
Seoul, Korea
delee@moasfotware.co.kr

Sung-Hwan Chi
Moasoft
Seoul, Korea
shji@moasfotware.co.kr

Do-Young Jang
Moasoft
Seoul, Korea
dyjang@moasfotware.co.kr

Han-Kil jung
Moasoft
Seoul, Korea
hkjung@moasoftware.co.kr

Radar design system and Stealth design system have been continuously developed. Radar cross section(RCS) is required in order to develop the systems, but it takes a lot of time for measuring RCS. Therefore, in general, M&S(modeling and simulation) is performed to predict target's RCS values. Nowadays, there are a lot of M&S for calculating RCS values such as WIPL-D, FEKO, HFSS-IE. Because each analysis method and performance simulation time for M&S tools is different, it is necessary to analysis the strength and weakness of each simulation. In this paper, we perform RCS M&S in the same environment using WIPL-D, FEKO and HFSS-IE, and compare the RCS data, simulation time and required computer resources in order to examine the reliability and efficient analysis for RCS.

Keyword: WIPL-D, HOBF, RCS, RAM(radar absorbing material)

I. Introduction

Radar design system and Stealth design system have been continuously developed. Radar cross section(RCS) is required in order to develop the systems. RCS is a measure of how detectable an object is by radar, and the target RCS is determined by target's geometry, size, and material. Stealth design system's goal is to reduce RCS, and RAM material is used to reduce RCS. In general, Aircraft or war vessels are required to reduce RCS, but it is difficult to measure their RCS because of their size. Therefore, EM M&S is preceded before measurement. M&S method can get RCS data in design stage, and they can also reduce time and money to get RCS data.

In this paper, we compared RCS data using different EM simulation tools such as WIPL-D, FEKO, and HFSS. We analyzed the time and the computer resource for simulation

II. Comparison RCS of Commercial Simulation Tools

A. RCS Simulation Condition for Simple Model

Figure 1 shows the geometry of simple model to run RCS simulations. The simple model is 1m x 1m x 0.1m, and we got the monostatic RCS data on XY-Plane. The simulation frequency is 1 GHz, and the RCS data is got in 1 degree interval. Table 2 shows the simulation cases. We had 5 cases such as PEC box, RAM volume box, PEC box & 2 mm RAM, Aluminum box and aluminum box & 2 mm RAM shield.

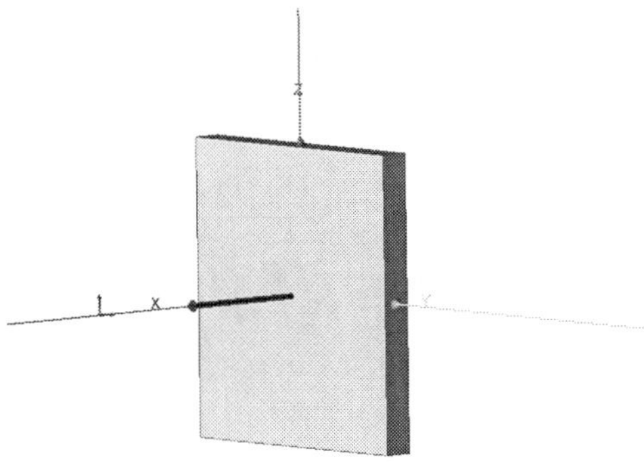

Fig. 1. RCS Target modeling

B. Analysis RCS Data for Simple Model

Figure 2 shows the RCS data for simple target depanding on simulation tools and simulation cases. As you can see, the RCS data are not different depending on simulation tools. However, the simulation is different each other. Table 3 shows the simulation time.

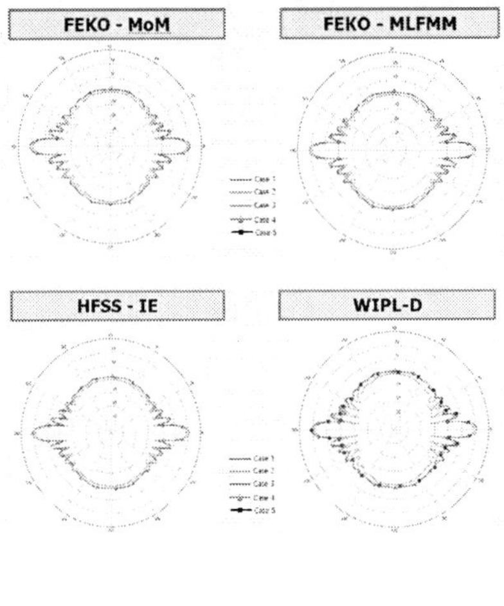

Identify applicable funding agency here. If none, delete this text box.

Fig. 2. RCS Target modeling

TABLE I. RCS SIMULATION TIME FOR SIMPLE MODEL

Case / Time	1	2	3	4	5
FEKO - MoM	2 min 5 sec	10 min 1 2 sec	2 min 11 sec	2 min 12 sec	x
FEKO -MLFMM	5 min 6 sec	1 hour	4 min 3 sec	5 min	Ram 200 Gbyte ne ed
HFSS – IE	1 min 12 sec	8 min 40 sec	3 min 40 sec	6 min	19 Hour s
WIPL-D	5.12 Sec	8.76 Sec	14 Sec	5.76 Sec	20.2 Sec

C. *Compare Aircraft RCS Data*

On the next step, we compared aircraft RCS data depending on EM simulation tools. Figure 3 shows the geometry of aircraft. The aircraft length is about 14 meters, and the model has PEC material with 2 mm RAM coating. We analyzed the aircraft RCS at 1 GHz using WIPL-D, FEKO and HFSS.

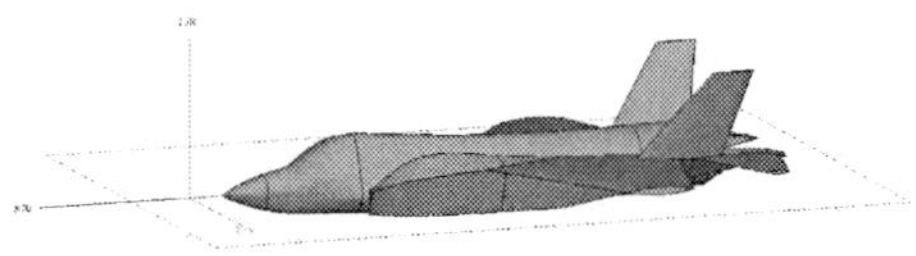

Fig. 3. Aircraft Geometry for RCS simulation

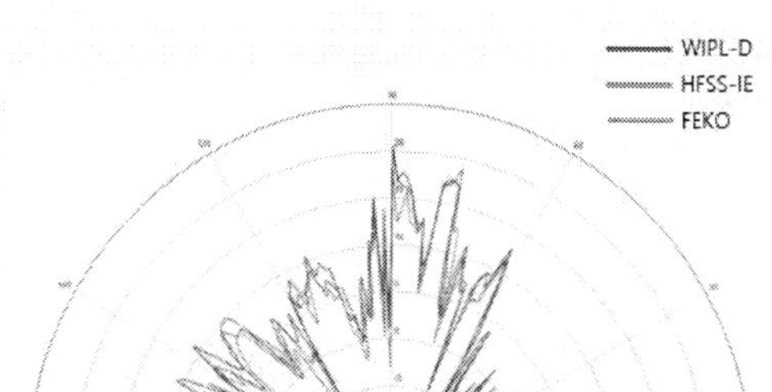

Fig. 4. The RCS of aircraft depending on simulation tools

TABLE II. RCS SIMULATION TIME FOR SIMPLE MODEL

Simulation	Time
WIPL-D	45 min
HFSS-IE	2 Hrs
FEKO-MLFMM	3 Hrs

Figure 4 shows RCS of aircraft. The RCS value of WIPL-D, HFSS-IE and FEKO at 180 degree are 16.1 dBsm, 16.7 dBsm, and 15.9 dBsm. Each RCS data are similar, but WIPL-D simulation time is 45 minutes , otherwise. FEKO simulation time is 3Hrs, HFSS-IE simulation time is 2Hrs.

III. CONCLUSION

In this paper, We compared RCS simulation data depending on EM simulation tools such as WIPL-D, FEKO and HFSS. The RCS data are similar to each EM simulation results, but Simulation time is that WIPL-D performed simulation fastest.

REFERENCES

[1] Byung-Jun Ahn, "A Study on the Recent Analysis Method for the RCS reduction for Naval Ships," The Journal of Korean Institute of Electromagnetic Engineering and Science , vol. 25, pp. 333-338, May 2014. *(references)*

[2] Han, Jun-Yong, Jung, In-Hwan, Lee, Jae-Wook, Lee, Young-Seung, Park, Seung-Keun, Cho, Choon-Sik, "Time-Efficient SE(Shielding Effectiveness) Prediction Method for Electrically Large Cavity" The Journal of Korean Institute of Electromagnetic Engineering and Science , vol. 25, pp. 333-338, May 2014. *(references)*

Polarimetric Weather Radar Calibration by Computational Electromagnetics

Djordje Mirkovic
Cooperative Institute for Mesoscale Meteorological Studies (OU)
The National Severe Storms Laboratory (NOAA)
Norman, OK
djordje.mirkovic@noaa.gov

Dusan S. Zrnic
The National Severe Storms Laboratory (NOAA)
Norman, OK
dusan.zrnic@noaa.gov

***Abstract*—Calibration of the polarimetric phased array radar is an ongoing challenge. Here we present an approach using computational electromagnetics.**

Keywords*— *polarimetric calibration, weather radar calibration.

I. INTRODUCTION

The current national weather radar surveillance network uses dual-polarized dish antennas. The network lifetime has been extended by about 20 years after which it may require replacement. Proposed successors include planar phased array radar (PPAR) and cylindrical phased array radar (CPAR). Either should provide the same quality of polarimetric data. In the current mode of operation (simultaneous transmission and reception) this requires 35dB cross-pol isolation to achieve differential reflectivity bias of less than 0.1dB and correlation coefficient bias less than 0.001 [1]. To achieve these requirements, the new generation PPAR requires calibration at every pointing direction [2].

II. PROBLEM OF CALIBRATION

The calibration issues concern orthogonality and orientation of the electric fields within the beam, the coupling between horizontal and vertical components (geometrical coupling) [1] [3], cross-polar (unwanted) radiation and matching of the H and V beams in beamwidth and pointing direction [1]. Received voltages are given by (1).This formula assumes that the cross-polar radiation pattern is coaxial with the copolar pattern and may be due to cross polar sides of the patch radiator and/or to the squinting of the electric field vector caused by geometry (i.e., pointing direction is out of the principal plane). The effective squinting angles ψ, γ determine the components of the electric field. This formulation yields nine calibration parameters [1], namely: antenna gains g_1, g_2; electric field squinting angles (i.e., angles off of intended "horizontal" and "vertical" components with respect to the horizontal and quasi-vertical direction) ψ, γ; radar system parameter C and calibration for port one and port two paths for same input on transmit $C_T e^{j\beta} = \frac{W_2}{W_1}$ (i.e., ratio of transmitted voltages at ports 1 and 2); and receive $C_R e^{j\xi} = \frac{V_2}{V_1}$ (ratio of received voltages at port 1 and port 2). In practice, the differential phase β consists of the part in the transmitter and part in the antenna. Similarly ξ has two components, one from the antenna the other from the receiver. Here, we will consider the antenna differential phases only.

III. CALIBRATION USING COMPUTATIONAL ELECTROMAGNETICS

The CEM may be used to obtain radiation properties of the large PPAR antenna. Herein, a polarimetric radar with 640 radiating elements is considered. We use simulation results to evaluate some of the biases in the polarimetric variables caused by the radar antenna patterns. Calibration parameters are calculated from the simulation results for antenna oriented according to Ludwig 2 definition. Thus E_φ and E_θ are copolar and cross-polar components of the radiated field Calibration parameters examined here are: $Gdiff = \frac{g_1}{g_2} = \frac{|f_{hh}|^2}{|f_{vv}|^2}$; $\beta = \frac{\arg(f_{vv}^{Tx})}{\arg(f_{hh}^{Tx})} + K_{backend}$. Where f_{hh}, f_{vv} determine values of the voltage radiation patterns at the beam center. The remaining $K_{backend}$ parameters depend only on the backend of the antenna are expected to be independent in the pointing direction.

IV. CALIBRATION PARAMETERS AND RADAR BIAS MEASUREMENTS

Data were collected with the TPD in light rain during spring 2016. The radar was scanning in the principal plane. In one case the broadside was pointing at the zenith (zenith mode) and in the other, it was tilted (3 to 5 deg) off the zenith (off zenith mode). In the zenith mode approximately 3mm thick water layer accumulated on top of the radome affecting results. Measurements were made in light rain wherein the expected differential reflectivity at zenith is zero and almost zero off zenith. In either case, the differential phase equals the system differential phase.

Here we illustrate and compare measured differential reflectivity Z_{DR} and differential phase of the radar system (Fig. 1) with model results. In the first column (Fig. 1 (a)& (d)) the principal plane is vertical whereas in the second row (Fig. 1 (b) & (e)) it is slightly tilted (3-5 degrees). Finally, in

$$\begin{vmatrix} V_1 \\ V_2 \end{vmatrix} = C \begin{vmatrix} (s_h \cos^2\gamma + s_v \sin^2\gamma) g_1 W_1 + (s_h \cos\gamma \sin\psi + s_v \sin\gamma \cos\psi)\sqrt{g_1}\sqrt{g_2} C_T e^{j\beta} W_1 \\ (s_h \cos\gamma \sin\psi + s_v \sin\gamma \cos\psi) C_T e^{j\xi} W_1 + (s_h \sin^2\gamma + s_v \cos^2\psi) g_2 C_T C_R e^{j(\beta+\xi)} W_1 \end{vmatrix} \quad (1)$$

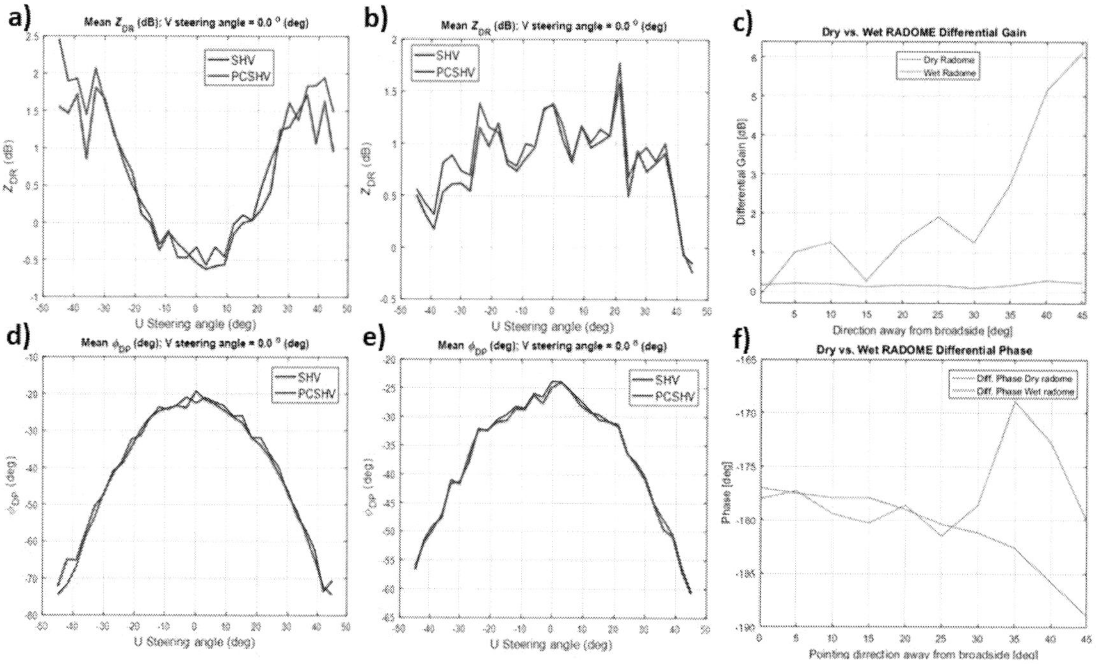

Fig. 1. - Differential reflectivity (top) and differential phase (bottom) in light rain showing the bias to polarimetric variables. First row for measured data when broadside is pointed at zenith, second row in case the principal plane is slightly off zenith, and for simulated antenna patters. First row represents the case of 3mm of water accumulated at the top of the radome. Whereas water was not present (except for droplets) in the latter case (second row). Simulation results consider "dry" (blue) and "wet" (red) radome.

the third row (Fig. 1 (c) & (d)) are the simulated results. Measurements are compared to the simulation of the TPD array (640 elements) and radar's single panel (64 elements) modeled in WIPL-D software. The single panel is expected to qualitatively replicate the behavior of the full antenna and thus we consider it first. The study of the full TPD antenna is ongoing.

The single panel was covered with "wet" and "dry" radome replicating the conditions in the zenith and off zenith modes. During weather surveillance, the radome would most likely be dry hence calibration for such case is required.

With antenna pointing to the zenith (Fig. 1 (a)), steering angle 0°) the Z_{DR} should be zero, but it is -0.5 dB. This clearly is system introduced bias. It increases with the pointing direction departing from the broadside value by approximately 2 dB at about 45 degrees. The simulation value of about 6dB (Fig. 1 (c)), is highly likely due to water thickness. But for dry radome, the bias is about 0.1dB and follows the same pattern. The increase of differential gain with beam steering is attributed to the radome which differently affects the two polarizations. The measured system bias changes its magnitude and shape (concave to convex) depending on mode from 1.3 to 0.5dB for an unknown reason.

Measurements of the differential phase Φ_{DP} are more consistent. At broadside system differential phase is about 20 degrees, whereas the electronic beam steering introduces the additional phase up to 50° for zenith pointing and 30° for off zenith mode. The simulated differential phase (Fig. 1 (f)) for "dry" radome agrees well with the measurements. Simulated value is about 15° (one-way) while measurement show about 30° (two-way). The results for "wet" radome are non-monotonic and do not depict measurements.

V. Conclusion

CEM tools have not been previously used to quantify the performance of phased array antennas meant for weather observations. Herein we demonstrated that polarimetric calibration parameters can, in principle, be obtained from the antenna model. We identified issues that should be addressed before the final quantitative analysis is carried out. Additionally, we identified the inconsistencies in the radar observations which should be reconciled in order to obtain high-quality. A calibration path is identified starting with a single panel model, followed by a populated proof of concept, and then the full operational size antenna. A set of hybrid CEM methods should be explored to find one that can achieve precise modeling of arrays with a few thousand elements expected in the operational arena.

References

[1] D. S. Zrnic, G. Zhang, and R. J. Doviak, "Bias correction and doppler measurement for polarimetric phased-array radar," *IEEE Trans. On Geosci. and Remote Sensing,* I 2, vol. 49. pp. 842-853, 2010.

[2] D. S. Zrnic, R. J. Doviak, G. Zhang, Y. Zhang, and C. Fulton, "Propagation and backscattering challenges for planar polarimetric phased array radars," in *AMS Radar Conference Proceedings*, Chicago, 2017.

[3] G. Zhang, R. J. Doviak, D. S. Zrnic, J. Crain, D. Steinman, and Y. Al-Rashid, "Phased array radar polarimetry for weather sensing: A theoretical formulation for bias corrections," *IEEE Trans. on Geoscience and Remote Sensing,* t. 47, vol. 11, pp. 3679-3689, 2009.

On Synthetic Aperture Radar Simulations using WIPL-D Pro

Nimrod Teneh
Airborne Systems & Radars Division
Elta Systems Ltd. Group & Subsidiary of IAI Ltd.
Israel
nteneh@elta.co.il

Branko Lj. Mrdakovic
WIPL-D d.o.o.
Gandijeva 7/32, 11073 Belgrade, Serbia,
branko.mrdakovic@wipl-d.com

***Abstract*—In this paper a design of a generic simulation environment for Synthetic Aperture Radar (SAR) applications based on WIPL-D Pro solver, is presented. We discuss the measurement scenario, simulation requirements and the computing complexity in terms of time consumption and hardware resources. An example of a generation of a SAR image of a fighter aircraft, based on its full-wave monostatic RCS simulations in a frequency range between 2 GHz and 3 GHz, is presented.**

Keywords—Synthetic Aperture Radar; EM Simulation;

I. INTRODUCTION

Synthetic Aperture Radar (SAR) is a technique which uses signal processing to improve the resolution beyond the limitation of physical antenna aperture [1]. In SAR, a physical movement of the actual antenna is used to synthesize electrically large antenna aperture.

In SAR processing a large number of measurements is performed along a certain aperture. The size of the aperture sets the size of the synthetic antenna. The larger synthetic antenna is, the higher angular resolution is obtained. On the other hand, high range resolution is achieved by working with wideband signals. Therefore, when performing EM SAR simulation, calculations must be performed on multiple frequencies using huge number of excitations.

Due to the electrical size of radar targets, its scattering analysis is usually performed by using high-frequency methods. However, an inherent characteristic of these methods is the limited accuracy. Applicability of these techniques in SAR systems is further restricted by the fact that simulation time linearly increases by increasing the number of transceiver positions.

Full-wave methods are generally highly accurate, but they are time consuming and require significant computational resources. In order to reduce these requirements, we used special techniques: quadrilateral mesh instead of triangular one [2] and higher order basis functions (HOBFs) [3]. For efficient solution of a large number of excitations, direct LU decomposition is used. Simulation time is further reduced by using parallel execution of the code on both, central processing units (CPUs) and graphical processing units (GPUs) [4]. All EM simulations are performed in WIPL-D software package [5].

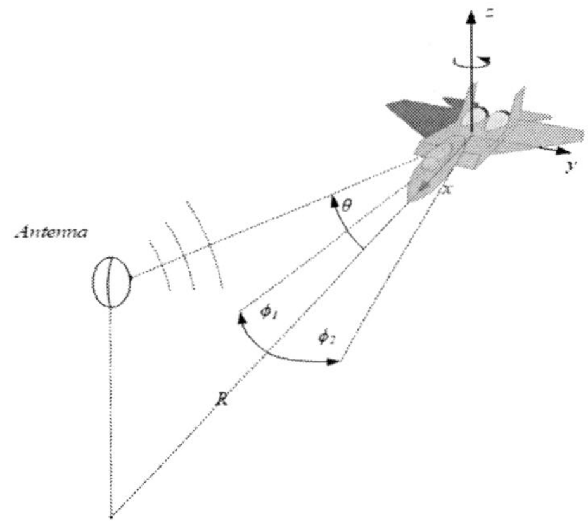

Fig. 1 – SAR measurement scenario.

II. MEASUREMENT SCENARIO

A sketch of the measurement scenario considered is shown in Fig.1.

Let us consider the received signal $S(f,\varphi)$, where f refers to the operating frequency, and φ refers to the aspect angle (the angle with respect to the target from which the measurement is performed). In addition, the area of interest must be located beyond the antenna's far-field lower bound in order to be compatible with the following simplified model:

- An electromagnetic plane wave propagates from the antenna to each of the points located in the scattering area under the investigation.
- The electromagnetic field impinges the scatterers and interacts with the surface. The reflectivity function $\alpha(x,y)$ represents the complex interaction between the electromagnetic wave and the scatterers.
- The scatterer distributes the impinging electromagnetic wave to all directions; a small portion of the signal is reflected back and received by the antenna.

Reflected field is a function of both, amplitude $A(\varphi,\theta)$ and phase, $k\cdot r$, of radar antenna radiation pattern. For most scenarios A may be neglected because the scattering area is small, with respect to the beam width. For this reason, instead of a real antenna model, uniform plane wave can be used as an excitation. Each measurement consists of the contribution from the entire area covered by the radar main beam, hence each measurement is expressed by integrating over the entire area.

It can be shown that the measured signal is the Fourier transform of the function $\alpha(x,y)$ [6]. This result is directly related to the pixel size of this algorithm:

$$dx = {}^{c}/_{(2 \cdot BW \cdot cos\theta)}$$
$$dy = {}^{\lambda}/_{(2 \cdot \Delta\Phi \cdot cos\theta)} \quad (1)$$

where c is the speed of light, BW is the signal bandwidth, λ is the operating wavelength, $\Delta\Phi$ is the size of the aperture and θ is the elevation angle. The length and width of the investigated area are set by the number of frequencies\aspect angles times the related pixel size.

III. Numerical Results

Calculation of a fighter's aircraft SAR image is depicted in Fig.2, and used as an example in this section. The length of the aircraft is 12 m, and its wingspan is 8.05 m.

Fig. 2 – Model of the analyzed fighter aircraft.

In order to obtain the resolution lower than 0.2 m, the central frequency is set to 2.5 GHz, with a signal bandwidth of 1 GHz. The angular aperture is set to ϕ=16°, while elevation angle is 20°. Monostatic RCS simulation is performed in 76 equidistant frequency points and 225 directions for each frequency. The total number of RCS results used for the creation of a SAR image is equal to $76 \times 225 = 17{,}100$.

In order to reduce a number of unknown coefficients, one (A)Symmetry plane is utilized. As (A)Symmetry plane is used, two models, the symmetrical and the anti-symmetrical, where each consist of half the number of unknowns, are simulated at each frequency. Additionally, the reference frequency is equal to the operating frequency in each frequency point. This way, simulation time is significantly reduced, as number of unknowns vary between 77,196 at 2 GHz and 141,820 at frequency of 3 GHz.

All simulations where carried out using the following computer configuration: Intel Xeon CPU E5-2660 v2 @2.2 GHz (2 processors), 256 GB of RAM, 7 hard-disk drives with I/O speed around 100 MB/s, 4 GPUs GTX 1080 Ti, Windows 10 Professional 64-bit. The Total simulation time is equal to 47 hours 41 min.

Comparison of the calculated SAR image and geometry of the aircraft is shown in the Figure 3. As can be seen, there is a very good correlation between the aircraft geometry and its SAR image.

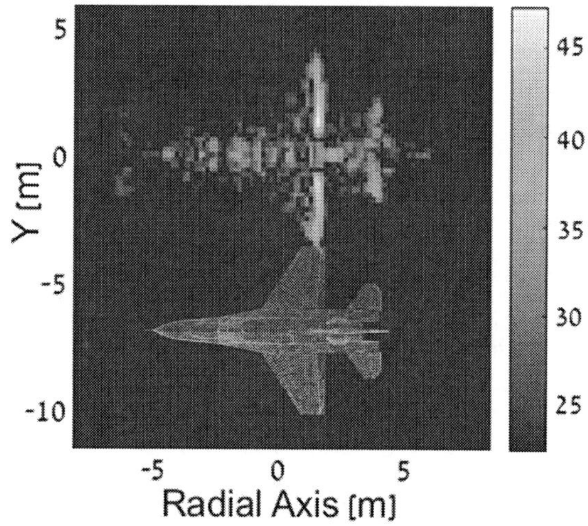

Fig. 3 – SAR image of the aircraft model.

IV. Conclusion

Calculation of SAR image of an electrically large structure is presented in this paper. The presented SAR image is in good agreement with actual shape of the target. The fact the required simulation time is relatively small, indicate that WIPL-D can be used for a very efficient analysis of SAR systems.

RCS simulation of a 12 m long fighter aircraft needed for construction of SAR image with resolution below 0.2 m and central operating frequency 2.5 GHz is performed on a desktop machine in approximately 2 days.

References

[1] Curlander, J. C. and R. N. McDounough, *Synthetic Aperture Radar*, Systems and Signal Processing, John Wiley & Sons, New York, 1991.

[2] B. M. Kolundzija, and A. R. Djordjevic, *Electromagnetic Modeling of Composite Metallic and Dielectric Structures*, Artech House, Norwood, 2002.

[3] B. M. Kolundzija, and B. D. Popovic, "Entire- Domain Galerkin Method for Analysis of Metallic Antennas and Scatterers," *IEE Proceedings-H*, vol.140, no.1, pp.1-10, Feb. 1993.

[4] B. Lj. Mrdakovic, M. M. Kostic, D. I. Olcan, and B. M. Kolundzija, "Acceleration of In-Core LU-Decomposition of Dense MoM Matrix by Parallel usage of Multiple GPUs," COMCAS 2017, November 13-15, 2017. Tel Aviv, Israel

[5] WIPL-D Pro CAD 2017, WIPL-D d.o.o, Belgrade, 2017.

[6] N. Levanon, *Radar Priciples*, New York, Wiley-Interscience, 1988.

A Wideband Antenna for Biotelemetry Applications: Design and Transmission Link Evaluation

Ala Alemaryeen and Sima Noghanian
Department of Electrical Engineering, University of North Dakota
Grand Forks, ND, USA
ala.alemaryeen@und.edu, sima.noghanian@und.edu

***Abstract*—In this paper, the design of a miniature wideband antenna for biotelemetry applications is presented. We propose a biocompatible antenna to be printed on the outer surface of a capsule. The size of the antenna in planar form is 2.52 *mm*³. The antenna shows a wide impedance bandwidth of 7.31 GHz (0.78 GHz – 8 GHz, for -10dB reflection coefficient) when implanted inside a simple three layer body model. The antenna gain values at 915 MHz and 2.45 GHz are -25.23 dBi and -27.51 dBi, respectively. The antenna resonance frequency is shown to be robust when implanted in a realistic anatomical body model. The performance of the communication link between the implanted antenna and an external half-wavelength dipole at 915 MHz and 2.45 GHz is also presented.**

Keywords—bandwidth enhancement, implantable antenna.

I. Introduction

Implantable medical devices (IMDs) have gained substantial attention due to their advantage in improving patient's quality of life. In biotelemetry, wireless links are needed for the communication between an implanted system and an external receiver unit. Antennas are the most important components to ensure robust wireless link performance. It is a great challenge to design an implantable antenna due to the complexity and variation of human tissues, which have an effect on the antenna propagation characteristics, i.e., frequency detuning may happen due to the loading effects of tissue covering the antennas. This necessitates the design of implantable antenna of a wide bandwidth characteristic to withstand the frequency shift when implanted inside tissues with different dielectric properties. Furthermore, biocompatibility and small implant size are another critical constraints that should be considered [1-3]. In this paper, we propose a wideband biocompatible small capsule antenna for biotelemetry applications. Numerical investigations were carried out using CST Microwave Studio software [4].

II. Implantable Antenna Design

The configuration of the proposed implantable antenna is shown in Fig. 1 (a). It consists of a conformal meandered antenna, to achieve miniaturization, designed on the outer wall surface of a capsule, with a diameter of 11 *mm* and length of 24 *mm*. It is assumed that the capsule inner volume will be utilized for the necessary electronic circuits and sensors. A flexible biocompatible material, ultem of 0.5 *mm* thickness with a relative permittivity (ε_r) and loss tangent ($\tan\delta$) of 3.15 and 0.0013 S/m, respectively, is used as the capsule substrate.

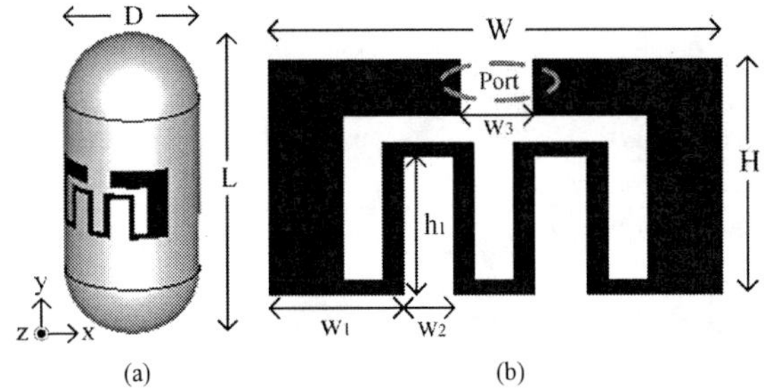

Fig. 1. Configuration of the proposed capsule antenna in: (a) conformal form and (b) planar form. Dimensions in *mm* are: L = 24, D = 11, W = 12, H = 6, h_1 = 3.5, w_1 = 3.5, w_2 = 1.5, and w_3 = 2.

This material is chosen because it has stable properties not affected by the variations of different parameters, such as temperature and frequency. For easy optimization of the antenna, the antenna is first embedded in a three-layer body model (named as Layered Model) that consisted of skin, fat and muscle body tissues of 2 *mm*, 8 *mm*, and 80 *mm* thicknesses, respectively. The dimensions of the body model are 100 × 100 × 90 *mm*³, and the depth of embedding the capsule is 40 mm. Properties of dispersive tissue layers are obtained from the material library in CST Microwave Studio software. The antenna in planar form measures 12 × 6 × 0.035 *mm*³ and the geometrical parameters of the antenna are shown in Fig. 1 (b).

When considering the influence of the electrical components of the implantable system on the antennas, the batteries are expected to have the most significant effects because of their size. Batteries are simply represented as a perfect electric conductor (PEC) cylinder with a length of 8 *mm* and diameter of 10 *mm* inside the capsule. This model is named as Layered_battery. Moreover, the proposed capsule antenna is analyzed in the anatomical Ella voxel model (without the battery) in two different locations: chest and shoulder, named as Ella_shoulder and Ella_chest, respectively. For the chest implanting the proposed antenna is envisioned as a pacemaker antenna, and for the shoulder implanting the application is for the patients suffering from osteoarthritis [1]. The Ella voxel model consists of various organs and represents a 26-year-old female with a height of 1.36 *m* and weight of 57.3 kg. In order to reduce the simulation time, we only imported the upper part of the human body torso, excluding the head, into our simulation model.

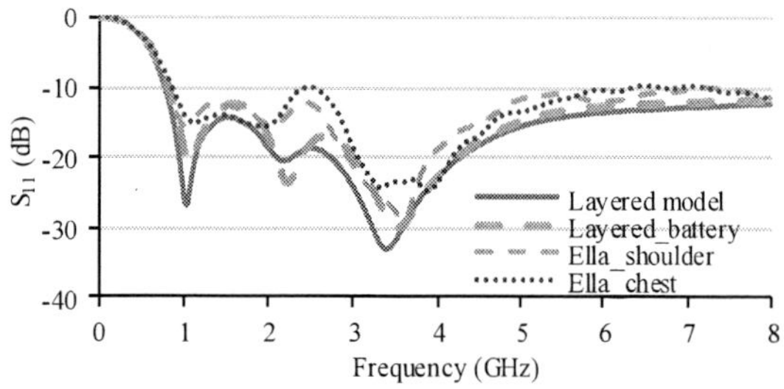

Fig. 2. Comparison of simulated reflection coefficients (S_{11}) of conformal capsule antenna for different simulations setups.

TABLE I. SUMMARY OF THE REALIZED GAIN OF CAPSULE ANTENNA

Scenario	915 MHz	2.45 GHz
Layered model	-25.23 dBi	-27.51 dBi
Layered_battery	-23.31 dBi	-25.32 dBi
Ella_shoulder	-21.77 dBi	-22.20 dBi
Ella_chest	-25.86 dBi	-28.78 dBi

III. RESULTS AND DISCUSSION

In order to test the robustness of the proposed antenna, reflection coefficients (S_{11}) for the aforementioned simulation setups are compared in Fig. 2. The antenna bandwidth ($S_{11} <$ -10 dB) of the layered model implantation case is about 7.31 GHz (0.78 GHz – 8 GHz). Integrating the battery causes a slight shift in the resonance frequencies. The implanted antennas in Ella's shoulder or chest also show a reduction in the S_{11} level and a detuning effect. The most noticeable reduction in the obtained bandwidth, which is about 800 MHz, is observed in the case of implanting antenna in Ella's chest. However, since the antenna is a wideband, these detuning effects do not cause a significant effect on the bandwidth variation. The antenna gain at the center frequencies of the 902.8 MHz – 928.0 MHz, and 2.40 GHz – 2.50 GHz ISM bands are summarized in Table I. These frequency bands are selected as they are commonly used for biotelemetry applications [1], [5]. From Table I, it is clear that the antenna gain is higher within ISM–915 MHz for all the studied cases.

For accurate assessment of the antenna performance for near/far-field communication in biotelemetry applications, where the near-field boundary is approximated at $\lambda/2\pi$ [6], the coupling strength (S_{12}) between an external half-wavelength dipole and the proposed capsule antenna implanted in the layered body model is evaluated for two scenarios. First, the free-space distance (s) of the external dipole is changed in the range of 10 *mm* – 70 *mm*, while the implanting depth (d) is 40 *mm*. Second, distance d is changed in a range of 10 *mm* – 70 *mm*, while s is 10 *mm*. The simulation setup is shown in Fig. 3 (a). For each of the studied frequency bands, a different dipole is adopted. As shown in Fig. 3 (b), the coupling strength at 915 MHz is higher than that at 2.45 GHz for both studied cases due to the larger obtained gain values at 915 MHz with changing d and s distances (results are not shown here due to space limitations and will be discussed during the presentation).

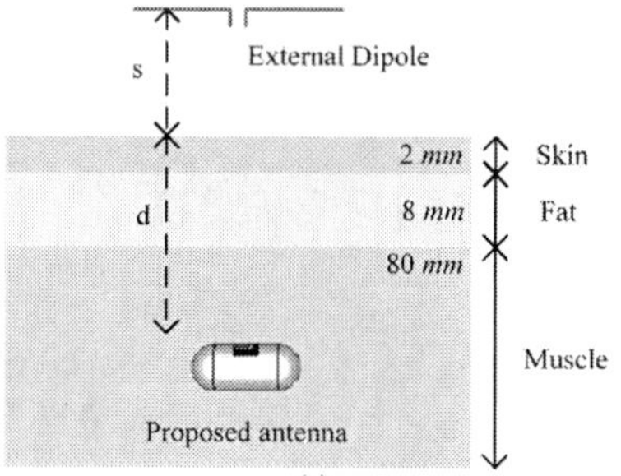

(a)

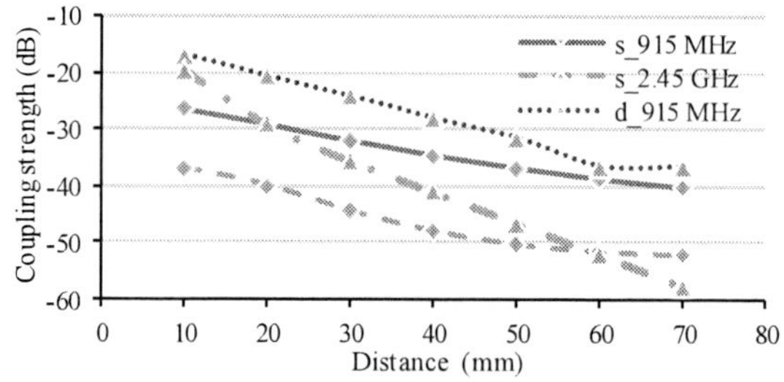

(b)

Fig. 3. Coupling strength for external half wavelength dipole; (a) simulation setup, (b) results for different free space distances *(s)* and implant depths *(d)*.

IV. CONCLUSION

The design and performance evaluation of a miniaturized wideband implantable capsule antenna is presented. The advantage of the wideband property of the proposed antenna is demonstrated through the performance evaluation of this antenna when it is implanted in a simplified layered body model and an anatomical realistic body model, as well as when it is integrated with a battery. Also, the near/far-field communication analysis is carried out at 915 MHz and 2.45 GHz for different free space distances of the receiver and different implant depths. Findings of this study suggest that the proposed capsule antenna support the functionality of wireless data transmission and wake-up receiver signal within 902.8 MHz–928.0 MHz and 2.40 GHz–2.50 GHz ISM bands, respectively. The wake-up receiver signal is necessary to save power by transmitting data only when is needed.

REFERENCES

[1] Z. Duan, Y. X. Guo, M. Je, and D. L. Kwong, "Design and in vitro test of a differentially fed dual-band implantable antenna operating at MICS and ISM Bands," IEEE Trans. Antennas Propag., vol. 62, no. 5, pp. 2430–2439, 2014.

[2] L. J. Xu, Y. X. Guo, and W. Wu, "Bandwidth enhancement of an implantable antenna," IEEE Antennas Wirel. Propag. Lett., vol. 14, pp. 1510–1513, 2015.

[3] A. Kiourti and K. S. Nikita, "Miniature scalp-implantable antennas for telemetry in the MICS and ISM bands: Design, safety considerations and link budget analysis," IEEE Trans. Antennas Propag., vol. 60, no. 8, pp. 3568–3575, 2012.

[4] CST Microwave Studio [Online]. Available: http/www.cst.com

[5] R. Das and H. Yoo, "A wideband circularly polarized conformal endoscopic antenna system for high-speed data transfer," IEEE Trans. Antennas Propag., vol. 65, no. 6, pp. 2816–2826, 2017.

[6] J. D. Kraus, "Antenna measurements," in Antennas for All Applications, 3rd ed., New York, NY, USA: McGraw-Hill, 2002.

Hybrid Power Transfer and Wireless Antenna System Design for Biomedical Implanted Devices

Reem Shadid
Electrical Engineering Department
University of North Dakota
Grand Forks, ND, 58202
reem.shadid@und.edu

Sima Noghanian
Electrical Engineering Department
University of North Dakota
Grand Forks, ND, 58202
sima.noghanian@und.edu

***Abstract*—In this paper, we present a hybrid system consisting of a high frequency (HF) coil (13.56 MHz), and an ultra-high frequency (UHF) antenna (905 MHz), integrated on an FR-4 substrate that provides a compact solution for simultaneous wireless power transfer and wireless communication for implanted medical devices. The challenge of minimizing the coupling effect between the coil and the antenna is addressed by optimizing their dimensions. The hybrid system was numerically modeled and the performance was tested at different depths inside a layered body tissue model. It is shown that the antennas' resonance frequencies of the external and implanted antennas, f_{rex} and f_{rim}, respectively, are stable and do not change by the depth of implanted antenna inside the tissue. Furthermore, transmission efficiency (η) at different distances is calculated. The system provides a good solution for the combination of power transfer and signal communication in a compact design.**

Keywords—Wireless power transfer; implanted biomedical devices; coupling effect.

I. Introduction

The advancement of wireless communication and biomedical implanted sensors brings the need of compact systems that combine the two functionalities in small form factor. Therefore, we are motivated to study the coupling effects when the wireless communication antennas are integrated with the wireless power transfer coils. Many solutions of wireless power transfer for implanted medical devices are presented in the literature. For example, in [1], an inductive link to transfer power and data to biomedical implantable devices using separate coils located on perpendicular plane is presented. In [2], the power is provided to an implanted neural recording system via inductive coupling in the HF band. There is also a system that transfers data via coupling at UHF band. However, the coupling effect between coils and antennas was not explained in [2]. In this paper, we propose a hybrid system that consists of a coil system working at 13.56 MHz, for power transfer, and a pair of antennas, working at 905 MHz, for data communication. To provide a compact design, the antenna and coil combination are printed on the same side of an FR-4 substrate. The main difficulty of this design is to minimize the coupling effect between the antenna and the coil. Therefore, via simulation, the optimum dimensions to keep the system compact while reducing the coupling effects were found. Moreover, we studied the influence of changing the spacing (S) between the external coil/antenna which will be referred as (EX) and the implanted one, which will be referred to as IM, on the f_{rex} and f_{rim}, as the IM antenna/coil setup is moved deeper into the tissue model. Also the efficiency (η) is calculated at each selected S.

This work was supported by North Dakota Department of Commerce through a Venture Phase I grant, and University of North Dakota and Applied Science University in Jordan.

II. Antenna and Coil Design

The proposed dual band design consists of an EX antenna/coil combination that is placed directly at the outer surface of the skin, whereas the IM antenna/coil combination is embedded in the muscle. We started the design by assuming that EX is at a distance of 15 *mm* from the skin layer. A layered body model consisting of three tissue layers: the skin layer (3 *mm*), the fat layer (7 *mm*) and the muscle layer (125 *mm*). The electromagnetic properties of each layer at each frequency were obtained from Institute of Applied Physics (IFAC) database [3] and are summarized in Table I. Both systems are assumed to be covered by a layer of silicone with the thickness of 100 μm. Fig. 1 shows each combination of the EX and IM. The details of each design are as follows:

A. Coil Design

The EX coil consists of a four turns spiral loop. The EX coil trace width (w_{ex}) is 1.6 *mm* and the space width (s_{ex}) is 1.4 *mm*. The coil is assumed to be printed on FR-4 substrate with 1.52 *mm* thickness. The IM coil is assumed to be placed inside the muscle. It consists of a five-turn spiral loop. The IM trace width (w_{im}) is 500 μm and the space width (s_{im}) is 300 μm. This coil is also designed on FR-4 substrate with 0.8 *mm* thickness. Both EX and IM coils have 35.56 μm copper thickness. Two matching capacitors elements are added in series with the EX coil and in parallel with the IM coil to make the resonance (C_{EX}=77.26 µF and C_{IM}=114.42 µF).

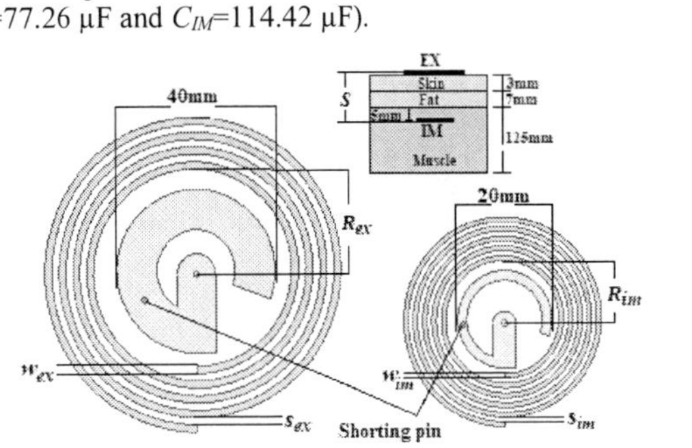

(a) (b)

Fig. 1. Coil and antenna design for (a) EX coil: w_{ex}=1.6 *mm*, s_{ex}=1.4 *mm* and R_{ex} [21to 30] *mm*, and (b) IM coil: w_{im}=500 μm, s_{im}=300 µm and R_{im} [10.5 to 14] *mm*.

TABLE I. Electromagnetic Properties at Different Frequencies

Frequency	**13.56 MHz**			**905 MHz**		
Parameter	Muscle	Fat	Skin	Muscle	Fat	Skin
ε_r	138.4	11.83	285.25	55	5.46	41.4
σ (S/m)	0.63	0.03	0.24	0.94	0.05	0.87

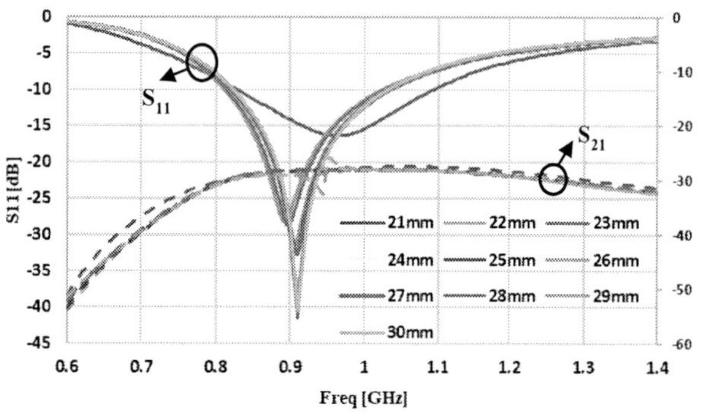

Fig. 2. S_{11} for EX antenna at different coil radii(R_{ex}) and S_{21} @ S= 15 mm.

B. Antennas Design

The antennas have a G-shape profile. The maximum outer diameter of the EX antenna is 40 *mm*, while the IM one that located inside the muscle layer is 20 *mm*. Both antennas have a shorting pin in the middle of the arc, the antenna is properly matched to 50 Ω and no matching elements have been added.

Antenna design was performed and simulated using Ansys HFSS. Ansys Maxwell and Ansys Simplorer were used to simulate the coil system design [4]. Initially the antennas were designed and simulated in the absence of the coils. The minimum reflection coefficients for the EX and IM antennas, S_{11} and S_{22}, respectively were achieved at 905 MHz, with -10 dB reflection coefficient bandwidth of 827 MHz – 1 GHz. In order to place the coil at a proper distance away from the antenna to minimize the interaction and coupling effects between the coil and the antenna, the value of the inner radius for EX and IM coils, R_{ex} and R_{im}, respectively, were optimized using the parametric tool solver in HFSS. First, the values of w_{ex} and s_{ex} were set then the value of R_{ex} was swept, starting from 21 *mm*, which is 1mm more than the radius of EX antenna, with the increments of 1 *mm*, up to maximum of 30 *mm*. The effects of the addition of coil on S_{11} and S_{22} were studied. Then the optimum value for R_{ex} was selected. Secondly, the same process was done for the IM coil by sweeping R_{im} from 10.5 *mm* to 14 *mm*, with 0.5 *mm* increments and the optimum value of R_{im} was selected though. Finally, the values of η and S_{21} for coil set and the antenna set were calculated at different distance between EX and IM combination of coils/antennas, for *S* range of 10 *mm* to 110 *mm*.

III. Results

Fig. 2 shows S_{11} and S_{21} versus frequency at different values of $R_{ex,}$ marked by different colors. The maximum coupling effects occurs at R_{ex} = 21 *mm* where f_{rex} was shifted to 970 MHz. This was expected since it is the closest distance between the EX coil and the antenna. The f_{rex} of 905 MHz was achieved at R_{ex} = 27 *mm*. S_{21} achieved its maximum value at (f_{rex} = 905 MHz). Fig. 3 shows S_{22} and S_{21} versus frequency, at different values of R_{im}. As expected the worst set-up of coupling case occurred at the closest distance between IM coil and antenna at 10.5 *mm*. Other values of R_{im} gave better results due to minimization of coupling effects when the separation of antenna and coil is increased. The best result was achieved at 11.5 *mm* and S_{21} achieved its maximum value at (f_{rim} = 905 MHz).

Table II shows the values of f_{rex} and f_{rim} at different value of *S* between the EX and IM combinations in the range of 10 *mm* to 110 *mm*. It is notable that the resonance frequency of the antenna does not change more than 10 MHz for the most cases. That indicates that the G-shape antenna is not affected by the *S* value between the EX and IM antennas.

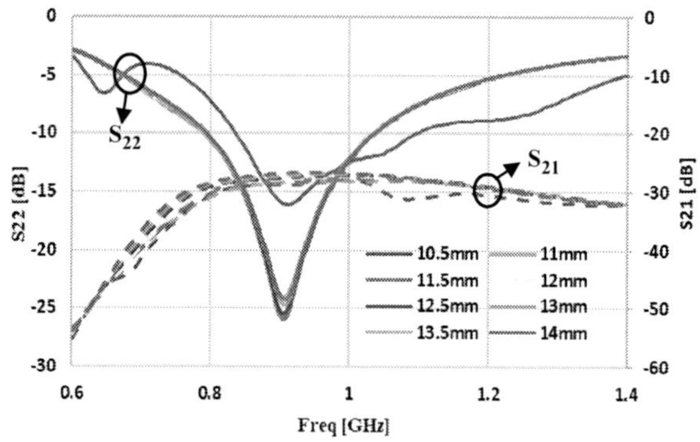

Fig. 3. S_{22} for the IM antenna at different coil radius (R_{im}).

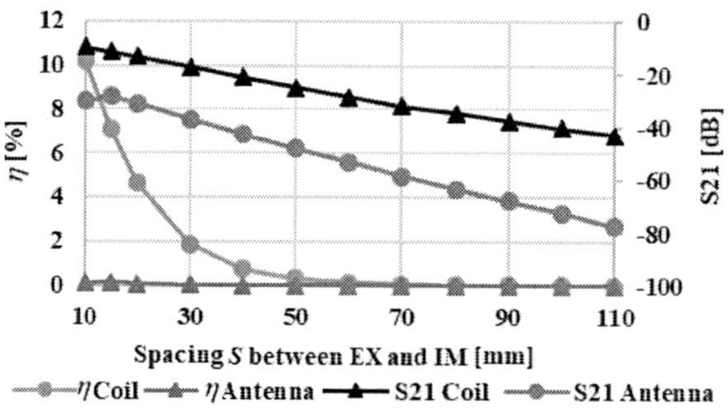

Fig. 4. η and S_{21} at different depths.

TABLE II. Resonance Frequencies' of Coils at Different *S*.

S[*mm*]	10	15	20	30	40	50	60
f_{rex} [MHz]	895	905	910	905	905	905	905
f_{rim} [MHz]	1115	905	900	905	905	910	905
***S*[*mm*]**	**70**	**80**	**90**	**100**	**110**		
f_{rex} [MHz]	905	905	905	905	905		
f_{rim} [MHz]	905	905	905	905	905		

In order to study the transmission efficiency of EX and IM combinations, we extracted S_{21} at 905MHz from simulations and calculated $\eta=|S_{21}|^2\times100\%$ for both bands at different *S* between EX and IM. Results are plotted in Fig. 4. As the distance between EX and IM increases the efficiency of both bands is approximately the same after 60 *mm*.

IV. Conclusion

In this paper, we investigated the design of a dual system for power and data transfer. The coils' dimensions used for power transfer were optimized to minimizes the coupling effect between coils and antennas working at 13.56 MHz and 905 MHz respectively. Moreover, we calculated η and S_{21} for the hybrid system at different implanting depths. The results show that this hybrid system provides a good combination for power transfer and signal communication.

References

[1] M. Ghovanloo and S. Atluri, "A wide-band power-efficient inductive wireless link for implantable microelectronic devices using multiple carriers," IEEE Trans. Circuits Syst. I Regul. Pap., vol. 54, no. 10, pp. 2211–2221, 2007.

[2] A. Sharma, E. Kampianakis, and M. S. Reynolds, "A Dual-band HF and UHF antenna system for implanted neural recording and stimulation devices," IEEE Antennas Wirel. Propag. Lett., vol. 16, pp. 493–496, 2017.

[3] "Institute of Applied Physics (IFAC)." [Online]. Available: http://niremf.ifac.cnr.it/tissprop/htmlclie/htmlclie.php

[4] "Ansys, Inc." [Online]. Available: www.ansoft.com

Circuitry Design and Magnetic Susceptibility Evaluation of 7T fMRI Implantable RF Coil

Rong Wang, Celia M. Dong, Ed X. Wu, Robert C. Roberts, Li Jun Jiang
Department of Electrical and Electronic Engineering
The University of Hong Kong
Pokfulam Road, Hong Kong
Email: wang1130@hku.hk

***Abstract*—Implantable coils have been widely utilized in functional magnetic resonance imaging (fMRI) owing to their superior signal to noise ratio. To effectively minimize the magnetic field distortion and image artifacts, the magnetic susceptibility of the implantable coil needs to be evaluated before practical use. In this work, we experimentally identify the magnetic susceptibility of each component of the implantable coil with the 7T Bruker NMR imaging scanner and provide useful guidelines for the following manufacturing. A 5×5 mm^2 implantable surface coil with a tunable frequency range is subsequently introduced for the 7T fMRI of the rat primary somatosensory cortex (S1FL). A detachable external tuning circuit for the implantable coil is employed to facilitate in-vivo measurements in the rat model.**

***Index Terms*—Implantable coil, magnetic susceptibility, fMRI**

I. Introduction

Radio frequency coils have become indispensable components for the magnetic resonance imaging (MRI) scanners owing to their ability to transmit RF pulse at the Larmor frequency and receive the free induction decay signal [1], [2]. The recent discovery that MRI could be utilized for sensing neural activity (also known as Functional MRI or fMRI) has greatly spurred the research and development of the miniaturized and implantable coils [3], [4]. In contrast with conventional T2-weighted MRI, fMRI sets stringent requirement of the magnetic susceptibility for the implantable coil since the fast image acquisition technique adopted such as echo planar imaging (EPI) is less tolerant of the magnetic field distortion induced by the implantable coil and tends to bring in susceptibility artifacts which diminish the quality of the retrieved image. Therefore, the magnetic susceptibility evaluation of each component of the implantable coil is crucial before system assembly and measurement. In this paper, a 5×5 mm^2 implantable planar coil is designed and manufactured for 7T fMRI of the rat S1FL cortex region. As shown in the flowchart of Fig. 1(a), after the circuitry design and simulation process, the magnetic susceptibility of all the components of the implantable coil are evaluated by capturing their EPI images within the cylindrical homogeneous saline phantom. The implantable coil is then carefully assembled following the guidelines offered by the magnetic susceptibility evaluation and finally connected with an external tuning circuit to experimentally function at 300 MHz, the Larmor frequency of 7T scanner.

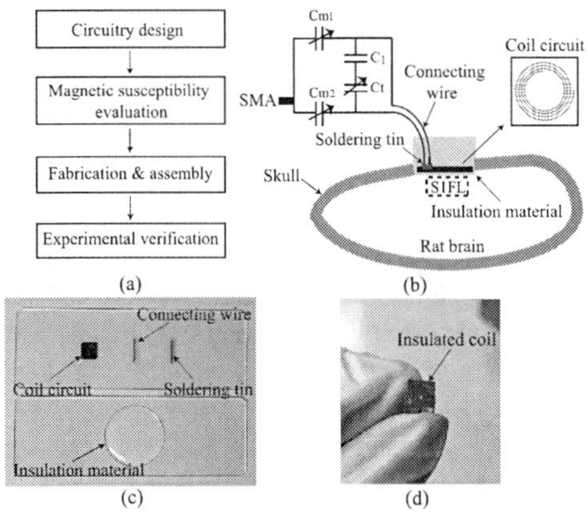

Fig. 1. (a) Flowchart of coil design. (b) Schematic diagram of the proposed implantable coil. (c) Samples of the coil components on glass slides. (d) Snapshot of the assembled coil.

II. Circuitry Design

The circuitry is mainly composed of an implantable coil and a tuning circuit. The proposed surface coil is constituted by four components, coil circuit, copper connecting wire, insulation material and soldering tin as shown in Fig. 1(b). The substrate of the coil circuit is 0.254 mm thick Rogers 5880 laminate. The insulation material is Polydimethylsiloxane (PDMS) which is exhaustively used in implantable devices for electrical sealing.

The simulated inductance and intrinsic resistance of the proposed 5×5 mm^2 four-turn planar coil (35 um thick copper trace, 0.127 mm trace width and spacing) are 67.2 nH and 0.38 Ω respectively, obtained from ANSYS Maxwell. Note that the Larmor frequency should be indicated in the simulation to obtain the additional resistance caused by the skin effect. The surface coil is then represented by an equivalent circuit in Agilent ADS simulator and the ranges of the variable matching and tuning capacitors C_m and C_t are further determined. In this design, the tuning circuit is constituted by a fixed capacitor C_1=2 pF and three identical trimmer capacitors C_{m1}, C_{m2} and C_t (tuning range: 1.8 to 4.5 pF, non-magnetic surface mount SGC3 series, manufactured by Sprague-Goodman).

III. MAGNETIC SUSCEPTIBILITY EVALUATION

Magnetic susceptibility χ_m is a measure indicating the magnetization extent of a material under external magnetic field. The magnetic induction $\mathbf{B}$ is related to χ_m by the relationship:

$$\mathbf{B} = \mu_0 (1 + \chi_m) \mathbf{H} \quad (1)$$

where μ_0 is vacuum permeability and $\mathbf{H}$ is the magnetic field strength. For implantable coil, the extra magnetic induction $\mathbf{B}$ induced by its magnetic susceptibility χ_m will distort the base magnetic induction $\mathbf{B}_0$ and vary the base Larmor frequency f_0 which is proportional to $\mathbf{B}_0$. The frequency deviation, in turn, produces signal loss and brings in susceptibility artifacts to the retrieved image. Compared with the time-consuming T2-weighted MRI process, fMRI sacrifices the magnetic susceptibility tolerance to reduce the image acquisition time and capture the instant change of the neural activity.

Therefore, for fMRI application, the evaluation of the magnetic susceptibility of the elements and materials that constitute the implantable coil should be conducted before the manufacture and assembly process. In this work, we take a piece of every coil construction component and place it on glass slide as shown in fig. 1(c). Both T2 and EPI images of every piece immersed in a cylindrical homogeneous saline phantom are captured by the high-field 7T Bruker NMR imaging scanner. The induced susceptibility artifacts of each component could be easily identified by comparing its T2 and EPI images in Fig. 2. The susceptibility artifacts produced by the soldering tin is more significant over the other three, visually indicated by the distorted EPI image of the glass slide underneath soldering tin. Thus, particular attention should be paid to the amount of the soldering tin during fabrication. The image of the assembled implantable coil is shown in Fig. 1 (d). The whole implantable surface coil is totally wrapped with PDMS and electrically insulated from the rat brain.

IV. MEASUREMENT

To facilitate the brain surgery for coil implantation, the implantable coil and the external tuning circuit are designed to

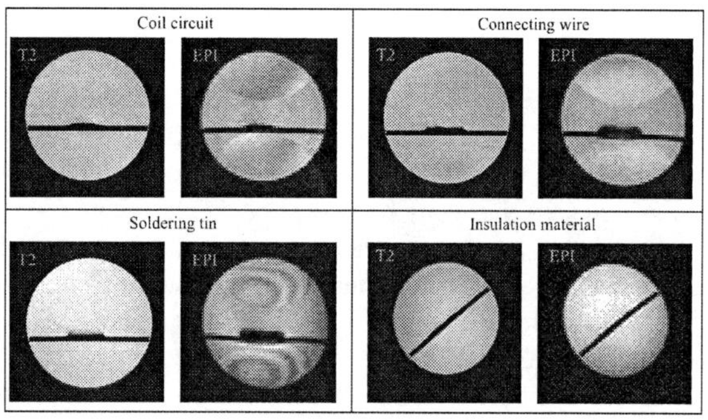

Fig. 2. T2 and EPI images of implantable coil components acquired by the high-field 7T Bruker NMR imaging scanner.

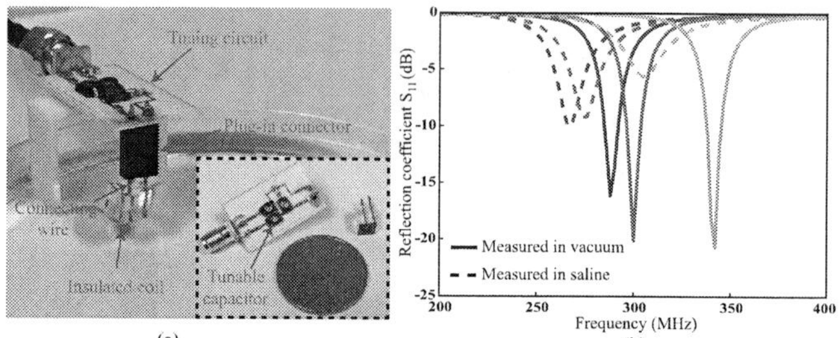

(a) (b)

Fig. 3. (a) Photograph of the implantable surface coil immersed in saline. The inset shows the detachable tuning circuit and coil. (b) Measured reflection coefficient and tunable frequency range in vacuum and saline.

be detachable with the aid of a plug-in detachable connector as shown in Fig. 3(a). In Fig. 3(b), the frequency tuning range is first measured in vacuum and the working frequency could be tuned to 300 MHz with S_{11} = -20.1 dB. A continuous range from 288 to 342 MHz is obtained (S_{11} < -15 dB) by tuning the variable capacitors. Furthermore, this tuning range is examinated in an extreme case when the sealed coil is immersed in saline since the permittivity of saline ($\varepsilon_r = 78.4$) is much larger than these of brain tissues, such as cerebral cortex and skull [5]. Here, the continuous tuning range shifts to 266 and 306 MHz and still covers the Larmor frequency of 300 MHz, validating the effectiveness of this surface coil for brain implantation.

V. CONCLUSION

This paper carries out both circuitry design and magnetic susceptibility evaluation of an implantable, tunable and detachable surface coil for the 7T fMRI of the rat cortex region. The experimentally identified magnetic susceptibility of each component provides useful guidelines for the implantable fMRI coil design and fabrication.

ACKNOWLEDGEMENT

This work is supported by the Seed Fund of University Grants Council of Hong Kong (No. AoE/P-04/08) and Hong Kong Research Grants Council grant (C7048-16G).

REFERENCES

[1] C. Massin, G. Boero, F. Vincent, J. Abenhaim, P-A. Besse, and R. S. Popovic, "High-Q factor RF planar microcoils for micro-scale NMR spectroscopy." *Sens. Actuators, A*, vol. 97, pp. 280-288, Apr. 2002.

[2] S. Eroglu, B.Gimi, B. Roman, G. Friedman, R. L. Magin, "NMR spiral surface microcoils: design, fabrication, and imaging." *Concepts in Magnetic Resonance Part B: Magnetic Resonance Engineering*, vol. 1, pp. 1-10, Apr. 2003.

[3] L. Renaud, M. Armenean, L. Berry, P. Kleimann, P. Morin, M. Pitaval, J. OBrien, M. Brunet, and H. Saint-Jalmes, "Implantable planar rf microcoils for NMR microspectroscopy." *Sens. Actuators, A*, vol. 99, pp. 244-248, Jun. 2002.

[4] M. Bilgen, I. Elshafiey, P. A. Narayana, "In vivo magnetic resonance microscopy of rat spinal cord at 7 T using implantable RF coils." *Magn. Reson. Med.*, vol. 46, pp. 1250-1253, Nov. 2001.

[5] S. Wood, T. S. Ibrahim, "Design and fabrication of a realistic anthropomorphic heterogeneous head phantom for MR purposes." *PloS one*, vol. 12, pp. 0183168, Aug. 2017.

Power Transfer Efficiency for Distance-Adaptive Wireless Power Transfer System

D.-G. Seo, S.-H. Ahn, J.-H. Kim, and W.-S. Lee*
Dept. of Elect. Eng./Eng. Res. Inst. (ERI)
Gyeongsang Nat'l Univ., Jinju 52828, Republic of Korea
*wsang@gnu.ac.kr

S.-T. Khang, S.-C. Chae, and J.-W. Yu
Dept. of Elect. Eng.
Korea Adv. Inst. of Sci. and Tech. (KAIST)
Daejeon 34141, Republic of Korea

***Abstract*—In this paper, a highly efficient distance-adaptive wireless power transfer system with automatic impedance tuning control at variable distances is proposed, and we compare the power transfer efficiency of wireless power transfer system at different operating conditions using the method of moments (MoM) technique. By sensing a reflected power and controlling impedance tuning networks, the proposed wireless power transfer system achieves the high and stable efficiency with regard to the variable operating distances. According to adaptive impedance matching algorithms under the minimum reflected power conditions, the proposed system achieves an improved power transfer efficiency of approximately maximum 160% within the operating distance.**

***Index Terms*—Distance-adaptive, power transfer efficiency (PTE), variable distances, wireless power transfer (WPT).**

I. Introduction

Wireless power transfer (WPT) technology transfers electrical energy using electromagnetic waves without electrical wires in various industries related to remote energy transfer, -sensors, digital IT consumer devices, and electric vehicles (EV) [1]. Due to the impedance matching characteristic of WPT systems that use coupled resonant antennas, WPT systems with different operating distances, variable impedance loads, and lateral misalignment between the transmitting and receiving antennas result in a significant degradation in power transfer efficiency (PTE) [2]–[4]. To achieve a highly efficient WPT, it is necessary for the system to be able to detect the location of the receiving device. In addition, in order to improve PTE for any transfer distance, adaptive frequency tracking was proposed, but it is not practical due to frequency regulation [5]. In this paper, a highly efficient WPT system with automatic impedance tuning control at variable operating distances is presented and by comparing the impedance matching algorithms under different conditions, its optimal performance is verified.

II. Proposed WPT System Configurations

The practical applications for the WPT with regard to the different mutual couplings between the transmitting and receiving antennas (i.e., variable operating distance and misalignments) are near-field communication (NFC), wireless charging pad, wireless electric vehicle charging, and medical implant. Using a method of moments (MoM) technique, the simulated transmission coefficient (S_{21}, related to the PTE) between the transmitting and receiving antenna with regard to the operating distance and the operating frequency in Fig. 1, respectively. The maximum PTE is obtained at the matching distance, and at other distances due to the impedance mismatching, the PTE is drastically degraded at operating distance. For a highly efficient WPT system, it is necessary to have a distance-adaptive impedance variation characteristic. By controlling an impedance tuning network, an impedance matching characteristic is obtained, and the PTE can be improved. To improve the WPT efficiency with

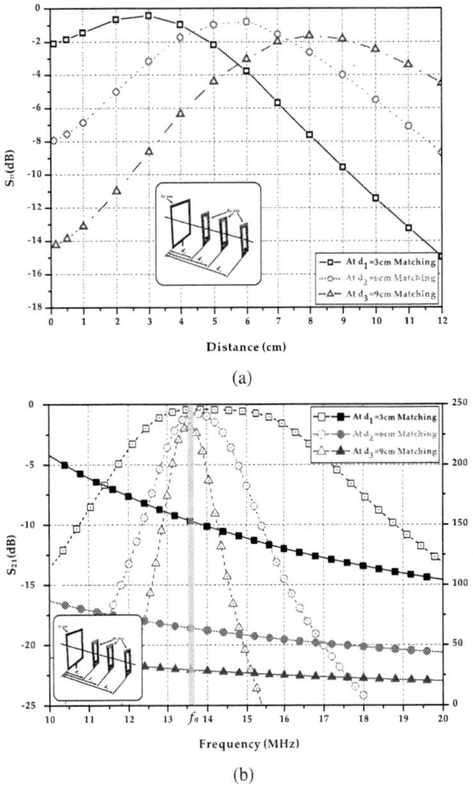

Fig. 1. The simulated transmission coefficient (S_{21}, related to the PTE) between the transmitting and receiving antennas with regard to the operating distance (a) and the operating frequency (b).

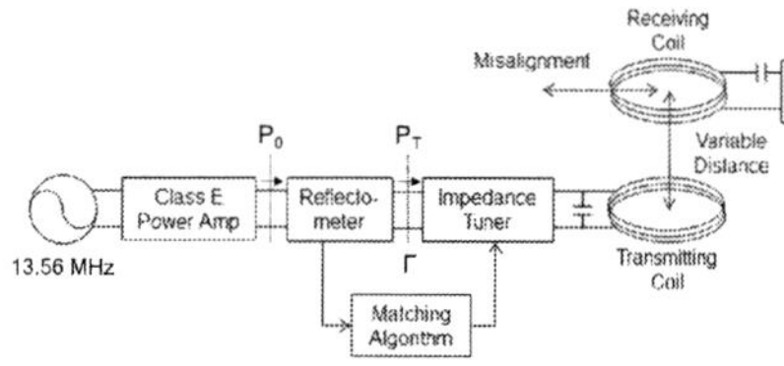

Fig. 2. The overall system block diagram for the proposed WPT system.

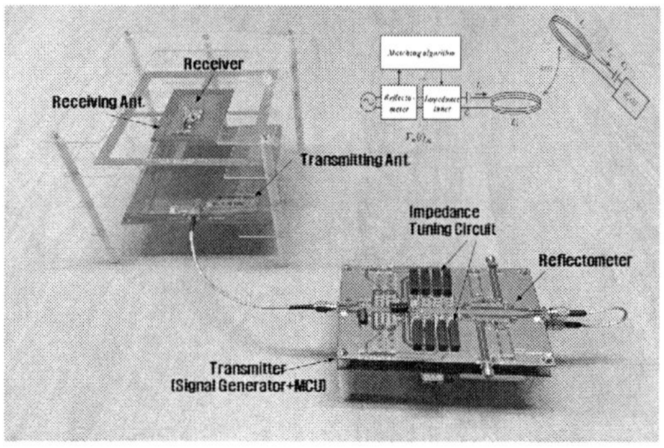

Fig. 3. The prototype of the proposed distance-adaptive WPT system.

variable distances, the distance-adaptive WPT system with automatic impedance tuning control is proposed in Fig. 2. The proposed system consists of resonant antennas for magnetic field generation, an impedance tuner (lumped network), a reflectometer to measure the reflection coefficient by detecting the reflected power, a matching algorithm for maximum PTE, and a signal source of 13.56 MHz (ISM band) with a Class-E power amplifier in Fig. 2.

III. Results And Discussion

To verify the PTE of the proposed WPT system with regard to the operating distances, we designed and implemented the proposed distance-adaptive WPT system with automatic impedance matching networks in Fig. 3. The simplified receiving device has a receiving antenna and a rectifying circuit with load. To investigate the power transfer link efficiency between the transmitting and receiving antennas, the coil antennas are designed and fabricated on an FR4 printed circuit board (PCB) substrate with a dielectric constant of 4.4 and thickness of 0.8 mm. Table I shows the received DC voltage and overall PTEs with regard to the fixed matching and proposed adaptive tuning conditions for the operating distance. The adaptive tuning conditions represent the maximum output power ($P_{0,max}$) at the output of the power amplifier, the maximum transmitting power ($P_{T,max}$), and the minimum reflection coefficient (minimum reflected power, min). If the WPT transmitting system has the maximum transmitting power condition ($P_{T,max}$), it can increase the received DC in the receiving device, but the overall PTE is less than the fixed matching condition of the impedance tuner. Within an operating distance of 3 cm to 9 cm, the minimum reflection coefficient condition displays an improved PTE of maximum approximately 160%.

TABLE I
THE PTE COMPARISON WITH REGARD TO THE OPERATING CONDITIONS

Conditions. (Dist: 3cm)	Γ	Voltage (V)	P_{in} (mW)	P_{out} (mW)	Efficiency (%)
Initial (Ref.)	0.691	10.5	163	110	68
Γ_{min}	0.541	11.6	149	135	90
$P_{0,max}$	-	10.2	1556	104	7
$P_{T,max}$	0.594	15.4	391	237	61
Conditions. (Dist: 6cm)	Γ	Voltage (V)	P_{in} (mW)	P_{out} (mW)	Efficiency (%)
Initial (Ref.)	0.832	5.55	133	31	23
Γ_{min}	0.499	9.95	204	99	48
$P_{0,max}$	-	7.25	1409	53	4
$P_{T,max}$	0.574	9.95	201	99	49
Conditions. (Dist: 9cm)	Γ	Voltage (V)	P_{in} (mW)	P_{out} (mW)	Efficiency (%)
Initial (Ref.)	0.878	2.45	127	6	5
Γ_{min}	0.500	5.0	191	25	13
$P_{0,max}$	-	3.6	1337	13	1
$P_{T,max}$	0.615	5.4	379	29	8

IV. Conclusion

We propose a highly efficient wireless power transfer system with automatic impedance tuning control for practical applications with variable operating distances. Under misalignment between the transmitting and receiving antenna or any operating distance, the proposed distance-adaptive WPT system achieves an improved PTE of maximum 160% by minimizing the reflection coefficient in the transmitting system. It can be useful in wireless charging without the response of the portable receiving device.

Acknowledgment

This work was supported in part by the Basic Science Research Program through the National Research Foundation (NRF) funded by the Ministry of Education under Grant NRF-2015R1D1A1A01056789, and in part by the Industrial Technology Innovation Program of the Korea Institute of Energy Technology Evaluation and Planning (KETEP), granted financial resource from the Ministry of Trade, Industry & Energy, under Grant 20172010106020.

References

[1] J.-M. Kim, M. Han, and H. Sohn, "Magnetic resonance-based wireless power transmission through concrete structures," *J. of Electrom. Eng. and Sci.*, vol. 15, no. 2, pp. 104110, Apr. 2015.
[2] K. Na, H. Jang, H. Ma, and F. Bien, "Tracking optimal efficiency of magnetic resonance wireless power transfer system for biomedical capsule endoscopy," *IEEE Trans. on Microw. Theo. and Tech.*, vol. 63, no. 1, pp. 295303, Jan. 2015.
[3] J. Lee, Y.-S. Lim, W.-J. Yang, and S.-O. Lim, "Wireless power transfer system adaptive to change in coil separation," *IEEE Trans. on Ant. and Prop.*, vol. 62, no. 2, pp. 889897, Feb. 2014.
[4] J. Kim and J. Jeong, "Range-adaptive wireless power transfer using multiloop and tunable matching techniques," *IEEE Trans. on Ind. Elect.*, vol. 62, no. 10, pp. 62336241, Oct. 2015.
[5] N. Y. Kim, K. Y. Kim, J. Choi, and C.-W. Kim, "Adaptive frequency with power-level tracking system for efficient magnetic resonance wireless power transfer," *Electr. Lett.*, vol. 48, no. 8, pp. 452454, Apr. 2012.

Novel Multiband Flamenco Fractal Antenna for Wearable WBAN Off-Body Communication Applications

Omar Masood Khan[1], Qamar Ul Islam[2], Raed M. Shubair[3], and Asimina Kiourti[4]
[1]Iqra University, Pakistan; [2]Institute of Space Technology, Pakistan
[3]Research Laboratory of Electronics (RLE), Massachusetts Institute of Technology (MIT), USA
[4]ElectroScience Laboratory, The Ohio State University, USA

Abstract— **Novel fractal geometry is presented in this paper termed as Flamenco for exhibiting multiband characteristics. The Flamenco fractal is iterated upto third order for attaining five resonances at 0.928 GHz, 3.56 GHz, 6.85 GHz, 8.12 GHz and 10.56 GHz covering Industrial, Scientific and Medical (ISM) band as well as Ultra-wide Band (UWB) for off-body Wireless Body Area Networks (WBAN) biomedical communications. The antenna is designed in monopole configuration along with microstrip stubs and slots embedded at the ground plane for providing frequency and bandwidth tuning and optimization of the desired resonances. Lower Specific Absorption Ratio (SAR) of 0.989 W/kg averaged over 1 g is achieved due to reduced size proposed fractal radiator. The gain patterns presented verifies the omni-directional radiations for the Flamenco fractal.**

Keywords-component; fractal antenna, Biomedical, WBAN, Off-body Communication

I. INTRODUCTION

Wireless body area networks provides significant breakthrough for providing vital communications for applications such as health monitoring, military and personal entertainment. Various configurations are studied over the past years such as coplanar waveguide fed ring strips is proposed in [1], with rectangular strip and microstrip stubs that are symmetrically attached with the ground plane for radiations in the UWB covering three frequencies of 3.19-4.57, 5.37-5.6 and 7.56-10.67 GHz, where the antenna characteristics are verified in the on-body communication environment. Biomedical implantable antenna system for dual band radiation is presented [2], in 13.56 MHz HF and 902-928 MHz UHF frequency bands for stimulation and neural recording devices. Separate antennas are used for implant and data transfer purposes, where the inductive coupling is used for providing power supply. PCB based metal frame antenna [3] is designed for wrist band devices healthcare monitoring biomedical applications. Circularly polarized printed loop antenna for implantable biomedical applications is designed for providing radiations in Industrial Scientific and Medical frequency bands [4]. Implantable on chip biomedical antenna can be designed using CMOS 0.18 um process for ISM band [5]. With the wideband design, antenna can be implanted with biocompatible thin and low loss coating. RF Inference reduction is required for thermal assessment of tissues for radiometry and heating in biomedical devices at 0.9 and 3.7 GHz [6]. Biomedical printed antenna for MIMO applications is designed for radiations in the MedRadio frequency band [7], consisting of two elements with mutual coupling below -26 dB is attained.

In this paper novel Flamenco fractal geometry is proposed for multiband radiations in the ISM and UWB bands for biomedical wearable off-body communication applications. The fractal antenna is fractalized upto third order and monopole configuration is adopted along with various slots and stubs embedded at the ground plane for bandwidth enhancement in the radiation bands. Parametric analysis is done for tuning various resonances. SAR value of 0.989 W/kg is achieved averaged over 1 g. Current density and radiation pattern plots are provided for the proposed antenna.

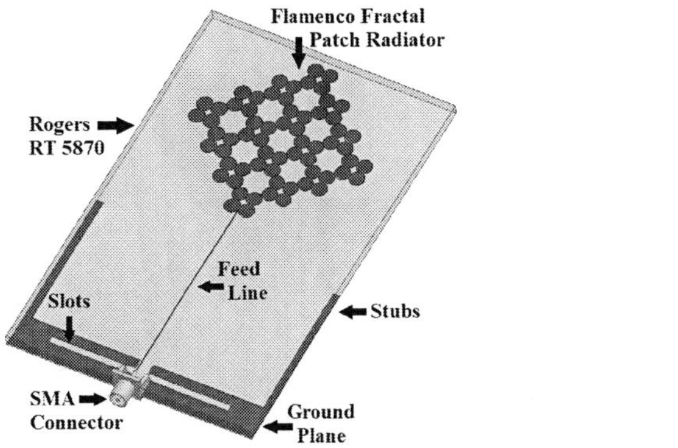

Fig. 1. Labeled prespective diagram of the proposed Flamenco fractal antenna

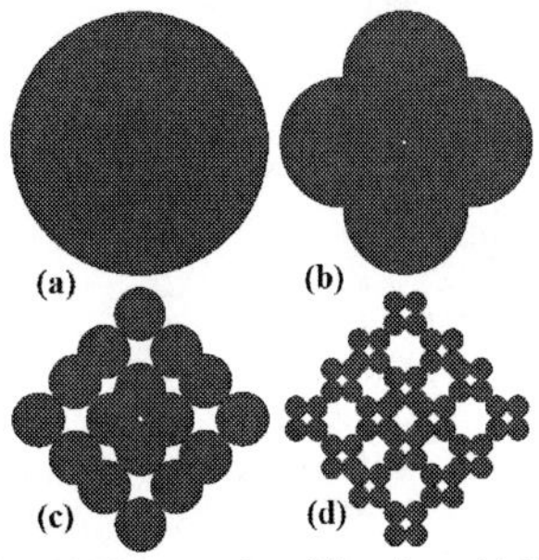

Fig. 2. Proposed novel Flamenco fractal iterations, (a) Unit Cell, (b) First Iteration, (c) Second Iteration, (d) Third Iteration

II. FLAMENCO FRACTAL ANTENNA DESIGN

The proposed novel Flamenco fractal antenna is presented in Fig. 1. The antenna consists of Flamenco fractal patch radiator of third order fed through microstrip transmission line placed on the top layer of the printed circuit board, with SMA connector soldered at the other end of the feed line. Rogers RT 5870 is used as substrate with height of 1.575 mm having dielectric constant of 2.33 and loss tangent of 0.0012. Flamenco fractal antenna is designed for achieving multiband band resonances covering ISM and UWB frequency bands for biomedical wearable off-body communication. The bottom layer consists of ground plane embedded with slots at the middle and stubs at the left and right edges for providing tuning capabilities for optimizing frequencies for the multibands and their corresponding bandwidths.

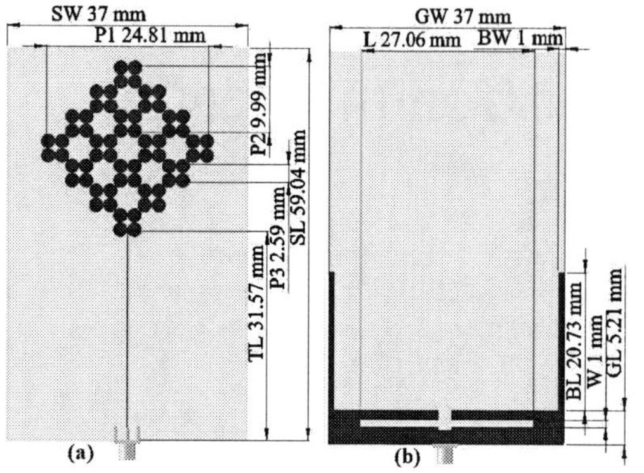

Fig. 3. Dimensions diagram of the proposed Flamenco fractal antenna, (a) Top Layer and (b) Bottom Layer

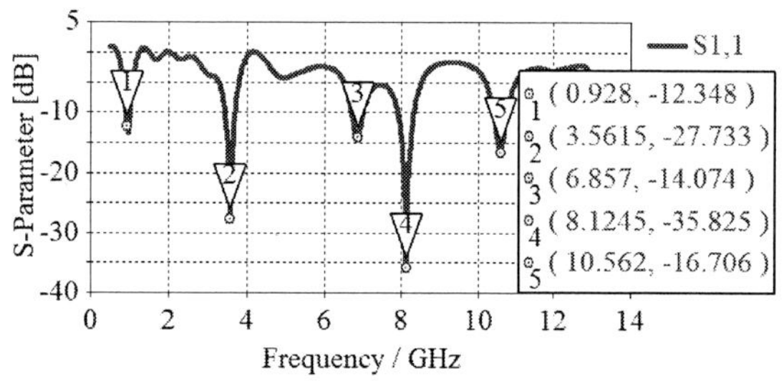

Fig. 4. Frequency Response of the Flamenco fractal antenna

The fractalization process for the generation of novel flamenco fractal geometry is demonstrated in Fig. 2 for its basic cell upto third iteration. The basic cell of the Flamenco fractal consists of circle as shown in Fig. 2a, that is used for the repeatability of pattern in higher order iterations as seen in Fig. 2b to 2d.

The dimensions for various segments of the optimized top and bottom layers of Flamenco fractal antenna is demonstrated in Figs. 3a and 3b respectively, consisting of radiating Flamenco fractal patch diameters constituting pattern repeatability and lengths and widths of ground plane, embedded slot, transmission line and symmetrically placed stubs at the left and right corner of the ground plane.

III. Simulation And Analysis

The proposed novel Flamenco fractal antenna is designed and analyzed in CST Microwave Studio. The antenna is designed for resonating at multiple frequencies for covering Industrial, Scientific and Medical (ISM) band as well as Ultra-Wideband (UWB) for wearable off-body Wireless Body Area Network medical applications. The frequency response is

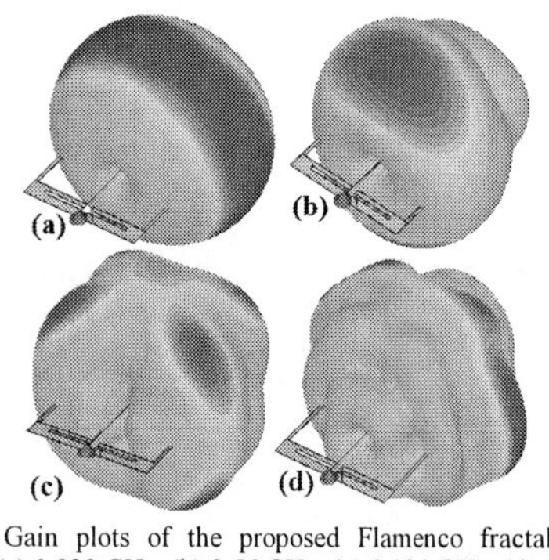

Fig. 5. 3D Gain plots of the proposed Flamenco fractal antenna at frequencies, (a) 0.928 GHz, (b) 3.56 GHz, (c) 8.124 GHz, (d) 10.56 GHz

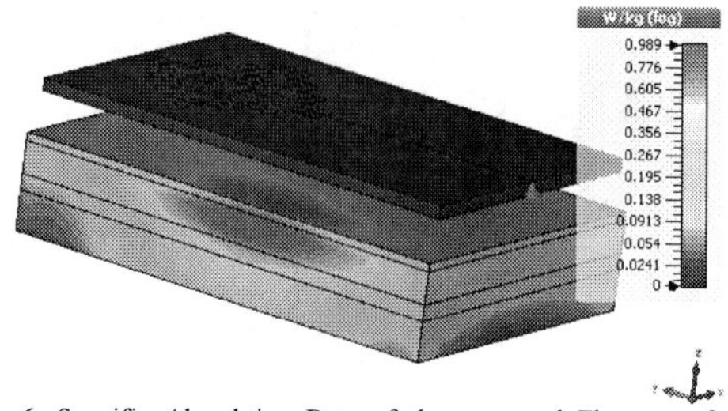

Fig. 6. Specific Absorbtion Rate of the proposed Flamenco fractal antenna over skin surface and internal body

presented in Fig. 4, with the first resonance covering 902-928 MHz ISM band, whereas the second, third, fourth and fifth resonances covering UWB at 3.56 GHz, 6.857 GHz, 8.12 GHz and 10.56 GHz respectively. The Flamenco fractal antenna is designed in monopole configuration for omni-directional radiation in multibands targeting the ISM and UWB medical bands. Three dimensional gain patterns of the proposed antenna are depicted in Fig. 5, exhibiting omni-directional patterns for 0.928 GHz, 3.56 GHz, 8.124 GHz and 10.56 GHz.

The SAR values are verified for the proposed Flamenco fractal antenna in CST as shown in Fig. 6. Nominal spacing of 5 mm is provided for antenna placement over skin tissue with corresponding layers of fat, muscle and bone, with simulations conducted at 902 MHz for the Industrial, Scientific and Medical (ISM) band. The standard of C95.1-1999 is applied with SAR averaged over 1 g of tissue and peak value of 0.989 W/kg is attained which is well within the maximum threshold of 1.6 W/kg.

IV. Conclusion

Novel Flamenco fractal antenna is proposed exhibiting multiband characteristics. The fractal iteration upto third order is achieved for attaining resonances for covering ISM as well as UWB medical bands. Lower levels of specific absorption rate upto 0.989 W/kg averaged over 1 g is achieved due to reduced size fractal geometry of the radiating element according to C95.1-1999 standards. The gain patterns verify omni-directional patterns for off-body WBAN communication applications.

References

[1] M. N. Shakib, M. Moghavvemi, and W. N. L. Mahadi, "Design of a Tri-band Off-body Antenna for WBAN Communication," *IEEE Antennas and Wireless Progagation Letters*, vol. 16 , pp. 210-213, 2017.

[2] A. Sharma, E. Kampianakis, and M. S. Reynolds, "A Dual-Band HF and UHF Antenna System for Implanted Neural Recording and Stimulation Devices," *IEEE Antennas and Wireless Progagation Letters*, vol. 16, pp. 493-496, 2017.

[3] Z. Duan, L.-J. Xu, and W. Geyi, "Metal frame repeater antenna with partial slotted ground for bandwidth enhancement of wristband devices," *IET Microwave, Antennas & Propagation*, vol. 11, no. 10, pp. 1438-1444, 2017.

[4] L.-J. Xu, Y.-X. Guo, and W. Wu, "Miniaturized Circularly Polarized loop Antenna for Biomedical Applications," *IEEE Transaction on Antennas and Propagation*, vol. 63, no. 3, pp. 922 - 930, March 2015.

[5] C. Liu, Y.-X. Guo, X. Liu, and S. Xiao, "An Integrated On-chip Implantable Antenna in 0.18μm CMOS Technology for Biomedical Applications," *IEEE Transaction on Antennas and Propagation*, vol. 63, no. 3, pp. 1167-1172, March 2016.

[6] M.-R. Tofighi, and J. R. Pardeshi, "Interference Enhanced Biomedical Antenna for Combined Heating and Radiometry Application," *IEEE Antennas and Wireless Progagation Letters*, vol. 16, pp. 1895 – 1898, 2017.

[7] S. Xiao, C. Liu, Y. Li, X. M. Yang, and X. Liu, "Small-Size Dual-Antenna Implantable System for Biotelemetry Devices," *IEEE Antennas and Wireless Progagation Letters*, vol. 15, pp. 1723 - 1726, 2016.

Multi-Bandwidth CPW-Fed Open End Square Loop Monopole Antenna for Energy Harvesting

Nermeen A. Eltresy, Dalia M. Elsheakh, and Esmat A. Abdallah
Microstrip Dept., Electronics Research Institute, El Dokki, Egypt
daliaelsheakh@eri.sci.eg

***Abstract*—Compact CPW-fed open end square loop monopole antenna is presented in this paper. The antenna can harvest at different radio frequencies. Multi band antenna operation has been created at 1.8, 1.9, 2.4 and 5.2 GHz. The multi-bandwidth coplanar waveguide antenna (MCPW) is designed and fabricated on a very thin and low-profile substrate.**

Keywords—Bandwidth, Coplanar waveguide antenna, Energy Harvesting.

I. INTRODUCTION

In recent years the wireless technology became the main subject for the rapid enormous changes in frequency allocation, policies and procedures of operations, and techniques to enhance the wireless system performance. Many of wired systems are converted into wireless, for example wired LAN is converted into a wireless. As a result of that an increased demand for multiple antennas covering different wireless communication bands on the same platform increased extremely. This makes the antenna more important day by day specially the multi-bandwidth antenna. As a result of that a multiband and broadband fractal patch antenna is presented in [1]. Four different planar multi-band antennas are designed, modeled, fabricated, and measured in [2]. A meandered planar inverted-F antenna introduced in [3] for LTE/GSM/UMTS multi band operation. In [4], a reconfigurable and multiband antenna is introduced for wireless and radar applications. Printed inverted F-antenna (PIFA) is a type of compact antenna. The design of compact multiband and environmental isolation for mobile phones represented in [5] using planar inverted-F antenna (PIFA). Ambient energy sources are widely used as a clean energy sources. The ambient energy is one of the environment friendly energy sources. It can be used for the production of electric energy. Ambient energy sources are using different energy harvesting methods [6], such as mechanical, optic, thermal energy extraction, and wireless energy harvesting. Wireless energy harvesting has proven to be one of the most promising solutions because of its simplicity, ease of implementation, and availability. The ability to harvest RF energy from ambient or dedicated sources enables the wireless charging of low power devices. The wireless energy harvesting system consists of three main subsystems. The first one is the receiving antenna, which is used to capture ambient radio frequency energy which will be converted to DC power. The second subsystem is the matching network between the antenna and the rectifier. The third subsystem is the rectification circuitry, which converts the input RF power into DC output power. An output DC filter (post rectification filter) is used to provide a DC to the load by separating the high-frequency components from the DC signal.

This paper presents a multi bandwidth antenna with a good response at 1.8 GHz, 1.9 GHz, 2.4 GHz and 5.2 GHz. The antenna consists of multi arm and each arm is responsible for a specific resonant frequency.

II. ANTENNA STRUCTURE AND GEOMETRY

The design of low profile coplanar waveguide (CPW) antenna using thin substrate and flexible of ROGERS (RO3003) with dielectric constant ε_r=3 and thickness 130 μm. The detailed structure of the multi-bandwidth flexible CPW-fed antenna is shown in Fig. 1. The antenna has area of $L \times W$=60×40 mm^2. Feeding line with width of W_f=5mm and length of L_f=18 mm is used to feed the antenna. The separation gap between the feeding line and the ground plane is g=0.3 mm. The ground plane has length of L_g =16 mm.

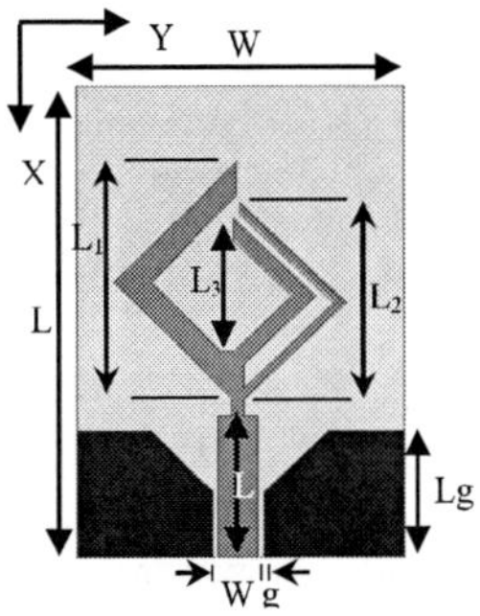

Fig. 1. The geometry of the proposed antenna.

III. DESIGN AND PARAMETRIC STUDY

A. Design Optimization Procedure

The design steps of the CPW antenna is shown in Fig. 2. The first assumed design is indicated in Fig. 2(a) which consists of a one arm CPW antenna, the arm length is L_1=29 mm that gives one resonant band at 1.8 GHz. Then another arm with length of L_2= 22 mm has been added to give resonant at 1.8 GHz, which is shown in Fig. 2(b). After that a third arm with length L_3=18.5 mm is added between the previous two arms, which drive resonant at 2.4 GHz.

Finally, a modified etched rectangular ground plane with angle $\alpha = 45^{o}$ is used to improve the impedance matching at the higher bands specially 5.2 GHz. The final design is shown in Fig. 2(d). Figure 3 indicates response of the design steps of the multiband proposed antenna which has the following impedance bandwidth (1.58-2.1 GHz), (2.35-2.48 GHz) and (4.6-5.8 GHz) according to -6dB reflection coefficient as a reference.

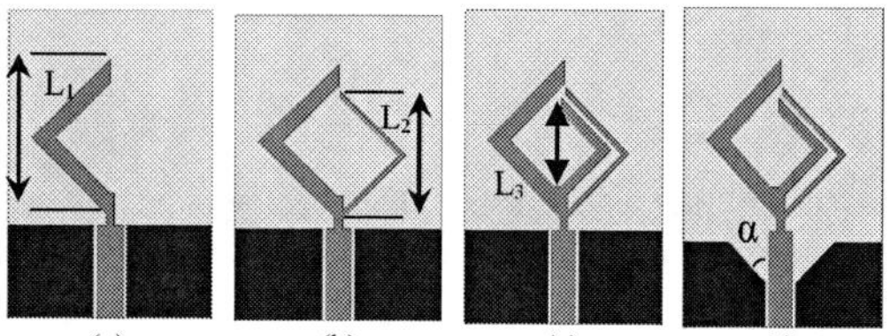

(a) (b) (c) (d)

Fig. 2. Design steps of the antenna.

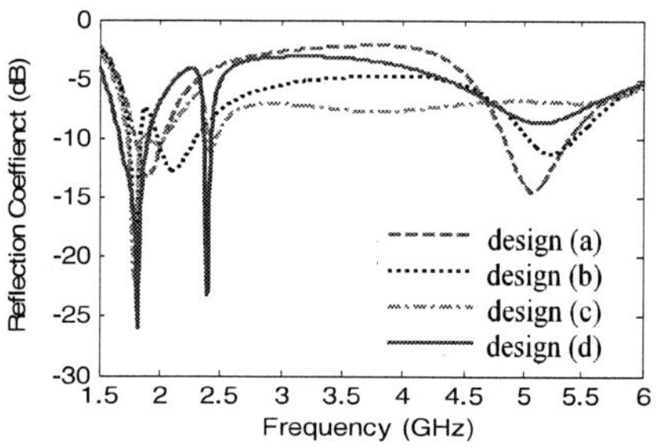

Fig. 3. Result of design steps of the antenna.

B. Current Distribution and Antenna Gain

The current distribution on the flexible multi-bandwidth CPW antenna at frequencies of 1.8, 1.9, 2.4, and 5.2 GHz is shown in Fig. 4, which indicates that each arm is responsible for a specific resonant frequency. This means that the largest arm gives 1.8 GHz resonant and the smallest arm gives 2.4 GHz resonant, as mentioned before in the design antenna procedure. The current distribution on the antenna at 5.2 GHz indicates that the etched ground plane in a tapered shape increases the antenna matching. The antenna radiation patterns at different frequencies in XY, XZ, and YZ are shown in Fig. 5. The antenna has a high gain at frequencies 1.8, 1.9, and 5.2 GHz.

IV. Implementation and Measured Results

The antenna has been manufactured and tested. The manufactured antenna is shown in Fig. 6. Fig. 7 shows the measurement result, which indicates a good agreement between CST, HFSS, and measured results.

V. Conclusion

Multi bandwidth coplanar waveguide fed open end square loop monopole antenna has been designed and optimized using both CST and HFSS electromagnetic packages. The detailed steps of the design have indicated. The antenna has been manufactured and measured. There is a good agreement between the simulated and measured results.

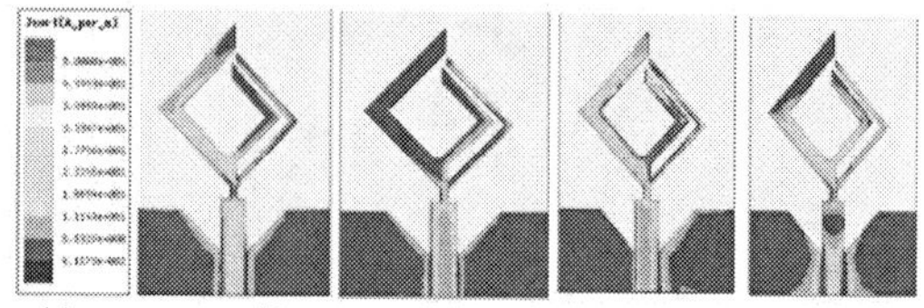

(a) (b) (c) (d)

Fig. 4. The current distribution at 1.8 GHz, 1.9 GHz, 2.4 GHz, and 5.2 GHz.

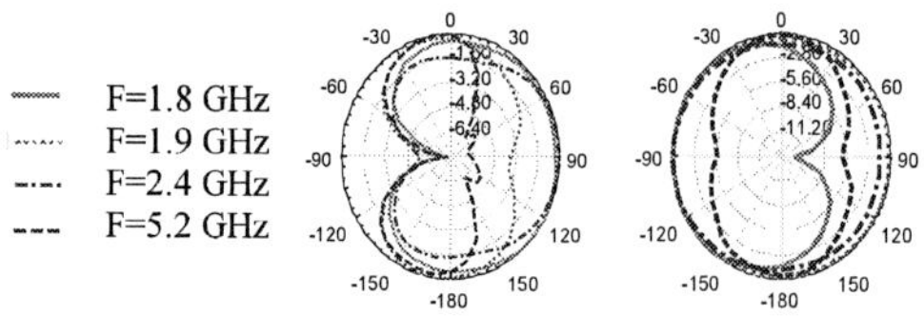

(a) E-plane (b) H-plane

Fig. 5. The radiation pattern of the antenna in E-plane, and H-plane at different frequencies 1.8, 1.9, 2.4, and 5.2 GHz.

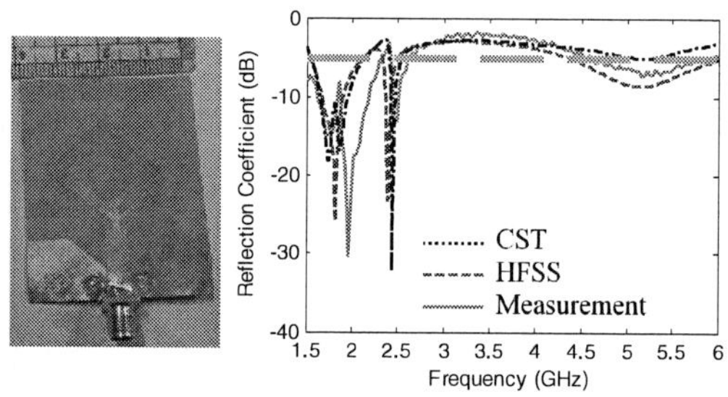

(a) (b)

Fig 6. a. Photo of fabricated antenna, b. Comparison between simulated and measured results.

References

[1] J. J. Huang, F. Q. Shan, and J. Z. She, "A Novel multiband and broadband fractal patch antenna," Progress In Electromagnetics Research Symposium, Cambridge, USA, March 26-29, 2006.

[2] A. Cáp, Z. Raida, E. H. Palmero and R. L. Ruiz. "Multi-band planar antennas: A comparative study," Radioengineering, vol. 14, no. 4, pp. 11-20, Dec. 2005.

[3] Y. Hong, J. Tak, J. Baek, B. Myeong, and J. Choi, "Design of a multiband antenna for LTE/GSM/UMTS band operation," International Journal of Antennas and Propagation, vol. 2014, pp. 1-9, 2014.

[4] N. Haider, D. Caratelli, and A. G. Yarovoy, "Recent developments in reconfigurable and multiband antenna technology," International Journal of Antennas and Propagation, vol. 2013, pp. 1-14, 2013.

[5] H. Tamaoka, H. Hamada, and T. Ueno, "A multiband antenna for mobile phones," Furukawa Review, no. 26, 2004.

[6] F. Yildiz, "Potential ambient energy-harvesting sources and techniques," The Journal of Technology Studies, vol. 35, no.1, pp. 40-48, 2009.

Quantum Electrodynamics of Optical Metasurfaces

Igor V. Bondarev
Department of Mathematics and Physics
North Carolina Central University
Durham, NC 27707, USA
ibondarev@nccu.edu

Vladimir M. Shalaev
School of Electrical and Computer Engineering
Birck Nanotechnology Center, Purdue University
West Lafayette, IN 47907, USA
shalaev@purdue.edu

***Abstract*—Recent theoretical and experimental development of optical metasurfaces has been able to address the major issues including high losses, cost-ineffective fabrication, and challenging integration that hamper the full-scale development of the metasurface technology. Future progress utilizing the quantum nature of light is likely to result in ultrathin metasurfaces with increased operational bandwidths and reduced losses. Here we discuss the simplest case of ultrathin plasmonic films as an example to show how quantum electrodynamics and understanding of quantum-dimensional effects therein can help uncover new functionalities of ultrathin metallic nanostructures.**

Keywords*—*nanomaterials, ultrathin films, plasmonics, QED.

I. Introduction

Current development of nanofabrication techniques makes it possible to design advanced plasmonic nanomaterials with optical properties on-demand [1], [2]. One type of such nanomaterials are optical metasurfaces [3]. By carefully controlling geometry, structural dimensions and material composition one can fabricate metasurfaces (MSs) for a variety of applications, including optoelectronics, microscopy, imaging, sensing, and probing the fundamentals of light-matter interactions at the nanoscale [4]-[7]. Depending on their material composition and thickness, metasurfaces can restructure the spectral and spatial distribution of both real and *vacuum* electromagnetic (EM) modes. While real modes can still be described semiclassically, the physical consequences of the EM vacuum restructuring can only be fully understood within the framework of medium-assisted quantum electrodynamics (QED) [8] — a rigorous quantized formalism valid *in the presence* of absorbing, dispersive and spatially confined media [9], [10] — to allow one to uncover new physics, new features and functionalities that make ultrathin (quasi-2D) optical MSs distinctly different from optical metamaterials, their 3D counterparts.

II. Medium-Assisted QED and Quantum Confinement

In presence of dispersing, absorbing and spatially confined media, the standard (vacuum) QED field quantization scheme fails to work in view of the fact that absorption makes the operator Maxwell equations non-Hermitian. As a consequence, their solutions cannot be expanded in power orthogonal modes, strictly speaking, and the concept of modes itself becomes more subtle. EM field quantization is necessary for the correct description of light-matter interaction scenarios with *virtual* (vacuum) photon excitations involved such as spontaneous emission and van der Waals interactions, mediated essentially by the virtual photon exchange [10].

Supported by NSF: ECCS-1306871 (I.V.B), DMR-1506775 (V.M.S.)

In the medium-assisted QED approach we employ herein for optical MSs, absorption and other EM relaxation processes are considered to create random charge fluctuations with their associated (medium-assisted) local fields being superposed on those of physical vacuum (no medium present), to give rise to the vacuum-type medium-assisted EM fields represented by the quantum field operators (Schrödinger picture, Gaussian units):

$$\hat{E}_\alpha(\mathbf{r},\omega)=i\frac{4\pi\omega^2}{c^2}\int d\mathbf{r}'\sum_{\lambda=x,y,z}G_{\alpha\lambda}(\mathbf{r},\mathbf{r}',\omega)\hat{J}_\lambda(\mathbf{r}',\omega)+\text{h.c.} \qquad (1)$$

Here, $\hat{J}_\lambda(\mathbf{r},\omega)=\sqrt{\hbar\,\mathrm{Im}\,\varepsilon_{\lambda\lambda}(\mathbf{r},\omega)/\pi}\,\hat{f}_\lambda(\mathbf{r},\omega)$ is the quantum noise current density operator responsible for the vacuum-type medium excitations annihilated (created) locally by operators $\hat{f}_\lambda\,(\hat{f}_\lambda^\dagger)$, $G_{\alpha\lambda}$ is a classical EM field Green's tensor calculated for a confined material system of interest under appropriate boundary conditions and the rest is commonly used quantities. Medium excitations are assumed to be of bosonic type so that $[\hat{f}_\alpha(\mathbf{r},\omega),\hat{f}_\lambda^\dagger(\mathbf{r}',\omega')]=\delta_{\alpha\lambda}\delta(\mathbf{r}-\mathbf{r}')\delta(\omega-\omega')$ as required by the Fluctuation-Dissipation Theorem and vacuum QED. Medium composition and medium confinement geometry are included in (1) by means of the dielectric response function $\varepsilon(\mathbf{r},\omega)$ and the Green's tensor, respectively. This makes the formalism extremely useful for calculating observables such as decay rates and Purcell factors for external emitters placed near MSs, which are proportional to the imaginary part of $G_{\alpha\lambda}(\mathbf{r},\mathbf{r},\omega)$, the main factor to represent the local density of photonic states (LDOS). The medium-assisted QED scheme can be extended to include nonlocal effects as well [11].

However, even though both medium composition and confinement geometry are included in the QED scheme above, there is one more important ingredient to add in. Metasurfaces are often based on ultrathin metallic films. In thin films [Fig. 1 (a)], the Coulomb interaction of charges strengthens with the thickness reduction [12] if the film dielectric constant (ε) is much larger than those of the film surroundings ($\varepsilon_{1,2}$). This is because the field produced by the confined charges outside of their confinement region starts playing a perceptible role with its size reduction. When $\varepsilon_{1,2} \ll \varepsilon$ and the in-plane inter-charge distance ρ is greater than the film thickness d, the increased 'outside' Coulomb contribution makes the interaction between the charges confined much stronger than that in homogeneous medium with the dielectric constant ε. In Fig. 1 (b), we see the pair Coulomb potential vary fast for $\varepsilon_1+\varepsilon_2 \ll \varepsilon$ and $d \ll \rho$ (the range of parameters for thin metal-semiconductor MSs), indicating strong spatial dispersion of the dielectric response function in (1) — a solely confinement related effect having nothing to do with the MS material inhomogeneity.

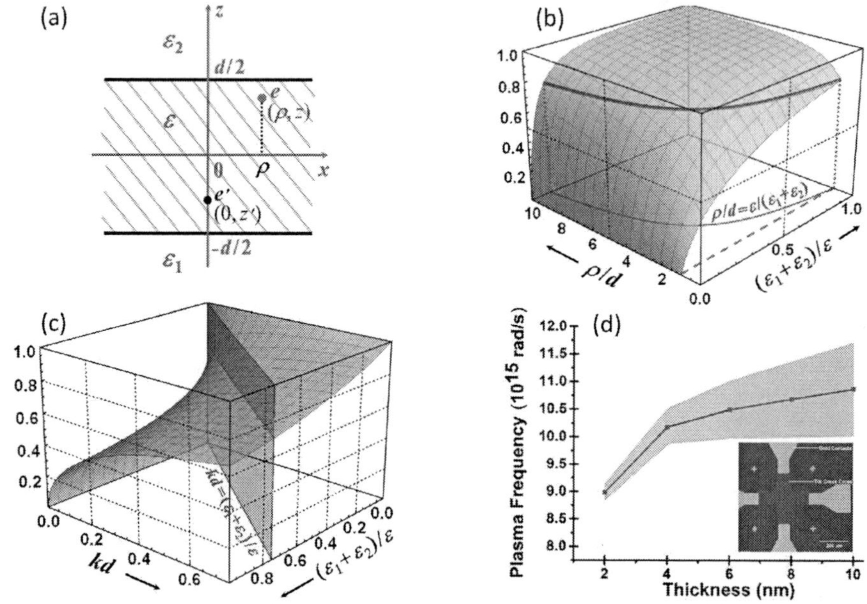

Fig. 1. (a) Schematic of the confined thin film geometry, and (b) the normalized Coulomb interaction (Keldysh [12]) potential, for finite thickness films. (c) Thin film plasma frequency normalized by the bulk plasma frequency one obtains using the Keldysh potential [13]. (d) Plasma frequency extracted from the ellipsometry measurements done on ultrathin TiN films (inset) of varied thicknesses fabricated at Purdue University [2]. See text and [13] for more details.

As an example, we have recently calculated plasma frequency spatial dispersion and the complex-valued dynamic dielectric response function for finite-thickness plasmonic films deposited on various substrates [13]. For the plasma frequency, in particular, we have:

$$\omega_p = \frac{\omega_p^{3D}}{\sqrt{1+(\varepsilon_1+\varepsilon_2)/\varepsilon kd}}. \qquad (2)$$

Here, k is the electron in-plane momentum absolute value and $\omega_p^{3D}=(4\pi e^2 N_{3D}/\varepsilon m^*)^{1/2}$ is the plasma frequency of the bulk electron gas with electron effective mass m^* and volumetric density N_{3D}. We see that if $(\varepsilon_1+\varepsilon_2)/\varepsilon kd \ll 1$ (thick MS case), then $\omega_p=\omega_p^{3D}$, whereas one has $\omega_p=[4\pi e^2 N_{2D}k/(\varepsilon_1+\varepsilon_2)m^*]^{1/2}$ in the opposite case of the infinitely thin MS ($N_{2D}=N_{3D}d$ is the surface electron density) in full agreement with the plasma frequency dependence of the 2D electron gas.

Fig. 1 (c) shows the ratio ω_p/ω_p^{3D} of (2) as a function of kd and $(\varepsilon_1+\varepsilon_2)/\varepsilon$. The thick/thin film regimes are separated by the vertical plane. While being constant for thick films, the plasma frequency is seen to acquire spatial dispersion typical of 2D materials such as graphene [14], gradually shifting to the red with the film thickness reduction. This explains recent plasma frequency measurements done on TiN films of varied thickness [2], shown in Fig. 1 (d), offering ways to tune spatial dispersion (and thereby magnetic permeability [15]) and other related optical properties of plasmonic films and metasurfaces — not only by varying their material composition but also by precisely controlling their thickness and choosing surrounding substrate and superstrate materials appropriately.

Acknowledgment

We acknowledge fruitful discussions with Alexandra Boltasseva and Harsha Reddy, College of Engineering and Birck Nanotechnology Center at Purdue University.

References

[1] J.-S. Huang, et al., "Atomically flat single-crystalline gold nanostructures for plasmonic nanocircuitrys," Nature Commun., vol. 1, 150, 2010.

[2] D. Shah, H. Reddy, N. Kinsey, V. M. Shalaev, and A. Boltasseva, "Optical properties of plasmonic ultrathin TiN films," Adv. Optical Mater., 1700065, 2017.

[3] A. V. Kildishev, A. Boltasseva, and V. M. Shalaev, "Planar photonics with metasurfaces," Science, vol. 339, 1232009, 2013.

[4] D. Rodrigo, et al., "Midinfrared plasmonic biosensing with graphene," Science, vol. 349, pp. 165–168, 2015.

[5] H. A. Atwater and A. Polman, "Plasmonics for improved photovoltaic devices," Nature Mater., vol. 9, pp. 205–213, 2010.

[6] M. W. Knight, H. Sobhani, P. Nordlander, and N. Halas, "Photodetection with active optical antennas, Science, vol. 332, pp. 702–704, 2011.

[7] F. H. L. Koppens, D. E. Chang, and F. J. García de Abajo, "Graphene plasmonics: A platform for strong light-matter interactions," Nano Lett., vol. 11, pp. 3370–3377, 2011.

[8] W. Vogel and D.-G. Welsch, Quantum Optics, 3rd ed., Berlin: Wiley-VCH, 2006, pp. 337–366.

[9] P. Ginzburg, "Cavity quantum electrodynamics in application to plasmonics and metamaterials," Rev. Phys., vol. 1, pp. 120–139, 2016.

[10] I. V. Bondarev and Ph. Lambin, "Near-field electrodynamics of atomically doped carbon nanotubes," in: Trends in Nanotubes Research, D. A. Martin, Ed. New York: Nova Science, 2006, pp. 153–201.

[11] C. Raabe, S. Scheel, and D.-G. Welsch, "Unified approach to QED in arbitrary linear media," Phys. Rev. A, vol. 75, 053813, 2007.

[12] L. V. Keldysh, "Coulomb interaction in thin semiconductor and semimetal films," Pis'ma Zh. Eksp. Teor. Fiz., vol. 29, pp. 716–719, 1979 [Engl. translation: JETP Lett., vol. 29, pp. 658–661, 1980].

[13] I. V. Bondarev and V. M. Shalaev, "Universal features of the optical properties of ultrathin plasmonic films," Optical Mater. Express, vol. 7, pp. 3731–3740, 2017.

[14] D. N. Basov, M. M. Fogler, A. Lanzara, F. Wang, and Y. Zhang, "Colloquium: Graphene spectroscopy," Rev. Mod. Phys., vol. 86, pp. 959–994, 2014.

[15] L. D. Landau and E. M. Lifshitz, Electrodynamics of Continuous Media, New York: Pergamon, 1984.

Asymmetric Band Structure Calculations Using the Plane Wave Expansion Method with Time-Modulated Permittivity

Adam Mock
School of Engineering and Technology
Science of Advanced Materials Program
Central Michigan University
Mount Pleasant, Michigan 48859
mock1ap@cmich.edu

Abstract—**In this work we show how the plane wave expansion method for calculating the band structure of materials with periodic electric permittivity may be extended to calculate the band structure of periodic materials that also possess a sinusoidal time-modulation. The numerical technique is applied to a structure possessing a synthetic linear momentum which causes unidirectional bandgaps to appear in the band structure. Such devices could be of use for tunable magnet-free isolators in integrated photonics platforms.**

I. Introduction

Electromagnetic devices that allow only one-way wave propagation have many practical uses including in optical isolators [1], antennas [2] and duplexed communication transceivers [3]. Any static linear electromagnetic device is time-reversible and therefore cannot be used for unidirectional wave propagation. However, incorporating a synthetic momentum into the system via directional time-modulation can break time-reversal symmetry and induce one-way electromagnetic wave propagation [4]. Most traditional computational techniques assume static material properties. However, some recent reports have detailed methods for incorporating a sinusoidal time-modulated permittivity into computational electromagnetic tools [5]. In this work we extend the plane wave expansion method for calculating the photonic band structure of static periodic structures to materials that have harmonically time-modulated electric permittivities. With this method we show how a directional spatio-temporal modulation results in an asymmetric (in wavevector) bandstructure that produces unidirectional wave propagation in a range of frequencies.

II. Method

This work is concerned with electric permittivities of the form $\varepsilon(z,t) = \varepsilon_a(z) + \varepsilon_b(z)\cos[2\pi\Omega t + \phi]$ where $\varepsilon_a(z+\Lambda) = \varepsilon_a(z)$ and $\varepsilon_b(z+\Lambda) = \varepsilon_b(z)$ are both periodic in Λ. For one-dimensional material variation, the Maxwell equations become:

$$\frac{\partial E_x(z,t)}{\partial z} = -\mu_0 \frac{\partial H_y(z,t)}{\partial t}, \tag{1a}$$

$$-\frac{\partial H_y(z,t)}{\partial z} = -\varepsilon_0 \frac{\partial}{\partial t}[\varepsilon(z,t)E_x(z,t)]. \tag{1b}$$

If the time derivative in (1b) is expanded, one obtains:

$$\begin{aligned}-\frac{\partial H_y(z,t)}{\partial z} &= -\varepsilon_0\{\varepsilon_a(z)\frac{\partial E_x(z,t)}{\partial t} + \\ &\varepsilon_b(z)\cos[\Omega t + \phi]\frac{\partial E_x(z,t)}{\partial t} - \\ &\varepsilon_b(z)\Omega\sin[\Omega t + \phi]E_x(z,t)\}.\end{aligned}$$

The spatial periodicity motivates the use of a Bloch form, and the time-modulation motivates inclusion of harmonics $\omega + n\Omega$ for integer n. Our ansatz for solution of Eqs. 1 is:

$$E_x(z,t) = \sum_{G,n} E_x(G,n)e^{i(k+G)z}e^{-i(\omega+n\Omega)t}, \tag{2a}$$

$$H_y(z,t) = \sum_{G,n} H_y(G,n)e^{i(k+G)z}e^{-i(\omega+n\Omega)t}, \tag{2b}$$

where $G = m2\pi/\Lambda$ for m integer. Combining Eqs. 2 with Eqs. 1 produces:

$$\mu_0(\omega + n\Omega)H_y(G,n) - GE_x(G,n) = kE_x(G,n), \tag{3a}$$

$$\begin{aligned}&-GH_y(G,n) + \varepsilon_0\sum_{G'}\{\varepsilon_a(G-G')(\omega_0 + n\Omega)E_x(G',n) \\ &+[e^{i\phi}E_x(G',n+1) + e^{-i\phi}E_x(G',n-1)] = kH_y(G,n),\end{aligned} \tag{3b}$$

which is an eigenvalue equation with eigenvalue k and eigenvector made up of the components $E_x(G,n)$ and $H_y(G,n)$. To obtain the bandstructure for these dynamic geometries, a range of frequency values is chosen, and for each frequency, the corresponding eigenvalue k is obtained.

III. Synthetic Momentum

To illustrate the physical properties of time-modulated periodic structures, consider the geometry shown in Fig. 1 (a). The structure consists of a repeating unit cell consisting of three layers each modulated by the same frequency but with relative phase offsets of $2\pi/3$. The phase sequence of 0, $2\pi/3$, $4\pi/3$ from left to right produces a non-zero overlap

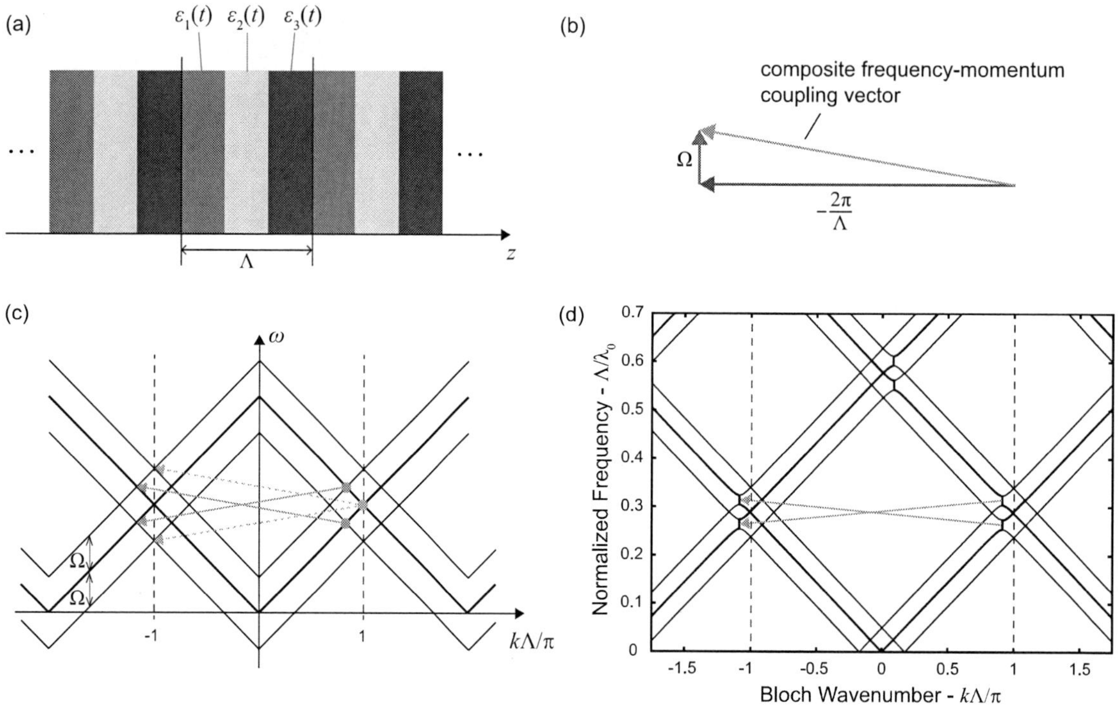

Fig. 1. (a) One-dimensional periodic structure with time-modulated permittivity. $\varepsilon_1(t) = 3.0 + 0.5\cos(\Omega t)$, $\varepsilon_2(t) = 3.0 + 0.5\cos(\Omega t + 2\pi/3)$ and $\varepsilon_3(t) = 3.0 + 0.5\cos(\Omega t + 4\pi/3)$. (b) Mode coupling vector in the spatio-temporally modulated system in (a). (c) The mode-coupling scheme in the empty lattice. The bold line is the fundamental band ($n = 0$) whereas the thin lines correspond to harmonics which is the fundamental band shifted vertically by $\pm n\Omega$ (only $n = 1$ is depicted). (d) The bandstructure of the dynamic geometry shown in (a) using the proposed numerical method.

with the continuous travelling wave modulation of the form $\cos(\Omega t + \frac{2\pi}{\Lambda}z)$ which produces a synthetic momentum pointing toward $-z$. Fig. 1 (b) shows the net momentum-frequency coupling vector. In a static periodic system, the coupling vector would be bidirectional, horizontal and of length $2\pi/\Lambda$. In the time-modulated system, it is unidirectional and tilted up by the amount Ω with concomitant length.

Fig. 1 (c) shows how the mode coupling works in this system. The empty lattice (a lattice with periodicity Λ and time-modulation frequency Ω but $\varepsilon_b \to 0$) is shown. Because of the directionality of the spatio-temporal modulation, the coupling vectors point only from right to left. The green arrows show couplings that result in photonic bandgaps. The green vectors couple band crossings that involve the fundamental band, and, therefore, bandgaps are expected to open at the green dots. The orange vectors show couplings between band crossings, but these bands belong to different order harmonics, and, therefore, no coupling occurs.

Fig. 1 (d) shows the band structure obtained using the proposed method. Indeed one sees bandgaps in the first Brillouin zone corresponding to the points highlighted in Fig. 1 (c). Specifically, there is a bandgap near $k\Lambda/\pi \lesssim 1.0$ but no bandgap near $k\Lambda/\pi \gtrsim -1.0$. This means that incident waves propagating along $+k$ at a frequency in the bandgap will be reflected; whereas, incident waves propagating along $-k$ at a frequency in the same frequency range will be transmitted as if there were no periodic perturbation to the electric permittivity at all. Due to the broken time-reversal symmetry, the band structure is clearly asymmetric in k. Technologically such a device could prove useful in tunable optical isolation particularly in magnet-free integrated photonics platforms.

In conclusion, a technique for calculating the band structure of harmonically time-modulated system is presented. We show how tailored time-modulation can impart a directional synthetic momentum to the field causing unidirectional propagation in these periodic materials.

References

[1] D. L. Sounas and A. Alù, "Angular-momentum-biased nanorings to realize magnetic-free integrated optical isolation," ACS Photonics, vol. 1, pp. 198–204, 2014.

[2] Y. Hadad, J. C. Soric, and A. Alù, "Breaking temporal symmetries for emission and absorption." Proceedings of the National Academy of Sciences, vol. 113, no. 13, p. 34713475, 2016.

[3] N. A. Estep, D. L. Sounas, J. Soric, and A. Alù, "Magnetic-free non-reciprocity and isolation based on parametrically modulated coupled-resonator loops," Nature Physics, vol. 10, pp. 923–927, 2014.

[4] S. Taravati, N. Chamanara, and C. Caloz, "Nonreciprocal electromagnetic scattering from a periodically space-time modulated slab and application to a quasi-sonic isolator," arXiv, p. 1705.06311, 2017.

[5] Y. Shi, W. Shin, and S. Fan, "Multi-frequency finite-difference frequency-domain algorithm for active nanophotonic device simulations," Optica, vol. 3, no. 11, pp. 1256–1259, 2016.

Ultra-thin, High-efficiency Mid-Infrared Huygens Metasurface Optics

Hanyu Zheng
Department of Materials Science & Engineering
Massachusetts Institute of Technology
Cambridge, MA, USA
hanyuz@mit.edu

Jun Ding
Department of Electrical & Computer Engineering
University of Massachusetts Lowell
Lowell, MA, USA
stevendingjun@gmail.com

Li Zhang
Department of Materials Science & Engineering
Massachusetts Institute of Technology
Cambridge, MA, USA
lzhang129@uestc.edu.cn

Hongtao Lin
Department of Materials Science & Engineering
Massachusetts Institute of Technology
Cambridge, MA, USA
hometown@mit.edu

Sensong An
Department of Electrical & Computer Engineering
University of Massachusetts Lowell
Lowell, MA, USA
sensong_an@student.uml.edu

Tian Gu
Department of Materials Science & Engineering
Massachusetts Institute of Technology
Cambridge, MA, USA
gutian@mit.edu

Hualiang Zhang
Department of Electrical & Computer Engineering
University of Massachusetts Lowell
Lowell, MA, USA
hualiang_zhang@uml.edu

Juejun Hu
Department of Materials Science & Engineering
Massachusetts Institute of Technology
Cambridge, MA, USA
hujuejun@mit.edu

***Abstract*—Mid-IR transmissive meta-optics are experimentally demonstrated, capitalizing on material innovations and a novel two-component Huygens metasurface design. We present, for the first time, diffraction limited focusing and subwavelength imaging in the mid-IR using transmissive meta-optics.**

Keywords—Metamaterials, metasurface, mid-infrared

I. INTRODUCTION

The mid-IR spectral regime, while of critical importance to many applications such as sensing and imaging, often presents a technical challenge due to the limited material options, inferior device performance, added processing complexity, and much higher component costs. Metasurfaces allow versatile manipulation of optical wavefront and thus offer unconventional optical properties with a flat form factor [1]. However, metasurfaces in the mid-IR inherit similar issues as conventional optics and have seen less advancement compared to their visible or NIR counterparts.

Here we present our recent results on a novel mid-IR Huygens metasurface (HMS) platform leveraging innovations on both material system and meta-atom designs [2]. A variety of meta-optical components operating near the mid-IR band of 5.2 μm were experimentally demonstrated. The meta-optical devices feature an ultra-thin profile ($\lambda_0/8$ in thickness) and measured optical efficiencies up to 75% in transmissive mode without AR coatings, both of which represent major improvements over state-of-the-arts. We also demonstrated, for the first time, diffraction-limited focusing and sub-wavelength imaging performance of mid-IR transmissive meta-lenses.

DARPA EXTREME Program.

II. HUYGENS METASURFACE DESIGN AND FABRICATION

A. Material and fabrication

Two novel aspects are leveraged to realize the high performance mid-IR metasurface platform: 1) a unique material combination of nanocrystalline PbTe (n = 5.0) and CaF2 (n = 1.4) (Fig. 1 (a)), which offers a gigantic index contrast, broadband mid-IR transparency up to 9 μm, and compatibility with wafer-scale, high-throughput fabrication, and 2) a novel two-component Huygens meta-atom design to achieve simultaneously full 2π phase coverage and near-unity optical transmission (Fig. 1 (b)). The size of a unit cell is 2.5 μm along both axes, less than half wavelength to eliminate undesired diffraction orders. Total thickness of the PbTe block is fixed at 650 nm, corresponding to 1/8 of the free-space wavelength (λ_0 = 5.2 μm), the smallest among dielectric metasurfaces reported to date. PbTe films with a thickness of 650 nm were thermally evaporated onto double-side polished CaF_2 substrates. The low-profile (with a maximum aspect ratio of merely 1.25) of the HMS structures allows them to be readily fabricated using a simple double-layer electron beam resist lift-off process.

B. Metasurface-enabled mid-IR flat optics

Several flat optical components based on the HMS metasurface are demonstrated. Fig. 1 shows a meta-optical beam deflector and the experimental and simulation results. It consists of 8 types of meta-atoms covering the 2π phase range and generating a step-wise phase profile resembling that of a traditional blazed grating to selectively enhance optical scattering into the first diffraction order while suppressing all

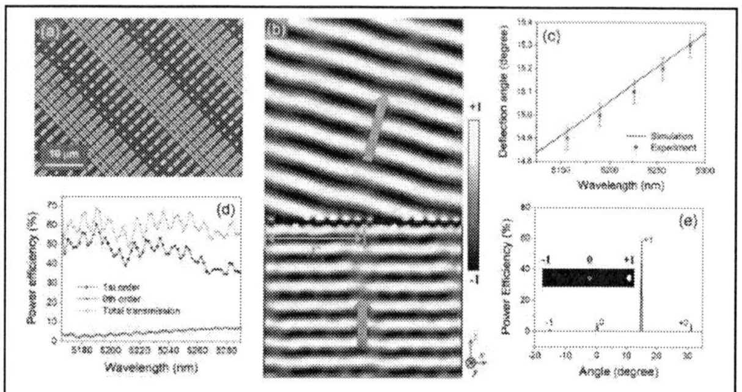

Fig. 1. (a) Top-view SEM image of the HMS beam deflector: the red box marks the unit cell; (b) simulated electric field profile when a plane wave at 5.2 μm wavelength is incident upon the metasurface from the substrate side, clearly showing the beam deflection effect; (c) simulated and experimentally evaluated wavelength dependence of the beam deflection angle; (d) experimentally measured spectra for total transmission (sum of all transmissive diffraction orders), 1st diffraction order (the blazed order) and 0th order (specular transmission) of the deflector; (e) angle-dependent output intensity from the device measured at 5.19 μm wavelength. Inset shows an infrared image of the diffracted beams at the same wavelength.

others. A peak absolute diffraction efficiency of 60% and an extinction ratio (ER) of 12 dB at 5.19 μm wavelength (Fig. 1e) are experimentally obtained, indicating significant performance enhancement over previously reported HMS beam deflectors at optical frequencies [3, 4].

The arbitrary wave front shaping capability of the HMS metasurface is further utilized to demonstrate aberration-free flat cylindrical and aspheric meta-lenses, in which the meta-atoms are arranged to impart 1D and 2D parabolic phase profiles, respectively. The cylindrical lens is designed and experimentally shown to have a focal length of 0.5 mm and a numerical aperture of 0.71. The optical transmittance through the lens is measured to be approximately 80% across the spectral range of 5.11 – 5.29 μm (Fig. 2 (a)). The optical intensity profile along the optical axis is measured and agrees well with the simulation results showing diffraction-limited focusing (Fig. 2 (b) &(c)).

The lens focusing characteristics were measured through the entire tuning range of our laser, showing diffraction limited focusing with near-unity Strehl ratios across the 5.11 – 5.405 μm band and focusing efficiencies of approximately 75% (Fig. 2 (e) - (g)). The imaging properties of the meta-lens is further characterized by using the meta-lens as an objective in an IR microscope at 5.2 μm wavelength and compared to a hypothetical aberration-free imaging system otherwise identical to the experimental setup (Fig. 2 (h) - (m)). The microscope can readily resolve bar targets with a gap width of 3.9 μm, consistent with a theoretical resolution limit of 3.4 μm, confirming that the HMS lens can indeed offer near-diffraction-limit, sub-wavelength imaging capability.

III. Conclusion

In summary, we have designed and experimentally implemented a transmissive Huygens meta-optics platform operating in the mid-IR. The devices we realized leveraging this platform uniquely combine a thin, deep sub-wavelength profile and superior optical performances, which benefit from

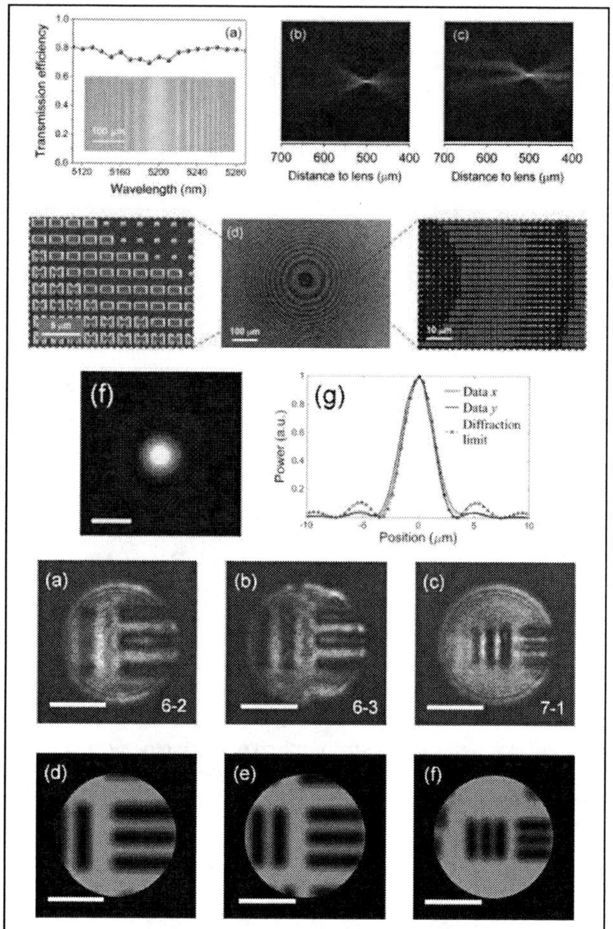

Fig. 2. Cylindrical meta-lens: (a) measured transmission efficiency; inset: top-view optical micrograph of the fabricated meta-lens.; (b) simulated and (c) measured intensity distributions near the lens focal spot at 5.2 □m. Aspheric meta-lens: (d) top-view SEM micrographs of the fabricated aspheric meta-lens; (e) & (f) measured focal spot profiles at 5.2 □m; (g) measured Strehl ratios vs. wavelength; (h-j) optical images of USAF-1951 resolution targets collected using the aspheric meta-lens as a microscope objective; (k-m) simulated images of the same bar targets acquired by a hypothetical aberration-free imaging system otherwise identical to the experimental setup. The scale bars correspond to 30 μm.

the ultra-high index and broadband transparency of chalcogenide materials, as well as the optically efficient two-component Huygens meta-atom design. The remarkable optical performance, SWaP advantages, and fabrication scalability of the meta-optics platform foresee their widespread adoption in future infrared optical systems.

[1] Yu, N. & Capasso, F. Flat optics with designer metasurfaces. *Nat Mater* **13**, 139-150 (2014).

[2] H. Zheng, *et al.* Ultra-thin, High-efficiency Mid-Infrared Transmissive Huygens Metasurface Optics, arXiv:1707.00760 (2017).

[3] Shalaev, M. I. *et al.* High-efficiency all-dielectric metasurfaces for ultracompact beam manipulation in transmission mode. *Nano Lett* **15**, 6261-6266 (2015).

[4] Pfeiffer, C. *et al.* Efficient light bending with isotropic metamaterial Huygens' surfaces. *Nano Lett* **14**, 2491-2497 (2014).

A High-Order Accurate FDTD Scheme for Maxwell's Equations on Overset Grids

Jordan B. Angel
Department of Mathematical Sciences
Rensselaer Polytechnic Institute
Troy, New York USA
angelj2@rpi.edu

Jeffrey W. Banks
Department of Mathematical Sciences
Rensselaer Polytechnic Institute
Troy, New York USA
banksj3@rpi.edu

William D. Henshaw
Department of Mathematical Sciences
Rensselaer Polytechnic Institute
Troy, New York USA
henshw@rpi.edu

Abstract—**An efficient and high-order accurate finite-difference time-domain (FDTD) scheme for solving Maxwell's equations on overset grids is described. Structured curvilinear boundary-fitted grids are used to accurately represent curved surfaces. These overlap with background Cartesian grids. Maxwell's equations for the electric field in second-order form are solved. Use of novel upwind schemes for the second-order form lead to stable discretization on non-orthogonal and overset grids. Use of structured and Cartesian grids together with high-order accurate approximations leads to a very efficient approach.**

Keywords— CHIMERA, FDTD, Maxwell's equations, overset grids, upwind schemes.

I. Introduction

We consider the solution of Maxwell's equations in second-order form using a finite difference approach based on that described in [1]. Overset grids are used to represent complex geometry using structured body-fitted curvilinear-grids to represent boundaries and interfaces and Cartesian background grids to cover the majority of the domain. The use of structured and Cartesian grids along with high-order accurate finite difference approximations leads to very efficient schemes. To provide stable and robust schemes on overset and non-orthogonal grids we use a novel upwind scheme for the second-order wave equation as recently described in [2]. The approach from [2] has now been extended to Maxwell equations on curvilinear and overset grids, and this extension is the subject of this paper (see [3] for further details).

For simplicity, consider the case of non-dispersive materials with constant material parameters. In the absence of external charges and currents, Maxwell's equations for the electric field $\mathbf{E}(\mathbf{x},t)$ takes the simple form of a vector wave equation,

$$\partial_t^2 \mathbf{E} = c^2 \Delta \mathbf{E}, \qquad \mathbf{x} \in \Omega. \tag{1}$$

These equations are augmented with initial conditions together with appropriate boundary and interface condition. Note that the second-order form requires one more boundary condition and this is taken as $\nabla \cdot \mathbf{E} = 0$. High-order finite difference schemes require additional numerical boundary conditions and these are derived using compatibility conditions [1].

This work was partially performed under DOE contracts from the ASCR Applied Math Program, and by the DARPA Defense Sciences Office.

II. Upwind Schemes for Wave Equations

We now briefly describe the form of the high-order upwind schemes for the second-order wave equation in curvilinear coordinates. We write the governing wave equation as an *exact difference equation* in conservation form:

$$\partial_t^2 U = LU(\mathbf{r},t) = \frac{1}{J}\partial_l F^l = \frac{1}{J} D_{+l} f^l(\mathbf{r} - \frac{\mathbf{h}_l}{2}, t), \tag{2}$$

$$D_{+l} f^l(\mathbf{r} - \frac{\mathbf{h}_l}{2}, t) \stackrel{\text{def}}{=} \frac{f^l(\mathbf{r} - \frac{\mathbf{h}_l}{2}, t) - f^l(\mathbf{r} - \mathbf{h}_l/2, t)}{\Delta h_l}. \tag{3}$$

Here U represents any component of $\mathbf{E}$, $\mathbf{h}_l$ represents a shift of size Δh_l in coordinate direction l, F^l is the *flux* defined in terms of the metrics $g^{\ell m}$ of the curvilinear grid,

$$F^l = Jc^2 g^{lm} \partial_m U, \quad g^{\ell m} = \frac{\partial r^\ell}{\partial x^\nu}\frac{\partial r^m}{\partial x^\nu}, \tag{4}$$

and $J = \det(\partial \mathbf{x}/\partial \mathbf{r})$. The new flux functions f^l, which are needed at the half points $\mathbf{r} \pm \mathbf{h}_l/2$, are defined in terms of the F^l and a linear operator $\mathcal{S}^l$, $f^l \stackrel{\text{def}}{=} \mathcal{S}^l F^l$ (no sum) so that,

$$\partial_l F^l(\mathbf{r},t) \stackrel{\text{def}}{=} D_{+l} f^l(\mathbf{r} - \frac{\mathbf{h}_l}{2}, t) = D_{+l}\mathcal{S}^l F^l(\mathbf{r} - \frac{\mathbf{h}_l}{2}, t) \tag{5}$$

is exact for smooth functions. The first few terms [1] of $\mathcal{S}^l$ are:

$$\mathcal{S}^l = I - \frac{h_l^2}{24}\partial_l^2 + \frac{7h_l^4}{5760}\partial_l^4 + \mathcal{O}(h_l^6). \tag{6}$$

To incorporate upwinding into our scheme we need to define an upwind flux. To do this we first convert to a first-order in time system by introducing the auxiliary variable $V \stackrel{\text{def}}{=} \partial_t U$. Integrating the equations over a time step Δt gives:

$$V(\mathbf{r}, t^{n+1}) = V(\mathbf{r}, t^n) + \frac{\Delta t}{J} D_{+l}\mathcal{F}_v^l(\mathbf{r} - \frac{\mathbf{h}_l}{2}, t^n) \tag{7}$$

$$U(\mathbf{r}, t^{n+1}) = U(\mathbf{r}, t^n) + \Delta t V(\mathbf{r}, t^n) + \frac{\Delta t^2}{J} D_{+l}\mathcal{F}_u^l(\mathbf{r} - \frac{\mathbf{h}_l}{2}, t^n), \tag{8}$$

[1] As a formal series, $\mathcal{S}^l = \alpha_\nu h_l^{2\nu}\partial_l^{2\nu}$ where $\alpha_\nu = B_{2\nu}(1/2)/(2\nu)!$ and $B_\nu(x)$ is the ν-th Bernoulli polynomial.

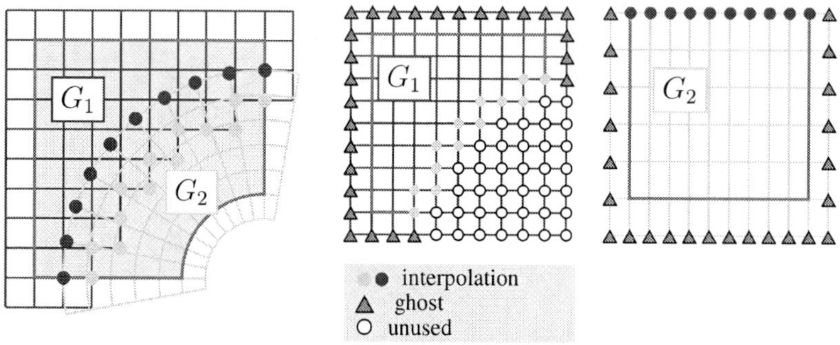

Fig. 1. Left: an overlapping grid consisting of two structured curvilinear component grids, $\mathbf{x} = G_1(\mathbf{r})$ and $\mathbf{x} = G_2(\mathbf{r})$. Middle and right: component grids for the square and annular grids in the unit square parameter space $\mathbf{r}$. Grid points are classified as discretization points, interpolation points or unused points. Ghost points are used to apply boundary conditions.

where we have defined the time-averaged flux functions,

$$\mathcal{F}^l_v(\mathbf{r} - \frac{\mathbf{h}_l}{2}, t^n) \stackrel{\text{def}}{=} \frac{1}{\Delta t}\int_0^{\Delta t} f^l(\mathbf{r} - \frac{\mathbf{h}_l}{2}, t^n + \tau)\mathrm{d}\tau \quad (9)$$

$$\mathcal{F}^l_u(\mathbf{r} - \frac{\mathbf{h}_l}{2}, t^n) \stackrel{\text{def}}{=} \frac{1}{\Delta t^2}\int_0^{\Delta t}\int_0^{\tau} f^l(\mathbf{r} - \frac{\mathbf{h}_l}{2}, t^n + \tau')\mathrm{d}\tau'. \quad (10)$$

We can find an upwind flux by considering waves propagating in l-th coordinate direction. This is done by the typical procedure of diagonalizing the system and setting up a generalized Riemann problem, here for left and right states of $\partial_l U$ and V, which we solve with an exact d'Alembert solution. Based on this upwind solution, we define our upwind numerical flux function,

$$\hat{f}^\ell(\mathbf{r_i} - \frac{\mathbf{h}_\ell}{2}, t^n + \tau) = f^\ell(\mathbf{r_i} - \frac{\mathbf{h}_\ell}{2}, t^n + \tau) + \frac{Jc\sqrt{g^{\ell\ell}}}{2}\left(\mathcal{S}^\ell V^L - \mathcal{S}^\ell V^R\right), \quad (11)$$

which takes the place of f^ℓ in the time-averaged flux functions. We have also introduced left and right biased expressions for V at the cell-face,

$$V^R = V(\mathbf{r_i} - \mathbf{h}_\ell/2, t^n + \tau) \quad (12)$$

$$V^L = V(\mathbf{r}_{\mathbf{i}-\mathbf{e}_\ell} + \mathbf{h}_\ell/2, t^n + \tau). \quad (13)$$

The difference of the discrete approximations of these left and right biased terms ultimately contributes the upwind dissipation.

III. Convergence Results

Here we present a convergence study for the scattering of a plane wave from a dielectric sphere using a fourth-order scheme. We discretize the physical space with a collection of structured, logically rectangular, component grids $\{G_k\}$ with each $\mathbf{x} = G_k(\mathbf{r})$ a smooth invertible map. See Fig. 1. The solution is communicated across grids by interpolation.

Fig. 2 shows an overlapping grid for the dielectric sphere and one component of the electric field for a typical computation. Table I shows max-norm convergence results for the fourth-order scheme. The left-most column is the target grid spacing h_j. Columns labeled by field components contain errors computed at $t = .1$ and columns labeled r denote the ratio of errors for successive refinements. The row labeled *Rate* shows the computed average rate of convergence. We observe the expected fourth-order convergence.

In-depth discussion, computational results, and results for stability on overlapping grids are presented in [3].

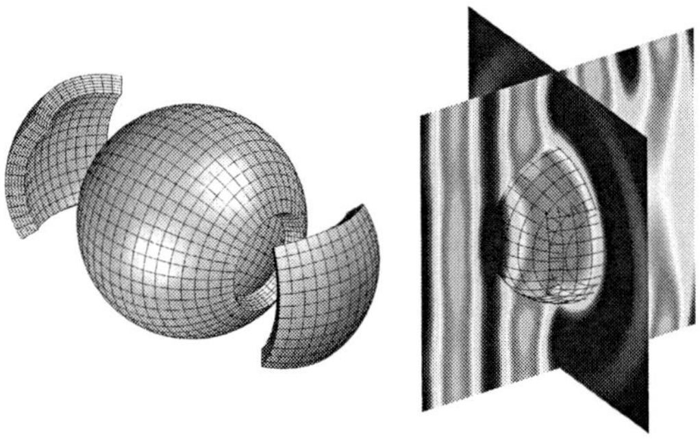

Fig. 2. Left: Exploded view of the composite grid used for the dielectric sphere. Right: E^y component of the electric field.

TABLE I
Max-Norm Error Convergence Study for the Fourth-Order Accurate Upwind Scheme

4th Order Max-norm Convergence

h_j	E_x	r	E_y	r	E_z	r
1/20	1.5e-3		5.8e-3		5.6e-4	
1/40	9.4e-5	16.3	1.9e-4	29.6	3.6e-5	15.7
1/80	6.1e-6	15.3	1.2e-5	15.6	2.2e-6	16.0
Rate		3.98		4.43		3.98

References

[1] W. D. Henshaw, "A high-order accurate parallel solver for Maxwell's equations on overlapping grids," SIAM J. Sci. Comput., vol. 28, no. 5, pp. 1730–1765, 2006.

[2] J. W. Banks and W. D. Henshaw, "Upwind schemes for the wave equation in second-order form," J. Comput. Phys., vol. 231, no. 17, pp. 5854–5889, 2012.

[3] J. B. Angel, J. W. Banks, and W. D. Henshaw, "High-order upwind schemes for the wave equation on overlapping grids: Maxwell's equations in second-order form," Journal of Computational Physics, vol. 352, no. Supplement C, pp. 534 – 567, 2018.

Challenges and Opportunities in Modeling and Optimization of 3D Optical Metasurfaces

D. Bruce Burckel, Aaron J. Pung, and Salvatore Campione
Sandia National Laboratories
Albuquerque, NM, USA
dbburck@sandia.gov, ajpung@sandia.gov, sncampi@sandia.gov

Abstract—**Planar meta-lenses, such as the v-antenna lens, are usually designed by varying two physical parameters of the v-antenna (arm length and central angle spread) and identifying a collection of antennas to discretize a modulo 2π phase swing with high transmission amplitude. Translation of the v-antenna structure into a vertically oriented antenna in a 2-dimensional array increases the necessary design parameter space, bringing to bear additional polarization and configurational possibilities which do not exist in the planar version. This talk will outline this increase in parameter space and the challenges and opportunities it presents.**

Keywords—3D Metamaterials, metasurfaces.

I. Introduction

As originally envisioned, the field of metamaterials concerned itself with the three-dimensional (3D) volumetric construction of artificial materials providing optical behaviors which could not be achieved using natural materials [1,2]. In the microwave and radio frequency portions of the electromagnetic spectrum such 3D artificial materials are readily constructed using macroscopic materials. Attempts to translate these results into the infrared (IR) and optical portions of the spectrum faced many challenges, foremost of which is the challenge of creating 3D structures with micrometer and sub-micrometer physical dimensions. Thus, most of the optical frequency metamaterial research has focused on planar (2D) [3] or stacked-planar (2.5 D) structures [4,5].

With the advancement of the generalized theory of refraction [6] and the subsequent realization of planar metasurface-inspired lenses [7,8], the interest in planar metasurfaces has increased substantially. Recently, we developed a method, membrane projection lithography (MPL), for the manufacture of 2D arrays of micron-scale 3D unit cells containing 3D meta-atoms [9,10]. Using MPL, unit cells with metallic and/or dielectric inclusions can be created in all three spatial directions, and makes fabrication of vertical structures straightforward. This ability forces an immediate departure from planar versions of standard meta-atoms [11]. At the same time, there is an opportunity to address some of the fundamental limitations of ultra-thin phase surfaces which plague planar meta-surface solutions [12]. The aim of this paper is to explore the impact that translation of canonical v-antennas used for planar meta-surface lenses to vertically oriented structures has on the meta-lens design space.

DARPA: DSO Extreme Agreement No. HR0011726711.

II. V-Antenna Lenses

A. Planar Meta-surface Lenses

The majority of planar meta-surface lenses employ a Fresnel zone plate architecture where the plane containing the meta-lens is divided into concentric radial zones which impose a quadratic phase profile on the incident plane wave such that propagation to the far field results in focusing to a point. The goal is to identify a series of planar meta-atoms to discretize the 0 to 2π phase space, representing the required quadratic phase modulo 2π. The ideal collection of meta-atoms will have high transmission while simultaneously spanning the 0-2π phase increment. Typically, a base nano-antenna design is chosen, such as a v-antenna, and full-wave simulations are performed while varying two physical parameters of the meta-atom, such as the arm length and central angle spread. Phase and amplitude maps are created, and a subset of meta-atoms is chosen to provide high transmission and the requisite phase increment.

B. 3D Meta-surface Lenses

The ability to rotate the antenna element in the vertical plane introduces several additional degrees of freedom which must be explored in order to find the optimal set of elements with which to discretize the 0-2π phase space. Not only can the arm lengths and arm central angle spread be varied, but the orientation of the v-antenna bisector can be rotated on the face of the vertical wall (Fig. 1). The vertical position of the antenna on the face of the unit cell can also be varied. This expansion of the degrees of design freedom for even "simple" meta-atoms such as the v-antenna drastically increases the space which must be explored and understood to identify optimal discretization elements, and gain an intuition for the complicated process space. Optimizing over such a large parameter space will invariably require advanced optimization methods as well as efficient forward solvers to model each iteration of the solution. This talk will explore this parameter space and our efforts to design meta-surfaces using these 3D structures.

Acknowledgment

Supported by the Laboratory Directed Research and Development program at Sandia National Laboratories, a multimission laboratory managed and operated by National Technology and Engineering Solutions of Sandia, LLC., a wholly owned subsidiary of Honeywell International, Inc., for the U.S. Department of Energy's National Nuclear Security Administration under contract DE-NA0003525. This work was performed, in part, at the Center for Integrated Nanotechnologies, an Office of Science User Facility operated for the U.S. Department of Energy (DOE) Office of Science by Los Alamos National Laboratory (Contract DE-AC52-06NA25396) and Sandia National Laboratories (Contract DE-NA-0003525). Partially supported by the Defense Advanced Research Projects Agency Defense Sciences Office (DSO) Program: DARPA/DSO EXTREME; Agreement No. HR0011726711.

REFERENCES

[1] J. B. Pendry, A. J. Holden, D. J. Robbins, and W. J. Stewart, "Magnetism from conductors and enhanced nonlinear phenomena," IEEE Trans. On Microwave Theory and Techniques, vol. 47, 1999, pp. 2075-2084.

[2] J. B. Pendry "Negative refraction makes a perfect lens," Phys. Rev. Lett., vol. 85, 2000, pp. 3966-3969.

[3] F. Falcone, T. Lopetegi, M. A. G. Laso, J. D. Baena, J. Bonache, M. Beruete, R. Marques, F. Martin, and M. Sorolla, "Babiniet principle applied to the design of metasurfaces and metamaterials," Phys. Rev. Lett., vol. 93, 2004, 197401.

[4] N. Liu, H. Liu, S. Zhu, and H. Giessen "Stereometamaterials," Nat. Photon., Vol. 3, 2009, pp. 157-162.

[5] G. Dolling, C. Enkrich, M. Wegener, J. F. Zhou, C. M. Soukoulis, and S. Linden, "Cut-wire pairs and plate pairs as magnetic atoms for optical metamaterials," Opt. Lett., vol. 30, 2005, pp. 3198-3200.

[6] N. Yu, P. Genevet, M. A. Kats, F. Aieta, J.-P. Tetienne, F. Capasso, and Z. Gaburro, "Light propagation with phase discontinuities: Generalized laws of reflection and refraction," Science, vol. 334, 2011, pp. 333-337.

[7] F. Aieta, P. Genevet, M. A. Kats, N. Yu, R. Blanchard, Z. Gaburro, and F. Capasso, "Aberation-free ultrathin flat lenses and axicons at telecom wavelengths based on plasmonic metasurfaces," Nano Letters, vol. 12, 2012, pp. 4932-4936.

[8] A. Arbabi, Y. Horie, A. J. Ball, M. Bagheri, and A. Faraon, "Subwavelength-thick lenses with high numerical apertures and large efficiency based on high-contrast transmitarrays," Nat. Comm., vol. 6, 2015, 7069.

[9] D. B. Burckel, J. R. Wendt, G. A. Ten Eyck, J. C. Ginn, A. R. Ellis, I. Brener, and M. B. Sinclair, "Micrometer-scale cubic unit cell 3D metamaterial layers," Advanced Materials, vol. 22, 2010, pp. 5053-5057.

[10] D. B. Burckel, P. J. Resnick, P. S. Finnegan, M. B. Sinclair, and P. S. Davids, "Micrometer-scale fabrication of complex three-dimensional lattice+basis structures in silicon," Optical Materials Express, vol. 5, 2015, pp. 2231-2239.

[11] D. B. Burckel, S. Campione, P. S. Davids, and M. B. Sinclair, "Three dimensional metafilms with dual channel unit cells," Applied Physics Letters, vol. 110, 2017, 143107.

[12] A. Arbabi and A. Faraon, "Fundamental limits of ultrathin metasurfaces," Scientific Reports, vol. 7, 2017, 43722.

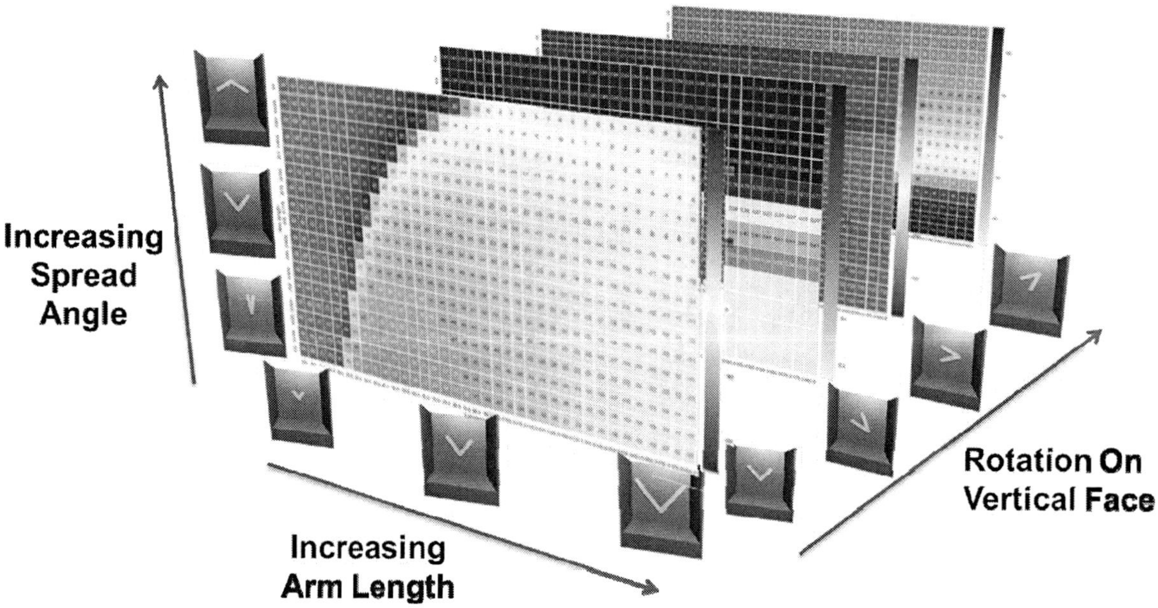

Fig. 1 Schematic representation of the available parameter space for design of 3D metafilms.

Inverse Design of Engineered Materials for Extreme Optical Devices

Sawyer D. Campbell, Danny Z. Zhu, Jogender Nagar, Ronald P. Jenkins, John A. Easum, Douglas H. Werner, and Pingjuan L. Werner
Department of Electrical Engineering
The Pennsylvania State University
University Park, PA 16802, USA
sdc22@psu.edu, dpz5045@psu.edu, jun163@psu.edu, rpj1@psu.edu, jae5377@psu.edu, dhw@psu.edu, plw7@psu.edu

***Abstract*—Optical devices based on engineered materials can achieve performances not possible with conventional design methodologies. However, these performances come at the cost of relatively unconstrained design spaces which necessitates the development of efficient optimization algorithms. Furthermore, engineered optical devices, as opposed to classical designs, may possess multifunctional behaviors which places additional demands on the optimization algorithms in order to maximize the performance. To this end, two custom state-of-the-art multi-objective optimization algorithms are presented and their application towards the inverse design of engineered materials for the realization of extreme optical devices is discussed.**

Keywords— nanoantennas; optimization; surrogate models; metamaterials.

I. Introduction

The design of an optical device can be extremely difficult due to a variety of factors, including, but not limited to, the tradeoffs that exist between competing design objectives, the constraints placed on the geometrical and material considerations, and the computational time required for design simulation. While the inverse design process is typically accelerated by greatly constraining the possible design space, this correspondingly constrains the possible solution space as well. Therefore, it is desirable to develop efficient ways to explore the wide solutions spaces of relatively unconstrained problems in order to find optimal solutions that meet all design objectives. To this end, state-of-the-art multi-objective optimization algorithms can be employed to efficiently find a Pareto set of solutions that simultaneously maximize the performance achievable between competing objectives. This is different than single objective optimization algorithms which yield only a single solution and provide no information to the user about the inherent performance tradeoffs that may exist for the given problem. The formal inverse design process for finding a device that satisfies a set of performance requirements given a set of design constrains is known as known as "system-by-design" (SBD) [1]. This procedure has successfully been employed to study the performance tradeoffs between highly directive nano-devices [2]. To further increase the speed of the inverse design process, these optimization algorithms can be accelerated with surrogate models [3,4] which are data-driven and physics-based models that provide rapid approximation of computationally expensive evaluations such as a full-wave simulation of a broadband engineered material (EnMat) enabled optical device. In this paper, a brief introduction to multi-objective optimization (MOO) and two custom MOO-algorithms as well as their potential for use in the efficient inverse design process of extreme EnMat optical devices is provided.

II. Optimization Algorithms

A. Multi-Objective Optimization

Optical devices typically need to satisfy a large number of often conflicting design objectives. Traditionally, single-objective optimizers have been employed with a weighted sum of these objectives which serves as the single cost function. However, choosing the appropriate weights for the individual objectives is very difficult in practice and the improper choice of weights may limit the percentage of the solution space that can be explored. Furthermore, this approach only provides the designer with a single solution. In comparison, multi-objective optimizers (MOO) [5] provide the user with a set of solutions called the Pareto front (see Fig. 1) which explicitly show the tradeoffs between design objectives.

Specifically, the Pareto front is the set of solutions for which simultaneous improvements in every objective lead to physically unrealizable designs. In simpler terms, for a given point on the Pareto front, to achieve better performance in one objective, one must sacrifice performance in at least one other

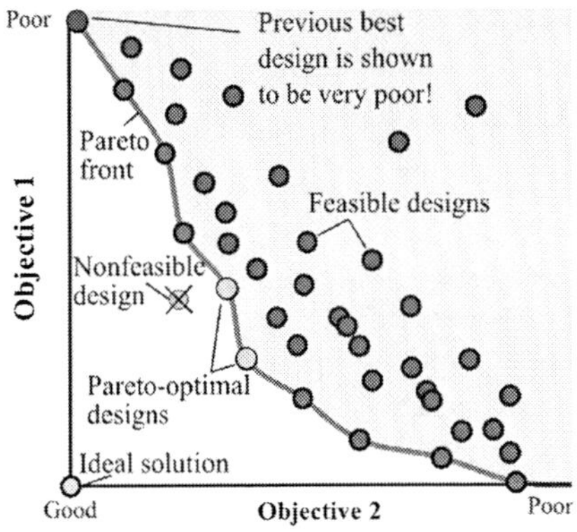

Fig. 1. Example Pareto front of design tradeoffs between two competing objectives.

objective. Knowledge of the Pareto front is very powerful as it can provide insight into the design tradeoffs and underlying physics of the given problem. Unfortunately, determination of the Pareto front can be difficult for complex and multimodal problems. Therefore, the choice of MOO algorithm is very important for the given problem.

B. Multi-Objective Optimization with Tolerance

Surrogate models have successfully been applied to a variety of engineering problems as a method to speed up computationally intensive simulations. For example, coarsely meshed full-wave simulations can be a surrogate for finely meshed simulations. Surrogate models are typically physics-based data-drive (*i.e.*, empirical) models that provide rapid approximation of a computationally-expensive function evaluation. Typically, surrogate models incorporate some form of statistical analysis or a "learn-by-example" approach. Therefore, one must train a surrogate model with intelligently chosen sample points. To enable a robust and fully-automated process, the Multi-Objective with Tolerances (MOTOL) algorithm has been developed [6]. MOTOL automatically generates surrogate models which approximate the potentially-hyper-dimensional response surfaces of multi-objective problems. At the same time, MOTOL explores the response surface to find solutions with the largest "tolerance hypervolumes" (*i.e.*, solutions that are the most robust to input variations).

MOTOL can be employed to explore a relatively-unconstrained design space based on a binary representation of Bezier surfaces to topologically optimize nanoantenna geometries while studying the tradeoffs between potential objectives such as transmission magnitude and phase including co- and cross-polarization behaviors, field enhancement, bandwidth, and field-of-view performances. While accelerating the inverse design process of such topologically-optimized nanoantenna architectures, MOTOL can simultaneously find manufacturable designs that are tolerant to input variations. An example topologically-optimized nanoatenna unit cell is given in Fig. 2.

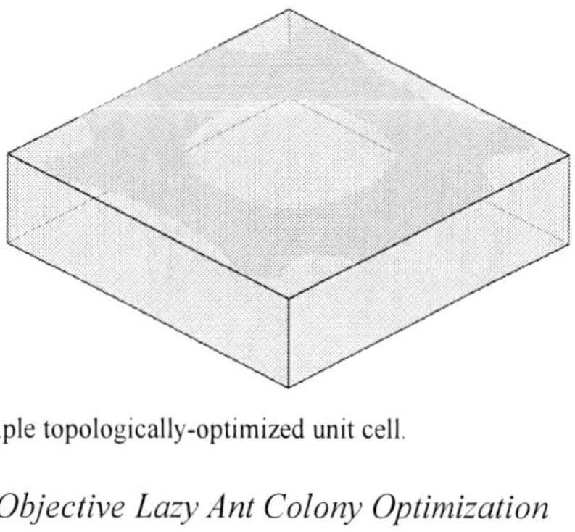

Fig. 2. Example topologically-optimized unit cell.

C. Multi-Objective Lazy Ant Colony Optimization

Another approach to designing engineered materials is through combinatorial optimization. One widely used evolutionary optimization algorithm that falls in this category is the Genetic Algorithm (GA). While GAs have proven to be effective for design of sub-wavelength unit cells in two dimensions, they are often impractical for 3D designs, due to the generation of non-contiguous structures that are not easily manufactured. An alternative to the GA, which leverages combinatorial optimization while still generating contiguous designs, is the Multi-Objective Lazy Ant Colony Optimization Algorithm (MOLACO) [7]. MOLACO is a member of the swarm intelligence family of optimization algorithms, and unlike traditional Ant Colony Optimization (ACO) techniques, MOLACO is adaptive and significantly increases the diversity of designs explored in the search space through the use of lazy ants and colony masking. While this algorithm can be applied to stochastically search any problem that can be represented by an arbitrary graph, making it suitable for a variety of problems (*i.e.*, artificial intelligence, routing and networking), for 3D engineered materials, it is most practical to use a gridded graph to describe spatial relationships of adjacent elements in a unit cell. Fig. 3 provides an example three-dimensional EnMat unit cell explored by MOLACO.

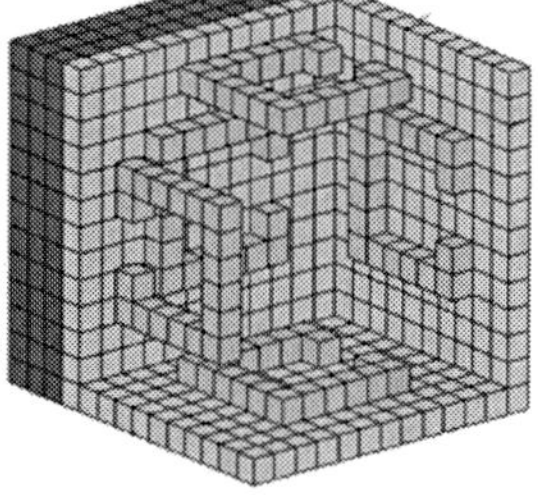

Fig. 3. Example three-dimensional unit cell using MOLACO.

ACKNOWLEDGMENTS

The authors acknowledge the financial support provided by the DARPA Extreme Optics and Imaging (EXTREME) program under contract number HR00111720032.

REFERENCES

[1] A. Massa, G. Oliveri, P. Rocca, and F. Viani, "System-by-design: A new paradigm for handling design complexity," 8th European Conf. on Antennas and Propagation, pp. 1180–1183, April 2014.

[2] J. Nagar, S. D. Campbell, Q. Ren, J. A. Easum, R. P. Jenkins, and D. H. Werner, "Multi-objective optimization aided metamaterials-by-design with application to highly directive nano-devices," IEEE Journal on Multiscale and Multiphysics Computational Techniques, vol. 2, no. 1, pp. 147-158 (Invited paper).

[3] S. D. Campbell, J. Nagar, D. E. Brocker, and D. H. Werner, "On the use of surrogate models in the analytical decompositions of refractive index gradients obtained through quasiconformal transformation optics," J. Opt., vol. 18, no. 4, April 2016.

[4] J. A. Easum, S. D. Campbell, J. Nagar, and D. H. Werner, "Analytical surrogate model for the aberrations of an arbitrary GRIN lens," Optics Express, vol. 24, no. 16, pp. 17805-17818, 2016.

[5] K. Deb, K. Sindhya, and J. Hakanen, "Multi-objective optimization," Decision Sciences: Theory and Practice, pp. 145-184, 2016.

[6] J. A. Easum, J. Nagar, P. L. Werner, and D. H. Werner, "Efficient multi-objective antenna optimization with tolerance analysis through the use of surrogate models," (submitted).

[7] D. Z. Zhu, P. L. Werner, and D. H. Werner, "Design and optimization of 3D frequency selective surfaces based on a multi-objective lazy ant colony optimization algorithm," IEEE Transactions on Antennas and Propagation, vol. 65, no. 12, pp. 7137-7149, December 2017.

Suppression of Anisotropic Birefringence in a Rectangular Waveguide

Gregory Mitchell
U.S. Army Research Laboratory
Adelphi, USA
gregory.a.mitchell1.civ@mail.mil

Abstract — **Birefringence is a known property of anisotropic media where incidence on an anisotropic boundary gives rise to two refracted waves. Typically, a 4th order polynomial solution for the propagating wave number arising from anisotropic dispersion relationships is the cause of birefringence in unbounded media. However, a rigorous derivation shows how unique properties of some rectangular waveguides serve to suppress birefringence when partially loaded with an anisotropic medium.**

Keywords— rectangular waveguide, anisotropic medium, anisotropic wave equation, birefringence

I. Introduction

Electromagnetic wave propagation in homogeneous anisotropic media has been well understood in optical media since the fifties. At optical frequencies, one relies on naturally occurring crystalline media with anisotropic properties. However, the development of low loss anisotropic magneto-dielectrics at microwave frequencies greatly expands the current application space for anisotropic media. This paper presents a rigorous derivation of the wave equation and dispersion relationships for anisotropic magneto-dielectric media. All results agree with those presented by Meng, et. al [1], [2]. Furthermore, setting $\underline{\underline{\mu}}_r = \underline{\underline{I}}$, where $\underline{\underline{I}}$ is the identity matrix, yields results that agree with those presented by Pozar and Graham for anisotropic dielectric media [3], [4].

Birefringence in anisotropic media results from a set of solutions to the 4th order polynomial solution for the propagation constant. Birefringence is a known property of anisotropic media resulting when an incident wave on the boundary of an anisotropic medium gives rise to two refracted waves. Finally, this paper derives properties of a rectangular waveguide that acts to suppress the property of birefringence in anisotropic media.

II. Anisotropic Wave Equation

To solve for the propagation wave number, k_z, a formulation of the anisotropic dispersion relationships for the electric field, $\underline{E}$, and magnetic field, $\underline{H}$, are needed. Starting with the anisotropic, time harmonic form of Maxwell's equations,

$$\nabla x \underline{E} = j\omega\mu_o \underline{\underline{\mu}}_r \cdot \underline{H}, \tag{1}$$

$$\nabla x \underline{H} = -j\omega\varepsilon_o \underline{\underline{\varepsilon}}_r \cdot \underline{E}, \tag{2}$$

we define $\underline{\underline{\mu}}_r$ and $\underline{\underline{\varepsilon}}_r$ as

$$\underline{\underline{\varepsilon}}_r = \begin{bmatrix} \varepsilon_x & 0 & 0 \\ 0 & \varepsilon_y & 0 \\ 0 & 0 & \varepsilon_z \end{bmatrix}, \tag{3}$$

$$\underline{\underline{\mu}}_r = \begin{bmatrix} \mu_x & 0 & 0 \\ 0 & \mu_y & 0 \\ 0 & 0 & \mu_z \end{bmatrix}. \tag{4}$$

Substituting equations (3) and (4) into (1) eliminates $\underline{H}$ yielding the wave equation satisfied by $\underline{E}$

$$\nabla x \underline{\underline{\mu}}_r^{-1} \cdot (\nabla x \underline{E}) = -k_o^2 \underline{\underline{\varepsilon}}_r \cdot \underline{E}. \tag{5}$$

Similarly, eliminating the $\underline{E}$ from (2) yields the wave equation satisfied by $\underline{H}$

$$\nabla x \underline{\underline{\varepsilon}}_r^{-1} \cdot (\nabla x \underline{H}) = k_o^2 \underline{\underline{\mu}}_r \cdot \underline{H}. \tag{6}$$

Equations (5) and (6) represent the vector wave equations in an anisotropic medium [1], [2].

Expanding and isolating the $\underline{x}_o$, $\underline{y}_o$, and $\underline{z}_o$ components of (5) and (6) solves for the transverse components of $\underline{E}$ and $\underline{H}$ in terms of E_z and H_z [2]

$$E_x = -\frac{j}{k_o^2\mu_y\varepsilon_x - k_z^2}\left(\omega\mu_o\mu_y \frac{dH_z}{dy} + k_z \frac{dE_z}{dx}\right), \tag{7}$$

$$E_y = \frac{j}{k_o^2\mu_x\varepsilon_y - k_z^2}\left(\omega\mu_o\mu_x \frac{dH_z}{dx} - k_z \frac{dE_z}{dy}\right), \tag{8}$$

$$H_x = \frac{j}{k_o^2\mu_x\varepsilon_y - k_z^2}\left(\omega\varepsilon_o\varepsilon_y \frac{dE_z}{dy} - k_z \frac{dH_z}{dx}\right), \tag{9}$$

$$H_y = -\frac{j}{k_o^2\mu_y\varepsilon_x - k_z^2}\left(\omega\varepsilon_o\varepsilon_x \frac{dE_z}{dx} + k_z \frac{dH_z}{dy}\right), \tag{10}$$

III. Anisotropic Dispersion Equations

The dispersion equation yields a second order differential equation for k_z in terms of either H_z or E_z. The solutions of k_z

that satisfy these equations quantifies the existence of birefringence or lack thereof in anisotropic media.

A. Dispersion Relationships for H_z and E_z

Expanding the left side of (6) yields the following relation for $\underline{H}$

$$\nabla x\left[\frac{\underline{x}_o}{\varepsilon_x}\left(\frac{dH_Z}{dy}-\frac{dH_Y}{dz}\right)+\frac{\underline{y}_o}{\varepsilon_y}\left(\frac{dH_X}{dz}-\frac{dH_Z}{dx}\right)+\frac{\underline{z}_o}{\varepsilon_z}\left(\frac{dH_Y}{dx}-\frac{dH_X}{dy}\right)\right]=k_o^2\underline{\mu}_r\cdot\underline{H} \quad (11)$$

Expanding the final cross product of (11) and taking the dot product of both sides with $\underline{z}_o$ will isolate the H_z component

$$-\frac{1}{\varepsilon_y}\frac{d^2H_z}{dx^2}-\frac{1}{\varepsilon_x}\frac{d^2H_z}{dy^2}+\frac{1}{\varepsilon_y}\frac{d^2H_x}{dxdz}+\frac{1}{\varepsilon_x}\frac{d^2H_y}{dydz}=k_o^2\mu_zH_z. \quad (12)$$

Now substituting the transverse magnetic field equations (9) and (10) into (12) yields the following dispersion equation in terms of H_z

$$\frac{k_o^2\mu_x}{k_o^2\mu_x\varepsilon_y-k_z^2}\frac{d^2H_z}{dx^2}+\frac{k_o^2\mu_y}{k_o^2\mu_y\varepsilon_x-k_z^2}\frac{d^2H_z}{dy^2}+k_o^2\mu_zH_z=0. \quad (13)$$

A similar procedure utilizing equations (5), (7), and (8) yields the following dispersion equation in terms of E_z

$$\frac{k_o^2\varepsilon_x}{k_o^2\mu_y\varepsilon_x-k_z^2}\frac{d^2E_z}{dx^2}+\frac{k_o^2\varepsilon_y}{k_o^2\mu_x\varepsilon_y-k_z^2}\frac{d^2E_z}{dy^2}+k_o^2\varepsilon_zE_z=0. \quad (14)$$

Equations (13) and (14) are consistent with the findings presented in references [3], [4].

IV. Suppression of Birefringence

Birefringence is a characteristic of anisotropic media where a single incident wave on the boundary of an anisotropic medium gives rise to two refracted waves as shown in Fig. 1 [4]. These two types of waves are known as the ordinary wave and the extraordinary wave. In an unbounded medium, assuming solutions to (14) based on the radiation condition and taking note that $d^2/dx^2=-k_x^2$ and $d/dy^2=-k_y^2$ yields

$$-\frac{k_o^2k_x^2\varepsilon_x}{k_o^2\mu_y\varepsilon_x-k_z^2}E_z-\frac{k_o^2\varepsilon_yk_y^2}{k_o^2\mu_x\varepsilon_y-k_z^2}E_z+k_o^2\varepsilon_zE_z=0. \quad (15)$$

Simplifying (15) and multiplying through by both denominators yields the following 4th order polynomial for k_z

$$k_z^4\mu_z+\left[k_x^2\mu_x+k_y^2\mu_y-(\varepsilon_x\mu_y+\varepsilon_y\mu_x)k_o^2\mu_z\right]k_z^2+\left[k_o^4\varepsilon_x\varepsilon_y\mu_x\mu_y\mu_z-k_o^2k_x\varepsilon_x\mu_y\mu_x-k_o^2\varepsilon_yk_y\mu_x\mu_y\right]=0. \quad (16)$$

A typical polynomial for k_z would be a 2nd order polynomial indicating a forward and backward propagating wave solution. However, the existence of a 4th order polynomial is indicative of birefringence in the medium.

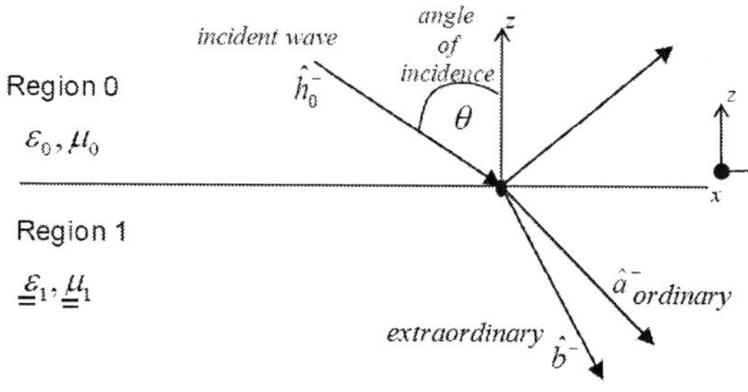

Fig. 1. A plane wave incident on an anisotropic medium [4].

For low order resonances, a rectangular waveguide suppresses the birefringence inherent to anisotropic media by suppressing propagation in the vertical direction of the waveguide. In other words, $k_y=0$ and $d^2/dy^2=0$ assuming the horizontal dimension of the waveguide is at least twice the size of the vertical dimension [3]. This simplifies (15) to

$$-\frac{k_o^2k_x^2\varepsilon_x}{k_o^2\mu_y\varepsilon_x-k_z^2}E_z+k_o^2\varepsilon_zE_z=0, \quad (17)$$

and results in the following 2nd order polynomial for k_z

$$k_z^2=\varepsilon_x\left(k_o^2\mu_y-\frac{k_x^2}{\varepsilon_z}\right). \quad (18)$$

The suppression of the k_y term in (15) yields a 2nd order differential equation for the wave number in the propagation direction, thereby eliminating the property of birefringence for this case.

V. Conclusions

This paper present a rigorous derivation of the wave equation and dispersion relationships for anisotropic magneto-dielectric media. Birefringence at the boundary of unbounded anisotropic media is unavoidable due to the existence of a 4th order polynomial solution for the wave number k_z. This 4th order solution arises directly from the anisotropic dispersion relationships for H_z and E_z derived previously. Finally, the suppression of the k_y term in a rectangular waveguide serves to suppress birefringence in some cases when loaded with an anisotropic medium.

References

[1] Meng, F. Y., Wu, Q., and Li, L. W., "Transmission Characteristics of Wave Modes in a Rectangular Waveguide filled with Anisotropic Metamaterial", *Applied Physics A: Materials Science and Processing*, vol. 94, pp. 747-753, 2009.

[2] Meng. F. Y., Wu, Q., and Fu, J. H., "Miniatured Rectangular Cavity Resonator based on Anisotropic Metamaterials Bilayer", *Wireless Prop. Lett.*, vol. 13, pp. 1624-1627, 2014.

[3] Pozar, D., "Radiation and Scattering from a Microstrip Patch on a Uniaxial Substrate", *IEEE Trans. on Ant. and Prop.*, vol. AP-35, no. 6, pp. 613-621, June 1987.

[4] Graham, J., "Arbitrarily Oriented Biaxlly Anisotropic Media: Wave Behvaior and Microstrip Antennas" (2012). *Electrical Engineering and Computer Science – Dissertations*. Syracuse, NY. Paper 320.

Performance Analysis for Linear Minimum Variance Adaptive Beamforming

1st Zhitao Yang
EECS
Wichita State University
Wichita, USA
zhitaoyang55@gmail.com

2nd Guanglei Zhang
EEIS
Harbin Institute of Technology
Harbin, China
guangleizhang201717@gmail.com

***Abstract*—As the dramatic advancement in array signal processing techniques, the phase array radar is widely used in different aspects. However, the electromagnetic environment becomes more and more complicated since there are more and more different kinds of electromagnetic interference. In order to suppress the interference, we propose an adaptive interference method based on linear minimum variance adaptive beamforming in this paper. The float round-off error is also analysed for the proposed method. The simulation results show that the proposed method has good performance in interference suppression.**

***Index Terms*—phase, radar, wireless, communication, beamforming, interference, suppression**

I. Introduction

The phase array radar has been widely used in military due to the dramatic advance in computer technique and signal processing technology [1]. Thus, the array signal processing technique becomes significantly important in the signal processing technology [2]. The major techniques in the array signal processing are the estimation for the direction of arrival and the adaptive digital beamforming [3]. The direction of arrival estimation locates the target by applying the space spectrum estimation into the array signal processing. The adaptive digital beamforming is actually the adaptive space filter which is very important for interference suppression [4]. However, the existing array signal processing has limitations. One of the serious issue is that most of the array signal processing is based on the antenna element level [5]. The antenna element level processing for the phase array radar needs a huge amount of receiving path since each antenna element has its own receiving path [6]. In order to reduce the number of receiving paths, the subarray level signal processing is introduced.

The most important part for the adaptive digital beamforming is the calculation of the weights for the subarray level processing. The adaptive digital beamforming suppresses the interference by adapting the weights in order to perform space filter [7]. In addition, the adaptive digital beamforming adapts the weights according to the different directions of the interference [8]. The phase array radar obtains the maximum signal and interference ratio by using adaptive digital beamforming techniques. However, the computation for the adaptive digital beamforming implementation is extreme complicated since the calculation for the adaptive weights needs to compute the inverse of the matrix which requires a huge amount of computation resources [9]. The real time processing becomes very challenging due to the huge amount of computation. In addition, the computation accumulative error from the float calculation makes the computation result accuracy decrease dramatically [10]. The simulation of the research work for adaptive digital beamforming are based on the computer where the data type is 64bit double float [11]. But in the industry, the computation for adaptive digital beamforming always adopts the 32bit float data type. The difference between the simulation and the implementation brings huge impact on the adaptive performance of the adaptive beamforming.

In this paper, in order to obtain better performance subarray level adaptive digital beamforming, we focus on the calculation of the weights and the computation performance analysis for the linear minimum variance adaptive beamforming approach with different kinds of data types.

The paper includes four sections. Section I shows the introduction. The derivation of the adaptive weights using linear minimum variance adaptive beamforming approach is introduced in section II. The simulation results are given in section III. Finally, the conclusion is shown in section IV.

II. The Derivation of the Weights

In this section, the details about the derivation of weights for the subarray level structure is introduced. The main idea is to use linear minimum variance adaptive beamforming approach to calculate the adaptive weight.

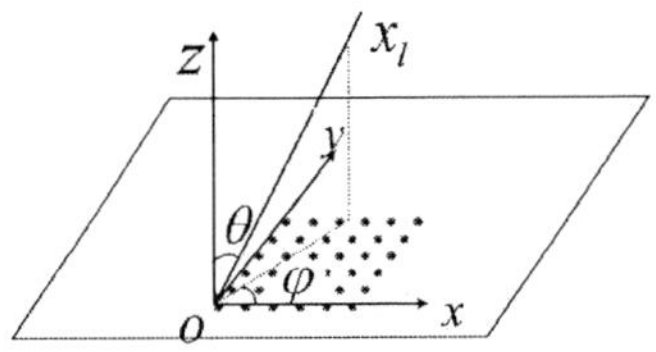

Fig. 1. Frame structure of CR networks.

First, the system model is introduced in order to further describe the derivation. As shown in 1, the plane array located in xoy is consisted of $N = N_1 \times N_2$ antenna elements. N_1 denotes the number of antenna elements on the x axis and

N_2 is the number of antenna elements on the y axis. The reference antenna element is located at $(0,0)$ where (x_n, y_n) denotes the coordinates of the nth $(n = 1, 2, \cdots, N)$ antenna element. The array is divided into M subarrays. The weights for the nth antenna element level is a_n. The direction of the beamforming is controlled by the phase shifter at the antenna element level.

Then, the derivation of the adaptive weights at the subarray level using linear minimum variance adaptive beamforming approach is introduced. The main idea of the approach is to obtain the adaptive weights for the minimum output power of the phase array when the gain at the expected direction of the signal is above the threshold τ. The formulation for the adaptive weights at the subarray level is

$$\begin{cases} minP(w_{CM}) = min(w_{CM}^H R_{sub} w_{CM}) \\ w_{CM}^H a_{sub}(\theta_0, \phi_0) = 1 \end{cases} \quad (1)$$

where (θ_0, ϕ_0) is the direction of the beamforming (the direction of the expected signal is $-90^\circ \leq \theta_0 \leq 90^\circ$). $a_{sub}(\theta_0, \phi_0)$ is the steering vectors of the beamforming with the arrival direction is (θ_0, ϕ_0)

$$a_{sub}(\theta_0, \phi_0) = T_{2D}^H a(\theta_0, \phi_0) \quad (2)$$

where $a(\theta_0, \phi_0) = exp{-}j2\pi[x_n \alpha(\theta_0, \phi_0) + y_n \beta(\theta_0, \phi_0)]/\lambda_{n=1,\cdots,N}$. The weights are obtained using lagrangian multiplier method

$$w_{CM} = \mu R_{sub}^{-1} a_{sub}(\theta_0, \phi_0) \quad (3)$$

where μ is a constant. The pattern of the array output is

$$y = w_{CM}^H a_{sub}(\theta, \phi) \quad (4)$$

where $a_{sub}(\theta, \phi)$ is the steering vector of the direction (θ, ϕ) at the subarray level.

III. The Simulation Results

In this section, the float error for linear minimum variance adaptive beamforming approach is given. In the simulation, the array is two-dimension phase array with 2.5GHz. The 100×30 array is divided into 16 subarrays which is 4×4. The antenna elements at the y direction is [10 5 5 10] and the weights at the antenna element level is $-40dB$ Taylor weights.

As shown in table I, BL denotes the bit length and PSL denotes the peak sidelobe power of azimuth. AAL represents the average power of the azimuth sidelobe and AML represents the mainlobe power of the azimuth direction. PPS and PAS denotes the pitch peak sidelobe power and pitch average sidelobe power respectively. PMW is the mainlobe bandwidth and INL is the null depth at the interference direction. In table I, it is clear to see that PSL, AAL and AML stays the same when the length of bits changes. The PPS also stays the same. From table , II, we can clearly see that PAS, PMW and INL is stable when the length of bits changes.

TABLE I

BL	PSL	AAL	AML	PPS
64bit	-14.9400	-35.7047	1.2	-15.445
32bit	-14.9361	-35.7033	1.2	-15.449
err	0.0039	0.0014	0	-0.0039

TABLE II

BL	PAS	PMW	INL
64bit	-23.7921	4.2	-130.0445
32bit	-26.572	4.2	-129.9169
err	-2.7801	0	0.1286

IV. Conclusion

In this paper, the adaptive interference suppression method based on linear minimum variance adaptive beamforming is proposed. The details about the derivation of the adaptive weights at the subarray level is shown. The proposed method generates a null point at the direction of the interference in order to suppression the interference. In addition, the float round-off error analysis is very important for the practical implementation of the adaptive interference.

References

[1] H. Subbaram and K. Abend, "Interference suppression via orthogonal projections: a performance analysis," *IEEE Transactions on Antennas and Propagation*, vol. 41, no. 9, pp. 1187–1194, Sep 1993.

[2] D. Wang and Z. Yang, "An novel spectrum sensing scheme combined with machine learning," in *2016 9th International Congress on Image and Signal Processing, BioMedical Engineering and Informatics (CISP-BMEI)*, Oct 2016, pp. 1293–1297.

[3] D. Wang, H. Hu, and Z. Yang, "Improved genetic algorithm for the configuration optimization of the sub arrays in phased array radar," in *2016 9th International Congress on Image and Signal Processing, BioMedical Engineering and Informatics (CISP-BMEI)*, Oct 2016, pp. 930–934.

[4] D. Wang, Y. Song, and Z. Yang, "A joint power adaptation and spectrum handoff scheme in mobile cognitive radio networks," in *2015 International Conference on Computing, Networking and Communications (ICNC)*, Feb 2015, pp. 1061–1065.

[5] I. P. Kirsteins and D. W. Tufts, "Adaptive detection using low rank approximation to a data matrix," *IEEE Transactions on Aerospace and Electronic Systems*, vol. 30, no. 1, pp. 55–67, Jan 1994.

[6] D. Wang and Z. Yang, "An advanced scheme with decision tree for the improvement of spectrum sensing efficiency in dynamic network," in *2016 9th International Congress on Image and Signal Processing, BioMedical Engineering and Informatics (CISP-BMEI)*, Oct 2016, pp. 1288–1292.

[7] W. Dan, H. Hang, and Q. Xin, "Space-time adaptive processing method at subarray level for broadband jammer suppression," in *2011 IEEE International Conference on Microwave Technology Computational Electromagnetics*, May 2011, pp. 281–284.

[8] D. Wang and Y. Song, "A novel distributed global time synchronization protocol in cognitive radio ad hoc networks," in *2015 IEEE Global Communications Conference (GLOBECOM)*, Dec 2015, pp. 1–6.

[9] D. Wang, Z. Yang, and Y. Song, "A novel spectrum sensing scheduling scheme for pu and su signal differentiation in cr networks," in *2015 IEEE International Conference on Communications (ICC)*, June 2015, pp. 5697–5702.

[10] S. Applebaum and D. Chapman, "Adaptive arrays with main beam constraints," *IEEE Transactions on Antennas and Propagation*, vol. 24, no. 5, pp. 650–662, Sep 1976.

[11] Z. Yang, Y. Song, and D. Wang, "An optimal operating frequency selection scheme in spectrum handoff for cognitive radio networks," in *2015 International Conference on Computing, Networking and Communications (ICNC)*, Feb 2015, pp. 1066–1070.

The Novel Normalized Method for Interference Suppression at Subarray Level

1st Zhitao Yang
EECS
Wichita State University
Wichita, USA
zhitaoyang55@gmail.com

2nd Guanglei Zhang
EEIS
Harbin Institute of Technology
Harbin, China
guangleizhang201717@gmail.com

***Abstract*—As the dramatic development of the computer and digital signal process techniques, the phase array radar becomes more and more important for many different kinds of military applications. In order to survive in the complicated electromagnetic environment with different kinds of interference, the adaptive digital beamformin is adopted to suppress the interference. In addition, the signal processing is performed at the subarray level in order to save the hardware resource cost. However, the sidelobe power of the antenna pattern dramatically increases since the output power of the noise for each subarray is different. In order to solve this issue, the normalized adaptive method is proposed to maintain the same output power for each subarray. The float round-off error is also analysed for the proposed method. The simulation results show that the proposed method has good performance.**

***Index Terms*—wireless, communication, phase, radar, signal, interference, suppression**

I. Introduction

With the dramatic development of the computer and digital signal process techniques, the phase array radar becomes more and more important for many different kinds of military applications [1]. Nowadays, the array signal processing becomes the significantly important part of the signal processing [2]. There are two major techniques in the array signal processing which are adaptive digital beamforming and direction of arrival estimation [3]. The adaptive digital beamforming helps to obtain good signal at the expected direction and filter the interference. Then, the optimal signal to interference plus noise ratio is obtained [4]. In order to maintain good mainlobe for the beamforming, the phase array radar usually is consisted of thousands of antennas [5]. This is a huge waste f hardware resources since each antenna has its own signal processing hardware path.

In order to reduce the cost, the phase array needs to be divided into subarrays. Then, the signal processing hardware path only needs to be adopted at subarray level. However, this brings a big challenge to the adaptive digital beamforming techniques [6]. Therefore, the weights for the adaptive digital beamforming at the subarray level should be provides. Actually, the weights of the amplitude are applied at the antenna element level in order to meet the sidelobe power requirement of the array before the adaptive digital beamforming is adopted in phase array radar [7]. Actually, the array signal processing still have some limitations. One of the limitation is that most of the existing array digital signal processing is based on antenna elemnt level. Therefore, we need to proposed a subarray level signal processing method using adaptive digital beamforming techniques.

The adaptive digital beamforming has huge computation complexity. This is because the inverse of the covariance matrix should be obtained in order to calculate the adaptive weights. Therefore, the key part of the adaptive digital beamforming is to choose proper adaptive weights. In addition, the computation for the inverse of the matrix is on the FPGA which makes the computation more difficult [8]. The float round-off error is accumulated during the complicated computation and results in the dramatic decrease in the accuracy of the final results [9]. The different length of bits has different impact on the computation accuracy. In order to make the implementation of the adaptive digital beamforming more practical, we need to analyse the bits length impact on the proposed method for the calculation of the adaptive weights.

In this paper, we analysis the float round-off error for the normalized adaptive method. The paper includes 4 sections. The introduction is shown in section I. Section II describes the derivation of the adaptive weights. In section III, the simulation results are shown. The conclusion is given in section IV.

II. The Derivation of the Adaptive Weights for the Proposed Normalized Adaptive Method

In this section, the normalized adaptive method is introduced. In order to suppress the interference [10], the weights are used at the antenna element level. The output power of the noise is different for each subarray since the number of antenna elements for each subarray is different. Thus, the output power of each subaaray is different. The sidelobe power of the antenna pattern dramatically increases compared with the static antenna pattern. In order to suppress the interference and maintain the low sidelobe power for the antenna pattern, the normalized adaptive method is proposed to make the output of the subarray stay the same.

First, the normalized matrix T_{2DL} is used to normalization for each subarray,

$$T_{2DL} = diag(c_m^{-1})_{m=0,\cdots,M-1} \quad (1)$$

where $c_m = (\sum_{j=p}^{Q} \omega_j^2)^{\frac{1}{2}}$ and P is the index of the first antenna element in the mth subarray. Q is the index of the last antenna element in the mth subarray. In addition, we only take the non-overlapped subaaray into consideration.

The interference and noise covariance matrix after the normalization at the subarray level is

$$R_{sub_norm} = T_{2DL}^H R_{sub} T_{2DL} \tag{2}$$

Then, the adaptive weights vector is obtained

$$\omega_{norm} = T_{2DL}^H R_{sub}^{-1} T_{2DL}^{-1} q \tag{3}$$

where T_{2DL}^{-1} is used to make the mainlobe amplitude of the antenna pattern stay the same. q is a M dimension vector that all the element is 1. When there is no interference, $R = R_0 = I_{N\times N}$. If the subarray is non-overlapped, $(R_{sub})_0 = diag(c_m)^2{}_{m=0,\cdots,M-1}$ and $(R_{subnorm})_0 = I_{M\times M}$. Therefore, the adaptive weights is $\omega_{norm} = q$ when there is no interference. This means the antenna pattern after the adaptive beamforming is the same with the static antenna pattern. Thus, the proposed method the beamforming using the proposed method could be used both in the environment with interference and no interference and no need to make changes.

Now, the float round-off error is introduced. Here the minimum number of the double accuracy and single accuracy is denoted by $eps(a^s)$ and $eps(a^d)$. The minimum number is usually related to the current accuracy and not stable. The minimum bumber brings different error window. We use the $[a^s]_s$ and $[a^d]_d$ to denote error window under single accuracy and double accuracy

$$\begin{cases} a \in [a^s]_s = [[a^s] - eps(a^s), a^s + eps(a^s)] \\ a \in [a^d]_d = [a^d - eps(a^d), a^d + eps(a^d)] \end{cases} \tag{4}$$

Due to the complicated calculation in the computer, the storage for the real number is always different from the original number. There are float round-off error. Thus, the parameter a in the calculation is a little bit different from the stored number a^h $(h = s, d)$. Therefore, it is very important to analysis the float round-off error impact on the final result.

III. The Simulation Results for the Proposed Normalized Method

In this section, the float error for linear minimum variance adaptive beamforming approach is given. In the simulation, the array is two-dimension phase array with 2.5GHz. The 100×30 array is divided into 16 subarrays which is 4×4. The antenna elements at the y direction is [10 5 5 10] and the weights at the antenna element level is $-40dB$ Taylor weights.

As shown in table I, BL denotes the bit length and PSL denotes the peak sidelobe power of azimuth. AAL represents the average power of the azimuth sidelobe and AML represents the mainlobe power of the azimuth direction. PPS and PAS denotes the pitch peak sidelobe power and pitch average sidelobe power respectively. PMW is the mainlobe bandwidth and INL is the null depth at the interference direction. In table I, it is clear to see that PSL, AAL and AML stays the same when the length of bits changes. The PPS also stays the same. From table , II, we can clearly see that PAS, PMW and INL is stable when the length of bits changes.

TABLE I

BL	PSL	AAL	AML	PPS
64bit	-14.9400	-35.7047	1.2	-15.445
32bit	-14.9361	-35.7033	1.2	-15.449
err	0.0039	0.0014	0	-0.0039

TABLE II

BL	PAS	PMW	INL
64bit	-23.7921	4.2	-130.0445
32bit	-26.572	4.2	-129.9169
err	-2.7801	0	0.1286

IV. Conclusion

In this paper, the normalized method is proposed to suppress the interference at the subarray level. This method helps to keep the output power of the subarray equal. Then, the performance of the array pattern is improved. The float round-off error analysis is also shown in the paper. The simulation results show the proposed method has good performance.

References

[1] J. Xin and A. Sano, "Directions-of-arrival estimation of cyclostationary signals in multipath propagation environment," in *Proceedings of the 11th IEEE Signal Processing Workshop on Statistical Signal Processing (Cat. No.01TH8563)*, 2001, pp. 524–527.

[2] D. Wang and Z. Yang, "An novel spectrum sensing scheme combined with machine learning," in *2016 9th International Congress on Image and Signal Processing, BioMedical Engineering and Informatics (CISP-BMEI)*, Oct 2016, pp. 1293–1297.

[3] D. Wang, H. Hu, and Z. Yang, "Improved genetic algorithm for the configuration optimization of the sub arrays in phased array radar," in *2016 9th International Congress on Image and Signal Processing, BioMedical Engineering and Informatics (CISP-BMEI)*, Oct 2016, pp. 930–934.

[4] D. Wang, Y. Song, and Z. Yang, "A joint power adaptation and spectrum handoff scheme in mobile cognitive radio networks," in *2015 International Conference on Computing, Networking and Communications (ICNC)*, Feb 2015, pp. 1061–1065.

[5] G. S. Bloom and S. W. Golomb, "Applications of numbered undirected graphs," *Proceedings of the IEEE*, vol. 65, no. 4, pp. 562–570, April 1977.

[6] D. Wang and Z. Yang, "An advanced scheme with decision tree for the improvement of spectrum sensing efficiency in dynamic network," in *2016 9th International Congress on Image and Signal Processing, BioMedical Engineering and Informatics (CISP-BMEI)*, Oct 2016, pp. 1288–1292.

[7] W. Dan, H. Hang, and Q. Xin, "Space-time adaptive processing method at subarray level for broadband jammer suppression," in *2011 IEEE International Conference on Microwave Technology Computational Electromagnetics*, May 2011, pp. 281–284.

[8] D. Wang and Y. Song, "A novel distributed global time synchronization protocol in cognitive radio ad hoc networks," in *2015 IEEE Global Communications Conference (GLOBECOM)*, Dec 2015, pp. 1–6.

[9] D. Wang, Z. Yang, and Y. Song, "A novel spectrum sensing scheduling scheme for pu and su signal differentiation in cr networks," in *2015 IEEE International Conference on Communications (ICC)*, June 2015, pp. 5697–5702.

[10] H. Subbaram and K. Abend, "Interference suppression via orthogonal projections: a performance analysis," *IEEE Transactions on Antennas and Propagation*, vol. 41, no. 9, pp. 1187–1194, Sep 1993.

The sidelobe power suppression for the aircraft circle phase array radar

Dan Wang
EECS
Wichita State University
Wichita, USA
dxwang@shockers.wichita.edu

***Abstract*—As the air force becomes more and more important, it is very important to improve the performance of object tracking. The circle phase array radar is adopted to improve the object tracking ability. However, it is very difficult to implement the circle phase array radar since it is a huge amount of antenna elements in the phase array radar. In this paper, we propose a novel method to help design the structure of the circle phase array radar and improve the performance of the circle phase array radar. The simulation results validate the proposed method.**

***Index Terms*—cancellation, radar, adaptive, interference**

I. Introduction

Nowadays, the air force becomes more and more important in the military. It is very important to have the aircraft radar to track the targets [1]. The aircraft radar has much larger scan range compared with the traditional ground radar. However, it is very difficult to implement the aircraft radar [2]. The antenna for aircraft radar is very difficult to design. The phase array radar antennas helps to solve this issue [3]. The phase array radar has the advantage in beamforming. The direction of the beamforming is controlled by the electric scan which is very fast [4]. Since the phase array radar is located at the front of the aircraft, it should be circle plane phase array structure. Therefore, it is very important to design the circle plane phase array radar. The phase array radar has huge amount of antenna elements [5]. If each antenna element has its own hardware signal processing path, it is a huge amount waste of money. Therefore, the circle plane phase array radar is divided into several subarrays and each subarray has its own hardware signal processing path [6]. Since the circle phase array radar is divided into subarrays, the sidelobe power of the array pattern increases a lot [7]. Therefore, we also need to decrease the sidelobe power when dividing the phase array radar into subarrays [9].

In this paper, we propose a novel method to divide the circle phase array into the subarrays and suppress the sidelobe power at the same time. There are 4 sections in the paper. The introduction is given in the section I. In section II, the system model and the proposed method is given. In section III, the simulation results are shown. The conclusion for the paper is given in section IV.

II. The System Model and the Proposed Method

In this section, the system model and the proposed method is introduced. First, the system model is show in Fig. 1. The antenna elements are put into the rectangle grids [6]. We assume all the antenna elements in the circle phase array radar are located at the xOy plane.

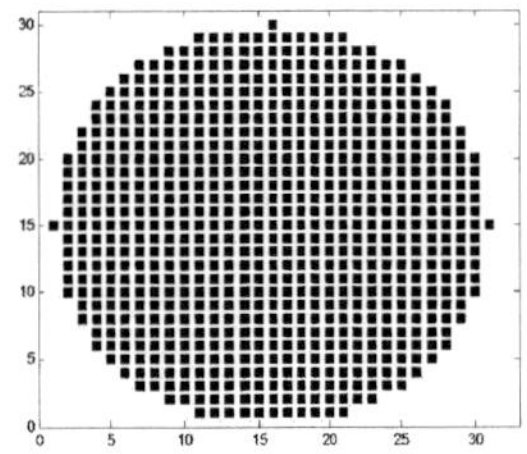

Fig. 1. The system model of the circle phase array radar.

As shown in Fig.1, the array structure is circle shape. The number of antenna elements in the diameter is N. The distance between the adjacent antenna elements is d. Then, we take a circle from the $N \times N$ array with the radius R, we have

$$R = \frac{N-1}{2} + \Delta \tag{1}$$

Then, the weights at the antenna element level is

$$\omega_d(m,n) = \begin{cases} 1 & d_0 < R \\ 0 & d_0 > R \end{cases} \tag{2}$$

where d_0 is the distance between the antenna elements and the circle central point [8]. Here, the coordinate of the circle central point is $(0, 0)$. The space phase difference between the adjacent antenna elements in the x direction is

$$\Delta\Phi_1 = \frac{2\pi}{\lambda} dx \tag{3}$$

The phase array difference between the adjacent antenna elements in the y direction is

$$\Delta\Phi_2 = \frac{2\pi}{\lambda} dy \tag{4}$$

where $x = sinvcosu$ and $y = sinvsinu$. The phase difference between the (i, j)th antenna element and the reference point is

$$\Delta\Phi_{ij} = i\Delta\Phi_1 + j\Delta\Phi_2 \tag{5}$$

Here, we propose a advanced genetic algorithm to divide the phase array into subarrays and suppress the sidelobe power at the same time. There are two major parts for the advanced genetic algorithm. First, the coding of the genetic algorithm is the random coding. Here, the distribution of the growth points are shown in Fig .3

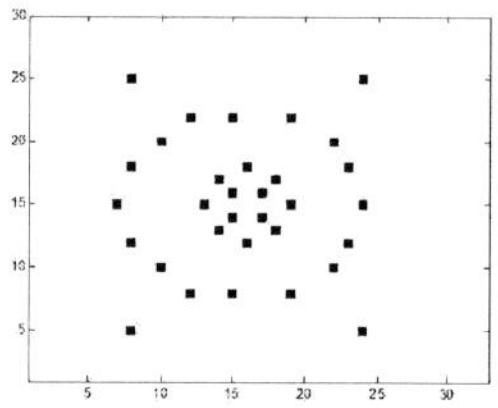

Fig. 2. The distribution of the growth points.

Second, we need to obtain the objective function for the advanced genetic algorithm. The coordinates for the circle phase array is shown in Fig.**??**

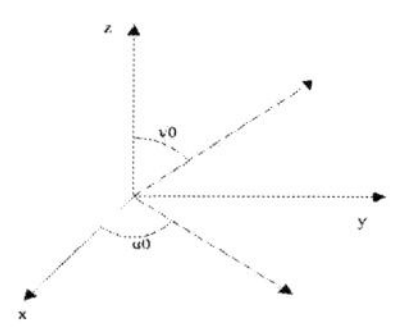

Fig. 3. The coordinates planes for the system.

We assume the phase difference between the antenna elements at the x direction and y direction is ϕ_{bi} and ϕ_{bj} respectively. We have

$$\Delta\Phi_{bij} = i\Delta\Phi_{bi} + j\Delta\Phi_{bj} \tag{6}$$

We assume the amplitude weight at the (i, j)th element is $A(i, j)$, the pattern at the antenna element level for the circle phase array is

$$F(u, v) = \sum_{i=0}^{N-1}\sum_{j=0}^{N-1} \omega_d(i, j)A(i, j)exp[-j(\Delta\Phi_{ij} - \Delta\Phi_{bij})] \tag{7}$$

Here, the objective function for the advanced genetic algorithm is the sidelobe of the u plane of the array pattern. The adaptive interference suppression array pattern is

$$f_1(u, v) = (\omega)^H[a_{sub}(u, v)a_{sub}(-u_0, v_0)] \tag{8}$$

where the product is Hardmard product.

III. Simulation Results

In this section, the simulation results are given. Here, the number of the antenna elements in the array is 708. The number of subarray is 32. The radius of the array is 15 times the half wavelength. The interference direction is $(1, 10)$. The JNR is 30dB.

As shown in Fig. 4, the elements with the same shape is in one subarray. The sidelobe power for the array structure is shown in Fig. 5. The sudelobe power after the optimization using our proposed method is much lower than that without the proposed method. Before the optimization, the sidelobe power in U plane is -16dB. The sidelobe power decreases to -27dB after the optimization. The sidelobe power is 11dB lower after the optimization.

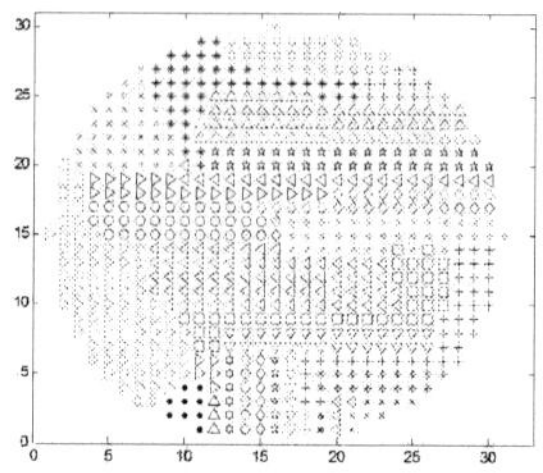

Fig. 4. The circle array structure.

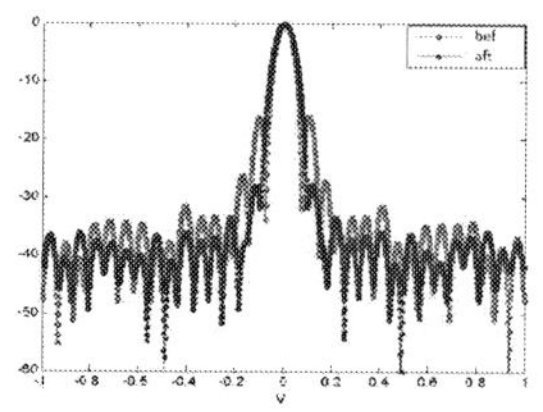

Fig. 5. The u plane of the array pattern.

IV. Conclusion

In this paper, we introduce a novel method to design the circle phase array for the aircraft radar. The number of signal processing path decreases dramatically. In addition, the sidelobe power of the array pattern using the proposed method is much lower than that without the proposed method. The array pattern after optimization has much better performance in receiving the signal and detect the expected signal.

References

[1] H. Subbaram and K. Abend, "Interference suppression via orthogonal projections: a performance analysis," *IEEE Transactions on Antennas and Propagation*, vol. 41, no. 9, pp. 1187–1194, Sep 1993.

[2] D. Wang and Z. Yang, "An novel spectrum sensing scheme combined with machine learning," in *2016 9th International Congress on Image and Signal Processing, BioMedical Engineering and Informatics (CISP-BMEI)*, Oct 2016, pp. 1293–1297.

[3] D. Wang, H. Hu, and Z. Yang, "Improved genetic algorithm for the configuration optimization of the sub arrays in phased array radar," in *2016 9th International Congress on Image and Signal Processing, BioMedical Engineering and Informatics (CISP-BMEI)*, Oct 2016, pp. 930–934.

[4] I. P. Kirsteins and D. W. Tufts, "Adaptive detection using low rank approximation to a data matrix," *IEEE Transactions on Aerospace and Electronic Systems*, vol. 30, no. 1, pp. 55–67, Jan 1994.

[5] D. Wang and Z. Yang, "An advanced scheme with decision tree for the improvement of spectrum sensing efficiency in dynamic network," in *2016 9th International Congress on Image and Signal Processing, BioMedical Engineering and Informatics (CISP-BMEI)*, Oct 2016, pp. 1288–1292.

[6] D. Wang and Y. Song, "A novel distributed global time synchronization protocol in cognitive radio ad hoc networks," in *2015 IEEE Global Communications Conference (GLOBECOM)*, Dec 2015, pp. 1–6.

[7] U. R. O. Nickel, "Subarray configurations for digital beamforming with low sidelobes and adaptive interference suppression," in *Proceedings International Radar Conference*, May 1995, pp. 714–719.

[8] S. Applebaum and D. Chapman, "Adaptive arrays with main beam constraints," *IEEE Transactions on Antennas and Propagation*, vol. 24, no. 5, pp. 650–662, Sep 1976.

[9] D. Wang, Y. Song, and Z. Yang, "A joint power adaptation and spectrum handoff scheme in mobile cognitive radio networks," in *2015 International Conference on Computing, Networking and Communications (ICNC)*, Feb 2015, pp. 1061–1065.

Supercapacitor Implementation for PV Power Generation System and Integration

Tunir Dey, Kowshik Dey, Greg Whelan and Abdullah Eroglu
Department of Electrical and Computer Engineering
Purdue University Fort Wayne
Fort Wayne, IN, US 46805

***Abstract*— Hybrid energy storage system configuration, novel to the authors' knowledge, is introduced. Interleaving the super capacitor between the electrostatically sensitive devices (ESDs) and DC-link capacitor enables the supercapacitor to directly handle all power demands in transient or steady state mode. Differentiation regarding the nature of the power demand is eliminated thus reducing the system's control complexity. Sliding-mode DC-DC control method is adapted to address the voltage variations and sustain the desired output voltage. The proposed system is implemented and verified via Matlab Simulink using a practical test case for household energy back up system. This new system can be integrated to PV power generation systems.**

Keywords—Supercapacitor, hybrid storage, smart grid, PV, grid integration.

I. Introduction

Hybrid energy storage systems have been well researched including various energy storage element combinations and configurations with several critical qualities [1-3]. It has been shown that an ESD and supercapacitor connected in parallel to a common dc bus is the commonly used configuration of the energy storage elements [4].

In this paper, hybrid energy storage system configuration, novel to the authors' knowledge is introduced. Interleaving the super capacitor between the ESD and DC-link capacitor the supercapacitor now directly handles all power demands, transient or steady state, and the ESD functions to maintain the super capacitor charge. Differentiation regarding the nature of the power demand is eliminated thus reducing the system's control complexity. The proposed hybrid system is shown in Fig. 1.

Due to the voltage-energy storage relationship characterizing any capacitor, the application of the adaptive sliding-mode DC-DC control design successfully addresses those voltage permutations to ensure the required output voltage. Bi-directional power flow, important to the continuous hybrid energy storage system operation, is fulfilled by this scheme as well. In addition, the proactive design streamlines implementation provided suitable response thresholds are initially available. Finally, continuous successful operation is fulfilled with supplemental protection controls, ensuring component life. The design's operation results were attained through simulation with Matlab's Simulink and the Simulink Power Systems toolkits.

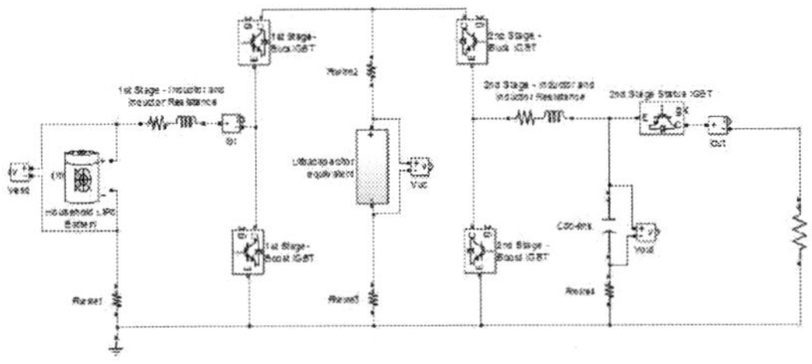

Fig. 1 – Hybrid storage system with supercapacitor

Such results are valid as the physical elements are defined by the fundamental component operation characteristic formulas. By following the design procedure, this system is applicable to any adequately defined situation.

II. Design and Simulation

Only through the application of the correct DC-DC control scheme, and related topology, could this configuration operate successfully. Such a control scheme is the selected Adaptive Sliding-Mode DC-DC Control shown in Fig. 2. Here-in a brief review of the control schemes properties condoning this configuration's successful operation, and the support thereof, is provided. This will begin with the benefits achieved by the reduced control structure. The computational burden in regards to the nature of the power demand with the parallel energy storage configuration made the control scheme's cumbersome. That is the leading improvement presented by the interleaved configuration.

The adaptive sliding-mode controller design is proactive and designed to achieve the correct response to a maximum transient load all transient loads of lesser magnitude fall within the same response design so that potential additional computation is eliminated. The goal of this controller, in regards to the DC-DC discrete switch operation, is to trigger an opposite output once a determined threshold away from the control variable surface of zero. Two complementary signals, one to each switch, result which influences the DC-DC converter operation to bring the output value towards its reference. Fulfilling the constraint inequalities expresses the controller's successful operation in the designed condition.

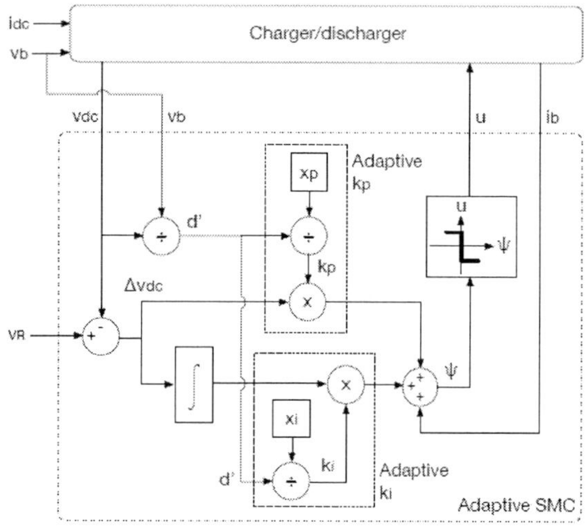

Fig. 2 - Sliding mode control for dc-dc converter

Implementing a bidirectional DC-DC converter implies no limitations in replacing the interleaved capacitor with the supercapacitor. The adaptive sliding-mode controller ensures reverse power flow capability. Maintaining the supercapacitor as the target for the boosted voltage provided by both stages allows for the fundamental control to be mirrored in regards to the boosted voltage target. With mirrored bidirectional DC-DC converters, the directions for power flow characterized by the battery current] oppose each other. The second stage control only requires a scaled input and the application of a DC-DC converter duty cycle characteristic to ensure the proper power flow direction and the buck output voltage from the super capacitor.

After careful consideration, the complimentary nature of the buck and boost DC-DC converter duty cycles was the key to this situation. The bucked voltage at the second stage output along with maintaining positive power flow dictated by the structure contradicted the goal. By simply scaling the output voltage to match the super-capacitor voltage and reconfiguring the control inputs to ensure calculated boost duty cycle compliment remained valid the duty cycle was fundamentally flipped so the bucked output voltage and power flow direction were achieved. The complementary nature with the input scaling effectively fools the control scheme into achieving a bucked output voltage through scaling the input to appear as the reverse.

To ensure reverse power flow, and system recharging, the IGBT which governs the first stage inductors magnetic field intensity required deactivation. Finally, as continuous operation is the fundamental goal for this system, over charge of the energy storage elements can result in a damaging, and potentially hazardous, scenario. Both energy storage elements can suffer failure from this situation: battery power storage reduction or worse and super-capacitor failure. Power flow corrects both potential scenario. As the supercapacitor boosted voltage should be selected in regards to its maximum rated voltage, implementation of an additional IGBT, following the DC-link capacitor, that is always on unless ESD complete state of charge estimate signal is true and the supercapacitor set voltage is present successfully eliminates overcharging that element. Reverse current is fundamental to the ESD state of charge estimate, a parameter of super capacitor overvoltage protection, so redundancy is not required. An ESD protection mechanism was implemented achieves ESD protection by using a running charge status comparison against the capacity rating to deactivate the first stage buck IGBT.

The simulation results are illustrated in Fig. 3. In Fig. 3, investigation for various combination of supercapacitor and inductors in the first and second stages show in Fig. 1 are given. It is shown that the proposed hybrid storage system keeps its stability during transients for various combinations.

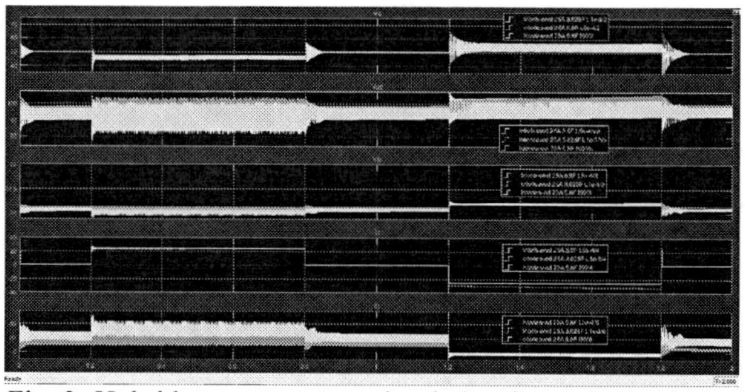

Fig. 3- Hybrid storage system simulation for various values of supercapactor and inductor values

III. CONCLUSION

A new hybrid energy storage system configuration using supercapacitors is discussed. Supercapacitor is implemented by interleaving it between the ESD and DC-link capacitor. The method used to implement the supercapacitor enables it to handle all power demands in transient or steady state mode. The proposed system is modeled and simulated by Matlab Simulink. It has been shown that it can successfully be integrated to PV power generation systems.

REFERENCES

[1] W. Hhuijian, Z. Jiancheng, "Research on Charging/Discharging ControlStrategy of Battery-Super Capacitor Hybrid Energy Storage System in Photovoltaic System" in IEEE 8th International Power Electronics and Motion Control Conference(IPEMC-ECCE Asia), 2016, pp. 2694-2698.

[2] F. S. Garcia, A. A. Ferreira, and J. A. Pomilio, "Control Strategy for Battery-Ultracapacitor Hybrid Energy Storage System" in Twenty-Fourth Annual IEEE Applied Power Electronics Conference and Exposition, 2009, pp. 826-832.

[3] D. Pavković, M. Lobrović, M. Hrgetić, and A. Komljenović, "A Design of DC Bus Control System for EVs Based on Battery/Ultracapacitor Hybrid Energy Storage" in IEEE International Electric Vehicle Conference (IEVC), 2014, pp. 1-8.

[4] D. Jianmin, X. Min, "Simulation Research on Hybrid Energy Storage System of Hybrid Electric Vehicle" in IEEE International Conference on Automation and Logistics, 2010, pp. 197-201.

[5] J. J. Awerbuch, C. R. Sullivan, "Control of Ultracapacitor-Battery Hybrid Power Source for Vehicular Applications" in IEEE Energy 2030 Conference, 2008, pp.1-7.

Design of Dual Band Rectifiers for Energy Harvesting Applications

Kowshik Dey, Tunir Dey, Rezwan Hussain and Abdullah Eroglu
Department of Electrical and Computer Engineering
Purdue University Fort Wayne
Fort Wayne, IN, US 46805

***Abstract*— Design, simulation and implementation of dual band radio frequency energy harvesting (RFEH) system operating at 900MHz and 1.8GHz is introduced. In the proposed design, RF-DC conversion system is designed to passively amplify the available voltage for rectification by developing a resonator with high quality factor. Passive amplification and rectification is implemented using a combination of clamper and peak detector. Harmonics presented in the rectified output voltage is eliminated by using matching network and filter. Energy harvesting system designed and simulated is then implemented and tested. Close agreement between analytical, simulation and measurement results are obtained.**

Keywords*— *Energy harvesting, radio frequency, dual band, rectanna, rectifier, matching network.

I. Introduction

Wireless sensor networks (WSNs) comprise of a set of active nodes which communicate with each other and a central node. In recent years WSNs have expanded to evolvement of a new area called Internet of Things (IoT) that investigates the connectivity and exchange of data between all physical devices in the network [1]. WSNs have been used in agriculture, healthcare, earth-sensing, industry and myriads of other applications. It is not uncommon to see that most of the time the sensor nodes are situated in hazardous locations with limited accessibility. Hence, these sensors at the nodes are typically powered by battery. Since, battery is limited form of energy source, they require periodic recharge or replacement which brings along the added cost of maintenance and replacement [2]. Disposal of battery is also a cumbersome task which is hazardous to the environment.

One way to overcome the power problem due to limited battery lifetime is to use a method called energy harvesting. Energy harvesting also known as power harvesting, or energy scavenging is the process of extracting energy from external sources using solar power, thermal energy, wind energy, salinity gradients, and kinetic energy which all can be referred as ambient energy. Energy harvester once extracts the energy in the ambient it then converts that energy to DC, rectifies the signal and powers wireless autonomous devices that might be part of larger networks [3-4]. The energy harvester systems have antenna, and impedance matching networks to interface the rectifier system as illustrated in Fig. 1. This system can energize any type of network that can operate with low power such as wireless sensor networks.

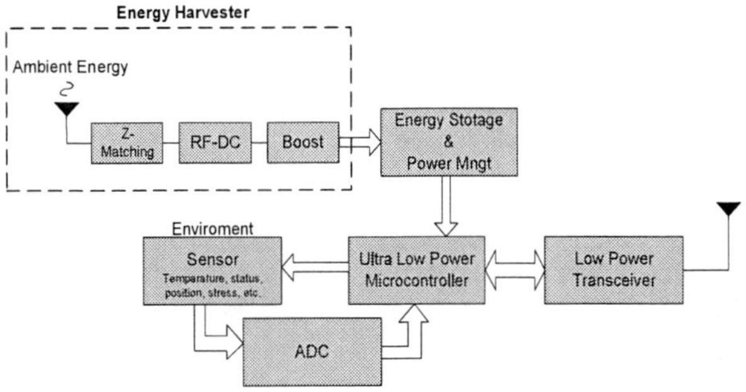

Fig. 1 - Block Diagram of RFEH

In this paper, design, simulation and implementation of dual band radio frequency energy harvesting system operating at 900MHz and 1.8GHz is introduced. The proposed energy harvester has integrated impedance matching network, filter and cascaded three stage rectifier which is based on voltage doubler circuit to convert RF-DC. The system is simulated with Agilent Design System (ADS) and implemented. It has been confirmed that the analytical, simulation and measurement results are all in agreement.

II. Design of Rectifier Circuit

Clampers or DC resonators hold the peak of a waveform at the desired DC level. In other words, it clamps the waveform either in positive or negative direction using diode with a capacitively coupled signal as shown in Fig. 2. The output voltage of the clamper circuit can be expressed as

$$V_{clamp} = 2V_p - V_{th} \tag{1}$$

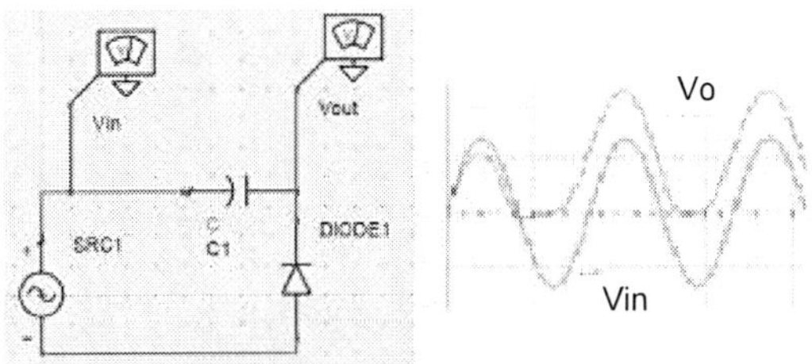

Fig. 2 – Voltage clamper circuit

Since the energy is considerably low in the ambient, we need to take into account the effect of diode threshold voltage, V_{th}. The diode should be capable of fast switching along with a very low threshold voltage required for conduction.

To produce a steady voltage from the rectifier we incorporate peak detector with clamper circuit. A peak detector is a series connection of a diode and a capacitor outputting a DC voltage equal to the peak value of the applied sinusoidal signal. The peak detector circuit with voltage waveforms are illustrated in Fig. 3.

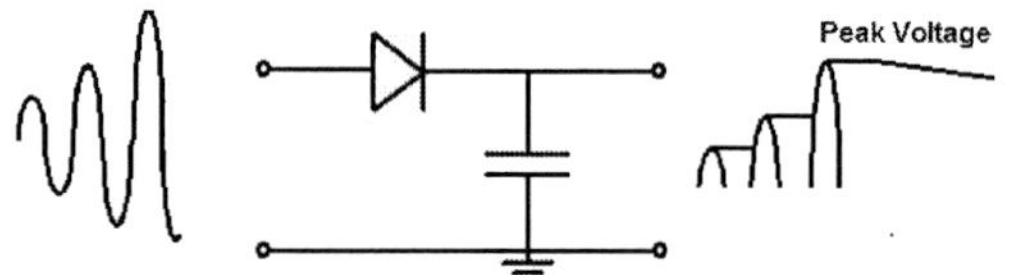

Fig. 3 – Peak detector circuit

The voltage output of the peak detector circuit is given as

$$V_{pkDetect} = V_{clamp} - V_{th} \quad (2)$$

The clamping and peak detector circuits can now be integrated to form single stage of the radio frequency energy harvesting (RFEH) system as shown in Fig. 4. The single stage RFEH can be cascaded to increase the amount of output voltage. In the proposed system, three stage RFEH is used to accomplish RF-DC conversion.

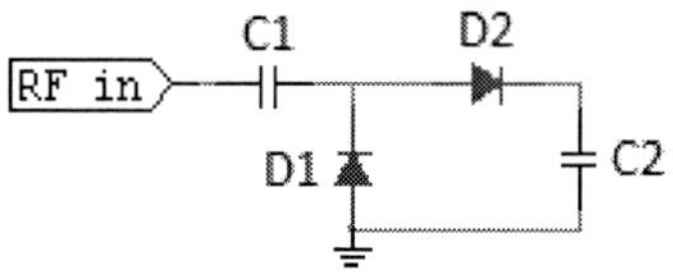

Fig. 4 – Single stage of RFEH

III. Simulation Results

The proposed three stage RFEH is designed and simulated as shown in Fig. 5. Harmonics are presented in the rectified output voltage. The design of novel three section matching network is developed to eliminate the harmonics. The three section matching network can match impedance at two distinct frequency without causing any complicacy. Fig. 6 shows the simulated output power in frequency domain where harmonics is present.

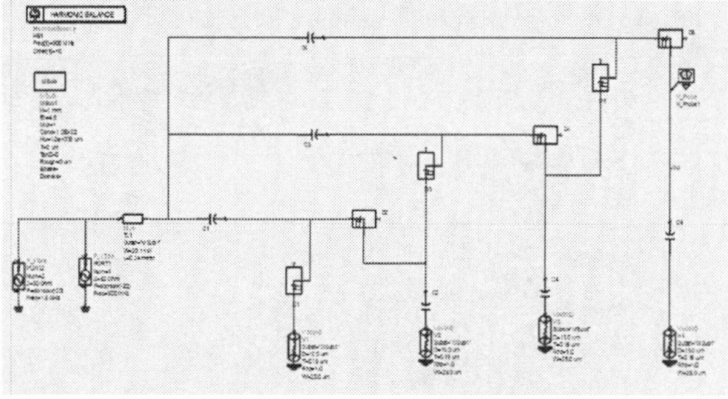

Fig. 5 – The complete RFEH system

Fig. 7 shows output spectrum without harmonics after the use of three section matching network.

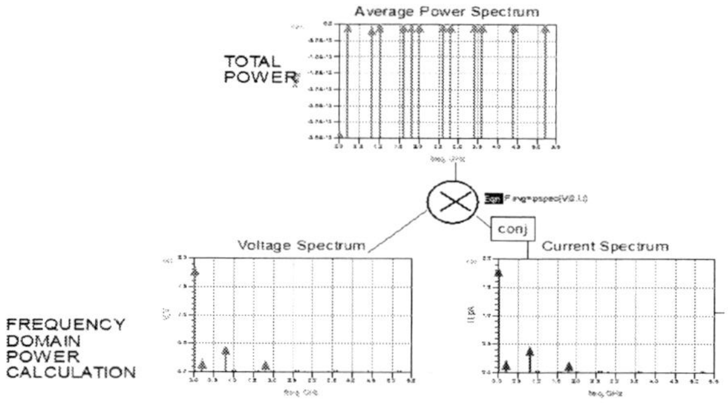

Fig. 6 - Frequency Spectrum of Output power

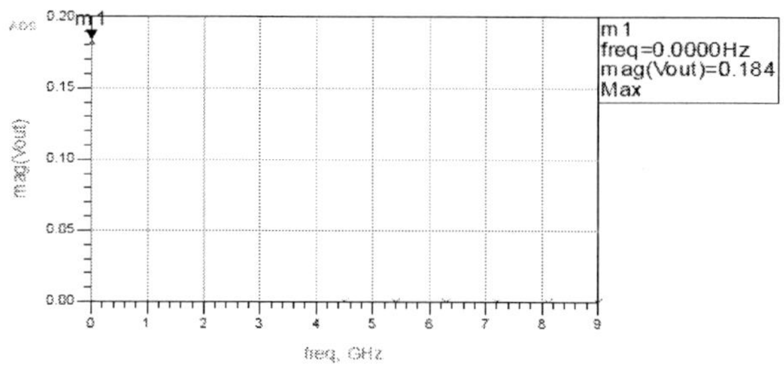

Fig. 7- Voltage spectrum showing elimination of harmonics from output.

IV. Conclusion

In this paper, design, simulation and implementation of dual band radio frequency energy harvesting (RFEH) system operating at 900MHz and 1.8GHz is introduced. The proposed harvesting system can passively amplify the available voltage for rectification using three stages of voltage doubler circuit. Passive amplification and rectification is implemented using a combination of clamper and peak detector. Harmonics presented in the rectified output voltage is eliminated by using matching network and filter. Energy harvesting system designed and simulated is then implemented and tested. Close agreement between analytical, simulation and measurement results are obtained

References

[1] L. Tan and N. Wang, ''Future Internet: The Internet of Things,'' in Proc. 3rd Int. Conf. Adv. Comput. Theory Eng. (ICACTE), vol. 5. Aug. 2010, pp. V5-376–V5-380

[2] Carli, D.; Brunelli, D.; Benini, L.; Ruggeri, M., "An effective multi-source energy harvester for low power applications," *Design, Automation & Test in Europe Conference & Exhibition (DATE), 2011* , vol., no., pp.1,6, 14-18 March 2011

[3] H. Li, C. Tian, and Z. D. Deng, "Energy harvesting from low frequency applications using piezoelectric materials," Applied Physics Reviews 1, 041301 ,2014.

[4] Vyas, R.; Nishimoto, Hiroshi; Tentzeris, Manos; Kawahara, Y.; Asami, T., "A battery-less, energy harvesting device for long range scavenging of wireless power from terrestrial TV broadcasts," in Microwave Symposium Digest (MTT), 2012 IEEE MTT-S International , vol., no., pp.1-3, 17-22 June 2012

A Highly Efficient Miniaturized Microwave Collector for Wireless Power Transmission

Safiullah Khan*, Thomas F. Eibert
Chair of High-Frequency Engineering, Department of Electrical and Computer Engineering,
Technical University of Munich, 80290 Munich, Germany,
safiullah.khan@tum.de*

***Abstract*—A metamaterial subwavelength structure is presented to capture incident electromagnetic waves at 6.75 GHz. Perfect impedance matching is implemented to channel the captured electromagnetic power to the load. The structure comprises a square loop resonator with an enclosed a T-type resonator. About 92.2 % of the incident power is captured from which 78.3 % of the energy is converted to real power in the resistive load of 490 Ω at 6.75 GHz. The total efficiency amounts to 72.2 %. Investigations for oblique angles of incidence show stability up to 45°.**

I. Introduction

Currently, fossil fuels, nuclear energy and renewable energy are the three major sources of power generation. Fossil fuels such as coal, natural gas and oil have been abundantly used since a long time. More recently, other means of power generation have been discovered. Fossil fuel reserves are limited and can not be solely relied upon. Similarly, power generated from nuclear energy is neither sustainable because of the radioactive waste nor renewable because of the scarce resources used for producing energy [1]. In such circumstances, power generated from renewable energy sources such as solar and wind are the best alternative solutions for clean and sustainable energy.

In addition to the day-night cycle limitation, using solar radiation directly on earth is subject to weather conditions and losses such as absorption, scattering and reflection. This means that the resource is not being used at its full potential. Therefore, the idea of space solar power satellite (SSPS) systems was proposed in 1968 [2]. In SSPS, energy from solar radiation is collected in space using photovoltaic systems and converted to microwave energy. The power is then transmitted to earth using microwave beams. On the earth station, large arrays of rectennas are positioned to receive the highly directive microwave beams and to convert it to real power. The choice of frequency depends on the low atmospheric losses and less heat losses (such as in the generation of laser).

Rectenna is a combination of an antenna and a rectifying circuit. Conventional antennas have some limitations, such as back scattering, the need of a dedicated impedance matching network, incident angle dependance, etc. because of which they are in general not favorable for wireless power transmission systems, where high efficiency is required. As an alternative, energy harvesting surfaces based on resonating structures are designed to achieve high end-to-end efficiency in SSPS systems.

Microwave beam incident on the resonating structure is absorbed and converted to power which is channeled through a via to the load. After conversion a rectifier circuit is used to filter DC power. In the conversion process, some of the energy is wasted as dielectric losses, metal losses and rectifier circuit losses. In order to obtain high end-to-end efficiency, both the conversion efficiency and filtering efficiency must be maximized. Therefore, the performance of the energy harvester is demonstrated by its absorption efficiency (amount of incident energy absorbed by the structure), conversion efficiency (amount of absorbed power which is dissipated by the load) and harvesting efficiency (ratio of output power to incident power). In addition to the performance indicators, some of the design challenges are perfect matching at the first interface (incident medium - resonant structure interface), harmonics suppression and wide incident angle stability.

A recently proposed metamaterial (MTM) design [3] is optimized for high efficiency and oblique incidence angle stability at a single resonance frequency. Previously, the structure had two absorption bands due to the combined effect of the resonance frequency of each constituent resonator and the mutual interactions between them. In the current design, both the resonators are physically joined such that a single absorption band is produced. Using a single absorption band reduces the losses due to metal and dielectric. It also increases the overall end-to-end efficiency. Hence, a single absorption band with higher efficiency would provide a more attractive solution for the SSPS system. The structure comprises a T-type resonator inside a square loop printed on a single layer

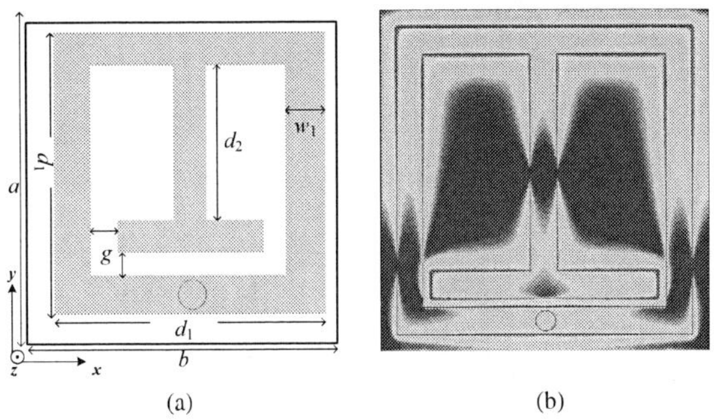

(a) (b)

Fig. 1. (a) MTM unit cell where a = 10 mm, b = 10 mm, d_1 = 9 mm, d_2 = 6.34 mm, w_1 = 0.8 mm, g = 0.26 mm, via= 0.6Ø. (b) Electric field distribution on a single unit cell at 6.75 GHz for normal incidence angle.

dielectric substrate Rogers RO3003 and backed by a copper ground. The substrate has permittivity $\epsilon = 3.0$, loss tangent 0.001 and thickness 0.254 mm. The via is located at the bottom of the structure, which channels the power to the resistive load. Fig. (a) shows the unit cell and its geometric parameters. CST Microwave studio has been used to simulate the design.

II. Result and Discussion

Since the structure is sensitive to an electric field vector along the y−axis, a plane wave with such an electric field vector is incident on the proposed unit cell structure with 0.5 Watt power per unit cell. The structure resonates at 6.75 GHz and its electric field distribution is shown in Fig. (b). Most of the energy is absorbed by the structure. The electric fields are stronger at the bottom and the top of the structure while parallel surface currents are induced in the vertical arms of the resonator which merge at the optimal location of the via. Anti-parallel currents are generated in the gap between the T-type resonator and the square loop at the bottom of the structure. For an electric field vector along the x−axis, the structure resonates at 5.85 GHz and all of the energy is lost with in the structure. At the first interface, the structure impedance must match the free space impedance for maximum absorption. This is achieved by identical permittivity and permeability. Fig. 2 shows the input impedance (Z_{in}), output impedance (Z_{out}) for maximum power delivered to the load and S-parameters. At resonance frequency, the impedance seen from the incident medium is $Z_{\text{in}} = (1.76 - j0.1)\,\Omega$ and the impedance seen from load is $Z_{\text{out}} = (1 + j0.02)\,\Omega$. In simulations, the load is only modelled with a resistive element of 490 Ω. Furthermore, it is observed that at harmonic frequencies Z_{out} is different than at the resonance frequency. Such mismatching prevents the reradiation of the harmonics produced by the rectifying circuit. The distribution of the absorbed power (P_{a}) in the structure and the load is illustrated in Fig. 3. It is seen that 78.3% of the total absorbed power is delivered to the load (P_{l}) which equals to 0.361 W. The losses due to dielectric (P_{d}) and metal (P_{m}) are 0.02 W and 0.07 W, respectively at 6.75 GHz.

Other important aspects in the analysis of the wave collector are the oblique incidence angle stability and the harvesting

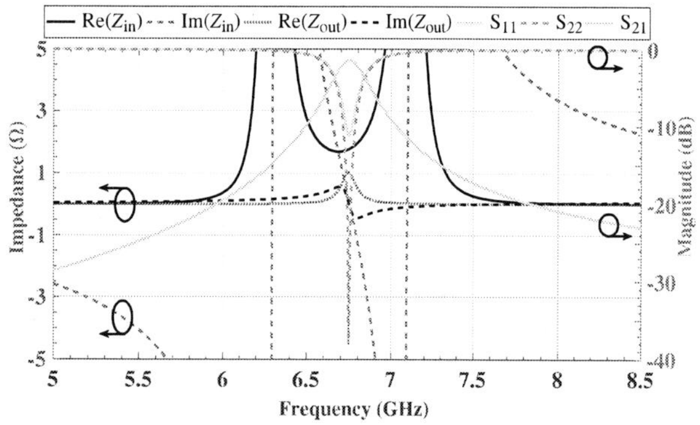

Fig. 2. Impedance, reflection and transmission of the structure as a function of frequency. Z_{in} and Z_{out} normalized with 376.73 Ω and 490 Ω, respectively.

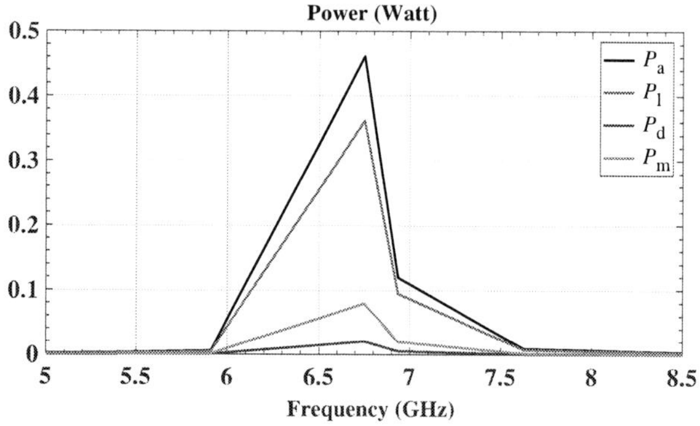

Fig. 3. Power distribution of the captured energy in the proposed unit cell. P_{a}, P_{l}, P_{d}, P_{m} are the power absorbed by the structure, power dissipated in resistive load, power losses in dielectric and power losses in metal, respectively.

efficiency. Table I depicts the change in the absorption and dissipation of the power along with the efficiencies for different incident angles. When the incidence angle is increased, the absorption power along with the dissipated power gradually decrease until 45° and from there onwards a significant loss due to reflection is observed. However, the conversion efficiency (C_{e}) remains almost the same for all presented incident angles. Conversion efficiency is the ratio of the power dissipated in the load to the absorbed power. Absorption efficiency (A_{e}) is the ratio of the power absorbed to the power incident on the surface of the structure. Harvesting efficiency (H_{e}) is the ratio of the power delivered to load to incident power ($H_{\text{e}} = \frac{A_{\text{e}}}{C_{\text{e}}}$).

TABLE I. Power and Efficiencies for Oblique Incidence Angles

	$\theta = 0°$	$\theta = 15°$	$\theta = 30°$	$\theta = 45°$	$\theta = 60°$
P_{a} in W	0.461	0.455	0.424	0.352	0.246
P_{l} in W	0.361	0.356	0.332	0.276	0.193
A_{e}	92.2%	91.0%	84.8%	70.4%	49.2%
C_{e}	78.3%	78.2%	78.301%	78.4%	78.5%
H_{e}	72.2%	71.2%	66.4%	55.2%	38.6%

III. Conclusion

A recently proposed meta-resonator for energy harvesting applications have been optimized to achieve higher efficiency at a single resonance frequency of 6.75 GHz. The harvesting efficiency has been increased from 48.16% to 72.2%. Also, the structure shows a stable response until 45° of incident angle.

Acknowledgment

The authors are grateful to Deutscher Akademischer Austauschdienst (DAAD), Germany for the support of this work.

References

[1] J. M. Pearce, "Limitations of nuclear power as a sustainable energy source," *Sustainability*, vol. 4, no. 6, pp. 1173–1187, 2012.

[2] P. E. Glaser, "Power from the sun: Its future," *Science*, vol. 162, no. 3856, pp. 857–861, 1968.

[3] S. Khan and T. F. Eibert, "A multi-resonant meta-absorber as an electromagnetic energy harvester," in *IEEE International Symposium on Antennas and Propagation and USNC-URSI Radio Science Meeting*, July 2017.

Harvesting of Aircraft Radar Altimeter Sidelobes for Low-Power Sensors

José Estrada, Philip Zurek and Zoya Popović
Department of Electrical, Computer and Energy Engineering
University of Colorado, Boulder, CO 80309, U.S.A.

***Abstract*—In this paper a harvesting system for powering low-power sensors from sidelobe power of an aircraft altimeter radar is presented. The rectenna is co-designed using full-wave field simulations and harmonic balance circuit simulations. A harvesting system is demonstrated and can produce a DC output power of -21 dBm from $2\,\mu\text{W/cm}^2$ incident power density at 4.3 GHz. The stored energy is sufficient for low-power sensor operation and validates the rectifier and antenna co-design.**

I. Introduction

Harvesting RF power from side-lobes of an aircraft altimeter can enable low-maintenance unattended sensing of various quantities relevant to aircraft structural health [1], [2]. Fig. 1 shows a photograph of the aircraft body with the position of the altimeter and potential placement of sensors. Altimeter antenna radiation patterns obtained from the manufacturer [3] show a gain of 10.4 dBi in the direction of ground and sidelobes with −13 dBi gain in the direction of the aircraft skin. The RF power density available ranges from $0.04\,\mu\text{W/cm}^2$ to $2.2\,\mu\text{W/cm}^2$ at 4.3 GHz and a distance of 30 cm from the altimeter's antenna [3], [4], [5]. Low-power structural integrity sensors can be powered by delivering $300\,\mu$J of energy every 10 minutes. The average power requirement at the DC side is then $P = 0.5\,\mu$W (-33 dBm).

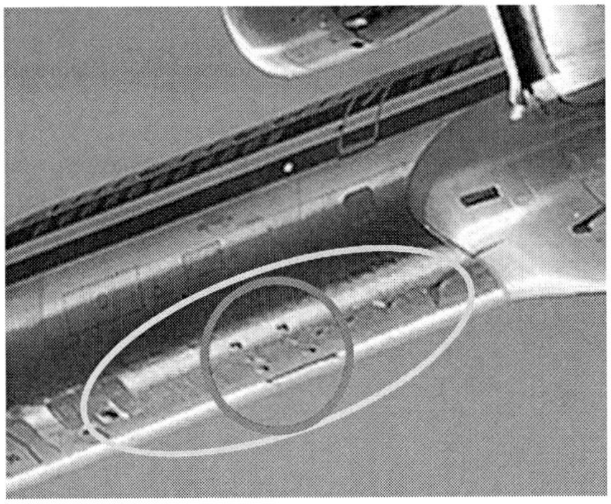

Fig. 1. Typical location of the altimeter radar on a commercial aircraft, the red circle shows the location of the altimeter antennas and the green oval is the approximate region where the harvesters can be located.

In this paper, we detail the co-design of the antenna, single-ended diode rectifier, and harvester power management, following the work in [5]. We experimentally demonstrate integration of a full system capable of harvesting the expected energy, thus validating rectenna design.

II. Rectenna Design

The rectenna uses a single SMS7630-061 GaAs Schottky diode as a half-wave rectifier connected in parallel with the antenna. The rectifier is simulated using harmonic balance (HB) source-pull analysis in National Instruments AWR. During the source pull simulations, the RF input impedance at the diode is swept, while the input power and DC load are varied. The contours of constant DC rectified power for a 5 kΩ DC load and at -15 dBm input power are shown in Fig. 2, indicating that the optimal complex antenna impedance under these conditions is $Z_a = (38 + j252)\,\Omega$.

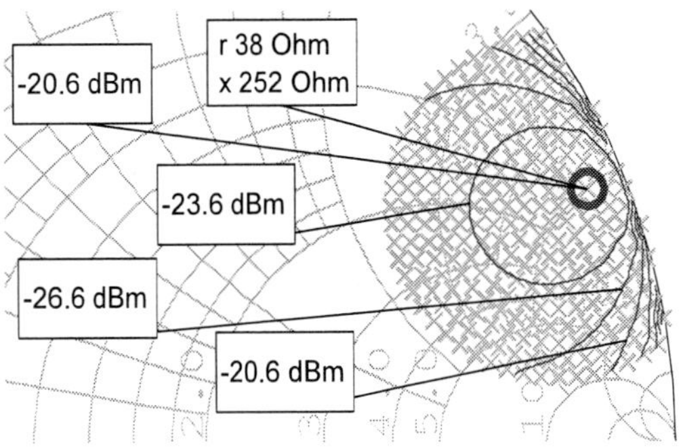

Fig. 2. Rectifier HB source-pull simulation results show contours of constant rectified power, in dBm, for -15 dBm input power and a DC load of 5 kΩ for the Skyworks SMS7630-061 GaAs Schottky diode.

The antenna is a radiating-edge fed linearly polarized rectangular patch antenna on a Rogers RO4350B™ substrate, designed for maximum power transfer to the rectifier. Ansys HFSS is used to design the feed point that directly matches the antenna feed point to the diode complex impedance, removing the need for a matching network. Fig. 3 shows the simulation results where the antenna impedance at 4.3 GHz is $Z_a = (30+j240)\,\Omega$ with an antenna gain of 5 dBi. The rectifier DC collection circuit uses the RF null of the patch as DC-RF isolation, further reducing the size and loss of the rectenna passive circuit. The DC power delivered by the rectenna at 4.3 GHz with an incident power density of $0.65\,\mu\text{W/cm}^2$ is -23.2 dBm

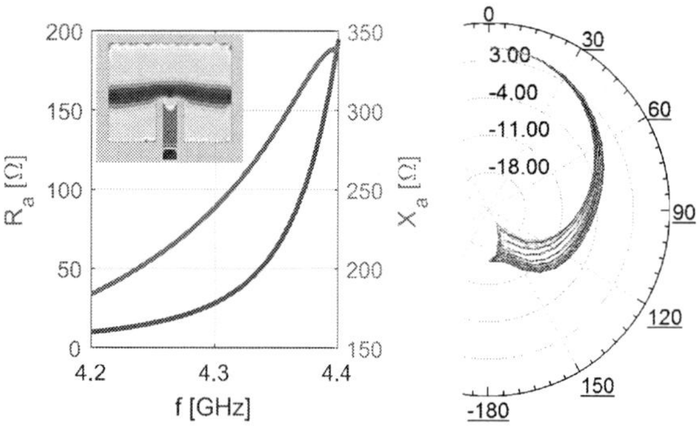

(a) (b)

Fig. 3. Antenna simulation results. (a) Antenna impedance showing both real and imaginary part and surface current density amplitude distribution. (b) Radiation pattern in θ and for a ϕ sweep.

Fig. 4. Harvesting system circuit diagram and photos of both the rectenna and the power management module.

III. Full Harvesting System

The voltage available from a single Schottky diode at low power levels is to small for most electronic functions, so some power management with voltage boosting is necessary. Additionally, when the available RF power varies, the optical DC load varies, so maximum power point tracking can be used to dynamically adapt the load for maximum power extraction [6], commonly used in, e.g., photo-voltaic systems [7]. In our case, the power variation is not substantial and the load seen by the rectifier is not dynamically adjusted but instead is fixed to the experimentally obtained $20\,\Omega$ optimum DC loading. Using a Texas Instruments BQ25504 PMM chip, the effective resistance seen by the rectifier is set to the optimum value. The BQ25504 chip also has a high efficiency boost converter used to get the voltage level to a more usable 3.2 V. The BQ25504 can efficiently manage microwatts of power and it also has a cold start up operation mode which can start with voltages as low as 330 mV. After the main boost charger turns on and efficient operation begins the system can work with input voltages as low as 80 mV.

A demo for the full harvesting system capable of charging a $100\,\mu$F capacitor (built into the EVM) or a $200\,\mu$F capacitance (a $100\,\mu$F capacitor in parallel with the built in one). A simple efficient circuit also allows the system to be configured to blink an LED for visual demonstration of harvested power. The experimental unit is shown in Fig. 4.

The energies stored in the two capacitors when charged to 3.2 V are $E_{100} = 512\,\mu$J and $E_{200} = 1024\,\mu$J, respectively. The time it takes for the system to fully charge the 100 and $200\,\mu$F capacitors from a fully discharged state (from cold-start operation) is 8 and 9 min, respectively. The module starts efficient operation when the output voltage reaches 1.7 V, which occurs after 7 and 8 min for the 100 and $200\,\mu$F capacitors, respectively. These measurements are performed with a $2\,\mu\mathrm{W/cm^2}$ incident field that is calibrated using an ETS HI-6005 electric field probe.

Another test is performed with an LED as the load. A $100\,\mu$F capacitor is charged to 3.2 V and then discharged through an LED to 1.8 V. While in efficient operation (the voltage is always above 1.7 V) and for an incident field of $2\,\mu\mathrm{W/cm^2}$, the LED turns on and off with a period of 20 s. Since the voltage drops to 1.8 V after each blink, the energy at the end of the cycle is $E' = 162\,\mu$J. This implies that the energy delivered after each blink is $\Delta E = 350\mu$J. The experiment shows that the energy that is specified to be delivered to a sensor every 10 min can be done every 20 s and the average harvested power is:

$$P = \frac{\Delta E}{T} = \frac{350\mu\mathrm{J}}{20\,\mathrm{s}} = 7.78\,\mu\mathrm{W} = -21\,\mathrm{dBm}.$$

In summary, the demonstrated energy harvesting from very low incident power levels at 4.3 GHz ($< 2\mu\mathrm{W/cm^2}$) is sufficient to power unattended sensors on an aircraft. These results validate the co-design methodology for the rectenna, which combines full-wave EM modeling and nonlinear circuit simulations.

Acknowledgment

The authors would like to thank Drs. Authi Narayanan and Alan Keith from Boeing Corporation for advice and support.

References

[1] B. Strauss, "The onboard commercial aircraft in-flight rf environment - measurements and implications," in *Electromagnetic Compatibility, 2006. EMC 2006. 2006 IEEE International Symposium on*, vol. 1, pp. 234–239, Aug. 2006.

[2] X. Zhao, H. Gao, G. Zhang, B. Ayhan, F. Yan, C. Kwan, and J. L. Rose, "Active health monitoring of an aircraft wing with embedded piezoelectric sensor/actuator network: I. Defect detection, localization and growth monitoring," *Smart Materials and Structures*, vol. 16, no. 4, p. 1208, 2007.

[3] www.ubcorp.com/product/microstrip-raa-ads43010-1a-1ac/.

[4] M. Vidmar, "Design improves 4.3-ghz radio altimeter accuracy," *Microwave & RF*.

[5] J. Estrada, I. Ramos, A. Narayan, A. Keith, and Z. Popovic, "Rf energy harvester in the proximity of an aircraft radar altimeter," in *2016 IEEE Wireless Power Transfer Conference (WPTC)*, pp. 1–4, May 2016.

[6] S. Dunbar and Z. Popovic, "Low-power electronics for energy harvesting sensors," *Wireless Power Transfer*, no. 1, pp. 35–43, 2014.

[7] T. Esram and P. L. Chapman, "Comparison of photovoltaic array maximum power point tracking techniques," *IEEE Transactions on Energy Conversion*, vol. 22, pp. 439–449, June 2007.

Focused Antenna Arrays for Wireless Power Transfer Applications

Payam Nayeri
Electrical Engineering Department
Colorado School of Mines, Golden, CO, USA
pnayeri@mines.edu

***Abstract*—Focused antenna arrays have the ability to concentrate their radiated power to a point. In this work, we study the advantages and benefits of these types of arrays for wireless power transfer applications. Through case studies, we demonstrate that focused arrays can significantly increase the total received power at the receiver and this capability can significantly enhance the efficiency of these wireless energy systems.**

Keywords—focused antennas, phased arrays, wireless energy harvesting, wireless power transfer.

I. Introduction

The rapid growth of wireless communication systems in recent years, combined with the growing popularity and applications of largescale, sensor-based wireless networks, as well as the Internet of Things (IoT), have created a strong demand to adopt inexpensive, green communication strategies. Most of these devices need to operate without batteries, or have the ability to recharge their battery wirelessly during operation, and as such require an energy harvesting circuit that captures wireless power and converts it to usable DC power. This paper investigates the advantages of focused antenna arrays for wireless power transfer applications.

II. Focused Antenna Arrays

Focused antennas can concentrate radiated electromagnetic power into a small spot in the nearfield of the antenna. These antennas have numerous applications in remote (non-contact) sensing, radar, medicine, and imaging systems, and therefore have received a great deal of attention over the years [1-4]. While different types of antennas, such as reflectors, lenses, and arrays, can be focused; arrays have the highest degree of design freedom, and therefore have received the most attention. Arrays can also offer the capability of movable focal point through electrical signals rather than mechanical movement by phase control at the elements [5-7].

To focus the radiated power of the array, the radiated waves from all elements of the array should add up in phase at the desired focusing point. Consider a linear array placed along the x-axis. At a focusing distance of F, the required phase shift for each element of the array is computed as:

$$\varphi_n = 2\pi \frac{f}{c} \sqrt{F^2 + x_n^{\,2}} \,. \qquad (1)$$

Here, f is the center design frequency, c is the speed of light, and x_n is the location of the nth element of the array. Assuming a linear array of isotropic radiators, the radiated electric fields of this array in the xz-plane can be computed using:

$$E(x,z) = \sum_{n=1}^{N} a_n e^{j\varphi_n} \frac{e^{-jkR_n}}{4\pi R_n}, \qquad (2)$$

where k is the wavenumber, a_n and φ_n are the amplitude and phase of the elements, and R_n is radial length from the source to the observation point based on the local coordinates of each element.

To study the focusing properties of antenna arrays, here we consider an 8-element linear array with a 20 dB Taylor taper with an element spacing of 26 mm placed at the center of the coordinate system along the x-axis. The array is designed to operate at 5.8 GHz and to focus its beam at 200 mm along the z-axis. The electric fields of the array are given in Fig. 1, where it can be seen that the antenna is indeed focusing its radiated power in the nearfield and the phase plot shows a zero phase at the desired focus point.

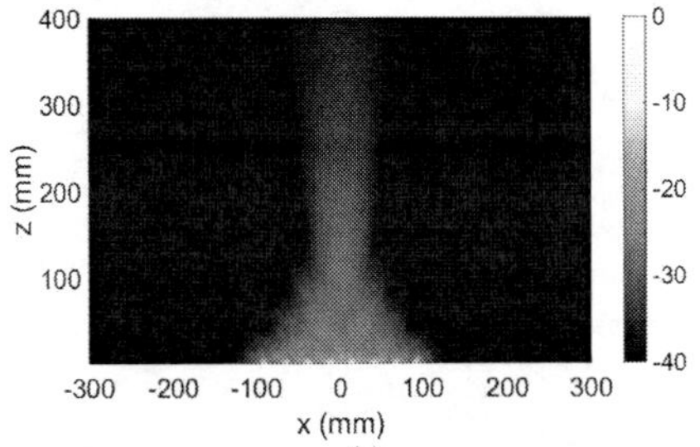

(a)

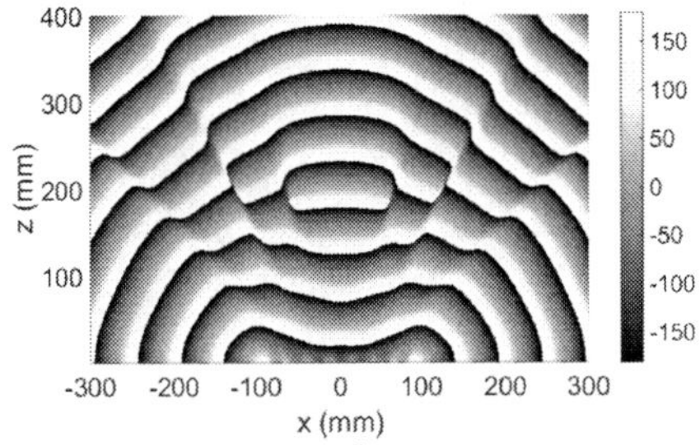

(b)

Fig. 1. Electric fields of a focused 8-element antenna array with isotropic radiators: (a) normalized amplitude in dB, and (b) phase in degrees.

III. Focused Arrays for Wireless Power Transfer

Efficient power transfer is achieved by selecting an appropriate scheme which is dependent on the distance between the receiver (Rx) and transmitter (Tx). In the reactive near-field zone, power is transferred via magneto-inductive coupling. At further distances, typically antennas are used to transmit the power into the far-field. In many instances, however, the Rx is in the radiative near-field region of the Tx, where the system efficiency can be improved by using focused antenna arrays. The use of focused array antennas not only serves to support the existing infrastructure of the IoT, but it allows for the development of more complex and capable wireless harvesting systems [4].

To study the advantages of focused arrays for wireless power transfer applications, here we study an 8-element linear dipole antenna array with the same array setup as in section II using the full-wave electromagnetic software FEKO [8]. The geometrical model of the antenna array is given in Fig. 2.

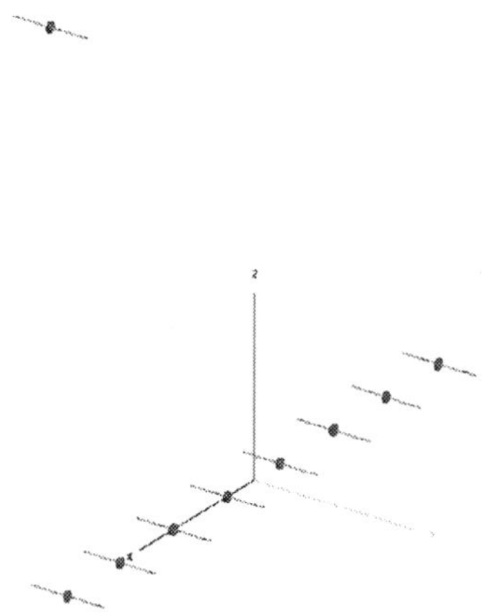

Fig. 2. An 8-element focused dipole array for wireless power transfer.

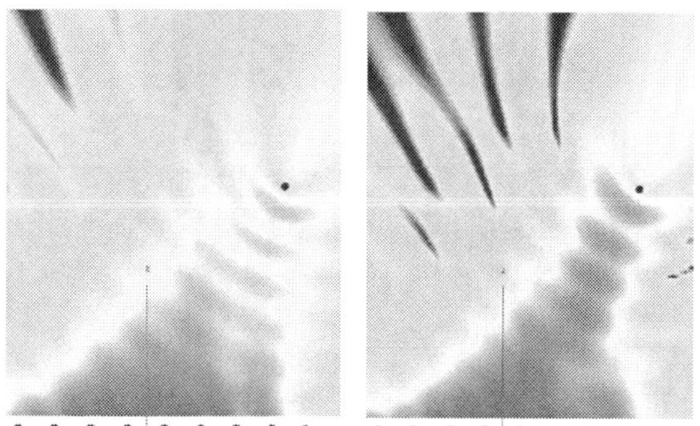

(a) (b)

Fig. 3. Magnitude of the electric fields: (a) array scans its beam to 30 degrees, and (b) array focuses its beam to a distance of 200 mm and 30° degrees.

In order to maximize transfered power, the array needs to scan its beam to the direction of the receiver. The receiver is located in the xz-plane at an angle of $\theta = 30°$ and a distance of 200 mm from the center of the coordinate system. We compare two cases: 1) the array scans its beam to 30°, and 2) the array focuses its beam to 200 mm and 30°. The electric fields at 5.8 GHz are given in Fig. 3 for both cases. Note that the much stronger electric field magnitude in the focused case is indicateive of a stronger coupling and will correspond to higher efficiency. To further verify this, the received power as a function of frequency is also given in Fig. 4, where note that the focused array increases the transferred power by almost 300 uWs at 5.8 GHz.

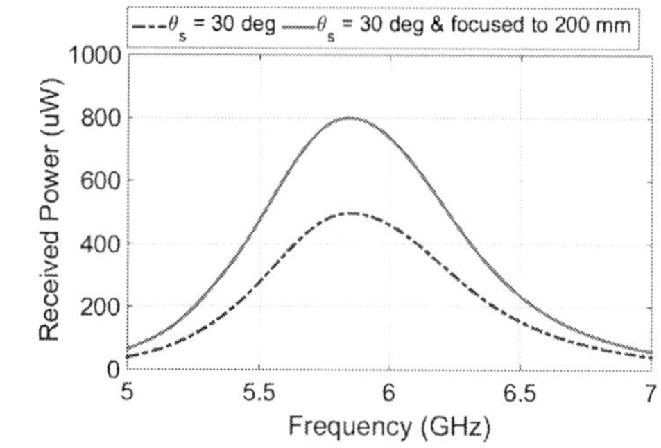

Fig. 4. Comparison between the received power when scanning and focusing the antenna array.

IV. Conclusions

In this work, we studied the advantages of focused antenna arrays for wireless power transfer and energy harvesting applications. Through case studies we demonstrate the improvement in wireless power transfer efficiency by using focused antenna arrays, and show that this capability can significantly enhance the efficiency of these systems.

References

[1] H. Lee, "5.8 GHz ISM band energy harvester utilizing Dickson charge pump," *17th International Symposium on Antenna Technology and Applied Electromagnetics* (ANTEM), Montreal, QC, 2016.

[2] P. Nintanavongsa, U. Muncuk, D. R. Lewis, and K. R. Chowdhury, "Design optimization and implementation for RF energy harvesting circuits," in *IEEE Journal on Emerging and Selected Topics in Circuits and Systems*, vol. 2, no. 1, pp. 24-33, Mar. 2012.

[3] Y. Huang, N. Shinohara, and T. Mitani, "Impedance matching in wireless power transfer," in *IEEE Transactions on Microwave Theory and Techniques*, vol. 65, no. 2, pp. 582-590, Feb. 2017.

[4] D. Schemmel and P. Nayeri, "A smart wireless energy harvesting system with adaptive beamforming and power management," *IEEE APS/USNC-URSI National Radio Science Meeting*, California, U.S., Jul. 2017.

[5] P. Nayeri, A. Z. Elsherbeni, R. L. Haupt, and F. Yang, "Near-field scanning characteristics of focused reflectarray antennas," *31st International Review of Progress in Applied Computational Electromagnetics*, Virginia, U.S., Mar. 2015.

[6] P. Nayeri, A. Z. Elsherbeni, and R. Haupt, "Broadband focusing using aperture-coupled microstrip patch array antennas," 9th *European Conference on Antennas & Propagation* (EuCAP 2015), Lisbon, Portugal, Apr. 2015.

[7] P. Nayeri, A. Z. Elsherbeni, and R. Haupt, "Phased array antenna limitations for ultra-wideband focusing," *IEEE International Conference on Antenna Measurements & Applications* (CAMA 2014), Antibes Juan-les-Pins, France, Nov. 2014.

[8] FEKO v 14.0, Altair Engineering, Inc.

A Multi-Linear Polarization Reconfigurable Plus Shaped Dipole Antenna for Wireless Energy Harvesting Applications

Ami Desai and Payam Nayeri

Electrical Engineering Department

Colorado School of Mines, Golden, CO 80401, USA

amiajaydesai@mymail.mines.edu, pnayeri@mines.edu

***Abstract*— A multi-linear polarization reconfigurable antenna consisting of a pair of printed dipole antennas with a plus shaped geometry is presented. The proposed design is based on the use of shorting pins and a coaxial feed network to obtain polarization reconfigurability. Specifically, two different polarization states have been obtained at 0° and 90°. Simulation results demonstrate a peak gain of 1.9 dBi at the center frequency. The proposed antenna is designed for 2.45 GHz and finds application in a variety of wireless energy harvesting and power transfer systems.**

Keywords—multi-linear polarization, polarization reconfigurable, printed dipole antenna, wireless energy harvesting, WLAN

I. INTRODUCTION

Polarization reconfigurable antennas have gained increasing attention due to their capabilities to improve the performance of communication systems, such as suppressing the fading losses caused by multipath effects and increasing the capacity of multiple input multiple-output systems [1]. To achieve the reconfigurability, mechanical [2], optical [3], or electronic [4] switches can be used. While many applications will benefit from circular polarization (CP), in general a linearly polarized signal received by a CP antenna will lose half the received power, hence for efficient wireless energy harvesting, linear polarization is more advantageous [5-6].

This paper presents a simple multilinear polarization-reconfigurable antenna. The antenna consists of a pair of printed dipoles forming a plus shaped configuration. One of the primary merits of the proposed antenna design is its simplicity. The antenna is designed for 2.45 GHz operation. Reconfigurable polarization is achieved by placing the shorting pin and coaxial feed network along x-axis for 0° polarization, while 90° polarization is obtained by placing the shorting pin and coaxial feed network along y-axis.

II. THE PRINTED DIPOLE ANTENNA

The geometry of a single printed dipole antenna is shown in Fig. 1. The dimensions for the substrate and ground plane are selected to be L_g = 62 mm and W_g = 10 mm, respectively. The radius of inner coaxial feed and the shorting pin are both 0.65 mm which is typical for panel mount SMA connectors. The width of the dipole arms (W) is set to 2 mm. A 62 mil Rogers Duroid 5880 laminate is used for the design (ε_r = 2.2, tan δ = 0.009), and analysis is conducted using Ansys HFSS [7].

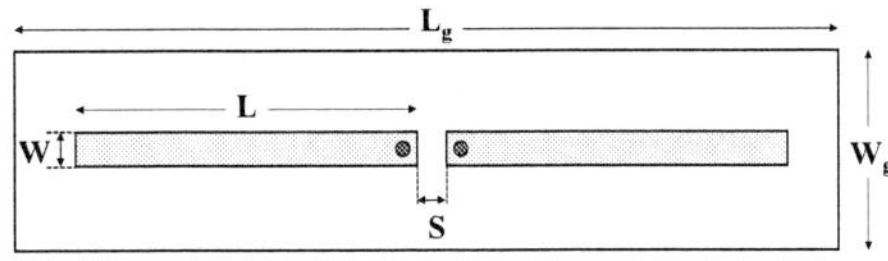

Fig. 1. Printed dipole antenna geometry.

Parametric studies are conducted to determine the optimal separation between the dipole arms (S) and length (L) of the dipole for 2.45 GHz operation. Fig. 2 shows $|S_{11}|$ as a function of frequency for different values of separation between the dipole arms with L = 27 mm. It can be seen that reducing the gap size results in a better matching. In practice however, smaller gap sizes will complicate the design of the plus shaped dipole which will be introduced in section III.

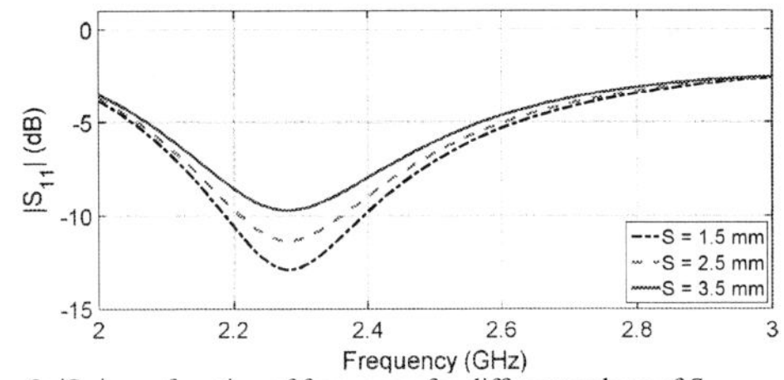

Fig. 2. $|S_{11}|$ as a function of frequency for different values of S.

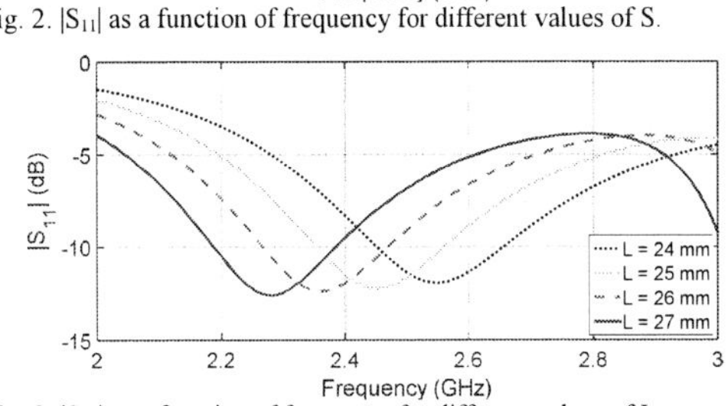

Fig. 3. $|S_{11}|$ as a function of frequency for different values of L.

A second parametric sweep is conducted on the dipole length to achieve the desired operating frequency of 2.45

GHz, while keeping the gap size S, equal to 2.5 mm . These results are given in Fig. 3, where it can be seen that the optimal length of L is 25 mm.

III. PLUS SHAPED POLARIZATION RECONFIGURABLE DIPOLE

Based on the above study on a single printed dipole antenna, different linear polarization configurations with desired angles can be obtained by creating more dipoles with rotated positions in the XY plane. The structure of the proposed plus shaped antenna is shown in Fig. 4, where two polarizations (0° and 90°) can be obtained. In this case, the ground plane is a square with a side length of 62 mm. The radius of coaxial feed and shorting pin are kept as before. Polarization in the x-direction (0°) is obtained by placing the feeding network along the X-axis while the polarization in the y-direction (90°) is obtained by placing the feed network along the Y-axis.

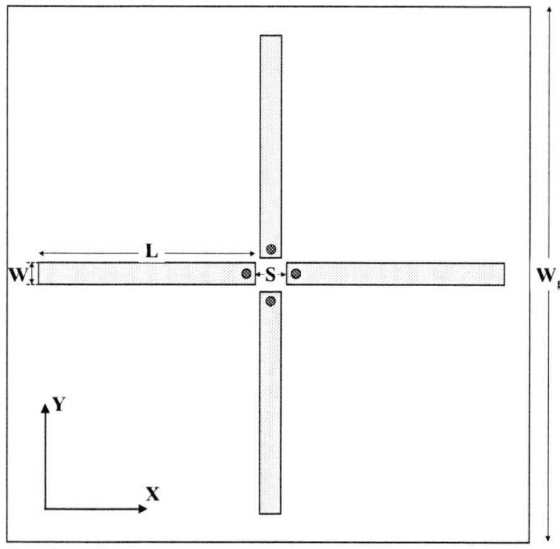

Fig. 4. Plus shaped antenna geometry.

Using the results from the previous section, the separation between the dipole arms (S) was set to 2.5 mm. Parametric studies on the length of the dipole arms (L) showed that the coupling between the two dipoles was not significant, thus the length of the dipole arms was kept at 25 mm. $|S_{11}|$ as a function of frequency along with the radiation patterns of the antenna at 2.45 GHz are given in Figs. 5 and 6 respectively. Due to symmetric nature of the antenna configuration, similar results are obtained for both polarizations. The electric surface currents on the dipole arms are also given in Fig. 7 for both polarizations.

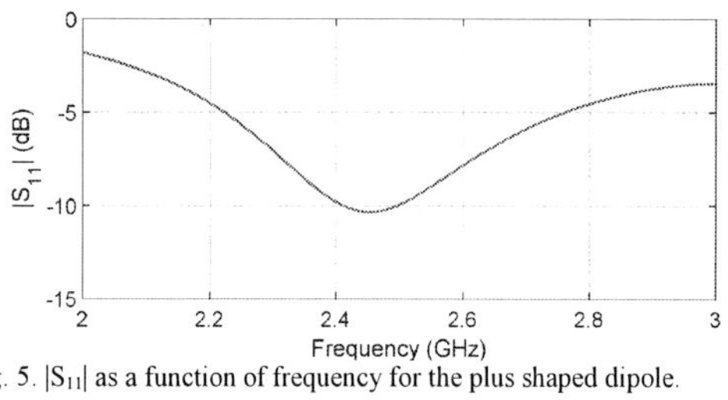

Fig. 5. $|S_{11}|$ as a function of frequency for the plus shaped dipole.

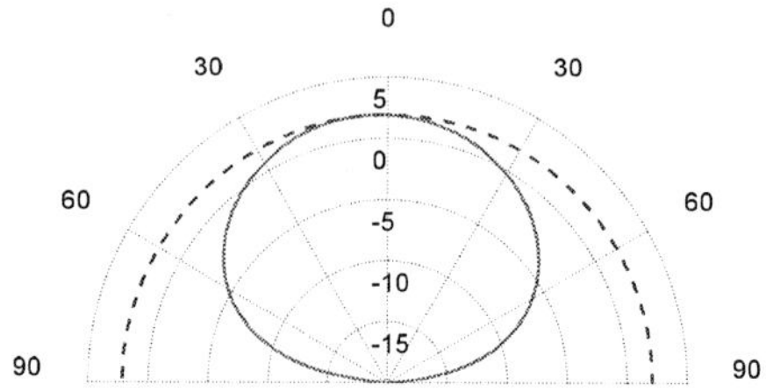

Fig. 6. Radiation pattern of the plus shaped antenna at 2.45 GHz. The solid red and dashed blue lines correspond to xz and yz planes, respectively.

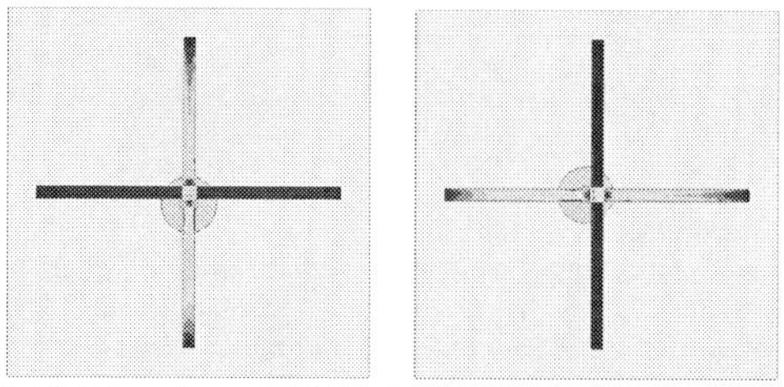

Fig. 7. Electric surface currents on the dipole arms for both polarization states at 2.45 GHz.

Electronic polarization reconfigurability can be achieved by using two pin diodes (SPST switches) in the feed network. Further discussion on electronic reconfiguration will be presented at the time of the conference.

IV. CONCLUSIONS

A multi-linear polarization reconfigurable antenna consisting of a pair of printed dipoles with a plus shaped configuration is demonstrated. A feed network consisting of two pairs of shorting pins and coaxial feeds is used to achieve reconfigurability. The proposed antenna is designed for 2.45 GHz operation in WLAN band and finds applications in wireless energy and power transfer systems.

REFERENCES

[1] M. K. Fries, M. Grani, and R. Vahldieck, "A reconfigurable slot antenna with switchable polarization," *IEEE Microw. Wireless Compon. Lett.*, vol. 13, pp. 490-492, Nov. 2003.

[2] G. Ruvio, M. J. Ammann, and Z. N. Chen, "Wideband reconfigurable rolled planar monopole antenna," *IEEE Transactions on Antennas and Propagation*, vol. 55, no. 6, pp. 1760–1767, Jun. 2007.

[3] C. J. Panagamuwa, A. C. Chauraya, and J. C. Vardaxoglou, "Frequency and beam reconfigurable antenna using photoconducting switches," *IEEE Transactions on Antennas and Propagation*, vol. 54, no. 2, pp. 449–454, Feb. 2006.

[4] S. Nikolaou, B. Kim, and P. Vryonides, "Reconfiguring antenna characteristics using PIN diodes," 3rd *European Conference on Antennas and Propagation* (EuCAP2009), Berlin, Germany, 2009.

[5] D. Schemmel and P. Nayeri, "A smart wireless energy harvesting system with adaptive beamforming and power management," *IEEE APS/USNC-URSI National Radio Science Meeting*, California, U.S., Jul. 2017.

[6] Z.-X. Yang, H.-C. Yang, J.-S. Hong, and Y. Li, "Bandwidth enhancement of a polarization-reconfigurable patch antenna with stair-slots on the ground," *IEEE Antennas Wireless Propag. Lett.*, vol. 13, pp. 579–592, 2014.

[7] Ansys HFSS, Ansys Inc, 2017.

Compact 24GHz Half-slot Antenna for Energy Combining

M. Aboualalaa[1,3], Adel B. Abdel-Rahman[1], and A. Allam[1]
[1]Electronics and Communications Engineering
[1]Egypt-Japan University of Science and Technology
Alexandria, Egypt
mohamed.ali@ejust.edu.eg

Ramesh K. Pokharel[2], Kuniaki Yoshitomi[2], and H. Elsadek[3]
[2]Electronics and Communications Engineering
[2]Kyushu University, Fukuoka, Japan
[3]Microstrip department
[3]Electronics Research Institute, Giza, Egypt

***Abstract*— A compact half-slot microstrip antenna is proposed in this paper. The antenna consists of microstrip line-fed half slot, and an open-circuited stub is connected to the microstrip feed line to adjust the matching at the operated frequency band. A half slot is used for miniaturization, as well as due to concentrating the field at only half slot; consequently, it decreases the resonance frequency and improves the antenna radiation characteristics. The antenna radiates at 24 GHz with measured fractional impedance bandwidth of 9%. The antenna gain at the resonant frequency is 5.2 dBi. The proposed antenna shows about 60% length reduction. Therefore, the proposed half slot antenna could be used for energy harvesting applications, at 24 GHz ISM band, due to its compact size with improved gain value. The proposed antenna was designed using ANSYS high-frequency structure simulator (HFSS). The simulated and measured results show good agreement.**

Keywords—Half-slot Antenna; ISM Band; Magnetic Wall; Open-circuited Stub; Rectenna; Slot antenna.

I. INTRODUCTION

The past few decades have witnessed dramatic development of wireless systems and low-power integrated electronic circuits, numerous research studies have been tended to study the possibility of powering these systems and circuits by the harvesting of RF ambient electromagnetic energy [1-3]. One of the most potential methods to harvest the RF energy is to use a rectenna (rectifying antenna). A rectenna mainly consists of a receiving antenna, filter, and a rectifying circuit. In this paper, the receiving antenna will be presented.

Broadly speaking, the RF input power level for energy harvesting circuits is slightly low. Consequently, various approaches have been proposed to cope with low input RF power. Many studies concentrate on the receiving antenna part to collect large input power as much as possible. Several studies have been using multiband antennas to harvest from different frequency bands [4], antennas with high gain also used with energy harvesters [5], EM wave and solar cell (SC) combinations [6], and rectenna arrays [7]. In this paper, a compact 24 GHz antenna is proposed for energy combining. Hence, this compact feature is very useful in rectenna array design to combine higher microwave power at 24 GHz ISM band.

In section II, the antenna configuration with geometrical parameters is illustrated. Antenna results (reflection and radiation characteristics) are discussed in section III. Conclusion is given in section V.

II. ANTENNA CONFIGURATION

Starting from conventional microstrip-fed rectangular slot antenna, with a magnetic wall at the slot center as shown in Fig 1 (a), our proposed design is introduced by using only a half slot fed by a microstrip line and open-circuited stub to adjust the antenna matching as shown in Fig. 1 (b). The antenna is simulated on a Rogers RT/Duroid 3003 substrate with a dielectric constant (ε_r) of 3, a thickness of 0.75 mm and a loss tangent (tan δ) of 0.0013. The antenna is compact not only owing to the use of half slot but also resulting from concentrating the current on only half slot that in turn decrease the operating frequency. The slot resonance frequency can be calculated from (1), where c is the speed of light in free space, and ε_{eff} is the effective dielectric constant for a slotline. Using half slot achives about 60% length reduction. Fig. 1 (b) and Fig. 1 (c) show the layout and the fabricated prototype of the proposed antenna, respectively; all geometrical parameters are illustrated in Fig. 1;

$$F = C/(Slot\ Length \times \sqrt{\varepsilon_{eff}}) \quad (1).$$

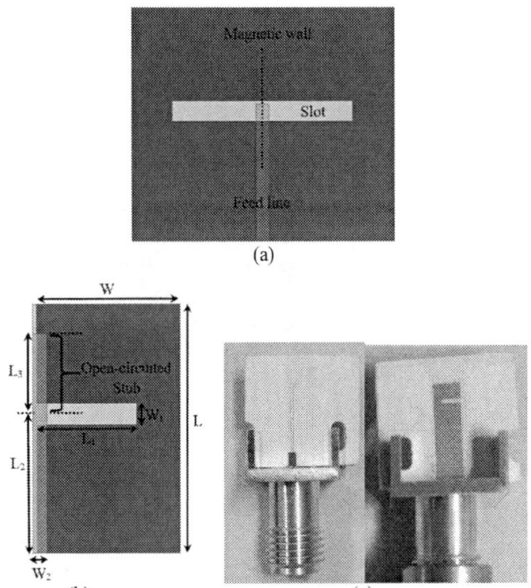

Fig. 1. The layout of the proposed antenna (a) slot antenna, (b) half slot geometry, and (c) photo of the fabricated prototype, L=3.4 mm, L_1=1.5 mm, L_2=2.1 mm, L_3=0.8 mm, W=2 mm, W_1=0.3 mm, W_2=0.2 mm.

III. Results and Discussion

A. Antenna Reflection Coefficient

Fig. 2 displays a good agreement between the simulated and measured return loss for the half slot antenna. As revealed from the figure, the antenna operates from 23.2 GHz to 25.4 GHz with impedance bandwidth of 2.2 GHz. The surface current distribution on the slot as well as half slot are shown in Figs. 4 (a) and 4 (b), respectively. The current is more concentrated on half slot than that of the full slot. Therefore, the resonant frequency is decreased. Fig. 3 illustrates the effect of the changing in the stub length on the antenna matching; stub length equal to 0.8 mm is chosen to achieve a good matching. The measurements are performed using the Agilent vector network analyzer (PNA-N5222A) which allows characterization up to 26.5 GHz. For soldering and connecting the connector, the feed line is extended in the fabricated prototype by $\lambda/2$, which in turn has a little effect on the measured results, where a K connector is used in the measurements.

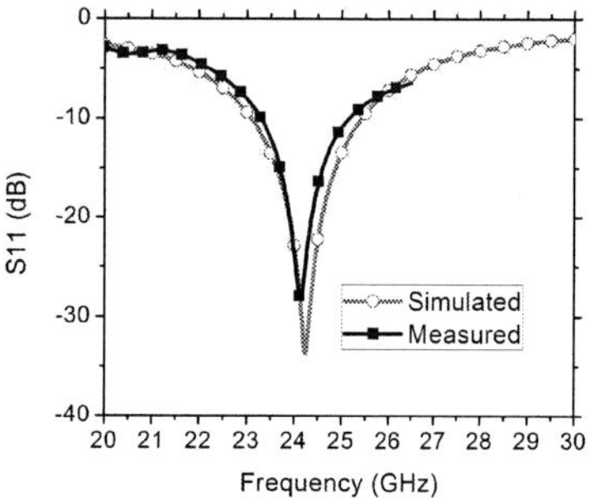

Fig. 2. Simulated and measured reflection coefficient.

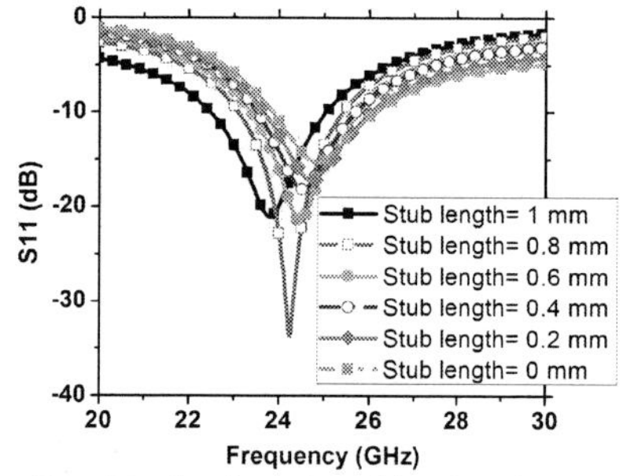

Fig. 3. The effect of the changing in the stub length on the antenna matching.

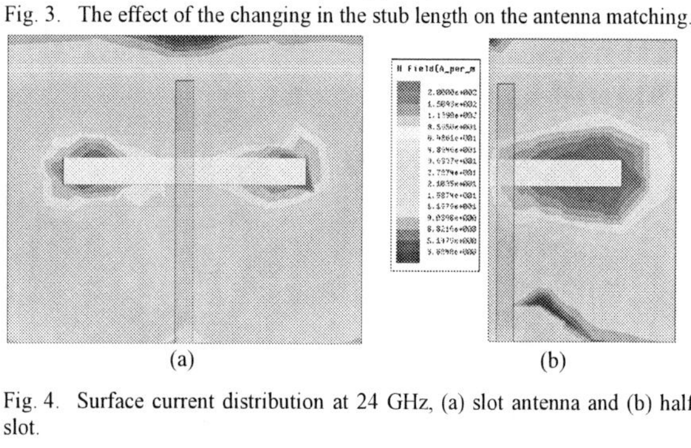

Fig. 4. Surface current distribution at 24 GHz, (a) slot antenna and (b) half slot.

This work is supported in part by a Grant-in-Aid for Scientific Research (C) (Grant No. JP 16K06301).

B. Radiation Characteristics

E-plane and H-plane at 24 GHz are shown in Fig. 5. The slot antenna shows the average gain about 3 dBi at 24 GHz, while the antenna gain in half slot case is around 5.2 dBi at the same frequency, this this due to confine the field in half slot. The antenna design has relatively stable radiation patterns over the whole frequency band, and the value of antenna radiation efficiency is around 90% over the operating frequency band.

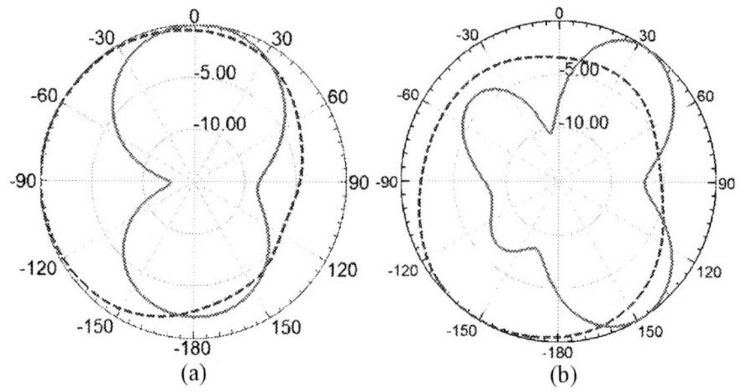

Fig. 5. E-plane "solid line", and H-plane "dashed line" at 24 GHz for (a) slot antenna and (b) half slot antenna.

IV. Conclusion

A compact 24 GHz half slot antenna with good radiation characteristics is presented in this paper. Due to the compact size and higher value of the antenna gain, compare with the conventional slot, it could be used in an antenna array for energy harvesting application to increase the harvested energy. The proposed receiving antenna operates at 24GHz with fractional bandwidth of 9%, antenna gain of 5.2 dBi, and average radiation efficiency of 90% over the frequency band.

References

[1] C. R. Valenta and G. D. Durgin, "Harvesting wireless power: Survey of energy-harvester conversion efficiency in far-field, wireless power transfer systems," IEEE Microw. Mag., vol. 15, no. 4, pp. 108–120, Jun. 2014.

[2] D. Pavone, A. Buonanno, M. D'Urso, and F. G. Corte, "Design considerations for radio frequency energy harvesting devices," Prog. Electromagn. Res. B, vol. 45, pp. 19–35, Jan. 2012.

[3] M. Arrawatia, M. S. Baghini, and G. Kumar, "Broadband bent triangular omnidirectional antenna for rf energy harvesting," *IEEE Antennas and Wireless Propag. Lett.*, vol. 15, pp. 36–39, Feb. 2016.

[4] V. Kuhn, C. Lahuec, F. Seguin, and C. Person, "A multi-band stacked RF energy harvester with RF-to-DC efficiency up to 84%," IEEE Trans. Microw. Theory Techn., vol. 63, no. 5, pp. 1768–1778, May 2015.

[5] M. Abou Al-alaa, A. B. Abdel-Rahman, A. Allam, H. A. Elsadek, and R. K. Pokharel, "Design of a dual-band microstrip antenna with enhanced gain for energy harvesting applications," IEEE Antennas and Wireless Propag. Lett., vol. 16, pp. 1622- 1626, 2017.

[6] A. Collado and A. Georgiadis, "Conformal hybrid solar and electromagnetic (EM) energy harvesting rectenna," in *IEEE Transact. on Circuits and Systems I*, vol. 60, no. 8, pp. 2225-2234, Aug. 2013.

[7] U. Olgun, C.-C. Chen, and J. L. Volakis, "Investigation of rectenna array configurations for enhanced RF power harvesting," IEEE Antenna Wireless Propag. Lett., vol. 10, pp. 262–265, 2011.

Analysis of Two/Four Coils WPT Systems for Embedded PLC Communications

Sami Barmada and Mauro Tucci
DESTEC
University of Pisa
Pisa, Italy
sami.barmada@unipi.it

Abstract—**In this contribution the authors investigate the possibility of improving the performances of a coupled Wireless Power Transfer (WPT) - Power Line Communications (PLC) system in case the WPT system is characterised by a four coils structure. The main idea is to use the so-called transmitting and receiving coil (the two "inner" coils) as access point for the PLC modems and use the drive and load loops (the two "outer" coils) as usual access point for power. The simulations results show that a higher wider band for communication is achieved with respect the previously proposed system.**

I. Introduction

Wireless Power Transfer (WPT) technology has lately gained a lot of attention as an alternative way to transmit power with respect to a cabled connection, see for instance [1]. In the last decade, Power Line Communication (PLC) has been recognised as a viable option for broadband communications. PLC technology uses power cables (where power is typically delivered at $50/60Hz$) to transmit high speed data; PLC communication is now considered one of the main possibility to transmit data in a smart grid environment (when, for instance, long distances do not allow wireless data transmission).

As an example, [2] shows how PLC can be used in the smart grid environment with special attention dedicated to home appliances and plug-in electric vehicles.

These two technologies are apparently colliding, since WPT transfers power wirelessly while PLC transmits data on a cabled connection originally designed for power. This has led the authors to the idea that a full integration between WPT and PLC could be a solution allowing the use of WPT without the need of changes to the pre-existing PLC system. In [3] a feasibility study of such system is proposed, in which a preliminary logic outline of the whole system is shown and the evaluation of the available channel capacity is performed based on a typical four coils system. In [4] an optimization procedure performed on the lumped equivalent circuit is presented, showing that such system can be properly designed taking into account both power and data transmission requirements. In addition, in [5] the full system (with coils and filters) have been designed and built showing the actual feasibility of the proposal.

[5] is specifically referring to a two coils WPT system, while in this contribution the authors investigate the possibility of using the inner coils as access points for data transmission retaining the usual access point for the power (i.e. the "outer coils").

II. Evaluation of the Theoretical Channel Capacity for Four Coils Systems

Fig. 1 shows the typical four coils WPT system with the drive and load loops (where the source and the load are connected) and the transmitting and receiving coils, that are used in order to increase the transmission distance (reducing k_{23}) retaining maximum power transfer. The inner coils have no access point and are often mounted on the same equipment as the relative loop.

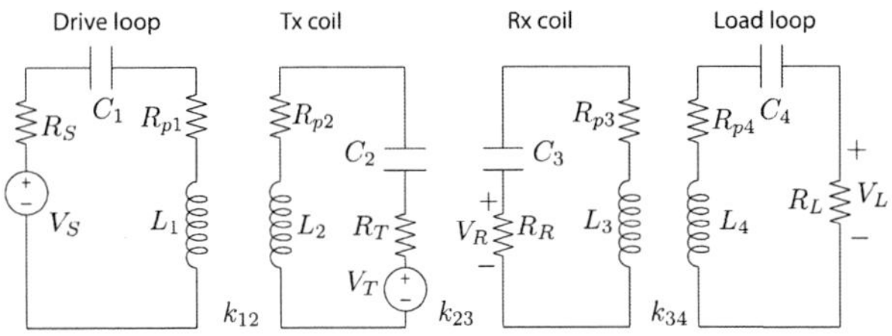

Fig. 1. Four coils equivalent.

Equations (1) and (2) show the transfer function between the load and the power source, with $R_R = R_T = V_T = 0$, i.e., with the system in its standard WPT state.

Equations (3) and (4) show the transfer function between the data receiver R_R and the data source V_T, in which the load and source resistances R_S and R_L are not excluded since data and power transmission take place at the same time. The reason why R_R and R_T are, on the contrary, excluded from the circuit in the previous evaluation comes from the fact that a filter to be placed on the coil is needed, with the aim of excluding the power dissipation at the resonant frequency of the power transfer:

$$\frac{\dot{V}_L}{\dot{V}_S} = R_L \frac{j\omega^3 k_{12} k_{23} k_{34} L_2 L_3 \sqrt{L_1 L_4}}{A\omega^4 + B\omega^2 + C}, \tag{1}$$

with

$$
\begin{aligned}
A &= k_{12}^2 k_{34}^2 L_1 L_2 L_3 L_4 \\
B &= k_{12}^2 L_1 L_2 \bar{Z}_3 \bar{Z}_4 + k_{23}^2 L_2 L_3 \bar{Z}_1 \bar{Z}_4 + k_{34}^2 L_3 L_4 \bar{Z}_1 \bar{Z}_2 \\
C &= \bar{Z}_1 \bar{Z}_2 \bar{Z}_3 \bar{Z}_4 \\
\bar{Z}_1 &= R_{p1} + R_S + j\omega L_1 - \frac{j}{\omega C_1} \\
\bar{Z}_2 &= R_{p2} + j\omega L_2 - \frac{j}{\omega C_2} \\
\bar{Z}_3 &= R_{p3} + j\omega L_3 - \frac{j}{\omega C_3} \\
\bar{Z}_4 &= R_{p4} + R_L + j\omega L_4 - \frac{j}{\omega C_4},
\end{aligned} \tag{2}
$$

$$
\frac{\dot{V}_R}{\dot{V}_T} = R_R \frac{j\omega k_{23} \bar{Z}_1 \bar{Z}_4 \sqrt{L_2 L_2}}{A\omega^4 + B\omega^2 + C}, \tag{3}
$$

with

$$
\begin{aligned}
A &= k_{12}^2 k_{34}^2 L_1 L_2 L_3 L_4 \\
B &= k_{12}^2 L_1 L_2 \bar{Z}_{3b} \bar{Z}_4 + k_{23}^2 L_2 L_3 \bar{Z}_1 \bar{Z}_4 + k_{34}^2 L_3 L_4 \bar{Z}_1 \bar{Z}_{2b} \\
C &= \bar{Z}_1 \bar{Z}_{2b} \bar{Z}_{3b} \bar{Z}_4 \\
\bar{Z}_{2b} &= R_{p2} + R_T + j\omega L_2 - \frac{j}{\omega C_2} \\
\bar{Z}_{3b} &= R_{p3} + R_S + j\omega L_3 - \frac{j}{\omega C_3}.
\end{aligned} \tag{4}
$$

TABLE I
CIRCUIT PARAMETERS.

Element	Unit	Value
$R_S = R_L = R_R = R_T$	Ω	50
$L_1 = L_4$	μH	1.0
$L_2 = L_3$	μH	20.0
$C_1 = C_4$	pF	235.0
$C_2 = C_3$	pF	12.6
$R_{p1} = R_{p4}$	Ω	0.25
$R_{p2} = R_{p3}$	Ω	1.0
$k_{12} = k_{34}$		0.1
k_{23}		$10^{-4} < k_{23} < 0.8$
f_0	MHz	10

The above equations have been evaluated for a circuit model whose parameters are reported in Table I; Fig. 2 shows the maximum value of the transfer function (for inner and outer access point) as a function of the coupling coefficient, while 3 shows the channel capacity (evaluated with a signal to noise ratio equal to 1) as a function of the coupling coefficient.

It is evident that from the power transfer point of view (i.e., maximum value of S_{21}) the usual power configuration (access point from the outer coils) outperforms the other one; on the contrary, taking into account the channel capacity (depending on the transfer function bandwidth), we can verify that access from the inner coils guarantees better performances for a wide range of k_{23} values.

III. CONCLUSION

The proposed study shows how a different selection of the access point of PLC modems in a four coils WPT system can increase bandwidth and offer better data transmission performances.

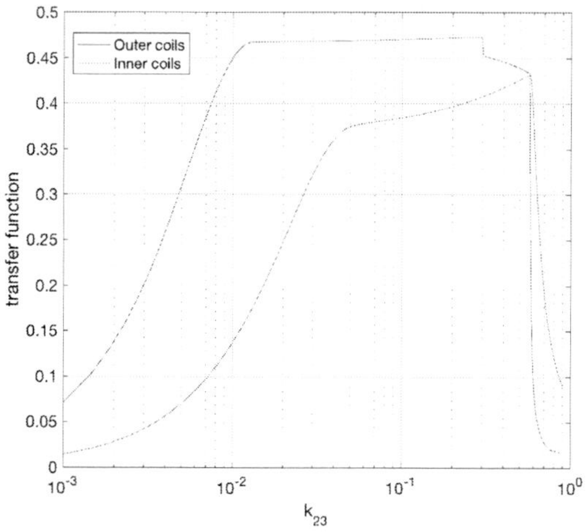

Fig. 2. Comparison between the maximum value of the transfer function.

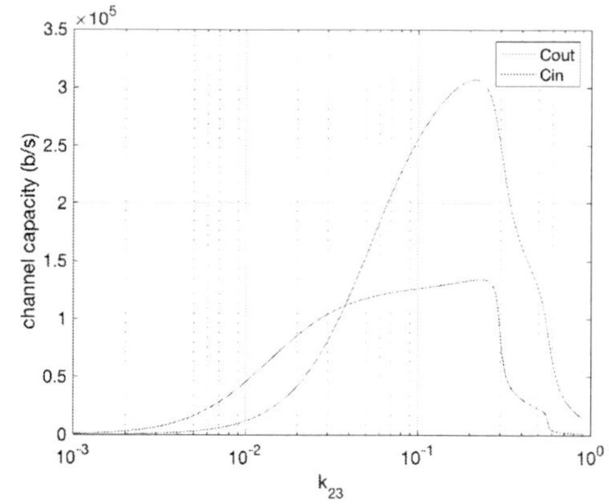

Fig. 3. Comparison between the channel capacity (S/N = 1).

REFERENCES

[1] A. Kurs, A. Karalis, R. Moffatt, J. Joannopoulos, P. Fisher, and M. Soljacic,: "Wireless power transfer via strongly coupled magnetic resonances", Science, vol. 317, no. 5834, pp. 83-86, Jul. 2007.

[2] S. Barmada, M. Tucci, M. Raugi, Y. Maryanka, and O. Amrani,: "PLC Systems for Electric Vehicles and Smart Grid Applications", Proceedings of IEEE International Symposium of Powerline Communications and its Applications (ISPLC), Johannesburg, South Africa, 2013, pp. 23 - 28.

[3] S. Barmada, M. Raugi, M. Tucci,: "Power line communication integrated in a Wireless Power Transfer system: A feasibility study", Proceedings of IEEE International Symposium of Powerline Communications and its Applications (ISPLC), Glasgow, UK, 2014, pp. 116 - 120.

[4] S. Barmada, M. Tucci,: "Optimization of a Magnetically Coupled Resonators System for Power Line Communication Integration", Proceedings of the IEEE Wireless Power Transfer Conference (WPTC), Boulder, CO, USA, 2015, pp. 1 - 4

[5] S. Barmada, M. Dionigi, P. Mezzanotte, M. Tucci,: "Design and Experimental Characterization of a Combined WPT - PLC System", Wireless Power Transfer, Cambridge, Vol. 4, No. 2, pp. 160 - 170, 2017.

On the Conforming Combination of the Electric and Magnetic Field Integral Equations

Ahmet F. Yilmaz and H. Arda Ülkü
Department of Electronics Engineering
Gebze Technical University
Gebze, Kocaeli, 41400, Turkey
{a.yilmaz, haulku}@gtu.edu.tr

***Abstract*—A scheme to conformingly combine the electric and magnetic field integral equations (EFIE and MFIE) is presented. Particularly the range space of the method of moments (MoM) matrix system for the mixed discretized MFIE is projected to the range space of the classically discretized EFIE and then combined with EFIE. As a result, an accurate, interior resonance free, and ideally combination factor independent matrix system for the combined field integral equation (CFIE) is obtained. Numerical examples that demonstrate the accuracy and combination factor dependence are presented.**

***Index Terms*—combined field integral equation (CFIE), interior resonance problem, mixed discretization**

I. Introduction

The dependence of the accuracy of the combined field integral equation (CFIE) to the combination factor has been a problem [1]–[4]. Conventionally, EFIE, MFIE and CFIE are discretized using the divergence conforming Rao-Wilton-Glisson (RWG) functions as the testing and basis functions, which is called the classically discretized CFIE (C-CFIE). It is shown in [5] that the accuracy of MFIE is limited due to this discretization scheme because the conforming testing is not satisfied. This problem can be remedied using the curl conforming Buffa-Christiansen-Chen-Wilton (BCCW) functions [6], [7] for testing, which is called the mixed discretization of MFIE. Based on the mixed discretization scheme, combining the classically discretized EFIE and mixed discretized MFIE, which is called mixed CFIE (M-CFIE) in this work, is proposed in [2]. The solution of M-CFIE provides more accurate results compared to C-CFIE, however due to the nonconformity of the testing function (range) spaces of EFIE and MFIE, the resulting matrix system supports interior resonances [3], [4].

In this work, an alternative formulation of CFIE that is obtained by conformingly combining the classically discretized EFIE and mixed discretized MFIE is presented. This formulation is originally developed in [4] and applied to the marching on-in-time solution of the time domain integral equations. In this work, the same approach is applied to the MoM solution of CFIE and two implementations are presented and compared. First, the range function space of the mixed discretized MFIE, i.e., curl conforming BCCW function space, is projected onto the range function space of the classical discretization of EFIE, i.e., divergence conforming RWG function space, and then combined with EFIE. This implementation is called the conforming CFIE via range space projection (RSP-CFIE). As the second implementation, the range space projection is directly formulated as an auxiliary equation and the resulting equation system that doubles the unknowns is solved. This implementation is called the conforming CFIE via auxiliary equation (AE-CFIE). A scheme similar to the latter implementation is presented in [3] where the magnetic and electric currents are used and the combination factor should be 0.5.

II. Formulation

Let S denote the surface of a perfect electrically conducting (PEC) scatterer and the current induced on S is modelled using the RWG functions $\mathbf{f}_n(\mathbf{r})$: $\mathbf{J}(\mathbf{r}) = \sum_{n=1}^{N} \{\mathbf{I}\}_n \mathbf{f}_n(\mathbf{r})$, where $\mathbf{I}$ holds the unknown coefficients. Substituting this expansion in EFIE and MFIE, and testing the resulting equations yield the MoM matrix systems where $\bar{\mathbf{Z}}_{\mathbf{f}}^{\mathrm{E}}$ and $\bar{\mathbf{Z}}_{\hat{\mathbf{n}}\times\mathbf{g}}^{\mathrm{H}}$ are the MoM matrices, and $\mathbf{V}_{\mathbf{f}}^{\mathrm{E}}$ and $\mathbf{V}_{\hat{\mathbf{n}}\times\mathbf{g}}^{\mathrm{H}}$ are the vectors of the tested electric and magnetic fields for classically discretized EFIE and mixed discretized MFIE. The elements of $\bar{\mathbf{Z}}_{\mathbf{f}}^{\mathrm{E}}$, $\bar{\mathbf{Z}}_{\hat{\mathbf{n}}\times\mathbf{g}}^{\mathrm{H}}$, $\mathbf{V}_{\mathbf{f}}^{\mathrm{E}}$, and $\mathbf{V}_{\hat{\mathbf{n}}\times\mathbf{g}}^{\mathrm{H}}$ are:

$$\{\bar{\mathbf{Z}}_{\mathbf{f}}^{\mathrm{E}}\}_{m,n} = \langle \mathbf{f}_m(\mathbf{r}), \mathcal{T}\{\mathbf{f}_n(\mathbf{r})\}\rangle, \tag{1}$$

$$\{\bar{\mathbf{Z}}_{\hat{\mathbf{n}}\times\mathbf{g}}^{\mathrm{H}}\}_{m,n} = \langle \hat{\mathbf{n}}(\mathbf{r}) \times \mathbf{g}_m(\mathbf{r}), \mathcal{K}\{\mathbf{f}_n(\mathbf{r})\}\rangle, \tag{2}$$

$$\{\mathbf{V}_{\mathbf{f}}^{\mathrm{E}}\}_m = \langle \mathbf{f}_m(\mathbf{r}), \mathbf{E}^{\mathrm{inc}}(\mathbf{r})\rangle, \tag{3}$$

$$\{\mathbf{V}_{\hat{\mathbf{n}}\times\mathbf{g}}^{\mathrm{H}}\}_m = \langle \hat{\mathbf{n}}(\mathbf{r}) \times \mathbf{g}_m(\mathbf{r}), \hat{\mathbf{n}}(\mathbf{r}) \times \mathbf{H}^{\mathrm{inc}}(\mathbf{r})\rangle, \tag{4}$$

where $\langle \mathbf{a}(\mathbf{r}), \mathbf{b}(\mathbf{r})\rangle = \int \mathbf{a}(\mathbf{r}) \cdot \mathbf{b}(\mathbf{r}) d\mathbf{r}$, $\mathbf{E}^{\mathrm{inc}}(\mathbf{r})$ and $\mathbf{H}^{\mathrm{inc}}(\mathbf{r})$ are the incident electric and magnetic field intensities, $\hat{\mathbf{n}}(\mathbf{r})$ is the unit normal vector of S, and $\hat{\mathbf{n}}(\mathbf{r}) \times \mathbf{g}_m(\mathbf{r})$ is the curl conforming BCCW functions. Operators $\mathcal{T}\{\cdot\}$ and $\mathcal{K}\{\cdot\}$ are defined as:

$$\mathcal{T}\{\mathbf{f}_n(\mathbf{r})\} = \frac{-j\omega\mu_0}{4\pi} \int_{S_n} \mathbf{f}_n(\mathbf{r}') \frac{e^{-jkR}}{R} d\mathbf{r}' + \frac{1}{4\pi j\omega\varepsilon_0} \nabla \int_{S_n} \nabla' \cdot \mathbf{f}_n(\mathbf{r}') \frac{e^{-jkR}}{R} d\mathbf{r}', \tag{5}$$

$$\mathcal{K}\{\mathbf{f}_n(\mathbf{r})\} = \frac{1}{2}\mathbf{f}_n(\mathbf{r}) - \hat{\mathbf{n}}(\mathbf{r}) \times \nabla \times \int_{S_n} \mathbf{f}_n(\mathbf{r}') \frac{e^{-jkR}}{R} d\mathbf{r}'. \tag{6}$$

Here $R = |\mathbf{r} - \mathbf{r}'|$ is the distance between the observation point $\mathbf{r}$, and the source point $\mathbf{r}'$, μ_0 and ε_0 are the permeability and permittivity of the background medium, $k = 2\pi f\sqrt{\varepsilon_0\mu_0}$, and f is the frequency.

To project the function space, the range of the MFIE operator acting on the discretized current density is assumed to be expanded by RWG functions:

$$\sum_{n=1}^{N} \mathcal{K}\{\mathbf{f}_n(\mathbf{r})\}\{\mathbf{I}\}_n \approx \sum_{m=1}^{N} \mathbf{f}_m(\mathbf{r})\{\mathbf{b}\}_m. \quad (7)$$

Testing (7) with the curl conforming BCCW functions $\hat{\mathbf{n}}(\mathbf{r}) \times \mathbf{g}_m(\mathbf{r})$, results in a matrix equation and the coefficients of the range space projected MFIE operator $\mathbf{b}$ found as:

$$\mathbf{b} = \bar{\mathbf{G}}^{-1}_{\hat{\mathbf{n}}\times\mathbf{g},\mathbf{f}} \bar{\mathbf{Z}}^{\mathrm{H}}_{\hat{\mathbf{n}}\times\mathbf{g}} \mathbf{I}, \quad (8)$$

where the element of the Gram matrix $\{\bar{\mathbf{G}}_{\hat{\mathbf{n}}\times\mathbf{g},\mathbf{f}}\}_{m,n} = \langle \hat{\mathbf{n}} \times \mathbf{g}_m(\mathbf{r}), \mathbf{f}_n(\mathbf{r})\rangle$ [6]. The same procedure can be repeated for the tested magnetic field. Then the expansion at the right hand side of (7) can be combined with EFIE as

$$\begin{aligned} \mathbf{V}^{\mathrm{C}} &= -\alpha\bar{\mathbf{Z}}^{\mathrm{E}}_{\mathbf{f}}\mathbf{I} + \eta_0(1-\alpha)\bar{\mathbf{G}}_{\mathbf{f},\mathbf{f}}\mathbf{b} \quad (9) \\ &= [-\alpha\bar{\mathbf{Z}}^{\mathrm{E}}_{\mathbf{f}} + \eta_0(1-\alpha)\bar{\mathbf{G}}_{\mathbf{f},\mathbf{f}}\bar{\mathbf{G}}^{-1}_{\hat{\mathbf{n}}\times\mathbf{g},\mathbf{f}}\bar{\mathbf{Z}}^{\mathrm{H}}_{\hat{\mathbf{n}}\times\mathbf{g}}]\mathbf{I}, \end{aligned}$$

where, $\mathbf{V}^{\mathrm{C}} = -\alpha\mathbf{V}^{\mathrm{E}}_{\mathbf{f}} + \eta_0(1-\alpha)\bar{\mathbf{G}}_{\mathbf{f},\mathbf{f}}\bar{\mathbf{G}}^{-1}_{\hat{\mathbf{n}}\times\mathbf{g},\mathbf{f}}\mathbf{V}^{\mathrm{H}}_{\hat{\mathbf{n}}\times\mathbf{g}}$, η_0 is the intrinsic impedance and α is the combination factor of CFIE. The element of the Gram matrix $\{\bar{\mathbf{G}}_{\mathbf{f},\mathbf{f}}\}_{m,n} = \langle \mathbf{f}_m(\mathbf{r}), \mathbf{f}_n(\mathbf{r})\rangle$. (9) provides range function space conformity for the combination of EFIE and MFIE (RSP-CFIE). In addition this formulation eliminates the interior resonance problem and solution of (9) is less dependent to the combination factor. However, solution of (9) using an iterative solver requires nested matrix solver calls: one for $\bar{\mathbf{G}}^{-1}_{\hat{\mathbf{n}}\times\mathbf{g},\mathbf{f}}$, one for the resulting matrix system in (9). Even though the $\bar{\mathbf{G}}_{\hat{\mathbf{n}}\times\mathbf{g},\mathbf{f}}$ is well-conditioned and sparse, the nested operations might cause saturation in the error of the iterative solver. Instead of solving (9) directly, the first line in (9) as the range space conforming CFIE and matrix equation in (8) as the auxiliary equation can be combined in a single matrix system (AE-CFIE):

$$\begin{bmatrix} \mathbf{V}^{\mathrm{C}} \\ 0 \end{bmatrix} = \begin{bmatrix} \bar{\mathbf{G}}_{\mathbf{f},\mathbf{f}} & -\alpha\bar{\mathbf{Z}}^{\mathrm{E}}_{\mathbf{f}} \\ \bar{\mathbf{G}}_{\hat{\mathbf{n}}\times\mathbf{g},\mathbf{f}} & -\eta_0(1-\alpha)\bar{\mathbf{Z}}^{\mathrm{H}}_{\hat{\mathbf{n}}\times\mathbf{g}} \end{bmatrix} \begin{bmatrix} \mathbf{b} \\ \mathbf{I} \end{bmatrix}. \quad (10)$$

This implementation doubles the unknowns, yet eliminates the nested matrix solver calls. In addition the matrix structure in (10) can be easily diagonally preconditioned.

III. Numerical Results

In this section a unit sphere discretized with 2430 RWG basis functions is analyzed to demonstrate the accuracy of the proposed scheme. An $\hat{\mathbf{x}}$ polarized plane wave propagating in $\hat{\mathbf{z}}$ direction is used as the excitation. A TFQMR iterative solver is employed to solve the MoM matrix systems. The tolerance is set to 10^{-10}. Note that for AE-CFIE the iterative solver saturates around 10^{-7} without reaching to 10^{-10}. In all figures, RMS errors are determined using the scattered electric fields in the far field obtained by the MoM solution and Mie series solution for $\theta \in [0, 180]^\circ$ and $\phi = 0^\circ$.

Fig. 1 plots the RMS error at $f = 130$ MHz for different values of the combination factor α. It is seen that the error values for RSP-CFIE (9) and AE-CFIE (10) are coinciding and do not vary drastically compared to the errors for C-CFIE and M-CFIE. Fig. 2 plots the RMS error for different frequencies. In this case the frequency is swept from 100 MHz to 200 MHz range and combination factor $\alpha = 0.5$. It is seen from Fig. 2 that the RSP-CFIE and AE-CFIE are resonance free and provide more accurate results. Although M-CFIE provides more accurate results than C-CFIE, solution is affected by interior resonances around 131 MHz and 186 MHz.

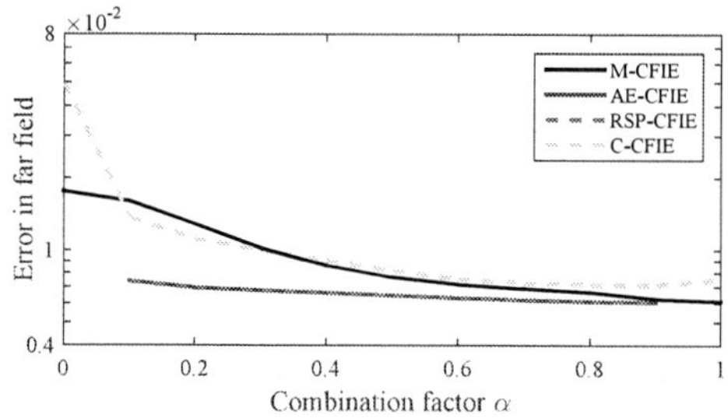

Fig. 1. The RMS error with respect to combination factor.

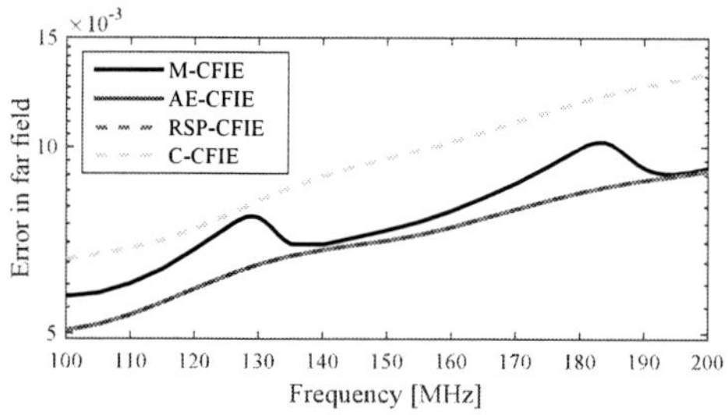

Fig. 2. The RMS error with respect to frequency.

Acknowledgement

This work is supported by the Scientific and Technical Research Council of Turkey (TUBITAK) under the Grant No. EEEAG-116E290.

References

[1] L. Gurel and O. Ergul, "Contamination of the accuracy of the combined-field integral equation with the discretization error of the magnetic-field integral equation," IEEE Trans. Antennas Propag., vol. 57, pp. 2650–2657, Sep. 2009.

[2] S. Yan, J. M. Jin, and Z. Nie, "Improving the accuracy of the second-kind Fredholm integral equations by using the Buffa-Christiansen functions," IEEE Trans. Antennas Propag., vol. 59, pp. 1299–1310, Apr. 2011.

[3] J. Kornprobst and T. F. Eibert, "An accurate combined source integral equation for perfect electrically conducting bodies," in Proc. IEEE Int. Symp. on Antennas and Propagation, pp. 1457–1458, July 2017.

[4] Y. Beghein *et al.*, "A space-time mixed Galerkin marching-on-in-time scheme for the time-domain combined field integral equation," IEEE Trans. Antennas Propag., vol. 61, pp. 1228–1238, Mar. 2013.

[5] K. Cools, F. P. Andriulli, D. D. Zutter, and E. Michielssen, "Accurate and conforming mixed discretization of the MFIE," IEEE Antennas Wireless Propag. Lett., vol. 10, pp. 528–531, 2011.

[6] F. P. Andriulli *et al.*, "A multiplicative Calderon preconditioner for the electric field integral equation," IEEE Trans. Antennas Propag., vol. 56, pp. 2398–2412, Aug. 2008.

[7] Q. Chen and D. R. Wilton, "Electromagnetic scattering by three-dimensional arbitrary complex material/conducting bodies," in Proc. IEEE Int. Symp. on Antennas and Propagation, pp. 590–593, vol.2, May 1990.

Coupled EM-Structural Analysis in Convected Coordinates

Daniel S. Weile
Department of Electrical and Computer Engineering
University of Delaware
Newark, DE 19711, USA
weile@udel.edu

David A. Hopkins and Brian M. Powers
RDRL-WMM-B
Army Research Laboratory, APG
Aberdeen, MD 21005, USA
david.a.hopkins.civ@mail.mil
brian.m.powers.civ@mail.mil

Abstract—**The form of Maxwell's equations when expressed in material coordinates has been debated for decades. The most commonly accepted formulation is known to be inconsistent, even to first order approximation. It has been shown that self-consistent formulations are possible when convected coordinates are used. In this presentation, we review these formulations. We then demonstrate their use in solving for the coupled EM/Structural response of a simple parallel plate capacitor bent into an arc.**

I. Introduction

The analysis of the response of structures to electromagnetically induced loads, and the converse problem of the effect of structural deformation upon electromagnetic fields are of fundamental interest. Numerous theories have been presented for the proper form of the equations [1], [2], [3], [4]. These theories all reduce to the same form for infinitesimal deformations. For finite deformations, they do not. In an earlier paper [5], we presented a theory based on the use of convected coordinates. We showed that the discrepancies arose from the failure to properly consider the role of relativity in the formulation of the transformations. Here we first provide a brief review of the convected coordinates approach. We then illustrate the utility of this approach by solving a simple coupled EM/Structural problem.

II. Convected Coordinates

Fundamental to continuum mechanics is the necessity of defining the relative motion of different parts of a deformable body [6]. The standard approach is to specify the current configuration of the body at some time t in the spatial (or *Eulerian*) frame in terms of the reference (or *Lagrangian*) coordinates which specify the initial configuration of the body. In [5], we showed that this relationship can be expressed, in Minkowski space-time by:

$$x^\alpha = \chi^\alpha(ct, X^I), \tag{1}$$

where $\alpha = 0,1,2,3$, x^0 is the time coordinate, $x^i, i = 1,2,3$ are the spatial coordinates, and $X^I, i = 1,2,3$ are the material coordinates. All of these coordinates have dimensions of length, with the time in seconds multiplied by the speed of light. Assuming the mapping is bijective, the inverse mapping exists. The mapping from spatial to convective coordinates $\tilde{x}$ is given by:

$$\tilde{x}^\alpha = \tilde{\chi}(x^\alpha). \tag{2}$$

In convective coordinates $\tilde{x}^I = X^I$ for $I \in \{1,2,3\}$. By choosing different forms of the time coordinate mapping, the transformations between the spatial and the convected electromagnetic variables can be expressed by either an asymmetric law (for a universal time mapping), or a symmetric law (time orthogonal mapping). Failure to recognize the consequences of this choice (or to properly reconcile mechanics and electromagnetics with relativity theory) accounts for the disparate theories previously presented.

In this notational system, a contravariant relativistic four-vector can be given by $v^\alpha, \alpha \in \{0,1,2,3\}$, and its length $|v|$ computed as:

$$|v|^2 = g_{\alpha\beta} v^\alpha v^\beta, \tag{3}$$

where summation on the right is implied by the usual Einstein convention.

The metric tensor expressed in convected coordinates is:

$$\tilde{g}_{\tilde{\alpha}\tilde{\beta}} = \frac{\partial x^\alpha}{\partial \tilde{x}^{\tilde{\alpha}}} \frac{\partial x^\beta}{\partial \tilde{x}^{\tilde{\beta}}} \eta_{\alpha\beta}, \tag{4}$$

where $\eta_{\alpha\beta}$ is the Minkowski metric with signature $(+---)$. The determinant of the metric is $\tilde{g} \doteq \det(\tilde{g}_{\tilde{\alpha}\tilde{\beta}})$.

III. Governing Equations

In convective coordinates, the Ampere-Maxwell-Gauss law is:

$$\frac{1}{\sqrt{-\tilde{g}}} \frac{\partial}{\partial \tilde{x}^{\tilde{\beta}}} (\sqrt{-\tilde{g}} \tilde{m}^{\tilde{\beta}\tilde{\alpha}}) = \tilde{j}^{\tilde{\alpha}}, \tag{5}$$

where the antisymmetric displacement tensor $\tilde{m}_{\tilde{\alpha}\tilde{\beta}}$ is given by:

$$\tilde{m}^{\tilde{i}0} = \frac{c\tilde{d}^{\tilde{i}}}{\sqrt{\tilde{g}_{00}}}, \tag{6}$$

$$\tilde{m}^{\tilde{i}\tilde{k}} = -\frac{\epsilon^{\tilde{i}\tilde{k}\tilde{l}} \tilde{h}_{\tilde{l}}}{\sqrt{-\tilde{g}}}, \tag{7}$$

where $\tilde{d}^{\tilde{i}}$ is the electric displacement, $\tilde{h}_{\tilde{i}}$ is the magnetic field and c is the speed of light as usual. The standard four current is represented by $\tilde{j}^{\tilde{\alpha}}$ [5].

The Faraday-Gauss Law in convective coordinates is:

$$\frac{\partial \tilde{n}_{\tilde{\alpha}\tilde{\beta}}}{\partial \tilde{x}^{\tilde{\theta}}} + \frac{\partial \tilde{n}_{\tilde{\beta}\tilde{\theta}}}{\partial \tilde{x}^{\tilde{\alpha}}} + \frac{\partial \tilde{n}_{\tilde{\theta}\tilde{\alpha}}}{\partial \tilde{x}^{\tilde{\beta}}} = 0, \tag{8}$$

where the electromagnetic tensor $\tilde{n}_{\tilde{\alpha}\tilde{\beta}}$ is:

$$\tilde{n}_{0\tilde{k}} = \frac{\tilde{e}_{\tilde{k}}}{c}, \tag{9}$$

$$\tilde{n}_{\tilde{i}\tilde{k}} = -\sqrt{\tilde{\mathrm{g}}}\,\epsilon_{\tilde{i}\tilde{k}\tilde{l}}\tilde{b}^{\tilde{l}}, \tag{10}$$

and $\tilde{\mathrm{g}}$ is the determinant of the normalized spatial metric given by $\tilde{\mathrm{g}}_{\tilde{i}\tilde{k}} = \tilde{g}_{\tilde{i}}\tilde{g}_{\tilde{k}} - \tilde{g}_{\tilde{i}\tilde{k}}$, and $\tilde{g}_{\tilde{i}} = \frac{\tilde{g}_{0\tilde{i}}}{\sqrt{\tilde{g}_{00}}}$.

Finally, the Cauchy equations of motion are [7]:

$$\frac{1}{\sqrt{-\tilde{\mathrm{G}}}}\frac{\partial}{\partial \tilde{x}^{\tilde{k}}}(\sqrt{-\tilde{\mathrm{G}}}\sigma^{\tilde{i}\tilde{k}}) + \sigma^{\tilde{l}\tilde{k}}\Gamma^{\tilde{i}}_{\tilde{l}\tilde{k}} + \rho b^{\tilde{i}} = \rho a^{\tilde{i}}, \tag{11}$$

where $\sigma^{\tilde{i}\tilde{k}}$ is the Cauchy stress, $b^{\tilde{i}}$ are the body forces, including the Lorentz force, $a^{\tilde{i}}$ is the particle acceleration of the body, $\tilde{\mathrm{G}}$ is the determinant of spatial submatrix of $\tilde{\mathrm{g}}_{\tilde{\alpha}\tilde{\beta}}$, and the $\Gamma^{\tilde{i}}_{\tilde{l}\tilde{k}}$ are the Christoffel symbols associated with metric $\tilde{g}$. Equations (5), (8) and (11), when combined with appropriate constitutive laws and boundary conditions constitute a complete set of equations for solving for the electromagnetic and structural variables.

In general, a closed-form solution to this set of equations cannot be found; consequently numerical solutions are sought. To simplify, we assume the field is two-dimensional and electrostatic, i.e., $\tilde{e}_{\tilde{i}} = \frac{\partial V}{\partial \tilde{x}^{\tilde{i}}} \doteq V_{,\tilde{i}}$. We also assume that the structural deformation is known. This completely decouples the problem, and reduces Equation (5) to Gauss's law for the electric field. Assuming $d^i = \epsilon^{ij}e_j$, and no free charge, we seek a weak form solution which leads to:

$$\int_{\tilde{v}} V_{,\tilde{i}}\frac{\partial \tilde{x}^{\tilde{i}}}{\partial x^i}\epsilon^{ij}\frac{\partial \tilde{x}^{\tilde{j}}}{\partial x^j}V_{,\tilde{j}}\,d\tilde{v} = 0. \tag{12}$$

Finally, if we assume that the permmitivity is isotropic, $\epsilon^{ij} = \epsilon\delta^{ij}$, where δ^{ij} is the Kronecker delta, Equation (12) reduces to:

$$\int_{\tilde{v}} \tilde{g}^{\tilde{i}\tilde{j}}V_{,\tilde{i}}V_{,\tilde{j}}\,d\tilde{v} = 0. \tag{13}$$

IV. Numerical Results

The simplest possible problem to analyze is a parallel plate capacitor bent into an arc. This is implemented by defining the structural deformation by:

$$u_x = \frac{k}{360}\left[\frac{2L}{\pi}\sin\left(\frac{\pi \tilde{\mathrm{x}}_1}{2L}\right) + \tilde{\mathrm{x}}_2\sin\left(\frac{\pi \tilde{\mathrm{x}}_1}{2L}\right) - \tilde{\mathrm{x}}_1\right], \tag{14}$$

$$u_y = \frac{k}{360}\left[\frac{2L}{\pi}\cos\left(\frac{\pi \tilde{\mathrm{x}}_1}{2L}\right) + \tilde{\mathrm{x}}_2\cos\left(\frac{\pi \tilde{\mathrm{x}}_1}{2L}\right) - \tilde{\mathrm{x}}_2\right], \tag{15}$$

where L is the length of the parallel plates, and $k \in \{0, 1, \ldots, 360\}$ is simply a parameter that defines the degree of deformation. The metric tensor, $\tilde{g}^{\tilde{i}\tilde{j}}$, can be computed exactly from Equations (14) and (15). Therefore the only unknown is the voltage, V. Plots of the electric field in the convected transverse coordinate as the bar is deformed are shown in Fig. 1.

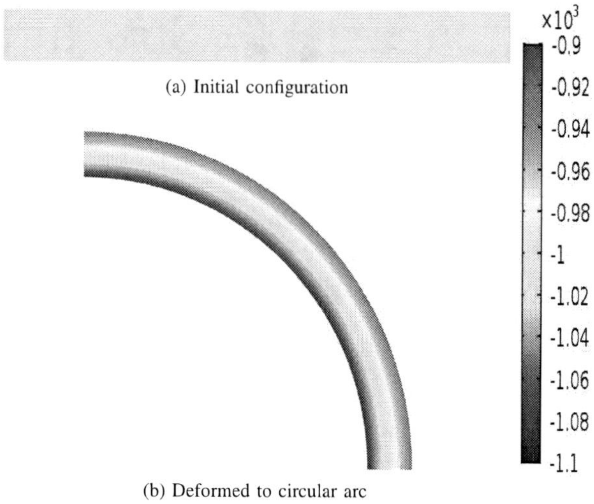

(a) Initial configuration

(b) Deformed to circular arc

Fig. 1. Transverse electric field, $\tilde{e}_{\tilde{2}}$, for finite deformation of a parallel plate capacitor.

V. Conclusions

The use of convective coordinates resolves inconsistencies in the coupling of Maxwell's equations with continuum mechanics. The more traditional formulations are recovered as special cases. Finally, we have presented a proof-of-principle solution to the finite deformation of a simple parallel plate capacitor. The solution agrees with known closed form solutions for this simple geometry.

References

[1] A. R. Dorfmann and R. W. Ogden, "Nonlinear electroelasticity," Acta Mechanica, vol. 174, no. 3–4, pp. 167–183, 2000.

[2] M. Lax and D. Nelson, "Maxwell equations in material form," Physical Review B, vol. 13, no. 4, pp. 1777–1784, 1976.

[3] J. S. Yang and R. C. Batra, "A theory of electroded thin thermopiezoelectric plates subject to large driving voltages," Journal of Applied Physics, vol. 76, no. 9, pp. 5411–5417, 1994.

[4] J. Clayton, "A non-linear model for elastic dielectric crystals with mobile vacancies," International Journal of Non-Linear Mechanics, vol. 44, no. 6, pp. 675–688, 2009.

[5] D. Weile, D. Hopkins, G. Gazonas, and B. Powers, "On the proper formulation of Maxwellian electrodynamics for continuum mechanics," Continuum Mechanics and Thermodynamics, vol. 26, no. 3, pp. 387–401, 2014.

[6] L. E. Malvern, Introduction to the Mechanics of a Continuous Medium. Englewood Cliffs, NJ: Prentice-Hall, Inc., 1969.

[7] R. Irgens, Continuum Mechanics. Berlin Heidelberg: Springer-Verlag, 2008.

A Study of Near-Field Imaging and Diagnostic Applications of Surface Equivalent Current Methods

Arslan Azhar and Thomas F. Eibert
Chair of High-Frequency Engineering
Deparmtent of Electrical and Computer Engineering
Technical University of Munich
80290 Munich, Germany
arslan.azhar@tum.de

Li Li
Shanghai Radio Equipement Institute
Shanghai, China
racky0213@sina.com

***Abstract*—The utilization of surface equivalent current (SEC) methods in near-field imaging and diagnostics of flat scatterers with fine details is discussed. Of special interest is the ability to identify and locate electrically small physical changes on the scatterers by analyzing the equivalent surface current densities obtained by transforming the observed near fields. Using two test objects as scattering targets for an incident plane wave at 77 GHz, it is shown that sub-wavelength physical changes can even be localized using SEC methods. Finally, the need for an appropriate excitation method and measurement setup is discussed in the light of experimental results.**

***Keywords*—antenna diagnostics, equivalent sources, near-field imaging.**

I. Introduction

A useful technique in RF diagnostics is the analysis of equivalent surface current distributions on a device-under-test (DUT) to identify any abnormal current flows. Modern computer technologies enable us to directly use the knowledge of the radiated or scattered fields to obtain (equivalent) source current densities on a surface enclosing a DUT by field transformations (inverse problem) [1]. Since a source current density is closely tied to the geometry of a DUT, an extension of surface current diagnostics is the profiling of physical features and defects in a DUT structure, especially when the DUT is not easily accessible for visual inspection. The resolution of the transformed images, among other factors, is limited by the operating frequency. Sub-wavelength physical variations can be detected if they result in reasonable changes in the surface current distribution.

To achieve sufficient flexibility for practical measurements, the diagnostics problem is posed as a scattering problem, where an incident wave illuminates a DUT. In this case, the unknowns can be the induced equivalent surface currents or scattering coefficient on the DUT and known are the scattered fields in a collection of observation locations.

The core computations in NF imaging are the numerical evaluations of the radiation or scattering integrals that relate the measured fields with the unknown sources through free-space Green's functions [2]. The integrals can be solved using an alternative and resource-efficient formulation of the method-of-moments based on the principles of the MLFMM (multilevel fast multipole method) [3]. Such capabilities are integrated in the state-of-the-art multifaceted FIAFTA (Fast Irregular Antenna Field Transformation Algorithm) which is utilized throughout this work [2].

In the following, the utilization of FIAFTA for NF imaging is discussed, where in particular two scattering examples are considered.

II. Near-Field Imaging with FIAFTA

The FIAFTA is suitable for practical NF imaging since the transformation algorithm is expected to: 1) deliver high resolution images, 2) use low memory and processing resources during the transformation, 3) quickly converge, and 4) enable flexible field measurements.

As a consequence of the Huygens principle of electromagnetic fields, a source region can be substituted by a (Huygens) surface with equivalent sources such that the fields outside the surface remain unaltered (sometimes also called the surface equivalence principle or SEP) [4]. Based on these concepts, the FIAFTA first transforms the measured fields into a set of equivalent current sources by minimizing the difference $\|\mathbf{Ax}-\mathbf{b}\|$ in least square manner, where the vector $\mathbf{b}$ contains the measured fields, the vector $\mathbf{x}$ contains the unknown sources, and $\mathbf{A}$ is the interaction matrix. A triangular mesh is used to discretize a user-defined surface for equivalent currents evaluation. Rao-Wilton-Glisson (RWG) basis functions model the equivalent currents on the mesh triangles [5],[6]. Finally, the FIAFTA can also perform NF-FF transformations by integrating the fields due to the equivalent currents in the far-field region.

III. Results and Discussion

To determine the NF imaging performance of the FIAFTA code, noise-free field measurements have been obtained from two CST Microwave Studio simulation models. Two planar test objects lying in the xy-plane are used as target, each one is illuminated by two incident plane waves with orthogonal polarizations (polarization vector along x and y-axis). The operating frequency is 77 GHz ($\lambda \approx 3.89$ mm). The ideal measurement surface that provides complete information about the induced currents on the DUT is a closed surface enclosing the DUT. However, we chose a planar surface in the simulations since planar measurements are more convenient and in general sufficient in practical situations.

This work was partially supported by the Science and Technology Commission of Shanghai Municipality under Grand NO. 17210730900.

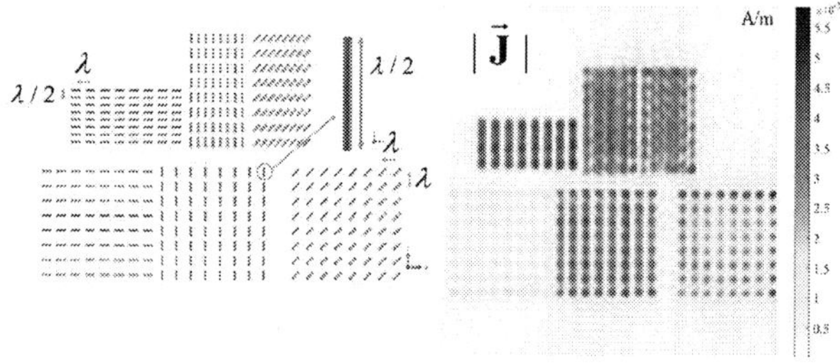

(a) Array of dipole-like PEC scatterers

(b) NF image of the scatterers in the form of surface equivalent current densities

Fig. 1. Geometry and equivalent current image for the first test object.

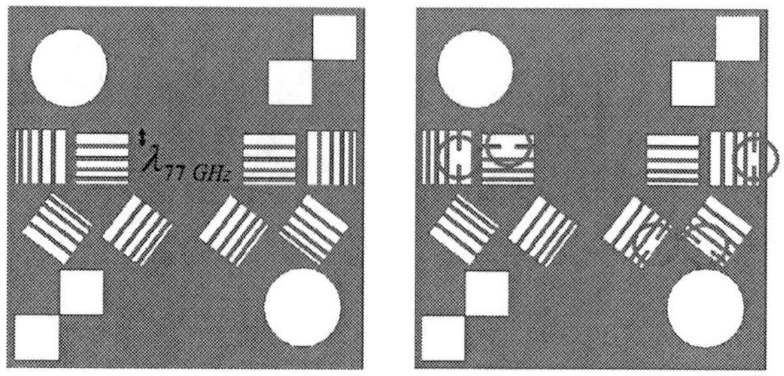

(a) Reference test plate

(b) Damaged test plate (note the breaks)

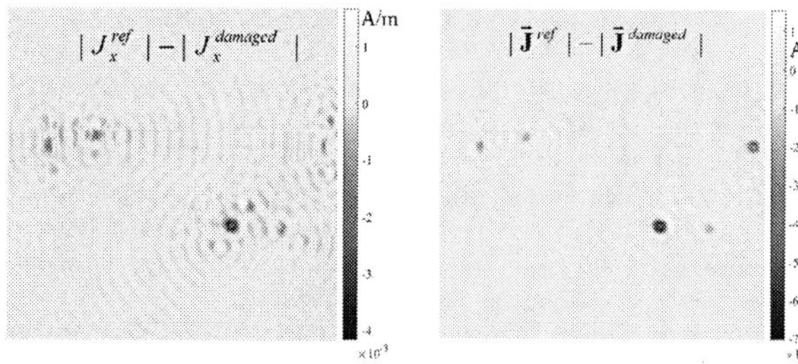

(c) Deviation of equivalent currents from the reference values due to damages (abs. of x component)

(d) Deviation of equivalent currents from the reference values due to damages (abs. of total component)

Fig. 2. PEC slotted test plate with 77 GHz incident plane. wave.

The first test object is an array of dipole-like PEC scatterers with three orientations in the xy-plane as shown in Fig. 1 (a). The inter-element clearance is $\lambda/2$ in the top-half while it is λ in the lower-half of the array. The propagation direction of the plane wave is inclined at 45° to the normal on xy plane. The scattered electric fields are observed on a z =18 mm plane in a (x,y) range with the dimensions of 275 mm by 244 mm (70λ by 63λ). The increment Δx and Δy are chosen to be 1 mm (over-sampled case). A 100 mm by 100 mm planar surface for the evaluation of the equivalent currents is placed parallel to the xy-plane and centered at the origin. For the discretization of the source plane, a mesh size of $\lambda/14$ is found to yield sharper NF images as compared to the mesh size of $\lambda/10$ (the latter is usually sufficient in case of NF-FF transformations). From the perspective of the transformation algorithm, this arrangement results in 445 376 unknowns versus 135 730 observation points. Fig. 1 (b) shows the transformed equivalent currents in the form of absolute total electric current densities. It is evident, that (a) a scatterer is only visible in the NF image if it has a reasonable strength of induced currents on it, and (b) the scattered fields due to the induced currents are captured on the observation plane. Hence, the careful choice of operating frequency, excitation method and measurement setup significantly improves the quality of the transformed.

In the second example, we replaced the scatterer array with a 100 mm by 100 mm planar PEC plate which has slots with different dimensions, see Fig. 2 (a,b) (note the slots with width < $\lambda/2$). The plane wave is normally incident to the test plate. The observation plane is 280 mm by 280 mm (72λ by 72λ) and it is centered at z=23.36 mm (6λ). The source mesh from previous example is used again so now we have 157 922 electric field observation points versus 445 376 unknowns. From Fig. 1(b), it can be seen that scatterers placed too close to each other are not readily distinguishable in the image. However, by introducing breaks in some electrically congested strips (Fig. 2 (b)) and by plotting the difference of equivalent current densities (broken vs. unbroken case), significant deviations are observed that exactly pin point the location of the breaks, Fig. 2 (c,d). Quantitatively, for the five breaks, a change in the absolute total electric current densities (relative to the peak value of the reference case) varies between 10 to 50%, see Fig. 2 (d).

IV. Conclusions

The three main factors that determine the quality of the NF imaging process using the FIAFTA are: 1) the choice of Huygens surface 2), surface current excitation, and 3) field measurement setup. Future work involves the NF imaging of complex 3-D scatterers using the surface equivalent current methods.

References

[1] Y. A. Lopez, F. L. Andres, M. R. Pino, and T. K. Sarkar, "An improved super-resolution source reconstruction method," *IEEE Transactions on Instrumentation and Measurement*, vol. 58, no. 11, pp. 3855-3866, Nov. 2009.

[2] T. F. Eibert, E. Kılıç, C. Lopez, R. A. M. Mauermayer, O. Neitz, and G. Schnattinger, "Electromagnetic field transformations for measurements and simulations," *Progress In Electromagnetics Research*, vol. 151, 127–150, 2015.

[3] W. C. Chew, E. Michielssen, J. M. Song, and J. M. Jin, *Fast and Efficient Algorithms in Computational Electromagnetics*, Artech House, Inc., 2001.

[4] J. M. Jin, *Theory and Computation of Electromagnetic Fields*, John Wiley & Sons, 2011.

[5] S. Rao, D. Wilton, and A. Glisson, "Electromagnetic scattering by surfaces of arbitrary shape," *IEEE Transactions on Antennas and Propagation*, vol. 30, no. 3, pp. 409-418, May 1982

[6] T. F. Eibert and C. H. Schmidt, "Multilevel fast multipole accelerated inverse equivalent current method employing Rao–Wilton–Glisson discretization of electric and magnetic surface currents," *IEEE Transactions on Antennas and Propagation*, vol. 57, no. 4, pp. 1178-1185, April 2009.

Mode Analysis of Waveguides in Layered Media

Aytaç Alparslan
Department of Electrical and Electronics Engineering
Trakya University, Edirne, Turkey
aytac@ieee.org

***Abstract*—In this paper, the mode analysis of realistic waveguides in multi layered geometries, which is among the most demanding problems in computational electromagnetics, is performed. Multiple multipole program (MMP) combined with layered media Green's functions is used to obtain the locations of the mode wave numbers on a complex plane bounded by the values given by the user. At an intermediate step of the MMP analysis, the approximate locations of the physical modes are obtained and then used to obtain exact locations of the corresponding modes. It is shown that the approximate locations taken from the MMP analysis provide a very precise starting point to determine the exact locations of the modes not only for MMP but also for all the well-known numerical methods, providing a guideline for the solution of the most demanding problems in the mode analysis. During the talk, advantages of the MMP analysis will be demonstrated by several numerical examples solved by different numerical techniques with and without the approximate location obtained from MMP.**

I. Introduction

Although sometimes assumed to be built in free space in the numerical analyses, waveguides are built in a layered geometry in realistic applications [1], [2]. The layered geometry is used primarily as the physical construction environment in which the circuits of various dimensions are designed. In the microwave regime, several wave types that can be seen only in layered media including: guided, surface and lateral waves that play a very important role in the design of devices. In the optical regime, the effects of such different wave types become even more important due to the highly lossy and dispersive nature of metals at such frequencies. Therefore a numerical tool that can efficiently include the salient features of layered media in the mode analysis of waveguides is desired in the computational electromagnetics society. In this talk such a numerical tool is introduced by combining multiple multipoles program (MMP) by layered media Green's functions [3]. Since all the physical features of the layered medium is included in the layered media Green's functions, i.e., the response of the layered medium in the presence of a point source, infinite domain approximation techniques such as perfectly matched layers (PMLs) and absorbing boundary conditions (ABCs) are eliminated and a very efficient technique for the mode analysis of waveguides in layered medium is obtained.

II. MMP and Layered Media

MMP is a boundary discretization method that can be used for the scattering and mode analyses of electromagnetic waves in arbitrary geometries. In MMP, boundary conditions introduced by the appropriate fundamental sources are fulfilled at specific points defined on the boundaries of the geometries in a least square sense. Therefore, the results obtained from the method can be compared with the analytical boundary conditions and the analytical error of the result can be directly calculated from the analysis which is one of the most important advantage of the method.

In MMP, the fundamental sources can take different forms depending on the analysis, geometrical specifications and the wavelength of the incident radiation. For structures built in layered media, the most suited fundamental sources are the layered media Green's functions, since all the physical effects of the layered media is already included in them. The most general setting for a layered geometry is shown in Fig. 1.

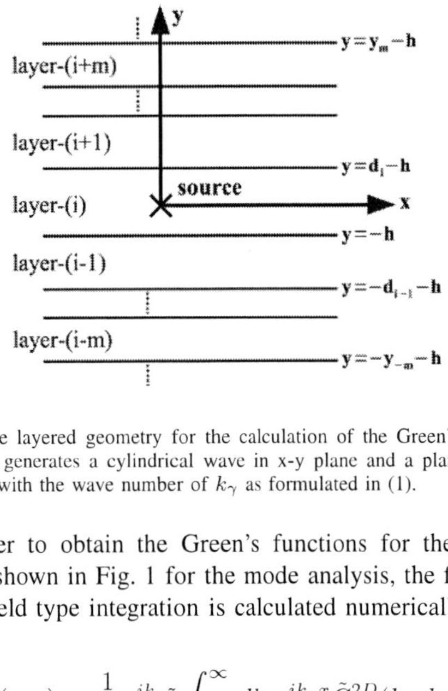

Fig. 1. The layered geometry for the calculation of the Green's function. The source generates a cylindrical wave in x-y plane and a plane wave in z-direction with the wave number of k_γ as formulated in (1).

In order to obtain the Green's functions for the layered medium shown in Fig. 1 for the mode analysis, the following Sommerfeld type integration is calculated numerically:

$$G^{2D}(x,y) = \frac{1}{2\pi}e^{ik_\gamma z}\int_{-\infty}^{\infty} dk_x e^{ik_x x}\tilde{G}^{2D}(k_x,k_\gamma), \quad (1)$$

where k_γ is the fixed propagation constant in z-direction, $\tilde{G}^{2D}(k_x,k_\gamma)$ is the spectral domain Green's function which includes all the transmission and reflection data for a given plane wave. Analyzing (1) with $e^{i\omega t}$ convention reveals that to obtain fields generated by a point source in a 2D layered geometry, all the plane waves going toward the location of the observation point should be summed up. Since the main objective of the mode analysis is to determine the wave number along the waveguide that maximizes the power flow, a plane wave that propagates in z-direction (along the waveguide) with k_γ is also included in (1) that fulfills the condition for wave numbers in layer-i:

$$\begin{aligned} k_i^2 &= k_\rho^2 + k_y^2 \\ k_i^2 &= k_x^2 + k_\gamma^2 + k_y^2. \end{aligned} \quad (2)$$

When $k_\gamma = 0$ in (2), the source generates plane waves only in x and y directions which sums up to be a cylindrical wave in the x-y plane. This kind of Green's functions are used for the in-plane scattering analysis of 2D structures in layered media.

III. Mode Analysis by MMP

As discussed above, the main objective of the mode analysis of waveguides is to find the complex wave number that maximizes the power flow along the waveguide. In the mode analysis by MMP, this task is performed both in a mathematical and in a physical way by the so called search function defined as:

$$f(k_\gamma) = \frac{Error(k_\gamma)}{Amplitude(k_\gamma)}, \quad (3)$$

where $Error(k_\gamma)$ is the average MMP mismatch error at the matching points defined on the boundaries of the waveguide and $Amplitude(k_\gamma)$ is the magnitude of the time averaged Poynting vector through the waveguide. Once the search function data is obtained on a given complex k_γ plane, the minimum locations reveal the approximate locations of the physical modes. By performing a fine search around these locations on can obtain the exact locations of the eigenvalues. The approximate location obtained from the search function can also be used as initial guess values in other numerical methods such as finite element method (FEM) or finite difference time domain method (FDTD).

As discussed above, different kinds of waves can be seen in a general layered medium. One of the most important wave type observed in layered media is the guided wave. Singularities in the spectral domain Green's functions (in k_γ plane) correspond to the wave numbers of guided waves along the boundaries of the layered medium (in $\rho = \sqrt{x^2 + z^2}$ direction). But since the search function in (3) is defined as a function of the wave number in z-direction (k_γ), the singularities in k_γ plane will be transformed into branch points and associated branch cuts due to the following double valued wave number relation:

$$k_\gamma = \sqrt{k_\rho^2 - k_x^2}. \quad (4)$$

As one can guess, having branch points and cuts on the complex k_γ plane makes it more difficult to find the minimum locations of the search functions, i.e., the modes of the waveguide. The main difficulty is due to the necessity of having a close enough initial guess for the mode search, not only for MMP analysis but for all the well known numerical methods used for the mode analysis.

IV. Numerical Results

As an example, before building a waveguide in a 3 layered geometry with the relative permittivity values starting from lowermost layer to top $\varepsilon_{r,1} = -0.80 + 5.52i$ (gold), $\varepsilon_{r,2} = 4.0$ $d_2 = 150$nm (thickness of the 2nd layer), $\varepsilon_{r,3} = 1$, the reflection coefficients for the TE and TM modes should be found as shown in Fig. 2 for $\lambda_0 = 380$nm.

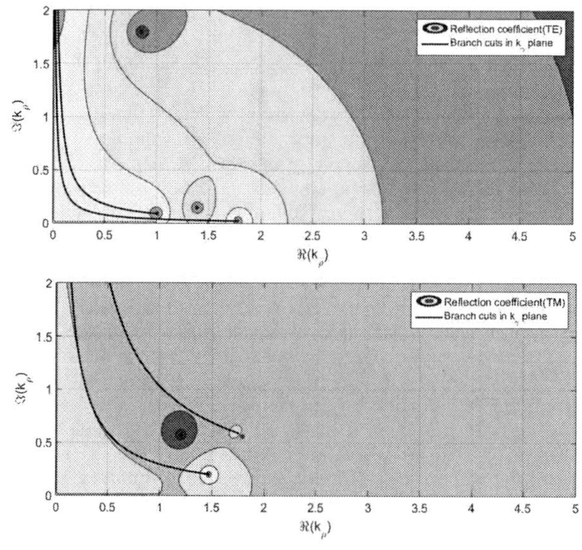

Fig. 2. The generalized reflection coefficients for the 3 layered geometry with $\varepsilon_{r,1} = -0.80 + 5.52i$ (gold), $\varepsilon_{r,2} = 4.0$ $d_2 = 150$nm (thickness of the 2nd layer), $\varepsilon_{r,3} = 1$ at $\lambda_0 = 380$nm. The singularities become branch points and cuts on the complex k_γ plane where the mode search is performed.

If a waveguide is built in the layered geometry analyzed above, the singularities in the reflection coefficients and the corresponding guided wave modes become very important and should be found before performing the full mode analysis. During the talk, several waveguide structures built in this layered geometry will be analyzed and the performance of different numerical metods will be compared.

V. Conclusion

In this talk, mode analysis of waveguides built in layered geometries is discussed. It is shown that guided waves supported by the layered geometry play a very important role in the mode analysis since they introduce new branch points and cuts on the complex search plane.

Acknowledgment

Financially supported by TÜBİTAK project no: 115C080.

References

[1] P. Berini, "Plasmon-polariton modes guided by a metal film of finite width bounded by different dielectrics," Opt. Express, vol. 7, no. 10, pp. 329–335, Nov. 2000. [Online]. Available: http://www.opticsexpress.org/abstract.cfm?URI=oe-7-10-329
[2] Y. Fang and M. Sun, "Nanoplasmonic waveguides: Towards applications in integrated nanophotonic circuits," Light: Science & Applications, Jun. 2015.
[3] A. Alparslan and C. Hafner, "Using layered geometry Green's functions in the multiple multipole program," J. Comput. Theor. Nanosci., vol. 8, no. 8, pp. 1600–1608, Aug. 2011.

Scattering Analysis of Silver Nanoparticles for Solar Cell Applications using Integral Equations

Ismail Enes Uysal
Physics Department, Bilkent University, Ankara, Turkey
Division of Computer, Electrical and Mathematical Science and Engineering, King Abdullah University of Science and Technology (KAUST), Thuwal, Saudi Arabia

Hakan Bagci
Division of Computer, Electrical and Mathematical Science and Engineering, King Abdullah University of Science and Technology (KAUST), Thuwal, Saudi Arabia

Huseyin Arda Ulku
Department of Electronics Engineering, Gebze Technical University, Kocaeli, Turkey

Oguz Gulseren
Physics Department, Bilkent University, Ankara, Turkey

***Abstract*—Plasmonic nanoparticles (NPs) can be used to improve the efficiency of solar cells. Analysis of electromagnetic scattering from NPs is often carried out under the assumptions that they reside in air and have "ideal" shapes (sphere, cube, etc.) However, in a realistic setup, nanoparticles are fabricated on a substrate and their shape and size cannot be controlled precisely. In this work, a surface integral equation solver is used to accurately characterize the scattering from a realistic system, where silver hemispheres of varying sizes are fabricated on an indium tin-oxide substrate. Results obtained by the solver are compared to the experimental results obtained for a similar system.**

Keywords—Electromagnetic scattering, plasmonics, solar cell, surface integral equations

I. Introduction

The efficiency of solar cells has been increasing steadily in the last two decades however significant improvements are still needed for them [1] to be able to compete with conventional energy sources. One way of increasing the efficiency of solar cells is to employ plasmonic nanoparticles (NPs) [2]. Ideally, NPs increase the efficiency by directing/focusing light energy into the active region of the solar cell. This means that NPs with high scattering cross section (SCS) but low absorption cross section (ACS) have to be designed and fabricated for enhanced efficiency.

SCS of an NP depends on the material, shape, and size as well as background medium it resides in. Scattering from various ideal NP geometries such as sphere, cylinder, cube, and tetrahedron has been analyzed using different numerical methods [2,3]. Oftentimes, in these scattering scenarios, a single ideally-shaped NP resides in an unbounded background medium. However, to accurately predict the output of a real experiment, simulations should take into account multiple non-ideally shaped NPs with varying sizes residing on a substrate.

In this work, electromagnetic scattering from a group of silver hemisphere-shaped NPs with varying radii, which are located on a dielectric substrate, is analyzed using a surface integral equation (SIE) solver [4]. Comparison of the SCS computed by the SIE solver to the experimental results demonstrates that simulations, which model multiple NPs with varying sizes and located on a substrate, yield more accurate results than those modeling a single NP that resides in air.

II. Formulation

The numerical scheme used in this work solves the well-known Poggio-Miller-Chan-Harrington-Wu-Tsai (PMCHWT) SIE [4,5]. The PMCHWT-SIE formulation makes use of the equivalence principle to represent volumes of the NPs and substrate in terms of equivalent electric and magnetic currents introduced on the surfaces of these volumes. The scattered electric and magnetic fields are constructed in the form of a spatial convolution of the equivalent current densities and the Green functions of the unbounded media with permeabilities and permittivities of the volumes. To numerically solve the PMCHWT-SIE, first, the equivalent current densities are expanded using Rao-Wilton-Glisson (RWG) basis functions [6]. These expansions are inserted into PMCHWT-SIE and the resulting equation is Galerkin-tested. This yields a matrix system, which is solved for the unknown coefficients of the current density expansions. Once the current-density expansion coefficients are known, the scattered electric and magnetic fields are computed in the far field region using these expansions. At the final step, SCS is obtained [5] by integrating these scattered fields over the solid angle spanning a sphere or a hemisphere.

III. Numerical Results

The PMCHWT-SIE solver, which is briefly described in Section II, is used to analyze scattering from a group of nine hemispheres with varying radii. The hemispheres are located on a dielectric substrate. This configuration represents silver NPs fabricated on an indium tin-oxide (ITO) substrate using the annealing technique [7]. In the simulations, the permittivity of the silver is calculated using the Johnson-Christy model [8] and relative permittivity of the ITO is 4.2. Dimensions of the substrate are 600 nm $\times$ 600 nm $\times$ 30 nm. Radii of the hemispheres change from 30 nm to 90 nm. The setup is excited by a plane wave normally incident on the substrate (from +z direction to −z direction). Fig. 1 shows the mesh discretizing the hemispheres and the substrate from top.

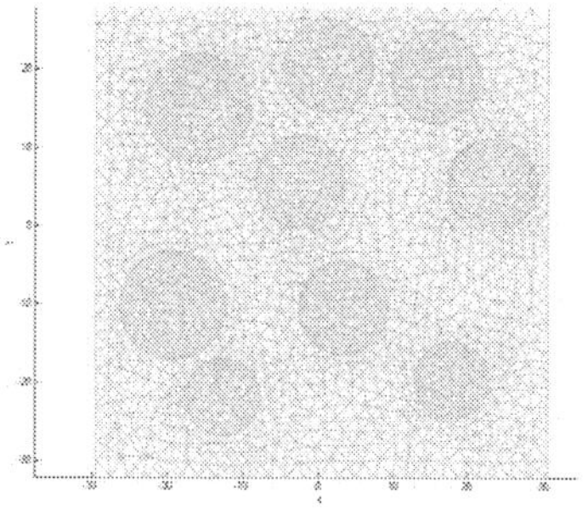

Fig. 1. Top view of the mesh discretizing the silver NPs and substrate.

This specific simulation model is inspired by the experimental setup, as described in [9], where reflection spectrum of the NPs is measured. In the simulations, as a measure of reflection, SCS is computed over the solid angle with theta spanning from 0^0 to 90^0 (hemisphere "sitting" at the top of the substrate). This is termed SCS-R. Similarly, as a measure of transmittance, SCS is computed over the solid angle with theta spanning from 90^0 to 180^0 (hemisphere "sitting" at the bottom of the substrate). This is termed SCS-T.

Fig. 2 plots SCS-R, SCS-T, and ACS of the setup described above versus the wavelength. SCS-T and SCS-R are very close to each other between 550 nm and 1200 nm. At lower wavelengths, they differ significantly. Overall ACS is lower than SCS-R and SCS-T and it even gets lower at wavelengths higher than 700 nm.

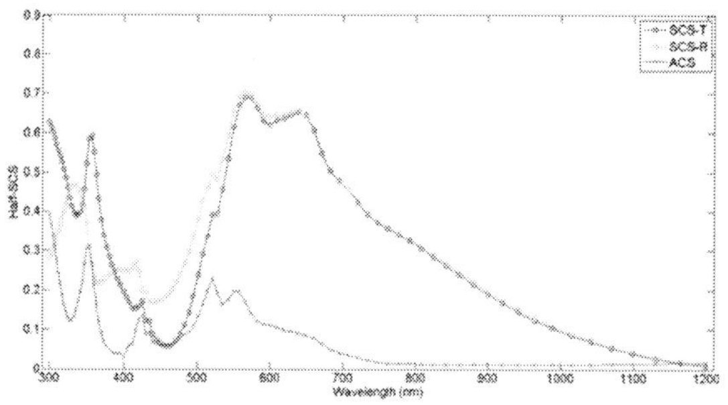

Fig. 2. SCS-R, SCS-T, and ACS computed by the PMCHWT-SIE solver for the setup with nine NPs.

The measured reflection of the silver NPs on ITO is provided in Fig. 2 in [9]. It has a single peak around 600 nm. Note that the experimental data is between 400 and 1000 nm. It is similar to SCS-R provided in Fig. 2, yet SCS-R has two very close peaks around 600 nm instead of a single and wider peak. This discrepancy might be due to the fact that the setup used by the PMCHWT-SIE solver does not incorporate the exact shape and size of NPs used in the experiments. Nevertheless, SCS-R of this setup is significantly closer to the experimental results than SCS-R of a single sphere or a hemisphere residing in vacuum as shown in Fig. 3.

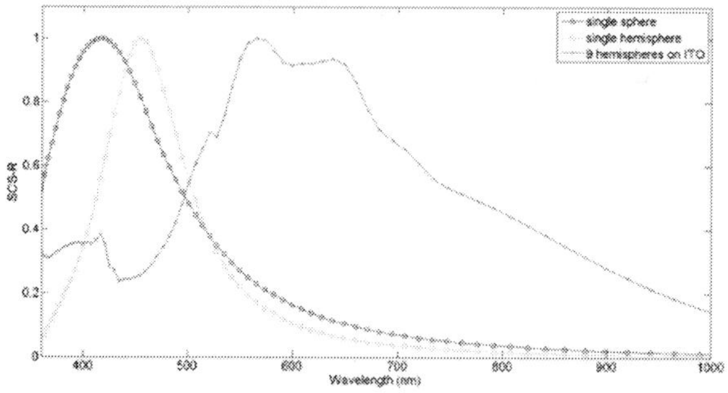

Fig. 3. SCS-R computed by the PMCHWT-SIE solver for the setup with nine NPs, a sphere in vacuum, and a hemisphere in vacuum.

IV. Conclusions

Carefully designed and fabricated NPs have the potential to boost up the efficiency of a solar cell by directing more light energy to the active region of the cell. This means that for increased efficiency, when NPs are placed on top of the cell, their SCS-T has to be increased while their SCS-R and ACS have to be decreased.

In this work, an accurate analysis of scattering from the silver NPs fabricated on an ITO substrate is carried out using a PMCHWT-SIE solver. Computed SCS-R is in good comparison with the measured reflection of the NPs as described in [9]. This clearly shows that electromagnetic interactions between the substrate and multiple particles have to be taken into account to obtain accurate results.

Acknowledgment

This work is partially supported by the Scientific and Technical Research Council of Turkey (TUBITAK) under the Grant No. 115F099. The authors I. E. Uysal and O. Gulseren would like to thank TUBITAK-ARDEB for their support.

References

[1] P. Mandal and S. Sharma, "Progress in plasmonic solar cell efficiency improvement: A status review," Renewable and Sustainable Energy Reviews, vol. 65, pp. 537-552, 2016.

[2] H. A. Atwater and A. Polman, "Plasmonics for improved photovoltaic devices," Nat. Mater., vol. 9, no. 3, pp. 205–213, 2010.

[3] D. C. Tzarouchis, P. Ylä-Oijala, T. Ala-Nissila, and A. Sihvol, "Shape effects on surface plasmons in spherical, cubic, and rod-shaped silver nanoparticles," Appl. Phys. A, 122:298, 2016.

[4] L. N. Medgyesi-Mitschang, J. M. Putnam, and M. B. Gedera, "Generalized method of moments for three-dimensional penetrable scatterers," JOSA A, vol. 11, no. 4, pp. 1383-1398, 1994.

[5] I. E. Uysal, H. A. Ulku, and H. Bagci, "Transient analysis of electromagnetic wave interactions on plasmonic nanostructures using a surface integral equation solver," J. Opt. Soc. Am. A, vol. 33, pp. 1747–1759, 2016.

[6] S. Rao, D.Wilton, and A. Glisson, "Electromagnetic scattering by surfaces of arbitrary shape," IEEE Trans. Antennas Propag., vol. 30, pp. 409–418, 1982.

[7] P. Albella, et. al., "Shape matters: Plasmonic nanoparticle shape enhances interaction with dielectric substrate," Nano Lett., vol. 11, pp. 3531–3537, 2011.

[8] P. B. Johnson and R. W. Christy, "Optical constants of the noble metals," Phys. Rev. B, vol. 6, pp. 4370–4379, 1972.

[9] I.Tanyeli, H. Nasser, F. Es, A. Bek, and R. Turan, "Effect of surface type on structural and optical properties of Ag nanoparticles formed by dewetting," Opt. Express, vol. 21, pp. A798–A807, 2013.

An FFT-Accelerated Inductance Extractor for Voxelized Structures

Abdulkadir C. Yucel and Hakan Bagci
Division of Computer, Electrical and Mathematical Science and Engineering
King Abdullah University of Science and Technology (KAUST)
Thuwal 23955-6900, Saudi Arabia
abdulkadir.yucel@kaust.edu.sa
hakan.bagci@kaust.edu.sa

Ioannis P. Georgakis and Athanasios G. Polimeridis
Center for Computational Data-Intensive Science and Engineering
Skolkovo Institute of Science and Technology
Moscow 143026, Russia
ioannis.georgakis@skolkovotech.ru
a.polimeridis@skoltech.ru

Jacob K. White
Department of Electrical Engineering and Computer Science
Massachusetts Institute of Technology
Cambridge, MA 02139, USA
white@mit.edu

***Abstract*—A fast Fourier transform (FFT)-accelerated integral equation solver for efficiently and accurately extracting inductance of structures discretized by voxels is described. This new solver called VoxHenry, unlike its predecessor FastHenry, can accurately account for the current flow around corners of structures using a carefully selected set of basis functions. VoxHenry solves the matrix system obtained upon discretization of the volume integral and current continuity equations iteratively. Matrix-vector multiplications required by the iterative solver are carried out using FFTs and the number of iterations is reduced using a sparse preconditioner. The accuracy and efficiency of VoxHenry are demonstrated via its application to inductance extraction of a circular coil.**

Keywords—Fast Fourier transform, inductance extraction, interconnects.

I. Introduction

The design of high-speed integrated circuits calls for efficient and accurate inductance extractors to produce circuit representations that can be used for signal timing, signal integrity, and cross-talk analyses. Inductance extractors that have been developed so far require structures to be discretized with volume filaments [1], tetrahedrons [2], or surface elements [3]. That said, there is a need for inductance extractors capable of working on structures discretized with voxels. Such an extractor would be extremely easy to incorporate into voxel-based virtual fabrication environments and suitable for modeling the structures during unit process steps of iterative design explorations. Additionally, its acceleration using fast Fourier transform (FFT) techniques [4]-[9] is straightforward.

In this work, an FFT-accelerated inductance extractor, named VoxHenry, is developed for solving a coupled system of volume integral and current continuity equations on voxelized structures. This new inductance extractor is more accurate and efficient than its predecessor FastHenry [1] thanks to algorithmic developments listed next. (i) VoxHenry expands the current density in terms of piecewise constant and linear basis functions permitting its accurate representation around corners. (ii) During the iterative solution of the matrix system obtained upon discretization, VoxHenry uses FFTs to expedite the matrix-vector multiplications. (iii) The number of iterations is reduced using a sparse preconditioner. Numerical results demonstrating the accuracy, efficiency, applicability of VoxHenry are provided.

I. P. Georgakis, A. G. Polimeridis, and J. White were supported by a grant from Skoltech as part of the Skoltech-MIT Next Generation Program.

II. Formulation

Let V represent the volume of a non-magnetic structure with conductivity σ, which resides in an unbounded background medium with permittivity ε_0 and permeability μ_0. The structure is excited by source(s) operated at frequency ω. The structure is discretized by K_t voxels of size Δd, $K_t = K_x \times K_y \times K_z$, where K_x, K_y, and K_z are the numbers of voxels along x, y, and z directions; Δd is selected to be equal to or less than the skin depth at ω. Let K denote the number of non-empty voxels (with non-zero σ), each of which has one node on each of its six surfaces; let M denote the total number of these nodes.

VoxHenry solves the coupled system of volume integral and current continuity equations:

$$\frac{\mathbf{J}(\mathbf{r})}{\sigma} + j\omega\frac{\mu_0}{4\pi}\int_V \frac{\mathbf{J}(\mathbf{r}')}{|\mathbf{r}-\mathbf{r}'|}dv' = -\nabla\phi(\mathbf{r}),\ \{\mathbf{r},\mathbf{r}'\}\in V \quad (1)$$

$$\nabla\cdot\mathbf{J}(\mathbf{r}) = 0, \quad (2)$$

where $\mathbf{J}(\mathbf{r})$ and $\phi(\mathbf{r})$ represent the current density and scalar potential. To solve (1) and (2), $\mathbf{J}(\mathbf{r})$ is expanded in terms of divergence-free basis functions as:

$$\mathbf{J}(\mathbf{r}) \approx \sum_{k=1}^{K}\sum_{i=1}^{5} I_k^i \mathbf{b}_k^i(\mathbf{r}) \quad (3)$$

where I_k^i is the unknown current coefficient,

$$\mathbf{b}_k^1(\mathbf{r}) = \hat{\mathbf{x}},\ \mathbf{b}_k^2(\mathbf{r}) = \hat{\mathbf{y}},\ \mathbf{b}_k^3(\mathbf{r}) = \hat{\mathbf{z}}, \quad (4)$$

$$\mathbf{b}_k^4(\mathbf{r}) = \Delta d^{-1}\left((x-x_k)\hat{\mathbf{x}} - (y-y_k)\hat{\mathbf{y}}\right), \quad (5)$$

$$\mathbf{b}_k^5(\mathbf{r}) = \Delta d^{-1}\left((x-x_k)\hat{\mathbf{x}} + (y-y_k)\hat{\mathbf{y}} - 2(z-z_k)\hat{\mathbf{z}}\right), \quad (6)$$

and (x_k, y_k, z_k) are the coordinates of center of kth voxel. Substituting (3) into (1), testing the resulting equation with $\mathbf{b}_l^j$, $j = 1,\ldots,5$, and enforcing (2) (in the form of normal current density continuity) across the voxel surfaces, yield a linear system of equations with dimensions $(5K+M)\times(5K+M)$:

$$\begin{bmatrix}\mathbf{V}\\ 0\end{bmatrix}=\begin{bmatrix}\bar{\mathbf{R}}+j\omega\bar{\mathbf{L}} & -\bar{\mathbf{A}}^{T}\\ \bar{\mathbf{A}} & 0\end{bmatrix}\begin{bmatrix}\mathbf{I}\\ \mathbf{\Phi}\end{bmatrix}. \tag{7}$$

Here, $\mathbf{V}$, $\mathbf{I}=[\mathbf{I}^1;\mathbf{I}^2;\mathbf{I}^3;\mathbf{I}^4;\mathbf{I}^5]$, and $\mathbf{\Phi}$ are the excitation vector and the vectors of unknown current and potential coefficients, respectively. The entries of sparse matrix $\bar{\mathbf{A}}_{mn}$, $n=1,\ldots,5K$, $m=1,\ldots,M$, are assigned as the value of nth basis function on m^{th} node, multiplied with ± 1. The entries of $\mathbf{V}$ are obtained by summing the columns of $\bar{\mathbf{A}}^T$ corresponding to the port nodes. Matrix $\bar{\mathbf{R}}$ consists of $K\times K$ diagonal blocks $\bar{\mathbf{R}}_{lk}^{ii}$ with entries $\sigma^{-1}\left\langle \mathbf{b}_k^i(\mathbf{r}),\mathbf{b}_k^i(\mathbf{r})\right\rangle_{V_k}$, $k=1,\ldots,K$, where $\langle\cdot,\cdot\rangle_{\Omega}$ denotes standard inner product with support Ω and V_k is the support of kth voxel. Similarly, matrix $\bar{\mathbf{L}}$ consists of $K\times K$ blocks $\bar{\mathbf{L}}_{lk}^{ji}$ with the entries:

$$\bar{\mathbf{L}}_{lk}^{ji}=\left\langle \mathbf{b}_l^j(\mathbf{r}),\frac{\mu_0}{4\pi}\int_{V_k}\frac{\mathbf{b}_k^i(\mathbf{r}')}{|\mathbf{r}-\mathbf{r}'|}dv'\right\rangle_{V_l}. \tag{8}$$

Blocks $\bar{\mathbf{L}}^{ji}$ are either zero or full matrices. The multiplication of full matrix $\bar{\mathbf{L}}^{ji}$ with $\mathbf{I}^i$, i.e., $\mathbf{C}^j=\bar{\mathbf{L}}^{ji}\mathbf{I}^i$, requires $O(K^2)$ operations and is reduced to $O(K_t\log K_t)$ using FFTs [4]-[9]:

$$\mathcal{C}^j=IFFT\left(\sum\nolimits_i\tilde{\mathcal{L}}^{ji}*FFT(\mathcal{I}^i)\right), \tag{9}$$

where $\tilde{\mathcal{L}}^{ji}=FFT(\mathcal{L}^{ji})$, $\mathcal{L}^{ji}$ is the circulant tensor with the entries computed using (8), $\mathcal{I}^i$ is a tensor formed by using current coefficients and zero padding, $\mathcal{C}^j$ is the resultant tensor that provides the entries of $\mathbf{C}^j$. Dimensions of all tensors are $2K_x\times 2K_y\times 2K_z$. Note that the multiplications of sparse matrices $\bar{\mathbf{A}}$ and $\bar{\mathbf{A}}^T$ with $\mathbf{I}$ and $\mathbf{\Phi}$, respectively, require only $O(K)$ operations. To ensure the rapid convergence of iterative solution of (7), a sparse preconditioner,

$$\bar{\mathbf{P}}=\begin{bmatrix}\bar{\mathbf{R}}+j\omega\bar{\mathbf{D}} & -\bar{\mathbf{A}}^{T}\\ \bar{\mathbf{A}} & 0\end{bmatrix}^{-1}, \tag{10}$$

is applied to matrix-vector multiplications; here $\bar{\mathbf{D}}=diag(\bar{\mathbf{L}})$.

III. Numerical Result

VoxHenry is used for extracting the inductance of a circular coil with conductivity of 5.8×10^7 S/m and loop and tube radii of $150\ \mu\text{m}$ and $5\ \mu\text{m}$. The coil positioned on the xy plane is excited from a spacing in the lower part of the coil between $x=155\ \mu\text{m}$ and $x=155.5\ \mu\text{m}$. Discretization parameters $\Delta d=0.5\ \mu\text{m}$, $5K=2969300$ and $M=1867528$. The inductance of the coil is computed at frequencies ranging from 1 Hz to 1 THz and compared to the values provided by an analytical formula [10] [Fig. 1 (a)]. An excellent match between results is observed. In addition, current distribution on the coil at 3GHz is plotted in Fig. 1 (b). For this problem, VoxHenry computes the inductance at one frequency point in 2.93 minutes.

IV. Conclusion

An FFT-accelerated inductance extractor, VoxHenry, and its application to a voxelized circular coil are presented. The filament-based approaches, such as FastHenry, can not model the 3D currents in a circular coil accurately and are not directly applicable to voxelized circular coils (without remeshing) due to reasons explained in [11].

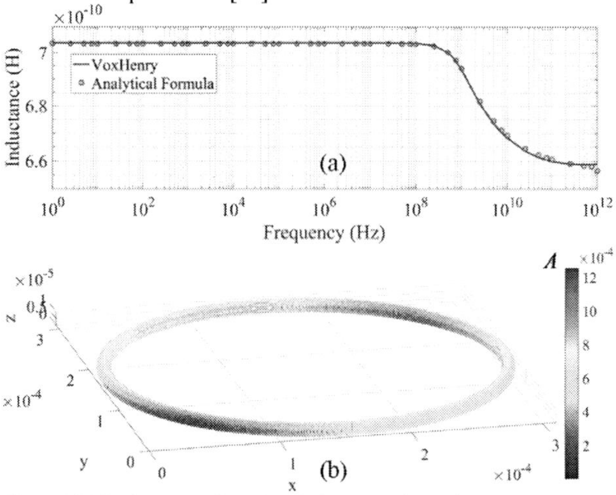

Fig. 1. (a) The frequency-dependent inductance of the circular coil. (b) The current distribution at 3 GHz.

References

[1] M. Kamon, M. J. Tsuk, and J. K. White, "FASTHENRY: A multipole-accelerated 3-D inductance extraction program," IEEE Trans. Microw. Theory Techn., vol. 42, pp. 1750-1758, 1994.

[2] K. Jackman and C. J. Fourie, "Tetrahedral modeling method for inductance extraction of complex 3-D superconducting structures," IEEE Trans. Appl. Supercond., vol. 26, no. 3, pp. 1-5, April 2016.

[3] M. Al-Qedra, J. Aronsson, and V. Okhmatovski, "Surface integral equation formulation for inductance extraction in 3-D interconnects," IEEE Microw. Compon. Lett., vol. 20, no. 5, pp. 250-252, May 2010.

[4] M. F. Catedra, E. Gago, and L. Nuno, "A numerical scheme to obtain the RCS of three-dimensional bodies of resonant size using the conjugate gradient method and the fast Fourier transform," IEEE Trans. Antennas Propagat., vol. 37, pp. 528-537, 1989.

[5] A. C. Yucel, L. J. Gomez and E. Michielssen, "Compression of translation operator tensors in FMM-FFT-accelerated SIE solvers via Tucker decomposition," IEEE Antennas Wireless Propag. Lett., vol. 16, pp. 2667-2670, 2017.

[6] A. G. Polimeridis, J. F. Villena, L. Daniel, and J. K. White, "Stable FFT-JVIE solvers for fast analysis of highly inhomogeneous dielectric objects," J. Comp. Phys., vol. 269, pp. 280-296, 2014.

[7] A. C. Yucel, "Uncertainty quantification for electromagnetic analysis via efficient collocation methods," Ph.D. thesis, University of Michigan, Ann Arbor, 2013.

[8] A. C. Yucel, L. J. Gomez, Y. Liu, H. Bagci, and E. Michielssen, "A FMM-FFT accelerated hybrid volume surface integral equation solver for electromagnetic analysis of re-entry space vehicles," in CNC-USNC/URSI National Radio Sci. Meet., 2014.

[9] A. C. Yucel, Y. Liu, H. Bagci, and E. Michielssen, "An FMM-FFT accelerated integral equation solver for characterizing electromagnetic wave propagation in mine tunnels and galleries loaded with conductors," in Proc CNC-USNC/URSI National Radio Sci. Meet., 2014.

[10] Radio Instruments and Measurements - Circular C74. Washington, DC: U.S. Government Printing Office, 1924.

[11] A. C. Yucel, I. Georgakis, A. G. Polimeridis, H. Bağcı, and J. White, "VoxHenry: A fast Fourier transform - accelerated 3D inductance extraction program for voxelized geometries," IEEE Trans. Microw. Theory Techn., in Press.

Versatile Nanoparticle Manipulation with Designer Thermoplasmonic Metasurface

Justus C. Ndukaife

Department of Electrical Engineering and Computer Science, and Vanderbilt Institute of Nanoscale Science and Engineering, Vanderbilt University, Nashville, TN, USA
justus.ndukaife@vanderbilt.edu

***Abstract*—The intrinsic loss in plasmonic systems has generally been considered to be detrimental for several device applications. Using this loss to advantage, we report thermoplasmonic metasurfaces for unprecedented control over nanoparticle manipulation and assembly. We report parallel assembly of quantum emitters on plasmonic nanoantennas, stand-off manipulation of particles, and size dependent arrangement of nanoparticles. Our platform opens up vistas of applications in structural material production, quantum photonics, and color printing.**

Keywords—metasurface, nano-assembly, quantum photonics, thermoplasmonics.

I. Introduction

Nanophotonic technologies call urgently for scalable, large scale, and low-cost production of sub-wavelength optical elements. A wide range of emerging technologies in diverse fields such as on-chip quantum light sources, photocatalytic energy generation with catalytic nanoparticles coupled to plasmonic resonators, and structural color printing would benefit from scalable production of sub-wavelength optical elements. To meet this need, we explore scalable patterning and directed assembly of nanoscale optical components. In our approach, we explore the interplay between near-field optical forces and electric-field induced forces such as electrohydrodynamic flow [1], dipolar Coulomb interaction, AC electro-osmosis [2], and heat-induced forces for directed self-assembly and patterning of nanoscale and sub-micron optical materials. These features provide flexibility, potential for high throughput assembly, and potential to fabricate seemingly complex structures. Inorder to elucidate the mechanisms that govern the nanoparticle transport and assembly process, we employ numerical simulations to solve the coupled multi-physics electromagnetic, heat transfer, and fluid dynamics problem. In this talk, I will discuss our latest results demonstrating the arrangement of nanoscale and submicron particles as a function of size, as well as schemes for both serial and parallel assembly of nanoscale and submicron functional nanoparticles on nanophotonic resonators.

II. Manipulation and Assembly of Nanoparticles with Thermoplasmonic Metasurfaces

A. Elucidating the Mechanism of Assembly

The thermoplasmonic metasurface comprise of an arrangement of sub-wavelength gold plasmonic nanostructures on a substrate. The plasmonic nanostructures could be made of nanopillars or nanoholes in a gold film. A microfluidic channel is constructed over the metasurface region and another substrate is placed over it, to create a parallel plate capacitor configuration, as depicted in Fig. 1. The illumination of the thermoplasmonic metasurface results in absorption of the incident light and conversion to heat. The heat generated is subsequently transferred to the surrounding fluid, thereby creating a thermal gradient in the fluid. The induced thermal gradient results in gradient in the fluid's permittivity, electrical conductivity and density. Applying an AC electric field under this condition of local inhomogeneity in the fluid's electrical properties creates volumetric body forces in the fluid, which in turn produces electrothermoplasmonic [3] microfluidic vortices. These vortices aid in the capture of suspended nanoparticles and transport them towards the region of the thermal hotspots created by the thermoplasmonic metasurface.

Additionally, the thermoplasmonic metasurface structure creates a distortion of the applied AC electric field. The tangential component of the AC electric field exerts forces on the induced charges in the electrical double layer sustained at the interface between the metasurface and the adjoining fluid medium. This creates an AC electro-osmotic flow. The strength of these are flows are dependent on the AC electric field frequency. By harnessing the interplay of these forces, we demonstrate several features including parallel directed assembly, stand-off manipulation of nanoparticles, and size-dependent assembly (Fig. 2) and arrangement of nanoparticles.

B. Experimental Platform and Observations

In this talk, I will discuss two experimental platforms that we have developed for directed assembly of nano-metric and sub-micron objects. An experimental result depicting the arrangement of 200 nm polystyrene beads is depicted in the inset of Fig. 2.

III. NUMERICAL SIMULATIONS

We employ numerical simulations via finite element analysis to model the mechanisms responsible for the assembly observed. To accomplish this, we are solving the time-independent electromagnetic wave-equation to ascertain the electromagnetic power dissipation density, which serves as a source term in the heat equation. We solve the heat equation to determine the temperature distribution in the fluid. Next, we solve the Navier-stokes equation to determine the velocity distribution in the fluid. These detailed numerical simulations will be used to explain the results.

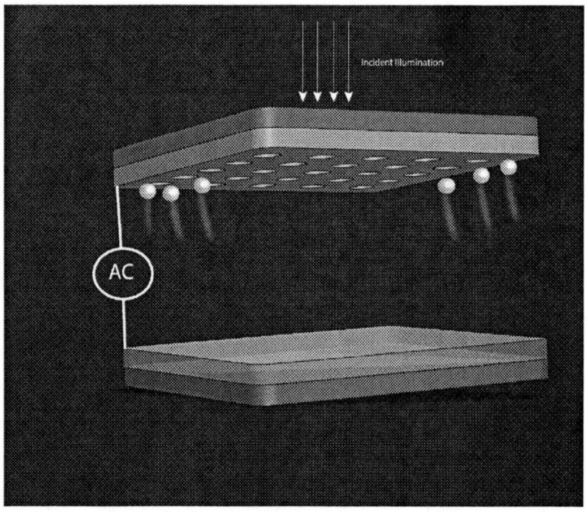

Fig. 1. Illustration of the thermoplasmonic metasurface platform that combines optical illumination of the nanohole array metasurface and applied AC electric field.

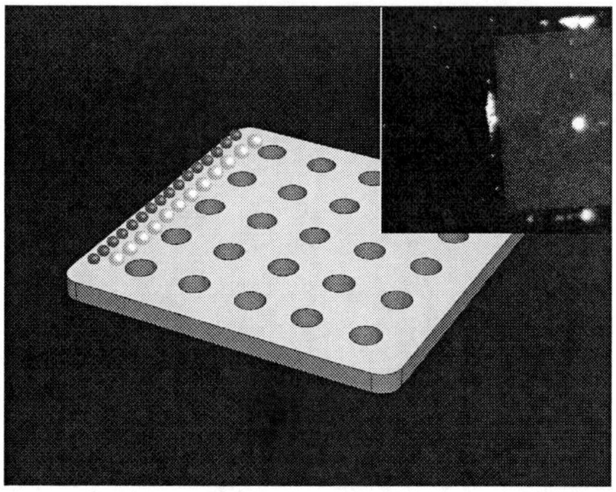

Fig. 2. Arrangement of nanoparticles according to their size in the vicinity of the thermoplasmonic metasurface. Larger particles are aligned closer to the thermoplasmonic metasurface than the smaller particles. This demonstrates the size selectivity of the platform. Inset is an experimental optical image showing the assembled nanoparticles.

REFERENCES

[1] S.R. Yeh, M. Seul, and B. I. Shraiman, "Assembly of ordered colloidal aggregrates by electric-field-induced fluid flow," Nature, vol. 386, no. 6620, pp. 57–59, Mar. 1997.

[2] T. M. Squires and M. Z. Bazant, "Induced-charge electro-osmosis," J. Fluid Mech, vol. 509, pp. 217–252, 2004.

[3] J. C. Ndukaife, A. V. Kildishev, A. G. A. Nnanna, V. M. Shalaev, S. T. Wereley, and A. Boltasseva, "Long-range and rapid transport of individual nano-objects by a hybrid electrothermoplasmonic nanotweezer," Nat. Nanotechnol., vol. 11, pp. 53–59, 2016.

Time Domain Modeling of Active Materials

(invited)

Shaimaa I. Azzam, Ludmila J. Prokopeva, and Alexander V. Kildishev
School of Electrical and Computer Engineering and Birck Nanotechnology Center
Purdue University, West Lafayette, IN 47907, USA
kildishev@purdue.edu

***Abstract*—This talk will overview the recent advances and details of time domain modeling of active materials. We focus on the multiphysics modeling of multi-level atomic systems coupled to full-wave time domain Maxwell's solver to include the transitions taking place in gain media. Different atomic systems, 2-level and higher, are reviewed and compared. The details of efficient and universal numerical implementation, as well as experimental characterization and calibration of the model are discussed. Also, we address simulation techniques that handle spontaneous emission and stochastic noise.**

Keywords — active materials, finite difference time domain, lasers, multi-level atomic systems, multiphysics, rate equations.

I. Introduction

Light propagation and interaction with active media has been the focus of many studies due to the broad spectrum of fascinating applications such as lasers, spasers, and light emitting diodes. A considerable effort has been excreted to develop numerical models that can accurately describe and design important gain-media based physical phenomena in the nanophotonic devices like loss compensation, lasing, reverse saturable absorption and other. Although simple analytical expressions for quantities like laser threshold can be obtained, accurate calculations for realistic systems require an accurate effective and experiment-calibrated numerical model. One of the most successful and accurate multiphysics methodologies is a semi-classical approach where the active medium is described quantum mechanically by a set of rate equations that accounts for the atomic transitions through a multi-level system, while the light propagation is described classically using the Maxwell equations. Such multi-level atomic systems can track the carrier population dynamics for each level along with induced macroscopic polarizations at each point of the computational domain, taking into account energy exchange between the atoms and fields, pumping, and nonradiative decays. In the historical context, examples of these multi-level atomic systems include, 2-level system, 3-level system, 4-level-1-electron system [1], 4-level-2-electron system [2, 3], 6-level systems [4], and 10-level system [5].

In this talk, we are drawing attention to the key differences between the modeling techniques related to each system briefly covering each model's strengths and weaknesses. Each of these models is well-suited to a specific class of applications, materials and/or device geometry, therefore, getting a detailed overview about the unique characteristics of each of these models is beneficial for making the right choice. Also, other important simulation details such as modeling the effects of stochastic noise [6] and random lasing [7] on active devices will be described.

The authors acknowledge the financial support by DARPA/DSO Extreme Optics and Imaging (EXTREME) Program, Award HR00111720032.

Once the mathematical model is chosen, there is a need for a universal yet effective numerical implementation with a calibration procedure to fit the dynamic parameters of the gain media to the data obtained from an experimental setup.

II. Multi-level Atomic Models

There has been a plethora of multi-level atomic models in the literature dealing with multiphysics numerical modeling of active materials. Here, we discuss the main structure behind these models. The molecule of a gain material is described quantum mechanically using a multi-level atomic model that incorporates all significant transitions (radiative and nonradiatvie). These transitions produce microscopic dipole moments that are then averaged to obtain the induced macroscopic polarizations satisfying a phase-relaxed Lorentz ordinary differential equation (ODE). The polarizations are coupled to the Maxwell equations through the electric flux density $\mathbf{D} = \varepsilon_0\mathbf{E} + \sum_{n=1}^{n_{max}} \mathbf{P}_n$, where $\mathbf{P}_n$ is the macroscopic polarizations due to n^{th} transition [1].

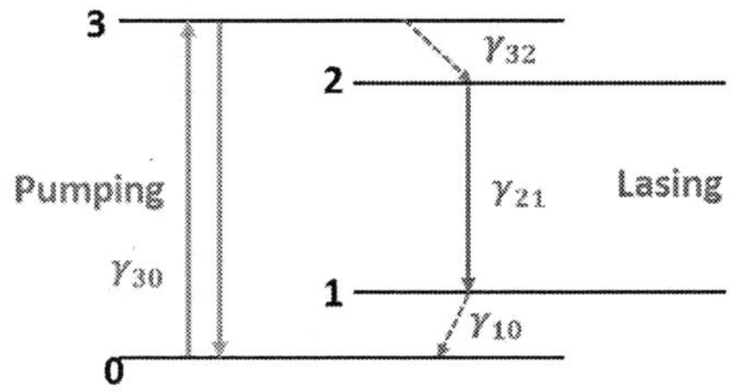

Fig. 1. Jablonski diagram of the allowed transitions in a four-level one-electron atomic model.

One example successfully tested and experimentally validated in our group for lasing is a 4-level-1-electron model described by the Jablonski diagram shown in Fig. 1, and the population kinetics defined by the rate equations:

$$\begin{cases} \dot{N}_3 = -\dfrac{N_3}{\tau_{32}} + \dfrac{1}{\hbar\omega_{30}}\mathbf{E}\cdot\left(\dot{\mathbf{P}}_{30} + \dfrac{\Delta\omega_{30}}{2}\mathbf{P}_{30}\right) \\ \dot{N}_2 = \dfrac{N_3}{\tau_{32}} - \dfrac{N_2}{\tau_{21}} + \dfrac{1}{\hbar\omega_{21}}\mathbf{E}\cdot\left(\dot{\mathbf{P}}_{21} + \dfrac{\Delta\omega_{21}}{2}\mathbf{P}_{21}\right) \\ \dot{N}_1 = \dfrac{N_2}{\tau_{21}} - \dfrac{N_1}{\tau_{10}} - \dfrac{1}{\hbar\omega_{21}}\mathbf{E}\cdot\left(\dot{\mathbf{P}}_{21} + \dfrac{\Delta\omega_{21}}{2}\mathbf{P}_{21}\right) \\ \dot{N}_0 = \dfrac{N_1}{\tau_{10}} - \dfrac{1}{\hbar\omega_{30}}\mathbf{E}\cdot\left(\dot{\mathbf{P}}_{30} + \dfrac{\Delta\omega_{30}}{2}\mathbf{P}_{30}\right) \end{cases}, \quad (1)$$

where N_i is population density at the ith level and Newton's notation for $\partial/\partial t$ is used. Life time between levels i and j is denoted as τ_{ij} and the energy difference between the two level corresponds to an angular frequency of ω_{ij}.

The macroscopic polarization vectors describing the 21 and 30 the transitions are given by a Lorentzian type ODE, where we add non-symmetry to the linewidth (observed experimentally) by adding the non-zero phase:

$$\ddot{\mathbf{P}}_{ij} + \Delta\omega_{ij}\dot{\mathbf{P}}_{ij} + \omega_{ij}^2\mathbf{P}_{ij} = k_{ij}\left(N_j - N_i\right)\left[\mathbf{E} + \nu_{ij}\dot{\mathbf{E}}\right], \quad (2)$$

where $ij \in \{21, 30\}$, $\Delta\omega_{ij}$ is the damping coefficient, and k_{ij} is the coupling factor between polarization $\mathbf{P}_{ij}$ and the **E**-field of light, and ν_{ij} is the non-zero phase correction coefficient. The Lorenzian lineshape in (2) is given just as an example, however, most of other schemes follow the general framework described by this representative sample.

The model has been successfully used to design and optimize various active devices and systems such as directional spaser arrays [8] and lasing in hyperbolic metamaterials [9]. A six-level system has also been developed to numerically simulate a lasing system using a more complicated organic laser dye with non-negligible split transitions [4]. To date, even more sophisticated models that account for dye bleaching have been proposed [5]. The full review of different systems and modeling techniques will be published elsewhere [10]. We also discuss the connection of the model to the classic density matrix formalism.

Another important aspect of the modeling of gain materials is fitting the kinetic parameters of the gain material such as lifetimes, dephasing time and coupling strength to the experimental results obtained from the optical characterization of the gain material samples. For example, some parameters of the dyes depend strongly on the host – not all combinations are covered in the literature, and, in principle, those values shall be experimentally fitted. To retrieve the parameters, additional pump-probe experiments and quantum yield characterization are required. For example, in Fig. 2 we show the results of fitting the parameters of a Rh800 dye in an epoxy solid film [1]. Different pulse durations and carrier wavelengths are used to ensure the proper retrieved values.

In addition, stochastic noise plays a non-negligible role in some structures and there have been several approaches to account for this noise with advanced numerical models in the time-domain [6], which are also covered as a part of our focused review of this multiphysics modeling framework.

CONCLUSION

A comprehensive overview of the time domain multiphysics approach to modeling active materials using carrier populations' kinetic equations will be given. Emphasis on the critical issues regarding each technique and how each technique compares vs. other methods will be highlighted. Other important aspects such as fitting of the numerical material models to the optical characterization of experimental samples of gain materials and realistic numerical implementation of quantum noise will be covered.

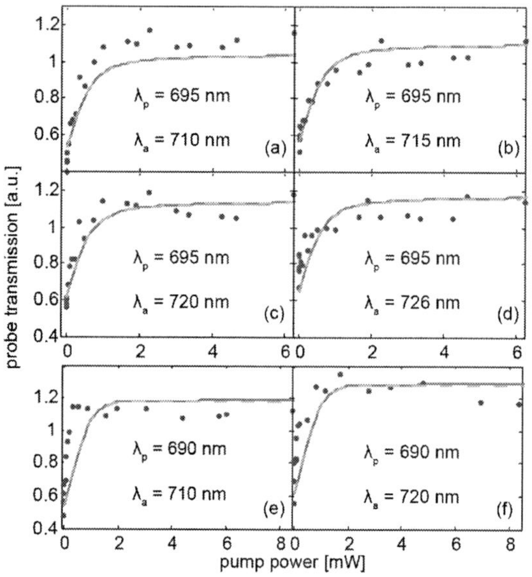

Fig. 2. Fitted transmission results performed with 2 ps (a-d) and 103 fs (e-f) pulse duration at different probing wavelengths.

REFERENCES

[1] J. Trieschmann, S. Xiao, L. J. Prokopeva, V. P. Drachev, and A. V. Kildishev, "Experimental retrieval of the kinetic parameters of a dye in a solid film," Optics Express, vol. 19, pp. 18253-18259, 2011.

[2] S. Chang and A. Taflove, "Finite-difference time-domain model of lasing action in a four-level two-electron atomic system," Optics Express, vol. 12, pp. 3827-3833, 2004.

[3] A. Taflove and S. C. Hagness, Computational Electrodynamics: The Finite-Difference Time-Domain Method, Artech House, p. 394, 2005.

[4] S. I. Azzam1, Z. Wang, J. Fang1, J. Liu, L. J. Prokopeva, N. Arnold, X. Meng, V.M. Shalaev, and A. V. Kildishev (unpublished).

[5] S. L. Chua, B. Zhen, J. Lee, J. Bravo-Abad, O. Shapira, and M. Soljačić, "Modeling of threshold and dynamics behavior of organic nanostructured lasers," Journal of Materials Chemistry C, vol. 2, pp. 1463-1473, 2014.

[6] J. Andreasen and H. Cao, "Finite-difference time-domain formulation of stochastic noise in macroscopic atomic systems," Journal of Lightwave Technology, vol. 27, pp. 4530-4535, 2009.

[7] X. Jiang, and C. M. Soukoulis, "Time dependent theory for random lasers," Physical Review Letters, vol. 85, pp. 70, 2000.

[8] X. Meng, J. Liu, A. V. Kildishev and V. M. Shalaev, "Highly directional spaser array for the red wavelength region," Laser & Photonics Reviews, vol. 8, pp. 896–903, 2014.

[9] R. Chandrasekar, Z. Wang, X. Meng, S. I. Azzam, M. Y. Shalaginov, A. Lagutchev, Y. L. Kim, A. Wei, A. V. Kildishev, A. Boltasseva, and V. M. Shalaev, "Lasing action with gold nanorod hyperbolic metamaterials," ACS Photonics, vol. 4, pp. 674–680, 2017.

[10] L. J. Prokopeva, S. I. Azzam, and A. V. Kildishev, Multiphysics Approach to Active Nanophotonics with Multi-Level Atomic Systems (unpublished).

Coupling Electron Transport with Maxwell Equations for Modelling Optically Tunable Photonic Elements

Michael Povolotskyi
Birck Nanotechnology Center
Purdue University
West Lafayette IN, USA
mpovolot@purdue.edu

Ludmila Prokopeva
School of ECE and
Birck Nanotechnology Center
Purdue University
West Lafayette IN, USA
lprokop@purdue.edu

Alexander Kildishev
School of ECE and
Birck Nanotechnology Center
Purdue University
West Lafayette IN, USA
kildisha@purdue.edu

***Abstract*—Numerical approach to modelling optically controlled photonic devices is presented. The model is based on a self-consistent solution of electron and hole transport equations, semiconductor Bloch equations and Maxwell equations.**

***Keywords*—hydrodynamic model, Maxwell equations, numerical modelling, semiconductor Bloch Equations.**

I. INTRODUCTION

We are now at a stage when electronic logic devices are reaching their limits, and optical devices are supposed to replace them, at least in some applications. Several solutions have been proposed in theoretical works, and the principle has been proven experimentally during the last 10 years. For traditional von Neumann paradigm, optics can offer multiple channel operation simultaneously and zero energy logic elements [1]. The technical problem with those solutions is that the optical elements have cm scales, require ideal laboratory conditions for functioning, and thus, are very far from becoming practical devices. To address this issue, one should look for nanoscale dynamic photonic components, operating at THz frequencies, to substitute glass prisms and lenses. One reason why such components are not available yet, is that there is no reliable design methodologies and tools for simulation of nanoscale dynamic photonic elements. The simulation engine should be able to describe electromagnetic wave propagation, interaction with media on the nanoscale along with non-equilibrium dynamics of electrons and lattice ions. We present a numerical model of light propagation in a solid state medium, where the response is computed based on microscopic non-equilibrium thermodynamic model.

II. MODEL

In the model light propagation equations are coupled with inter-band dipole transition dynamics in semiconductors and thermodynamics of electron and hole gas.

A. Electron Transport Model

Evolution of electrons and holes is described using hydrodynamic model [2]. The model considers conservation of particles, momentum and energy in the electron/hole gas under the light excitation. The position dependent quantities of the model are particle densities, drift velocities and temperatures for electrons and holes, respectively. They are determined from the conservation laws.

1) Conservation of Particles

In terms of electron and hole densities n_e and n_h, drift velocities $\mathbf{v}_e$ and $\mathbf{v}_h$ the particle conservation reads:

$$\partial_t n_e + \nabla(n_e \mathbf{v}_e) = G - R; \partial_t n_h + \nabla(n_h \mathbf{v}_h) = G - R, \qquad (1)$$

where G and R are generation and recombination rates.

2) Conservation of Momentum

Conservation of momentum considers the Lorentz force $\mathbf{F}$, pressure of the electron/hole gas p, momentum relaxation with the time constant τ, and gain/loss of momentum due to generation and recombination. Assuming the parabolic bands, the equation for the drift velocity $\mathbf{v}$ reads:

$$\begin{aligned} m_e \partial_t \mathbf{v}_e + m_e \mathbf{v}_e \nabla \mathbf{v}_e - \mathbf{F}_e + \frac{\nabla p_e}{n_e} &= -\frac{m_e \mathbf{v}}{\tau_{e,v}} + \frac{(G-R) m_e \mathbf{v}_e}{n_e} \\ m_h \partial_t \mathbf{v}_h + m_h \mathbf{v}_h \nabla \mathbf{v}_h - \mathbf{F}_h + \frac{\nabla p_h}{n_h} &= -\frac{m_h \mathbf{v}}{\tau_{h,v}} + \frac{(G-R) m_h \mathbf{v}_h}{n_h}. \end{aligned} \qquad (2)$$

3) Conservation of Energy

The local temperatures can be determined from the particle energy w conservation law. The energy is changed due to the Lorentz force and the gas pressure. The energy excess over the equilibrium energy w_0, which corresponds to the lattice temperature, leads to the energy relaxation. Finally, the energy is added to the system by the generation of electrons and holes. Hence, the single particle energy balance for electron and hole reads:

$$\begin{aligned} \partial_t w_e + \mathbf{v}_e \nabla w_e - \mathbf{F}_e \mathbf{v}_e + \frac{1}{n_e} \nabla(\mathbf{v}_e p_e) &= -\frac{w_e - w_e^0}{\tau_{e,w}} + \frac{(G-R) w_e}{n_e} \\ \partial_t w_e + \mathbf{v}_h \nabla w_h - \mathbf{F}_h \mathbf{v}_h + \frac{1}{n_h} \nabla(\mathbf{v}_h p_h) &= -\frac{w_h - w_h^0}{\tau_{h,w}} + \frac{(G-R) w_h}{n_h}. \end{aligned} \qquad (3)$$

The generation/recombination rates G and R have both non-radiative (Shockley-Read-Hall and Auger) and radiative contributions: $G - R = (G-R)_{\text{non-rad}} + (G-R)_{\text{rad}}$.

To close the equation system (1-3), it is assumed that the particles have local 'drifted' Fermi Dirac distribution. E.g., for

Partially supported by DARPA/DSO Extreme Optics and Imaging (EXTREME) Program, Award HR00111720032.

an electron, the probability to occupy a state at position **r** and wave vector **k** reads:

$$f_e(\mathbf{r},\mathbf{k}) = \left(1+\exp\left(\left(E_c - E_f + \tfrac{(\hbar\mathbf{k}-m\mathbf{v})^2}{2m}\right)\Big/\left(k_{\mathrm{B}}T\right)\right)\right)^{-1}, \quad (4)$$

where E_c is the band edge energy, E_f and T are local chemical potential and temperature, and **v** is the average (drift) velocity of the gas at point **r**. Then, the particle pressure and energy can be expressed in terms of temperature and drift velocity:

$$p = k_{\mathrm{B}} n T_h;\ w = \tfrac{3}{2} k_{\mathrm{B}} T_h + \tfrac{1}{2} m\mathbf{v}^2, \quad (5)$$

where T_h is the hydrodynamic temperature. It depends on the degeneracy of the gas and is related to the thermodynamic temperature T from Eq. (1), as follows [3]:

$$T_h = T\frac{2}{3}\frac{F_{3/2}((E_f - E_0)/(k_{\mathrm{B}}T))}{F_{1/2}((E_f - E_0)/(k_{\mathrm{B}}T))}, \quad (6)$$

where $F_j(\eta)$ is the Fermi integral of the order j.

B. Radiative Generation-Recombination Processes

Generation recombination processes are described by semiconductor Bloch equations [4]. Direct dipole transitions between valence and conduction band for different electron wave vectors **k** give contribution to both radiative generation/recombination rates and polarization **P**:

$$\left(G-R\right)_{\mathrm{rad}} = -2\frac{2}{(2\pi)^3}\mathrm{Im}\left(\int \frac{\mathbf{d}(\mathbf{k})\mathbf{E}(t)}{\hbar} Q_{\mathbf{k}}^{*}(t)d^3\mathbf{k}\right)$$
$$\mathbf{P} = 2\frac{2}{(2\pi)^3}\mathrm{Re}\left(\int \mathbf{d}(\mathbf{k},t)Q_{\mathbf{k}}(t)d^3\mathbf{k}\right), \quad (7)$$

where $\mathbf{d}(\mathbf{k})$ is the dipole moment of the transition, $\mathbf{E}(t)$ is the electric field and $Q_{\mathbf{k}}(t)$ is the dimensionless polarization contribution, found from the Bloch equation:

$$i\hbar d_t Q_{\mathbf{k}}(t) = \left(E_e(\mathbf{k}) - E_h(\mathbf{k})\right)Q_{\mathbf{k}}(t) +$$
$$\left(n_e(\mathbf{k},t) - n_h(\mathbf{k},t)\right)\mathbf{d}(k)\mathbf{E}(t) - \frac{i\hbar}{\tau_r}Q_{\mathbf{k}}(t), \quad (8)$$

where $E_{e,h}(\mathbf{k})$ is the energy of electrons and holes, τ_r is the relaxation time. The model neglects quantum correlations between particles, such as exciton effects.

C. Electromagnetic Field Equations

The microscopic Maxwell equations are written with assumption that the medium polarization can be divided in two contributions: the interband and the intraband. The intraband polarization is described by the electron/hole charge and current densities from the transport model, and the interband polarization is from the semiconductor Bloch equations (7,8). The Maxwell equations, essential for the case, are:

$$\nabla(\mathbf{E}+4\pi\mathbf{P}) = 4\pi e\left(n_h - n_e + N_D^+ - N_A^-\right)$$
$$c\nabla\times\mathbf{H} = 4\pi e\left(n_h\mathbf{v}_h - n_e\mathbf{v}_e\right) + \partial_t\left(\mathbf{E}+4\pi\mathbf{P}\right), \quad (9)$$

where N_D^+ and N_A^- are concentrations of the ionized donors and acceptors.

III. Numerical Implementation

The transport equations (Sec. II.A) are solved on a finite element mesh using the libMesh library [5]. The time integration is done by a 1st order implicit scheme. The corresponding linear systems are solved by PETSC linear solver [6]. The major carrier density in a doped semiconductor is by many orders bigger that the minor carrier density. Therefore, instead of density, the chemical potential from (1) is used as a variable for major carriers. The Bloch equations (Sec. II.B) are reduced to a set of ODEs for each wave vector and space coordinates. They are integrated by an explicit 2nd order scheme. All equations are then coupled to a time domain Maxwell's solver, where a standard 2nd order leap-frog scheme is used, while the material dispersion outside of the transport domain is implemented using the Generalized Dispersive Material model approach [7].

Example of electron transport simulations under the optical excitation is shown in Fig. 1. The non-equilibrium carrier concentration leads to the heating of the electron gas and creates a flux of electrons from the excitation area.

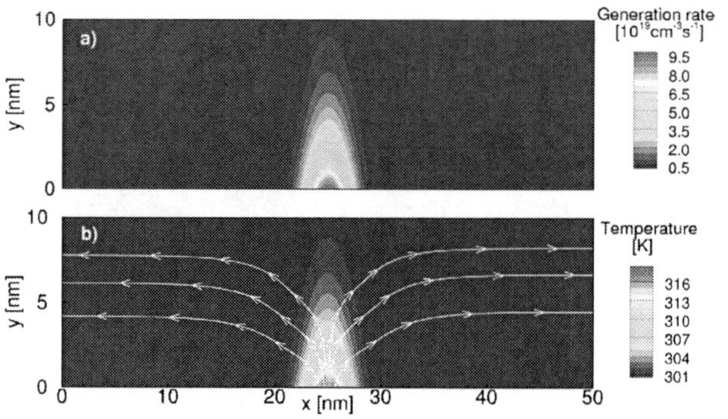

Fig. 1. Simulation result of electron transport under localized optical excitation. a) Color map of the optical excitation rate, and b) color map of the electron temperature. White stream lines show flux of electrons.

References

[1] H. J. Caulfield and S. Dolev, "Why future supercomputing requires optics," Nature Photonics 4, 261-263, 2010.

[2] D. L. Woolard, *et al.*, "Hydrodynamic electron-transport model: Nonparabolic corrections to the streaming terms," Physical Review B 44, 11119–11131, 1991.

[3] A. Leone, *et al.*, "Hydrodynamic simulation of semiconductor devices operating at low temperature," IEEE Trans. On Computer-Aid. Des. Of Int. Cir. And Systems 13(11), 1400–1408, 1994.

[4] R.V. Baltz, "Semiconductor Bloch equations," Chapter 27 in Semiconductor Optics by C. F. Klingshirn, 4th Edition, Springer, 2012.

[5] B. S. Kirk, *et al.*, "libMesh: A C++ Library for Parallel Adaptive Mesh Refinmaent/Coarsening Simulations," Engineering with Computers 22, 237-254, 2006.

[6] S. Balay, *et al.*, PETSc Web page, http://www.mcs.anl.gov/petsc

[7] L. J. Prokopeva, J. D. Borneman, and A. V. Kildishev, "Optical dispersion models for time-domain modeling of metal-dielectric nanostructures", IEEE Transactions on Magnetics, 47(5), 1150-1153, 2011.

Efficient Multiphysics and Multiscale FDTD Methods for Terahertz Plasmonic Devices

Shubhendu Bhardwaj
Electrical and Computer Engineering
Florida International University
10555, W. Flagler Street, Miami, FL, USA
sbhardwa@fiu.edu

***Abstract*—Modeling terahertz plasmonic devices is a multiphysics and multiscale problem. Due to high mesh density in the electron transport regions, the simulation times are long. In this work, we develop hybrid coupled finite difference time domain (FDTD) methods for fast design of terahertz plasmonic devices. The methods employ implicit solution (using Alternate Direction Implicit), coupled with hydrodynamic modeling for plasmonic applications. The theory, simulation and time-improvement related results will be presented at the conference.**

Keywords—FDTD, graphene, HEMT, hydrodynamic, plasmonic modeling , terahertz.

I. Introduction

2D electron-gas based terahertz electronics has gained interest for terahertz operations such as mixing and detection. Underlying phenomenon in these devices is plasma-wave oscillations in the 2D electron gas (2DEG) channel [1]. These 2DEG based devices can be modeled using multiphysics modeling tool that integrates the electromagnetic propagation effects and electron transport effects within the devices [2]. This is often accomplished using finite difference time domain (FDTD) based coupled models that integrate hydrodynamic equations in their solution.

A typical 2DEG-channel has an electron density of 10^{11} to $10^{13} cm^{-2}$. Therefore, the plasmonic wavelengths would be 10 to 1000 times smaller than that the free-space. This requires a mesh-size in the order of $\lambda/5000$. As per Courant-Friedrich-Levy (CFL) condition, FDTD time-step for this simulation is 10^{-17}s. This results in long simulations times using traditional FDTD coupled hydrodynamic equations.

In this work, the time-efficiency of the traditional FDTD based model [2] is improved using unconditionally stable FDTD algorithms. First, we present Alternating Direction Implicit (ADI) FDTD method [3] coupled with hydrodynamic equations for terahertz plasmonic applications. Secondly, an iterative-ADI based FDTD method [4] coupled with hydrodynamic equations, is presented for efficient yet accurate modeling. These methods are referred to as ADI-FDTD-HD and it-ADI-FDTD-HD, respectively.

II. Governing Equations for Multiphysics Modeling

Solution requires modeling of electrodynamic fields via

$$\nabla \times \vec{H} = \frac{\partial \vec{D}}{\partial t} + \vec{J} + \sigma \vec{E}, \quad \text{and} \qquad (1)$$

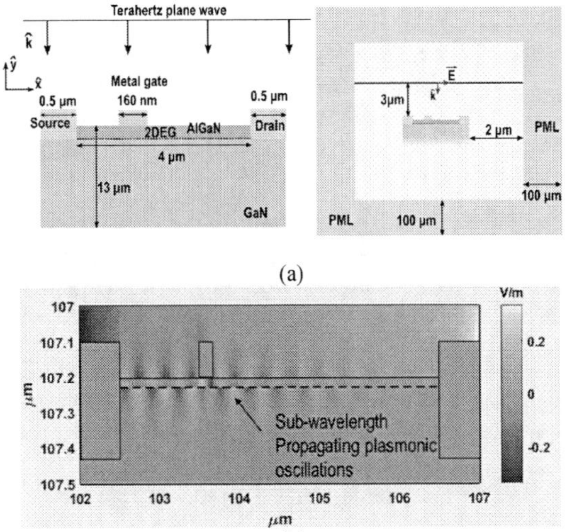

(b)

Fig. 1. GaN/AlGaN High Electron Mobility Transistor (HEMT) model used for the performance evaluation of the algorithms. Left: Schematic showing device-dimensions and excitation-method. Right: Simulation domain and position of PML boundaries. (b) Plasmonic field obtained at t=3ps, propagating away from discontinuity.

$$\nabla \times \vec{E} = -\frac{\partial \vec{B}}{\partial t} - \sigma^* \vec{H}. \qquad (2)$$

For 2D TE$_Z$ solution, electric field $\vec{E} = \hat{x}E_x + \hat{y}E_y$ is used. Electrical and magnetic conductivity parameters, i.e. σ and σ^*, are used for the modeling of anisotropic, perfectly matched layer surrounding the domain. Electron transport in the channel is modelled via hydrodynamic equations, given by,

$$\frac{\partial n_{sh}}{\partial t} + \frac{\partial j}{\partial x} = 0, \quad \text{and} \qquad (3)$$

$$\frac{\partial j}{\partial t} + v\frac{\partial j}{\partial x} + \frac{j \partial v}{\partial x} = -\frac{qnE_x}{m_e} - \frac{j}{\tau} - \frac{KT}{m_e}. \qquad (4)$$

Here n_{sh} is the sheet carrier density, j ($= n_{sh}v$) is the sheet current and v is the electron velocity within the 2DEG channel. τ refers to the momentum relaxation time and m_e is the effective electron mass. q = 1.6×10−19 C is the charge-magnitude of a single electron. T is the electron temperature in the channel and K is the Boltzmann constant.

III. ADI-FDTD-HD AND IT-ADI-FDTD-HD METHODS

Note that solution of hydrodynamic equations is carried by upwind discretization, similar to prior work in [2] and will not be discussed here. The distinction of this work, i.e. use of ADI-FDTD and it-ADI-FDTD methods is briefly explained in the following.

A. ADI-FDTD-HD Method

The ADI-FDTD approach uses a splitting-operator applied on the electrodynamic equations to yield an implicit form of difference equations [3, 4]. Notably, these equations are tridiagonal and can be solved at a small computational cost. In the meantime, the time-steps can be arbitrarily large, reducing the simulation-times. In ADI-FDTD method, the accuracy is perturbed by a second order terms (which is truncated so as to achieve a tridiagonal system of linear implicit equations [5]). This error term (so-called splitting error or truncation error) is proportional to Δt^2 and second order spacial derivative of field [3] (Δt is the time-step).

B. Iterative ADI-FDTD-HD Method

The iterative method uses the basic ADI-FDTD method with added iterative corrections to correct ignored Δt^2 term [4]. Note that it-ADI-FDTD and ADI-FDTD are both $O(\Delta t^2)$ accurate. However, iterative method has more accuracy due to correction of additionally truncated term of the ADI method. The added iterations come at some time-cost, but overall performance is maintained over the traditional FDTD-HD method.

IV. PERFORMANCE COMPARISON

For performance bench-marking, we modeled a gallium nitride (GaN) based High Electron Mobility Transistor (HEMT) device under the influence of an incident terahertz plane-wave excitation (freq. = 5 THz) (Fig. 1). A small gate discontinuity is used for coupling of the incident terahertz waves to the 2DEG channel. The channel and media parameters are chosen as $n_{sh} = 5 \times 10^{12}\ cm^{-2}$, $\epsilon_r = 9.5$, $m_e = 0.2m_o$ and $\tau = 1.14$ ps (considering low temperature operation). The cell-size along x-axis was chosen to be $\Delta x = 4$ nm in the channel area. The minimum mesh of $\Delta y = 1$ nm was used in vertical direction. For outside the channel regions, non-uniform meshing scheme was used, resulting in 1460 and 740 cells respectively in the horizontal and vertical directions. Simulation is allowed to run for 3 ps.

For comparison, the obtained channel-currents are plotted in Fig. 2. The simulation-cases considered here are *CN*=300, <*CN*=300, *it*=3>, <*CN*=300, *it*=7>. Here *CN* refers to Courant Number and *it* refers to the number of iterations used for the iterative case. That is, *CN*=300 case is for ADI-FDTD-HD algorithm and rest are for it-ADI-FDT-HD method. As shown in the plot, in ADI-FDTD-HD method the solution diverges from the reference data, however errors are recovered by adding more and more iterations. Specifically, for 7 iterations the solution converges to the reference solution. Here, the reference solution corresponds to the Yee's FDTD method [6].

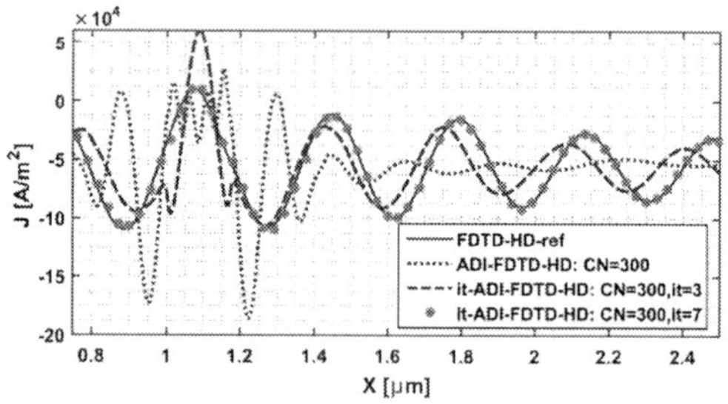

Fig. 2. Channel current recorded at 3 ps using ADI-FDTD and iterative ADI-FDTD methods. Courant Numbers (*CN*) and iteration count (*it*) are varied for different simulation cases.

Table I. TIME COMPARISON FOR IT-ADI-FDTD-HD METHODS

	ΔT (s)	CPU-Time Per Time-Step (s)	CPU-Time Total (Hrs)
FDTD-HD	3.24×10^{-18}	0.35	90
it-ADI-FDTD-HD (*CN*=100, *it*=2)	3.24×10^{-16}	15.17	39.14
it-ADI-FDTD-HD (*CN*=200, *it*=4)	6.48×10^{-16}	30.25	19.16
it-ADI-FDTD-HD (*CN*=300, *it*=7)	9.72×10^{-16}	53.11	43.64

Comparison of total simulation times for various scenarios are shown in Table I. As shown *CN*=300, *it*=7 case takes only half of total simulation time taken by the original reference case. Thus, high degree of accuracy if achieved with almost 50% decrease in simulation times. Note that CPU-time for ADI-FDTD-HD cases may also be calculated by simply dividing the it-ADI-FDTD-HD's CPU time by corresponding *it* count.

V. CONCLUSIONS

We have proposed efficient method for multiphysics modeling using iterative-ADI-FDTD methods. For the devices under consideration, the total simulation time was reduced by a factor of 0.42 using it-ADI-FDTD-HD method, while nominal 3% error was registered. Overall, we maintained the accuracy-levels with significant time-cost advantages as compared to traditional explicit-FDTD modeling.

REFERENCES

[1] M. Dyakonov and M. Shur, "Detection, mixing, and frequency multiplication of terahertz radiation by two-dimensional electronic fluid," *IEEE Transactions on Electron Devices*, vol. 43, no. 3, pp. 380–387, Mar. 1996.

[2] S. Bhardwaj, N. K. Nahar, S. Rajan, and J. L. Volakis, "Numerical analysis of terahertz emissions from an ungated hemt using full-wave hydrodynamic model," *IEEE Transactions on Electron Devices*, vol. 63, no. 3, pp. 990–996, 2016.

[3] T. Namiki, "A new FDTD algorithm based on alternating-direction implicit method," *IEEE Transactions on Microwave Theory and Techniques*, vol. 47, no. 10, pp. 2003–2007, 1999.

[4] S. Wang, F. L. Teixeira, and J. Chen, "An iterative ADI-FDTD with reduced splitting error," *IEEE Microwave and Wireless Components Letters*, vol. 15, no. 2, pp. 92–94, 2005.

[5] S. G. Garcia, Tae-Woo Lee and S. C. Hagness, "On the accuracy of the ADI-FDTD method," in *IEEE Antennas and Wireless Propagation Letters*, vol. 1, pp. 31-34, 2002.

[6] Taflove, Allen, and Susan C. Hagness. "Computational Electrodynamics: the finite-difference time-domain method". Artech house, 2005.

Frequency-Domain versus Time-Domain Analysis of Slow-light Mesophotonic Waveguides: Theoretical Insights for Practically Realizable Devices

Stavroula Foteinopoulou
Electrical and Computer Engineering Dept. (ECE)
Univ. of New Mexico
Albuquerque, NM 87131, USA
sfoteino@unm.edu

***Abstract*— Slow-light mesophotonic waveguides have gained increasing interest in the recent years owing to their potential for time-delay control of optical signals, crucial for all-optical circuitry, as well as EM energy storage and field enhancement which is important for driving a stronger light-matter interaction. Yet, the design of such systems has hitherto been predominantly directed by modal-type of analyses in frequency domain. We discuss here why frequency domain analysis fails for real systems, leading to mistaken predictions for the effective propagation speed of the EM signal. In particular, by utilizing a time-domain analysis we demonstrate a slow-light paradigm waveguide system which contradicts the widespread notion that the group-index is generally a good measure of the light's speed effective slow-down factor within the waveguide. In particular, our counterexample shows that it is entirely possible when two modes are compared that it would be the one with the lower group index to yield effectively the larger light slow-down factor. We analyze the salient characteristics of the modes with the higher light slow-down-factor merit to understand how to enable slow light in practical platforms. Our results suggest that in order for a large group index to practically effect a large slow-down factor it should be accompanied by a large modal index bandwidth. This can occur when both the group velocity and the group-velocity dispersion are simultaneously near-zero.**

Keywords—finite difference time domain method, group index, group velocity, group velocity dispersion, left-handed materials, negative-index media, slow light, wave dispersion.

I. INTRODUCTION

Electromagnetic (EM) modeling methods fall within two large classes: frequency-domain methods and time-domain methods. In the former methods, the EM wave solutions are sought for a fixed frequency, ω. This can be done numerically, for example with the Finite Difference Frequency Domain (FDFD) method [1-3], or analytically for simple geometries [4-7]. These frequency-domain methods generally provide important information for a system's response to incoming EM waves. However, they fail to accurately predict the time-dependent response to realistic source excitations that are not necessarily perfect monochromatic plane waves. Indeed, it is possible to construct the response of the system in time-domain by utilizing frequency-domain methods together with rigorous-modal matching analysis [8]. However, this can get increasingly tedious or difficult as structures or EM-wave launch geometries get more complicated. A brute-force method

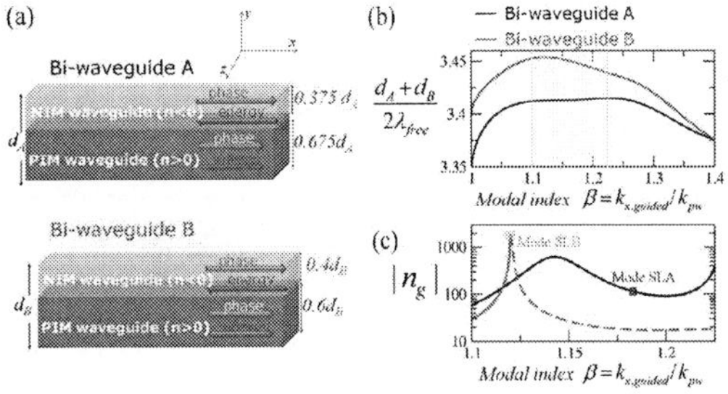

Fig. 1. (a) The bi-waveguide with the size parameters indicated for the two different designs. (b) The wave dispersion for the two bi-waveguide designs, A and B. The frequency is expressed in dimensionless units, by multiplying the inverse of the free-space wavelength, λ_{free}, with the average of the width of the two waveguide designs. The wavevector along the waveguide direction, $k_{x,guided}$, is also scaled with the free-space plane-wave wavevector, k_{pw}. The ratio of the two gives the dimensionless parameter, β, which represents the modal index of the guided mode [11]. (c) Magnitude of the group index, $|n_g|$, versus the modal index, β, for the two waveguide modes seen in (b) in logarithmic scale. Note: dashed lines have been used where the group index becomes negative.

for time-domain analysis is certainly attractive. The most popular method for time-domain analysis is the Finite-Difference-Time-Domain (FDTD) [9]. Free from any assumptions for simplifications, it can model actual experimental set-ups. We discuss here why for slow-light-waveguide [10] problems the FDTD is uniquely suited for designing structures that practically demonstrate a large light propagation slow-down factor. In particular, we present in the following a counter-example where a frequency-domain analysis alone clearly fails to accurately quantify the effective slow-down factor for the propagating slow waveguide mode.

II. RESULTS AND DISCUSSION

In Fig. 1 (a) we show such waveguide counterexample. It comprises a top Negative-Index-Medium (NIM) waveguide and a bottom Positive-Index-Medium (PIM) waveguide. We consider two different designs, A and B, as shown in Fig. 1 (a). Waveguide A, has a width of d_A=4.54 μm, while waveguide B has a width of d_A=5.675 μm. The dispersion relation of the guided mode, i.e., the frequency versus the wave vector along the guide direction, x, is depicted in Fig. 1 (b). Both frequency and wave vector are represented in dimensionless units [see caption of Fig. 1]. This dimensionless scaled wave vector, β, is known as modal index [11]. Note a single guided-mode band is present for each design; this is an inherent property of the NIM-PIM heterostructure [12]. We recognize the existence of a mode where the guided mode dispersion flattens for both waveguide designs, i.e., has a large light slow-down factor as represented by the magnitude of the group index, $|n_g|$, depicted in Fig. 1 (c). The modes of interest for waveguide A and waveguide B are designated in the figure with the blue box (mode SLA) and green box (mode SLB) respectively.

We subsequently put the aforementioned frequency-domain predictions under test with a time-domain analysis with the FDTD method. Time-domain analysis captures how EM pulses would travel through the waveguide. Actually, a "trapped rainbow" waveguide phenomenon that was predicted with a ray-optical frequency-domain analysis [7] was later shown to be unfeasible with a rigorous time-domain analysis by Sailing He et al. [8], concurring with further experimental evidence [8]. In the FDTD, we use a numerical Otto configuration set-up [13, 14] yielding an evanescent wave that further excites the guided mode in the bi-waveguide system.

We show the results in Fig. 2. The prism of the Otto configuration, fixes the modal index to $\beta_0=n_{prism}\sin(45^0)$, as EM boundary condition mandate the wavevector along the x-direction to be conserved. The refractive index of the prism, n_{prism}, is set to a fictitious value so that the modal index of modes SLA and SLB is achieved in each case. However, the input EM wave, launched from the left side of the prism, has a Gaussian beam waist, which implies a spread $\Delta\beta$ around the β_0 value. This means, that modes in the vicinity of SLA and SLB will be simultaneously excited. Additionally, for the case of mode SLB, some of these are backward, i.e., have a negative group index [see dotted-line in Fig. 1 (c)]. As a result, EM energy can in principle travel both along the +x and –x

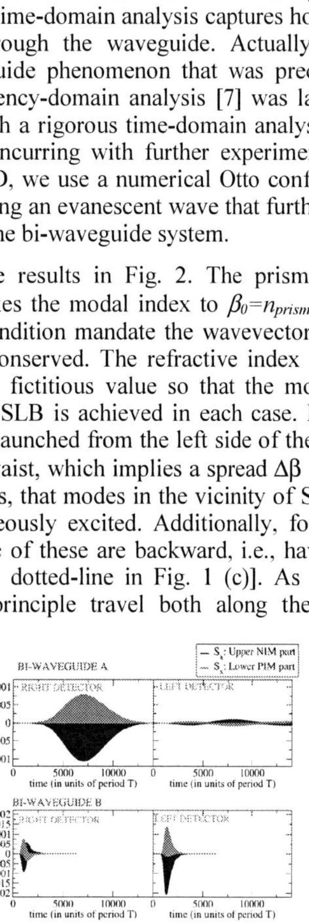

Fig. 2. The Poynting vector along the waveguide direction, x, monitored with time in the FDTD. The averaged values in the upper NIM part (black lines) and in the lower PIM (red lines) are shown. The right (left) detector monitors are placed at a distance of 13.62 μm from the right (left) corner of the excitation prism [5].

directions. So detector monitors are placed in the FDTD simulation both at the left and right side of the prism.

We show in Fig. 2 the time-dependent Poynting vector along the x-direction, S_x, monitored at these detectors. For design A the signal predominantly propagates in the $+x$ direction, with some energy propagating in the $-x$ direction; this is because the spread $\Delta\beta$ inevitably introduces some negative β values. The situation for design B is more complicated as the spread $\Delta\beta$ additionally enables both forward and backward modes with a higher group velocity with a modal index in the vicinity of β_0. For design A, an analysis [5, 15] of the pulsed signal propagation yields an effective slow down factor of ~300. Unlike design A, a similar analysis shows that for design B the effective slow down factor varies with the distance from the prism edge between ~8 and 40. All-in all the time-domain excitation of mode SLA yields a much slower effective propagation speed in comparison to that of mode SLB despite the fact that the group index of mode SLB is about one order of magnitude higher. These results suggest that a flat group-index versus modal index profile together with a large group index are required to obtain an effectively large slow-down factor. This can occur when both the group velocity and the group-velocity dispersion are simultaneously near-zero.

REFERENCES

[1] E. I. Smirnova, C. Chen, M. A. Shapiro, J. R. Sirigiri, and R. J. Temkin, "Simulation of photonic band gaps in metal rod lattices for microwave applications," J. Appl. Phys., vol. 91, pp. 960-968, 2002.

[2] S. Foteinopoulou, M. Kafesaki, E.N. Economou, and C. M. Soukoulis, "Backward surface waves at photonic crystals," Phys. Rev. B, vol. 75, pp. 245116-1-6, 2007.

[3] G. Veronis, Finite-difference Frequency-Domain Technique, Encyclopedia of Nanotechnology, Springer, pp. 843-852, 2012.

[4] C. Vandenbem, S. Foteinopoulou, J. P. Vigneron, and V. Lousse, "Guided waves in a bilayer film made of right- and left-handed materials," presented at Photonic Metamaterials: From Random to Periodic: Topical Meeting and Tabletop Exhibit, Grand Island, Bahamas, June 5–8, 2006, Paper WD5.

[5] S. Foteinopoulou and J.-P. Vigneron, "Extended slow-light field enhancement in positive-index/negative-index heterostructures," Phys. Rev. B, vol. 88, pp. 195144-1-8, 2013.

[6] S. Foteinopoulou, "Electromagnetic energy accumulation in mesophotonic slow-light waveguides," published in 19th International Conference on Transparent Optical Networks (ICTON), IEEE, pp. 1-4, 2017.

[7] K. L. Tsakmakidis, A. D. Boardman, and O. Hess, "Trapped rainbow storage of light in metamaterials," Nature, vol. 450, pp. 397-401, 2007.

[8] S. He, Y. He, and Y. Jin, "Revealing the truth about 'trapped rainbow' storage of light in metamaterials," Scientific Reports, vol. 2, pp. 583-1-9, 2012.

[9] A. Taflove, Computational Electrodynamics: The Finite Difference Time-Domain Method, Artech House, Boston, 1995.

[10] K. L. Tsakmakidis, O. Hess, R. W. Boyd, and X. Zhang, "Ultraslow waves on the nanoscale," Science, vol. 358, pp. eaan5196-1-11, 2017; and references therein.

[11] J. C. Knight, "Photonic crystal fibers," Nature, vol. 424, pp. 847–851, 2003.

[12] A. Alu and N. Engheta, "Guided modes in a waveguide filled with a pair of single-negative (SNG), double-negative (DNG), and/or double-positive (DPS) layers," IEEE Trans. Microwave Theory Tech., vol. 52, pp. 199-210, 2004.

[13] S. Foteinopoulou, G. Kenanakis, N. Katsarakis, I. Tsiapa, M. Kafesaki, E. N. Economou, and C. M. Soukoulis, "Experimental verification of backward wave propagation at photonic crystal surfaces," Appl. Phys. Lett., vol. 91, pp. 214102-1-3, 2007.

[14] A. Otto, "Excitation of nonradiative surface plasma waves in silver by the method of frustrated total reflection," Z. Phys., vol. 216, 398-410, Aug. 1968.

[15] J. Peatross, S. A. Glasgow, and M. Ware, "Average energy flow of optical pulses in dispersive media," Phys. Rev. Lett., vol. 84, pp. 2370 - 2373, 2000.

Estimation of 1090 MHz Signal Environment on Airport Surface by using Multilateration System

Junichi Honda, Yasuyuki Kakubari, and Takuya Otsuyama
Surveillance and Communications Department
Electronic Navigation Research Institute (ENRI)
National Institute of Maritime, Port and Aviation Technology
Chofu, Tokyo 182-0012 Japan
j-honda@enri.go.jp

***Abstract*—This paper presents the estimation of a 1090 MHz signal environment on an airport surface. Secondary surveillance radar and its applications share the 1030 MHz and 1090 MHz frequency bands. Many aircraft emit signals lying in the same frequency band; the consequent increase in the signal amount causes saturation and results in performance degradation. To meet aviation requirements, it is important to manage the signal amount. In this paper, we focus on the 1090 MHz signals and propose an estimation method for the signal amount on an airport surface by using a multilateration system.**

***Index Terms*—secondary surveillance radar, multilateration, ATCRBS, Mode S, 1090 MHz, signal amount.**

I. INTRODUCTION

Secondary surveillance radar (SSR) has become one of the main surveillance systems in civil aviation, and multiraterration (MLAT), wide area MLAT and automatic dependent surveillance - broadcast have been developed so far as SSR applications. These systems use the 1030/1090 MHz frequency bands and share the bands with each other [1]. Therefore, as the demand for aircraft increases, the signal environment becomes increasingly saturated. To ensure the safe operation of aircraft, the signal amount and signal rate should be appropriately managed.

The purpose of this study is to estimate the current signal environment for the 1030/1090 MHz frequency and thereby evaluate the future signal environment. In addition, we consider the environment of distorted signals which affect the detection rate. In this paper, focusing on 1090 MHz, we propose an estimation method for analyzing signal environment on airport surface. Currently, we are investigating a new MLAT system by using radio-over-fiber (RoF) technology [2]. A prototype system has been deployed at Sendai Airport, Japan. The proposed method to acquire signal data uses receiver units implemented in the MLAT system. By comparing the signal data between receivers, we analyze the signal amount, signal rate, and amount of distorted signals on the airport surface. In this paper, we first introduce the experimental system for gathering 1090 MHz signals and then discuss the estimation method for the signal environment. Finally, we show the signal amount and distorted signals from an air traffic control radar beacon system (ATCRBS) and Mode S, which are signals employed in 1090 MHz [3].

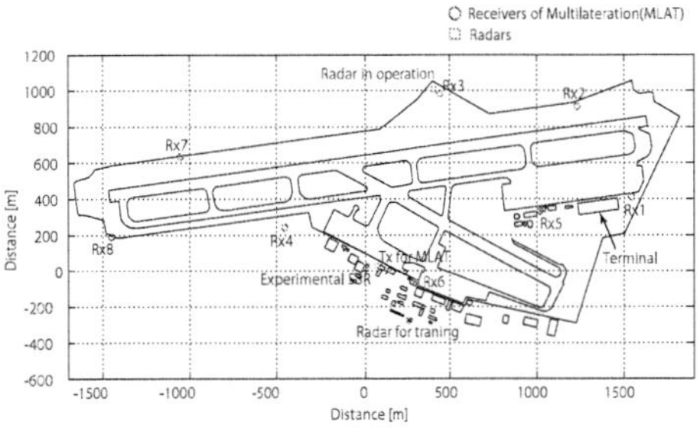

Fig. 1. Experimental environment in Sendai airport.

II. ESTIMATION METHOD FOR SIGNAL ENVIRONMENT

To obtain 1090 MHz signals, an MLAT system is employed. ENRI has developed a new MLAT system called optical-fiber-connected passive surveillance (OCTPASS) [2], and this system has been deployed at Sendai Airport, which is a midsize airport in Japan. OCTPASS has eight receiver units connected to a central signal processing unit through an optical fiber network. The received signals are transmitted to the central processing unit by RoF technology, which facilitates the transmission of RF signals over long distances by amplitude modulation in the optical region. Consequently, OCTPASS directly processes the RF signals at the central processing unit. Our method to analyze the 1090 MHz signals uses the characteristics of OCTPASS.

Fig. 1 shows an experimental environment in Sendai Airport. As shown in the figure, eight OCTPASS receivers are located in the airport. In addition, three transmitters exist. The first is used for actual operations, the second for trainees, and the third for our experimental system. The signal amount at this airport is anticipated to be larger than that at other same-sized airports because of the use of three transmitters.

Next, we describe the method to count the number of 1090 MHz signals. All the received RF signals are transmitted to the central processing unit, which groups the signals collected within an arbitrary time gate. Therefore, we can count and compare the signals at the same arrival time. Whenever a receiver unit detects a signal, the signal is added to the statistical signal amount in the airport even if the signal is not

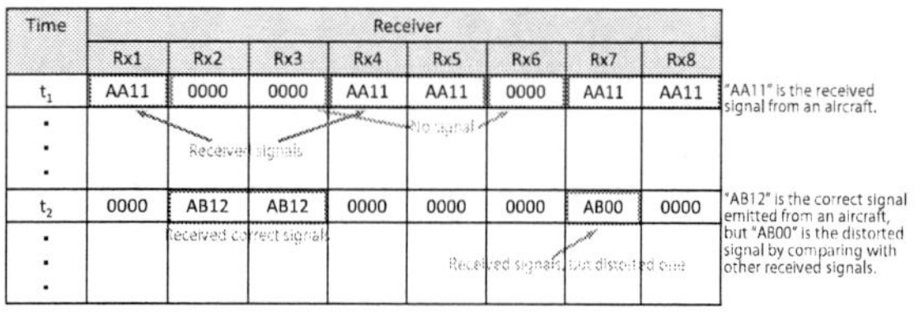

Fig. 2. Distinction between received signals.

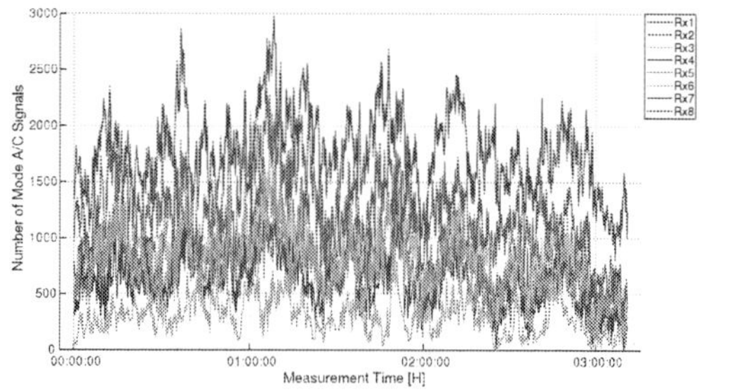

Fig. 3. Signal amount for ATCRBS.

decoded. On the other hand, distorted signals are counted by comparing all received signals. If a received signal is different from other received signals, it is regarded as a distorted signal. Fig. 2 is an example for distinguishing received signals.

III. Estimated Signal Amount and Distorted Signals

We analyzed ATCRBS and Mode S signals in 1090 MHz frequency band. Fig. 3 shows the signal amount for ATCRBS. The figure indicates that the signal amount depends on the receiver position. The data points represent the averaged value for 10 s. The maximum value is approximately 3,000/s. The maximum number of signals is obtained by Rx7, and the minimum by Rx6. The signal amount is large for Rx7 because it is located in a relatively open area, whereas the signal amount for Rx6 is small because it is located around the buildings such as hanger and is shadowed by the airport terminal. Fig. 4 shows the signal amount for Mode S. As shown in this figure, the signal amount is less than 1/10th that of ATCRBS. The time dependence characteristics are the almost same as those shown in Fig. 3.

Finally, we analyzed the distorted signals. In this paper, we present the result for ATCRBS only because of page limitations. Fig. 5 shows the estimated amount of distorted signals based on the data shown in Fig. 3. As an example, we compare the signals from Rx7 at 1:00. The number of distorted signals is approximately 450, and the total received signals is approximately 1,750 from Fig. 3. Therefore, the rate of distorted signals is approximately 25%. The rate of distorted signals depends on the receiver allocation, but in this airport, the performance of a normal MLAT system that requires decoded signals, might become worse.

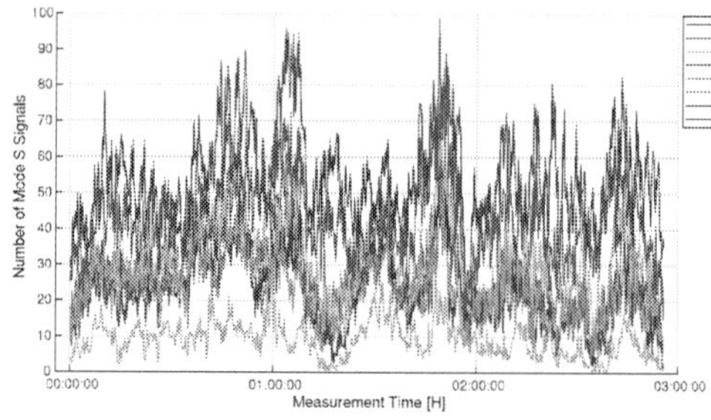

Fig. 4. Signal amount for Mode S.

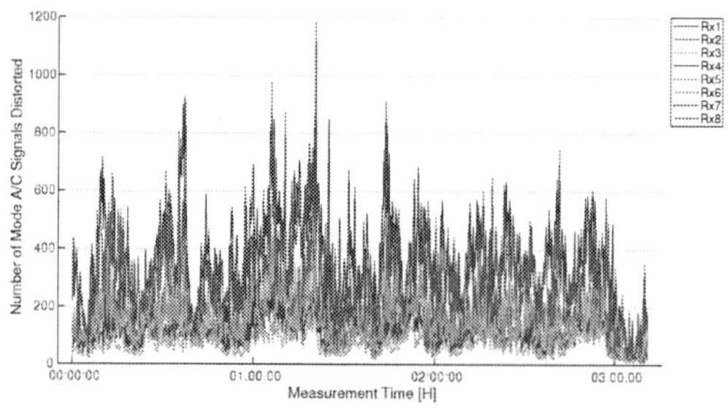

Fig. 5. Amount of distorted signals for ATCRBS.

IV. Conclusion

In this paper, we have introduced an estimation method for analyzing a 1090 MHz signal environment in an airport. The proposed method uses the OCTPASS system, with several receiver units deployed in the airport; these receiver units are connected by RoF technology. By transmitting RF signals to the central processing unit, we can easily estimate the received signal amount and number of distorted signals. The signal amount depends on receiver allocation. The signal amount for Mode S is considerably less than that for ATCRBS. Moreover, the number of distorted signals is found to be approximately 1/4th that of normal signals.

In future, we intend to analyze other experimental data obtained on other dates and predict the expectancy values for future signal amounts. We also intend to evaluate the performance of OCTPASS by comparing its results with those of the normal MLAT.

Acknowledgment

The work was supported in part by a Grant-in-Aid for Young Scientists (B) (16K18072) from the Japan Society for Promotion of Science.

References

[1] ICAO, Aeronautical Telecommunications, Annex 10, Volume 4 Surveillance and Collision Avoidance Systems, 4th edition, 2007.

[2] T. Koga, et al., "Results of Evaluation of Multilatelation with Radio on Fiber Connection," *IEICE Technical Report SANE*, vol.106, no.1, pp.273-278, April 2006.

[3] RTCA, Minimum Operational Performance Standards for Air Traffic Control Radar Beacon System / Mode Select (ATCRBS / Mode S) Airborne Equipment, DO-181E, March 2011.

A Novel Compact Microstrip Bandstop Filter (BSF) Using Spurline & Stepped-Impedance Resonator (SIR)

Hamad.G. Alrwuili, T.S.Kalkur
Department of Electrical and Computer Engineering
University of Colorado, Colorado Springs
CO 80933-7150
halrwuil@uccs.edu, tkalkur@uccs.edu

***Abstract*—This paper presents a novel microstrip design to increase the bandwidth of spurline bandstop filter (BSF). This design combines between conventional spurline section and stepped impedance resonator (SIR) in one filter. The compact structure of bandstop filter is designed by using microstrip transmission lines at 2.4 GHz. The proposed filter has a better and wider bandwidth with S21 from 2.1 GHz to 2.64 GHz at -20 dB rejection band while the conventional spurline has a bandwidth from 2.3 GHz to 2.4 GHz. The performance of the proposed filter is simulated by Agilent ADS with a good rejection band at -80 dB.**

Keywords— Band Stop Filter (BSF), Spurline Filter, Stepped Impedance Resonator (SIR), and ADS.

I. Introduction

Microstrip bandstop filters are used widely to suppress unwanted signals in the RF/microwave applications. They are utilized to stop the interference of undesired signals in receiver and transmitter devices[1]. Microstrip lines are one of the most common transmission systems for high frequency signals[2]. Microstrip lines also have a compatible structure with integrated circuits for low frequencies[2]. It can be easily miniaturized and integrated with both passive and active microwave devices[3]. The conventional bandstop filter design is mostly achieved by using shunt open stubs, coupled lines, and stepped impedance resonators (SIRs)[4]. Recently, the development of these type of filters has become a field of study that attracts many researchers. Spurline technique is one of the most important methods that used to improve the performance of the bandstop filter. Spurline sections provide inherently compact characteristics and better rejection band performance[5]. They are used to moderate bandwidth of the order 10%[6]. They can simply be embedded into microstrip transmission lines which compose filter, couplers, and other devices[7]. They can be embedded into microwave circuit without any increasing of the patch size[6]. Spurline filters provide a very compact structure with significantly less radiation comparing with traditional shun-stub and coupled filters[6]. This paper presents a novel design structure to improve the performance of the spurline filter. The proposed filter combines the spurline section with the stepped impedance resonator (SIR) to create a better and wider rejection bandstop filter at 2.4 GHz. The model of the compact bandstop filter is designed by the advanced design system 2015 (ADS) according to synthesis equations.

II. Characteristics and Filter Development

A. Compact Spurline Filter with a SIR

Figure 1 shows the development of a compact filter design by using a conventional spurline filter and stepped impedance resonator. The conventional spurline filter in figure 1 (a) was designed utilizing a coupled line method at 2.4 GHz. The stepped impedance resonator was designed at 2.4 GHz then integrated with a spurline section as seen in figure 1 (b).

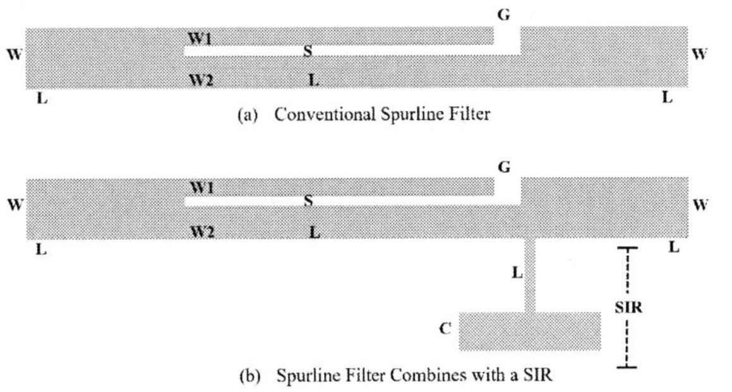

Figure 1. Compact Spurline Filter & SIR

B. ADS Modeling of the Compacte Filter

The modeling of the proposed filter has been designed by using the Advanced Design System (ADS) 2015. FR-4 substrate has been used to design the new model with the specification that is shown in figure 2. The physical length of the spurline section is given as $\lambda/4$. Figure 2 shows the characteristics of the conventional spurline filter at 2.4 GHz.

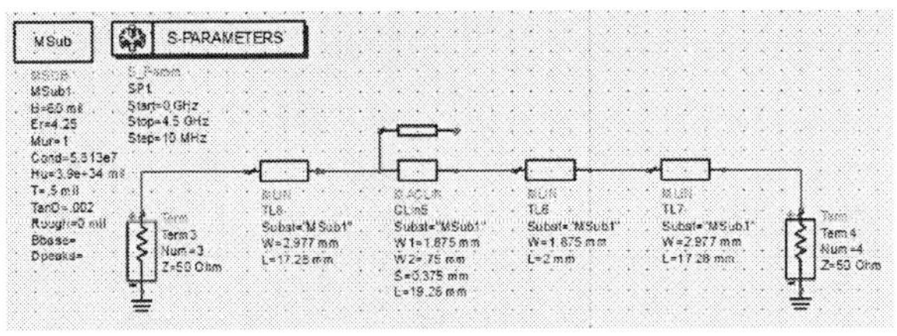

Figure 2. ADS Modeling of Conventional Spurline Filter

The compact design of the spurline filter with SIR is shown in figure 3 at the same center frequency.

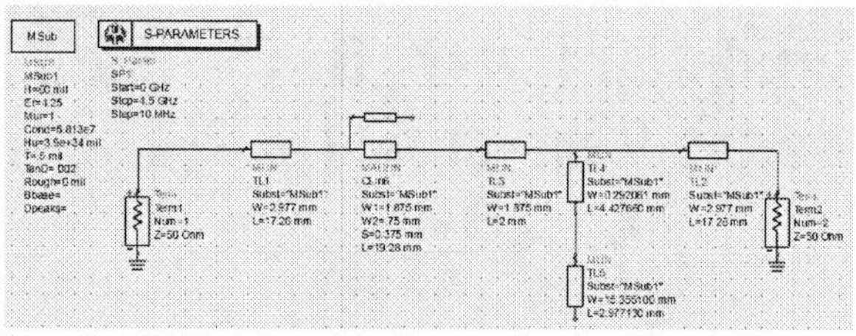

Figure 3. ADS Modeling of the Compact Spurline Filter & SIR

III. Experimental Results

Figures 4, 5, and 6 show the comparison of the results from the conventional spurline filter with the new spurline filter that was compacted with SIR at 2.4 GHz. The results consist of a measured variation of scattering parameters S11 and S21. The new compact design shows a wider bandwidth from 2.1 GHz to 2.64 GHz with a good rejection band less than 20 dB.

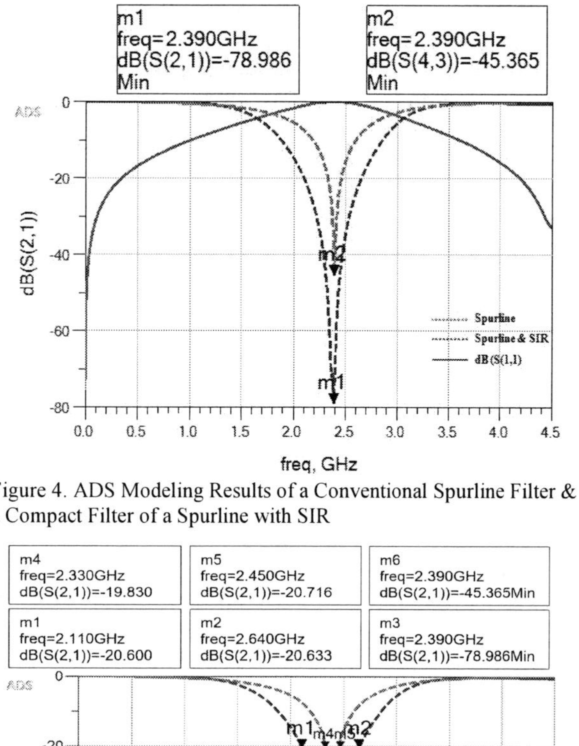

Figure 4. ADS Modeling Results of a Conventional Spurline Filter & a Compact Filter of a Spurline with SIR

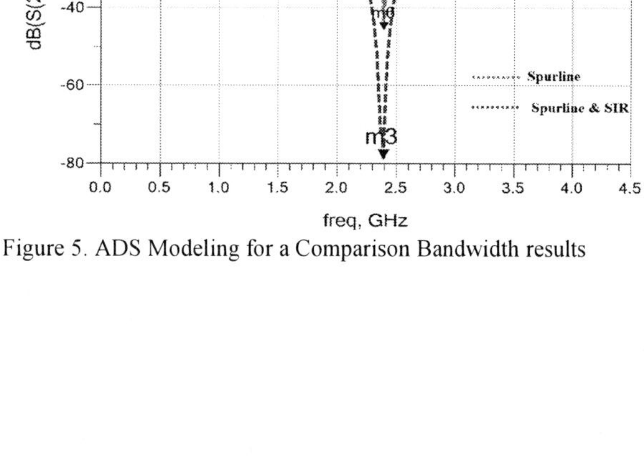

Figure 5. ADS Modeling for a Comparison Bandwidth results

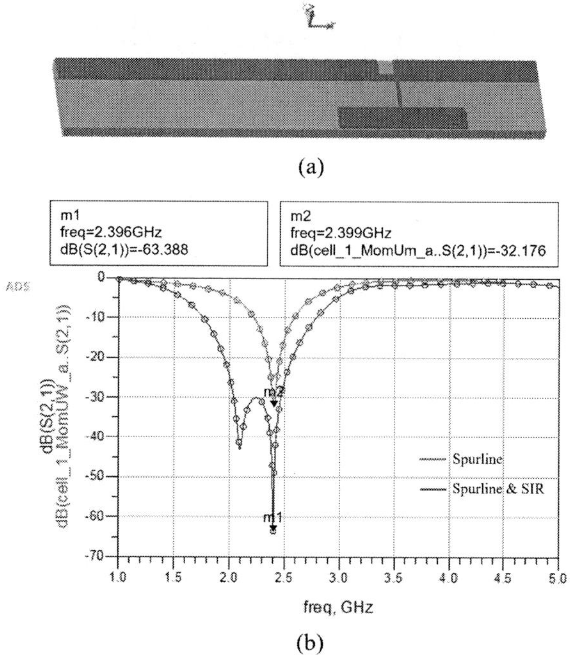

Figure 6. ADS Modeling Result for the Compact filter of Spurline with SIR; (a) Momentum design (b) Signal response

IV. Conclusion

A novel compact design of the spurline bandstop filter (BSF) with a stepped impedance resonator has been presented in this paper. The modeling of the proposed filter was designed at 2.4 GHz by using the Advanced Design System (ADS). The proposed filter shows a better rejection performance with a wider bandwidth comparing to a conventional spurline filter. The bandwidth of the new compact filter increased from 2.1 GHz to 2.64 GHz while the bandwidth of the conventional spurline filter started from 2.3 GHz to 2.4 GHz at the same center frequency. The bandwidth of the compact spurline filter has been improved by using a stepped impedance resonator.

References

[1] K.-S. Chin and C.-K. Lung, "Miniaturized microstrip dual-band bandstop filters using tri-section stepped-impedance resonators," *Prog. Electromagn. Res. C*, vol. 10, pp. 37–48, 2009.

[2] Z. Awang, *Microwave Systems Design*. Singapore: Springer Singapore, 2014.

[3] D. M. Pozar, *Microwave engineering*, 4th ed. Hoboken, NJ: Wiley, 2012.

[4] Y. Liu, H. Zheng, and C. Sun, "A tunable compact bandstop filter using meander spurline and folding open stubs," in *Consumer Electronics, Communications and Networks (CECNet), 2012 2nd International Conference on*, 2012, pp. 115–118.

[5] L. Ke, W. Wenping, Z. Lei, and M. Xiaohan, "Microstrip bandstop filter using open stub and spurline," in *Microwave Technology & Computational Electromagnetics (ICMTCE), 2011 IEEE International Conference on*, 2011, pp. 233–236.

[6] Hany Fathy Hammad, "DUAL AND BROAD BAND ANTENNAS USING SPUR-LINE FILTERS FOR COMMUNICATION SYSTEMS," Queen's University, Kingston, Ontario, Canada, 1997.

[7] J. H. Krishna, "Compact spiral folded spurline for low-frequency applications," *Electron. Lett.*, vol. 47, no. 15, p. 1, 2011.

High-density Compact Chipless RFID Tag for Item-level Tagging

Ayesha Habib, Hafsa Anam, Yasar Amin
ACTSENA Research Group,
University of Engineering and Technology (UET),
Taxila, Pakistan
ayesha.habib@uettaxila.edu.pk

Hannu Tenhunen
TUCS, Department of Information Technology,
University of Turku,
Turku-20520, Finland

***Abstract*— This paper presents 36-bit compact passive chipless RFID tag. The bowtie shape based tag structure is loaded with 36 slots. The tag is capable of yielding high data density. The overall tag dimension is 27mm x 26mm. The tag structure is optimized and analyzed for three different substrates, i.e., FR-4, Taconic TLX-0, and Rogers RT5880. Each loaded slot in tag structure has different length and hence yields resonance at particular frequencies. The response of the tag is observed through radar cross section (RCS) parameter. The 36-bit tag design can tag 2^{36} objects/items. The passive chipless RFID tag produces resonances in the frequency band of 4-13GHz for FR-4 substrate and 5-15.5GHz using Taconic TLX-0 and Rogers RT5880 substrates. The ultimate cost-effective, compact chipless RFID tag can be deployed in various industrial applications. In future, further improvements can be made to integrate the concept of 'green electronics.'**

***Keywords*— radio frequency identification (RFID), radar cross section (RCS), backscattering, electromagnetic waves.**

I. Introduction

RFID (Radio- frequency identification) is proven to be a potential candidate for item-level tagging. It is an emerging technology with non-line of sight communication [1]. Due to its reliability and low-cost, it has been deployed in a wide range of applications such as asset tracking, supply chain management, and logistics [2, 3]. It has been predicted that by 2019, the expected products to be sold are 10 trillion [4]. RFID is a wireless technology and relies on RF waves for transmission of information [5]. The proposed tag structure is using frequency encoding approach for data encoding. In this paper, 36-bit chipless RFID tag is designed and optimized for different substrates, i.e., FR-4, Taconic TLX-0, and Rogers RT5880. The passive chipless RFID tag comprises of the bowtie-shaped slotted structure. Each slot having different length corresponds to unique resonance. The tag has data capacity of 2^{36} = 68,719,476,736. The frequency band of operation using FR-4 substrate is 4-13 GHz and 5-15.5 GHz for both Taconic TLX-0 and Rogers RT5880. Numerous researches have been made for the enhancement of data capacity [6, 7], but the novelty of the proposed work relies on achieving high-data density while remaining in a compact size. The urge towards low-cost identification has been fulfilled by deploying chipless RFID technology [8].

II. Working Principle

RFID is a wireless technology that involves automatic identification and tracking of tagged objects using electromagnetic waves [9]. The tag structure is designed and optimized for data capacity of 36 bits using CST STUDIO SUITE®. To observe the RCS response of tag, the tag is needed to be placed at far field distance which is calculated by Fraunhofer distance formula [10], given as;

$$R = \frac{2D^2}{\lambda}, \qquad (1)$$

'*D*' is the largest dimension and 'λ' is the wavelength.

III. Tag Design

The proposed chipless tag is loaded with 36 slots in a tag dimension of 27mm x 26mm. Slots are designed in such a way that the position of the metal gap in one patch corresponds to slot in another patch to avoid the mutual coupling between resonators as shown in Fig. 1. Each slot of varying length produces dip at a different frequency. All slots from *S1* to *S34* are 0.3mm wide. The slot widths of *S35* and *S36* are 0.6mm and 0.4mm, respectively. The non-uniformity in slot and metal widths is to improve the resonance dips.

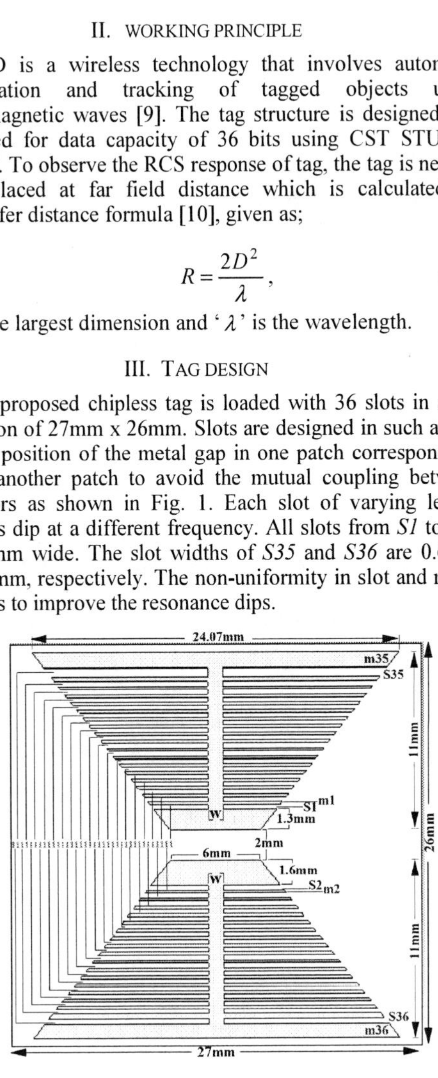

Fig. 1. The layout of proposed tag design.

IV. Results and Discussion

The proposed passive chipless tag having 36-bit data capacity can tag a number of items. The tag is analyzed for three different substrates of different electrical properties. The tag design using a FR-4 substrate with copper as conducting material is referred as Tag-A. Absence and presence of notch corresponds to '0' and '1' bit, respectively. The 36-bit RCS response of Tag-A is observed in the frequency range of 4-13GHz. Using Taconic TLX-0 as substrate and copper as conducting material the tag design is referred as Tag-B. The Tag B is producing 36-bit data in the frequency band of 5-15.5GHz. The Tag-C represents the tag design with Rogers RT5880 as substrate and copper as a radiator. It has been observed that with the change in permittivity there is a shift in resonances. With decreasing permittivity values, a right shift in resonances has been observed which can be seen from comparison graph in Fig. 2.

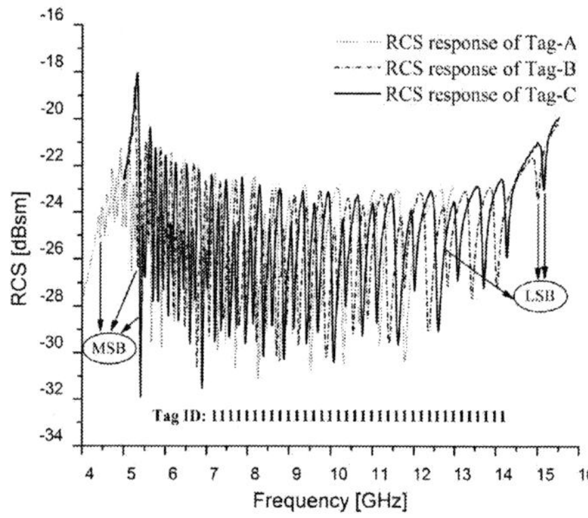

Fig. 2. Comparison graph of all tags.

Multiple tag ID's can be generated by opting the 'shortening of slot' approach. The Tag-D shows one of the ID's in 2^{36} combinations by shortening three slots (*S3*, *S6*, and *S10*) in tag design. The shorted tag structure along with its RCS response is shown in Fig. 3.

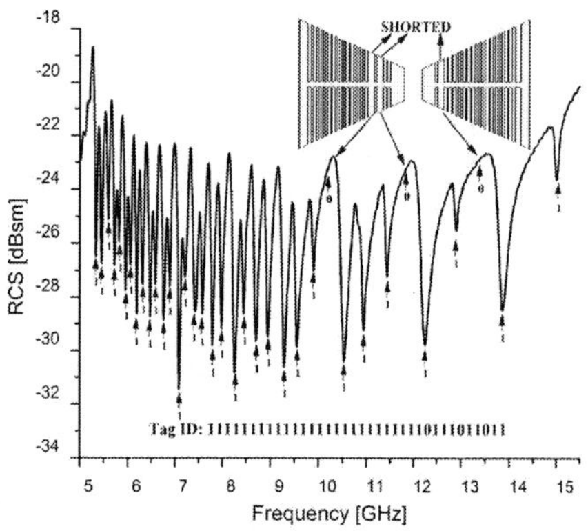

Fig. 3. Simulated RCS response of Tag-D.

V. Conclusion

This paper presents a compact passive chipless RFID tag with high data encoding capacity of 36 bits. It has been analyzed that such high density in compact size relies on using the concept of placement of slots with metal gaps alternate to each other, in alternate patches. There are different dielectric permittivities for different substrates, therefore due to change in electrical characteristics of the substrate, there is variation in RCS response. These changes in electrical properties produce a shift in overall resonances. Moreover, efficient bandwidth utilization has been observed. This chipless RFID tag with its compact size and passive nature along with dense data transmission is a cost-effective solution towards item level tagging. In future, the design can be optimized for sensing applications.

Acknowledgment

This work was financially supported by Vinnova (The Swedish Governmental Agency for Innovation Systems) and University of Engineering and Technology Taxila, Pakistan through the Vinn Excellence Centers program and ACTSENA research group funding, respectively.

References

[1] J. Wang, Y. Wang, and X. Guan, "An indoor localization system based on backscatter RFID tag," 2016 IEEE Wireless Communications and Networking Conference, Doha, Qatar, 2016, pp. 1-6, Apr. 2016.

[2] P. Yang, W. Wu, M. Moniri, and C. C. Chibelushi, "Efficient object localization using sparsely distributed passive RFID tags," in IEEE Transactions on Industrial Electronics, vol. 60, no. 12, pp. 5914-5924, Dec. 2013.

[3] R. Nair, E. Perret and S. Tedjini, "Temporal multi-frequency encoding technique for chipless RFID applications," Microwave Symposium Digest (MTT), 2012 IEEE MTT-S International, Montreal, QC, Canada, 2012, pp. 1-3, Aug. 2012.

[4] IdTechEx, "IDTechEx, printed and chipless RFID forecasts, technologies & players," 2009–2019. [Online]. Available: http://www.idtechex.com

[5] S. Preradovic and N. C. Karmakar, "Chipless RFID: Bar code of the future," IEEE Microwave Magazine, vol. 11, pp. 87-97, 2010.

[6] R. Rezaiesarlak, and M. Manteghi, "Complex-natural-resonance-based design of chipless RFID tag for high-density data", IEEE Transactions on Antennas and Propagation, vol. 62, pp. 898-904, Nov. 2013.

[7] A. Habib, M. A. Azam, Y. Amin, and H. Tenhunen, "Chipless slot resonators for IoT system identification," 2016 IEEE International Conference on Electro Information Technology (EIT), Grand Forks, ND, 2016, pp. 0341-0344, Aug. 2016.

[8] M. R. Al Shareef, M. A. Ashraf, O. M. Haraz, H. M. Behairy, and S. Alshebili, "Time analysis of frequency coded chipless RFID tag based on CPW multi-band resonators," 2016 17th International Symposium on Antenna Technology and Applied Electromagnetics (ANTEM), Montreal, QC, Canada, 2016, pp. 1-2, Aug 2016.

[9] C. Yang, W. Shen, and X. Wang, "Applications of internet of things in manufacturing," 2016 IEEE 20th International Conference on Computer Supported Cooperative Work in Design (CSCWD), Nanchang, China, 2016, pp. 670-675, May 2016.

[10] N. Javed, A. Habib, Y. Amin, J. Loo, A. Akram, and H. Tenhunen, "Directly printable moisture sensor tag for intelligent packaging," in IEEE Sensors Journal, vol. 16, no. 16, pp. 6147-6148, Aug. 15, 2016.

Design Method for Wide-Beam Waveguide Antenna

Chong-Hwan Park
Dept. of radio science and engineering
Chungnam National University
Daejeon, Republic of Korea
jhpark0223@cnu.ac.kr

Seung-Real Ryu
Dept. of radio science and engineering
Korea Automotive Technology Institute
Daejeon, Republic of Korea
syryu@katech.re.kr

Jae-Yoon Shin
Dept. of radio science and engineering
Chungnam National University
Daejeon, Republic of Korea
sjy2321@cnu.ac.kr

Dong-Su Choi
Dept. of radio science and engineering
Chungnam National University
Daejeon, Republic of Korea
onlypray4u@cnu.ac.kr

Jong-Myung Woo
Dept. of radio science and engineering
Chungnam National University
Daejeon, Republic of Korea
jmwoo@cnu.ac.kr

***Abstract*— In this study, we developed a new-concept for a dual-cover radar antenna that uses a basic TE_{01} mode rectangular waveguide, and proposed a method to increase the HPBW (Half Power Beam Width) of the E-plane. As a result, we secured over 144 degrees of HPBW at the E-plane, and were able to dual-cover in a horizontal plane when designed antenna was arrayed in a pentagon.**

Keywords—Antenna, Radar, Array, Wide beam width

I. INTRODUCTION

The antennas installed on battleships generally cover 90° of beam scanning angle per plane, covering 360° in four planes. The stability and reliability of the radar are low, since these antennas have a disadvantage that when one plane is damaged or malfunctions, it is unable to detect in that 90° range.

To solve this problem, if antennas with a beam scanning angle of 144° per plane are arrayed in a pentagon, they could cover 720° in combination. In this system, if one side system is disabled, the antennas on both sides are able to cover for them with their radiation pattern, enhancing stability and reliability.

Therefore, we designed the wide-beam waveguide antenna, which can perform a dual-beam scan cover when arrayed in five planes, and uses a rectangular waveguide to acquire over 144° of HPBW at the E-plane.

II. A NEW CONCEPT OF THE DUAL-COVER RADAR ANTENNA

Fig. 1 shows the direction-finding angle of a typical square-array antenna installed on battleships. The antennas arrayed on each plane have 90° of beam scanning angle as, shown in Fig. 1(a). It is possible to detect 360° using four planes. However, if one antenna is damaged or malfunctions due to an enemy attack, we have a 90° blind spot. To prevent this low reliability, we added one more plane and secured 144° of scanning beam width on each side, to maintain over 720° of beam scanning angle. In this case, it is possible to accomplish beam-directing with other array sides even if one side is disabled, increasing the stability and reliability.

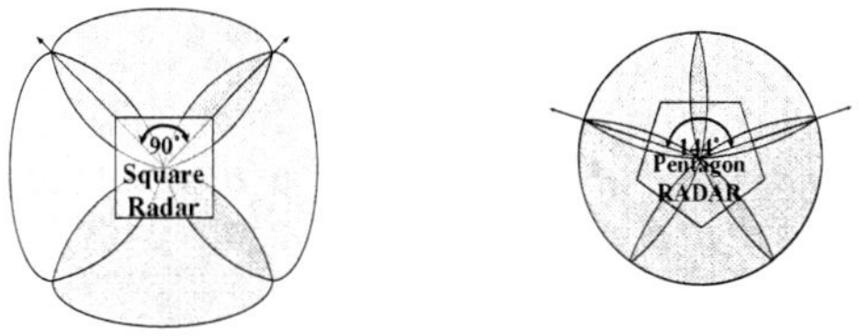

(a) Square array radar; covering 360° (b) Proposed pentagon array radar; covering 720°

Fig. 1 Beam width variation with the number of array planes.

III. DESIGN PROCESS OF THE PROPOSED ANTENNA

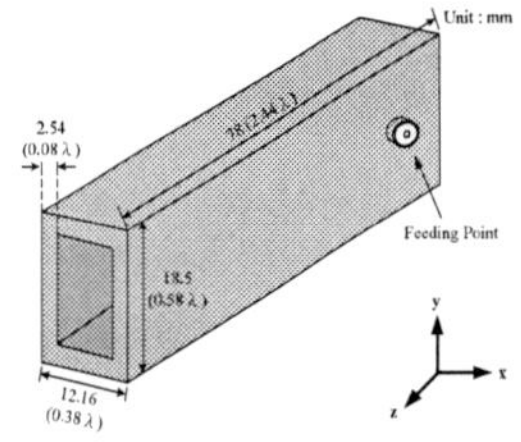

(a) Structure

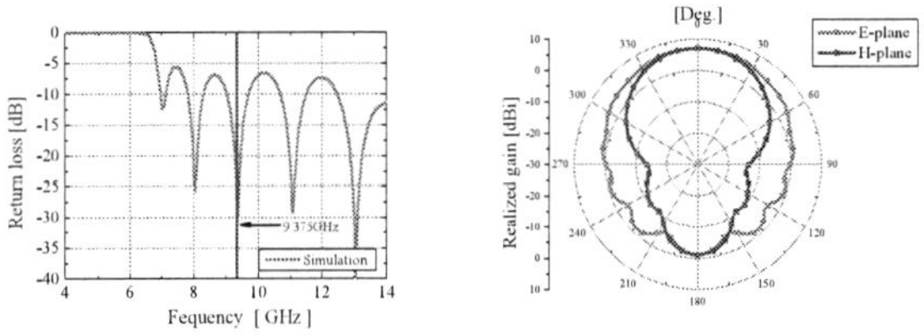

(b) Return loss (c) radiation patterns

Fig. 2. Structure and basic characteristics of the WR-90 basic waveguide.

The structure and basic characteristics of the WR-90 basic waveguide on the center frequency of the X-band are shown in

Fig. 2 [1]. The structure of the waveguide is shown in Fig. 2(a), the return loss is shown in Fig. 2(b), and Fig. 2(c) shows the radiation patterns that display that the HPBW on the E-plane and H-plane are 104.2° and 63.2°, respectively. Since the HPBW of the E-plane is wider than that of the H-plane, the antenna was designed with various parameters to increase the HPBW of the E-plane.

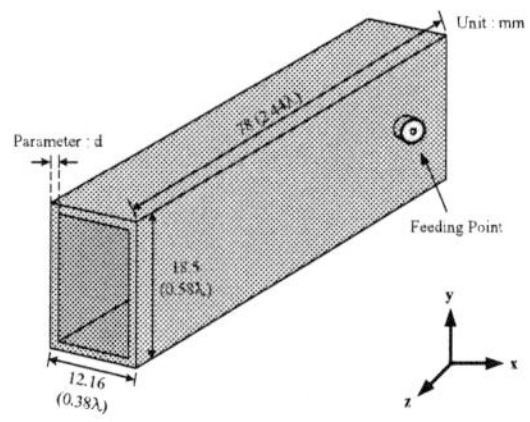

(a) Structure

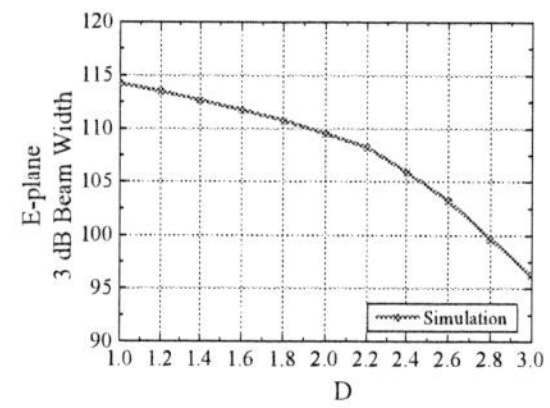

(b) Beam width of the E-plane due to the thickness of waveguide

Fig. 3. Structure and characteristic variation with the thickness of the wave guide.

Fig. 3 shows the variation of the HPBW with the thickness of the waveguide. Fig. 3(a) shows the structure with the change in the thickness. Fig. 3(b) shows the variation of the HPBW on the E-plane by increasing the thickness of the waveguide from 1 to 3 mm in intervals of 0.5 mm. The maximum HPBW on the E-plane was 114° when the thickness was 1 mm. The HPBW increases as the thickness decreases.

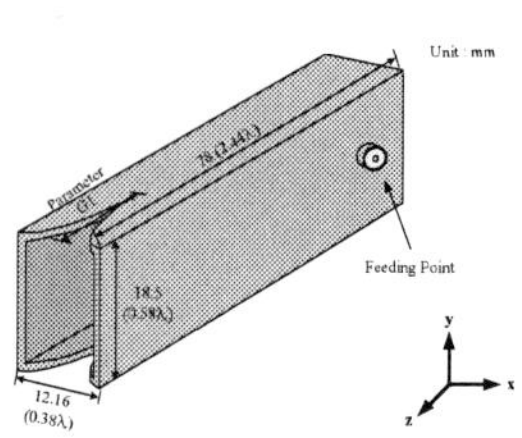

(a) Structure

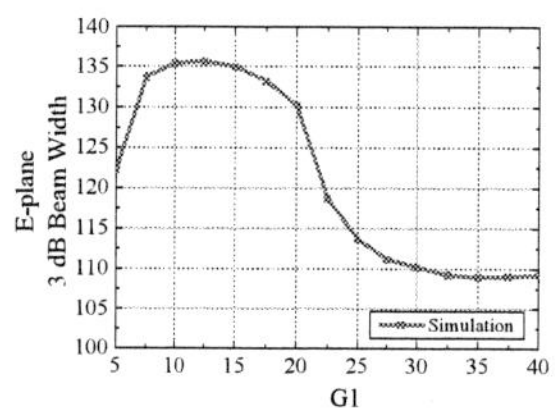

(b) Beam width of the E-plane due to the depth of the tapering on the x-axis plane of the waveguide

Fig. 4. Structure and characteristics variation with the depth of the tapering on the x-axis plane of the waveguide.

Additionally, we analyzed the change of HPBW by adding tapering on the x-axis planes of the waveguide. Fig. 4(a) shows the structure with tapering, and Fig. 4(b) shows the HPBW of the E-plane varying with the parameter G1. The maximum HPBW of 135.6° was measured when G1 was12.5 mm. It appears that the beam width becomes narrower after a certain point. This is because until G1 is increased to a certain length, the leakage of the electric field increases because of tapering, resulting in a contribution to beam widening. However, if G1 is longer than a certain length, the HPBW becomes narrower due to the effect of increasing magnetic field energy volume.

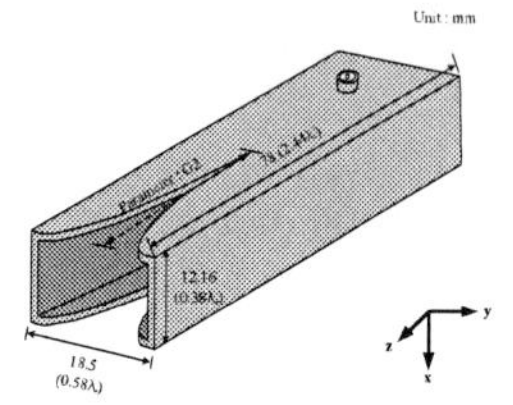

(a) Structure

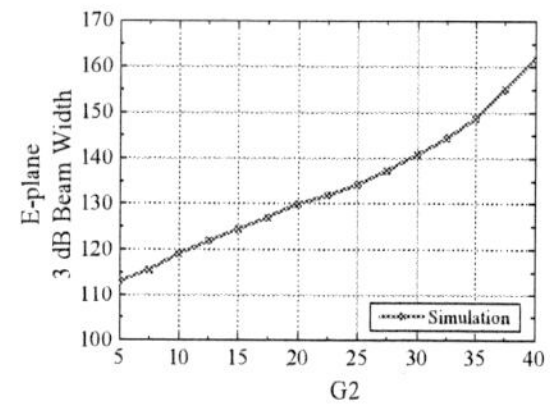

(b) Variation of the beam width of the E-plane with the depth of tapering on the y-axis plane of the waveguide

Fig. 5. Structure and characteristic variation with the depth of tapering on the x-axis plane of the waveguide.

Furthermore, we evaluated the variation of the HPBW by adding tapering on the y-axis planes of the waveguide. Fig. 5(a) shows the structure with tapering on the y-axis planes, and Fig. 5(b) shows the HPBW of the E-plane with variation of the parameter G2. The beam width characteristic reached the goal of 144° when the parameter G2 was over 32.5 mm. The HPBW becomes wider as G2 increases. When this E-plane pattern is arrayed in a pentagon, a dual-beam cover pattern is possible in the horizontal plane. This is considered to be due to the fact that the side plane of the waveguide acts as the radiation pattern, and the apertures are directed to the left and right sides, thereby achieving a wide-angle beam.

IV. Conclusion

The HPBW of the E-plane was analyzed according to the thickness of the waveguide, and by adding tapering on both sides of the waveguide for the newly proposed dual-beam cover radar antenna. The beam width became wider when the thickness decreased, and the maximum was 114°. Further, a maximum HPBW of 135.6° was obtained when tapering was added to the x-axis planes. Finally, when more than 32.5 mm of tapering was added to the y-axis planes of the waveguide, a maximum HPBW of over 144° was acquired, which is suitable for the newly proposed dual-cover radar.

References

[1] D.M. Pozar, *"Microwave Engineering 4th"*, Wiley Interscience, 2003.

[2] Balanis, *"Antenna Theory Analysis and Design 3rd"*, Wiley Interscience, 2005.

Recent Developments in the Application of Contactless Inductive Flow Tomography

Matthias Ratajczak
Helmholtz-Zentrum Dresden-Rossendorf
Institute of Fluid Dynamics
Dresden, Germany
m.ratajczak@hzdr.de

Thomas Wondrak
Helmholtz-Zentrum Dresden-Rossendorf
Institute of Fluid Dynamics
Dresden, Germany
t.wondrak@hzdr.de

Frank Stefani
Helmholtz-Zentrum Dresden-Rossendorf
Institute of Fluid Dynamics
Dresden, Germany
f.stefani@hzdr.de

Abstract—**In many industrial processes dealing with liquid metals or semiconductors, the quality of the resulting product is directly affected by the flow of the melt. These melts are often too hot or too aggressive for direct flow measurement with conventional techniques. One candidate for a feasible application to metallurgical processes is the contactless inductive flow tomography (CIFT), which works by exposing the melt to a magnetic excitation field, measuring the flow-induced perturbances to that field and solving the underlying inverse problem. This paper gives an overview about the theory of CIFT and its application in small-scale models of continuous casting under the influence of a strong static magnetic field.**

Index Terms—**tomography, continuous casting, inverse problems, magnetic field measurement**

I. Introduction

More than 95 % of today's steel is produced by means of continuous casting, making it the most relevant casting method. During this process liquid metal flows from a tundish through a submerged entry nozzle (SEN) into a mould, which consists of enclosing water-cooled copper walls. A solid steel shell is formed at the inside of the mould walls, and the resulting strand with the still molten core is pulled out at the bottom of the mould and solidifies completely. After complete solidification, the cast steel can be processed further.

Especially in the casting of slabs, only the so-called double roll flow structure is expected to yield optimum results, while other flow profiles (like the chaotic-unstable flow) are associated with various kinds of defects, like slag entrainment, segregation or pinholes [1]. In industry electromagnetic brakes (EMBr) are often used because it is expected that their strong DC magnetic flux has a stabilizing and decelerating effect on the flow, reducing the likelihood of defects. However, lab scale experiments [2] as well as simulations [3] suggest that the effect of an EMBr in continuous casting is more complex, and strongly dependent on electrical boundary conditions.

For operators of continuous casters, an immediate feedback from the flow would therefore be highly benefecial. Yet, today's market-ready flow measurement techniques fail when it comes to measuring the global flow structure in hot or chemically agressive melts. One promising candidate for such a scenario is the contactless inductive flow tomography (CIFT) [4], [5] which relies on contactless measurement of the flow-induced perturbances of an applied magnetic field, and solving the underlying inverse problem in order to infer the global flow structure in the mould.

In this paper we will first delineate the basic theory of CIFT. After that the paper is concerned with a cold lab-scale model of a casting mould under the influence of an EMBr. In contrast to previous experiments [6], the EMBr was positioned so that the maximum flux was applied just below the bottom of the nozzle outlet.

II. Theory

We start by assuming a non-magnetic fluid with constant electrical conductivity σ and velocity $\mathbf{v}$, located inside a non-conducting container. The fluid has a volume V and surface S, and is exposed to a magnetic field $\mathbf{B}$, which is either steady or has a very low frequency. Then, according to Ohm's law for moving conductors, currents are induced in the fluid, which give rise to a new magnetic field $\mathbf{b}$:

$$\begin{aligned}\mathbf{b}(\mathbf{r}) =& \frac{\mu_0\sigma}{4\pi}\iiint\limits_V \frac{[\mathbf{v}(\mathbf{r}')\times\mathbf{B}(\mathbf{r}')]\times(\mathbf{r}-\mathbf{r}')}{|\mathbf{r}-\mathbf{r}'|^3}dV' \\ &- \frac{\mu_0\sigma}{4\pi}\oint\!\!\oint\limits_S \varphi(\mathbf{s}')\frac{\mathbf{n}(\mathbf{s}')\times(\mathbf{r}-\mathbf{s}')}{|\mathbf{r}-\mathbf{s}'|^3}dS' .\end{aligned} \tag{1}$$

Here $\mathbf{r}$ describes a position in space, and $\mathbf{n}$ denotes a normal vector at position $\mathbf{s}$ on surface S. The surface potential is denoted by φ and can be described as follows:

$$\begin{aligned}\varphi(\mathbf{s}) =& \frac{1}{2\pi}\iiint\limits_V \frac{[\mathbf{v}(\mathbf{r}')\times\mathbf{B}(\mathbf{r}')]\cdot(\mathbf{s}-\mathbf{r}')}{|\mathbf{s}-\mathbf{r}'|^3}dV' \\ &- \frac{1}{2\pi}\oint\!\!\oint\limits_S \varphi(\mathbf{s}')\frac{\mathbf{n}(\mathbf{s}')\cdot(\mathbf{s}-\mathbf{s}')}{|\mathbf{s}-\mathbf{s}'|^3}dS' .\end{aligned} \tag{2}$$

In general, the magnetic field $\mathbf{B}$ is the sum of the induced field $\mathbf{b}$ and the excitation field $\mathbf{B}_0$. However, by calculating the magnetic Reynolds number Rm one can show that in continuous casting $\mathbf{b}$ is much smaller than $\mathbf{B}_0$, and can therefore be neglected in $\mathbf{B}$ [6], yielding a linear inverse problem. The intrinsic non-uniqueness is solved by jointly applying Tikhonov's regularization, penalizing high velocities in our case, and the L-curve method, where the residual is traced over the mean squared velocities for different values of the regularization parameter [7]. The optimal solution with a

Figure 1. The Mini-LIMMCAST mould (M) with the EMBr (E) and the CIFT excitation coil (X) and sensors (S)

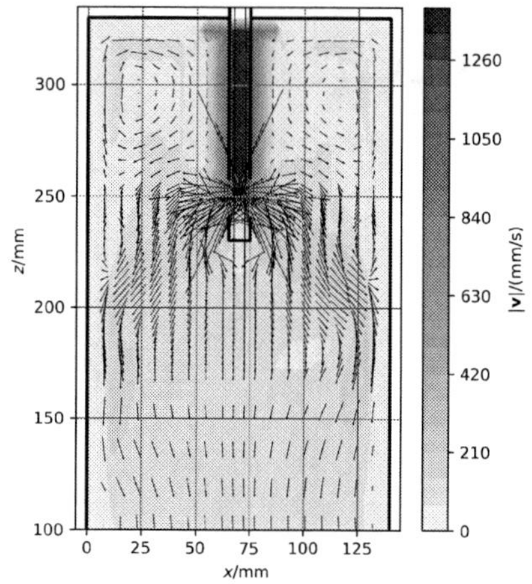

Figure 2. Typical reconstruction with the EMBr in low position, but switched off

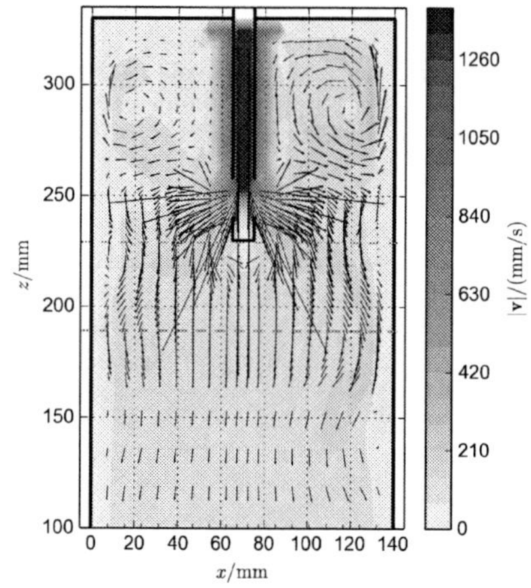

Figure 3. Time-averaged flow reconstruction the EMBr in low position, generating a field of $310\,\mathrm{mT}$. The red dashed lines indicate the area of the maximum EMBr flux.

small residual and sensible velocities can be found at the point of maximum curvature of the curve. The integral equation system is then solved by minimizing the quadratic functional

$$F[\mathbf{v}] = F_{B_0}[\mathbf{v}] + F_{\mathrm{div}}[\mathbf{v}] + F_{\mathrm{pen}}[\mathbf{v}] + F_{2D}[\mathbf{v}] + F_{\mathrm{inlet}}[\mathbf{v}], \quad (3)$$

where the separate functionals (a) minimize the deviations between the modelled and measured fields, (b) ensure divergence-free flows, (c) apply the Tikhonov penalty function, (d) force a 2D-flow for slab casting and (e) set inlet velocities in the area of the entry nozzle. The basic coupled integral equation system (1) and (2) has been extended to account for conducting walls and AC excitation [8], as well as gradiometric sensors [6] (the latter two increasing robustness against noise). The accuracy and comparison of CIFT with the well-established ultrasonic doppler velocimetry technique is beyond the scope of this paper, but can be studied in [5] for the same mould but without the EMBr.

III. Experimental Results

Modelling experiments of the flow in a continuous casting mould can be conducted at the Mini-LIMMCAST facility [9]. We used an acrylic glass model of a slab mould with dimensions $(140 \times 35 \times 335)\,\mathrm{mm}^3$, filled with the eutectic alloy GaInSn, which is liquid at room temperature. The mould is surrounded by an EMBr which creates a maximum flux of $310\,\mathrm{mT}$ at an area just below the nozzle outlets (see Figure 1). It is important to note that the amplitude of the excitation field is minimal in the area of maximum EMBr flux, because of the high μ_r of the EMBr pole shoes. In this new, low EMBr position, the jet is located in an area with larger excitation field amplitude, which leads to different flow structures and simultaneously enhances reconstruction accuracy. An experimental run with the EMBr switched off resulted in a CIFT-reconstructed flow as depicted in Figure 2, where the diagonal jet from the nozzle and the upper rolls on both sides are clearly visible. As soon as we switch on the EMBr (Figure 3), changes in the average flow structure become apparent, with an intensified upper roll and a more vertically oriented jet. Additionally, regular superimposed flow oscillations occur.

IV. Conclusion

CIFT has been applied to cold small-scale models of continuous casting moulds, even under the influence of strong static fields. A new implementation of the reconstruction code with linear elements is on the way. While there are still many challenges to be overcome, it is expected that in the future CIFT will enable industrial operators to discern relevant flow structures in their processes in real-time.

References

[1] P. H. Dauby, Revue de Metallurgie, vol. 109, pp. 113–136, 2012.
[2] K. Timmel, et al., Met. Mat. Trans. B, vol. 42, pp. 68–80, 2011.
[3] R. Chaudhary, et al., Met. Mat. Trans. B, vol. 43, pp. 532–553, 2012.
[4] F. Stefani, et al., Phys. Rev. E, vol. 70, ID 056306, 2004.
[5] T. Wondrak, et al., Met. Mat. Trans. B, vol. 42, 1202–1210, 2011.
[6] M. Ratajczak, et al., Phil. Trans. Roy. Soc. A, vol. 374, ID 20150330, 2016.
[7] P. C. Hansen, SIAM Review, vol. 34, pp. 561–580, 1992.
[8] M. Ratajczak, et al., IEEE Sensors Conference, Busan, Republic of Corea, 2015.
[9] K. Timmel, et al., ISIJ Int., vol. 50, 1134–1141, 2010.

Simulation Model to Predict EM Scattering due to Different Parameters of Dust/Sandstorm

Sharif Iqbal Mitu Sheikh
EE Department, KFUPM
Dhahran, Suadi Arabia
sheikhsi@kfupm.edu.sa

Mahfuz Ullah
EE Department, KFUPM
Dhahran, Suadi Arabia
g201205260@kfupm.edu.sa

Abstract— **During a severe sand storm, maintaining the link budget of wireless channels require accurate modeling of EM scattering. Existing models used to predict the electromagnetic (EM) attenuation due to dust/sand particles are mostly based on visibility measurement. Since visibility is not constant throughout the sand storm, the attenuation models need a correction factor to include horizontal and vertical intensity variation of the dust/sand particles. This paper presents a simulation model, where EM attenuation due to different size and concentration of the dust/sand particles can be separately investigated. Simulated results are verified with controlled laboratory based experiments and existing data from well known references.**

Keywords—Attenuation, Dust, Sand, Simulation model

I. Introduction

Severe sand storm affects the quality of wireless communication channels due to EM scattering from the suspended particles. Average duration of these storms is 2-3 hours, but sometimes they could last for several days [1]. The particles are considered to be dust if the diameter is up to 90 μm and sand if they are between 100–200 μm [2]. Majority of the terrestrial radio relays or satellite links are affected by dust particles, as they can reach to a height of several thousand feet [3]. But, relatively larger sand particles can only rise to several meters and affect ground level communication between mobile and car based devices. Visibility measurements are widely used to indicate the level of the storm. If visibility at the epicenter of the storm is less than 500 meter, it is considered to be a severe sand storm [4,5]. The presence of moisture and/or electrical charges within dust/sand particles are also known to affect the propagation of micro/millimeter-wave signals [6,7].

Several models exist in the literature to predict the attenuation and phase-shift of EM wave due to severe dust/sand storms. The propagation constant is an important electrical parameter, as it expresses the attenuation and phase shift properties of wave. Popular expression for propagation constant, derived by Chu, can be written as [2],

$$K_{V,H}(\varphi) = k_0 + \frac{2\pi}{k_0}\int_0^{\infty} f_{V,H}(\varphi, r)\, N(r)\, dr, \qquad (1)$$

where, k_0 is the propagation constant in free space, $N(r)$ is the particle size distribution per unit volume having radii in the specified region, φ is the elevation angle of the incident radiation and $f_{V,H}(\varphi,r)$ is the scattering amplitude for vertical/horizontal polarization. Well known attenuation models that followed include the works of Goldhirsh [3], Dong [4] improved this model to predict EM scattering from dust/sand storm for millimeter wave band. To include Mea scattering from DS particles with sizes comparable to wavelength, Ahmed [5] formulated a separate attenuation expression. The affect of moister contents within the particles are investigated by Haddad [6], whereas the affects of partially charged particles are considered by Li [7]. Note measured visibility values in multiple locations of the storm are essential in above models, which are often difficult and dangerous to obtain. In addition visibility also varies in horizontal direction of the storm as it depends on the concentration of dust/sand particles. So the attenuation models needed a correction factor to include the horizontal and vertical intensity variation of the particles. The work of El-Sheikh included the concept of layered distribution of sand/dust with each layer having constant particle concentration or visibility value. He has introduced an adjustment factor that accounts for the vertical intensity variation of the sand/dust storm [8,9]. Harb also proposed an attenuation model, where vertical intensity variation of the visibility is used to better predict EM attenuation [10]. Unfortunately, the theoretical models based on layered concentrations are not be experimentally verified. In this research work, a validated simulation model is used to predict EM scattering due to layered concentration of sand particles. This required predicted attenuation due to different size and concentration of dust/sand particles within the storm.

II. Design and Analysis

The proposed simulation model is shown in Fig. 1. It consists of a scaled rectangular sample-holder (12x12x20 cm^3) excited with X-band horn antennas. Scaled samples with known particle sizes and concentrations are placed within the sample-holder to predict the attenuation and scattering of propagating EM wave. Once the simulated result is validated using controlled laboratory experiment, the scaled simulation model can be used to predict EM attenuation due to changing size and concentration of dust/sand particles.

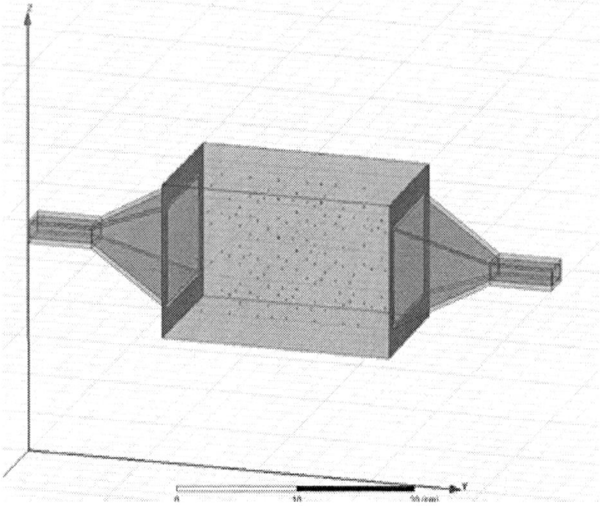

Fig. 1. Scaled simulation model of rectangular sample-holder filled with air-sand mixture and excited by horn antennas.

The controlled experimental setup used in the lab is shown in Fig. 2. Note that multiple blower and filtered air vent are used to introduce controlled sand storm within the 60x60x80 cm^3 rectangular sample-holder. Sand samples are separated using sieve analysis technique to collect sand samples with diameters of 90 and 150 μm. Horn antennas are used to excite a randomly selected 9 GHz signal, propagating through the air-sand mixture. A vector network analyzer is used to record the S-parameters of the EM wave propagating through different size and concentration of the sand samples. An experimentally observed attenuation of 0.04 dB/m is observed for 150 μm sand sample with volume ratio of 39506 between the rectangle sample-holder and total amount uniformly distributed of sand particles.

Solving the equivalent simulation model with 150 μm diameter sand particles and a volume ratio of 39506 requires extensive computer resources. So a cluster of 6.6 sand particles with relatively larger diameter of 1mm is used. To maintain volume ratio within the scaled 12x12x20 cm^3 simulation sample-holder, the calculated number of particles is found to be 135. The uniformly distributed 135 sand samples within the scaled simulation sample-holder is shown in Fig. 1. For a propagating signal with frequency of 9-GHz, the simulated un-scaled results displayed an attenuation of 0.034 dB/m. This value concurs with the EM attenuation reported in reference [6] for a propagating signal of 9 GHz through a similar sand storm. The difference in measured (0.04 dB/m) and simulated (0.034 dB/m) results is mainly due to non-uniformity of the air-sand mixture within the sample-holder of the experimental setup. Even after using optimally located blowers and filtered air-vents, authors found it difficult to create a perfectly controlled sand storm.

The simulation model is then used to investigate the attenuation due to changing particle size and concentration. For a fixed concentration of 135 sand-particles, Fig. 3 displays the S_{21} responses resulted from increasing particle sizes. The attenuation due to sand particles are calculated by subtracting the losses due to air-only media from that of air-sand media, shown in the figure. Note that very low attenuation is demonstrated by dust particles with relatively smaller radius compared to larger sand particles.

Fig. 2. Calibrated laboratory setup to create a controlled sand storm and measure the attenuation of the propagating 9 GHz signal.

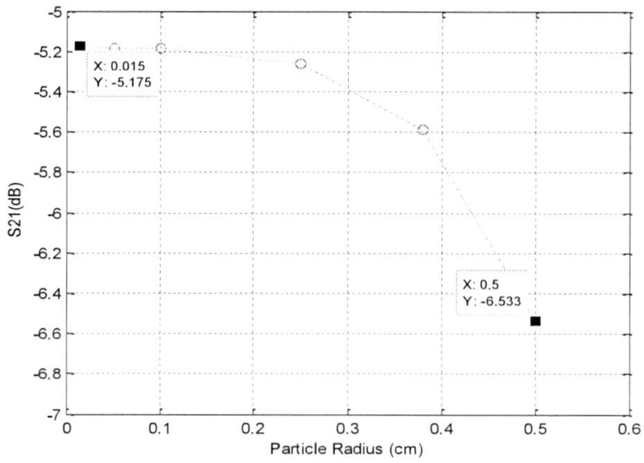

Fig. 3. S_{21} for sand concentration of 135 sand-spheres/sample-holder.

This is because increasing the sand particles increases the effective permittivity of the propagating media in addition to increase in scattering of EM waves. Fig. 4 plots the change in transmission (S_{21}) response with increasing sand concentration for scaled particle radiuses (R) of 0.05cm to 0.38cm. Note that R=0.05cm and 0.1cm particles shows insignificant change in insertion loss due to very low volume ratio, whereas R=0.25cm and 0.38cm demonstrates an increases EM attenuation with increasing concentration.

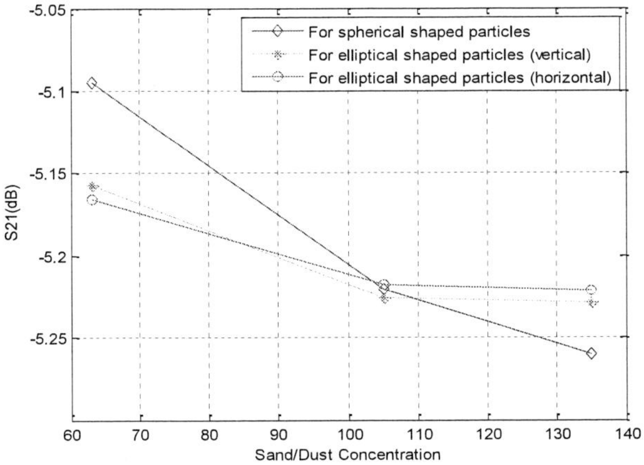

Fig. 4. Comparison for elliptical and spherical shaped sand particles

III. Conclusion

A scaled simulation model for estimating EM scattering through sandstorm is presented. The attenuation predicted by the software model is validated using data available in the literature and controlled laboratory experiment. For a 9 GHz signal, propagating through a known concentration of 150 μm sand particles, the model predicted an attenuation of 0.035 dB/m. The simulated results also demonstrated how the EM scattering is affected by some of the parameters of the sand storm.

Acknowledgment

The authors would like to acknowledge the support provided by the Deanship of Scientific Research at King Fahd University of Petroleum and Minerals (KFUPM) under Research Grant RG-1417-1/1417-2.

References

[1] A.J. ANSARI, and B.G. EVANS, "Microwave propagation in sand and dust storms", IEE Proc. F, Commun., Radar & Signal Processing, 1982, 129, pp. 315-322.

[2] T. S. Chu, "Effect of sand storms on microwave propagation," Bell Syst. Tech. J., vol. 58, pp. 549–555, 1979.

[3] J. Goldhirsh, "Attenuation and backscatter from a derived two-dimensional dust storm model, "IEEE Trans. Antennas Propagation, vol. 49, no. 12, pp. 1703–1711, Dec. 2001.

[4] X.Y. Dong, H.Y. Chen, D.H. Guo, "Microwave and Millimeter-Wave attenuation in sand and dust storms", IEEE ANTENNAS AND WIRELESS PROPAGATION LETTERS, VOL. 10, 2011.

[5] A. S. Ahmed, A. Ali, and M. A. Alhaider, "Airborne dust size analysis for tropospheric propagation of millimetric waves into dust storms," IEEE Trans. Geosci. Remote Sens., vol. 25, no. 5, pp. 593–599, September, 1987.

[6] S. HADDAD, M.J.H. SALMAN, and R.K. JHA, "Effects of dust/ sand storms on some aspect s of microwave propagation", URSE Commission F. Belgium, pp. 153-161, 1983.

[7] X. Li, L. Xingcai, and Z. Xiaojing, "Attenuation of an electromagnetic wave by charged dust particles in a sandstorm," Applied Optics, vol. 49, no. 35, pp. 6756-6761, 2010.

[8] E. A. A. El-Sheikh, M. R. Islam, J. Chebil, S. Bashir, and A. F. Ismail, "Preliminary analysis of dust effects on microwave propagation measured in Sudan," Proc. ICOM, pp. 1–7, 2013.

[9] E. A. A. El-Sheikh etal, "Dust Storm Attenuation Modeling Based on Measurements in Sudan", IEEE Trans on Antenna and Propagation, vol. 65, no. 8, pp. 4200-4208, 2017.

[10] K. Harb, S. Abdillah, and S. Abdul-Jauwad, "Dust amp; Sand (DUSA) storms impact on LEO satellite microwave radio links," Advanced Satellite Multimedia Systems Conference and the 13th Signal Processing for Space Communications Workshop (ASMS/SPSC), pp. 442-447, 2014.

Examination on a Self-Mixing Circuit

Congying Chen, Adalbert Beyer
Department of Electrical Engineering and Informatics
Duisburg-Essen University
Campus Duisburg, Germany
a.beyer@ieee.org

Winfried Simon, Rüdiger Follmann, Peter Waldow

IMST GmbH
Kamp-Lintfort, Germany
simon@imst.de

Dominique Schreurs
Department of Electrical Engineering (ESAT)
KU Leuven,
Leuven, Belgium
dominique.schreurs@kuleuven.be

Abstract—**In this paper, a self-mixing circuit is introduced, in which, a large local oscillator (LO) signal at the input will pump the device into non-linear regime, whereas the radio frequency (RF) input signal should be connected to the output port, of which the conductance will be changed by the LO drive. Both, simulations and measurements are performed for verifying the technique used.**

Keywords— bias network, conversion loss, FET models, self-mixing circuit, stability analysis.

I. Introduction

In microwave and millimeter wave transceivers the mixer plays a key role [1]. Very often a resistive mixer is a good choice. This type of mixer based on field effect transistor was reported first in [2]. Also, this type of mixer is capable of operating with low LO power [3].

In a FET resistive mixer, it must be ensured that the transistor operates in its linear ohmic region, implying zero bias voltage (DC bias) at the drain port. In this configuration, the LO signal is applied at the gate. The intermediate frequency (IF) (or RF) signal is applied at the drain, whereas the RF (or (IF)) signal is collected by filtering from the drain. The LO signal is applied for modulating the channel resistance of the transistor [1, 4].

In this study, a self-mixing circuit as a mixer unit [5] is used. The equivalent circuit diagram is shown in Fig. 1.

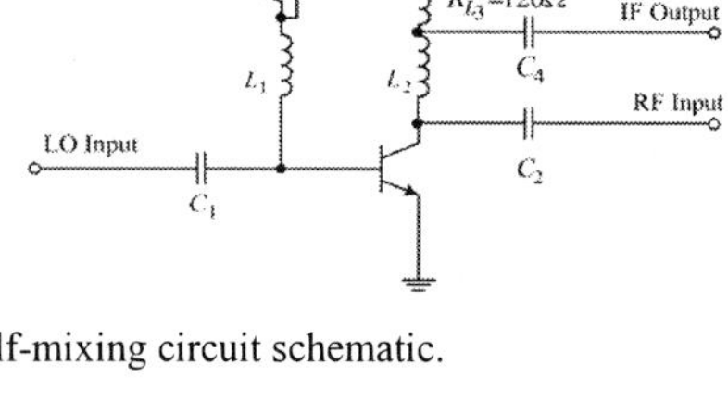

Fig. 1. Self-mixing circuit schematic.

The mixer unit under examination includes three ports. The fundamental difference with the resistive mixer configuration is that the device's drain port is DC biased in the proposed design. Using the theory and experience for amplifier design operating in the lower frequency band, a 10 GHz self-mixing circuit [6] is developed in this work.

II. Circuit Design and Initial Characterization

In this design, the low noise GaAs HEMT MGF 4953A is chosen as the active device for achieving sufficient gain. The Advanced Design System (ADS) template for FET DC characteristics can directly produce the required DC curves. As a result, V_{ds} = 2 V and I_D = 10 mA operating point is chosen. In addition, V_{gs} = - 0.35 V is selected.

A. Bias Network

To minimize the high-frequency signal that flows through the circuit towards the DC source, the bias must present a low resistance at DC. For this purpose, a quarter-wavelength radial stub and a series quarter-wavelength transmission line is adopted (see Fig. 2).

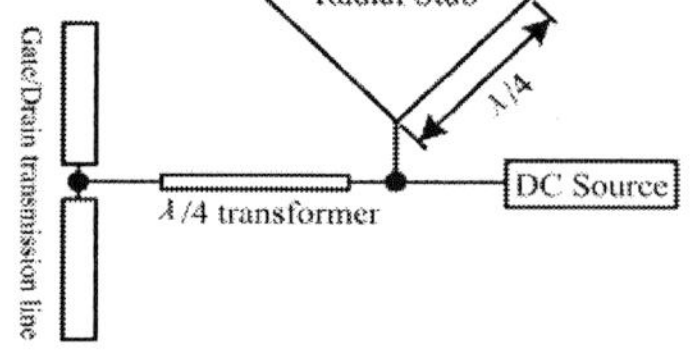

Fig. 2. Bias stub concept.

In order to get excellent reflection behavior, an S-parameters optimization is necessary (s. Fig. 3). As a result, the magnitude of S_{11} is extremely low at the center frequency, and S_{21} is almost 0 dB at the operating frequency. Thus, the transmission line loaded by the bias circuit has nearly no reflection and excellent transmission characteristics.

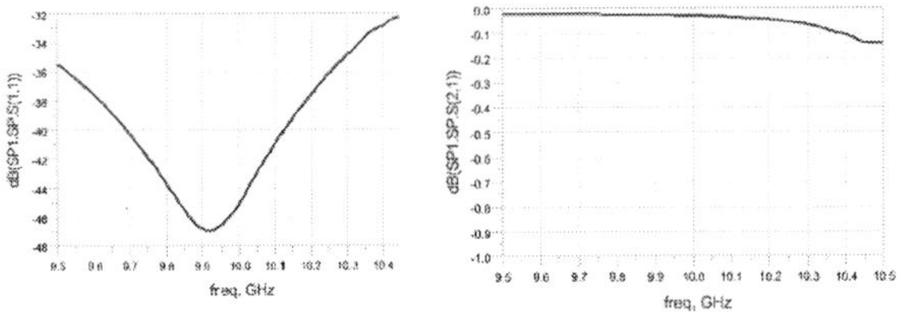

(a) (b)

Fig. 3. Simulation of the transmission properties of the bias circuit. ((a): magnitude of S_{11}, and, (b): magnitude of S_{21}.)

B. Stability Analysis

At first, the stability factor of this circuit is calculated by the *S*-parameters analysis in ADS. The results show that the stability factor at 10 GHz is larger than 1. Sometimes rather large curve shift may occur when only a narrow band (9.5 GHz – 10.5 GHz) is considered. Therefore, the popular method of adding a series resistance to increase the stability is chosen [5]. Fig. 4 shows the improved stability factor, which is larger than 1 across the 5-15 GHz frequency range.

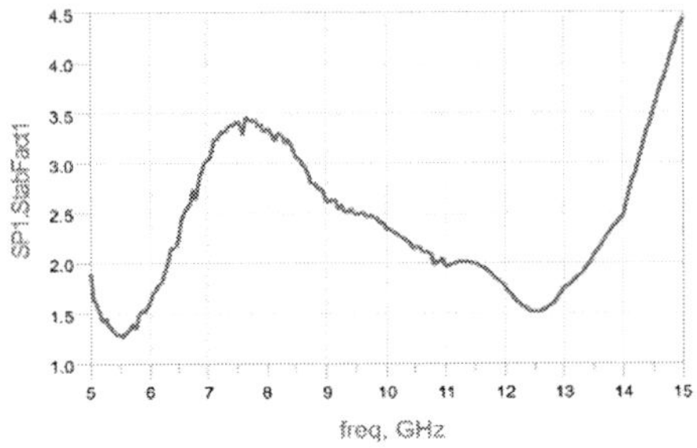

Fig. 4. Improved stability factor.

C. Input and Output Matching

The input and output matching networks can be designed. by adopting a single stub topology and by using the matching synthesis tool available in ADS.

To check the performance of the practical circuit, *S*-parameters measurements using a vector network analyzer are performed. Results of S_{11} and S_{22} are shown in Fig. 5.

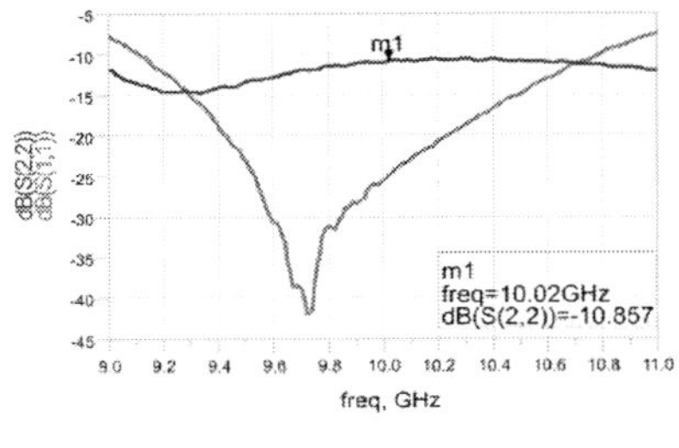

Fig. 5. Measured magnitude of reflection characteristics of the fabricated amplifier. (S_{11} and S_{22}).

The magnitude of S_{22} is shifted slightly to the lower frequencies and is less than -11 dB across the entirely frequency range. The S_{22} might cause a reflection loss of nearly 30% of the RF signal in the mixer circuit.

D. Additional Results

The measurement suggests 0 dBm input power as the 1dB-compression point. The inflection point of linear and nonlinear range can also be read from this measurement as being -6dBm, i.e., the LO signal must be at least -6 dBm to pump the transistor into nonlinear range.

The circuit's output conductance *g* can be extracted by a 50 Ohm-open measurement. The calculated *g* is related to the input voltage, which is the LO signal in the considered design. The values of *g* are varying between 15.9 mS and 17.2 mS by changing the input power from –30 dBm to –3 dBm.

E. Conversion Loss Measurement

There are several methods for measuring conversion loss [3]. In this study, results are obtained by spectrum analyzer measurements. For measuring the conversion loss directly by using a spectrum analyzer, a capacitor C_4 (see Fig. 1) is needed to block the DC bias at the output port, for the reason that the input port of a spectrum analyzer allows no DC.

Meanwhile, the RF signal is always near –62.8 dBm at the IF output, which will improbably influence the IF signal. This also means that an IF signal close to -60 dBm is hard to be extracted. The conversion loss will be decreased from 25 dB to 11 dB by setting larger LO drive. On this topic, additional results will be given and discussed in final manuscript.

III. Conclusion

In this work, a self-mixing circuit is examined, in which a large LO signal at the input pumps the device into nonlinear regime, so that the strongly varying output conductance can be used to achieve down conversion of the small RF input signal. The output conductance (RF input conductance) of the circuit, IF output impedance and conversion loss are simulated and measured in order to investigate the characteristics of the self-mixing circuit. The results are promising such that the developed circuit can be used for practical purposes, e.g. in Doppler sensors, as the mixer in the receiver

References

[1] M. Varonen, M. Kärkkäinen, J. Riska, P. Kangaslahti, and K. A. I. Halonen, "Resistive HEMT Mixers for 60-GHz Broad-Band Telecommunication," IEEE Trans. MTT , vol. 53, no. 4, pp. 1322-1330, Apr. 2005.

[2] S. A. Maas, "A GaAs MESFET mixer with very low intermodulation," IEEE Trans. MTT, vol. 35, no. 4, pp. 435–429, Apr. 1987.

[3] S. Maas, Nonlinear Microwave and RF Circuits, 2nd ed. Norwood, MA: Artech House, 2003.

[4] M. Kimishima, T. Ataka, and H. Okabe, "A family of Q, V, and W-band monolithic resistive mixers," IEEE MTT-S Int. Microwave Symp., pp. 115–118, May 2001.

[5] S. A. Maas, Microwave Mixers, Artech House, Dedham, MA, 1986.

[6] W. H. Cantrell, W. A. Davis, V. Hwang, and T. Itoh, "Quasi-optical HEMT and MESFET self-oscillating mixers," IEEE Trans. MTT., vol. 36, no. 12, pp. 1701-1705, Dec. 1988.

Circulant Preconditioning in the Volume Integral Equation Method for Nanophotonics

Samuel Groth
Research Laboratory of Electronics
Massachusetts Institute of Technology
Cambridge, USA
samgroth@mit.edu

Jacob White
Electrical Engineering and Computer Science
Massachusetts Institute of Technology
Cambridge, USA
white@mit.edu

Athanasios Polimeridis
Computational Prototyping Group
Skoltech
Moscow, Russia
a.polimeridis@skoltech.ru

***Abstract*—Wave propagation problems arising in nanophotonics can be considered high frequency, however typically this high frequency behavior is confined to one main propagation direction. It is well known that EM solvers employing iterative methods are slow to converge for high-frequency problems and thus require effective preconditioners. Here we employ a frequency-domain volume integral equation method based on a voxelized discretization. This leads to a three-level Toeplitz system. We make a circulant approximation to this matrix along only the long dimension and show that this proves to be an extremely effective preconditioner for a range of nanophotonics problems.**

Keywords—circulant preconditioning, high frequency, nanophotonics, Toeplitz matrix, volume integral equation.

I. Introduction

The volume integral equation method (VIEM), as implemented in MARIE [1], relies on a voxelized discretization. From such a uniform discretization results the matrix system:

$$\mathbf{Tx} = \mathbf{b}, \tag{1}$$

where $\mathbf{T}$ is a three-level block-Toeplitz Toeplitz-block matrix. The matrix-vector product with a Toeplitz matrix can be executed in $\mathcal{O}(n \log n)$ operations with $\mathcal{O}(n)$ storage using the FFT, where n is the number of unknowns. Hence, employing an iterative solver can lead to EM problems being solved extremely efficiently via the VIEM [2].

However, for high-frequency problems such as those arising in nanophotonics applications, iterative solvers can stagnate leading to long solve times. Therefore, one must precondition. A popular preconditioning technique for Toeplitz systems is to approximate $\mathbf{T}$ by a *circulant matrix* $\mathbf{C}$ [3], which is diagonalized by the FFT, hence inverted cheaply. It has been shown that, for the preconditioned system,

$$\mathbf{C}^{-1}\mathbf{Tx} = \mathbf{C}^{-1}\mathbf{b}, \tag{2}$$

GMRES converges superlinearly [3]. However, it was also shown that this is only true in one dimension [4].

This work was supported by a grant from Skoltech as part of the Skoltech-MIT Next Generation Program.

Nanophotonics problems are in three dimensions, but often one of the dimensions is much greater than the other two. For example, consider the directional coupler in Fig. 1. Typical dimensions for each of the waveguides in this geometry are:

$$(x, y, z) \approx (5 \times 10^{-7}, 2.2 \times 10^{-7}, Z)\text{m}, \tag{3}$$

where Z can range from 10^{-5}m to 10^{-3}m. The wavelength inside the waveguide is 4.5×10^{-7}m, hence Z can be up to thousands of wavelengths.

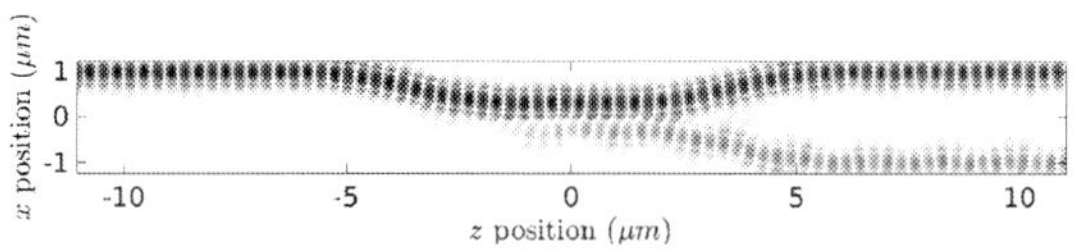

Fig. 1. Directional coupler. Mode enters the top waveguide at the left and is partially coupled to the bottom waveguide.

We show that a circulant approximation to the multi-level Toeplitz matrix made *only* in the z-direction leads to an effective preconditioner. The resulting preconditioned system is solved in a small number of iterations independent of Z. We first demonstrate this for a straight uniform waveguide, then we generalize to non-uniform and curved structures such Bragg gratings and directional couplers where the Toeplitz structure of the matrix is distorted.

II. Volume Integral Equation Method

Consider the propagation of time-harmonic (with $e^{j\omega t}$ dependence) electromagnetic waves with angular frequency ω through a dielectric object occupying a bounded domain Ω in $\mathbb{R}^3$. The electric and magnetic properties are defined as:

$$\begin{aligned} \epsilon = \epsilon_0,\ \mu = \mu_0 \quad \text{in } \mathbb{R}^3\backslash\Omega, \\ \epsilon = \epsilon_r(\mathbf{r})\epsilon_0,\ \mu = \mu_0 \quad \text{in } \Omega, \end{aligned} \tag{4}$$

where ϵ_0 and μ_0 are the free-space permittivity and permeability, respectively. For *silicon* nanophotonics, $\epsilon_r(\mathbf{r}) \approx 12$.

The total field is $\mathbf{e} = \mathbf{e}_{\text{inc}} + \mathbf{e}_{\text{sca}}$, where the scattered field can be written in terms of polarization currents $\mathbf{j}$ as:

$$\mathbf{e}_{\text{sca}} = \frac{1}{c_e}(\mathcal{N} - \mathcal{I})\mathbf{j}, \tag{5}$$

where $c_e := j\omega\epsilon_0$, $\mathcal{I}$ is the identity operator, and $\mathcal{N}$ is the integro-differential operator,

$$\mathcal{N}f := \nabla \times \nabla \times \int_\Omega \frac{\mathrm{e}^{-jk_0|\mathbf{r}-\mathbf{r}'|}}{4\pi|\mathbf{r}-\mathbf{r}'|} f(\mathbf{r}')\mathrm{d}\mathbf{r}',\ k_0 = \omega\sqrt{\epsilon_0\mu_0}. \tag{6}$$

The equivalent current densitiy is given in terms of $\mathbf{e}$ as:

$$\mathbf{j}(\mathbf{r}) = c_e(\epsilon_r(\mathbf{r}) - 1)\mathbf{e}(\mathbf{r}). \tag{7}$$

The integral equation we solve for the unknown currents is:

$$\left(\mathcal{I} - \left(\frac{\epsilon_r(\mathbf{r}) - 1}{\epsilon_r(\mathbf{r})}\right)\mathcal{N}\right)\mathbf{j} = c_e\left(\frac{\epsilon_r(\mathbf{r}) - 1}{\epsilon_r(\mathbf{r})}\right)\mathbf{e}_{\text{inc}}. \tag{8}$$

III. Circulant Approximation of Toeplitz Matrices

Recall an $n \times n$ matrix $\mathbf{T}_n = [t_{ij}]_{ij=0}^{n-1}$ is Toeplitz if

$$t_{ij} = t_{i-j},\ 0 \le i, j \le n-1; \tag{9}$$

$\mathbf{C}_n = [c_{ij}]_{ij=0}^{n-1}$ is circulant if,

$$c_{ij} = c_{i-j(\text{mod } n)},\ 0 \le i, j \le n-1. \tag{10}$$

We employ the Chan circulant preconditioner [3] $\widetilde{\mathbf{C}}$ which minimizes $||\widetilde{\mathbf{C}} - \mathbf{T}||_F$ in the Frobenius norm. The entries c_j of $\widetilde{\mathbf{C}}$ are given by:

$$c_j = \begin{cases} \frac{n-j}{n}t_j + \frac{j}{n}t_{-(n-j)} & ,0 \le j \le n-1, \\ c_{n+j} & ,-(n-1) \le j < 0. \end{cases}$$

Our matrix is in fact multi-level Toeplitz - it consists of three levels of Toeplitz matrix corresponding to the three dimensions of the problem. We use this circulant approximation for the level corresponding to the long z-direction.

IV. Numerical Results

We present results for a straight uniform waveguide and a Bragg grating. The waveguide is the "ideal" case since the geometry does not vary in the z-direction, hence the matrix is a pristine multi-level Toeplitz matrix. The Bragg grating is non-uniform, hence the underlying matrix is Toeplitz save for missing rows and columns corresponding to the air voxels of the indentations. For both we look at the iteration count and solve time with and without the preconditioner.

A. Uniform Waveguide

Fig. 2 shows the performance of GMRES for a waveguide of length 100 wavelengths. Observe the stagnation of GMRES without a preconditioner. The number of iterations is 608 and solve time 320s. With the preconditioner, we observe no such stagnation. GMRES converges in 16 iterations with a solve time of 2.9s. The preconditioner assembly here took 2.8s.

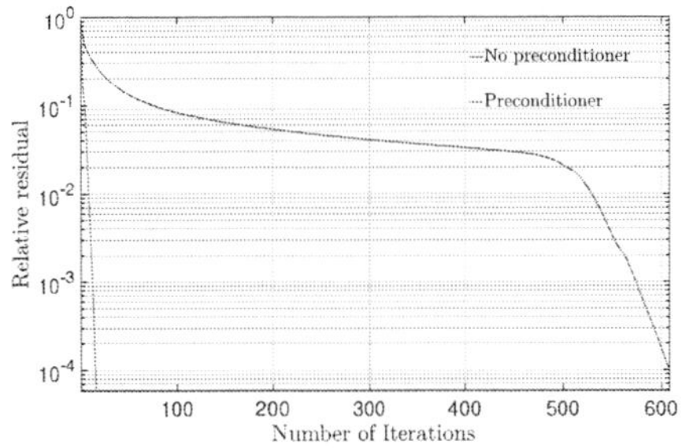

Fig. 2. Convergence history of unpreconditioned and preconditioned GMRES for uniform waveguide of length $Z = 4.5 \times 10^{-5}$ ($\approx$ 100 wavelengths).

B. Bragg Grating

For this non-uniform structure, we observe that our preconditioner still performs excellently. We see in Fig. 4 that the number of iterations increases slowly, from 30 to 65 as the length is increased from 7 wavelengths to 142 wavelength. This is a dramatic improvement over using no preconditioner.

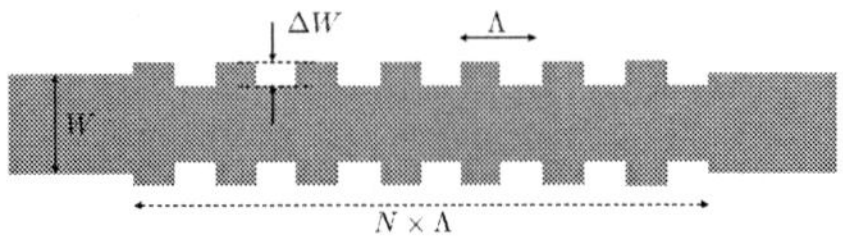

Fig. 3. Bragg grating with width W, corrugation depth ΔW, period Λ, and number of periods N.

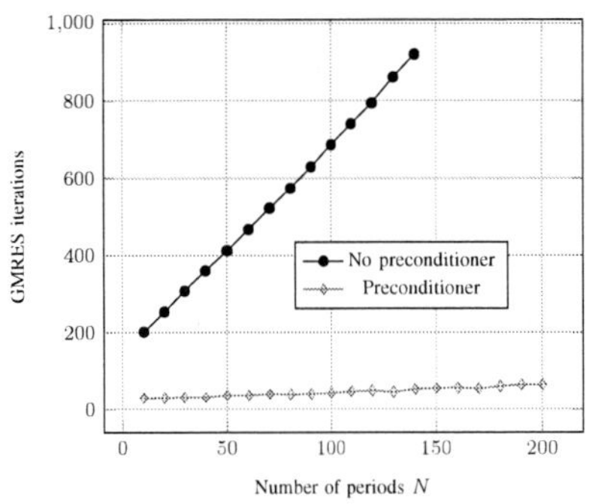

Fig. 4. GMRES iteration count against number of periods in Bragg grating. Linear growth without preconditioner. Close to constant with preconditioner.

References

[1] A. Polimeridis, J. F. Villena, L. Daniel, and J. White, "Stable FFT-JVIE solvers for fast analysis of highly inhomogeneous dielectric objects," J. Comp. Phys., 269, pp. 280–296, 2014.

[2] N. A. Ozdemir and J. F. Lee, "IE-FFT algorithm for a nonconformal volume integral equation for electromagnetic scattering from dielectric objects," IEEE Trans. Magn., 44, pp. 1398–1401, 2008.

[3] T. Chan, "An optimal preconditioner for Toeplitz systems," SIAM J. Sci. Statist. Comput., 9, pp. 766–771, 1988.

[4] S. S. Capizzano and E. Tyrtyshnikov, "Any circulant-like preconditioner for multilevel matrices is not superlinear," SIAM J. Matrix Anal. Appl., 21 (2), pp. 431–439, 2000.

On Complexity Reduction in Solution of Scattering Problems on Well-Conducting 3D Objects With Surface-Volume-Surface EFIE

Jamiu Mojolagbe
Dept. of Electrical and
Computer Engineering
University of Manitoba
Winnipeg, R3T5V6, Canada
Email: chenz313@myumanitoba.ca

Reza Gholami
Dept. of Electrical and
Computer Engineering
University of Manitoba
Winnipeg, R3T5V6, Canada
Email: gholamir@myumanitoba.ca

Vladimir Okhmatovski
Dept. of Electrical and
Computer Engineering
University of Manitoba
Winnipeg, R3T5V6, Canada
Email: vladimir.okhmatovski@umanitoba.ca

***Abstract*—The Surface-Volume-Surface Electric Field Integral Equation (SVS-EFIE) is applicable to the solution of the scattering problems on both lossless dielectric and highly conducting metal objects. When solution of scattering and radiation problems on metal objects is sought the rapidly attenuating field behaviour due to skin-effect can be exploited to reduce complexity of the Method of Moments (MoM) discretized SVS-EFIE. Among these strategies is the removal of the volume mesh corresponding to the part of the scatterer in which field is expected to attenuate below certain threshold and truncation of the range in MoM interactions due to their attenuation governed by the metal medium Green's function. The qualitative description of these techniques is provided as well as numerical results demonstrating their validity.**

I. Introduction

Solution of the scattering and radiation problems on well conducting penetrable objects has important applications in analysis of plasmonic structures, antenna design, high-speed interconnects and various other areas. Solution of such problems is performed through either direct discretization of the partial differential equations of the electromagnetics using finite-element method (FEM) and finite-difference schemes or through casting the pertinent boundary value problems into a form of surface integral equations (IEs).

In this work we demonstrate solution of the scattering and radiation problems with a SVS-EFIE [1]–[4]. It represents the field inside the metal (or equivalently volumetric polarization current dominated by the current of conductivity) via single source surface integral of the fictitious electric current on the boundary with the rapidly attenuating Green's function of the metal medium. The internal field only reaches the areas within a few skin depths away from the surface. It is then subsequently translated to the tangential component of the scattered field on its boundary. The physics of field attenuation through the volume of the metal produces patterns of significant sparsity in the matrices of the MoM discretized SVS-EFIE. It also allows for removal of the internal volume of the scatterer in which the field is attenuated below a certain threshold. The above described effects are illustrated through comparison of the MoM SVS-EFIE solution of the problem of radial electric dipole radiation in the vicinity of a $10\mu m$ radius lead sphere at 10GHz.

II. SVS-EFIE for Scattering on 3D Metal Object

In the case of a time-harmonic scattering of the incident field $\boldsymbol{E}^{\text{inc}}$ impinging on a metal object with V and surface ∂V situated in free space, the same SVS-EFIE formulation (1) holds as in the case of dielectric object 3D. The detailed description of it and it's MoM discretization can be found in [3]. In SVS-EFIE (1) $\overline{\overline{G}}_{e\epsilon}$ is the following electric field dyadic Green's function of the metal medium

$$\overline{\overline{G}}_{e\epsilon}(\boldsymbol{r},\boldsymbol{r}') = \left(\frac{\nabla\nabla}{k_0^2\epsilon} + \overline{\overline{I}}\right) G_\epsilon(\boldsymbol{r},\boldsymbol{r}'), \tag{2}$$

where $G_\epsilon(\boldsymbol{r},\boldsymbol{r}') = \frac{e^{-ik_\epsilon|\boldsymbol{r}-\boldsymbol{r}'|}}{4\pi|\boldsymbol{r}-\boldsymbol{r}'|}$ is the corresponding 3D scalar Green's function, $k_\epsilon = k_0\sqrt{\epsilon}$ is its wave number, and $\epsilon = \varepsilon - \sigma/(j\omega\varepsilon_0)$ is the complex relative permittivity of the metal material, σ being it's conductivity. The Green's function $\overline{\overline{G}}_{e0}$ is (1) is the electric field dyadic Green's function of free space. In SVS-EFIE (1) the integral operator

$$\boldsymbol{E}(\boldsymbol{r}) = -i\omega\mu_0 \oint_{\partial V} \overline{\overline{G}}_{e\epsilon}(\boldsymbol{r},\boldsymbol{r}')\cdot\boldsymbol{J}(\boldsymbol{r}')ds', \quad \boldsymbol{r}\in V\setminus\partial V, \tag{3}$$

translates the auxiliary electric current $\boldsymbol{J}$ from the surface of the scatterer to the electric field in its volume through the dyadic Green's function $\overline{\overline{G}}_{e\epsilon}$ of the homogeneous metal medium. Due to the fact that the depth of the field penetration into the volume of scatterer is governed by the skin-effect the field can be treated as negligible in the inner part V_i of the volume residing several skin-depths away from the surface. Hence, this inner part of the volume V_i can be removed from the mesh while the error in the resultant field computations is controlled through the depth of penetration past which the field is treated as negligible. To demonstrate this effect we consider radiation of the radial electric dipole situated above north pole of a metal sphere $30um$ away from its center at 10GHz. The

$$i\omega\mu_0 \hat{\mathbf{t}}\cdot\left(-\oint_{\partial V}\overline{\overline{G}}_{e\epsilon}(\boldsymbol{r},\boldsymbol{r}'')\cdot\boldsymbol{J}(\boldsymbol{r}'')ds'' + k_0^2(\epsilon-1)\int_V \overline{\overline{G}}_{e0}(\boldsymbol{r},\boldsymbol{r}')\cdot\oint_{\partial V}\overline{\overline{G}}_{e\epsilon}(\boldsymbol{r}',\boldsymbol{r}'')\cdot \boldsymbol{J}(\boldsymbol{r}'')ds''dv'\right) = \hat{\mathbf{t}}\cdot\boldsymbol{E}^{\mathrm{inc}}(\boldsymbol{r}), \quad \boldsymbol{r}\in\partial V. \quad (1)$$

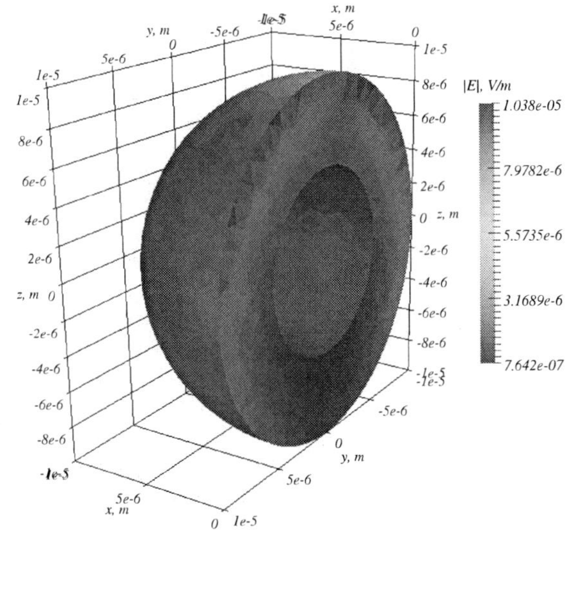

Fig. 1. Magnitude of the electric field in lead sphere of radius $10um$ obtained via MoM solution of SVS-EFIE due to radial electric dipole at 10GHz. The inner volume of the sphere is removed due to skin-effect field attenuation.

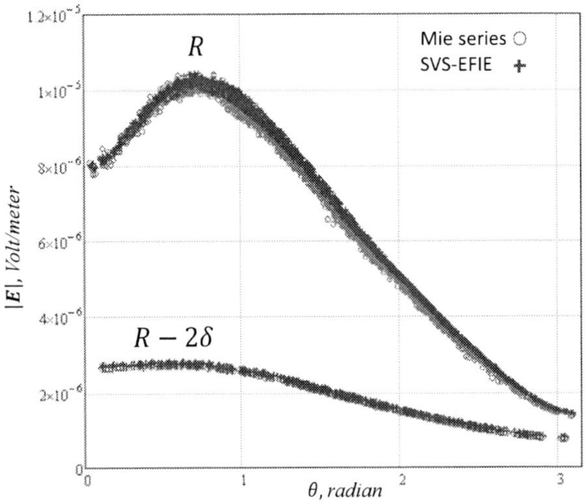

Fig. 2. Magnitude of the electric field in lead sphere of radius $10um$ obtained via MoM solution of SVS-EFIE due to radial electric dipole at 10GHz as a function of the polar angle θ at the centers of tetrahedrons nearest to the outer radius R of the hollow sphere (Fig. 1) and nearest to the radius $R - 2\delta$ of the volume removed from the sphere due to skin-effect attenuation. The Mie series results are provided for comparison.

sphere has the radius $R = 10um$ and is made of lead with conductivity $\sigma = 10^6$S/m. The skin-depth at this frequency is $\delta = 2.37um$. We performed computations of the field in the case of the entire sphere and the sphere with removed inner spherical volume V_i or radius $R_i = R - 2\delta$ as shown in Fig. 1. The behaviour of the magnitude of the electric field $|\boldsymbol{E}|$ as a function of the polar angle θ at the centers of the tetrahedrons in $11,774$ element volumetric mesh nearest to the outer radius of the sphere R and the radius of mesh truncation R_i is shown in Fig. 2. For comparison the analytic Mie series solution at the centers of the same tetrahedrons is shown also for the case of complete sphere with no inner volume removal. One can observe the closeness in the SVS-EFIE solution with partially removed volume to the Mie series solution on the full sphere.

The skin-effect based field attenuation also produces sparsity in the MoM matrices of the discretized SVS-EFIE. This sparsity is the higher the large is the size of the scatterer compared to the skin-depth. This effect was discussed in details in the case 2D SVS-EFIE formulation in [4].

III. Conclusion

The paper describes two strategies for reduction of computational complexity associated with Method of Moment (MoM) solution of the Surface-Volume-Surface Electric Field Integral Equation (SVS-EFIE) for the problems of scattering and radiation of the electromagnetic field on 3D penetrable metal objects. The strategies include the approach based on removal of the volumetric mesh elements in the regions of weak field penetration and utilization of the sparsity in the matrices of the MoM discretized SVS-EFIE.

References

[1] A. Menshov, et.al., "New single-source surface integral equations for scattering on penetrable cylinders and current flow modeling in 2-D conductors," *IEEE Trans. Microw. Theory Techn.*, vol. 61, no. 1, pp. 341–350, Jan. 2013.

[2] F. L. S. Hosseini, et.al. "New vector single-source surface integral equation for scattering problems on dielectric objects in 2D," *IEEE Trans. Antennas Propag.*, vol. 65, no. 7, pp. 3794–3799, Jul. 2017.

[3] F. L. S. Hosseini, et.al. "Novel single-source integral equation for scattering problems by 3D dielectric objects," *IEEE Trans. Antennas Propag.*, vol. 66, no. 2, pp. 797–807, Feb. 2018.

[4] S. Zheng, et.al. "New single-source surface integral equation for magneto-quasi-static characterization of transmission lines situated in multilayered media," *IEEE Trans. Microw. Theory Techn.*, vol. 64, no. 12, pp. 4341–4351, Dec. 2016.

Linear-Complexity Direct Integral Equation Solver with Explicit Accuracy Control for Large-Scale Interconnect Extraction

Miaomiao Ma and Dan Jiao
School of Electrical and Computer Engineering, Purdue University
West Lafayette, IN 47907, USA, djiao@purdue.edu

***Abstract*—In this paper, we develop new linear-complexity direct matrix solutions for large-scale integral equation based interconnect extraction, including both factorization and inversion algorithms. These algorithms have explicitly controlled accuracy, while taking less CPU time than existing direct solvers. Rapid direct solutions of millions of unknowns have been obtained on a single CPU core with explicit accuracy control.**

***Index Terms*—Direct solvers, interconnect extraction, integral-equation-based methods, linear complexity.**

I. Introduction

Integral-equation (IE) based solvers have been particularly popular in interconnect extraction because they can reduce the problem dimension by one, and they avoid the use of absorbing boundary conditions. Many fast integral equation solvers for interconnect extraction are iterative solvers [1], [2]. They have significantly reduced one dense matrix-vector multiplication from the brute-force $O(N^2)$ to $O(N)$ complexity, where N is matrix size. However, due to the number of right hand sides N_{rhs}, and the number of iterations N_{it}, the overall complexity of an iterative solver is $O(N_{rhs}N_{it}N)$. When handling complicated materials in multiple scales, the iteration number can be huge and the convergence of an iterative solver may not be guaranteed either. The performance of an iterative solver is further degraded when multiple inputs and outputs are encountered or many what-if analyses have to be performed.

In this work, we develop a new fast direct solver that has a linear complexity for large-scale interconnect extraction. Compared to our previous work in [3], this new solver has a directly controlled accuracy. The proposed direct solver has been applied to extract interconnect capacitance parameters as well as to perform a full-wave interconnect analysis. The solver exhibits a clear $O(N)$ complexity in factorization, inversion, solution time, memory, and with a strictly controlled accuracy. Comparisons with state of the art $\mathcal{H}^2$-based direct solvers for interconnect extraction have also demonstrated the superior performance of the proposed solver.

II. Proposed Direct Solver

Consider an $\mathcal{H}^2$-representation of the IE operator, one example of which is illustrated in Fig. 1 (a). Starting from the leaf level, for leaf cluster $i = 1$, we first obtain:

$$(\widetilde{\mathbf{Q}}_i)_{\#i\times\#i} = [(\mathbf{V}_i^{\perp})_{\#i\times(\#i-k)} \quad (\mathbf{V}_i)_{\#i\times k}], \tag{1}$$

in which $\mathbf{V}_i$ is the unitary cluster basis, $(\mathbf{V}_i^{\perp})^H\mathbf{V}_i = 0$, k is the rank, and $\#i$ denotes the cardinality of cluster i. Thus, we have:

$$\widetilde{\mathbf{Q}}_i^H \times \mathbf{V}_i = \begin{bmatrix}\mathbf{0}_{(\#i-k)\times k}\\ \mathbf{I}_{k\times k}\end{bmatrix}; \tag{2}$$

$$\mathbf{V}_i^T \times \overline{\widetilde{\mathbf{Q}}}_i = [\mathbf{0}_{k\times(\#i-k)} \quad \mathbf{I}_{k\times k}]. \tag{3}$$

Let $\mathbf{Q}_i$ be a block diagonal matrix whose i-th diagonal block is $\widetilde{\mathbf{Q}}_i$, and other blocks are identity matrices. An operation of $\mathbf{Q}_i^H\mathbf{Z}\overline{\mathbf{Q}}_i$ will zero out the first $(\#i - k)$ rows of the admissible blocks formed by row cluster i, as well as their transpose entries in $\mathbf{Z}$. These zeros are shown as white blocks in Fig. 1 (b) for cluster $i = 1$. Next, we perform a partial LU factorization of $\mathbf{Q}_i^H\mathbf{Z}\overline{\mathbf{Q}}_i$ to eliminate the first $(\#i - k)$ unknowns of cluster i, denoted by set i'. We obtain:

$$\mathbf{Q}_i^H\mathbf{Z}\overline{\mathbf{Q}}_i = \begin{bmatrix}\mathbf{Z}_{i'i'} & \mathbf{Z}_{i'c}\\ \mathbf{Z}_{ci'} & \mathbf{Z}_{cc}\end{bmatrix} = \begin{bmatrix}\mathbf{L}_{i'i'} & \mathbf{0}\\ \mathbf{Z}_{ci'}\mathbf{U}_{i'i'}^{-1} & \mathbf{I}\end{bmatrix}\begin{bmatrix}\mathbf{I} & \mathbf{0}\\ \mathbf{0} & \widetilde{\mathbf{Z}}_{cc}\end{bmatrix}\begin{bmatrix}\mathbf{U}_{i'i'} & \mathbf{L}_{i'i'}^{-1}\mathbf{Z}_{i'c}\\ \mathbf{0} & \mathbf{I}\end{bmatrix}, \tag{4}$$

where $\widetilde{\mathbf{Z}}_{cc} = \mathbf{Z}_{cc} - \mathbf{Z}_{ci'}\mathbf{U}_{i'i'}^{-1}\mathbf{L}_{i'i'}^{-1}\mathbf{Z}_{i'c}$ is the Schur complement. The above can be written in short as:

$$\mathbf{Q}_i^H\mathbf{Z}\overline{\mathbf{Q}}_i = \mathbf{L}_i(\mathbf{Z}_{cur})\mathbf{U}_i, \tag{5}$$

where $\mathbf{Z}_{cur}$ is the center matrix that remains to be factorized. Because of zeros in the admissible blocks, the $\mathbf{Z}_{i'c}$ and $\mathbf{Z}_{ci'}$ only consist of the inadmissible blocks formed by cluster i, the number of which is bounded by constant C_{sp}. Hence, the storage and computation of $\mathbf{L}_i$ and $\mathbf{U}_i$ only involve C_{sp} blocks of $leafsize$. Thereby the cost is constant at the leaf level. Meanwhile, the Schur complement $\widetilde{\mathbf{Z}}_{cc}$ only introduces $O(C_{sp}^2)$ fill-in blocks in the remaining matrix to be factorized, $\mathbf{Z}_{cur}$, which is shown in Fig. 1 (c) as blocks marked in light or dark blue. Hence, the number of fill-in blocks generated is also a constant. If the fill-in block is added upon an original inadmissible block, as the block marked in dark blue in Fig. 1 (c), we add the fill-in directly to the original inadmissible block. If the fill-in appears in an admissible block, shown as a light blue block in Fig. 1 (c), we store the fill-in

This work was supported by a grant from NSF under award No. 1619062 and a grant from DARPA under award HR0011-14-1-0057.

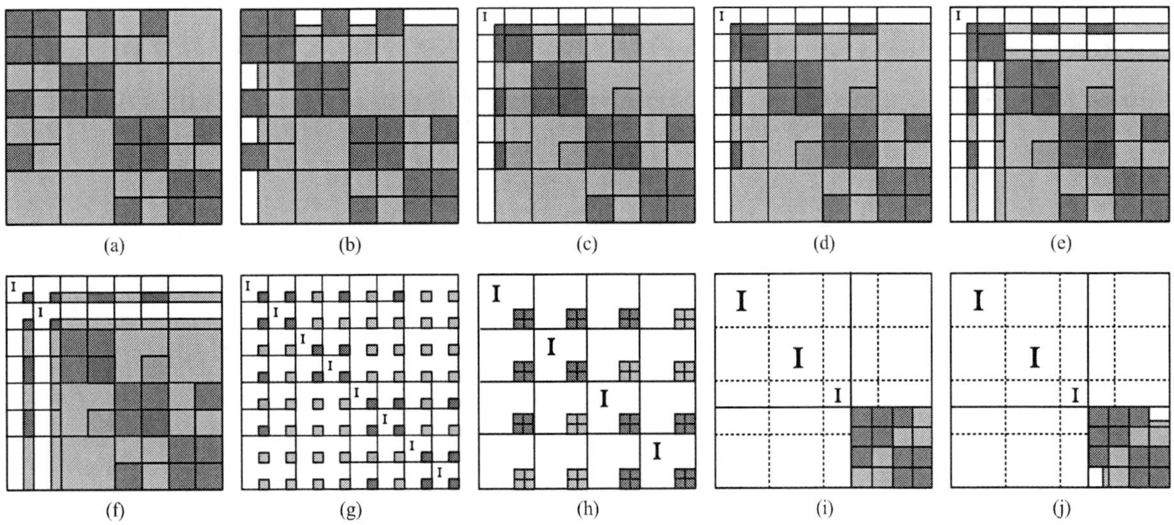

Fig. 1. (a) $\mathcal{H}^2$-matrix structure. (b) $\mathbf{Q}_1^H\mathbf{Z}\overline{\mathbf{Q}}_1$. (c) Partial LU factorization for cluster 1. (d) Update cluster basis of cluster 2. (e) $\mathbf{Q}_2^H\mathbf{Z}\overline{\mathbf{Q}}_2$. (f) Partial LU factorization for cluster 2. (g) $\mathcal{H}^2$-matrix after leaf level elimination. (h) Merging to next level. (i) Ancestor level structure. (j) Ancestor level $\mathbf{Q}_t^H\mathbf{Z}\overline{\mathbf{Q}}_t$.

temporarily in $\mathbf{F}_{j,k_m}$ $(m = 1, 2, ..., O(C_{sp}))$, where j denotes the row cluster index, and k_m denotes the column cluster index of the fill-in block. No computation involving $\mathbf{F}_{j,k_m}$ is needed yet until row cluster j is reached during the factorization. If multiple fill-in blocks are generated at the same admissible block, the new one is added upon the old $\mathbf{F}_{j,k_m}$. Next, we proceed to the second leaf cluster $i = 2$ and others to factorize $\mathbf{Z}_{cur}$ that remains to be factorized. All the operations are the same as those done to the first cluster. The only difference is that before constructing (1), we first update cluster basis $\mathbf{V}_i$ based on accuracy ϵ_{acc} to account for the contributions of fill-ins. After all the leaf-level computation, we obtain a matrix shown in Fig. 1 (g), which is current $\mathbf{Z}_{cur}$ left to be factorized. This structure is not only true for $l = L - 1$ level, i.e., one level above the leaf level, but also true for every non-leaf level l. After merging and permutation, we obtain the matrix at next level, shown in Fig. 1 (j), which again is an $\mathcal{H}^2$-matrix. The same procedure at the leaf level can then be applied at this level and thereafter. Overall, the proposed direct solution is a one-way bottom-up traversal of the $\mathcal{H}^2$-tree, the complexity of which has been proved to be linear.

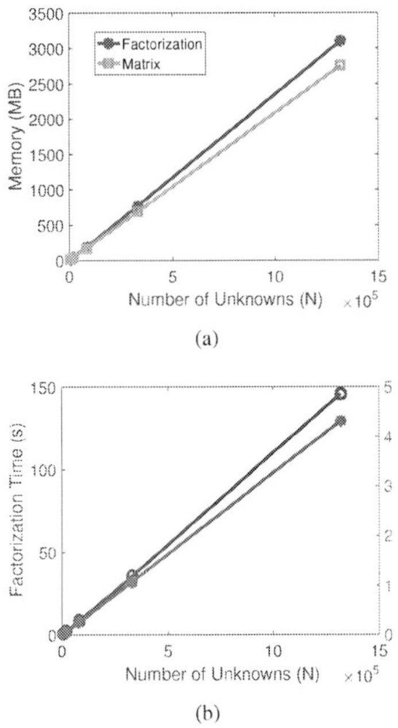

Fig. 2. Simulation of a suite of large-scale on-chip buses. (a) Memory complexity. (b) Time complexity.

III. Numerical Results

The first example is the capacitance extraction of a 2-layer cross bus structure [3]. We simulate a suite of such structures with bus number from 16 to 512. The total time of the last case having 4,206,592 unknowns for all 512 right hand sides is only 2.62 hours using the proposed direct solver; whereas the time of FastCap [1] is 210.44 hours, and that of [3] is 6.69 hours. Second example is a full-wave volume IE simulation of on-chip interconnects. A suite of large-scale on-chip bus structures from a 4×4 to 64×64 are simulated at 30 GHz. The dimensions of each bus are $1\mu m \times 1\mu m \times 20\mu m$, with the horizontal spacing being $20\mu m$, and the vertical spacing $40\mu m$. The conductivity of the metal is $5.8 \times 10^7 S/m$. The total number of unknowns ranges from 5,152 to 1,318,912. For the $\mathcal{H}^2$-tree construction, we set $leafsize$ to be 25 and $\eta = 1$, with $\epsilon_{\mathcal{H}^2} = 1e-4$. The $\epsilon_{acc} = 1e-4$ is used in the direct solution. In Fig. 2 (a), we plot the memory cost of both storing the original matrix, and that for factorizing the matrix. In Fig. 2 (b), we plot both factorization time and solution time for one right hand side as a function of N. Clear linear complexities can be observed. The accuracy is assessed by relative residual and found to be 0.001% for all the unknown cases.

References

[1] K. Nabors and J. White, "Fastcap: A multipole accelerated 3-D capacitance extraction program," IEEE Trans. on CAD, pp. 1447-1459, 1991.

[2] W. Shi, J. Liu, N. Kakani and T. Yu, "A fast hierarchical algorithm for 3-D capacitance extraction," IEEE Trans. on CAD, pp. 330-336, 2002.

[3] W. Chai and D. Jiao, "Dense matrix inversion of linear complexity for integral-equation based large scale 3-D capacitance extraction," IEEE Trans. Microw. Theory Techn., vol. 59, no. 10, pp. 2404-2421, Oct. 2013.

Optical Couplers for Sharply Bended Nanowires: Sensitivity to Coupler Nanoparticles

Aşkın Altınoklu and Özgür Ergül
Department of Electrical and Electronics Engineering
Middle East Technical University
Ankara, Turkey
ozergul@metu.edu.tr

Abstract—**We consider optical couplers that consists of optimal arrangements of nanoparticles to improve the transmission abilities of nanowire systems with sharp bends. Previously, it was shown that absence/existence of nanoparticles in a given grid can be optimized such that the power transmission can significantly be increased without smoothing the bend. In this contribution, we present the sensitivity of coupler performances to the particle geometries. Numerical results demonstrate a high dependency of coupler characteristics to particle types due to strong plasmonic interactions at short distances. These findings further support the need for case-dependent optimization.**

I. Introduction

Nanowires are natural components of nano-optical systems as they enable long-distance transmission of electromagnetic power via surface plasmons [1]–[7]. When they are straight, smooth, and perfectly aligned, nanowires have excellent transmission abilities for long distances with respect to the operating wavelength [2],[6]. When they are bended, however, reflection and diffraction at the bend regions may significantly reduce the efficiency [3]. To alleviate this problem, optical couplers can be used to improve the power transmission, especially when smooth bending is not desired to avoid inefficient usage of the available space. Recently, we showed that robust couplers involving nanoparticles can be designed such that the transmission can be improved significantly even through very sharp corners [7]. The designs were obtained via optimization with genetic algorithms (GAs) supported by full-wave solutions with surface integral equations and the multilevel fast multipole algorithm (MLFMA).

It is well known that plasmonic properties of metals at optical frequencies lead to complex interactions and very different responses to excitations, in comparison to the behaviors of metals at the lower (radio and microwave) frequencies. For example, when nanostructures are close to each other, the extraordinary coupling between them leads to useful abilities, particularly for energy harvesting, focusing, and optical sensing. At the same time, these strong interactions may increase the sensitivity of the designs to geometric properties. In this contribution, we further investigate optical couplers involving nanoparticles and their optimal designs to improve the power transmission through sharp corners. We show that the geometries of particles can significantly change the characteristics of a coupler, while new optimizations may be required depending on geometric deformations.

II. Simulation and Optimization Environment

The transmission problems involving nanowires and couplers (nanoparticles) are modeled as three-dimensional structures and formulated by using surface integral equations in the frequency domain. There are diverse choices for the formulation [8]–[10], while we prefer the electric and magnetic current combined-field integral equation (JMCFIE) [11] or the modified combined tangential formulation (MCTF) [12] for fast and accurate solutions depending on the frequency. The surfaces and integral equations are discretized by using triangles and the Rao-Wilton-Glisson functions. The complex permittivity values of the metals are extracted from experimental data [13]. The problems are solved iteratively, while the required matrix-vector multiplications are performed via MLFMA. In addition, electromagnetic interactions in plasmonic media (e.g., inside nanowires) are truncated to improve the efficiency without sacrificing the accuracy [14].

III. Coupler Problems and Optimizations

We consider transmission lines involving nanowires with sharp (e.g., 90°) bends. As shown in Fig. 1, a given transmission line is excited from one side and the power density is observed at an output frame at the other side. A coupler is designed and located at the corner such that the power density at the output is maximized. Optimization problems are solved by employing GAs, while the required trials are performed as three-dimensional simulations via the MLFMA implementation. The couplers are designed by considering

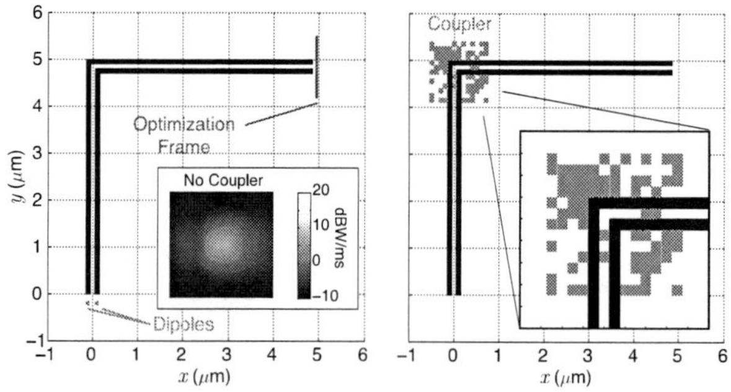

Fig. 1. An optimization problem involving a transmission line (a pair of Ag nanowires) with a 90° sharp bend. An optimal coupler that consists of $90 \times 90 \times 90$ nm cubic nanoparticles is also depicted.

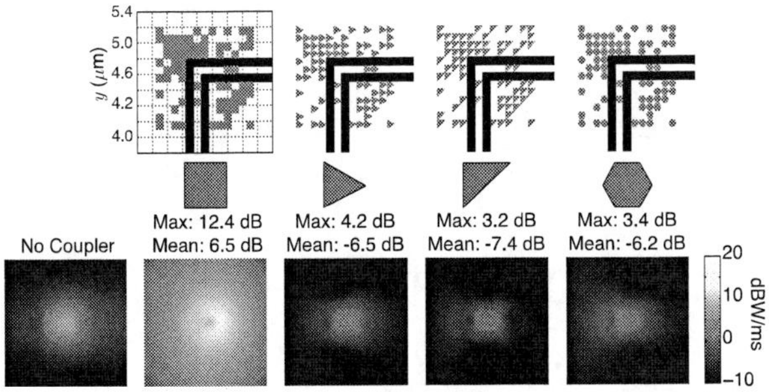

Fig. 2. The power density at the output frame when a designed coupler involving cubic nanoparticles is used, in comparison to the no-coupler case. Results for three other couplers using the same arrangement of nanoparticles with different particle geometries are also shown.

an initial grid of nanoparticles and deciding which particles need to be kept/extracted to maximize the cost functions (e.g., average/maximum of power density at the output). The GA implementation is integrated with the MLFMA implementation by employing dynamic accuracy control in order the reduce the optimization time. In addition, embarrassing parallelism is used by assigning simultaneous MLFMA solutions to multiple cores.

IV. Numerical Examples and Conclusions

For numerical examples, we consider a pair of 10 μm silver nanowires with 90° sharp bends at the middle, as shown in Fig. 1. Each nanowire has 0.1×0.1 μm square cross section. The transmission line is excited by a pair of Hertzian dipoles located on one side at 0.2 μm from the nanowires. The output frame is selected as a 1.3×1.3 μm square area at 0.1 μm distance from the nanowires. The frequency is selected as 250 THz, at which the relative permittivity of Ag is approximately $-60.8 + 4.31i$. Fig. 1 also depicts the power density at the output frame when no coupler is used.

Fig. 2 presents the power density at the output frame when a coupler is designed by using $90 \times 90 \times 90$ nm Ag cubes. In this optimization (and also for the following ones), the maximum power at the output frame is maximized. In addition to the result for the optimal coupler, those obtained by using different types of particles (triangular and hexagonal prisms) with the same configuration (the optimized arrangement using cubic particles) are shown. It can be observed that changing the geometry of the particle significantly deteriorates the performance of the coupler. Fig. 3 presents designed couplers with different types of nanoparticles when an optimization is performed for each particle type. It can be observed that (1) the maximum power density can significantly be increased (compared to the no-coupler case) for all particle types and (2) the optimal arrangement of nanoparticles strongly depends on the particle type. It is remarkable that cubic particles also lead to a larger value for the mean power, while this was not particularly required in the related optimization.

Numerical experiments, some of which are included in this short paper, demonstrate that the particle geometry is an extremely important parameter in optical couplers involving

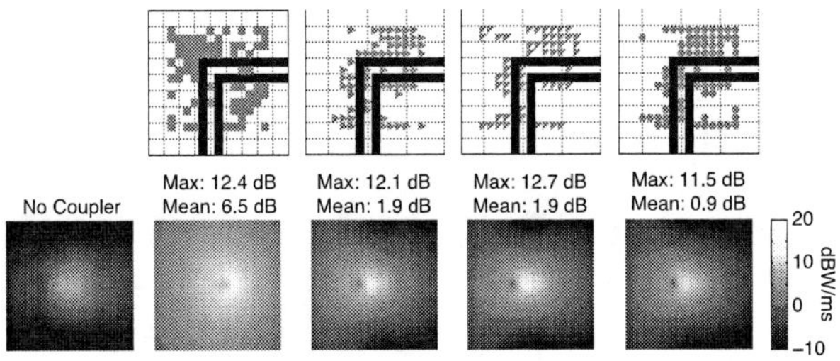

Fig. 3. The power density at the output frame when four designed couplers involving different types of nanoparticles are used.

array arrangements of nanoparticles. In this context, possible effects of fabrication errors (deformation of nanoparticles) to the performance of the designed couplers are under investigation.

Acknowledgement

This work was supported by the Scientific and Technical Research Council of Turkey (TUBITAK) under the Research Grant 114E498 and by the Turkish Academy of Sciences (TUBA) in the framework of the Young Scientist Award Program.

References

[1] X. Wang, C. J. Summers, and Z. L. Wang, "Large-scale hexagonal-patterned growth of aligned ZnO nanorods for nano-optoelectronics and nanosensor arrays," Nano Lett., vol. 4, no. 3, pp. 423–426, Jan. 2004.

[2] A. W. Sanders, et al., "Observation of plasmon propagation, redirection, and fan-out in silver nanowires," Nano Lett., vol. 6, no. 8, pp. 1822–1826, Jun. 2006.

[3] W. Wang, et al., "Light propagation in curved silver nanowire plasmonic waveguides," Nano Lett., vol. 11, no. 4, pp. 1603–1608, Mar. 2011.

[4] S. M. Bergin, et al., "The effect of nanowire length and diameter on the properties of transparent, conducting nanowire films," Nanoscale, vol. 4, no. 6, pp. 1996–2004, Feb. 2012.

[5] Y. Huang, et al., "Nanowire-supported plasmonic waveguide for remote excitation of surface-enhanced Raman scattering," Light: Science and Applications, vol. 3, no. 199, Aug. 2014.

[6] H. A. Şatana, B. Karaosmanoğlu, and Ö. Ergül, "A comparative study of nanowire arrays for maximum power transmission," in Nanowires, K. Maaz, Ed. InTech, 2017.

[7] Y. E. Tunçyürek, B. Karaosmanoğlu, and Ö. Ergül, "Computational design of optical couplers for bended nanowire transmission lines," ACES J., vol. 32, no. 7, pp. 562–568, Jul. 2017.

[8] Ö. Ergül and L. Gürel, "Comparison of integral-equation formulations for the fast and accurate solution of scattering problems involving dielectric objects with the multilevel fast multipole algorithm," IEEE Trans. Antennas Propag., vol. 57, no. 1, pp. 176–187, Jan. 2009.

[9] M. G. Araujo, et al., "Comparison of surface integral equation formulations for electromagnetic analysis of plasmonic nanoscatterers," Opt. Exp., vol. 20, no. 8, pp. 9161–9171, Apr. 2012.

[10] D. M. Solis, J. M. Taboada, and F. Obelleiro, "Surface integral equation method of moments with multiregion basis functions applied to plasmonics," IEEE Trans. Antennas Propag., vol. 63, no. 5, pp. 2141–2152, May 2015.

[11] P. Ylä-Oijala, M. Taskinen, and S. Järvenpää, "Surface integral equation formulations for solving electromagnetic scattering problems with iterative methods," Radio Sci., vol. 40, no. 6002, Dec. 2005.

[12] B. Karaosmanoğlu, A. Yılmaz, and Ö. Ergül, "A comparative study of surface integral equations for accurate and efficient analysis of plasmonic structures," IEEE Trans. Antennas Propag., vol. 65, no. 6, pp. 3049–3057, Jun. 2017.

[13] P. B. Johnson and R. W. Christy, "Optical constants of the noble metals," Phys. Rev. B, vol. 6, no. 12, pp. 4370–4379, Dec. 1972.

[14] B. Karaosmanoğlu, et al., "Solutions of plasmonic structures using the multilevel fast multipole algorithm," Special Issue on Challenges in RF and Microwave Defense Engineering, Int. J. RF Microwave Comput.-Aided. Eng., vol. 26, no. 4, pp. 335–341, May 2016.

Analytical Evaluation of Matrix Elements of Electromagnetic Integral Equations with RWG basis Functions for Arbitrarily Oriented Pairs of Triangular Surface Elements

Elizabeth Bleszynski*, Marek Bleszynski, and Thomas Jaroszewicz
Monopole Research, Thousand Oaks, CA 91360
* elizabeth@monopoleresearch.com

***Abstract*—We present an approach to calculation of matrix elements for arbitrarily oriented planar surface elements, based on reduction of the surface integrals to line integrals over perimeters of the elements. The described method is a generalization of our previous developments applicable to parallel geometry elements; it utilizes a representation of the Helmholtz-equation Green function in terms of an auxiliary function acted upon by a differential operator involving tangential gradients in *two different planes*. Integration by parts allows then reduction of surface- to line integrals with nonsingular integrands. The latter integrals can be either evaluated as standard quadratures or expressed analytically, in every order of expansion in the wave number k, in closed form.**

The method can be applied to all operators arising in Maxwell equations and in similar problems in acoustics and elastodynamics, offering significant advantages in accuracy and the computational cost.

***Index Terms*—Integral equations, Moment methods, Numerical analysis.**

We have previously [1] presented a procedure for the evaluation of matrix elements of the kernels of electromagnetic surface integral equation operators sandwiched between the surface Rao-Wilton-Glisson (RWG) [2] supported on *parallel* triangles. In contrast to the majority of methods [3] used in computation of matrix elements of singular Green functions (singularity subtraction, e.g., [4] and singularity cancellation e.g., [5], [6], [7]), the method was based on a representation of the relevant Green function as a two-dimensional Laplacian of an auxiliary function, allowing integrating by parts and expressing surface integrals as line integrals with nonsingular integrands.

We have subsequently [8] generalized our approach to problems involving non-parallel surface elements by representing the Green function $g(k,R) = \exp(\mathrm{i}\,kR)/(4\pi R)$ as:

$$g\big(k,|\boldsymbol{R}_1-\boldsymbol{R}_2|\big) = \big\{\boldsymbol{\nabla}_1\cdot \hat{M}_a\,\boldsymbol{\nabla}_2\big\}\,\Phi^{(1)}(k,a,\boldsymbol{R}_1-\boldsymbol{R}_2), \quad (1)$$

involving a bilinear form of two tangential gradient operators $\boldsymbol{\nabla}_1$ and $\boldsymbol{\nabla}_2$ acting on the coordinates $\boldsymbol{R}_1$ and $\boldsymbol{R}_2$ of points in *two different, non-parallel, planes* Π_1 and Π_2, containing the considered triangles T_1 and T_2; $\hat{M}_a = \mathrm{diag}(1, 1-a)$ is a (2×2) matrix acting in the space of tangential components of the points $\boldsymbol{R}_1$ and $\boldsymbol{R}_2$ in the respective planes (Fig. 1).

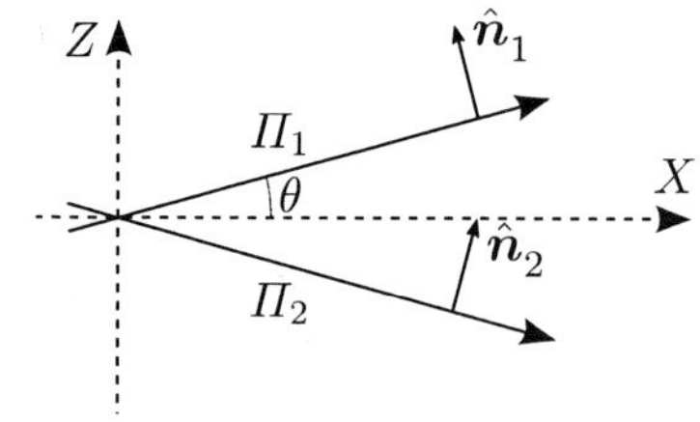

Fig. 1. Geometry of two intersecting planes, Π_1 and Π_2 with the indicated normal vectors $\hat{\boldsymbol{n}}_1$ and $\hat{\boldsymbol{n}}_2$, and the global Cartesian coordinate system $\mathscr{S} = (X, Y, Z)$.

Having determined the auxiliary function $\Phi^{(1)}$, we can convert the double surface integral of the Green function over the two flat triangles to the line integral over their perimeters,

$$\begin{aligned}&\int_{T_1}\mathrm{d}S(\boldsymbol{R}_1)\int_{T_2}\mathrm{d}S(\boldsymbol{R}_2)\;g(k,|\boldsymbol{R}_1-\boldsymbol{R}_2|) \\ &= \oint_{\partial T_1}\mathrm{d}l_1\oint_{\partial T_2}\mathrm{d}l_2\,\{\hat{\boldsymbol{u}}_1\cdot\hat{M}_a\,\boldsymbol{u}_2\}\;\Phi^{(1)}(k,a,\boldsymbol{R}_1-\boldsymbol{R}_2),\end{aligned} \quad (2)$$

with $\hat{\boldsymbol{u}}_1$ and $\hat{\boldsymbol{u}}_2$ representing unit vectors perpendicular to the perimeter lines, located in the planes Π_1 and Π_2. Analogous procedures can be applied to other integral-equation kernels, in particular those involving the tensor and vector Green functions, and to polynomial trial and test functions (including RWG basis functions). In those cases it is, generally, necessary to consider representations involving higher powers of the differential operator in Eq. (1) and, possibly, gradients of such representations.

In the present paper we describe a procedure for constructing a set of auxiliary functions which allow us to convert expressions for matrix elements of both tensor and vector Green functions from surface to line integrals. The final result for matrix elements are given in terms of line integrals over triangle perimeters with simple and nonsingular integrands. The line integrals can be further evaluated analytically. However, the computation cost of evaluating the obtained analytical expression may be comparable to the cost of quadratures.

The outline of our procedure is as follows:

1. We first choose a suitable global Cartesian coordinate system $\mathscr{S} = (X, Y, Z)$, as shown in Fig. 1, with: the axis $\hat{\boldsymbol{Y}}$ coinciding with the line of intersection of the planes Π_1 and Π_2 and the $\hat{\boldsymbol{Z}}$ axis along the mean normal to the planes. In such a coordinate system we denote the vector representing the difference of two points, $\boldsymbol{R}_1$ and $\boldsymbol{R}_2$ on the individual triangles with

$$\boldsymbol{R} \equiv \boldsymbol{R}_1 - \boldsymbol{R}_2 = (\boldsymbol{\rho}, s) = (t, y, s)\,; \tag{3}$$

this expression *defines* the variables t, y, s used in the following.

2. The above definition of geometrical parameters allows us to relatively easily evaluate the auxiliary function $\Phi^{(1)}(a, k; \rho, s)$, as well as its generalizations. Indeed, it can be shown that, in the variables $(\boldsymbol{\rho}, s)$, Eq. (1) is equivalent to the d'Alembert-type equation:

$$\begin{aligned}\left[-(1-a)\,\frac{\partial}{\rho\,\partial\rho}\,\frac{\rho\,\partial}{\partial\rho} + a\,\partial_s^2\right]\,\Phi^{(1)}(a, k; \rho, s) \\ = g(k; \rho, s)\,,\end{aligned} \tag{4}$$

where the r.h.s. is the original Green function $g(k; \boldsymbol{R})$ also expressed in terms of the coordinates $\boldsymbol{R}$.

3. The d'Alembert equation (4) can be then solved in the Fourier domain and closed-form results can be obtained to all orders in the expansion of $\Phi^{(1)}$ in powers of k, by using methods similar to those in evaluating Feynman diagrams. That fact that the function $\Phi^{(1)}$ is defined only up to a solution of the homogeneous d'Alembert equation can be exploited in choosing a solution having the most advantageous regularity, symmetry, etc., properties.

The simplest example of a closed-form expression is the lowest-order, $\mathcal{O}(k^0)$, term in the expansion,

$$\begin{aligned}&\Phi^{(1)}(a, k; \boldsymbol{r}_1(\boldsymbol{R}), \boldsymbol{r}_2(\boldsymbol{R})) \equiv \Phi^{(1)}(a, k; \rho, s) \\ &= -\frac{(\rho^2+s^2)^{1/2}}{8\pi\,(1-a)^{1/2}}\,\Phi_0^{(1)}\left(a, \frac{s^2}{\rho^2+s^2}\right) + \mathcal{O}(k)\,,\end{aligned} \tag{5}$$

where the coefficient function $\widehat{\Phi}_0^{(1)}$ (as well as higher-order coefficients) depend only on a and a single variable $\sigma := s^2/(\rho^2+s^2)$. Explicitly,

$$\begin{aligned}&\Phi_0^{(1)}(a, \sigma) \\ &= 2\,\mathrm{Re}\left\{\sqrt{1-a} - \sqrt{\sigma - a} + \frac{1}{2}\,\sqrt{1-a}\,\sqrt{\sigma}\,\ln\lambda(a,\sigma)\right\},\end{aligned} \tag{6}$$

with

$$\lambda(a, \sigma) = \frac{\sqrt{(1-a)\,\sigma} + \sqrt{\sigma - a}}{\sqrt{(1-a)\,\sigma} - \sqrt{\sigma - a}}\,. \tag{7}$$

4. Expressions for the matrix elements are given in terms of line integrals (2), and their generalizations. Such integrals can be relatively easily implemented numerically without a need for any specialized integration quadratures.

5. It is also possible to evaluate line integrals analytically in any order in k, with closed-form expressions involving elementary functions only.

A line integral such as (2) is a sum of integrals over pairs of triangles' edges. For each pair, coordinates of the integration points can be parameterized edges as linear functions of normalized length parameters $\xi_1, \xi_2 \in [0, 1]$. Hence, s is a linear function and ρ^2 a quadratic function of ξ_1, ξ_2. Formulae of the type of Eq. (5), with σ expressed in terms of s and ρ, involve factors $s = a_0 + a_1\xi_1 + a_2\xi_2 \equiv L(\xi_1, \xi_2)$ and $s \pm \sqrt{(s^2 - a\rho^2)/(1-a)} = L(\xi_1, \xi_2) \pm \sqrt{Q(\xi_1, \xi_2)}$ with $Q = A_0 + B_1\xi_1 + B_2\xi_2 + C_1\xi_1^2 + C_2\xi_2^2 + C_{12}\xi_1\xi_2$. It can be then easily verified that the integral of (5) reduces to the integrals of the type:

$$\begin{aligned}J_1 &= \int_0^1 \mathrm{d}\xi_1 \int_0^1 \mathrm{d}\xi_2\,\sqrt{Q(\xi_1, \xi_2)} \quad \text{and} \\ J_2 &= \int_0^1 \mathrm{d}\xi_1 \int_0^1 \mathrm{d}\xi_2\,L(\xi_1, \xi_2)\,\ln\!\left[L(\xi_1, \xi_2) + \sqrt{Q(\xi_1, \xi_2)}\right],\end{aligned} \tag{8}$$

expressible in terms of elementary functions. Nevertheless, since the actual formulae contain a large number of terms (which, moreover, partly cancel in the limit $a \to 0$), special precautions are required in their numerical implementation.

In order to illustrate differences and advantages of the proposed method relative to other approaches we carried out extensive numerical calculations demonstrating the method's accuracy and efficiency. Representative numerical examples will be presented and discussed at the conference.

ACKNOWLEDGMENTS

This material is based upon work supported by the U. S. Air Force Office of Scientific Research under award number FA 9550-16-C-0014.

REFERENCES

[1] E. H. Bleszynski, M. K. Bleszynski, and T. Jaroszewicz, "Reduction of singular surface integrals to nonsingular line integrals in integral equations for planar geometries," *IEEE Transactions on Antennas and Propagation*, vol. 64, no. 11, pp. 4760–4769, 2016.

[2] S. M. Rao, D. R. Wilton, and A. W. Glisson, "Electromagnetic scattering by surfaces of arbitrary shape," *IEEE Transactions on Antennas and Propagation*, vol. AP-30, pp. 409–418, 1982.

[3] A. Tzoulis and T. F. Eibert, "Review of singular potential integrals for method of moments solutions of surface integral equations," *Advances in Radio Science*, vol. 2, pp. 93–99, 2004.

[4] I. Hänninen, M. Taskinen, and J. Sarvas, "Singularity subtraction integral formulae for surface integral equations with RWG, rooftop and hybrid basis functions," *Progress in Electromagnetics Research*, vol. 63, pp. 243–278, 2006.

[5] M. G. Duffy, "Quadrature over a pyramid or cube of integrands with a singularity at a vertex," *SIAM Journal on Numerical Analysis*, vol. 19, no. 6, pp. 1260–1262, 1982.

[6] M. A. Khayat and D. R. Wilton, "Numerical evaluation of singular and near-singular potential integrals," *IEEE Transactions on Antennas and Propagation*, vol. 53, pp. 3180–3190, 2005.

[7] M. M. Botha, "A family of augmented Duffy transformations for near-singularity cancellation quadrature," *IEEE Transactions on Antennas and Propagation*, vol. 61, no. 6, pp. 3123–3134, 2013.

[8] E. Bleszynski, M. Bleszynski, and T. Jaroszewicz, "Conversion of singular surface integrals for to line integrals with nonsingular integrands for non-planar configurations of rwg basis functions," in *2017 IEEE/ACES International Conference on Applied Computational Electromagnetics*. IEEE, 2017.

Coupled Modeling and Experimental Investigation of RF-Induced Heating near Ablation Catheters under 1.5T MRI

Qi Zeng, Jingshen Liu, and Jianfeng Zheng
Electrical and Computer Engineering
University of Houston
Houston, Tx
{qzeng, jliu44, jzheng3}@uh.edu

Tom Lloyd
Imricor Medical Systems
Burnsville, MN
tom.lloyd@imricor.com

Leonardo M. Angelone and Wolfgang Kainz
Center for Device and Radiological Health
US Food and Drug Administration
Silver Spring, MD
{Leonardo.Angelone, Wolfgang.Kainz}@fda.hhs.gov

Ji Chen
Electrical and Computer Engineering
University of Houston
Houston, TX
jchen23@central.uh.edu

***Abstract*—RF-induced heating of ablation catheters under 1.5T magnetic resonance image (MRI) is studied using combined computational modeling and bench testing. The transfer function of ablation catheters are measured experimentally without simplification. A high-resolution anatomical human model was then used to simulate clinical MRI RF exposure environment. The upper limit of the temperature rise was calculated around two types of catheters, namely a single wire catheter and twin wire catheter. Four different insertion depths between 17.5 cm to 70 cm inside human body model were evaluated, simulating procedure for brain or cardiac ablation. A temperature hotspot was observed around the tip of the catheter with an estimated maximum temperature rise higher than 100°C for the single lead catheter and around 94°C for twin lead catheter, with patient landmark varying from -200 mm to 1000 mm with respect to human eye-center. Three experiments were conducted in a standard phantom to validate this coupled method and it showed a good agreement between direct measurements and predicted heating results.**

Keywords—RF-induced heating, MRI safety, Ablation Catheters

I. Introduction

Magnetic resonance imaging (MRI) is a widely used diagnostic imaging technique for soft tissue imaging . However, due to the possible safety issues related to electromagnetic and magnetic field interactions between interventional devices and MRI, most interventional procedures are currently instead based on x-ray – guided imaging. One of the major concerns is the radiofrequency (RF) induced heating of tissue near the tip of the interventional device. It is thus important to be able to evaluate the induced heating near catheter electrodes when a catheter is exposed to the RF field generated by an MRI. Current approaches used to evaluate RF-induced heating for fully implanted medical leads are often based on a combination of computational modeling and in-vivo animal testing [1]. This method is most clinically relevant, but it is expensive and time-consuming. Another approach is based on measurement of the transfer function of the device [2]. Among the specific implementation of the transfer function method, the forward method cannot be used when an interventional device is partially implanted with a portion of the device is inside the human body and the remaining portion exposed in air. Both the permittivity and conductivity of human tissue are usually several tens of times higher than for air. In order to obtain accurate measurement results when applying the transfer function method, the excitation along the catheter needs to be uniform and highly focused, which is difficult to maintain in practice. If the behavior of the excitation waveform cannot be guaranteed, the resolution and accuracy of the measurement results will be impacted.

Considering such limitations, we propose a method based on combined computational modeling and experimental measurements to investigate the RF-induced heating near ablation catheters [3]. This method measures the transfer function of the catheter using the reciprocity theorem and applies the electric field distribution evaluated by the high-resolution anatomical human models to achieve accurate RF-heating device characterization.

II. Materials and Methods

A. Test Object

The RF-induced heating near a generic conventional ablation catheter is studied in this work. This catheter can be used as a drug delivery device and/or to perform catheter ablation procedures. The catheter is 120 cm in length and its inner conductor is covered by an insulated tube. Two types of catheters are studied, one is referred to as 'single wire' catheter and the other one is referred to as 'dual wire' catheter. The single wire catheter has only one inner conductor and a single electrode, while the dual wire catheter has two inner conductors and two electrodes. In the dual wire catheter, the conductor connected to a distal electrode referred to as 'tip', and the second electrode is connected to a proximal electrode referred to as 'ring'.

B. Electrode Trajectories and Landmark

An adult male human body model (Duke, from the Virtual Family, including over 70 anatomical structures) was used for the study [4]. To consider several possible scenarios, four trajectories in the human body were considered as shown in

Fig. 1. The insertion depth of the catheter can vary from 17.5 cm to 70 cm. As shown in the figure, the trajectories 1 and 2 were used to simulate human brain surgery with insertion depths of 17.5 cm and 35 cm (insertion point at skull location); trajectories 3 and 4 modeled paths for cardiac surgery with insertion depths of 52.5 cm and 70 cm (insertion point at groin location). The RF-induced heating for both catheter types were investigated for all four trajectories, for a total of eight cases (i.e., Four insertion depths and two catheters). Different patient landmark positions ranging between -200 mm to 1000 mm relative to human eye-center were studied to cover most of the clinical scanning conditions.

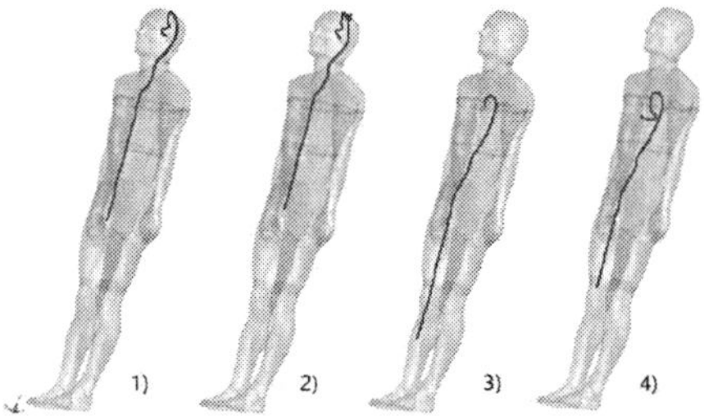

Fig. 1. Ablation catheter implanted trajectories in the Duke model. Trajectory 1) and 2) are for human brain surgery with insertion depth 17.5cm and 35cm. Trajectory 3) and 4) are for cardiac surgery with insertion depth 52.5cm and 70cm.

C. *Transfer Function Method*

The transfer function method based on the reciprocity theory is the state-of-art-method to evaluate the RF-induced heating near ablation catheters. For a specific medical elongated structure, the temperature rise near the device tip can be evaluated following the approach described in [3]:

$$\Delta T_{tip} = \left| \int H(l) \cdot E_l(l) dl \right|^2 . \tag{1}$$

where $E_l(l)$ is the incident tangential electric field along the catheter. This E-field is obtained using a full-wave simulation in the Duke model without the catheter. $H(l)$ is the transfer function of the catheter which is measured in the ASTM phantom. The transfer function relates the incident electric field to the RF induced heating near the tip of the catheter. The transfer function varies with different insertion depths. During the measurement of the transfer functions, different lengths from the device tip were submerged into the gel to simulate the clinically relevant insertion depths. Following the reciprocity procedure, an excitation source was placed near the device tip and the induced current along the catheter was measured along the catheter. This measurement configuration can provide a stable and accurate device characterization.

III. Results and Validation

The transfer functions for two types of catheters with four different insertion depths were obtained. Based on the simulation results obtained from the Duke model, the temperature rise near the implanted ablation catheter in the Duke model under 1.5T MRI RF coil were extracted and shown in Fig. 2.

Temperature rise around the single wire catheter was higher than those from the dual wire catheter, regardless of the insertion depth and patient landmark. The maximum temperature rise can be higher than 100°C. This result is a conservative estimate, because the blood circulation and tissue metabolic are not considered. The temperature rises for trajectories 1 and 2 at landmark 200 mm to 400 mm were more than ten times higher than those for trajectories 3 and 4. This is because at these landmarks the trunk is centered in the coil (with the leg still outside the coil), and thus the electric field inside the RF coil along the device is much higher than the fields outside the coil.

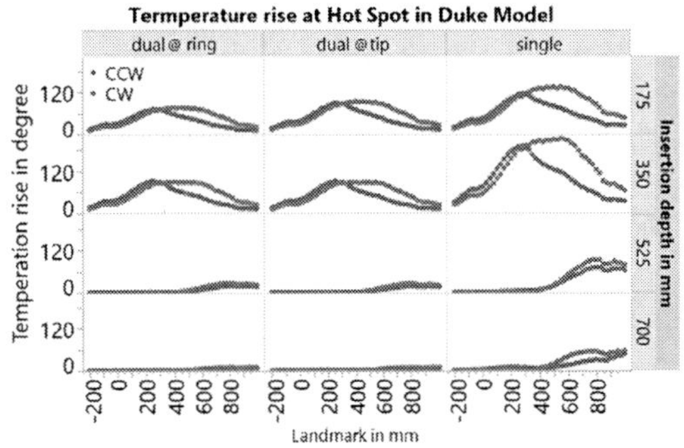

Fig. 2. Temperature Rise around the ablation catheter in the Duke model under 1.5T MRI RF coil.

Finally, the temperature rise near the single wire catheter with three implant trajectories in the ASTM phantom were both measured and predicted by the transfer function method, to validate our method. The insertion depth for these trajectories was 17.5 cm, 35 cm, and 52.5 cm, of which 52.5 cm was the worst case for all the insertion depths studied. The validation results are shown in the following table. As one can see from table I, the temperature rise predicted by our approach were validated by direct measurement, thus further confirming the accuracy and efficiency of the transfer function approach.

TABLE I. VALIDATION RESULT OF 1.5 T RF-INDUCED HEATING (Unit: Degree Celsius)

	Trajectory 1	Trajectory 2	Trajectory 3
Measured	16.6	9.2	3.5
Predicted	16.6	9.3	4.2

Disclaimer: The mention of commercial products, their sources, or their use in connection with material reported herein is not to be construed as either an actual or implied endorsement of such products by the Department of Health and Human Services.

References

[1] R. Luechinger *et al.*, "In Vivo Heating of Pacemaker Leads During Magnetic Resonance Imaging," *Eur. Heart J.*, vol. 26, no. 4, pp. 376–383, 2005.

[2] S. M. Park, R. Kamondetdacha, and J. A. Nyenhuis, "Calculation of MRI-induced Heating of an Implanted Medical Lead Wire with an Electric Field Transfer Function," *J. Magn. Reson. Imaging*, vol. 26, pp. 1278–1285, 2007.

[3] S. Feng, R. Qiang, W. Kainz, D. Jackson, and J. Chen, "Efficient Evaluation of MRI-Induced Electric Fields in the Vicinity of Implantable Lead," *2013 Texas Symp. Wirel. Microw. Circuits Syst.*, pp. 1–4, 2013.

[4] A. Christ *et al.*, "The Virtual Family--Development of Surface-Based Anatomical Models of Two Adults and Two Children for Dosimetric Simulations.," *Phys. Med. Biol.*, vol. 55, no. 2, pp. N23–N38, 2010.

Hyperthermia Study in Cancer Treatment

H. F. Guarnizo Mendez
Electronics Engineering
Universidad El Bosque
Bogotá, Colombia
hguarnizo@unbosque.edu.co

J. J. Pantoja
Electronics Engineering
Universidad Nacional de Colombia -Sede Bogotá
Bogotá, Colombia
jjpantojaa@unal.edu.co

M. A. Polochè Arango
Electronics Engineering
Universidad de San Buenaventura
Bogotá, Colombia
mpoloche@usbbog.edu.co

***Abstract*—This paper assess initial collateral effects of the use of hyperthermia in breast cancer treatment by means of an electromagnetic simulation. The breast model was radiated by microwaves with a waveguide at 2.45 GHz and the power density distribution inside the breast was calculated. A comparison between the power density in the tumor and other breast tissues (skin, fat, and muscle) is presented. Results show that the location of the microwave applicator is a factor that determines the unwanted overheating of tissues close the tumor.**

Keywords— Electromagnetic fields, cancer cell, heat flow, hyperthermia, radiation, simulation, tissues.

I. Introduction

Cancer is a disease that largely affects senior population worldwide. Cancerous tumors can affect different tissues and can be located in different parts of the body. To tackle these diseases, researchers from different areas have developed in recent years treatments such as surgery, radiotherapy, chemotherapy, immunotherapy, stem cell transplantation, and targeted medicine therapies. Along with the mentioned methods, another method known as hyperthermia (or thermal therapy) is being evaluated in clinical studies. Hyperthermia is a method in which body tissues that present tumors are exposed to high temperatures in order to destroy the tumor or cancer cells, but without significantly affecting healthy tissues. This technique is currently under study in human patients [1].

One of the main challenges in the treatment of non-invasive electromagnetic (EM) hyperthermia is to focus the EM energy over cancerous tissue and avoid damage to normal tissue [2] [3]. In EM hyperthermia, it is essential to obtain a temperature of 35°C to 45°C in the affected area [4], [5]. For this reason, it is important to know the temperature and power density distributions to obtain a more effective microwave heating and avoid unwanted heating in other tissues. In [6]– [9], the temperature distribution over to 3D breast model is presented. In [9], the use of a radiation frequency of 2.45 GHz is justified based in the electrical properties of the breast tissues.

In this paper, the power density distribution dissipated in a breast radiated by microwaves at 2.45 GHz is analyzed to determine overexposure zones and the influence of the applicator position. In particular, the characteristics used in the electromagnetic simulation are presented in detail, and the power density was obtained from case when the waveguide is located at 90° over the breast and when it is located at 45° over the breast.

II. Methodology

The electromagnetic simulation was carried out using the finite element method (FEM) solver of ANSYS Electronics®. The breast model radius was of 6.5 cm and tumor was modeled like a cube width, high and large 0.8 cm and the simulation setup is presented in the Table I.

TABLE I. HFSS Configuration Setup

Properties	Values
Maximum number of passes	10
Maximum delta S	0.01
Maximum converged passes	3
Order of basis function	Mixed order

The maximum delta S values and maximum converged passes values were chosen to improve the mesh accuracy and to improve the convergence of the simulation. Mixed order basis function was chosen because the breast has different tissues and different electrical properties (permittivity (ε) and conductivity (σ)). Mixed order assigns base function elements based on the need greater precision in different parts of the model. Mixed order uses a higher order where more precision is required, and a lower order where the fields are weaker.

Table II shows the electrical properties of the breast tissues used in the electromagnetic simulation based in the properties reported in [10] and [11] for a frequency of 2.45 GHz.

TABLE II. Electrical Properties of the Breast Tissues

Tissue	Permittivity	Conductivity (S/m)
Muscle	52.7	1.7
Tumor	56	1.8
Fat	5.3	0.3
Skin	38	1.5
Lobes	35	1

III. Results

Two locations of the applicator were considered as shown in Fig. 1. First, the waveguide was placed at 90° to consider as case where the location of the tumor is not aligned with the applicator. Then, the waveguide was placed at 45° over the breast to consider alignment between the applicator and the tumor. The WR340 waveguide was exited with the TE_{10} mode and 1 W. The power density obtained inside the breast for both cases is presented in Fig. 2.

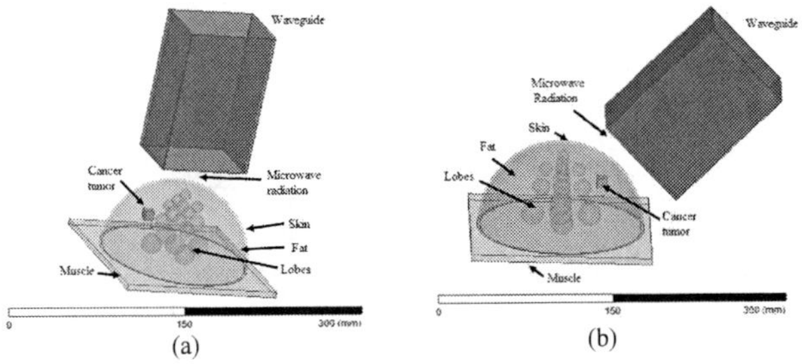

Fig. 1. 3D model, (a) waveguide at 90° over the breast, (b) waveguide at 45° over the breast.

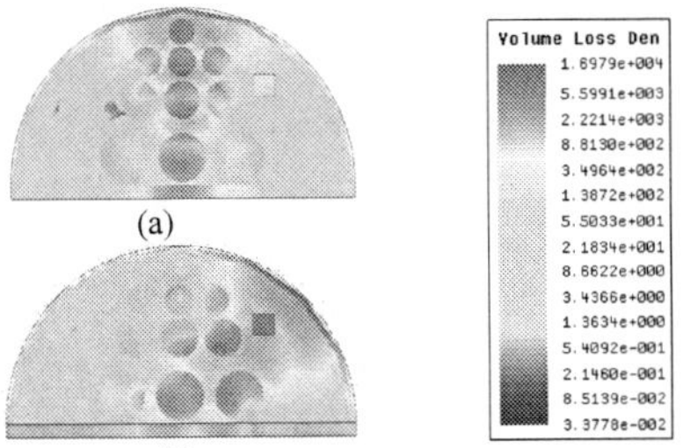

Fig. 2. Power density in the breast model, (a) waveguide at 90° over the breast, (b) waveguide at 45° over the breast.

As shown in Fig. 2(a) when the waveguide is 90° over the breast, the highest concentration of power density (~5.6 kW/m^3) is found in the lobes located directly below of the waveguide. The tumor as well as the tissues near the center of breast have the second highest concentration (~350 kW/m^3) of power density. Fig. 2(b) shows that when the waveguide is located at 45° over the breast, the highest concentration of power density is found initially over skin and the tumor. It can also be observed that the fat and lobes near the tumor have a concentration of power density very close to that of the tumor. The power density used in treatments against cancer can be harmful to the healthy tissues, because, high temperatures can generate cell death in healthy tissues. However, these treatments its search that the electromagnetic radiation and likewise the power density originating by the applicator mainly focused on the tissue affected by the cancer.

As mentioned above, in treatment against cancer, it is necessary to raise the tissue temperature between 40°C and 45°C; the applicators used in the treatments are fed with powers between 8W and 300 W, the power density used in the treatment varies depending on the power used in the applicator, the desired temperature in the treatment and the exposure time of the electromagnetic waves is between 5 minutes to 30 minutes. Based on the above, from the power density obtained in the tissue, the corresponding treatment, the duration and the repetitions of the exposures must be determined to achieve the desired temperatures.

IV. Conclusions

From the presented results it can be concluded that the skin is the tissue that dissipates the highest power density in both cases. To improve the effectiveness of the treatment with hyperthermia, the location of the applicator has a relevant variable. Therefore, it is important to precisely determine the location of the tumor by means of a previous diagnosis because a misalignment between the applicator and the tumor can cause unwanted deterioration of nearby cells and even the desired temperature in the tumor could be obtained for the treatment. By previously locating the tumor, electromagnetic radiation in healthy cells can be avoided in some percentage.

References

[1] A. Chichel, J Skowronek, M. Kubaszewska, and M. Kanikowski, "Hyperthermia – description of a method and a review of clinical applications", Reports of Practical Oncology & Radiotherapy, vol. 12, iss. 5, pp. 267-275, September–October 2007.

[2] M. Converse, E. J. Bond, B. D. Van Veen, and S. C. Hagness, "A Computational Study of Ultra-Wideband Versus Narrowband Microwave Hyperthermia for Breast Cancer Treatment," IEEE Transactions on Microwave Theory and Techniques, pp. 2169-2180, vol. 54, May 2006.

[3] E. Neufeld, M. Pauildes, M. Capstick, G. van Rhoon, and N. Kuster "Recent Advances in Hyperthermia Cancer Treatment" IEEE Asia-Pacific International Symposium on Electromagnetic Compatibility, pp. 389-392, April 2010.

[4] J. Van der Zee, "Heating the patient: A promising approach," Annals of Oncology, 13, 1173-84, August 2002.

[5] J. Kim, S. Gang, Y. Kwon, and C. Cheon, "A Study of Microwave Hyperthermia for Breast Cancer Treatment using Cavity Applicator," IEEE Antennas and Propagation Society International Symposium, pp. 249-252, June 2007.

[6] B. Bai, X. Yin, D. Xie, and Y. Zhang "FDTD-based Temperature Distribution Computation of Microwave Hyperthermia for Breast Cancer," 14th Biennial IEEE Conference on Electromagnetic Field Computation (CEFC), May 2010.

[7] P. T. Nguyen, and A. M. Abbosh "Focusing Techniques in Breast Cancer Treatment Using Non-invasive Microwave Hyperthermia," International Symposium on Antennas and Propagation (ISAP), November 2015.

[8] P. T. Nguyen, A. M. Abbosh, and S. Crozier "Realistic Simulation Environment to Test Microwave Hyperthermia Treatment of Breast Cancer," IEEE Antennas and Propagation Society International Symposium, pp. 1188-1189, July 2014.

[9] I. Merunka, O. Fiser, L. Vojackova, J. Vrba, and D. Vrba "Utilization potential of balanced antipodal Vivaldi antenna for microwave hyperthermia treatment of breast cancer," The 8th European Conference on Antennas and Propagation (EuCAP 2014), pp. 706–710, April 2014.

[10] E. Porter, J. Fakhoury, R. Oprisor, M. Coates, and M. Popovic "Improved Tissue Phantoms for Experimental Validation of Microwave Breast Cancer Detection," Proceedings of the Fourth European Conference on Antennas and Propagation (EuCAP), pp. 1-5, April 2010.

[11] Handbook of Biomedical Telemetry, First Edition. Edited by K. S. Nikita. © 2014 John Wiley & Sons, Inc., Published by John Wiley & Sons, Inc., pp. 551, August 2014.

Co-simulation of a Reactor Assisted by Microwaves

Carlos Rivera, John J. Pantoja, and Felix Vega
Department of Electrical and Electronic Engineering
Universidad Nacional de Colombia -Sede Bogotá
Bogotá, Colombia
cariverag@unal.edu.co, jjpantojaa@unal.edu.co

***Abstract*— In this paper, the design and analysis of a chemical reactor assisted by microwaves is presented. A co-simulation that links the electromagnetic and thermal phenomena presented in the reactor is performed to obtain the power density and temperature distributions. The results show that a matching network is required to obtain a maximum transfer of power.**

Keywords—co-simulation, microwave assisted processing, microwave heating, thermal simulation.

I. Introduction

The heating of materials using medium and high power microwaves is being widely used in chemical, food, and other industries due to its speed and efficiency [1]. Microwave heating is used in different industrial processes such as plastic sealing, and material heating and drying Novel uses such as plague elimination and food sterilization [2], have been also proposed.

The power and the operation frequency are determined by the drying or heating rate, while the type of applicator is determined by the size and geometry of the material [1]. In addition, applicators must be adapted to the operation condition and process. For liquids, for example, the material commonly flows through tubular sections. The optimization of applicators in this kind of scenarios require the use of electromagnetic simulations.

This paper describes the design of a microwave applicator used to assist a chemical reaction based in electromagnetic and thermal simulations. The electromagnetic simulation is used to match the applicator to the reactor and to calculate the power density distribution in the material. The thermal simulation is performed to estimate the temperature distribution produced by the microwaves in the material.

II. Methodology

Although multimode type configurations are commonly used for heating applications [3], we decided to use the fundamental mode TE10 because the material under test is continuously flowing through the heating zone and presents high losses. The material of interest has the following characteristics: relative permittivity ε_r=37.4, relative permeability μ_r=1, and electrical conductivity σ=0.000107 S/m.

The reactor was modeled in CST Microwave Studio® representing its main components and real dimensions. Fig. 1 shows the reactor represented by a cylinder and the applicator composed by a waveguide, an iris, and a conical aperture. First, an electromagnetic simulation was performed to determine the iris dimensions. Then, an electromagnetic and thermal co-simulation was performed in CST to estimate the temperature distribution achieved in the material.

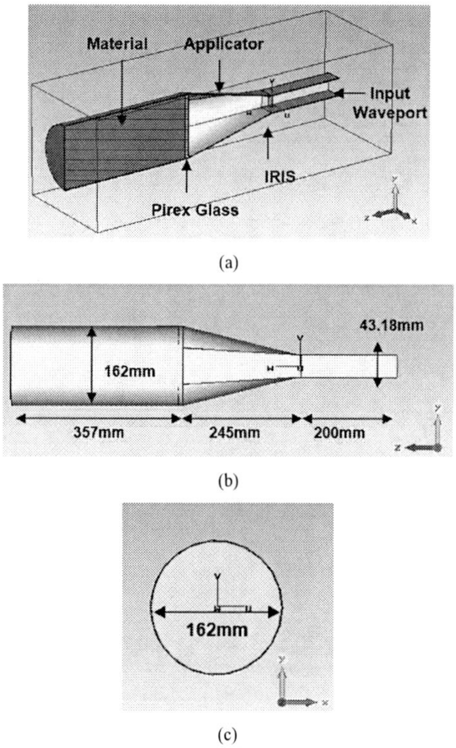

Fig. 1. Model of the reactor and the microwave applicator. (a) Modeled components, (b) side view, and (c) crosssection.

The thermal co-simulation in CST [4-6] requires first the calculation of the electromagnetic fields induced in the materials to obtain the volume power density and the surface power density generated in the dielectrics and metallic sheets, respectively. These power densities, also called thermal losses, together with the thermal material properties and the thermal boundaries are the inputs of the thermal simulation task. Since the electromagnetic field solver and the thermal solver use hexahedral grid, both computations can be performed within a single project [5].

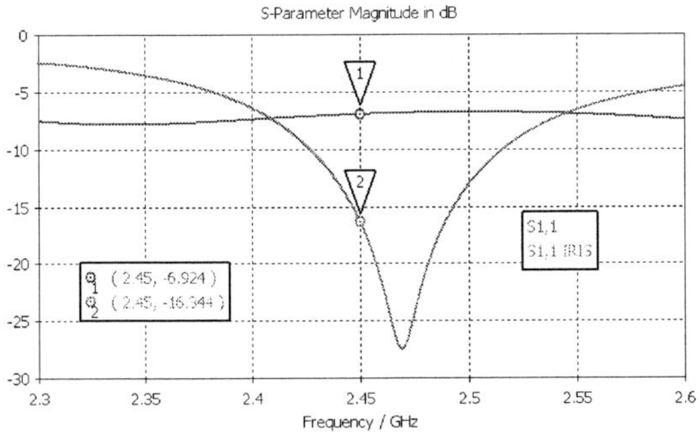

Fig. 2. Simulated S11 parameter with and without the coupling IRIS.

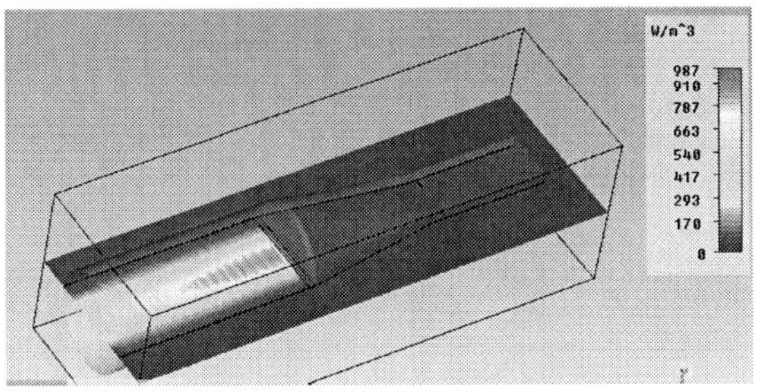

Fig. 3. Power density distribution simulated for 1 kW input power.

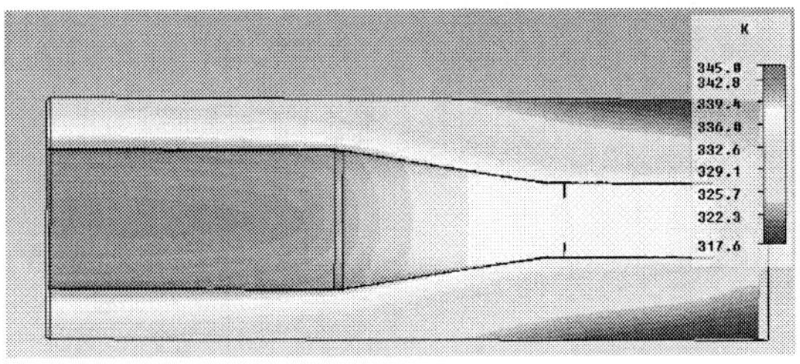

Fig. 4. Temperature distribution calculated for 1 kW input power.

The boundary conditions used in the electromagnetic simulation were configured open with additional space for the lateral sections normal to x and y axes and for the area of the waveguide port. For the zone where the reactor ends, a border of the PML type was implemented. The metallic elements were represented by aluminum sheets with finite electric conductivity; thereby, their surface losses are included in the thermal simulation.

A coupling network between the input port and conical applicator was designed to reduce reflections in the excitation port. For this, an inductive IRIS was implemented [7], as shown Fig. 1 (a). Fig. 2 presents the results of the reflection coefficient obtained in the simulation with and without the inductive IRIS. Fig. 2 shows that the iris produces an adequate impedance matching between the input port and the applicator.

III. Results

Once the applicator was matched to the waveguide port, the transfer power performance and the energy conversion was assessed using co-simulation. First, the analysis power was scaled by a factor of 2000 to represent an available a power value of 1 kW in the source. This value was chosen because is the nominal output power of the available microwave source.

Therefore, the power density in the material simulated inside the reactor was obtained. Fig. 3 shows that the central area of the reactor presents most of loss density, as expected due to the TE10 excitation mode in the waveguide. Using the power density calculated with the electromagnetic simulation, a thermal analysis was performed. Fig. 4 shows the temperature distribution of the material in the reactor, where it can be seen that the maximum temperature value is obtained in the area where the heated material is located. The maximum temperature calculated is 345K (71.85 °C).

IV. Conclusions

The design and simulation of the electromagnetic and thermal behavior of a reactor assisted with microwaves is presented. The electromagnetic simulation shows that an acceptable level of return losses was achieved, which is interpreted as a good transfer of the microwave power from the input waveguide port to the reactor. On the other hand, the results of the thermal simulation show that the studied material dissipates the microwave power, reached temperatures of 345K (71.85 °C).

In the presented analysis two simplifications were considered. First, the change of the material properties with the temperature was neglected. This variation can be considered including an iterative procedure in the co-simulation. In addition, the material is continuously flowing through the reactor but the performed analysis is static. Work is in progress to characterize the dependence of the material permittivity with the temperature and to determine the effect of the material movement in the results.

References

[1] M. Mehdizadeh, Microwave/RF Applicators and Probes for Material Heating, Sensing, and Plasma Generation, A Design Guide. Oxford, UK: Elsevier, 2009.

[2] A. L. Brody, "Advances in Microwave Pasteurization and Sterilization," IFT Food-Technology, vol. 6(2), Feb. 2011.

[3] P. Plaza□Gonzalez, J. Monzo□Cabrera, J. Catala□Civera, and D. Sanchez□Hernandez, "New approach for the prediction of the electric field distribution in multimode microwaveheating applicators with mode stirrers," IEEE Trans. Magn., 40(3), 1672□1678, 2004.

[4] T. Isenlik and K. Yegin, "Tutorial on the design of hole-slot-type cavity magnetron using CST particle studio," IEEE Trans. Plasma Sci., vol. 41, no. 2, pp. 296–304, Feb. 2013.

[5] R. Hemamalini, P. R. R. Rao, K. V. Rao, S. K. Datta, C. Bhattacharya and S. Kamath, "Thermal co-simulation of coaxial RF window and connector of a TWT," *IEEE International Vacuum Electronics Conference*, Monterey, CA, 2014, pp. 259-260.

[6] CST Studio Suite documentation. Computer Simulation Technology (CST) GmbH.: www.cst.de

[7] N. Marcuvitz, Waveguide Handbook, vol. 10, MIT Rad. Lab. Ser., New York, McGraw Hill, 1951.

Simulation and Fabrication of BST FBAR Resonator

Abdulhamid Matoug, Daw Asderah, and T.S. Kalkur
Department of Electrical and Computer Engineering
University of Colorado Colorado Springs
Colorado Springs, CO 80918, USA
amatoug@uccs.edu

Abstract*— In this paper a switchable and tunable bulk acoustic wave (BAW) resonator based on Barium Strontium Titanite (Ba0.75Sr0.25TiO3) with MOD deposition on high resistivity Sapphire substrate was implemented using six layers of Silicon dioxide and Tantalum oxide as Bragg reflector. Finite Element Modeling was used for simulation of the resonator to obtain the return loss S11 and both series and parallel resonant frequencies and compared with the result of fabricated resonator.

***Keywords*— BST, BAW resonator, Bragg reflector, MOD.**

I. INTRODUCTION

Resonators are used to control the incoming and outgoing signals, traditionally are generally of four types: LC resonators, ceramic resonators, microstrip resonators, acoustic wave resonators (surface acoustic wave SAW and bulk acoustic resonator (BAW) [3]. Thin film bulk acoustic wave resonator devices based on ferroelectric perovskite materials are of great interest for various applications such as tunable filters, and voltage controlled oscillators design for digital wireless communications [1][2]. Recently, the conventional RF devices that are used in RF frontend receiver were replaced by bulk acoustic component based on piezoelectric materials [4]. Classical surface mount based FBAR resonator structure is composed of a piezoelectric plate between two metal electrodes as shown in fig (3-b) [2]. The piezoelectric layer is typically composed of aluminum nitride (AlN), Zinc oxide (ZnO), or barium strontium titanite (BTO) [2]. However, AlN based resonators are fixed frequency devices, and are not tunable and switchable [4]. High dielectric constant ferroelectric materials such as barium titanite (BTO), strontium titanite (STO) and barium strontium titanite (BST) can be widely used in reconfigurable frontend receivers because they are switchable and tunable [1]. Tunable thin film BST bulk resonator have many applications in wireless communication as tunable filter in cell phone, owing to their significant advantages over surface acoustic wave devices because of their small size, high quality factor, permittivity, tunability, sharp filter skirt, and relatively low loss[1][3].

II. BAW RESONATOR DESIGN AND MODELING

There are two main popular 1D models that are used for BAW design, physical models (Mason model) and the equivalent circuit (Butterworth Van Dyke) model. BVD is a lumped element model which is a practical approach for designing resonators and filters by representing the electrode losses, piezoelectric characteristics and parasitic effect [4]. Figure 1 shows the equivalent circuit of the resonator. The following equations are used to model electromechanical and parasitic characteristics.

$$C_s = \frac{\varepsilon_T \varepsilon_0 A}{BST_{thickness}} \quad (1)$$

Where the active area A is 15 μm by 10μm, and C_s is the physical plate capacitance.

$$C_m = \frac{8C_s k_{eff}^2}{\pi^2 - 8k_{eff}^2} \quad (2)$$

$$L_m = \frac{\pi^2}{8k_{eff}^2 (2\pi f_s)^2 C_s} \quad (3)$$

$$R_m = \frac{2\pi f_s L_m}{Q_s} \quad (4)$$

The FBAR was designed at 5 GHz with electromechanical coefficient of 0.062. The static arms Cm, L_m, and R_m are calculated from the three equations above. The simulated result of the resonator based on mBVD equivalent circuit shown in Figure 1 using ADS is illustrated in Figure 2. The simulated result of the resonator shows the return loss is -15.663 dB at the frequency 5.144GHz while the series and parallel resonance frequencies are 4.988 GHz, and 5.162 GHz respectively.

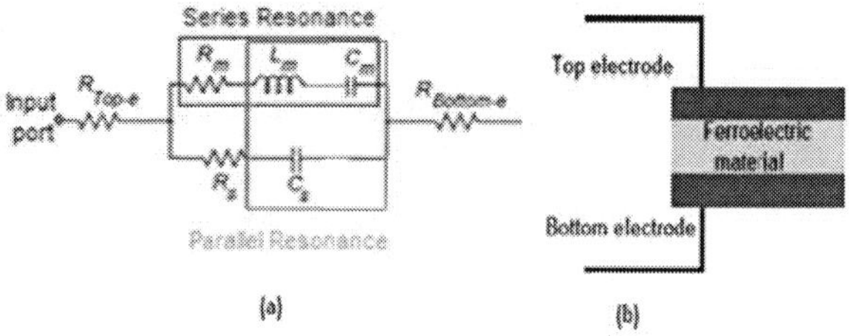

Fig. 1. a- Equivalent circuit of BAW SMR using mBVD model b- 1D structure of BAW resonator [4]

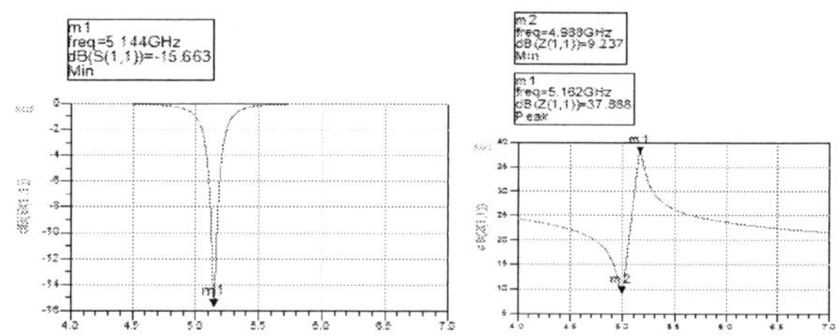

Fig. 2. Simulated S11 and impedance using mBVD equivalent circuit

III. Fabrication of BAW Resonator and Measurements

The Bragg reflector for the SMR BAW structure is made of multiple pairs of quarter-wave layers of high and low acoustic impedance as shown in figure 1. SMR BAW resonator was fabricated on the top of sapphire wafer of thickness (500μm). Alternating 3 layers of SiO2 and tantalum oxide were coated on this wafer. The total thickness of each layer is 280nm and 180 nm for silicon dioxide and tantalum oxide respectively. The bottom electrode with titanium 20nm thickness and platinum 100nm thickness were deposited on the wafer by DC magnetron sputtering in argon environment. Spin-on metalorganic (MOD) Ba0.75Sr0.25TiO3 (BST) was deposited on the wafer with total thickness 180nm and annealed at a temperature of 800 C for 30 minutes in oxygen environment. The top electrode platinum of thickness 100nm was deposited on this wafer by DC magnetron sputtering. Figure 3 shows the micrograph of fabricated resonator and figure 4 shows the return loss of switchable resonator. The result shows that at frequency 4.75 GHz the return loss is -8.77 and the series resonance frequency fr was found to be 4.65 GHz and the parallel resonance frequency fp was found to be 4.780 GHz.

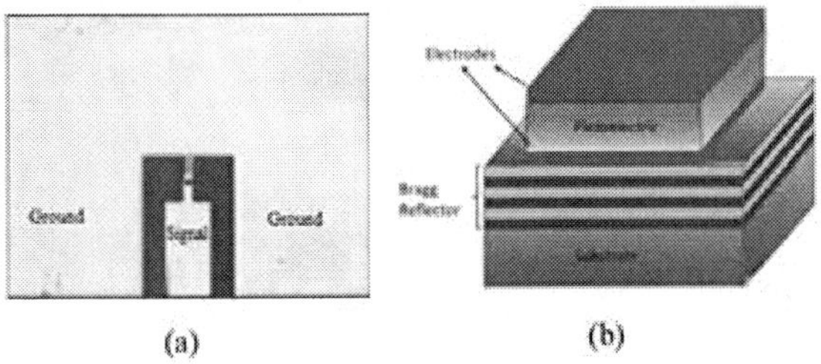

Figure 3 (a) fabricated BAW resonator (b) SMR BAW resonator

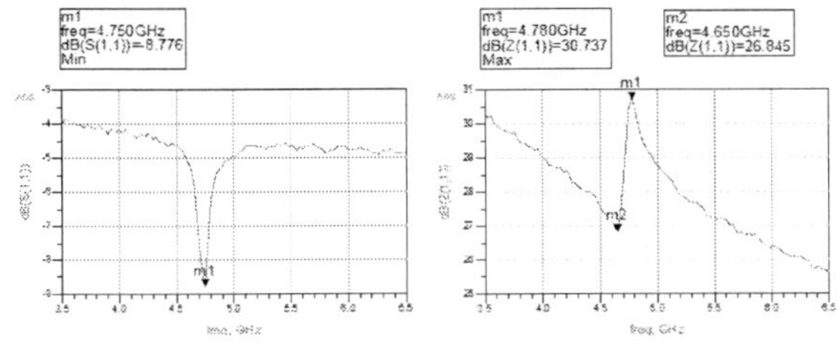

Fig. 4. measured S11 and impedance with applied 8V.

TABLE I. Acoustic parameters of SMR materials

Layer	Density (g/cm3)	Acoustic impedance (Kg/m2s)	Acoustic velocity (m/s)	Dielectric constant (Ɛr)	Thickness (nm)
Sapphire	2.6	25.5e6	9800	9.3	500
SiO_2	2.65	12.6e6	5100	3.9	280
Ta_2O_5	8.2	34e6	4100	25	180
platinum	21.4	80.2e6	3737	7	100
titanium	4.48	27.3e6	6070	10	20
BST	6.2	33.5e6	6500	200	180

IV. FEM 3D Modeling and Result

A three-dimensional finite element model of thin film bulk acoustic wave resonator was developed to investigate the return loss and both parallel and series resonance frequencies and finally compared with fabricated result. Table 1 shows the parameters used for the finite element model of BST based FBAR resonator. Figure 5(a) shows 3D structure of the BAW and (b) shows the impedance and return loss versus frequency. The design of BAW is composed of six layers of silicon dioxide and tantalum oxide as Bragg reflector and BST plate between two platinum electrodes on sapphire substrate with the same thicknesses of the fabricated resonator with the parameters shown in table I.

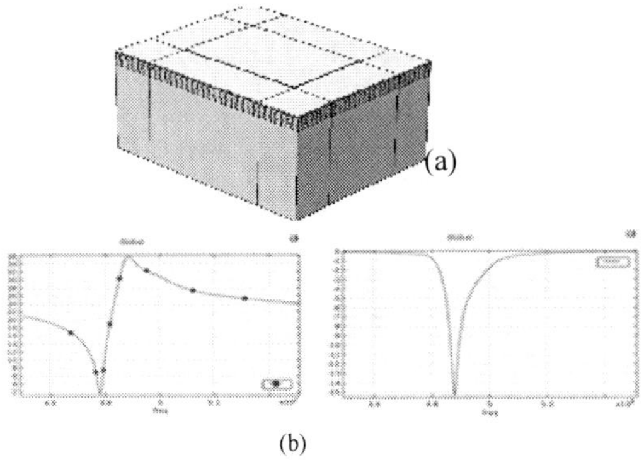

Fig. 5 (a) 3D of BAW (b) return loss and impedance

V. Conclusion

In conclusion, a tunable and switchable BST solidly mounted bulk acoustic wave resonator has been demonstrated. The return loss at frequency 4.75 GHz is -8.77 dB. In FEM the return loss is -15.6 dB at frequency 4.88 GHz and the series resonance frequency fr was found to be 4.78 GHz and the parallel resonance frequency fp was found to be 4.9 GHz.

References

[1] Almonir Mansour, T. S. Kalkur, "switchable and Tunable BAW Duplexer Based on ferroelectric Material," IEEE Transaction on Ultrasonic, Ferroelectric, and frequency Control, VOL. 63, NO. 12, December 2016.

[2] M.Terzieva, D.Gaydazhiev, B. Nikolova "2D Multiphysics Frequency Simulation of Thin-Film Bulk Acoustic Wave Resonator," IEEE International Spring Seminar on Electronic Technology, 2017.

[3] T. Kalkur, Amonir Mansour, "Tunable and switchable resonator and filters based on ferroelectric BST thin films for wireless communications". IEEE p 5-8, July 29, 2015.

[4] Almonir Mansour, and Thomas Kalkur, "High quality factor, low temperature dependency SMR FBAR based on BST using MOD deposition method" IEEE Tranaction on Ultrasonic, Ferroelectric, and frequency Control, VOL. 64, NO. 2, February 2017.

A Tunable Microstrip Bandstop Filter Using Compact Spiral Folded Spurline For RF Microwave Systems

Hamad.G. Alrwuili, T.S.Kalkur
Department of Electrical and Computer Engineering
University of Colorado, Colorado Springs
CO 80933-7150
halrwuil@uccs.edu, tkalkur@uccs.edu

***Abstract*— This paper briefly describes the design principle of a tunable compact spurline bandstop filter using a spiral folded resonator. A compact rejection bandstop filter (BSF) is designed by using a conventional microstrip coupled line methodology at 2.4 GHz. The physical length has been reduced up to 75% with a good tunability results in comparing with a traditional spurline filter. Spurline section is loaded with a p-n junction varactor diode to make tunability from 1.8 GHz to 2.2GHz by applying a DC control voltage from 0V to 10V. The tunable design provides a satisfactory result for simulation and fabrication filter circuits. The modeling of the proposed filter is simulated and fabricated by Advanced Design System (ADS).**

Keywords*— *Band Stop Filter (BSF), Spurline filter and ADS.

I. Introduction

Microstrip bandstop filters are used widely in modern communication systems because of their effective suppression of spurious signals. They are utilized to stop the interference of undesired electromagnetic signals. The conventional microstrip bandstop filter is mostly designed by utilizing shunt open stubs, coupled lines and stepped impedance resonators (SIRs) [1], [2]. Recently, spurline sections have become one of the most attractive methodologies that used to improve the performance of microstrip bandstop filters. Microstrip spurline filters are used widely in RF/microwave applications because of their inherently compact characteristics and suitable rejection performance[3]. The coupled line of spurline structure is connected from the input port only to the feed of microstrip[4]. It is acting like a quarter-wavelength stub that causes a notch effect in the transmission RF signals. Spurline filter is one of the microstrip bandstop filters with moderate bandwidth of about 10%[5]. It can simply be embedded into the microstrip lines that compose filters, couplers and other devices[4], [5]. They can be implemented into microwave circuits without any penalty of increasing the patch size[4], [5]. Spurline filters radiate significantly less than traditional shun-stub and coupled filters with a very compact structure[5]. This paper proposes a tunable bandstop filter using a compact spiral folded spurline methodology. Spurline physical length had been reduced from 18.6 mm to 4.5mm by using spiral folded structure. The tunable bandstop filter has been designed by embedding diode varactor into the transmission line. The spiral folded filter is designed and fabricated according to synthesis equations, and design curves are provided.

II. Characteristics and Filter Development

A. Compact Spiral Folded Spurline Filter

Figure 1 shows the development of a new structure design using a spurline conventional filter with the new spiral folded structure. A FR-4 microstrip substrate has been selected to design the spurline folded filter by using advanced design system (ADS) software as shown in figure 2.

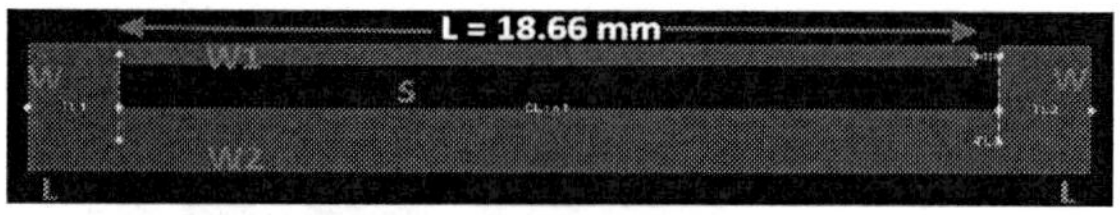

(a) Conventional Spurline Filter

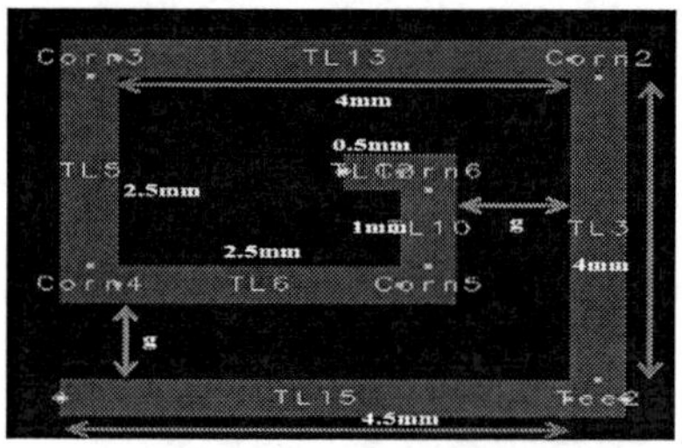

(b) Spurline Spiral Folded Filter

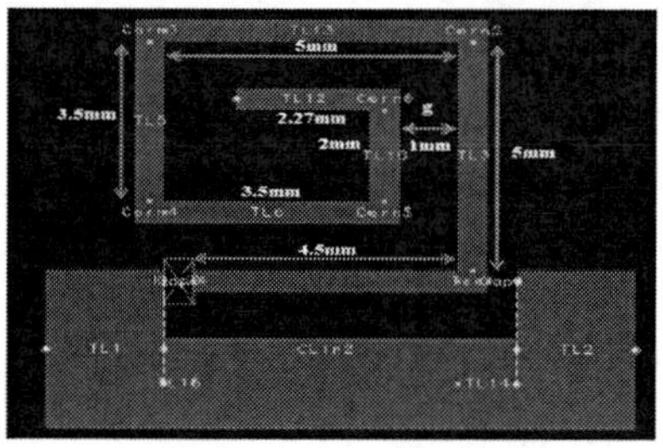

(c) Tunable Spurline Spiral Folded

Figure 1. A tunable compact spurline Bandstop Filter

The conventional spurline filter in Figure 1 (a) was designed based on the coupled line method using microstrip transmission lines with a rejection band at 2.4 GHz. The proposed spiral folded filter in Figure 1 (b) and (c) can be designed using spurline section that is used in the spurline conventional filter with the characteristics that shown in Figure2.

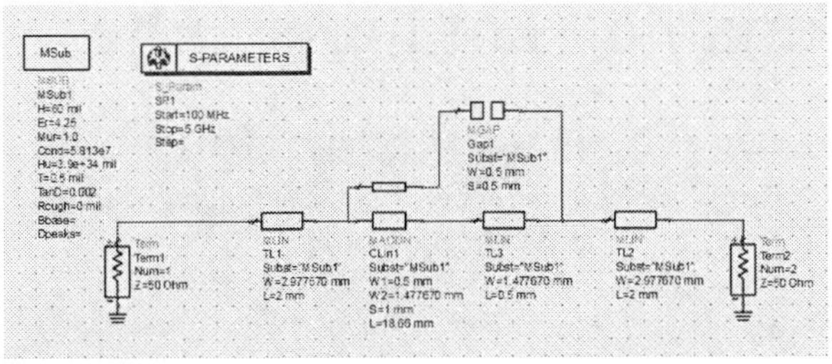

Figure 2. ADS Simulation and Modeling for the Conventional Spurline Filter

B. *A tunable spurline spiral folded filter*

A tunable compact spurline filter design is achieved by embedding a SMV1233 Varactor Diode (Sky-Works Co.) into the transmission line as shown in Figure 1 (c). Embedding varactor diode into the spiral folded filter will cause some changes to the physical length of the spurline section as shown in Figure 1 (c). These changes must be considered while using the ADS momentum features to make the final layout of the BSF. Figure 3 shows the fabrication comparison between the conventional spurline filter and the compact design of the spiral folded filter.

(a) Conventional Spurline Filter

(b) Compact Spiral Folded Filter

Figure 3. Fabrication of the Spurline BSF

III. Experimental Results

Figure 4 shows the measured variation of scattering parameters S11 and S21 with frequency for the fabricated folded spurline filter using Agilent Technology Vector network analyzer for various applied voltages to the varactor diode. The notch frequency could be tuned from 1.8GHz to 2.2 GHz with an applied control voltage 0 to 10 V. The notch depth was about -13db. The reduction in length of the spurline was about 75%.

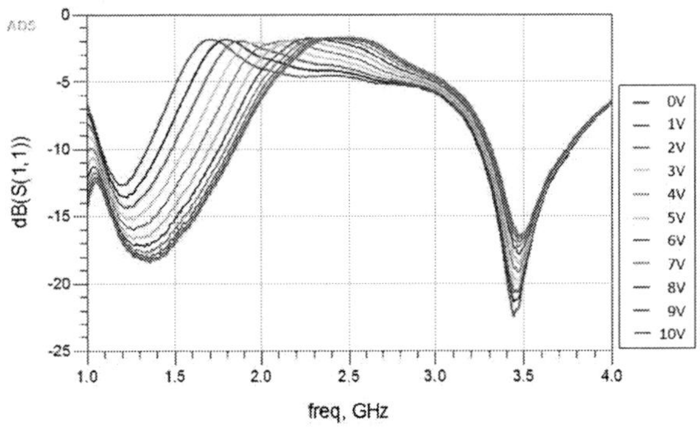

(a) Tunable Result dB(S(1,1))

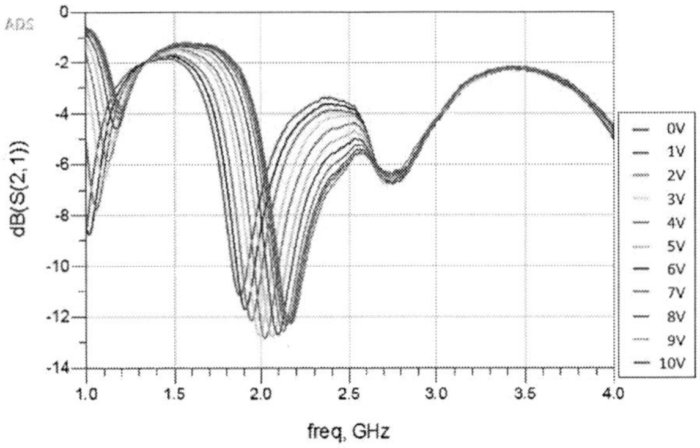

(b) Tunable Result dB(S(2,1))

Figure 4. Tunable Results for BSF Using Spiral Folded Spurline Filter

IV. Conclusion

A compact spiral folded spurline design has been presented in this paper for the tunable bandstop filter. Filter physical length has been reduced by 75% by using a compact design of spurline spiral folded methodology. The notch frequency of the filter can be tuned from 1.8 GHz to 2.2 GHz by embedding a p-n varactor diode into spurline section with a DC control voltage from 0 V to 10 V.

References

[1] Y. Liu, H. Zheng, and C. Sun, "A tunable compact bandstop filter using meander spurline and folding open stubs," in *Consumer Electronics, Communications and Networks (CECNet), 2012 2nd International Conference on*, 2012, pp. 115–118.

[2] K.-S. Chin and C.-K. Lung, "Miniaturized microstrip dual-band bandstop filters using tri-section stepped-impedance resonators," *Prog. Electromagn. Res. C*, vol. 10, pp. 37–48, 2009.

[3] L. Ke, W. Wenping, Z. Lei, and M. Xiaohan, "Microstrip bandstop filter using open stub and spurline," in *Microwave Technology & Computational Electromagnetics (ICMTCE), 2011 IEEE International Conference on*, 2011, pp. 233–236.

[4] J. H. Krishna, "Compact spiral folded spurline for low-frequency applications," *Electron. Lett.*, vol. 47, no. 15, p. 1, 2011.

[5] Hany Fathy Hammad, "DUAL AND BROAD BAND ANTENNAS USING SPUR-LINE FILTERS FOR COMMUNICATION SYSTEMS," Queen's University, Kingston, Ontario, Canada, 1997.

A Balanced Dual-Band Tunable Bandpass Filter

Dubari Borah
Department of Electrical and Computer Engineering
University of Colorado
Colorado Springs, USA
dborah@uccs.edu

Thottam S. Kalkur
Department of Electrical and Computer Engineering
University of Colorado
Colorado Springs, USA
tkalkur@uccs.edu

***Abstract*—This paper presents a balanced tunable non-resonating node (NRN) based dual-band filter which produces a bandpass response under differential mode (DM) and a wide stopband under common mode (CM) excitation. Using one uniform impedance resonator and two assymetrical stepped impedance resonators (SIR) for CM operation, a flat stopband with five transmission zeros can be achieved. The lengths and widths of the SIR line sections are adjusted to achieve required transmission zeros and rejection level in the CM stopband. For demonstration, a varactor loaded balanced dual-band tunable prototype is designed and implemented.**

***Index Terms*—CM, DM, insertion loss, return loss, stopband.**

I. Introduction

Nowadays, electronically tunable/reconfigurable dual-band microwave filter is becoming a popular topic for research and development owing to their widespread applications in reconfigurable communication system [1], [2]. However, these filters generally operate under complex electromagnetic environment because of which differential mode (balanced) tunable filters are more desirable than single-ended systems [2].

So far, many efforts have been made to develop single-band tunable balanced bandpass filters (BPF) [1]–[4] and wideband balanced filters [5], [6]. In [1]–[4], different elements such as resistance, capacitance or varactor are loaded at the middle of a tunable resonator to misalign CM resonant frequencies. In [5] and [6], two quarter-wavelength or half-wavelength open stubs of equal impedance are added respectively in the central plane to enhance DM selectivity as well as to attain design freedom of CM stopband of a wideband BPF. An analysis incorporating non-resonating nodes (NRN) is presented in [7] to independently control the center frequencies and bandwidths of a multi-band BPF. However, to the best of our knowledge, no work has been introduced in the previous publications regarding tunable multi-band BPF which operates in differential mode.

In this paper, a novel dual-band balanced BPF with tunability of center frequencies is presented. Varactors are used to tune the resonant frequencies of the two passbands. In the symmetrical plane, two open stubs of different dimensions are introduced to obtain a maximum of five transmission zeros when excited by a common-mode signal. This helps to achieve a wide common mode stopband with high level of suppression. Moreover, this structure can be extrapolated to any number of passbands.

II. Proposed Design

A. Filter Configuration

Fig. 1 (a) depicts the schematic of the proposed filter which consists of six NRN based dual-band bandpass sections with three branch-line stubs. The first and third branch-lines have two additional open-circuited stubs attached to them, on the horizontal symmetrical plane. These stubs are marked by (θ_B,Z_B) and (θ_A,Z_A) respectively. For tuning purpose,varactors C_1 and C_2 are connected to the resonators (θ_{R1}, Z_{R1}) and (θ_{R2}, Z_{R2}) respectively.

B. Differential-mode Operation

If the circuit is excited differentially by any of the paired ports, Port 1 and 1′ or Port 2 and 2′, the horizontal symmetrical plane acts as a perfect electric wall (PEW). As a result of this, the open stubs connected to the first and third vertical lines are short-circuited and have no effect on the DM resonant frequencies (Fig. 1 (b)).

C. Common-mode Operation

While the circuit is excited by a common-mode signal, the horizontal symmetrical plane behaves as a perfect magnetic wall (PMW). The open-circuited stubs along the plane appear with impedances Z_A and Z_B (Fig. 1 (c)) for which the line pairs (θ_1, Z_1), (θ_A, Z_A) on the right hand side and (θ_1, Z_1), (θ_B, Z_B) on the left hand side form two SIRs respectively. Each of these two SIRs produces one pair of transmission zeros in the common-mode stopband.

In [5] and [6], they used two SIRs having line sections of equal length and equal impedance, to obtain a wide common-mode stopband for a wideband balanced BPF. In that case, the transmission zeros produced by the two SIRs overlap, resulting in a total of three stopband transmission zeros (one for the central open stub which has a uniform impedance). However, for a dualband balanced filter, if the differential passbands are not very close to each other, three transmission zeros are not sufficient to achieve a wide stopband in common-mode operation. To increase the number of stopband transmission zeros, both SIRs should have either different impedance ratio ($Z_1/Z_A \neq Z_1/Z_B$) or different length ratio ($\theta_1/\theta_A \neq \theta_1/\theta_B$). Either of these two methods prevents overlapping of the zeros and increases the number of zeros from three to five. For the SIRs having different impedance ratio (but same length ratio), the transmission zeros can be calculated by using the

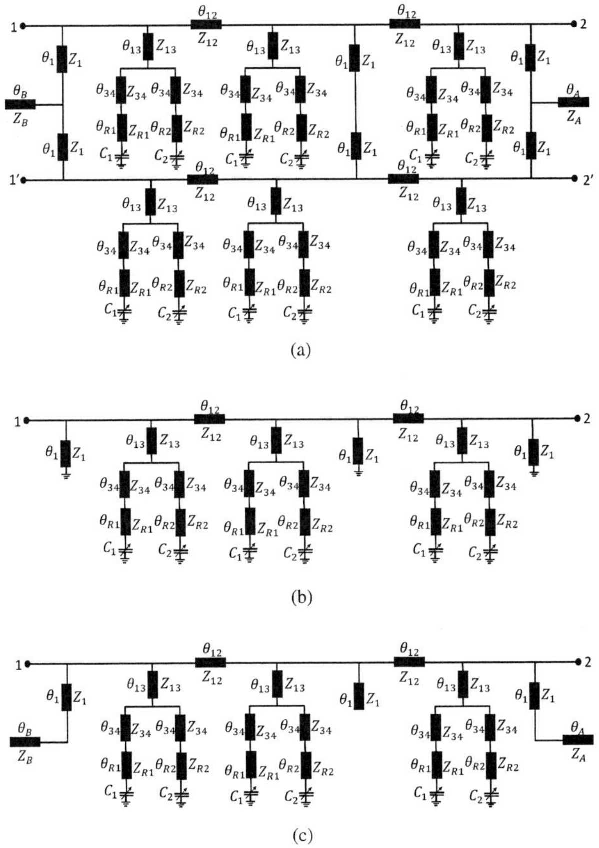

Fig. 1. (a) Structure of the proposed design. (b) DM equivalent circuit. (c) CM equivalent circuit.

formulas in [8]. Incorporating both impedance ratio and length ratio together, a wide common-mode stopband with desired rejection level can be achieved.

III. Results and Discussion

For demonstration, a microstrip-line balanced dual-band tunable filter is designed on Rogers RO4003 substrate with a relative dielectric constant 3.38, dielectric thickness 1.52mm and dielectric loss tangent 0.0027. The prototype shown in Fig. 2 has been built and its characterization is under progress. Here, $\theta_1 = \theta_{12} = 25$, $\theta_{13} = 32$, $\theta_{34} = 25$, $\theta_{R1} = 22$, $\theta_{R2} = 15$, $\theta_A = 18$, $\theta_B = 27$, $W_1 = 10$, $W_{12} = W_{34} = W_{R1} = W_{R2} = 1$, $W_{13} = W_A = W_B = 6$ (all in mm). The filter utilizes SMV1234-011LF varactor model from Skyworks for tuning the center frequencies of the two passbands. From the simulated response of the filter in Fig. 3, the tuning range of the two differential passbands are 1.07 − 1.26GHz and 1.8 − 1.93GHz respectively. The DM return loss for both passbands is found to be 25-30dB. Also, the design exhibits a wide common mode stopband which contains five transmission zeros (two of them are in close proximity) as well as a sharp rejection level of 40dB or more, in the whole tuning range.

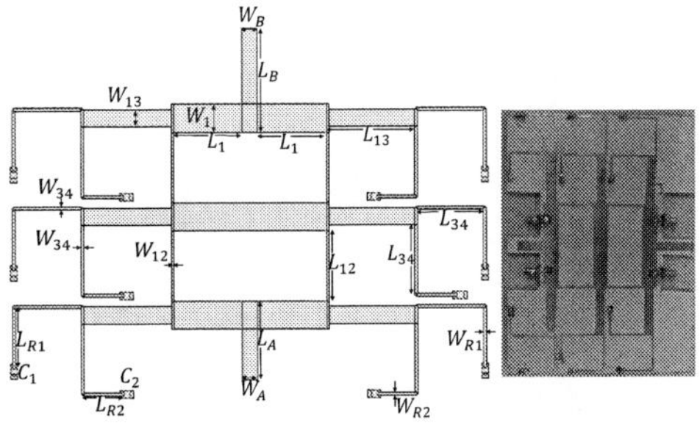

Fig. 2. Physical layout and photograph of the fabricated prototype for the proposed design.

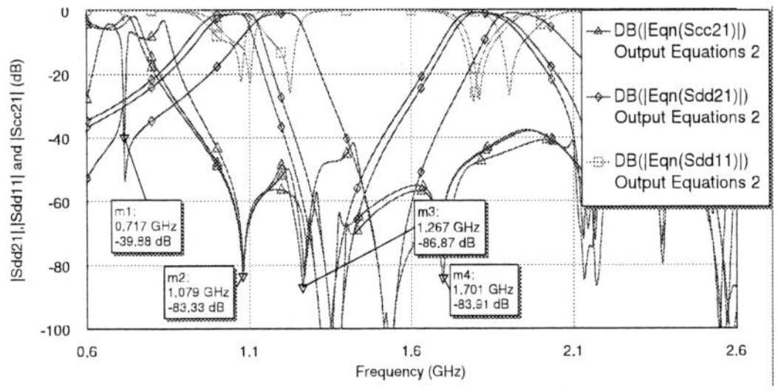

Fig. 3. DM insertion loss (Sdd21), DM return loss (Sdd11) and CM insertion loss (Scc21) of the proposed design.

IV. Conclusion

A dual-band balanced reconfigurable filter is successfully proposed and designed in this letter. It is found that by adjusting the lengths and widths of the open circuited stubs in the symmetrical plane of the proposed filter, the common-mode transmission zeros can be easily adjusted. This gives design freedom of a wide common-mode stopband without deteriorating the differential mode operation.

References

[1] W. Zhou and J. Chen, "High-selectivity tunable balanced bandpass filter with constant absolute bandwidth," IEEE Transactions on Circuits and Systems II: Express Briefs, vol. 64, no. 8, pp. 917-921, 2017.

[2] J. Mao, J. Chen, Y. Ma, and W. Che, "Tunable differential-mode bandpass filters with wide tuning range and high common-mode suppression," IET Microwaves, Antennas & Propagation, vol. 8, no. 6, pp. 437-444, 2014.

[3] S. Zhang, Z. Chen, Q. Chu, and S. Member, "Compact tunable balanced bandpass filter with novel multi-mode resonator," IEEE Microwave and Wireless Components Letters, vol. 27, no. 1, pp. 43-45, 2017.

[4] X. Zhao, L. Gao, and J. Xu, "Tunable balanced bandpass filter with high common-mode suppression," Electronics Letters, vol. 51, no. 24, pp. 2021-2023, 2015.

[5] T. B. Lim and L. Zhu, "A differential-mode wideband bandpass filter on microstrip line for UWB application." IEEE Microwave and Wireless Components Letters, vol. 19, no. 10, pp. 632-634, 2009.

[6] Z. Ouyang and Q. Chu, "A wideband balanced filter with 3/4, stepped-impedance resonator," 2015 Asia-Pacific Microwave Conference (APMC).

[7] R. Gomez-Garcia, A. Guyette, D. Psychogiou, E. Naglich, and D. Peroulis, "Quasi-elliptic multi-band filters with center-frequency and bandwidth tunability," IEEE Microwave and Wireless Components Letters, vol. 26, no. 3, pp. 192-194, 2016.

[8] F. Chen, R. Li, J. Qiu, and Q. Chu, "Sharp-rejection wideband bandstop filter using stepped impedance resonators," IEEE Transactions on Components, Packaging and Manufacturing Technology, vol. 7, no. 3, pp. 444-449, 2017.

UHF-Band Bandpass Filters With Fully-Reconfigurable Transfer Function

Dakotah J. Simpson
Dept. of Electrical, Computer, & Energy Engineering
University of Colorado Boulder
Boulder, USA
Dakotah.Simpson@colorado.edu

Roberto Gómez-García
Dept. of Signal Theory & Telecommunications
University of Alcalá
Alcalá de Henares, Spain
roberto.gomez.garcia@ieee.org

Dimitra Psychogiou
Dept. of Electrical, Computer, & Energy Engineering
University of Colorado Boulder
Boulder, USA
Dimitra.Psychogiou@colorado.edu

***Abstract*—This paper presents a lumped-element bandpass filter (BPF) with multiple levels of transfer-function tunability including bandwidth (BW), center frequency, and intrinsic RF switching. The reported filter is based on a cascaded-resonator structure that exhibits three poles and two transmission zeros (TZs). Transfer-function reconfigurability is achieved by only tuning the filter's resonators via variable capacitors which results in less in-band insertion-loss (IL) variation and better linearity than in conventional filter schemes in which coupling controllability is required. For practical-validation purposes, a lumped-element BPF prototype was designed, built, and measured in the UHF band. It exhibits center-frequency tunability of 1.63:1, BW tunability of 7.3:1 and minimum in-band IL in the range 1.26-3.96 dB.**

Keywords—Bandpass filter (BPF), lumped-element filter, reconfigurable filter, tunable filter.

I. INTRODUCTION

Recent advances in wireless communication systems call for RF front-ends that are able to cover a wide range of communication bands and support alternative types of communication standards [1]. In order to facilitate their deployment, the realization of programmable RF hardware is of critical importance. Among the required developments, bandpass filters (BPFs) with multiple levels of transfer-function tunability are highly desired to select the signal of interest and suppress the undesired noise and RF interference.

Whereas there exists a large number of tunable filter concepts in which frequency tunability is addressed [2], the number of filter designs in which multiple levels of transfer-function adaptivity is achieved is limited; with the exception of a few BPF topologies in which the filter's bandwidth (BW) is tuned by reconfiguring the magnitude and phase of its impedance inverters [3]. However, it results in excessive levels of in-band insertion loss (IL). For example, the lowest-loss filter of the three presented in [3] exhibits an IL of 7 dB in the narrow-BW states. Recently, the authors reported on a filter concept that facilitates multiple levels of transfer-function tunability including center frequency, BW, and intrinsic RF switching. The preceding functionality is achieved at the same filter volume with significantly improved RF performance in terms of IL and tuning range due to the lack of tuning elements in the impedance inverters. This BPF concept was validated in microstrip technology in [4], which would result in large size for the lower part of the microwave band (e.g., UHF range).

The authors would like to acknowledge Lockheed Martin for supporting this work under award 4102673517.01

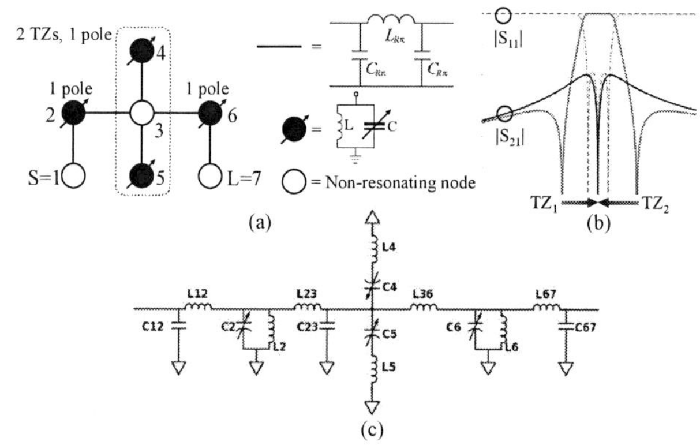

Fig. 1. Fully-reconfigurable filter concept. (a) Coupling-matrix diagram. (b) Conceptual transfer functions for both bandpass filtering mode and intrinsic switching. (c) Circuit schematic.

In this paper, we built upon our previous work and report on a miniaturized fully-reconfigurable UHF-band BPF. It exhibits transfer-function tunability in terms of center frequency, BW, and intrinsic RF switching. The proposed filter is realized using commercially-available lumped elements (LEs) so that the microstrip-line size constrains at the UHF range are avoided. Thin-film trimmer capacitors are incorporated within its volume to achieve the desired adaptive RF characteristics.

II. THEORETICAL FOUNDATIONS

The concept of the fully-reconfigurable BPF is shown in Figs. 1 (a) and (b) in terms of coupling-matrix diagram and conceptual transfer function [4]. It is based on four resonators that are connected through impedance inverters and result in three poles and two transmission zeros (TZs). By reconfiguring the location of the TZs, the transfer function can be tuned in BW and it can be intrinsically switched-off as shown in Fig. 1 (b). Furthermore, it can be controlled in frequency by simultaneously reconfiguring the location of its poles and TZs. Using as a reference the coupling-matrix diagram in Fig. 1 (a), nodes 2 and 6 interact with the source and load and contribute to one pole each. Furthermore, nodes 3, 4, and 5 interact with each other to create a "TZ-generation cell", as outlined in blue in Fig. 1 (a). This cell is responsible for producing two TZs (one on each side of the passband) and one additional pole. The two TZs are located at the resonant frequencies of resonators 4

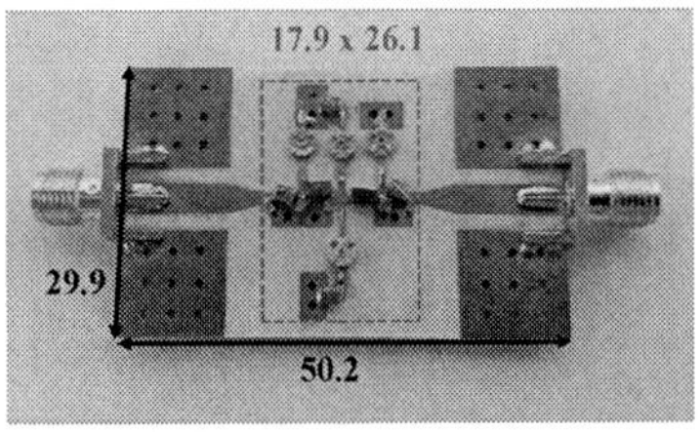

Fig. 2. Manufactured prototype (dimensions in mm). All static capacitors are are from Johanson 251R14S series: C_{12}=2pF, C_{23}=2.2pF, and C_{67}=1pF. All variable capacitors are from Johanson 9402 series: C_2=C_6=2.5 to 10pF, and C_4=C_5=1 to 5pF. All inductors are from Coilcraft: L_{12}=L_4=L_5=L_{67}=23nH (0908SQ23N), L_2=L_6=14nH (0807SQ14N), and L_{23}=L_{36}=27nH (1206CS270).

and 5 and the pole is positioned at the frequency at which the two input admittances, looking into nodes 4 and 5 from node 3, are mutually canceled. If nodes 4 and 5 are tuned to have the same resonant frequency, the TZs are placed at the same location and the transmission response is intrinsically-switched off. A practical realization scheme for the BPF concept includes LE impedance inverters—realized by their π-type circuit equivalent using the methodology in [5]—and parallel LC resonators. Reconfigurability is achieved by incorporating variable capacitors within each resonator.

III. Experimental Validation

To validate the design principles of the fully-reconfigurable BPF concept, a UHF-band LE prototype was designed, manufactured, and characterized in the frequency range 0.6-1.0 GHz. The BPF design was performed using as a basis the design methodology in Section II and with post-layout simulations in ADS, Keysight. A photograph of the BPF prototype is shown in Fig. 2. It was built on a Rogers 4003 substrate (h=1.52 mm, ε_r=3.55). Its measured characteristics were obtained with a Keysight N5224A PNA and are summarized in Fig. 3. In particular, Fig. 3 (a) shows a comparison between the electromagnetically-(EM)-simulated and RF-measured responses of one state which, as can be seen, are in fair agreement. Figs. 3 (b)-(d) respectively demonstrate the reconfiguration capabilities of the devised fully-reconfigurable BPF concept in terms of intrinsic RF switching, BW, and center-frequency tuning. As it can be seen, a BW tuning of 17-124 MHz (7.3:1 tuning ratio) at a center frequency of 800 MHz, and a center-frequency tuning of 575-938 MHz (1.63:1 tuning ratio) for a constant bandwidth of 50 MHz are achieved. The minimum in-band IL was measured around 3.96 dB and 1.26 dB for BW states of 17 MHz and 124 MHz, respectively, and varies less than 0.15 dB as the center frequency is tuned. These states correspond to an effective Q_{eff} of 230 and 128, respectively. The aforementioned characteristics demonstrate the ability of the BPF concept for multiple levels of tunability.

IV. Conclusion

A fully-reconfigurable UHF-band LE BPF has been reported. It is based on four frequency-reconfigurable resonators and static impedance inverters that result in three poles and two TZs. By reconfiguring the center frequency of its constituent resonators, the transfer function can be tuned in frequency and in BW and it can be intrinsically-switched off.

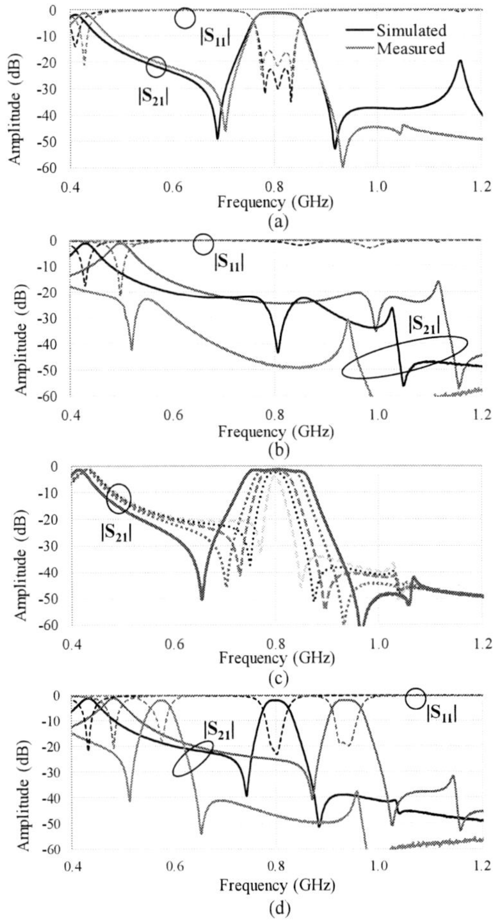

Fig. 3. (a) Comparison of the EM-simulated and RF-measured power transmission ($|S_{21}|$) and reflection ($|S_{11}|$) responses of one bandpass state. (b) RF-measured responses of various intrinsically-switched states. (c) RF-measured BW tunability, and (d) RF-measured center-frequency tunability.

The proposed BPF concept has been experimentally validated with an UHF-band prototype featuring BW tunability of 7.3:1 and center-frequency tuning of 1.6:1.

References

[1] W. J. Chappell, E. J. Naglich, C. Maxey, and A. C. Guyette, "Putting the radio in "software-defined radio": Hardware developments for adaptable RF systems," Proc. IEEE, vol. 102, no. 3, pp. 307–320, Mar. 2014.

[2] X. G. Huang, J.-Q. Zhang, Y.-Q. Lin, and Q. Y. Xiang, "Design of a six-pole tunable band-pass filter with constant absolute bandwidth," 2016 Progress in Electromagnetic Research Symposium (PIERS), Shanghai, pp. 3507–3510, 2016.

[3] C. Schuster, et al., "Performance analysis of reconfigurable bandpass filters with continuously tunable center frequency and bandwidth," in IEEE Trans. Microw. Theory Techn., Early Access, pp. 1–12, 2017.

[4] R. Gómez-García, J. M. Muñoz-Ferreras, and D. Psychogiou, "Fully-reconfigurable bandpass filter with static couplings and intrinsic-switching capabilities," 2017 IEEE MTT-S Int. Microw. Symp., Honolulu, HI, USA, pp. 914–917, 2017.

[5] D. Kuylenstierna, S. E. Gunnarsson, and H. Zirath, "Lumped-element quadrature power splitters using mixed right/left-handed transmission lines," in IEEE Trans. Microw. Theory Techn., vol. 53, no. 8, pp. 2616–2621, Aug. 2005.

Investigation of the RCS of Wind Turbine Rotor Blades

Sebastian Hegler, Klaus Wolf, Christoph Statz, Niels Neumann, Dirk Plettemeier

Dresden University of Technology,
Chair for RF Engineering,
Dresden, Germany
Email: sebastian.hegler@tu-dresden.de

***Abstract*—Wind turbines are a key element for the production of renewable energy. However, their huge size as well as the rotating components cause radar clutter in air traffic and weather surveillance radars operating in the frequency range 1 GHz–10 GHz. This paper reports on simulation setups and results of wind turbines and different rotor blade designs.**

I. Introduction

Wind turbines are a key element for the further increase of renewable energy generation. In addition to large off-shore locations, further allotments of on-shore locations as well as "repowering" (i.e., the replacement of older generator generations by newer ones with increased performance and/or efficiency) projects will be needed in order to fulfil the goals of reducing the carbon footprint prescribed by the German *Climate Protection Plan*[1].

To reach these goals, lots of requirements have to be met, including those in the domain of radar EMI compatibility. Wind turbines are known to cause significant radar backscattering in the frequency bands allotted to air traffic surveillance and weather surveillance radars (WSR) operating in the L, S, C, and X bands (see Fig. 1)[2, 3]. Therefore, currently, large safety zones radius around radar locations are reserved, and cannot be allotted to on-shore wind farms.

In order to ease these requirements, an investigation of radar backscattering of wind turbine generators and wind farms and possible mitigation strategies is to be undertaken.

II. Wind Turbine and Rotor Blade Models

State-of-the-art wind turbines have a rotor diameter of 120 m or more, and roughly the same tower height (including the nacelle), and therefore make extremely large radar targets. Both numbers are expected to grow: power yield is proportional to

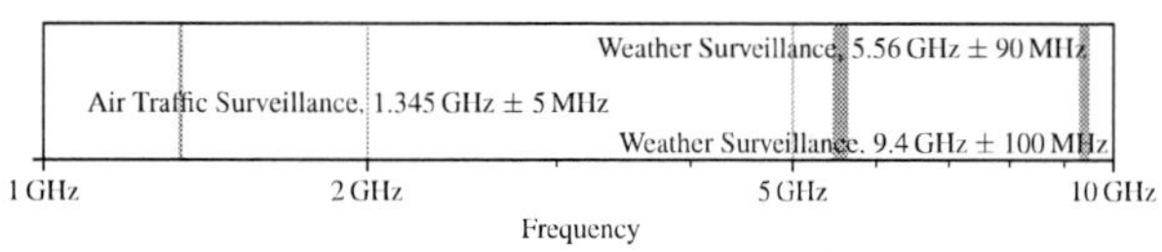

Fig. 1: Frequency ranges of air traffic surveillance and weather surveillance radars in the range 1 GHz–10 GHz.

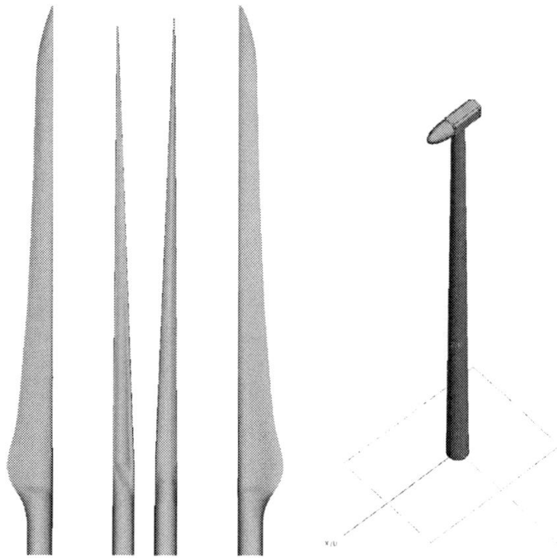

(a) The investigated wind turbine blades. Design V1 innermost, design V2 outermost.

(b) Non-rotating parts of the wind turbine.

Fig. 2: CAD models.

the area covered by the rotating rotor assembly, and air flows much less turbulently in higher altitudes.

The non-rotating parts are kept simple. The tower is modelled as a simple cone with non-zero top radius, the nacelle as a box with rounded corners, and the hub as a prolate semi-sphere. The tower's height was chosen to be 114 m.

In order to investigate different blade geometries, different models were created, shown in Figure 2a. The first version blade (V1) is quite simple, built from a single NACA airfoil profile extruded and shrunk over the total length. The second blade (V2) is more sophisticated, built of several NACA and DU[4] profiles, including aerodynamic wing twist.

III. Simulation Results

Simulations were performed using a well-known commercial Method of Moments (MoM) software package. In order to keep simulation times in a reasonable range, the frequency was chosen as 1.345 GHz, the center frequency of L-band

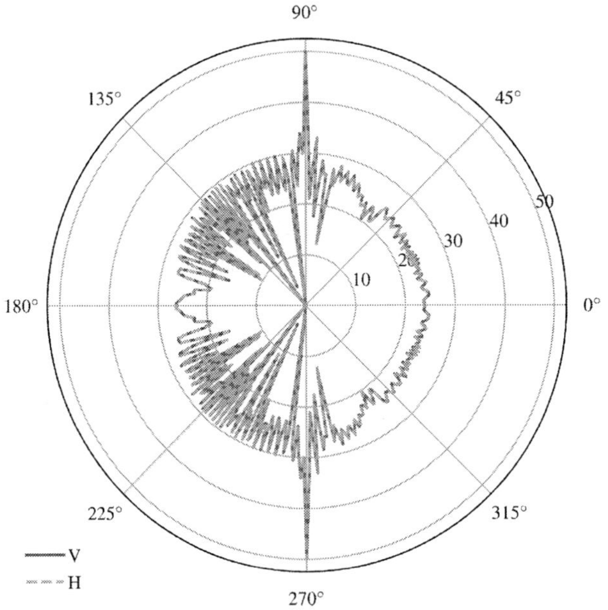

Fig. 3: Monostatic RCS in the x-y plane, in dB m^2, of the non-rotating parts.

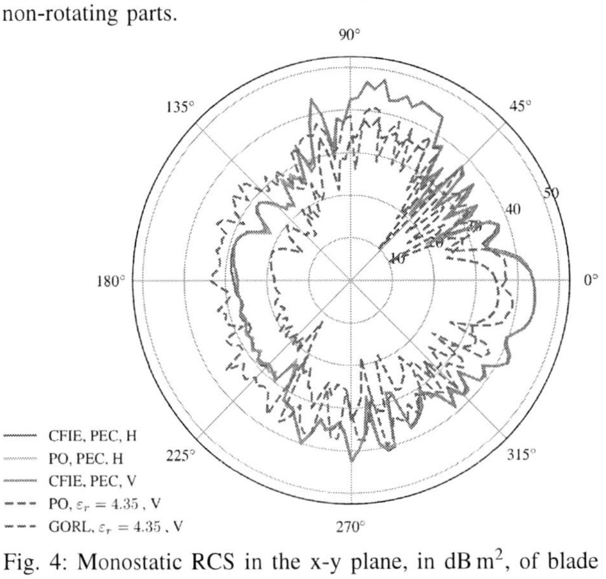

Fig. 4: Monostatic RCS in the x-y plane, in dB m^2, of blade V2.

air traffic surveillance systems. The Fast Multipole Method (FMM) solver was chosen, and where possible, the combined field integral equation (CFIE).

A. Non-rotating Parts

Simulation results of the non-rotating parts (see Fig. 2b) are shown in Fig. 3. As can be seen, the monostatic RCS is symmetric, as would be expected by the model. The material was chosen to be perfectly electrically conducting (PEC), which is warranted by the fact that these parts are mostly made of steel. Also, the V and H polarizations do not show significant differences. The spikes at 90° and 270° can be attributed to the nacelle's sides, which form huge planar reflectors.

B. Blade V2

Blade V2 was simulated in several different configurations, with different numerical methods. The monostatic RCS is shown in Figure 4, with the blade placed along the z axis and the blade's leading edge pointing towards +x. CCW rotation in Figure 4 goes to the blade's lower side first. As can be seen, for PEC material the Physical Optics (PO) and CFIE solvers yield – expectedly – nearly identical results. The V and H polarizations do not differ much. Also, the blade's RCS is larger than that of the non-rotating parts most of the time, which can only be attributed to the relatively complex shape.

A point of concern is the disagreement between the PO and the Geometric Optics/Ray Launching (GORL) results when using dielectric material with a permittivity $\varepsilon_r = 4.35$ for glass fiber reinforced plastic (GRP), where the PO results seem to underreport the backscattering significantly. However, using a FMM solver, which would yield the most reliable results, for dielectric media is currently computationally infeasible.

IV. Conclusions and Further Work

The RCS of the non-rotating parts of a wind turbine can be computed by current technology. The rotating parts, especially when using a realistic setup with lightweight construction materials such as GRP, pose a problem. Also, a very important factor, namely the Doppler shift introduced due to the rapid blade movement, cannot easily be characterized by these methods.

In order to better understand the backscattering behavior of wind turbine rotor blades, a laboratory measurement setup is currently being built. It will allow the measurement of the monostatic RCS of built-to-scale rotor blade models of 1 m and 2.5 m length, made of GRP, in the frequency range of 60 GHz–300 GHz. It will possibly also enable measurement of the Doppler shift by enabling rotational movement of the blades.

Acknowledgements

This research was funded by the German Federal Ministry for Economic Affairs and Energy under grant number 0325727B.

References

[1] "Klimaschutzplan 2050 – Die deutsche Klimaschutzlangfriststrategie." [Online]. Available: https://www.bmub.bund.de/fileadmin/Daten_BMU/Download_PDF/Klimaschutz/klimaschutzplan_2050_bf.pdf

[2] United States Departement of Defence, "The Effect of Windmill Farms on Military Readiness," United States Departement of Defence, Tech. Rep., 2006.

[3] "The Effects of Wind Turbine Farms on ATC Radar," UK Ministry of Defence, Tech. Rep., 2005.

[4] W. A. Timmer and R. P. J. O. M. Van Rooij, "Summary of the Delft University wind turbine dedicated airfoils," *Transactions – American Society Of Mechanical Engineers*, vol. 125, no. 4, pp. 488–496, 2003.

Design of a Cost-Effective Analog Lock-In Amplifier Using Phase Sensitive Detector

Fardin Humayun
RMIT University
Melbourne, Australia
humayun.fardin@gmail.com

Riasat Khan
New Mexico State University
Las Cruces, NM, USA
rkhan@nmsu.edu

Shatil Saadman
and Rezwanul Haque
Islamic University of Technology
Gazipur, Bangladesh

***Abstract*—The measurement of a physical quantity in the presence of noise is a typical situation in research science. A lock-in amplifier is an electronic measurement device which has the capability of detecting, amplifying, extracting and measuring small signals buried within noise sources. This noise source can typically be thousands of times greater than the original signal. This paper details the procedure of building a simple and cost-effective analog lock-in amplifier. Some approaches have been investigated in designing this lock-in amplifier, taking into consideration the efficiency, expense, and practicality of the design. The final design is simulated in NI Multisim program and then executed in a practical circuit using basic, inexpensive electronic components. Using the essential technique of phase sensitive detection, the lock-in amplifier can provide extensive improvements on the signal-to-noise ratio. The simulation output presents very accurate results showing the functionality of the lock-in amplifier. The practical output also shows a compelling result with the presence of minor fluctuations in the amplitude of the signal.**

***Index Terms*—Lock-In Amplifier, Low Pass Filter, NI Multisim, Phase Sensitive Detection, Signal-to-Noise Ratio.**

I. Introduction

A lock-in amplifier is an electronic device having dual capabilities, used to measure the amplitude of weak signals contained within a noisy environment, and also to extract weak signals from an extremely noisy source [1]. The lock-in amplifier makes use of an important technique known as the "phase sensitive detection" which is mainly used on signals having a low SNR [2]. These signals typically have an SNR value of less than 1, indicating that the signal of concern is completely or partially masked by noise.

The first step to design a lock-in amplifier is to amplify the input signal using a specific op-amp circuit selectively. During this amplification stage, any noise component present with the signal also gets amplified and furthermore the op-amp has its noise factor which gets added to the signal. Some form of noise elimination (outside the bandwidth of the signal) also takes place at this stage due to the presence of pre-detection filter circuits. The next stage of the amplification process involves the most important step where the phase sensitive detection takes place [2]. In this step, the original signal and the reference signal, both maintaining the same phase, are synchronously demodulated using a "demodulator." The demodulation is a dominant and powerful method of differentiating and discriminating against random noise figures. This is because the phase locking property of the design provides demodulation of only the phase-locked signals in this multiplication process, thereby ignoring any other unwanted signals that are out of phase. The final step involves passing the output signal from the demodulator through a low pass filter to obtain the original signal of concern.

In this paper, an analog lock-in amplifier is implemented by first using suitable circuit designs through simulations of the software NI Multisim. In the next step, a real circuit is built based on the most efficient simulated design obtained from NI Multisim. The circuit has been made using essential electronic components to justify the cost of the lock-in amplifier because practically, lock-in amplifiers can be extremely expensive [3]. But due to a trade-off between cost and efficiency, the proposed design using basic electronic components did not provide highly efficient performance. Finally, the performance of the analog lock-in amplifier circuit is evaluated.

II. Phase Sensitive Detection

The two signals entering the demodulator where the synchronous demodulation takes place is assumed to be $V_{sig}sin(\omega_r t + \theta_{sig})$ from the input signal and $V_L sin(\omega_L t + \theta_{ref})$ from the reference signal. V_{sig} is the input signal amplitude, and V_L is the reference signal amplitude. The output of this process is the product of the two sine waves as shown by (1),

$$V_{psd} = V_{sig}V_L sin(\omega_r t + \theta_{sig}) sin(\omega_L t + \theta_{ref}) \quad (1)$$

V_{psd} is considered as the output which consists of two AC signals, one at the difference of frequency $(\omega_r - \omega_L)$ and one at the sum of frequency $(\omega_r + \omega_L)$. If the output is passed through a low pass filter, it will technically remove all AC signals. The difference frequency component will be represented as a DC signal if ω_r equals ω_L. The filtered output of this is shown by (2),

$$V_{psd} = \frac{1}{2} V_{sig} V_L cos(\theta_{sig} - \theta_{ref}) \quad (2)$$

This produces a DC signal having a fundamental frequency which is twice that of the original signal. Adjusting the reference signal phase θ_{ref} can make θ equal to zero which will produce an optimum output. Conversely, a phase difference angle of 90^0 will not produce any DC output. Hence the signals must always be in phase for the efficient operation of the device.

III. Results and Discussion

A. *Software Simulation Results*

The lock-in amplifier is setup without using the notch filter which is now replaced with a low pass filter acting as the pre-detection filter. This has been done to reduce the load of the input which is fed into the demodulator. The trans-amplifier circuit is generating the noise signal and adding it to a sine wave which has similar properties as before. The output of this design simulated in NI Multisim is shown in Fig. 1. The signal at the top indicates the original signal produced by the signal generator. This signal is then added to the noise generated by the Zener circuit to provide the signal in the middle. The SNR of this signal is 0.1 which means it is completely obscured by the noise source. The wave at the bottom shows the final extracted output from the lock-in amplifier.

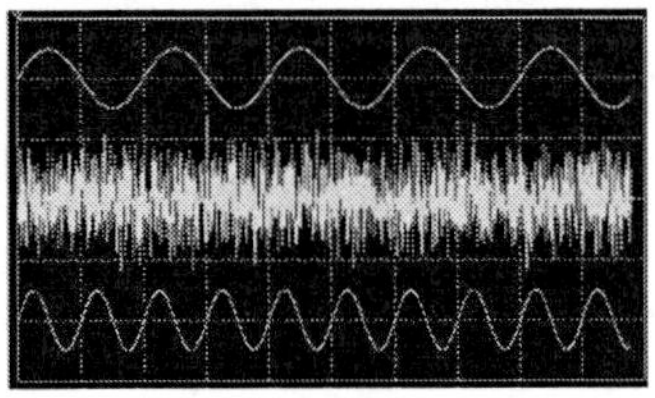

Fig. 1. Output of the lock-in amplifier simulated in NI Multisim.

B. *Hardware Circuit Results*

Next, the circuit is implemented on a breadboard using basic electronic components. The input to the system is provided through a function generator, much like the one used for the software simulation. The signal fed into the system is a sine wave having a frequency of approximately 1 kHz. A DC power supply of 5V is used to power up the circuit. A digital oscilloscope is used to check the output of each stage and finally the output of the lock-in amplifier as a whole system. First, the original signal before and after the selective amplification stage is recorded in the oscilloscope and the screenshot of the result is shown in Fig. 2. Channel 1 shows the processed signal, and channel 2 shows the original signal that was fed into the lock-in amplifier system.

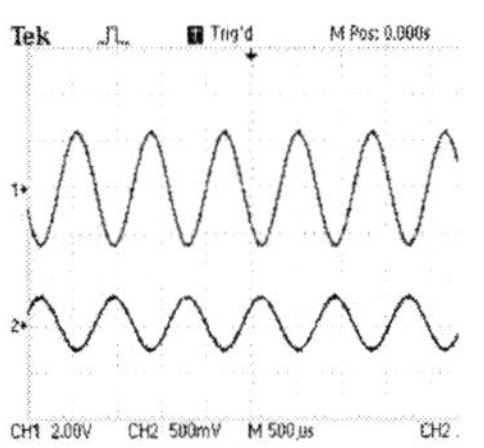

Fig. 2. Original signal before and after the selective amplification stage.

Finally, a noisy signal is provided to the lock-in amplifier to verify and test the performance of the practical circuit. A signal, completely buried within noise and having an SNR of 0.1, is fed into the lock-in amplifier design and the screenshot of the output is shown in Fig. 3. The output of the lock-in amplifier shows a signal which has been extracted and amplified from the obscuring noise source.

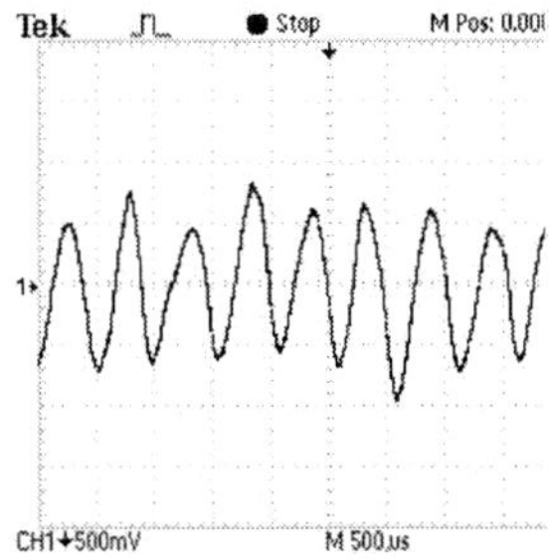

Fig. 3. Extracted output of the lock-in amplifier.

IV. Conclusion

In this paper, a cost-effective analog lock-in amplifier is designed in both NI Multisim design software and practical circuit. The results are compared to check the stability and performance of the real circuit. The software simulation shows an efficient and accurate result, exactly how the theory described the output of a lock-in amplifier. The practical hardware circuit also shows a compelling result at the output except for some very minor negligible fluctuations present in the final waveform. The main reason for the difference in the output signal is the unfeasibility of a zero degree phase shift of the reference signal with the original signal. The implementation and procedures for the phase sensitive detector of a lock-in amplifier are different for an analog and a digital approach. Digital signal processing instruments and devices will basically always show a better performance when compared with their analog versions. In this paper, an analog lock-in amplifier gives a better response compared to a digital one because of higher dynamic reserve or operating frequency, true analog output signals, and experiment with dual demodulation process. Last of all in this paper, the cost of the designed analog lock-in amplifier is compared to a digital one. A simple digital dual phase lock-in amplifier costs nearly about 300 times than the designed analog one. The trade-off between cost and efficiency is indicated as the designed analog lock-in amplifier definitely does not provide an equal performance to the digital one.

References

[1] J. A. F. Ferreira and A. Petraglia, "Analog integrated lock-in amplifier for optical sensors," *IEEE Instrumentation Measurement Magazine*, vol. 20, no. 2, pp. 43–50, April 2017.

[2] B. Akin, U. Orguner, H. A. Toliyat, and M. Rayner, "Phase-sensitive detection of motor fault signatures in the presence of noise," *IEEE Transactions on Industrial Electronics*, vol. 55, no. 6, pp. 2539–2550, June 2008.

[3] A. D. Marcellis, E. Palange, N. Liberatore, and S. Mengali, "Low-cost portable 1 mhz lock-in amplifier for fast measurements of pulsed signals in sensing applications," *IEEE Sensors Letters*, vol. 1, no. 4, pp. 1–4, Aug 2017.

The Novel Adaptive Method for Interference Suppression

1st Zhitao Yang
EECS
Wichita State University
Wichita, USA
zhitaoyang55@gmail.com

2nd Guanglei Zhang
EEIS
Harbin Institute of Technology
Harbin, China
guangleizhang201717@gmail.com

***Abstract*—As the dramatic advancement in array signal processing and the computer techniques, the phase array radar becomes more and more popular. However, the electromagnetic environment is more and more complicated with different kinds of interference. The ability to suppress the interference becomes the most important consideration for the phase array radar. In this paper, the mismatch optimal detector method is proposed to suppress the interference at the subarray level. In addition, the float round-off error analysis is given. The simulation results show that the proposed method has good performance in interference suppression.**

***Index Terms*—wireless, optimal, subarray, beamforming, communication, phase, adaptive**

I. Introduction

As the dramatic development in array signal processing techniques, the phase array radar is widely used in different aspects of military [1]. The phase array radar has the beamforming that scans both at pitch and azimuth direction. As for the phase array radar, there are thousands of antenna elements [2]. The subarray level adaptive digital beamforming technique is adopted to reduce the cost of the hardware resource and obtain good signal at expected direction [3]. The most important part of the adaptive digital beamforming is the derivation of the adaptive weightes. It is actually very difficult to obtain the adaptive weights because of the huge complicated complexity [4]. Therefore, we need to propose a adaptive weights derivation method to help to reduce the calculation complexity. In addition, during the computation of the adaptive weights, the data needs to be transfer to binary data first and the computation is baed on the binary data [5]. The data generated by the complicated computation is not accurately stored and the final result is not accurate [6]. This makes the adaptive digital beamforming technique not accurate for the interference suppression. The main impact is from the calculation of the inverse for the matrix.

Most of the decimal number is not accurately stored in the computer. Each float storage brings machine error due to the bit length. Then, the inaccurate result is used for the further calculation. Thus, the float round-off error is accumulated more and more. Since the float round-off error for each calculation is very small to affect the result accuracy [7], the float round-off error is always ignored. However, the accumulated float round-off error should not be ignored. For example, we have the computation $f(\alpha)$ and the only data is α. The computation is consisted of basic calculation on α. The real number is stored inaccurate due to the float round-off error. We assume α is denoted by $\alpha^h(h = s, d)$ in the computer. α^s is the single precision for α where α^d is the double precision for α. Since there is float round-off error citedan-02, the stored value $\alpha^h(h = s, d)$ is not exact the same as the original α. α should be in the window which is consisted of two float numbers close to α^h. Therefore, it is significantly important to analyse the impact of float round-off error.

In this paper, we analyse the performance of mismatched optimum detector method under different bit length. The paper includes 4 sections. In section I, the introduction is shown. The derivation of the adaptive weights using subspace projection method is shown. In section III, the simulation results are given to analyse the performance under different bit length. The conclusion is given in section IV.

II. The Derivation of the Adaptive Weights for the Proposed Method

In this section, the details about the proposed mismatched optimum detector method is introduced. The subarray level adaptive weights method is usually used to suppress the interference [8], but the sidelobe power increases a lot compared with the sidelobe power of the static antenna pattern [9]. The sidelobe power becomes much higher if there is no interference in the adaptive method. In order to solve this issue, we propose a mismatch control vector to calibrate the interference and noise covariance matrix at the subarray level.

First, the system model is shown in figure 1. As shown in figure 1, the phase shifter at the antenna level is used to control the direction of the beam and form the steering vector [10]. In addition, as for the weights at the antenna element level, the Taylor weight is adopted for sum beam and Bayliss weight is used for differentiation beam to control the sidelobe power of the static antenna pattern. The adaptive weights are used at the subarray level to suppress the interference.

Then, the mismatch control vector is introduced. We have $(R_{sub})_0$

$$a(\theta_0, \phi_0) = (R_{sub})_0 q \tag{1}$$

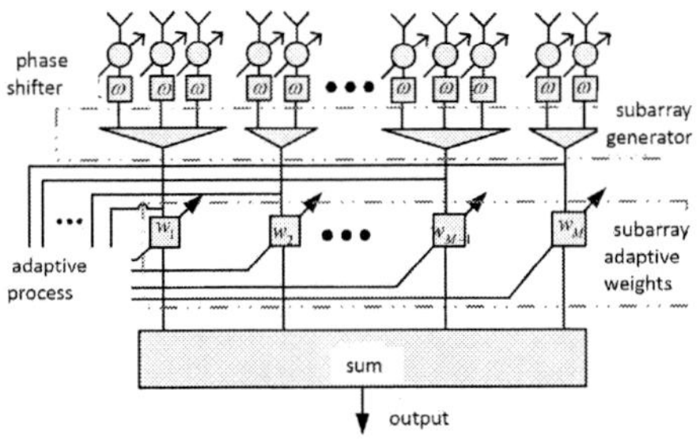

Fig. 1. subarray level weights structure.

where q is the M column vector and all the elements is 1. As for the weights, we have

$$\omega_{CM} = \mu R_{sub}^{-1} \alpha_{sub}(\theta_0, \phi_0) \tag{2}$$

where μ is the constant and $\alpha(\theta_0, \phi_0) = exp{-j2\pi[x_n\alpha(\theta_0, \phi_0) + y_n\beta(\theta_0, \phi_0)]/\lambda}_{n=1,\cdots,N}$. Then, the adaptive weights for the proposed method is

$$\omega_{mod} = \mu R_{sub}^{-1}(R_{sub})_0 q \tag{3}$$

when there is no interference, we have $R_{sub} = (R_s ub)_0$. Then, we have

$$\omega_{mod} = \mu R_{sub}^{-1}(R_{sub})_0 q = \mu q \tag{4}$$

where the weight for each subarray is μ. The adaptive antenna pattern is the same as the static antenna pattern, which means the mismatch optimal detector method suppresses the interference efficiently.

III. The Simulation Results

In this section, the performance of the proposed mismatch optimal detector method is shown and the float round-off error is also given. First, the parameters for the simulation is given in table 1. The subarray structure stays the same and the subarray shape is rectangle with 4×4 antenna elements in each subarray. The number of subarray is different. Here, 7 scenario is considered. The number of subarray changes from 16 to 100 and the number of antenna elements changes from 256 to 1000.

Table1 matrix dimension and sub array division (same sub array structure)

matrix dimension	16	25	36	49	64	81	100
subarray(number)	4*4=16	5*5=25	6*6=36	7*7=49	8*8=64	9*9=81	10*10=100
total elements	256	400	576	784	1024	1296	1600

As shown in table 2, the peak sidelobe power, average sidelobe power, mainlbe width and interference null depth is given. It can be clearly seen that the float round-off error in peak sidelobe and average sodelobe power is very small. As for the mainlobe width, it is the same with 32 bit and 64 bit. The interference null depth has large float round-off error.

Table 1. 32 bit length. MOD performance(the subarray structure is the same)

parameter	length	matrix dimension						
		16	25	36	49	64	81	100
Peak sidelobe (dB)	64bit	-36.9041	-38.4202	-36.3605	-39.7335	-37.1441	-37.0603	-38.846
	32bit	-36.9092	-38.4224	-36.33	-39.6667	-37.1065	-36.9958	-38.958
	error	0.0051	0.0022	-0.0305	-0.0668	-0.0376	-0.0645	0.112
Average sidelobe (dB)	64bit	-42.9504	-42.5543	-41.9979	-42.4868	-43.7788	-43.4427	-44.8779
	32bit	-42.9844	-42.5548	-41.9975	-42.4475	-43.8	-43.4386	-44.8786
	error	0.0340	0.0005	-0.0004	-0.0393	0.0212	-0.0041	0.0007
Mainlobe width (°)	64bit	9.2	7.2	6.0	5.0	4.4	4.0	3.6
	32bit	9.2	7.2	6.0	5.0	4.4	4.0	3.6
Interference null depth (dB)	64bit	-149.4729	-153.8362	-145.8902	-171.1729	-150.5158	-158.8119	-156.7939
	32bit	-139.9422	-137.5873	-134.5682	-133.7086	-132.599	-131.926	-133.0426
	error	-9.5307	-16.2489	-11.3220	-37.4643	-17.9168	-26.8859	-23.7513

IV. Conclusion

In this paper, the mismatch optimal detector method is proposed and the details about the derivation for the proposed method is provided. The proposed method is very important for the interference suppression at the subarray level for phase array radar. In addition, the float round-off error is also analysed in the paper. The float round-off error analysis is a good guidance for the practical implementation.

References

[1] D. Wang and Z. Yang, "An novel spectrum sensing scheme combined with machine learning," in *2016 9th International Congress on Image and Signal Processing, BioMedical Engineering and Informatics (CISP-BMEI)*, Oct 2016, pp. 1293–1297.

[2] H. Subbaram and K. Abend, "Interference suppression via orthogonal projections: a performance analysis," *IEEE Transactions on Antennas and Propagation*, vol. 41, no. 9, pp. 1187–1194, Sep 1993.

[3] D. Wang, H. Hu, and Z. Yang, "Improved genetic algorithm for the configuration optimization of the sub arrays in phased array radar," in *2016 9th International Congress on Image and Signal Processing, BioMedical Engineering and Informatics (CISP-BMEI)*, Oct 2016, pp. 930–934.

[4] I. P. Kirsteins and D. W. Tufts, "Adaptive detection using low rank approximation to a data matrix," *IEEE Transactions on Aerospace and Electronic Systems*, vol. 30, no. 1, pp. 55–67, Jan 1994.

[5] D. Wang, H. Hu, and Z. Yang, "The pareto rank algorithm for the division of the sub arrays for the phase array radar," in *2016 9th International Congress on Image and Signal Processing, BioMedical Engineering and Informatics (CISP-BMEI)*, Oct 2016, pp. 945–949.

[6] D. Wang and Z. Yang, "An advanced scheme with decision tree for the improvement of spectrum sensing efficiency in dynamic network," in *2016 9th International Congress on Image and Signal Processing, BioMedical Engineering and Informatics (CISP-BMEI)*, Oct 2016, pp. 1288–1292.

[7] D. Wang and Y. Song, "A novel distributed global time synchronization protocol in cognitive radio ad hoc networks," in *2015 IEEE Global Communications Conference (GLOBECOM)*, Dec 2015, pp. 1–6.

[8] G. S. Bloom and S. W. Golomb, "Applications of numbered undirected graphs," *Proceedings of the IEEE*, vol. 65, no. 4, pp. 562–570, April 1977.

[9] D. Wang, Y. Song, and Z. Yang, "A joint power adaptation and spectrum handoff scheme in mobile cognitive radio networks," in *2015 International Conference on Computing, Networking and Communications (ICNC)*, Feb 2015, pp. 1061–1065.

[10] W. Dan, H. Hang, and Q. Xin, "Space-time adaptive processing method at subarray level for broadband jammer suppression," in *2011 IEEE International Conference on Microwave Technology Computational Electromagnetics*, May 2011, pp. 281–284.

Advanced Subspace Projection Method for Interference Suppression in Phase Array Radar

1st Zhitao Yang
EECS
Wichita State University
Wichita, USA
zhitaoyang55@gmail.com

2nd Guanglei Zhang
EEIS
Harbin Institute of Technology
Harbin, China
guangleizhang55@gmail.com

***Abstract*—As the dramatic development of the radar system, the phase array radar is widely used in military. There are more and more techniques adopted to improve the performance of the phase array radar. The most important part for the phase array radar is the ability to suppress the interference under the complicated electromagnetic environment with different kind of interference. In this paper, a novel method is proposed for interference suppression at the subarray level and the float round-off error for the proposed method is shown. The simulation results show that the proposed method has good performance.**

***Index Terms*—wireless, radar, adaptive, interference, suppression**

I. Introduction

As the dramatic development of the radar system, the phase array radar is widely used in military [1]. The performance of the radar system needs to be dramatically improved since the electromagnetic environment is becoming more and more complicated. The detection performance of the radar system decreases dramatically because the interference is received by the antenna [2]. The interference suppression ability is very important to the radar system. The adaptive digital beamforming is used to improve the interference suppression ability of the radar system [3]. The adaptive digital beamforming technique adapts the parameters according to the interference.

In the past, the amplitude weights and array structure design is used to suppress the interference in order to meet the requirements of the sidelobe power of the antenna pattern [4]. However, the interference at the sidelobe still has impact on the expected signal extraction when the active interference is very big. The return expected signal is always very weak compared with the interference signal from the transmitters. The power of the interference signal is tens dB higher than the expected signal [5]. Then, the expected signal cannot be correctly extracted from the received signal even the -40dB Taylor weights are used [6]. Therefore, the weights of the array needs to be adapted in order to have the null depth at the direction of the interference [7]. Since the direction of the interference changes all the time, the weights of the array needs to be adapted in order to filter the changing interference. However, the array signal processing techniques still have limitation [8]. One of the most important limitation is that most of the processing is based on the antenna element level. Each antenna element needs to have its own receiving path which brings in a lot of waste in hardware resources [9].

Therefore, the signal processing on subarray level is needed for the phase array radar with large scale of antenna elements [10]. The construction of the subarrays also has great impact on the antenna pattern. If the number of antenna elements in one subarray is too small, the hardware resources is wasted [11]. If the number of antenna elements in one subarray is too large, the period of the grating lobe is too short [12]. Then, the performance of the antenna array dramatically decreases. Therefore, we also need to consider the subarray constructions. Another issue is the float round-off error. In the calculation of the adaptive weights [13], the float round-off error is accumulated. In order to make the adaptive weights more practical, we also need to take the float round-off error into consideration.

In this paper, the performance analysis for the subspace projection method with different subarray numbers and bit length is given. The paper includes 4 sections. In section I, the introduction is shown. In section 2, the derivation of the adaptive weights for mismatched optimum detective method is shown. The validation results is shown in section III. In section IV, the conclusion is given.

II. The Derivation of the Weights for the Proposed Subspace Projection Method

In this section, the details about the derivation of weights for the subarray level structure is introduced. The main idea is to make the adaptive array pattern same as the static array pattern when there is no interference and decrease the sidelobe power when there is interference. Therefore, we do not need to change the mode between the environment with interference and environment without interference. The main idea of the proposed method is to select three proper subspace and perform processing in the subspace separately in order to control the array pattern. There are three major steps for the proposed method.

First, we try to obtain the first subspace. The static antenna pattern is obtained by combining the subarray level output and the M dimension column vector q that all the elements are 1. Then, Ψ_1 is the subspace that is orthographic with Ψ_1 where $\Psi^H q = 0$. The performance of the static antenna pattern decreases when there is no interference. The main reason for this is because the Ψ_1 is parallel to $\Psi_1^H(R_{sub})_0 q$. The control for the adaptive array pattern is obtained if we drop this subspace. The last step is to get the weights. We assume Ω_1 is the subspace of the Ψ_1 which is orthotropic to $\Psi_1^H(R_{sub})_0 q$. This means Ω_1 meets the requirement that $\Omega^H \Psi^H (R_{sub})_0 q = 0$. Then, we only need to perform the adaptive processing in the $M-2$ dimension. The minimum interference and noise power for the subspace Ω_1 is obtained. Then we have

$$w_{M-2} = [R_{sub-ssp}(3:M, 3:M)]^{-1} R_{sub-ssp}(3:M, 1) \quad (1)$$

where $R_{sub-ssp}(3:M, 1)$ denotes the third column to the Mth column of the interference and noise covariance matrix at the subarray level. We have

$$R_{sub-ssp} = \begin{bmatrix} 1 & 0 \\ 0 & T_w^H \end{bmatrix} \begin{bmatrix} q^H \\ \Psi^H \end{bmatrix} R_{sub} \begin{bmatrix} q & \Psi \end{bmatrix} \begin{bmatrix} 1 & 0 \\ 0 & T_w \end{bmatrix} \quad (2)$$

where

$$T_w = \begin{bmatrix} \Psi^H (R_{sub})_0 q & \Omega_1 \end{bmatrix} \quad (3)$$

Then, the adaptive weights is obtained

$$w_{ssp} = T_{ssp} \begin{bmatrix} 1 & 0 & -w_{w-2} \end{bmatrix}^T \quad (4)$$

where we have

$$T_{ssp} = \begin{bmatrix} q & \Psi\Psi^H (R_{sub})_0 q & \Psi\Omega \end{bmatrix} \quad (5)$$

In the common case, we have

$$R_{sub-ssp}(3:M, 1) = \Omega^H \Psi^H R_{sub} q \quad (6)$$

where $R_{sub} = (R_{sub})_0$ when there is no interference. We have $w_{ssp} = q$ and $R_{sub-ssp}(3:M, 1) = 0$. This means the weights for the proposed method is 1 when there is no interference. Therefore, the adaptive array pattern is the same with the static array pattern when there is no interference.

III. Simulation Results

In this section, the simulation results for the proposed method is given. The results are shown for different number of subarrays in the phase array radar.

As shown in table 1, the number of antenna elements in the subarray stays the same and the subarray shape is rectangle with 4×4 antenna elements in each subarray. In addition, there is float round-off error for the peak sidelobe power and average sidelobe power. As for the mainlobe width, there is no foat round-off error. Moreover, the array pattern for the proposed method has good sidelobe and mainlobe performance.

IV. Conclusion

In this paper, we propose a novel method to adaptively suppression the interference at the subarray level. The proposed method has good performance at the interference suppression and helps to save a lot of hardware resources cost since it is performed at the subarray level. In addition, in order to make the implementation more accuracy, the float round-off error analysis is given for the proposed method.

Table 1. the performance of the proposed method

result	length	Matrix dimension						
		16	25	36	49	64	81	100
Peak sidelobe (dB)	64bit	-36.0253	-35.687	-37.1342	-35.5524	-36.6902	-37.3373	-37.8703
	32bit	-33.9535	-23.3673	-35.0077	-35.566	-32.8083	-31.9243	-24.7068
	error	-2.0718	-12.3197	-2.1265	0.0136	-3.8819	-5.413	-13.1635
Average sidelobe (dB)	64bit	-44.0793	-43.0647	-43.3373	-44.4748	-44.2779	-44.2397	-44.2274
	32bit	-42.884	-37.7143	-41.4365	-43.5016	-39.8112	-41.4226	-35.4754
	error	-1.1953	-5.3504	-1.9008	-0.9732	-4.4667	-2.8171	-8.752
Mainlobe width (°)	64bit	4.8	4.8	4.8	4.8	4.8	4.8	4.8
	32bit	4.8	4.8	4.8	4.8	4.8	4.8	4.8
Interference null depth (dB)	64bit	-141.2781	-144.2163	-139.1824	-125.469	-109.5691	-85.4486	-73.4237
	32bit	na	na	na	na	na	na	na

References

[1] H. Subbaram and K. Abend, "Interference suppression via orthogonal projections: a performance analysis," *IEEE Transactions on Antennas and Propagation*, vol. 41, no. 9, pp. 1187–1194, Sep 1993.

[2] I. P. Kirsteins and D. W. Tufts, "Adaptive detection using low rank approximation to a data matrix," *IEEE Transactions on Aerospace and Electronic Systems*, vol. 30, no. 1, pp. 55–67, Jan 1994.

[3] D. Wang and Z. Yang, "An novel spectrum sensing scheme combined with machine learning," in *2016 9th International Congress on Image and Signal Processing, BioMedical Engineering and Informatics (CISP-BMEI)*, Oct 2016, pp. 1293–1297.

[4] D. Wang, H. Hu, and Z. Yang, "Improved genetic algorithm for the configuration optimization of the sub arrays in phased array radar," in *2016 9th International Congress on Image and Signal Processing, BioMedical Engineering and Informatics (CISP-BMEI)*, Oct 2016, pp. 930–934.

[5] D. Wang and Y. Song, "A novel distributed global time synchronization protocol in cognitive radio ad hoc networks," in *2015 IEEE Global Communications Conference (GLOBECOM)*, Dec 2015, pp. 1–6.

[6] G. S. Bloom and S. W. Golomb, "Applications of numbered undirected graphs," *Proceedings of the IEEE*, vol. 65, no. 4, pp. 562–570, April 1977.

[7] D. Wang and Z. Yang, "An advanced scheme with decision tree for the improvement of spectrum sensing efficiency in dynamic network," in *2016 9th International Congress on Image and Signal Processing, BioMedical Engineering and Informatics (CISP-BMEI)*, Oct 2016, pp. 1288–1292.

[8] D. Wang, H. Hu, and Z. Yang, "The pareto rank algorithm for the division of the sub arrays for the phase array radar," in *2016 9th International Congress on Image and Signal Processing, BioMedical Engineering and Informatics (CISP-BMEI)*, Oct 2016, pp. 945–949.

[9] D. Wang, Z. Yang, and Y. Song, "A novel spectrum sensing scheduling scheme for pu and su signal differentiation in cr networks," in *2015 IEEE International Conference on Communications (ICC)*, June 2015, pp. 5697–5702.

[10] U. R. O. Nickel, "Subarray configurations for digital beamforming with low sidelobes and adaptive interference suppression," in *Proceedings International Radar Conference*, May 1995, pp. 714–719.

[11] Z. Yang, Y. Song, and D. Wang, "An optimal operating frequency selection scheme in spectrum handoff for cognitive radio networks," in *2015 International Conference on Computing, Networking and Communications (ICNC)*, Feb 2015, pp. 1066–1070.

[12] D. Wang, Y. Song, and Z. Yang, "A joint power adaptation and spectrum handoff scheme in mobile cognitive radio networks," in *2015 International Conference on Computing, Networking and Communications (ICNC)*, Feb 2015, pp. 1061–1065.

[13] L. Griffiths and C. Jim, "An alternative approach to linearly constrained adaptive beamforming," *IEEE Transactions on Antennas and Propagation*, vol. 30, no. 1, pp. 27–34, Jan 1982.

The Adaptive Interference Suppression Method Based on Householder At Subarray Level

1st Dan Wang
EECS
Wichita State University
Wichita, USA
dxwang@shockers.wichita.edu

2nd Guanglei Zhang
EEIS
Harbin Institute of Technology
Harbin, China
guangleizhang55@gmail.com

***Abstract*—As the phase array meets the complicated with different kind of interference, it is very important to improve the interference suppression performance of the phase array radar. In this paper, we propose a novel adaptive method for the interference suppression for phase array radar at the subarray level. In addition, the analysis for float round-off error is also given. The simulation results show the proposed method has good performance.**

***Index Terms*—cancellation, radar, adaptive, interference, wireless**

I. Introduction

As the electromagnetic environment becomes more and more complicated with different kind of interference, the performance of the radar system dramatically decreases due to the interference. There are existing work focused on amplitude weights and array structure design to improve the radar performance in interference suppression [1]. The main goal is to decrease the sidelobe power of the array pattern. However, the interference at the sidelobe still has impact on the expected signal extraction when the interference is very strong active interference [2]. In radar system, the signal from the oobject reflection is very small compared with the interference [3]. The interference power is much higher than the expected signal. Therefore, the interference at the sidelobe is higher than the expected signal power at the mainlobe [4]. The expected signal is impossible to be extracted from the received signal.

Therefore, we need to adapt the weights for the array to form a huge null depth at the interference direction [5]. In addition, the environment for the radar systems keep changing and the weights should be adapted according to the environment changes [6]. The adaptive process is needed to meet the requirement. However, the current array signal process has some limitations. One of the important limitation is that most of the array signal processing is based on the antenna element level [7]. Each antenna element has its own receiving path. This is a huge amount of hardware resource waste when the radar has a lot of antenna elements [8]. In order to reduce the cost, the signal process is performed at the subarray level. The adjacent antenna elements are formed into one subarray and each subarray has its own receiving path [9]. But the grating lobe gets into the mainlobe and brings dramatic decrease at the antenna performance. Therefore, we have to consider the subarray division and the adaptive interference suppression for the phase array radar
citeother-06.

In this paper, we propose a general sidelobe cancellation method at the subarray level to perform the interference suppression. The paper includes 4 sections. In section I, the introduction is shown. In section 2, the derivation of the adaptive weights for the proposed method is shown. The validation results is shown in section III. In section IV, the conclusion is given.

II. The Derivation of the Weights for the Proposed Adaptive Methods

In this section, the details about the derivation for the weights of the adaptive method based on the Householder transform is introduced. The main idea of the method is to use the strictly orthogonal method to obtain signal block matrix. The performance of the proposed method is the same as the direct subarray level weights structure using linear minimum variance method [10]. As for the narrow band forming device, the constraint is actually a inner product $\omega_{lcmv}^H a_{sub}(\theta_0, \phi_0) = 1$, ω_{lcmv} is the common adaptive weights vector and $a_{sub}(\theta_0, \phi_0)$ is the steering vector at the subarray level [11]. Then, the multiple linear constraint is obtained,

$$C_a^H w_{lcmv} = g \tag{1}$$

where matrix C_a is the linear constraint matrix. The vector g is the gain vector with the constant elements value. We assume the number of constraints is L. The dimension of C_a is $M \times L$ and g is a L dimension column vector. The matrix C_a has L linear constraint condition. We have

$$\begin{bmatrix} a_{sub}(\theta) & a_{sub}(\theta_1, \phi_1) \end{bmatrix}^H w_{lcmv} = \begin{bmatrix} 1 \\ 0 \end{bmatrix} \tag{2}$$

In order to improve the power of the expected signal at the direction (θ_0, ϕ_0) and suppress the known interference at the direction (θ_1, ϕ_1), the constraint is adopted at the narrow band beamforming device.

Then, we define $M \times (M - L)$ dimension matrix C. We have

$$C^H a_{sub}(\theta_0, \phi_0) = 0 \tag{3}$$

where C is the block matrix. C is adopted to block the expected signal from the received signal. Therefore, we only need to obtain the orthogonal matrix of the expected signal steering vector $a_{sub}(\theta_0, \phi_0)$. We assume

$$k = [1, 0, \cdots, 0]^T_{M-1} \tag{4}$$

$$\mu = \frac{\alpha_{sub}(\theta_0, \phi_0) - ||\alpha_{sub(\theta_0, \phi_0)}||_2 k}{||\alpha_{sub}(\theta_0, \phi_0) - ||\alpha_{sub}(\theta_0, \phi_0)||_2 k||_2} \tag{5}$$

Then, the transfer matrix based on Householder is obtained

$$H = I - 2\mu\mu^T \tag{6}$$

where the first column vector of the transfer matrix H has the beam direction $\alpha_{sub}(\theta_0, \phi_0)$. The remaining $M - 1$ column vectors is orthogonal to $\alpha_{sub}(\theta_0, \phi_0)$. Then we have

$$C = H \begin{bmatrix} 0 & \cdots & 0 & 0 \\ 1 & \cdots & 0 & 0 \\ \vdots & \vdots & \vdots & \vdots \\ 0 & \cdots & 1 & 0 \\ 0 & \cdots & 0 & 1 \end{bmatrix}_{M \times (M-1)} \tag{7}$$

Then, we have

$$\omega_\alpha = (C^H R_{sub} C)^{-1} C^H R_{sub} \omega_q \tag{8}$$

The output power signal and noise interference ratio is obtained

$$SINR = \frac{(\omega_q - C\omega_\alpha)^H \alpha_{sub}(\theta_0, \phi_0) P_s \alpha^H_{sub}(\theta_0, \phi_0)(\omega_q - C\omega_\alpha)}{(\omega_q - C\omega_\alpha)^H R^H_{sub}(\omega_q - C\omega_\alpha)} \tag{9}$$

III. Simulation Results

In this section, the performance of the proposed method is shown and the float round-off error is also given. First, the parameters for the simulation is given in table 1. The number of subarray is different. Here, 7 scenario is considered. The number of subarray changes from 16 to 100 and the number of antenna elements changes from 256 to 1000.

Table 1. The performance for the proposed method

parameter	length	Matrix dimension						
		16	25	36	49	64	81	100
Peak sidelobe (dB)	64bit	-14.7783	-13.1674	-13.5673	-13.5627	-13.6684	-13.7331	-13.5576
	32bit	-14.7919	-13.165	-13.5636	-13.564	-13.6784	-13.7232	-13.6732
	error	0.0136	-0.0024	-0.0037	0.0013	0.0100	-0.0099	0.1156
Average sidelobe (dB)	64bit	-19.0521	-25.7353	-22.9257	-23.698	-27.2509	-25.0409	-28.22
	32bit	-19.0624	-25.7175	-22.9204	-23.7022	-27.3272	-25.0062	-28.8462
	error	0.0103	-0.0187	-0.0053	0.0042	0.0763	-0.0347	0.6262
Mainobe width(°)	64bit	7.2	5.6	4.6	3.8	3.2	2.8	2.6
	32bit	7.2	5.6	4.6	3.8	3.2	2.8	2.6
Interference null depth (dB)	64bit	-142.1413	-121.4897	-129.279	-135.8315	-133.2694	-158.0997	-139.2786
	32bit	-118.9075	-84.6702	-82.0558	-88.8043	-72.0748	-76.6974	-60.527
	error	-23.2338	-36.8195	-47.2232	-47.0272	-61.1946	-81.4023	-78.7516

In this section, the simulation results for the proposed method is given. The results are shown for the performance of the array pattern at the azimuth, pitch and interference direction using the proposed method. As shown in table 1, the array pattern has good performance at the azimuth peak sidelobe power, the azimuth average sidelobe power, the azimuth mainlobe width, the pitch peak sidelobe power, the pitch average sidelobe power, the pitch mainlobe width and the null depth at the interference direction. In addition, the bit length has huge impact on the interference null depth. The performance changes when the number of antenna elements in the phase array radar increases.

IV. Conclusion

In this paper, we propose a novel method to adaptively suppression the interference at the subarray level. The details about the adaptive weights derivation for the proposed adaptive interference suppression method is shown in the paper. The proposed method has good array pattern performance at the azimuth direction sidelobe power and mainlobe width, pitch direction sidelobe power and mainlobe width and interference null depth. In addition, the float round-off error analysis is also shown for the proposed method. The bit length has huge impact on the interference null depth.

References

[1] H. Subbaram and K. Abend, "Interference suppression via orthogonal projections: a performance analysis," *IEEE Transactions on Antennas and Propagation*, vol. 41, no. 9, pp. 1187–1194, Sep 1993.

[2] D. Wang and Z. Yang, "An novel spectrum sensing scheme combined with machine learning," in *2016 9th International Congress on Image and Signal Processing, BioMedical Engineering and Informatics (CISP-BMEI)*, Oct 2016, pp. 1293–1297.

[3] D. Wang, H. Hu, and Z. Yang, "Improved genetic algorithm for the configuration optimization of the sub arrays in phased array radar," in *2016 9th International Congress on Image and Signal Processing, BioMedical Engineering and Informatics (CISP-BMEI)*, Oct 2016, pp. 930–934.

[4] D. Wang, Y. Song, and Z. Yang, "A joint power adaptation and spectrum handoff scheme in mobile cognitive radio networks," in *2015 International Conference on Computing, Networking and Communications (ICNC)*, Feb 2015, pp. 1061–1065.

[5] I. P. Kirsteins and D. W. Tufts, "Adaptive detection using low rank approximation to a data matrix," *IEEE Transactions on Aerospace and Electronic Systems*, vol. 30, no. 1, pp. 55–67, Jan 1994.

[6] U. R. O. Nickel, "Subarray configurations for digital beamforming with low sidelobes and adaptive interference suppression," in *Proceedings International Radar Conference*, May 1995, pp. 714–719.

[7] D. Wang and Z. Yang, "An advanced scheme with decision tree for the improvement of spectrum sensing efficiency in dynamic network," in *2016 9th International Congress on Image and Signal Processing, BioMedical Engineering and Informatics (CISP-BMEI)*, Oct 2016, pp. 1288–1292.

[8] W. Dan, H. Hang, and Q. Xin, "Space-time adaptive processing method at subarray level for broadband jammer suppression," in *2011 IEEE International Conference on Microwave Technology Computational Electromagnetics*, May 2011, pp. 281–284.

[9] Y. Zhitao, H. Hang, W. Dan, and Q. Weicheng, "Advanced optimization for subarray structure in electronic warfare environment," in *2013 IEEE INTERNATIONAL CONFERENCE ON MICROWAVE TECHNOLOGY COMPUTATIONAL ELECTROMAGNETICS*, Aug 2013, pp. 30–34.

[10] D. Wang and Y. Song, "A novel distributed global time synchronization protocol in cognitive radio ad hoc networks," in *2015 IEEE Global Communications Conference (GLOBECOM)*, Dec 2015, pp. 1–6.

[11] D. Wang, Z. Yang, and Y. Song, "A novel spectrum sensing scheduling scheme for pu and su signal differentiation in cr networks," in *2015 IEEE International Conference on Communications (ICC)*, June 2015, pp. 5697–5702.

Massively Parallel Frequency Domain Electromagnetic Simulation Codes

William L. Langston, Joseph Kotulski, Rebecca Coats, Roy Jorgenson, S. Adam Blake, Salvatore Campione, Aaron Pung, and Brian Zinser
Department of Electromagnetic Theory
Sandia National Laboratories
Albuquerque, USA
{wllangs, jdkotul, rscoats, rejorge, sablake, sncampi, ajpung, bzinser}@sandia.gov

***Abstract*—This paper provides an overview of the electromagnetic frequency domain simulation capabilities of the Electromagnetic Theory department at Sandia National Laboratories via a description of two of its codes. EIGER is a Method of Moments code for electromagnetic simulations, but it only runs on traditional CPUs, not on new architectures. Gemma is in development to replace EIGER and will run on many architectures, including CPUs, GPUs, and MICs, by leveraging the Kokkos library.**

Keywords—electromagnetics, GPU, Kokkos, MIC, moment method, performance portability.

I. Introduction

The Electromagnetic (EM) Theory department at Sandia National Laboratories (SNL) requires several codes to support its analysists. The ideal code returns results quickly, handles a wide variety of problems across an extreme band of frequencies, and produces high accuracy results. The Boundary Element Method (BEM) version of the Method of Moments (MoM) for solving integral equations satisfies these criteria by reducing the dimensionality of the problem to be solved while producing high accuracy results on the boundary, which yeilds accurate results elsewhere with post processing. Next generation platforms (NGPs) promise the ability to reduce the turnaround time without degrading the accuracy. As such, the present production code EIGER is being rewritten into a new code Gemma to leverage the computational efficiency of the NGPs [1]. The rewrite will include the development of new algorithms that leverage the NGPs and better analytic models.

II. EIGER

EIGER (Electromagnetic Interactions GenERalized) is a massively parallel EM simulation code that uses MoM to solve electrodynamic and electrostatic problems. EIGER was originally written in FORTRAN 90 and underwent a partial rewrite in the early 2000's to leverage MPI for intra- and internode parallelism.

EIGER supports a wide variety of problems, including scattering, coupling, layered media, and 1D and 2D periodic problems [2]. Excitations can be from plane wave or voltage sources. Geometries can be made up of wires and/or bodies, which can be perfect electrical conductors (PECs) or dielectrics, following the PMCHWT formulation for dielectrics [3-6]. Specific examples where these features are used include modeling metamaterials and antennas as well as aircraft bodies [7].

EIGER utilizes RWG basis functions in filling a dense, complex-valued matrix for the electric field integral equation (EFIE), magnetic field integral equation (MFIE), or combined field integral equation (CFIE) where the CFIE avoids the internal resonance problems of the EFIE and MFIE. Singular and near-singular integrals are handled by a radial-angular transformation [8]. EIGER then solves the matrix via LU factorization, GMRES, or conjugate gradient. Simulation geometry is typically meshed using at least 10 elements per wavelength. Each element contributes to a dense, complex-value matrix. The storage requirement for this matrix is the limiting favtor for simulating high frequencies.

III. Gemma

Gemma is a C++ rewrite of EIGER for NGPs. Using the Kokkos library for performance portability, it can be compiled for CPU, GPU, or MIC by changing a single flag [9]. Kokkos is a lightweight wrapper around OpenMP, CUDA, and other back-ends that implement thread level parallelism. It also provides a multidimensional array that is indexed layout left (column major) for GPUs or layout right (row major) for CPUs to ensure proper coalesced memory access and caching, respectively. Algorithms written with Kokkos can take advantage of multiple levels of parallelism and memory as well as utilize several different types of execution resources at the same time. While Kokkos manages parallel threads on a single node, MPI will be used for internode parallelism.

Currently, Gemma solves the dense, complex-valued matrix equation using LU factorization or an iterative solver, such as GMRES, from Trilinos's Belos library [10]. For the iterative solve, Gemma uses a Sparse Approximate Inverse (SpAI) preconditioner [11]. The sparse approximation is constructed using an octree based on distance between unknowns; the matrix entries decay exponentially with distance. The relationships between octree leaf sizes, the frequency, and internal resonance have not been studied extensively. Calculating the inverse of the sparse approximation yields a suitable preconditioner for the linear system.

Sandia National Laboratories is a multimission laboratory managed and operated by National Technology and Engineering Solutions of Sandia, LLC., a wholly owned subsidiary of Honeywell International, Inc., for the U.S. Department of Energy's National Nuclear Security Administration under contract DE-NA-0003525.

Gemma can presently perform scattering calculations from an incident plane wave. An example is discussed below. Developing Gemma will continue by first implementing the MFIE, CFIE, dielectrics, and wire and slot subcell models needed for electromagnetic coupling problems. Broadly, Gemma will include all the features in EIGER, though the algorithms will be modified where performance gains can be obtained for the new architectures. In addition, new features will be developed for Gemma. These include interfacing with a circuit solver Xyce [12] and advanced solver technologies such as hybrid methods, fast multipole methods, and adaptive cross approximation.

IV. Validation

The Electromagnetic Code Consortium (EMCC) provides a set of measurement data for specific geometries and incident plane waves for code validation [13]. The EMCC problems are run with EIGER, Gemma, and FEKO's MoM solver, FEKO being used for comparison when agreement with EMCC data is poor. Being a partial reimplementation of EIGER, EIGER and Gemma produce indistinguishable results, up to a prescribed level of numerical accuracy.

As an example, Fig. 1 shows the measured and calculated radar cross section (RCS) for a cone-sphere with the mesh pictured at the center of the figure. For all three codes, the geometry was meshed with 10 elements per wavelength; FEKO was allowed to refine the mesh as it deemed necessary while EIGER and Gemma used a mesh produced by the CUBIT meshing software and have no adaptive refinement capabilities [14]. Further refining the mesh did not change the character of the results. Fig. 1 shows EIGER and Gemma obtaining excellent agreement with FEKO and good agreement with experiment.

V. Summary

While EIGER meets the current needs of the EM theory department at SNL, it cannot run efficiently on MICs and it cannot run on GPUs. Gemma meets future needs by utilizing the Kokkos library to run well on all desired high-performance computing (HPC) architectures. By using Kokkos, Gemma will be low maintenance. First, it will be written once for all platforms. Second, Kokkos, not Gemma, will implement any new architectures as a new backend that can be selected at compile time. In short, Gemma will provide analysts with high accuracy results quickly on a variety of HPC architectures for a minimal amount of programming effort.

Acknowledgment

We thank Rafael Schleder for his work projecting the RCS results on to a polar coordinate system.

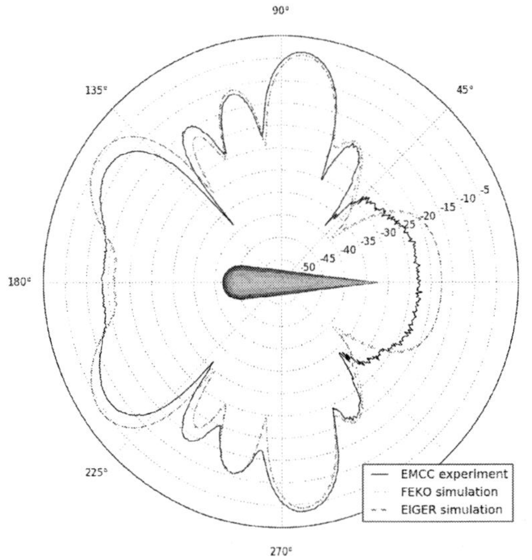

Fig. 1. Monostatic RCS (dB per square meter) of a cone-sphere from multiple angles due to an incident plane wave of 869 MHz. Being indistinguishable in this plot, EIGER and Gemma are both represented by the dashed red line.

References

[1] D. R. Wilton, W. A. Johnson, R. Jorgenson, R. Sharpe, and J. Rockway, "EIGER: A new generation of computational electromagnetics tools," ElectroSft: Software for EE Analysis and Design, Miniato, Italy, pp. 28-30, May 1996.

[2] C. Lertsirimit, D. R. Jackson, and D. R. Wilton, "An efficient hybrid method for calculating the EMC coupling to a device on a printed circuit board inside a cavity by a wire penetrating an aperture," Electromagnetics, vol. 25, iss. 7-8, 2005.

[3] J. Poggio and E. K. Miller, "Integral equation solutions of three-dimensional scattering problems," in R. Mittra (ed.), Computer Techniques for Electromagnetics, Oxford, UK, Pergamon Press, 1973.

[4] Y. Chang, R. F. Harrington, "A surface formulation for characteristic modes of material bodies", *IEEE Trans. Antennas Propag.*, vol. 25, no. 6, pp. 789-795, Nov. 1977.

[5] T.-K. Wu, L. L. Tsai, "Scattering from arbitrarily-shaped lossy dielectric bodies of revolution", *Radio Sci.*, vol. 12, no. 5, pp. 709-718, Sep./Oct. 1977.

[6] J. R. Mautz and R. F. Harrington, "Electromagnetic Scattering from a Homogeneous Material Body of Revolution," Archiv fur Elektronik und Ubertragungstechnik, vol. 33, pp. 71-80, 1979.

[7] L. I. Basilio, W. L. Langston, L. K. Warne, W. A. Johnson, and M. B. Sinclair, "Full-wave simulation of a three-dimensional metamaterial prism," Microw. Opt. Technol. Lett., vol. 57, pp. 537–540, March 2015.

[8] M. A. Khayat, D. R. Wilton, and P. W. Fink, "An improved transformation and optimized sampling scheme for the numerical evaluation of singular and near-singular potentials," IEEE Antennas Wireless Propag. Lett., vol. 7, pp. 377–380, 2008.

[9] H. Edwards, C. Trott, and D. Sunderland, "Kokkos: Enabling manycore performance portability through polymorphic memory access patterns," J. Parallel Distrib. Comput., vol. 74, no. 12, pp. 3202-3216, 2014.

[10] E. Bavier, M. Hoemmen, S. Rajamanickam, and H. Thornquist, "Amesos2 and Belos: Direct and iterative solvers for large sparse systems," Scientific Programming, vol. 20, iss. 3, 2012.

[11] M. Bettencourt, B. Zinser, R. Jorgenson, and J. Kotulski, "Performance portable sparse approximate inverse preconditioner for EFIE equations," CEM, 2017, in press.

[12] E. Keiter, et al., "Xyce parallel electronic simulator users' guide, version 6.7," Albuquerque, NM: Sandia National Laboratories, 2017.

[13] A. Woo, H. Wang, M. Schuh, and M. Sanders, "Benchmark radar targets for the validation of computational electromagnetics programs," IEEE Antennas and Propag. Mag., vol. 35, no. 1, pp. 84-89, February 1993.

[14] "CUBIT Geometry and Mesh Generation Toolkit 15.3 User Documentation", Sandia report SAND2017-6895, 2017.

The Parallel Implementation and Accuracy of Matrix Compression in the Method of Moments code EIGER

Joseph D. Kotulski
Electromagnetic Theory
Sandia National Laboratories
Albuquerque, NM USA
jdkotul@sandia.gov

***Abstract*—This paper describes the implementation of the adaptive cross approximation(ACA) in the method of moments code EIGER. This purely algebraic method provides a mechanism to reduce memory usage and overall computation time. In addition, this work has been targeted for massively parallel platforms to extend the viable frequency range for electromagnetic compatibility and interference problems.**

Keywords—electromagnetic boundary element formulation, method of moments, fast integral equation methods, matrix compression

I. INTRODUCTION

The integral equations solved by the Method of Moments (MOM) are an invaluable tool to analyze and then predict the response of systems to electromagnetic environments[1]. Since there is a memory limitation prohibiting the storage of the full matrix for problems large with respect to frequency, alternative techniques have been identified to circumvent this restriction. These alternative techniques are based on methods that use the reduction of the degrees of freedom for the far zone interactions to decrease the storage requirement. The method to be examined is matrix compression using the adaptive cross approximation(ACA)[2], implemented in EIGER[3].

II. FORMULATION

A. Approximation to the Matrix Equation

The electric and magnetic field integral equations are cast using the standard Stratton-Chu formulation. They are combined to avoid the interior resonance problem associated with closed surfaces using a coupling parameter of 0.5. Once the equations are defined, the Rao-Wilton-Glisson expansions are used for the currents on the surface of the scatterer. Following the application of Galerkin's method a system of linear equations is formed.

$$\sum_{n=1}^{N} Z_{mn} I_n = V_m \qquad m = 1,2,\ldots,N \qquad , \qquad (1)$$

where N is the number of unknowns. The ACA method and other "compression" techniques have theoretical basis from the work of Bucci and Franceschetti[4]. Simply stated - separated clusters of unknowns (on elements) have a reduced order to adequately describe their interactions. From the moment method point of view a cluster of elements containing m test elements interacting with a cluster of n source elements can be described by a matrix that has less then $m \; x \; n$ contributions. With this thought in mind the matrix equation can be written as:

$$Z_{nxn} I_n = V_m \Rightarrow (Z_{near} + Z_{far}) I = V \qquad . \qquad (2)$$

Where

$$Z_{near} = \sum_{j=1}^{MOM\_blocks} Z_j^{mom} \text{ and } Z_{far} = \sum_{i=1}^{COM\_blocks} \widetilde{Z}_i^{com} \qquad . \qquad (3)$$

The *MOM* blocks are full matrix blocks representing the interaction between a group of testing and source functions which are computed in the standard way. The *COM*(compressed) blocks represent the interaction between a group of testing functions and source functions approximated via the ACA. The steps include the identification of the interaction blocks and then the computation of the blocks. The blocks are identified by encapsulating the entire geometry into a group (identified as a box) which is then sub-divided by using an oct-tree (Figure 1). The box at the lowest level of the oct-tree should be large enough allow compression of the block (box to box) interaction.

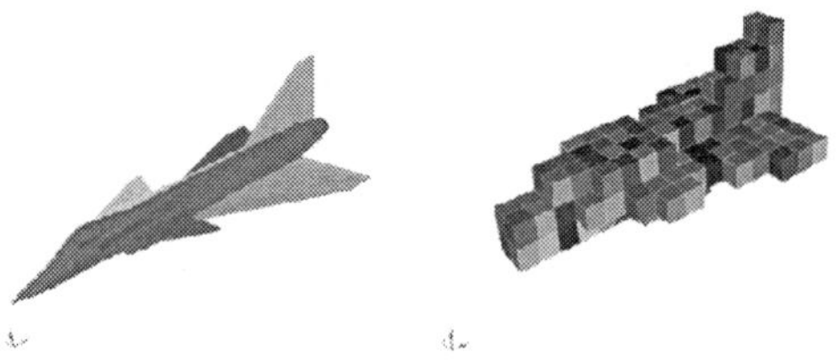

Figure 1. An example of a meshed object and corresponding oct-tree boxes used for the compression algorithm.

Sandia National Laboratories is a multimission laboratory managed and operated by National Technology and Engineering Solutions of Sandia, LLC., a wholly owned subsidiary of Honeywell International, Inc., for the U.S. Department of Energy's National Nuclear Security Administration under contract DE-NA-0003525.

Each compressed block is described as

$$\widetilde{Z}_i^{m\times n} = U_i^{m\times r} V_i^{r\times n} = \sum_{j=1}^{r} u_j^{m\times 1} v_j^{1\times n} \quad . \tag{4}$$

The algorithm is described in detail by Zhao et. al[2]. The key feature consists of building a low-rank matrix in an iterative fashion without building the entire matrix block. At each iteration, the Frobenius norm of the new approximation is compared to the calculated value of the approximate matrix multiplied by an error criterion.

$$\|u_k\| \cdot \|v_k\| \leq \varepsilon \left\| \widetilde{Z}^{(k)} \right\| \tag{5}$$

Where ε is the compression tolerance used in the algorithm. When this criterion is met the for the k'th iteration the process stops, a compressed form of the matrix is obtained, and the memory storage is now $(m+n) \times r$ elements instead of $m \times n$.

The matrix fill algorithm for the blocks (*MOM* and *COM*) has been implemented for use on parallel computing platforms. To efficiently perform this operation a load-balancing scheme has been used in the distribution of the different blocks to multiple processors based on the size of the different blocks. It is straightforward to load-balance the MOM blocks due to the knowledge of the sizes of the blocks. The distribution of the *COM* blocks are based on an estimate of their size from the work of Bucci and Franceschetti[4].

Now with the matrix blocks computed equation 1 can be solved using an iterative solver. Two such solvers have been implemented and tested – generalized minimum residual method(GMRES) and the transpose free quasi-minimal residual method (TFQMR). The results shown here are for the GMRES algorithm with restart[5].

B. *Parallel Considerations*

Two different algorithms were used to distribute the matrix fill for both *MOM* and *COM* blocks to the different processors. First, a simplified technique was employed that only used the number of blocks without regard to the size of work in each block. The rule for this algorithm was that no processor would have no more, or less, than one block with respect to any of the other processors. This implementation resulted in a highly imbalanced time for the matrix fill on the different processors. To improve this the computational workload in each block was calculated for the *MOM* blocks and estimated for the *COM* blocks using [4]. This resulted in a very balanced fill for the matrix blocks.

III. RESULTS

The algorithm was applied to the VFY-218 with a grid density that would be used for up to 1.2 GHz (~940,000 unknowns). This problem was also solved using LU decomposition for comparison. The job statistics are shown in Table 1 and are for a compression tolerance (ε) of 1.5e-03 and a solver tolerance of 1.e-06 using the GMRES solver. The incident plane wave electric field is polarized in the phi direction and is incident on the nose of the aircraft.

Table 1.Job Statistics for the Vfy-218 (934,128 unknowns).

Solution Method	Memory Used (GB)	Solution Time(hours)	Number of Processors
Direct Solve(LU)	13962	4.6	5040
ACA (GMRES)	436	13.5	80

The comparison of the bistatic RCS between the direct solve and using ACA is shown in Figure 2.

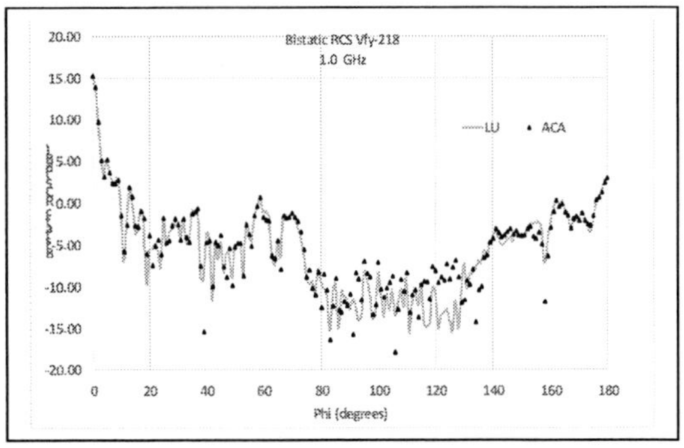

Figure 2. Comparison of bistatic RCS for the VFY-218 at 1GHz for the LU and ACA solution.

IV. CONCLUSIONS

This paper demonstrates the utility of the method of moments when coupled with the ACA and an iterative solver. Further work is continuing to improve the solution accuracy, developing methods of evaluating the accuracy, and solver efficiency.

REFERENCES

[1] J. Poggio and E. K. Miller, "Integral equation solutions of three-dimensional scattering problems," in R. Mittra (ed.), Computer Techniques for Electromagnetics, Oxford, UK, Pergamon Press, 1973.

[2] K. Zhao, M. N. Vouvakis, J.-F. Lee, "The adaptive cross approximation for accelarated method of moments compiuttation of EMC problem," IEEE Trans. Electromagnetic Compat., vol 47, pp. 763-773,Nov. 2005.

[3] D. R. Wilton, W. A. Johnson, R. Jorgenson, R. Sharpe, J. Rockway, "EIGER: a new generation of computational electromagnetics tools," ElectroSft: Software for EE Analysis and Design, Miniato, Italy, pp. 28-30, May 1996.

[4] O. Bucci and Giorgio Franceschetti, "On the degrees of freedom of scattered fields," IEEE Trans,. Antennas and Prop., vol 30, pp. 918-926, July 1989.

[5] Y. Saad, Iterative Methods for Sparse Linear Systems, Sec. Ed., SIAM, 2003, pp. 164-184.

HIPERCONE FDTD: Vectorized Highly Scalable Full-Wave Electromagnetic Solver

Sergei Belousov
Kintech Lab Ltd.
Moscow, Russia
belousov@kintechlab.com

Sergey Khilkov
HiPerCone Ltd.
Moscow, Russia
khilkov@hipercone.com

Vadim Levchenko
Keldysh Institute of Applied Mathematics
Moscow, Russia
lev@keldysh.ru

Anastasia Perepelkina
Keldysh Institute of Applied Mathematics
Moscow, Russia
mogmi@narod.ru

Ilya Valuev
HiPerCone Ltd.
Moscow, Russia
valuev@hipercone.com

***Abstract*—In this paper we introduce a novel full-wave electromagnetic solver based on the Finite-Difference Time Domain method, which is extremely efficient in terms of CPU performance and scalability. These features of the HIPERCONE solver are attained by the use of asynchronous mesh updates, localization of data in the fast memory, and parallelism at all levels including vectorization. The algorithms in the solver are used to achieve the performance up to 1–2 orders of magnitude higher than the traditional approaches. Unlike the traditional memory-bound electromagnetic solvers, the maximal performance rate of HIPERCONE FDTD in terms of mesh cell updates per second is reached for large meshes occupying or even exceeding the total available CPU RAM. Therefore, the HIPERCONE solver is especially advantageous in solving large-scale problems. In this work we describe the algorithmic background of the simulation method and give an example of a typical large application which benefits from the solver's performance.**

***Index Terms*—code optimization, FDTD, memory efficiency, parallelism, scalability, vectoriztion.**

I. Introduction

Full-wave simulations of electromagnetic devices often require large meshes and are computationally expensive. Thus, for testing device designs a solver performance becomes the key feature. For example, a typical full-wave modeling of OLED in 3D domain by the Finite-Difference Time-Domain (FDTD) method requires about 80 GB of mesh data and 10^{11} Yee cell updates in total [1].

According to the roofline model [2] the performance is limited either by the peak flop rate of the computer (compute-bound) or by the memory bandwidth (memory-bound). In most cases the algorithms for full-wave electromagnetic simulations, including the finite difference and finite element methods both for the time and frequency domains, are memory bound. In order to get faster code we have to increase the flop/byte ratio of our algorithm. Another problem is achieving scalability of the computation with the increase of the problem size. This requires efficient data transfers between computing units (parallel scalability) and efficient use of the computer memory hierarchy (memory scalability). We have developed an approach to constructing an algorithm for the conventional FDTD scheme which is both memory efficient, and highly scalable on all levels of computer parallelism including vectorization, multi-core and multi node levels.

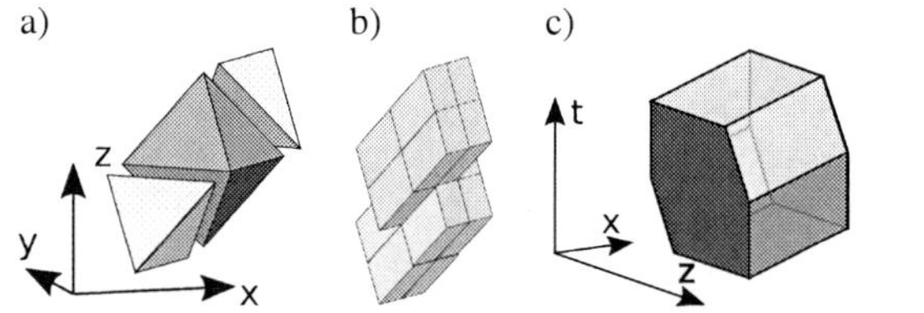

Fig. 1. (a) Candy xyz projection decomposed into octahedron and two tetrahedrons; (b) candies xyz projections for H and E fields; (c) candy xzt projection.

II. Technology Background

In the HIPERCONE FDTD code the updates of field values are performed according to the Maxwell equations in a Yee cell with a regular stencil of 2nd or 4th order in space and 2nd order in time. This determines the dependency graph in 4D domain. Each individual field update (an event in our model 4D space-time) may be attributed to some 4D hyperconic domain of influence or dependence. Performing hypercone-based computation and keeping track of the 4D domains compact in computer memory allows to construct a class of asynchronous algorithms, which are called Locally Recursive non-Locally Asynchronous (LRnLA) algorithms [3]. Among the many possibilities, each type of 4D decomposition is more or less efficient depending on the computer architecture and the scheme stencil. Different decompositions (ConeFold, DiamondTorre) were successfully applied earlier to electromagnetic and acoustic FDTD simulations [4], [5] for multi-CPU and multi-GPU architectures.

Recently, a new LRnLA algorithm DiamondCandy was proposed [6]. It provides superior data access locality in 3D space and is suitable for building vectorized updates with tunable vector size. We use local vectorization approach where the components of the CPU or GPU vector correspond to positions adjacent in space. This requires some extra vector transformations in the updates, however increases the re-use of data and keeps the vector conformal to local material properties.

We implement the LRnLA algorithm DiamondCandy into universal multi-purpose electromagnetic solver. The solver functionality is based on the parallel EMTL library [7]. The

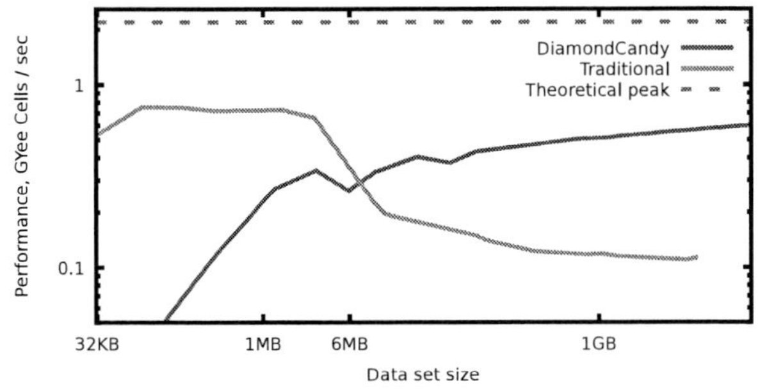

Fig. 2. Performance test results for 4th order double-precision electromagnetic FDTD on Intel Core i5-6400 (4 cores with AVX2, 3.3GHz frequency). Peak performance is the maximum performance of the processor mesured in flops divided by the number of operations for one Yee cell update.

library was designed for many-core CPUs and clusters and implements most of the state of the art FDTD techniques including dispersive media, subpixel smoothing, periodic and PML boundaries, near to far field transformation. The new HIPERCONE solver overperforms the EMTL library up to a factor of 15 for large meshes and has no relevant limitations on problem size and geometry.

The efficiency of the new DiamondCandy algorithm for the FDTD simulation in HIPERCONE has been tested. Here we present the results for the desktop computer with Intel Core i5-6400 (Fig. 2). We compare the traditional algorithm (not LRnLA, data synchronization takes place on each time step for the whole mesh) with the new DiamondCandy. As usual, the performance of traditional algorithm drops when the data size exceeds L3 cache capacity (6MB). The use of DiamondCandy provides greater performance for large problem sizes, and only large size performance is important for the relevant practical purposes. Since both vectorization and many-core parallelism are used, the performance of up to 30% from peak is achieved. It is 6 times greater than the results of the traditional algorithm.

III. Large Problem Example

As a characteristic test case for the developed FDTD code, we consider modeling of optical characteristics of an organic light emitting diode (OLED) with the corrugated cathode. Corrugation helps extract the emission out of the device, which is largely coupled to the surface plasmon polariton (SPPs) modes otherwise [8]. This problem is computationally challenging due to the great attenuation length of the SPPs (greater than 10 microns) and the large field gradients at the metallic interface, necessitating a very fine mesh resolution. In the test case, we consider a 20 by 20 microns fragment of the OLED with the thickness of 1 micron excluding the substrate. The mesh step is 5 nm, which corresponds to the computational volume size of $3.2 \cdot 10^9$ Yee cells. We compute the angular distribution of the outgoing radiation intensity for the vertically oriented emitters in the emitting layer and compare the results for the flat and corrugated cathode. In

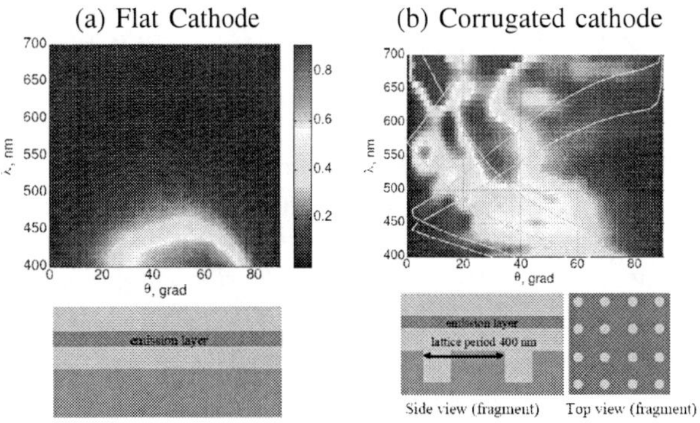

Fig. 3. Angular distribution of radiation from an OLED (see text), computed with the FDTD code, for (a) the flat, unstructured metallic cathode; (b) the corrugated cathode. The schematic of the OLED layers in the vicinity of the cathode is shown for both cases. Note the green curves corresponding the analytically computed dispersion of the surface plasmons on the 2D periodic corrugation.

Fig. 3 (b), we observe the distinctive signature of the surface plasmon scattering: intensity peaks corresponding to the Bragg scattering of the surface plasmons by the 2D periodic lattice of corrugations. In contrast, in Fig. 3 (a), no such peaks are observed due to the coupling of the emission to the nonradiative surface plasmon modes.

IV. Conclusion

We present a new multipurpose FDTD solver HIPERCONE-FDTD. It is efficient since it uses the new LRnLA algorithm DiamondCandy which optimizes the data locality and parallel scalability for the FDTD cross stencil, and uses all available methods of parallelism, including vectorization.

References

[1] A. Zakirov, S. Belousov, I. Valuev, V. Levchenko, A. Perepelkina, and Y. Zempo, "Using memory-efficient algorithm for large-scale time-domain modeling of surface plasmon polaritons propagation in organic light emitting diodes," *Journal of Physics: Conference Series*, vol. 905, no. 1, p. 012030, 2017. [Online]. Available: http://stacks.iop.org/1742-6596/905/i=1/a=012030

[2] S. Williams, A. Waterman, and D. Patterson, "Roofline: an insightful visual performance model for multicore architectures," *Communications of the ACM*, vol. 52, no. 4, pp. 65–76, 2009.

[3] V. D. Levchenko, "Asynchronous parallel algorithms as a way to archive effective ness of computations (in Russian)," *J. of Inf. Tech. and Comp. Systems*, no. 1, p. 68, 2005.

[4] V. Levchenko, A. Perepelkina, and A. Zakirov, "DiamondTorre algorithm for high-performance wave modeling," *Computation*, vol. 4, no. 3, p. 29, 2016.

[5] A. Zakirov, V. Levchenko, A. Perepelkina, and Y. Zempo, "High performance FDTD algorithm for GPGPU supercomputers," in *Journal of Physics: Conference Series*, vol. 759, no. 1. IOP Publishing, 2016, p. 012100.

[6] A. Perepelkina and V. Levchenko, "The DiamondCandy algorithm for maximum performance vectorized cross-stencil computation," *to be published.*

[7] A. Deinega, S. Belousov, and I. Valuev, "Transfer-matrix approach for finite-difference time-domain simulation of periodic structures," *Phys. Rev. E*, vol. 88, p. 053305, Nov 2013. [Online]. Available: https://link.aps.org/doi/10.1103/PhysRevE.88.053305

[8] S. Belousov, M. Bogdanova, and A. Teslyuk, "Outcoupling efficiency of OLEDs with 2D periodical corrugation at the cathode," *Journal of Physics D: Applied Physics*, vol. 49, no. 8, p. 085102, 2016. [Online]. Available: http://stacks.iop.org/0022-3727/49/i=8/a=085102

Dual Resonance Proximity Coupled Patch Antenna

Bahadır KILIÇ and Taha İMECİ
Department of Electrical Engineering
International University of Sarajevo
Sarajevo, Bosnia and Herzegovina
simeci@ius.edu.ba

Mustafa İMECİ
Department of Electrical and Electronics Engineering
Ankara Yildirim Beyazit University, Ankara, Turkey

Oğuzhan Salih GÜNGÖR
Department of Electrical and Electronics Engineering
Selcuk University, Konya, Turkey

Negar Majidi
Department of Electrical and Electronics Engineering
Ozyegin University, Istanbul, Turkey

Mohammad Rahim Sobhani
Department of Electrical and Computer Engineering
University of Alberta, Edmonton, Canada

***Abstract*—In this paper there are four different shape of proximity patch antennas (straight, trimmed, trapezoid and ribbon). The minimum input match achieved with the straight proximity patch antenna as -39.68 dB. The maximum gain is achieved with the ribbon proximity patch antenna as 12.1 dB. Simulation and measurement results are presented. There is a perfect match with simulated and measured gain. The antenna is first demonstrated example of working with four different geometries, having satisfactory gain and input match.**

Keywords*—*bandwidth, gain, patch antenna, proximity, return loss, ribbon, trapezoid.

I. Introduction

The four antennas that will be explained in this article have a midband between 3,15 and 3,56 GHz and bandwidth of 0.19 and 0.23 GHz, which are typically used in various applications like military, satellite communications or wireless. This work explains the design and test of a proximity coupled patch antennas constructed from relatively high quality dielectric material. Two dielectric substrates are used such that the feed line is between the two substrates and the radiating patch is on top of the other substrate [1]. The purpose of this work is to make a comparative study on the technique that helps to overcome the bandwidth constraint of microstrip patch antennas and to propose the better technique by taking different consideration such as the antenna gain, bandwidth and related issues [2]. Basic ideas about microstrip patch antenna, its working principle and important parameters have been discussed. The paper explained the analysis and designs a typical patch antenna that helps describing its narrow bandwidth problem as well. A paper shows improving the bandwidth of proximity coupled stacked microstrip patch antennas [3]. The results obtained clearly indicate the main factors that affect the bandwidth of a particular microstrip antenna are thickness of the dielectric substrate, the size of the metallic patch, the dielectric constant of the dielectric substrate, the feed type to be used (as seen in the non-contacting feed techniques) and the coupling level to some extent [4]. Aperture coupling is also used in [5] for this purpose. Most efficient part of the gain enhancement is maintained by changing the geometries of the slots [5].

II. Design Details

The work is done by using a high frequency electromagnetic simulator called Sonnet Suites [6]. In order to meet the required design specifications, important parameters need to be optimized. Better results could be obtained after several iteration steps. All antennas are placed on 290 x 290 mm box. The material used for the substrates is Rogers RT5880 (ε_r = 2.2). The thickness of the dielectric layers is used as 0.8 mm. Feeding line dimensions are 145.9 x 2.6 mm. Edge feeding is used.

A. The Straight Proximity Patch Antenna

The dimension of antenna is 27 x 39 mm. The minimum return loss was achieved with this antenna among all four antennas. The minimum return loss achieved is -39,68 dB and the maximum gain of 8.05 dB is achieved at 3.56 GHz.

B. The Trimmed Proximity Patch Antenna

The trimmed antenna is a different form of the straight proximity patch antenna. Short sides are angled as 3° with both ways. 41.52 x 27.03 mm and 1,315 mm sliding are dimensions of this antenna. The minimum return loss achieved is -29,07 dB and the maximum gain of 8.25 dB is achieved at 3.52 GHz.

C. The Trapezoid Proximity Patch Antenna

The height of the antenna is 27 mm. Opposite sides of the antenna measures are 45 x 30 mm. The shape of the antenna is isosceles trapezoid. Isosceles zones both have 15° contraction. The minimum return loss achieved is -14.63 dB and the maximum gain of 7.98 dB is achieved at 3.448 GHz.

D. The Ribbon Proximity Patch Antenna

The maximum gain was achieved with this antenna among all four antennas. The maximum gain is 12,10 dB at 10.2 GHz. The minimum return loss achieved is -17.55 dB at 3.15 GHz. The height of the antenna is 27 mm and opposite edges of the antenna measures are 40 x 40 mm.

III. Evaluation of Design Performance

The most important result about the ribbon proximity patch antenna is dual resonance. The ribbon proximity patch antenna has dual resonance with high gain. As it is seen in the literature, this kind of antenna has better solutions in communication. Return loss of the ribbon antenna at 3.15 GHz is 17.55 dB and at 10.2 GHz is 14.96 dB. The ribbon proximity coupled patch antenna has a gain of 7.21 dB at 3.15 GHz at $\theta = 0^{\circ}$ and it has also a gain of 12.10 dB at 10.2 GHz with $\theta = 0^{\circ}$.

IV. Fabrication

The straight antenna was fabricated due to its easiest structure among others. Top view is in Fig. 1. 3D view of straight antenna is in Fig. 3. Fig. 2 shows the input match and Fig. 4 shows the radiation pattern comparison of the simulated and measured antenna. There is only a small frequency shift between the simulated and measured input match. Furthermore, the gain has perfect match at $\Theta=0^{\circ}$.

Fig. 1. Top layer view of the manufactured antenna.

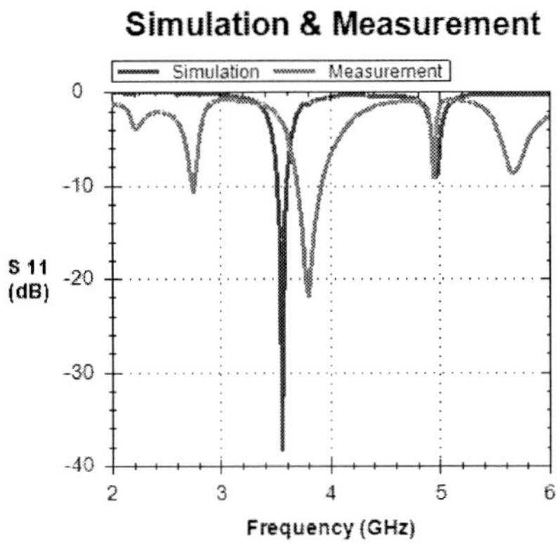

Fig. 2. S11 comparison of the antenna.

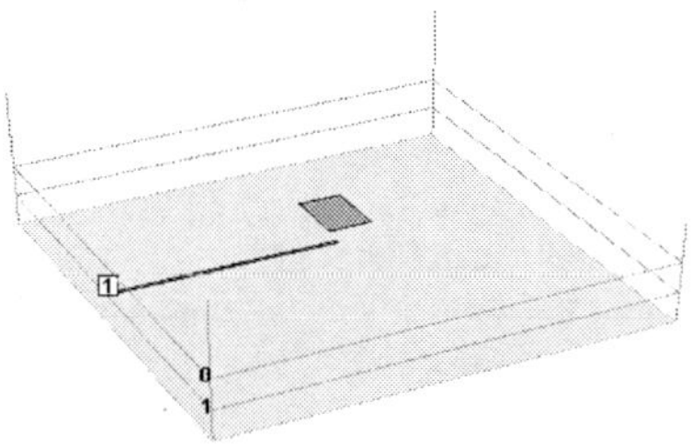

Fig. 3. 3D view of straight proximity coupled patch antenna.

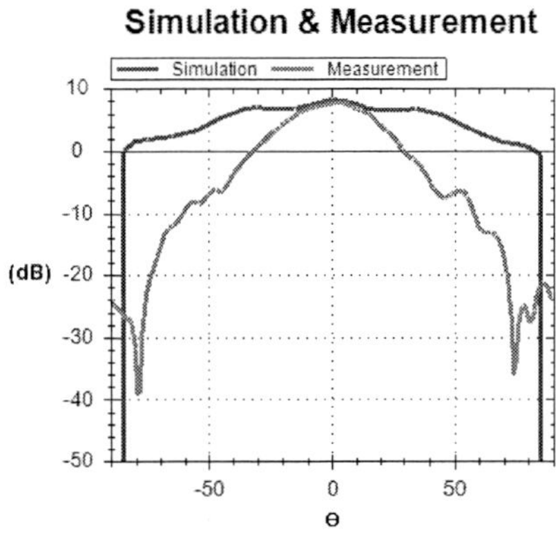

Fig. 4. Gain Comparison of the antenna.

V. Conclusion

In this work, four different geometries of proximity coupled patch antenna has been designed, simulated, built and tested. Dual resonance has been achieved with the ribbon shaped proximity patch antenna. The minimum return loss achieved is -39,68 dB with the straight proximity patch antenna at 3.56 GHz. The maximum gain is achieved 12.10 dB at 10.2 GHz with ribbon proximity patch antenna. Measurement result of straight patch antenna as follows: S11 = -21 dB at 3.79 GHz and Gain = 7.3 dB.

Acknowledgement

We would like to thank Ahmet KIRLILAR, İsmail Hakkı BATUM and Erhan HALAVUT for their support during fabrication and measurements at ASELSAN A.Ş., which is an affiliated company of Turkish Armed Forces Foundation.

References

[1] Z. Hailu, "Comparative study on bandwidth enhancement techniques of microstrip patch antenna," Thesis. pp. 1-86, January 2008.

[2] K. Wong, Compact and Broad Band Microstrip Antennas, John Wiley & Sons Inc., 2002.

[3] W. S. T. Rowe and R. B. Waterhouse, "Investigation into the performance of proximity coupled stacked patches," IEEE Antennas and Propagation, vol. 54 pp. 1693-1698, June 2006.

[4] R. Sastry and K. J. Sankar, "Proximity coupled rectangular microstrip antenna with X-slot for WLAN application," Global Journal of Researches in Engineering: Electrical and Electronics Engineering, vol. 14, no. 1, pp. 1360-1370, Janurary 2014.

[5] M. Ali, A. Kachouri, and M. Samet, "Novel design of a compact proximity coupled feed antenna," International Journal of Computer Science Issues, vol. 9, no. 3, pp. 419-426, January 2012.

[6] Sonnet Suites, version: 13.56, www.sonnetsoftware.com, 2014.

Design of a Quad Element Patch Antenna at 5.8 GHz

Negar Majidi and Goksen Goksenin Yaralioglu
Department of Electrical and Electronic Engineering
Ozyegin University, Istanbul, Turkey
negar.majidi@ozu.edu.tr

Mohammad Rahim Sobhani
Department of Electrical and Computer Engineering
University of Alberta, Edmonton, Canada

Taha Imeci
Department of Electrical Engineering
International University of Sarajevo
Sarajevo, Bosnia and Herzegovina

***Abstract*—This paper presents simulation and experimental verification of a quad microstrip patch antenna that operates at 5.8 GHz. Sonnet antenna design software was used to simulate the performance of the antenna. To reduce the design's complexity and the computational load, the antenna and the feeding lines were simulated separately. An optimization was done for each subpart to get the optimum desired results. Finally, all the subparts were merged and the final structure was simulated to check the performance. A prototype of the antenna was fabricated on a double sided PCB substrate (relative permittivity=10.2, thickness=1.28 mm) using a PCB milling machine. The s_{11} of -14 dB and -18.8 dB and maximum gain of 6.2 dB and 4.2 dB were obtained, from the simulation and experimental measurements, respectively.**

Keywords*—*2x2 Microstrip Patch Antenna, 5.8 GHz Antenna, Quad Microstrip Patch Antenna.

I. Introduction

Nowadays, microstrip patch antennas are frequently used in telecommunication products due to their low cost, low profile, light weight, and easiness of fabrication and integration [1-3]. Literately, when the microstrip patch antenna is excited, the electrical charges are accumulated at the edge of the patches. These electrical charges make curved fringing fields and therefore these fields at edge of the microstrip antenna generate electromagnetic radiation [4, 5]. Therefore, the parameters such as frequency, input impedance and gain of the antenna depend on the geometrical shape and the feeding type as well as the physical properties of the substrate [6]. The frequency band of 5.8 GHz is especially important for FPV (First Person View) applications where the transmitter could be placed in a remotely controlled device where small antenna dimensions are desirable.

In this paper we designed an antenna to operate at 5.8 GHz, optimizing all the geometrical shape and feeding type of a 2x2 array. For the antenna, the architecture presented in [7, 8] was used where a 2x2 array of microstrip patch antennas were simulated. The shape and feeding lines were changed and redesigned to operate the antenna at 5.8 GHz. An inset-fed feeding method was chosen which provides an effortless way of impedance control [9-11].

II. Design Procedure

Fig. 1 shows the geometry of the 2x2 microstrip patch antenna that was designed in this paper. The antenna input was a via placed at the center as shown in the Fig. 1. The input was coupled to the antenna patches through a 2 stage Binomial feeding line to achieve good impedance matching. Dimensions of the patch antennas were calculated using analytical equations and then few optimizations were done to get the optimum dimensions. In order to reduce the proposed antenna size, a substrate with high ε_r of 10.2 with thickness of 1.28 (ROGERS, RO3010) was used for the simulations and the prototype.

As a start point, the patches were simulated with inset feeds. The simulations were started with known theoretical equations for the rectangular single patch antenna. The dimensions and the feed lines were optimized using Sonnet Suite. Then 4 of these single patch antennas were combined through feed lines and the central input via. A 100 mm thick of air layer was added during the Sonnet simulations such that the whole antenna was placed in a 100 x 400 x 300 mm insulation box. Finally, an optimization was done to adjust the dimensions of the whole antenna to reach the lowest reflection coefficient as much as possible. The final dimensions are shown in Fig. 1.

III. Results

Based on the simulations, the maximum gain of 6.2 dB on the side lobes, and s_{11} of -14 dB were achieved at the operation frequency of 5.8 GHz. Obtaining these satisfying results from the simulations lead us to fabricate the antenna. Thus, the antenna was fabricated on the specified substrate (ROGERS, RO3010) as shown in Fig. 2, following by a practical measurement of the antenna performance. The measurements for the prototype antenna and the simulation results are shown in Fig. 3. There is a good agreement between the measurements and the simulations. However, the slightly differences can be attributed to the inaccuracies during the fabrication and measurement process.

A simulation for the current density over the antenna patches also was done as illustrated in Fig. 4. The microstrip patch antennas emit electromagnetic waves at the outer edges of the antennas; therefore, the current density along the perimeter of the patch antenna should be higher compared to the other parts. Fig. 4 illustrates the JXY Magnitude for the current density in Amps/Meter unit.

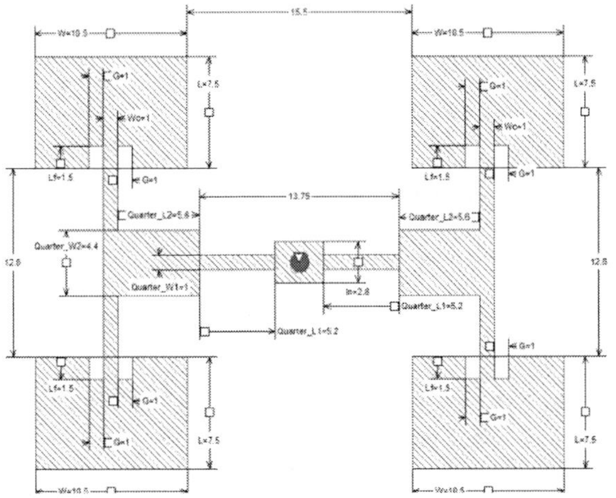

Fig. 1. Proposed 2x2 mictrostrip patch antenna with via feeding. The antenna was put inside a box with multiple times of the antenna's exact size (box size of 400 x 300 mm and air height of 100 mm at top).

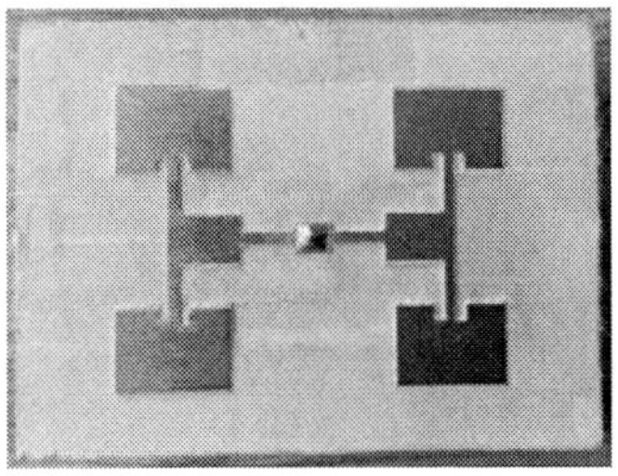

Fig. 2. The fabricated antenna on the RO3010 substrate using drilling machine.

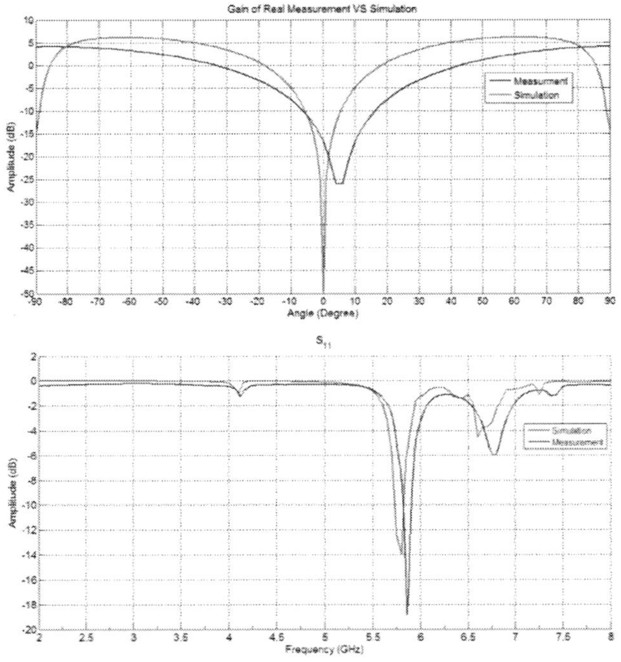

Fig. 3. Comparison of the gain (top) and reflection (bottom) for the antenna.

IV. Conclusion

In this work, a 2x2 mictrostrip patch antenna was designed and fabricated a 5.8 GHz that only occupies 2.7 cm by 3.6 cm. The measured gain of 4.2 dB and S_{11} of -18.8 dB were obtained for the antenna. Slight differences between the simulation and measurements are due to the inaccuracy of the drilling machine that was used to build the antenna. The results can be further optimized by using high performance workstations to execute the sequential optimization algorithms. Also, a precise antenna can be machined using laser based fabrication methods.

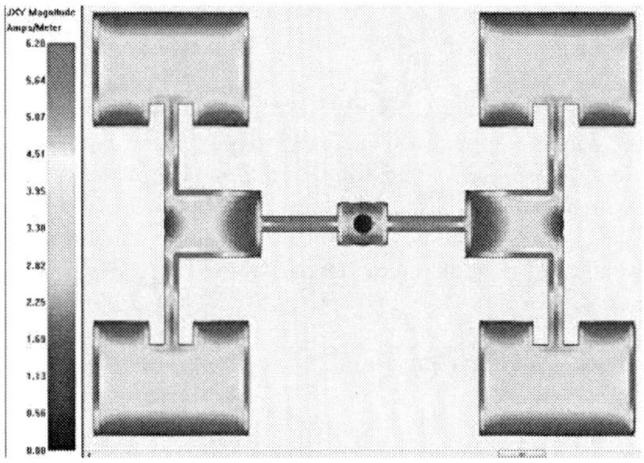

Fig. 4. Current density of the antenna operating at 5.8 GHz.

Acknowledgment

The authors thank Mert Karaca from Ozyegin University who has assisted us during the antenna fabrication, and Omer Yilmaz and Fatma Zengin from TUBITAK for the measurements support.

References

[1] J. R. James and P. S. Hall, Handbook of Microstrip Antennas, Peter Peregrinus, London, UK, 1989.

[2] J. Q. Howell, "Microstrip antennas," IEEE Trans. Antennas Propagation Magazine, vol. AP-23, pp. 90-93, 1975.

[3] R. Garg, P. Bhartia, I. Bahl, and A. Ittipiboon, Microstrip Antenna Design Handbook, London, Artech House, 2001.

[4] P. S. Nakar, "Design of a compact microstrip patch antenna for use in wireless/cellular devices," Florida State University, pp. 20-45, 2004.

[5] A. F. Alsager, "Design and analysis of microstrip patch antenna arrays," University College of Boras, 2011.

[6] J. R. Ojha and M. Peters, Patch Antennas and Microstrip Lines, Microwave and Millimeter Wave Technologies Modern UWB Antennas and Equipment, I. Mini (Ed.), ISBN: 978-953-7619-67-1.

[7] C. K. Ghosh and S. K. Parui, "Design and study of a 2x2 microstrip patch antenna array for WLAN/MIMO application," 2009 International Conference on Emerging Trends in Electronic and Photonic Devices & Systems (ELECTRO-2009).

[8] C. Ninan, C. H. Shekhar, and M. Radhakrishna, "Design and optimization of a 2x2 directional microstrip patch antenna," Communications in Computer and Information Science, July 2013.

[9] S. Rajan, "Design and analysis of rectangular microstrip patch antenna using inset feed technique for wireless application," IJIRSET, vol. 4, spec. iss. 4, April 2015.

[10] M. S. R. Mohd Shah, M. Z. A. Abdul Aziz, M. K. Suaidi, and M. K. A Rahim, Dual Linearly Polarized Microstrip Array Antenna, Trends in Telecommunications Technologies, C. J. Bouras (Ed.), ISBN: 978-953-307-072-8.

[11] M. A. Matin and A. I. Sayeed, "A design rule for inset-fed rectangular microstrip patch antenna," WSEAS Transactions on Communications, vol. 9, iss. 1, January 2010, ISDN: 1109-2742.

Design and Analysis of a Bandpass Hairpin Filter

Rafsan Ahmed and Shpetim Emiri
Department of Electrical Engineering
Antalya Science University
Antalya, Turkey
rafsan.ahmed@std.antalya.edu.tr,
shpetim.emiri@std.antalya.edu.tr

Ş. Taha İmeci
Department of Electrical Engineering
International University of Sarajevo
Sarajevo, Bosnia and Hersegovina
simeci@ius.edu.ba

***Abstract*— Design, simulation and analysis of an angled hairpin filter was introduced through this paper. The proposed frequency band was 3-4 GHz. The simulated design and parametric studies complied with the initial proposed design and a bandpass signal between 3.05–3.96 GHz frequency range was achieved. Main contribution is to have uneven and angled legs of U-shaped hairpin elements.**

Keywords* — *bandpass filter, hairpin filter, microstrip, parametric study.

I. Introduction

The hairpin filter is a classic design example of a minimized microstrip filter. It is used in modern wireless technology. The specifications of the proposed filter were as following:

- Dielectric constant $\varepsilon r = 4.4$ (FR-4),
- Substrate thickness = 200mils (air) 63mils (dielectric),
- Bandpass frequency range of 3-4 GHz,
- The filter box space was optimum at 1200mm x 800mm.

An angled hairpin filter was proposed in comparison with a straight filter [1] and through several studies the following designs were chosen as starting reference [1-3]. Fig. 1 has the top view.

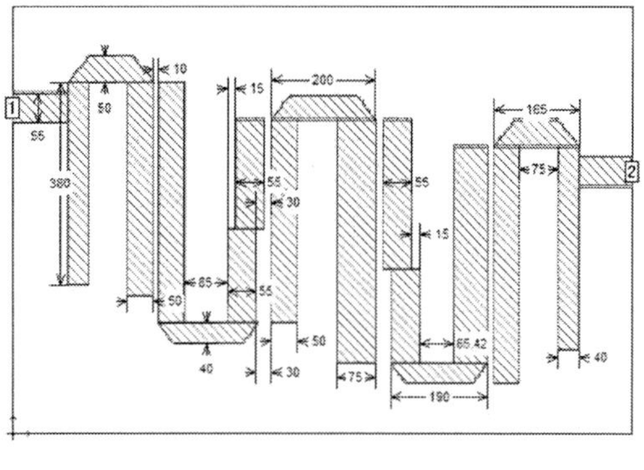

Fig. 1. Top view of the proposed hairpin filter.

Another microstrip hairpin band pass filter is designed to have a fractional bandwidth of 20% at mid frequency of 2GHz in [4]. The filter parameters were varied and the results were analyzed. These variations were based on the theory that the intermediate gap between lines are directly related to the filter bandwidth [5, 6]. Slight variations of the filter parameters resulted in different output bandwidth for the filter. Through trial and error the filter design in Fig. 1 was obtained. The design in Fig. 1 shows the simulation carried out in Sonnet Suites [7].

II. Simulation and Output Data

Fig. 2 has the S-parameter of the proposed microstrip hairpin filter.

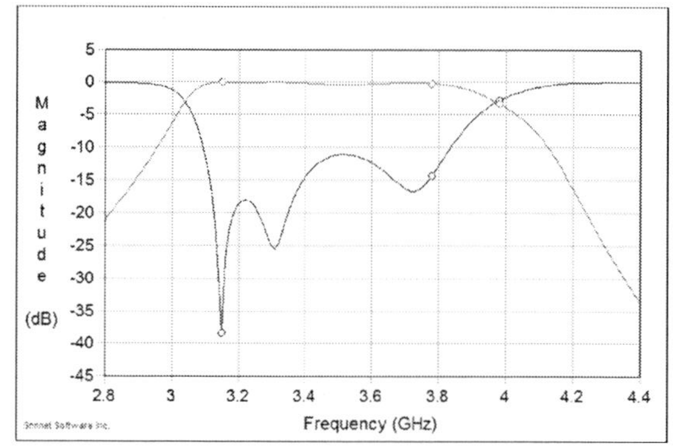

Fig. 2. Frequency vs magnitude output graph of the hairpin filter.

As seen in the graph, the hairpin filter passes a frequency range between 3.05-3.96 GHz. This output range is very close to the expected output band of 3-4 GHz. The input match is well below -11 dB through the passband of the filter.

III. Parametric Study and Variations

The physical parameters of the hairpin filter were varied to observe the output. Varying the length of the strips, the distance between them or the angle resulted in deviations in the output value and bandwidth of the hairpin filter. The following subsections describe the results observed from varying the angle, varying the space between broken edges and variation in length.

A. Varying Angle

The angle of the hairpin filter was varied by changing the height of the right edges of the three pins in the middle. The resulting data is given below.

TABLE I. Output Frequency When Angle is Varied

Length Difference (mm)	Output Frequency Min (GHz)	Output frequency Max (GHz)	Max Magnitude (dB)
5	3.04	3.97	-11.60
10	3.05	3.97	-11.96
25	3.06	3.97	-6.90
50	3.06	3.97	-2.74

Increasing the angle of the filter results in a lower dB output. Further increase in angle is not optimum.

B. Varying Space Between Broken Edges

The right edge of the second pin and the left edge of the fourth pin have "broken" edges or have two microstrips joined together to form one edge. The spacing between the edges were studied for variations in the output.

TABLE II. Output Frequency When Spacing Between Broken Edges are Varied

Length Difference (mm)	Output Frequency Min (GHz)	Output Frequency Max (GHz)	Max Magnitude (dB)
5	3.12	3.88	-11.67
10	3.09	3.93	-11.60
20	2.99	4.08	-10.11
25	2.91	4.06	-7.15

Increasing the space between the broken edges increases the overall frequency range. However, the magnitude also increases significantly. Therefore the 15mm space between the edges is optimum.

C. Variation in Length of the Broken Edges

The broken edges are not symmetrical. The fourth pin edge is longer than the second to maintain the angle. The effects of varying the length of the broken edges were studied for variations in the output.

TABLE III. Output Frequency When Top Edge Lengths of the Broken Edges are Varied

length difference (mm)	Output frequency min (GHz)	Output frequency max (GHz)	Max magnitude (dB)
15	2.94	3.82	-7.56
5	3.01	3.91	-11.65
-5	3.09	4.02	-10.41
-15	3.15	4.08	-9.74

TABLE IV. Output Frequency When Bottom Edge Lengths of the Broken Edges are Varied

Length Difference (mm)	Output Frequency Min (GHz)	Output Frequency Max (GHz)	Max Magnitude (dB)
15	2.97	3.84	-8.99
5	3.05	3.93	-11.42
-5	3.07	4.00	-10.71
-15	3.11	4.06	-10.06

Varying the length of the edges change the magnitude but the output bandwidth also deviates from the original specified bandwidth.

IV. Conclusion

The proposed angled hairpin filter was designed and analyzed for a range of 3-4 GHz. The simulation results suggested that the obtained angled hairpin filter successfully passes a frequency range between 3.05-4.00 GHz. The parametric studies that were conducted show how variations in different parameters resulted in different bandwidth or lengths that deviated from expected results.

References

[1] B. Dana, "The design, fabrication and measurement of microstrip filters and coupler circuits," High Frequency Electronics, pp. 22-30, 2002.

[2] D. K. Cheng, "Field and wave electromagnetics," Addision-Wesley Publishing Company, Second Edition, pp. 435-437, 1989.

[3] R. Pathak, "Characterizing losses in transmission lines," University of Wisconsin-Madison, WI, 2005.

[4] N. Parikh, P. Katare, K. Kathal, N. Patel, and G. Chaitanya, "Design and analysis of hairpin micro-strip line band pass filter," International Journal of Innovative Research in Electrical, Electronics, Instrumentation and Control Engineering, vol. 3, Iss. 5, 2015.

[5] G. Mathei, L. Young, and E. M. T. Jones, Microwave Filters Impedance Matching Network and Coupling Structures", Artech House, Boston, MA, 1980.

[6] P. Wade, "Recipes for printed hairpin filters", W1GHz: www.W1GHz.com, 2011.

[7] Sonnet Suites, ver. 16, Sonnet Software Inc., North Syracuse, NY.

Microstrip Patch Antenna with Triangular Slits

Anıl Elakaş, Gürhan Ali İmrak and Mert Şencan
Department of Electrical & Electronics Engineering,
Istanbul Commerce University,
Istanbul, Turkey

Ş. Taha Imeci
Department of Electrical Engineering, International
University of Sarajevo, Sarajevo, Bosnia and Hersegovina
Tahsin Durak
Department of Technology, NSU, Norfolk, VA

Abstract— **In this paper, a microstrip patch antenna with triangular slits is presented. The proposed patch antenna, with operating frequency of 9.5 GHz, is targeted. Simulation is carried out using Sonnet Suites 13.52. Antenna has 9.683 dB gain at 9.5 GHz with corresponding reflection coefficient of -15 dB. The measurements of the fabricated patch antenna corroborate the simulation results well.**

Keywords— Asymmetric triangular slit, gain, microstrip patch antenna.

I. Introduction

Microstrip patch antennas (MPAs) have sparked tremendous research efforts with great prospects and they have been widely integrated into many wireless applications. The salient features of MPAs have made them the ultimate candidates for applications, such as spaceborn systems, radar or satellite systems, where lightweight and cost-effective antennas with low-profile and simple geometrical structure for ease of fabrication and installation are required. With the ever-increasing need for mobile communication and the emergence of many systems, it is important to design broadband antennas to cover a wide frequency range. The design of an efficient wide band small size antenna, for recent wireless applications, is a major challenge. Microstrip patch antennas have found extensive application in wireless communication system owing to their advantages such as low profile, conformability, low-cost fabrication and ease of integration with feed networks [1].

The operation frequency of the reference antenna is 2.285 GHz. The size of the antenna is 80 mm X 80 mm. The coaxial probe feeding technique is used. Reference antenna has a parasitic element strip under the main part and antenna has 4 asymmetric triangular slits [2].

In this paper, the parasitic element strip in the reference antenna was removed, the number of slits was reduced from 4 to 2 and the feed position was moved to the middle of the antenna. The size of the antenna is reduced to 21.6 mm X 21.6 mm and simulation air thickness is 10 mm. As a result of the analysis, operation frequency is 9.5 GHz. Slits angle was changed to optimize the maximum gain.

The rest of this paper is organized as follow: the design steps are described in section II, results and conclusion are presented in section III of the paper.

II. Design Steps

The geometrical shape of the triangular microstrip patch antenna with triangular slits design in the first step is as shown in Fig 1. The size of the antenna is 43 mm x 42.5 mm and the box size is 700 mm X 700 mm.

In the second stage, the design in Fig. 2 was created by optimizing triangular slit measurements and determining the feed point location again. As a result of the simulation, S11 value was measured as -10.06 dB at 2.3 GHz and -19.56 dB at 4.7 GHz, antenna gain was measured as 4.82 dB at 2.3 GHz and 7.30 dB at 4.7 GHz.

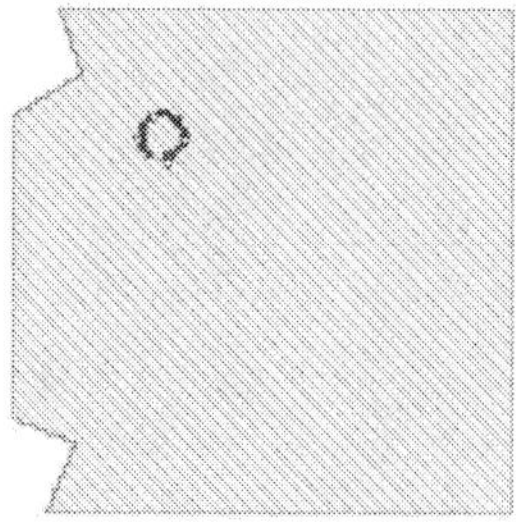

Fig. 1. First design.

Fig. 2. Second design.

At the third step, the final design in Fig. 3 was created by reducing the antenna size and changing the feed position. The proposed patch antenna with triangular slits is designed using RT/duroit 6002 substrate with dielectric constant of 2.94, thickness $h=0.76mm$ and loss tangent of 0.0012.

As a result of successive iteration of simulations, the S11 value is measured as -19.6589 dB and the antenna gain is measured as 9.683 dB at 9.5 GHz, and the reverse polarity value is measured as -6.03 dB. Fabricated antenna is shown in Fig. 4.

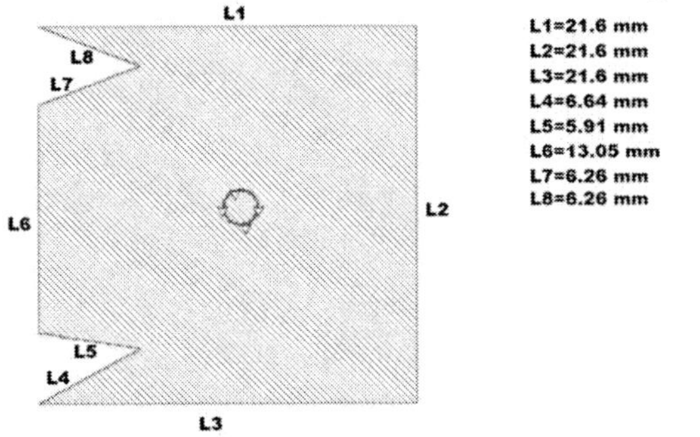

Fig. 3. Final Design.

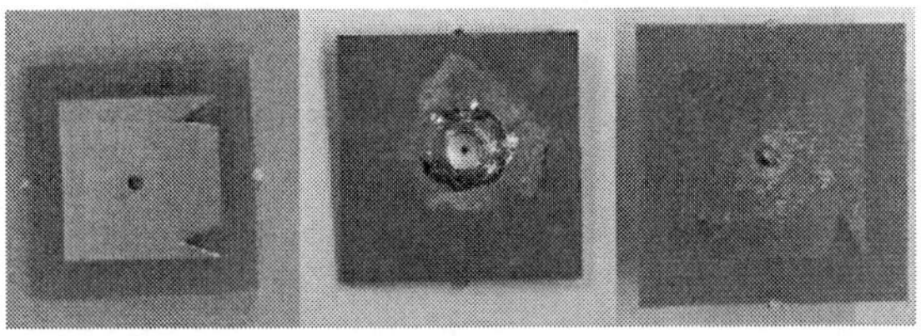

Fig. 4. Fabricated and measured antenna.

The S11 value obtained as a result of the final design is shown in Fig. 5.

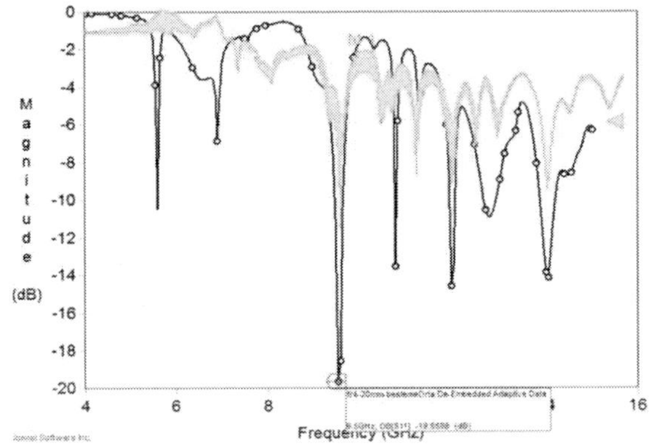

Fig. 5. Input match (|S11|) of the proposed antenna.

E Theta - E Phi radiation diagram occurred at resonance frequency at 9.5 GHz is given in Fig. 6. Measurement setup is shown in Fig. 7.

III. Results and Conclusion

Analysis was performed in Sonnet software program. The frequency range between 0-15 GHz. In this paper, a triangular shaped double-slit microstrip patch antenna with resonance at 9.5 GHz frequency was designed and simulated results are given. As a result of studies on the geometry of the slit, optimum dimensions have been determined. According to the results of simulations made by taking air thickness 10 mm and insulation thickness 1.6 mm, simulated and measured S11 were matched well 9.5 GHz, where measured S11 is slightly lower -15 dB and gain 9.683 dB at 9.5 GHz.

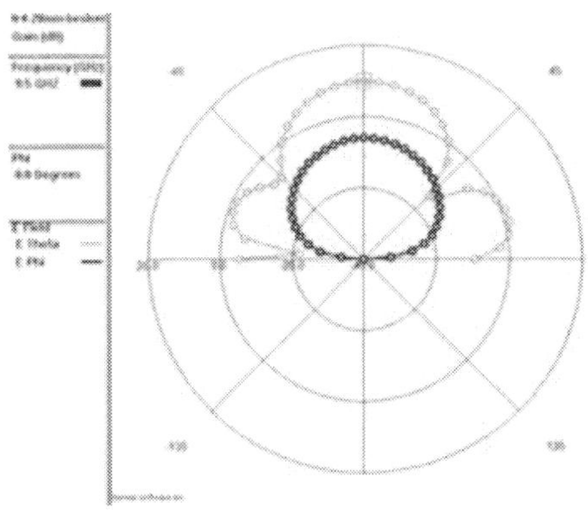

Fig. 6. E Theta – E Phi radiation pattern of patch antenna at 9.5 GHz.

Fig. 7. Measurement setup.

The flux density at 9.5 GHz is given in Figure 8.

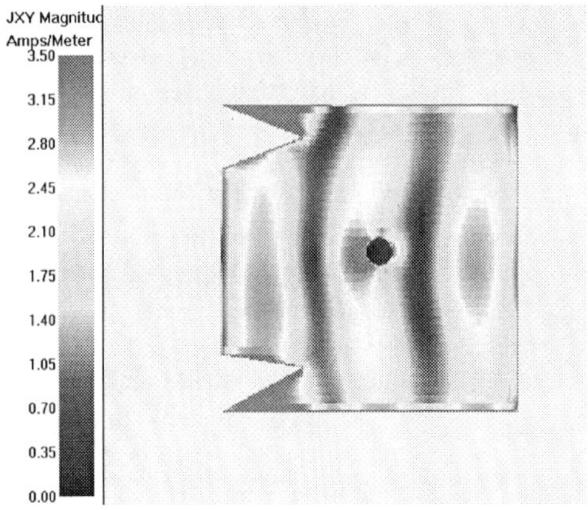

Fig. 8. The flux density at 9.5GHz.

References

[1] C. A. Balanis, Antenna Theory Analysis and Design, 2nd edition, John Wiley & Sons, Inc., 1997.

[2] M. T. Islam, M. Cho, M. Samsuzzaman, and S. Kibria, "Compact antenna for small satellite applications," IEEE Antennas and Propagation Magazine, vol. 57, no. 2, pp. 30-36, April 2015.

[3] Sonnet Suites, version 13.52, www.SONNETSOFTWARE.com

Circular Shaped Microstrip Patch Antenna at 14.6 GHz

Furkan Atalah
Istanbul Commerce University, Istanbul, Turkey
Mustafa Imeci
Yildirim Beyazit University, Ankara, Turkey
Oguzhan Gungor
Selcuk University, Konya, Turkey

S. Taha Imeci
Department of Electrical Engineering,
International University of Sarajevo, Sarajevo,
Bosnia and Hersegovina
Tahsin Durak
Department of Technology, NSU, Norfolk, VA

***Abstract*— In this paper, a circular shaped ground-fed patch antenna is designed, simulated, built and tested. The operating antenna frequency is 14.6 GHz with -15.68 dB input and 8.14 dB gain. Furthermore, the antenna does not only have a circular shaped build but also is supported with a triangle, square and column shapes.**

Keywords*— *Circular shaped Antenna, micro strip patch antenna, single resonance.

I. Introduction

The recent revolution in electronic circuits pressured the antenna designers to come up with small, lightweight and low cost radiating structures. This requirement led to the invention of several antenna structures, of which, printed microstrip antenna received a lot attention in recent years [1]. Due to their low-profile and conformable geometry, they are widely used as embedded antennas in handheld wireless devices and military equipment [2]. However, intensive research is required to improve the inherent disadvantages of this antenna, such as: narrow bandwidth, low efficiency, spurious feed radiation, poor polarization purity and limited power capacity [3]. During the design process, the motivations involved in selecting different antenna components are as follows: Microstrip antennas can be incorporated in various geometries, such as: rectangular, circular, triangular, annular patches and others [4]. Circular patch is the second most popular shape and can be easily analyzed and modified to produce a range of impedance values, radiation patterns and frequencies of operation. Among the four most popular feed techniques, coax-fed method has low spurious feed radiation and is easy to match [5].

II. Design Steps

The size of the antenna is 20.00 X 31.06 mm. Substrate material is FR- 4 and the thickness of it is 1 mm (ε_r= 4.4, dielectric loss tangent =0.0018 mm). The thickness of air is taken as 3 times of the thickness of the FR-4, (3 mm). The top view of the antenna is in Fig. 1, and Table 1 shows the antenna parameters and the values.

TABLE I. Antenna Parameters and Values

Dimension	Length		
A	1.5mm	F	5mm
B	6mm	G	5.8mm
C	4.3mm	H	8.3mm
D	11mm	I	1.2mm
E	2.5mm	J	19.3mm
		K	8mm

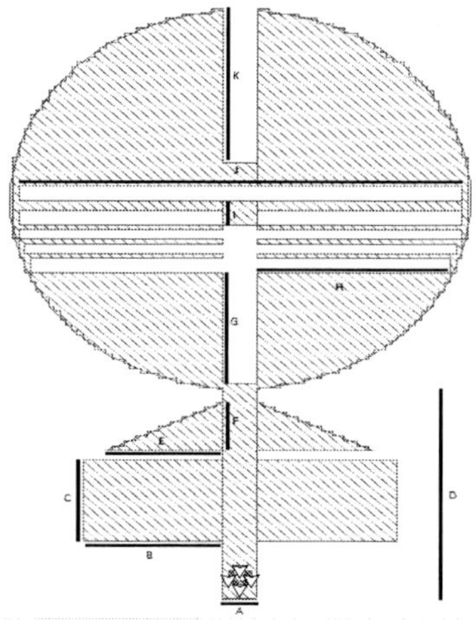

Fig. 1. Top view of the fabricated circular antenna.

III. Simulation and Parametric Study

In the earlier designs,only circular shape and a standard port was used, but there was no gain even though a -35 dB return loss is achieved at 14.6 GHz. Furthermore, changing the feeding location and adding triangular and rectangular shapes to design lowered the resonances, also high gains are maintained. In Fig. 2, input reflection coefficient, S_{11} is shown at 14.6 GHz, and -15.69 dB magnitude was found as simulation and -13.9 dB as measurement. In Fig. 3, gain graph is shown and +8.14 dB simulated and 6.1 dB measured result was found at 14.6 GHz. Fig. 4 has the manufactured antenna. Table II shows variations of gap between slits.

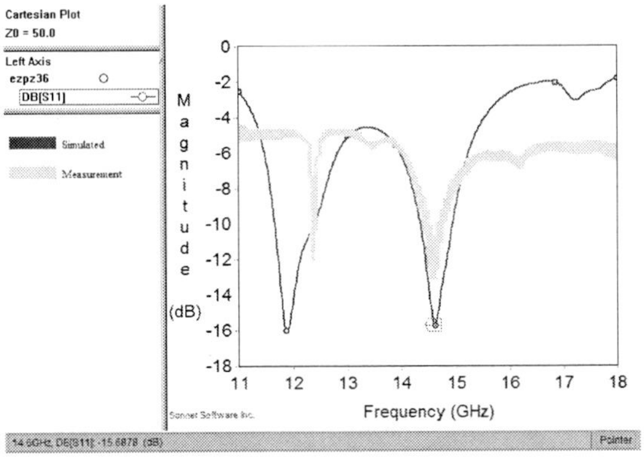

Fig. 2. S11 graph.

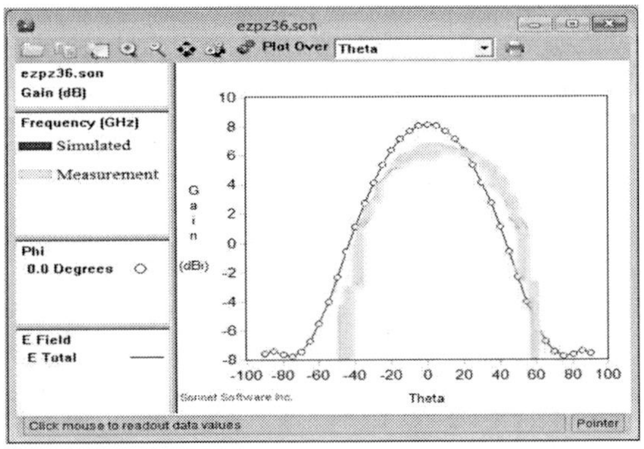

Fig 3. Radiation pattern (gain) graph.

Fig. 4. Top view of produced antenna

IV. Conclusion

Our aim is to find higher gain values for fabrication of circular shaped patch antenna for single band operations by simulating with different geometrical values mentioned in the article. Throughout our design steps in this conclusion part of this project we can say that designing circular ring shaped antenna is not easy due to limitations, dielectric material type, gain - frequency relation, feeding type and technique. Even small changes on the antenna may have drastic outcomes, these changes have to be noted each time and avoid being applied again to cause further confusion during design. It should also be noted that in circular ring shaped patch antennas making slits, gaps inside of circular ring and pincering current to the sides by increasing the length of slits and gaps increases gain.

By varying the thickness, different parameters of the designed antenna can be optimized. Proposed antenna can be used in different applications such as in wireless communication and S band applications.

TABLE II. Frequency-Gain-Input Match with Modified Gap

Gap between slits :	Frequencies	Gain (dB)	Input Match (dB)
0.25	*10.5 GHz*	*6.35*	*−16.8*
	11.3 GHz	*7.22*	*−14.72*
0.5	*10.7 GHz*	*6.68*	*−15.77*
	11.9 GHz	*7.32*	*−10.5*
0.75	*11.9 GHz*	*6.88*	*−8.5*
	14.6 GHz	*8.14*	*−15.69*
1	*12.7 GHz*	*5.33*	*−8.45*
	13.5 GHz	*5.77*	*−9.25*
	14.44 GHz	*6.11*	*−18.22*

References

[1] A. Dalli, L. Zenkouar, and S. Bri, "Comparison of circular sector and rectangular patch antenna arrays in C-Band," Journal of Electromagnetic Analysis and Applications, vol. 4, no. 11 pp. 457-467, 2012.

[2] S. Malisuwan, J. Sivaraks, N. Madan, and N. Suriyakrai, "Design of microstrip patch antenna for Ku-band satellite communication applications," International Journal of Computer and Communication Engineering, vol. 3, no. 6, November 2014.

[3] A. Thakur, M. Chauhan and M. Kumar, "Effect of substrate relative dielectric constant on bandwidth characteristics of line feed rectangular patch antenna," International Journal of Engineering Science Invention Research & Development, vol. 1, iss. 10, e-ISSSN: 2349-6185, April 2015.

[4] A. Deshmukh, V. Pandit, R. Colaco and R. Doshi "Dual band dual polarized modified circular microstrip antenna," International Conference on Circuits, Systems, Communication and Information Technology Applications (CSCITA), 2014.

[5] R. Garg, P. Bhatia, I. Bhal and A. Ittipibon, Microstrip Antenna Design Handbook, Artech House, 2001.

E-Shaped Patch Antenna at 4.87 GHz

Ezgi Kucuk and Burak Bayram
Department of Electrical & Electronics Engineering,
Istanbul Commerce University,
Istanbul, Turkey
Ezgikucuk1994@gmail.com, brk.bayrm@gmail.com

S. Taha Imeci
Department of Electrical Engineering, International University of Sarajevo, Sarajevo, Bosnia and Hersegovina
simeci@ius.edu.ba
Tahsin Durak
Department of Technology, NSU, Norfolk, VA
tahsind@gmail.com

Abstract— **This paper represents designing & analysis of E-shape microstrip patch antenna for wireless communication. Low volume, low profile configuration, easily mounted, light weight, low fabrication cost is the advantages of this antenna. The operating frequencies of antenna are 2.97 GHz and 4.85 GHz, the substrate FR4 is used for proposed antenna with dielectric constant 4.2 and thickness of 1.7mm. Two parallel slots are cut to perturb the surface current path, which provides a bandwidth of 11%. The E-shape has return loss of -28 dB of and -14.03 dB at operating frequencies 2.97 GHz and 4.85 GHz respectively. Designing and simulation of this antenna has been done by the help of HFSS Software. This antenna is fed by a co-axial probe feeding. In this paper, the effects of different types of antenna parameters studied.**

Keywords— Co-axial feed antenna, compact wireless antenna, E-shaped antenna, micro strip patch antenna, patch antenna, U slot antenna.

I. Introduction

In the recent world, the demand for low weight, cheap, low profile and efficient antennas is increasing microstrip patch antenna and are more popular for meeting these requirement in several applications. The main problem encountered with these such kind of patch antennas is high value of return loss and smaller impedance bandwidth, but theses problem can be solved by using some new designing approaches [1].

The microstrip patch antenna offers the advantages of low profile, ease of fabrication, and compatibility with integrated circuit technology. They can be designed to operate over a large range of frequencies (1- 40 GHz) and easily combine to form linear or planar arrays [2].

A microstrip patch antenna is types of antennas that offers a low profile, i.e., thin and easily manufacture ability, which provides great advantages over traditional. An E-shaped patch antenna is easily formed by cutting two slots from a rectangular shape. By cutting the slots from a patch, gain, return loss and bandwidth of microstrip antenna can be improved. The increased development of wireless communications, the urgency to design low volume, compact, low profile planar configuration and wideband multi-frequency planar antennas become highly desirable. Narrow bandwidth is a serious limitation of these microstrip patch antennas. Different techniques are used to overcome this narrow bandwidth limitation. These techniques include increasing the thickness of the dielectric substrate, decreasing dielectric constant and using parasitic patches [3].

For the E-shaped patch antenna, two parallel slots are incorporated to introduce a second resonant mode, resulting in a dual band antenna. If the feed point is located at the tip of the center arm as in [3–5], the second resonant mode will be introduced at a lower frequency than the fundamental resonant mode [4].

Research on microstrip antenna in the 21st century aims at size reduction, increasing gain, wide bandwidth, multiple functionality and system-level integration. Significant research work has been reported on increasing the gain and bandwidth of microstrip antennas [3-5]. In this paper, an attempt has been made to design a single band microstrip antenna without any geometrical complexities [5].

Fig. 1. Top view of the fabricated circular antenna.

II. Design Steps

The size of the antenna is 17.0 X 18.0mm. Substrate material is FR- 4 and the thickness of it is 1 mm (εr = 4.01, dielectric loss tangent = 0.0018). The thickness of air is taken as 3 times of the thickness of the FR-4, (3 mm). Top view of the fabricated and measured antenna is shown in Fig. 1.

III. SIMULATION AND PARAMETRIC STUDY

Analyses were performed in the Sonnet software program. The frequency range is between 1 - 10 GHz. In two different frequency values, -10dB or lower magnitude values were obtained. When the magnitude of S11 is -15.35 dB, gain is +7.27 dB. At 2.97 GHz. In second analysis, frequency was 4.87 GHz and S11 was -12.65 dB and gain is +8.86 dB. Results are provided in Table I. When compared with the first antenna, the size of the antenna is changed from 15.0 X 16.8 mm to 17.0 X 18.0 mm. Also change the port position. In Fig. 2, gain-frequency graph is shown and +8.79 gain is found at 4.85 GHz. In Fig. 3, S11 graph is shown and at 4.85 GHz, -14.03 dB magnitude was found.

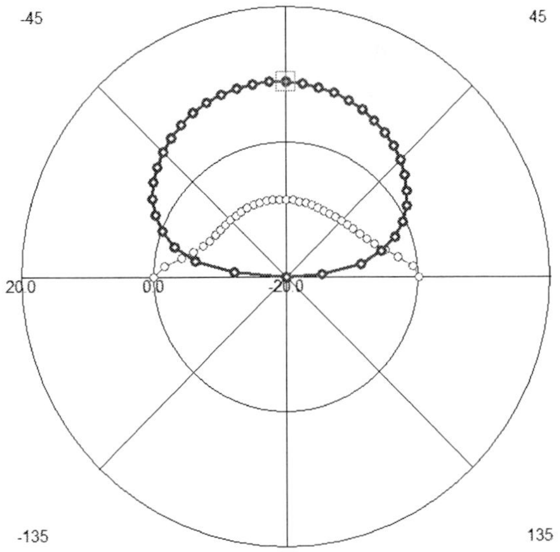

Fig. 2. Radiation pattern.

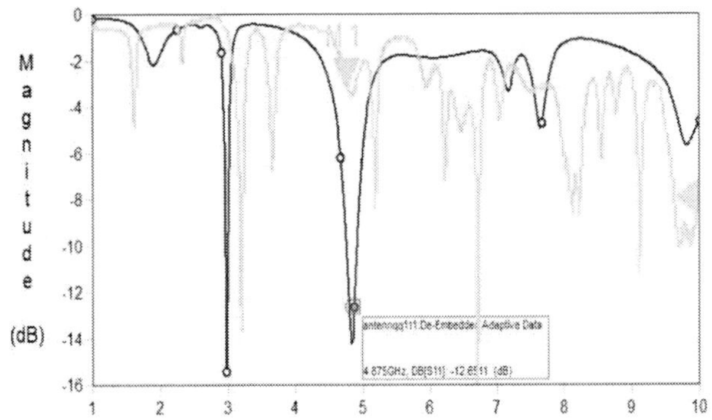

Fig. 3. Input match (S11).

IV. CONCLUSION

In this work, E type patch antenna was designed, simulated and fabricated. Compared to the first analysis, in the second analysis there was an increase in the gain value. So, when the frequency is at 2.97 GHz, S11 is -15.35 dB and the gain value is found as +7.27 dB. In the second analysis when the frequency is at 4.85 GHz, S11 is -14.03 dB and the gain is found as +8.79 dB. Two different analyses were compared in this article. We are also in the process of measuring the fabricated antenna for further studies on single band operations.

TABLE I. RESULTS AND COMPARISONS

Frequency	*S11*	*Gain*
4.87 GHz	-12.65 dB	8.86 dB
2.97 GHz	-15.35 dB	7.27 dB
4.0 GHz	-0.92 dB	6.91 dB
6.22 GHz	-1.80 dB	4.93 dB

ACKNOWLEDGMENT

We would like to thank Sonnet Software for their services.

REFERENCES

[1] International Journal of Scientific Research Engineering & Technology (IJSRET).

[2] R. Divya and M. Priya, "Design and characterization of E-shape microstrip patch antenna for wireless communication," International Journal of Advanced Trends in Computer Science and Engineering, vol. 2, no. 2, March 2013.

[3] A. Yadav, B. Chauhan, and A. Jain, "Microstrip symmetrical E-shape patch antenna for the wireless communication systems," International Journal of Emerging Technology and Advanced Engineering, vol. 2, iss. 12, December 2012.

[4] B.-K. Ang and B.-K. Chung, "A wideband E-shaped microstrip patch antenna for 5-6 GHz wireless communications," Faculty of Engineering Multimedia University, Cyberjaya, Malaysia, 2007.

[5] P. Tomar, J. K. Bhutto, and S. Rankawat, "Effect of feed position for same E-type microstrip patch antenna," International Journal of Electronics and Communication Engineering, vol. 7, no. 1, 2014.

Roof Shaped Rectangular Slotted Patch Antenna at 18.3 GHz

Melis Ecem Koca
Department of Electrical & Electronics Engineering,
Istanbul Commerce University, Istanbul, Turkey
melis.koca@hotmail.com

Tahsin Durak
Department of Technology, NSU, Norfolk, VA
tahsind@gmail.com

S. Taha Imeci
Department of Electrical Engineering,
International University of Sarajevo, Sarajevo,
Bosnia and Hersegovina
simeci@ius.edu.ba

***Abstract*— This paper proposes a compact sized, high frequency microstrip patch antenna with probe feeding. The patch of the antenna is pentagonal shaped which has a rectangular slot in the upper-center. Main contribution of the paper is to perturbe the side edges of the patch and to add a rectangular slot. Parametric study of those two-substrade change was investigated. The proposed structures were simulated by using the Sonnet Suites, a planar 3D electromagnetic simulation software which gave S11 value of -14.12 dB and gain value of 6.33 dB at 18.3 GHz.**

Keywords*— *Mobile equipment, rectangular slot, roof shaped, Single band, wireless communication.

I. Introduction

With the advancements of mobile and wireless technologies, the consumer market is demanding compact size handsets with multiple functions. Microstrip antennas are a suitable candidate for these applications due to their inherent properties including low weight, low manufacturing cost, conformability and low profile in comparison to conventional antennas [1]. Pentagonal geometry is one of the various shapes for microstrip antennas capable of circular polarization operation that has been reported in literature, but it can be also used for linear polarization [2]. Electrically thick dielectrics increase bandwidth, but also introduce impedance matching challenges [3]. Slotted microstrip antenna possesses better bandwidth, return loss, gain and directivity when compared with non-slotted microstrip patch antenna [4]. The limitations of MSA such as narrow bandwidth, low gain and low efficiency can be minimized by selecting a proper substrate material, as permittivity of substrate is the critical parameter to control bandwidth, radiation pattern, and efficiency of patch antenna [5].

II. Design Steps

The size of the antenna is 6.4 X 6.4mm. Substrate material is Rogers RT6002 and the thickness of it is 0.762 mm (ε_r= 2.94, dielectric loss tangent = 0.0012). The thickness of air is taken as 3 times of the thickness of the Rogers RT6002, (3 mm). Fig. 1 shows the picture of the fabricated antenna.

Fig. 1. Picture of the fabricated antenna.

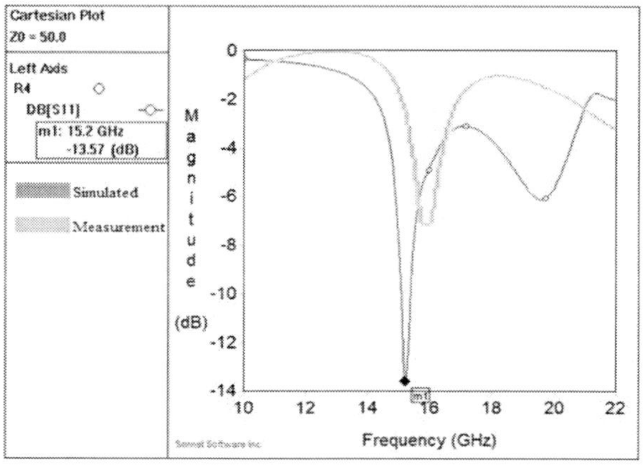

Fig. 2. S11 graph.

III. Simulation and Parametric Study

Analyses were performed in the Sonnet software program v13.52. The frequency range is between 15.5 - 20 GHz. In two different frequency values, obtained magnitude values were -10dB below. When the magnitude of S11 is -14.12 dB, gain is 6.33 dB at 18.3 GHz. In second analysis, frequency was 14.7 GHz and S11 was -24.5 dB and the antenna's gain is 4.18 dB.

In Fig. 2, S11-frequency graph is shown and -14.12 magnitude is found at 18.3 GHz. In Fig. 3, gain-frequency Graph is shown and +6.33 gain is found at 18.3 GHz. Table I provides frequency gain input match verses modified gap. Table II provides the list of variables changed and their values.

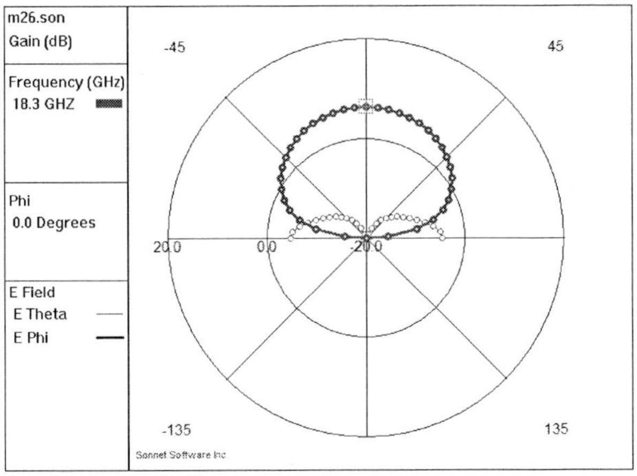

Fig. 3. Radiation pattern (gain) graph.

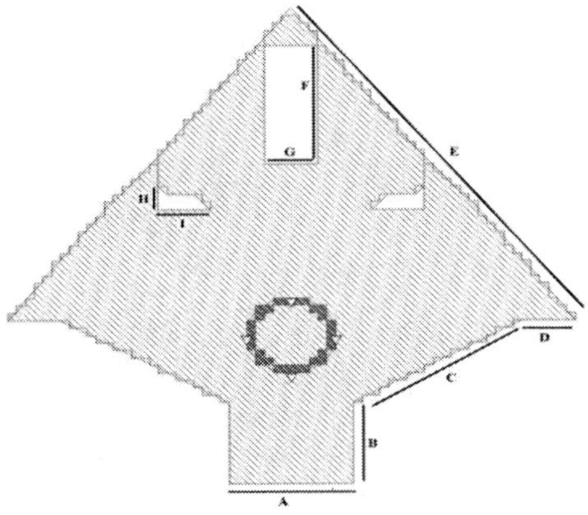

Fig. 4. Top view of the manufactured antenna and it's parameters.

IV. Conclusion

In this work, perturbed pentagonal cross-slotted patch

TABLE I. Frequency-Gain-Input Match with Modified Gap

Variable	Value
A	1.4 mm
B	1.1 mm
C	2.2 mm
D	0.6 mm
E	5.3 mm
F	1.6 mm
G	0.6 mm
H	0.3 mm
I	0.6 mm

antenna was designed, simulated and fabricated. Compared to the first analysis, in the second analysis there was a decrease in the gain value. So, when the frequency is at 18.3 GHz, S11 is -14.12 dB and the gain value is found as + 6.33 dB. In the second analysis when the frequency is at 14.7 GHz, S11 value is -24.5 dB and the gain is found as +4.18 dB. Two different analyses were compared in this article. We are also in the process of measuring the fabricated antenna for further studies on single band operations.

TABLE II. Changing Parameters

Variable	Freq. (GHz)	S11 (dB)	Gain (dB)
B = 2.1mm	22.7	-18.7	1.92
B = 0.1mm	20.2	-12.0	6.27
C = 2.7mm	16.6	-16.15	6.11
D = 1.6mm	23.4	-18.6	3.92
E = 5.8mm	25.2	-23.3	4.24

Acknowledgment

We would like to thank Sonnet Software for their services.

References

[1] B. Sharma, V. Sharma, D. Bharadwaj, K. B. Sharma, V. K. Saxena, J. S. Saini, and D. Bhatnagar, "Broadband dual frequency pentagonal microstrip antenna for wireless communication systems," Proceedings of International Conference on Microwave - 08, 2008.

[2] M. Tecpoyotl-Torres and J. G. Vera-Dimas, "Dual band pentagonal microstrip antenna for Wi-Fi applications," 2010 IEEE Electronics, Robotics and Automotive Mechanics Conference, pp. 255, 2010.

[3] R. Garg, P. Bhartia, I. Bahl, and A. Ittipiboon, Microstrip Antenna Design Handbook. Artech House, 2001.

[4] M. John, B. Manoj, and S. Rodrigues, "Design of slotted rectangular microstrip patch antenna operated in ISM band using RT-Duroid substrate," International Conference on Electrical, Electronics, and Optimization Techniques (ICEEOT), 2016.

[5] S. D. Mahamine, R. S. Parbat, S. H. Bodake, and M. P. Aher, "Effects of different substrates on rectangular microstrip patch antenna for S-band," 2016 International Conference on Automatic Control and Dynamic Optimization Techniques (ICACDOT), 2016.

Effect of Random Antenna Element Displacements on Sparse-UCA-Root-MUSIC Direction-of-Arrival Estimation

Veronique Inghelbrecht*
veronique.inghelbrecht@ugent.be

Jo Verhaevert+
jo.verhaevert@ugent.be

Tanja Van Hecke+
tanja.vanhecke@ugent.be

Dries Vande Ginste+
dries.vandeginste@ugent.be

Hendrik Rogier+
hendrik.rogier@ugent.be

Marc Moeneclaey*
marc.moeneclaey@ugent.be

Herwig Bruneel*
hb@telin.ugent.be

***Abstract*—We leverage a generalized polynomial chaos (GPoC) expansion to model the effect of correlated random antenna element displacements in a uniform circular antenna array (UCA) on the probability density function of the estimated directions-of-arrival (DOAs). To limit the number of antenna array realizations to be evaluated through full-wave simulations, we determine the GPoC expansion coefficients based on the stochastic collocation method. The method yields a speedup factor of about 40 compared to the Monte-Carlo approach, for a UCA with two displaced antenna elements and for DOA estimates obtained via the sparse-UCA-root-MUSIC algorithm.**

***Index Terms*—Antenna arrays, direction-of-arrival estimation, stochastic collocation method (SCM)**

I. Introduction

Most algorithms for direction-of-arrival (DOA) estimation using circular antenna arrays (UCAs) exploit the circular symmetry of the array. When random antenna displacements break this symmetry, these algorithms experience a significant performance loss. In this letter, we apply the stochastic collocation method (SCM) to obtain the mean square error (MSE) of the DOA estimates. The procedure is illustrated by relying on the Sparse UCA Root-MUSIC [1] DOA estimation algorithm. This algorithm can compensate for mutual coupling by incorporating all relevant phase modes of the active elements patterns of the antenna arrays.

II. Sparse UCA Root-MUSIC Algorithm for a UCA with Antenna Displacements

The nominal UCA consists of N identical antenna elements distributed over a circle with radius R. The phase center of each antenna element is located in the xy-plane, at azimuth angles $\varphi_n = (n-1)\frac{2\pi}{N}$ with $n = 1, 2, \ldots, N$. The number of incoming plane waves equals K, with corresponding elevation and azimuth angles (θ_k, φ_k), $k = 1, ..., K$. In order to account for the antenna element displacements, we adjust the received signals $\mathbf{x}$ as follows [2]:

$$\mathbf{x}(t) = \mathbf{A}_{displ}\mathbf{s}(t) + \mathbf{v}(t), \ t = 0, 1, 2, \ldots \tag{1}$$

where $\mathbf{s}(t) \in \mathbb{R}^{K\times 1}$ is the transmitted signal vector at time instant t, $\mathbf{x}(t) \in \mathbb{C}^{N\times 1}$ is the received signal vector and $\mathbf{v}(t) \in \mathbb{C}^{N\times 1}$ is assumed to be a spatially uncorrelated additive white Gaussian noise vector. The signal-to-noise ratio SNR (in dB) is defined as:

$$\text{SNR} = 10\log_{10}\left(\frac{E\left\{||\mathbf{A}\mathbf{s}(t)||^2\right\}}{E\left\{||\mathbf{v}(t)||^2\right\}}\right), \tag{2}$$

with $\mathbf{A}$ the element-manifold matrix of the nominal UCA. The k-th column of the $(N \times K)$ matrix $\mathbf{A}_{displ}$ equals the element-space manifold vector $\mathbf{a}_{displ}(\theta_k, \varphi_k)$, determined by the DOA (θ_k, φ_k) of the k-th plane wave. $\mathbf{A}_{displ}$ incorporates both the effects of the displacements of the antenna elements, as well as the mutual coupling effects, and can be found using a electromagnetic field simulator such as 4NEC2. On the received signals (1), we apply the sparse UCA Root-MUSIC algorithm [1], assuming a perfect UCA configuration.

III. Stochastic Collocation Method

In order to investigate the influence of Gaussian random displacements, we apply the SCM method [3]. First, we apply a Karhunen-Loève transform [4] to decorrelate the Gaussian random variables: the vector $\mathbf{u}$ of O correlated displacements with covariance matrix $\mathbf{\Sigma}$ is related to a vector $\boldsymbol{\eta}$ of O statistically independent variables through $\mathbf{u} = \sqrt{2}\mathbf{V}\sqrt{\mathbf{\Lambda}}\boldsymbol{\eta}$, where the columns of $\mathbf{V}$ are the eigenvectors of $\mathbf{\Sigma}$, and $\mathbf{\Lambda}$ is the diagonal matrix containing the corresponding eigenvalues. Consider a vector $\mathbf{y}(\mathbf{u})$ depending on the displacement vector $\mathbf{u}$. We can rely on the Askey scheme [5] to approximate $\mathbf{y}(\sqrt{2}\mathbf{V}\sqrt{\mathbf{\Lambda}}\boldsymbol{\eta})$ as a truncated polynomial expansion of the variables $\boldsymbol{\eta}$:

$$\mathbf{y}(\sqrt{2}\mathbf{V}\sqrt{\mathbf{\Lambda}}\boldsymbol{\eta}) \approx \sum_{i_1,\ldots,i_O} \mathbf{y}_{i_1,\ldots,i_O} H_{i_1}(\eta_1)\ldots H_{i_O}(\eta_O), \tag{3}$$

This research was partially funded by the Inter-University Attraction Poles Program initiated by the Belgian Science Policy Office.

* Dep. of TELIN, Ghent University.
+ Dep. of INTEC, Ghent University.

where $H_i(v)$ represents the Hermite polynonial of degree i, and the summation index i_l ranges from 0 to P_l ($l = 1, ..., O$); hence, the expansion (3) has a degree $P_{tot} = P_1 + ... + P_O$. Considering that the Hermite polynomials satisfy $\int H_i(v)H_j(v)e^{-v^2}dv = \delta_{i,j}$ with $\delta_{i,j}$ representing the Kronecker delta function, it follows that the coefficients $\mathbf{y}_{i_1,...,i_O}$ in (3) are given by:

$$\mathbf{y}_{i_1,...,i_O} = \int \mathbf{y}(\sqrt{2}\mathbf{V}\sqrt{\mathbf{\Lambda}}\boldsymbol{\eta})H_{i_1}(\eta_1)...H_{i_O}(\eta_O)p(\boldsymbol{\eta})\mathrm{d}\boldsymbol{\eta}. \quad (4)$$

We approximate the integral (4) by cubature formulas with weight function $e^{-|\boldsymbol{\eta}|^2}$ ([6]). Note that, if we want to calculate the mean of $\mathbf{y}(\mathbf{u})$, we can evaluate it as $E[\mathbf{y}(\mathbf{u})] = \sum_{k=1}^{Q} w_k \mathbf{y}(\mathbf{u_k})$, with $\mathbf{u}_k$ the Q quadrature points, and w_k the corresponding weights ([6]). Consequently, if the vector $\mathbf{y}(\mathbf{u}) = [y_1(\mathbf{u}), \dots y_K(\mathbf{u})]$ represents the MSE of the K DOA estimates:

$$y_i(\mathbf{u}) = E_{\boldsymbol{v}}[(\theta_i - \hat{\theta}_i)^2|\mathbf{u}] \ , \ i = 1, \dots, K \ , \quad (5)$$

for a certain value of the displacement vector $\mathbf{u}$ (averaged over different values of the noise vector $\mathbf{v}$), we obtain the MSE averaged over both the displacement vector and the noise vector as:

$$\mathrm{MSE} = E[(\theta_i - \hat{\theta}_i)^2] = \sum_{k=1}^{Q} w_k E_{\boldsymbol{v}}[(\theta_i - \hat{\theta}_i)^2|\mathbf{u}_k]. \quad (6)$$

IV. Numerical Results

Consider a uniform circular array consisting of nine dipole antenna elements tuned to 2.45 GHz (dipole length $l = \lambda/2 = 6.12$cm). All antennas are terminated by a load $Z_0 = 73\Omega$. In the center of the circle, there is a short-circuited dipole with length $l = \lambda/2$, representing a platform effect. The nine array elements are uniformly distributed on a circle with radius $\lambda/2$. We consider $K = 3$ uncorrelated sources, each transmitting pseudorandom bit sequences of length 500, using BPSK modulation. These signals are impinging on the UCA along the same elevation angle $\theta = 90°$ and along the azimuth angles $[20°, 200°, 285°]$. The signals are received in the presence of additive white Gaussian noise $\mathbf{v}(t)$. We consider the case where the first and second antenna element have random radial displacements u_1 and u_2, while the other antenna elements remain at their nominal positions. These random variables are assumed to be multivariate Gaussian distributed with zero mean, correlation coefficient $\rho = 0.8$, and standard deviation σ.

In Fig. 1, we have plotted the MSE of the first true DOA=20° as a function of the signal to noise ratio (SNR) and for different values of the dispersion. To obtain the mean square error, we apply two different methods: Monte-Carlo (M-C) simulation and the two-dimensional SCM theory. For the M-C method, based on 10000 realizations of $(u_1, u_2, \mathbf{v})$, we estimate the 3 DOAs and calculate the corresponding MSE. We compare this with the two-dimensional SCM theory that relies on the cubature formulas for the plane with $Q = 44$ quadrature points. In each of these quadrature points (u_1, u_2)

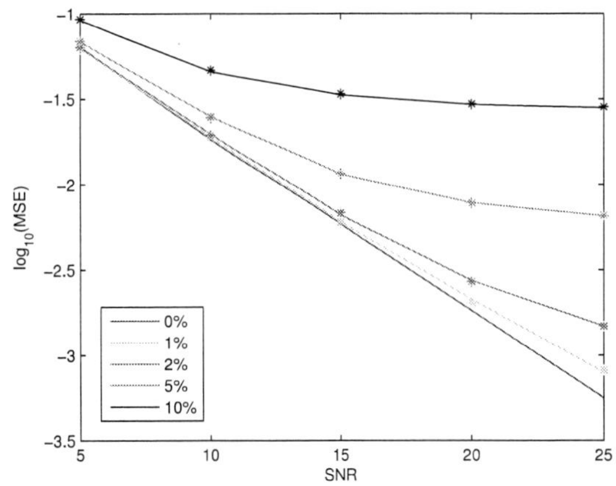

Fig. 1. The $\log_{10}(\mathrm{MSE})$ as a function of SNR, obtained with M-C (solid line) method and SCM (asterisk) for a radial displacement of the first two antenna elements, (u_1, u_2) Gaussian distributed with standard deviation $[0\%, 1\%, 2\%, 5\%, 10\%]$ of the radius.

we calculate the MSE averaged over 1000 values of the noise vector $\mathbf{v}$ (5), to finally obtain the MSE given by (6). Note that, for the SCM-method, we have to calculate the matrix $\mathbf{A}_{displ}$ only in the 44 quadrature points, whereas for the M-C method, we need to calculate $\mathbf{A}_{displ}$ for all 10000 realizations. Due to cost of an electromagnetic field simulation, the calculation of the $\mathbf{A}_{displ}$ is by far more time consuming than applying the Sparse-UCA-Root-MUSIC algorithm. We observe from Fig. 1 that the displacements give rise to a MSE floor, which increases with increasing standard deviation of the displacement. The results from M-C simulation and SCM theory match very well.

V. Conclusions

We have investigated an UCA, subject to correlated Gaussian random displacements. We have applied the SCM method and the M-C method to obtain the $\log_{10}(\mathrm{MSE})$ as a function of the SNR. Comparison of the SCM to the M-C method demonstrates that the SCM method accurately predicts the performance of the DOA estimates, with a reduction in CPU time by a factor of 40.

References

[1] R. Goossens and H. Rogier, "UCA Root-MUSIC with sparse uniform circular arrays," IEEE Trans. Signal Process., vol. 56, pp. 4095–4099, Aug. 2008.

[2] A. Balanis, *Antenna Theory Analysis and Design*. Hoboken, New Jersey: A John Wiley & Sons, 2005.

[3] V. Inghelbrecht, J. Verhaevert, T. Van Hecke, H. Rogier, M. Moeneclaey, and H. Bruneel, "Stochastic framework for evaluating the effect of displaced antenna elements on DOA estimation," IEEE Antennas and Wireless Propagation Letters, vol. 16, pp. 262–265, 2017.

[4] T. El-Moselhy, *Field Solver Technologies for Variation-Aware Interconnect Parasitic Extraction*, 2005.

[5] D. Xiu, "Fast numerical methods for stochastic computations: A review," Communications in Computational Physics, vol. 5, no. 2-4, pp. 242–272, Feb. 2009.

[6] R. Cools, L. Pluym, and D. Laurie, "Cubpack++: A C++ package for automatic two-dimensional cubature," ACM Transactions on Mathematical Software (TOMS), vol. 23, no. 1, pp. 1–15, Mar. 1997.

Designing Experiments to Reduce Uncertainty in Point Source Locations in the Helmholtz Equation

Troy Butler
Department of Mathematical and Statistical Sciences
University of Colorado Denver, Denver, USA, troy.butler@ucdenver.edu

***Abstract*—We show how a recently developed approach to formulating and solving stochastic inverse problems can be combined with an expected information gain to determine the physical placement of sensors that optimally reduce the uncertainty in the point source location for the inhomogeneous Helmholtz equation.**

I. Introduction

Key information about parameter values for models of physical systems are often subject to uncertainty. It may be possible to infer parameter values using experimental data on observable model quantities of interest (QoI). However, experimental data are often polluted by measurement errors representing additional uncertainties. This suggests we must formulate and solve stochastic inverse problems (SIPs) whose solutions quantify uncertainties in terms of probabilities. When experimental resources are limited so that it is only possible to obtain data on a relatively small number of observable QoI, it becomes important to design experiments in an optimal way in order to maximize the impact of each experiment on the solution to the SIP. In this context, we refer to an experimental design as determining a specific QoI and the optimal experimental design (OED) as defining the particular QoI for which we will obtain experimental (noisy) data in order to solve a SIP.

In this summary paper, we use the Kullback-Leibler (KL) divergence [1] to quantify the *information gained* by using a particular QoI to construct a posterior density solving a SIP. Recent work suggests that the consistent Bayesian approach [2] allows for efficient computations of the expected KL divergence (i.e., the expected information gain) in order to determine the OED [3]. To make these concepts both concrete and of interest to the intended audience, we consider the inhomogeneous Helmholtz equation where the physical location of a point-source is uncertain and two sensors may be placed anywhere in the physical domain.

II. Helmholtz and Optimal Experimental Design

A. The Inhomogeneous Helmholtz Equation

The equation considered in this work is:

$$\nabla^2 E(x) + k^2 E(x) = -f(x;\lambda),\ x \in \Omega \subset \mathbb{R}^2. \qquad (1)$$

Here, we take $\Omega = [0,1]^2$ and $k = 15$, we assume homogeneous Dirichlet boundary conditions, and f represents a point source located at $\lambda = (\lambda_1, \lambda_2) \subset \Lambda := [0, 0.2]^2$ with the exact values of these parameters λ_1 and λ_2 considered uncertain. We use the open-source finite element library FEniCS [4] to solve (1) using a uniform triangular mesh defined from a 100×100 grid and linear elements. We assume that the QoI are defined by placing a sensor anywhere within the physical domain Ω to record $E(x)$. For computational simplicity, we discretize the space of potential QoI using a grid of 39×39 uniformly spaced interior points in Ω. We interpolate other QoI values on the interior of this grid and we show the response of all the (error-free) QoI for a single random sample $\lambda \in [0, 0.2]^2$ is shown in Fig. 1.

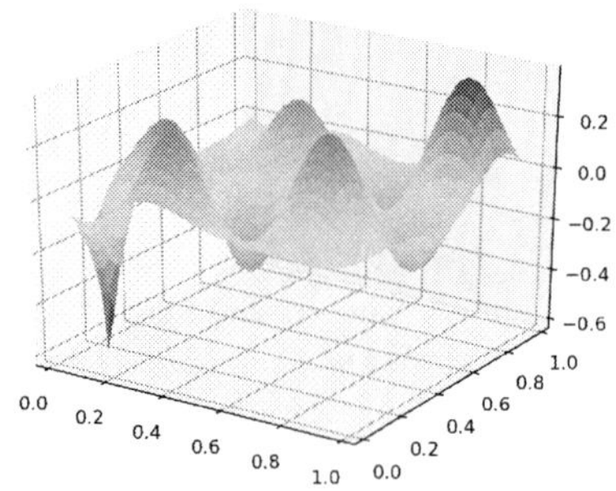

Fig. 1. $E(x)$ on interior of Ω for a single random sample $\lambda \in [0, 0.2]^2$.

B. Consistent Bayesian Inference

We let Λ denote the space of all possible parameter values and $\mathcal{D}$ the space of all possible QoI values for a specific QoI map denoted by Q. Given a prior probability density function (pdf) $\pi_\Lambda^{\text{prior}}$ on Λ and an observed data pdf $\pi_\mathcal{D}^{\text{obs}}$ on $\mathcal{D}$, it was proven in [1] that the *posterior pdf*, $\pi_\Lambda^{\text{post}}$, defined by:

$$\pi_\Lambda^{\text{post}}(\lambda) = \pi_\Lambda^{\text{prior}}(\lambda) \frac{\pi_\mathcal{D}^{\text{obs}}(Q(\lambda))}{\pi_\mathcal{D}^{Q(\text{prior})}(Q(\lambda))}, \qquad (2)$$

is unique and stable with respect to perturbations in either the observed data or specification of the prior. Here, $\pi_\mathcal{D}^{Q(\text{prior})}$ denotes the push-forward density of $\pi_\Lambda^{\text{prior}}$, i.e., $\pi_\mathcal{D}^{Q(\text{prior})}$ is obtained by propagating $\pi_\Lambda^{\text{prior}}$ through the QoI map Q. Moreover, $\pi_\Lambda^{\text{post}}$ is consistent in the sense that the push-forward density of $\pi_\Lambda^{\text{post}}$ through Q gives $\pi_\mathcal{D}^{\text{obs}}$. Clearly, the choice of Q plays a role in solving the SIP as evidenced by the form of the solution in (2). Moreover, different choices of Q may define completely different data spaces $\mathcal{D}$ for which the accuracy or availability of experimental data may vary significantly.

C. Optimal Experimental Design

Conceptually, an experimental design defining a QoI map Q is considered informative if the posterior is significantly different from the prior probability measure. We use the KL divergence to quantify this difference, which is commonly used in the Bayesian OED community [3]. The KL divergence of $\pi_\Lambda^{\text{post}}$ from $\pi_\Lambda^{\text{prior}}$, denoted KL_Q to emphasize the role that the map Q plays in determining $\pi_\Lambda^{\text{post}}$, is given by:

$$KL_Q(\pi_\Lambda^{\text{prior}} : \pi_\Lambda^{\text{post}}) := \int_\Lambda \pi_\Lambda^{\text{post}} \log\left(\frac{\pi_\Lambda^{\text{post}}}{\pi_\Lambda^{\text{prior}}}\right) d\mu_\Lambda. \quad (3)$$

For simplicity, we assume that any $\pi_\mathcal{D}^{\text{obs}}$ has a $N(d,1)$ distribution where $d \in \mathcal{D}$ is the mean datum recorded for the particular QoI. Hyper-parameters can also be incorporated into the analysis, e.g., to describe uncertainties in the standard deviation of the measurements. Using the assumed parametric form, the possible $\pi_\mathcal{D}^{\text{obs}}$ are easily indexed by $d \in \mathcal{D}$, and we write $\pi_\mathcal{D}^{\text{obs}}(Q(\lambda); d)$, $\pi_\Lambda^{\text{post}}(\lambda; d)$, and $KL_Q(d)$ to make the dependence of these quantities on $d \in \mathcal{D}$ more explicit. The push-forward $\pi_\mathcal{D}^{Q(\text{prior})}$ is useful in assessing relatively likelihoods for the $d \in \mathcal{D}$ prior to collecting experimental data, i.e., we expect a priori that some $d \in \mathcal{D}$ are more likely than others. Therefore, we use the push-forward of the prior to compute the EIG. This utilizes both the prior knowledge of the parameters and the choice of map Q. The EIG, denoted $\mathbb{E}(KL_Q)$, is then given as:

$$\mathbb{E}(KL_Q) := \int_\mathcal{D} KL_Q(d)\pi_\mathcal{D}^{Q(\text{prior})}(d)d\mu_\mathcal{D}. \quad (4)$$

Given a space of possible QoI maps, denoted by $\mathcal{Q}$, we then define the OED as the map Q that maximizes the EIG, i.e., the OED is given by:

$$Q^{\text{opt}} := \arg\max_{Q\in\mathcal{Q}} \mathbb{E}(KL_Q). \quad (5)$$

III. Numerical Results and Discussion

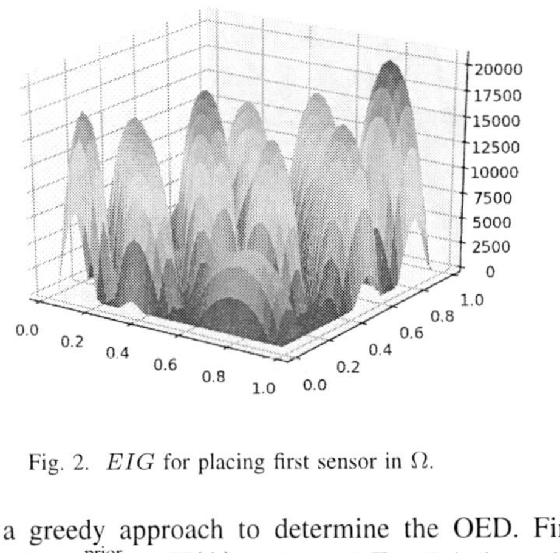

Fig. 2. *EIG* for placing first sensor in Ω.

We use a greedy approach to determine the OED. First, we assume that $\pi_\Lambda^{\text{prior}} \sim U(\Lambda)$ and use $1E+2$ independent identically distributed samples in Λ, and their corresponding QoI values in $\mathcal{D}$, to estimate the EIG in (4) for placing a single sensor somewhere in the 39×39 interior grid of Ω mentioned above. We plot the results in Fig. 2. While there are many local maxima, there is a clear global maximum at $(0.85, 0.85)$ near the upper right corner of Ω. This maximum occurs in a typical location for the maximum recorded $E(x)$ response (e.g., see Fig. 1), which is also on the opposite corner of the physical domain from the possible location of the point source in $[0, 0.2]^2$. Fixing this as the first QoI,

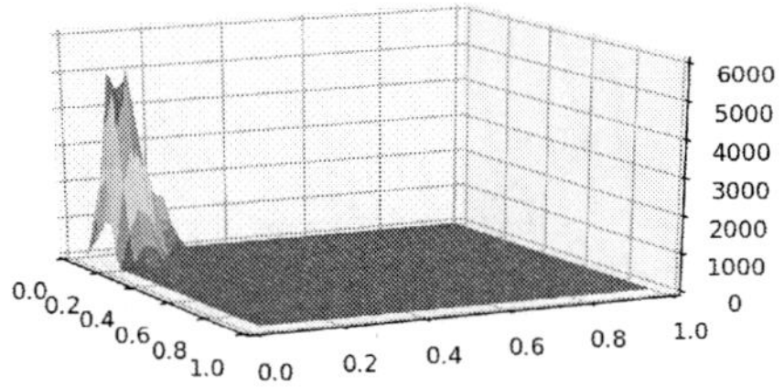

Fig. 3. *EIG* for placing second sensor in Ω.

we then proceed with the greedy approach by repeating the computations to determine the maximal EIG for a vector-valued QoI map where the first sensor is fixed at $(0.85, 0.85)$. We plot these results in Fig. 3 and observe that any maxima for the EIG now only occur in a single location due to the information gained from placing the first sensor. Moreover, the global maximum occurs at $(.175, .075)$, which is within the physical area $[0, 0.2]^2$ where the point source is allowed to vary.

IV. Conclusions

We demonstrated how the optimal placement of a single sensor should be far away from the possible locations of point sources in order to maximize EIG, and only the second sensor should be placed near where the point sources are restricted. Such results, which may seem counter-intuitive, demonstrate the importance of combining probability models with physics to quantify system behavior and uncertainties when deciding which measurement data are most likely to reduce uncertainties.

V. Acknowledgment

This material is based upon work supported by the U.S. Department of Energy Office of Science, Office of Advanced Scientific Computing Research, Applied Mathematics program under Award Number DOE-SC00009279 as part of the DiaMonD Multifaceted Mathematics Integrated Capability Center.

References

[1] T. van Erven and P. Harrermoes, "Renyi divergence and Kullback-Leibler divergence," IEEE Transactions on Information Theory, pp. 3797–3820, vol. 60, 2014.

[2] T. Butler, J. Jakeman, and T. Wildey, "A consistent Bayesian formulation for stochastic inverse problems based on push-forward measures," arXiv:1704.00680, pp. 1–25, 2017, unpublished.

[3] S. N. Walsh, T. M. Wildey, and J. D. Jakeman, "Optimal experimental design using a consistent Bayesian approach", ASME J. Risk Uncertainty Part B., 2017, 4(1):011005–011005-19. doi:10.1115/1.4037457.

[4] M. S. Alnaes, et al., "The FEniCS Project Version 1.5," Archive of Numerical Software, vol. 3, 2015.

Accurate and Efficient Bayesian Parameter Inversion Based on Low-Fidelity Model Solutions

Yaning Liu
Department of Mathematical & Statistical Sciences
University of Colorado Denver
Denver, Colorado, USA
yaning.liu@ucdenver.edu

***Abstract*—We propose an efficient Bayesian parameter inversion technique that utilizes the implicit particle filter to characterize the posterior distribution, and a multi-scale surrogate modeling method called the proper orthogonal decomposition mapping method to provide high-fidelity solutions to the forward model by conducting only low-fidelity simulations. The proposed method is applied to the nonlinear Burgers equation, widely used to model electromagnetic waves, with stochastic viscosity and periodic solutions.**

***Index Terms*—Bayesian parameter inversion, implicit particle filters, proper orthogonal decomposition mapping method, surrogate modeling.**

I. Introduction

Bayesian parameter inversion (BPI) techniques are desirable for estimating model parameter, since they consider the uncertainty associated with the inversion in the form of a posterior distribution. As a widely used BPI technique, the Markov Chain Monte Carlo (MCMC) method is robust for estimating posterior information; however, the efficiency of MCMC can be low due to its acceptance-rejection nature. The particle filtering (PF) method, as an alternative to MCMC, has many advantages. Recently, a particular PF method, the implicit particle filter (IPF), was developed in [1], which can alleviate or prevent the so-called "weight collapse" phenomenon. It has been shown, by [2] for instance, that IPF can outperform state-of-the-art MCMC for some applications.

Surrogate models, also known as reduced order models, serving as efficient approximations for computationally expensive models, have been used in BPI, including IPF [2], to improve efficiency. One particular technique, called the proper orthogonal decomposition mapping method (PODMM) [3], can approximate a fine-resolution solution from a coarse-resolution solution, which is significantly more inexpensive to obtain.

In this paper, we consider BPI with an IPF for the one-dimensional Burgers equation with stochastic viscosity. To further improve the efficiency, we couple PODMM with IPF by building a multi-scale surrogate mapping to accurately approximate the solutions to the Burgers equation.

II. Methodology

A. Implicit Particle Filters

IPFs are based on importance sampling, where an importance distribution is constructed by computing the maximizer of the posterior $p(\boldsymbol{\theta}|\boldsymbol{D})$, i.e., the maximum a posteriori (MAP) of the parameters $\boldsymbol{\theta}$ given the data D, which can be found by minimizing the objective function:

$$F(\boldsymbol{\theta}) = -\log\left(p(\boldsymbol{\theta})p(\boldsymbol{D}|\boldsymbol{\theta})\right),$$

where $p(\boldsymbol{\theta})$ and $p(\boldsymbol{D}|\boldsymbol{\theta})$ are the prior distribution and the likelihood functions, respectively. Once the minimization problem is solved, one generates samples in the neighborhood of the minimizer $\boldsymbol{\mu} = \arg\min F$ as follows. A sequence of reference variables $\{\boldsymbol{\xi}_i\}_{i=1}^N$ are first sampled from a reference probability distribution $g(\boldsymbol{\xi})$, and subsequently each target posterior sample $\boldsymbol{\theta_i}$ is obtained by solving,

$$F(\boldsymbol{\theta}_i) - \phi = G(\boldsymbol{\xi}_i) - \gamma, \tag{1}$$

where $\phi = \min_{\boldsymbol{\theta}} F$, $G(\boldsymbol{\xi}) = -\log\left(g(\boldsymbol{\xi})\right)$ and $\gamma = \min_{\boldsymbol{\xi}} G$. If we replace $F(\boldsymbol{\theta})$ by its second-order Taylor expansion around the MAP $\boldsymbol{\mu}$, $F_0(\boldsymbol{\theta})$, and use a standard Gaussian reference variable, then the solution to (1) takes the simpler form:

$$\boldsymbol{\theta}_i = \boldsymbol{\mu} + L^{-T}\boldsymbol{\xi}_i, \tag{2}$$

where L is a lower triangular matrix obtained from the Cholesky decomposition of the Hessian matrix around $\boldsymbol{\mu}$. The sample weights are,

$$w_i \propto \exp\left(F_0(\boldsymbol{\theta_i}) - F(\boldsymbol{\theta_i})\right). \tag{3}$$

The posteriors are then represented by the ensemble of weighted samples $\{(\boldsymbol{\theta}_i, w_i)\}_{i=1}^N$.

B. Proper Orthogonal Decomposition Mapping Method

PODMM maps $\boldsymbol{g} = [g_1, \ldots, g_{\mathcal{N}_g}]^T$, the coarse-resolution solutions, to fine-resolution solutions $\boldsymbol{f} = [f_1, \ldots, f_{\mathcal{N}_f}]^T$, where $\mathcal{N}_g$ and $\mathcal{N}_f$ are the respective degrees of freedom. Suppose N coarse- and fine-resolution solutions, $\{\boldsymbol{g}_1, \ldots, \boldsymbol{g}_N\}$ and $\{\boldsymbol{f}_1, \ldots, \boldsymbol{f}_N\}$ are available for the training process. We first form the data matrix $\boldsymbol{W}^{\text{PODMM}}$ given by:

$$\boldsymbol{W}^{\text{PODMM}} = \begin{bmatrix} \boldsymbol{f}_1 - \bar{\boldsymbol{f}} & \cdots & \boldsymbol{f}_N - \bar{\boldsymbol{f}} \\ \boldsymbol{g}_1 - \bar{\boldsymbol{g}} & \cdots & \boldsymbol{g}_N - \bar{\boldsymbol{g}} \end{bmatrix},$$

where $\bar{\boldsymbol{f}}$ and $\bar{\boldsymbol{g}}$ are the averages of $\{\boldsymbol{f}_i\}_{i=1}^N$ and $\{\boldsymbol{g}_i\}_{i=1}^N$ respectively. We then determine M right singular vectors, $\boldsymbol{V} = \{\boldsymbol{v}_1, \ldots, \boldsymbol{v}_M\}$ corresponding to the M largest singular values

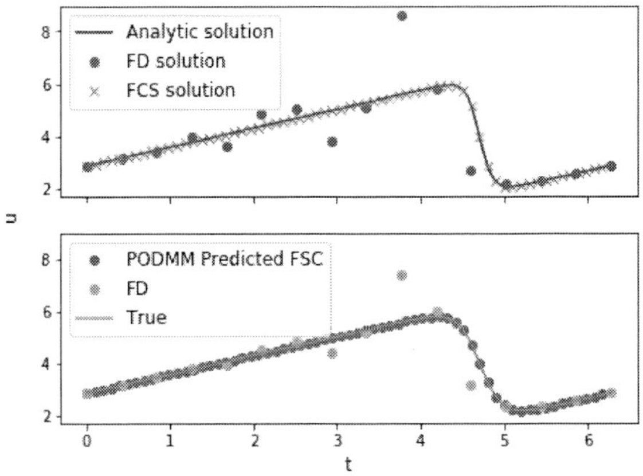

Fig. 1. Top: Analytic, FD and FCS solutions for Burgers equation with $\nu = 0.2$; bottom: Analytic, FD and PODMM-predicted FCS solutions for the case $\nu = 0.302$.

for $\boldsymbol{W}^{\text{PODMM}}$. The proper orthogonal decomposition (POD) bases are $\boldsymbol{\xi}_i = \boldsymbol{W}^{\text{PODMM}}\boldsymbol{v}_i, i = 1, \ldots, M$. Split $\boldsymbol{\xi}_i$ into,

$$\boldsymbol{\xi}_i = \begin{bmatrix} \boldsymbol{\xi}_i^f \\ \boldsymbol{\xi}_i^g \end{bmatrix}.$$

For any given coarse-resolution $\boldsymbol{g} \notin \{\boldsymbol{g}_1, \ldots, \boldsymbol{g}_N\}$, we can predict the corresponding fine-resolution $\boldsymbol{f}$ by,

$$\boldsymbol{f} = \bar{\boldsymbol{f}} + \sum_{i=1}^{M} \gamma_i \boldsymbol{\xi}_i^f,$$

where $\gamma = \{\gamma_1, \ldots, \gamma_m\}$ is the solution to the least-squares problem,

$$\arg\min_{\gamma} \left\| \boldsymbol{g} - \bar{\boldsymbol{g}} - \sum_{i=1}^{M} \gamma_i \boldsymbol{\xi}_i^g \right\|_2$$

III. Results and Discussion

Consider the one-dimensional Burgers equation,

$$\frac{\partial u}{\partial t} + \frac{1}{2}\frac{\partial u^2}{\partial x} - \nu \frac{\partial^2 u}{\partial x^2} = 0,$$

where the viscosity ν is a random variable. We consider a periodic solution with an infinite number of N-wave solutions.

The coarse-resolution solutions are obtained from a second-order finite difference (FD) spatial discretization on a grid of 16 points, while the fine-resolution solutions are computed by a Fourier spectral collocation (FSC) method with 64 spatial collocation points.

TABLE I
Statistical moments of the prior and posterior densities

	mean	variance	skewness	kurtosis
prior	0.4	0.04	0.0	0.0
PODMM posterior	0.2517	9.5645E-4	0.1168	2.8127
FSC posterior	0.2517	9.5645E-4	0.1168	2.8127

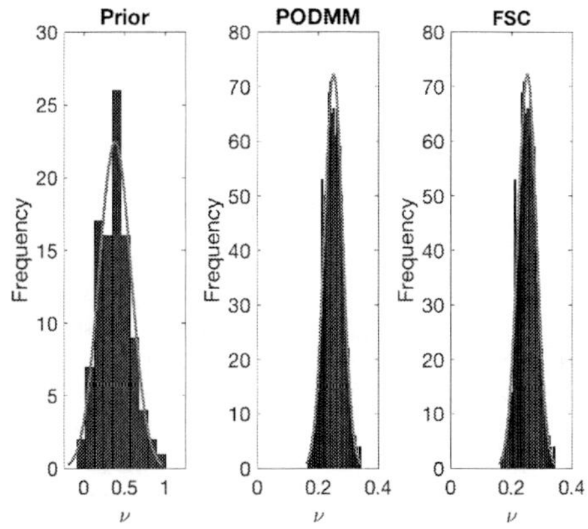

Fig. 2. Prior density and posterior densities estimated by IPF using PODMM and FCS.

Fig. 1 (top) shows the analytical, FD, and FCS solutions corresponding to $\nu = 0.2$. The FD solution oscillates around the shock, while the FCS solution resolves the transition zone well.

To test the performance of PODMM surrogate model in IPF, we consider a synthetic test case, where the FCS solution corresponding to $\nu = 0.2$ is perturbed by a Gaussian noise with mean 0 and 10% of the solution as the standard deviation. The prior distribution for the viscosity is also taken as Gaussian: $\mathcal{N}(0.4, 0.2^2)$. A set of 64 training data $\boldsymbol{g}_i, \boldsymbol{f}_i, i = 1, \ldots, 64$ is generated to construct the PODMM surrogate.

Fig. 1 (bottom) demonstrates that the PODMM-predicted FSC fine-resolution solution corresponding to $\nu = 0.302$ is in good agreement with the analytical solution.

We now show the posterior distributions of ν generated by the FCS and PODMM-predicted FCS solutions in the IPF. Fig. 2 shows that the probability densities estimated from the samples for the two solutions are nearly indistinguishable (middle and right). Also shown is the prior normal distribution (left), which is significantly different from the posteriors. To confirm it, the statistical moments of these distributions are given in Table I.

As a result, we have achieved high accuracy in estimating the posterior using the PODMM surrogate model, while saving significant computational time. The computational cost of the fine-resolution FCS solution in our example is about 10 times that of the FD solution, while the cost of PODMM prediction is negligible.

References

[1] A. J. Chorin and X. Tu, "Implicit sampling for particle filters," Proc. Natl. Acad. Sci. 106 (41), pp. 17249–17254.

[2] Y. Liu, G. S. H. Pau, and S. Finsterle, "Implicit sampling combined with reduced order modeling for the inversion of vadose zone hydrological data," Comput. Geosci., vol. 108, pp. 21–32, 2017.

[3] G. S. H. Pau, C. Shen, W. J. Riley, and Y. Liu, "Accurate and efficient prediction of fine-resolution hydrologic and carbon dynamic simulations from coarse-resolution models," Water Resour. Res., vol. 52, pp. 791–812.

Multi-Fidelity Approach for Polynomial Chaos Based Statistical Analysis of Microwave Networks

Aditi K. Prasad and Sourajeet Roy

Department of Electrical and Computer Engineering, Colorado State University, Fort Collins, Colorado, CO 80253 USA

Abstract — **In this paper, a novel polynomial chaos based approach for the fast statistical analysis of complex microwave structures is proposed. This approach leverages a highly efficient closed form low-fidelity model elicited from the high-dimensional model representation (HDMR) of the network. By cross-cutting the efficiency of this low-fidelity model with the accuracy of general high-fidelity simulations, the accuracy-CPU cost tradeoff for the statistical analysis can be achieved.**

I. Introduction

The generalized polynomial chaos (PC) theory is a widely accepted numerical approach for statistical analysis of circuits and systems [1]-[3]. In this approach, the uncertainty in a network response is modeled as a linear combination of polynomial basis functions of the input network parameters [1]-[3]. The coefficients of the expansion form the new unknowns of the network and can be evaluated via repeated black box solutions of the original network model [2],[3]. The main drawback with PC approaches is that the number of coefficients to be evaluated increases in a polynomial manner with the number of random parameters or dimensions. As a result, classical PC approaches are computationally prohibitive for statistical analysis of high-dimensional problems.

This paper presents a more efficient alternative to the traditional PC approaches. First, a closed form low-fidelity model of the network response is constructed using unidimensional PC expansions elicited from the first order terms of a high-dimensional model representation (HDMR). This low-fidelity model can be used to analytically emulate the network response at a fraction of the CPU costs required for a rigorous high-fidelity simulation. However, this efficiency comes at the cost of the low accuracy of the model caused by the negligence of the higher order HDMR terms. Next, a nonintrusive linear regression approach to evaluate the PC coefficients of the full-blown expansion is adopted. In this regression approach, the majority of the deterministic black box network solutions are determined by probing the closed-form low-fidelity model. In order to compensate for the lower accuracy of the low-fidelity model, only a limited number of high-fidelity simulations of the network response are added. In effect, the efficiency of the low-fidelity model is cross-cut with the accuracy of high-fidelity simulations. Notably the fraction of low-fidelity solutions to high-fidelity simulations can be easily tuned for the optimal accuracy-CPU cost tradeoff.

II. Development of Proposed Multi-Fidelity Approach

A general microwave network is considered where the input uncertainty is represented by n mutually uncorrelated random dimensions $\boldsymbol{\lambda}=[\lambda_1,\lambda_2,..\lambda_n]$. Traditional PC approaches model the resultant uncertainty in the unknown current/voltage responses, $\mathbf{X}(t,\boldsymbol{\lambda})$, using a linear combination of orthogonal polynomials as:

$$\mathbf{X}(t,\boldsymbol{\lambda})=\sum_{k=0}^{P}\mathbf{X}_k(t)\boldsymbol{\Phi}_k(\boldsymbol{\lambda}), \tag{1}$$

where $\Phi_k(\boldsymbol{\lambda})$ is the kth degree multivariate polynomial, $\mathbf{X}_k(t)$ is the corresponding coefficient, and the number of terms $P+1 = (n+m)!/(n!m!)$, m being the maximum degree of the expansion. In this paper, a high dimensional model representation (HDMR) of the network of (1) is considered where any response $x(t,\boldsymbol{\lambda})\in \mathbf{X}(t,\boldsymbol{\lambda})$ can be represented as a hierarchical superposition of functions describing the interactions among the random dimensions as: [4]

$$x(t,\boldsymbol{\lambda})=x_0(t)+\sum_{i=1}^{n}x_i(t,\lambda_i)+\sum_{1\le i,j\le n}x_i(t,\lambda_i,\lambda_j)+\ldots+x_{12\ldots n}(t,\lambda_i\ldots\lambda_n). \tag{2}$$

In (2), x_0 is the mean value of $x(t,\boldsymbol{\lambda})$, $x_i(t,\lambda_i)$ represents the contribution of λ_i to $x(t,\boldsymbol{\lambda})$ acting alone, $x_{ij}(t,\lambda_i, \lambda_j)$ represents the pairwise contribution of λ_i and λ_j to $x(t,\boldsymbol{\lambda})$ etc. The first order terms of (2) can be expressed using cut-HDMR [4] as:

$$x_i(t,\lambda_i)=x(t,\boldsymbol{\lambda})\big|_{\boldsymbol{\lambda}^{(0)}\setminus\lambda_i}-x_0(t), \tag{3}$$

where $\boldsymbol{\lambda}^{(0)}\setminus\lambda_i$ represents the vector where all $\boldsymbol{\lambda}$ except λ_i is 0. These first order terms can now be modeled as 1D PC expansions:

$$x_i(t,\lambda_i)\approx\sum_{k=1}^{m}x_k^{(i)}(t)\phi_k(\lambda_i), \tag{4}$$

where $x_i^{(k)}(t)$ represents the kth coefficient and ϕ_k is the corresponding 1D basis. The coefficients of (4) can be evaluated using the pseudo-spectral collocation technique in conjunction with (3) [3]. Now, neglecting the higher order HDMR terms of (2), a low-fidelity PC representation of the response $x(t,\boldsymbol{\lambda})$ is obtained as:

$$x(t,\boldsymbol{\lambda})\approx x_0(t)+\sum_{i=1}^{n}\sum_{k=1}^{m}x_k^{(i)}(t)\phi_k(\lambda_i). \tag{5}$$

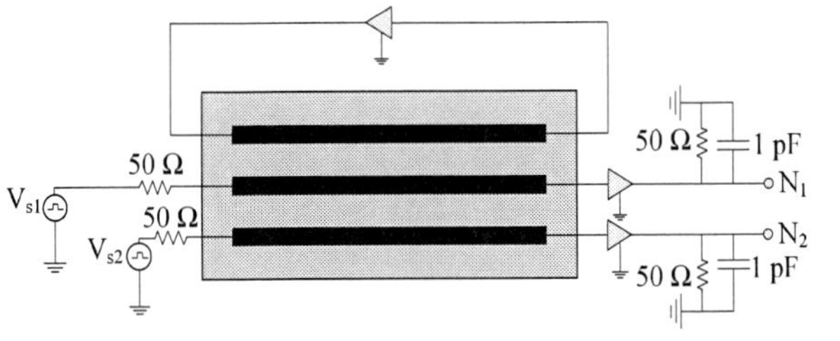

Fig. 1. Coupled transmission line network schematic.

TABLE I
CHARACTERISTICS OF RANDOM PARAMETERS OF NETWORK OF FIG. 1

Random Parameters	Mean	Relative SD
ε_r (Relative permittivity of dielectric)	4.4	10%
σ (Metal conductivity)	5.8e7	
t (Thickness of metal)	5 μm	
w (Width of transmission lines)	180 μm	
h_1 (TL_1 height)	50 μm	
h_2 (TL_2 height)	70 μm	
h_3 (TL_3 height)	60 μm	
s (line spacing)	90 μm	
len (NMOS channel length)	0.1 μm	
wid (NMOS channel width)	10 μm	

The model of (5) is closed form in nature and can be used to analytically emulate the response instead of using a rigorous and time consuming high-fidelity simulation.

Next, to recover the coefficients of (1), the linear regression approach is chosen which typically requires $K = 2(P+1)$ black box model simulations of the network response [2]. In this paper, an iterative algorithm is used to find the fraction of K simulations performed using the low-fidelity model. This algorithm begins by initially assuming that all K simulations are performed using the low-fidelity model of (5). Thereafter, the number of high-fidelity network simulations is increased in steps of k nodes per iteration and the PC coefficients are reevaluated. The value of k is kept small enough (k = 10% of K) to minimize any overshoot beyond the optimal number of high-fidelity simulations. As the number of high-fidelity simulations increases per iteration relative to the number of low-fidelity simulations, the resultant improvement in the accuracy of the response variance is computed as:

$$\eta = \int_0^{T_{\max}} \left(\sum_{i=1}^{P+1} \left(\hat{x}_i^{(r)}\right)^2 - \sum_{i=1}^{P+1} \left(\hat{x}_i^{(r-1)}\right)^2 \right) dt \Bigg/ \int_0^{T_{\max}} \sum_{i=1}^{P+1} \left(\hat{x}_i^{(r)}\right)^2 dt, \quad (6)$$

where $\hat{x}$ are the computed PC coefficients and the superscript r is the iteration count. As the iteration count increases, the error in the numerator of η steadily decreases. Once the value of η falls below a prescribed tolerance, the iterations are halted.

III. NUMERICAL RESULT AND DISCUSSION

To validate the proposed approach, the multicondutor transmission line (MTL) network of Fig. 1 is considered. The

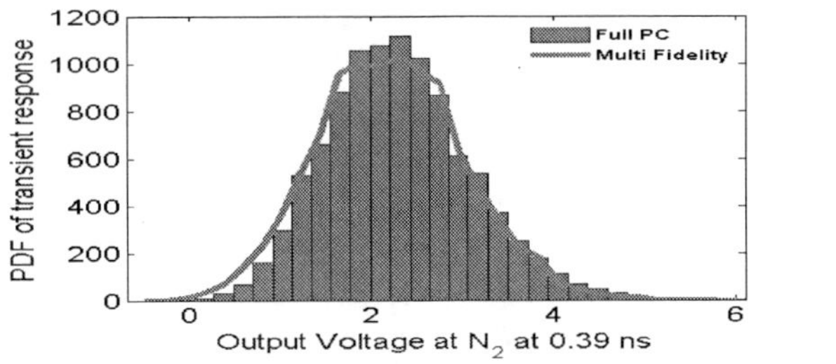

Fig. 2. Probability distribution function of transient response at node N_2 at timepoint of maximum standard deviation (t = 0.39 ns).

MTLs are terminated with cascode amplifiers modeled using SPICE level-49 CMOS transistors. The input waveform to lines 2 and 3 are trapezoidal pulses with rise/fall time T_r = 0.1 ns, pulse width T_w = 1 ns, and amplitude 5V. The uncertainty in the network is introduced via n = 10 random variables whose characteristics are shown in Table I. For this example, a Hermite PC expansion of degree m = 3 is required. The uncertainty quantification of the network is performed using two PC approaches – the proposed multi-fidelity approach and the traditional linear regression approach of [2]. The low-fidelity model requires only $(m+1)n+1$ = 41 SPICE simulations. In the multi-fidelity stage, only 30% of the $2(P+1)$ = 572 regression nodes (i.e., 171 nodes) requires a high-fidelity SPICE simulation translating to a speedup of more than 5 times over the traditional linear regression approach. The probability density of the transient response at N_2 evaluated at the time point when the standard deviation is maximum (0.39 ns) using the above methods and 10,000 samples is compared in Fig. 2. Despite the speedup, the proposed approach exhibits good accuracy relative to the traditional linear regression approach.

IV. CONCLUSION

In this paper, a new multi-fidelity approach is proposed for the fast evaluation of PC coefficients. In the future, this work can be extended to include epistemic uncertainties that arise due to lack of knowledge of the network parameters.

REFERENCES

[1] P. Manfredi, D. Vande Ginste, D. De Zutter, and F. Canavero, "Stochastic modeling of nonlinear circuits via SPICE-compatible spectral equivalents," *IEEE Trans. Circuits Syst.*, vol. 61, no. 7, pp. 2057–2065, Jul. 2014.

[2] A. K. Prasad, M. Ahadi, and S. Roy, "Multidimensional uncertainty quantification of microwave/RF networks using linear regression and optimal design of experiments," *IEEE Trans. Microwave Theory Techn.*,vol. 64, no. 8, pp. 2433-2446, Aug. 2016.

[3] A. C. Yucel, H. Bagci, and E. Michielssen, "An ME-PC enhanced HDMR method for efficient statistical analysis of multiconductor transmission line networks," *IEEE Trans. Comp., Packag. and Manuf. Technol.*, vol. 5, no. 5, pp. 685-696, May 2015.

[4] H. Rabitz and O. F. Alis, "General formulation of high-dimensional model representations," *Journal of Math. Chem.*, vol. 50, no. 2-3, pp. 197-233,1999.

Augmented Surrogates for Predictive Extrapolation in Electromagnetics

Varis Carey
Department of Mathematical and Statistical Sciences
University of Colorado Denver
varis.carey@ucdenver.edu

Abstract—**Surrogate models are a popular solution for predictive science of complex models with restricted computational budgets. We introduce the augmented surrogate, an adaption allowing both extrapolation and cost reduction for training the surrogate, and give an illustrative example for a prediction scenario for the Helmholtz problem.**

I. Introduction

Prediction under uncertainty is often an expensive and complicated process. The tradeoff between the computational cost of complex models and the loss of predictive accuracy associated with simpler models is a modern challenge in the field of uncertainty quantification(UQ).

The traditional approach to prediction, with or without extrapolation, is to sample the model parameter input space $\theta = \theta_1, \theta_2, \ldots, \theta_d$, evaluate the model, and return a quantity of interest (QoI) $Q(\theta)$. Most realistic QoI maps are nonlinear in the QoI map(even if the governing PDE is linear), so the probability distribution function(pdf) of $Q(\theta)$ will have to be estimate in a non-parametric way, typically by kernel density estimation. The mean-integrated squared error of the approximate pdf converges with a rate of $\mathcal{O}(N^{-2/(d+4)})$, where N is the number of samples of the model and d is the dimension of the input space. As each sample typically involves a PDE solve and subsequent post-processing, this process quickly becomes exorbitantly expensive. One panacea for this cost is dimension reduction, trying to discover a reduced set of (potentially mapped) variables $\hat{\theta}_1, \hat{\theta}_2, \ldots, \hat{\theta}_l$, $l < d$. Most methods for this process (for an expensive model) usually explore the d-dimensional parameter space in some systematic, structured manner.

A surrogate model replaces the large cost of the model solve with a fast, explicit function evaluation. The surrogate model is constructed via interpolation or regression on a modest number of potentially deterministic traning samples M. The error from insufficient samples in the kernel density estimation is exchanged for the error between the true QoI $Q(\theta)$ and surrogate QoI $Q_S(\theta)$[1]. Sparse grid approaches [2], [3] give roughly the same error(modulo a factor of n^{d-1}, where d is the dimension and n is the number of training points)) as traditional tensor-product surrogates. However, the number of samples is $\mathcal{O}(2^n n^{d-1})$, instead of the full grid cost of $\mathcal{O}(2^{nd})$. These savings and accuracy can potentailly be increased by adopting adaptive sparse grid surrogates[2].

In predictive extrapolation, the target scenario for $Q(\theta)$ is often sufficiently expensive to even make the surrogate approach tenuous. One strategy in this situation is to construct the surrogate using a sequence of lower-fidelity models to construct $\tilde{Q}(\theta)$, and then train the surrogate[4]. This often requires a good characterization of the error between $Q(\theta)$ and $\tilde{Q}(\theta)$. Another approach is to add deterministic parameters that describes "nearby" scenarios, s.t. $Q(\theta) = A(\theta, k_1, k_2, \ldots, k_r)$, k_i fixed. We call the determanistic parameters k_i augmentation parameters, and the surrogate model A_S of A, the augmented surrogate. Moderate gains are achieved when the number of augmentation parameters is small and the cost of sampling A outside of the prediction scenario Q is much cheaper. If the gradient of A with respect to θ is only weakly dependent on the augmentation parameters, great savings can be achieved.

We will now demonstrate this approach on an inhomogeneous Helmholtz problem, using the wavenumber k as the augmentation parameter.

II. Augmented Surrogates for Helmholtz

A. *Inhomogeneous Helmholtz Prediction Scenario*

Let $u(x)$, $x \in \Omega = [0,1] \times [0,1]$, satisfy

$$-\Delta u - k^2 u = f(x, \theta), \quad u = 0, u \in \partial\Omega,$$

$$f(x) = \delta(x - x_1) + \delta(x - x_2), \quad x_1 = (\theta_1, \theta_2), \quad x_2 = (\theta_3, \theta_4),$$

and $\theta_i = \mathcal{U}[-.1 + c_i, .1 + c_i]$, c_i known. We let $Q(u, \theta) = u(\hat{x})$, $\hat{x} = (.75, .75)$.

For $k = 30$ a typical solution is plotted in Figure 1; for "unpolluted" asympototic accuracy we require $k^2 h \leq 1$, where h is the (finite element) mesh size; it is possible to reduce this pollution affect (to $kh \leq 1$) by using non-standard, multiscale FEM[5].

Thes prediction scenario is four-dimensional; a traditional sparse grid showing the training points in two-dimensions in shown in Figure 2. A typical tensor-product surrogate with the same accuracy would require 49 as opposed to 17 samples.

There are two fundmental assumptions in the construction of an augmented surrogate of a n-dimensional predictive scenario $Q(\theta_1, \theta_2, \ldots, \theta_n)$.

1) There exists small number m of (usually deterministic) parameters $d_1, d_2, \ldots, d_m$ that characterize nearby n-dimensional predictive scenarios $\tilde{Q}_i(\theta_1, \theta_2, \ldots, \theta_n)$.

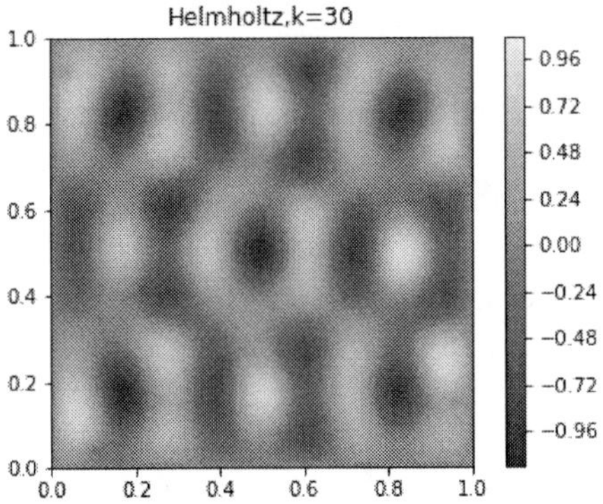

Fig. 1. Model realization for prediction scenario

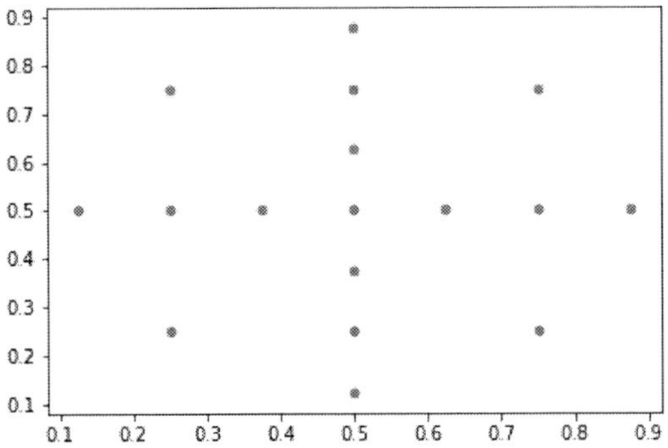

Fig. 2. Two dimensional sparse grid traning points for level 3

2) The cost of a sample from the nearby scenario, $C_{\tilde{Q}_i}$, is much less than the cost C_Q of a sample from the desired prediction scenario.

The *augmented surrogate* is a surrogate model $A(\theta, d)$ constructed on training data $\{(\theta, d), \hat{Q}(\theta, d)\}$ in the $m + n$-dimensional parameter space.

We may employ any of the sparse grid designs discussed in the Introduction. The very nature of the augmented surrogate suggests two strategies: adaptive sparse grids, or unstructured surrogates based on radial basis functions.

An adaptive sparse grid method: The classical sparse grid method is dimension agnostic[2]. All interactions of the same order are treated equally. Often, a small subset of variables and interactions contributes significantly to the variability of the function $Q(\theta, d)$. If the variability in the θ-dimensions is greater than the variability in the scenario parameters($\{d_i\}$) then the overall cost of constructing the larger dimensional surrogate is actually less, due to the cheaper computational cost of $\tilde{Q}_i$.

We modify the greedy algorithm for constructing h-adaptive generalized sparse grid (h-GSG) in [3]. The hierarchical surpluses for the current sparse grid are modified with a cost weight $W_C(d_1, d_2, \ldots, d_m)$ that approximates the relative cost of simulating the added sparse grid point, and a m-dimensional distance metric that penalizes sparse grid samples that are too far away from the prediction scenario $Q(\theta)$. This encourages parameter exploration in θ_i-dimensions at inexpensive simulation levels, while rewarding coarse grid points that reduce the local surrogate error near the prediction scenario $Q(\theta)$. If efficient gradients in parameter space are availabe(*e.g.* adjoint-based methods [6]) then a gradient-informed candiate point for hierarchic surplus calculation may be selected.

	Max Rel. Error	Min Rel. Error	Mean Rel. Error
Sparse Grid Surrogate	.1425	.0567	.0836
Augmented Surrogate	.1638	.0372	.0537

TABLE I
SURROGATE RESULTS ON TEST DATA

III. Numerical Results

We illustrate the augmented surrogate approach for our Helmholtz prediction scenario corresponding to $k = 40$, and use $k = 20$, which leads to an effective simulation cost that is roughly sixteen times cheaper in two spatial dimensions. We compare a non-adaptive surrogate for prediction that uses 9 training points(dimension 4, level 2) with an adaptive augmented surrogate (5 dimensions, total alloted cost = 144 runs at $k = 20$). After training both surrogates, we compare predictive accuracy (fixing $k = 40$ in the augmented surrogate) on 10 randomly selected points in the four-dimensional prediction scenario. We summarize the results in Table I.

IV. Conclusions

We present an augmented surrogate approach for uncertainty quantification and predictive extrapolation for the Helmholtz problem. We are currently applying this technique to the study of turbulent transport in electrostatic and electromagnetic kinetic simulations of tokamak fusion plasmas, where a single sample in the prediction scenario requires a two day run on the entirety of a DOE leadership-class computing facility(Oak Ridge's Titan).

References

[1] T. Butler, C. Dawson, and T. Wildey, "Propagation of uncertainties using improved surrogate models," *SIAM/ASA Journal on Uncertainty Quantification*, vol. 1, no. 1, pp. 164–191, 2013.

[2] H.-J. Bungartz and M. Griebel, "Sparse grids," *Acta Numerica*, vol. 13, p. 147269, 2004.

[3] J. D. Jakeman and S. G. Roberts, "Local and dimension adaptive sparse grid interpolation and quadrature," *CoRR*, vol. abs/1110.0010, 2011.

[4] B. Peherstorfer, K. Willcox, and M. Gunzburger, "Survey of multifidelity methods in uncertainty propagation, inference, and optimization," *Technical Report, Aerospace Computational Design Laboratory*, no. TR-16-1, 2016.

[5] D. Peterseim, "Eliminating the pollution effect in helmholtz problems by local subscale correction," *Mathematics of Computation*, vol. 86, 11 2014.

[6] M. B. Giles and E. Süli, "Adjoint methods for pdes: a posteriori error analysis and postprocessing by duality," *Acta Numerica*, vol. 11, p. 145236, 2002.

Vector Parabolic Equation Modeling of Wireless Propagation in Tunnels with Statistically Rough Surface Walls

Xingqi Zhang* and Costas D. Sarris
The Edward S. Rogers Sr. Department of Electrical and Computer Engineering
University of Toronto, Toronto, ON, Canada
xingqi.zhang@mail.utoronto.ca, costas.sarris@utoronto.ca

***Abstract*—Vector parabolic equation (VPE) methods can be employed to model wave propagation in tunnel environments with high accuracy and computational efficiency. However, the relevant literature is rather limited in terms of modeling wall roughness, a statistical source of additional and often significant path loss. We present a comprehensive approach to embed wall roughness in VPE and demonstrate its validity through comparisons to experimental data.**

I. Introduction

The study of electromagnetic wave propagation in railway and mine tunnels is of great practical interest for the deployment of reliable wireless communication systems in such environments [1], [2]. Although it is often disregarded, surface roughness of tunnel walls can play an important role, as an additional source of path loss.

In [1], an analytical model is developed by Emslie et al. to estimate the excess loss caused by wall roughness. However, the analysis is limited to the dominant mode in canonical waveguides. In addition to waveguide models, the vector parabolic equation (VPE) [3], [4] has emerged as a more versatile propagation modeling technique, especially for tunnels. It is by far more efficient than ray or full-wave methods, while accounting for arbitrary tunnel cross-section and variations in ground elevation.

Research on modeling wall roughness with VPE has been limited so far to small scale roughness in canonical geometries [5]. This paper presents a new approach to incorporating roughness into VPE, which can be applied to arbitrary tunnel geometries and large-scale surface roughness. Validation is provided by comparisons with measured data in realistic guideway scenarios.

II. Statistical Modeling of Rough Surface Walls

A. *Parametrization of Random Rough Surface*

Surface roughness is the local variation of the tunnel wall relative to a mean surface level. Due to lack of complete knowledge of realistic rough surfaces, it is natural to adopt a probabilistic framework, where the height variation of the rough surface is modeled as a random process.

The Karhunen-Loève (KL) expansion is a widely-used technique to represent and parametrize random processes. Let $s(\xi,\omega)$ represent the random process characterizing the height variation of a rough surface:

$$s(\xi,\omega) = \overline{s}(\xi) + \sigma_s \sum_{m=1}^{\infty} \sqrt{\lambda_m} f_m(\xi) Y_m(\omega), \qquad (1)$$

where $\overline{s}(\xi)$ is mean surface height and σ_s is the height deviation. For any fixed ω, $s(\xi,\cdot)$ is a deterministic function representing a realization of the surface geometry; $\omega \in \Omega$ indicates a realization in the probability space Ω; and at a given location ξ, $s(\cdot,\omega)$ is a random variable representing the uncertain height of the surface at this location. $Y_m(\omega)\,(m \geq 1)$ are independent random variables, and λ_m and $f_m(\xi)$ are eigenvalues and eigenfunctions of Fredholm equations:

$$\int_0^L \rho_s(\xi_1,\xi_2) f_m(\xi_2)\, \mathrm{d}\xi_2 = \lambda_m f_m(\xi_1), \qquad (2)$$

where L is the total length of the rough surface and $\rho_s(\xi_1,\xi_2)$ is the correlation function.

B. *Cross-Section Rough Surface Walls*

First, a rough surface is generated according to Eqn. (1). Then, as shown in Fig. 1, the generated surface is mapped to the cross-section geometry of the tunnel, where ξ can be expressed as a function of angle θ_0. For every point near the wall, the normal angle and the distance to the wall are

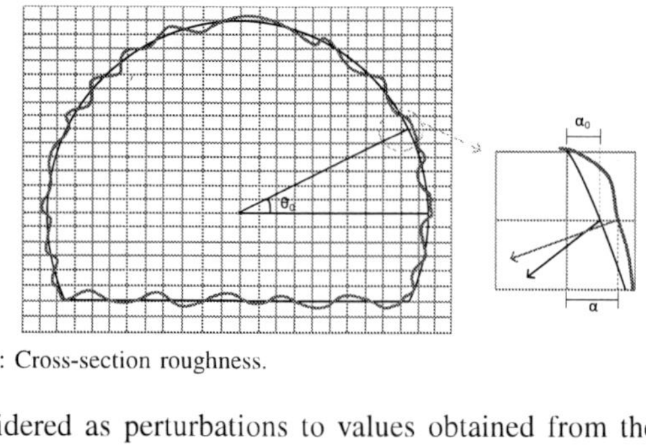

Fig. 1: Cross-section roughness.

considered as perturbations to values obtained from the case with smooth surface wall:

$$\theta = \pi/2 - \tan^{-1}(s'(\xi(\theta_0,\omega))), \qquad (3a)$$

$$\alpha = \alpha_0 + s(\xi(\theta_0,\omega)), \qquad (3b)$$

θ_0 and θ are the normal angles correspond to a smooth surface and a rough surface, respectively; α_0 and α are the distances to the smooth and rough surface walls, respectively.

C. *Longitudinal Rough Surface Walls*

A two-dimensional cut of a tunnel with rough surface walls is shown in Fig. 2. First, the top and bottom rough surfaces are generated according to Eqn. (1). Then, their profiles are approximated using staircase fitting. Each gray bar in Fig. 2 represents one short tunnel section with a length equal to the mesh cell size ($\sim \lambda/10$) along the propagation direction. At the end of each short section, the fields generated on that plane are used as initial conditions for the next section.

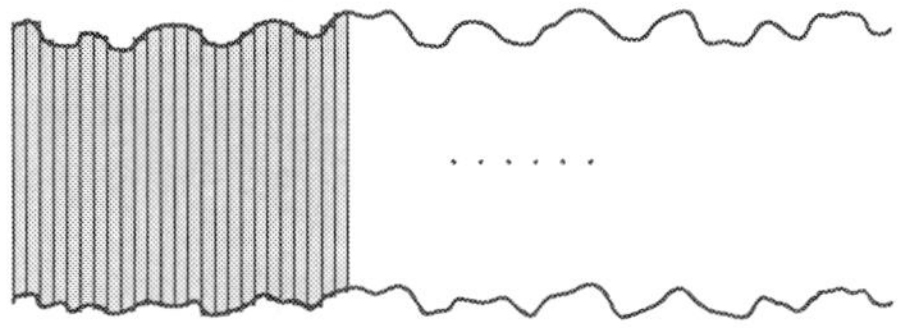

Fig. 2: Staircase fitting of the longitudinal rough surface profile.

III. Numerical Examples

In this section, first, the proposed approach is compared with known theoretical solutions and results in [5] for the case of a canonical waveguide. Then, a realistic mine tunnel geometry is considered.

A. *Canonical Waveguide*

The analytical expressions for the excess loss due to roughness can be found using ray tracing techniques, as outlined in Emslie et al. [1]. The excess loss (in dB) caused by surface roughness for a rectangular waveguide is:

$$L_{\text{rough}} = 4.343\pi^2{\sigma_s}^2\lambda\left(\frac{1}{d_1^4}+\frac{1}{d_2^4}\right)z, \tag{4}$$

where d_1 and d_2 are the width and height of the tunnel, respectively; z is the distance along the propagation direction; σ_s is the height deviation of the rough surface and λ is the free-space wavelength.

For verification, the cross-section dimensions of the tunnel are chosen to correspond with the coal mine tunnel studied in [1], where the width is 2.3 m and the height is 2.1 m. The operating frequency is 1 GHz and the fundamental mode, EH_{11}, with horizontal polarization is used as the initial field. Regarding the rough surface, the height deviation is 0.1 m and the correlation length is 2.5 m. The electrical parameters of the surrounding walls are set to $\varepsilon_r = 12$ and $\sigma_0 = 0.02$ S/m.

The attenuation factors obtained from the proposed approach, analytical solutions, and the method in [5], are summarized in Table I. It can be seen that the excess loss obtained from the proposed approach has a better agreement with the analytical result.

TABLE I: Comparison of the Attenuation Factors

Unit: dB/km	Smooth Surface	Rough Surface	Excess Loss
Analytical	31.0	38.0	7.0
Method in [5]	29.8	36.1	6.3
This work	30.0	37.0	7.0

B. *Morina-Amerika Mine Tunnel*

The tunnel under consideration here is a mine tunnel, which was previously studied in [6]. The cross-section dimensions are 2.3 m×2.1 m. A vertically polarized omnidirectional monopole antenna operating at 860 MHz is employed. The transmitter is mounted on an anchored wooden rod with a height of 1.2 m, as shown in Fig. 3. The receiving antenna is a vertically polarized half-wave dipole antenna placed at the center of the tunnel. Further details for the measurement setup can be found in [6].

The height deviation for the bilateral and top rough surface walls is chosen to be 0.4 m and the correlation length is set to be 2.5 m. The ground is assumed to be smooth. A comparison of the received power is shown in Fig. 3. As can be seen, the obtained simulated results have a good agreement with the measured data.

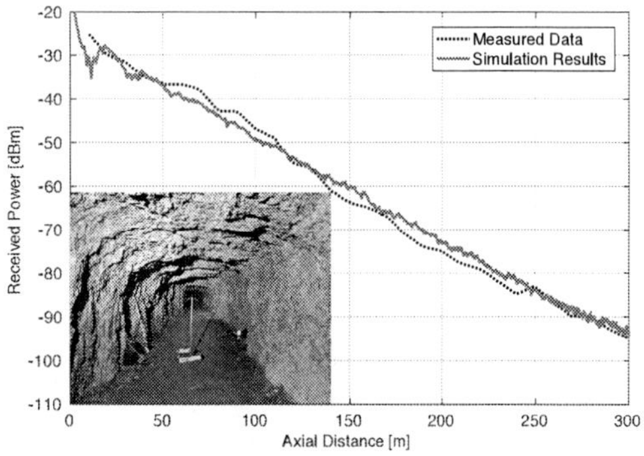

Fig. 3: Comparison between simulated received power and measured data. Source of on-site photo: [6].

References

[1] A. Emslie, R. Lagace, and P. Strong, "Theory of the propagation of UHF radio waves in coal mine tunnels," IEEE Trans. Antennas Propag., vol. 23, no. 2, pp. 192–205, Mar. 1975.

[2] X. Zhang, N. Sood, J. K. Siu, and C. D. Sarris, "A hybrid ray-tracing/vector parabolic equation method for propagation modeling in train communication channels," IEEE Trans. Antennas Propag., vol. 64, no. 5, pp. 1840–1849, May 2016.

[3] X. Zhang and C. D. Sarris, "Error analysis and comparative study of numerical methods for the parabolic equation applied to tunnel propagation modeling," IEEE Trans. Antennas Propag., vol. 63, no. 7, pp. 3025–3034, Jul. 2015.

[4] ——, "A Gaussian beam approximation approach for embedding antennas into vector parabolic equation based wireless channel propagation models," IEEE Trans. Antennas Propag., vol. 65, no. 2, pp. 1840–1849, Feb. 2017.

[5] R. Martelly and R. Janaswamy, "Modeling radio transmission loss in curved, branched and rough-walled tunnels with the ADI-PE method," IEEE Trans. Antennas Propag., vol. 58, no. 6, pp. 2037–2045, Jun. 2010.

[6] M. Rak and P. Pechac, "UHF propagation in caves and subterranean galleries," IEEE Trans. Antennas Propag., vol. 55, no. 4, pp. 1134–1138, Apr. 2007.

Ridge Approximation and Dimension Reduction for an Acoustic Scattering Model

Paul G. Constantine and Jeffrey M. Hokanson
Department of Computer Science
University of Colorado Boulder
Boulder, Colorado 80309
{paul.constantine,jeffrey.hokanson}@colorado.edu

Drew P. Kouri
Optimization and Uncertainty Quantification
Sandia National Laboratories
Albuquerque, NM 87185
dpkouri@sandia.gov

***Abstract*—Problems in uncertainty quantification (UQ) suffer from the curse of dimensionality. One approach to address this issue is to identify and exploit low-dimensional structure in the underlying model. In this paper, we show that low-dimensional active subspaces are *not* present in a particular model arising from acoustic scattering. This suggests that UQ techniques based on active subspaces are not appropriate for this problem.**

I. Introduction

Uncertainty quantification (UQ) seeks to characterize uncertainty in the output of a complex physical model given a characterization of the uncertainty on the model inputs. Such characterization is challenging when the number of inputs is large due to the *curse of dimensionality*. The only way to bypass the curse of dimensionality is to identify and exploit low-dimensional structure in the map from input parameters to model predictions. Denote a generic deterministic map from inputs to an output quantity of interest (QoI) by $f : \mathbb{R}^M \to \mathbb{R}$. The particular low-dimensional structure that we study, called *ridge structure*, can be loosely described as $f(\boldsymbol{\xi}) \approx g(\boldsymbol{A}^T\boldsymbol{\xi})$ for some matrix $\boldsymbol{A} \in \mathbb{R}^{M\times N}$ with $N < M$ and $g : \mathbb{R}^N \to \mathbb{R}$. This description suggests that the model prediction varies primarily along directions defined by the columns of $\boldsymbol{A}$. When such structure exists in a model, UQ can proceed on the coordinates $\boldsymbol{A}^T\boldsymbol{\xi}$, which is a form of dimension reduction. In this paper, we show numerical evidence that such structure does *not* exist in a UQ problem arising from a Helmholtz-based model for acoustic scattering with a random wave number. The absence of this structure is interesting given how prevalent such structures are in physics-based models [1, Chapter 5].

We pursue two numerical techniques for assessing the presence of ridge structure. The first is based on *active subspaces* [1], which are eigenspaces of the matrix

$$\boldsymbol{C} = \mathbb{E}\left[\nabla f(\boldsymbol{\xi})\,\nabla f(\boldsymbol{\xi})^T\right], \tag{1}$$

This work was supported by the Department of Defense, Defense Advanced Research Project Agency's program Enabling Quantification of Uncertainty in Physical Systems. Sandia National Laboratories is a multimission laboratory managed and operated by National Technology and Engineering Solutions of Sandia, LLC, a wholly owned subsidiary of Honeywell International, Inc., for the US Department of Energy's National Nuclear Security Administration under contract DE-NA0003525.

where the expectation is with respect to the given measure on $\boldsymbol{\xi}$. The null space of $\boldsymbol{C}$ identifies directions along which f is constant. Rapid decay in eigenvalues reveals ridge structure, where the important directions are the associated eigenvectors. When gradients are available as a subroutine, we can approximate $\boldsymbol{C}$ and its eigenpairs with simple Monte Carlo. The second approach we use to assess ridge structure is discrete least-squares. Let $(\boldsymbol{\xi}_i, f(\boldsymbol{\xi}_i))$ be given input/output pairs, and consider the nonlinear least-squares problem,

$$\underset{\boldsymbol{U}\in\mathbb{G},g\in\mathbb{P}_k}{\text{minimize}} \sum_{i=1}^{n} \left(f(\boldsymbol{\xi}_i) - g(\boldsymbol{U}^T\boldsymbol{\xi}_i)\right)^2, \tag{2}$$

where $\mathbb{G}$ is the Grassmann manifold of N-dimensional subspaces, and $\mathbb{P}_k$ is the set of polynomials of total degree k in N variables. We call this approach *ridge approximation* [2].

II. A Helmholtz Model for Acoustic Scattering

The model is motivated by direct field acoustic testing (DFAT) [3]. DFAT is a nondestructive method for testing components of engineered systems. The typical setup for DFAT experiments is: (i) surround the component with speakers; (ii) bombard the component with acoustic pressure; and (iii) measure the vibrational response with, e.g., accelerometers. The accelerometer data can then be used to infer material properties of the component. An important QoI in DFAT is the deviation of the acoustic pressure field inside the component from a target pressure field. We model the acoustic pressure field as the solution to Helmholtz equation with random refractive index. See [4] for DFAT optimal control problems constrained by Helmholtz equation.

We consider an idealized DFAT example in the physical domain $D = (-5,5)^2$. Let $D_R = \{x \in D : \|x\|_2 \leq 2\}$ define the component subdomain and $\bar{w}(x)$ denote the target pressure profile. Let $D_C = \{x \in D : 2.5 \leq \|x\|_2 \leq 2.6\}$ denote the speaker subdomain. Fig. 1 depicts the experimental setup. The QoI is

$$J(u) = \frac{1}{2}\int_{D_R} (u(x) - \bar{w}(x))\overline{(u(x) - \bar{w}(x))}\mathrm{d}x, \tag{3}$$

where u is an acoustic pressure field. The uncertain wave number is $k(x) = 10$ if $x \notin D_R$ and $k(x) = 10\,(1 + \varepsilon(x))$ if $x \in D_R$, where ε is the uncertain refractive index.

We model ε by the truncated Karhunen-Loève expansion $\varepsilon(x) = \sum_{m=1}^{M} \phi_m(x)\, \xi_m$, with $M = 40$ terms. Here, $\boldsymbol{\xi} = [\xi_1, \ldots, \xi_m]^T$ is a vector of uncorrelated Gaussian random variables with mean zero and unit variance. This model for refractive index has zero mean, and the basis $\{\phi_m\}$ is derived from eigenpairs of the squared-exponential covariance kernel $0.01^2 \exp(-(x-x')^2/L)$ with correlation length $L > 0$. The acoustic source $s : D \to \mathbb{C}$ is $(1+i)$ in D_C and 0 elsewhere. The acoustic pressure field $u = u(x)$ solves the Helmholtz equation:

$$-\Delta u - k^2 u = s \text{ in } D, \qquad \frac{\partial u}{\partial n} = i k_0 u \text{ on } \partial D. \qquad (4)$$

The real and imaginary components of the desired wave pressure $\bar{w}(x)$ are plotted in Fig. 1 with $k_0 = 10$. We discretize

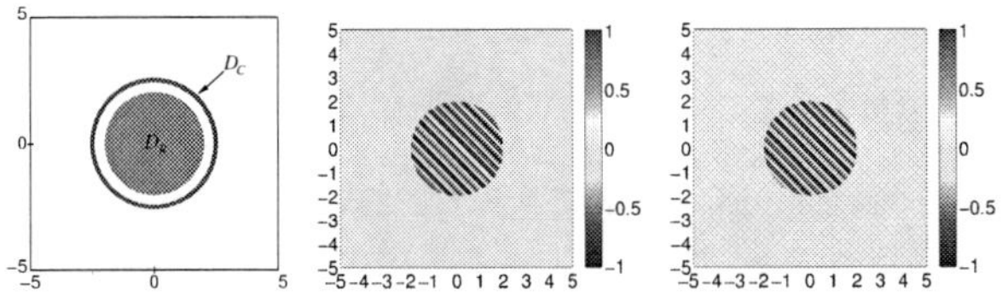

Fig. 1. Speaker subdomain, D_C, and component subdomain, D_R (left). Real (center) and imaginary (right) parts of the desired state, $\bar{w}$.

(4) in space using continuous Q1 finite elements on a uniform mesh of 200×200 quadrilaterals.

III. Numerical Results

The first test we apply to the DFAT QoI (3) as a function of the 40 refractive index coefficients $\boldsymbol{\xi}$ is to randomly sweep the parameter space along random directions to assess smoothness. Fig. 2 shows three representative sweeps revealing that the QoI is smooth but oscillatory. Fig. 3 shows the first 11 eigenvalues of a 20 000-sample estimate of $\boldsymbol{C}$ from (1) and bootstrap-based estimates of the subspace errors. The order-of-magnitude gap between the first and second eigenvalues suggests 1-d ridge structure. Fig. 4 shows a shadow plot (right) of the QoI versus one linear combination of $\boldsymbol{\xi}$ computed as in (2) with a 10 000-sample subset. The leftmost plot shows the 40 components of the computed direction with 10 different data subsets; the plot suggests that computation of these weights is stable. The shadow plot shows that the QoI varies in more than one direction, since the plotted data does *not* look like it comes from a univariate function.

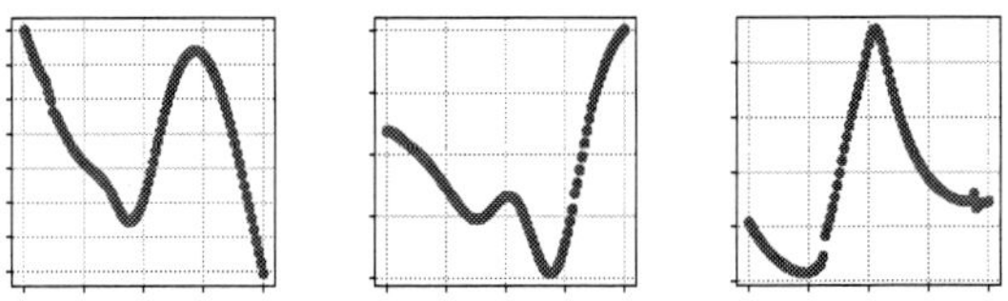

Fig. 2. Random 1d sweeps of the QoI.

Table I shows the 2-norm error in a 10 000-sample testing set for a variety of polynomial degrees and subspace dimensions in (2). The slow decrease in error as degree increases

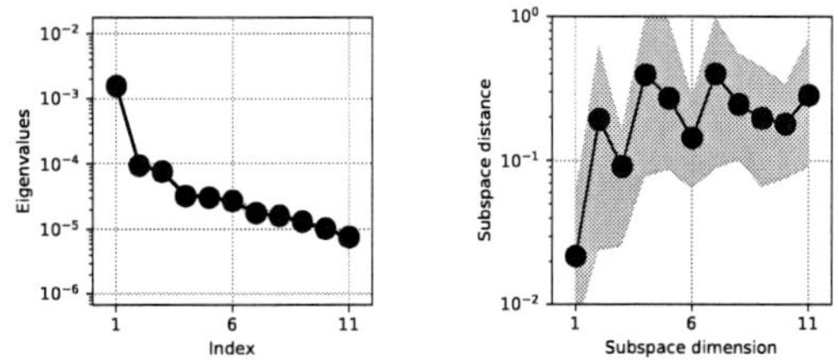

Fig. 3. First 11 eigenvalues (left) of $\boldsymbol{C}$ from (1) and bootstrap-based estimates of Monte Carlo subspace errors (right).

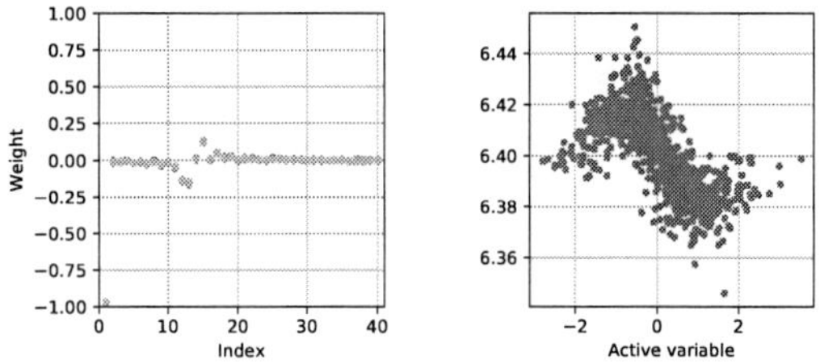

Fig. 4. One-d shadow plot (right) and associated weights (left).

TABLE I
Testing Error in Ridge Approximation (2).

deg \ dim	1	2	3	4	5
2	1.14e+0	1.14e+0	1.13e+0	1.13e+0	1.13e+0
3	9.89e-1	9.63e-1	9.56e-1	9.52e-1	9.50e-1
4	9.72e-1	9.48e-1	9.28e-1	9.25e-1	9.17e-1
5	9.12e-1	8.73e-1	8.52e-1	8.66e-1	8.53e-1

and dimension increases provides further evidence that low-dimensional ridge structure is *not* present in the QoI as a function of the 40 input parameters.

IV. Conclusion

We have determined that a particular QoI from a particular acoustic scattering model as a function of 40 coefficients parameterizing the refractive index does *not* contain low-dimensional ridge structure. This result may help decide among available methods for quantifying uncertainty. One might expect that the responses in related scattering problems might exhibit similar, intrinsically high-dimensional structure.

References

[1] P. G. Constantine, *Active Subspaces: Emerging Ideas in Dimension Reduction for Parameter Studies*. SIAM, Philadelphia, 2015. [Online]. Available: https://doi.org/10.1137/1.9781611973860
[2] P. G. Constantine, A. Eftekhari, J. Hokanson, and R. A. Ward, "A near-stationary subspace for ridge approximation," *Computer Methods in Applied Mechanics and Engineering*, vol. 326, pp. 402–421, 2017. [Online]. Available: https://doi.org/10.1016/j.cma.2017.07.038
[3] P. Larkin and M. Whalen, "Direct, near field acoustic testing," SAE, Tech. Rep., 1999, technical Paper 1999–01–5553.
[4] D. P. Kouri, M. Heinkenschloss, D. Ridzal, and B. G. van Bloemen Waanders, "A trust-region algorithm with adaptive stochastic collocation for PDE optimization under uncertainty," *SIAM Journal on Scientific Computing*, vol. 35, no. 4, pp. A1847–A1879, 2013. [Online]. Available: https://doi.org/10.1137/120892362

Wavelet Model of Multivariate Prior Covariance

Aimé Fournier
Department of Mathematical and Statistical Sciences, University of Colorado Denver, Colorado, USA
aime.fournier@ucdenver.edu

***Abstract*—Initialization of numerical weather-prediction models uses data assimilation to specify an optimal *analysis* state derived from *observations* and the model *background* state. The associated covariance structures are crucial factors. The full *background-error covariance* (BEC) matrix would contain a number of entries of order the square of the nominal degrees of freedom, which for realistic models is prohibitive even to store, let alone compute with. To obtain the ideal diagonal BEC would require solving an intractably large eigenvector problem. A reasonable approach is to approximate the eigenvectors by appropriate known functions, then construct diagonal BEC values accordingly. Until now, the Weather Research and Forecasting (WRF) model data assimilation (WRFDA) used recursive filters for the horizontal factors of these functions. Here an option is introduced to replace those with a little-known wavelet type, the wavelet Parseval frame (i.e., left-invertible transform that preserves the sum of squares). The wavelet option has strong theoretical and empirical support in the reviewed literature. The pseudo-single observation tests presented here exhibit improved representation of horizontal spatial heterogeneity and anisotropy compared to recursive filters, comparable to the realism of the ensemble method, but at much less computational cost.**

***Index Terms*—Bayes methods, covariance matrices, data assimilation, discrete wavelet transforms, state estimation.**

I. Introduction

Numerical weather predictions and weather observations are steadily increasing in spatio-temporal resolution and complexity, so data assimilation (DA) must better represent multi-scale structures. Theorems and experiments in the literature strongly suggest that enabling the background covariance to be both scale-selective and location-dependent using wavelets should greatly improve that representation. Background-error covariance quantifies the contribution to uncertainty of a forecast informed by observations from the uncertainty of the uninformed forecast.

The wavelet approach described below was developed at NCAR [2]. Suppose one has a putatively random field $x[\mathbf{r}]$ on coordinates $\mathbf{r} := (r^1, \ldots, r^d)^\mathrm{t} \in \mathbb{R}^d$, and samples it at N_a points along each coordinate r^a. The result is a random vector $\mathbf{x} := (x[\mathbf{r}_1], \ldots, x[\mathbf{r}_N])^\mathrm{t}$ of length $N := \prod_{a=1}^d N_a$. Its spatial covariance matrix is $B_{m,n} := \langle x^\star[\mathbf{r}_m] x^\star[\mathbf{r}_n] \rangle$, where $\mathbf{x}^\star := \mathbf{x} - \langle \mathbf{x} \rangle$ is deviation of $\mathbf{x}$ from its mean $\langle \mathbf{x} \rangle$. By well known theorems, if $B_{m,n}$ decays as a function of index separation $|m-n|$ sufficiently quickly, they yield sparse wavelet-matrix representations $\widetilde{\mathsf{B}}$. That is, $\widetilde{\mathsf{B}}$ will exhibit $\mathcal{O}[N \log N]$ [1, eq. 4.26] or $\mathcal{O}[N]$ significant entries [1, remark 4.4]. Similar theorems for more general locally stationary fields $x[\mathbf{r}]$ exist [4]. Mutually correlated fields $x_{\underset{\sim}{f}}$, $f = 1, \ldots, F$ imply cross-field covariance matrix blocks $\mathsf{B}_{f,g}$ that are sparse if the block-$\mathsf{B}_{f,g}$ entries decay as $B_{m,n}$ does. This sparseness reduces $\widetilde{\mathsf{B}}_{f,g}$ multiplication cost from $\mathcal{O}\left[N^3\right]$ to $\mathcal{O}\left[N\right]$.

Supported by NSF award DMS-1216481 and previously, NCAR.

II. Analysis and Modeling Methods

A. Horizontal 2D Wavelet Parseval Frame Analysis

1) One-dimensional wavelet Parseval frame analysis: Consider a sequence $x_n = x[r_n]$ of any number N of function values at uniform coordinates r_n. The so-called *aperiodic* discrete wavelet transform of [6, pp. 226–234], [7, p. 70] is better described as a 1D wavelet Parseval frame. As a frame, it maps the x_n to a sequence of $\widetilde{N} > N$ scaling-function and wavelet coefficients $\widetilde{x}_i := \sum_{n=0}^{N-1} W_{n,i}^N x_n$, and back again (injectivity), $x_n = \sum_{i=0}^{\widetilde{N}-1} W_{n,i}^N \widetilde{x}_i$. A *Parseval* frame is isometric: $\sum_{n=0}^{N-1} x_n^2 = \sum_{i=0}^{\widetilde{N}-1} \widetilde{x}_i^2$. The $\widetilde{N}$ discrete wavelets $W_{n,i}^N$ used in this code are complete, $\mathsf{W}^N \mathsf{W}^{N\mathrm{t}} = \mathsf{I}_N$, but are not orthogonal, $\mathsf{W}^{N\mathrm{t}} \mathsf{W}^N \neq \mathsf{I}_{\widetilde{N}}$ is a projection onto the N-hyperplane of valid wavelet-coefficient vectors in $\mathbb{R}^{\widetilde{N}}$.

These wavelets eliminate the usual severe restriction to a dyadic number $N \to 2^L \in \{2, 4, 8, \ldots\}$ of points along r_n. That is, starting from a (possibly nondyadic) index $i_0 := N$, a partition of the data is defined by three index sequences in L bands: i_ℓ, $\check{\imath}_\ell$, $\bar{\imath}_\ell$ (low-pass, high-pass and aggregate length [3, eqs. A4, A5, A6]); ultimately resulting in transform length $\widetilde{N} := \bar{\imath}_0$. Following [6, corollary 15.3], one concludes that the excess data-storage cost $\widetilde{N} - N \leq (2^L - 1)(Q-1)$ is small, assuming one fixes $L \ll \log_2 N$, where Q (even) is the length of the low-pass filter [3, eq. A1]. Whereas the index n only describes spatial location (e.g., $r_n = n r_N / N$), the index:

$$i \in \{\bar{\imath}_\ell, \ldots, \bar{\imath}_\ell + \check{\imath}_\ell - 1\} \subsetneq \{Q, \ldots, \widetilde{N} - 1\}, \quad (1)$$

at band $\ell \in \{1, \ldots, L\}$ describes both wavenumber band-center and bandwidth $\propto \check{\imath}_\ell / r_N$, and spatial location $r_{i,\ell} := (i - \bar{\imath}_\ell + \frac{1}{2}) r_N / \check{\imath}_\ell$. Furthermore, the smoothness of $x[r]$ is characterized by the collection of $\widetilde{x}_i$ for which $r \approx r_{i,\ell}$. No periodicity or any boundary condition is assumed. No interpolation is required. The vectors $\widetilde{\mathbf{x}} \equiv \mathsf{W}^{N\mathrm{t}} \mathbf{x} \in \mathbb{R}^{\widetilde{N}}$ and $\mathbf{x} = \mathsf{W}^N \widetilde{\mathbf{x}} \in \mathbb{R}^N$ are computed by a sparse recursive hierarchy on L bands; but in the frame case, each sparse coarsening and detailing filter matrix has a specific nondyadic size. Three-dimensional functions $\mathbf{z}_{\underset{\sim}{f}} \in \mathbb{R}^{N_1 N_2 K}$ are horizontally transformed using $N_1 N_2 K \times \widetilde{N}_1 \widetilde{N}_2 K$ tensor triple-products $\mathsf{W} := \mathsf{I}_K \otimes \mathsf{W}^{N_2} \otimes \mathsf{W}^{N_1}$ etc.

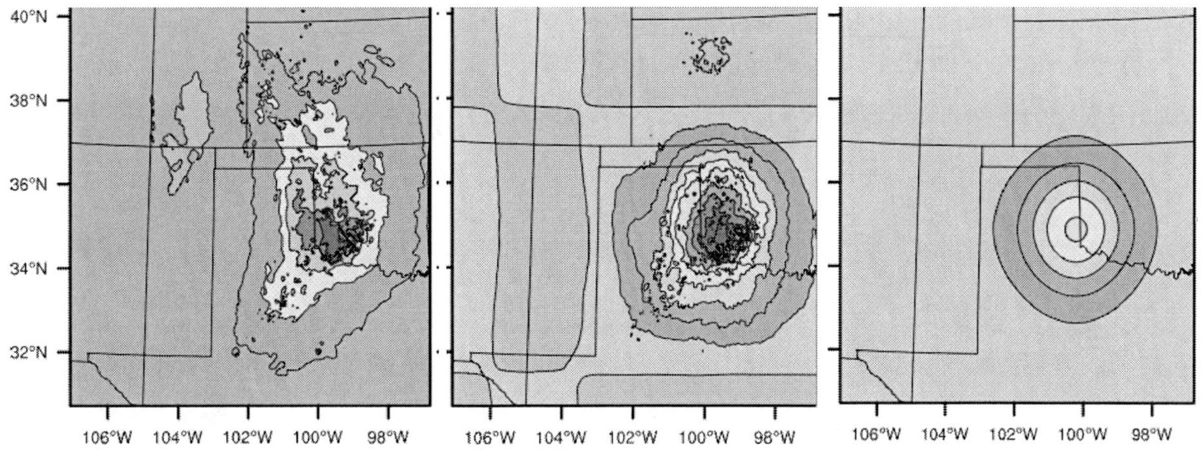

Fig. 1. Pseudo-single observation test temperature (K, eq. 3) on level $\eta_{k'} = 0.28$ as a function of longitude $r^1_{\mathbf{n}}$ (abscissa) and latitude $r^2_{\mathbf{n}}$ (ordinate). (Left) pure-ensemble estimate [3, eq. 22], contour interval (CI) 0.2K. (Center) $L = 7$ Coifman $Q = 30$ wavelet estimate (2), CI 0.1K. (Right) Homogeneous recursive-filter estimate, CI 0.1K [5, sec. 3c]. Red corresponds to 0.9K. Reference coordinates: $r^1_{\mathbf{n}'} = 100^\circ$W; $r^2_{\mathbf{n}'} = 35^\circ$N.

B. Background-error Covariance Model: Horizontal Control-variable Transform

The 3D, F-variate meteorological analysis increment $\mathbf{x} \in \mathbb{R}^{N_1 N_2 N_3 F}$ is the difference between model and background states. The background cost function $J_{\mathrm{b}} := \mathbf{x}^{\mathrm{t}}\mathsf{B}^{+}\mathbf{x}$, where $(\,)^{+}$ denotes the pseudo-inverse. To compute J_{b}, introduce the usual control-variable ($\mathbf{v} \in \mathbb{R}^{\widetilde{N}}$) transforms $\mathbf{x} =: \mathsf{U}_{\mathrm{p}}\mathsf{U}_{\mathrm{v}}\mathbf{z}$ and $\mathbf{z} =: \mathsf{U}_{\mathrm{h}}\mathbf{v} \in \mathbb{R}^{N}$ [5, eq. 10], where U_{h} is to $N_1 N_2$ horizontal locations from $\widetilde{N}_1\widetilde{N}_2$ modes and $\widetilde{N} := \widetilde{N}_1\widetilde{N}_2 KF > N := N_1 N_2 KF$. Unconventionally, possibly $\widetilde{N}_1\widetilde{N}_2 K \neq N_1 N_2 N_3$. The standardization assertion $\langle \mathbf{v}^{\star}\mathbf{v}^{\star\mathrm{t}}\rangle \approx \mathsf{I}_{\widetilde{N}}$ and definition $\mathsf{B}_{\mathrm{h}} := \mathsf{U}_{\mathrm{h}}\mathsf{U}_{\mathrm{h}}^{\mathrm{t}}$ imply that:

$$\mathsf{B} := \mathsf{U}_{\mathrm{p}}\mathsf{U}_{\mathrm{v}}\mathsf{B}_{\mathrm{h}}\mathsf{U}_{\mathrm{v}}^{\mathrm{t}}\mathsf{U}_{\mathrm{p}}^{\mathrm{t}} \approx \langle \mathbf{x}^{\star}\mathbf{x}^{\star\mathrm{t}}\rangle, \tag{2}$$

approximates the background-error covariance. The horizontal covariance B_{h} approximation accuracy is derived by [3, eqs. 13–17]. The approximation may be interpreted as the columns of $\mathsf{U}_{\mathrm{h}}\Sigma_{\mathrm{w}}^{-1}$ approximating eigenvectors of $\langle \mathbf{z}^{\star}\mathbf{z}^{\star\mathrm{t}}\rangle$, so that (2) implies approximate eigenvalues in Σ_{w}^{2}. As a corollary, $J_{\mathrm{b}} = \mathbf{v}^{\mathrm{t}}\Pi\mathbf{v} = \mathbf{v}^{\mathrm{t}}\mathbf{v}$ if $\mathbf{v} = \Pi\mathbf{v}$, where $\Pi := \mathsf{U}_{\mathrm{h}}^{\mathrm{t}}(\mathsf{U}_{\mathrm{h}}\mathsf{U}_{\mathrm{h}}^{\mathrm{t}})^{-1}\mathsf{U}_{\mathrm{h}}$ is the projection on the N-hyperplane row$[\mathsf{U}_{\mathrm{h}}] \subsetneq \mathbb{R}^{\widetilde{N}}$. An idealized covariance B_{i} may be defined *exactly without approximation* so that in general, only departures of B_{h} from B_{i} are approximated [3, eq. 18].

III. Results

A. Pseudo-single Observation Tests

Given a single observation innovation $\triangle T_{\mathbf{n}',k'}$ on level $\eta_{k'}$ with error $\varDelta$, the resulting analysis increment to field $\mathbf{x}_b$ is merely column $(\mathbf{n}', k', f)_{x_f = T}$ of the scaled B-matrix:

$$T_{\mathbf{n},k} = \left.\frac{B_{(\mathbf{n},k,f),(\mathbf{n}',k',f)}}{B_{(\mathbf{n}',k',f),(\mathbf{n}',k',f)} + \varDelta^2}\right|_{x_f = T} \triangle T_{\mathbf{n}',k'}. \tag{3}$$

Examples are shown in Fig. 1. In Fig. 1 the parameters are $\triangle T_{\mathbf{n}',k'} = \varDelta = 1$K,$N_{\mathrm{e}} = 30$, $N_1 N_2 = 351 \times 451$ and $N_3 = K = 5$. In Fig. 1 (a), note the multiscale anisotropic features such as the SW-NE structures over north Texas. Comparing with other estimates, one sees that the new B represents heterogeneity and anisotropy, but still localizes. Recall that compared to the pure-ensemble, the new wavelet B is much less expensive at a cost of only $\mathcal{O}[L^2 N_1 N_2]$.

IV. Summary

Wavelets have great potential for DA applications, based on their well-known analytical properties and recent applications to DA [3, and citations therein]. A tensor-product wavelet Parseval frame was implemented that allows any size of data, and conserves the sum-of-squares and reconstruction to machine precision. A new background-error covariance matrix B was implemented by incorporating this wavelet Parseval frame into the horizontal control-variable transform. Pseudo-single-observation tests indicate better representation of heterogeneity and anisotropy than recursive filters, for less computational cost than ensemble methods.

References

[1] G. Beylkin, R. Coifman, and V. Rokhlin, 1991: "Fast wavelet transforms and numerical algorithms I," *Comm. Pure Appl. Math.*, **44**, 141–183.

[2] A. Fournier, 2009: "Development of wavelet compression for WRF," *AFWA Cloud Analysis Workshop*, doi:10.13140/RG.2.1.2167.1523.

[3] A. Fournier, 2016: "Wavelet model of background-error covariance in the Weather Research & Forecasting model," doi: 10.13140/RG.2.2.23851.03365.

[4] S. Mallat, G. Papanicolaou, and Z. Zhang, 1998: "Adaptive covariance estimation of locally stationary processes," *Ann. Statist.*, **26 (1)**, 1–47, doi:10.1214/aos/1030563977.

[5] Y. Michel and T. Auligné, 2010: "Inhomogeneous background error modeling and estimation over Antarctica," *Mon. Wea. Rev.*

[6] M. V. Wickerhauser, 1991: "INRIA lectures on wavelet packet algorithms," *Problémes Non-Linéaires Appliqués, Ondelettes et Paquets D'Ondes*, P.-L. Lions, Ed., INRIA, 31–99.

[7] M. V. Wickerhauser, 1994: *Adapted Wavelet Analysis from Theory to Software*. AK Peters, Ltd., Wellesley, Massachusetts, xii + 486 pp.

A Cost-Effective Far-Field Antenna Pattern Measurement System

Kyle Patel
Department of Electrical Engineering
Colorado School of Mines
Golden, CO 80401 USA
kypatel@mines.edu

Robert Jones
Department of Electrical Engineering
Colorado School of Mines
Golden, CO 80401 USA
rojones@mines.edu

Atef Elsherbeni
Department of Electrical Engineering
Colorado School of Mines
Golden, CO 80401 USA
aelsherb@mines.edu

***Abstract*— A low-cost far-field antenna measurement solution is developed and presented. In an increasingly wireless society, it is important to be able to characterize antennas. Unfortunately, determining antenna radiation pattern characteristics is an involved and often expensive process. The presented system provides a complete combination of hardware and software that can be used for far-field pattern measurements of an antenna operating in the 700 MHz to 18 GHz range. This would allow institutions and groups with few resources to be able to characterize the radiation pattern of antennas for many emerging applications.**

***Keywords*— Anechoic chamber, Antenna pattern measurement, Far-field measurement, Low cost.**

I. Introduction

Antennas are typically characterized by their impedance bandwidth and their radiation qualities. The impedance bandwidth is easily determined through a one-port measurement with a VNA, however, the radiation qualities of an antenna require specialized ranges to ascertain [1-2]. These ranges typically consist of a standard antenna that is used to determine the radiation parameters of an unknown antenna. The distance between the two antenna must meet the far-field criteria for accurate measurements [3].

There are many types of such far-field ranges, however, the one this paper focuses on is an implementation of a system that works within an anechoic chamber.

The proposed system consists of electrical hardware, mechanical fixtures, and in-house software as explained in the following sections. The far-field measurement is conducted by analyzing S21 data taken using a Keysight VNA connected to a source fixture and an antenna-under-test (AUT) fixture spaced approximately three meters apart. There is one rotary table for the source antenna, typically a horn, and two rotary tables for the AUT. These rotary tables allow the system to perform S21 measurements as a function of multiple angles and frequencies. An example dipole antenna pattern measurement with this system can be seen in Fig. 1. The pattern is asymmetrical because the measurement was conducted without calibration or absorbers lining the anechoic chamber at the time of this writing.

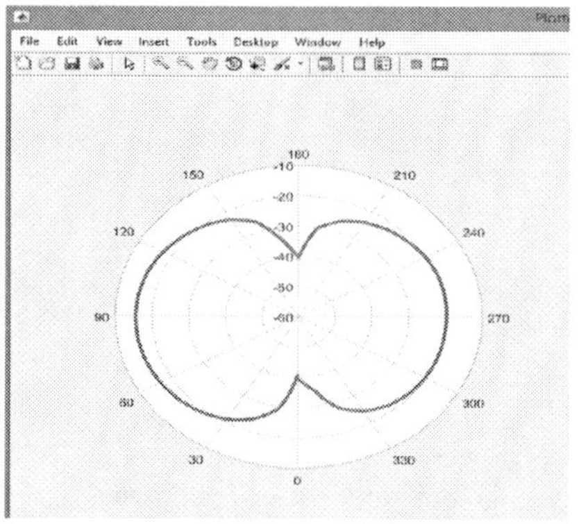

Fig. 1. The measured y-z plane pattern cut of a z-directed half-wavelength dipole antenna [4].

II. Electronic Hardware

Several pieces of equipment facilitate the measurement process. The system components are shown in Fig. 2. There are two LNAs, one at the output of port 1 and one at the input of port 2. The software automatically powers the LNAs through a programmable BK-Precision power supply. Three Velmex rotary tables are used, one on the source side, and two on the AUT side. These rotary tables allow for two axes of rotations at the AUT and one axis of rotation at the source antenna. There are also two Pololu linear actuators that allow for horizontal and vertical alignment of the source antenna with the AUT.

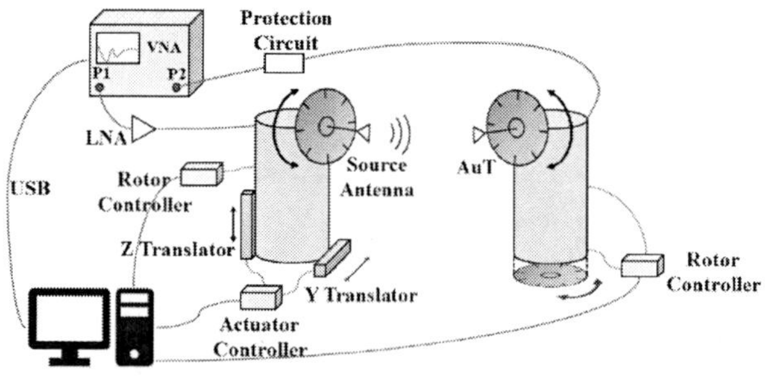

Fig. 2. Schematic for the designed antenna pattern measurement system [4].

In this design, there is a novel protection mechanism that is optional to the base functionality of the system but adds to the robustness of the overall system. This protection circuit was added to protect the VNA receiver from damage due to high power levels which may occur with novice users. This circuit essentially consists of a limiter and detector diode. The detector diode serves to notify the software and operator that a hazardous condition has been reached and halts the measurement until it is reviewed. This equipment can be seen on the control table in Fig. 3.

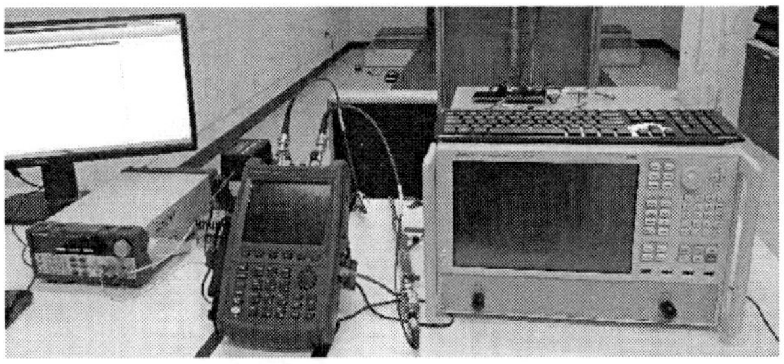

Fig. 3. Control table featuring all necessary electronic hardware.

III. Mechanical Fixtures

The fixtures shown in Fig. 4 that hold the source and AUT were designed using MDF plywood, which was chosen for its low cost, relative strength, and machining ease. Furthermore, MDF plywood would not reflect electromagnetic waves as much as metal materials such as aluminum, which would disturb the measurement results. The AUT fixture allows for different antenna to be easily mounted. The fixtures are also designed to be easily taken apart so that maintenance and inspection can be done in a short amount of time.

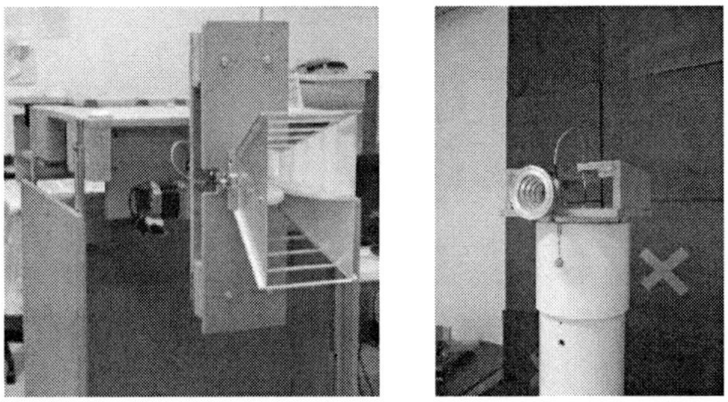

Fig. 4. Source fixture with source horn (left) and AUT fixture with mounted dipole antenna (right).

IV. Software

The developed software consists of a main GUI written in MATLAB and custom C# drivers that communicate with SCPI-enabled programmable power supplies and Keysight ENA/Fieldfox series VNAs [4]. This software allows for complete setup and control of the measurement. The software was designed to be modular so it could be easily upgraded and adapted to different equipment.

V. Future Enhancement

Currently, the alignment of the source antenna with the AUT is done manually. An automated system for alignment utilizing lasers is in progress. Furthermore, the fixtures can be greatly improved by moving away from the MDF that was used and instead utilizing 3D printed plastics and belts to make them more compact, lightweight, and robust. Lastly, the linear actuators are to be replaced with geared stepper motors for better positional accuracy of the source fixture.

VI. Precautions

Most groups who try to make their first antenna pattern measurement system will underestimate how important it is to have a defined and consistent antenna mounting scheme. There are many kinds of antennas which may potentially require measuring different planes, so it is important to always define measurement sweeps in a consistent manner for clarity of measurement results across operators and antennas. This is directly related to how each group decides to mount their rotary tables, as no single combination of rotary table placements is necessarily more correct over another especially when one is measuring many different types of antennas. Depending on where one chooses to locate their rotary tables, they may or may not get pure ϕ or θ plane cuts of their antenna, which is important to take into consideration when defining measurements and analyzing data.

VII. Cost

The presented system provides antenna far-field measurement capability at low cost. The total costs is less than \$10,000. A majority of this cost can be further reduced by utilizing less precise rotary tables for which the software and fixtures can easily be adapted to. This of course does not include the costs for a two port VNA and absorbers for the chamber, which are a significant cost of any antenna pattern measurement system. However, one may not need to buy an expensive VNA like the ones used in this system. Depending on the user's needs, one could opt for one of the growing consumer and affordable VNAs on the market, which would reduce entry costs significantly. These other VNAs can easily be adapted to the controller software due to its modularity.

VIII. Conclusion

Cost effective antenna measurement system is developed. Components, associated cost, and precautions in developing the system are presented.

References

[1] R. C. Johnson, Antenna Engineering Handbook, New York: McGraw-Hill, Inc., 1993.

[2] J. S. Hollis, T. J. Lyon, and L. Clayton Jr, Microwave Antenna Measurements, Atlanta, GA: Scientific-Atlanta, Inc., 1970.

[3] C. A. Balanis, Antenna Theory Analysis and Design, New York: John Wiley & Sons, Inc., 1997.

[4] K. Patel, "Design of an Antenna Measurement System," M.S. Thesis, Elect. Eng. Dept., Colorado School of Mines, Golden, CO, 2017.

Efficient Modeling of Antennas with Finite Conductivity using Calderón Preconditioning

Michiel Gossye, Dries Vande Ginste, Daniël De Zutter, and Hendrik Rogier
IDLab/Electromagnetics Group, Department of Information Technology
Ghent University/imec, Belgium
Michiel.Gossye@UGent.be

***Abstract*—A Calderón preconditioner for a novel single-source integral equation, which allows the simulation of high dielectric contrasts and lossy conductors, is introduced. It is shown that this preconditioner avoids breakdown when simulating scattering problems including high permittivities. This is corroborated by a numerical example of a receiving copper dipole antenna.**

I. Introduction

In recent research, Calderón preconditioners (CPs) were developed to resolve dense mesh breakdown problems that occur when solving boundary integral equations (BIEs). This preconditioner is based on the self-regularization effect of the electric field integral operator (EFIO) [1]. In [2], such a preconditioner was developed for the Poggio-Miller-Chang-Harrington-Wu-Tsai (PMCHWT) equation, resolving the dense mesh breakdown of this operator. However, for high dielectric contrasts, this preconditioner is not able to stabilize the system matrix [3]. Therefore, the accurate simulation of high contrasts including lossy conductors still remains an active research topic. In this contribution, a Calderón preconditioner for a novel single-source equation is introduced that resolves dense mesh breakdown at high dielectric contrasts. In Section II, the theoretical framework and spectral analysis of this method are described. These results are then validated by a numerical example of a lossy dipole antenna in Section III.

II. Theory

Assume a homogeneous object (characterized by ε', μ' and k'), embedded in a homogeneous background medium (characterized by ε, μ and k), as shown in Fig. 1 (a). An incident time-harmonic ($e^{j\omega t}$ time dependence) electromagnetic field $(\mathbf{E}^{in}, \mathbf{H}^{in})$ impinges on this object, generating a scattered field $(\mathbf{E}^{sc}, \mathbf{H}^{sc})$. Consider next the equivalent situation in Fig. 1 (b), where the material inside the object is replaced by that of the external region. Furthermore, a magnetic virtual current $\mathbf{m}$ residing on the boundary of the object is introduced. This current, which is to be determined, must generate the same scattered fields as in the original problem. After introduction of the Poincaré-Steklov operator $\mathcal{P}$, satisfying the property $\mathcal{P}(-\hat{\boldsymbol{n}} \times \boldsymbol{e}) = \hat{\boldsymbol{n}} \times \boldsymbol{h}$, and by imposing continuity of the electromagnetic fields on the object boundary Γ, we find the following single-source matrix equation:

$$\begin{bmatrix} \mathcal{K} + \frac{1}{2} & -1 \\ \frac{\mathcal{T}}{\eta} & -\mathcal{P} \end{bmatrix} \cdot \begin{bmatrix} \boldsymbol{m} \\ -\boldsymbol{u}_n \times \boldsymbol{E} \end{bmatrix} = \begin{bmatrix} \boldsymbol{u}_n \times \boldsymbol{E}^{in} \\ -\boldsymbol{u}_n \times \boldsymbol{H}^{in} \end{bmatrix}, \qquad (1)$$

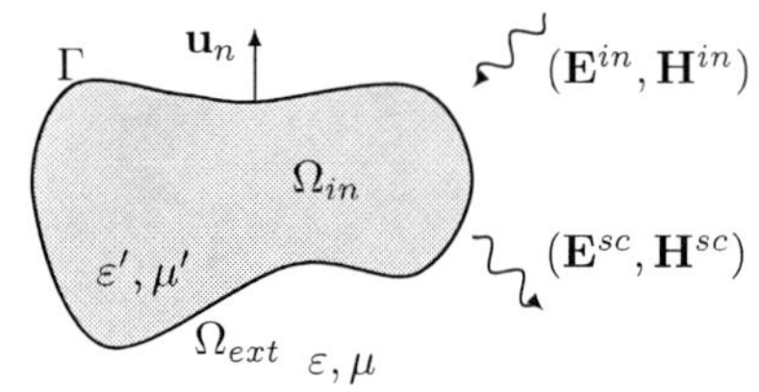

(a) Original problem

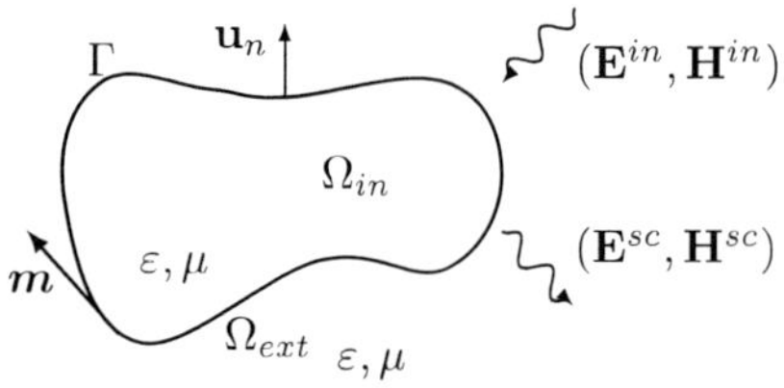

(b) Equivalent problem

Fig. 1. In (a), a homogeneous object Ω_{in} is embedded in a homogeneous background medium Ω_{ext}. Interaction of the incident field $(\boldsymbol{E}^{in}, \boldsymbol{H}^{in})$ results in a scattered field $(\boldsymbol{E}^{sc}, \boldsymbol{H}^{sc})$. In (b), the object is filled with the medium of Ω_{ext} and a surface current density $\mathbf{m}$, generating $(\boldsymbol{E}^{sc}, \boldsymbol{H}^{sc})$, is introduced on Γ.

with $\mathcal{T}$ and $\mathcal{K}$ the electric and magnetic field integral operator of Ω_{ext} [2], $\eta = \sqrt{\mu/\varepsilon}$ the impedance of Ω_{ext}, and $\boldsymbol{u}_n \times \boldsymbol{E}$ the total tangential electric field on the boundary. Next, we left multiply (1) with the following Calderón preconditioner:

$$\begin{bmatrix} 1 & 0 \\ 0 & -\eta' \mathcal{T}' \end{bmatrix}, \qquad (2)$$

with η' and $\mathcal{T}'$ the impedance and the EFIO of Ω_{int}, respectively. This results, after discretization, in:

$$\begin{bmatrix} K + \frac{1}{2}G & -G \\ -\frac{\eta'}{\eta} T' \cdot (-G^T)^{-1} \cdot T & K' + \frac{1}{2}G \end{bmatrix} \cdot \begin{bmatrix} \boldsymbol{M} \\ \boldsymbol{E}_t \end{bmatrix} = \begin{bmatrix} \boldsymbol{E}_t^i \\ \eta' T' (-G^T)^{-1} \boldsymbol{H}_t^i \end{bmatrix}. \qquad (3)$$

The vectors $\boldsymbol{M}$ and $\boldsymbol{E}_t$ in (3) collect the coefficients after expanding $\boldsymbol{m}$ and $-\boldsymbol{u}_n \times \boldsymbol{E}$ in Rao-Wilton-Glisson (RWG) functions. Furthermore, T and $\boldsymbol{H}_t^i$ are tested with rotated RWG basis functions, while K, K', $\boldsymbol{E}_t^i$ and the Gramian matrix G are tested with rotated Buffa-Christiansen (BC) [4] functions. T' is expanded and tested with BC and rotated BC functions, respectively.

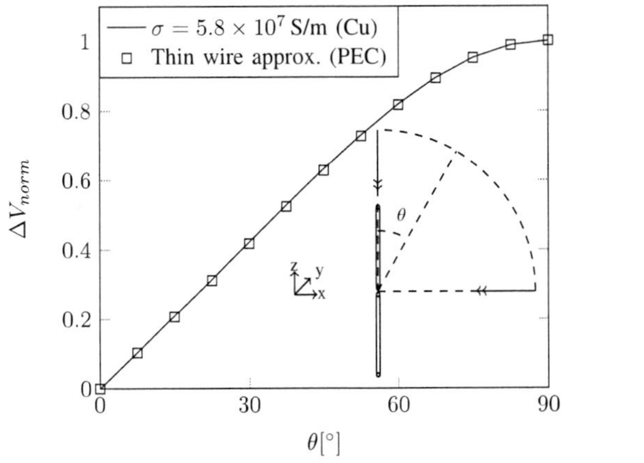

Fig. 2. Normalized voltage difference between the terminals of a copper dipole antenna with axis along the z-axis, at a frequency of 100 MHz. The antenna has a total length of $\lambda/2$, a radius of $\lambda/100$, a terminal gap of $\lambda/150$ and 2552 mesh elements. The incident wave is given by $\boldsymbol{E}^{in} = (cos(\theta)\boldsymbol{u}_x - sin(\theta)\boldsymbol{u}_z)e^{jk(sin(\theta)x+cos(\theta)z)}$ (as depicted in the schematic inset). The data are compared to the analytical approximation of a perfectly conducting thin wire antenna.

The convergence time of the iterative solution of (3) depends on the eigenvalue distribution of the system matrix [5]. It can be proven [6] that the eigenvalue accumulation points of the system matrix in (3) are given by:

$$\lambda_{1,\pm} = \frac{1}{2} \pm \frac{1}{2}\sqrt{\frac{\varepsilon}{\varepsilon'}}j, \tag{4}$$

and

$$\lambda_{2,\pm} = \frac{1}{2} \pm \frac{1}{2}\sqrt{\frac{\mu'}{\mu}}j. \tag{5}$$

If non-magnetic materials are assumed, one observes that the accumulation points only tend to zero or infinity when $\varepsilon \to 0$ or $\varepsilon \to -1$. Hence, in most practical engineering situations such as antenna design, which includes modeling of high dielectric contrast and conductive media, this formulation is well-conditioned.

III. Example

As a numerical validation of the formulation in (3), we consider a copper dipole antenna at a frequency of 100 MHz (inset of Fig. 2). The antenna has a total length of $\lambda/2$ and a radius of $\lambda/100$. The gap between the rods equals $\lambda/150$. In Fig. 2, the simulated voltage difference between the terminals is shown as a function of the angle of incidence of the incoming plane wave. This result is validated by the analytical thin wire approximation. The open-circuit voltage of the copper dipole shows a root mean square (rms) difference of 0.3 % compared to this reference solution.

In Fig. 3, the number of iterations until convergence (rms error $< 10^{-10}$) and the condition number of the system matrix are given as a function of the number of unknowns for both the method proposed in this paper and for the CP-PMCHWT equation. On the one hand, it can be seen that the number

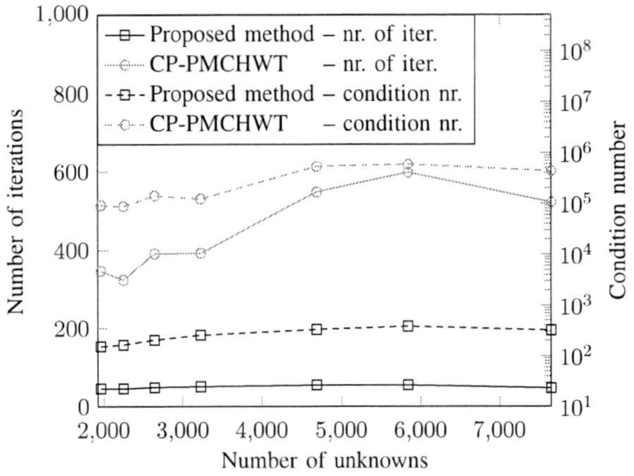

Fig. 3. Iterations until convergence (left y-axis) and condition number (right y-axis) as a function of the number of unknowns for the copper dipole antenna of Fig. 2 for an incident field $\boldsymbol{E}^{in} = \boldsymbol{u}_x e^{jkz}$, for the proposed method and for the CP-PMCHWT equation.

of iterations (≈ 50) and the condition number (≈ 300) of the proposed method remain at a stable low value for an increasing number of unknowns, validating the claim that dense mesh breakdown does not occur. The CP-PMCHWT method on the other hand suffers from ill-conditioning, resulting in longer convergence times.

IV. Conclusion

In this paper, a Calderón preconditioner for a novel single-source method that resolves the breakdown problem at high dielectric contrasts is presented. A receiving, copper dipole antenna is considered. The results demonstrate the practical applicability of the proposed method to antenna design and other scattering problems.

Acknowledgment

The authors thank the Research Foundation Flanders (FWO) for supporting this research.

References

[1] F. P. Andriulli, K. Cools, H. Bağci, F. Olyslager, A. Buffa, S. Christiansen and E. Michielssen, "A multiplicative Calderón preconditioner for the Electric Field Integral Equation," IEEE Trans. Antennas Propag., vol. 56, no. 8, pp. 2398–2412, Aug. 2008.

[2] K. Cools, F. P. Andriulli and E. Michielssen, "A Calderón multiplicative preconditioner for the PMCHWT integral equation," IEEE Trans. Antennas Propag., vol. 59, no. 12, pp. 4579–4587, Dec. 2011.

[3] Pasi Ylä-Oijala and Sami P. Kiminki, "Challenges in developing efficient Calderón preconditioners for resonating or high material contrast penetrable objects," J. Comput. Appl. Math., vol. 289, pp. 296–305, Dec. 2015.

[4] A. Buffa and S. H. Christiansen, "A dual finite element complex on the barycentric refinement," Math. Comput. , vol. 76, no. 260, pp. 1743–1769, 2007.

[5] P. Yla-Oijala and M. Taskinen, "Application of combined field Integral equation for electromagnetic scattering by dielectric and composite objects," IEEE Trans. Antennas Propag., vol. 53, pp. 1168–1173, Mar. 2005.

[6] M. Gossye, M. Huynen, D. Vande Ginste, D. De Zutter and H. Rogier, "A Calderón Preconditioner for High Dielectric Contrast Media", IEEE Trans. Antennas Propag., in press.

Domain Decomposition Method for Scattering from an Aircraft with Jet Engine Inlet Cavity

Miodrag Tasic and Branko Kolundzija
Chair of General Electrical Engineering
School of Electrical Engineering
Belgrade, Serbia
tasic@etf.rs, kol@etf.rs

Tomislav Milosevic
Applications/Technical Support
WIPL-D d.o.o.
Belgrade, Serbia
tomislav.milosevic@wipl-d.com

***Abstract*—Monostatic radar cross section (RCS) of an aircraft is analyzed using iterative domain decomposition method (DDM). The model of the (99 wavelengths long) aircraft is made of perfect electric conductor (PEC). Inlet cavity of the jet engine is included in the model. The inlet has realistic shape, whereas cavity is closed with a PEC on the outlet side. Corresponding model without the inlet is also analyzed—the inlet contour is smoothed, and then it is closed with a PEC. Method of moments (MoM) solution is used as a reference. It is shown that DDM solution converges faster for the model without the inlet, but the convergence for the model with the inlet is also satisfying.**

Keywords*—*domain decomposition method, jet engine inlet, method of moments, monostatic radar cross section.

I. Introduction

It is shown that jet engines have significant influence on the monostatic radar cross section (RCS) of aircrafts. A jet engine alone is difficult for electromagnetic (EM) analysis, because its inlet cavity acts like resonant structure, and it features geometrically complex, fine details (e.g., blades). Thus, asymptotic techniques (like ray tracing) cannot provide sufficient accuracy, whereas numerically exact methods (like the Method of Moments—MoM and the Finite Element Method—FEM) are limited by their computational cost. In the last decade of 20th century different strategies were used for jet engine analysis [1]. Recently, domain decomposition methods (DDMs) coupled with accelerators such as the multilevel fast multipole algorithm (MLFMA) show as good candidates for such analysis [2].

A novel iterative DDM is introduced in [3]. The entire model is decomposed into subdomains. Solution is obtained as a linear combination of the subdomain solutions from the current iteration and from all previous iterations. Original excitation is used for the subdomain solutions in 0th iteration, whereas the subdomains are excited with the residual error in the subsequent iterations. The weighting coefficients of the linear combination are determined in a way to minimize residual error of the MoM system of equations. The method does not store or invert entire MoM matrix, so it is more efficient than the MoM.

In this paper the DDM method from [3] is used to obtain the monostatic RCS of the geometrically realistic aircraft model, made of perfect electric conductor (PEC). The model includes the inlet cavity, but without fan blades / non-trivial outlet terminations. The cavity is ended with a simple PEC wall. To illustrate the influence of the inlet on the convergence speed, we will also analyze the model without the inlet.

II. Numerical Results and Comments

The model of an aircraft is shown in Fig. 1. The model is symmetric, so only the half of the model is shown. Enlarged details of the model with and without the inlet are shown in inset figures up. The model without the inlet has smooth inlet contoure, in order to simplify meshing of the PEC cover of the cavity. The uniform automatic domain decomposition [3] results in 48 subdomains, as illustrated in inset figure right. As a result, the cavity does not belong to a single subdomain. The monostatic RCS, σ, is calculated in the symmetry plane (205 incident waves are used). The normalized RCS (σ/λ^2) is shown in the graphs. Analysis is performed at the single frequency of 2 GHz, where the model is 99 wavelengths long. The EM simulator WIPL-D Pro [4] is used for the MoM analysis. The MoM discretization of the model with the inlet, using higher order bases, results in 142,520 unknowns.

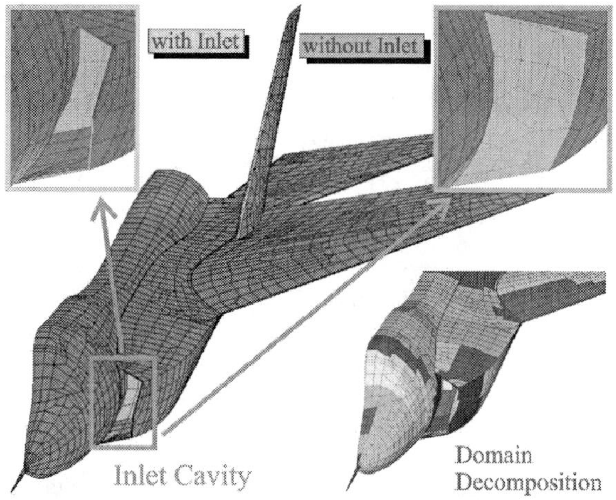

Fig. 1. A half of the symmetric aircraft model with/without inlet (inset up), and automatic domain decomposition of the model (inset right).

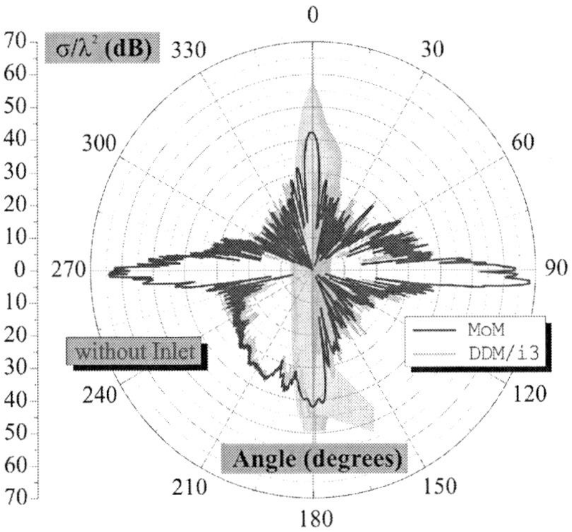

Fig. 2. The monostatic RCS for the model without the inlet, MoM solution vs. DDM solution in 3rd iteration.

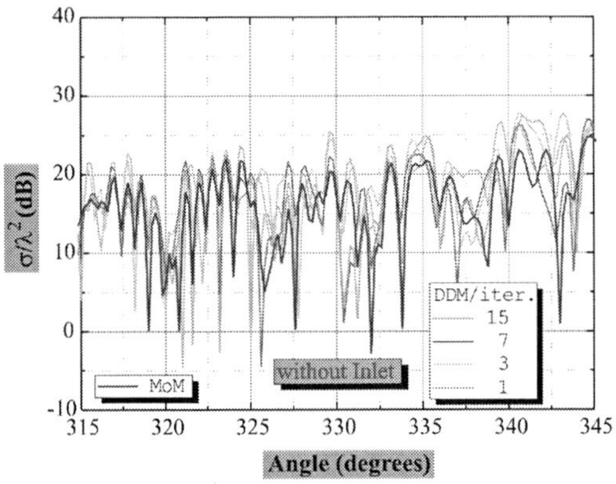

Fig. 3. The monostatic RCS for the model without the inlet, MoM solution vs. DDM solutions in 1st/3rd/7th/15h iteration.

The normalized monostatic RCS for the model without/with the inlet is shown in Figs. 2 and 3 / Figs. 4 and 5. The inlet significantly changes RCS in the zone where incident waves enter the inlet cavity. The DDM solution for the model without the inlet converges very fast—very good matching with the MoM result is obtained in just a few iterations. The convergence of the model with the inlet is somewhat slower. In particular, the most critical is incidence around 330 degrees. This zone is extracted in Figs. 3 and 5.

The CPU time and the storage are similar for both models. The MoM analysis CPU time / the MoM matrix storage is ~17 hours / 151.3 GB. The CPU time for the DDM after the iteration 3/7 is ~1.5/3.3 hours. The DDM matrix storage after the iteration 3/7 is 0.056 GB/0.225 GB.

Generally, the DDM behaves well for different object shapes, but automatically decomposed resonant cavities can cause the slower convergence.

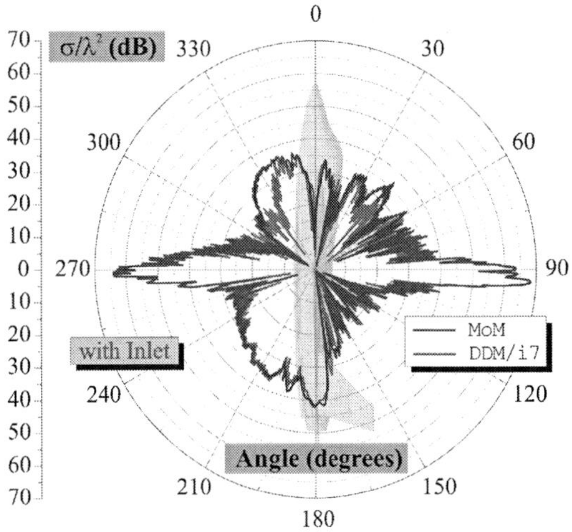

Fig. 4. The monostatic RCS for the model with the inlet, MoM solution vs. DDM solution in 7th iteration.

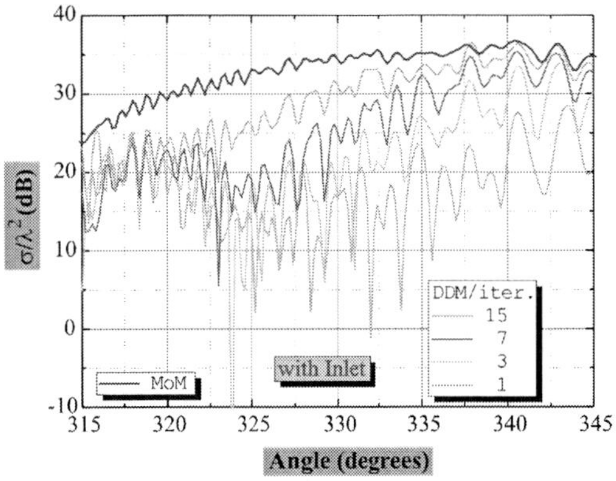

Fig. 5. The monostatic RCS for the model with the inlet, MoM solution vs. DDM solutions in 1st/3rd/7th/15h iteration.

In the future work we will try to improve the convergence of the models with the inlets by treating the inlet cavity as a single subdomain.

REFERENCES

[1] H. T. Anastassu, "A review of electromagnetic scattering analysis for inlets cavities and ppen ducts", IEEE Antennas and Propagation Magazine, vol. 45, no. 6, pp. 27-40, 2003.

[2] E. Garcia, C. Delgado, I. G. Diego, and M. F. Catedra, "An iterative solution for electrically large problems combining the characteristic basis function method and the multilevel fast multipole algorithm," IEEE Trans. Antennas Propag., vol. 56, no. 8, pp. 2363-2371, 2008.

[3] M. Tasic and B. Kolundzija, "Iterative MoM-based technique for evaluation of bistatic RCS of electrically large scatterers," Microwave review - Mikrotalasna revija, vol. 22, no. 2, Dec. 2016.

[4] https://www.wipl-d.com/

Improved Shaping of Reflector Antennas using a New Minimax Initialization Strategy

Anders Eltved* and Martin S. Andersen
DTU Compute, Technical University of Denmark
Kongens Lyngby, Denmark
*Email: aelt@dtu.dk

Oscar Borries
TICRA
Copenhagen, Denmark

Abstract—**Numerical optimization is an essential part of the design process when shaping a contoured beam reflector antenna to produce a required coverage. The minimax formulation that has been used for decades generally results in a nonconvex problem, and since the evaluation of a design is costly, local optimization is typically used in practice. An inherent challenge with the minimax formulation is that it often leads to multiple local minima. As a result, the quality of the final design obtained via local optimization depends strongly on the initial design.**

To address the sensitivity to the initial design, we investigate the use of initialization based on a different problem formulation. In particular, we first solve a one-sided nonlinear least-squares problem to improve an initial design, and the resulting design is then used as initialization of a minimax algorithm. We use this strategy to shape a reflector antenna starting from different initial shapes, and our results show that the initialization strategy improves the coverage with five out of six initial guesses.

I. Introduction

For many modern communications satellites, the design of contoured beam reflector antennas involves the use of optimization to shape the reflector to produce a desired coverage. The performance of a reflector system is simulated using Physical Optics (PO) which is sometimes augmented by Physical Theory of Diffraction (PTD) to account for the effects from the reflector edges. Using these techniques, the gain, cross-polar performance, and other relevant quantities can be evaluated for a specific design.

To optimize the design, it is common to consider the minimax problem where the objective is to maximize the minimum gain in the coverage, or equivalently, maximizing the guaranteed gain in the coverage. The minimax problem has been studied extensively [1], and good local optimization algorithms exist for solving the problem [2], [3]. However, with local optimization algorithms, the solution depends on an initial guess which is usually provided by the user. In practice, the antenna designer comes up with an initial design which is then improved by the optimization algorithm.

Unfortunately, the minimax formulation can have many local minima, and hence local optimization algorithms can be sensitive to the initial guess; if the antenna designer provides a poor initial design, the final design after optimization may not be improved much. Multi-start methods (doing multiple local optimizations from various starting points) and global optimization methods can improve this situation, but evaluating the performance of a design, which is done in each iteration of the optimization, can take hours in some applications, making these approaches too computationally expensive. In practice, the user often decides on a maximum number of function evaluations and the optimization is terminated if this number is exceeded even if the usual stopping criteria are not satisfied.

In this study, we present an alternative optimization problem to solve — the one-sided nonlinear least-squares (one-sided LS) problem — and an algorithm for finding a (local) minimum. Given a maximum number of function evaluations, $k_{\max}$, to be used in the optimization, we propose the following strategy: (i) the initial design is first improved by optimizing the one-sided LS formulation using at most $k_{\max}/2$ iterations (one iteration corresponds to one function evaluation), and (ii) the resulting design is then optimized using the minimax algorithm with a cap on the number of iterations such that the total number of function evaluations is at most $k_{\max}$.

II. Method

In the following, we will assume that $x \in \mathbb{R}^n$ is a vector of n parameters that define the design of the reflector antenna (e.g., the elements of x can represent spline coefficients of a shaped surface, the position or excitation of feeds and arrays, etc.). For each of the m points in the coverage we define a residual function:

$$r_i(x) = w_i(g_i - f_i(x)), \tag{1}$$

where $f_i(x)$ is a function that measures the performance of the current design, g_i is a performance goal, and w_i is a weight that determines the importance of meeting the performance goal at the ith point. To ensure that a design can be realized, it is often necessary to put constraints on x (e.g., restricting the curvature of the reflector to avoid having to bend the metal surface of the reflector too much, or restricting the position of a feed such that it does not coincide with other components on the structure). Here we consider linear constraints represented by the set $\mathcal{C} = \{x \in \mathbb{R}^n \mid Cx + d \geq 0\}$, where $C \in \mathbb{R}^{p \times n}$, $d \in \mathbb{R}^p$, p is the number of constraints, and the inequality is element-wise. The minimax problem can now be formulated as:

$$\underset{x \in \mathcal{C}}{\text{minimize}} \quad \max_i \, r_i(x), \tag{2}$$

and the one-sided LS problem is given by:

$$\underset{x\in\mathcal{C}}{\text{minimize}} \quad \sum_{i=1}^{m} \max\{0, r_i(x)\}^2, \tag{3}$$

Notice that all positive residuals are penalized in the one-sided LS formulation; this is sensible since a positive residual implies that the goal is not attained at the given point. As mentioned in the introduction, there are efficient algorithms for optimizing (2) locally, and in the next section, we outline a method for local optimization of (3).

III. Algorithm

To optimize (3), we consider the equivalent problem:

$$\begin{array}{ll} \underset{x\in\mathcal{C}, u\in\mathbb{R}^m}{\text{minimize}} & \|u\|^2 \\ \text{subject to} & u_i \geq r_i(x),\ u_i \geq 0, \qquad i = 1, \ldots, m, \end{array} \tag{4}$$

where u is a vector of auxiliary variables. This problem has a quadratic objective function, but due to the possibly nonconvex constraints $u_i \geq r_i(x)$, it is still intractable to find a global minimum. Thus, we use a trust-region method [4] to search for a local minimum. At a current iterate, x^k, we linearize the residual functions in (4), and find a candidate for the next iterate, $x^{k+1} = x^k + \Delta x$, by solving the trust-region subproblem:

$$\begin{array}{ll} \underset{\Delta x\in\mathbb{R}^n, u\in\mathbb{R}^m}{\text{minimize}} & \|u\|^2 \\ \text{subject to} & C\Delta x + d^k \geq 0 \\ & u \geq r^k + J^k \Delta x \\ & u \geq 0,\ \delta^k \geq \|\Delta x\|_\infty, \end{array} \tag{5}$$

where $\delta^k > 0$ is the trust-region radius, $r^k = r(x^k)$, and:

$$d^k = Cx^k + d,\ J^k = \left[\nabla r_1(x^k) \ \cdots \ \nabla r_m(x^k)\right]^T. \tag{6}$$

The problem (5) is a convex quadratic problem with linear constraints (since the ∞-norm is linearly representable) which we solve with an interior-point method [5].

IV. Results

To illustrate the effect of the initialization strategy, we consider a case where the objective is to shape a reflector for illumination of the continental United States (the US excluding Alaska and Hawaii). We have $n = 783$ variables (spline coefficients of a reflector surface) and optimize the coverage over $m = 810$ points starting from six different initial shapes. The initial shapes were created by de-focusing the reflector such that the initial guesses become progressively worse: guess 1 is expected to produce the best results and initial guess 6 is expected to produce the worst results. We did not impose constraints on x (i.e., $p = 0$). An example of the coverage obtained with the minimax algorithm initialized with initial guess 2 is shown in Fig. 1.

In our experiments, we limited the number of function evaluations ($k_{\max}$) to 500, and for each of the six initial guesses we did two experiments. In the first experiment, we

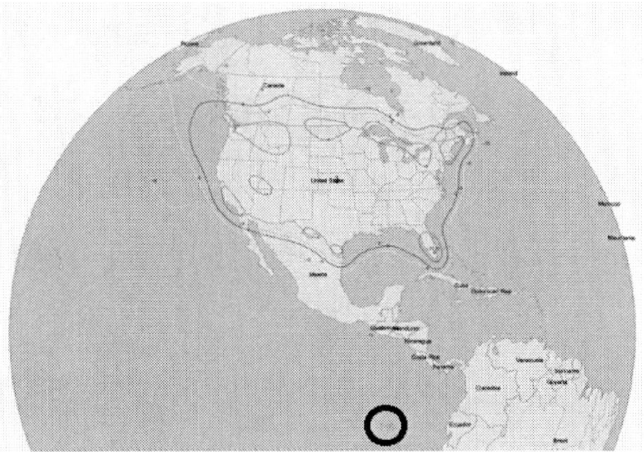

Fig. 1. Contours of coverage optimized using the minimax algorithm. The peak gain of around 33 dB is at the cross in Florida. The Nadir direction of the satellite is shown in the black circle.

TABLE I. Value of Maximal Residual in dB After 500 Iterations. The 6 Initial Guesses Become Progressively Worse: 1 is a Good (Green) Initial Guess and 6 is a Poor (Red) Initial Guess.

Initial Guess	1	2	3	4	5	6
Minimax only	-0.074	0.090	0.826	2.019	4.149	9.360
OLS+minimax	-0.074	-0.004	0.417	1.952	4.103	7.690
Difference	0.000	0.094	0.409	0.067	0.046	1.67

applied the one-sided LS algorithm for 250 iterations (or until a stopping criteria is met), followed by the minimax algorithm for the remaining iterations. In the second experiment, we used only the minimax algorithm for 500 iterations. Our results are summarized in Table I; recall that smaller residuals are better. The results clearly show that the initialization strategy can improve the minimum gain in the coverage: the gain is improved for initial guesses 2-6, and the result remains the same for initial guess 1. Considering the maximal residual — it measures how far we are from reaching the goal value — the absolute improvement is largest for initial guess 6 (1.67 dB), where there is much room for improvement, and the relative improvement is largest for initial guess 3 (49.5%).

V. Conclusion

The use of one-sided least-squares for initializing the minimax algorithm can lead to improved results: in our numerical experiments, the initialization strategy led to an improved design with five out of six initial guesses.

References

[1] V. Demyanov and V. Molozemov, Introduction to Minimax. Wiley: New York, 1974.

[2] J. Hald, "Two stage algorithms for linearly constrained minimax optimization," Ph.D. dissertation, Technical University of Denmark, 1984.

[3] K. Madsen and H. Schjær-Jacobsen, "Linearly constrained minimax optimization," Mathematical Programming, vol. 14, no. 1, 1978.

[4] A. Conn, N. Gould, and P. Toint, Trust Region Methods. Society for Industrial and Applied Mathematics, 2000.

[5] J. Nocedal and S. Wright, "Quadratic programming," in Numerical Optimization, 2nd ed. Springer-Verlag New York, 2006, ch. 16.

Fast and Rigorous Method for Solving Low-Frequency Breakdown in Full-Wave Finite-Element-Based Solution of General Lossy Problems

Li Xue and Dan Jiao
School of Electrical and Computer Engineering, Purdue University
West Lafayette, IN 47907, USA, djiao@purdue.edu

***Abstract*—A rigorous and fast method is developed to overcome the low-frequency breakdown in the finite-element-based analysis of general lossy problems, where both dielectrics and conductors can be lossy and arbitrarily inhomogeneous. The method is equally valid at high frequencies without any need for changing the formulation. In this method, a full-wave finite-element solution is first decomposed into two components: nullspace component and its complementary one. Each component is then found without breakdown from high down to any low frequency. Both nullspace and its complementary space are analytically generated in this work for an arbitrary mesh, thus incurring *no* computational cost. From the proposed method, the frequency dependence of a full-wave finite-element solution at low frequencies is also explicitly revealed for general inhomogeneous lossy problems. Numerical results have validated the accuracy and efficiency of the proposed method.**

***Index Terms*—Conductor loss, finite-element solvers, full-wave solvers, lossy problems, low-frequency breakdown.**

I. Introduction

A full-wave finite-element-based solution of Maxwell's equations breaks down at low frequencies. This problem is especially severe when dealing with VLSI circuit problems, because the breakdown frequency falls right in the range of circuit operating frequencies [1]. Therefore, it is important to solve the low-frequency breakdown problem. Among existing methods for solving the problem, one class of methods stitches a static- or quasistatic-based electromagnetic solver with a full-wave-based electromagnetic solver. However, this approach requires deciding at which frequency to switch between different solvers. It also fails to handle the scenario where the solution of Maxwell's equations is not a static solution, while a full-wave solver still breaks down. Another class is to extend the validity of full-wave solvers to low frequencies. Existing approaches that belong to this category utilize low-frequency approximations. For example, the tree-cotree splitting [2] was used to provide an approximate Helmholtz decomposition for edge elements in finite-element-based methods. In addition, while lossless problems are extensively studied, the lossy problems are seldom examined for overcoming the low-frequency breakdown. In [3], a method without using any low-frequency approximation is proposed to solve the breakdown problem involving lossy conductors embedded in inhomogeneous dielectrics. For cases where conductivity is space dependent, whose value can also be small like that in lossy dielectrics, the formulations of [3] are not applicable. In addition, eigenvalue solutions are involved in [3], which can be expensive for simulating large-scale problems.

This work was supported by a grant from NSF under award No. 1619062 and a grant from DARPA under award HR0011-14-1-0057.

In this work, we propose a method to obtain a rigorous full-wave finite-element-based solution of general lossy problems from high frequencies all the way down to DC, where the dielectric and conductor loss can co-exist and both can be inhomogeneously distributed in space. In addition, the column space we use to decompose a full-wave solution is generated analytically without solving an eigenvalue problem, thus significantly speeding up computation.

II. Proposed Method

A full-wave finite-element-method (FEM) based analysis of a general lossy problem results in the following matrix equation in frequency domain:

$$(\mathbf{S} + j\omega\mathbf{R} - \omega^2\mathbf{T})x = j\omega b, \tag{1}$$

where $\mathbf{S}$ is a stiffness matrix, $\mathbf{R}$ is related to conductivity, $\mathbf{T}$ is a mass matrix, and b denotes a current source vector.

The solution of (1), x, can be expanded in the column space of $\mathbf{V}_0$ and $\mathbf{V}_h$, where $\mathbf{V}_0$ is the nullspace of $\mathbf{S}$ and $\mathbf{V}_h$ is the complementary space of $\mathbf{V}_0$. Both of them can be generated analytically as follows. The number of column vectors in $\mathbf{V}_0$ is $nd - 1$, where nd is the number of nodes in an FEM mesh. Take an arbitrary j-th column vector of $\mathbf{V}_0$ as an example. It corresponds to node j, and having only a few number of nonzero entries, whose number is equal to the number of edges connected to node j. If the edge basis (normalized using edge length l_i) along an edge enters the node, then $1/l_i$ appears in the row entry corresponding to the edge basis in the nullspace vector; otherwise, $-1/l_i$ appears. Certainly, an opposite convention can also be used. As for $\mathbf{V}_h$, it is the cycle space of an FEM mesh, which is orthogonal to $\mathbf{V}_0$. The number of column vectors in $\mathbf{V}_h$ is the number of cycles in an FEM mesh. Each $\mathbf{V}_h$ vector can be generated by encircling an independent cycle of a mesh. If the edge basis's direction is the same as a pre-defined cycle direction, l_i appears in the row corresponding to the edge; otherwise, $-l_i$ appears.

Using the analytically generated $\mathbf{V}_0$ and $\mathbf{V}_h$, x can be written as:

$$x = \mathbf{V}_0 x_0 + \mathbf{V}_h x_h, \tag{2}$$

where x_0 and x_h are, respectively, the unknown coefficient vectors of $\mathbf{V}_0$ and $\mathbf{V}_h$. To solve x_0, substituting (2) into (1), and multiplying both sides of (1) by $\mathbf{V}_0^T$, we obtain:

$$\mathbf{V}_0^T(\mathbf{R}+j\omega\mathbf{T})\mathbf{V}_0 x_0 = \mathbf{V}_0^T b - \mathbf{V}_0^T(\mathbf{R}+j\omega\mathbf{T})\mathbf{V}_h x_h, \tag{3}$$

which can be compactly written as:

$$(\mathbf{R}_0 + j\omega\mathbf{T}_0)x_0 = \mathbf{V}_0^T b - \mathbf{V}_0^T(\mathbf{R}+j\omega\mathbf{T})\mathbf{V}_h x_h, \tag{4}$$

where $\mathbf{T}_0 = \mathbf{V}_0^T\mathbf{T}\mathbf{V}_0$ and $\mathbf{R}_0 = \mathbf{V}_0^T\mathbf{R}\mathbf{V}_0$. The solution of (4) can still break down at low frequencies because the $j\omega\mathbf{T}_0$ term will be neglected due to finite machine precision, and the system matrix of (4) becomes singular. In order to solve this problem, we further decompose x_0 into the space of $\mathbf{X}_0$ and $\mathbf{X}_h$, where $\mathbf{X}_0$ is the nullspace of $\mathbf{R}_0$ and $\mathbf{X}_h$ is the orthogonal space of $\mathbf{X}_0$. $\mathbf{X}_0$ and $\mathbf{X}_h$ again can be generated analytically. The solution x_0, thus, can be written as $x_0 = \mathbf{X}_0 u_0 + \mathbf{X}_h u_h$. To find $\tilde{\mathbf{X}}_h$ such that $\mathbf{X}_0^T\mathbf{T}_0\tilde{\mathbf{X}}_h = 0$, we can set $\tilde{\mathbf{X}}_h = \mathbf{T}_0^{-1}\mathbf{X}_h$. Using $\tilde{\mathbf{X}}_h$, the system for solving u_0 can be decoupled from that for solving u_h. Multiplying $\mathbf{X}_0^T$ on both sides of (4), we obtain:

$$j\omega\mathbf{X}_0^T\mathbf{T}_0\mathbf{X}_0 u_0 = \mathbf{X}_0^T\mathbf{V}_0^T b - \mathbf{X}_0^T\mathbf{V}_0^T(\mathbf{R}+j\omega\mathbf{T})\mathbf{V}_h x_h. \tag{5}$$

Similarly, multiplying $\tilde{\mathbf{X}}_h^T$ on both sides of (4), we have:

$$\begin{aligned}&\tilde{\mathbf{X}}_h^T(\mathbf{R}_0 + j\omega\mathbf{T}_0)\tilde{\mathbf{X}}_h u_h = \\ &\tilde{\mathbf{X}}_h^T\mathbf{V}_0^T b - \tilde{\mathbf{X}}_h^T\mathbf{V}_0^T(\mathbf{R}+j\omega\mathbf{T})\mathbf{V}_h x_h.\end{aligned} \tag{6}$$

To find x_h of (2), we multiply both sides of (1) by $\mathbf{V}_h^T$, obtaining:

$$\begin{aligned}&\mathbf{V}_h^T(\mathbf{S}+j\omega\mathbf{R}-\omega^2\mathbf{T})\mathbf{V}_h x_h \\ &= j\omega\mathbf{V}_h^T b - \mathbf{V}_h^T(j\omega\mathbf{R}-\omega^2\mathbf{T})\mathbf{V}_0(\mathbf{X}_0 u_0 + \tilde{\mathbf{X}}_h u_h).\end{aligned} \tag{7}$$

Combining (5), (6) and (7), we obtain the final system of equations to solve all components of the field solution, u_0, u_h, and x_h:

$$\begin{bmatrix} j\omega\mathbf{X}_0^T\mathbf{T}_0\mathbf{X}_0 & 0 & \mathbf{A}_{00,h} \\ 0 & \tilde{\mathbf{X}}_h^T(\mathbf{R}_0+j\omega\mathbf{T}_0)\tilde{\mathbf{X}}_h & \mathbf{A}_{0h,h} \\ \mathbf{A}_{00,h}^T & \mathbf{A}_{0h,h}^T & \mathbf{V}_h^T(\mathbf{S}/(j\omega)+\mathbf{R}+j\omega\mathbf{T})\mathbf{V}_h \end{bmatrix}\begin{bmatrix} u_0 \\ u_h \\ x_h \end{bmatrix} = \begin{bmatrix} \mathbf{X}_0^T\mathbf{V}_0^T b \\ \tilde{\mathbf{X}}_h^T\mathbf{V}_0^T b \\ \mathbf{V}_h^T b \end{bmatrix}, \tag{8}$$

where $\mathbf{A}_{00,h} = \mathbf{X}_0^T\mathbf{V}_0^T(\mathbf{R}+j\omega\mathbf{T})\mathbf{V}_h$, and $\mathbf{A}_{0h,h} = \tilde{\mathbf{X}}_h^T\mathbf{V}_0^T(\mathbf{R}+j\omega\mathbf{T})\mathbf{V}_h$. Notice that the matrices involved in (8) are sparse, due to analytical construction of $\mathbf{V}_0$, $\mathbf{V}_h$, $\mathbf{X}_0$, and $\mathbf{X}_h$. Furthermore, the solution of (8) does not break down at low frequencies, and also is equally valid at high frequencies. In addition, we can find an explicit frequency dependence of each component of the field solution from (8).

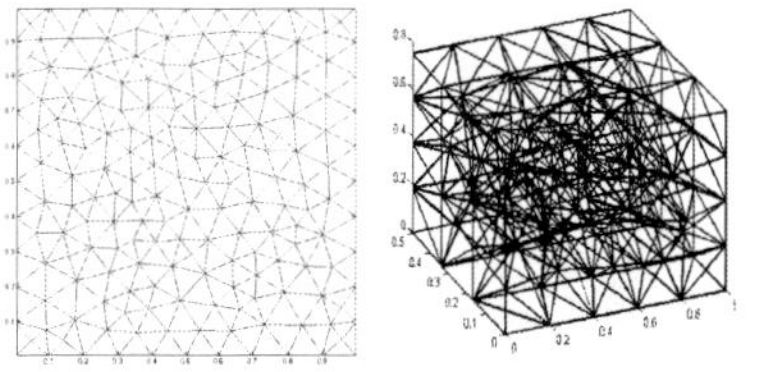

(a) (b)

Fig. 1. (a) A triangular mesh (length unit mm) and (b) a tetrahedral mesh.

TABLE I
THE VERIFICATION OF $\mathbf{V}_0$ AND $\mathbf{V}_h$

	Nullspace Size of $\mathbf{S}$	Size of $\mathbf{V}_0$	$\frac{\|\mathbf{S}\mathbf{V}_0\|}{\|\mathbf{S}\|\|\mathbf{V}_0\|}$	$\|\mathbf{V}_0^T\mathbf{V}_h\|$
Triangular mesh	164	164	4.0543e-17	3.6093e-16
Tetrahedral mesh	70	70	4.9443e-17	4.9809e-16

III. NUMERICAL RESULTS

First, we verify the correctness of the $\mathbf{V}_0$ and $\mathbf{V}_h$ generated by the proposed algorithm. We use two meshes shown in Fig. 1 (a) and Fig. 1 (b) as examples. The fourth column in Table I shows $\frac{\|\mathbf{S}\mathbf{V}_0\|}{\|\mathbf{S}\|\|\mathbf{V}_0\|}$, which verifies that $\mathbf{V}_0$ is the nullspace of $\mathbf{S}$. The fifth column shows the norm of $\mathbf{V}_0^T\mathbf{V}_h$, which proves that the two are orthogonal. Next, we examine the capability of the proposed solution in overcoming the low-frequency breakdown. A 3-D lossy problem discretized into a tetrahedron mesh is considered. The solution error is plotted in Fig. 2 from 10^{-20} to 10 GHz. The solution error is calculated as $\frac{\|x-x_r\|}{\|x_r\|}$, where x is the solution from this method and x_r is the solution from [3]. As can be seen from Fig. 2, the proposed method is accurate at both high and low frequencies. Furthermore, it is much faster because the cost of generating the nullspace and its complementary space is avoided.

REFERENCES

[1] J. Zhu and D. Jiao, "A theoretically rigorous full-wave finite-element-based solution of Maxwell's equations from DC to high frequencies," *IEEE Transactions on Advanced Packaging*, vol. 33, no. 4, pp. 1043-1050, Nov. 2010.

[2] S. H. Lee and J. M. Jin, "Application of the treecotree splitting for improving matrix conditioning in the fullwave finiteelement analysis of highspeed circuits," *Microwave and Optical Technology Letters*, vol. 50, no. 6, pp. 1476-1481, 2008.

[3] J. Zhu and D. Jiao, "A rigorous solution to the low-frequency breakdown in full-wave finite-element-based analysis of general problems involving inhomogeneous lossless/lossy dielectrics and nonideal conductors," *IEEE Transactions on Microwave Theory and Techniques*, vol. 59, no. 12, pp. 3294-3306, 2011.

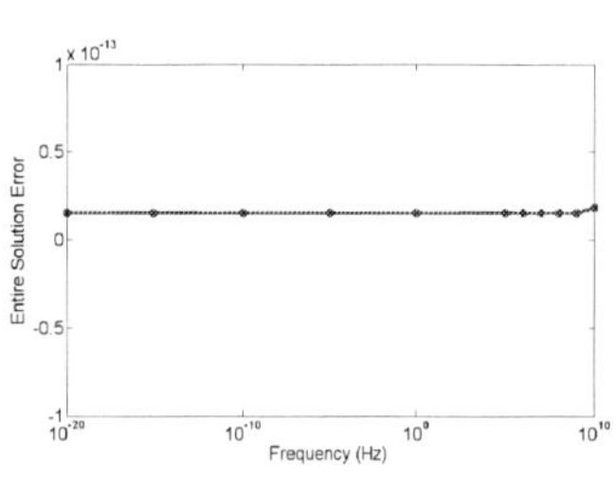

Fig. 2. Entire solution error for a 3-D lossy problem.

Design and Optimization of Two-Dimensional Nano-Arrays for Beam Steering

Aşkın Altınoklu, N. Rasoolzadeh, and Özgür Ergül
Department of Electrical and Electronics Engineering
Middle East Technical University
Ankara, Turkey
ozergul@metu.edu.tr

***Abstract*—We consider design and optimization of nano-arrays involving two-dimensional arrangements of nanoparticles. Similar to their counterparts used at the lower frequencies, nanoantennas can be arranged periodically to achieve directive and/or controllable radiation patterns at optical frequencies. While nanoantenna geometries are usually simple due to restrictions in nanoscale fabrications, their robust analysis still requires accurate simulation tools that model strong plasmonic interactions between particles. We use a full-wave optimization environment based on heuristic algorithms and surface integral equations to optimize two-dimensional nano-arrays and to shape their radiation patterns for nano-optical applications.**

I. Introduction

Nanoantennas are well-known devices of nano-optical systems [1],[2] that are developed and used for a variety of applications, such as energy harvesting, optical communication, and sensing. Both numerical [3] and experimental [4] studies demonstrate interesting properties of nanoantennas, such as strong field enhancement, thanks to the plasmonic properties of metals at optical frequencies. Similar to their counterparts at the lower frequencies, arranging nanoantennas in array forms provides further capabilities [5],[6], such as controllability of radiation characteristics. This study is devoted to the design of nanoantenna arrays for beam-steering applications.

As presented in [6], linear arrangements of nanoparticles, such as nano-cubes, provide an ability to control scattering and radiation. For example, a well-designed array can direct the radiation of an isotropic source to desired directions, while suppressing the radiation at other directions. For the best radiation characteristics, the number of elements, their sizes, and the distances between them can be optimized. On the other hand, if a steering ability is required, two-dimensional arrays can be more suitable since they are more compact and their rotation around an isotropic source can be easier. In this work, we present the design of such two-dimensional arrays by using a full-wave simulation and optimization environment. We show that, by using very compact arrays, it is possible to control the overall radiation by directing the main beam to a desired direction, or more importantly, to multiple directions.

II. Simulation and Optimization Environment

We consider two-dimensional arrays involving nanoparticles, particularly silver (Ag) nano-cubes arranged periodically. The plasmonic properties of the metals at optical frequencies are taken into account by using surface integral equations for penetrable bodies. In the frequency domain, the permittivity values, which are typically complex numbers with negative real parts, are extracted from available measurement data. The arrays are modeled as finite (e.g., $n \times n$) three-dimensional structures that are excited by a main source (e.g., a dipole at the center) located in free space. The radiation problems are solved iteratively by using the multilevel fast multipole algorithm designed for plasmonic objects [7].

In order to design nano-arrays, we perform on/off optimization, i.e., the array elements are kept/extracted to obtain the desired radiation characteristics. An in-house implementation of GAs is employed due to its easier usage for multi-purpose optimization trials. The main excitation is kept in a gap at the center of the structure such that the array can be rotated to steer the created beam or beams. Once an optimal configuration for a desired radiation characteristics is found, it is further exposed to sensitivity analysis. This is particularly essential to estimate the deteriorations on the performance of an optimal structure when it is fabricated. In addition, we perform extensive tests on the sensitivity of radiations to missing array elements to identify critical ones.

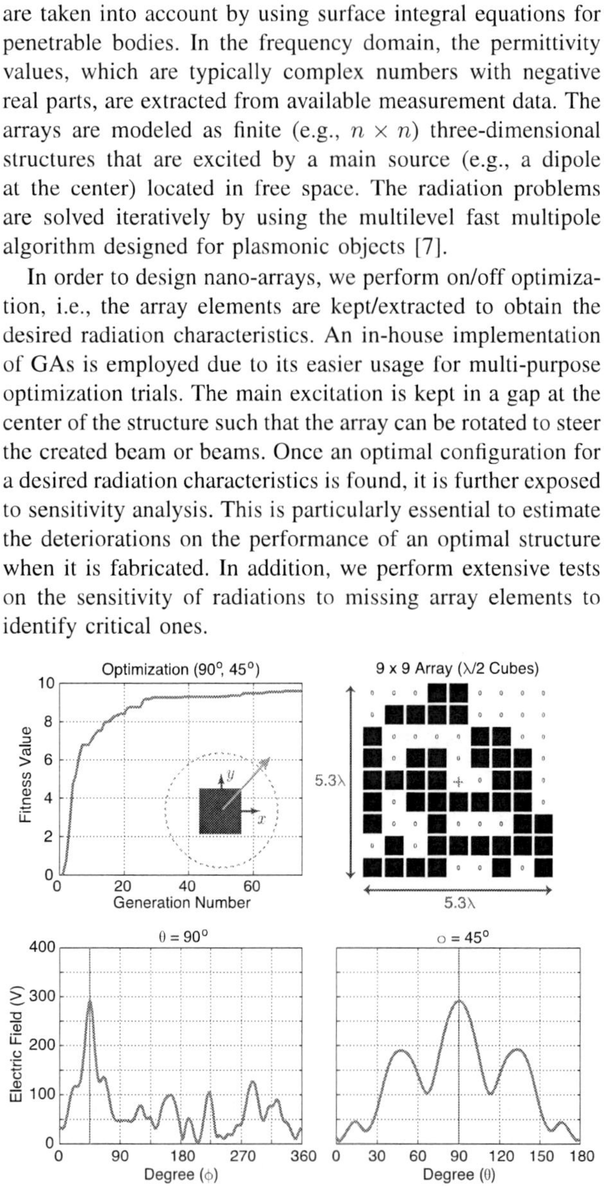

Fig. 1. The result of an optimization when the radiation is maximized at a single direction ($\theta = 90^\circ$ and $\phi = 45^\circ$).

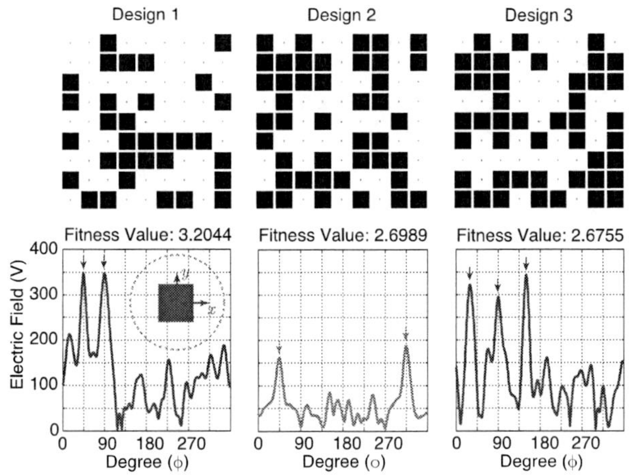

Fig. 2. Optimization results when the radiation is maximized at multiple directions.

III. Numerical Examples

As numerical examples, we consider two-dimensional nano-arrays involving a total of 80 Ag nano-cubes arranged as a 9×9 grid on the x-y plane. The nano-cubes have dimensions of $750 \times 750 \times 750$ nm, while the center-to-center distance is 900 nm. The structures are investigated at 200 THz, at which the cube edges correspond to $\lambda/2$ while the overall size is $5.3\lambda \times 5.3\lambda$. The relative permittivity of Ag at this frequency is approximately $-96+7.5i$. The arrays are excited by a Hertzian dipole oriented in the z direction and located at the center of the array (the cube-free space). Fig. 1 presents the results of an optimization when the radiation is maximized at $\theta = 90°$ and $\phi = 45°$. The radiation pattern of the array is investigated on the $\theta = 90°$ and $\phi = 45°$ planes, while the value of the electric field intensity at the desired direction is maximized with respect to the other values on these planes. Fig. 1 depicts the optimal array configuration (kept nano-cubes), as well as the far-zone electric field intensity on the related planes. The maximization at the desired direction is clearly observed.

Fig. 2 presents three examples to multi-beam optimizations, i.e., when the radiation pattern of the overall structure is maximized simultaneously at two or three directions. The fitness value is defined as the mean of the far-zone electric field intensity values at these directions normalized by the values at the other directions on the same ($\theta = 90°$) plane. The designs that provide the best radiation patterns are also depicted under titles Design 1, Design 2, and Design 3. The optimization directions are shown with small arrows in the electric-field plots. We observe quite successful results with maximized radiations at the desired directions. We emphasize that once a nano-array is optimized, the same pattern can be rotated and the beams can be steered by physically rotating the array while the main source is fixed.

When a nano-array is optimized and designed, a further analysis is required to test the feasibility of the design and to identify major performance parameters. Fig. 3 presents such an analysis, where the importance of each nano-cube of an

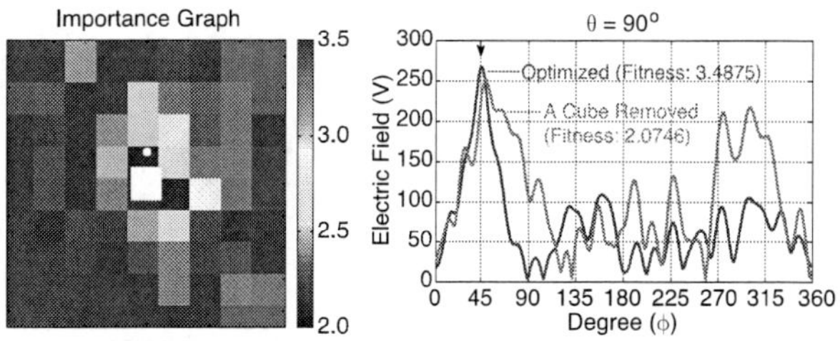

Fig. 3. The importance graph for an optimized nano-array that maximizes the radiation at a single direction. The fitness value is re-calculated when each nano-cube is added (if it was absent in the design) or extracted (if it was kept in the design).

optimized nano-array is investigated. This nano-array is designed to provide a single beam at $\theta = 90°$ and $\phi = 45°$. The color plot shows the value of the fitness function (originally 3.4875 for the optimized array) when each nano-cube decision is inverted (kept/extracted becomes extracted/kept) while all others remain the same. It can be observed that some of the nano-cubes are more critical; especially, two nano-cube locations close to the source location are extremely important. When these locations, which are originally empty, become filled, the fitness value drops down to 2. Fig. 3 also depicts the radiation patterns of the optimized and modified (when only one critical nano-cube is added) structures, where the deterioration of the pattern is clearly observed.

As shown in the numerical examples, two-dimensional nano-arrays can provide a great control ability on the radiation characteristics at optical frequencies. Extensions to three-dimensional structures for a full spherical steering is under investigation.

Acknowledgement

This work was supported by the Scientific and Technical Research Council of Turkey (TUBITAK) under the Research Grant 114E498 and by the Turkish Academy of Sciences (TUBA) in the framework of the Young Scientist Award Program.

References

[1] D. P. Fromm, et al., "Gap-dependent optical coupling of single bowtie nanoantennas resonant in the visible," Nano Lett., vol. 4, no. 5, pp. 957–961, Mar. 2004.
[2] P. J. Schuck, et al., "Improving the mismatch between light and nanoscale objects with gold bowtie nanoantennas," Phys. Rev. Lett., vol. 94, no. 017402, Jan. 2005.
[3] D. M. Solis, et al., "Optimization of an optical wireless nanolink using directive nanoantennas," Opt. Exp., vol. 21, no. 2, pp. 2369–2377, 2013.
[4] H. Chen, et al., "Design, fabrication, and characterization of near-IR gold bowtie nanoantenna arrays," Phys. Chem. C, vol. 118, no. 35, pp. 20553–20558, Aug. 2014.
[5] M. Alavirad, L. Roy, and P. Berini, "Optimization of plasmonic nanodipole antenna arrays for sensing applications," IEEE J. Sel. Top. Quantum Electron., vol. 20, no. 3, May/June 2014.
[6] A. Altınoklu and Ö. Ergül, "Computational analysis and full-wave optimizations of nanoantenna arrays for desired scattering and radiation characteristics," in Proc. URSI General Assembly and Scientific Symp. (URSI-GASS), 2017.
[7] A. Çekinmez, B. Karaosmanoğlu, and Ö. Ergül, "Integral-equation formulations of plasmonic problems in the visible spectrum and beyond," in Dynamical Systems - Analytical and Computational Techniques, M. Reyhanoglu, Ed. InTech, 2017, pp. 191–214.

Pattern Synthesis of Irregular Antenna Arrays with Small Element-Counts

Robert P. Scheeler
FIRST RF Corporation
Boulder, CO, USA
rscheeler@firstrf.com

James L. McDonald
FIRST RF Corporation
Boulder, CO, USA
jmcdonald@firstrf.com

Arian C. Lalezari
FIRST RF Corporation
Boulder, CO, USA
alalezari@firstrf.com

Joseph R. Mruk
FIRST RF Corporation
Boulder, CO, USA
jmruk@firstrf.com

***Abstract*—This paper details the procedure for synthesis of arbitrary patterns from an irregular antenna array with few elements. The procedure involves determining the embedded radiation pattern for each antenna element and the mutual coupling matrix for calculating the active reflection coefficients. Patterns are synthesized through a least-squares method. The procedure is demonstrated with an array of UHF antennas to form linearly and circularly polarized radiation patterns.**

Keywords*—*irregular antenna array, pattern synthesis, small array.

I. Introduction

As wireless sensor and system technologies advance, there is a need to integrate these new technologies on space constrained platforms. This leads to many different antennas of varying polarizations and operational frequencies being mounted near each other [1,2]. Ideally, these systems would be isolated from one another and, therefore, would have a marginal impact on the performance of their neighboring systems. However, when these antennas operate over the same frequency band they couple to each other forming an irregular array.

There has been significant interest in multi-antenna MIMO techniques that leverage multiple apertures to perform transmit and receive beam forming, interference mitigation, and spatial multiplexing [3]. To accomplish these functions, a method to determine how to excite the antenna elements to form the desired beam shape is required. It is also desirable to determine the active impedance of each element over the field of regard to limit potential damage to active RF components in the system. In this paper, a radiation pattern synthesis method is presented that allows for full characterization of an arbitrary array of antennas on a finite platform. Superposition of the radiated fields of the embedded element simulation is used to determine the phase excitation required at each antenna element to achieve maximum gain at any location in space in any desired polarization. Lastly, a method to calculate the active impedance of each beam state over the field of regard for different polarizations is also presented by means of the mutual coupling matrix.

II. Synthesis Procedure

The apertures must first be characterized before a beam may be synthesized. Generally, for medium to large regularly spaced arrays, the simulation and measurement procedure involves infinite array unit cell simulation, and a single representative embedded element simulation [4]. For small irregular arrays like that seen in Fig. 1, these techniques do not apply, and, due to their finite nature, lend themselves to a more thorough characterization procedure.

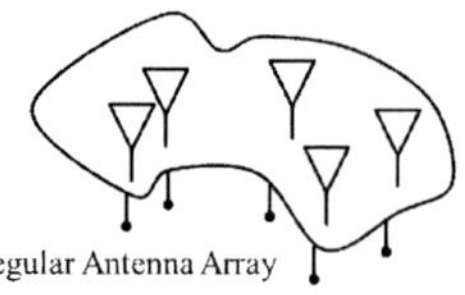

Fig. 1. Finite irregularly spaced antenna array.

A. Antenna Array Charcterization

The characterization of the antenna array requires only measured or simulated individual embedded element patterns. In this paper, the embedded element pattern is considered to be the radiation pattern of a single antenna while all other elements are terminated in their system impedance, which is generally 50Ω. The embedded radiation pattern of each element is the only information necessary to synthesize an arbitrarily polarized beam. The mutual coupling matrix is necessary for calculating active impedance. This is determined through measurement or simulation by determining the scattering matrix.

B. Pattern Synthesis and Active Impedance

The most general way to optimize a beam for a given single spatial location (θ_i, φ_i) is to determine the amplitude and phase for each antenna in the desired polarization and weight the excitation amplitude and phase accordingly. While this approach is valid, a more general optimization technique can be applied to optimize multiple spatial and polarimetric points. A least-squares method can be applied to optimize the excitation for a desired far-field pattern at different points [5], the simplest case being a maximization of the gain in a single direction. The matrix equation to optimize takes the form of

$$\mathbf{D}=\mathbf{F}\mathbf{A}, \tag{1}$$

where **D** represents the desired far-field pattern. **F** is the transfer function where each column represents the embedded pattern from each antenna in the array, and the rows correspond to the desired pattern and spatial point in **D**, and **A** is the complex element weight. The least-squares solution can be found by calculating the Moore-Penrose pseudoinverse $\mathbf{F}^{+}$, and solving for **A** as

$$\mathbf{A}=\mathbf{F}^{+}\mathbf{D}. \tag{2}$$

The formation of the desired pattern requires determining the complex radiation pattern of the desired polarization from each antenna. In this way, the excitation can be optimized both spatially and polarimetrically. However, in practice, the array architecture will limit the performance and diversity of the synthesized pattern in terms of the spatial and polarimetric sampling. Finally, with the excitation determined, the corresponding active reflection coefficients can be found. Utilizing the $N\times N$ scattering matrix for an N element array, active reflection coefficient at the mth port is

$$\Gamma_m = \sum_{n=1}^{N} S_{mn}\frac{V_n}{V_m}, \tag{3}$$

where V_n and V_m are the complex excitations at the nth and m^{th} ports respectively.

III. Simulated Example

To illustrate how to apply this technique, a simplified array of four antenna elements operating in the UHF-Band was simulated using FEKO (MoM) as shown in Fig. 2. Two elements are vertical monopoles, and the other two elements are crossed dipoles. The monopoles represent elements used for UHF line-of-sight communications, and the crossed-dipoles can form a MUOS SATCOM pattern.

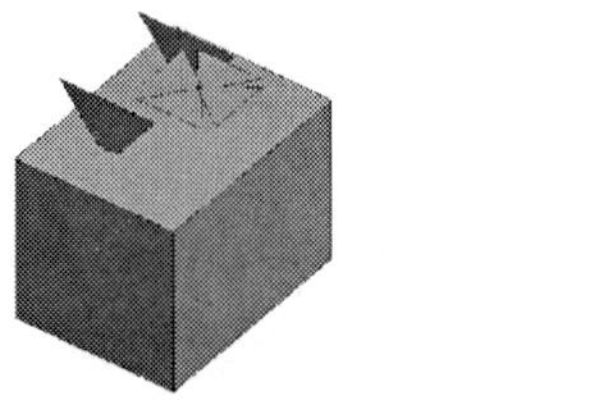

Fig. 2. FEKO model consisting of two monopole UHF line-of-sight antennas, and two orthogonal dipoles for a MUOS SATCOM pattern.

To characterize the array, four separate simulations were carried out. Each antenna was excited, while the others were terminated in 50Ω. The realized gain patterns were saved for each antenna element. Finally, the array scattering matrix was determined.

First, the pattern was optimized at (θ=50°, φ=90°) for vertical polarization. The resulting gain over frequency is shown in Fig. 3 demonstrating the peak achievable gain at that location is between 3 and 5 dBi. Extending this technique spatially in a conic sweep, the peak gain at each desired location is determined demonstrating the scanning envelope. Fig. 4 shows the envelope gain for a vertically polarized beam and a right-hand circularly polarized beam demonstrating a gain between 2 and 7 dBi.

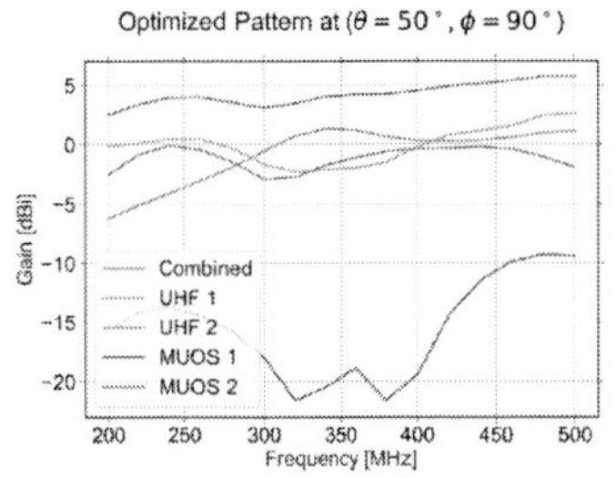

Fig. 3. Peak gain at (θ=50°, φ=90°) and the constituent patterns for a vertically polarized pattern.

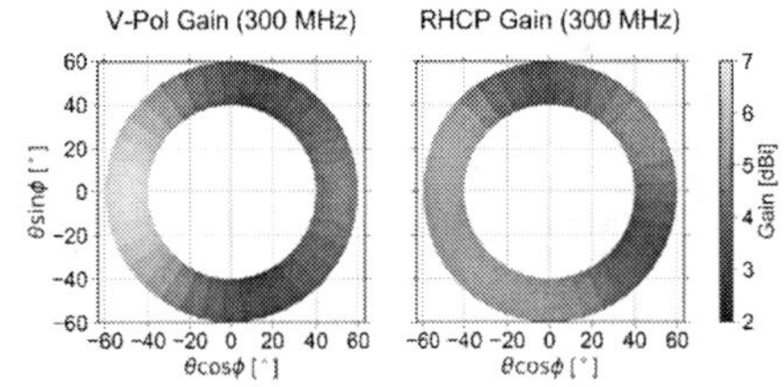

Fig. 4. Envelope gain optimized for the vertically polarized beam (left) and right-hand circularly polarized beam (right) demonstrating a gain between 2 and 7 dBi .

IV. Conclusions

This paper has detailed the pattern synthesis from irregular small element-count arrays. The method can be applied in the same fashion to both measured and simulated data, and can synthesize spatial and polarimetric peaks and nulls. The method was applied to a simplified model in simulation demonstrating vertically polarized, and RHCP beams. Additionally, a method to compute the active reflection coefficients was described.

References

[1] K. Allsebrook and C. Ribble, "VHF Cosight Interference Challenges and Solutions for the United States Marine Corps' Expeditionary Fighting Vehicle Program," IEEE Millitary Communications Conference (MILCOM 2004), vol. 1, pp. 548–554, Nov. 2004.

[2] S. Karlsson, M. Grenvall, A. Kvick, L. Eugensson, F. Grahn, and L. Pettersson, "Co-site Interference Analysis and Antenna System Integration on a Swedish Combat Vehicle Platform," IEEE Military Communications Conference (MILCOM 2013), vol. 1, pp. 369–374, Nov. 2013.

[3] L. Pucker, "Finding MIMO: A Proposed Model for Incorporating Multiple Input, Multiple Output Technology into Sofware Defined Radios," Proceedings of the SDR 05 Technical Conference and Product Exposition, pp. 1–6, 2005.

[4] R. J. Mailloux, Phased Array Antenna Handbook (Artech House Antennas and Propagation Library). Artech House, 2005.

[5] B. D. Carlson and D. Willner, "Antenna pattern synthesis using weighted least squares," IEE Proceedings H - Microwaves, Antennas and Propagation, vol. 139, no. 1, pp. 11-16, Feb. 1992.

The General Sidelobe Cancellation Based on Linear Minimum Variance At Subarray Level

1st Dan Wang
EECS
Wichita State University
Wichita, USA
dxwang@shockers.wichita.edu

2nd Guanglei Zhang
EEIS
Harbin Institute of Technology
Harbin, China
guangleizhang55@gmail.com

***Abstract*—As the electromagnetic environment becomes more and more complicated with different kind of interference, it is very important to suppress interference for the electromagnetic devices. In this paper, we propose a novel adaptive method for the interference suppression for phase array radar at the subarray level. In addition, the analysis for float round-off error is also given. The simulation results show the proposed method has good performance.**

***Index Terms*—cancellation, radar, adaptive, interference, suppression**

I. Introduction

As the electromagnetic environment becomes more and more complicated with different kind of interference, it is very important to suppress interference for the electromagnetic devices [1]. The phase array radar is widely used since the beam direction is controlled by the phase shifter [2]. The array signal processing for the phase array radar is based on the antenna element level [3]. As for the phase array radar, it is a huge amount of hardware resource cost due to the huge number of antenna elements. Therefore, the array signal process at the subarray level is adopted to help reduce the hardware cost. However, there are very few works focused on subarray array signal processing [4]. There are still a lot of issues to be solved. One of the most important issue is the interference suppression at the subarray level [5]. In order to perform interference suppression at the subarray level [6], the subarray division and interference suppression is considered. There are some existing works focused on the subarray division for the large scale phase array radar [7]. The interference suppression is considered when performing subarray division [8]. Two kinds of inhomogeneous subarray structure based on the line array is proposed. The main idea is that the distance between the central of two adjacent subarray has no constraints. The array pattern of the inhomogeneous subarray structure has no grating lobe compared with the homogeneous subarray structure. Then, the interference suppression should be considered [9]. In this paper, we propose a adaptive interference suppression method. In addition, the float round-off error analysis is also shown since it is very important for the practical implementation.

In this paper, we propose a general sidelobe cancellation method at the subarray level to perform the interference suppression. The paper includes 4 sections. In section I, the introduction is shown. In section 2, the derivation of the adaptive weights for the proposed method is shown. The validation results is shown in section III. In section IV, the conclusion is given.

II. The Derivation of the Weights for the Proposed General Sidelobe Cancellation Method

In this section, the proposed novel general sidelobe cancellation method is shown in this paper. The maximum signal interference and noise ratio is obtained by using linear minimum variance rule [7]. The existing work is focused on the method about how to transfer the constrains optimization into non constrain optimization at the antenna element level [10]. We proposed the general sidelobe cancellation method which is at the subarray level [11]. As for the narrow band forming device, the constraint is actually a inner product $\omega_{lcmv}^{H} a_{sub}(\theta_0, \phi_0) = 1$, ω_{lcmv} is the common adaptive weights vector and $a_{sub}(\theta_0, \phi_0)$ is the steering vector at the subarray level [12]. Then, the multiple linear constraint is obtained,

$$C_a^H w_{lcmv} = g \tag{1}$$

where matrix C_a is the linear constraint matrix. The vector g is the gain vector with the constant elements value. We assume the number of constraints is L. The dimension of C_a is $M \times L$ and g is a L dimension column vector. The matrix C_a has L linear constraint condition. We have

$$\left[\begin{array}{cc} a_{sub}(\theta) & a_{sub}(\theta_1, \phi_1) \end{array}\right]^H w_{lcmv} = \left[\begin{array}{c} 1 \\ 0 \end{array}\right] \tag{2}$$

In order to improve the power of the expected signal at the direction (θ_0, ϕ_0) and suppress the known interference at the direction (θ_1, ϕ_1), the constraint is adopted at the narrow band beamforming device.

Then, we define $M \times (M - L)$ dimension matrix C. We have

$$\begin{cases} C^H C_a = & 0 \\ C_a^H C = & 0 \end{cases} \tag{3}$$

Then, we assume

$$U = \left[\begin{array}{c} C_a \vdots C \end{array}\right] \tag{4}$$

where U is non-singular matrix. U^{-1} is the inverse matrix of U. The $M \times 1$ beamforming weights is

$$w_{lcmv} = Uq \tag{5}$$

Then, the $M \times 1$ dimension q is

$$q = U^{-1} w_{lcmv} \tag{6}$$

The q is written as

$$q = \begin{bmatrix} v \\ \cdots \\ -w_a \end{bmatrix} \tag{7}$$

where w_a is a $(L-P) \times 1$ vector. w_a is the non-constraint part of w_{lcmv}. v is a $L \times 1$ vector. Then, we have

$$w_{lcmv} = \begin{bmatrix} C_a & \vdots & C \end{bmatrix} \begin{bmatrix} v \\ \vdots \\ -w_a \end{bmatrix} = C_a v - C w_a \tag{8}$$

Then, we have

$$C_a^H C_a v - C_a^H C w_a = g \tag{9}$$

The following equation is obtained

$$C_a^H C_a v = g \tag{10}$$

Then, the vector v is obtained

$$v = (c_a^H C_a)^{-1} g \tag{11}$$

Therefore, v is dependent from w_a which means the multiple constraints has no impact on the w_a. The other part of w_{lcmv} is

$$w_q = C_a v = C_a (C_a^H C_a)^{-1} g \tag{12}$$

where w_q is orthographic to matrix C. Then, the linear constraint minimum variance adaptive weights is

$$w_{lcmv} = w_q - C w_a \tag{13}$$

The part of w_{lcmv} which meets the constraint is w_q and the other part is w_a. w_a is the free degree of the design for beamforming device. The block matrix is

$$C = \begin{bmatrix} 1 & -1 & 0 & \cdots & 0 \\ 0 & 1 & -1 & \cdots & 0 \\ \vdots & \vdots & \vdots & \vdots & \vdots \\ 0 & \cdots & 0 & 1 & -1 \end{bmatrix}_{L \times (L-1)} \tag{14}$$

III. Simulation Results

In this section, the simulation results for the proposed method is given. The results are shown for the performance of the array pattern at the azimuth, pitch and interference direction using the proposed method. As shown in table 1, the array pattern has good performance at the azimuth peak sidelobe power, the azimuth average sidelobe power, the azimuth mainlobe width, the pitch peak sidelobe power, the pitch average sidelobe power, the pitch mainlobe width and the null depth at the interference direction. In addition, the bit length also has no impact on the proposed method.

Table 1. the performance of the proposed method

Bit length	GSLC					GSLC	
	APSL	AASL	AMLW	PPSL	PASL	PMLW	IND
64bit	-9.6650	-29.5143	1	-13.1174	-22.4228	4	-124.2822
32bit	-9.6634	-29.514	1	-13.1029	-22.4189	4	-124.2621
error	0.0016	0.0003	0	0.0154	0.0039	0	0.0201

IV. Conclusion

In this paper, we propose a novel method to adaptively suppression the interference at the subarray level. The details about the adaptive weights derivation for the proposed general sidelobe cancellation method is shown in the paper. The proposed method has good array pattern performance at the azimuth direction sidelobe power and mainlobe width, pitch direction sidelobe power and mainlobe width and interference null depth. In addition, the float round-off error almost has no impact on the proposed method according to the simulation results.

References

[1] H. Subbaram and K. Abend, "Interference suppression via orthogonal projections: a performance analysis," *IEEE Transactions on Antennas and Propagation*, vol. 41, no. 9, pp. 1187–1194, Sep 1993.

[2] D. Wang and Z. Yang, "An novel spectrum sensing scheme combined with machine learning," in *2016 9th International Congress on Image and Signal Processing, BioMedical Engineering and Informatics (CISP-BMEI)*, Oct 2016, pp. 1293–1297.

[3] D. Wang, H. Hu, and Z. Yang, "Improved genetic algorithm for the configuration optimization of the sub arrays in phased array radar," in *2016 9th International Congress on Image and Signal Processing, BioMedical Engineering and Informatics (CISP-BMEI)*, Oct 2016, pp. 930–934.

[4] I. P. Kirsteins and D. W. Tufts, "Adaptive detection using low rank approximation to a data matrix," *IEEE Transactions on Aerospace and Electronic Systems*, vol. 30, no. 1, pp. 55–67, Jan 1994.

[5] D. Wang, H. Hu, and Z. Yang, "The pareto rank algorithm for the division of the sub arrays for the phase array radar," in *2016 9th International Congress on Image and Signal Processing, BioMedical Engineering and Informatics (CISP-BMEI)*, Oct 2016, pp. 945–949.

[6] D. Wang and Z. Yang, "An advanced scheme with decision tree for the improvement of spectrum sensing efficiency in dynamic network," in *2016 9th International Congress on Image and Signal Processing, BioMedical Engineering and Informatics (CISP-BMEI)*, Oct 2016, pp. 1288–1292.

[7] D. Wang and Y. Song, "A novel distributed global time synchronization protocol in cognitive radio ad hoc networks," in *2015 IEEE Global Communications Conference (GLOBECOM)*, Dec 2015, pp. 1–6.

[8] S. Applebaum and D. Chapman, "Adaptive arrays with main beam constraints," *IEEE Transactions on Antennas and Propagation*, vol. 24, no. 5, pp. 650–662, Sep 1976.

[9] D. Wang, Y. Song, and Z. Yang, "A joint power adaptation and spectrum handoff scheme in mobile cognitive radio networks," in *2015 International Conference on Computing, Networking and Communications (ICNC)*, Feb 2015, pp. 1061–1065.

[10] D. Wang, Z. Yang, and Y. Song, "A novel spectrum sensing scheduling scheme for pu and su signal differentiation in cr networks," in *2015 IEEE International Conference on Communications (ICC)*, June 2015, pp. 5697–5702.

[11] L. Brennan, J. Mallett, and I. Reed, "Adaptive arrays in airborne mti radar," *IEEE Transactions on Antennas and Propagation*, vol. 24, no. 5, pp. 607–615, Sep 1976.

[12] Z. Yang, Y. Song, and D. Wang, "An optimal operating frequency selection scheme in spectrum handoff for cognitive radio networks," in *2015 International Conference on Computing, Networking and Communications (ICNC)*, Feb 2015, pp. 1066–1070.

Design Concepts for Broadband Antenna Arrays with Constant Half-Power Beamwidth

Christopher Gay
Dpt. of Electrical, Computer, & Energy Engineering
University of Colorado Boulder
Boulder, USA

Matthew Cullen
Dpt. of Electrical, Computer, & Energy Engineering
University of Colorado Boulder
Boulder, USA

Dimitra Psychogiou
Dpt. of Electrical, Computer, & Energy Engineering
University of Colorado Boulder
Boulder, USA

***Abstract*—This paper reports on the design of broadband antenna arrays with constant half-power beamwidth (HPBW). The proposed concept is based on non-uniformly spaced and non-uniformly-fed radiating elements using frequency-selective feeding networks. As opposed to conventional feeding schemes, it facilitates the realization of constant HPBW within two octaves of bandwidth. For proof-of-concept demonstration purposes, the radiation characteristics of a five-element array are studied for frequencies between 1-4 GHz. The proposed frequency-selective feeding scheme allows for HPBW of 45°±2° and HPBW variation of 9.3 % to be obtained within the entire 1-4 GHz range.**

Keywords—Antenna arrays, broadband antenna, constant beamwidth, frequency-selective feed network, linear antenna arrays.

I. INTRODUCTION

Recent advances in wireless communication and radar systems are increasingly calling for RF transceivers with multi-standard operability across multiple octaves of bandwidth (BW). In order to facilitate their deployment, RF hardware with broadband characteristics needs to be developed. This is particularly important for the antenna elements of these systems, due to their input-reflection and radiation characteristics being frequency dependent. Recent research efforts in broadband antenna design are mostly focusing on single antenna elements (e.g, vivaldi, spiral and broadband monopoles) and optimize their bandwidth (BW) for low input reflection (<10 dB) [1]. However, their radiation pattern characteristics and most importantly their half-power beamwidth (HPBW) vary significantly with frequency and in particular for BWs >1.5-2:1. These effects are even more pronounced when these elements are used in antenna array configurations [2], [3]. This is shown in the example case of a conventional uniformly-fed and uniformly-spaced five-element antenna array—shaped by ideal $\lambda/2$ dipole elements (omni-directional radiation pattern cut) that are aligned on the x-axis—in Fig. 1. As can be seen, its HPBW varies between 54°-26° (108 %) for frequencies between 1-2 GHz and between 54°-13° (315 %) for a frequency BW of 4:1, making this antenna configuration unsuitable for practical use.

Taking into consideration the aforementioned limitations, this paper presents a study on the radiation pattern characteristics of a five-element antenna array and a design methodology for achieving constant HPBW. The proposed approach is based on: i) feeding networks with frequency dependent characteristics [2]—non-uniform feed—and ii) non-uniform element spacing, which result in a constant HPBW to be obtained within a 4:1 BW. Despite the fact that this concept is shown for a five-element antenna array, it can be readily extended to larger numbers of elements or alternative levels of HPBW.

This work was supported by Lockheed Martin under award OCG6415B

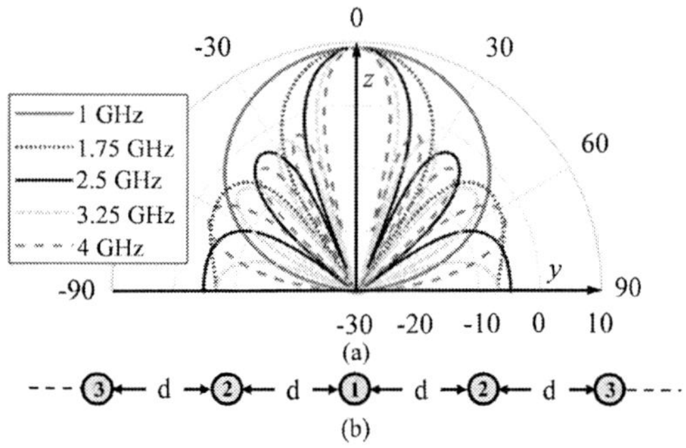

Fig. 1. Five-element array with uniformly-spaced and uniformly-fed elements. (a) Gain patterns (due to symmetry along the y-axis only half of the zy plane is shown). (b) Array configuration (d= 6 cm, i.e., 0.2λ at 1 GHz).

II. ARRAYS WITH CONSTANT HALF-POWER BEAMWIDTH

A. Uniformly-spaced and non-uniformly-fed antenna elements

Taking into consideration that the HPBW of an antenna array depends on the antenna element spacing (d), a three-element array can provide the same radiation pattern characteristics at a frequency f_0 and $2f_0$ if the spacing of its outer elements is altered from 2d to d. This property can be exploited for the realization of a five-element antenna array as a combination of two distinct

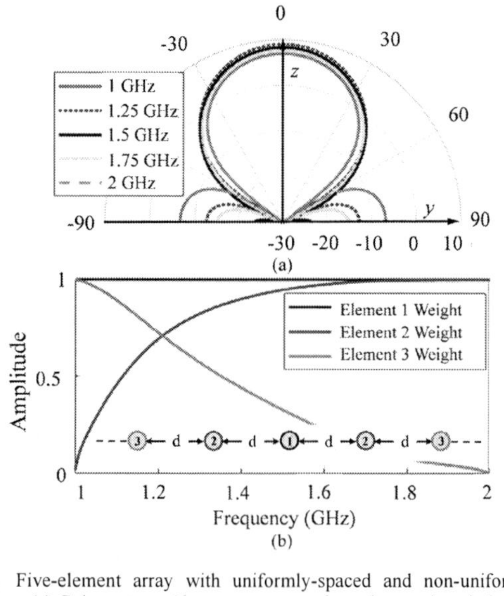

Fig. 2. Five-element array with uniformly-spaced and non-uniformly-fed elements. (a) Gain patterns (due to symmetry along the y-axis only half of the zy plane is shown). (b) Normalized voltage weights and antenna configuration (d= 6 cm, i.e., 0.2λ at 1 GHz).

sets of three-element arrays—one shaped by elements 1 and 2 and the other by elements 1 and 3—and is expected to result in identical HPBW characteristics at two frequencies that are separated by one octave, Fig. 2. It is apparent that switching between different sets of three-element arrays may result in constant HPBW within the entire frequency range between f_0 and $2f_0$ (2:1) or even to a wider BW. However, the practical realization of such an antenna configuration may result in increased levels of complexity and size. As an alternative solution to the aforementioned practical limitations, non-uniform feeding schemes can be considered. This is illustrated in Fig. 2 for the case of a uniformly-spaced five-element antenna array—shaped by two three-element arrays that share the central element—whose inner element (1) is constantly fed whereas its outer elements (2,3) are fed in a non-uniform fashion. In particular, in the proposed feeding scheme, the power is gradually shifted from the outer array elements to the inner ones as a function of frequency with the goal of maintaining constant HPBW and low side-lobe level (<-8 dBc). In this manner, an almost constant HPBW of 46°±2° (9 % variation) and gain between 7-9 dBi can be obtained. The normalized voltage weights in Fig. 2 (b) have been obtained using finite difference interior-point optimization in Matlab that is programmed to minimize the HPBW variation for a given BW, side-lobe level and gain variation. It is apparent that if wider BWs need to be realized, additional sets of three-element arrays need to be added, e.g., three—seven-element array—for a BW of 3:1.

B. Non-uniformly-spaced and non-uniformly-fed elements

With the purpose of increasing BW without having to increase the number of antenna elements, we consider the case of an antenna array with non-uniformly-spaced and non-uniformly-fed elements as shown in Fig. 3. In relation to the antenna array of Section II A., the five-element antenna array is designed as follows. The elements of the three-element array that comprises elements 1 and 2 (high-frequency array) are set at a distance $d_1=0.4\lambda$ at f_{max}, and the elements of the three-element array that comprises elements 1 and 3 (low-frequency array) are set at a distance $d_2=0.4\lambda$ at f_{min}—1 GHz in this case. Optimization is performed in order to specify f_{max} for which constant HPBW can be obtained for side-lobe-levels <-8dBc and gain variation between 7-9 dBi. The optimization results of this study are summarized in Fig. 3. As it can be seen, a constant HPBW of 45°±2° (9 %) can be obtained across a 4:1 BW as opposed to a HPBW variation of 315 % in the conventional uniformly-spaced and uniformly-fed array in Fig. 1. This proves the applicability of the proposed antenna array design methodology for the realization of constant HPBW within two octaves. It should be noted that larger BWs can be obtained in the five-element configuration if higher side-lobe levels are to be allowed. Fig. 4 shows a comparison of the three different methods for designing a five-element array in terms of gain and HPBW. It can be seen that the antenna arrays with constant HPBW exhibit less gain at almost all frequencies due to their elements not being continuously fed. The maximum gain deviation from the gain of the uniformly-fed array appears at frequencies at which only three out of the five elements are fed, e.g., at 1 and 2 GHz in the non-uniformly fed array and 1 and 4 GHz in the non-uniformly-fed and non-uniformly-spaced array.

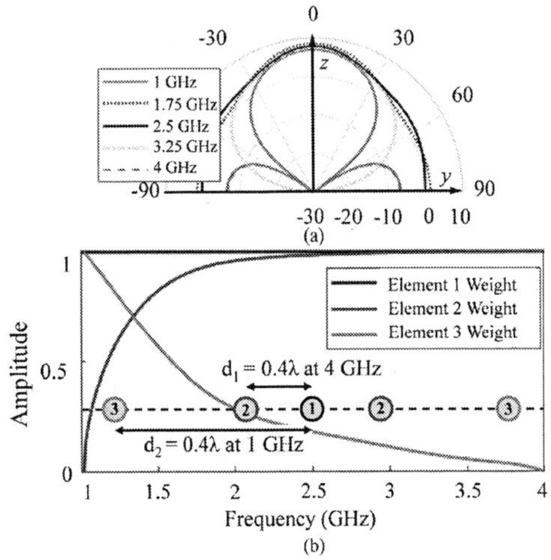

Fig. 3. Five-element array with non-uniformly-spaced and non-uniformly-fed elements. (a) Gain patterns (due to symmetry along the y-axis only half of the zy plane is shown). (b) Normalized voltage weights and antenna configuration.

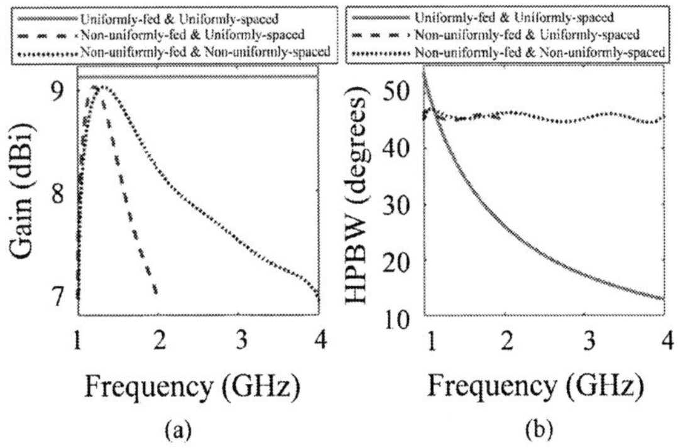

Fig. 4. (a) Gain and (b) HPBW

III. CONCLUSION

This paper presented a methodology for the design of broadband antenna arrays with constant HPBW. The proposed approach is based on non-uniformly spaced and non-uniformly-fed radiating elements using frequency-selective feeding networks. As opposed to conventional feeding schemes, it facilitates the realization of constant HPBW within two octaves of bandwidth. For proof-of-concept demonstration purposes, the radiation characteristics of a five-element array are studied between 1-4 GHz. The proposed frequency-selective feeding scheme allows for HPBW of 45°±2° and HPBW variation of just 9 % to be obtained within the entire 1-4 GHz range.

REFERENCES

[1] R. Natarajan, J. V. George, M. Kanagasabai, and A. K. Shrivastav, "A compact antipodal Vivaldi antenna for UWB applications," IEEE Antennas Wireless Propag. Lett., 2015.

[2] K. Wincza and S. Gruszczynski, "Broadband scalable antenna arrays with constant beamwidths fed by frequency-selective networks," IEEE Trans. Antennas Propag., vol. 64, no. 7, pp. 2936-2943, Jul. 2016.

[3] S. S. Holland, D. H. Schaubert, and M. N. Vouvakis, "A 7-21 GHz dual-polarized planar ultrawideband modular antenna (PUMA) array," IEEE Trans. Antennas Propag., vol. 60, no. 10, pp. 4589-4660, Oct. 2012.

Comparison of an Isotropic Point Source and a Spherically Distributed Antenna Array

Kristopher Buchanan[1], Timi Adeyemi[1], Carlos Flores-Molina[1], Sara Wheeland[1], and Steven Weiss[2]

Space and Naval Warfare Systems Center Pacific (SSC Pacific)[1]: Electromagnetics Technology Branch, San Diego CA, USA

Adelphi Laboratory Center[2]: Antennas and RF Technology Integration Branch, 2800 Powder Mill Rd, Adelphi, MD 20783, USA

***Abstract*—This work investigates beam pattern behavior of an isotropic point source and a collection of sources distributed amongst a spherical volume. Pattern behavior is also compared to the tapering of a plane wave expansion of spherical waves demonstrating self-adjoint characteristics. Beampatterns of atomic like orbitals and Zernike polynomials are provided as connections to common applications.**

***Index Terms*—Distributed beamforming.**

I. Introduction

The expected beampattern for any geometrically bound topology has been shown in [1] by taking the expected value of the power pattern $|\bar{F}(\Psi)^2|$ across the unit interval [-1, 1]. Hence, for a volumetric random variable x this provides the characteristic functions (1), which are orthogonal in all three axes and uncorrelated. Hence, the analysis involves the characteristic functions of the aperture distribution [1-3]:

$$\bar{U} = \tfrac{1}{N} + \left(1 - \tfrac{1}{N}\right)\Lambda|u|^2 \Lambda|v|^2 \Lambda|w|^2 = \tfrac{1}{N} + \left(1 - \tfrac{1}{N}\right)\Lambda\left|\vec{\Psi}\right|^2 \quad (1)$$

A. Spherical Waves in Unbounded Space

The characteristic modes of the spherical harmonics are derived from the Helmholtz equation (2) in unbounded space,

$$\left(\nabla^2 + k^2\right)G_k = -\delta\left(\vec{r} - \vec{r}\,'\right) = -\frac{\delta\left(r - r'\right)\delta\left(\theta - \theta'\right)\delta\left(\phi - \phi'\right)}{rr'\sin\theta} \quad .(2)$$
$$G_k\left(\vec{r},\vec{r}\,'\right) = G_k\left(\vec{r} - \vec{r}\,'\right) = jh_0^{(1)}\left(jk\left|r - r'\right|\right)/4\pi = G_k\left(\vec{r}\,',\vec{r}\right)$$

The fundamental solution (2) is a point source and implies the self-adjointness property such that $G_k\left(\vec{r},\vec{r}\,'\right) = G_k\left(\vec{r}\,',\vec{r}\right)$. In other words, a spherical wave converges to a plane wave in the far field and vice versa. An expansion of (2) as a scalar plane wave composed of scalar spherical waves can also be written as (3). From the orthogonality property of the spherical harmonics, outgoing waves are composed from multipole coefficients derived from the pattern multiplication of spherical Hankel, Bessel and spherical harmonics (4):

$$G_k\left(\vec{r}_1,\vec{r}_2\right) = jk\sum_{l=0}^{\infty}\begin{Bmatrix} j_l\left(kr_1\right)h_l^{(1)}\left(kr_2\right)\ \left[r_1 < r_2\right] \\ j_l\left(kr_2\right)h_l^{(1)}\left(kr_1\right)\ \left[r_1 > r_2\right]\end{Bmatrix}\sum_{m=-l}^{l} Y_l^m\left(\theta_1,\phi_1\right) Y_l^{m*}\left(\theta_2,\phi_2\right) \quad (3)$$

$$G_k\left(\vec{r},\vec{r}\,'\right) = jk\sum_{l=0,\infty} j_l\left(kr_<\right)h_l^{(1)}\left(kr_>\right)\sum_{m=-l,+l} Y_{lm}^*\left(\theta',\phi'\right)Y_{l,m}\left(\theta,\phi\right)$$
$$\neg\oint Y_{lm}^*\left(\theta,\phi\right)G_k\left(\vec{r},\vec{r}\,'\right)d\Omega = jkh_l^{(1)}\left(kr\right)j_l\left(kr'\right)Y_{lm}^*\left(\theta',\phi'\right) \quad .(4)$$

In the far field the term $|\vec{r} - \vec{r}\,'| \approx r' - \vec{n}\cdot\vec{r}$, where $\vec{n}$ is a unit vector pointing in the direction of $\vec{r}\,'$. $h_l^{(1)}\left(kr\right)$ can be reduced in its asymptotic form such that:

$$\frac{e^{j\vec{k}\cdot\vec{r}}}{4\pi r}e^{-j\vec{k}\cdot\vec{r}\,'} = jk\frac{e^{jkr}}{kr}\sum_{l=0}^{\infty}\left(-j\right)^{l+1} j_l\left(kr'\right)\sum_{m=-l,+l} Y_{lm}^*\left(\theta',\phi'\right)Y_{l,m}\left(\theta,\phi\right) .(5)$$

The scalar plane wave expansion (6) is obtained by canceling the factor exp(jkr)/r, taking the complex conjugate, and rewriting via the well-known addition theorem (7):

$$e^{j\vec{k}\cdot\vec{r}\,'} = 4\pi\sum_{l=0}^{\infty} j^l j_l\left(kr'\right)\sum_{m=-l,+l} Y_{lm}^*\left(\theta',\phi'\right)Y_{l,m}\left(\theta,\phi\right), \quad (6)$$

$$e^{j\vec{k}\cdot\vec{r}\,'} = \sum_{l=0}^{\infty} j^l\left(2l+1\right)j_l\left(kr'\right)P_l\left(\cos\psi\right)$$
$$= \sum_{l=0}^{\infty} j^l\sqrt{4\pi\left(2l+1\right)}j_l\left(kr'\right)Y_{l0}\left(\psi\right), \quad (7)$$
$$Y_{l0}\left(\psi\right) = P_l\left(\cos\psi\right)\sqrt{\left(2l+1\right)/4\pi},\ \psi = \hat{r}\cdot\hat{r}\,'$$

B. Zernike Polynomials and Spherical Harmonics

It is possible to create patterns with multiple beams using complex orthogonal phase variations. A nominal example in *UV-space* is provided in Fig. 1.

Distributed orthogonality of this behavior is applied to the plane wave expansion of ψ and angular (θ, ϕ) spaces of Fig 2 and 3, respectively. Fig. 2 demonstrates ψ *-spaces* with rotationally symmetric attributes whereas Fig. 3 demonstrates the self-adjoint properties of spherically distributed arrays (SDA). For example, a spherical wave converges to a plane wave as the modal order increases whereas the point source converges to a spherical wave.

The Legendre polynomials, which are orthogonal to the L^2 inner product on the interval $-1 \le x \le 1$, are the eigenfunctions of the Hermitian differential operator. They arise naturally in multipole expansions analogous to the monopole, dipole and higher moments of the spherical harmonic solutions, yielding the beampattern characteristics in Fig. 4. Furthermore, achievable pattern behavior is verified from HFSS simulations using 32 monopole element radiators steered at the meridian elevation angle in a normalized spherical aperture, A/λ=2.78 for select orbital distributions.

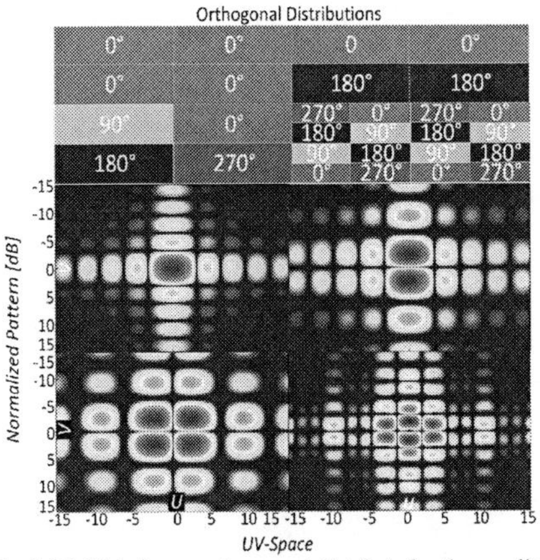

Fig. 1. Multiple beam patterns and distributed orthogonality.

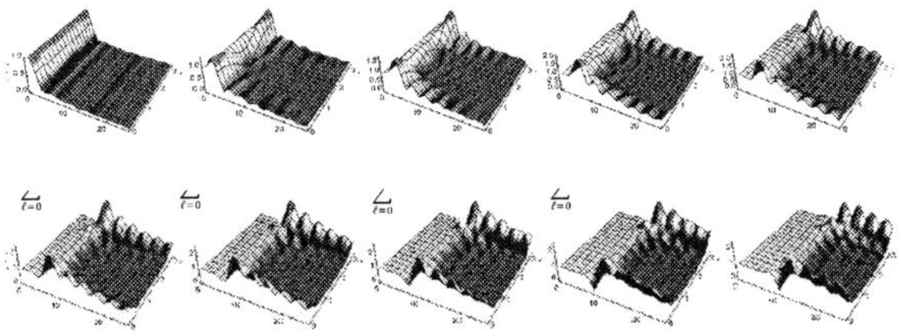

Fig. 2. Plane wave expansion in UV – space.

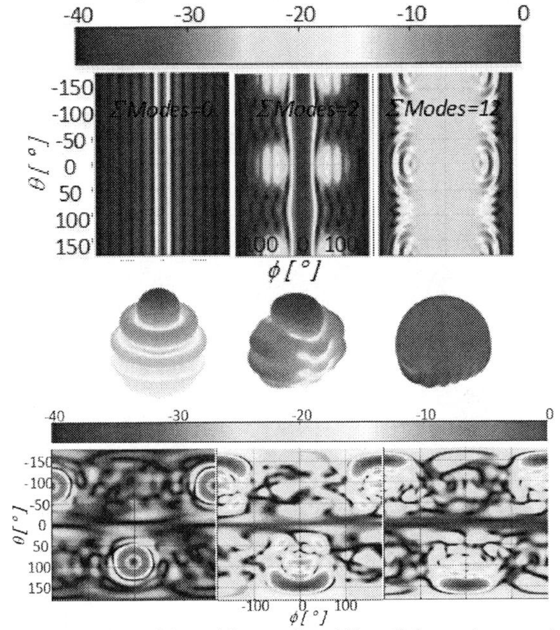

Fig. 3. Comparison of the modal summation of (6) applied to a point source in angular space, top and SDA, bottom.

The three-dimensional Zernike polynomials are likewise composed of angular solutions of an orthogonal sequence defined on the unit sphere. In two-dimensional space, Zernike polynomials are commonly used in optics to describe aberrations of the cornea or lens from the nominal spherical shape (resulting in refraction errors). Examples include a circularly distributed array (CDA) as illustrated in Fig. 5. Closed form solutions of the patterns are provided in [2].

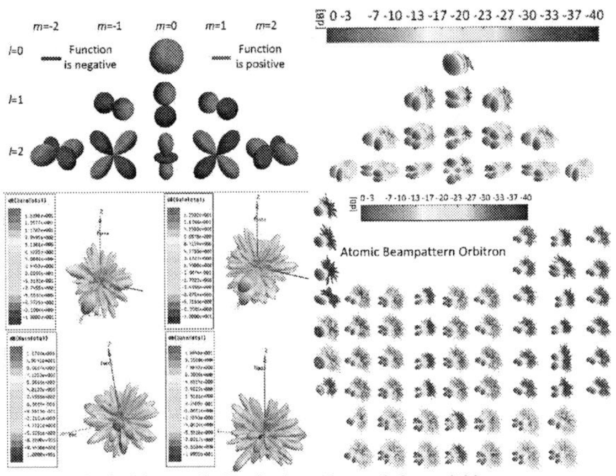

Fig. 4. Spherical harmonic distributions Y_{nm} top-left; modal beampatterns top-right; simulated patterns $Y_{00,}$ Y_{01}; Y_{02} , and Y_{03}, bottom-left; atomic like orbital patterns bottom-right.

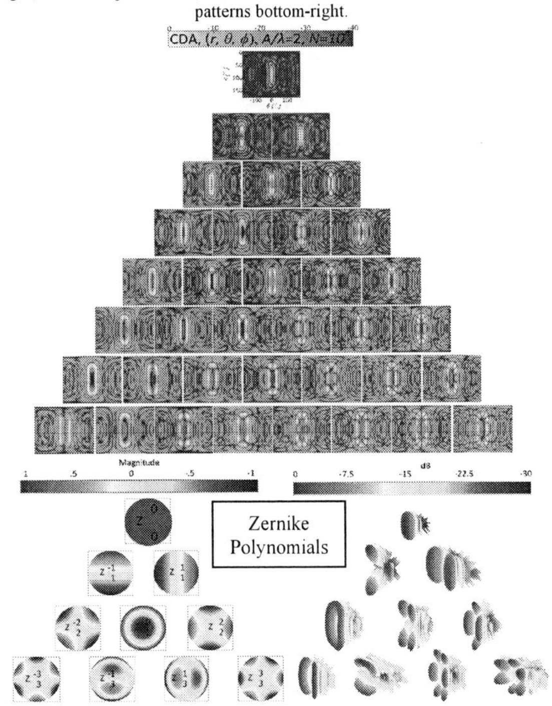

Fig. 5. Characteristic modes of the Zernike polynomials; topographical – top; distributions, bottom-left; three dimensional modal patterns, bottom-right.

References

[1] B. D. Steinberg, Principles of Aperture & Array System Design, New York: Wiley, 1976.

[2] K. R. Buchanan, "Theory and applications of aperiodic (random) phased arrays," Ph.D. dissertation, Dept. Elect. & Com. Eng., Texas A&M University, TX, 2014.

[3] K. Buchanan and G. Huff, "A stochastic mathematical framework for the analysis of spherically bound random arrays," *IEEE Trans. Antennas Propag.*, vol. 62., pp. 3002-3011, June 2014.